GRUBER'S
FOURTH EDITION
COMPLETE PREPARATION FOR THE
SAT*
BY GARY R. GRUBER, PH.D.

FEATURING
CRITICAL THINKING SKILLS

* SAT is a registered trademark of the College Entrance Examination Board. The College Entrance Examination Board is not associated with and does not endorse this book.

PERENNIAL LIBRARY

Harper & Row, Publishers, New York
Grand Rapids, Philadelphia, St. Louis, San Francisco
London, Singapore, Sydney, Tokyo, Toronto

GRUBER'S COMPLETE PREPARATION FOR THE SAT (*Fourth Edition*). Copyright © 1990, 1988, 1987, 1986, 1985 by Gary R. Gruber and Edward C. Gruber. All rights reserved. Printed in the United States of America. No part of this book may be used or reproduced in any manner whatsoever without written permission except in the case of brief quotations embodied in critical articles and reviews. For information address Harper & Row, Publishers, Inc., 10 East 53rd Street, New York, NY 10022.

Library of Congress Cataloging-in-Publication Data

Gruber, Gary R.
   [Complete preparation for the SAT]
   Gruber's complete preparation for the SAT : featuring critical thinking skills / by Gary R. Gruber — 4th ed.
     p.   cm.
   ISBN 0-06-463732-8 (pbk.)
   1. Scholastic aptitude tests—Study guides.   I. Title.   II. Title: Complete preparation for the SAT.
LB2353.57.G778   1990
378.1′664—dc20   89-46095

91 92 93 94 MPC 10 9 8 7 6 5 4

The Author Has Something Important to Tell You About How to Raise Your SAT Score

WHAT ARE CRITICAL THINKING SKILLS?

First of all, I believe that intelligence can be taught. Intelligence, simply defined, is the aptitude or ability to reason things out. I am convinced that *you can learn to think logically* and figure things out better and faster, *particularly in regard to SAT Math and Verbal problems*. But someone must give you the tools. Let us call these tools *strategies*. And that's what Critical Thinking Skills are all about—*strategies*.

LEARN THE STRATEGIES TO GET MORE POINTS

The Critical Thinking Skills (beginning on page 67) will sharpen your reasoning ability so that you can increase your score up to 300 points on each part of the Scholastic Aptitude Test.

These Critical Thinking Skills—5 General strategies, 25 Math strategies and 25 Verbal strategies—course right through this book. The Explanatory Answers for the 7 Practice Tests in the book direct you to those strategies which may be used to answer specific types of SAT questions. We can readily prove that the strategies in Part 2 of this book are usable for approximately 90% of the questions that have appeared in recent official SAT exams. *Each additional correct answer gives you approximately 10 points*. It is obvious, then, that your *learning* and *using* the 55 easy-to-understand strategies in this book will very likely raise your SAT score substantially.

ARE THE PRACTICE TESTS IN THIS BOOK LIKE AN ACTUAL SAT?

If you compare any one of the 7 Practice Tests in this book with an actual *recent* SAT, you will find the book test very much like the *actual* test in regard to *format*, *question-types*, and *level of difficulty*. Recent official SAT exams have been published by the College Board and are available for purchase—"10 SATs," for example. Compare our book tests with one of the official tests.

Documentary evidence is readily available to prove conclusively that no other commercial SAT book has Practice Tests that follow the actual SAT as closely as the 7 Practice Tests in this book.

BUILDING UP YOUR VOCABULARY WILL MAKE A BIG DIFFERENCE ON YOUR TEST

This book includes three vital sections to build up your vocabulary:

1. 3400-Word List
2. 100 Vocabulary Tests
3. 366 Latin and Greek roots, prefixes, and suffixes

It is very important for you to study this word-building instructional material. You will find that *many, many words* in the 3400-Word List will actually show up in the Antonym, Analogies, Sentence Completion, and Reading Comprehension sections of the Verbal part of your SAT. We repeat that each additional correct answer adds approximately 10 points to your score. Knowing the meanings of the words in the 3400-Word List will thus help you considerably to "rake in" those precious points.

EXAMPLE

The following 22 words appeared as the stem words of Antonym questions in a recent SAT. (There are 25 Antonym questions in every SAT.)

affirmation	haphazard	irk	monitor	retention
commodious	harrowing	maladroit	mottled	rue
defer	incongruity	misanthrope	nonentity	sheepish
derangement	insuperable	mobile	placate	stamina
	inter		prevalent	

A student earns approximately 10 points for each correct answer.

All of the 22 words above also appear in the Gruber SAT 3400-Word List. Accordingly, if a student had studied thoroughly the SAT 3400-Word List before taking that particular SAT, he would have earned 220 points by simply knowing the meanings of the foregoing 22 words.

SEE PAGE 124 FOR ADDITIONAL EXAMPLES TO PROVE THAT STUDYING OUR 3400-WORD LIST IS VITAL FOR EXTRA POINTS.

STUDY THE 366 LATIN AND GREEK ROOTS, PREFIXES AND SUFFIXES

We have developed a list of roots, prefixes, and suffixes which contain the 50 prefixes and roots that give you the meaning of over 150,000 words. Learning all 366 will increase your vocabulary immensely.

THE EXPLANATORY ANSWERS TO QUESTIONS ARE KEYED TO SPECIFIC STRATEGIES AND BASIC SKILLS

The Explanatory Answers in this book are far from skimpy—so unlike other SAT books. Our detailed answers will direct you to the strategy which will help you to arrive at a correct answer quickly. In addition, the Math solutions in the book refer directly to the 150-page Math Refresher section, particularly useful in case your Math skills are "rusty."

LIFT THAT SAT SCORE DON'T FOLLOW THE DOWN-TREND

You have probably read or heard about the latest College Board statistics that alarmingly reveal that the average score on the Verbal section of the SAT has dropped to 427 from 478, while the average score on the Math section has fallen to 476 from 502. You can reverse that down-trend for yourself. How? Simply do what this book directs you to do. You'll never regret it.

—**Gary Gruber**

Contents

INTRODUCTION

I. Important Facts about the SAT

WHAT IS THE SAT?

The Scholastic Aptitude Test (SAT) is a three-hour college entrance test which has 6 sections timed 30 minutes each. It contains 60 counted math questions in two math sections and 85 counted verbal questions in two verbal sections. Another section contains grammar questions which do not count toward the SAT score and is only used for college first-year English class placement purposes. It is advisable not to prepare for this grammar part, especially since it does not count toward the SAT score. There is also an experimental section which contains either grammar, math, or verbal questions but does not count toward any score.

HOW IS THE SAT SCORED?

The SAT is scored from 200 to 800 on both parts, verbal and math.

WHAT IS THE NATIONAL AVERAGE SCORE?

The average national SAT score for the 1988–89 school year was 427 for the verbal and 476 for the math.

HOW MUCH IS EACH QUESTION WORTH IN SAT POINTS?

On the SAT you get a *raw* score (the number of correct answers minus a small penalty for incorrect ones). You also get a *scaled* score which is derived from the raw score. This scaled score is your actual SAT score. Each additional question you get right can increase your score by about 10 more points.

WHAT VERBAL BACKGROUND MUST I HAVE?

The reading and vocabulary level is at a 10th to 12th grade level, but strategies presented here will help you even if you are at a lower grade level.

WHAT MATH BACKGROUND MUST I HAVE?

The SAT includes questions related to only first-year elementary algebra and plane geometry. However, if you use common sense and rely on just a handful of geometric formulas, you really don't need to have taken a full course in geometry. If you have not taken algebra you should still be able to answer many of the math questions using the strategies presented.

WHEN IS GUESSING ADVISABLE?

There is a penalty of approximately 2.5 SAT points for each wrong answer in a 5-choice type question, and about a 3.3 SAT points penalty for each wrong answer in a 4-choice type question. Guessing is advisable if you can eliminate one or more choices. However, if you cannot eliminate any choices, and you guess, because you have a 1 in 5 chance (with 5 choice questions) and a 1 in 4 chance (for 4 choice questions), the effective penalty is not 2.5–3.5 points, but more like 0.5–0.8 points. It is sometimes thought advisable not to leave any answer blank so that you don't risk mismarking your answer sheet, even if you have to guess at an answer.

SHOULD YOU TAKE AN ADMINISTERED ACTUAL SAT FOR PRACTICE?

Yes, but only if you will learn from your mistakes by seeing what strategies you should have used on your exam. For a student to take the SAT merely for its own sake is a waste of time and may in fact reinforce bad methods and habits.

CAN YOU GET BACK THE SAT WITH YOUR ANSWERS AND THE CORRECT ONES AFTER YOU TAKE IT? HOW CAN YOU MAKE USE OF THIS SERVICE?

The SAT is disclosed (sent back to the student on request with a $10.00 payment) 4 of the 7 times it is given through the year. Very few people take advantage of this fact or use the disclosed SAT to see what mistakes they've made and what strategies they could have used on the questions.

This Question and Answer Service usually is available for SAT tests taken in the following dates:

May (Saturday & Sunday)	January (Saturday)
November (Saturday)	March (Saturday)

To receive an order form for test results write College Board, ATP, P.O. Box 6203, Princeton, New Jersey, 08541-6203.

HOW DO OTHER EXAMS COMPARE WITH THE SAT? CAN YOU USE THE STRATEGIES IN THIS BOOK?

Most other exams are modeled after the SAT, and so the strategies used here are definitely useful when taking them. For example, the GRE (Graduate Records Examination for entrance into graduate school) has questions which use the identical stretegies used on the SAT. The questions are just worded at a slightly higher level. The ACT (American College Testing Program), another college entrance exam, was changed in the Fall of 1989 to reflect strategies that are used on the SAT.

HOW DOES THE GRUBER PREPARATION METHOD DIFFER FROM OTHER PROGRAMS?

Many other SAT programs try to use "quick fix" methods or subscribe to rote memorization. So-called "quick fix" methods can be detrimental to effective preparation because the SAT people constantly change questions to prevent "gimmick" approaches. Rote memorization methods do not enable you to answer the variety of questions that appear in the SAT exam. In over twenty-five years of experience writing preparation books for the SAT, we have developed and honed the critical thinking skills and strategies that are based on all standardized test construction. So, while this method immediately improves your performance on the SAT, it also provides you with the confidence to tackle problems in all areas of study for the rest of your life.

II. Useful Steps for Using This Book

1) Learn the Five General Strategies for test-taking on page 67.
2) Take the Diagnostic SAT Pre-Test on page 1 and score yourself according to the instructions.
3) For those problems or questions which you answered incorrectly or were uncertain of, see the explanatory answers beginning on page 32, and make sure that you learn the strategies keyed to the questions, beginning on page 69.

FOR VOCABULARY BUILDING

4) Learn the special Latin and Greek prefixes, roots, and suffixes beginning on page 198. This will significantly build your vocabulary.
5) Study 100 words per day from the 3400 Word List. At least 70% of all SAT antonym questions on each recent SAT examination have been found on this list. That's 175 SAT points.
6) Take the Vocabulary Tests beginning on page 169.

FOR MATH AREA BASIC SKILLS HELP

7) For the basic math skills keyed to the questions, study the SAT Math Refresher section.

NOW

8) Take the remaining six practice SAT tests, score yourself, and go over your answers with the explanatory answers. Always refer to the associated strategies and basic skills for questions you answered incorrectly or were not sure how to do.

Format of a Recent Scholastic Aptitude Test

6 SECTIONS OF THE SAT*	NUMBER OF QUESTIONS	NUMBER OF MINUTES
SECTION 1: VERBAL ABILITY		
Antonyms	15 ⎫	
Analogies	10 ⎪ 45	30
Sentence Completions	10 ⎪	
Reading Comprehension	10 ⎭	
SECTION 2: MATH ABILITY		
Regular Math	25	30
SECTION 3: STANDARD WRITTEN ENGLISH ABILITY**		
Grammar and Usage	35 ⎫ 50	30
Sentence Correction	15 ⎭	
SECTION 4: VERBAL ABILITY		
Antonyms	10 ⎫	
Analogies	10 ⎪ 40	30
Sentence Completions	5 ⎪	
Reading Comprehension	15 ⎭	
SECTION 5: MATH ABILITY		
Regular Math	15 ⎫ 35	30
Quantitative Comparison	20 ⎭	
SECTION 6: MATH ABILITY***	25 or 35	
or		30
VERBAL ABILITY***	40 or 45	

TOTAL MINUTES = 180
(3 HOURS)

*The order of the sections on the actual test varies since the SAT has several different forms.

**The Standard Written English Test does *not* count toward your SAT scores. The purpose of the test is to help the college you attend choose a course that is appropriate for your ability.

***One of the six sections is experimental. If there are three Math sections or three Verbal sections in the test, then one of these three sections is experimental. An experimental section does *not* count in your SAT score. You cannot tell which of the six sections of the test is experimental.

1

DIAGNOSTIC SAT PRE-TEST

Don't Waste Any Time! Take This SAT Pre-Test Before You Do Anything Else!

This SAT Pre-Test is very much like the actual SAT. It follows the genuine SAT very closely. Taking this Diagnostic Pre-Test is like taking the actual SAT. Following is the purpose of taking this Pre-Test:

1) to find out what you are *weak* in and what you are *strong* in
2) to know where to concentrate your efforts in order to be fully prepared for the actual test.

Taking this Pre-Test will prove to be a very valuable TIME SAVER for you. Why waste time studying what you already know? Spend your time profitably by studying what you *don't* know. That is what this Pre-Test will tell you.

In this book, we do not waste precious pages. We get right down to the business of helping you to increase your SAT scores.

Other SAT preparation books place their emphasis on drill—drill—drill. We do not believe that drill work is of primary importance in preparing for the SAT exam. Drill has its place. In fact, this book contains a great variety of drill material—2500 SAT-type multiple-choice questions (Verbal and Math), practically all of which have explanatory answers. But drill work must be coordinated with learning Critical Thinking Skills. These skills will help you to think clearly and critically so that you will be able to answer many more SAT questions correctly.

After you finish the Pre-Test, you will come to Part 2 of this book—"Using Critical Thinking Skills to Score High on the SAT," beginning on page 67.

Ready? Start taking the Pre-Test. It's just like the real thing.

Answer Sheet—Practice Test 1
(Diagnostic SAT Pre-Test)

SECTION 1: VERBAL ABILITY

1 Ⓐ Ⓑ Ⓒ Ⓓ Ⓔ   10 Ⓐ Ⓑ Ⓒ Ⓓ Ⓔ   19 Ⓐ Ⓑ Ⓒ Ⓓ Ⓔ   28 Ⓐ Ⓑ Ⓒ Ⓓ Ⓔ   37 Ⓐ Ⓑ Ⓒ Ⓓ Ⓔ
2 Ⓐ Ⓑ Ⓒ Ⓓ Ⓔ   11 Ⓐ Ⓑ Ⓒ Ⓓ Ⓔ   20 Ⓐ Ⓑ Ⓒ Ⓓ Ⓔ   29 Ⓐ Ⓑ Ⓒ Ⓓ Ⓔ   38 Ⓐ Ⓑ Ⓒ Ⓓ Ⓔ
3 Ⓐ Ⓑ Ⓒ Ⓓ Ⓔ   12 Ⓐ Ⓑ Ⓒ Ⓓ Ⓔ   21 Ⓐ Ⓑ Ⓒ Ⓓ Ⓔ   30 Ⓐ Ⓑ Ⓒ Ⓓ Ⓔ   39 Ⓐ Ⓑ Ⓒ Ⓓ Ⓔ
4 Ⓐ Ⓑ Ⓒ Ⓓ Ⓔ   13 Ⓐ Ⓑ Ⓒ Ⓓ Ⓔ   22 Ⓐ Ⓑ Ⓒ Ⓓ Ⓔ   31 Ⓐ Ⓑ Ⓒ Ⓓ Ⓔ   40 Ⓐ Ⓑ Ⓒ Ⓓ Ⓔ
5 Ⓐ Ⓑ Ⓒ Ⓓ Ⓔ   14 Ⓐ Ⓑ Ⓒ Ⓓ Ⓔ   23 Ⓐ Ⓑ Ⓒ Ⓓ Ⓔ   32 Ⓐ Ⓑ Ⓒ Ⓓ Ⓔ   41 Ⓐ Ⓑ Ⓒ Ⓓ Ⓔ
6 Ⓐ Ⓑ Ⓒ Ⓓ Ⓔ   15 Ⓐ Ⓑ Ⓒ Ⓓ Ⓔ   24 Ⓐ Ⓑ Ⓒ Ⓓ Ⓔ   33 Ⓐ Ⓑ Ⓒ Ⓓ Ⓔ   42 Ⓐ Ⓑ Ⓒ Ⓓ Ⓔ
7 Ⓐ Ⓑ Ⓒ Ⓓ Ⓔ   16 Ⓐ Ⓑ Ⓒ Ⓓ Ⓔ   25 Ⓐ Ⓑ Ⓒ Ⓓ Ⓔ   34 Ⓐ Ⓑ Ⓒ Ⓓ Ⓔ   43 Ⓐ Ⓑ Ⓒ Ⓓ Ⓔ
8 Ⓐ Ⓑ Ⓒ Ⓓ Ⓔ   17 Ⓐ Ⓑ Ⓒ Ⓓ Ⓔ   26 Ⓐ Ⓑ Ⓒ Ⓓ Ⓔ   35 Ⓐ Ⓑ Ⓒ Ⓓ Ⓔ   44 Ⓐ Ⓑ Ⓒ Ⓓ Ⓔ
9 Ⓐ Ⓑ Ⓒ Ⓓ Ⓔ   18 Ⓐ Ⓑ Ⓒ Ⓓ Ⓔ   27 Ⓐ Ⓑ Ⓒ Ⓓ Ⓔ   36 Ⓐ Ⓑ Ⓒ Ⓓ Ⓔ   45 Ⓐ Ⓑ Ⓒ Ⓓ Ⓔ

SECTION 2: MATH ABILITY

1 Ⓐ Ⓑ Ⓒ Ⓓ Ⓔ   6 Ⓐ Ⓑ Ⓒ Ⓓ Ⓔ   11 Ⓐ Ⓑ Ⓒ Ⓓ Ⓔ   16 Ⓐ Ⓑ Ⓒ Ⓓ Ⓔ   21 Ⓐ Ⓑ Ⓒ Ⓓ Ⓔ
2 Ⓐ Ⓑ Ⓒ Ⓓ Ⓔ   7 Ⓐ Ⓑ Ⓒ Ⓓ Ⓔ   12 Ⓐ Ⓑ Ⓒ Ⓓ Ⓔ   17 Ⓐ Ⓑ Ⓒ Ⓓ Ⓔ   22 Ⓐ Ⓑ Ⓒ Ⓓ Ⓔ
3 Ⓐ Ⓑ Ⓒ Ⓓ Ⓔ   8 Ⓐ Ⓑ Ⓒ Ⓓ Ⓔ   13 Ⓐ Ⓑ Ⓒ Ⓓ Ⓔ   18 Ⓐ Ⓑ Ⓒ Ⓓ Ⓔ   23 Ⓐ Ⓑ Ⓒ Ⓓ Ⓔ
4 Ⓐ Ⓑ Ⓒ Ⓓ Ⓔ   9 Ⓐ Ⓑ Ⓒ Ⓓ Ⓔ   14 Ⓐ Ⓑ Ⓒ Ⓓ Ⓔ   19 Ⓐ Ⓑ Ⓒ Ⓓ Ⓔ   24 Ⓐ Ⓑ Ⓒ Ⓓ Ⓔ
5 Ⓐ Ⓑ Ⓒ Ⓓ Ⓔ   10 Ⓐ Ⓑ Ⓒ Ⓓ Ⓔ   15 Ⓐ Ⓑ Ⓒ Ⓓ Ⓔ   20 Ⓐ Ⓑ Ⓒ Ⓓ Ⓔ   25 Ⓐ Ⓑ Ⓒ Ⓓ Ⓔ

SECTION 3: STANDARD WRITTEN ENGLISH

1 Ⓐ Ⓑ Ⓒ Ⓓ Ⓔ   11 Ⓐ Ⓑ Ⓒ Ⓓ Ⓔ   21 Ⓐ Ⓑ Ⓒ Ⓓ Ⓔ   31 Ⓐ Ⓑ Ⓒ Ⓓ Ⓔ   41 Ⓐ Ⓑ Ⓒ Ⓓ Ⓔ
2 Ⓐ Ⓑ Ⓒ Ⓓ Ⓔ   12 Ⓐ Ⓑ Ⓒ Ⓓ Ⓔ   22 Ⓐ Ⓑ Ⓒ Ⓓ Ⓔ   32 Ⓐ Ⓑ Ⓒ Ⓓ Ⓔ   42 Ⓐ Ⓑ Ⓒ Ⓓ Ⓔ
3 Ⓐ Ⓑ Ⓒ Ⓓ Ⓔ   13 Ⓐ Ⓑ Ⓒ Ⓓ Ⓔ   23 Ⓐ Ⓑ Ⓒ Ⓓ Ⓔ   33 Ⓐ Ⓑ Ⓒ Ⓓ Ⓔ   43 Ⓐ Ⓑ Ⓒ Ⓓ Ⓔ
4 Ⓐ Ⓑ Ⓒ Ⓓ Ⓔ   14 Ⓐ Ⓑ Ⓒ Ⓓ Ⓔ   24 Ⓐ Ⓑ Ⓒ Ⓓ Ⓔ   34 Ⓐ Ⓑ Ⓒ Ⓓ Ⓔ   44 Ⓐ Ⓑ Ⓒ Ⓓ Ⓔ
5 Ⓐ Ⓑ Ⓒ Ⓓ Ⓔ   15 Ⓐ Ⓑ Ⓒ Ⓓ Ⓔ   25 Ⓐ Ⓑ Ⓒ Ⓓ Ⓔ   35 Ⓐ Ⓑ Ⓒ Ⓓ Ⓔ   45 Ⓐ Ⓑ Ⓒ Ⓓ Ⓔ
6 Ⓐ Ⓑ Ⓒ Ⓓ Ⓔ   16 Ⓐ Ⓑ Ⓒ Ⓓ Ⓔ   26 Ⓐ Ⓑ Ⓒ Ⓓ Ⓔ   36 Ⓐ Ⓑ Ⓒ Ⓓ Ⓔ   46 Ⓐ Ⓑ Ⓒ Ⓓ Ⓔ
7 Ⓐ Ⓑ Ⓒ Ⓓ Ⓔ   17 Ⓐ Ⓑ Ⓒ Ⓓ Ⓔ   27 Ⓐ Ⓑ Ⓒ Ⓓ Ⓔ   37 Ⓐ Ⓑ Ⓒ Ⓓ Ⓔ   47 Ⓐ Ⓑ Ⓒ Ⓓ Ⓔ
8 Ⓐ Ⓑ Ⓒ Ⓓ Ⓔ   18 Ⓐ Ⓑ Ⓒ Ⓓ Ⓔ   28 Ⓐ Ⓑ Ⓒ Ⓓ Ⓔ   38 Ⓐ Ⓑ Ⓒ Ⓓ Ⓔ   48 Ⓐ Ⓑ Ⓒ Ⓓ Ⓔ
9 Ⓐ Ⓑ Ⓒ Ⓓ Ⓔ   19 Ⓐ Ⓑ Ⓒ Ⓓ Ⓔ   29 Ⓐ Ⓑ Ⓒ Ⓓ Ⓔ   39 Ⓐ Ⓑ Ⓒ Ⓓ Ⓔ   49 Ⓐ Ⓑ Ⓒ Ⓓ Ⓔ
10 Ⓐ Ⓑ Ⓒ Ⓓ Ⓔ   20 Ⓐ Ⓑ Ⓒ Ⓓ Ⓔ   30 Ⓐ Ⓑ Ⓒ Ⓓ Ⓔ   40 Ⓐ Ⓑ Ⓒ Ⓓ Ⓔ   50 Ⓐ Ⓑ Ⓒ Ⓓ Ⓔ

SECTION 4: VERBAL ABILITY

1 Ⓐ Ⓑ Ⓒ Ⓓ Ⓔ   9 Ⓐ Ⓑ Ⓒ Ⓓ Ⓔ   17 Ⓐ Ⓑ Ⓒ Ⓓ Ⓔ   25 Ⓐ Ⓑ Ⓒ Ⓓ Ⓔ   33 Ⓐ Ⓑ Ⓒ Ⓓ Ⓔ
2 Ⓐ Ⓑ Ⓒ Ⓓ Ⓔ   10 Ⓐ Ⓑ Ⓒ Ⓓ Ⓔ   18 Ⓐ Ⓑ Ⓒ Ⓓ Ⓔ   26 Ⓐ Ⓑ Ⓒ Ⓓ Ⓔ   34 Ⓐ Ⓑ Ⓒ Ⓓ Ⓔ
3 Ⓐ Ⓑ Ⓒ Ⓓ Ⓔ   11 Ⓐ Ⓑ Ⓒ Ⓓ Ⓔ   19 Ⓐ Ⓑ Ⓒ Ⓓ Ⓔ   27 Ⓐ Ⓑ Ⓒ Ⓓ Ⓔ   35 Ⓐ Ⓑ Ⓒ Ⓓ Ⓔ
4 Ⓐ Ⓑ Ⓒ Ⓓ Ⓔ   12 Ⓐ Ⓑ Ⓒ Ⓓ Ⓔ   20 Ⓐ Ⓑ Ⓒ Ⓓ Ⓔ   28 Ⓐ Ⓑ Ⓒ Ⓓ Ⓔ   36 Ⓐ Ⓑ Ⓒ Ⓓ Ⓔ
5 Ⓐ Ⓑ Ⓒ Ⓓ Ⓔ   13 Ⓐ Ⓑ Ⓒ Ⓓ Ⓔ   21 Ⓐ Ⓑ Ⓒ Ⓓ Ⓔ   29 Ⓐ Ⓑ Ⓒ Ⓓ Ⓔ   37 Ⓐ Ⓑ Ⓒ Ⓓ Ⓔ
6 Ⓐ Ⓑ Ⓒ Ⓓ Ⓔ   14 Ⓐ Ⓑ Ⓒ Ⓓ Ⓔ   22 Ⓐ Ⓑ Ⓒ Ⓓ Ⓔ   30 Ⓐ Ⓑ Ⓒ Ⓓ Ⓔ   38 Ⓐ Ⓑ Ⓒ Ⓓ Ⓔ
7 Ⓐ Ⓑ Ⓒ Ⓓ Ⓔ   15 Ⓐ Ⓑ Ⓒ Ⓓ Ⓔ   23 Ⓐ Ⓑ Ⓒ Ⓓ Ⓔ   31 Ⓐ Ⓑ Ⓒ Ⓓ Ⓔ   39 Ⓐ Ⓑ Ⓒ Ⓓ Ⓔ
8 Ⓐ Ⓑ Ⓒ Ⓓ Ⓔ   16 Ⓐ Ⓑ Ⓒ Ⓓ Ⓔ   24 Ⓐ Ⓑ Ⓒ Ⓓ Ⓔ   32 Ⓐ Ⓑ Ⓒ Ⓓ Ⓔ   40 Ⓐ Ⓑ Ⓒ Ⓓ Ⓔ

SECTION 5: MATH ABILITY

1 Ⓐ Ⓑ Ⓒ Ⓓ Ⓔ   8 Ⓐ Ⓑ Ⓒ Ⓓ Ⓔ   15 Ⓐ Ⓑ Ⓒ Ⓓ Ⓔ   22 Ⓐ Ⓑ Ⓒ Ⓓ Ⓔ   29 Ⓐ Ⓑ Ⓒ Ⓓ Ⓔ
2 Ⓐ Ⓑ Ⓒ Ⓓ Ⓔ   9 Ⓐ Ⓑ Ⓒ Ⓓ Ⓔ   16 Ⓐ Ⓑ Ⓒ Ⓓ Ⓔ   23 Ⓐ Ⓑ Ⓒ Ⓓ Ⓔ   30 Ⓐ Ⓑ Ⓒ Ⓓ Ⓔ
3 Ⓐ Ⓑ Ⓒ Ⓓ Ⓔ   10 Ⓐ Ⓑ Ⓒ Ⓓ Ⓔ   17 Ⓐ Ⓑ Ⓒ Ⓓ Ⓔ   24 Ⓐ Ⓑ Ⓒ Ⓓ Ⓔ   31 Ⓐ Ⓑ Ⓒ Ⓓ Ⓔ
4 Ⓐ Ⓑ Ⓒ Ⓓ Ⓔ   11 Ⓐ Ⓑ Ⓒ Ⓓ Ⓔ   18 Ⓐ Ⓑ Ⓒ Ⓓ Ⓔ   25 Ⓐ Ⓑ Ⓒ Ⓓ Ⓔ   32 Ⓐ Ⓑ Ⓒ Ⓓ Ⓔ
5 Ⓐ Ⓑ Ⓒ Ⓓ Ⓔ   12 Ⓐ Ⓑ Ⓒ Ⓓ Ⓔ   19 Ⓐ Ⓑ Ⓒ Ⓓ Ⓔ   26 Ⓐ Ⓑ Ⓒ Ⓓ Ⓔ   33 Ⓐ Ⓑ Ⓒ Ⓓ Ⓔ
6 Ⓐ Ⓑ Ⓒ Ⓓ Ⓔ   13 Ⓐ Ⓑ Ⓒ Ⓓ Ⓔ   20 Ⓐ Ⓑ Ⓒ Ⓓ Ⓔ   27 Ⓐ Ⓑ Ⓒ Ⓓ Ⓔ   34 Ⓐ Ⓑ Ⓒ Ⓓ Ⓔ
7 Ⓐ Ⓑ Ⓒ Ⓓ Ⓔ   14 Ⓐ Ⓑ Ⓒ Ⓓ Ⓔ   21 Ⓐ Ⓑ Ⓒ Ⓓ Ⓔ   28 Ⓐ Ⓑ Ⓒ Ⓓ Ⓔ   35 Ⓐ Ⓑ Ⓒ Ⓓ Ⓔ

SECTION 6: MATH ABILITY

1 Ⓐ Ⓑ Ⓒ Ⓓ Ⓔ   6 Ⓐ Ⓑ Ⓒ Ⓓ Ⓔ   11 Ⓐ Ⓑ Ⓒ Ⓓ Ⓔ   16 Ⓐ Ⓑ Ⓒ Ⓓ Ⓔ   21 Ⓐ Ⓑ Ⓒ Ⓓ Ⓔ
2 Ⓐ Ⓑ Ⓒ Ⓓ Ⓔ   7 Ⓐ Ⓑ Ⓒ Ⓓ Ⓔ   12 Ⓐ Ⓑ Ⓒ Ⓓ Ⓔ   17 Ⓐ Ⓑ Ⓒ Ⓓ Ⓔ   22 Ⓐ Ⓑ Ⓒ Ⓓ Ⓔ
3 Ⓐ Ⓑ Ⓒ Ⓓ Ⓔ   8 Ⓐ Ⓑ Ⓒ Ⓓ Ⓔ   13 Ⓐ Ⓑ Ⓒ Ⓓ Ⓔ   18 Ⓐ Ⓑ Ⓒ Ⓓ Ⓔ   23 Ⓐ Ⓑ Ⓒ Ⓓ Ⓔ
4 Ⓐ Ⓑ Ⓒ Ⓓ Ⓔ   9 Ⓐ Ⓑ Ⓒ Ⓓ Ⓔ   14 Ⓐ Ⓑ Ⓒ Ⓓ Ⓔ   19 Ⓐ Ⓑ Ⓒ Ⓓ Ⓔ   24 Ⓐ Ⓑ Ⓒ Ⓓ Ⓔ
5 Ⓐ Ⓑ Ⓒ Ⓓ Ⓔ   10 Ⓐ Ⓑ Ⓒ Ⓓ Ⓔ   15 Ⓐ Ⓑ Ⓒ Ⓓ Ⓔ   20 Ⓐ Ⓑ Ⓒ Ⓓ Ⓔ   25 Ⓐ Ⓑ Ⓒ Ⓓ Ⓔ

SAT Practice Test 1
[Full-Length Diagnostic Pre-Test]

SECTION 1   VERBAL ABILITY
30 MINUTES   45 QUESTIONS

For each question in this section, choose the best answer and blacken the corresponding space on the answer sheet.

Each question below consists of a word in capital letters, followed by five lettered words or phrases. Choose the word or phrase that is most nearly *opposite* in meaning to the word in capital letters. Since some of the questions require you to distinguish fine shades of meaning, consider all the choices before deciding which is best.

Example:

GOOD: (A) sour   (B) bad   (C) red
(D) hot   (E) ugly

Ⓐ ● Ⓒ Ⓓ Ⓔ

1. BENEVOLENT: (A) opposing   (B) observant
(C) superficial   (D) miserly   (E) sociable

2. TRITE: (A) vague   (B) unique   (C) proper
(D) temporary   (E) urgent

3. DISSENSION: (A) feeling   (B) concealment
(C) stretching   (D) confusion   (E) harmony

4. REPRISAL: (A) approval   (B) survival
(C) assistance   (D) inactivity   (E) tolerance

5. VINDICATE: (A) simplify   (B) vanquish
(C) anger   (D) satisfy   (E) accuse

6. LIVID: (A) effective   (B) modern
(C) fantastic   (D) inhumane   (E) glowing

7. BOORISH: (A) modest   (B) needless
(C) quiet   (D) civilized   (E) experienced

8. CONSOLIDATION: (A) liquid   (B) reform
(C) division   (D) discrimination
(E) disappearance

9. INCLEMENT: (A) unwilling   (B) misty
(C) impure   (D) occupied   (E) mild

10. BERATE: (A) guide   (B) praise   (C) irritate
(D) underrate   (E) explain

11. PROFICIENCY: (A) mistreatment   (B) success
(C) disadvantage   (D) incompetence
(E) generosity

12. DEARTH: (A) urgency   (B) familiarity
(C) cleanliness   (D) boldness   (E) abundance

13. GHASTLY: (A) pleasant   (B) useful
(C) informed   (D) lavish   (E) ghostly

14. EXUDE: (A) urge   (B) depart   (C) block
(D) applaud   (E) encounter

15. GARISH: (A) simple   (B) tolerant
(C) rewarding   (D) favorable
(E) harmonious

Each sentence below has one or two blanks, each blank indicating that something has been omitted. Beneath the sentence are five lettered words or sets of words. Choose the word or set of words that *best* fits the meaning of the sentence as a whole.

Example:

Although its publicity has been _____, the film itself is intelligent, well-acted, handsomely produced, and altogether _____.

(A) tasteless . . . respectable
(B) extensive . . . moderate
(C) sophisticated . . . amateur
(D) risqué . . . crude
(E) perfect . . . spectacular

● Ⓑ Ⓒ Ⓓ Ⓔ

16. The fact that many professional athletes are getting million-dollar contracts while college professors are averaging $30,000 a year seemed to him _____ and unjust.

(A) economic   (B) ironic   (C) factual
(D) equitable   (E) fascinating

17. Because the majority of the evening cable TV programs available dealt with violence and sex, the parents decided that the programs were _____ for the children to watch.

(A) exclusive   (B) acceptable
(C) instructive   (D) inappropriate
(E) unnecessary

18. The novel *Uncle Tom's Cabin*, which effectively _____ the unfairness toward Black people, was a major influence in _____ the anti-slavery movement.

(A) portrayed . . . strengthening
(B) attacked . . . pacifying
(C) glamorized . . . launching
(D) viewed . . . appraising
(E) exposed . . . condemning

19. Having written 140 books to date, he may well be considered one of the most _____ novelists of the century.

(A) eccentric   (B) controversial
(C) easygoing   (D) unheralded
(E) prolific

20. The articles that he wrote ran the gamut from the serious to the lighthearted, from objective to the _____, from the innocuous to the _____.

(A) constant . . . evil
(B) casual . . . realistic
(C) ridiculous . . . remote
(D) argumentative . . . hostile
(E) incapacitated . . . conditioned

Each passage below is followed by questions based on its content. Answer all questions following a passage on the basis of what is *stated* or *implied* in that passage.

The snow falls gently on our quiet meadow sloping down to Penobscot Bay, with spruce trees back against the gray of the water. A raven croaks from a nearby treetop. Two gulls sail over the house and squawk
5 unintelligibly together. The only other sounds are the wood fire snapping, the kettle steaming on the stove and Pusso purring.

There is no phone to ring, no radio to turn on, no television to watch. We need don no city disguise and
10 ride subways, catch trains, attend cocktail parties or dinners. We can choose and make our own music, reread our favorite books, wear our old clothes, eat when and what we like from a well-stocked root cellar, or happily abstain from food, if we wish, the whole day.
15 There is wood to cut, snow to shovel, mail to answer, but all in our own good time. No one is pushing, no one shoving, no one ordering about. There is no job to lose; we make our own jobs. Free men? Almost.

A neighbor may amble in on snowshoes and bring us
20 word of his horse's health or wife's pregnancy. Over a glass of cider we may talk of snowmobile incursions or hunters' depredations. He may bring us a huge cabbage he has grown and we send him back with a bottle of our rosehips juice and a knitted doll for his little
25 daughter. In our chat beside the fire we will probably not touch on the outside world, though we are not unaware of what stirs the nation.

The newspaper, reaching us by mail, brings us echoes of an inconsequential election between two
30 shadow-boxing candidates for an office no one should covet. We read that two high officials, the Episcopal Bishop of New York and the chief of the Soviet delegation to the United Nations, have separately been held up in daylight and robbed by armed men in Central
35 Park. We learn that invaders are entering classrooms in Manhattan's public schools and at knife or gunpoint relieving teachers of their cash and trinkets before their open-mouthed pupils.

We thank our lucky stars that we live out in the wilderness, that we are not on congested streets and 40 highways or clustered in high-rise city rookeries, with jangling noise and turmoil all about, that we are not in smog, that we can drink clean clear water, not fluoridized or chlorinated, from our bubbling spring, that our homegrown food is not stale, preserved or 45 embalmed and bought from the supermarket.

We are thankful for what the wilderness makes possible. Peace, progress, prosperity? We prefer peace, quiet, and frugality.

21. The general feeling running through the passage is one of

(A) guarded resentment
(B) tolerable boredom
(C) restless indecision
(D) peaceful satisfaction
(E) marked indifference

22. Which of the following is the most appropriate title for the passage?

(A) Winter in the Country
(B) The Frills Aren't Needed
(C) Peace, Progress, and Prosperity
(D) Life Goes On
(E) A Lack of Conveniences

23. The author's reference to "an inconsequential election between two shadow-boxing candidates" (lines 29–30) indicates that the author

(A) has no faith in politicians
(B) is opposed to professional prizefighting
(C) does not believe in having any elections
(D) prefers that people should govern themselves
(E) is of the opinion that all elections are fixed

24. The author states or implies that

(A) there is no work to be done
(B) he is a completely free man
(C) his wife is pregnant
(D) he reads no newspapers
(E) he has a farm

25. The location of the author's home is likely in the state of

(A) Nevada   (B) Florida   (C) Maine
(D) Louisiana   (E) Georgia

The discoveries made by scientific geniuses, from Archimedes through Einstein, have repeatedly revolutionized both our world and the way we see it. Yet no one really knows how the mind of a genius works. Most
5 people think that a very high IQ sets the great scientist apart. They assume that flashes of profound insight like Einstein's are the product of mental processes, so arcane, that they must be inaccessible to more ordinary minds.
10 But a growing number of researchers in psychology, psychiatry, and the history of science are investigating the way geniuses think. The researchers are beginning to give us tantalizing glimpses of the mental universe that can produce the discoveries of an Einstein, an
15 Edison, a DaVinci—or a Nobel prizewinner.
Surprisingly, most researchers agree that the important variable in genius is not the IQ but creativity. Testers start with 135 as the beginning of the "genius" category, but the researchers seem to feel that, while
20 an IQ above a certain point—about 120—is very helpful for a scientist, having an IQ that goes much higher is not crucial for producing a work of genius. All human beings have at least four types of intelligence. The great scientist possesses the ability to move back and
25 forth among them—the logical-mathematical, the spatial which includes visual perception, the linguistic, and the bodily-kinesthetic.
Some corroboration of these categories comes from the reports of scientists who describe thought processes
30 centered around images, sensations, or words. Einstein reported a special "feeling at the tips of the fingers" that told him which path to take through a problem. The idea for a self-starting electric motor came to Nikola Tesla one evening as he was reciting a
35 poem by Goethe and watching a sunset. Suddenly he imagined a magnetic field rapidly rotating inside a circle of electro-magnets.
The IQ test predicts fairly accurately how well a person will do in school and how quickly he will master
40 knowledge, but genius involves more than knowledge. The genius has the capacity to leap significantly beyond his present knowledge and produces something new. To do this, he sees the relationship between facts or pieces of information in a new or unusual way.
45 The scientist solves a problem by shifting from one intelligence to another, although the logical-mathematical intelligence is dominant. Creative individuals seem to be marked by a special fluidity of mind.

They may be able to think of a problem verbally, logically, and also spatially.
50 Paradoxically, fluid thinking may be connected to another generally agreed upon trait of the scientific genius—persistence, or unusually strong motivation to work on a problem. Persistence kept Einstein looking for the solution to the question of the relationship
55 between the law of gravity and his special theory of relativity. Yet surely creative fluidity enabled him to come up with a whole new field that included both special relativity and gravitation.
Many scientists have the ability to stick with a prob-
60 lem even when they appear not to be working on it. Werner Heisenberg discovered quantum mechanics one night during a vacation he had taken to recuperate from the mental jumble he had fallen into trying to solve the atomic-spectra problem.
65

26. Which statement is true, according to the passage?

(A) The law of gravity followed the publication of Einstein's theory of relativity.
(B) Nikola Tesla learned about magnets from his research of the works of Goethe.
(C) Archimedes and Einstein lived in the same century.
(D) Most scientists have IQ scores above 120.
(E) We ought to refer to intelligences rather than intelligence.

27. The author believes that, among the four intelligences he cites, the most important one is

(A) spatial   (B) bodily-kinesthetic
(C) linguistic   (D) logical-mathematical
(E) not singled out

28. The author focuses on the circumstances surrounding the work of great scientists in order to show that

(A) scientific geniuses are usually eccentric in their behavior
(B) the various types of intelligence have come into play during their work
(C) scientists often give the impression that they are relaxing when they are really working on a problem
(D) a scientist must be a happy man to do his best work
(E) great scientific discoveries are almost always accidental

29. The passage can best be described as

    (A) a comparison of how the average individual and the great scientist think
    (B) an account of the unexpected things that led to great discoveries by scientists
    (C) an explanation of the way scientific geniuses really think
    (D) a criticism of intelligence tests as they are given today
    (E) a lesson clarifying scientific concepts such as quantum mechanics and relativity

30. The paragraph suggests that a college football star who is majoring in literature is quite likely to have which intelligences to a high degree?

    I. logical-mathematical
    II. spatial
    III. linguistic
    IV. bodily-kinesthetic

    (A) I only
    (B) II only
    (C) III only
    (D) I, II, and III only
    (E) II, III, and IV only

Select the word or set of words that best completes each of the following sentences.

31. Because auto repair places have such _____ rates, many community colleges have _____ courses in automotive mechanics.

    (A) shattering . . . planned
    (B) exorbitant . . . instituted
    (C) impertinent . . . discussed
    (D) reasonable . . . introduced
    (E) intolerable . . . discontinued

32. Though Socrates was _____ by his students who found truth in his teachings, his philosophy constituted _____ to the existent government.

    (A) accepted . . . a benefit
    (B) denied . . . an innovation
    (C) appraised . . . an exception
    (D) slighted . . . a challenge
    (E) revered . . . a threat

33. It is unthinkable for a prestigious conductor to agree to include _____ musicians in his orchestra.

    (A) capable   (B) seasoned   (C) mediocre
    (D) recommended   (E) professional

34. Mindful that his hardworking parents _____ to give him an education, Lopez, now wealthy, contributes _____ to scholarship funds for the needy.

    (A) planned . . . needlessly
    (B) skimped . . . profitably
    (C) squandered . . . sparingly
    (D) struggled . . . generously
    (E) regaled . . . regretfully

35. Being _____ person, he insisted at the conference that when he spoke he was not to be interrupted.

    (A) a successful   (B) a delightful
    (C) a headstrong   (D) an understanding
    (E) a solitary

Each question below consists of a related pair of words or phrases, followed by five lettered pairs of words or phrases. Select the lettered pair that *best* expresses a relationship similar to that expressed in the original pair.

Example:

> YAWN : BOREDOM :: (A) dream : sleep
> (B) anger : madness   (C) smile : amusement
> (D) face : expression   (E) impatience : rebellion
> Ⓐ Ⓑ ● Ⓓ Ⓔ

36. COLLAGE : ARTIST ::

    (A) opera : musician
    (B) novel : author
    (C) decision : umpire
    (D) interest : spectator
    (E) graduation : student

37. PARLEY : DISCUSS ::

    (A) restaurant : dine   (B) ballpark : cheer
    (C) motel : park   (D) school : discipline
    (E) park : walk

38. AGENDA : CONFERENCE ::

    (A) teacher : class   (B) agency : assignment
    (C) map : trip   (D) man : woman
    (E) executive : employee

39. EROSION : RAVINE ::

    (A) sand : pearl   (B) derrick : equipment
    (C) swelling : protrusion   (D) drilling : hole
    (E) mountain : peak

40. TURTLE : REPTILE ::

    (A) oak : tree   (B) leaf : branch
    (C) trout : fish   (D) snake : rattle
    (E) oyster : clam

41. PROFLIGATE : MORAL ::

(A) crook : fearful   (B) carpenter : patient
(C) lawyer : placid   (D) miser : generous
(E) profiteer : understanding

42. DISORGANIZED : SYSTEM ::

(A) greedy : money
(B) traitorous : loyalty
(C) athletic : intelligence
(D) conservative : party
(E) retired : hope

43. FRUSTRATE : DRIVE ::

(A) supervise : penalty   (B) guide : goal
(C) alert : warning   (D) reprimand : offense
(E) swindle : property

44. REBEL : CHANGE ::

(A) soldier : conflict   (B) gambler : profit
(C) coach : advice   (D) baby : attention
(E) architect : blueprint

45. INFERENCES : DISCERNING ::

(A) successes : enterprising
(B) insults : obnoxious
(C) agreements : competitive
(D) observations : social-minded
(E) warnings : suspicious

S T O P

IF YOU FINISH BEFORE TIME IS CALLED, YOU MAY CHECK YOUR WORK ON
THIS SECTION ONLY.
DO NOT WORK ON ANY OTHER SECTION IN THE TEST.

SECTION 2 MATH ABILITY
30 MINUTES 25 QUESTIONS

In this section solve each problem, using any available space on the page for scratchwork. Then decide which is the best of the choices given and blacken the corresponding space on the answer sheet.

The following information is for your reference in solving some of the problems.

Circle of radius r: Area $= \pi r^2$; Circumference $= 2\pi r$
The number of degrees of arc in a circle is 360.
The measure in degrees of a straight angle is 180.

Triangle: The sum of the measures in degrees of the angles of a triangle is 180.

If $\angle CDA$ is a right angle, then

(1) area of $\triangle ABC = \dfrac{AB \times CD}{2}$

(2) $AC^2 = AD^2 + DC^2$

Definitions of symbols:
= is equal to
≠ is unequal to
< is less than
> is greater than
≦ is less than or equal to
≧ is greater than or equal to
∥ is parallel to
⊥ is perpendicular to

Note: Figures which accompany problems in this test are intended to provide information useful in solving the problems. They are drawn as accurately as possible EXCEPT when it is stated in a specific problem that its figure is not drawn to scale. All figures lie in a plane unless otherwise indicated. All numbers used are real numbers.

Questions 1–2 refer to the following definition.

$$ⓍⓍ = \frac{x+1}{x-2}$$

for all positive numbers x, where $x \neq 2$.

1. If x is a positive number and $x \neq 2$, then which of the following is equal to $\dfrac{1}{3}\left(\dfrac{1}{Ⓧ}\right)$?

(A) $\dfrac{x-2}{x+4}$ (B) $\dfrac{x-2}{3(x+1)}$ (C) $\dfrac{3(x-2)}{x+1}$

(D) $\dfrac{x+1}{x-2}$ (E) $\dfrac{3(x+1)}{x-2}$

2. If $x = 7$, find $Ⓧ7$.

(A) $\dfrac{8}{5}$ (B) $\dfrac{8}{7}$ (C) 1 (D) $\dfrac{1}{2}$ (E) 0

3. If the sum of $2r$ and $2r + 3$ is less than 11, which of the following is a possible value of r?

(A) 11 (B) 10 (C) 3 (D) 2 (E) 1

4. At 8:00 a.m. the outside temperature was $-15°F$. At 11:00 a.m. the temperature was $0°F$. If the temperature continues to rise at the same uniform rate, what will the temperature be at 5:00 p.m. on the same day?

(A) $-15°F$ (B) $-5°F$ (C) $0°F$
(D) $15°F$ (E) $30°F$

5. Find the value of $x + x^3 + x^5 + x^6$ if $x = -1$.

(A) -4 (B) -2 (C) 1 (D) 2 (E) 4

6. There are some flags hanging in a horizontal row. Starting at one end of the row, the U.S. flag is 25th. Starting at the other end of the row, the U.S. flag is 13th. How many flags are in the row?

(A) 36 (B) 37 (C) 38 (D) 39 (E) 40

Questions 7–8 refer to the following definition.

Let $\boxed{n}\!\!>$ represent the greatest even integer less than n that divides n, for any positive integer n.

For example, $\boxed{24}\!\!> = 12$

7. $\boxed{20}\!\!> =$

(A) 2 (B) 4 (C) 5 (D) 10 (E) 20

8. Which of the following is not defined?

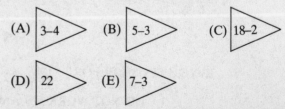

9. If $55,555 = y + 50,505$ find the value of $50,505 - 10y$.

 (A) -5.05　(B) 0　(C) 5
 (D) 5.05　(E) 50.5

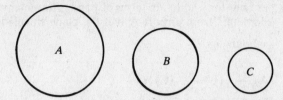

10. In the figure above, there are three circles, A, B, and C. The area of A is three times B and the area of B is three times C. If the area of B is 1, find the sum of the areas of A, B, and C.

 (A) 3　(B) $3\frac{1}{3}$　(C) $4\frac{1}{3}$　(D) 5　(E) $6\frac{1}{3}$

11. $\left[\left(3a^3b^2\right)^3\right]^2 =$

 (A) $27a^9b^6$　(B) $54a^9b^6$　(C) $729a^9b^6$
 (D) $729a^{18}b^{12}$　(E) $729a^{54}b^{16}$

Note: Figure is not drawn to scale.

12. In the figure above, two concentric circles with center P are shown. PQR, a radius of the larger circle, equals 9. PQ, a radius of the smaller circle, equals 4. If a circle L (not shown) is drawn with center at R and Q on its circumference. Find the radius of circle L.

 (A) 13　(B) 5　(C) 4　(D) 2
 (E) It cannot be determined from the information given.

13. Given that $\frac{a}{b}$ is less than 1, $a > 0$, $b > 0$. Which of the following must be greater than 1?

 (A) $\frac{a}{2b}$　(B) $\frac{b}{2a}$　(C) $\frac{\sqrt{b}}{a}$

 (D) $\frac{b}{a}$　(E) $\left(\frac{a}{b}\right)^2$

14. Given that $\left(\frac{3}{10}\right)^2$ is equal to p hundredths. Find the value of p.

 (A) 5　(B) 6　(C) 9　(D) 12　(E) 32

Note: Figure is not drawn to scale.

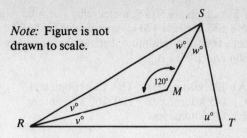

15. If $\angle RST = 80°$, find u.

 (A) 45　(B) 50　(C) 60　(D) 75　(E) 90

16. Find the circumference of a circle that has the same area as a square that has perimeter 2π.

 (A) $2\sqrt{2}$　(B) $\pi\sqrt{\pi}$　(C) $\frac{\pi}{2}$

 (D) $\frac{\sqrt{2}}{\pi}$　(E) 2

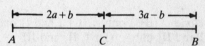

17. Given ACB is a straight line segment and C is the midpoint of AB. If the two segments have the lengths shown above, then

 (A) $a = -2b$　(B) $a = -\frac{2}{5}b$　(C) $a = \frac{2}{5}b$
 (D) $a = b$　(E) $a = 2b$

18. Bus A averages 40 kilometers per gallon of fuel. Bus B averages 50 kilometers per gallon of fuel. If the price of fuel is $3 per gallon, how much less would an 800 kilometer trip cost for Bus B than for Bus A?

 (A) $18　(B) $16　(C) $14　(D) $12
 (E) $10

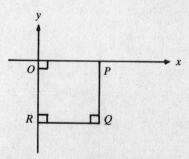

19. $OR = RQ$ in the figure above. If the coordinates of Q are $(5, m)$, find the value of m.

 (A) -5　(B) $-\sqrt{5}$　(C) 0
 (D) $\sqrt{5}$　(E) 5

20. If Masonville is 50 kilometers due north of Adamston and Elvira is 120 kilometers due east of Adamston, then the minimum distance between Masonville and Elvira is

(A) 125 kilometers   (B) 130 kilometers
(C) 145 kilometers   (D) 160 kilometers
(E) 170 kilometers

21. How many different pairs of parallel edges are there on a rectangular solid?

(A) 4   (B) 6   (C) 8   (D) 12   (E) 18

22. If $\frac{a}{b} = \frac{1}{4}$, where a is a positive integer, which of the following is a possible value of $\frac{a^2}{b}$?

I. $\frac{1}{4}$

II. $\frac{1}{2}$

III. 1

(A) None   (B) I only   (C) I and II only
(D) I and III only   (E) I, II, and III

23. Given $3x + y = 17$ and $x + 3y = -1$. Find the value of $3x + 3y$.

(A) 12   (B) 16   (C) 22   (D) 28   (E) 40

24. A plane left airport A and has traveled x kilometers per hour for y hours. In terms of x and y, how many kilometers from airport A had the plane traveled $\frac{2}{3}y$ hours ago?

(A) $\frac{xy}{6}$ (B) $\frac{xy}{3}$ (C) xy

(D) $\frac{3xy}{2}$ (E) $\frac{xy}{12}$

25. The average (arithmetic mean) of k scores is 20. The average of 10 of these scores is 15. Find the average of the remaining scores in terms of k.

(A) $\frac{20k + 150}{10}$ (B) $\frac{20k - 150}{10}$ (C) $\frac{150 - 20k}{10}$

(D) $\frac{150 - 20k}{k - 10}$ (E) $\frac{20k - 150}{k - 10}$

S T O P

IF YOU FINISH BEFORE TIME IS CALLED, YOU MAY CHECK YOUR WORK ON
THIS SECTION ONLY.
DO NOT WORK ON ANY OTHER SECTION IN THE TEST.

SECTION 3   STANDARD WRITTEN ENGLISH TEST

30 MINUTES   50 QUESTIONS

The questions in this section measure skills that are important to writing well. In particular, they test your ability to recognize and use language that is clear, effective, and correct according to the requirements of standard written English, the kind of English found in most college textbooks.

Directions: The following sentences contain problems in grammar, usage, diction (choice of words), and idiom.

Some sentences are correct.
No sentence contains more than one error.

You will find that the error, if there is one, is underlined and lettered. Assume that elements of the sentence that are not underlined are correct and cannot be changed. In choosing answers, follow the requirements of standard written English.

If there is an error, select the one underlined part that must be changed to make the sentence correct and blacken the corresponding space on your answer sheet.

If there is no error, blacken answer space Ⓔ.

EXAMPLE: SAMPLE ANSWER

The region has a climate so severe that plants   Ⓐ Ⓑ ● Ⓓ Ⓔ
                        A
growing there rarely had been more than twelve
     B   C
inches high. No error
       D   E

---

1. Even before he became the youngest player to win
        A
the Wimbledon men's singles championship,
                        B
Boris Becker had sensed that his life would
                    C
no longer be the same. No error
        D   E

2. If any signer of the Constitution was to return to life
                              A
for a day, his opinion of our amendments would be
     B   C   D
interesting. No error
              E

3. The dean of the college, together with some other
                    A   B
faculty members, are planning a conference for
                    C
the purpose of laying down certain regulations.
                    D
No error.
     E

4. If one lives in Florida one day and in Iceland the
              A   B
next, he is certain to feel the change in temperature.
        C   D
No error.
     E

5. Now that the stress of examinations and interviews
        A
are over, we can all relax for awhile. No error.
   B   C   D   E

6. The industrial trend is in the direction of more
                    A   B   C
machines and less people. No error.
              D   E

7. The American standard of living is still higher
                                    A   B
than most of the other countries of the world.
   C   D
No error.
     E

8. At last, late in the afternoon, a long line of flags and
        A   B
colored umbrellas were seen moving toward the
                    C   D
gate of the palace. No error.
                    E

9. Due to the failure of the air-cooling system, many in
   A
the audience had left the meeting before the prin-
              B   C
cipal speaker arrived. No error.
                    D   E

10. Psychologists and psychiatrists will tell us that it is of
    $\overline{\text{A}}$
    utmost importance that a disturbed child receive
    $\overline{\text{B}}$ $\overline{\text{C}}$
    professional attention as soon as possible. No error.
    $\overline{\text{D}}$ $\overline{\text{E}}$

11. After waiting in line for three hours, much to our
    $\overline{\text{A}}$ $\overline{\text{B}}$ $\overline{\text{C}}$
    disgust, the tickets had been sold out when we
    $\overline{\text{C}}$ $\overline{\text{D}}$
    reached the window. No error.
                     $\overline{\text{E}}$

12. That angry outburst of Father's last night was so
    $\overline{\text{A}}$
    annoying that it resulted in our guests packing up
    $\overline{\text{B}}$ $\overline{\text{C}}$
    and leaving this morning. No error.
    $\overline{\text{D}}$ $\overline{\text{E}}$

13. Sharp advances last week in the wholesale price of
    $\overline{\text{A}}$
    beef is a strong indication of higher meat costs to
    $\overline{\text{B}}$ $\overline{\text{C}}$
    come, but so far retail prices continue favorable.
                                        $\overline{\text{D}}$
    No error.
    $\overline{\text{E}}$

14. An acquaintance with the memoirs of Elizabeth
    Barrett Browning and Robert Browning enable us
                                     $\overline{\text{A}}$
    to appreciate the depth of influence that two people
                     $\overline{\text{B}}$
    of talent can have on each other. No error.
                     $\overline{\text{C}}$ $\overline{\text{D}}$ $\overline{\text{E}}$

15. The supervisor was advised to give the assignment
                     $\overline{\text{A}}$
    to whomever he believed had a strong sense of
    $\overline{\text{B}}$ $\overline{\text{C}}$
    responsibility, and the courage of his conviction.
                                   $\overline{\text{D}}$
    No error.
    $\overline{\text{E}}$

16. If he would have lain quietly as instructed by the
       $\overline{\text{A}}$ $\overline{\text{B}}$
    doctor, he might not have had a second heart attack.
              $\overline{\text{C}}$ $\overline{\text{D}}$
    No error.
    $\overline{\text{E}}$

17. The founder and, for many years, the guiding spirit
                     $\overline{\text{A}}$ $\overline{\text{B}}$
    of the "Kenyon Review" is John Crowe Ransom,
    who you must know as an outstanding American
    $\overline{\text{C}}$ $\overline{\text{D}}$
    critic. No error.
           $\overline{\text{E}}$

18. Though you may not agree with the philosophy of
    $\overline{\text{A}}$ $\overline{\text{B}}$
    Malcolm X, you must admit that he had tremendous
                                   $\overline{\text{C}}$
    influence over a great many followers. No error.
             $\overline{\text{D}}$ $\overline{\text{E}}$

19. There is no objection to him joining the party
                             $\overline{\text{A}}$
    provided he is willing to fit in with the plans of the
    $\overline{\text{B}}$ $\overline{\text{C}}$
    group and is ready and able to do his share of the
                     $\overline{\text{D}}$
    work. No error.
          $\overline{\text{E}}$

20. Ceremonies were opened by a drum and bugle
    $\overline{\text{A}}$ $\overline{\text{B}}$
    corps of Chinese children parading up Mott Street
                                        $\overline{\text{C}}$
    in colorful uniforms. No error.
    $\overline{\text{D}}$ $\overline{\text{E}}$

21. The reason most Americans don't pay much atten-
                     $\overline{\text{A}}$ $\overline{\text{B}}$
    tion to rising African nationalism is because they
           $\overline{\text{C}}$ $\overline{\text{D}}$
    really do not know modern Africa. No error.
                                        $\overline{\text{E}}$

22. There remains many reasons for the animosity that
             $\overline{\text{A}}$ $\overline{\text{B}}$
    exists between the Arab countries and Israel.
    $\overline{\text{C}}$ $\overline{\text{D}}$
    No error.
    $\overline{\text{E}}$

23. The Federal Aviation Administration ordered an
                                        $\overline{\text{A}}$
    emergency inspection of several Pan American
                             $\overline{\text{B}}$
    planes on account of a Pan American Boeing 707
    $\overline{\text{C}}$
    had crashed on Bali, in Indonesia. No error.
    $\overline{\text{D}}$ $\overline{\text{E}}$

24. A gang of armed thieves, directed by a young
             $\overline{\text{A}}$
    woman, has raided the mansion of a gold-mining
             $\overline{\text{B}}$ $\overline{\text{C}}$
    millionaire near Dublin late last night.
                             $\overline{\text{D}}$
    No error.
    $\overline{\text{E}}$

25. I had a male chauvinist pig dream that the women
    $\overline{\text{A}}$ $\overline{\text{B}}$
    of the world rose up and denounced the women's
                     $\overline{\text{C}}$ $\overline{\text{D}}$
    liberation movement. No error.
                        $\overline{\text{E}}$

Directions: In each of the following sentences, some part or all of the sentence is underlined. Below each sentence you will find five ways of phrasing the underlined part. Select the answer that produces the most effective sentence, one that is clear and exact, without awkwardness or ambiguity, and blacken the corresponding space on your answer sheet. In choosing answers, follow the requirements of standard written English. Choose the answer that best expresses the meaning of the original sentence.

Answer (A) is always the same as the underlined part. Choose answer (A) if you think that the original sentence needs no revision.

EXAMPLE:

SAMPLE ANSWER

Laura Ingalls Wilder published her first book and she was sixty-five years old then.
(A) and she was sixty-five years old then
(B) when she was sixty-five years old
(C) at age sixty-five years old
(D) upon reaching sixty-five years
(E) at the time when she was sixty-five

---

26. Such of his novels as was humorous were successful.

   (A) Such of his novels as was humorous were successful.
   (B) Such of his novels as were humorous were successful.
   (C) His novels such as were humorous were successful.
   (D) His novels were successful and humorous.
   (E) Novels such as his humorous ones were successful.

27. Being that the plane was grounded, we stayed over till the next morning so that we could get the first flight out.

   (A) Being that the plane was grounded, we stayed over
   (B) In view of the fact that the plane was grounded, we stayed over
   (C) Since the plane was grounded, we stayed over
   (D) Because the plane was grounded, we stood over
   (E) On account of the plane being grounded, we stayed over

28. He never has and he never will keep his word

   (A) He never has and he never will
   (B) He has never yet and never will
   (C) He has not ever and he will not
   (D) He never has or will
   (E) He never has kept and he never will

29. The teacher felt badly because she had scolded the bright child who was restless for want of something to do.

   (A) felt badly because she had scolded the bright child
   (B) felt badly why she had scolded the bright child
   (C) felt bad because she had scolded the bright child
   (D) felt bad by scolding the bright child
   (E) had felt badly because she scolded the bright child

30. This book does not describe the struggle of the Blacks to win their voting rights that I bought.

   (A) does not describe the struggle of the Blacks to win their voting rights that I bought
   (B) does not describe the Black struggle to win their voting rights that I bought
   (C) does not, although I bought it, describe the struggle of the Blacks to win their voting rights
   (D) which I bought does not describe the struggle to win for Blacks their voting rights
   (E) that I bought does not describe the struggle of the Blacks to win their voting rights

31. Barbara cannot help but think that she will win a college scholarship.

   (A) Barbara cannot help but think
   (B) Barbara cannot help but to think
   (C) Barbara cannot help not to think
   (D) Barbara can help but think
   (E) Barbara cannot but help thinking

32. In spite of Tom wanting to study, his sister made him wash the dishes.

    (A) Tom wanting to study
    (B) the fact that Tom wanted to study
    (C) Tom's need to study
    (D) Tom's wanting to study
    (E) Tom studying

33. The old sea captain told my wife and me many interesting yarns about his many voyages.

    (A) my wife and me
    (B) me and my wife
    (C) my wife and I
    (D) I and my wife
    (E) my wife along with me

34. A great many students from several universities are planning to, if the weather is favorable, attend next Saturday's mass rally in Washington.

    (A) are planning to, if the weather is favorable, attend next Saturday's mass rally in Washington
    (B) are planning, if the weather is favorable, to attend next Saturday's mass rally in Washington
    (C) are planning to attend, if the weather is favorable, next Saturday's mass rally in Washington
    (D) are planning to attend next Saturday's mass rally in Washington, if the weather is favorable
    (E) are, if the weather is favorable, planning to attend next Saturday's mass rally in Washington

35. Jane's body movements are like those of a dancer.

    (A) like those of a dancer
    (B) the same as a dancer
    (C) like a dancer
    (D) a dancer's
    (E) like those of a dancer's

36. This is one restaurant I won't patronize because I was served a fried egg by the waitress that was rotten.

    (A) I was served a fried egg by the waitress that was rotten
    (B) I was served by the waitress a fried egg that was rotten
    (C) a fried egg was served to me by the waitress that was rotten
    (D) the waitress served me a fried egg that was rotten
    (E) a rotten fried egg was served to me by the waitress

37. Watching the familiar story unfold on the screen, he was glad that he read the book with such painstaking attention to detail.

    (A) that he read the book with such painstaking attention to detail.
    (B) that he had read the book with such painstaking attention to detail.
    (C) that he read the book with such attention to particulars.
    (D) that he read the book with such intense effort.
    (E) that he paid so much attention to the plot of the book.

38. If anyone requested tea instead of coffee, it was a simple matter to serve it to them from the teapot at the rear of the table.

    (A) it was a simple matter to serve it to them
    (B) it was easy to serve them
    (C) it was a simple matter to serve them
    (D) it was a simple matter to serve it to him
    (E) he could serve himself

39. He bought some bread, butter, cheese and decided not to eat them until the evening.

    (A) some bread, butter, cheese and decided
    (B) some bread, butter, cheese and then decided
    (C) a little bread, butter, cheese and decided
    (D) some bread, butter, cheese, deciding
    (E) some bread, butter, and cheese and decided

40. The things the children liked best were swimming in the river and to watch the horses being groomed by the trainer.

    (A) swimming in the river and to watch the horses being groomed by the trainer.
    (B) swimming in the river and to watch the trainer grooming the horses.
    (C) that they liked to swim in the river and watch the horses being groomed by the trainer.
    (D) swimming in the river and watching the horses being groomed by the trainer.
    (E) to swim in the river and watching the horses being groomed by the trainer.

Note: The remaining questions are like those at the beginning of the section.

Directions: For each sentence in which you find an error, select the one underlined part that must be changed to make the sentence correct and blacken the corresponding space on your answer sheet.

If there is no error, blacken answer space Ⓔ.

EXAMPLE:

The region has a climate so severe that plants
                             A

growing there rarely had been more than twelve
    B   C

inches high. No error
    D   E

SAMPLE ANSWER

Ⓐ Ⓑ ● Ⓓ Ⓔ

---

41. On April 8, 1974, Henry Aaron hit his 715th home
     A   B
run, and breaking Babe Ruth's record. No error.
     C   D   E

42. Since their attempt at a reconciliation has ended
                A   B
in failure, Elizabeth Taylor and Richard Burton will
  C
file for divorcing. No error.
    D   E

43. The long lines of cars at gasoline stations have dis-
      A
appeared like as if there were never an energy crisis.
     B   C   D
No error.
  E

44. The residents of the town of Hillsborough, where
Patricia Hearst's parents live, is getting lessons
    A   B   C
on how to protect themselves from kidnapping.
  D
No error.
  E

45. The man told his son to take the car to the service
     A   B   C
station because it needed gasoline. No error.
      D   E

46. The man who's temper is under control at all times is
      A   B   C
likely to think clearly and to accomplish more in his
  D
business and social relations. No error.
             E

47. Whether nineteenth century classics should be
                      A
taught in school today has become a matter of con-
  A   B   C
troversy for students and teachers alike. No error.
               D   E

48. Neither George Foreman or millions of others
              A   B
believed that Muhammad Ali would win the
                 C
heavyweight title by an eighth-round knockout.
              D
No error.
  E

49. Bob wanted to finish his homework completely be-
                     A
fore his mother had come home from her sister's
   B   C   D
house. No error.
     E

50. Inflation together with the high interest rates and
soaring oil prices are hurting the nation's economy
   A   B   C
very seriously. No error.
    D   E

S T O P

IF YOU FINISH BEFORE TIME IS CALLED, YOU MAY CHECK YOUR WORK
ON THIS SECTION ONLY.
DO NOT WORK ON ANY OTHER SECTION IN THE TEST.

SECTION 4   VERBAL ABILITY
30 MINUTES   40 QUESTIONS

For each question in this section, choose the best answer and blacken the corresponding space on the answer sheet.

Each question below consists of a word in capital letters, followed by five lettered words or phrases. Choose the word or phrase that is most nearly *opposite* in meaning to the word in capital letters. Since some of the questions require you to distinguish fine shades of meaning, consider all the choices before deciding which is best.

Example:

GOOD: (A) sour   (B) bad   (C) red
(D) hot   (E) ugly

(A) ● (C) (D) (E)

1. DUBIOUS: (A) exact   (B) lofty
   (C) sincere   (D) dutiful   (E) certain

2. COARSE: (A) well-dressed   (B) polished
   (C) disciplined   (D) friendly   (E) prominent

3. BELLIGERENT: (A) creative   (B) irreligious
   (C) tranquil   (D) practical   (E) ambitious

4. ATROCIOUS: (A) calm   (B) smooth
   (C) skillful   (D) considerate   (E) sluggish

5. SOMBER: (A) exposed   (B) satisfactory
   (C) cheerful   (D) awake   (E) alert

6. GRUELING: (A) acceptable   (B) refreshing
   (C) helpful   (D) interesting   (E) simple

7. PRESTIGE: (A) profit   (B) scorn
   (C) dullness   (D) disadvantage
   (E) indifference

8. TACITURN: (A) obscene   (B) shrewd
   (C) impolite   (D) complimentary   (E) talkative

9. VALIANT: (A) cowardly   (B) extraordinary
   (C) ailing   (D) violent   (E) excitable

10. INSIPID: (A) selective   (B) reckless
    (C) tasteful   (D) fortunate   (E) conscious

Each sentence below has one or two blanks, each blank indicating that something has been omitted. Beneath the sentence are five lettered words or sets of words. Choose the word or set of words that *best* fits the meaning of the sentence as a whole.

Example:

Although its publicity has been _____, the film itself is intelligent, well-acted, handsomely produced, and altogether _____.

(A) tasteless . . . respectable
(B) extensive . . . moderate
(C) sophisticated . . . amateur
(D) risqué . . . crude
(E) perfect . . . spectacular

● (B) (C) (D) (E)

11. The low-cost apartment buildings, new and well-managed, are _____ to those accustomed to living in tenements _____ by shady characters.

(A) a boon . . . haunted
(B) a specter . . . inhabited
(C) an exodus . . . frequented
(D) an example . . . viewed
(E) a surprise . . . approached

12. Before the inflation _____, one could have had a complete meal in a restaurant for a dollar, including the tip, whereas today a hotdog, coffee, and dessert would _____ add up to two or three times that much.

(A) spiral . . . indubitably
(B) cancellation . . . rapidly
(C) problem . . . improbably
(D) abundance . . . consequently
(E) incidence . . . radically

13. Although the death of his dog had saddened him markedly, his computer designing skills remained completely _____.

(A) twisted   (B) unaffected   (C) incapable
(D) repaired   (E) demolished

14. A sense of fairness _____ that the punishment should fit the crime; yet, in actual practice, judicial decisions _____ greatly for the same type of criminal offense.

(A) assumes . . . coincide
(B) relegates . . . deviate
(C) accumulates . . . simplify
(D) insists . . . compromise
(E) dictates . . . vary

15. The guerrillas were so _____ that the general had to develop various strategies to trap them.

(A) distant   (B) wild   (C) unreasonable
(D) elusive   (E) cruel

Each question below consists of a related pair of words or phrases, followed by five lettered pairs of words or phrases. Select the lettered pair that *best* expresses a relationship similar to that expressed in the original pair.

Example:

> YAWN : BOREDOM :: (A) dream : sleep
> (B) anger : madness   (C) smile : amusement
> (D) face : expression   (E) impatience : rebellion
>   Ⓐ Ⓑ ● Ⓓ Ⓔ

16. VIRTUOUS : TRUST ::

(A) kindly : avoid
(B) honest : encounter
(C) intellectual : study
(D) shady : suspect
(E) simple : greet

17. EMBARRASS : HUMILIATE ::

(A) labor : succeed
(B) bicker : argue
(C) reduce : enlarge
(D) spank : whip
(E) pilfer : steal

18. AUTHENTICITY : COUNTERFEIT ::

(A) argument : contradictory
(B) reliability : erratic
(C) anticipation : solemn
(D) reserve : reticent
(E) mobility : energetic

19. COT : BED ::

(A) hotel : motel
(B) tissue : handkerchief
(C) lesson : composition
(D) hand : finger
(E) tea : lemon

20. PARAGRAPH : ESSAY ::

(A) question : response
(B) saddle : horse
(C) act : play
(D) performance : applause
(E) author : book

21. PROVERB : PITHY ::

(A) novel : acclaimed
(B) poem : ribald
(C) accident : tragic
(D) wedding : humorous
(E) snowflake : white

22. SCOLD : DENOUNCE ::

(A) mutter : jabber
(B) advocate : support
(C) squander : spend
(D) exhaust : refresh
(E) injure : maim

23. INTEGRITY : CORRUPTED ::

(A) disguise : recognized
(B) accusation : freed
(C) appearance : seen
(D) simplicity : admired
(E) nonchalance : bored

24. ETERNAL : DURATION ::

(A) temporary : time
(B) weak : control
(C) harmonious : music
(D) dry : water
(E) omnipotent : power

25. SUBMISSIVE : DEFIANCE ::

(A) agile : alertness
(B) courageous : fear
(C) doubtful : indecision
(D) confident : poise
(E) violent : rebellion

Each passage below is followed by questions based on its content. Answer all questions following a passage on the basis of what is *stated* or *implied* in that passage.

Many factors unite to make the battle of Gettysburg not only the turning point of the Civil War, but also the most dramatic event in American military history. It has everything to render it engrossing to the historian
5 and his followers: the white-hot fierceness of civil strife; the dominating figure of Robert E. Lee; and a desperately crucial quality which penetrated the consciousness of the men in the battle lines of both sides. Possibly more has been written about this engagement
10 than about even the battle of Waterloo. No famous battle can ever be completely re-created for a later generation, but loose ends have been gathered up over the years and false impressions have been corrected about what went on at Gettysburg during the first three
15 days of July, 1863.

During those three days, the South came within a hair's-breadth of winning the battle and the war. By those who like to speculate about such matters, its failure to do so has frequently been attributed to des-
20 tiny or chance—even the hand of God, wearying of the Southern cause at Gettysburg as he had wearied of Napoleon's at Waterloo.

Among the innumerable "ifs" of Gettysburg, a certain few would rank high on the list of any partisan of
25 the South: if, for example, Stonewall Jackson had survived to be Lee's right-hand man just once more; and if Lee's correspondence had not been captured on July 2.

The biggest of all such speculations, however, inevitably revolves around the strange case of the missing
30 Jeb Stuart. The absence of his cavalry, as pointed out later by Lee himself, deprived the Army of Northern Virginia of its ears and eyes, slowing its march into Pennsylvania and allowing Meade's Union forces to intercept it at Gettysburg. Not until the eve of the last
35 day of battle did the errant Stuart arrive. Originally assigned to the task of harassing Hooker and impeding his pursuit of Lee's invasion forces, Stuart had been scheduled to rejoin the latter long before the possibility of any general engagement. The fact that he did not do
40 so, whether because of vagueness in Stuart's orders or his own bad judgment, provided a major stumbling block for Lee's campaign.

26. According to the passage,

   (A) God prevented the South from winning the battle of Gettysburg
   (B) the battle of Gettysburg had more dramatic impact than any other battle ever fought
   (C) General Lee died heroically as his forces went down to defeat
   (D) Lee's qualities as a leader have enshrined him in the affections of all Americans
   (E) Hooker was an officer who fought on the Union side

27. Which of the following is the most suitable title for this passage?

   (A) High Tide at Gettysburg
   (B) My Kingdom for a Horse
   (C) A General for the Ages
   (D) A Lost Cause
   (E) General Robert E. Lee

28. According to the passage, the battle of Gettysburg would have been won by the South if

   (A) Lee's forces had taken the battle more seriously
   (B) Lee had used the military strategies of Napoleon
   (C) the weather had favored the South
   (D) certain unexpected events had not taken place
   (E) Lee's brigadier generals and colonels had been more experienced

As soon as his wife had driven off, Ethan took his coat and cap from the peg. Mattie was washing up the dishes, humming one of the dance tunes of the night before. He said "So long, Matt," and she answered gaily "So long, Ethan"; and that was all.   5

It was warm and bright in the kitchen. The sun slanted through the south window on the girl's moving figure, on the cat dozing in a chair, and on the geraniums brought in from the doorway, where Ethan had planted them in the summer to "make a garden" for 10 Mattie. He would have liked to linger on, watching her tidy up and then settle down to her sewing; but he wanted still more to get the hauling done and be back at the farm before night.

All the way down to the village he continued to 15 think of his return to Mattie. The kitchen was a poor place, not "spruce" and shining as his mother had kept it in his boyhood; but it was surprising what a homelike look the mere fact of Zeena's absence gave it. And he pictured what it would be like that evening, when he 20 and Mattie were there after supper. For the first time they would be alone together indoors, and they would sit there, one on each side of the stove, like a married couple, he in his stocking feet and smoking his pipe, she laughing and talking in that funny way she had, 25 which was always as new to him as if he had never heard her before.

The sweetness of the picture, and the relief of knowing that his fears of "trouble" with Zeena were unfounded, sent up his spirits with a rush, and he, who 30 was usually so silent, whistled and sang aloud as he drove through the snowy fields. There was in him a slumbering spark of sociability which the long New England winters has not yet extinguished. By nature grave and inarticulate, he admired recklessness and 35 gaiety in others and was warmed to the marrow by friendly human intercourse.

29. According to the passage,

   (A) Ethan preferred to watch and stay with Mattie than do anything else
   (B) Ethan's wife was no longer living with him
   (C) Ethan had lived in the house even before he was married
   (D) Mattie and Ethan were contemplating marriage
   (E) Ethan was generally a sociable type of person

30. The word "spruce" in line 17 means

   (A) supplied with adequate kitchen utensils
   (B) having attractive plants in various places
   (C) well lit and airy
   (D) having a neat and trim appearance
   (E) roomy and comfortable

31. We may infer from the passage that Ethan was the kind of person who was generally

   (A) faithful and loving
   (B) sensitive to his surroundings
   (C) eager to please other people
   (D) inclined to avoid responsibilities
   (E) hard to trust

To the world when it was half a thousand years younger, the outlines of all things seemed more clearly marked than to us. The contrast between suffering and joy, between adversity and happiness, appeared more
5 striking. All experience had yet to the minds of men the directness and absoluteness of the pleasure and pain of child-life. Every event, every action, was still embodied in expressive and solemn forms, which raised them to the dignity of a ritual.
10 Misfortunes and poverty were more afflicting than at present; it was more difficult to guard against them, and to find solace. Illness and health presented a more striking contrast; the cold and darkness of winter were more real evils. Honors and riches were relished with
15 greater avidity and contrasted more vividly with surrounding misery. We, at the present day, can hardly understand the keenness with which a fur coat, a good fire on the hearth, a soft bed, a glass of wine, were formerly enjoyed.
20 Then, again, all things in life were of a proud or cruel publicity. Lepers sounded their rattles and went about in processions, beggars exhibited their deformity and their misery in churches. Every order and estate, every rank and profession, was distinguished by its
25 costume. The great lords never moved about without a glorious display of arms and liveries, exciting fear and envy. Executions and other public acts of justice, hawking, marriages and funerals, were all announced by cries and processions, songs and music. The lover
30 wore the colors of his lady; companions the emblem of their brotherhood; parties and servants the badges of their lords. Between town and country, too, the contrast was very marked. A medieval town did not lose itself in extensive suburbs of factories and villas; girded by its walls, it stood forth as a compact whole, bristling 35 with innumerable turrets. However tall and threatening the houses of noblemen or merchants might be, in the aspect of the town, the lofty mass of the churches always remained dominant.

The contrast between silence and sound, darkness 40 and light, like that between summer and winter, was more strongly marked than it is in our lives. The modern town hardly knows silence or darkness in their purity, nor the effect of a solitary light or a single distant cry. 45

All things presenting themselves to the mind in violent contrasts and impressive forms, lent a tone of excitement and passion to everyday life and tended to produce that perpetual oscillation between despair and distracted joy, between cruelty and pious tenderness 50 which characterize life in the Middle Ages.

32. Conditions like those described in the passage would most likely have occurred about

   (A) 55 A.D.   (B) 755 A.D.   (C) 1055 A.D.
   (D) 1455 A.D.   (E) 1755 A.D.

33. The phrase "with greater avidity" in line 15 is best interpreted to mean with greater

   (A) desire   (B) sadness   (C) terror
   (D) silence   (E) disappointment

34. In the passage, all of the following are stated or implied about towns in the Middle Ages except

   (A) Towns had no suburbs.
   (B) Towns were always quite noisy.
   (C) Towns served as places of defense.
   (D) Towns always had large churches.
   (E) Merchants lived in the towns.

35. The author's main purpose in the passage is to

   (A) describe the miseries of the period
   (B) show how life was centered on the town
   (C) emphasize the violent course of life at the time
   (D) point out how the upper classes mistreated the lower classes
   (E) indicate how religious people were in those days

36. According to the passage, people at that time, as compared with people today, were

   (A) worse off
   (B) better off
   (C) less intelligent
   (D) more subdued
   (E) more sensitive to certain events

The universe began with the primordial "Big Bang" 20 billion years ago and has been expanding from that unimaginable first explosion ever since. The sun, Earth, and other planets were formed about four and a
5 half billion years ago. Life arose in the planet's early seas a billion years or less thereafter. Whether these first universal events were blind effects of natural processes or evidence of the purpose of a Creator is a matter of individual determination.

10 Science can find no force in nature that might account for the beginning of the universe—nor can it find any evidence that the universe even existed before that first moment. But there is overwhelming evidence supporting the natural progression of all the later ma-
15 jor steps. The first brains appeared in fish only about 450 million years ago, but these were modest nerve-circuits to maintain balance and muscle control and to give simple "good-bad" responses to signals of odor and light. Intelligence, involving memory and more
20 complex judgmental responses to the world, was not yet born. It began with the mammal-like reptiles who reached their zenith about 250 million years ago. It developed further among the first true mammals who hid out in small scurrying nocturnal forms for 100
25 million years while the great dinosaurs ruled the earth. The mammals needed acute hearing, smell, memory, and judgment as well as agility to survive. All of these required better brains.

The long upward path of intelligence on earth con-
30 tinued as changing conditions called forth more sophisticated responses from brains that grew increasingly large and potent. The long process climaxed, of course, with the appearance of humans only a million or so years ago. The modern human brain is the single most
35 complex and powerful thing that has yet arisen in the whole panorama of life on earth.

37. With which of the following is the passage primarily concerned?

(A) Telling how the universe evolved from its origin to the present time
(B) Comparing the intelligence of fish, dinosaurs, and man
(C) Exemplifying the "survival of the fittest" theory of evolution
(D) Proving that science can find no force in nature to account for the beginning of the universe
(E) Discussing the evolutionary process that led to man's superior brain

38. In this passage, the author tells the reader

(A) how life came about in the beginning years of our Earth
(B) when life with a brain made its first appearance
(C) why dinosaurs disappeared from the earth
(D) the reason that animal life has two different sexes
(E) the location on a current map where the human race began

39. In regard to the following three items listed, for which of them are we able to depend upon scientific investigation to explain *why* it (they) came about?

    I. the advent of man
    II. the origin of the universe
    III. the first signs of intelligence

(A) II only
(B) I and II only
(C) I and III only
(D) II and III only
(E) I, II, and III

40. Which of the following representative types of individual would be *least* likely to accept whatever the author has stated in the passage?

(A) a sports writer
(B) a church minister
(C) a typical businessman
(D) an average student
(E) a government employee

S T O P

IF YOU FINISH BEFORE TIME IS CALLED, YOU MAY CHECK YOUR WORK ON
THIS SECTION ONLY.
DO NOT WORK ON ANY OTHER SECTION IN THE TEST.

SECTION 5 MATH ABILITY
30 MINUTES 35 QUESTIONS

In this section solve each problem, using any available space on the page for scratchwork. Then decide which is the best of the choices given and blacken the corresponding space on the answer sheet.

The following information is for your reference in solving some of the problems.

Circle of radius r: Area $= \pi r^2$; Circumference $= 2\pi r$
The number of degrees of arc in a circle is 360.
The measure in degrees of a straight angle is 180.

Definitions of symbols:
$=$ is equal to $\leq$ is less than or equal to
$\neq$ is unequal to $\geq$ is greater than or equal to
$<$ is less than $\parallel$ is parallel to
$>$ is greater than $\perp$ is perpendicular to

Triangle: The sum of the measures in degrees of the angles of a triangle is 180.

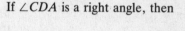

If $\angle CDA$ is a right angle, then

(1) area of $\triangle ABC = \dfrac{AB \times CD}{2}$

(2) $AC^2 = AD^2 + DC^2$

Note: Figures which accompany problems in this test are intended to provide information useful in solving the problems. They are drawn as accurately as possible EXCEPT when it is stated in a specific problem that its figure is not drawn to scale. All figures lie in a plane unless otherwise indicated. All numbers used are real numbers.

---

1. If a and b are positive integers and $ab = 64$, what is the smallest possible value of $a + b$?

   (A) 65 (B) 34 (C) 20 (D) 16 (E) 8

2. $\sqrt{\dfrac{3}{\sqrt{9}}} =$

   (A) 1 (B) $\sqrt{3}$ (C) $\dfrac{3}{\sqrt{3}}$
   (D) 3 (E) $3\sqrt{3}$

3.
$$\begin{array}{r} AB \\ + BA \\ \hline 66 \end{array}$$

   If $0 < A < 6$ and $0 < B < 6$ in the addition problem above, how many different integer values of A are possible?

   (A) Two (B) Three (C) Four
   (D) Five (E) Six

4. Given $r = a + b$ and $s = b - a$. When $a = 5$ and $b = 4$, find the value of $r - s$.

   (A) 8 (B) 9 (C) 10 (D) 18 (E) 81

Questions 5–6 refer to the following chart.

Number of Shirts	Total Price
1	$12.00
Box of 3	$22.50
Box of 6	$43.40

5. Which of the following is the closest approximation of the lowest cost per shirt, when a box of shirts is purchased?

   (A) $7.10 (B) $7.20 (C) $7.30
   (D) $7.40 (E) $7.50

6. If exactly 11 shirts are to be purchased, what is the minimum amount of money which must be spent?

   (A) $65.90 (B) $89.90 (C) $91.50
   (D) $103.40 (E) $132.00

7. If $5x^2 - 15x = 0$ and $x \neq 0$, find the value of x.

   (A) -10 (B) -3 (C) 10
   (D) 5 (E) 3

Questions 8–27 each consist of two quantities, one in Column A and one in Column B. You are to compare the two quantities and on the answer sheet blacken space

A if the quantity in Column A is greater;
B if the quantity in Column B is greater;
C if the two quantities are equal;
D if the relationship cannot be determined from the information given.

Notes: 1. In certain questions, information concerning one or both of the quantities to be compared is centered above the two columns.
2. In a given question, a symbol that appears in both columns represents the same thing in Column A is it does in Column B.
3. Letters such as x, n, and k stand for real numbers.

EXAMPLES		
Column A	Column B	Answers
E1. 2×6	$2 + 6$	● Ⓑ Ⓒ Ⓓ

E2. $180 - x$	y	Ⓐ Ⓑ ● Ⓓ
E3. $p - q$	$q - p$	Ⓐ Ⓑ Ⓒ ●

Column A	Column B

8. $4a > 3b$

         a b

9.   John flips a quarter coin twice.

The chances of John getting 2 tails | The chances of John getting no tails

10. $4.8 + 3.6 + 8$ | $\dfrac{95.9 + 94.8}{10}$

11. 3^9 | 1^{27}

12. y is an integer

        10 | The maximum value of $9 - y^2$

13. $\dfrac{a}{7} = \dfrac{b}{1}$

        a | $7b$

14. 6×7^{15} | 7×6^{15}

Column A	Column B

15. In solving an equation, Mary made a mistake in her final step. Instead of adding 20 to what she had obtained so far, Mary subtracted 15. She made no other errors.

Mary's answer to the question | The correct answer to the question

16. The regular price of a car is p dollars.

The price of the car after a 20 percent discount | $0.80p$ dollars

17. $y^2 - 11y + 30 = 0$

        y | 7

18. There are x boys in high school A. The number of girls in high school A is 8 less than 4 times the number of boys

The number of girls in high school A | $4x - 8$

SUMMARY DIRECTIONS FOR COMPARISON QUESTIONS

Answer: A if the quantity in Column A is greater;
          B if the quantity in Column B is greater;
          C if the two quantities are equal;
          D if the relationship cannot be determined from the information given.

Column A	Column B

19. r, s and t are equal to 6, 5 and 4, but not necessarily in that order. $s < r$

| $s + t - r$ | 4 |

---

20. A solid figure has equal faces. The volume of the solid is 125.

| The number of faces of the solid | 5 |

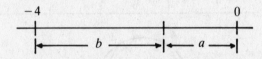

21. a and b are each lengths of segments on the number line shown above.

| $4 - a$ | b |

22.

$$\frac{5}{6} < y < \frac{6}{5}$$

| y | $\dfrac{8}{7}$ |

23.

| $\dfrac{2}{\dfrac{9}{5} - 1}$ | 3 |

---

24.   100 centimeters = 1 meter

| The area of a square that has a side of length 5 meters | 100 times the area of a square that has a side of length 5 centimeters |

Column A	Column B

25. a and b are positive.

$$b > a$$

| $b^2 - a$ | $b^2 - a^2$ |

26.

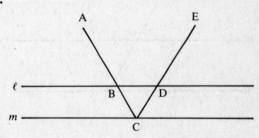

<u>Note:</u> Figure not drawn to scale. Line ℓ || Line m. Line segments AC and EC intersect Line ℓ at B and D respectively.

| The length of BC | The length of DC |

27.

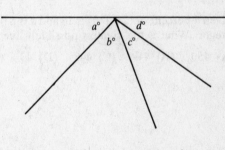

$a = c = d$ and $\dfrac{c}{b} = \dfrac{1}{3}$

| b | 80 |

Solve each of the remaining problems in this section using any available space for scratchwork. Then decide which is the best of the choices given and blacken the corresponding space on the answer sheet.

28. Given the sum of two angles of a quadrilateral is 90°. Find the average (arithmetic mean) of the measures of the other two angles.

(A) 60   (B) 90   (C) 135   (D) 155   (E) 180

29. Find x if $(10^3 + 7)^2 = 1,000,000 + x$.

(A) 49   (B) 7,049   (C) 14,007
(D) 14,049   (E) 70,049

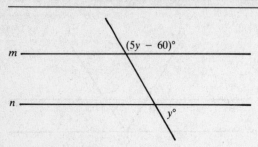

30. $m \parallel n$ in the figure above. Find y.

(A) 10   (B) 20   (C) 40   (D) 65   (E) 175

31. The ratio of $3\frac{1}{3}$ hours to 11 hours is equal to

(A) $\dfrac{3}{110}$ (B) $\dfrac{3}{13}$ (C) $\dfrac{3}{11}$ (D) $\dfrac{10}{33}$ (E) $\dfrac{10}{13}$

32. Given 4 percent of $(2a + b)$ is 18 and a is a positive integer. What is the greatest possible value of b?

(A) 450   (B) 449   (C) 448   (D) 43   (E) 8

33. A square has an area of R^2. An equilateral triangle has a perimeter of E. If r is the perimeter of the square and e is a side of the equilateral triangle, then, in terms of R and E, $e + r =$

(A) $\dfrac{E + R}{7}$ (B) $\dfrac{4R + 3E}{3}$ (C) $\dfrac{3E + 4R}{12}$

(D) $\dfrac{12E + R}{3}$ (E) $\dfrac{E + 12R}{3}$

34. Using the formula $C = \dfrac{5}{9}(F - 32)$, if the Celsius (C) temperature increased 35°, by how many degrees would the Fahrenheit (F) temperature be increased?

(A) $19\dfrac{4}{9}°$ (B) 31°   (C) 51°   (D) 63°   (E) 82°

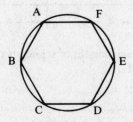

35. Equilateral polygon ABCDEF is inscribed in the circle. If the length of arc BAF is 14π, find the length of the diameter of the circle.

(A) 7   (B) 14   (C) 7π (D) 21   (E) 42

S T O P

IF YOU FINISH BEFORE TIME IS CALLED, YOU MAY CHECK YOUR WORK ON
THIS SECTION ONLY.
DO NOT WORK ON ANY OTHER SECTION IN THE TEST.

SECTION 6   MATH ABILITY
30 MINUTES   25 QUESTIONS

In this section solve each problem, using any available space on the page for scratchwork. Then decide which is the best of the choices given and blacken the corresponding space on the answer sheet.

The following information is for your reference in solving some of the problems.

Circle of radius r: Area $= \pi r^2$; Circumference $= 2\pi r$
  The number of degrees of arc in a circle is 360.
The measure in degrees of a straight angle is 180.

Definitions of symbols:
$=$ is equal to	$\leqq$ is less than or equal to
$\neq$ is unequal to	$\geqq$ is greater than or equal to
$<$ is less than	$\parallel$ is parallel to
$>$ is greater than	$\perp$ is perpendicular to

Triangle: The sum of the measures in degrees of the angles of a triangle is 180.

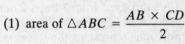

If $\angle CDA$ is a right angle, then

(1) area of $\triangle ABC = \dfrac{AB \times CD}{2}$

(2) $AC^2 = AD^2 + DC^2$

Note: Figures which accompany problems in this test are intended to provide information useful in solving the problems. They are drawn as accurately as possible EXCEPT when it is stated in a specific problem that its figure is not drawn to scale. All figures lie in a plane unless otherwise indicated. All numbers used are real numbers.

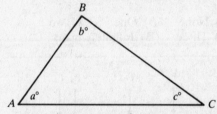

Note: Figure is not drawn to scale

1. In triangle ABC, if $a > c$ which of the following is true?

    (A) $BC = AC$ (B) $AB > BC$ (C) $AC > AB$
    (D) $BC > AB$ (E) $BC > AC$

2. Which combination of the following statements can be used to demonstrate that x is positive?

     I. $x > y$
     II. $1 < y$

    (A) I alone but not II
    (B) II alone but not I
    (C) I and II taken together but neither taken alone
    (D) Both I alone and II alone
    (E) Neither I nor II nor both

3. Find 25 percent of 25 percent of 2.

    (A) $\frac{1}{16}$ (B) $\frac{1}{8}$ (C) $\frac{1}{4}$ (D) $\frac{1}{2}$ (E) 1

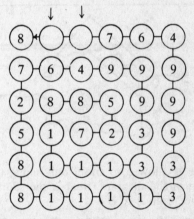

4. The pattern in the figure shown above is repeated every 16 digits. Which of the following number pairs, when placed below the arrows in the sequence above, will continue the pattern of the sequence?

    (A) 9, 4   (B) 5, 2   (C) 1, 1
    (D) 7, 2   (E) 1, 3

5. Three trucks weigh 5, 7, and 14 tons, respectively. What is the difference in weight between the heaviest truck and the average (arithmetic mean) weight of the three trucks?

    (A) 10 tons   (B) $8\frac{2}{3}$ tons   (C) $7\frac{1}{3}$ tons

    (D) 7 tons   (E) $5\frac{1}{3}$ tons

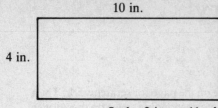

10 in.

4 in.

Scale: 2 in. = 11 yd.

6. In the scale drawing of the rectangular field shown above, what is the actual area, in square yards, of the field?

(A) 77   (B) 440   (C) 605
(D) 1210   (E) 2420

7. 4 is subtracted from 3 times a number, n, and this result is divided by 3. Which of the following expressions represents the statement above concerning n?

(A) $\frac{1}{3}(3n - 4)$ (B) $\frac{1}{3}[(n + 3) - 4]$

(C) $\frac{4}{3} - 3n$ (D) $3(3n - 4)$

(E) $\frac{n}{3} + \frac{4}{3}$

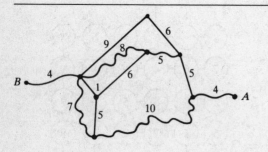

8. If one is allowed to travel only along the paths shown in the diagram, what is the shortest path distance from A to B?

(A) 18   (B) 21   (C) 24   (D) 27   (E) 28

9. Which of the following inequalities below could be *true* about a and b if ab is negative?

(A) $a < b < 0$ (B) $b < a < 0$
(C) $a < 0 < b$ (D) $0 < a < b$
(E) $0 < b < a$

10. If $pq = \frac{1}{r}$, $r = 4$ and $p = \frac{1}{20}$, find the value of q.

(A) 5   (B) $\frac{1}{24}$ (C) $\frac{1}{5}$ (D) $\frac{1}{80}$ (E) 80

11. If two cubes have edges of 1 and 2, what is the sum of their volumes?

(A) 1   (B) 3   (C) 8   (D) 9   (E) 27

12. If the numerical value of the binomial coefficient $\binom{n}{2}$ is given by the formula $\frac{n(n - 1)}{2}$, then the numerical value of $\binom{15}{2}$ is

(A) 60   (B) 90   (C) 105   (D) 175   (E) 210

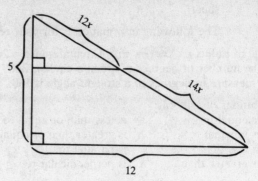

13. If the segments shown in the diagram have the indicated lengths, find the value of x

(A) 13   (B) 12   (C) 5   (D) 2   (E) $\frac{1}{2}$

14. How many integers x satisfy $-\frac{1}{2} < \frac{x}{3} < -\frac{1}{4}$

(A) None   (B) One   (C) Two
(D) Three   (E) Infinitely many

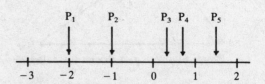

15. For the five numbers marked above by arrows, the best approximation to their product is

(A) $\frac{1}{3}$ (B) $\frac{2}{3}$ (C) $\frac{3}{2}$ (D) 3   (E) -3

16. If K is the sum of three consecutive even integers and y is the sum of the greatest three consecutive *odd* integers that precede the least of the three even integers, express y in terms of K.

(A) $y = K - 5$ (B) $y = K - 10$
(C) $y = K - 15$ (D) $y = K - 20$
(E) It cannot be determined from the information given.

17. At one instant, two meteors are 2500 kilometers apart and traveling toward each other in straight paths along the imaginary line joining them. One meteor has a velocity of 300 meters per second while the other travels at 700 meters per second. Assuming that their velocities are constant and that they continue along the same paths, how many seconds elapse from the first instant to the time of their collision? (1 kilometer = 1000 meters)

(A) 250   (B) 500   (C) 1250
(D) 2500   (E) 5000

18. The chickens on a certain farm consumed 600 pounds of feed in half a year. During that time the total number of eggs laid was 5000. If the feed cost $1.25 per pound then the feed cost per egg was

(A) $0.0750   (B) $0.1250   (C) $0.15
(D) $0.25   (E) $0.3333

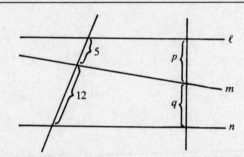

19. Lines ℓ and n are parallel to each other, but line m is parallel to neither of the other two. Find $\dfrac{p}{q}$ if $p + q = 13$.

(A) $\dfrac{13}{5}$ (B) $\dfrac{12}{5}$ (C) $\dfrac{7}{6}$ (D) $\dfrac{1}{5}$

(E) It cannot be determined from the information given.

20. Let $x = \sqrt{\dfrac{1}{9} + \left(\dfrac{1}{3} + \dfrac{1}{9} + \dfrac{1}{27} + \dfrac{1}{81}\right)}$

An equivalent expression for x is

(A) $\dfrac{1}{9}$ (B) $\dfrac{\sqrt{3}}{3}$ (C) $\dfrac{1}{81}$ (D) $\dfrac{1}{3\sqrt{3}}$ (E) $\dfrac{7}{9}$

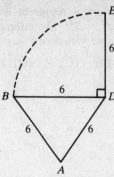

21. Arc BE is a quartercircle with radius 6 and C, which is not shown, is an arbitrary point on arc BE. If $AB = BD = AD = 6$, then all of the possible values of the perimeter P of the quadrilateral $ABCD$ are

(A) $P = 18$ (B) $12 < P \le 18$ (C) $18 < P \le 24$
(D) $18 < P \le 18 + 6\sqrt{2}$ (E) $18 < P \le 30$

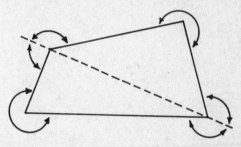

22. The arrows in the diagram above represent all of the exterior angles of the figure. The sum of the degree measures of these angles is

(A) 720   (B) 1080   (C) 1440   (D) 1800
(E) It cannot be determined from the information given.

23. In the watch shown above, the normal numbers 1, 2, 3, . . . , 12 have been replaced by the letters A, B, C, . . . , L. In terms of these letters, a correct reading of the time shown would be

(A) I minutes after L   (B) 3E minutes before A
(C) 5C minutes after L   (D) I minutes before A
(E) None of the above

24. The letters r and s represent numbers satisfying $r^2 = 9$ and $s^2 = 25$. The difference between the greatest possible values of $s - r$ and $r - s$ is

(A) 16   (B) 8   (C) 5   (D) 3   (E) 0

25. 27 equal cubes, each with a side of length r, are arranged so as to form a single larger cube with a volume of 81. If the larger cube has a side of length s, then r divided by s equals

(A) $\frac{1}{3}$ (B) $\frac{1}{\sqrt{3}}$ (C) $\frac{1}{2}$ (D) $\frac{1}{8}$ (E) $\frac{1}{27}$

S T O P

IF YOU FINISH BEFORE TIME IS CALLED, YOU MAY CHECK YOUR WORK ON
THIS SECTION ONLY.
DO NOT WORK ON ANY OTHER SECTION IN THE TEST.

HOW DID YOU DO ON THIS TEST?

STEP 1. Go to the Answer Key on page 32.

STEP 2. For your "raw score," count your correct answers in each of the test parts of the test you have just taken:

Verbal (Section 1 and 4 combined) _____.

Math (Sections 2, 5, and 6 combined) _____.

Standard Written English (Section 3) _____.

STEP 3. Get your "scaled score" for the test by referring to the Raw Score/Scaled Score Conversion Tables on pages 64–66.

THERE'S ALWAYS ROOM FOR IMPROVEMENT!

ANSWER KEY FOR PRACTICE TEST 1
(DIAGNOSTIC SAT PRE-TEST)

Section 1—Verbal

1. D	8. C	15. A	22. B	29. C	36. B	43. E
2. B	9. E	16. B	23. A	30. E	37. A	44. B
3. E	10. B	17. D	24. E	31. B	38. C	45. A
4. C	11. D	18. A	25. C	32. E	39. D	
5. E	12. E	19. E	26. E	33. C	40. C	
6. E	13. A	20. D	27. D	34. D	41. D	
7. D	14. C	21. D	28. B	35. C	42. B	

Section 2—Math

1. B	5. B	9. C	13. D	17. E	21. E	25. E
2. A	6. B	10. C	14. C	18. D	22. E	
3. E	7. D	11. D	15. C	19. A	23. A	
4. E	8. A	12. B	16. B	20. B	24. B	

Section 3—Standard Written English

1. E	9. A	17. C	25. E	33. A	41. C	49. C
2. A	10. E	18. E	26. B	34. D	42. D	50. B
3. C	11. C	19. A	27. C	35. A	43. B	
4. E	12. B	20. D	28. E	36. D	44. C	
5. B	13. B	21. D	29. C	37. B	45. D	
6. D	14. A	22. A	30. E	38. D	46. A	
7. C	15. B	23. C	31. A	39. E	47. E	
8. C	16. A	24. B	32. D	40. D	48. A	

Section 4—Verbal

1. E	7. B	13. B	19. B	25. B	31. B	37. E
2. B	8. E	14. E	20. C	26. E	32. D	38. B
3. C	9. A	15. D	21. E	27. A	33. A	39. C
4. D	10. C	16. D	22. E	28. D	34. B	40. B
5. C	11. A	17. D	23. A	29. C	35. C	
6. B	12. A	18. B	24. E	30. D	36. E	

Section 5—Math

1. D	6. B	11. A	16. C	21. C	26. D	31. D
2. A	7. E	12. A	17. B	22. D	27. A	32. C
3. D	8. D	13. C	18. C	23. B	28. C	33. E
4. C	9. C	14. A	19. D	24. A	29. D	34. D
5. B	10. B	15. B	20. D	25. D	30. C	35. E

Section 6—Math

1. D	5. E	9. C	13. E	17. D	21. D	25. A
2. C	6. D	10. A	14. B	18. C	22. B	
3. B	7. A	11. D	15. B	19. E	23. B	
4. B	8. C	12. C	16. C	20. E	24. E	

EXPLANATORY ANSWERS FOR DIAGNOSTIC SAT PRE-TEST (PRACTICE TEST 1)

Section 1: Verbal Ability

> As you read these Explanatory Answers, you are advised to refer to "Using Critical Thinking Skills in Verbal Questions" (beginning on page 90) whenever a specific Strategy is referred to in the answer. Of particular importance are the following Master Verbal Strategies:
>
> Sentence Completion Master Strategy 1—page 94.
> Sentence Completion Master Strategy 2—page 95.
> Analogies Master Strategy 1—page 90.
> Antonyms Master Strategy 1—page 99.
> Reading Comprehension Master Strategy 2—page 109.

1. **(D)** Choice D is correct. See **Antonym Strategies 1, 2.** *Benevolent* means *generous; kindly.* The opposite of *benevolent* is *miserly.*

2. **(B)** Choice B is correct. *Trite* means *worn out; stale; commonplace.* The opposite of *trite* is *unique.*

3. **(E)** Choice E is correct. See **Antonym Strategies 1, 2.** *Dissension* means *disagreement; violent quarreling.* The opposite of *dissension* is *harmony.*

4. **(C)** Choice C is correct. See **Antonym Strategy 1.** *Reprisal* means *retaliation; revenge.* The opposite of *reprisal* is *assistance.*

5. **(E)** Choice E is correct. *Vindicate* means *to clear of guilt* or *blame.* The opposite of *vindicate* is *accuse.*

6. **(E)** Choice E is correct. *Livid* means *pale* or *ashen,* as with rage. The opposite of *livid* is *glowing.*

7. **(D)** Choice D is correct. See **Antonym Strategy 3.** *Boorish* means *rude; ill-mannered.* The opposite of *boorish* is *civilized.*

8. **(C)** Choice C is correct. See **Antonym Strategies 1, 3.** *Consolidation* means the *act of combining;* a *merger.* The opposite of *consolidation* is *division.*

9. **(E)** Choice E is correct. *Inclement* means *harsh; unfavorable; severe.* The opposite of *inclement* is *mild.*

10. **(B)** Choice B is correct. *Berate* means *to scold severely.* The opposite of *berate* is *to praise.*

11. **(D)** Choice D is correct. See **Antonym Strategies 1, 2.** *Proficiency* means *skill; competency.* The opposite of *proficiency* is *incompetence.*

12. **(E)** Choice E is correct. *Dearth* means *scarcity; lack.* The opposite of *dearth* is *abundance.*

13. **(A)** Choice A is correct. See **Antonym Strategy 2.** *Ghastly* means *horrible; dreadful.* The opposite of *ghastly* is *pleasant.*

14. **(C)** Choice C is correct. See **Antonym Strategy 1.** *Exude* means *to discharge; to ooze.* The opposite of *exude* is *to block.*

15. **(A)** Choice A is correct. *Garish* means *gaudy; loud* and *flashy.* The opposite of *garish* is *simple.*

16. **(B)** Choice B is correct. See **Sentence Completion Strategy 1.** The word "ironic" (meaning "incompatible," "incongruous") completes the sentence so that it makes good sense. The other choices don't do that.

17. **(D)** Choice D is correct. **See Sentence Completion Strategy 4.** The first word "Because" is a *result indicator.* We can then expect some action to take place after the information about what the evening cable TV programs deal with. The expected action is that parents will consider such programs "inappropriate." Accordingly, only Choice D is correct.

18. **(A)** Choice A is correct. See **Sentence Completion Strategy 2.** Examine the first word of each choice. Choice (C) glamorized . . . and Choice (D) viewed . . . do *not* make good sense because a word does not effectively glamorize or effectively view unfairness. Now consider the other choices. Choice (A) portrayed . . . strengthening, is the only choice which has a word pair which makes sentence sense.

19. **(E)** Choice E is correct. See **Sentence Completion Strategy 1.** The word "prolific" (meaning "producing abundant works or results") completes the sentence so that it makes good sense. The other choices do *not* do that.

20. **(D)** Choice D is correct. Although this is a two-blank question, we should use **Sentence Completion Strategy 1** (primarily used for one-blank questions). Note that we have a set of three opposites: from the "serious" to the "lighthearted," from the "objective" to the "argumentative," and from the "innocuous" (meaning *harmless, innocent*) to the "hostile." The other choices do *not* have this opposite pattern.

21. **(D)** Choice D is correct. The author is definitely satisfied and happy with the simple life he and his partner are leading. See lines such as the following: "We thank our lucky stars that we live out in the wilderness." (lines 39–40) "We are thankful for what the wilderness makes possible." (lines 47–48) Choices A, B, C, and E are incorrect because the author gives no indication that the lifestyle, as he describes it, is marked by resentment, boredom, indecision, or indifference.

22. **(B)** Choice B is correct. Throughout the passage, the author is showing that frills are not necessary for a happy life. Example: "There is no phone to ring, no radio to turn on, no television to watch." (lines 8–9) Choices A and D are incorrect because they are much too general. Choice C is an inappropriate title because progress and prosperity are not of interest to the author. Choice E is an inappropriate title because the author is not concerned about conveniences such as a phone, radio, or television. He has what he needs—"peace, quiet, and frugality." (line 49)

23. **(A)** Choice A is correct. The author indicates that the typical election is inconsequential—that is, unproductive, of no use. One may conclude, then, that the author has no faith in the typical candidates who run for office. Choices B, C, D, and E are incorrect because the author does not express these sentiments in the passage—although he may agree with those choices.

24. **(E)** Choice E is correct. The author must have a farm because he says: ". . . our homegrown food is not stale, preserved or embalmed and bought from the supermarket." (lines 45–46) Choice A is incorrect because the author states: "There is wood to cut, snow to shovel . . ." (line 15) Choice B is incorrect. See lines 16–18: "No one is pushing, no one is shoving . . . we make our own jobs. Free men? Almost." Therefore, the author is not *completely* a free man. Choice C is incorrect because it is his neighbor's wife who may be pregnant. (Lines 19–20) Choice D is incorrect. See line 28: "The newspaper reaching us by mail . . ."

25. **(C)** Choice C is correct. Maine is the only one of the five states listed that would likely have snow (line 1) and spruce (evergreen) trees. (line 2) Therefore, Choices A, B, D, and E are incorrect.

26. **(E)** Choice E is correct. See lines 22–23: "All human beings have at least four types of intelligence." Choice A is incorrect. See lines 54–57: "Persistence kept Einstein looking for the solution to the question of the relationship between the law of gravity and his special theory of relativity." Isaac Newton (1642–1727) formulated the law of gravitation. Choice B is incorrect. The passage simply states: "The idea for the self-starting electric motor came to Nikola Tesla one evening as he was reciting a poem by Goethe and watching a sunset." (Lines 33–35) Choice C is incorrect. The author indicates a span of time when he states: "The discoveries made by scientific geniuses from Archimedes through Einstein . . ." (lines 1–2). Archimedes was an ancient Greek mathematician, physicist, and inventor (287–212 B.C.) While Einstein was, of course, a modern scientist (1879–1955). Choice D is incorrect. The passage states: ". . . while an IQ above a certain point—about 120—is very helpful for a scientist (it) is not crucial for producing a work of genius." (lines 19–22) The passage does not specifically say that most scientists have IQ scores above 120.

27. **(D)** Choice D is correct. See lines 45–47: "The scientist solves a problem by shifting from one intelligence to another, although the logical-mathematical intelligence is dominant." Accordingly, Choices A, B, C, and E are incorrect.

28. **(B)** Choice B is correct. When the author describes the work experiences of Einstein and Tesla, he refers to their use of one or more of the four types of intelligence. Moreover, lines 28–30 state: "Some corroboration of these (four intelligence) categories comes from the reports of scientists who describe thought processes centered around images, sensations, or words." Choices A, C, D, and E are incorrect because the author does not refer to these choices in the passage.

29. **(C)** Choice C is correct. The author indicates that great scientists use to advantage four intelligences—logical-mathematical, spatial, linguistic, and bodily-kinesthetic. See lines 23–27: "The great scientist possesses the ability to move back and forth among them—the logical-mathematical, the spatial which includes visual perception, the linguistic, and the bodily-kinesthetic." Choices B and D are brought out in the passage but not at any length. Therefore, Choices B and D are incorrect. Choice A is incorrect because the author nowhere compares the thinking of the average individual and that of the great scientist. Choice E is incorrect because, though the concepts are mentioned, they certainly are not clarified in the passage.

30. **(E)** Choice E is correct. As a football star, he would certainly have to have a high level of (a) spatial intelligence [II] which involves space sensitivity as well as visual perception, and (b) bodily-kinesthetic intelligence [IV] which involves the movement of muscles, tendons, and joints. As a literature major, he would certainly have to have a high level of linguistic intelligence [III] which involves the ability to read, write, speak, and listen. Whether he would have logical-mathematical intelligence to a high degree is questionable. It follows that Choices A, B, C, and D are incorrect.

31. **(B)** Choice B is correct. See **Sentence Completion Strategy 2.** Examine the first word of each choice. Choice (A) *shattering . . .* and Choice (C) *impertinent . . .* do *not* make sense because rates at a repair place are not aptly called shattering or impertinent. Now consider the other choices. Choices D and E do *not* make sense in the sentence. Choice (B) *exorbitant . . . instituted does* make sense.

32. **(E)** Choice E is correct. See **Sentence Completion Strategy 2.** Examine the first word of each choice. Choice (B) *denied . . .* and Choice (D) *slighted . . .* do *not* make sense because students who found truth in Socrates' teachings would not deny or slight him. Now consider the other choices. Choice (A) *accepted . . . a benefit,* and Choice (C) *appraised . . . an exception,* do not make sense in the sentence. Choice (E) *revered . . . a threat, does* make sense in the sentence.

33. **(C)** Choice C is correct. See **Sentence Completion Strategy 1.** The word "mediocre" (meaning "average," "ordinary") completes the sentence so that it makes good sense. The other choices do *no* do that.

34. **(D)** Choice D is correct. See **Sentence Completion Strategy 2.** Examine the first words of each choice. We eliminate Choice (C) *squandered* and Choice (E) *regaled* because hardworking parents do *not* squander (spend money recklessly) or regale (entertain) to give their son an education. Now consider the other choices. The word pairs of Choice A and Choice B do *not* make sense in the sentence. Choice (D) *struggled . . . generously, does* make good sense.

35. **(C)** Choice C is correct. See **Sentence Completion Strategy 4.** The main clause of the sentence—"he insisted . . . not be interrupted"—supports the idea expressed in the first three words of the sentence. Accordingly, Choice (C) *headstrong* (meaning stubborn) is the only correct choice.

36. **(B)** Choice B is correct. A collage is an artistic composition of pieces of printed material. A novel is a work of literature done by an author.

(Action to Object relationship)

37. **(A)** Choice A is correct. A parley is primarily a place to have a discussion or conference. A restaurant is primarily a place to dine.

(Place relationship)

38. **(C)** Choice C is correct. An agenda is a guide or outline of things to be discussed at a conference. A map is a guide or representation to help a person find his way on a trip.

(Purpose relationship)

39. **(D)** Choice D is correct. Erosion means wearing away. Erosion by something like water can cause a deep, narrow passage in the earth's surface. This passage or opening is called a ravine. Drilling causes an opening (in the form of a hole) if it is done in a substance like wood.

(Cause and Effect relationship)

40. **(C)** Choice C is correct. A turtle is part of the reptile family. A trout is part of the fish family. This is a Part : Whole analogy type. You might have chosen A which is also a Part : Whole analogy. However, reptiles and fish are associated with the "animal kingdom" while oak and tree are associated with the "vegetable kingdom." Therefore, Choice A is incorrect. Also see **Analogy Strategy 4.**

(Part-Whole relationship)

41. **(D)** Choice D is correct. A profligate is recklessly wasteful, wildly extravagant, and inclined to vice. Accordingly, a profligate is *not* a moral person. A miser is obviously *not* a generous person.

(Association relationship)

42. **(B)** Choice B is correct. A disorganized person is without system. A traitorous person is without loyalty.

(Opposite relationship)

43. **(E)** Choice E is correct. When we frustrate a person, we deprive him of drive—in this case, meaning motivation, initiative, aggressiveness. When we swindle a person, we deprive him of property or money. Also see **Analogy Strategy 5.**

(Cause and Effect relationship)

44. **(B)** Choice B is correct. A rebel's purpose is to bring about a change—in government, for example. A gambler's purpose is to bring about a profit—by winning money in a card game for example. Also see **Analogy Strategy 5.**

(Purpose relationship)

45. **(A)** Choice A is correct. Inferences are likely to be made by the person who is discerning. Successes are likely to be scored by the person who is enterprising.

(Association relationship)

EXPLANATORY ANSWERS FOR
PRACTICE TEST 1 (continued)

Section 2: Math Ability

As you read these solutions, you are advised to do two things if you answered the Math question incorrectly:

1) When a specific Strategy is referred to in the solution, study that strategy, which you will find in "Using Critical Thinking Skills in Math Questions" (beginning on page 69).

2) When the solution directs you to the "Math Refresher" (beginning on page 205)—for example, Math Refresher #305—study the 305 Math principle to get a clear idea of the Math operation that was necessary for you to know in order to answer the question correctly.

1. **(B)** Choice B is correct. **(Use Strategy 11: Use new definitions carefully.)**

$$Given:\ \widehat{x} = \frac{x+1}{x-2}$$

$$\frac{1}{\widehat{x}} = \frac{1}{\frac{x+1}{x-2}}$$

$$\frac{1}{\widehat{x}} = \frac{x-2}{x+1} \qquad \boxed{1}$$

(Use Strategy 13: Find unknowns by multiplication.)

Multiply $\boxed{1}$ by $\frac{1}{3}$. We get

$$\frac{1}{3}\left(\frac{1}{\widehat{x}}\right) = \frac{1}{3}\left(\frac{x-2}{x+1}\right)$$

$$\frac{1}{3}\left(\frac{1}{\widehat{x}}\right) = \frac{x-2}{3(x+1)}$$

(Math Refresher #431)

2. **(A)** Choice A is correct. **(Use Strategy 11: Use new definitions carefully.)**

$$Given:\ \widehat{x} = \frac{x+1}{x-2} \qquad \boxed{1}$$

$$\widehat{7} = \frac{7+1}{7-2}$$

$$\widehat{7} = \frac{8}{5}$$

(Math Refresher #431)

3. **(E)** Choice E is correct. **(Use Strategy 2: Translate from words to algebra.)**

$$2r + 2r + 3 < 11$$
$$4r + 3 < 11$$
$$4r < 8$$
$$r < 2 \qquad \boxed{1}$$

(Use Strategy 8: When all choices must be tested, start with E.) Choice E, 1, meets the condition in $\boxed{1}$.

(Math Refresher #422)

4. **(E)** Choice E is correct.

$$Given:\ \text{Temperature at 11:00 a.m.} = \quad 0°F \quad \boxed{1}$$
$$\text{Temperature at\ 8:00 a.m.} = -15°F \quad \boxed{2}$$
$$Let\ x = \text{Temperature at 5:00 p.m.} \qquad \boxed{3}$$

$$y = \text{Temperature rise} \qquad \boxed{4}$$

(Use Strategy 13: Find unknowns by subtracting.)
Subtract $\boxed{2}$ from $\boxed{1}$. We get

$$\text{Temperature rise in 3 hours} = 15°F \quad \boxed{5}$$

Subtract the times in $\boxed{1}$ and $\boxed{3}$. We get

$$\text{Time change} = 6 \text{ hours} \qquad \boxed{6}$$

Use $\boxed{4}$, $\boxed{5}$ and $\boxed{6}$ to find temperature rise from 11:00 a.m. to 5:00 p.m. We get

$$\frac{3 \text{ hours}}{6 \text{ hours}} = \frac{15°F}{y}$$

$$3y = 6 \times 15°F$$
$$y = 30°F$$

Use $\boxed{1}$, $\boxed{3}$ and $\boxed{7}$ to find the final temperature.

$$x = 0°F + 30°F$$
$$x = 30°F$$

(Math Refresher #120)

5. **(B)** Choice B is correct

$$Given:\ x + x^3 + x^5 + x^6 \qquad \boxed{1}$$
$$x = -1 \qquad \boxed{2}$$

Substitute $\boxed{2}$ into $\boxed{1}$. We get

$$-1 + (-1)^3 + (-1)^5 + (-1)^6 =$$
$$-1 - 1 - 1 + 1 \qquad = -2$$

(Math Refresher #431)

6. **(B)** Choice B is correct. **(Use Strategy 16: The obvious may be tricky!)**

Method 1: Given:
The U.S. flag is 25th from one end. $\boxed{1}$
The U.S. flag is 13th from the other end. $\boxed{2}$

At first glance it may appear that adding $\boxed{1}$ and $\boxed{2}$, $25 + 13 = 38$ will be the correct answer. This is WRONG!
    The U.S. flag is being counted twice: Once as the 25th and again as the 13th from the other end. The correct answer is

$$25 + 13 - 1 = 37.$$

Method 2:

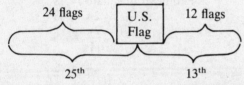

$$24 + 12 + \text{U.S. Flag} = 36 + \text{U.S. Flag} = 37$$

(Logical Reasoning)

7. **(D)** Choice D is correct. **(Use Strategy 11: Use new definitions carefully.)**

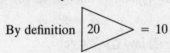

(Math Refresher #603 and # 607)

8. **(A)** Choice A is correct. **(Use Strategy 11: Use new definitions carefully.)**

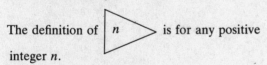

(Math Refresher #431)

9. **(C)** Choice C is correct. **(Use Strategy 17: Use the given information effectively.)**

$$Given:\ 55,555 = y + 50505$$
$$5050 = y \qquad \boxed{1}$$
We need: $50505 - 10y$ $\qquad \boxed{2}$

Substitute $\boxed{1}$ into $\boxed{2}$. We get

$$50505 - 10(5050) =$$
$$50505 - 50500 \quad =$$
$$5$$

(Math Refresher #406)

10. **(C)** Choice C is correct. **(Use Strategy 2: Translate from words to algebra.)**

$$Given:\ \text{Area B} = 1 \qquad \boxed{1}$$
$$\text{Area A} = 3(\text{Area B}) \qquad \boxed{2}$$
$$\text{Area B} = 3(\text{Area C}) \qquad \boxed{3}$$

Substitute $\boxed{1}$ into $\boxed{2}$. We get

$$\text{Area A} = 3(1) = 3 \qquad \boxed{4}$$

Substitute $\boxed{1}$ into $\boxed{3}$. We get

$$1 = 3(\text{Area C})$$
$$\frac{1}{3} = \text{Area C} \qquad \boxed{5}$$

Using $\boxed{1}$, $\boxed{4}$ and $\boxed{5}$, we have

Sum of areas A, B and C $= 3 + 1 + \dfrac{1}{3}$

Sum of areas A, B and C $= 4\dfrac{1}{3}$

(Math Refresher #200)

11. **(D)** Choice D is correct. **(Use Strategy 17: Use the given information effectively.)**

$$[(3a^3b^2)^3]^2 =$$
$$(3a^3b^2)^6 = 3^6 a^{18} b^{12}$$

Checking the choices, we find only Choice D has $a^{18}b^{12}$ and must be correct.
Note: We did not have to calculate 3^6!

(Math Refresher #429)

12. **(B)** Choice B is correct.

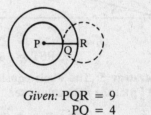

$$Given:\ PQR = 9 \qquad \boxed{1}$$
$$PQ = 4 \qquad \boxed{2}$$

(Use Strategy 3: The whole equals the sum of its parts.) From the diagram, we see that

$$PQR = PQ + QR \qquad \boxed{3}$$

Substitute $\boxed{1}$ and $\boxed{2}$ into $\boxed{3}$. We get

$$9 = 4 + QR$$
$$5 = QR$$

QR is the radius of a circle with center R and Q on its circumference. (See dot circle in diagram)

(Math Refresher #524)

13. **(D)** Choice D is correct. **(Use Strategy 6: Know how to manipulate inequalities.)**

$$Given: \frac{a}{b} < 1 \qquad \boxed{1}$$
$$a > 0 \qquad \boxed{2}$$
$$b > 0 \qquad \boxed{3}$$

Multiply $\boxed{1}$ by b. We get

$$\not b\left(\frac{a}{\not b}\right) < b\left(1\right)$$
$$a < b \qquad \boxed{4}$$

Divide $\boxed{4}$ by a. We get

$$\frac{a}{a} < \frac{b}{a}$$
$$1 < \frac{b}{a}$$

or

$$\frac{b}{a} > 1$$

(Math Refresher #422)

14. **(C)** Choice C is correct. **(Use Strategy 17: Use the given information effectively.)**

$$\left(\frac{3}{10}\right)^2 = \frac{9}{100}$$

Thus $\left(\frac{3}{10}\right)^2 = 9$ hundredths.

(Math Refresher #429)

15. **(C)** Choice C is correct.

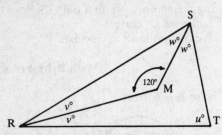

$$Given: \angle\ M = 120° \qquad \boxed{1}$$
$$\angle\ RST = 80° \qquad \boxed{2}$$

(Use Strategy 3: The whole equals the sum of its parts.) From the diagram we see that

$$\angle\ RST = w + w \qquad \boxed{3}$$

Substitute $\boxed{2}$ into $\boxed{3}$. We get

$$80° = w + w$$
$$80° = 2w$$
$$40° = w \qquad \boxed{4}$$

We know that in triangle RMS

$$v + w + 120° = 180° \qquad \boxed{5}$$

Substituting $\boxed{4}$ into $\boxed{5}$, we get

$$v + 40° + 120° = 180°$$
$$v + 160° = 180°$$
$$v = 20° \qquad \boxed{6}$$

From the diagram we see that

$$\angle\ SRT = v + v \qquad \boxed{7}$$

Substitute $\boxed{6}$ into $\boxed{7}$. We get

$$\angle\ SRT = 20° + 20°$$
$$\angle\ SRT = 40° \qquad \boxed{8}$$

We know that in triangle RST

$$\angle\ RST + \angle\ SRT + u = 180° \qquad \boxed{9}$$

Substitute $\boxed{2}$ and $\boxed{8}$ into $\boxed{9}$. We get

$$80° + 40° + u = 180°$$
$$120° + u = 180°$$
$$u = 60°$$

(Math Refresher #505)

16. **(B)** Choice B is correct. **(Use Strategy 2: Translate from words to algebra.)**

$$Given:\ \text{Square has perimeter } 2\pi \qquad \boxed{1}$$
Let S = side of square.
We know Perimeter of a square = 4S $\boxed{2}$

Substitute $\boxed{1}$ into $\boxed{2}$. We get

$$\text{Perimeter of square} = 4S$$
$$2\pi = 4S$$
$$\frac{2\pi}{4} = S$$
$$\frac{\pi}{2} = S \qquad \boxed{3}$$

We are given that area of circle = $\boxed{4}$
area of square
We know that: area of circle = πr^2 $\boxed{5}$
area of square $= S^2$ $\boxed{6}$

Substituting $\boxed{5}$ and $\boxed{6}$ into $\boxed{4}$, we get

$$\pi r^2 = S^2 \qquad \boxed{7}$$

Substitute $\boxed{3}$ into $\boxed{7}$. We get

$$\pi r^2 = \left(\frac{\pi}{2}\right)^2$$
$$\pi r^2 = \frac{\pi^2}{4}$$
$$r^2 = \frac{\pi^2}{4\pi}$$
$$r^2 = \frac{\pi}{4}$$
$$r = \sqrt{\frac{\pi}{4}} = \frac{\sqrt{\pi}}{2} \qquad \boxed{8}$$

We know the circumference of a circle = $2\pi r$ $\boxed{9}$
Substitute $\boxed{8}$ into $\boxed{9}$. We have

$$\text{Circumference} = \not 2\pi\left(\frac{\sqrt{\pi}}{\not 2}\right)$$
$$\text{Circumference} = \pi\sqrt{\pi}$$

(Math Refresher #303 and #310)

17. **(E)** Choice E is correct

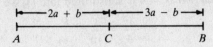

Given: C is the midpoint of AB
Thus, AC = CB ☐1
Substitute the lengths from the diagram into ☐1. We have

$$2a + b = 3a - b$$
$$b = a - b$$
$$2b = a$$

(Math Refresher #431)

18. **(D)** Choice D is correct

Given: Bus A averages $\dfrac{40km}{gallon}$ ☐1

Bus B averages $\dfrac{50km}{gallon}$ ☐2

Trip distance = 800 km ☐3

Fuel cost $= \dfrac{\$3}{gallon}$ ☐4

(Use Strategy 10: Know how to use units.) Divide ☐3 by ☐1. We get

$$\frac{800km}{\frac{40km}{gallon}} = \frac{800}{40} \text{ gallons} = 20 \text{ gallons used by Bus A} \quad ☐5$$

Divide ☐3 by ☐2. We get

$$\frac{800km}{\frac{50km}{gallon}} = \frac{800}{50} \text{ gallons} = 16 \text{ gallons used by Bus B} \quad ☐6$$

Multiply ☐5 by ☐4. We get

20 gallons × $\dfrac{\$3}{gallon}$ = \$60 cost for fuel for Bus A ☐7

Multiply ☐6 by ☐4. We get

16 gallons × $\dfrac{\$3}{gallon}$ = \$48 cost for fuel for Bus B ☐8

(Use Strategy 13: Find unknowns by subtracting.)
Subtract ☐8 from ☐7. We get \$60 − \$48 = \$12 difference in the fuel costs between Bus A and Bus B for an 800 km trip.

(Math Refresher #202)

19. **(A)** Choice A is correct.

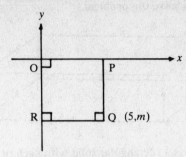

Given: OR = RQ ☐1
Coordinates of Q = (5,*m*) ☐2

From ☐2, we get RQ = 5 ☐3

Substitute ☐3 into ☐1. We get

$$OR = 5$$

(Use Strategy 16: The obvious may be tricky!) Since Q is below the *x*-axis, its *y*-coordinate is negative. Thus $m = -5$.

(Math Refresher #410)

20. **(B)** Choice B is correct. **(Use Strategy 14: Draw lines to help solve the problem.)**

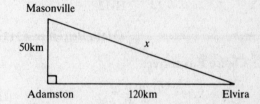

The given information translates into the diagram above. **(Use Strategy 18: Remember the special right triangles.)** The triangle above is a multiple of the special 5, 12, 13 right triangle

$$50 = 10(5)$$
$$120 = 10(12)$$
$$\text{Thus, } x = 10(13) = 130km.$$

(Note: The Pythagorean Theorem could also have been used: $50^2 + 120^2 = x^2$)

(Math Refresher #509)

21. **(E)** Choice E is correct. **(Use Strategy 14: Draw lines to help solve the problem.)**

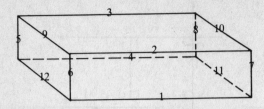

Above is a rectangular solid with each of its edges numbered 1 through 12, respectively. There are 3 groups of 4 parallel edges each.

$$1, 2, 3 \text{ and } 4 \text{ are parallel.}$$
$$5, 6, 7 \text{ and } 8 \text{ are parallel.}$$
$$9, 10, 11 \text{ and } 12 \text{ are parallel.}$$

For each group, there are 6 different pairs of edges. Thus, $3 \times 6 = 18$ different pairs of edges in all. Below is a listing of all the pairs:

1-2	2-3	5-6	6-7
1-3	2-4	5-7	6-8
1-4	3-4	5-8	7-8

9-10	10-11
9-11	10-12
9-12	11-12

(Math Refresher #312)

22. **(E)** Choice E is correct.

$$\text{Given: } \frac{a}{b} = \frac{1}{4} \qquad \boxed{1}$$

(Use Strategy 13: Find unknowns by multiplying.) Multiply $\boxed{1}$ by b. We have

$$\cancel{b}\left(\frac{a}{\cancel{b}}\right) = b\left(\frac{1}{4}\right)$$

$$a = \frac{b}{4} \qquad \boxed{2}$$

Squaring both sides of $\boxed{2}$, we get

$$a^2 = \frac{b^2}{16} \qquad \boxed{3}$$

(Use Strategy 13: Find unknowns by dividing.) Divide $\boxed{3}$ by b. We get

$$\frac{a^2}{b} = \frac{\frac{b^2}{16}}{b} \qquad \boxed{4}$$

$$\frac{a^2}{b} = \frac{b}{16}$$

(Use Strategy 7: Use numerics to help find the answer.) If $b = 4$ is substituted into $\boxed{4}$ we have

$$\frac{a^2}{4} = \frac{4}{16} = \frac{1}{4}$$

If $a = 1$ then $\frac{a}{b} = \frac{1}{4}$ and $\frac{a^2}{b} = \frac{1}{4}$

Thus, Choice I is satisfied. If $b = 8$ and $a = 2$ are substituted into $\boxed{4}$, we get

$$\frac{a}{b} = \frac{2}{8} = \frac{1}{4} \text{ and } \frac{a^2}{b} = \frac{2^2}{8} = \frac{4}{8} = \frac{1}{2}$$

Thus, Choice II is satisfied. If $b = 16$ and $a = 4$ are substituted into $\boxed{4}$, we have

$$\frac{a}{b} = \frac{4}{16} = \frac{1}{4} \text{ and } \frac{a^2}{b} = \frac{4^2}{16} = \frac{16}{16} = 1$$

Thus Choice III is satisfied.

(Math Refresher #111 and #112)

23. **(A)** Choice A is correct.

$$\text{Given: } 3x + y = 17 \qquad \boxed{1}$$
$$x + 3y = -1 \qquad \boxed{2}$$

(Use Strategy 13: Find unknowns by adding.) Adding $\boxed{1}$ and $\boxed{2}$, we get

$$4x + 4y = 16 \qquad \boxed{3}$$

(Use Strategy 13: Find unknowns by division.) Divide $\boxed{3}$ by 4. We have

$$x + y = 4 \qquad \boxed{4}$$

(Use Strategy 13: Find unknowns by multiplying.) Multiply $\boxed{4}$ by 3. We get

$$3x + 3y = 12$$

(Math Refresher #407)

24. **(B)** Choice B is correct. **(Use Strategy 2: Translate from words to algebra.)**

$$\text{Given: Rate of plane} = x \frac{\text{km}}{\text{hour}} \quad \boxed{1}$$

$$\text{Time of flight} = y \text{ hours} \quad \boxed{2}$$

Need: Distance plane had flown $\frac{2}{3} y$ hours ago $\quad \boxed{3}$

Subtracting $\boxed{3}$ from $\boxed{2}$, we get

Time plane had flown $\frac{2}{3} y$ hours ago $= y - \frac{2}{3} y$

Time plane had flown $\frac{2}{3} y$ hours ago $= \frac{1}{3} y$ hours $\quad \boxed{4}$

(Use Strategy 9: Know the rate, time and distance relationship.)

We know: Rate × Time = Distance $\quad \boxed{5}$
Substitute $\boxed{1}$ and $\boxed{4}$ into $\boxed{5}$. We get

$$x \frac{\text{km}}{\text{hour}} \times \frac{1}{3} y \text{ hours} = \text{Distance}$$

$\frac{xy}{3} = $ Distance plane had flown $\frac{2}{3} y$ hours ago.

(Math Refresher #201 and #202)

25. **(E)** Choice E is correct.

$\left(\text{Use Strategy 5: Average} = \dfrac{\text{Sum of values}}{\text{Total number of values}} \right)$

We know that Average $= \dfrac{\text{Sum of values}}{\text{Total number of values}} \quad \boxed{1}$

Given: Average of k scores is 20 $\quad \boxed{2}$
Substitute $\boxed{2}$ into $\boxed{1}$. We get

$$20 = \frac{\text{Sum of } k \text{ values}}{k}$$

$20k = $ Sum of k values $\quad \boxed{3}$
Given: Average of 10 of these scores is 15. $\boxed{4}$

Substitute $\boxed{4}$ into $\boxed{1}$. We have

$$15 = \frac{\text{Sum of 10 scores}}{10}$$

$150 = $ Sum of 10 scores $\quad \boxed{5}$
There are $k - 10$ scores remaining. $\quad \boxed{6}$

(Use Strategy 3: The whole equals the sum of its parts.)

We know: Sum of 10 scores + Sum of remaining scores

$= $ Sum of k scores $\quad \boxed{7}$

Substituting $\boxed{3}$ and $\boxed{5}$ into $\boxed{7}$, we get

$150 + $ Sum of remaining scores $= 20k$
Sum of remaining scores $= 20k - 150$ $\quad \boxed{8}$

Substituting $\boxed{6}$ and $\boxed{8}$ into $\boxed{1}$, we get

Average of remaining scores $= \dfrac{20k - 150}{k - 10}$

(Math Refresher #601)

EXPLANATORY ANSWERS FOR PRACTICE TEST 1 (continued)

Section 3: Standard Written English

> Section 3 does not count toward your SAT score. This Standard Written English section is used only for Freshman English placement when you get to college. However, you are advised to improve yourself in grammar and usage, and also in sentence structure. If you do well in the Standard Written English Test, you will be placed more advantageously in your college Freshman English class.

1. **(E)** All underlined parts are correct.

2. **(A)** "If any signer of the Constitution *were* to return to life . . ."
The verb in the "if clause" of a present contrary-to-fact conditional statement must have a past subjunctive form (*were*).

3. **(C)** "The dean of the college . . . *is* planning . . ."
The subject of the sentence (*dean*) is singular. Therefore, the verb must be singular (*is planning*).

4. **(E)** All underlined parts are correct.

5. **(B)** "Now that the stress . . . *is* over . . ."
The subject of the subordinate clause is singular (*stress*). Accordingly, the verb of the clause must be singular (*is*—not *are*). Incidentally, *examinations* and *interviews* are not subjects—they are objects of the preposition *of*.

6. **(D)** ". . . of more machines and *fewer* people."
We use *fewer* for persons and things that may be counted. We use *less* for bulk or mass.

7. **(C)** ". . . than *that of most* of the other countries of the world."
We must have paralellism so that the word *standard* in the main clause of the sentence acts as an antecedent for the pronoun *that* in the subordinate clause. As the original sentence reads, the American standard of living is still higher than the countries themselves.

8. **(C)** ". . . a long line of flags . . . *was* seen . . ."
The subject of the sentence is singular (*line*). Therefore, the verb must be singular (*was seen*).

9. **(A)** "*Because of* the failure . . ."
Never start a sentence with *Due to*.

10. **(E)** All underlined parts are correct.

11. **(C)** "After waiting in line for three hours, the tickets had, *much to our disgust*, been sold out when we reached the window."
Avoid squinting constructions—that is, modifiers that are so placed that the reader cannot tell whether they are modifying the words immediately preceding the construction, or the words immediately following the construction.

12. **(B)** ". . . resulted in our *guests'* packing up . . ."
A noun or pronoun immediately preceding a gerund is in the possessive case. Note that the noun *guests* followed by an apostrophe is possessive.

13. **(B)** "Sharp advances . . . *are* . . ."
Since the subject of the sentence is plural (*advances*), the verb must be plural (*are*).

14. **(A)** "An acquaintance with the memoirs . . . *enables* us . . ."
Since the subject of the sentence is singular (*acquaintance*), the verb must be singular (*enables*).

15. **(B)** ". . . to *whoever* . . . had a strong sense . . ."
The subject of the subordinate clause is *whoever* and it takes a nominative form (*whoever*—not *whomever*) since it is a subject. Incidentally, the expression *he believed* is parenthetical so that it has no grammatical relationship with the rest of the sentence.

16. **(A)** "If he *had lain* . . ."
The verb in the "if clause" of a past contrary-to-fact conditional statement must take the *had lain* form—not the *would have lain* form.

17. **(C)** ". . . John Crowe Ransom, *whom* you must know as an outstanding American critic."
The direct object of the subordinate clause—or of any clause or sentence—must be in the objective case and, accordingly, must take the objective form (*whom*—not *who*).

18. **(E)** All underlined parts are correct.

19. **(A)** "There is no objection to *his* joining . . .
We have here a pronoun that is acting as the subject of the gerund *joining*. As a subject of the gerund, the pronoun must be in the possessive case (*his*).

20. **(D)** ". . . of Chinese children parading *in colorful uniforms* up Mott Street."
In the original sentence, *in colorful uniforms* was a misplaced modifier.

21. **(D)** "The reason . . . is *that* . . ."
We must say *the reason is that*—not *the reason is because*.

22. **(A)** "There *remain* many reasons . . ."
The word "There" in this sentence is an expletive or introductory adverb. The subject of the sentence ("reasons") must agree with the verb ("remain") in number.

23. **(C)** ". . . *because* a Pan American Boeing 707 had crashed . . ."
The word group *on account of* has the function of a preposition. We need a subordinate conjunction (*because*) here in order to introduce the clause.

24. **(B)** ". . . *raided* the mansion . . ."
The past tense (*raided*)—not the present perfect tense (*has raided*)—is necessary because the sentence has a specific past time reference (*last night*).

25. **(E)** All underlined parts are correct.

26. **(B)** Choice A is incorrect because the plural verb ("were") is necessary. The reason for the plural verb is that the subject "as" acts as a relative pronoun whose antecedent is the plural noun "novels." Choice B is correct. Choice C is awkward. Choice D changes the meaning of the original sentence—so does Choice E.

27. **(C)** Choice A is incorrect—never start a sentence with "being that." Choice B is too wordy. Choice C is correct. Choice D is incorrect because we "stayed"—not "stood." Choice E is incorrect because "on account of" may never be used as a subordinate conjunction.

28. **(E)** Avoid improper ellipsis. Choices A, B, C, and D are incorrect for this reason. Choice E is correct. The word "kept" must be included since the second part of the sentence uses another form of the verb ("keep").

29. **(C)** Choice A is incorrect because the copulative verb "felt" takes a predicate adjective ("bad")—not an adverb ("badly"). Choice B is incorrect for the same reason. Moreover, we don't say "felt bad why." Choice C is correct. Choice D is incorrect because the verbal phrase "by scolding" is awkward in this context. Choice E is incorrect because of the

use of "badly" and because the past perfect form of the verb ("had felt") is wrong in this time sequence.

30. **(E)** Choices A, B, and C are incorrect because the part of the sentence that deals with the buying of the book is in the wrong position. Choice D is incorrect because the meaning of the original sentence has been changed. According to this choice, others besides Blacks have been struggling. Choice E is correct.

31. **(A)** Choice A is correct. The other choices are unidiomatic.

32. **(D)** Choice A is incorrect because the possessive form of the noun ("Tom's") must be used to modify the gerund ("wanting"). Choice B is too wordy. Choice C changes the meaning of the original sentence. Choice D is correct. Choice E is incorrect for the same reason that Choice A is incorrect. Also, Choice E changes the meaning of the original sentence.

33. **(A)** Choice A is correct. Choice B is incorrect because "wife" should precede "me." Choice C is incorrect because the object form "me" (not the nominative form "I") should be used as the indirect object. Choice D is incorrect for the reasons given above for Choices B and C. Choice E is too roundabout.

34. **(D)** Choices A, B, C, and E are incorrect because of the misplacement of the subordinate clause ("if the weather is favorable"). Choice D is correct.

35. **(A)** Choices B and C are incorrect because of improper ellipsis. The words "those of" are necessary in these choices. Choice D is incorrect because the "body movements" are not "a dancer's." The possessive use of "dancer's" is incorrect in Choice E.

36. **(D)** The clause "that was rotten" is misplaced in Choices A, B, and C. Choice D is correct. Choice E is incorrect because the passive use of the verb is not as effective as the active use, in this context.

37. **(B)** Choice A uses wrong tense sequence. Since the reading of the book took place before the watching of the picture, the reading should be expressed in the past perfect tense, which shows action prior to the simple past tense. Choice B corrects the error with the use of the past perfect tense, "had read," instead of the past tense, "read." Choices C, D, and E do not correct the mistake, and Choice E in addition changes the meaning.

38. **(D)** Choice A is wrong because the word "them," being plural, cannot properly take the singular antecedent, "anyone." Choices B and C do not correct this error. Choice D corrects it by substituting "him" for "them." Choice E, while correcting the error, changes the meaning of the sentence.

39. **(E)** Choice A contains a "false series," meaning that the word "and" connects the three words in the series—bread, butter, cheese—with a wholly different clause, instead of with a similar fourth word. The series, therefore, needs its own "and" to complete it. Only Choice E furnishes this additional "and."

40. **(D)** Choice A violates the principle of parallel structure. If the first thing the children liked was "swimming" (a gerund), then the second thing they liked should be, not "to watch" (an infinitive), but "watching" (the gerund). Choice B does not improve the sentence. Choice C repeats the beginning of the sentence with the repetitious words "that they liked." Choice D is correct. Choice E simply reverses the gerund and the infinitive without correcting the error.

41. **(C)** "... *breaking* Babe Ruth's record."
The unnecessary conjunction *and* makes the sentence awkward.

42. **(D)** "... will file *for divorce*."
The idiom is "to file for divorce"—not "to file for divorcing."

43. **(B)** "... disappeared *as if* ..."
The correct expression is "as if"—not "like as if." Incidentally, Choice C (*were*) is correct because it is the correct form of the contrary-to-fact conditional.

44. **(C)** "... *are* getting lessons ..."
The subject (*residents*) is plural. Therefore the verb (*are getting*) must be plural.

45. **(D)** "... because *the car* needed gasoline. The pronoun *it* has an indefinite antecedent. We cannot tell whether *it* refers to the car or the service station. Accordingly, we must be specific by using *car* instead of *it*.

46. **(A)** "The man *whose* temper is under control ..."
The contraction (*who's* meaning *who is*) is obviously incorrect here. We need the possessive pronoun-adjective *whose* to modify the noun (*temper*).

47. **(E)** All underlined parts are correct.

48. **(A)** "Neither George Foreman *nor* millions of others ..."
Neither must be paired with *nor* (not with *or*).

49. **(C)** "... before his mother *came* home ..."
The past perfect tense (*had come*) is used for a past action that occurs before another past action. The mother's coming home did not occur before Bob wanted to finish his homework. Therefore, the past tense (*came*) should be used—not the past perfect tense (*had come*).

50. **(B)** "Inflation together with the high interest rates and soaring oil prices *is hurting* ..."
The subject of the sentence is *Inflation*. This is a singular subject so the verb must be singular—*is hurting* (not *are hurting*). The words *rates* and *prices* are not parts of the subject.

EXPLANATORY ANSWERS FOR PRACTICE TEST 1 (continued)

Section 4: Verbal Ability

1. **(E)** Choice E is correct. See **Antonym Strategy 3.** *Dubious* means *doubtful; questionable.* The opposite of *dubious* is *certain.*

2. **(B)** Choice B is correct. See **Antonym Strategy 3.** *Coarse* means *crude; lacking delicacy.* The opposite of *coarse* is *polished.*

3. **(C)** Choice C is correct. See **Antonym Strategy 2.** *Belligerent* means *warlike; quarrelsome.* The opposite of *belligerent* is *tranquil.*

4. **(D)** Choice D is correct. See **Antonym Strategy 2.** *Atrocious* means *cruel, brutal.* The opposite of *atrocious* is *considerate.*

5. **(C)** Choice C is correct. See **Antonym Strategy 2.** *Somber* means *dark; gloomy.* The opposite of *somber* is *cheerful.*

6. **(B)** Choice B is correct. See **Antonym Strategy 2.** *Grueling* means *exhausting.* The opposite of *grueling* is *refreshing.*

7. **(B)** Choice B is correct. *Prestige* means *importance; influence.* The opposite of *prestige* is *scorn.*

8. **(E)** Choice E is correct. *Taciturn* means *speaking very little; silent.* The opposite of *taciturn* is *talkative.*

9. **(A)** Choice A is correct. *Valiant* means *brave.* The opposite of *valiant* is *cowardly.*

10. **(C)** Choice C is correct. See **Antonym Strategy 2.** *Insipid* means *tasteless; dull.* The opposite of *insipid* is *tasteful.*

11. **(A)** Choice A is correct. See **Sentence Completion Strategy 2.** Examine the first word of each choice. Choice (B) a specter . . . and Choice (C) an exodus . . . , do *not* make sense because a nice apartment building is not a specter (ghost) or an exodus (a departure). Now consider the other choices. Choice (A) a boon . . . haunted, is the only choice which makes sense in the sentence. The word "haunted" here means "visited frequently."

12. **(A)** Choice A is correct. See **Sentence Completion Strategy 2.** Examine the first word of each choice. Choice (B) cancellation . . . and Choice (D) abundance . . . , do *not* make sense because we do not refer to an inflation cancellation or an inflation abundance. Now consider the other choices. Choice (A) spiral . . . indubitably (meaning unquestionably, certainly) is the only choice which has a word pair which makes sentence sense.

13. **(B)** Choice B is correct. See **Sentence Completion Strategy 4.** The first word "although" is an *opposition indicator.* After the subordinate clause "although . . . markedly," we can expect an opposing idea in the main clause which follows and completes the sentence. Choice (B) unaffected, gives us the word that brings out the opposition thought that we expect in the sentence. Choices A, C, D, and E do not give us a sentence that makes sense.

14. **(E)** Choice E is correct. See **Sentence Completion Strategy 2.** Examine the first word of each choice. Choice (B) relegates (meaning to banish or to assign to a lower position) . . . and Choice (C) accumulates . . . , do *not* make sense since we do not say that a sense of fairness relegates or accumulates. Now consider the other choices. Choice (E) dictates . . . varies, is the only choice which makes sentence sense.

15. **(D)** Choice D is correct. See **Sentence Completion Strategy 1.** The word "elusive" means "cleverly or skillfully; able to avoid being caught." Therefore, Choice (D) elusive, is the only correct choice.

16. **(D)** Choice D is correct. One is likely to trust a person who is virtuous. One is likely to suspect a person who is shady. Also see Analogy Strategy 5.

    (Association relationship)

17. **(D)** Choice D is correct. To embarrass is to cause a person to feel ill at ease; to humiliate is to humble or disgrace a person. To spank is a light form of punishment; to whip is a severe form of punishment. We have in this analogy a matter of Degree. Choice B may seem correct but it is incorrect. To bicker and to argue both mean to quarrel. There is no difference of intensity here. Also see Analogy Strategy 4.

    (Degree relationship)

18. **(B)** Choice B is correct. Something that is counterfeit does not have authenticity. Someone who is erratic does not have reliability.

    (Association relationship)

19. **(B)** Choice B is correct. A cot is used instead of a bed. A tissue is used instead of a handkerchief.

    (Purpose relationship)

20. **(C)** Choice C is correct. A paragraph is a necessary part of the whole essay. An act is a necessary part of the whole play. You might have chosen Choice (B) saddle : horse, which is incorrect because a saddle is *not* a necessary or indispensable part of the horse. Also see **Analogy Strategy 4.**

(Part-Whole relationship)

21. **(E)** Choice E is correct. It is a characteristic of a proverb to be pithy—that is, short and to the point. It is a characteristic of snow to be white. The other choices do not have this characteristic or association relationship *consistently*. Also see **Analogy Strategy 4.**

(Association relationship)

22. **(E)** Choice E is correct. The word scold means to reprimand or to find fault with another person. The word denounce means to speak out strongly against another person or condemn him openly. Therefore, denounce is a stronger form than scold. To maim means to injure seriously. Therefore, to maim is a stronger form than to injure. We have in this question a Degree relationship. Note that there is also a Degree relationship in Choice C since to squander means to spend recklessly. But Choice C is incorrect because the order of words is reversed. If the choice were spend : squander, this choice would also be correct. See **Analogy Strategy 3.**

(Degree relationship)

23. **(A)** Choice A is correct. A person's integrity would prevent him from being corrupted. A person's disguise would prevent him from being recognized. We have here an opposite relationship and also cause and effect relationship in a negative way. Choice C sounds correct but it is *not* correct. A person's simplicity might cause him to be admired, but we do not have the negative situation that we have in the capitalized pair and in the correct Choice A. See **Analogy Strategy 4.**

(Opposite and Cause and Effect relationship)

24. **(E)** Choice E is correct. Something that is eternal has endless duration. Something or someone who is omnipotent has full or endless power.

(Degree relationship)

25. **(B)** Choice B is correct. A person who is submissive is not likely to show defiance. A person who is courageous is not likely to show fear. We have here an Opposite relationship in a negative way. Choice D may seem correct because a person who is confident is likely to have poise. However, this relationship is not expressed in a negative way, so Choice D is incorrect.

(Opposite relationship)

26. **(E)** Choice E is correct. Hooker must have been an officer on the Union side because Jeb Stuart, who led a Confederate cavalry contingent, was "assigned to the task of harassing Hooker and impeding his pursuit of Lee's invasion forces." (Lines 36–37) Choice A is incorrect. The passage states: "By those who like to speculate . . . (the South's) failure to do so (win the battle in the first three days) has frequently been attributed to destiny or chance—even the hand of God." (Lines 17–20) Others—not the author—have held God responsible for the South's defeat. Choice B is incorrect. The author confines his statement about the battle's tremendous impact to "American military history." (Line 3) Choice C is incorrect. The passage does not state or imply that General Lee died in battle. Choice D is incorrect because, though the statement may be true, the passage does not offer any opinion about Lee's place in the hearts of all Americans.

27. **(A)** Choice A is correct. The term "high tide" means the highest point—in this case, a point of greatest progress. The South was never closer to winning the Civil War as it was at the battle of Gettysburg. As the passage states, the battle of Gettysburg was the turning point of the Civil War. From that point on, the Confederate Army was on the downgrade. Choice B is incorrect. The reference is to Shakespeare's title character Richard III who, in desperation, exclaims that he is willing to give his kingdom for a horse. The situation of King Richard is irrelevant to the passage. Choice C is incorrect. Lee has been accepted as a "General for the Ages" but the passage does not deal exclusively with the Confederate general. Choices D and E are incorrect because they are too general.

28. **(D)** Choice D is correct. The passage states: "Among the innumerable 'ifs' of Gettysburg, a certain few would reach high on the list . . ." The passage goes on to mention the capture of Lee's correspondence and the failure of Stuart's cavalry unit to appear on time. Choices B, C, and E are incorrect because these matters—Napoleon's military strategy, the weather at Gettysburg, and the work of Lee's brigadier generals and colonels—are not mentioned in the passage. Choice A is incorrect because the passage speaks of the "desperately crucial quality which penetrated the consciousness of the men in the battle lines on both sides." (Lines 7–8)

29. **(C)** Choice C is correct. See lines 16–18: "The kitchen . . . as his mother had kept it in his boyhood." Choice A is incorrect. See lines 11–14: "He would have liked . . . at the farm before night." Choice B is incorrect. Although the passage indicates that Ethan's wife "had driven off" (line 1) and refers to the "fact of Zeena's absence," the passage does not state or imply that Ethan's wife was no longer living with him. Choice D is incorrect. The passage *does* show that Ethan had a feeling for Mattie. See lines 21–24: "For the first time . . . like a

married couple." However, nowhere does the passage indicate that Mattie and Ethan were planning to get married. Choice E is incorrect. See lines 32–37: "There was in him . . . friendly human intercourse."

30. **(D)** Choice D is correct. The word "spruce" is derived from the word "Prussia." Prussian leather was noted for its fineness. Therefore, "spruce" as it describes the kitchen means "neat and trim." Choice A, B, C, and E are, accordingly, incorrect.

31. **(B)** Choice B is correct. See lines 32–37: "There was in him . . . friendly human intercourse." Choice A is incorrect. Although there are indications in the passage that Ethan *could be* faithful and loving to Mattie, there is no indication in the passage that he was *generally* faithful and loving. Choices C and D are incorrect because the passage does not show that Ethan is either eager to please other people or that he is inclined to avoid responsibilities. Although the passage may imply that Ethan is going to be unfaithful while his wife is away, the passage does not indicate that Ethan is a *generally* hard person to trust. Therefore, Choice E is incorrect.

32. **(D)** Choice D is correct. Line 1 ("To the world when it was half a thousand years younger . . .") indicates that the author is describing the world roughly 500 hundred years ago. Choice D—1455 A.D.—is therefore the closest date. Although Choice C is also in the Middle Ages, it is almost a thousand years ago. So it is an incorrect choice. Choices A, B, and E are obviously incorrect choices.

33. **(A)** Choice A is correct. We can see that "with greater avidity" is an adverbial phrase telling the reader how "honors and riches" were enjoyed and desired. See lines 16–19: "We, at the present day . . . formerly enjoyed." The reader thus learns that even simple pleasures such as a glass of wine were more keenly enjoyed then. Choices B, C, D, and E are incorrect because the passage does *not* state or imply that "with greater avidity" means "with greater sadness *or* terror *or* silence *or* disappointment."

34. **(B)** Choice B is not true—therefore it is the correct choice. See lines 40–42: "The contrast between silence and sound . . . than it is in our lives." The next sentence states that the modern town hardly knows silence. These two sentences together imply that the typical town of the Middle Ages did have periods of silence.
Choice A is true—therefore an incorrect choice. See lines 33–34: "A medieval town . . . in extensive suburbs of factories and villas."
Choice C is true—therefore an incorrect choice. See lines 35–36: ". . . it (a medieval town) stood forth . . . with innumerable turrets."
Choice D is true—therefore an incorrect choice. See line 38: ". . . the lofty mass of the churches always remained dominant."

Choice E is true—therefore an incorrect choice. See lines 36–38: "However tall . . . in the aspect of the town."

35. **(C)** Choice C is correct. Throughout the passage, the author is indicating the strong, rough, uncontrolled forces that pervaded the period. See, for example, the following references. Lines 10–11: "Misfortunes and poverty were more afflicting than at present." Lines 20–21: "Then, again, all things in life . . . cruel publicity." Lines 27–29: "Executions . . . songs and music." Therefore, Choice C is correct. Choice A is incorrect because the passage speaks of joys as well as miseries. See lines 16–19: "We, at the present day . . . formerly enjoyed." Choice B is incorrect for this reason: Although the author contrasts town and country, he gives no indication as to which was dominant in that society. Therefore, Choice B is incorrect. Choice D is incorrect. The author contrasts how it felt to be rich or poor but he does not indicate that the rich mistreated the poor. Choice E is incorrect because the pious nature of the people in the Middle Ages is only one of the many elements discussed in the passage.

36. **(E)** Choice E is correct. See lines 5–7: "All experience . . . pain of child-life." Throughout the passage, this theme is illustrated with specific examples. Choices A and B are incorrect because they are one-sided. In the passage, many conditions that may make the Middle Ages seem worse than today are matched with conditions that may make the Middle Ages seem better than today. Choice C is incorrect because nowhere in the passage is intelligence mentioned or implied. Choice D is incorrect because the third paragraph indicates that, far from being subdued, people went about their lives with a great deal of show and pageantry.

37. **(E)** Choice E is correct. Except for the first part of the passage that tells about the beginning of the universe and the start of life, the passage, for the most part, deals with how the "changing conditions [on earth] called forth more sophisticated responses from brains that grew increasingly large and potent." [lines 30–32] Also see lines 32–36: "The long process climaxed . . . life on earth." Choice A is incorrect because it deals only with the introductory part of the passage. Choice B is incorrect because the author really does not compare various intelligences. He describes them. Choice C is incorrect because the only reference the author makes to the "survival of the fittest" is in lines 26–28: "The mammals needed . . . better brains." Choice D is incorrect because the passage is not primarily about the beginning of the universe.

38. **(B)** Choice B is correct. See lines 15–19: "The first brains appeared in fish . . . odor and light." Choice A, C, D, and E are incorrect because the author does not include an answer for these choices anywhere in the passage. Consider Choice A. The passage tells the reader *when*—not *how*—life came

about in the beginning years of our earth. Also consider Choice C. A student may infer from the passage that dinosaurs disappeared from the earth because their brains were inferior to those of the mammals. However, this inference is unjustified because it might have been the height and bulkiness of the dinosaurs that proved a handicap in surviving.

39. **(C)** Choice C is correct. First let us consider each of the three items listed.
Item I is true. See lines 32–37: "The long process [the development of intelligence on earth] climaxed . . . the whole panorama of life on earth."
Item III is true. See lines 19–22: "Intelligence . . . 250 million years ago."

Item II is not true. See lines 10–11: "Science can find . . . beginning of the universe."
Accordingly, Choice C is the correct choice.

40. **(B)** Choice B is correct. See lines 5–9: "Life arose . . . purpose of a Creator is a matter of individual determination." Among the representative types mentioned in the choices, there would, no doubt, be some religiously inclined persons in each of the A, C, D, and E groups who would refuse to accept what the author states in lines 5–9. However, it is more *likely* that a church minister would reject what the author states in these lines. Therefore, Choices A, C, D, and E are incorrect.

EXPLANATORY ANSWERS FOR
PRACTICE TEST 1 (continued)

Section 5: Math Ability

1. **(D)** Choice D is correct.

Given: $ab = 64$ and a and b are
positive integers $\boxed{1}$

(Use Strategy 7: Use numerics to help find the answer.)

If $a = 64$, $b = 1$, then $\boxed{1}$ is satisfied
and $a + b = 65$ $\boxed{2}$
If $a = 32$, $b = 2$, then $\boxed{1}$ is satisfied
and $a + b = 34$ $\boxed{3}$
If $a = 16$, $b = 4$, then $\boxed{1}$ is satisfied
and $a + b = 20$ $\boxed{4}$
If $a = 8$, $b = 8$, then $\boxed{1}$ is satisfied
and $a + b = 16$ $\boxed{5}$

The only other pairs of values that satisfy $\boxed{1}$ are each of the above pairs of values reversed for a and b. Thus $\boxed{5}$, $a + b = 16$, is the smallest value of $a + b$.

(Math Refresher #431)

2. **(A)** Choice A is correct.

$$\sqrt{\frac{3}{\sqrt{9}}} = \sqrt{\frac{3}{3}}$$
$$= \sqrt{1}$$
$$= 1$$

(Math Refresher #430)

3. **(D)** Choice D is correct.

Given: AB $\quad 0 < A < 6$ $\boxed{1}$
$+ BA$ $\quad 0 < B < 6$ $\boxed{2}$
66 $\boxed{3}$

(Use Strategy 17: Use the given information effectively.) From $\boxed{3}$ we see that
$$B + A = 6 \qquad \boxed{4}$$

(Use Strategy 7: Use numerics to help find the answer.) Conditions $\boxed{1}$, $\boxed{2}$ and $\boxed{4}$ can be satisfied when:

$A = 1, B = 5$
$A = 2, B = 4$
$A = 3, B = 3$
$A = 4, B = 2$
$A = 5, B = 1$

Thus, there are five possible values of A.

(Math Refresher #431)

4. **(C)** Choice C is correct.

Given: $r = a + b$ $\boxed{1}$
$s = b - a$ $\boxed{2}$

(Use Strategy 13: Find unknowns by subtracting.) Subtract $\boxed{2}$ from $\boxed{1}$. We get

$$r - s = a + b - (b - a)$$
$$= a + b - b + a$$
$$r - s = 2a \qquad \boxed{3}$$

Given: $a = 5$, $b = 4$ $\boxed{4}$

Substitute $\boxed{4}$ into $\boxed{3}$. We have

$$r - s = 2a$$
$$= 2(5)$$
$$r - s = 10$$

(Math Refresher #407)

5. **(B)** Choice B is correct.

Number of Shirts	Total Price
1	$12.00
Box of 3	$22.50
Box of 6	$43.40

From the chart above, we know

$$6 \text{ shirts} = \$43.40 \qquad \boxed{1}$$

(Use Strategy 13: Find unknowns by division.) Dividing $\boxed{1}$ by 6, we get

$$\frac{6 \text{ shirts}}{6} = \frac{\$43.40}{6}$$
$$1 \text{ shirt} = \$ 7.23\overline{3}$$

Cost per shirt $\approx \$7.20$

(Math Refresher #406)

6. **(B)** Choice B is correct. [See chart in Question 5 on page 49.]
(Use Strategy 17: Use the given information effectively.) From the chart above, we see

Box of 6 shirts = $43.40

Price per shirt $= \dfrac{\$43.40}{6} = 7.23\overline{3}$ ☐1

Box of 3 shirts = $22.50

Price per shirt $= \dfrac{\$22.50}{3} = \$7.50$ ☐2

1 shirt = $12.00
Price per shirt = $12.00 ☐3

From ☐1, ☐2 and ☐3 we see the best price per shirt is for a box of 6; then a box of 3; and finally a single shirt. To buy 11 shirts at *minimum* cost we need

1 Box of 6	=	$43.40	☐4
1 Box of 3	=	$22.50	☐5
2 single shirts =	{	$12.00	☐6
		$12.00	☐7

(Use Strategy 13: Find unknowns by adding.) Adding ☐4, ☐5, ☐6 and ☐7, we get

Minimum cost of 11 shirts = $89.90

(Math Refresher #406)

7. **(E)** Choice E is correct.

Given: $5x^2 - 15x = 0$ ☐1
$x \neq 0$ ☐2

Factoring ☐1, we get

$5x(x - 3) = 0$
$5x = 0$ or $x - 3 = 0$
$x = 0$ or $x = 3$ ☐3

Applying ☐2 to ☐3, we get

$x = 3$

(Math Refresher #407)

8. **(D)** Choice D is correct.

Given: $4a > 3b$ ☐1

(Use Strategy C: Use numerics if it appears that the answer can't be determined.)

Let $a = 1$ and $b = 1$ ☐2
Then $4a = 4(1) = 4$ and $3b = 3(1) = 3$
and ☐1 is satisfied.

Let $a = 2$ and $b = 1$ ☐3
Then $4a = 4(2) = 8$ and $3b = 3(1) = 3$
and ☐1 is satisfied.

From ☐2 and ☐3 we see that two different relationships are possible. Thus, the answer can't be determined from the given information.

(Math Refresher #431)

9. **(C)** Choice C is correct.

Given: John flips a quarter coin twice ☐1

Column A	Column B
The chances of John getting 2 tails	The chances of John getting no tails

(Use Strategy 17: Use the given information effectively.) Applying ☐1, we get

Chances of a tail $= \dfrac{1}{2}$ ☐2

Chances of no tail $= \dfrac{1}{2}$ ☐3

Using ☐2 and ☐3, the columns become

Column A	Column B
$\left(\dfrac{1}{2}\right)\left(\dfrac{1}{2}\right)$	$\left(\dfrac{1}{2}\right)\left(\dfrac{1}{2}\right)$

(Logical Reasoning)

10. **(B)** Choice B is correct.

Column A	Column B
$4.8 + 3.6 + 8 =$	$95.9 + 94.8$ =
16.4	$\dfrac{}{10}$
	$\dfrac{190.7}{10} = 19.07$

(Decimal Addition)

11. **(A)** Choice A is correct.

Column A	Column B
3^9	1^{27}

Column B, $1^{27} = 1$. It is obvious that Column A, 3^9 is larger than 1.

(Math Refresher #429)

12. **(A)** Choice A is correct.

y is an integer ☐1

Column A	Column B
10	The maximum value of $9 - y^2$ ☐2

(Use Strategy 17: Use the given information effectively.) Since y^2 is being subtracted from 9 in Column B, $9 - y^2$ will be maximum when y^2 is minimum. Using ☐1, y^2 will be minimum when $y = 0$ (Any non-zero integer squared is positive.)

Thus $y^2 = 0$ ☐3

Substituting ☐3 into ☐2, the columns become

10	$9 - 0 =$
10	9

(Math Refresher #429 and #431)

13. **(C)** Choice C is correct.

$$\text{Given: } \frac{a}{7} = \frac{b}{1} \qquad \boxed{1}$$

Column A	Column B	
a	$7b$	$\boxed{2}$

(Use Strategy E: Get the columns and given to look the same.) (Use Strategy 13: Find unknowns by division.) Divide each part of $\boxed{2}$ by 7. The columns become

$\dfrac{a}{7}$	$\dfrac{7b}{7}$	
$\dfrac{a}{7}$	$\dfrac{b}{1}$	$\boxed{3}$

$\boxed{3}$ and $\boxed{1}$ are identical. Thus, Choice C is correct.

(Math Refresher #406)

14. **(A)** Choice A is correct.

Column A	Column B
6×7^{15}	7×6^{15}

(Use Strategy B: Cancel positive quantities from both columns by division.) Divide both columns by 6×7. We get

$\dfrac{6 \times 7^{15}}{6 \times 7}$	$\dfrac{7 \times 6^{15}}{6 \times 7}$
$= \dfrac{7^{15}}{7}$	$\dfrac{6^{15}}{6}$
7^{14}	6^{14}

Thus, Column A is larger.

(Math Refresher #429)

15. **(B)** Choice B is correct. **(Use Strategy 2: Translate from words to algebra.)**

Let x = what Mary has obtained so far	$\boxed{1}$
Then $x - 15$ = Mary's answer	$\boxed{2}$
$x + 20$ = Correct answer	$\boxed{3}$

Column A	Column B	
Mary's answer to the question	The correct answer to the question	$\boxed{4}$

Substituting $\boxed{2}$ and $\boxed{3}$ into $\boxed{4}$, the columns become

$x - 15$	$x + 20$

(Use Strategy A: Cancel equal things from both columns by subtracting.) Subtract x from both columns. We get

-15	$+20$

(Math Refresher #406)

16. **(C)** Choice C is correct.

Given: The regular price of a car is p dollars.

(Use Strategy 2: Know how to find a percent less than a given amount.)

Column A	Column B
The price of the car after a 20 percent discount =	$0.80\,p$ dollars

$$p - \left(\frac{20}{100}\right)p =$$
$$p - .20p =$$

$0.80\,p$ dollars	$0.80\,p$ dollars

(Math Refresher #114 and #119)

17. **(B)** Choice B is correct.

$$\text{Given: } y^2 - 11y + 30 = 0 \qquad \boxed{1}$$

(Use Strategy 17: Use the given information effectively.) Factoring $\boxed{1}$, we have

$$(y - 6)(y - 5) = 0$$
$$y = 6 \text{ or } y = 5 \qquad \boxed{2}$$

Column A	Column B	
y	7	$\boxed{3}$

Substituting each value from $\boxed{2}$ into $\boxed{3}$, we have

5	7
or	
6	7

In both cases, Column B is larger.

(Math Refresher #409)

18. **(C)** Choice C is correct. **(Use Strategy 2: Translate from words to algebra.)**

Given: x = number of boys in highschool A

The number of girls = $4x - 8$	$\boxed{1}$

Column A	Column B	
The number of girls in highschool A	$4x - 8$	$\boxed{2}$

Substituting $\boxed{1}$ into $\boxed{2}$, the columns become

$4x - 8$	$4x - 8$

(Math Refresher #406)

19. **(D)** Choice D is correct. **(Use Strategy C: Use numerics if it appears that the answer can't be determined.)**

Column A	Column B	
$s + t - r$	4	$\boxed{1}$

Given: $s < r$ and r, s and t are equal to 6, 5, 4, but not necessarily in that order $\boxed{2}$

Let $s = 4$, $r = 5$ and $t = 6$. The columns become

$\dfrac{4 + 6 - 5}{5}$	4	$\boxed{3}$

Let $s = 4$, $r = 6$, $t = 5$. The columns become

$\dfrac{4 + 5 - 6}{3}$	4	$\boxed{4}$

From $\boxed{3}$ and $\boxed{4}$ we see that two different relationships are possible. Thus, the answer can't be determined from the given information.

(Math Refresher #431)

20. **(D)** Choice D is correct.

Given: A solid figure has equal faces. The volume of the solid is 125.

Column A	Column B
The number of faces of the solid	5

(Use Strategy 17: Use the given information effectively.) Equal faces and a volume of 125 are not enough information to determine the number of faces!

(Logical Reasoning)

21. **(C)** Choice C is correct.

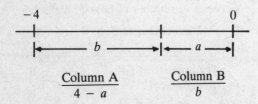

Column A	Column B
$4 - a$	b

(Use Strategy D: Make comparison simpler by adding.) Add a to both columns:

Column A	Column B
$4 - a + a$	$b + a$
4	$b + a$

(Use Strategy 3: The whole equals the sum of its parts.) From the numberline we see that

$b + a = 4$ (The distance from 0 to -4 is 4 units)

(Math Refresher #410)

22. **(D)** Choice D is correct.

Given: $\dfrac{5}{6} < y < \dfrac{6}{5}$

This becomes

$\dfrac{5}{6} < y < 1\dfrac{1}{5}$ $\boxed{1}$

Column A	Column B
y	$\dfrac{8}{7} = 1\dfrac{1}{7}$

(Use Strategy C: Use numerics if it appears that the answer can't be determined.)
Let $y = 1$, which satisfies $\boxed{1}$. The columns become

1	$1\dfrac{1}{7}$	$\boxed{2}$

Now let $y = 1\dfrac{1}{6}$, which satisfies $\boxed{1}$.

The columns become

$1\dfrac{1}{6}$	$1\dfrac{1}{7}$	$\boxed{3}$

From $\boxed{2}$ and $\boxed{3}$ we see that two different relationships are possible. Thus, the answer can't be determined from the information given.

(Math Refresher #111 and #431)

23. **(B)** Choice B is correct.

Column A	Column B
$\dfrac{2}{\dfrac{9}{5} - 1}$	3

(Use Strategy D: Make a comparison simpler by multiplying.)
Multiply Column A by $\dfrac{9}{5} - 1$. We get:

Column A	Column B
2	$3\left(\dfrac{9}{5} - 1\right)$
2	$\dfrac{27}{5} - 3$
2	$\dfrac{27}{5} - \dfrac{15}{5}$
2	$\dfrac{12}{5}$
2	$2\dfrac{2}{5}$

(Math Refresher #111)

24. **(A)** Choice A is correct.

Given: 100 centimeters = 1 meter ⊡1

(Use Strategy 10: Know how to use units.)

Column A

Side of square = 5 meters ⊡2
Using ⊡1, we have
Side of square = 5 meters × $\dfrac{100 \text{ centimeters}}{1 \text{ meter}}$

Side of square = 500 centimeters ⊡3
Area of square = (side)^2 ⊡4
Substituting ⊡3 into ⊡4, we get
Area of square = (500 centimeters)^2
Area of square = 250000 centimeters^2 ⊡5

Column B

Side of square = 5 centimeters ⊡6
Substituting ⊡6 into ⊡4, we get
Area of square = (5 centimeters)^2
Area of square = 25 centimeters^2 ⊡7
Multiplying ⊡7 by 100, we get
100 × Area of square = 100 × 25 centimeters^2
100 × Area of square = 2500 centimeters^2 ⊡8

Comparing ⊡5 and ⊡8, we see that Column A is larger.

(Math Refresher #121 and #303)

25. **(D)** Choice D is correct.

Given: a and b are positive ⊡1
  $b > a$ ⊡2

(Use Strategy A: Cancel expressions common to both columns by subtraction.)

Cancel b^2 from both columns:

Column A	Column B
$\cancel{b^2} - a$	$\cancel{b^2} - a^2$

(Use Strategy D: To make a comparison simpler, divide both columns by the same quantity, making sure that quantity is not negative or 0.)

Divide by a:

Column A	Column B
$\dfrac{-a}{a}$	$\dfrac{-a^2}{a}$
-1	$-a$

(Use Strategy C: Use numbers in place of variables.)
Let $a = 1$: Column A = Column B
Now let $a = 2$: Column A > Column B
Two different results are possible so Choice D is correct.

(Math Refresher #429 and #431)

26. **(D)** Choice D is correct.

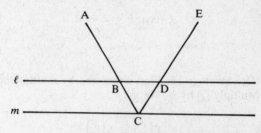

Given: $\ell \parallel m$ (parallel sign)

No information is supplied regarding the angle that AC or EC makes with m. **(Use Strategy 14: Draw lines to help solve the problem.)** Redraw AC at a different angle

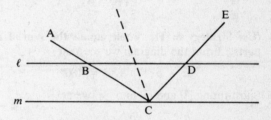

In the above diagram BC > CD ⊡1

Redraw EC at a different angle

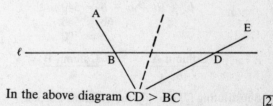

In the above diagram CD > BC ⊡2

Since two different results are possible, the answer can't be determined from the information given.

(Math Refresher #504)

27. **(A)** Choice A is correct.

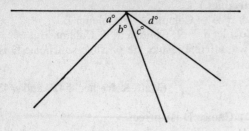

Given: $a = c = d$ [1]

$$\frac{c}{b} = \frac{1}{3}$$ [2]

(Use Strategy 13: Find unknowns by multiplying.)
Multiply [2] by b. We get

$$\not{b}\left(\frac{c}{\not{b}}\right) = b\left(\frac{1}{3}\right)$$

$$c = \frac{b}{3}$$ [3]

Substituting [3] into [1], we have

$$a = \frac{b}{3}, d = \frac{b}{3}$$ [4]

(Use Strategy 3: The whole equals the sum of its parts.) From the diagram we see that

$$a + b + c + d = 180°$$ [5]

Substituting [3] and [4] into [5], we get

$$\frac{b}{3} + b + \frac{b}{3} + \frac{b}{3} = 180°$$ [6]

(Use Strategy 13: Find unknowns by multiplying.)
Multiply [6] by 3. We get

$$b + 3b + b + b = 540°$$
$$6b = 540°$$
$$b = 90°$$ [7]

Column A	Column B	
b	80	[8]

Substituting [7] into [8], the columns become

90	80

(Math Refresher #111, #406, and #501)

28. **(C)** Choice C is correct. **(Use Strategy 3: The whole equals the sum of its parts.)**

The sum of the four angles in a quadrilateral $= 360°$ [1]

Given: the sum of two angles $= 90°$ [2]

Let a and b represent the two
remaining angles. [3]

Substituting [2] and [3] into [1], we get

$$90° + a + b = 360°$$
$$a + b = 270°$$ [4]

$$\left(\text{Use Strategy 5: Average} = \frac{\text{Sum of values}}{\text{Total number of values}}\right)$$

Average of a and $b = \dfrac{a + b}{2}$ [5]

Applying [5] to [4], we get

$$\frac{a + b}{2} = \frac{270°}{2}$$

Average of $a + b = 135°$

(Math Refresher #521)

29. **(D)** Choice D is correct. **(Use Strategy 4: Remember classic expressions.)**

Given $(10^3 + 7)^2 = 1,000,000 + x$ [1]
Remember $(x + y)^2 = x^2 + 2xy + y^2$ [2]

Apply [2] to the left side of [1]. We get

$$(10^3)^2 + 2(10^3)(7) + (7)^2 = 10^6 + x$$
$$10^6 + 14(10^3) + 49 = 10^6 + x$$ [3]

(Use Strategy 1: Cancel numbers on both sides of an equation.) Cancel 10^6, from both sides of [3]. We get

$$\not{10^6} + 14(10^3) + 49 = \not{10^6} + x$$
$$14,000 + 49 = x$$
$$14,049 = x$$

(Math Refresher #406 and #409)

30. **(C)** Choice C is correct.

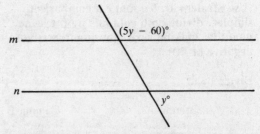

(Use Strategy 17: Use the given information effectively.)

Given: $m \| n$ [1]

From [1] we know that the two angles are supplementary. Thus,

$$(5y - 60)° + y° = 180°$$
$$6y - 60 = 180°$$
$$6y = 240°$$
$$y = 40°$$

(Math Refresher #504)

31. **(D)** Choice D is correct. **(Use Strategy 2: Translate from words to algebra.)**

The ratio of $3\frac{1}{3}$ hours to 11 hours =

$$\frac{3\frac{1}{3}\text{ hours}}{11\text{ hours}} =$$

$$\frac{\dfrac{10}{3}}{11} \qquad \boxed{1}$$

(Use Strategy 13: Find unknowns by multiplication.)

Multiply $\boxed{1}$ by $\left(\dfrac{3}{3}\right)$, we get

$$\left(\frac{3}{3}\right)\frac{\dfrac{10}{3}}{11} =$$

$$\frac{10}{33}$$

(Math Refresher #112)

32. **(C)** Choice C is correct. **(Use Strategy 2: Translate from words to algebra.)**

We have: $\dfrac{4}{100} \times (2a + b) = 18 \qquad \boxed{1}$

(Use Strategy 13: Find unknowns by multiplication.) Multiply $\boxed{1}$ by $\dfrac{100}{4}$. We get

$$\frac{100}{4}\left(\frac{4}{100} \times (2a + b)\right) = \frac{100}{4}\left(18\right)$$

(Use Strategy 19: Factor and reduce)

$$2a + b = \frac{\cancel{4} \times 25}{\cancel{4}}\left(18\right)$$

$$2a + b = 450$$
$$b = 450 - 2a \qquad \boxed{2}$$

(Use Strategy 17: Use the given information effectively.)

b will be greatest when a is smallest. $\qquad \boxed{3}$
Given: a is a positive integer $\qquad \boxed{4}$

Applying $\boxed{4}$ to $\boxed{3}$, we get

$$a = 1 \qquad \boxed{5}$$

Substituting $\boxed{5}$ into $\boxed{2}$, we have

$$b = 450 - 2(1)$$
$$= 450 - 2$$
$$b = 448$$

(Math Refresher #406)

33. **(E)** Choice E is correct.

Given: Area of square $= R^2 \qquad \boxed{1}$
Perimeter of equilateral triangle $= E \qquad \boxed{2}$
Perimeter of square $= r \qquad \boxed{3}$
Side of equilateral triangle $= e \qquad \boxed{4}$

(Use Strategy 17: Use the given information effectively.)

We know Perimeter of square $= 4(\text{side}) \qquad \boxed{5}$
We know Area of square $= (\text{side})^2 \qquad \boxed{6}$
Substituting $\boxed{1}$ into $\boxed{6}$, we get

$$R^2 = (\text{side})^2$$
$$R = \text{side} \qquad \boxed{7}$$

Substituting $\boxed{7}$ and $\boxed{3}$ into $\boxed{5}$, we have

$$r = 4(R)$$
$$r = 4R \qquad \boxed{8}$$

We know Perimeter of
equilateral triangle $= 3(\text{side}) \qquad \boxed{9}$

Substituting $\boxed{2}$ and $\boxed{4}$ into $\boxed{9}$, we get

$$E = 3(e)$$
$$E = 3e$$
$$\frac{E}{3} = e \qquad \boxed{10}$$

We need $e + r \qquad \boxed{11}$

(Use Strategy 13: Find unknowns by addition.) Add $\boxed{8}$ and $\boxed{10}$ to get $\boxed{11}$. We have

$$e + r = \frac{E}{3} + 4R$$

$$= \frac{E}{3} + 4R\left(\frac{3}{3}\right)$$

$$\frac{E}{3} + \frac{12R}{3}$$

$$e + r = \frac{E + 12R}{3}$$

(Math Refresher #303 and #308)

34. **(D)** Choice D is correct.

$$\text{Given: } C = \frac{5}{9}(F - 32) \qquad \boxed{1}$$

Call the number of degrees that the Fahrenheit temperature (F°) increases, x.

Now use Strategy 17: Use the given information effectively.

The Centigrade temperature (C°) is given as

$$C = \frac{5}{9}(F - 32) \qquad \boxed{1}$$

When the Centigrade temperature increases by 35°, the Fahrenheit temperature increases by x°, so we get:

$$C + 35 = \frac{5}{9}[(F + x) - 32]$$

$$C + 35 = \frac{5}{9}F + \frac{5}{9}x - \frac{5}{9}(32) \qquad \boxed{2}$$

Now use Strategy 13: Find unknowns by subtraction.

Subtract $\boxed{1}$ from $\boxed{2}$:

$$C + 35 = \frac{5}{9}F + \frac{5}{9}x - \frac{5}{9}(32) \qquad \boxed{2}$$
$$-C \quad\quad = \frac{5}{9}F - \frac{5}{9}(32) \qquad\qquad \boxed{1}$$
$$\overline{\qquad\qquad\qquad\qquad\qquad\qquad}$$
$$35 = \frac{5}{9}x \qquad \boxed{3}$$

Multiply $\boxed{3}$ by 9:

$$35 \times 9 = 5x \qquad \boxed{4}$$

Use Strategy 19: Don't multiply when reducing can be done first.

Divide $\boxed{4}$ by 5:

$$\frac{35 \times 9}{5} = x \qquad \boxed{5}$$

Now reduce $\frac{35}{5}$ to get 7 and we get for $\boxed{5}$

$$7 \times 9 = x$$

$$63 = x$$

(Math Refresher #406)

35. **(E)** Choice E is correct.

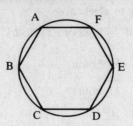

$$\text{Given: } \overset{\frown}{BAF} = 14\pi \qquad \boxed{1}$$

ABCDEF is equilateral $\qquad \boxed{2}$

From $\boxed{2}$ we know that all 6 sides are = $\qquad \boxed{3}$
From $\boxed{3}$ we know that all 6 arcs are equal. $\qquad \boxed{4}$
From $\boxed{1}$ and $\boxed{4}$ we find

$$\overset{\frown}{AB} = \overset{\frown}{BC} = \overset{\frown}{CD} = \overset{\frown}{DE} = \overset{\frown}{EF} = \overset{\frown}{FA} = 7\pi \quad \boxed{5}$$

(Use Strategy 3: The whole equals the sum of its parts.)

Circumference of circle =

$$6 \times 7\pi \text{ (since there are 6 arcs)} \qquad \boxed{6}$$

We know circumference $= 2\pi r \qquad \boxed{7}$

Using $\boxed{6}$ and $\boxed{7}$, we get

$$2\pi r = 6 \times 7\pi$$
$$2\pi r = 42\pi$$
$$2r = 42 \qquad \boxed{8}$$

We know diameter $= 2 \times$ radius $\qquad \boxed{9}$
So diameter $= 42$

(Math Refresher #310 and #524)

EXPLANATORY ANSWERS FOR
PRACTICE TEST 1 (continued)

Section 6: Math Ability

1. **(D)** Choice D is correct. **(Use Strategy 18: Remember triangle inequality facts.)** From basic geometry, we know that, since $m \sphericalangle BAC > m \sphericalangle BCA$, then leg opposite $\sphericalangle BAC >$ leg opposite $\sphericalangle BCA$ or

$$BC > AB$$

(Triangle inequality facts)

2. **(C)** Choice C is correct. **(Use Strategy 6: Know how to manipulate inequalities.)** We want to know which of the following

$$x > y \qquad \boxed{1}$$
$$1 < y \qquad \boxed{2}$$

is enough information to conclude that

$$x > 0 \qquad \boxed{3}$$

$\boxed{1}$ alone is not enough to determine $\boxed{3}$ because $0 > x > y$ could be true. (Note: x is greater than y, but they both could be negative.)

$\boxed{2}$ alone is not enough to determine $\boxed{3}$ because we don't know whether x is greater than, less than, or equal to y.

However, if we use $\boxed{1}$ and $\boxed{2}$ together, we can compare the two:

$$1 < y \text{ is the same as } y > 1$$

Therefore, $x > y$ with $y > 1$ yields:

$$x > 1 \qquad \boxed{4}$$

Since $1 > 0$ is always true, then from $\boxed{4}$

$$x > 0 \text{ is always true}$$

(Math Refresher #419)

3. **(B)** Choice B is correct. **(Use Strategy 2: Remember the definition of percent.)** 25 percent of 2 is

$$\frac{25}{100} \times 2$$

Thus, 25 percent of 25 percent of 2 is

$$\frac{25}{100} \times \frac{25}{100} \times 2 = \frac{1}{4} \times \frac{1}{4} \times 2$$
$$= \frac{2}{16}$$
$$= \frac{1}{8}$$

(Math Refresher #114)

4. **(B)** Choice B is correct. **(Use Strategy 17: Use the given information effectively.)** The pattern begins at the center of the diagram with the digits

$$7, 2, 5, 8, 8, 1, 1, 1, 1,$$
$$3, 3, 9, 9, 9, 4, 6$$

These 16 digits are continuously repeated. Thus, we are looking for the two numbers immediately following the "7" and immediately before the "8." The two numbers are 2, 5.

(Logical Reasoning)

5. **(E)** Choice E is correct. We want to find the weight of the heaviest truck *minus* the average weight of the three trucks $\qquad \boxed{1}$

$$\left(\text{Use Strategy 5: Average } \frac{= \text{ Total of values}}{\text{Total number of values}} \right)$$

From the definition of arithmetic mean, average weight of the three trucks

$$= \frac{5 + 7 + 14}{3}$$
$$= \frac{26}{3} = 8\frac{2}{3} \text{ tons} \qquad \boxed{2}$$

We are given the weight of the heaviest truck $= 14$ tons $\qquad \boxed{3}$

Substituting $\boxed{2}$ and $\boxed{3}$ into $\boxed{1}$, the answer is

$$14 - 8\frac{2}{3} = 5\frac{1}{3} \text{ tons}$$

(Math Refresher #601)

6. **(D)** Choice D is correct. **(See Strategy 17: Use the given information effectively.)**

$$Given:\ 2\ in. = 11\ yd. \qquad \boxed{1}$$
$$length = 10\ inches \qquad \boxed{2}$$
$$width = 4\ inches \qquad \boxed{3}$$

(Use Strategy 10: Know how to use units.)

Use $\boxed{1}$ and $\boxed{2}$ to form: $\dfrac{2\ in.}{11\ yd.} = \dfrac{10\ in.}{x}$

Cross-multiplying we get
$$(2\ in.)(x) = (10\ in.)(11\ yd.)$$
$$2x = (10)(11\ yd.)$$
$$x = 55\ yd.$$

$$length = 55\ yd.$$

Use $\boxed{1}$ and $\boxed{3}$ to form: $\dfrac{2\ in.}{11\ yd.} = \dfrac{4\ in.}{x}$

Cross-multiplying we get
$$(2\ in.)(x) = (4\ in.)(11\ yd.)$$
$$2x = (4)(11\ yd.)$$
$$x = 22\ yd.$$

$$width = 22\ yd.$$

Actual area $= L \times W = (55\ yd.)(22\ yd.)$
$$= 1210\ sq.\ yds.$$

(Math Refresher #120, #121, and #304)

7. **(A)** Choice A is correct. **(Use Strategy 2: Translate from words to algebra.)** 4 is subtracted from 3 times a number translates to $3n - 4$.
This result is divided by 3 translates to $\dfrac{3n - 4}{3}$

$$\frac{3n - 4}{3} = \frac{1}{3}(3n - 4)$$

(Math Refresher #200)

8. **(C)** Choice C is correct. There is one path such that the total distance from A to B is 24. For all other paths, the total distance between A and B is greater than 24.

(Logical Reasoning)

9. **(C)** Choice C is correct. **(Use Strategy 6: Know how to manipulate inequalities.)** When a and b are of opposite sign, then

$$ab < 0$$

Clearly, Choice C is correct. In all of the other choices, a and b have the same sign.

(Math Refresher #425)

10. **(A)** Choice A is correct. **(Use Strategy 17: Use the given information effectively.)**

$$Given:\ r = 4 \qquad \boxed{1}$$
$$p = \frac{1}{20} \qquad \boxed{2}$$
$$pq = \frac{1}{r} \qquad \boxed{3}$$

Substitute $\boxed{1}$ and $\boxed{2}$ into $\boxed{3}$

$$\frac{1}{20}q = \frac{1}{4} \qquad \boxed{4}$$

Multiplying $\boxed{4}$ by 20,
$$q = 5$$

(Math Refresher #431 and #406)

11. **(D)** Choice D is correct.

$$Volume\ of\ cube = (side)^3$$

Thus, the volume of a cube whose edge has length of $1 = 1^3 = 1$.
The volume of a cube whose edge has the length of $2 = 2^3 = 8$. Thus the sum of the volumes of the two cubes $= 8 + 1 = 9$.

(Math Refresher #313)

12. **(C)** Choice C is correct. **(Use Strategy 11: Use new definitions carefully. These problems are generally easy.)**

$$Given:\ \binom{n}{2} = \frac{n(n - 1)}{2}$$

$$Thus\ \binom{15}{2} = \frac{15(15 - 1)}{2}$$

$$= \frac{15(14)}{2}$$

$$= 105$$

(Math Refresher #431)

13. **(E)** Choice E is correct.

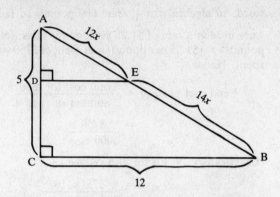

Method 1: **(Use Strategy 18: Remember right triangle facts.)** Triangle B C A is a right triangle, so we can use the Pythagorean Theorem:

$$(AB)^2 = (AC)^2 + (BC)^2$$
$$(12x + 14x)^2 = 5^2 + 12^2$$
$$(26x)^2 = 25 + 144$$
$$676x^2 = 169$$
$$x^2 = \frac{169}{676}$$

(Use Strategy 19: Factor and reduce.)

$$x^2 = \frac{13 \times 13}{13 \times 13 \times 4} = \frac{1}{4}$$

$$x = \frac{1}{2}$$

Method 2: **(Use Strategy 18: Remember special right triangles.)** Triangle B C A is a right triangle with legs 5 and 12. 5, 12, 13 is a special right triangle. Thus, AB must = 13

$$\text{Therefore } 12x + 14x = 13$$
$$26x = 13$$

$$x = \frac{13}{26}$$

$$x = \frac{1}{2}$$

(Math Refresher #509 and #406)

14. **(B)** Choice B is correct. **(Use Strategy 6: Know how to manipulate inequalities.)**

Multiply string of inequalities

$-\frac{1}{2} < \frac{x}{3} < -\frac{1}{4}$, by 3 to get x alone:

$$3\left[-\frac{1}{2} < \frac{x}{3} < -\frac{1}{4}\right] =$$

$$-\frac{3}{2} < x < -\frac{3}{4} \qquad \boxed{1}$$

Only one integer, $x = -1$ will satisfy $\boxed{1}$

15. **(B)** Choice B is correct. **(Use Strategy 17: Use the given information effectively.)** By looking at the diagram, we have

$$P_1 = -2$$
$$P_2 = -1$$

We can approximate the other numbers by looking at their positions on the number line:

$$P_3 \approx \frac{1}{3}$$

$$P_4 \approx \frac{2}{3}$$

$$P_5 \approx \frac{3}{2}$$

Thus,

$$P_1 \, P_2 \, P_3 \, P_4 \, P_5 \approx (-2)(-1)\left(\frac{1}{3}\right)\left(\frac{2}{3}\right)\left(\frac{3}{2}\right)$$

$$P_1 \, P_2 \, P_3 \, P_4 \, P_5 \approx \frac{2}{3}$$

(Math Refresher #410)

16. **(C)** Choice C is correct. **(Use Strategy 2: Translate from words to algebra.)** Let the 3 consecutive even integers be

$$x, x + 2, x + 4 \qquad \boxed{1}$$

where x is even. We are told that

$$\begin{aligned} x + x + 2 + x + 4 &= K \\ \text{or} \qquad 3x + 6 &= K \qquad \boxed{2} \end{aligned}$$

From $\boxed{1}$, we know that

$$x - 5, x - 3, x - 1$$

must be the 3 consecutive odd integers immediately preceding x. We are told that

$$\begin{aligned} x - 5 + x - 3 + x - 1 &= y \\ \text{or} \qquad 3x - 9 &= y \qquad \boxed{3} \end{aligned}$$

(Use Strategy 13: Find unknown expressions by subtraction.) Subtracting $\boxed{3}$ from $\boxed{2}$,

$$\begin{aligned} 15 &= K - y \\ \text{or} \quad y &= K - 15 \end{aligned}$$

(Math Refresher #200 and #406)

17. **(D)** Choice D is correct.

Given:

Meteor 1 travels at 300 meters/second	$\boxed{1}$
Meteor 2 travels at 700 meters/second	$\boxed{2}$

Draw a diagram:

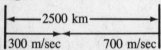

Let t be the time it takes meteors to meet. Call x the distance Meteor 1 travels. Then $2500 - x$ is the distance Meteor 2 travels.
(Use Strategy 9: Know Rate, Time, and Distance relationship.)

$$\begin{aligned} \text{Rate} \times \text{Time} &= \text{Distance} \\ 300 \text{ m/sec} \times t &= x \qquad \boxed{3} \\ 700 \text{ m/sec} \times t &= 2500 - x \qquad \boxed{4} \end{aligned}$$

(Use Strategy 13: Find unknowns by addition.)
Add $\boxed{3}$ and $\boxed{4}$

$$\begin{aligned} (300 \text{ m/sec})t + (700 \text{ m/sec})t &= 2500 \text{ km} \\ (1000 \text{ m/sec})t &= 2500 \text{ km} \qquad \boxed{5} \end{aligned}$$

(Use Strategy 10: Know how to use units.)

$$1 \text{ km} = 1000 \text{ m} \qquad \boxed{6}$$

Substitute $\boxed{6}$ in $\boxed{5}$:

$$(1000 \text{ m/sec})t = 2500(1000)\text{m} \qquad \boxed{7}$$

Divide $\boxed{7}$ by 1000m:

$$\begin{aligned} t/\text{sec} &= 2500 \\ t &= 2500 \text{ sec} \end{aligned}$$

(Math Refresher #121, #201, and #202)

18. **(C)** Choice C is correct. **(Use Strategy 2: Translate words to algebra.)** In $\frac{1}{2}$ year, 600 pounds of feed were used at a rate of $1.25 per pound. Thus, (600 pounds) × ($1.25 per pound) was spent or $750 was spent. Hence,

$$\begin{aligned} \text{Feed cost per egg} &= \frac{\text{Total cost for feed}}{\text{number of eggs}} \\ &= \frac{\$750}{5000 \text{ eggs}} \end{aligned}$$

(Use Strategy 19: Factor and reduce.)

$$\begin{aligned} &= \frac{\$75 \times 10}{500 \times 10 \text{ eggs}} \\ &= \frac{\$25 \times 3}{25 \times 20 \text{ eggs}} \\ &= \frac{\$3}{20} \text{ per egg} \\ &= \$0.15 \text{ per egg} \end{aligned}$$

(Math Refresher #200 and #601)

19. **(E)** Choice E is correct. Since we know only that $\overleftrightarrow{m}$ is not parallel to either $\overleftrightarrow{\ell}$ or $\overleftrightarrow{n}$, both of the following situations could be true. **(Use Strategy 17: Use the given information effectively.)**

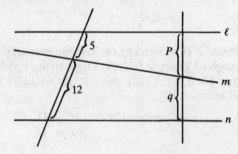

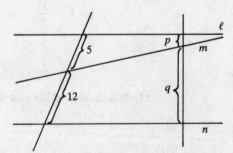

(Note: $p + q = 13$ is still true in both cases in the drawings above.) Clearly, the value of $\frac{p}{q}$ is different for each case. Hence, $\frac{p}{q}$ cannot be determined unless we know more about $\overleftrightarrow{m}$.

(Logical Reasoning)

20. **(E)** Choice E is correct. **(Use Strategy 17: Use the given information effectively.)**

$$x = \sqrt{\frac{1}{9} + \left(\frac{1}{3} + \frac{1}{9} + \frac{1}{27} + \frac{1}{81}\right)}$$

The common denominator for all the fractions is 81.

We have: $x = \sqrt{\frac{9}{81} + \frac{27}{81} + \frac{9}{81} + \frac{3}{81} + \frac{1}{81}}$

$$= \sqrt{\frac{9 + 27 + 9 + 3 + 1}{81}}$$

$$= \sqrt{\frac{49}{81}}$$

$$= \frac{7}{9}$$

(Math Refresher #110 and #430)

21. **(D)** Choice D is correct.

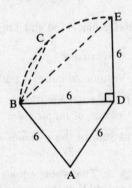

(Use Strategy 14: Draw lines where appropriate.)

Given: $AB = BD = AD = 6$ $\boxed{1}$

C can be any point on arc $\overparen{BE}$, not just where it appears in the drawing above. For any point C on arc $\overparen{BE}$

$$CD = 6 \qquad \boxed{2}$$
because CD = radius of the arc.

(Use Strategy 3: The whole equals the sum of its parts.) We want to find P = perimeter of

$$ABCD = AB + BC + CD + AD \qquad \boxed{3}$$

Substituting $\boxed{2}$ and $\boxed{1}$ into $\boxed{3}$,

$$P = 18 + BC \qquad \boxed{4}$$

We cannot find BC, but we can find the highest and lowest possible values for BC. Clearly, since BC is a side of a quadrilateral,

$$BC > 0 \qquad \boxed{5}$$

By looking at the diagram, we see that the highest possible value of BC occurs when C coincides with E.

$$BC \leq BE \qquad \boxed{6}$$

must be true. BE can easily be found. ΔEDB is similar to one of the standard triangles discussed before. **(Use Strategy 18: Remember special right triangles.)**

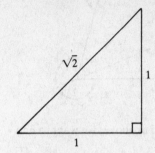

Corresponding sides of similar triangles are proportional, so that

$$\frac{\sqrt{2}}{1} = \frac{BE}{6}$$
or
$$BE = 6\sqrt{2} \qquad \boxed{7}$$

Substituting $\boxed{7}$ into $\boxed{6}$,

$$BC \leq 6\sqrt{2} \qquad \boxed{8}$$

Comparing $\boxed{4}$ and $\boxed{8}$,

$$P = 18 + BC \leq 18 + 6\sqrt{2} \qquad \boxed{9}$$

Comparing $\boxed{4}$ and $\boxed{5}$,

$$P = 18 + BC > 18 \qquad \boxed{10}$$

From $\boxed{9}$ and $\boxed{10}$ together,

$$18 < P \leq 18 + 6\sqrt{2}$$

(Math Refresher #431, #507, #509, and #510)

22. **(B)** Choice B is correct.

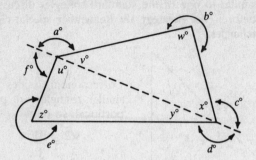

With the diagram labeled as above, we want to find

$$a + b + c + d + e + f \qquad \boxed{1}$$

(Use Strategy 3: The whole equals the sum of its parts.) Looking at the diagram, we see

$$a + f + u + v = 360 \qquad \boxed{2}$$
$$b + w = 360 \qquad \boxed{3}$$
$$c + d + x + y = 360 \qquad \boxed{4}$$
$$e + z = 360 \qquad \boxed{5}$$

(Use Strategy 13: Find unknown quantities by addition.) Adding equations $\boxed{2}$ through $\boxed{5}$,

$$a + b + c + d + e + f$$
$$+ u + v + w + x + y + z$$
$$= 1440 \qquad \boxed{6}$$

Since the sum of the measures of the angles of a triangle is 180, then

$$v + w + x = 180 \qquad \boxed{7}$$
$$u + y + z = 180 \qquad \boxed{8}$$

Substituting $\boxed{7}$ and $\boxed{8}$ into $\boxed{6}$

$$a + b + c + d + e + f + 180 + 180 = 1440$$
$$\text{or } a + b + c + d + e + f = 1080$$

(Math Refresher #526, #505, and #406)

23. **(B)** Choice B is correct. **(Use Strategy 11: Use new definitions carefully.)**

Given: $\qquad$ A, B, C, . . . , L = $\qquad \boxed{1}$
1, 2, 3, ... 12 (respectively)

The time on the watch is 15 minutes before 1. $\boxed{2}$

From $\boxed{1}$, we know that

$$E = 5 \text{ and } A = 1 \qquad \boxed{3}$$

Substituting $\boxed{3}$ into $\boxed{2}$, we have

3E minutes before A.

(Math Refresher #431)

24. **(E)** Choice E is correct.

Given: $\qquad\qquad r^2 = 9 \qquad \boxed{1}$
$$s^2 = 25 \qquad \boxed{2}$$

(Use Strategy 17: Use the given information effectively.) From $\boxed{1}$ and $\boxed{2}$, we have

$$r = 3 \text{ or } -3 \qquad \boxed{3}$$
$$s = 5 \text{ or } -5 \qquad \boxed{4}$$

The greatest possible value of $s - r$ occurs when s is a maximum and r is a minimum or

$$5 - (-3) = 8 \qquad \boxed{5}$$

The greatest possible value of $r - s$ occurs when r is a maximum and s is a minimum or

$$3 - (-5) = 8 \qquad \boxed{6}$$

The answer to this question is the difference between $\boxed{5}$ and $\boxed{6}$:

$$8 - 8 = 0$$

(Math Refresher #430 and Logical Reasoning)

25. **(A)** Choice A is correct.

$$\text{Volume of cube} = (\text{side})^3$$

Thus, Volume of each small cube = $r^3 \qquad \boxed{1}$
Volume of larger cube = $s^3 \qquad \boxed{2}$

and Sum of the volumes of the
$$27 \text{ cubes} = 27r^3 \qquad \boxed{3}$$

(Use Strategy 3: The whole equals the sum of its parts.) We are told that the sum of the Volumes of the 27 cubes = the Volume of the larger cube

$$= 81 \qquad \boxed{4}$$

From $\boxed{2}$, $\boxed{3}$, and $\boxed{4}$ together, we have

$$27r^3 = 81 \qquad \boxed{5}$$
$$s^3 = 81 \qquad \boxed{6}$$

(Use Strategy 13: Find unknown expressions by division.) Dividing $\boxed{5}$ by $\boxed{6}$, we get

$$27\frac{r^3}{s^3} = 1 \qquad \boxed{7}$$

Multiplying $\boxed{7}$ by $\frac{1}{27}$, we get

$$\frac{r^3}{s^3} = \frac{1}{27}$$
$$\text{or } \frac{r}{s} = \frac{1}{3}$$

(Math Refresher #313 and #406)

What You Must Do Now to Raise Your SAT Score

1. Go back to the SAT Diagnostic Pre-Test which you have just taken.
   a) Count the number of correct answers that you had for the Verbal part and for the Math part of the Pre-Test.
   b) Determine your Scaled Score for each part by referring to the Raw Score/Scaled Score Conversion Tables on pages 64–66. These results will give you a good idea about whether or not you ought to study hard in order to achieve a certain score on the actual SAT.
   c) Using your Pre-Test correct answer count as a basis, indicate for yourself your areas of strength and weakness as revealed by the "Self-Appraisal Chart" on page 66.
2. Eliminate your weaknesses in each of the SAT test areas (as revealed in the "Self-Appraisal Chart") by taking the following Giant Steps toward SAT success:

VERBAL PART

GIANT STEP 1

Take advantage of the Verbal Strategies that begin on page 90. Read again the Explanatory Answer for each of the Verbal questions that you got wrong. Refer to the Verbal Strategy that applies to each of your incorrect answers. Learn each of these Verbal Strategies thoroughly. These strategies are crucial if you want to raise your SAT Verbal score substantially.

GIANT STEP 2

Improve your vocabulary by doing the following:

(1) Study the SAT 3400-Word List beginning on page 123.

(2) Take the 100 SAT-type "tough word" Vocabulary Tests beginning on page 169.

(3) Study "Increasing Your Vocabulary with Latin and Greek Roots, Prefixes, and Suffixes" beginning on page 198.

(4) Read as widely as possible—not only novels. Nonfiction is important too . . . and don't forget to read newspapers and magazines.

(5) Listen to people who speak well. Tune in to worthwhile TV programs also.

(6) Use the dictionary frequently and extensively—at home, on the bus, at work, etc.

(7) Play word games—for example, crossword puzzles, anagrams, and Scrabble. Another game is to compose your own Antonym, Analogy, and Sentence Completion questions. Try them on your friends.

MATH PART

GIANT STEP 3

Make good use of the Math Strategies that begin on page 70. Read again the solutions for each Math question that you answered incorrectly. Refer to the Math Strategy that applies to each of your incorrect answers. Learn each of these Math Strategies thoroughly. We repeat that these strategies are crucial if you want to raise your SAT Math score substantially.

GIANT STEP 4

For each Math question that you got wrong in the Pre-Test, note the reference to the Math Refresher section on page 205. This reference will explain clearly the mathematical principle involved in the solution of the question you answered incorrectly. Learn that particular mathematical principle thoroughly.

3. After you have done some of the tasks you have been advised to do in the suggestions above, proceed to Practice Test 2, beginning on page 359. (We consider the Pre-Test that you have already taken as Practice Test 1.)

After taking Practice Test 2, concentrate on the weaknesses that still remain.

4. Continue the foregoing procedures for Practice Tests 3, 4, 5, and 6—and finally for the SAT Post-Test (Practice Test 7).

If you do the job *right* and follow the steps listed above, you are likely to raise your SAT score on both the Verbal and the Math part of the test 50 points—maybe 100 points—and even more.

> I am the master of my fate;
> I am the captain of my soul.
>
> —From the poem "Invictus"
> by William Ernest Henley

RAW SCORE/SCALED SCORE CONVERSION TABLES FOR THE PRACTICE TEST YOU HAVE JUST TAKEN

The College Board will send you your SAT results about six weeks after you have taken the test. The report will include two separate scores—Verbal and Math. Each score consists of three digits, from 200 to 800. These scores are your so-called scaled scores which constitute an important factor in a college's acceptance decision. The report will also include your score for the Standard Written English Test, which is *not* part of the SAT score.

This Scaled Score is derived by a statistical process from the Raw Score. The Raw Score is the number of questions you answered correctly, with a penalty for each incorrectly answered question. For each incorrectly answered Verbal or Regular Math question, there is a deduction of ¼ of a question. For each incorrectly answered Quantitative Comparison Math question (which has 4 choices), there is a deduction of ⅓ of a question. A Scaled Score of 500 is equivalent to a 50th percentile ranking—that is, about half of those taking the test scored better than you and half scored below you.

The following unofficial Raw Score/Scaled Score Tables will give you a rough idea of what your Scaled Score should be for the SAT Practice Test which you have just taken.

Math Part
(For Practice Tests 1, 3, 5, 7)

RAW SCORE	SCALED SCORE	RAW SCORE	SCALED SCORE	RAW SCORE	SCALED SCORE
85	800	66	610	47	420
84	790	65	600	46	410
83	780	64	590	45	400
82	770	63	580	44	390
81	760	62	570	43	380
80	750	61	560	42	370
79	740	60	550	41	360
78	730	59	540	40	350
77	720	58	530	39	340
76	710	57	520	38	330
75	700	56	510	37	320
74	690	55	500	36	310
73	680	54	490	35	300
72	670	53	480	34	290
71	660	52	470	33	280
70	650	51	460	32	270
69	640	50	450	31	260
68	630	49	440	30	250
67	620	48	430	29 and below	240 and below

Math Part
(For Practice Tests 2, 4, 6)

RAW SCORE	SCALED SCORE	RAW SCORE	SCALED SCORE	RAW SCORE	SCALED SCORE
95	800	73	620	51	460
94	790	72	610	50	450
93	780	71	610	49	440
92	770	70	600	48	430
91	760	69	600	47	420
90	750	68	590	46	410
89	740	67	590	45	400
88	730	66	580	44	390
87	720	65	580	43	380
86	710	64	570	42	370
85	700	63	560	41	360
84	690	62	550	40	350
83	680	61	540	39	340
82	670	60	530	38	330
81	660	59	520	37	320
80	650	58	510	36	310
79	650	57	500	35	300
78	640	56	490	34	290
77	640	55	490	33	280
76	630	54	480	32	270
75	630	53	480	31	260
74	620	52	470	30	250
				29 *and below*	240 *and below*

Verbal Part

RAW SCORE	SCALED SCORE	RAW SCORE	SCALED SCORE	RAW SCORE	SCALED SCORE
85	800	59	580	33	410
84	790	58	580	32	410
83	780	57	570	31	400
82	770	56	570	30	390
81	760	55	560	29	380
80	750	54	560	28	380
79	740	53	550	27	370
78	730	52	550	26	360
77	720	51	540	25	350
76	710	50	530	24	350
75	700	49	530	23	340
74	690	48	520	22	330
73	680	47	520	21	330
72	670	46	510	20	320
71	660	45	500	19	310
70	650	44	490	18	300
69	640	43	480	17	300
68	630	42	470	16	290
67	620	41	470	15	280
66	620	40	460	14	280
65	610	39	460	13	270
64	610	38	450	12	260
63	600	37	440	11	250
62	600	36	430	10	250
61	590	35	420	9	240
60	590	34	420	8 *and below*	230 and below

Standard Written English Score Table*

RAW SCORE	SCALED SCORE	RAW SCORE	SCALED SCORE
50	80	33	57.5
49	79	32	55
48	78.5	31	52.5
47	78	30	50
46	77.5	29	48
45	77	28	46
44	76	27	44
43	75	26	42
42	74	25	40
41	73	24	38
40	72	23	36
39	71	22	34
38	70	21	32
37	67.5	20	30
36	65	19	28
35	62.5	18	26
34	60	17	25
		16 *and below*	24 *and below*

*The Standard Written English Test does *not* count toward your SAT scores.

CHART FOR SELF-APPRAISAL BASED ON THE PRACTICE TEST YOU HAVE JUST TAKEN

The Self-Appraisal Chart below tells you quickly where your SAT strengths and weaknesses lie. Check or circle the appropriate box in accordance with the number of your correct answers for each area of the Practice Test you have just taken.

	Anto-nyms	Anal-ogies	Sentence Comple-tions	Reading Compre-hension	85 Math Questions*	95 Math Questions*
EXCELLENT	23–25	17–20	14–15	21–25	76–85	86–95
GOOD	19–22	14–16	12–13	16–20	64–75	72–85
FAIR	14–18	10–13	10–11	11–15	50–63	58–71
POOR	9–13	6–9	6–9	7–10	30–49	38–57
VERY POOR	0–8	0–5	0–5	0–6	0–29	0–37

*Some SAT forms may have 85 math questions, while other forms may have 95 Math questions.

PART 2

USING CRITICAL THINKING SKILLS TO SCORE HIGH ON THE SAT

5 General Strategies

GENERAL STRATEGIES FOR TAKING THE SAT EXAMINATION

Before studying the 50 specific strategies for the Math and Verbal Questions, you will find it useful to review the following Five General Strategies for taking the SAT Examination.

Strategy 1:
DON'T RUSH INTO GETTING AN ANSWER WITHOUT THINKING. BE CAREFUL IF YOUR ANSWER COMES TOO EASILY, ESPECIALLY IF THE QUESTION IS TOWARD THE END OF THE SECTION.

Beware of Choice A If You Get the Answer Fast or Without Really Thinking

Everybody panics when they take an exam like the SAT. And what happens is that they rush into getting answers. That's OK, except that you have to think carefully. If a problem looks too easy, beware! And, especially beware of the Choice A answer. It's usually a "lure" choice for those who rush into getting an answer without critically thinking about it. Here's an example:

Below is a picture of a digital clock. The clock shows that the time is 6:06. Consider all the times on the clock where the hour digit is the same as the minute digit like in the clock shown below. Another such "double" time would be 8:08 or 9:09. What is the *smallest* time period between any two such doubles?

(A) 61 minutes
(B) 11 minutes
(C) 60 minutes
(D) 101 minutes
(E) 49 minutes

6:06

Did you subtract 8:08 from 7:07 and get 1 hour and 1 minute (61 minutes)? If you did you probably chose choice A. The *lure choice*. Think—do you really believe that the test maker would give you such an easy question? The fact that you figured it out so easily and saw that Choice A was your answer should make you think twice. The thing you have to realize is that there is another possibility: 12:12 to 1:01 gives 49 minutes and so Choice E is correct.

Here's another example illustrating the Choice A lure:

What is the opposite of UNWITTING?

(A) intelligent
(B) conscious
(C) annoying
(D) excited
(E) fearless

Many of you would select Choice A (the lure choice). But think carefully. An unwitting person doesn't have his wits about him—he is therefore unconscious, not unintelligent. The opposite of unconscious is conscious (Choice B).

So, in summary, if you get the answer fast and without doing much thinking, and it's a Choice A answer, think again. You may have fallen for the Choice A lure.

NOTE: Choice A is often a "lure choice" for

---

those who quickly get an answer without doing any real thinking. However, you should certainly realize that Choice A answers can occur, especially if there is no "lure choice."

Strategy 2:
KNOW AND LEARN THE DIRECTIONS TO THE QUESTION TYPES BEFORE YOU TAKE THE ACTUAL TEST

Never Spend Time Reading Directions During the Test or Doing Sample Questions That Don't Count

All SAT tests are standardized. For example, all the Analogy questions have the same directions from test to test as do the Sentence Completions, the Antonym questions, etc. So it's a good idea to learn these sets of directions and familiarize yourself with their types of questions early in the game before you take your actual SAT.

Here's an example of a set of SAT directions, together with an accompanying example for the Sentence Completion type of questions.

Each sentence below has one or two blanks, each blank indicating that something has been omitted. Beneath the sentence are five lettered words or sets of words. Choose the word or set of words that *best* fits the meaning of the sentence as a whole.

Although its publicity has been _____ , the film itself is intelligent, well-acted, handsomely produced, and altogether _____ .

(A) tasteless . . . respectable
(B) extensive . . . moderate
(C) sophisticated . . . amateur
(D) risqué . . . crude
(E) perfect . . . spectacular

If on your actual test you spend time reading these directions and/or answering the sample question, you will waste valuable time.

As you go through my course, you will get familiar with all the question types so that you won't have to read their directions on the actual test.

Strategy 3:
IT MAY BE WISER NOT TO LEAVE AN ANSWER BLANK

The Penalty for Guessing Is Much Smaller Than You Would Expect

On the SAT you lose a percentage of points if you guess and get the wrong answer. Of course, you should always try to eliminate choices. You'll find that, after going through this book, you'll have a better chance of eliminating wrong answers. However, if you cannot eliminate any choice in a question and have no idea of

how to arrive at an answer, you might want to pick any answer and go on to the next question.

There are two reasons for this:
1. You don't want to risk mismarking a future answer by leaving a previous answer blank.
2. Even though there is a penalty for guessing, the penalty is much smaller than you'd expect and this way you have at least a chance of getting the question right. Suppose, for example, that you have a five-choice question:

From a probablistic point of view, it is very likely that you would get one question right and four wrong (you have a 1 in 5 chance of getting a five-choice question right) if you randomly guess at the answers. Since ¼ point is taken off for each wrong five choice question, you've gotten $1 - \frac{1}{4} \times 4 = 0$ points, because you've gotten 1 question right and four wrong. Thus you break even. So the moral is whether you randomly guess at questions you're not sure of at all or whether you leave those question answers blank, it doesn't make a difference in the long run!

Strategy 4:
WRITE AS MUCH AS YOU WANT IN YOUR TEST BOOKLET

Test Booklets Aren't Graded—So Use Them As You Would Scrap Paper

Many students are afraid to mark up their test booklets. But, the booklets are not graded! Make any marks you want. In fact, some of the strategies demand that you extend or draw lines in geometry questions or label diagrams, or circle incorrect answers, etc. That's why when I see computer programs that only show the questions on a screen and prevent the student from marking a diagram or circling an answer, I realize that such programs prevent the student from using many powerful strategies. *So write all you want on your test booklet—use your test paper as you would scrap paper.*

Strategy 5:
USE YOUR OWN CODING SYSTEM TO TELL YOU WHICH QUESTIONS TO RETURN TO

If You Have Extra Time After Completing a Test Section, You'll Know Exactly Which Questions Need More Attention

When you are sure that you have answered a question correctly, mark your question paper with ✔. For questions you are not sure of but for which you have eliminated some of the choices, use ?. For questions that you're not sure of at all or for which you have not been able to eliminate any choices, use ??. This will give you a bird's-eye view of what questions you should return to, if you have time left after completing a particular test section.

50 Easy-to-Learn Strategies

25 MATH STRATEGIES + 25 VERBAL STRATEGIES

Critical thinking is the ability to think clearly in order to solve problems and answer questions of all types. SAT questions, for example—both Math and Verbal!

Educators who are deeply involved in research on Critical Thinking Skills tell us that such skills are straightforward, practical, teachable, and learnable.

The 25 Math strategies and 25 Verbal strategies in this section are Critical Thinking Skills. These strategies have the potential to raise your SAT scores dramatically. A realistic estimate is anywhere from approximately 50 points to 300 points in each part of the test—Verbal and Math. Since each correct SAT question gives you an additional 10 points on the average, it is reasonable to assume that, if you can learn and then use these valuable SAT strategies, you can boost your SAT scores phenomenally!

If a student leaves a question *unanswered,* he automatically loses 10 points.

If a student *answers* the question and gets an *incorrect* answer, an additional penalty of ¼ of a question or 2½ points is charged against him.

BE SURE TO LEARN AND USE THE STRATEGIES WHICH FOLLOW!

MATH STRATEGY 1

Using Critical Thinking Skills in Math Questions*

CANCEL NUMBERS AND EXPRESSIONS WHICH APPEAR ON BOTH SIDES OF AN EQUATION

You will save precious time by using this strategy. You won't have to make any long calculations.

EXAMPLE 1

If $P \times \frac{11}{14} = \frac{11}{14} \times \frac{8}{9}$, then $P =$

(A) $\frac{8}{9}$ (B) $\frac{9}{8}$ (C) 11   (D) 14   (E) 8

Choice A is correct. Do not multiply $\frac{11}{14} \times \frac{8}{9}$!

Cancel the common $\frac{11}{14}$:

$$P \times \frac{11}{\cancel{14}} = \frac{\cancel{11}}{\cancel{14}} \times \frac{8}{9}$$

$$P = \frac{8}{9} \ (Answer)$$

EXAMPLE 2

If $y + \frac{7}{13} + \frac{6}{19} = \frac{3}{5} + \frac{7}{13} + \frac{6}{19}$, then $y =$

(A) $\frac{6}{19}$ (B) $\frac{13}{32}$ (C) $\frac{7}{13}$ (D) $\frac{3}{5}$ (E) $\frac{211}{247}$

Choice **D** is correct. *Do not add the fractions* $\frac{3}{5} + \frac{7}{13} + \frac{6}{19}$!You will waste a lot of time! There is a much shorter way to do the problem. Cancel $\frac{7}{13} + \frac{6}{19}$ from both sides of the equation. Thus,

$$y + \frac{\cancel{7}}{\cancel{13}} + \frac{\cancel{6}}{\cancel{19}} = \frac{3}{5} + \frac{\cancel{7}}{\cancel{13}} + \frac{\cancel{6}}{\cancel{19}}$$

$$y = \frac{3}{5} \ (Answer)$$

---

*Math Strategies 1–19 refer to Regular Math questions.
Math Strategies A–F refer to Quantitative Comparison questions.

TRANSLATE ENGLISH WORDS INTO MATHEMATICAL EXPRESSIONS

Many of the SAT problems are word problems. Being able to translate word problems from English into mathematical expressions or equations will help you to score high on the test. The following table translates some commonly used words into their mathematical equivalents:

TRANSLATION TABLE

Words	Math Way to Say It
is, are, was, has, cost	$=$
percent	$\dfrac{}{100}$ (the percent number over 100)
which, what	x (or any other variable)
x <u>and</u> y	$x + y$
y units more than x	$x + y$
y units less than x	$x - y$
x units less than y	$y - x$
the sum of x and y	$x + y$
the difference between x and y	$x - y$
the product of x and y	xy
the quotient of x and y (x divided by y)	$x \div y$ or $\dfrac{x}{y}$
<u>of</u> (used with percents or fractions)	$\times$ (multiply)
the square of x	x^2
older than	$+$
younger than	$-$
y years ago	$- y$
y years from now	$+ y$
c times as old as John	$c \times$ (John's age)
the percent increase of x with respect to y (if $x > y$)	$\dfrac{x - y}{y} \times 100$
the percent of increase	$\dfrac{\text{amount of increase}}{\text{original amount}} \times 100$
the percent decrease of x with respect to y (if $x < y$)	$\dfrac{y - x}{y} \times 100$
the percent of decrease	$\dfrac{\text{amount of decrease}}{\text{original amount}} \times 100$
n percent greater than x	$x + \left(\dfrac{n}{100}\right) x$
n percent less than x	$x - \left(\dfrac{n}{100}\right) x$

By knowing this table, you will find word problems much easier to do.

EXAMPLE 1

Sarah is twice as old as John. Six years ago, Sarah was 4 times as old as John was then. How old is John now?

(A) 3   (B) 18   (C) 20   (D) 9
(E) impossible to determine

Choice D is correct. Translate:

Sarah is twice as old as John.
  ↓   ↓   ↓   ↓
  S   =   2   ×   J

$$S = 2J \qquad \boxed{1}$$

Six years ago Sarah was 4 times as old as John was then
   ↓   ↓   ↓   ↓   ↓
  −6   S = 4   ×   (J − 6)

This becomes S − 6 = 4(J − 6) $\boxed{2}$

Substituting $\boxed{1}$ into $\boxed{2}$:

$$2J - 6 = 4(J - 6)$$
$$2J - 6 = 4J - 24$$
$$18 = 2J$$
$$9 = J \qquad (Answer)$$

EXAMPLE 2

200 is what percent of 20?

(A) $\dfrac{1}{10}$ (B) 10   (C) 100   (D) 1000   (E) 10000

Choice D is correct. Translate:

200 is what percent of 20
 ↓   ↓   ↓   ↓   ↓   ↓
200 = x $\frac{}{100}$ × 20

$$200 = \frac{x}{100}(20)$$

Divide by 20: $10 = \dfrac{x}{100}$

Multiply by 100: $1000 = x$ (*Answer*)

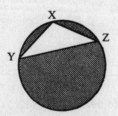

MATH STRATEGY 3

KNOW HOW TO FIND UNKNOWN QUANTITIES (AREAS, LENGTHS, ARC AND ANGLE MEASUREMENTS) FROM KNOWN QUANTITIES (THE WHOLE EQUALS THE SUM OF ITS PARTS)

This strategy is very helpful in many types of geometry problems. A very important equation to remember is

The whole = the sum of its parts $\boxed{1}$

Equation $\boxed{1}$ is often disguised in many forms, as seen in the following examples:

EXAMPLE 1

In the diagram above, △*XYZ* has been inscribed in a circle. If the circle encloses an area of 64, and the area of △*XYZ* is 15, then what is the area of the shaded region?

(A) 25   (B) 36   (C) 49   (D) 79
(E) It cannot be determined from the information given.

Choice C is correct, Use equation $\boxed{1}$. Here, the whole refers to the area within the circle, and the parts refer to the areas of the shaded region and the triangle. Thus,

Area within circle =
Area of shaded region +
Area of △*XYZ*

64 = Area of shaded region + 15

or Area of shaded region = 64 − 15 = 49
(*Answer*)

EXAMPLE 2

In the diagram below, $\overline{AE}$ is a straight line, and F is a point on $\overline{AE}$. Find an expression for m ∢ DFE.

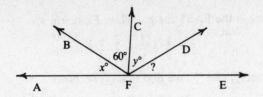

(A) $x + y - 60$ (B) $x + y + 60$ (C) $90 - x - y$
(D) $120 - x - y$ (E) $180 - x - y$

Choice D is correct. Use equation ①. Here, the whole refers to the straight angle, ∢ AFE, and its parts refer to ∢AFB, ∢BFC, ∢CFD, and ∢DFE. Thus,

$$m\angle AFE = m\angle AFB + m\angle BFC + m\angle CFD + m\angle DFE$$
$$180 = x + 60 + y + m\angle DFE$$

or
$$m\angle DFE = 180 - x - 60 - y$$
$$m\angle DFE = 120 - x - y \quad (Answer)$$

EXAMPLE 3

In the diagram below, AB = m, BC = n, and AD = 10. Find an expression for CD.

(Note: Diagram represents a straight line.)

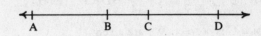

(A) $10 - mn$ (B) $10 - m - n$
(C) $m - n + 10$ (D) $m + n - 10$
(E) $m + n + 10$

Choice B is correct. Use equation ①. Here, the whole refers to AD, and its parts refer to AB, BC, and CD. Thus,

$$AD = AB + BC + CD$$
$$10 = m + n + CD$$

or
$$CD = 10 - m - n \quad (Answer)$$

MATH STRATEGY 4

REMEMBER CLASSIC EXPRESSIONS SUCH AS
$x^2 - y^2,\ x^2 + 2xy + y^2,\ x^2 - 2xy + y^2,\ \dfrac{x + y}{xy}$

Memorize the following factorizations and expressions:

$$x^2 - y^2 = (x + y)(x - y) \qquad \boxed{\text{Equation 1}}$$

$$x^2 + 2xy + y^2 = (x + y)(x + y) = (x + y)^2 \qquad \boxed{\text{Equation 2}}$$

$$x^2 - 2xy + y^2 = (x - y)(x - y) = (x - y)^2 \qquad \boxed{\text{Equation 3}}$$

$$\frac{x + y}{xy} = \frac{1}{x} + \frac{1}{y} \qquad x, y \neq 0 \qquad \boxed{\text{Equation 4}}$$

EXAMPLE 1

$$66^2 + 2(34)(66) + 34^2 =$$

(A) 9950 (B) 9860 (C) 10000
(D) 4730 (E) 5000

Choice C is correct. Note that $66^2 + 2(34)(66) + 34^2$ is of the form

$$a^2 + 2ab + b^2$$

where $a = 66$ and $b = 34$

But from equation 1,

$$a^2 + 2ab + b^2 = (a + b)(a + b) = \qquad \boxed{1}$$
$$(a + b)^2$$

Substitute 66 for a and 34 for b in $\boxed{1}$:

$$66^2 + 2(34)(66) + 34^2 =$$
$$(66 + 34)(66 + 34) =$$
$$100 \times 100 =$$
$$10,000 \qquad (Answer)$$

EXAMPLE 2

If $(x + y) = 9$ and $xy = 14$, find $\dfrac{1}{x} + \dfrac{1}{y}$.

(Note: $x, y > 0$)

(A) $\dfrac{1}{9}$ (B) $\dfrac{2}{7}$ (C) $\dfrac{9}{14}$ (D) 5 (E) 9

Choice C is correct. We are given:

$(x + y) = 9$ ①
$xy = 14$ ②
$x, y > 0$ ③

I hope that you did not solve ② for x (or y), and then substitute it into ①. If you did you obtained a quadratic equation.

Here is the FAST method. Use Equation 4:

$$\frac{1}{x} + \frac{1}{y} = \frac{x + y}{xy} \qquad ④$$

From ① and ②, we find that ④ becomes

$$\frac{1}{x} + \frac{1}{y} = \frac{9}{14} \quad (Answer)$$

MATH STRATEGY **5**

KNOW HOW TO MANIPULATE AVERAGES

Almost all problems involving averages can be solved by remembering that

$$\text{Average} = \frac{\text{Sum of the individual quantities or measurements}}{\text{Number of quantities or measurements}}$$

(Note: Average is also called Arithmetic Mean.)

EXAMPLE

The average height of 3 students is 68 inches. If two of the students have heights of 70 inches and 72 inches respectively, then what is the height (in inches) of the third student?

(A) 60 (B) 62 (C) 64
(D) 65 (E) 66

Choice B is correct. Recall that

$$\text{Average} = \frac{\text{Sum of the individual measurements}}{\text{Number of measurements}}$$

Let x = height (in inches) of the third student. Thus,

$$68 = \frac{70 + 72 + x}{3}$$

Multiplying by 3,

$$204 = 70 + 72 + x$$
$$\text{or } 204 = 142 + x$$
$$\text{or } x = 62 \text{ inches } (Answer)$$

MATH STRATEGY 6

KNOW HOW TO MANIPULATE INEQUALITIES

Most problems involving inequalities can be solved by remembering one of the following statements.

If $x > y$, then $x + z > y + z$	Statement 1
If $x > y$ and $w > z$, then $x + w > y + z$	Statement 2
If $w > 0$ and $x > y$, then $wx > wy$	Statement 3
If $w < 0$ and $x > y$, then $wx < wy$	Statement 4
If $x > y$ and $y > z$, then $x > z$	Statement 5
$x > y$ is the same as $y < x$	Statement 6
$a < x < b$ is the same as both $a < x$ and $x < b$	Statement 7
If $x > y > 0$ and $w > z > 0$, then $xw > yz$	Statement 8
If $x > 0$ and $z = x + y$, then $z > y$	Statement 9

Note that Statement 1 and Statement 2 are also true if all the ">" signs are changed to "<" signs.

If $x < 0$ then $\begin{cases} x^n < 0 \text{ if } n \text{ is odd} \\ x^n > 0 \text{ if } n \text{ is even} \end{cases}$

Statement 10

Statement 11

EXAMPLE

If $0 < x < 1$, then which of the following must be true?

I. $2x < 2$
II. $x - 1 < 0$
III. $x^2 < x$

(A) I only   (B) II only   (C) I and II only
(D) II and III only   (E) I, II, and III

Choice E is correct. We are told that $0 < x < 1$. Using Statement 7, we have

$$0 < x \qquad \boxed{1}$$
$$x < 1 \qquad \boxed{2}$$

For Item I, we multiply $\boxed{2}$ by 2. See
Statement 3

$$2x < 2$$

Thus, Item I is true.

For Item II, we add -1 to both sides of $\boxed{2}$.

See Statement 1 to get

$$x - 1 < 0$$

Thus Item II is true.

For Item III, we multiply $\boxed{2}$ by x.

See Statement 3 to get

$$x^2 < x$$

Thus, Item III is true.

All items are true, so Choice E is correct.

USE SPECIFIC NUMERICAL EXAMPLES TO PROVE OR DISPROVE YOUR GUESS

When you do not want to do a lot of algebra, or when you are unable to prove what you think is the answer, you may want to substitute numbers.

EXAMPLE

The sum of the cubes of any two consecutive positive integers is always

(A) an odd integer
(B) an even integer
(C) the cube of an integer
(D) the square of an integer
(E) the product of an integer and 3

Choice A is correct. Try specific numbers. Call consecutive positive integers 1 and 2.

Sum of cubes:

$$1^3 + 2^3 = 1 + 8 = 9$$

You have now eliminated choices B and C. You are left with choices A, D, and E.

Now try two other consecutive integers: 2 and 3

$$2^3 + 3^3 = 8 + 27 = 35$$

Choice A is acceptable. Choice D is false. Choice E is false.

Thus, Choice A is the only choice remaining.

WHEN EACH CHOICE MUST BE TESTED, START WITH CHOICE E AND WORK BACKWARDS

If you must check each choice for the correct answer, start with Choice E and work backwards. The reason for this is that the test-maker of a question in which each choice must be tested often puts the correct answer as Choice D or E. In this way, the careless student must check all or most of the choices before finding the correct one.

EXAMPLE 1

If p is a positive integer, which *could* be an odd integer?

(A) $2p + 2$ (B) $p^3 - p$ (C) $p^2 + p$
(D) $p^2 - p$ (E) $7p - 3$

Choice E is correct. Start with Choice E first since you have to *test* out the choices.

Method 1: Try a number for p. Let $p = 1$. Then (starting with choice E)
$7p - 3 = 7(1) - 3 = 4$. 4 is even so try another number for p to see whether $7p - 3$ is odd. Let $p = 2$.

$7p - 3 = 7(2) - 3 = 11$. 11 is odd. Therefore, Choice E is correct.

Method 2: Look at Choice E. $7p$ could be even or odd, depending on what p is. If p is even, $7p$ is even. If p is odd, $7p$ is odd. Accordingly, $7p - 3$ is either even or odd. Thus, Choice E is correct.

Note: By using either Method 1 or Method 2, it is not necessary to test the other choices.

EXAMPLE 2

If $y = x^2 + 3$, then for which value of x is y divisible by 7?

(A) 3   (B) 4   (C) 7   (D) 8   (E) 5

Choice E is correct. Since you must check all of the choices, start with Choice E:

$$y = 5^2 + 3 = 25 + 3 = 28$$

28 is divisible by 7 (*Answer*)

If you had started with Choice A, you would have had to test four choices, instead of one choice before finding the correct answer.

KNOW HOW TO SOLVE PROBLEMS USING
THE FORMULA R × T = D

Almost every problem involving motion can be solved using the formula
$$R \times T = D$$
or
$$\text{rate} \times \text{time} = \text{distance}$$

EXAMPLE

The diagram below shows two paths: Path 1 is 10 miles long and Path 2 is 12 miles long. If person X runs along Path 1 at 5 miles per hour and person Y runs along Path 2 at y miles per hour, and if it takes exactly the same amount of time for both runners to run their whole path, then what is the value of y?

A   Path 1   B

C   Path 2   D

(A) 2   (B) $4\frac{1}{6}$ (C) 6   (D) 20   (E) 24

Choice C is correct. Let T = Time (in hours) for either runner to run the whole path.

Using $R \times T = D$, for Person X, we have
$$(5\text{mi./hr.})(T \text{ hours}) = 10 \text{ miles}$$
or $5T = 10$ or
$$T = 2 \qquad \boxed{1}$$

For Person Y, we have
$$(y \text{ mi./hr.})(T \text{ hours}) = 12 \text{ miles}$$
or $yT = 12$
Using $\boxed{1}$ $y(2) = 12$ or $y = 6$

MATH STRATEGY 10.

KNOW HOW TO USE UNITS OF TIME, DISTANCE, AREA, OR VOLUME TO FIND OR CHECK YOUR ANSWER.

By knowing what the units in your answer must be, you will often have an easier time finding or checking your answer. A very helpful thing to do is to treat the units of time or space as variables (like "*x*" or "*y*"). Thus, you should substitute, multiply, or divide these units as if they were ordinary variables. The following examples illustrate this idea.

EXAMPLE 1

What is the distance in miles covered by a car which traveled at 50 miles per hour for 5 hours?

(A) 10 (B) 45 (C) 55
(D) 200 (E) 250

Choice E is correct. Although this is an easy "R × T = D" problem, it illustrates this strategy very well.
Recall that

$$\text{rate} \times \text{time} = \text{distance}$$
$$(50 \text{ mi./hr.})(5 \text{ hours}) = \text{distance}$$

Notice that when I substituted into R × T = D, *I kept the units of rate and time* (miles/hour and hours). Now I will *treat these units as if they were ordinary variables.* Thus,

$$\text{distance} = (50 \text{ mi./hr.})(5 \text{ hours})$$

I have canceled the variable "hour(s)" from the numerator and denominator of the right side of the equation. Hence,

$$\text{distance} = 250 \text{ miles}$$

The distance has units of "miles" as I would expect. In fact, if the units in my answer had been "miles/hour" or "hours," then I would have been in error.

Thus, *the general procedure* for problems using this strategy is:

Step 1. Keep the units given in the question.
Step 2. Treat the units as ordinary variables.
Step 3. Make sure the answer has units that you would expect.

EXAMPLE 2

How many inches is equivalent to 2 yards, 2 feet, and 7 inches?

(A) 11 (B) 37 (C) 55
(D) 81 (E) 103

Choice E is correct.
Remember that

| 1 yard = 3 feet | ① |
| 1 foot = 12 inches | ② |

Treat the units of length as variables! Divide ① by 1 yard, and ② by 1 foot, to get

$$1 = \frac{3 \text{ feet}}{1 \text{ yard}} \qquad ③$$

$$1 = \frac{12 \text{ inches}}{1 \text{ foot}} \qquad ④$$

We can multiply any expression by 1, and get the same value. Thus, 2 yards + 7 inches = (2 yards)(1)(1) + (2 feet)(1) + 7 inches. ⑤
Substituting ③ and ④ into ⑤, 2 yards + 2 feet + 7 inches.

$$= 2 \text{ yards} \left(\frac{3 \text{ feet}}{\text{yard}} \right)\left(\frac{12 \text{ inches}}{\text{foot}} \right) + 2 \text{ feet} \left(\frac{12 \text{ inches}}{\text{foot}} \right)$$
$$+ 7 \text{ inches}$$
$$= 72 \text{ inches} + 24 \text{ inches} + 7 \text{ inches}$$
$$= 103 \text{ inches}$$

Notice that the answer is in "inches" as I expected. If the answer had come out in "yards" or "feet," then I would have been in error.

USE NEW DEFINITIONS AND FUNCTIONS CAREFULLY

Some SAT questions use new symbols, functions, or definitions that were created in the question. At first glance, these questions may seem difficult because you are not familiar with the new symbol, function, or definition. *However, most of these questions can be solved through simple substitution or application of a simple definition.*

EXAMPLE 1

If the symbol ϕ is defined by the equation

$$a\phi b = a - b - ab$$

for all a and b, then $\left(-\dfrac{1}{3}\right)\phi(-3) =$

(A) $\dfrac{5}{3}$ (B) $\dfrac{11}{3}$ (C) $-\dfrac{13}{3}$ (D) -4 (E) -5

Choice A is correct. All that is required is substitution:

$$a\phi b = a - b - ab$$

$$\left(-\dfrac{1}{3}\right)\phi(-3)$$

Substitute $-\dfrac{1}{3}$ for a and

$$-3 \text{ for } b \text{ in } a - b - ab:$$

$$\left(-\dfrac{1}{3}\right)\phi(-3) = -\dfrac{1}{3} - (-3) - \left(-\dfrac{1}{3}\right)(-3)$$

$$= -\dfrac{1}{3} + 3 - 1$$

$$= 2 - \dfrac{1}{3}$$

$$= \dfrac{5}{3} \; (Answer)$$

EXAMPLE 2

Let $\boxed{x} = \begin{cases} \dfrac{5}{2}(x + 1) & \text{if } x \text{ is an odd integer} \\ \dfrac{5}{2}x & \text{if } x \text{ is an even integer} \end{cases}$

Find $\boxed{2y}$, where y is an integer.

(A) $\dfrac{5}{2}y$ (B) $5y$ (C) $\dfrac{5}{2}y + 1$

(D) $5y + \dfrac{5}{2}$ (E) $5y + 5$

Choice B is correct. All we have to do is to substitute $2y$ into the definition of $\boxed{x}$. In order to know which definition of $\boxed{x}$ to use, we want to know if $2y$ is even. Since y is an integer, then $2y$ is an even integer. Thus,

$$\boxed{2y} = \dfrac{5}{2}(2y)$$

or

$$\boxed{2y} = 5y \; (Answer)$$

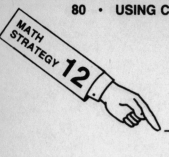

MATH STRATEGY **12**

TRY NOT TO MAKE TEDIOUS CALCULATIONS SINCE THERE IS USUALLY AN EASIER WAY

In many of the examples given in these strategies, it has been explicitly stated that one should not calculate complicated quantities. In some of the examples, we have demonstrated a fast and a slow way of solving the same problem. On the actual exam, if you find that your solution to a problem involves a tedious and complicated method, then you are probably doing the problem in a long, hard way. Almost always there will be an easier way. Here is another example of this principle.

EXAMPLE 1

If $y^8 = 4$ and $y^7 = \dfrac{3}{x}$,

what is the value of y in terms of x?

(A) $\dfrac{4x}{3}$ (B) $\dfrac{3x}{4}$ (C) $\dfrac{4}{x}$ (D) $\dfrac{x}{4}$ (E) $\dfrac{12}{x}$

Choice A is correct. Just divide the two equations:

$$y^8 = 4$$

$$y^7 = \frac{3}{x}$$

$$\frac{y^8}{y^7} = \frac{4}{\dfrac{3}{x}}$$

$$y = 4 \times \frac{x}{3}$$

$$y = \frac{4x}{3} \ (Answer)$$

EXAMPLE 2

If $x = 1 + 2 + 2^2 + 2^3 + 2^4 + 2^5 + 2^6 + 2^7$
$+ 2^8 + 2^9$
and $y = 1 + 2x$, then $y - x =$

(A) 2^7 (B) 2^8 (C) 2^9 (D) 2^{10} (E) 2^{11}

Choice D is correct. I hope you did not calculate $1 + 2 + \ldots\ldots 2^9$. If you did, then you found that $x = 1023$ and $y = 2047$ and $y - x = 1024$.

Here is the FAST method. Instead of making these tedious calculations, observe that since

$$x = 1 + 2 + 2^2 + 2^3 + 2^4 + 2^5 + 2^6 \\ + 2^7 + 2^8 + 2^9 \qquad \boxed{1}$$

then $2x = 2 + 2^2 + 2^3 + 2^4 + 2^5 + 2^6 + 2^7$
$+ 2^8 + 2^9 + 2^{10}$ $\boxed{2}$

and $y = 1 + 2x = 1 + 2 + 2^2 + 2^3 + 2^4$
$+ 2^5 + 2^6 + 2^7 + 2^8 + 2^9 + 2^{10}$ $\boxed{3}$

Thus, calculating $\boxed{3} - \boxed{1}$, we get

$y - x = 1 + 2 + 2^2 + 2^3 + 2^4 + 2^5 + 2^6 + 2^7$
$\qquad + 2^8 + 2^9 + 2^{10}$

$- \qquad (1 + 2 + 2^2 + 2^3 + 2^4 + 2^5 + 2^6 + 2^7$
$\qquad + 2^8 + 2^9)$

$= 2^{10} \ (Answer)$

KNOW HOW TO FIND UNKNOWN EXPRESSIONS BY ADDING, SUBTRACTING, MULTIPLYING, OR DIVIDING EQUATIONS OR EXPRESSIONS

When you want to calculate composite quantities like $x + 3y$ or $m - n$, you can often do it by adding, subtracting, multiplying, or dividing the right equations or expressions.

EXAMPLE 1

If $4x + 5y = 10$ and $x + 3y = 8$,
then $\dfrac{5x + 8y}{3} =$

(A) 18   (B) 12   (C) 9   (D) 6   (E) 15

Choice D is correct. Don't solve for x, then for y.
Try to get the quantity $\dfrac{5x + 8y}{3}$ by adding or subtracting the equations. In this case, *add* equations.

$$\begin{array}{r} 4x + 5y = 10 \\ +\ \ x + 3y = \ 8 \\ \hline 5x + 8y = 18 \end{array}$$

Now divide by 3:

$$\frac{5x + 8y}{3} = \frac{18}{3} = 6 \ (Answer)$$

EXAMPLE 2

If $25x + 8y = 149$ and $16x + 3y = 89$, then

$$\frac{9x + 5y}{5} =$$

(A) 12   (B) 15   (C) 30   (D) 45   (E) 60

Choice A is correct. We are told

$$25x + 8y = 149 \ \boxed{1}$$
$$16x + 3y = \ \ 89 \ \boxed{2}$$

The long way to do this problem is to solve $\boxed{1}$ and $\boxed{2}$ for x and y, and then substitute these values into $\dfrac{9x + 5y}{5}$

The fast way to do this problem is to subtract $\boxed{2}$ from $\boxed{1}$ and get

$$9x + 5y = 60 \ \boxed{3}$$

Now all we have to do is to divide $\boxed{3}$ by 5

$$\frac{9x + 5y}{5} = 12 \ (Answer)$$

EXAMPLE 3

If $21x + 39y = 18$, then $7x + 13y =$

(A) 3   (B) 6   (C) 7   (D) 9
(E) It cannot be determined from the information given.

Choice B is correct. We are given

$$21x + 39y = 18 \ \boxed{1}$$

Divide $\boxed{1}$ by 3

$$7x + 13y = 6 \ (Answer)$$

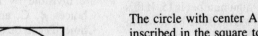

DRAW OR EXTEND LINES IN A DIAGRAM TO MAKE A A PROBLEM EASIER; LABEL UNKNOWN QUANTITIES

EXAMPLE 1

The circle with center A and radius AB is inscribed in the square to the left. AB is extended to C. What is the ratio of AB to AC?

(A) $\sqrt{2}$ (B) $\dfrac{\sqrt{2}}{4}$ (C) $\dfrac{\sqrt{2} - 1}{2}$

(D) $\dfrac{\sqrt{2}}{2}$ (E) none of these

Choice D is correct. Always draw or extend lines to get more information. Also label unknown lengths, angles or arcs with letters.

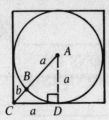

Label $AB = a$ and $BC = b$.
Draw perpendicular AD. Note it is just the radius, a. CD also $= a$.

We want to find $\dfrac{AB}{AC} = \dfrac{a}{a + b}$

Now $\triangle ADC$ is an isosceles right triangle so $AD = CD = a$.

By the Pythagorean Theorem,
$a^2 + a^2 = (a + b)^2$ where $a + b$ is hypotenuse of right triangle.

We get: $2a^2 = (a + b)^2$
Divide by $(a + b)^2$:

$$\frac{2a^2}{(a + b)^2} = 1$$

Divide by 2:

$$\frac{a^2}{(a + b)^2} = \frac{1}{2}$$

Take square roots of both sides:

$$\frac{a}{(a + b)} = \frac{1}{\sqrt{2}} =$$

$$= \frac{1}{\sqrt{2}}\left(\frac{\sqrt{2}}{\sqrt{2}}\right)$$

$$= \frac{\sqrt{2}}{2} \text{ (Answer)}$$

MATH STRATEGY 15.

EXAMPLE 2

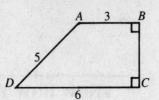

What is the perimeter of the above figure if B and C are right angles?

(A) 14   (B) 16   (C) 18   (D) 20
(E) It cannot be determined.

Choice C is correct.

Draw perpendicular AE. Label side $BC = h$. You can see that $AE = h$.

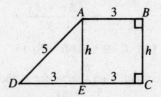

$ABCE$ is a rectangle, so $CE = 3$. This makes $ED = 3$ since the whole $DC = 6$.

Now use the Pythagorean Theorem for triangle AED:

$$\begin{aligned}
h^2 + 3^2 &= 5^2 \\
h^2 &= 5^2 - 3^2 \\
h^2 &= 25 - 9 \\
h^2 &= 16 \\
h &= 4
\end{aligned}$$

So the perimeter is $3 + h + 6 + 5 = 3 + 4 + 6 + 5 = 18$ (*Answer*)

KNOW HOW TO ELIMINATE CERTAIN CHOICES

Instead of working out a lot of algebra, you may be able to eliminate several of the choices at first glance. Thus, you can save yourself a lot of work. The key is to remember to use pieces of the given information to eliminate several of the choices at once.

EXAMPLE

The sum of the digits of a three-digit number is 15. If this number is not divisible by 2, but is divisible by 5, which of the following is the number?

   (A) 384   (B) 465   (C) 635   (D) 681   (E) 780

Choice B is correct. Use pieces of the given information to eliminate several of the choices.

Which numbers are divisible by 2? Choices A and E are divisible by 2 and, thus, can be eliminated. Of Choices B, C, and D, which are <u>not</u> divisible by 5? Choice D can be eliminated. We are left with Choices B and C.

Only Choice B (465) has the sum of its digits equal to 15. Thus, 465 is the only number which satisfies all the pieces of the given information.

If you learn to use this method well, you can save loads of time.

WATCH OUT FOR QUESTIONS WHICH SEEM VERY EASY BUT WHICH CAN BE TRICKY—BEWARE OF CHOICE A AS A "LURE CHOICE"

When questions appear to be solved very easily, think again! Watch out especially for the "lure" Choice A.

EXAMPLE 1

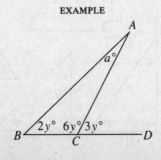

6:06

The diagram above shows a digital clock whose hour digit is the same as the minutes digit. Consider each time when the same number appears for both the hour and the minutes as a "double time" situation. What is the shortest elapsed time period between the appearance of one double time and an immediately succeeding double time?

(A) 61 minutes   (B) 11 minutes   (C) 60 minutes
(D) 101 minutes   (E) 49 minutes

Choice E is correct. Did you think that just by subtracting something like 8:08 from 9:09 you would get the answer (1 hour and 1 minute = 61

minutes)? That's Choice A which is wrong. So beware, because your answer came too easily for a test like the SAT. You must realize that there is another possibility of double time occurrence—12:12 and 1:01 whose difference is 49 minutes. This is Choice E, the correct answer.

EXAMPLE 2

The letters d and m are integral digits in a certain number system. If $0 \le d \le m$, how many different, possible values are there for d?

(A) m (B) $m - 1$ (C) $m - 2$
(D) $m + 1$ (E) $m + 2$

Choice D is correct. Did you think that the answer was m? Do not be careless! The list 1, 2, 3,...,m contains m elements. If 0 is included in the list, then there are $m + 1$ elements. Hence, if $0 \le d \le m$ where d is integral, then d can have $m + 1$ different values.

USE THE GIVEN INFORMATION EFFECTIVELY (AND IGNORE IRRELEVANT INFORMATION)

You should always use first the piece of information which tells you the most, or gives you a useful idea, or which brings you closest to the answer.

EXAMPLE

In the figure at the left, side BC of triangle ABC is extended to D. What is the value of a?

(A) 15   (B) 17   (C) 20   (D) 24   (E) 30

Choice C is correct.

Use the piece of information that will give you something definite. You might have first thought of using the fact that the sum of the angles of a triangle = 180°. However that will give you

$$a + 2y + 6y = 180$$

That's not very useful. However if you use the fact that the sum of the angles in a straight angle is 180 we get:

$$6y + 3y = 180$$

and we get $9y = 180$

$$y = 20.$$

Now we have gotten something useful.
At this point, we can use the fact that the sum of the angles in a triangle is 180.

$$a + 2y + 6y = 180$$

Substituting 20 for y, we get

$$a + 2(20) + 6(20) = 180$$

$$a = 20 \qquad (Answer)$$

MATH
STRATEGY 18.

KNOW AND USE FACTS ABOUT TRIANGLES

By remembering these facts about triangles, you can often save yourself a lot of time and trouble.

I.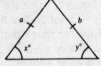

If $a = b$, then $x = y$
If $x = y$, then $a = b$

III.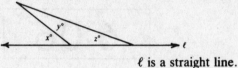

ℓ is a straight line.
Then, $x = y + z$

II.

In a right triangle,
$c^2 = a^2 + b^2$
and $x° + y° = 90°$

IV.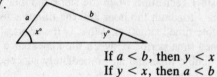

If $a < b$, then $y < x$
If $y < x$, then $a < b$

V.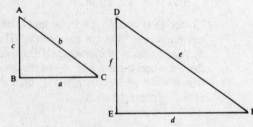

If $\triangle ABC \sim DEF$, then

$m \angle A = m \angle D, m \angle B = m \angle E, m \angle C = m \angle F$

and $\dfrac{a}{d} = \dfrac{b}{e} = \dfrac{c}{f}$

VI.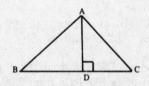

$\angle A + \angle B + \angle C = 180°$

Area of $\triangle ABC = \dfrac{AD \times BC}{2}$

VII. Memorize the following standard triangles:

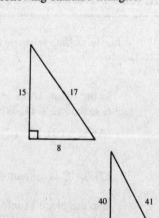

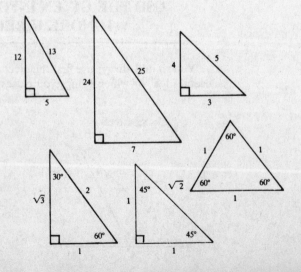

EXAMPLE

In the diagram below, what is the value of x?

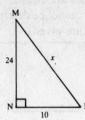

(A) 20   (B) 25   (C) 26   (D) 45   (E) 48

Choice C is correct.

Method 1: Use II on page 83.
Then,

$$x^2 = 24^2 + 10^2$$
$$= 576 + 100$$
$$= 676$$

Thus, $x = 26$ (*Answer*)

Method 2: Look at VI on page 83. Notice that $\triangle$MNP is similar to one of the standard triangles:

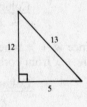 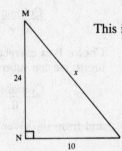

This is true because

$$\frac{12}{24} = \frac{5}{10} \text{ (Look at V)}$$

Hence, $\frac{12}{24} = \frac{13}{x}$ or $x = 26$ (*Answer*)

MATH STRATEGY 19

WHEN CALCULATING ANSWERS, NEVER MULTIPLY AND/OR DO LONG DIVISION, IF REDUCING CAN BE DONE FIRST

EXAMPLE

If $w = \dfrac{81 \times 150}{45 \times 40}$, then $w =$

(A) 3   (B) $6\frac{3}{4}$ (C) $7\frac{1}{4}$ (D) 9   (E) $20\frac{1}{4}$

$\left.\begin{array}{l}\textit{Do not} \\ \textit{multiply in} \\ \textit{this case}\end{array}\right\}$ 81×150 and 45×40 to get

$$\frac{12150}{1800}$$

Factor first $\dfrac{\overset{81}{\overbrace{9 \times 9}} \times \overset{150}{\overbrace{15 \times 10}}}{\underset{45}{\underbrace{9 \times 5}} \times \underset{40}{\underbrace{4 \times 10}}}$

Then cancel like factors in numerator and denominator

$$\frac{\cancel{9} \times 9 \times 15 \times \cancel{10}}{\cancel{9} \times 5 \times 4 \times \cancel{10}}$$

Reduce further $\dfrac{9 \times \cancel{5} \times 3}{\cancel{5} \times 4}$

Then simplify

$$\frac{27}{4} = 6\frac{3}{4} \text{ (\textit{Answer})}$$

Thus, Choice B is correct.

SUMMARY DIRECTIONS FOR COMPARISON QUESTIONS

Choose A if the quantity in Column A is greater;	Choose C if the two quantities are equal;
Choose B if the quantity in Column B is greater;	Choose D if the relationship cannot be determined from the information given.

MATH STRATEGY A

CANCEL NUMBERS OR EXPRESSIONS COMMON TO BOTH COLUMNS BY AN ADDITION OR SUBTRACTION

If the same expression or number appears in both columns, we can then subtract it from both columns.

EXAMPLE 1

Column A	Column B
$\frac{1}{2} + \frac{1}{6} + \frac{1}{17}$	$\frac{1}{17} + \frac{1}{2} + \frac{1}{7}$

Choice A is correct.
Don't add fractions in columns! Cancel common quantities:

Column A	Column B
$\cancel{\frac{1}{2}} + \frac{1}{6} + \cancel{\frac{1}{17}}$	$\cancel{\frac{1}{17}} + \cancel{\frac{1}{2}} + \frac{1}{7}$
$\frac{1}{6}$	$\frac{1}{7}$

Column A > Column B.

EXAMPLE 2

$$y > 0$$

Column A	Column B
$w + x$	$w + x + y$

Choice B is correct. Since $w + x$ appears in both columns, we can subtract $w + x$ from both columns to get

Column A	Column B
0	y

and from the given information we knew that $y > 0$.

MATH STRATEGY B

CANCEL NUMBERS OR EXPRESSIONS (POSITIVE QUANTITIES ONLY!!) COMMON TO BOTH COLUMNS BY MULTIPLICATION OR DIVISION

If the same expression or number (positive quantities only which may be multiplied by other expressions) appears in both columns, we can then divide it from both columns. NEVER divide both columns by zero or a negative number.

EXAMPLE 1

Column A	Column B
$24 \times 46 \times 35$	$46 \times 24 \times 36$

Column B is greater.
Don't multiply out! Cancel 24×46 from both columns (by dividing both columns by 24×46).

Column A	Column B
$\cancel{24} \times \cancel{46} \times 35$	$\cancel{46} \times \cancel{24} \times 36$

Column A < Column B.

EXAMPLE 2

$$m > 1$$
$$n > 0$$

Column A	Column B
mn	n

Choice A is correct. Since $n > 0$ and n appears in both columns, we can divide it from both columns to get

Column A	Column B
m	1

and we are given that $m > 1$.

SUMMARY DIRECTIONS FOR COMPARISON QUESTIONS

Choose A if the quantity in Column A is greater;
Choose B if the quantity in Column B is greater;

Choose C if the two quantities are equal;
Choose D if the relationship cannot be determined
from the information given.

WHEN A COMPARISON OF THE TWO COLUMNS IS DIFFICULT, USE NUMBERS IN PLACE OF VARIABLES

Sometimes by using numbers in place of variables, you can show that different comparisons exist, making choice D correct.

EXAMPLE 1

Column A	Column B
$a, b > 1$	
$\dfrac{a}{b}$	$\dfrac{b}{a}$

Choice D is correct. Let us take numerical examples which satisfy $a, b > 1$

CASE 1

$a = 6, b = 3$ Then the columns become

Column A	Column B
$\dfrac{6}{3} = 2$	$\dfrac{3}{6} = \dfrac{1}{2}$

and the quantity in Column A is greater.

CASE 2

$a = 4, b = 12$

Then the columns become

Column A	Column B
$\dfrac{4}{12} = \dfrac{1}{3}$	$\dfrac{12}{4} = 3$

and the quantity in *Column B is greater*.

In one case, Column A > Column B. In the second case, Column B > Column A. Thus, a definite comparison *cannot* be made.

EXAMPLE 2

Column A	Column B
$a > 0$	
$\dfrac{1}{a}$	a

Choice D is correct.
Often you can find a number for the variable which makes the columns equal. Then all you have to find is another number which will make them unequal. In the above example, choose $a = 1$. This makes the columns equal. You can see that any other value of a, like $a = 100$, will make the columns unequal. Thus, a definite relation *cannot* be obtained.

TO MAKE A COMPARISON SIMPLER—ESPECIALLY OF FRACTIONS—MULTIPLY, DIVIDE, ADD TO, OR SUBTRACT FROM BOTH COLUMNS BY A QUANTITY (NEVER MULTIPLY OR DIVIDE BY ZERO OR BY A NEGATIVE NUMBER)

EXAMPLE 1

Column A	Column B
1	$\dfrac{\frac{7}{9}}{\frac{9}{7}}$

Choice A is correct.
Don't divide 7/9 by 9/7. Multiply both columns by 9/7

to get rid of the complicated fraction in Column B:

Column A	Column B
$1 \times 9/7$	$\dfrac{7/9}{\cancel{9/7}} \times \cancel{9/7}$
9/7	7/9

Column A > Column B.

SUMMARY DIRECTIONS FOR COMPARISON QUESTIONS

Choose A if the quantity in Column A is greater;	Choose C if the two quantities are equal;
Choose B if the quantity in Column B is greater;	Choose D if the relationship cannot be determined from the information given.

EXAMPLE 2

Column A	Column B

$$-1 \quad 0 \quad a \quad 3 \quad 8$$

a	$8 - a$

Choice B is correct.
Get rid of the minus sign by *adding a* to both columns:

Column A	Column B
$a + a$	$8 - a + a$
$2a$	8

Divide by 2: a 4

Now look at the diagram: $a < 3$, so $a < 4$.
Column A < Column B.

EXAMPLE 3

Column A	Column B
$\sqrt{19} - \sqrt{3}$	$\sqrt{16}$

Choice B is correct. First, get rid of the minus sign by adding $\sqrt{3}$ to both columns.

Column A	Column B
$\sqrt{19}$	$\sqrt{16} + \sqrt{3}$

Now *square* both columns:

Column A	Column B
$(\sqrt{19})^2$	$(\sqrt{16} + \sqrt{3})^2$
19	$16 + 3 + 2\sqrt{16}\sqrt{3}$
19	$19 + 2\sqrt{16}\sqrt{3}$

Cancel the 19's:

Column A	Column B
0	$2\sqrt{16}\sqrt{3}$

Column B > Column A

MATH STRATEGY E

TRY TO GET THE COLUMNS AND THE GIVEN TO LOOK SIMILAR

The quantities to be compared in the columns and the information given may look different. Whenever it is possible, you should try to get the columns to look like what is given, or try to get the given to look like what is in the columns.

EXAMPLE 1

Column A	Column B

$$m > n$$
$$n > p$$

m	p

Choice A is correct. We want to compare m and p. However, the given information,

$$m > n \quad \boxed{1}$$
$$n > p \quad \boxed{2}$$

does not directly relate to m and p. So we should try to get the given information to look similar to what we want to compare. By comparing $\boxed{1}$ and $\boxed{2}$ we have

$$m > p$$

This is the piece of crinformation we need to compare the two columns. Clearly, Choice A is correct.

EXAMPLE 2

Column A	Column B

$$-5 < x < +5$$

-6	$-x$

Choice B is correct.
Try to get the given to look like what's in the columns.

Multiply the given by -1. You get

$$-1(-5 < x < +5) \rightarrow +5 > -x > -5$$

remembering to reverse the inequality signs when multiplying by a negative number.

Now we found $-x > -5$. Now look at the columns:

If $-x > -5$, surely

$$-x > -6 \text{ and Column A} < \text{Column B.}$$

SUMMARY DIRECTIONS FOR COMPARISON QUESTIONS

Choose A if the quantity in Column A is greater;
Choose B if the quantity in Column B is greater;
Choose C if the two quantities are equal;
Choose D if the relationship cannot be determined from the information given.

MATH STRATEGY F

USE THE CHOICE C METHOD WHEN STRAIGHTFORWARD COMPUTATIONS MUST BE MADE

This strategy should be used only if you must guess the answer or if you do not have the time to work out tedious arithmetic. When the answer to a problem requires only a straightforward computation and if there are very specific numbers (like 17 or 23) involved in the problem, Choice C is almost always correct. The reason is that the test-maker has a logical reason to make Choice C the answer. We see this in the following problem.

EXAMPLE 1

Column A	Column B
$5x + 12 = 27$	
x	3

Choice C is correct. Look at all the specific numbers that are involved in this question: 5, 12, 27, and 3. These numbers were not accidentally chosen! The solution to this problem involves a straightforward calculation!

$$5x + 12 = 27 \quad \boxed{1}$$
$$5x = 15$$
$$x = 3$$

Why did the test-maker want Choice C as the answer? The reason is that if you could not solve $\boxed{1}$, then you guessed what x should be. You probably guessed that x is some number greater than 3 or less than 3. In addition, if you made a mistake solving $\boxed{1}$, then you obtained a value for x that was greater than 3 or less than 3. Either way, you wrote Choice A or B as your answer. You may even have written Choice D if you could not do the problem correctly. Thus, the test-maker felt that only someone who really knew how to solve the problem would write Choice C. Let us look at another problem.

EXAMPLE 2

Column A	Column B

Last year, Jack had 60 marbles. This year Jack has 75 marbles.

The percent increase in the number of marbles Jack had since last year.   25%

Choice C is correct. Look at all the specific numbers in this problem: 60, 75, and 25. These numbers were not accidentally chosen! The solution to this problem involves a straightforward computation:

The percent increase in the number of marbles Jack had since last year =

$$\frac{\text{Number of marbles Jack has now} - \text{Number of marbles Jack had last year}}{\text{Number of marbles Jack had last year}} \times 100$$

$$= \frac{75 - 60}{60} \times 100$$
$$= \frac{15}{60} \times 100$$
$$= 25\% \ (Answer)$$

Anyone who guessed the answer or who made a mistake in the above calculation probably wrote A, B, or D as his answer. Only someone who really solved the problem correctly was able to get the right answer.

EXAMPLE 3

Column A	Column B
The length of the hypotenuse of a right triangle whose legs are 7 inches and 24 inches long.	The length of the hypotenuse of a right triangle whose legs are 15 inches and 20 inches long.

Choice C is correct. Look at all the specific numbers in this question: 7, 24, 15, and 20. These numbers were not accidentally chosen! The solution to this problem involves straightforward calculation!

$$(\text{hypotenuse})^2 = (\text{first leg})^2 + (\text{second leg})^2$$

Thus, for column A,

$$(\text{hypotenuse})^2 = 7^2 + 24^2$$
$$= 49 + 576$$
$$= 625$$

hypotenuse in Column A = 25 $\boxed{1}$

For Column B

$$(\text{hypotenuse})^2 = 15^2 + 20^2$$
$$= 225 + 400$$
$$= 625$$

hypotenuse in Column B = 25 $\boxed{2}$

From $\boxed{1}$ and $\boxed{2}$ the answer is clear. Anyone who guessed the answer or who made a mistake in the above calculation probably wrote A, B, or D as his answer. Only someone who really solved the problem correctly was able to get the right answer.

Using Critical Thinking Skills in Verbal Questions

5 ANALOGY STRATEGIES

ANALOGY STRATEGY 1

ALWAYS EXPRESS AN ANALOGY IN SENTENCE FORM*

Without looking at the answer choices, try to establish an exact relationship between the CAPITALIZED pair of words. When you do establish the relationship, *express it in sentence form*. Then use that same sentence form in the choices to get the correct answer.

EXAMPLE 1

ROBBERY : THIEF::

(A) diamond : vault
(B) crime : prison
(C) hostage : kidnapper
(D) capture : convict
(E) forgery : counterfeiter

EXPLANATORY ANSWER

Choice E is correct. Put the capitalized words in the form of a sentence: ROBBERY is committed by a THIEF. Now put the choice E words into the same sentence form: forgery is committed by a counterfeiter.

By using this analogy strategy, you can immediately eliminate all wrong choices simply by applying the sentence form method with all the choices:

(A) A diamond is committed by a vault. NO!
(B) A crime is committed by a prison. NO!
(C) A hostage is committed by a kidnapper. NO!
(D) A capture is committed by a convict. NO!
(E) A forgery is committed by a counterfeiter. YES!

(Action to Person relationship)

EXAMPLE 2

CLOCK : TIME::

(A) minute : hour
(B) dimension : space
(C) distance : meter
(D) thermometer : temperature
(E) gravity : weight

EXPLANATORY ANSWER

Choice D is correct. A CLOCK is used to tell or determine the TIME. A thermometer is used to tell or determine the temperature. The other choices do not lend themselves to this sentence relationship.

(Purpose relationship)

*Strategy 1 is considered the Master Analogy Strategy because it can be used effectively in every Analogy question. However, it is important that you learn the other Analogy Strategies also since they can often be used to double-check your answers.

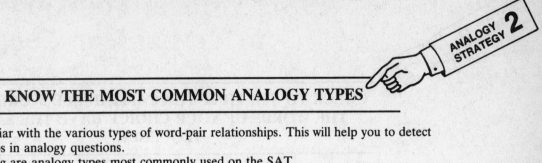

KNOW THE MOST COMMON ANALOGY TYPES

Be familiar with the various types of word-pair relationships. This will help you to detect relationships in analogy questions.

Following are analogy types most commonly used on the SAT.

Analogy Type	Example
PART : WHOLE	LEG : BODY
PURPOSE	SCISSORS : CUT
DEGREE	GRIN : LAUGH
OPPOSITES	COY : AGGRESSIVE
CHARACTERISTIC	SANDPAPER : ROUGH
CAUSE : EFFECT	PRACTICE : IMPROVEMENT
ASSOCIATION	COW : MILK
ACTION : SITUATION	RUN : MARATHON
ACTION : OBJECT	SHOOT: RIFLE
RESULT	TRIAL : JUDGMENT
PLACE : PERSON	SCHOOL : TEACHER

Note: Some Analogy types may be used in reverse. You may have WHOLE : PART, EFFECT : CAUSE, etc.

EXAMPLE 1

DRIZZLE : RAIN ::

  (A) diamond : ruby
  (B) novel : autobiography
  (C) lightning : thunderstorm
  (D) blizzard : avalanche
  (E) surprise : shock

EXPLANATORY ANSWER

Choice E is correct. A DRIZZLE is a fine, gentle falling of water drops from the sky. RAIN has a greater intensity of such falling of water drops. You have here a relationship of Degree. A shock is an emotional disturbance and is more extreme than a surprise is. In other words, when a person is shocked, he is more violently upset than when he is merely surprised.

(Degree relationship)

EXAMPLE 2

SALUTATION : FAREWELL ::

  (A) birth : death
  (B) army : navy
  (C) noon : midnight
  (D) friendship : divorce
  (E) plane : bus

EXPLANATORY ANSWER

Choice A is correct. We have here an Opposite analogy of a certain type—a *beginning-end* analogy. A SALUTATION may be the beginning of a letter—"Dear Sir" for example; or it could be a greeting such as "Hello." A FAREWELL expresses the end of something such as a visit. A farewell expression is "goodbye." It is obvious that *birth* and *death* represent a beginning and an end.

(Opposites relationship)

EXAMPLE 3

WRITE : PENCIL ::

  (A) hammer : nail
  (B) inflate : tire
  (C) open : door
  (D) fly : kite
  (E) wash : hose

EXPLANATORY ANSWER

Choice E is correct. We WRITE with a PENCIL and we wash with a hose. The other choices are incorrect because one does *not* hammer *with* a nail, or inflate *with* a tire, or open *with* a door, or fly *with* a kite.

(Action to Object relationship)

EXAMPLE 4

TENSION : HEADACHE ::

  (A) disposition : anger
  (B) volt : electricity
  (C) virus : malady
  (D) tree : leaf
  (E) mistake : correction

EXPLANATORY ANSWER

Choice C is correct. TENSION is likely to cause a HEADACHE and a virus is likely to cause a malady or disease.

(Cause and Effect relationship)

CHECK TO SEE THAT THE CAPITALIZED WORDS AND THE WORDS OF YOUR CHOICE HAVE THE SAME SEQUENCE

Be sure that the one-two position of the capitalized words is the same as the one-two position of the words of the answer you have chosen. Beware of the choice that would be correct if the words of that choice were reversed.

EXAMPLE 1

ANGER : INSULT ::

(A) business : judgment
(B) admiration : happiness
(C) conduct : behavior
(D) appreciation : kindness
(E) willingness : refusal

EXPLANATORY ANSWER

Choice D is correct. We have here a Cause and Effect analogy. However, the effect word (ANGER) is presented first and the cause word (INSULT) is presented second. So we really have an Effect-Cause relationship here. Anger on the part of one person is likely the effect of an insult on the part of another person. Choice D (appreciation : kindness) has the same Effect-Cause relationship. Appreciation on the part of one person is likely the effect of kindness on the part of the other person. Note the position of the words in Choice B (admiration : happiness). It is true that happiness on the part of one person is likely caused by admiration on the part of another person. In order to follow through with the ANGER : INSULT position, we would have to change Choice B to happiness : admiration.

(Effect—Cause relationship)

EXAMPLE 2

HOSPITAL : NURSE ::

(A) college : professor
(B) theater : dramatist
(C) artist : studio
(D) drugs : pharmacist
(E) cathedral : architect

EXPLANATORY ANSWER

Choice A is correct. A hospital is a place where a nurse works. A college is a place where a professor works. Note the position of the words in Choice C—artist : studio. It is true that an artist works in a studio. In order to follow through with the HOSPITAL : NURSE position, we would have to change Choice C to studio : artist.

(Place—Worker relationship)

MAKE SURE TO GET THE *EXACT* RELATIONSHIP OF THE CAPITALIZED WORDS AND YOUR CHOICE TO ELIMINATE ALL INCORRECT CHOICES

Two or more of the answer choices may, at first glance, show a relationship *similar* to the relationship of the capitalized pair of words. It is necessary to go back to the capitalized pair of words sometimes in order to establish an *exact* relationship. Then find the choice which has the two words with the *very same* relationship as that of the capitalized words.

EXAMPLE 1

MOTH : CLOTHING : :

   (A) sheep : wool
   (B) butterfly : wood
   (C) puncture : tire
   (D) run : stocking
   (E) termite : house

EXPLANATORY ANSWER

Choice E is correct. A MOTH makes a hole in CLOTHING. A puncture makes a hole in a tire (Choice C). A termite makes a hole in a house (Choice E). You must now get the <u>exact</u> relationship of the capitalized words. A MOTH is a <u>living thing</u> which makes a hole in clothing. A termite is a <u>living thing</u> which makes a hole in a house. A puncture is <u>not</u> a living thing.

(Cause and Effect relationship)

EXAMPLE 2

JUROR : JUDGE ::

   (A) criminal : sentence
   (B) broom : sweep
   (C) umpire : oust
   (D) decision : vacillate
   (E) doctor : cure

EXPLANATORY ANSWER

Choice E is correct. A juror's purpose is to JUDGE (decide) whether a person is innocent or guilty, right or wrong, etc. A doctor's purpose is to cure a person. Note that Choice B—broom : sweep is also a Purpose analogy. However, you must observe that a juror is a *person* and a doctor is a *person*. But a broom is *not* a person—it is a thing. Accordingly, Choice B is incorrect.

(Purpose relationship)

BE AWARE THAT CERTAIN WORDS MAY HAVE TWO DIFFERENT MEANINGS

Sometimes a word may have two different meanings. If you find it difficult to establish a relationship between the capitalized pair of words and a pair of words among the choices, study carefully the capitalized pair to get its *precise* relationship. With this in mind, try to get the same *precise*, relationship while keeping in mind that certain words have more than one meaning.

EXAMPLE 1

STRIKE : PRODUCTION ::

   (A) manufacture : merchandise
   (B) injure : repair
   (C) employ : inflation
   (D) collide : car
   (E) vaccinate : disease

EXPLANATORY ANSWER

Choice E is correct. In this question, STRIKE is a verb which means to stop work. Employees strike to stop production. A doctor vaccinates to prevent (or stop) a disease. We have here a Purpose analogy. The word "strike" can also mean to hit or collide with—but not in this question.

(Purpose relationship)

EXAMPLE 2

BULB : PLANT ::

   (A) leaf : tree   (B) tadpole : frog
   (C) biology : chemistry   (D) pupil : teacher
   (E) switch : light

EXPLANATORY ANSWER

Choice B is correct. A bulb has the biological meaning of an underground stem or bud here—not the meaning of an object that you put into an electric lamp. A bulb, then, grows into a plant and a tadpole grows into a frog. We have here a Degree of Development relationship— or a Part-Whole relationship (partially developed —wholly developed).

(Degree relationship and Part: Whole relationship)

SENT. COMPL. STRATEGY 1.

4 SENTENCE COMPLETION STRATEGIES

FOR A SENTENCE WITH ONLY ONE BLANK, FILL THE BLANK WITH EACH CHOICE TO SEE THE BEST FIT*

Before you decide which is the best choice, fill the blank with each of the five answer choices, to see which word will fit best into the sentence as a whole.

EXAMPLE 1

He believed that while there is serious unemployment in our auto industry, we should not _____ foreign cars.

   (A) discuss   (B) regulate   (C) research
   (D) import   (E) disallow

EXPLANATORY ANSWER

Choice D is correct. The word "import" means to bring in from another country or place. The sentence now makes good sense. The competition resulting from importation of foreign cars reduces the demand for American-made cars. This throws many American auto workers out of jobs.

EXAMPLE 2

His attempt to _____ his guilt was betrayed by the tremor of his hand as he picked up the paper.

   (A) extenuate   (B) determine   (C) conceal
   (D) intensify   (E) display

EXPLANATORY ANSWER

Choice C is correct. The word "conceal" means to keep secret or to hide. The sentence now makes good sense. The nervousness caused by his guilty conscience is shown by the shaking of his hand. He is thus prevented in his attempt to hide his guilt.

*Strategy 1 is considered the Master Strategy for *one-blank* Sentence Completion questions because it can be used effectively to answer *every* *one-blank* Sentence Completion question. However, it is important that you learn all of the other Sentence Completion Strategies since they can be used to double-check your answers.

FOR A SENTENCE WITH TWO BLANKS BEGIN BY ELIMINATING THE INITIAL WORDS THAT DON'T MAKE SENSE IN THE SENTENCE*

This strategy consists of 2 steps.

Step 1. Find out which "first words" of the choices make sense in the first blank of the sentence. Don't consider the second word of each pair yet. *Eliminate those choices that contain "first words" that don't make sense in the sentence.*

Step 2. Now consider the *remaining* choices by filling in the pair of words for each choice.

EXAMPLE 1

The salesmen in that clothing store are so _____ that it is impossible to even look at a garment without being _____ by their efforts to convince you to purchase.

(A) offensive . . . considerate
(B) persistent . . . harassed
(C) extensive . . . induced
(D) immune . . . aided
(E) intriguing . . . evaluated

EXPLANATORY ANSWER

Choice B is correct.

STEP 1 [ELIMINATION]

We have eliminated Choice (C) extensive . . . induced because saying salesmen who are "extensive" does not make sense here. We have eliminated Choice (D) immune . . . aided because salesmen who are "immune" does not make sense here.

STEP 2 [REMAINING CHOICES]

This leaves us with these remaining choices to be considered. Choice (A) offensive . . . considerate. The sentence *does not* make sense. Choice (B) persistent . . . harassed. The sentence *does* make sense. Choice (E) intriguing . . . evaluated. The sentence *does not* make sense.

EXAMPLE 2

Television in our society is watched so _____ that intellectuals who detest the "idiot box" are _____.

(A) reluctantly . . . offended
(B) stealthily . . . ashamed
(C) frequently . . . revolted
(D) intensely . . . exultant
(E) noisily . . . amazed

EXPLANATORY ANSWER

Choice C is correct. We have eliminated Choice A because television is not watched reluctantly in our society. We have eliminated Choice B because television is not watched stealthily in our society. We have eliminated Choice E because it is not common for the viewer to watch television noisily. This leaves us with these remaining choices to be considered. Choice D—intensely . . . exultant. The sentence does *not* make sense. Choice C—frequently . . . revolted. The sentence *does* make sense.

---

*Strategy 2 is considered the Master Strategy for *two-blank* Sentence Completion questions because it can be used effectively to answer every *two-blank* Sentence Completion question. However, it is important to learn all of the other Sentence Completion Strategies since they can be used to double-check your answers.

TRY TO COMPLETE THE SENTENCE IN YOUR OWN WORDS BEFORE LOOKING AT THE CHOICES

This strategy often works well especially with one-blank sentences. You may be able to fill in the blank with a word of your own that makes good sense. Then look at the answer choices to see whether any of the choices has the same meaning as your own word.

EXAMPLE 1

Many buildings with historical significance are now being _____ instead of being torn down.

   (A) built (B) forgotten (C) destroyed
   (D) praised (E) repaired

EXPLANATORY ANSWER

Choice E is correct. The key words "instead of" constitute an *opposite indicator*. The words give us a good clue—we should fill the blank with an antonym (opposite) for "torn down." If you used the strategy of trying to complete the sentence *before* looking at the five choices, you might have come up with any of the following appropriate words:

    remodeled   remade
    reconstructed   renovated

These words all mean the same as the correct Choice E word ⟶ repaired.

EXAMPLE 2

Wishing to _____ the upset passenger who found a nail in his steak, the stewardess offered him a complimentary bottle of champagne.

   (A) appease (B) berate (C) disregard
   (D) reinstate (E) acknowledge

EXPLANATORY ANSWER

Choice A is correct. Since the passenger was upset, the stewardess wished to do something to make him feel better. If you used the strategy of trying to complete the sentence *before* looking at the five choices, you might have come up with the following words that would have the meaning of "to make someone feel better":

    pacify   satisfy
    soothe   conciliate
         relieve

These words all mean the same as the Choice A word ⟶ appease.

PAY CLOSE ATTENTION TO THE KEY WORDS IN THE SENTENCE

A key word may indicate what is happening in the sentence. Here are some examples of key words and what these words may indicate.

Key Word	Indicating
although however in spite of rather than nevertheless on the other hand but	OPPOSITION

Key Word	Indicating
moreover besides additionally furthermore in fact	SUPPORT

Key Word	Indicating
therefore consequently accordingly because when so	RESULT

There are many other words—in addition to the above—that can act as key words to help you considerably in getting the right answer. A key word frequently appears in the sentence. Watch for it!

EXAMPLE 1

Richard Wagner was frequently intolerant; moreover, his strange behavior caused most of his acquaintances to _____ the composer whenever possible.

    (A) contradict   (B) interrogate   (C) shun
    (D) revere   (E) tolerate

EXPLANATORY ANSWER

Choice C is correct. The word "moreover" is a *support indicator* in this sentence. As we try each choice word in the blank, we find that shun (avoid) is the only logical word that fits. You might have selected Choice A ("contradict") but very few would seek to contradict Wagner because most of his acquaintances tried to avoid him.

EXAMPLE 2

The dinosaurs were feared by all other forms of life because they were much larger and stronger, but their bulkiness_____their ability to adjust to new situations.

    (A) improved   (B) welcomed   (C) explained
    (D) interrupted   (E) limited

EXPLANATORY ANSWER

Choice E is correct. The word "but" is an *opposition indicator* in this sentence. As we try each choice word in the blank, we find that "limited" is the only word that fits. You might have chosen Choice D ("interrupted") because it does have some opposition sense. However, "their bulkiness" would not *interrupt* their ability to adjust. So Choice D is incorrect.

EXAMPLE 3

Until we are able to improve substantially the _____ status of the underprivileged in our country, a substantial _____ in our crime rate is remote.

    (A) burdensome . . . harmony
    (B) beneficial . . . gloom
    (C) financial . . . reduction
    (D) remarkable . . . puzzle
    (E) questionable . . . disappointment

EXPLANATORY ANSWER

Choice C is correct. The word "Until" is a *result indicator*. As we try the first word of each choice in the first blank, we find that "burdensome," "financial," and "questionable" all make sense up till the second part of the sentence. We, therefore, eliminate Choices B and D. Now let us try both words in Choice A, C, and E. We then find that we can eliminate Choices A and E as not making sense in the entire sentence. This leaves us with the correct Choice C, which *does* bring out the result of what is stated in the first part of the sentence.

7 ANTONYM STRATEGIES

ANTONYM STRATEGY 1

USE ROOTS, PREFIXES, AND SUFFIXES TO GET THE MEANINGS OF WORDS

You can increase your vocabulary tremendously by learning Latin and Greek roots, prefixes, and suffixes. 60% of all the words in our English language are derived from Latin and Greek. By learning certain Latin and Greek roots, prefixes, and suffixes, you will be able to understand the meanings of over 100,000 additional English words. See "Word Building with Roots, Prefixes, and Suffixes" beginning on page 198.

EXAMPLE 1

PROFICIENT: (A) antiseptic (B) unwilling (C) inconsiderate (D) retarded (E) awkward

EXPLANATORY ANSWERS

Choice E is correct. The prefix PRO means *forward, for the purpose of.* The root FIC means *to make* or *to do.* Therefore, PROFICIENT literally means *doing something in a forward way.* The definition of *proficient* is *skillful, adept, capable.* The antonym of *proficient* is, accordingly, *awkward, incapable.*

EXAMPLE 2

DELUDE: (A) include (B) guide (C) reply (D) upgrade (E) welcome

EXPLANATORY ANSWER

Choice B is correct. The prefix DE means *downward, against.* The root LUD means *to play* (a game). Therefore, DELUDE literally means *to play a game against.* The definition of *delude* is *to deceive, to mislead.* The antonym of *delude* is accordingly *to guide.*

EXAMPLE 3

LAUDATORY: (A) vacating (B) satisfactory (C) revoking (D) faultfinding (E) silent

EXPLANATORY ANSWER

Choice D is correct. The root LAUD means *praise.* The suffix ORY means a *tendency toward.* Therefore, LAUDATORY means having a *tendency toward praising someone.* The definition of *laudatory* is *praising.* The antonym of laudatory is, accordingly, *faultfinding.*

EXAMPLE 4

SUBSTANTIATE: (A) reveal (B) intimidate (C) disprove (D) integrate (E) assist

EXPLANATORY ANSWER

Choice C is correct. The prefix SUB means *under.* The root STA means *to stand.* The suffix ATE is a verb form indicating *the act of.* Therefore, SUBSTANTIATE literally means *to perform the act of standing under.* The definition of *substantiate* is *to support* with proof or evidence. The antonym is, accordingly, *disprove.*

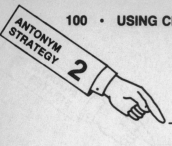

ANTONYM STRATEGY **2**

ATTEND TO THE SOUND OF THE CAPITALIZED WORD AND THE SENSE IT GIVES YOU, AND LOOK FOR A CHOICE WHICH IMPARTS AN *OPPOSITE* SOUND AND SENSE.

If, for example, the capitalized word sounds harsh, such as "obstreperous," look for a word that has an opposite, positive or softer sound such as "pleasantly quiet or docile." The sense of the word "obstreperous" can also be seen as negative—as opposed to a positive quality of "docile".

EXAMPLE 1

BELLIGERENCY: (A) pain   (B) silence
(C) homeliness   (D) elegance   (E) peace

EXPLANATORY ANSWER

Choice E is correct. The word BELLIGERENCY imparts a tone of forcefulness or confusion and means warlike. The opposite would be calmness or peacefulness. The closest choices are choice B or E with E a little closer to the opposite in tone for the CAPITALIZED word. Of course, if you knew the root BELLI means "war" you could see the opposite as (E) peace.

EXAMPLE 2

DEGRADE: (A) startle   (B) elevate
(C) encircle   (D) replace   (E) assemble

EXPLANATORY ANSWER

Choice B is correct. Here you can think of the DE in DEGRADES as a prefix which is negative (bad) and means *down* and in fact DEGRADE does mean debase or lower. So you should look for an opposite which would be a word with a *positive* (good) meaning. The best word from the choices is (B) elevate.

EXAMPLE 3

OBFUSCATION: (A) illumination   (B) irritation
(C) conviction   (D) minor offense
(E) stable environment

EXPLANATORY ANSWER

Choice A is correct. The prefix OB is usually negative as in obstacle or obliterate and in fact OBFUSCATE means darken or obscure. So since we are looking for an opposite, you would look for a *positive* word. Choices A and E are positive, and you would go for the more positive of the two, which is Choice A.

EXAMPLE 4

MUNIFICENCE: (A) disloyalty   (B) stinginess
(C) dispersion   (D) simplicity   (E) vehemence

EXPLANATORY ANSWER

Choice B is correct because MUNIFICENCE means generosity. Many of the words ending in ENCE like OPULENCE, EFFERVESCENCE, LUMINESCENCE, QUINTESSENCE, etc., represent or describe something big or bright. So the opposite of one of these words would denote something small or dark. The choices which are best are (B) stinginess and (D) simplicity. Here it is a matter of random choice if you have to guess (between B and D). However, you have a 50–50 chance of success.

EXAMPLE 5

DETRIMENT: (A) recurrence   (B) disclosure
(C) resemblance   (D) enhancement
(E) postponement

EXPLANATORY ANSWER

Choice D is correct. The prefix DE can also mean against and is negative and DETRIMENT means something that causes damage or loss. So you should look for a positive word. The only one is *enhancement*.

EXAMPLE 6

UNDERSTATE: (A) embroider   (B) initiate
(C) distort   (D) pacify   (E) reiterate

EXPLANATORY ANSWER

Choice A is correct. UNDERSTATE means something said in a restrained or downplayed manner. You see "under" in UNDERSTATE so look for a choice that gives you the impression of something that is "over" as in "overstated". The only choice is (A) embroider, which means to embellish.

EXAMPLE 7

DISHEARTEN: (A) engage (B) encourage
(C) predict (D) dismember (E) misinform

EXPLANATORY ANSWER

Choice B is correct. You see "HEART" in DIS-HEARTEN and the DIS is negative or means "not to," or "not to have heart," and dishearten does mean to discourage. So you want to look for a *positive* word. (B) encourage fits the bill.

EXAMPLE 8

FIREBRAND: (A) an intellect (B) one who is charitable (C) ones who makes peace
(D) a philanthropist (E) one who is dishonest

EXPLANATORY ANSWER

Choice C is correct. You see FIRE in FIREBRAND. So think of something fiery or dangerous. The opposite of FIREBRAND must be something that's calm or safe. The best choice is choice C, whereas a FIRE-BRAND is someone who causes trouble.

ANTONYM STRATEGY 3

USE WORD ASSOCIATIONS TO DETERMINE WORD MEANINGS AND THEIR OPPOSITES

Looking at the root or part of any capitalized word may suggest an association with another word that looks similar and whose meaning you know; this word's meaning may give you a clue as to which choice is the exact opposite of the capitalized word. For example, extricate reminds us of the word "extract" the opposite of which is put together.

EXAMPLE 1

(Remember, you are looking for opposites)

THERMAL: (A) improving (B) possible
(C) beginning (D) reduce (E) frigid

EXPLANATORY ANSWER

Choice E is correct. Here you may associate the word THERMAL with THERMOMETER. A thermometer measures temperature, so it usually measures something that is warm or cold. Look for a choice that has something to do with temperature. Since THERMAL means caused by or producing heat, the only one is (E), frigid.

EXAMPLE 2

STASIS: (A) stoppage (B) reduction
(C) depletion (D) fluctuation (E) completion

EXPLANATORY ANSWER

Choice D is correct. Think of STATIC or STATION-ARY. The opposite would be moving or fluctuating since STASIS means stopping or retarding movement.

EXAMPLE 3

APPEASE: (A) criticize (B) analyze
(C) correct (D) incense (E) develop

EXPLANATORY ANSWER

Choice D is correct. Appease means to placate. Think of PEACE in APPEASE. The opposite would be violent or incense.

EXAMPLE 4

COMMISERATION: (A) undeserved reward
(B) lack of sympathy (C) unexpected success
(D) absence of talent (E) inexplicable danger

EXPLANATORY ANSWER

Choice B is correct. Think of MISERY in the word COMMISERATION. Commiseration means the sharing of misery. Choice B is the only appropriate choice.

EXAMPLE 5

JOCULAR: (A) unintentional (B) exotic
(C) muscular (D) exaggerated (E) serious

EXPLANATORY ANSWER

Choice E is correct. Think of JOKE in the word JOC-ULAR, which means given to joking. The opposite would be serious.

EXAMPLE 6

ELONGATE: (A) melt   (B) wind   (C) confuse
(D) smooth   (E) shorten

EXPLANATORY ANSWER

Choice E is correct. Think of the word LONG in ELONGATE, which means to lengthen. The opposite would be short or shorten.

EXAMPLE 7

SLOTHFUL: (A) permanent   (B) ambitious
(C) average   (D) truthful   (E) plentiful

EXPLANATORY ANSWER

Choice B is correct. Think of SLOTH, a very, very slow animal. So SLOTHFUL, which means lazy or sluggish, must be slow and unambitious. The opposite would be ambitious.

EXAMPLE 8

FORTITUDE: (A) timidity   (B) conservatism
(C) placidity   (D) laxness   (E) ambition

EXPLANATORY ANSWER

Choice A is correct. FORTITUDE means strength in the face of adversity; you should think of FORT or FORTIFY as something strong. The opposite would be weak or timid.

EXAMPLE 9

LUCID: (A) underlying   (B) complex
(C) luxurious   (D) tight   (E) general

EXPLANATORY ANSWER

Choice B is correct. LUCID means easily understood or clear; you should think of LUCITE, a clear plastic. The opposite of clear is hard to see through or complex.

TRY TO ANSWER BEFORE YOU SEE THE CHOICES

Before you look at the answer choices, decide upon a word which would be the antonym (opposite) of the capitalized word in the question. Then look at the answer choices and see whether your own word means the same as any of the five word choices.

EXAMPLE 1

POTENT: (A) imposing   (B) pertinent
(C) feeble   (D) comparable   (E) frantic

EXPLANATORY ANSWER

Choice C is correct. The word POTENT means *strong, powerful, mighty, influential*. If you used the strategy of trying to get your *own word* which was *opposite* in meaning, you might have come up with any of the following words which are antonyms of the four words above:

powerless	ineffectual
weak	ineffective
	impotent

These words all mean the same as the correct Choice C—*feeble*.

EXAMPLE 2

RECEDE: (A) accede   (B) settle   (C) surrender
(D) advance   (E) reform

EXPLANATORY ANSWER

Choice D is correct. The word RECEDE means *moving back, retreating, withdrawing*. We get the meaning from the prefix "re" meaning *back* and the root "ced" meaning *to go*. If you used the strategy of trying to get your *own word* which was *opposite* in meaning, you might have come up with any of the following words which are antonyms of the 3 definitions above:

proceed	go forward
progress	push ahead

These words all mean the same as the correct Choice D—*advance*.

EXAMPLE 3

OBLIVIOUS: (A) apologetic   (B) circular
(C) praiseworthy   (D) glorious   (E) mindful

EXPLANATORY ANSWER

Choice E is correct. The word OBLIVIOUS means *forgetful, thoughtless, careless*. If you used the strategy of trying to get your *own word* which was *opposite* in meaning, you might have come up with any of the following words which are antonyms of the three words above:

aware	noticing	alert

These words all mean the same as the correct Choice E—*mindful*.

EXAMPLE 4

RESTITUTION: (A) activity   (B) loss
(C) stability   (D) recognition   (E) cure

EXPLANATORY ANSWER

Choice B is correct. The word RESTITUTION means *restoring, returning, compensating*. We get the meaning from the prefix "re" meaning *back*; the root "stit" meaning *to set, to place, to stand*; and the suffix "ion" meaning *the act of*. The literal meaning of RESTITUTION is therefore *the act of placing or putting back*. If you used the strategy of trying to get your own word which is *opposite* in meaning you might have come up with any of the following words which are antonyms of RESTITUTION:

damage	denial
injury	deprivation

These words all mean the same as the correct Choice B—*loss*.

WATCH FOR SHADES OF MEANING
IN THE CHOICE WORDS

Sometimes you will find two answer choices that *both seem correct*. Look for the choice *that is most nearly opposite* to the meaning of the capitalized word. Watch for shades of meaning to determine which is the *most nearly* opposite choice.

EXAMPLE 1

OSTENTATIOUS: (A) lazy   (B) motionless
(C) contented   (D) ambitious   (E) modest

EXPLANATORY ANSWER

Choice E is correct. The word OSTENTATIOUS means *pretentious, boasting, showing off*. The *opposite* meaning of OSTENTATIOUS can be found among these words:

shy	quiet
humble	reserved
unpretentious	

The above words all mean the same as the correct Choice E—*modest*. Note that Choice B (motionless) may seem to be the opposite of OSTENTATIOUS. However, consider a *motionless* female modeling very showy clothes. She is OSTENTATIOUS, even though she is *motionless*. Accordingly, Choice B is incorrect.

EXAMPLE 2

ASSIDUOUSLY: (A) incorrectly   (B) brilliantly
(C) stupidly   (D) heedlessly   (E) willingly

EXPLANATORY ANSWERS

Choice D is correct. The word ASSIDUOUSLY means *diligently, devotedly, carefully*. The *opposite* meaning of ASSIDUOUSLY can be found among these words:

carelessly   inattentively   sloppily

The above words all mean about the same as Choice D—*heedlessly*. Note that Choice C (stupidly) may seem to be the opposite of ASSIDUOUSLY. However, a *careless* or *sloppy* person is not necessarily a *stupid* person. So Choice C is incorrect.

EXAMPLE 3

AUSTERE: (A) sensible   (B) willful
(C) inflexible   (D) affable   (E) generous

EXPLANATORY ANSWER

Choice D is correct. The word AUSTERE means *stern, hard, severe, strict*. The *opposite* meaning of AUSTERE can be found among these words:

mild	amiable
bland	gentle
kindly	

The above words all mean about the same as Choice D—*affable*. Note that Choice E (generous) may seem to be the opposite of AUSTERE. However, an austere person may also be a generous person. So Choice D is correct.

EXAMPLE 4

DECOROUS: (A) deceitful   (B) unseemly
(C) placid   (D) uneducated   (E) candid

EXPLANATORY ANSWER

Choice B is correct. The word DECOROUS means *polite, dignified, proper*. The *opposite* meaning of DECOROUS can be found among these words:

bad-mannered	undignified
immodest	disorderly
impolite	

The above words all mean about the same as Choice B—*unseemly*. Note that Choice D (uneducated) may seem to be the opposite of DECOROUS. However, an uneducated person may behave with dignity and appear proper. Therefore, Choice D is incorrect.

BE SURE THAT THE CAPITALIZED WORD HAS THE SAME PART OF SPEECH AS THE CHOICE WORD

It is possible for the capitalized word to have two different parts of speech. In such a case, check the part of speech of the five choices. The capitalized word must have the same part of speech that the choices have.

EXAMPLE 1

SCALE: (A) soothe   (B) reduce   (C) escalate
(D) descend   (E) weigh

EXPLANATORY ANSWER

Choice D is correct. First of all, you have to determine what part of speech the word SCALE is. Is it a noun or is it a verb? To answer this question, you must examine the choices, all of which are verbs. Now you go back to the capitalized word SCALE. As a verb, it means to climb up or to ascend. The *opposite* of these meanings is to climb down or to descend (Choice D).

EXAMPLE 2

CHAMPION: (A) oppose   (B) retreat   (C) alter
(D) defeat   (E) swim

EXPLANATORY ANSWER

Choice A is correct. First, you have to determine what part of speech the word CHAMPION is. To do this, you examine the choices, all of which are verbs. Now you go back to the capitalized word CHAMPION. As a verb, it means to defend or support (a cause or a person). The *opposite* of these meanings is *to oppose* (Choice A).

EXAMPLE 3

EXHAUST: (A) tire   (B) change   (C) refill
(D) inhale   (E) fume

EXPLANATORY ANSWER

Choice C is correct. First of all, you have to determine what part of speech the word EXHAUST is. To do so, you examine the choices. Note that Choice A (tire), Choice B (change), Choice C (refill), and Choice E (fume) may be either *nouns* or *verbs*. However, Choice D (inhale) may be *only a verb*. Therefore, we must conclude that all five choices and the question stem EXHAUST are *verbs*. Reason: The actual SAT Antonym questions *always* have the *same part of speech* throughout the question. Now go back to the capitalized word EXHAUST. As a verb it means *to empty*, *to use up*, *to consume*. The opposite of these meanings is *to refill*. (Choice C).

EXAMPLE 4

CONTEST: (A) correct   (B) accept   (C) examine
(D) dispute   (E) retest

EXPLANATORY ANSWER

Choice B is correct. First of all, you have to determine what part of speech the word CONTEST is. Is it a noun or a verb? To answer this question, you must examine the choices. Choice A ("correct") may be an adjective or a verb. Choices B, C, and E are all verbs. Choice D ("dispute") may be a noun or a verb. Therefore, we must conclude that all five choices and the question stem CONTEST are *verbs*. Reason: The actual SAT Antonym questions *always* have the *same part of speech* throughout the question. Now go back to the capitalized word CONTEST. As a verb it means *to compete* or *to oppose*. The *opposite* of these meanings is *to accept*. (Choice B).

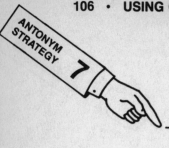

ANTONYM
STRATEGY

7

IF THE CAPITALIZED WORD HAS TWO DIFFERENT MEANINGS, MATCH ONE MEANING CORRECTLY WITH YOUR CHOICE

The capitalized word may have two different meanings. In this case, keep in mind the two meanings when you are deciding which answer choice is correct.

EXAMPLE 1

SANCTION: (A) denial   (B) evil
(C) difference   (D) inadequacy   (E) doubt

EXPLANATORY ANSWERS

Choice A is correct. In this question, SANCTION means *approval* or *support*. [SANCTION has another meaning—a *penalty* for not complying with what is specified in a law or decree.] The *opposite* of approval is *denial* (Choice A).

EXAMPLE 2

SLEEPER: (A) harmless drug   (B) moving train
(C) sure winner   (D) successful businessman
(E) bright person

EXPLANATORY ANSWER

Choice C is correct. In this question, SLEEPER means something like a race horse or a book that, for some time, has indicated little chance of success, but then shows clear signs of being a winner. [SLEEPER may also refer to a person or an animal that sleeps—but not in this case.] The *opposite* of sleeper is *sure winner*. (Choice C).

EXAMPLE 3

RETREAT: (A) welcome   (B) bedlam
(C) consideration   (D) friendship   (E) insult

EXPLANATORY ANSWER

Choice B is correct. In this question, RETREAT means a quiet or private place; a period of solitude or retirement. [RETREAT has another meaning—the act of going backward or withdrawing—but not in this case.] The *opposite* of RETREAT is *bedlam* (Choice B) which means a place or situation of *noisy uproar and confusion*.

EXAMPLE 4

STERILE: (A) restless   (B) agile   (C) wounded
(D) fertile   (E) hostile

EXPLANATORY ANSWER

Choice D is correct. In this question STERILE means *unproductive, barren, impotent, infertile*. [STERILE has another meaning—*free from germs, uncontaminated*—but not in this case.] The *opposite* of STERILE is *fertile*. (Choice D).

9 READING COMPREHENSION STRATEGIES

This section of Reading Comprehension Strategies includes several passages. These passages, though somewhat shorter than the passages that appear on the actual SAT and in the 7 SAT Practice Tests in this book, illustrate the general nature of the "real" SAT reading passages.

Each of the 9 Reading Comprehension Strategies that follow is accompanied by at least two different passages followed by questions and explanatory answers in order to explain how the strategy is used.

READ. COMP. STRATEGY 1

AS YOU READ EACH QUESTION, DETERMINE THE TYPE: MAIN IDEA, DETECTING DETAILS, INFERENCE, TONE/MOOD

Here are the 4 major abilities tested in Reading Comprehension questions:

1. **Main Idea.** Selection of the main thought of a passage; ability to judge the general significance of a passage; ability to select the best title of a passage.
2. **Detecting Details.** Ability to understand the writer's explicit statements; to get the literal meaning of what is written; to identify details.
3. **Inferential Reasoning.** Ability to weave together the ideas of a passage and to see their relationships; to draw correct inferences; to go beyond literal interpretation to the implications of the statements.
4. **Tone/Mood.** Ability to determine from the passage the tone or mood which is dominant in the passage—humorous, serious, sad, mysterious, etc.

Example 1

The fight crowd is a beast that lurks in the darkness behind the fringe of white light shed over the first six rows by the incandescents atop the ring, and is not to be trusted with pop bottles or other hardware.

5   People who go to prize fights are sadistic.

When two prominent pugilists are scheduled to pummel one another in public on a summer's evening, men and women file into the stadium in the guise of human beings, and thereafter become a part of a gray
10 thing that squats in the dark until, at the conclusion of the bloodletting, they may be seen leaving the arena in the same guise they wore when they entered.

As a rule, the mob that gathers to see men fight is unjust, vindictive, swept by intense, unreasoning
15 hatreds, proud of its swift recognition of what it believes to be sportsmanship. It is quick to greet the purely phony move of the boxer who extends his gloves to his rival, who has slipped or been pushed to the floor, and to reward this stimulating but still baloney
20 gesture with a pattering of hands which indicates the following: "You are a good sport. We recognize that you are a good sport, and we know a sporting gesture when we see one. Therefore we are all good sports, too. Hurrah for us!"
25   The same crowd doesn't see the same boxer stick his thumb in his opponent's eye or try to cut him with the laces of his glove, butt him or dig him a low one when

the referee isn't in a position to see. It roots consistently for the smaller man, and never for a moment considers the desperate psychological dilemma of the 30 larger of the two. It howls with glee at a good finisher making his kill. The Roman hordes were more civilized. Their gladiators asked them whether the final blow should be administered or not. The main attraction at the modern prize fight is the spectacle of a man 35 clubbing a helpless and vanquished opponent into complete insensibility. The referee who stops a bout to save a slugged and punch-drunken man from the final ignominy is hissed by the assembled sportsmen.

QUESTIONS

1. The tone of the passage is chiefly

   (A) disgusted   (B) jovial   (C) matter-of-fact
   (D) satiric   (E) devil-may-care

2. Which group of words from the passage best indicates the author's opinion?

   (A) "referee," "opponent," "finisher"
   (B) "gladiators," "slugged," "sporting gesture"
   (C) "stimulating," "hissing," "pattering"
   (D) "beast," "lurks," "gray thing"
   (E) "dilemma," "hordes," "spectacle"

3. Apparently, the author believes that boxing crowds find the referee both

(A) gentlemanly and boring
(B) entertaining and essential
(C) blind and careless
(D) humorous and threatening
(E) necessary and bothersome

EXPLANATORY ANSWERS

1. **(A)** Choice A is correct. The author is obviously much offended (disgusted) by the inhuman attitude of the crowd watching the boxing match. For example, see these lines:
Line 1: "The crowd is a beast."
Line 5: "People who go to prize fights are sadistic."
Lines 13–14: ". . . the mob that gathers to see men fight is unjust, vindictive, swept by intense hatreds."
Lines 32–33: "The Roman hordes were more civilized."
To answer this question, you must be able to determine the tone which is dominant in the passage. Accordingly, this is a TONE/MOOD type of question.

2. **(D)** Choice D is correct. The author's opinion is clearly one of disgust and discouragement because of the behavior of the fight crowd. Accordingly, you would expect the author to use words that were condemnatory, like "beast"—and gloom-filled words like "lurks" and "gray thing." To answer this question, you must see relationships between words and feelings. So, we have here an INFERENTIAL REASONING question-type.

3. **(E)** Choice E is correct. Lines 25–28 show that the referee is *necessary*: "The same crowd doesn't see the same boxer stick his thumb into his opponent's eye . . . when the referee isn't in a position to see." Lines 37–39 show that the referee is bothersome: "The referee who stops a bout . . . is hissed by the assembled sportsmen." To answer this question, the student must have the ability to understand the writer's specific statements. Accordingly, this is a DETECTING DETAILS type of question.

Example 2

Mist continues to obscure the horizon, but above us the sky is suddenly awash with lavender light. At once the geese respond. Now, as well as their cries, a beating roar rolls across the water as if five thousand house-
5 wives have taken it into their heads to shake out blankets all at one time. Ten thousand housewives. It keeps up—the invisible rhythmic beating of all those goose wings—for what seems a long time. Even Lonnie is held motionless with suspense.
10 Then the geese begin to rise. One, two, three hundred—then a thousand at a time—in long horizontal lines that unfurl like pennants across the sky. The horizon actually darkens as they pass. It goes on and on like that, flock after flock, for three or four minutes, each new contingent announcing its ascent with an 15 accelerating roar of cries and wingbeats. Then gradually the intervals between flights become longer. I think the spectacle is over, until yet another flock lifts up, following the others in a gradual turn toward the northeastern quadrant of the refuge. 20
Finally the sun emerges from the mist; the mist itself thins a little, uncovering the black line of willows on the other side of the wildlife preserve. I remember to close my mouth—which has been open for some time—and inadvertently shut two or three mosquitoes inside. 25 Only a few straggling geese oar their way across the sun's red surface. Lonnie wears an exasperated, proprietary expression, as if he had produced and directed the show himself and had just received a bad review. "It would have been better with more light," he says; 30 "I can't always guarantee just when they'll start moving." I assure him I thought it was a fantastic sight. "Well," he rumbles, "I guess it wasn't too bad."

QUESTIONS

1. In the descriptive phrase, "shake out blankets all at one time" (lines 5–6), the author is appealing chiefly to the reader's

(A) background   (B) sight   (C) emotions
(D) thoughts   (E) hearing

2. The mood created by the author is one of

(A) tranquility   (B) excitement   (C) sadness
(D) bewilderment   (E) unconcern

3. The main idea expressed by the author about the geese is that they

(A) are spectacular to watch
(B) are unpredictable
(C) disturb the environment
(D) produce a lot of noise
(E) fly in large flocks

4. Judging from the passage, the reader can conclude that

(A) the speaker dislikes nature's inconveniences
(B) the geese's timing is predictable
(C) Lonnie has had the experience before
(D) both observers are hunters
(E) the author and Lonnie are the same person

EXPLANATORY ANSWERS

1. **(E)** Choice E is correct. See lines 3–6: ". . . a beating roar rolls across the water . . . shake out blankets all at one time." The author, with these words, is no doubt appealing to the reader's hearing. To answer this question, the reader has to identify those words dealing with sound and noise. Therefore, we have here a DETECTING DETAILS type of question. It is also an INFERENTIAL REASONING question-type in that the "sound" words such as "beating" and "roar" lead the reader to infer that the author is appealing to the auditory (hearing) sense.

2. **(B)** Choice B is correct. Excitement courses right through this passage. Here are examples:
Lines 7–8: ". . . the invisible rhythmic beating of all those goose wings."
Lines 8–9: "Even Lonnie is held motionless with suspense."
Lines 10–11: "Then the geese begin to rise . . . a thousand at a time."
Lines 14–16: ". . . flock after flock . . . roar of cries and wingbeats."

To answer this question, you must determine the dominant tone in this passage. Therefore, we have here a TONE/MOOD question-type.

3. **(A)** Choice A is correct. The word "spectacular" means *dramatic, thrilling, impressive*. There is considerable action expressed throughout the passage. Sometimes there is a lull—then the action begins again. See lines 17–19: "I think the spectacle is over, until yet another flock lifts up, following the others." To answer this question, you must have the ability to judge the general significance of the passage. Accordingly, we have here a MAIN IDEA type of question.

4. **(C)** Choice C is correct. See lines 27–32: "Lonnie wears an exasperated proprietary expression . . . when they will start moving." To answer this question, you must be able to draw a correct inference. Therefore, we have here an INFERENTIAL REASONING type of question.

UNDERLINE THE KEY PARTS OF THE READING PASSAGE*

The underlinings will help you to answer questions. Reason: Practically every question will ask you to detect

a) the main idea
or
b) information that is specifically mentioned in the passage
or
c) information that is implied (not directly stated) in the passage
or
d) the tone or mood of the passage

If you find out quickly what the question is aiming for, you will more easily arrive at the correct answer by referring to your underlinings in the passage.

Example 1

That one citizen is as good as another is a favorite American axiom, supposed to express the very essence of our Constitution and way of life. But just what do we mean when we utter that platitude? One surgeon is not
5 as good as another. One plumber is not as good as another. We soon become aware of this when we require the attention of either. Yet in political and economic matters we appear to have reached a point where knowledge and specialized training count for
10 very little. A newspaper reporter is sent out on the street to collect the views of various passers-by on such a question as "Should the United States defend El Salvador?" The answer of the bar-fly who doesn't even know where the country is located, or that it is a country, is quoted in the next edition just as solemnly 15 as that of the college teacher of history. With the basic tenets of democracy—that all men are born free and equal and are entitled to life, liberty, and the pursuit of happiness—no decent American can possibly take issue. But that the opinion of one citizen on a technical 20 subject is just as authoritative as that of another is manifestly absurd. And to accept the opinions of all comers as having the same value is surely to encourage a cult of mediocrity.

*Strategy 2 is considered the Master Reading Comprehension Strategy because it can be used effectively in every Reading Comprehension question. However, it is important that you learn the other Reading Comprehension Strategies since they can often be used to double-check your answers.

QUESTIONS

1. Which phrase best expresses the main idea of this passage?

   (A) the myth of equality
   (B) a distinction about equality
   (C) the essence of the Constitution
   (D) a technical subject
   (E) knowledge and specialized training

2. The author most probably included the example of the question on El Salvador (lines 12–13) in order to

   (A) move the reader to rage
   (B) show that he is opposed to opinion sampling
   (C) show that he has thoroughly researched his project
   (D) explain the kind of opinion sampling he objects to
   (E) provide a humorous but temporary diversion from his main point

3. The author would be most likely to agree that

   (A) some men are born to be masters; others are born to be servants
   (B) the Constitution has little relevance for today's world
   (C) one should never express an opinion on a specialized subject unless he is an expert in that subject
   (D) every opinion should be treated equally
   (E) all opinions should not be given equal weight

EXPLANATORY ANSWERS

1. **(B)** Choice B is correct. See lines 1–7: "That one citizen . . . attention of either." These lines indicate that there is quite a distinction about equality when we are dealing with all the American people.

2. **(D)** Choice D is correct. See lines 10–16: "A newspaper reporter . . . college teacher of history." These lines show that the author probably included the example of the question of El Salvador in order to explain the kind of opinion sampling he objects to.

3. **(E)** Choice E is correct. See lines 20–24: "But that the opinion . . . to encourage a cult of mediocrity." Accordingly, the author would be most likely to agree that all opinions should *not* be given equal weight.

Example 2

She walked along the river until a policeman stopped her. It was one o'clock, he said. Not the best time to be walking alone by the side of a half-frozen river. He smiled at her, then offered to walk her home. It was the first day of the new year, 1946, eight and a 5 half months after the British tanks had rumbled into Bergen-Belsen.

That February, my mother turned twenty-six. It was difficult for strangers to believe that she had ever been a concentration camp inmate. Her face was smooth 10 and round. She wore lipstick and applied mascara to her large dark eyes. She dressed fashionably. But when she looked into the mirror in the mornings before leaving for work, my mother saw a shell, a mannequin who moved and spoke but who bore only a superficial 15 resemblance to her real self. The people closest to her had vanished. She had no proof that they were truly dead. No eyewitnesses had survived to vouch for her husband's death. There was no one living who had seen her parents die. The lack of confirmation haunted her. 20 At night before she went to sleep and during the day as she stood pinning dresses she wondered if, by some chance, her parents had gotten past the Germans or had crawled out of the mass grave into which they had been shot and were living, old and helpless, some- 25 where in Poland. What if only one of them had died? What if they had survived and had died of cold or hunger after she had been liberated, while she was in Celle* dancing with British officers?

She did not talk to anyone about these things. No 30 one, she thought, wanted to hear them. She woke up in the mornings, went to work, bought groceries, went to the Jewish Community Center and to the housing office like a robot.

*Celle is a small town in Germany.

QUESTIONS

1. The policeman stopped the author's mother from walking along the river because

   (A) the river was dangerous
   (B) it was the wrong time of day
   (C) it was still wartime
   (D) it was too cold
   (E) she looked suspicious

2. The author states that his mother thought about her parents when she

   (A) walked along the river
   (B) thought about death
   (C) danced with the officers
   (D) arose in the morning
   (E) was at work

3. When the author mentions his mother's dancing with the British officers, he implies that his mother

(A) compared her dancing to the suffering of her parents
(B) had clearly put her troubles behind her
(C) felt it was her duty to dance with them
(D) felt guilty about dancing
(E) regained the self-confidence she once had

EXPLANATORY ANSWERS

1. **(B)** Choice B is correct. See lines 1–4: "She walked along . . . offered to walk her home." The policeman's telling her that it was not the best time to be walking alone indicates clearly that "it was the wrong time of day."

2. **(E)** Choice E is correct. Refer to lines 21–29: ". . . during the day . . . dancing with the British officers."

3. **(D)** Choice D is correct. See lines 27–29: "What if they had survived . . . dancing with British officers?"

READ. COMP. STRATEGY **3**

LOOK BACK AT THE PASSAGE WHEN IN DOUBT

Sometimes while you are answering a question, you are not quite sure whether it is the correct answer. Often, the underlinings that you have made in the reading passage will help you to determine whether a certain choice is the only correct choice.

Example 1

Despite the many categories of the historian, there are only two ages of man. The first age, the age from the beginnings of recorded time to the present, is the age of the cave man. It is the age of war. It is today. The
5 second age, still only a prospect, is the age of civilized man. The test of civilized man will be represented by his ability to use his inventiveness for his own good by substituting world law for world anarchy. That second age is still within the reach of the individual in our time.
10 It is not a part-time job, however. It calls for total awareness, total commitment.

QUESTION

1. The author's attitude toward the possibility of man's reaching the age of civilization is one of

(A) limited hope
(B) complete despair
(C) marked uncertainty
(D) untempered complacency
(E) extreme anger

EXPLANATORY ANSWER

1. **(A)** Choice A is correct. An important idea that you might have underlined is expressed in lines 8–9: "That second age is still within the reach of the individual in our time."

Example 2

All museum adepts are familiar with examples of *ostrakoi*, the oystershells used in balloting. As a matter of fact, these "oystershells" are usually shards of pottery, conveniently glazed to enable the voter to express his wishes in writing. In the Agora a great number of 5 these have come to light, bearing the thrilling name, Themistocles. Into rival jars were dropped the ballots for or against his banishment. On account of the huge vote taken on that memorable date, it was to be expected that many ostrakoi would be found, but the 10 interest of this collection is that a number of these ballots are inscribed in an *identical* handwriting. There is nothing mysterious about it! The Boss was on the job, then as now. He prepared these ballots and voters cast them—no doubt for the consideration of an obol 15 or two. *The ballot box was stuffed.*

How is the glory of the American boss diminished! A vile imitation, he. His methods as old as Time!

QUESTION

1. The title below that best expresses the ideas of this passage is

(A) An Odd Method of Voting
(B) Themistocles, An Early Dictator
(C) Democracy in the Past
(D) Political Trickery—Past and Present
(E) The Diminishing American Politician

EXPLANATORY ANSWER

1. **(D)** Choice D is correct. An important idea that you might have underlined is expressed in lines 13–14: "The Boss was on the job, then and now."

Example 3

But the weather predictions which an almanac always contains are, we believe, mostly wasted on the farmer. He can take a squint at the moon before turning in. He can "smell" snow or tell if the wind is shifting
5 dangerously east. He can register forebodingly an extra twinge in a rheumatic shoulder. With any of these to go by, he can be reasonably sure of tomorrow's weather. He can return the almanac to the nail behind the door and put a last stick of wood in the stove. For an
10 almanac, a zero night or a morning's drifted road—none of these has changed much since Poor Richard wrote his stuff and barns were built along the Delaware.

READ. COMP.
STRATEGY
4.

QUESTION

1. The author implies that, in predicting weather, there is considerable value in

(A) reading the almanac
(B) placing the last stick of wood in the stove
(C) sleeping with one eye on the moon
(D) keeping an almanac behind the door
(E) noting rheumatic pains

EXPLANATORY ANSWER

1. **(E)** Choice E is correct. Important ideas that you might have underlined are the following:
Line 3: "He can take a squint at the moon."
Line 4: "He can smell snow shifting."
Lines 4–5: "He can register forebodingly an extra twinge in a rheumatic shoulder."
These underlinings will reveal that, in predicting weather, the quote in lines 4–5 gives you the correct answer.

BEFORE YOU START ANSWERING THE QUESTIONS, READ THE PASSAGE *CAREFULLY*.

A great advantage of careful reading of the passage is that you will, thereby, get a very good idea of what the passage is about. If a particular sentence is not clear to you as you read, then re-read that sentence to get a better idea of what the author is trying to say.

Example 1

The American Revolution is the only one in modern history which, rather than devouring the intellectuals who prepared it, carried them to power. Most of the signatories of the Declaration of Independence were
5 intellectuals. This tradition is ingrained in America, whose greatest statesmen have been intellectuals—Jefferson and Lincoln, for example. These statesmen performed their political function, but at the same time they felt a more universal responsibility, and they
10 actively defined this responsibility. Thanks to them there is in America a living school of political science. In fact, it is at the moment the only one perfectly adapted to the emergencies of the contemporary world, and one which can be victoriously opposed to
15 communism. A European who follows American politics will be struck by the constant reference in the press and from the platform to this political philosophy, to the historical events through which it was best expressed, to the great statesmen who were its best repre-
20 sentatives.

[Underlining important ideas as you are reading this passage is strongly urged.]

QUESTIONS

1. The title below that best expresses the ideas of this passage is

(A) Fathers of the American Revolution
(B) Jefferson and Lincoln—Ideal Statesmen
(C) The Basis of American Political Philosophy
(D) Democracy versus Communism
(E) The Responsibilities of Statesmen

2. According to the passage, intellectuals who pave the way for revolutions are usually

(A) honored   (B) misunderstood
(C) destroyed   (D) forgotten
(E) elected to office

3. Which statement is true according to the passage?

(A) America is a land of intellectuals.
(B) The signers of the Declaration of Independence were all well educated.
(C) Jefferson and Lincoln were revolutionaries.
(D) Adaptability is a characteristic of American political science.
(E) Europeans are confused by American politics.

EXPLANATORY ANSWERS

1. **(C)** Choice C is correct. Throughout this passage, the author speaks about the basis of American political philosophy. For example, see lines 5–11: "This tradition is ingrained in America . . . a living school of political science."

2. **(C)** Choice C is correct. See lines 1–3: "The American Revolution is the only one . . . carried them to power." These lines may be interpreted to mean that intellectuals who pave the way for revolutions—other than the American Revolution—are usually destroyed.

3. **(D)** Choice D is correct. The word "adaptability" is the ability to adapt—to adjust to a specified use or situation. Now see lines 11–15: ". . . there is in America . . . opposed to communism."

Example 2

The microscopic vegetables of the sea, of which the diatoms are most important, make the mineral wealth of the water available to the animals. Feeding directly on the diatoms and other groups of minute unicellular
5 algae are the marine protozoa, many crustaceans, the young of crabs, barnacles, sea worms, and fishes. Hordes of small carnivores, the first link in the chain of flesh eaters, move among these peaceful grazers. There are fierce little dragons half an inch long, the
10 sharp-jawed arrowworms. There are gooseberrylike comb jellies, armed with grasping tentacles, and there are the shrimplike euphausiids that strain food from the water with their bristly appendages. Since they drift where the currents carry them, with no power or will to
15 oppose that of the sea, this strange community of creatures and the marine plants that sustain them are called plankton, a word derived from the Greek, meaning wandering.

[Underlining important ideas as you are reading this passage is strongly urged.]

QUESTIONS

1. According to the passage, diatoms are a kind of

   (A) mineral   (B) alga   (C) crustacean
   (D) protozoan   (E) fish

2. Which characteristic of diatoms does the passage emphasize?

   (A) size   (B) feeding habits   (C) activeness
   (D) numerousness   (E) cellular structure

EXPLANATORY ANSWERS

1. **(B)** Choice B is correct. See lines 3–5: "Feeding directly on the diatoms . . . minute unicellular algae are the marine protozoa. . . ." These lines indicate that diatoms are a kind of alga.

2. **(A)** Choice A is correct. See lines 1–5: "The microscopic vegetables of the sea . . . minute unicellular algae . . ." In these lines, the words "microscopic" and "minute" emphasize the small size of the diatoms.

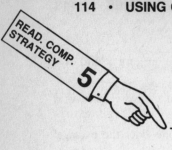

GET THE MEANINGS OF "TOUGH" WORDS BY USING THE CONTEXT METHOD

Suppose you don't know the meaning of a certain word in a passage. Then try to determine the meaning of that word from the context—that is, from the words that are close in position to that word whose meaning you don't know. Knowing the meanings of difficult words in the passage will help you to better understand the passage as a whole.

Example 1

Like all insects, it wears its skeleton on the outside—a marvelous chemical compound called chitin which sheathes the whole of its body. This flexible armor is tremendously tough, light and shatterproof,
5 and resistant to alkali and acid compounds which would eat the clothing, flesh and bones of man. To it are attached muscles so arranged around catapult-like hind legs as to enable the hopper to hop, if so diminutive a term can describe so prodigious a leap as ten or
10 twelve feet—about 150 times the length of the one-inch or so long insect. The equivalent feat for a man would be a casual jump, from a standing position, over the Washington Monument.

QUESTIONS

1. The word "sheathes" (line 3) means

   (A) strips   (B) provides   (C) exposes
   (D) encases   (E) excites

2. The word "prodigious" (line 9) means

   (A) productive   (B) frightening   (C) criminal
   (D) enjoyable   (E) enormous

EXPLANATORY ANSWERS

1. **(D)** Choice D is correct. The words in line 1: "it wears a skeleton on the outside" give us the idea that "sheathes" probably means "covers" or "encases."

2. **(E)** Choice E is correct. See the surrounding words in lines 8–11: ". . . enable the hopper to hop . . . so prodigious a leap as ten or twelve feet—about 150 times the length of the one-inch or so long insect." We may easily imply that the word "prodigious" means "great in size"; "enormous."

Example 2

Since the days when the thirteen colonies, each so jealous of its sovereignty, got together to fight the British soldiers, the American people have exhibited a tendency—a genius to maintain widely divergent viewpoints in normal times, but to unite and agree in times 5 of stress. One reason the federal system has survived is that is has demonstrated this same tendency. Most of the time the three coequal divisions of the general government tend to compete. In crises they tend to cooperate. And not only during a war. A singular 10 instance of cooperation took place in the opening days of the first administration of Franklin D. Roosevelt, when the harmonious efforts of Executive and Legislature to arrest the havoc of depression brought the term *rubber-stamp Congress* into the headlines. On the 15 other hand, when in 1937 Roosevelt attempted to bend the judiciary to the will of the executive by "packing" the Supreme Court, Congress rebelled. This frequently proved flexibility—this capacity of both people and government to shift from competition to coopera- 20 tion and back again as circumstances warrant—suggests that the federal system will be found equal to the very real dangers of the present world situation.

QUESTIONS

1. The word "havoc" (line 14) means

   (A) possession   (B) benefit   (C) destruction
   (D) symptom   (E) enjoyment

2. The word "divergent" (line 4) means

   (A) interesting   (B) discussed   (C) flexible
   (D) differing   (E) appreciated

EXPLANATORY ANSWERS

1. **(C)** Choice C is correct. The prepositional phrase "of depression" which modifies "havoc" should indicate that this word has an unfavorable meaning. The only choice that has an unfavorable meaning is Choice C—"destruction."

2. **(D)** Choice D is correct. See lines 3–6: ". . . the American people . . . widely divergent viewpoints . . . but to unite and agree in times of stress." The word "but" in this sentence is an *opposite* indicator. We may, therefore, assume that a "divergent viewpoint" is a "differing" one from the idea expressed in the words "to unite and agree in times of stress."

READ. COMP. STRATEGY 6

CIRCLE TRANSITIONAL WORDS IN THE PASSAGE

There are certain transitional words—also called "bridge" or "key" words—that will help you to discover logical connections in a reading passage. *Circling* these transitional words will help you to get a better understanding of the passage.

Here are examples of commonly used transitional words and what these words may indicate.

Transitional Word	Indicating
although however in spite of rather than nevertheless on the other hand but	OPPOSITION

Key Word	Indicating
moreover besides additionally furthermore in fact	SUPPORT

Key Word	Indicating
therefore consequently accordingly because when so	RESULT

Example 1

Somewhere between 1860 and 1890, the dominant emphasis in American literature was radically changed. But it is obvious that this change was not necessarily a matter of conscious concern to all writers. 5In fact, many writers may seen to have been actually unaware of the shifting emphasis. Moreover, it is not possible to trace the steady march of the realistic emphasis from its first feeble notes to its dominant trumpet-note of unquestioned leadership. The progress of 10realism is, to change the figure, rather that of a small stream, receiving accessions from its tributaries at unequal points along its course, its progress now and then balked by the sand bars of opposition or the diffusing marshes of error and compromise. Again, it is ap-15parent that any attempt to classify rigidly, as romanticists or realists, the writers of this period is doomed to failure, since it is not by virtue of the writer's conscious espousal of the romantic or realistic creed that he does much of his best work, but by virtue of that writer's 20sincere surrender to the atmosphere of the subject.

QUESTIONS

1. The title that best expresses the ideas of this passage is

    (A) Classifying American Writers
    (B) Leaders in American Fiction
    (C) The Sincerity of Writers
    (D) The Values of Realism
    (E) The Rise of Realism

2. Which characteristic of writers does the author praise?

    (A) their ability to compromise
    (B) their allegiance to a "school"
    (C) their opposition to change
    (D) their awareness of literary trends
    (E) their intellectual honesty

EXPLANATORY ANSWERS

1. (E) Choice E is correct. Note some of the transitional words that will help you to interpret the passage: "but" (line 3); "in fact" (line 5); "moreover" (line 6); "again" (line 14). A better understanding of the passage should indicate to you that the main idea (title)—"The Rise of Realism"—is emphasized throughout the passage.

2. (E) Choice E is correct. See lines 17–20: ". . . since it is not by virtue of . . . but by virtue of the writer's sincere . . . of the subject." The transitional word "but" helps us to arrive at the correct answer which is "their intellectual honesty."

Example 2

A humorous remark or situation is, furthermore, always a pleasure. We can go back to it and laugh at it again and again. One does not tire of the *Pickwick Papers*, or of the humor of Mark Twain, any more than the child tires of a nursery tale which he knows by5 heart. Humor is a feeling and feelings can be revived. But wit, being an intellectual and not an emotional impression, suffers by repetition. A witticism is really an item of knowledge. Wit, again, is distinctly a gregarious quality; whereas humor may abide in the breast of10 a hermit. Those who live by themselves almost always have a dry humor. Wit is a city, humor a country, product. Wit is the accomplishment of persons who are busy with ideas; it is the fruit of intellectual cultivation and abounds in coffeehouses, in salons, and in literary15 clubs. But humor is the gift of those who are concerned with persons rather than ideas, and it flourishes chiefly in the middle and lower classes.

QUESTION

1. It is probable that the paragraph preceding this one discussed the

    (A) *Pickwick Papers*
    (B) characteristics of literature
    (C) characteristics of human nature
    (D) characteristics of humor
    (E) nature of human feelings

EXPLANATORY ANSWER

1. (D) Choice D is correct. See lines 1–2: "A humorous remark or situation is, furthermore, always a pleasure." The transitional word "furthermore" means "in addition." We may, therefore, assume that something dealing with humor has been discussed in the previous paragraph.

DON'T ANSWER A QUESTION ON THE BASIS OF YOUR OWN OPINION

Answer each question on the basis of the information given or suggested in the passage itself. Your own views or judgments may sometimes conflict with what the author of the passage is expressing. Answer the question according to what the author believes.

Example 1

The drama critic, on the other hand, has no such advantages. He cannot be selective; he must cover everything that is offered for public scrutiny in the principal playhouses of the city where he works. The 5 column space that seemed, yesterday, so pitifully inadequate to contain his comments on *Long Day's Journey Into Night* is roughly the same as that which yawns today for his verdict on some inane comedy that has chanced to find for itself a numskull backer with five 10 hundred thousand dollars to lose. This state of affairs may help to explain why the New York theater reviewers are so often, and so unjustly, stigmatized as baleful and destructive fiends. They spend most of their professional lives attempting to pronounce intelligent 15 judgments on plays that have no aspiration to intelligence. It is hardly surprising that they lash out occasionally; in fact, what amazes me about them is that they do not lash out more violently and more frequently. As Shaw said of his fellow-critics in the nine- 20 ties, they are "a culpably indulgent body of men." Imagine the verbal excoriations that would be inflicted if Lionel Trilling, or someone of comparable eminence, were called on to review five books a month of which three were novelettes composed of criminal con- 25 fessions. The butchers of Broadway would seem lambs by comparison.

QUESTIONS

1. In writing this passage, the author's purpose seems to have been to

(A) comment on the poor quality of our plays
(B) show why book reviewing is easier than play reviewing.
(C) point up the opinions of Shaw
(D) show new trends in literary criticism
(E) defend the work of the play critic

2. The passage suggests that, as a play, *Long Day's Journey Into Night* was

(A) inconsequential   (B) worthwhile
(C) poorly written   (D) much too long
(E) pleasant to view

EXPLANATORY ANSWERS

1. **(E)** Choice E is correct. Throughout the passage, the author is defending the work of the play critic. See, for example, lines 10–16: "This state of affairs . . . plays that have no aspiration to intelligence." Be sure that you do not answer a question on the basis of your own views. You yourself may believe that the plays presented on the stage today are of poor quality (Choice A) generally. The question, however, asks about the *author's opinion*—not yours.

2. **(B)** Choice B is correct. See lines 4–10: "The column space . . . dollars to lose." You yourself may believe that *Long Day's Journey Into Night* is a bad play. (Choice A or C or D). But remember—the author's opinion, and not yours, is asked for.

Example 2

History has long made a point of the fact that the magnificent flowering of ancient civilization rested upon the institution of slavery, which released opportunity at the top for the art and literature which became the glory of antiquity. In a way, the mechanization of 5 the present-day world produces the condition of the ancient in that the enormous development of labor-saving devices and of contrivances which amplify the capacities of mankind affords the base for the leisure necessary to widespread cultural pursuits. Mechaniza- 10 tion is the present-day slave power, with the difference that in the mechanized society there is no group of the community which does not share in the benefits of its inventions.

QUESTION

1. The author's attitude toward mechanization is one of

(A) awe (B) acceptance (C) distrust
(D) fear (E) devotion

EXPLANATORY ANSWER

1. **(B)** Choice B is correct. Throughout the passage, the author's attitude toward mechanization is one of acceptance. Such acceptance on the part of the author is indicated particularly in lines 10–14: "Mechanization is . . . the benefits of its inventions." You yourself may have a feeling of distrust (Choice C) or fear (Choice D) toward mechanization. But the author does not have such feelings.

READ. COMP. STRATEGY 8.

AFTER READING THE PASSAGE, READ EACH QUESTION *CAREFULLY*

Be sure that you read *with care* not only the stem (beginning) of a question, but also *each* of the five choices. Some students select a choice just because it is a true statement—or because it answers a part of a question. This can get you into trouble.

Example 1

The modern biographer's task becomes one of discovering the "dynamics" of the personality he is studying rather than allowing the reader to deduce that personality from documents. If he achieves a reason-
5 able likeness, he need not fear too much that the unearthing of still more material will alter the picture he has drawn; it should add dimension to it, but not change its lineaments appreciably. After all, he has had more than enough material to permit him to reach
10 conclusions and to paint his portrait. With this abundance of material he can select moments of high drama and find episodes to illustrate character and make for vividness. In any event, biographers, I think, must recognize that the writing of a life may not be as "scien-
15 tific" or as "definitive" as we have pretended. Biography partakes of a large part of the subjective side of man; and we must remember that those who walked abroad in our time may have one appearance for us— but will seem quite different to posterity.

QUESTION

1. According to the author, which is the real task of the modern biographer?

(A) interpreting the character revealed to him by study of the presently available data
(B) viewing the life of the subject in the biographer's own image
(C) leaving to the reader the task of interpreting the character from contradictory evidence
(D) collecting facts and setting them down in chronological order
(E) being willing to wait until all the facts on his subject have been uncovered

EXPLANATORY ANSWER

1. **(A)** Choice A is correct. See lines 1–8: "The modern biographer's task . . . but not change its lineaments appreciably." The word "dynamics" is used here to refer to the physical and moral forces which exerted influence on the main character of the biography. The lines quoted indicate that the author believes that the real task of the biographer is to study the *presently available data*. Choice D may also appear to be a correct choice since a biographer is likely to consider his job to be collecting facts and setting them down in chronological order. But the passage does not directly state that a biographer has such a procedure.

Example 2

Although patience is the most important quality a treasure hunter can have, the trade demands a certain amount of courage too. I have my share of guts, but make no boast about ignoring the hazards of diving. As all good divers know, the business of plunging into an 5 alien world with an artificial air supply as your only link to the world above can be as dangerous as stepping into a den of lions. Most of the danger rests within the diver himself.

The devil-may-care diver who shows great bravado 10 underwater is the worst risk of all. He may lose his bearings in the glimmering dim light which penetrates the sea and become separated from his diving companions. He may dive too deep, too long and suffer painful, sometimes fatal, bends.

15

QUESTION

1. According to the author, an underwater treasure hunter needs, above all, to be

   (A) self-reliant   (B) adventuresome
   (C) mentally alert   (D) patient
   (E) physically fit

EXPLANATORY ANSWER

1. **(D)** Choice D is correct. See lines 1–3: "Although patience is the most important . . . courage too." Choice E ("physically fit") may also appear to be a correct choice since an underwater diver certainly has to be physically fit. Nevertheless, the passage nowhere states this directly.

READ. COMP. STRATEGY **9**

INCREASE YOUR VOCABULARY TO BOOST YOUR READING COMPREHENSION SCORE

1.   You can increase your vocabulary tremendously by learning Latin and Greek roots, prefixes, and suffixes. Knowing the meanings of difficult words will thereby help you to understand a passage better.

   60% of all the words in our English language are derived from Latin and Greek. By learning certain Latin and Greek roots, prefixes, and suffixes, you will be able to understand the meanings of over 100,000 additional English words. See "Word Building with Roots, Prefixes, and Suffixes" beginning on page 194.

2. This book also includes "A 3400 SAT Word List" beginning on page 119. This Word List will prove to be a powerful vocabulary builder for you.

   There are other steps—in addition to the two steps explained above—to increase your vocabulary. Here they are:

3. Take vocabulary tests like the 100 SAT-type "tough word" vocabulary tests beginning on page 165.
4. Read as widely as possible—novels, nonfiction, newspapers, magazines.
5. Listen to people who speak well. Many TV programs have very fine speakers. You can pick up many new words listening to such programs.
6. Get into the habit of using the dictionary often. Why not carry a pocket-size dictionary with you?
7. Play word games—crossword puzzles will really build up your vocabulary.

Example 1

   Acting, like much writing, is probably a compensation for and release from the strain of some profound maladjustment of the psyche. The actor lives most intensely by proxy. He has to be somebody else to be
5 himself. But it is all done openly and for our delight. The dangerous man, the enemy of nonattachment or any other wise way of life, is the born actor who has never found his way into the Theater, who never uses a stage door, who does not take a call and then wipe the
10 paint off his face. It is the intrusion of this temperament into political life, in which at this day it most emphatically does not belong, that works half the mischief in the world. In every country you may see them rise, the actors who will not use the Theater, and always they
15 bring down disaster from the angry gods who like to see mountebanks in their proper place.

QUESTIONS

1. The meaning of "maladjustment" (line 3) is a

   (A) replacement of one thing for another
   (B) profitable experience in business
   (C) consideration for the feelings of others
   (D) disregard of advice offered by others
   (E) poor relationship with one's environment

2. The meaning of "psyche" (line 3) is

   (A) person   (B) mind   (C) personality
   (D) psychology   (E) physique

3. The meaning of "intrusion" (line 10) is

(A) entering without being welcome
(B) acceptance after considering the facts
(C) interest that has developed after a period of time
(D) fear as the result of imagination
(E) refusing to obey a command

4. The meaning of "mountebanks" (line 16) is

(A) mountain climbers (B) cashiers
(C) high peaks (D) fakers
(E) mortals

EXPLANATORY ANSWERS

1. **(E)** Choice E is correct. The prefix "mal" means bad. Obviously a maladjustment is a bad adjustment—that is, a poor relationship with one's environment.

2. **(B)** Choice B is correct. The root "psyche" means the mind functioning as the center of thought, feeling, and behavior.

3. **(A)** Choice A is correct. The prefix "in" means "into" in this case. The root "trud, trus" means "pushing into"—or entering without being welcome.

4. **(D)** Choice D is correct. The root "mont" means "to climb." The root "banc" means a "bench." A mountebank means literally "one who climbs on a bench." The actual meaning of mountebank is a quack (faker) who sells useless medicines from a platform in a public place.

Example 2

The American Museum of Natural History has long portrayed various aspects of man. Primitive cultures have been shown through habitat groups and displays of man's tools, utensils, and art. In more recent years, there has been a tendency to delineate man's place in 5 nature, displaying his destructive and constructive activities on the earth he inhabits. Now, for the first time, the Museum has taken man apart, enlarged the delicate mechanisms that make him run, and examined him as a biological phenomenon. 10

In the new Hall of the Biology of Man, Museum technicians have created a series of displays that are instructive to a degree never before achieved in an exhibit hall. Using new techniques and new materials, they have been able to produce movement as well as 15 form and color. It is a human belief that beauty is only skin deep. But nature has proved to be a master designer, not only in the matter of man's bilateral symmetry but also in the marvelous packaging job that has arranged all man's organs and systems within his skin- 20 covered case. When these are taken out of the case, greatly enlarged and given color, they reveal form and design that give the lie to that old saw. Visitors will be surprised to discover that man's insides, too, are beautiful. 25

QUESTIONS

1. The meaning of "bilateral" (line 18) is

(A) biological (B) two-sided (C) natural
(D) harmonious (E) technical

2. The meaning of "symmetry" (line 18) is

(A) simplicity (B) obstinacy (C) sincerity
(D) appearance (E) proportion

EXPLANATORY ANSWERS

1. **(B)** Choice B is correct. The prefix "bi" means "two." The root "latus" means "side." Therefore, "bilateral" means "two-sided."

2. **(E)** Choice E is correct. The prefix "sym" means "together." The root "metr" means "measure." The word "symmetry," therefore, means "proportion," "harmonious relation of parts," "balance."

3

VOCABULARY BUILDING THAT IS GUARANTEED TO RAISE YOUR SAT SCORE

Knowing Word Meanings is Essential for a Higher SAT Score

Improving your vocabulary is essential if you want to get a high score on the Verbal part of the SAT. We shall explain why this is so.

The Verbal part of the SAT consists of four different question-types: Antonyms, Analogies, Sentence Completions, and Reading Comprehension. Almost all SAT exam-takers come across many "tough" words in the Verbal part, whose meanings they do not know. These students, thereby, lose many, many points because, if they do not know the meanings of the words in the questions, they aren't able to answer the questions confidently—and so, they are likely to answer incorrectly.

Every correct answer on the SAT gives you approximately 10 points. The 25 questions on the SAT Antonyms part of the test always contain several "tough" words. In addition, the 20 Analogies questions and the 15 Sentence Completion questions also contain quite a number of "tough" words whose meanings you will have to know in order to answer these questions correctly.

We must also bring to your attention the fact that several "tough" words show up in the 6 Reading Comprehension passages of every SAT exam. Knowing the meanings of these difficult words will, of course, help you to understand the passages better. It follows that knowing what the passages are all about will give you many more correct answers for the 25 Reading Comprehension questions that appear in the SAT—*and each correct answer nets you approximately 10 points.*

7 STEPS TO WORD POWER

STEP 1. Study vocabulary lists. You have in this book just the list you need for SAT preparation. The "SAT 3400-Word List" begins on page 123.

STEP 2. Take vocabulary tests. "100 Tests to Strengthen Your Vocabulary" begins on page 169.

STEP 3. Learn those Latin and Greek roots, prefixes, and suffixes which make up many English words. It has been estimated that more than half of all English words come from Latin and Greek. "Word Building with Roots, Prefixes, and Suffixes" begins on page 198.

STEP 4. Have a college-level dictionary at home. Carry a pocket dictionary when you are moving about. Refer to a dictionary whenever you are not sure of the meaning of a word.

STEP 5. Read—read—read. By reading a great deal, you will encounter new and valuable words. You will learn the meanings of many of these words by context—that is, you will perceive a clear connection between a new word and the words that surround that word. In this way, you will learn the meaning of that new word.

STEP 6. Listen to what is worthwhile listening to. Listen to good radio and TV programs. Listen to people who speak well. Go to selected movies and plays. Just as you will increase your vocabulary by reading widely, you will increase your vocabulary by listening to English that is spoken well.

STEP 7. Play word games like crossword puzzles, anagrams, and Scrabble.

NO ONE CAN DISPUTE THIS FACT!

You will pile up SAT points by taking advantage of the valuable Vocabulary Building study and practice materials that are offered to you in the following pages of this chapter.

YOU DON'T HAVE TO LEARN THE MEANING OF EVERY WORD IN THE SAT 3400-WORD LIST

Go as far into the alphabetized groups as time permits. Use the VOCABULARY LEARNING STEPS listed on the next page. If you cannot learn the meanings of all the words in the 3400-Word List, don't fret. Whatever words you have added to your vocabulary, *before* you take the actual test, will raise your SAT Verbal score substantially. Keep in mind that **every correct Antonym answer will give you approximately 10 more points.**

SAT 3400-Word List

EVERY NEW WORD THAT YOU LEARN IN THIS SAT WORD-LIST CAN

HELP YOU TO ADD 10 EXTRA POINTS TO YOUR SAT VERBAL SCORE

VOCABULARY LEARNING STEPS

STEP 1. Conceal each definition with a card as you go down the column.

STEP 2. *Jot down each word whose meaning you do not know.* Then make up a flash card for each word you did not know.
Write the synonym (meaning) on the back of the card.

STEP 3. Study the flash cards that you have made up.

STEP 4. After you have studied the DID-NOT-KNOW flash cards, give yourself a flash card test.
Put aside the flash cards for the words you did know.

STEP 5. For each word you still do not know, write a sentence which includes the word you still have not learned well.

STEP 6. Now test yourself again on the DID-NOT-KNOW flash cards referred to in Step 5 above.
Put aside your flash cards for the words you did know.

STEP 7. Study the new reduced pile of DID-NOT-KNOW flash cards.

STEP 8. Give yourself a flash card test on this new reduced DID-NOT-KNOW pile.

STEP 9. Keep reducing your DID-NOT-KNOW flash card pile until you have no DID-NOT-KNOW words.

IMPORTANT

Do not throw your flash cards away. Keep the cards for reinforcement testing in the future.

RECENT ACTUAL SATs PROVE THAT STUDYING OUR 3400-WORD LIST IS VITAL FOR EXTRA POINTS

EXAMPLE 1

The following 18 words appeared as the stem words of Antonym questions in the January 1990 SAT:

arcane	exotic	infidel	mirth	valid
assuage	explicit	iniquity	penury	verity
chide	fusion	laconic	puny	
exhume	gargantuan	migratory	spartan	

A student earns approximately 10 points for each correct answer.

All of the 18 words above also appear in the **Gruber SAT** 3400-Word List. Accordingly, if a student studied thoroughly the SAT 3400-Word List before taking the January 1990 SAT, the student would have earned 180 points simply by knowing the meanings of the foregoing 18 words.

EXAMPLE 2

Here are 18 words that appeared as the stem words of Antonym questions in the May 1989 SAT:

abandon	ethereal	palatial	ruthless	stultify
acumen	festive	pessimistic	shortage	toxin
contentious	impertinence	prostrate	stalwart	turbulent
dismal	migrate	raze		

These words constitute 72% of the 25 Antonym questions that appeared in the May 1989 SAT.

All of the 18 words above also appear in the Gruber SAT 3400-Word List. Therefore, studying this 3400-Word List before taking the May 1989 SAT would have assured the student of 180 extra points just by knowing the meanings of the 18 words listed above.

EXAMPLE 3

The following 19 words appeared as the stem words of Antonym questions in the January 1989 SAT:

(There are 25 Antonym questions in every SAT.)

abridge	cachophonous	desultory	humility	pulverized
acrimonious	convivial	diatribe	intractable	somber
askew	cursory	emollient	luminous	tantamount
assent	daunt	exotic	myriad	

A student earns approximately 10 points for each correct answer.

All of the 19 words above also appear in the Gruber SAT 3400-Word List. Accordingly, if a student studied thoroughly the SAT 3400-Word List before taking the January 1989 SAT, he would have earned 190 points by simply knowing the meanings of the foregoing 19 words.

ABACK – AZURE

aback (preceded by *taken*) surprised; startled

abandon to leave; to give up; to discontinue

abase to humiliate; to humble; to lower

abash ashamed; embarrassed

abate to lessen; to decrease

abdicate to yield; to give up

abduct to take away; to kidnap

aberration abnormality; deviation

abet to aid; to encourage

abeyance a temporary postponement

abhor to hate; to detest

abide (*two meanings*) to remain; to put up with

abject miserable; wretched

abjure to give up (rights);

ablution a washing; cleansing

abnegate to deny; to reject

abolition doing away with; putting an end to

abominate to detest; to dislike strongly

aborigine original inhabitant

abortive unsuccessful

abound to be large in number

aboveboard honest; frank; open

abrade to wear away

abridge to shorten

abrogate to abolish; to repeal

abscond to leave secretly; to flee

absolve to free from responsibility

abstemious moderate or sparing in eating or drinking

abstinence self-denial; resisting tempting foods

abstract (*two meanings*) a summary (*noun*); to remove (*verb*)

abstruse hard to understand

absurd ridiculous; unreasonable

abut to touch; to rest on or against

abysmal wretched; extremely bad

abyss a bottomless pit; anything infinite

academic (*two meanings*) pertaining to school; theoretical or unrealistic

accede to agree to

accelerate to speed up; to move faster

accessible easy to approach; open

access approach; admittance

accessory something additional

acclaim to greet with approval

acclimate to adapt; to get used to

acclivity upward slope

accolade honor; award; approval

accommodate to make fit; to help

accomplice a partner in crime

accord agreement

accost to approach and speak to

accoutrement equipment; outfit

accredit to approve; to certify

accretion an increase; an addition

accrue to gather; to accumulate

acerbic sharp or bitter in smell or taste

Achilles' heel a weakness

acknowledge to admit; to confess

acme highest point; peak

acoustics branch of physics dealing with sound

acquiesce to agree; to consent

acquit to free of guilt; to clear

acrid bitter to the taste or smell; sarcastic

acrimonious harsh in speech or behavior

acronym word formed from initials

acrophobia fear of heights

actuate to put into motion or action

acumen mental keenness; shrewdness

acute sharp; keen

ad infinitum endlessly; forever

ad lib to act or speak without preparation

adage a familiar saying

adamant stubborn; unyielding

adapt to adjust; to change

addendum something added as a supplement

addled confused

adduce to give an example in proving something

adept highly skilled

adherent (*two meanings*) sticking fast (*adjective*); a follower or a supporter (*noun*)

adipose fatty

adjacent near; close; adjoining

adjudicate to judge

adjunct   a subordinate; an assistant

admonish   to warn

ado   fuss; trouble

adonis   a very handsome man

adorn   to dress up; to decorate

adroit   skillful; clever

adulation   excessive praise or flattery

adulterate   to make impure

advent   an arrival; a coming

adventitious   accidental; nonessential

adversary   enemy; opponent

adversity   a misfortune; distress

advocate   to recommend; to defend

aegis   a shield; protection; sponsorship

aesthetic   pertaining to beauty

affable   friendly; agreeable

affectation   a phony attitude; insincerity

affiliate   to associate or to unite with

affinity   attraction to

affirmation   a statement that something is true

affix   to attach

affliction   great suffering; hardship

affluence   wealth

affront   an insult

aftermath   outcome; result

agape   open-mouthed; surprised

agenda   a list or program of things to be done

aggrandize   to enlarge or to expand

aggravate   to worsen an already bad situation;
   to intensify

aggregate   to collect; to gather together

aghast   shocked; terrified

agile   able to move quickly

agitate   to upset; to stir up

agnostic   one who doubts the existence of God

agoraphobia   fear of open places

agrarian   pertaining to farmers and agriculture

ague   a fever; plague

alacrity   liveliness; willingness

albatross   (*two meanings*)   a seabird;
   a constant burden

albeit   although

alchemy   chemistry of the Middle Ages

alias   an assumed name

alien   strange; foreign

alienate   to make others unfriendly to you

alimentary   furnishing food or nourishment

allay   to relieve or to calm

alleged   so-called; supposed

allegory   a symbolic work of literature

allegro   rapid; quick

alleviate   to lessen; to relieve

allocate   to set aside for a specific purpose

allude   to hint at; to refer to indirectly

alluring   tempting; fascinating; charming

alluvial   pertaining to a deposit of sand formed by
   flowing water

aloft   up in the air; high

aloof   reserved; cool; indifferent

alter   to change

altercation   an argument; a disagreement

altruism   unselfishness; concern for others

amalgamate   to combine; to unite; to blend

amass   to accumulate; to collect

amazon   a big, strong, masculine woman

ambidextrous   equally skillful with either hand

ambient   surrounding; on all sides

ambiguous   unclear; open to more than
   one interpretation

ambivalence   conflicting feelings toward something
   or someone

ambrosial   pleasing to the taste or smell

ambulatory   moving about; capable of walking

ambuscade   hidden or secret attack

ameliorate   to improve; to make better

amenable   agreeable; responsive

amend   to change; to alter

amenities   courtesies; social graces; pleasantries

amiable   friendly; pleasant

amicable   friendly; agreeable

amiss   wrong; faulty; improper

amity   friendship

amnesty   official pardon for an offense

amoral   lacking a sense of right and wrong

amorous   loving

amorphous   shapeless

amphibious   able to live on both land and water

ample   roomy; abundant

amplify   to make larger or greater

amulet   a charm worn to keep evil away

anachronism   something out of place or time

analgesic   drug that relieves pain

analogy   similarity or comparison

anarchy   absence of government

anathema   a curse; a person or thing to be avoided

ancillary   helping; subordinate

anecdote   a short, entertaining story

anent   regarding; concerning

anguish   great suffering or grief

anhydrous   without water

animadversion   criticism; comment that opposes

animate   to give life to

animosity   hatred; hostility

animus   hostile feeling

annals   historical records

anneal   to heat and then cool; to toughen

annihilate   to totally destroy

annuity   specified income payable at stated intervals

annul   to cancel; to do away with

anomalous   abnormal; inconsistent

anon   soon

anoxia   lack of oxygen

antecedent   that which goes before something else

antediluvian   very old-fashioned; primitive

anterior   located in front or forward

anteroom   a lobby or waiting room

anthem   song of praise

anthology   collection of literary works

anthropoid   resembling man

anthropomorphic   attributing human form to objects, gods, etc.

antic   playful or silly act; prank

anticlimax   something unimportant coming after something important

antidote   a remedy; a counteractive

antipathy   intense dislike

antipodes   opposite sides (of the earth)

antiquated   ancient; extremely old

antithesis   an exact opposite

apathy   indifference; lack of feeling

ape   (*two meanings*)   a monkey (*noun*); to imitate or to mimic (*verb*)

aperture   an opening; a gap

apex   the highest point; summit

aphasia   loss of the ability to speak

aphorism   brief saying; proverb

apiary   place where bees are kept

aplomb   self-confidence; poise

apocryphal   doubtful; not authentic

apogee   farthest point away from the earth

apoplexy   sudden loss of consciousness; paralysis

apostate   one who gives up his beliefs

apothecary   druggist

apothegm   brief instructive saying

apotheosis   glorification of a person to the rank of God

appall   to frighten; to cause loss of courage

apparel   clothing; attire

apparition   a ghost

appease   to soothe; to satisfy

appellation   a name

append   to attach; to add

apposite   appropriate

apprehend   (*two meanings*)   to seize; to understand

apprehensive   fearful; anxious

apprise   to inform

approbation   approval

appropriate   to take possession of (*verb*); suitable (*adjective*)

appurtenance   something added to another more important thing

apropos   relevant; appropriate; fitting

aptitude   ability

aquatic   pertaining to water

aquiline   like an eagle; curved or hooked

arable   good for farming

arbiter   a judge; an umpire

arbitrary   partial; biased

arbor   a shaded area

arcane   mysterious

archaic   out-dated; old-fashioned

archeology   study of remains of past cultures

archetype   original; first of its kind

archipelago   group of islands

archives   public records and documents

ardent   intensely enthusiastic

arduous   difficult; strenuous

aria   a solo in an opera

arid   dry

armistice   a truce; suspension of hostilities

aromatic   pleasant-smelling

arraign   to accuse

arrant   notorious; downright

array   an orderly arrangement

arrears   (preceded by *in*) in debt

arrogant   proud; haughty

arroyo   a deep ditch caused by running water

arson   illegal burning of property

artful   cunning; tricky; crafty

articulate   to speak clearly

artifact   a handmade object

artifice   trick; deception

artisan   one skilled in arts and crafts

ascendant   rising

ascertain   to find out; to determine

ascetic   one who denies his body pleasure and comfort

ascribe   to attribute; to credit as to a cause or source

aseptic   without bacteria

asinine   stupid; silly

askance   (preceded by *to look*) sidewise; suspiciously

askew   crooked; out of position

asperity   harshness; roughness

aspersion   a damaging remark

aspire   to desire; to have an ambition

assail   to attack; to assault

assay   to test; to try

assent   to agree; to accept

assess   to estimate the value of

assertive   confident; positive

assiduity   diligence; care

assimilate   to absorb

assuage   to calm; to make less severe

asteroid   a very small planet

astral   pertaining to the stars

astray   in the wrong direction

astringent   substance that contracts blood vessels or shrinks tissue

astute   shrewd; very smart

asunder   into separate parts

asylum   a safe place; a refuge

atavistic   going back to behavior found in a remote ancestor

atheist   one who denies God's existence

atlas   book of maps

atone   to make up for; to repent

atrocious   cruel; brutal

atrophy   to waste away; to become useless

attenuated   decreased; weakened

attest   to confirm; to declare to be correct

attribute   (*two meanings*) to credit or assign to (*verb*); a characteristic or trait (*noun*)

attrition   a wearing down or away; a decline

atypical   abnormal; not usual

au courant   up-to-date; fully informed

audacity   boldness; daring

audible   capable of being heard

audit   to examine accounts

augment   to increase; to make greater

augur   to predict

august   majestic; worthy of respect; impressive

aura   a radiance; a glow

aural   pertaining to the sense of hearing

auroral   rosy; pertaining to the dawn

auspices   approval; support

auspicious   favorable

austere   severe; stern; self-disciplined

authenticate   to confirm; to make acceptable

authoritative   dictatorial; having power

autocratic   arrogant; unlimited in authority

automaton   self-operating machine; robot

autonomy   self-rule

autumnal   mature; declining

auxiliary   giving assistance; subordinate

avarice   greed

avenge   to get even; to take revenge

aver   to declare; to state firmly

averse   reluctant; not willing

aversion   intense dislike

avert   to prevent; to turn away

aviary   place where birds are kept

avid   enthusiastic

avocation   a hobby; not one's regular work

avoirdupois   heaviness; weight

avow   to declare openly

avuncular   like an uncle

awe   (*in awe of*) great admiration for or fear of

awry   twisted to one side; in the wrong direction

axiom   true statement; established principle

azure   blue

BACCHANALIAN – BUTTRESS

bacchanalian   wild with drunkenness

badger   to nag; to annoy

badinage   playful, teasing talk

baffle   to confuse; to bewilder

bagatelle   thing of little value; trifle

bait   (*two meanings*)   to entrap or to seduce (*verb*); a decoy (*noun*)

baleful   harmful; menacing; pernicious

balk   to stop short

balm   something that calms or soothes

balmy   (*two meanings*)   mild and refreshing; mentally unstable (*slang*)

banal   common; ordinary; trite

bandy   to exchange (*as words*)

bane   cause of ruin, harm, or distress

banter   teasing; good-natured joking

barb   a pointed part, as of an arrow or fishhook

barbarous   uncultured; crude

bard   a poet

bark   a boat or sailing vessel

baroque   overdecorated; showy

barrage   heavy attack

barrister   lawyer (*British*)

bask   to lie in or be exposed to warmth

bastion   a strong defense; a fort

bauble   showy but useless thing; trinket

bawdy   indecent; humorously obscene

bayou   marshy body of water

beacon   a light used for warning or guiding

beatitude   state of bliss

bedlam   (*two meanings*)   a madhouse; a noisy uproar

befuddle   to confuse; to perplex

beget   to produce

begrudge   to resent another's success or enjoyment

beguile   to deceive; to charm

behemoth   huge animal

beholden   obligated; indebted

belated   delayed or detained

beleaguer   to encircle (with an army); to annoy

belittle   to put down; to humiliate

belligerent   warlike; quarrelsome

bellow   to yell loudly

benediction   blessing

benefactor   one who helps or supports another

beneficiary   one who receives benefits or profits

benevolent   generous; kindly

benign   harmless; gentle

benignant   kindly; gentle

bequeath   to hand down; to pass on to

berate   to scold severely

bereave   to leave in a sad or lonely state; to deprive by force

berserk   frenzied; violently destructive

beseech   to beg; appeal to

beset   to attack

besiege   to overwhelm; to close in on

besmirch   to make dirty

bestial   savage; brutal

bestow   to give or present

bestride   to mount (a horse)

betrothed   engaged; pledged to marry

bevy   a large group

bewitch   to cast a spell on; to charm; to fascinate

bias   preference; prejudice

bibliophile   lover of books

bibulous   absorbent; fond of alcoholic beverages

bicker   to quarrel

bide   (*one's time*) to wait for a favorable opportunity

biennial   occurring every two years

bigot   a narrow-minded, prejudiced person

bilious   bad-tempered; cross

bilk   to cheat; to swindle

binge   a spree; wild party

biped   two-legged animal

bivouac   temporary shelter

bizarre   weird; strange

blanch   to whiten; to make pale

bland   mild; tasteless; dull

blandishment   flattery

blasé   bored with life; unexcited; indifferent

blasphemy   disrespect for holy places, people, or things; irreverence

blatant   annoyingly conspicuous; offensively noisy and loud

blazon   to display; to proclaim

bleak   unsheltered; gloomy

bleary   blurred; dimmed

blight   destruction; withering; disease

bliss   extreme happiness

blithe   carefree; light-hearted

bludgeon   a short, heavy club

blunt   (*two meanings*)   abrupt in speech or manner; having a dull edge

blurt   (*out*) to utter suddenly or indiscreetly

bluster   to speak noisily; to boast

bode   to indicate in advance, as an omen does

bog   (*two meanings*)   a swamp (*noun*); to sink or become stuck in (*verb*)

bogus   false; fake

bolster   to prop up; to support

bolt   to dash out suddenly; to discontinue support of

bombastic   using impressive but meaningless language

bon mot   witty remark

bona fide   genuine; in good faith

bondage   slavery

boon   a benefit; a blessing; a favor

boor   a rude or impolite person

booty   stolen money or goods

boreal   northern

borne   carried; put up with

botch   to mess up; to perform clumsily

bountiful   plentiful; abundant

bounty   reward; generosity

bourgeoisie   middle class

bovine   pertaining to cows or cattle

bowdlerize   to censor; to remove offensive passages of a play, novel, etc.

braggart   one who boasts

brandish   to shake or wave a weapon aggressively

brash   offensively bold; rude

bravado   a show of courage; false bravery

brawn   muscular strength

brazen   shameless or impudent

breach   a violation; a gap

breadth   width

brethren   brothers

brevity   briefness

brigand   a robber

brine   salt water

brisk   lively; quick

bristling   showing irritation

broach   to introduce (a subject)

brochure   a pamphlet

bronchial   pertaining to the windpipe

browbeat   to bully; to intimidate

bruit   to spread the news

brunt   shock, force, or impact, as of a blow

brusque   abrupt in manner, blunt; rough

buccaneer   a pirate

bucolic   pertaining to the countryside; rural

buffoon   clown or fool

bugbear   something causing fear

bulbous   swollen; shaped like a bulb

bulwark   a strong defense

bumptious   conceited; arrogant

bungle   to do things clumsily or badly

buoy   (*two meanings*)   a floating object (*noun*); to encourage (*verb*)

buoyant   (*two meanings*)   able to float; lighthearted and lively

bureaucracy   system of government through departments

burgeon   to flourish; to grow rapidly

burlesque   a speech or action that treats a serious subject with ridicule

burly   muscular; husky

burnish   to polish

buttress   any prop or support

CABAL – CYNOSURE

cabal   a small, secret group

cache   a hiding place

cacophony   harsh or unpleasant sound

cadaverous   pale; ghastly; corpselike

cadence   rhythm; beat

caesura   pause

cajole   to coax; to persuade

calamitous   causing trouble or misery; disastrous

caliber   degree of worth

calligraphy   fancy handwriting

callous   unyielding; insensitive

callow   young and inexperienced

calumny   a false accusation; slander

camaraderie   loyalty; friendship

canard   a false story, report, or rumor

candor   honesty; openness; frankness

canine   pertaining to dogs

canny   shrewd

canon   rule; law; standard

cant   insincere statements usually made in a singsong tone

cantankerous   bad-tempered; quarrelsome

canter   smooth, easy pace; gallop

canvass   to make a survey

capacious   spacious; roomy

capitulate   to surrender

capricious   erratic; impulsive

captious   hard to please; faultfinding

captivate   to capture; to charm; to fascinate

carapace   shell; hard, protective covering

carcinogenic   causing cancer

cardinal   principal; chief

careen   to swerve; to dip to one side

caricature   an exaggerated portrayal

carnage   slaughter; massacre

carnal   sensual; sexual

carnivorous   flesh-eating

carouse   to engage in a noisy, drunken party

carp   (*two meanings*)   a type of fish (*noun*); to complain (*verb*)

carrion   decaying flesh

carte blanche   freedom to use one's own judgment

cartel   association of business firms

cartographer   mapmaker

cascade   a waterfall

caste   social class

castigate   to punish

casualty   (*two meanings*)   an accident; one who is hurt in an accident

cataclysm   a violent change

catacomb   underground burial place

catalyst   person or thing that speeds up a result

cataract   (*two meanings*)   large waterfall; abnormality of the eye

catastrophe   disaster; calamity

cathartic   cleansing

catholic   universal; wide-ranging

caucus   a private meeting

caustic   sarcastic; severely critical; corrosive

cauterize   to burn

cavalcade   a procession; a sequence of events

cavalier   a haughty and casually indifferent person

caveat   a warning

cavil   to quibble; to argue

cavort   to leap about; to frolic

celerity   speed; swiftness

celestial   heavenly

celibate   unmarried

censure   to criticize sharply

centrifugal   moving away from the center

cerebration   thinking; using one's brain

certitude   sureness; certainty

cessation   a stopping; a discontinuance

chafe   to irritate; to annoy

chaff   worthless matter

chagrin   embarrassment; complete loss of courage

chameleon   a lizard which is able to change its skin color; a changeable or fickle person

champ   (*verb*) to bite impatiently; to show impatience (*to champ at the bit*)

chaos   complete disorder

charisma   great appeal or attraction

charlatan   a fake; a quack

charnel   cemetery; tomb

chary   (*of*) careful; cautious

chasm   a wide gap

chaste   pure; virtuous

chastise   to punish; to purify

chattel   slave

chauvinism   fanatical devotion to one's country, sex, religion, etc.

cherub   angel; an innocent person

chic   stylish; fashionable

chicanery   trickery; deception

chide   to scold

chimerical   imaginary; fantastic; unreal

chirography   art of handwriting

chivalrous   courteous; courageous; loyal

choleric   easily angered

chronic   long-lasting

churlish   rude; ill-bred

cipher   person or thing of no value; zero

circuitous   roundabout; indirect

circumlocution   roundabout way of speaking

circumscribe   to encircle; to limit or confine

circumspect   cautious; careful

circumvent   to surround or entrap; to go around or by-pass

citadel   a fortress

cite   to quote a passage, book, author, etc; to refer to an example

civility   politeness

clairvoyant   having great insight; keenly perceptive

clamber   to climb with effort or difficulty

clamor   noise

clandestine   secretive; private

clangor   harsh ringing sound

clarify   to make clear

clarion   clear and shrill

claustrophobia   fear of enclosed spaces

cleave   (*two meanings*)   to split something apart; to stick or cling to something

cleft   split; divided

clemency   mercy; leniency

cliché   a trite or worn-out expression

clientele   customers

climax   highest point

clime   climate; region

clique   a small, exclusive group

cloistered   secluded; confined

clout   (*colloquial*) power; influence

cloven   divided; split

coadjutor   assistant; helper

coalesce   to blend; to merge; to fuse

coddle   to treat tenderly

coerce   to force

coffer   a strongbox

cog   a gear tooth; a minor part

cogent   convincing

cogitate   to think; to consider carefully

cognate   related; relevant

cognizant   aware

cognomen   family name; last name

coherent   logically connected; consistent

cohesive   tending to stick

cohort   colleague; associate; partner

coincide   to occur simultaneously

collaborate   to work together; to cooperate

collage   collection of various bits and pieces (*usually artistic*)

collate   to put together in order

collateral   security for payment of a loan

colloquial   informal

colloquy   conversation

collusion   conspiracy; agreement to commit a wrongful act

colossal   huge; enormous

combative   eager to fight; argumentative

combustible   capable of catching fire easily

comely   attractive

commemorative   honoring; remembering

commence   to begin

commendation   praise

commensurate   proportionate

commiserate   to express pity for

commodious   roomy; spacious

communal   shared; pertaining to a group of people

compact   (*two meanings*)   firmly packed (*adjective*); a treaty (*noun*)

compassion   pity; sympathy

compatible   agreeable; harmonious

compel   to force

compendium   brief summary

compensatory paying back; making up for

complacent self-satisfied

complement (*note spelling*) to make whole; to complete

compliant yielding; submissive

complicity partnership in a wrongful act

components ingredients; elements

composure calmness of mind or manner

compulsory required

compunction uneasiness; remorse

compute to calculate; to estimate

concave hollow; curved inward

concede to admit; to grant

concentrate (*two meanings*) to think deeply; to increase in strength or degree

concentric having a common center

conception (*two meanings*) a beginning; original idea or plan

concession allowance; the act of yielding

conciliate to soothe the anger of; to win over

concise brief and to the point

conclave secret meeting

concoct to invent; to devise

concomitant accompanying; attending

concord agreement; harmony

concourse a crowd; a wide street

concur to agree

condescend to lower oneself to an inferior's level

condign deserved; suitable

condiment seasoning; spices

condolence expression of sorrow

condone to excuse; to overlook

conducive tending to or leading to

conduit pipe or tube through which fluid or electricity passes

confidant a close, trusted friend

configuration shape; arrangement

confiscate to seize by way of penalty

conflagration a large and destructive fire

confluent merging; flowing together

conformity agreement; doing the same as others

confounded confused; amazed

congeal to freeze solid; to thicken

congenial friendly; agreeable

congenital existing at birth

conglomerate mass; cluster; corporation

congregate to gather; to assemble

congruent in agreement

coniferous bearing cones (*pertaining to trees*)

conjecture to guess

conjugal pertaining to marriage

conjure to call upon or to command a devil or spirit to practice magic; cast a spell on

connivance pretended ignorance of another's wrongdoing; conspiracy

connoisseur an expert

connote to suggest or imply

connubial pertaining to marriage

consanguinity close relationship, usually by blood

consecrate to make holy

consensus general agreement, especially of opinion

console (*two meanings*) a musical panel or unit (*noun*); to comfort (*verb*)

consolidate to combine; to make or become solid

consonant in agreement or harmony

consort (*two meanings*) a husband or wife (*noun*); to associate or join (*verb*)

consternation sudden confusion; panic

constituents voters; supporters

constraints restrictions; limits

constrict to shrink; to bind

construe to analyze; to interpret

consummate to complete (*verb*); perfect (*adjective*)

contagious likely to spread; infectious

contaminant substance that pollutes or infects

contemn to regard with scorn or contempt

contemporary happening in the same time period; current

contemptuous scornful

contentious ready to argue; quarrelsome

contest (*three meanings*) a competitive game (*noun*); to dispute (*verb*); to compete (*verb*)

contiguous nearby; neighboring

contingent possible

contort to twist; to distort

contraband smuggled or stolen goods

contrary opposite

contravene to go against; to oppose

contretemps an embarrassing occurrence

contrite sorrowful; penitent

controversial debatable; questionable

contumacious   disobedient; obstinate

contumely   rudeness

contusion   a bruise

conundrum   a riddle

convalesce   to recover from an illness

convene   to come together; to assemble

conventional   ordinary; usual

converge   to come together; to meet in a point or line

conversant   being familiar with

converse   (*two meanings*)   to talk to someone (*verb*); the opposite (*noun*)

convex   curving outward

conveyance   a vehicle

convivial   sociable; friendly

convoke   to call together

convoluted   twisted; coiled

cope   (*with*) to deal with; to contend with

copious   plentiful; abundant

coquetry   flirtation

cordial   friendly; courteous

cornucopia   horn of plenty; abundance

corollary   inference; deduction; consequence

corona   crown; bright circle

corporeal   pertaining to the body

corpulent   fat; fleshy

corroborate   to strengthen; to confirm

corrosive   eating away, as an acid

corrugated   wrinkled; ridged; furrowed

cortege   funeral procession; group of followers

cosmic   pertaining to the universe; vast

cosmopolitan   worldly-wise; universal

coterie   close circle of friends

countenance   (*two meanings*)   the face (*noun*); to permit, tolerate, or approve (*verb*)

countermand   to cancel an order

counterpart   duplicate; copy

coup   a brilliant move; a successful and sudden attack

courier   messenger

covenant   an agreement; a contract

covert   hidden; secretive

covet   to desire

cower   to tremble in fear

coy   shy; modest

cozen   to trick

crafty   sly; tricky

crass   stupid; unrefined

crave   to desire strongly

craven   cowardly

credence   belief; trust

credible   believable

credulity   readiness to believe; gullibility

creed   a religious belief

crescendo   gradual increase in intensity or loudness

crestfallen   dejected; humbled

crevice   an opening; a crack

cringe   to shrink back, as in fear

criterion   measure of value; standard of judging

crone   hag; withered old woman

crony   close friend

crotchety   grouchy; eccentric

crucial   extremely important; decisive

crucible   a severe test or trial

crux   the essential part

cryptic   mysterious; secretive

crystallize   to settle; to take on a definite form

cubicle   small compartment

cudgel   club; thick stick

cue   a hint; a signal

cuisine   style of cooking

culinary   pertaining to cooking

cull   to select; to pick

culminate   to result in; to reach the highest point

culpable   blameworthy

cumbersome   heavy; hard to handle because of size or weight

cumulative   collected; accumulated

cupidity   greed

curb   to control; to check

curry   to try to win favor by flattery

cursive   running or flowing

cursory   superficial; hasty

curtail   to cut short

cynic   one who is critical; a fault-finder

cynosure   center of attention

DAIS – DYSPHASIA

dais platform; speaker's stand

dale valley

dally to waste time

dank chilly and wet

dappled spotted

dastardly sneaking and cowardly; shameful

daub to smear; to cover over with paint, etc.

daunt to discourage

dawdle to waste time; to idle

de facto in fact; in reality

deadlock a standstill; a tie

dearth a scarcity or lack

debacle a complete failure; total collapse

debase to lower in rank; to humiliate

debauch to corrupt

debilitate to weaken

debonair pleasant; courteous; charming

debris fragments; litter; rubble

debut first public appearance

decadence moral deterioration

decant to pour off (a liquid)

decapitate to behead

decelerate to slow down

deciduous not permanent; passing

decipher decode; figure out the meaning of

declaim to speak dramatically

declivity downward slope

decompose to decay; to break up into parts

decorum appropriate social behavior

decoy a person or thing that entices or lures, as into danger

decrepit broken down by age or disease

decry to speak out against

deduce to reason out; to infer

deem to think; to believe; to judge

defalcate to misuse funds; to embezzle

defamatory damaging another's reputation with false remarks

default to fail to pay a debt or to perform a task

defection desertion

defer to postpone; to put off

deference respect

defile to pollute; to corrupt

definitive comprehensive; complete

deflect to turn aside; to bend

defoliate to strip of leaves

defray to pay the cost of

deft skillful

defunct no longer in existence; extinct

degrade to lower in degree or quality

deify to idolize; to make god-like

deign to lower oneself before an inferior

delectable delicious; very pleasing

delete to leave out; to cross out

deleterious harmful

delineate to describe; to depict

delirium condition of mental disturbance; wild excitement

delude to deceive; to mislead

deluge a flood; a rush

delve to search; to investigate

demagogue a popular leader who appeals to the emotions

demean to degrade; to lower

demeanor behavior

demented deranged; insane

demesne region; area

demigod a person who is partly a god and partly human

demise death; ending

demography study of population trends

demolish to tear down

demoralize to discourage; to cause to lose spirit

demur to object; to take exception to

demure shy

denigrate to ruin the reputation of; to blacken

denizen occupant; inhabitant; resident

denomination the name or designation for a class of persons, such as a religious group

denouement outcome; result

denounce to publicly condemn

depict to portray; to represent

depilate to remove hair from

deplete to use up gradually (resources, strength, etc.)

deplore   to regret

deploy   to place troops in position

depose   to remove from office

depraved   sinful; immoral

deprecate   to disapprove of

depreciate   to lessen in value

deranged   insane

derelict   (*three meanings*)   abandoned (*adjective*); negligent (*adjective*); a vagrant or bum (*noun*)

deride   to ridicule

derision   ridicule

dermatology   study of skin diseases

derogatory   belittling

descry   to discover

desecrate   to damage a holy place

desiccate   to dry up; to wither

desist   to cease or stop

desolate   lonely; deserted

despicable   contemptible; hateful

despise   to scorn; to regard with disgust

despoil   to rob; to plunder

despondent   depressed; dejected

despot   a dictator

destitute   poor; lacking

desuetude   condition of disuse; extinction

desultory   wandering from subject to subject; rambling

détente   a lessening of tension or hostility

deter   to discourage; to hinder

detergent   a cleansing agent

detonate   explode

detoxify   remove the poison from

detract   to take away; to diminish

detriment   harm; damage

devastate   to destroy; to overwhelm

deviate   to turn aside; to digress

devious   sly; underhand

devoid   completely without

devotee   an enthusiastic follower

devout   religious; pious; sincere

dexterity   skill; cleverness

diabolical   devilish; cruel

diadem   crown

dialectic   logical discussion

diaphanous   transparent; very sheer and light

diatribe   bitter criticism

dichotomy   division into two parts

dicker   to bargain; to argue over prices

diction   style of speaking

dictum   a positive statement

didactic   instructive; inclined to lecture others too much

diffident   shy; modest

diffuse   to spread; to scatter

digress   to wander off the subject

dilapidated   broken down; falling apart

dilate   to expand; to become wider

dilatory   slow or late in doing things

dilemma   a troubling situation

dilettante   a dabbler in the fine arts; one who is not an expert

diligent   hard-working; industrious

diminutive   small

dint   power; force

dipsomaniac   a drunkard

dire   dreadful; causing disaster

dirge   a funeral song or hymn

disarray   disorder; confusion

disavow   to disown; to deny; to repudiate

disburse   to pay out

discern   to distinguish; to recognize; to perceive

disciple   a follower

disclaimer   denial; renunciation

disclose   to reveal; to make known

discomfiture   frustration; confusion

disconcert   to upset; to embarrass

disconsolate   without hope

discordant   disagreeing; harsh-sounding

discount   (*two meanings*)   reduction (*noun*); to disregard (*verb*)

discountenance   to disapprove of

discourse   conversation; lecture

discredit   to disgrace; to cast doubt on

discreet   showing good judgment; cautious

discrepancy   inconsistency; difference

discrete   separate; not attached

discretion   good judgment

discrimination   (*two meanings*)   prejudice; ability to distinguish

discursive   rambling; wandering

disdain   to scorn

disgruntled   unhappy; discontented

dishearten   to discourage; to depress

disheveled   untidy

disinter   to uncover; to dig up

disinterested   impartial; not prejudiced

dismal   gloomy; depressing

dismantle   to take apart

dismember   to cut or pull off limbs

disparage   to belittle; to put down

disparity   inequality; difference

dispassionate   calm; impartial

dispel   to drive away

disperse   to scatter

disputatious   fond of arguing

disreputable   having a bad reputation

dissection   cutting apart; analysis

dissemble   to conceal; to pretend

disseminate   to scatter; to spread

dissension   disagreement; opposition

dissertation   a written essay

dissident   disagreeing

dissimulate   to hide one's feelings

dissipate   to waste; to scatter

dissociate   to break ties with; to part company

dissolute   immoral; unrestrained

dissonant   out of harmony

dissuade   to advise or urge against

distend   to expand; to swell; to stretch out

distort   to twist out of shape

distraught   troubled

dither   (preceded by *in a*) nervously excited or confused

diurnal   daily

divergent   varying; different

divers   several

diverse   different

divest   to deprive

divination   the act of foretelling the future

divulge   to reveal; to make known

docile   obedient; submissive

doddering   shaky; senile

doff   to throw off or away

doggedly   stubbornly

dogmatic   having a definite opinion; authoritative

doldrums   low spirits

dole   to distribute; to give out sparingly

doleful   sorrowful

dolorous   mournful; sad

dolt   a dull, stupid person

domicile   home; residence

donnybrook   rough, rowdy fight

dormant   asleep; inactive

dorsal   pertaining to the back

dossier   a complete group of documents containing detailed information

dotage   feeblemindedness of old age

doughty   courageous; worthy

dour   gloomy

douse   to put out (a fire); to extinguish

dowdy   shabby; untidy

downtrodden   trampled on; suppressed

doyen   senior or eldest member

Draconian   severe; cruel

dregs   leftovers

drivel   childish nonsense; stupid talk

droll   amusing in an odd way

drone   (*three meanings*)   a male bee (*noun*); an idle person (*noun*); to talk on and on monotonously (*verb*)

dross   waste matter

drudgery   hard, tiresome work

dual   consisting of two people, items, or parts

dubious   doubtful; questionable

ductile   capable of being molded or shaped

dudgeon   anger, resentment

dulcet   pleasing to the ear

dulcimer   a type of zither

dupe   to trick; to deceive

duplicity   deceit; double-dealing; dishonesty

duress   force

dutiful   obedient

dwindle   to shrink; to become smaller

dynamo   a powerful person

dyspepsia   poor digestion

dysphasia   difficulty in speaking

EARNEST – EXULT

earnest   sincere; serious

earthy   realistic; coarse

ebb   to slowly decrease

ebullient   enthusiastic

eccentric   odd; out of the ordinary

ecclesiastical   pertaining to the church

echelon   rank of authority; level of power

éclat   brilliance; fame

eclectic   selecting; choosing from various sources

eclipse   to overshadow; to outshine

ecology   study of the environment

ecstatic   extremely happy

edifice   structure; building

edify   to improve someone morally; to instruct

educe   to draw or bring out

eerie   weird; mysterious

efface   to erase; to wipe out

effectual   effective; adequate

effeminate   unmanly; womanly; soft and weak

effervescent   bubbly; spirited

effete   worn-out; barren

efficacy   power to produce an effect

effigy   a likeness; an image

efflorescent   blossoming; flowering

effluent   flowing out

effrontery   shameful boldness

effulgent   shining forth brilliantly; radiant

effusion   a pouring out; an uncontrolled display of emotion

egalitarian   pertaining to belief in the equality of all men

ego   a feeling of self-importance

egotism   selfishness; boasting about oneself

egregious   remarkably bad; outrageous

egress   exit (*noun and verb*)

ejaculation   an exclamation

eject   to throw out

elapse   to pass; to slip away

elated   overjoyed

electrify   to thrill

elegy   a sad or mournful poem

elicit   to draw forth; to cause to be revealed

elite   the choice or best of a group of persons

elixir   remedy

ellipsis   the omission in a sentence of a word or words

eloquent   convincing or forceful in speech

elucidate   to make clear

elude   to avoid; to escape notice

elusive   difficult to grasp

elysian   blissful; heavenly

emaciated   abnormally thin

emanate   to come forth; to send forth

emancipate   to set free

embark   (*on*) begin a journey or an endeavor

embellish   to decorate

embezzle   to steal

embroil   to involve in trouble; to complicate

embryonic   undeveloped; in an early stage

emendation   correction

emetic   causing vomiting

eminent   famous; renowned

emissary   one sent on a special mission

emit   to send out; to give forth

emollient   something that soothes or softens

emolument   profit; gain

empathy   understanding another's feelings

empirical   based on experience rather than theory

emulate   to imitate

emulous   jealous; envious

enamored   (*of*) in love with

enclave   a country, or part of a country, surrounded by another country

encomium   an expression of high praise

encompass   to include; to surround

encore   a repeat performance

encroach   (*upon*) to trespass; to intrude

encumbrance   hindrance; obstruction

encyclopedic   filled with knowledge; comprehensive

endearment   an expression of affection

endemic   confined to a particular country or area

energize   to rouse into activity

enervate   to weaken

enfranchise   to give the right to vote

engender   to produce

engrossed   completely absorbed in

engulf   to overwhelm

enhance   to increase in value or beauty; to improve

enigma   a puzzling situation; dilemma

enigmatic   mysterious; puzzling

enlighten   to inform; to reveal truths

enmity   hostility; hatred

ennui   boredom

enormity   an outrageous and immoral act

enrapture   to delight beyond measure

ensconce   to hide; to conceal; to settle comfortably

ensue   to follow; to result from

enthrall   to charm; to captivate

entice   to attract; to tempt

entity   independent being

entomology   study of insects

entourage   a group of personal attendants

entranced   filled with delight or wonder

entreaty   a request; a plea

entrenched   firmly established; dug in

entrepreneur   successful businessman; promoter

enunciate   to pronounce words clearly

environs   surroundings

envisage   to imagine; to form a mental picture

envoy   messenger; agent

eon   extremely long period of time

ephemeral   temporary; short-lived

epic   a long poem about heroic occurrences

epicure   one who seeks pleasure in fine foods

epigram   witty saying

epilogue   closing part of a speech or literary work

epiphany   appearance of a deity (god); revelation

epistle   a letter

epitaph   inscription on a tomb

epithet   a descriptive word or phrase

epitome   a typical example; a summary or condensed account

epoch   particular period of history

equanimity   calmness; evenness of temperament

equestrian   a horseback rider

equilibrium   balance; stability

equine   pertaining to horses

equinox   the time when day and night are of equal length

equipoise   balance

equitable   fair; just

equity   fairness; justice; impartiality

equivocal   doubtful; ambiguous

equivocate   to confuse by speaking in ambiguous terms

eradicate   to erase; to wipe out

ergo   therefore

erode   to wear away

erotic   pertaining to sexual love

err   to make a mistake

errant   wandering (*in search of adventure*); straying from what is right

erratic   irregular; abnormal

erroneous   mistaken; wrong

ersatz   artificial; inferior substitute

erstwhile   formerly; in the past

erudite   scholarly; learned

escalate   to increase; to grow rapidly; to intensify

escapade   a reckless adventure

escarpment   steep cliff

eschew   to avoid; to keep away from

escrow   (preceded by *in*) money deposited with a third person pending fulfillment of a condition

esoteric   for a select few; not generally known

espionage   spying

espouse   to support (*a cause*)

essay   (*verb*) to try; to attempt

estival   pertaining to summer

estranged   separated; alienated

ethereal   spiritual; airy

ethnic   pertaining to a particular race or culture

etymology   the origin and development of words

eugenics   science of improving the human race

eulogy   praise for a dead person

euphemism   substitution of a pleasant expression for an unpleasant one

euphonious   having a pleasant sound; harmonious

euphoria   a feeling of well-being

euthanasia   mercy killing

evanescent   temporary; fleeting

evasive   not straightforward; tricky

eventuate   to result; to happen finally

evict to expel; to throw out

evince to show clearly

evoke to call forth; to produce

evolve to develop gradually

exacerbate to aggravate; to make more violent

exact (two meanings) accurate (adjective); to demand or to require (verb)

exalt to raise in position; to praise

exasperate to irritate; to annoy extremely

excise (two meanings) a tax on liquor, tobacco, etc. (noun); to cut out or off (verb)

excoriate (two meanings) to scrape the skin off; to criticize sharply

excruciating unbearably painful

exculpate to free from blame; to vindicate

execrate to curse

exemplary worthy of imitation

exhilaration liveliness; high spirits

exhort to warn

exhume to bring out of the earth; to reveal

exigent urgent; critical

exiguous scanty; small in quantity

exodus a departure; a going out

exonerate to free from guilt or blame

exorbitant excessive; unreasonable

exorcise to drive out an evil spirit

exotic foreign; excitingly strange

expatiate to enlarge upon; to speak or write at length

expatriate a person who is banished from, or leaves, his native country

expectorate to spit out

expedient practical; advantageous

expedite to speed up; to make easy

expendable replaceable

expiate to atone for

explicate explain in detail; make clear

explicit clear; unambiguous; direct

exploit to use for one's own advantage

expound to explain; to interpret

expressly especially; particularly

expunge to erase

expurgate to remove offensive passages; to cleanse

extant still in existence

extemporaneous offhand; done without preparation

extenuating less serious

extinct no longer in existence

extirpate to destroy; to remove completely

extol to praise

extort to obtain by force

extradite to give up a prisoner to another authority

extraneous unrelated; not essential

extrapolate to estimate; to infer

extricate to set free; to disentangle

extrinsic external; coming from outside

extrovert an outgoing person

exuberant full of enthusiasm

exude to discharge; to ooze

exult to rejoice

FABRICATE – FUTILE

fabricate (two meanings) to construct; to lie

fabulous incredible; imaginative

facade outward appearance

facet aspect

facetious joking; sarcastic

facile easy; effortless

facilitate to make easy

facsimile an exact copy; a duplicate

faction a minority within a larger group

factious causing disagreement

factitious artificial

factotum an employee who can do all kinds of work

faculty power; ability; skill

fallacious misleading; deceptive

fallible capable of error

fallow inactive; unproductive

falter to stumble; to hesitate

fanatic a person with uncontrolled enthusiasm

fanciful unreal; imaginative; unpredictable

fanfare noisy or showy display

farcical absurd; ridiculous

fastidious hard to please

fatal   causing death

fatalistic   believing that all things in life are inevitable

fathom   (*two meanings*)   nautical measure of 6 feet in depth (*noun*); to comprehend (*verb*)

fatuous   foolish

fauna   animals of a certain area

fawn   (*two meanings*)   a young deer (*noun*); to act slavishly submissive (*verb*)

faze   to disturb; to discourage

fealty   loyalty; devotion

feasible   capable of being accomplished; suitable

feat   deed or accomplishment

febrile   feverish

fecund   fertile; productive

feign   to pretend

feint   a false show; a pretended blow

feisty   quick-tempered or quarrelsome

felicity   happiness

feline   pertaining to cats

fell   (*two meanings*)   to knock down (verb); fierce or cruel (adjective)

felon   a criminal

felonious   treacherous; base; villainous

ferment   a state of agitation or excitement

ferret   (*two meanings*)   a small animal of the weasel family (*noun*); to search or drive out (*verb*)

fervent   eager; earnest

fervid   very emotional

fester   to rot

festive   joyous; merry

fete   to honor; to entertain

fetid   foul-smelling

fetish   object with magical power; object that receives respect or devotion

fetter   to confine; to put into chains

fiasco   a total disaster

fiat   an official order

fickle   changeable in affections; unfaithful

fictitious   false; not genuine

fidelity   faithfulness

figment   something imagined

filch   to steal

filial   like a son or daughter

finale   the climax; end

finesse   diplomacy; tact

finicky   extremely particular; fussy

finite   limited; measurable

firebrand   one who stirs up a revolution

firmament   sky; heavens

fiscal   pertaining to finances

fissure   opening; groove; split

fitful   irregular; occurring in spurts

flabbergasted   astonished; made speechless

flaccid   flabby

flag   (*two meanings*)   a banner (*noun*); to droop or to slow down (*verb*)

flaggelate   to whip

flagrant   scandalous; shocking

flail   to strike freely and wildly

flair   a knack; a natural talent

flamboyant   showy; conspicuous

flaunt   to boast; to show off

flay   (*two meanings*)   to strip the skin off; to criticize sharply

fledgling   a young, inexperienced person

fleece   (*two meanings*)   wool of a lamb (*noun*); to swindle (*verb*)

flexible   bendable

flinch   to draw back; to cringe

flippant   treating serious matters lightly

flora   plant life of a certain area

florid   flowery; ornate

flotilla   small fleet of ships

flotsam   floating cargo or wreckage

flout   to mock; to ridicule

fluctuate   to move back and forth; to vary

fluent   flowing; able to speak and/or write easily and clearly

fluster   to upset; to confuse

fluvial   pertaining to a river

flux   state of continual change

foible   a weakness; minor fault

foil   (*two meanings*)   to prevent the success of a plan (*verb*); a person who, by contrast, makes another person seem better (*noun*)

foist   (*on*) to pass off merchandise which is inferior

folderol   nonsense

folly   a foolish action

foment   to stir up; to instigate

foolhardy   foolish; reckless

fop   an excessively vain man

foray   a sudden attack

forbearance   patience; restraint

forebear   ancestor

foreboding   a warning; an omen

foregone   long past

forensic   pertaining to a formal discussion or debate

forerunner   ancestor; predecessor

foreshadow   to hint

forestall   to prevent by action in advance; to anticipate

forfeit   to give up

forgo   to do without; to give up

formidable   dreadful; discouraging

forte   strong point

forthright   direct; frank

fortitude   strength; courage

fortnight   two weeks; fourteen days

fortuitous   lucky; by chance

foster   to nourish; to encourage

fracas   a loud quarrel

fractious   irritable; quarrelsome; stubborn

fracture   to break or to crack

frailty   a weakness; a defect

franchise   special right or privilege

fraternal   brotherly

fraudulent   dishonest; cheating

fraught   (with) filled

fray   (*two meanings*)   a noisy quarrel (*noun*); to unravel or to come apart (*verb*)

frenetic   frantic; wild

frenzy   madness; fury

freshet   a fresh water stream

fretful   worried; irritated

friction   (*two meanings*)   a rubbing together (*noun*); conflict or disagreement (*noun*)

frigid   extremely cold

frivolous   trivial; silly

frowzy   dirty; unkempt

frugal   economical; thrifty

fruition   fulfillment; realization

fruitless   barren; yielding no results

frustrate   to prevent; to discourage

fugacious   pertaining to the passing of time

fulminate   to explode; to denounce

fulsome   disgusting; sickening; repulsive

furor   rage; frenzy; fury

furtive   stealthy; secretive

fusion   a union; merging

futile   useless

GADFLY – GYRATE

---

gadfly   a person who annoys others

gaff   a hook

gainsay   to deny; to contradict

gait   manner of walking

gala   festive

galaxy   a group of stars; any large and brilliant assemblage of persons

gall   bitterness

gallant   polite; noble

galvanize   to stimulate; to startle into sudden activity

gambit   strategy; an opening one uses to advantage

gambol   to frolic; to romp about

gamut   the whole range or extent

gape   to stare with open mouth

garble   to distort

gargantuan   gigantic; huge

garish   tastelessly gaudy

garland   a wreath of flowers

garner   to gather; to acquire

garnish   to decorate; to trim

garrulous   talkative

gauche   awkward; tactless

gaudy   flashy; showy

gaunt   thin and bony; bleak and barren

gazebo   an open structure with an enjoyable view

gazette   newspaper

gelid   very cold; frozen

genealogy   family history

generate   to produce; to originate

generic   general; not specific; pertaining to a class

genesis   origin; beginning

genial   warm; friendly

genocide   killing of a race of people

genre   an art form or class

genteel   polite; refined

gentry   upper class people

genuflect   to kneel; to bend the knee

germane   relevant; fitting

gerontology   the study of older people and their problems

gesticulation   lively or excited gesture

ghastly   horrible; dreadful

ghoul   grave robber; ogre

gibberish   silly, unintelligible talk

gibbet   gallows from which criminals are hanged

gibe   to scoff; to ridicule

giddy   dizzy; flighty; whirling

gild   to cover with gold

gingerly   carefully; cautiously

gird   to encircle

gist   main point; essence

glazed   glassy; smooth; shiny

glean   to gather patiently and with great effort

glee   joy

glib   fluent; smooth

glissade   a skillful glide over snow or ice in descending a mountain

glitch   a malfunction; an error

gloaming   twilight; dusk

gloat   to look at or think about with great satisfaction

glower   to frown; to stare angrily at

glum   sad; gloomy

glutinous   gluey; sticky

glutton   one who eats or drinks too much

gnarled   knotty; twisted; roughened

gnome   a legendary dwarf-like creature

goad   to encourage; to spur on

gorge   (*two meanings*)   a deep valley with steep sides (*noun*); to eat or to swallow greedily (*verb*)

gory   bloody

gossamer   light; flimsy; fine

Gothic   medieval; mysterious

gouge   (*two meanings*)   to dig out; to swindle or overcharge

gourmand   a glutton; a person who eats excessively

gourmet   an expert of fine food and drink

gradient   a slope; a ramp

granary   a storehouse for grain

grandiloquent   pretentious; speaking in a pompous style

grandiose   impressive; showy

graphic   giving a clear and effective picture

grapple   to grip and hold; to struggle

grate   (*two meanings*)   to grind to shreds; to irritate

gratify   to please; to satisfy

gratis   without payment; free

gratuitous   free of cost; unnecessary

grave   serious; somber

gregarious   sociable; friendly

grievous   causing grief or sorrow; distressing

grim   fierce; stern

grimace   a distorted face; an expression of disapproval

grime   dirt

gripe   complaint

grisly   horrible; gruesome; ghastly

grit   stubborn courage

gross   extreme; vulgar

grotesque   absurd; distorted

grotto   a cave

grovel   to lower oneself to please another

grudging   resentful; reluctant

grueling   exhausting

gruff   rough or harsh in manner

guile   deceit; trickery

guileless   sincere

guise   a false appearance

gull   to trick; to deceive

gullible   easily deceived; too trusting

gumption   courage and initiative

gustatory   pertaining to the sense of taste

gusto   hearty enjoyment

gusty   windy; stormy

guttural   pertaining to the throat

gyrate   to rotate; to spin

HABITAT – HYPOTHESIS

habitat   dwelling

hackneyed   trite; commonplace; overused

haggard   worn out from sleeplessness, grief, etc.

haggle   to bargain over a price

halcyon   calm

hale   healthy

hallmark   a symbol of high quality

hallow   to make holy; to bless

hallucination   illusion; a false notion

hamper   to hinder; to keep someone from acting freely

haphazard   dependent upon mere chance

hapless   unlucky

harangue   long speech

harass   to annoy; to bother

harbinger   an omen or sign

harbor   (*two meanings*)   a body of water providing ships with protection from winds, waves, etc. (*noun*); to conceal or hide (*verb*)

hardy   courageous; sturdy

harlequin   a clown

harpy   a greedy, grasping person; a scolding, nagging, bad-tempered woman

harrowing   upsetting; distressing

harry   to worry; to torment

hart   a male deer

haughty   snobbish; arrogant

haunt   to appear as a spirit or ghost; to visit frequently; to disturb or distress

haven   a safe place

havoc   great destruction

hazard   risk; danger

headlong   recklessly; impulsively

headstrong   stubborn; willful

hearsay   rumor; gossip

hearth   fireplace

hector   to bully

hedonist   a pleasure-seeker

heedless   careless; unmindful

hefty   large and powerful; heavy

hegemony   leadership or strong influence

hegira   flight; escape

heinous   hateful; abominable

hemophilia   tendency toward bleeding

herald   to announce; to usher in

herbivorous   feeding on vegetation

herculean   tremendous in size, strength, or difficulty

heresy   rejection of a religious belief

hermetic   airtight; tightly sealed

heterodox   departing from acceptable beliefs

heterogeneous   different; unlike; dissimilar

heyday   period of success

hiatus   pause or gap

hibernate   to be inactive, especially during the winter

hierarchy   a ranking, one above the other

hilarity   gaiety; joy

hircine   goat-like

hirsute   hairy; bearded

histrionic   theatrical; overly dramatic

hoard   to store away; to accumulate

hoary   white with age or frost

hoax   a practical joke

hobgoblin   a frightening apparition; something that causes fear

hodgepodge   mixture

hogwash   meaningless or insincere talk

hoi polloi   common people; the masses

holocaust   complete destruction

homage   respect; honor

homily   a sermon

homogenous   composed of parts all of the same kind

homophonic   sounding alike

hone   to sharpen

hoodwink   to deceive

hoot   to shout in disapproval

horde   a crowd of people

horticulture   the science of gardening

hospice   shelter

hovel   a dirty, wretched living place

hover   to keep lingering about; to wait near at hand

hubris   excessive pride or self-confidence

hue   a color; a shade

humane   kind; compassionate

humbug   trick; hoax

humdrum monotonous; routine

humid moist

humility lowliness; meekness

humus black soil for fertilizing

hurtle to dash; speed; run

husbandry the science of raising crops; careful management

hybrid mixed; assorted

hydrophobia fear of water; rabies

hymeneal pertaining to marriage

hyperbole extreme exaggeration

hypercritical overcritical; faultfinding

hypochondriac a person with imaginary ailments

hypocrite one who pretends to be someone or something he is not

hypothesis an assumption; a theory

ICHTHYOLOGY – ITINERANT

---

ichthyology study of fish

icon a statue or idol

iconoclast a rebel; one who breaks with tradition

idealist one with very high standards

idiosyncrasy a peculiar personality trait

idolatry excessive or blind adoration; worship of idols

idyllic charmingly simple or poetic

igneous pertaining to fire

ignoble dishonorable

ignominious shameful; disgraceful

ignoramus a stupid person

ilk type; sort; kind

illicit unlawful; illegal

illiterate uneducated

illumine to brighten; to inspire

illusion fake impression

illustrious distinguished; bright

imbibe to drink; to absorb

imbroglio a difficult or confusing situation

imbue to fill completely; to penetrate

immaculate spotless; pure

imminent likely to happen; threatening

immolate to kill someone as a sacrificial victim, usually by fire

immortal not subject to death

immunity freedom from disease

immutable unchangeable

impair to weaken; to cause to become worse

impale to pierce with a sharp stake through the body

impalpable vague; not understandable

impartial without prejudice

impasse a dead-end; a problem without a solution

impeach to accuse

impeccable flawless; without fault

impecunious without money; penniless

impede to hinder; to obstruct

impediment a barrier; an obstruction

impel push into motion; urge

impending likely to happen soon

imperative extremely necessary

imperious domineering; haughty

impermeable not permitting passage

impertinent rude; disrespectful

imperturbable steady; calm

impervious not capable of being affected; hardened

impetuous acting without thought; impulsive

impetus a stimulus; a moving force

impinge to strike; to collide; to encroach

impious disrespectful toward God

implacable unbending; inflexible; merciless

implausible unbelievable

implement (*two meanings*) a tool (*noun*); to carry out or put into practice (*verb*)

implication an indirect indication; a statement that suggests something

implicit suggested, but not plainly expressed

imply to suggest

import (*two meanings*) significance; meaning (*noun*); to bring in from a foreign country (*verb*)

importune to persistently ask; to beg

impostor a person who goes about under an assumed name or character

impotent powerless; lacking strength

imprecation a curse

impregnable unconquerable

impromptu without preparation; offhand

impropriety pertaining to something that is not proper or suitable

improvident wasteful

improvise to do without preparation

impudent disrespectful; shameless

impugn to attack a person with words; to challenge a person in regard to motives

impunity freedom from punishment

impute to accuse a person of some wrong doing; to attribute a fault or a crime to a person

inadvertent unintentional

inalienable not able to be transferred to another

inane silly; meaningless

inanimate lifeless; dull; dead

inarticulate pertaining to speech that is not clear or understandable

incandescent very bright; shining

incapacitated disabled; unable to function

incarcerate to imprison

incarnadine blood-red; flesh-colored

incarnate in human form

incendiary causing fire; stirring up trouble

incense to inflame; to enrage

incentive something that incites to action

inception beginning; start

incessant continuous; without pause

inchoate at an early stage; just beginning

incipient beginning to exist or appear

incisive sharp; keen

incite to urge to action; to stir up

inclement (*usually refers to weather*) harsh; unfavorable; severe

incognito disguised

incoherent rambling; not logically connected

incongruous unsuited; inappropriate

inconsequential unimportant

incontrovertible certain; undeniable

incorrigible bad beyond correction or reform

incredulous skeptical; disbelieving

increment an increase; a gain

incriminate to charge with a crime; to connect or relate to a wrongdoing

incubus nightmare

inculcate (*in* or *upon*) to teach earnestly; to influence someone to accept an idea

incumbent (*two meanings*) resting or lying down (*adjective*); one who holds a political office (*noun*)

incur to bring upon oneself; to run into some undesirable consequence

incursion a raid; an invasion

indefatigable incapable of being tired out

indelible incapable of being erased

indemnify to insure; to repay

indicative signifying; implying

indict to charge with a crime; to accuse of a wrongdoing

indigenous native to a particular area; inborn

indigent extremely poor

indignant angry as a result of unjust treatment

indisputable unquestionable; without doubt

indissoluble permanent

indoctrinate to teach someone principles or beliefs

indolent lazy

indomitable unconquerable; unyielding

indubitable unquestionable; certain

induce to cause; to bring about

indulgence gentle treatment; tolerance

inebriated drunk

inefffable not able to be described; unspeakable

ineluctable inevitable; inescapable

inept unfit; bungling; inefficient

inert without power to move; inactive

inevitable unavoidable; sure to happen

inexorable unyielding

infallible certain; without mistakes

infamous having an extremely bad reputation; destestable

infantile childish; immature

infectious passing on a disease with germs; likely to spread; contagious

infer to conclude; to derive by reasoning

infernal hellish; fiendish; diabolical

infidel unbeliever

infinitesimal exceedingly small; minute (pronounced *my-newt*)

infirmity weakness; feebleness

inflated puffed up; swollen

influx a flowing in

infraction the breaking of a law or rule

infringe (*on* or *upon*) to break a law; to violate; to trespass

ingenious   clever

ingenuous   simple; innocent; naive

ingrate   ungrateful person

ingratiate   (*oneself*) to work one's way into another's favor

inherent   inborn

inhibition   restraint; reserve

inimical   harmful; unfriendly

inimitable   not able to be imitated or equaled

iniquity   wickedness

initiate   to begin

injunction   a command; an order

inkling   a hint

innate   inborn; existing from birth

innocuous   harmless

innovate   to introduce a new idea

innuendo   indirect remark; hint

inordinate   unusual; excessive

insatiable   unable to be satisfied

inscrutable   mysterious; difficult to understand

insidious   treacherous

insightful   having a penetrating understanding of things; mentally alert and sharp

insinuate   to hint; to suggest

insipid   tasteless; dull

insolent   boldly disrespectful

insolvent   bankrupt; unable to pay creditors

insomnia   sleeplessness

insouciant   carefree; happy-go-lucky

instigate   to provoke; to stir up

insubordinate   disobedient

insular   pertaining to an island; detached; isolated

insuperable   unconquerable

insurgence   rebellion; action against authority

insurrection   uprising; rebellion

intact   entire; left whole; sound

integral   essential; whole

integrate   unify; to bring together into a whole

integrity   honesty; sincerity

intellectual   intelligent; having mental capacity to a high degree

intelligentsia   highly educated, cultured people

inter   to bury

interdict   to prohibit; to ban

interim   meantime; period of time between

interlocutor   one who takes part in a conversation

interloper   an intruder

interlude   a period of time between two events

interminable   endless

intermittent   starting and stopping; periodic

interpolate   to insert between; to estimate

interpose   to place between

interregnum   pause; interval; any period during which a nation is without a permanent ruler

interrogate   to question

interstellar   between or among stars

intervene   to come between

intimate   (*two meanings*)   private or personal (*adjective*); to imply (*verb*)

intimidate   make afraid; threaten

intolerant   bigoted; narrow-minded

intractable   hard to manage

intransigent   stubborn; refusing to give in

intrepid   fearless; courageous

intricate   complex; hard to understand

intrinsic   essential; pertaining to a necessary part of something

introspective   looking into oneself

introvert   a person who is concerned with his own thoughts or feelings

intuitive   insightful; knowing by a hidden sense

inundate   to fill to overflowing; to flood

inured   (*to*) accustomed to

invalidate   deprive of legal value; to make null and void

invariably   constantly; uniformly; without changing

invective   strong verbal abuse

inveigh   (*against*) to make a bitter verbal attack

inveigle   trick; lure; deceive

invert   to turn inside out or upside down

inveterate   firmly established; deep-rooted

invidious   causing resentment; offensive

invigorate   to fill with energy

invincible   not able to be defeated; unconquerable

invoke   to call upon

invulnerable   not able to be hurt; immune to attack

iota   a small quantity

irascible   easily angered

ire   anger; wrath

iridescent   displaying a wide range of colors like those of the rainbow

irksome   annoying; bothersome

ironic   contrary to what was expected

irrational   senseless; unreasonable

irreconcilable   unable to agree

irredeemable   hopeless; unable to be brought back

irremediable   unable to be corrected or cured

irreparable   beyond repair

irrepressible   unable to be controlled or restrained

irresolute   indecisive; doubtful; undecided

irreverent   disrespectful

irrevocable   final; unchangeable

itinerant   traveling from place to place

JADED – KNUCKLE

jaded   tired; worn out; dulled

jargon   vocabulary peculiar to a particular trade or group of people; meaningless talk; gibberish

jaundiced   (*two meanings*)   pertaining to a yellowed skin; prejudiced

jaunt   short trip; excursion

jaunty   carefree; confident

jeer   to sneer; to mock

jeopardy   danger

jest   to joke; to make light of

jetsam   goods cast overboard to lighten a ship

jettison   to throw goods overboard

jilt   to reject; to cast off

jingoism   extreme patriotism

jinx   to bring bad luck to

jocose   joking; humorous

jocular   humorous

jostle   to bump; to push

jovial   jolly; good-natured

jubilation   celebration; rejoicing

judicious   wise; showing sound judgment

juggernaut   a terrible, destructive force

jugular   pertaining to the throat or neck

juncture   a point of time; a crisis

junket   a pleasure trip; an excursion

junta   a small group ruling a country

jurisprudence   science of law

jut   to stick out; to project

juxtapose   to place side by side

kaleidoscopic   constantly changing

ken   range of knowledge

kindle   to set on fire; to excite

kindred   relatives; family, tribe, or race

kinetic   pertaining to motion

kismet   destiny; fate

kleptomania   a compulsion to steal

knave   a tricky, deceitful person

knead   to work dough, clay, etc. into a uniform mixture

knell   the sound made by a bell rung slowly for a death or funeral

knoll   a small rounded hill

knuckle   (*under*) to yield; (*down*) to apply oneself vigorously

LABYRINTHINE – LUXURIANT

labyrinthine   complicated; intricate

lacerate   to tear (*flesh*) roughly; to mangle

lachrymose   tearful

lackadaisical   uninterested; listless

lackey   slavish follower

lackluster   lacking brilliance or liveliness; dull or vapid

laconic   using few words; concise

lactic   pertaining to milk

laden   burdened; loaded

laggard   a slow person; one who falls behind

laity   religious worshipers who are not clergy

lambent   softly bright or radiant; running or moving lightly over a surface

lament   to mourn

laminated   covered with thin sheets, often plastic

lampoon   a sharp, often harmful satire

languid   sluggish; drooping from weakness

languish   to become weak or feeble

lank   long and slender

lapidary   a dealer in precious stones

larceny   theft

largess   gifts that have been given generously

lascivious   lustful or lewd; inciting sexual desire

lassitude   a feeling of weakness and weariness

latent   present, but hidden

lateral   to the side; sideways

latitude   freedom; margin

laudable   praiseworthy

laureate   worthy of praise or honor

lave   to wash or bathe

lavish   very generous; extravagant

lax   careless or negligent

leeway   room for freedom of action; margin

legerdemain   sleight of hand; deception

lenient   mild; lax; permissive

leonine   lion-like; fierce; authoritative

lesion   an injury; a wound

lethal   deadly; fatal

lethargic   dull; slow-moving; sluggish

leviathan   anything vast or huge; a sea monster

levity   lightness of body or spirit; lack of seriousness

levy   to impose and collect taxes

lewd   pertaining to lust or sexual desire

lexicon   dictionary

liaison   a bond; a connection; an illicit relationship between a man and a woman

libation   a drink; a beverage

libel   a false statement in written form

liberal   giving freely; not strict

libertine   one who leads an immoral life

libretto   the words of an opera

licentious   lawless; immoral; lewd

liege   lord; master

lieu   (*in lieu of*) in place of; instead of

lilliputian   tiny; narrow-minded

limber   easily bent; flexible

limpid   clear; transparent

lineage   ancestry; descent

lineaments   facial features

linguistic   pertaining to language

lionize   to treat as a celebrity

liquidate   (*two meanings*)   to get rid of by killing; to wind up the affairs of a business

lissome   moving gracefully; agile or active

listless   feeling no interest in anything; indifferent

literal   exact; precise; word for word

lithe   graceful; flexible

litigation   lawsuit

livid   darkened or discolored; pale from anger or embarrassment

loath   reluctant; unwilling

loathe   to hate; to feel disgust for

locus   place

lode   a rich source of supply such as a mineral deposit

lofty   very high; formal; proud

logistics   military operations dealing with the supply and maintenance of equipment

loiter   to linger; to hang around

loll   to lean or lounge about; to droop

longevity   a long life

lope   to move along with a swinging walk

loquacious   talkative

lot   fate

lout   an awkward, stupid person

lowly   humble; ordinary

lucent   giving off light; shining

lucid   clear; easy to understand; rational or sane

lucrative   profitable; producing wealth or riches

ludicrous   ridiculous

lugubrious   sad; mournful

lull   to soothe or calm

luminous   bright

lunacy   insanity; madness

lunar   pertaining to the moon

lupine   wolflike; fierce

lurch   to move suddenly forward

lurid   shocking; glowing; sensational

lurk   to lie concealed in waiting; to stay hidden

lush   abundant; rich

lustrous   shining; bright

luxuriant   rich; extravagant

MACABRE – MYTHICAL

macabre   horrible; gruesome

Machiavellian   deceitful; tricky

machination   evil design

macroscopic   visible to the naked eye

maelstrom   whirlpool

magnanimous   generous

magnate   important person in any field

magnitude   size; extent

maim   to cripple; to deprive of the use of some part of the body

maladroit   clumsy; unskillful; awkward

malady   disease; illness

malaise   discomfort; uneasiness

malapropism   word humorously misused

malcontent   one who is dissatisfied

malediction   curse

malefactor   wrong-doer; villain

malevolent   showing ill will or hatred; very dangerous; harmful

malfeasance   wrongdoing

malicious   spiteful; vengeful

malign   to speak badly of

malignant   evil; deadly

malingerer   one who pretends to be sick to avoid work

malleable   capable of being changed; adaptable

malodorous   bad-smelling; stinking

mammoth   huge; enormous

manacle   handcuff; restraint

mandarin   influential person

mandate   an order; a command

mandatory   required; obligatory

mangle   to cut, slash, or crush so as to disfigure

mangy   shabby; filthy

manifest   evident; obvious

manifold   many; varied

manipulate   (*two meanings*)   to handle or manage with skill; to influence a person in a bad way

manumit   to set free

maraud   to raid; to plunder

marital   pertaining to marriage

maritime   pertaining to the sea

marquee   a rooflike shelter, such as glass, projecting above an outer door

martial   warlike

martinet   a strict disciplinarian

martyr   one who suffers for a cause

marvel   to be amazed; to wonder

masochist   one who enjoys his own pain and suffering

massive   huge; bulky

masticate   to chew

maternal   motherly

matriarchy   a social organization in which the mother is the head of the family

matrix   a place of origin

maudlin   excessively sentimental

maul   to injure; to handle roughly

mausoleum   large tomb for many bodies

maverick   a rebel; a nonconformist

mawkish   sickeningly sweet; overly sentimental

maxim   a proverb or saying

meager   inadequate; of poor quality

mean   (*three meanings*)   nasty or offensive (*adjective*); inferior or low (*adjective*); an average (*noun*)

meander   to wander aimlessly

meddlesome   interfering; curious

mediate   to settle a dispute; to act as a go-between

mediocre   ordinary; average; neither good nor bad

meditate   to think deeply; to ponder

medley   a mixture; a musical selection combining parts from various sources

megalomania   false impression of one's own greatness; tendency to exaggerate

melancholy   sad; depressed

melee   noisy fight

mellifluous   smoothly flowing; sweet-sounding

melodramatic   overly emotional

memento   remembrance; a souvenir

menace   a threat; a danger

ménage   household; domestic establishment

menagerie   collection of wild or strange animals

mendacious   lying; false

mendicant   a beggar

menial   low; degrading

mentor   adviser

mercantile   pertaining to merchants; commercial

mercenary   motivated only by a desire for money

mercurial   changeable; fickle; erratic

meretricious   gaudy; showy; attractive in a cheap, flashy way

mesa   a flat-topped elevation of land with steep rock walls

mesmerize   to hypnotize

metamorphosis   a change; a transformation

metaphor   comparison (without *like* or *as*)

metaphysics   pert. to beyond what is natural

mete   (*out*) to distribute in portions

meteoric   momentarily dazzling; swift

meteorology   study of weather and climate

meticulous   excessively careful; finicky

metropolis   large city

mettle   courage; spirit

miasma   pollution; poisonous environment

microcosm   a miniature world

mien   manner; bearing

migratory   wandering; moving from place to place

milieu   environment; setting

militant   ready and willing to fight

millennium   a thousand years

mimic   to imitate

minion   a devoted follower; a highly regarded person

minuscule   very small

minute   (*two meanings*)   sixtieth part of an hour (pronounced *min-ut*); very small and insignificant (pronounced *mine-yute*)

minutiae   insignificant details; trivia

mirage   an apparition or illusion

mire   (*two meanings*)   wet, swampy ground (*noun*); to involve in difficulties (*verb*)

mirth   joy; amusement; laughter

misanthrope   hater of mankind

misapprehension   a misunderstanding

miscegenation   mixture of races, especially through marriage

mischance   unlucky accident; bad luck

misconstrue   misinterpret; misjudge

miscreant   a vicious person; a villain

misdemeanor   a criminal offense less serious than a felony

misgiving   doubt; suspicion

misnomer   an error in listing the name of a person

misogamy   hatred of marriage

misogynist   woman-hater

missive   letter

mitigate   to make less severe; to become milder

mnemonic   pertaining to memory

mobile   movable; flexible

mock   to ridicule; to insult; to lower in esteem

modicum   a small amount

modish   fashionable; stylish

modulate   to soften; to tone down

mogul   powerful person

molest   to disturb; to bother

mollify   to pacify; to calm; to appease

molt   to shed, such as feathers and skin

molten   melted

momentous   very important

monarchy   government by one ruler

monastic   pertaining to a monk; self-denying

monetary   pertaining to money

monitor   one who watches or warns

monograph   a paper, book, etc. written about a single subject

monolithic   unyielding; unified

monologue   long speech by one person

monotheism   belief in one god

monumental   great; important

moot   doubtful; debatable

moratorium   delay; postponement

morbid   depressing; gruesome

mordant   sarcastic; biting

mores   customs; traditions; morals

moribund   dying

morose   gloomy; ill-humored

mortal   destined to die; causing death

mortify   to embarrass; to humiliate

motif   theme; central idea

motley   diverse; assorted; having different colors

mottled   spotted; blotched; streaked

mountebank   a phony; a fraud; a charlatan

muddle   to confuse; to mix up

mulct   to punish with a fine; to obtain money by extortion

mull   (*over*) to study or think about

multifarious   varied; having many parts

mundane   worldly

munificent   generous

murky   dark; unclear; gloomy

muse   to think deeply

muster   to gather together

musty   stale; moldy

mute   silent

mutilate   to disfigure; to cripple

mutinous   rebellious

muzzle   to restrain; to gag

myopic   near-sighted; having a limited point of view

myriad   infinitely vast in number

myrmidon   an unquestioning follower

mythical   imaginary; fictitious

NABOB – NUTRIMENT

nabob   a very wealthy or powerful person

nadir   lowest point

naive   simple; unsophisticated

narcissistic   conceited; vain

nascent   coming into being; being born

natation   the act or art of swimming

nativity   birth

naught   nothing

nautical   pertaining to ships, sailors, navigation

nebulous   hazy; vague; uncertain

necromancy   magic, especially that practiced by a witch

nefarious   wicked

negate   to deny; to make ineffective

negligent   careless

nemesis   something that a person cannot conquer or achieve

neologism   new use of a word

neophyte   a beginner; a novice

nepotism   favoritism shown toward relatives

nether   lower; under

nettle   to irritate; to annoy

neutralize   to make ineffective; to counteract

nexus   connection, tie, or link among the units of a group

nicety   delicacy; subtlety

niche   recess or hollow in a wall

niggardly   stingy; miserly

niggle   to spend excessive time on unimportant details

nihilism   total rejection of established laws

nimble   quick and light in motion

nirvana   place of great peace or happiness

nocturnal   pertaining to the night

nodule   a small, rounded mass or lump

noisome   foul-smelling; harmful or injurious

nomadic   wandering; homeless

nomenclature   a set of names or terms

nominal   in name only; not in fact

non sequitur   something that does not logically follow

nonage   a period of immaturity

nonchalant   unconcerned; casual

noncommittal   having no definite point of view

nonentity   person or thing of little importance

nonpareil   unequaled; unrivaled

nonplus   to confuse; to perplex

nostalgia   homesickness; longing for the past

nostrum   quack medicine; supposed cure-all

notorious   having a bad reputation; infamous

novice   a beginner

noxious   harmful

nuance   delicate variation in meaning, tone, color, etc.

nub   a lump or small piece

nubile   suitable for marriage, in regard to age and physical development

nugatory   worthless; invalid

nullify   to make useless or ineffective

numismatist   coin collector

nuptial   pertaining to marriage

nurture   to feed; to sustain

nutriment   food; nourishment

OAF – OVOID

oaf   a dunce or blockhead

oasis   a place which offers a pleasant relief

obdurate   stubborn; hard-hearted

obeisance   a bow or similar gesture expressing deep respect

obese   very fat

obfuscate   to confuse; to bewilder; to perplex

oblation   an offering for religious or charitable purposes

obligatory   required; mandatory

oblique   slanted; indirect

obliterate   to erase; to do away with

oblivious   forgetful; unmindful

obloquy   strong disapproval; bad reputation resulting from public criticism

obnoxious   objectionable; offensive

obscurant   a person who tries to prevent the spread of knowledge

obscure   dim; not clear; not easily understood

obsequious   excessively submissive; overly attentive

obsequy   a funeral rite or ceremony

obsess   to control the thoughts or feelings of a person

obsolescent   going out of use; becoming extinct

obstinate   stubborn

obstreperous   boisterous; unruly

obtrude   to push something toward or upon a person

obtuse   slow to comprehend

obviate   to prevent

occidental   western; opposite of oriental

occlude   to close; to shut; to block out

occult   hidden; secret; mysterious

ocular   pertaining to sight

odious   disgusting; hateful

odoriferous   giving off a pleasant smell

odyssey   a long journey

offal   garbage; waste parts

officious   meddling; interfering

ogle   to look at with desire

ogre   monster; hideous being

olfactory   pertaining to smell

oligarchy   government in which power is in the hands of only a few individuals

Olympian   majestic

omen   an event which indicates the future

ominous   threatening; indicating evil or harm

omnifarious   of all kinds

omnipotent   all-powerful

omniscient   all-knowing

omnivorous   eating any kind of food; absorbing everything

onerous   burdensome; heavy

onslaught   a furious attack

onus   a burden; a responsibility

opaque   not transparent; not letting light pass through

opiate   narcotic; causing sleep or relief

opportunist   one who takes advantage of a situation

oppress   to rule harshly; tyrannize

opprobrious   shameful; disgraceful

opt   (*for*) to choose

optimist   one who sees the good side of things

optimum   the best; most favorable

opulent   rich; luxurious

oracular   mysterious; predicting

oration   a speech delivered on a special occasion

orbit   a curved path, such as a planet takes around the sun

ordain   to order; to establish; to arrange

ordeal   difficult or painful experience; a primitive form of trial

ordinance   law; regulation

organic   fundamental; essential

orient   (*two meanings*)   an area of the Far East, such as Asia (*noun*); to adjust or adapt to (*verb*)

orifice   mouth; opening

ornate   showy; highly decorated

ornithology   study of birds

orthodox   accepting the usual or traditional beliefs

orthography   correct spelling

oscillate to swing or move back and forth, like a pendulum

ossify to change into bone; to become rigid

ostensible apparent; conspicuous

ostentatious showing off; boastful

ostracize to banish; to exclude

oust to drive out; to expel

outwit to trick; to get the better of

overt open; aboveboard; not hidden

ovine of or like a sheep

ovoid egg-shaped

PACIFY – PYRRHIC

pacify to calm down

pact an agreement

paean song of praise or joy

palatable pleasant to the taste

palatial magnificent

paleontology study of prehistoric life

pall (*two meanings*) something that covers or conceals (*noun*); to become wearisome or unpleasant (*verb*)

palliate to ease; to lessen

pallid pale; dull

palpable obvious; capable of being touched or felt

palpitate to beat rapidly; to tremble

palsy muscle paralysis

paltry trivial; worthless

panacea a cure-all; an answer for all problems

panache self-confidence; a showy manner

pandemic general; widespread

pandemonium wild disorder; confusion

panegyric an expression of praise

pang a sharp pain

panoply suit of armor; any protective covering

panorama unlimited view; comprehensive survey

parable a simple story giving a moral or religious lesson

paradigm a model; an example

paradox a statement that seems contradictory, but probably true

paragon a model of excellence or perfection

parameter boundary; limits

paramount chief; supreme

paranoia mental disorder characterized by a feeling of being persecuted

paraphernalia personal belongings; equipment

paraphrase to reword; to restate

parched dried up; extremely thirsty

pariah an outcast

parity equality; similarity

parley discussion; conference

parlous dangerous

parochial local; narrow; limited

parody a work which imitates another in a ridiculous manner

paroxysm a sudden outburst; a fit

parrot to repeat or imitate without understanding

parry to avoid something such as a thrust or blow

parsimonious stingy; miserly

partisan a strong supporter of a cause

passé old fashioned; out-of-date

passive submissive; unresisting

pastoral pertaining to the country; rural

patent (*two meanings*) a government protection for an inventor (*noun*); evident or obvious (*adjective*)

paternal fatherly

pathogenic causing disease

pathos pity; deep feeling

patriarch an early Biblical person regarded as one of the fathers of the human race

patrician aristocratic

patrimony inherited right; heritage

patronage the control of power to make appointments to government jobs

patronize (*two meanings*) to be a customer; to talk down to

paucity scarcity; lack

peccadillo a minor offense

pectoral pertaining to the chest

peculate to steal; to embezzle

pecuniary pertaining to money

pedagogue a schoolteacher

pedantic tending to show off one's learning

pedestrian (*two meanings*) one who walks (*noun*); ordinary or dull (*adjective*)

pedigree a record of ancestors; a line of descent

peer (*two meanings*) an equal (*noun*); to look closely (*verb*)

peerless without equal; unmatched

peevish hard to please; irritable

pejorative having a negative effect; insulting

pellucid transparent; clear

pelt (*two meanings*) skin of a fur-bearing animal (*noun*); to throw things at (*verb*)

penal pertaining to punishment

penchant a strong liking for; an inclination

pendant anything that hangs or is suspended

penitent expressing sorrow for sin or wrongdoing

pensive dreamily thoughtful

penury extreme poverty

peon common worker

perceive to observe

perceptible observable; recognizable

perdition damnation; ruin; hell

peregrinate to travel from place to place

peremptory decisive; final; not open to debate

perennial lasting for a long time; perpetual

perfidious deceitful; treacherous; unfaithful

perforce of necessity

perfunctory done without care; routine

perigee point nearest to the earth

perilous dangerous; risky

periphery outside boundary; unimportant aspects of a subject

periphrastic said in a roundabout way

perjury making a false statement while under oath

permeate to spread throughout

pernicious deadly; destructive

peroration the concluding part of a speech

perpetrate to do something evil; to be guilty of

perpetuate to cause to continue

perplexity confusion

perquisite something additional to regular pay

persevere to endure; to continue

personification giving human qualities to a non-human being

perspicacity keenness of judgment

perspicuity clearness, as of a statement

pert bold; saucy

pertinent relevant; to the point

perturb to unsettle; to disturb

peruse to read carefully

pervade to spread throughout; to pass through

perverse contrary; cranky

pervert to lead astray; to corrupt

pessimist one who sees the worst in everything

petrify to turn to rock; to paralyze with fear

petrology study of rocks

petty unimportant; minor

petulant irritable; rude

phalanx closely massed body of persons

phenomenon extraordinary person, thing, or event

philander to engage in various love affairs

philanthropy a desire to help mankind; generosity

philately stamp collecting

philippic a bitter verbal attack

philistine uncultured; common

phlegmatic unemotional; cool; not easily excited

phobia intense fear

phoenix a bird which symbolizes immortality

picaresque pertaining to an adventurous wanderer

piddling trifling; petty

piecemeal bit by bit; gradually

pied many-colored; variegated

piety reverence; devotion

pigment dye; coloring matter

pilgrimage a journey to a holy place

pillage to rob by violence

pillory to expose to public ridicule or abuse

pinnacle peak; highest point

pious religious

piquant stimulating to the taste; exciting interest

pique to irritate or annoy

piscine of or like a fish

pitfall unexpected difficulty; a trap

pithy concise; to the point

pittance small share or amount

pivotal central; crucial

placard small poster

placate to soothe; to calm

placebo harmless phony medicine; something said or done to soothe

placid   calm

plagiarism   claiming another's work to be one's own

plague   (*two meanings*)   a contagious disease (*noun*); to torment; to trouble (*verb*)

plaintive   sorrowful; sad

platitude   a dull or trite remark

platonic   spiritual; free from sensual desire

plaudit   applause; (in the plural) any expression of approval

plausible   apparently true, fair, or reasonable

plebeian   pertaining to a member of the lower classes

plenary   full; complete; absolute

plethora   abundance

pliant   easily bent; adaptable

plight   a sad or dangerous situation

ploy   a gimmick; a trick

pluck   (*two meanings*)   to pull at (*verb*); courage (*noun*)

plumb   to test; to measure

plunder   to rob; to take by force

plutocracy   rule by the wealthy class

poach   to trespass

podium   a platform

poignant   keenly distressing; affecting the emotions

polarize   to separate into opposing groups

polemic   a controversy or argument

politic   diplomatic; shrewd

poltroon   a coward

polychromatic   many-colored

polyglot   speaking or writing several languages

polymorphic   having many forms

polytheism   belief in many gods

pomp   brilliant show or display

ponder   to think deeply; to consider carefully

ponderous   heavy; burdensome

porcine   of or like a pig

portable   capable of being carried

portal   door; gate; entrance

portentous   warning; foreshadowing

portly   stout; large

posterity   future generations

posthumous   occurring after death

postulate   to assume without proof; to take for granted

potable   drinkable

potent   powerful; strong

potentate   ruler; monarch

potential   capacity for being or becoming something

potion   a drink

potpourri   a mixture

pragmatic   practical

prate   to talk extensively and pointlessly; to babble

precarious   uncertain; dangerous; risky

precede   to be, come, or go before

precedent   an act that may be used as an example in the future

precept   a rule of conduct

precipice   cliff

precipitate   to bring about an action suddenly

precipitous   extremely steep

précis   brief summary

preclude   to prevent; to shut out

precocious   prematurely developed

precursor   a forerunner; predecessor

predatory   living by plunder, exploitation, etc.

predicate   to declare; to assert

predilection   a liking; preference; inclination

predispose   to make susceptible

preeminent   standing out above all others

preen   to dress oneself carefully or smartly

prehensile   adapted for seizing or grasping something

prelude   an introduction

premeditate   to plan beforehand

premier   first in importance or time

premise   statement from which a conclusion is drawn

premonition   forewarning; hunch

preponderance   superiority in quantity or power; dominance

preposterous   absurd; ridiculous

prerogative   privilege or right

presage   to indicate or warn in advance

prescience   knowledge of things before they happen

presentiment   anticipation, especially of something evil

prestige   influence; importance

presumptuous   boldly assuming

pretentious   showy; putting on airs

preternatural   abnormal; beyond what is natural

pretext   a false reason or motive; an excuse

prevail   to succeed; to gain the advantage

prevaricate   to lie

prim   formal; proper

primary   first; chief

primeval   of the earliest times or ages

primogeniture   state of being the first born

primordial   first; original

primp   to dress up in a fussy way

prismatic   many-colored

pristine   uncorrupted; in its original state

privation   loss or lack of something essential

privy   (to) having knowledge of something private or secret

probe   to investigate; to examine

probity   honesty; integrity

proclivity   inclination; tendency

procrastinate   to postpone; to delay

procreate   to beget or produce

procrustean   designed to get conformity at any cost

procure   to obtain; to secure

prod   to urge; to poke or jab

prodigal   wasteful

prodigious   enormous; vast

profane   showing disrespect for sacred things

profess   to acknowledge; to admit frankly

proffer   to offer

proficiency   skill; competency

profligate   shamelessly immoral; extremely wasteful

profound   very deep

profuse   abundant

progeny   descendants

prognosticate   to predict; to foretell

projectile   a bullet, shell, grenade, etc. for firing from a gun

proletarian   one who belongs to the working class

proliferate   to expand; to increase

prolific   productive; fertile

prolix   tediously long and wordy

prologue   introduction

promenade   a stroll or a walk; an area used for walking

promiscuous   sexually loose

promontory   piece of land that juts out

promulgate   to announce; to advocate

prone   reclining; lying flat; inclined

propagate   to spread; to multiply

propensity   inclination; tendency

prophetic   predicting

propinquity   nearness; closeness

propitious   favorable

proponent   a person who supports a cause or doctrine

propriety   conformity; appropriateness

prosaic   dull; commonplace; unimaginative

proscribe   to denounce; exile

proselyte   a person who has changed from one religion to another; a convert

prospectus   a report describing a forthcoming project

prostrate   lying flat; thrown or fallen to the ground

protagonist   main character

protean   changeable; variable

protégé   one who has been guided or instructed by another

protocol   the etiquette observed by diplomats

prototype   the original; first of its kind; a model

protract   to draw out; to prolong

protrude   to stick out; to project

proverbial   well-known

provident   having foresight

provincial   countrified; narrow; limited

provisional   temporary

proviso   a condition; a stipulation

provoke   to anger; to irritate; to annoy

prowess   skill; strength; daring

proximity   nearness in place or time

proxy   one who acts in place of another

prude   an overly proper person

prudence   caution; good judgment

prune   to cut off or lop off such as twigs, branches, or roots

prurient   lustful; obscene; lewd

pseudo   false; counterfeit

pseudonym   a fake or assumed name

psyche   the human soul or spirit

puerile   childish; immature

pugilist   a boxer

pugnacious   eager to fight; quarrelsome

puissant   powerful; strong

pulchritude   beauty

pulmonary   pertaining to the lungs

pulverize   crush or grind into powder; totally destroy

pummel   to beat or thrash with the fists

pun   the use of words alike in sound but different in meaning

punctilious   very exact; precise

pundit   a learned man; an expert or authority

pungent   having a sharp taste or smell; severely critical or sarcastic

punitive   pertaining to punishment

puny   weak; inferior

purge   to cleanse; to purify

puritanical   strict; rigid; harsh

purloin   to steal

purport   to claim to be

purvey   to furnish; to supply

pusillanimous   cowardly; fearful

putative   supposed; believed

putrefy   to rot; to decay

pyre   a funeral fire in which the corpse is burned

pyretic   pertaining to fever

pyromaniac   one who likes to start fires; arsonist

Pyrrhic victory   success gained at too high a cost

QUACK – QUOTIDIAN

quack   an untrained doctor; a pretender to any skill

quadruped   a four-footed animal

quaff   to gulp; to drink in large quantities

quagmire   a swamp; a difficult situation

quail   to lose courage; to shrink with fear

quaint   strange or unusual in a pleasing or amusing way

qualm   a feeling of uneasiness

quandary   a puzzling situation; a dilemma

quarry   an animal that is being hunted down

quash   to cancel; to set aside (as an indictment)

quasi   resembling; seeming

quaver   to tremble; to shake

quay   a wharf

queasy   uneasy; nauseated

quell   to subdue; to calm down

querulous   complaining

query   a question

quest   a search

queue   a line of people waiting their turn

quibble   petty objection or argument

quiddity   essential quality

quidnunc   a gossip or busybody

quiescent   at rest; motionless

quietus   finishing stroke; anything that ends an activity

quintessence   the pure and concentrated essence of something

quip   a witty or sarcastic remark

quirk   a peculiar characteristic of a person ; a sudden twist or turn

quiver   to tremble; to shake

quixotic   extremely idealistic; romantic; not practical

quizzical   odd; questioning; puzzled

quotidian   daily

RABBLE – RUTHLESS

rabble   mob; disorderly crowd

rabid   intense; furious or raging; mad

rack   to torment; to torture

raconteur   storyteller

radical   extreme; complete; violent

rail   (*at* or *against*) to complain bitterly

raillery   good-humored ridicule

raiment   clothing; garments

rakish   carefree; lively

rambunctious   restless; hard to control

ramification   a result; a consequence; a branch

rampant   widespread; raging

ramshackle   shaky; ready to fall apart

rancid   having a bad taste or smell; stale; repulsive

rancor   bitter resentment; hatred

rankle   to cause irritation; to fester

rant   to speak in a loud or violent manner

rapacious   taking by force; greedy

rapport   a close relationship; harmony

rapt   completely absorbed in; overcome with joy, love, etc.

rarefy   to make less dense; to refine

rash   (*two meanings*)   a skin irritation (*noun*); reckless or daring (*adjective*)

raspy   harsh; grating

ratify   to officially approve of

ratiocinate   to reason

ration   a fixed portion; a share

rational   sensible; reasonable

rationalize   to make an excuse for

raucous   irritating or harsh in sound

ravage   to damage; ruin

ravenous   extremely hungry; greedy

raze   to destroy; to level to the ground

realm   kingdom; region

rebuff   to refuse; to snub

rebuke   to scold; to blame

rebuttal   contradiction; opposing argument

recalcitrant   disobedient; hard to manage

recant   to withdraw or disavow a statement or opinion

recapitulate   to summarize; repeat briefly

recede   to go or move back; to withdraw

recess   (*two meanings*)   a cut or notch in something; a pause or rest

recidivist   a person who goes back to crime

recipient   one who receives

reciprocal   interchangeable; mutual

reciprocate   to give in return

recluse   hermit; one who shuts himself off from the world

recoil   to retreat; to draw back

reconcile   to bring into agreement or harmony

recondite   difficult to understand; profound

reconnoiter   to survey; to check out in advance

recount   to tell or relate, as a story

recreant   coward; traitor

recrimination   countercharge

rectify   to correct; to make right

rectitude   honesty; moral uprightness

recumbent   lying down; reclining

recuperate   to get well

recur   to happen again

redemption   deliverance from sin; a rescue

redolent   having a pleasant odor

redoubtable   formidable; commanding respect

redress   to set right; to remedy

redundant   repetitious; unnecessary

reek   to give off; emit

refractory   stubborn; hard to manage

refulgent   shining; glowing

refurbish   to make new; to freshen up

refute   to prove wrong, such as an opinion

regal   pertaining to a king; splendid

regale   to entertain

regenerate   to re-create; to reform morally; to replace a lost part of the body

regent   one who governs

regicide   the killing of a king

regime   a system of government

regimen   a regular system (of exercise, diet, etc.)

regressive   moving in a backward direction

regurgitate   to rush or surge back, as undigested food

rehabilitate   to restore to useful life

reimburse   to pay back

reiterate   to repeat

rejuvenate   to make young again

relegate   to banish; to assign to an inferior position

relentless   unyielding

relevant   significant; pertaining to the subject

relinquish   to give up; to let go

relish   to enjoy; to take delight in

remediable   capable of being corrected

remedial   intended to correct

reminisce   to remember

remiss   negligent

remission   a lessening; a forgiveness as of sins or offenses

remonstrate   to protest; to complain

remorse   regret for wrongdoing

remuneration   payment for a service

renaissance   rebirth; renewal; revival

renal   pertaining to the kidneys

rend   to split; to tear apart

rendezvous   a meeting; appointment

renegade   a deserter; a traitor

renege   to go back on one's word

renounce   to give up (a belief)

renovate   to make new; to repair

reparation   compensation; something done to make up for a wrong or injury done

repartee   a quick, witty reply

repast   a meal

repellent   something that drives away or wards off (insects, etc.)

repercussion   reaction; after-effect

repertoire   special skills or talents one possesses; collection

repine   to complain; to fret

replenish   to fill up again

replete   well-filled

repose   to rest; to sleep

reprehensible   deserving criticism or blame; shameful

repress   to control; to subdue

reprimand   to scold

reprisal   retaliation; revenge

reproach   to blame; to scold

reprobate   a wicked person

reproof   a rebuke

repudiate   to reject; to disown

repugnant   distasteful; disgusting

repulse   to drive back; to repel

reputed   supposed to be

requiem   funeral hymn; mass for the dead

requisite   required or necessary; indispensable

requite   to make a return or repayment

rescind   to cancel; to repeal

residue   that which remains

resilient   recovering quickly; elastic

resolute   very determined

resonance   fullness of sound

resourceful   able to deal effectively with problems

respite   a delay; a rest

resplendent   shining brightly; dazzling

restitution   repayment; a giving back

restive   restless; uneasy; impatient

restrain   to hold back; to control

résumé   a summary

resurge   to rise again

resurrection   revival; rebirth

resuscitate   to revive from apparent death or from unconsciousness

retaliation   revenge; repayment for an evil act

retentive   having a good memory; remembering

reticent   silent or reserved in manner

retinue   body of attendants or followers

retort   a short, witty reply

retract   to take back (a statement); to withdraw

retrench   to cut down or reduce expenses

retribution   deserved punishment

retrieve   to get or bring back

retroactive   applying to a period before a certain law was passed

retrogressive   going backwards; becoming worse

retrospect   (preceded by *in*) looking back on past events

revelation   something made known; a disclosure

revelry   noisy merrymaking

reverberate   to echo; to resound

revere   to honor; to respect

reverie   a daydream

revile   to abuse; to slander

rhetorical   concerned with mere style or effect

ribald   vulgar; indecent

rife   frequently occurring; widespread

rift   a break or split

righteous   behaving justly or morally

rigorous   strict

risible   laughable; funny

risqué   daring or indecent; not proper

rite   a religious ceremony; a solemn act

robust   strong; hearty

rogue   a dishonest person; a scoundrel

rollicking   jolly; carefree

roster   a list

rote   (preceded with *by*) from memory, without thought for meaning

rotund   round; fat

rout   overwhelming defeat

rudimentary   elementary; basic

rue   to regret; to be sorrowful

ruffian   hoodlum; lawless person

ruffle   (*two meanings*)   a wrinkle or a ripple (*noun*); to irritate or to annoy (*verb*)

ruminate   to consider carefully; to meditate on

rupture   to break apart; to burst

ruse   a skillful trick or deception

rustic   pertaining to the country

rustle   (*two meanings*)   to steal; to make a swishing sound

ruthless   cruel; merciless

SACCHARINE – SYNTHETIC

---

saccharine   overly sweet

sacrilege   the violation of anything sacred

sacrosanct   extremely holy

sadistic   deriving pleasure from inflicting pain on others

saga   a long story of adventure

sagacious   wise

sage   a wise person

salacious   obscene; lusty

salient   significant; conspicuous

saline   salty

sallow   sickly pale

salubrious   healthful

salutary   healthful; wholesome

salutatory   a welcoming address, as at a graduation

salvage   to rescue; to save from destruction

sanctimonious   hypocritical in regard to religious belief

sanction   to authorize; to give permission

sangfroid   calmness; composure

sanguinary   bloody

sanguine   cheerful; optimistic

sapient   wise

sardonic   mocking; scornful

sartorial   pertaining to clothes or tailoring

satiated   satisfied; filled up

satirical   sarcastic; ironic

saturate   to soak; to fill up

saturnine   gloomy; sluggish

saunter   to stroll; to walk leisurely

savant   a person of extensive learning

savoir faire   tact; knowledge of just what to do in any situation

savor   to enjoy, as by taste or smell

scant   inadequate in size or amount

scapegoat   one who takes the blame for others

scathing   extremely severe or harsh, such as a remark

schism   a split or break

scintilla   a tiny amount; a speck

scintillate   to sparkle; to twinkle

scion   an offspring; a descendant

scoff   to ridicule

scope   range; extent

scourge   a whip or a lash; a person or thing that punishes or destroys

scrupulous   honest; ethical; precise

scrutinize   to examine closely

scurrilous   coarsely abusive; vulgar

scurry   run about; to hurry

scuttle   to sink (a ship); to abandon

sear   to burn; to scorch

sebaceous   fatty

seclude   to keep apart; to isolate

secrete   to hide or conceal

secular   worldly; non-religious

sedate   quiet; calm; serious

sedentary   sitting most of the time

sediment   material that settles on the bottom; residue

sedition   rebellion

sedulous   hard-working; industrious; diligent

seedy   run-down; shabby

seethe   to boil; to be violently agitated

seismic   pertaining to earthquakes

semblance   outward appearance

senile   pertaining to mental weakness due to old age

sensate   pertaining to feeling

sensual   pertaining to enjoyment of food and sex

sensuous   pertaining to enjoyment of art, music, etc.

sententious   concise; including proverbs and brief remarks

sentient   conscious; capable of feeling

sentinel a guard

sepulcher tomb; burial vault

sequel an event or literary work that follows a previous one

sequester to separate; to set aside

seraphic angelic; pure

serendipity a talent for making desirable discoveries by accident

serene calm; peaceful

serpentine winding

serrated having tooth-like edges

servile like a slave

servitude slavery; bondage

sever to cut in two; to separate

shackle to keep prisoner; to restrain

sham a pretense

shambles a slaughterhouse; great disorder

shard a fragment

sheepish embarrassed; bashful

shibboleth a slogan; a password

shiftless lazy; inefficient

shoal a shallow place in the water; a reef

shortcomings defects; deficiencies

shrew a nagging, bad-tempered woman

shroud a cloth or sheet in which a corpse is wrapped for burial

sibilant hissing

sibling a brother or sister

simian pertaining to an ape or monkey

simile a comparison using *like* or *as*

simony the sin of buying or selling church benefits

simper to smile in a silly way

simulacrum an image; a likeness

simulate to pretend; to imitate

simultaneous occurring at the same time

sinecure job with no responsibility

sinewy tough; firm; strong

singular extraordinary; remarkable; exceptional

sinister threatening evil; ominous

sinuous curving; winding

siren an attractive but dangerous woman

skeptic one who doubts

skinflint stingy person; miser

skittish restless; excitable; nervous

skulduggery trickery; deception

skulk to sneak around; to lie in hiding

slacken become loose; to relax

slake to lessen (thirst, desire, anger, etc.) by satisfying; to quench

slander to make a false statement against someone

slattern an untidy woman

sleazy cheap; flimsy

sleek smooth and shiny

slither to slide or glide

slothful lazy

slough (*off*) to discard; to shed

slovenly untidy; dirty; careless

smirk to smile in an affected or offensive way

smite to strike forcefully

smolder to burn without flame; to keep feelings concealed

smug self-satisfied

snare to trap

sneer to look at with contempt; to scorn; to deride

snicker to laugh in a half-suppressed way

snippet a small fragment

snivel to whine; to complain

sober not drunk; serious

sobriquet nickname; assumed name

sodden soaked; damp

sojourn a brief stay or visit

solace comfort

solar pertaining to the sun

solecism ungrammatical usage; an error or inconsistency

solicit to ask; to seek; to try to get an order in business

solicitude concern; anxiety

soliloquy act of talking to oneself

solipsistic pertaining to the theory that only oneself exists or can be proved to exist

solitude loneliness

solon a wise man

solvent (*two meanings*) having the ability to pay a debt (*adjective*); a substance that dissolves another (*noun*)

somber dark; gloomy

somnambulate walk in one's sleep

somniferous causing sleep

somnolent drowsy; sleepy

sonorous   producing a deep, rich sound

sophistry   a deceptive, tricky argument

sophomoric   immature; pretentious

soporific   causing sleep

sordid   dirty; filthy

sot   a drunkard

sobriquet   nickname; assumed name

sovereign   a monarch or other supreme ruler

spacious   roomy; convenient

Spartan   warlike; brave; disciplined

spasm   a sudden burst of energy

specious   not genuine; pleasing to the eye but deceptive

specter   a ghost; a phantom

speculate   (*two meanings*)   to meditate; to participate in a risky business transaction

sphinx   person who is difficult to understand

splenetic   bad-tempered; irritable

sporadic   infrequent; irregular

spry   full of life; active

spume   foam

spurious   deceitful; counterfeit

spurn   to reject

squalid   filthy; dirty

staccato   made up of short, abrupt sounds

stagnant   not flowing; stale; sluggish

staid   sedate; settled

stalemate   a deadlock; a draw

stalwart   strong; sturdy

stamina   endurance; resistance to fatigue

stance   attitude; posture

stark   complete; harsh; severe

static   inactive; motionless

stationary   standing still; not moving

statute   law; rule

steadfast   firm in purpose; dependable; constant

stench   a foul smell

stentorian   very loud

stereotyped   not original; commonplace

sterling   of high quality; excellent

stigma   mark of disgrace

stilted   artificially formal

stint   to be sparing; to conserve

stipend   salary

stipulate   to specify; to arrange definitely

stoic   showing no emotion; indifferent to pleasure or pain

stolid   impassive; having little emotion

strait   a position of difficulty; a narrow passage of water

stratagem   a plan, scheme, or trick

strew   to spread about; to scatter

striated   striped; marked with lines

stricture   negative criticism; a restriction

strident   harsh sounding; loud and shrill

stringent   strict; tight

strut   to walk in a proud manner; to show off

stultify   make absurd or ridiculous; render worthless

stupefy   to stun; to amaze

stygian   dark; gloomy

stymie   to hinder; to block

suave   polished; sophisticated

sub rosa   secretly; confidentially

subaqueous   underwater

subjective   not objective; personal

subjugate   to conquer

sublimate   to make a person act noble or moral

sublime   majestic; elevated or lofty in thought

subliminal   subconscious; unaware

submissive   yielding; humbly obedient

subordinate   of lower rank

suborn   to hire for an unlawful act

subsequent   following; occurring later

subservient   submissive; helpful, in an inferior capacity

subside   to become quiet; to settle down

subsidiary   auxiliary; supplementary; serving to assist

substantiate   to prove; to confirm; to support

subterfuge   trickery; deceit

subterranean   underground

subversive   tending to overthrow or undermine

succinct   concise; brief and to the point

succor   assistance; help; relief

succulent   juicy

succumb   to yield; to give in

suffrage   the right to vote

sullen   gloomy; showing irritation

sully   to soil, stain, or tarnish

sultry hot and moist

sumptuous luxurious; lavish; extravagant

sundry various; assorted

superannuated retired because of old age

supercilious proud; haughty

superficial on the surface; shallow

superfluous excessive; unnecessary

supernal heavenly

supernumerary extra; more than necessary

supersede to take the place of

supervene to take place or occur unexpectedly

supine lying on the back

supplant to replace

supple flexible

suppliant begging; asking humbly

supplicate to pray humbly; to beg

surfeit an excessive amount

surly rude; bad-tempered

surmise to guess

surmount to go beyond; to overcome

surreptitious acting in a sneaky way

surrogate substitute

surveillance supervision; close watch

sustenance nourishment

susurration whispering; murmuring

suture to join together, as with stitches

svelte slender; graceful

swarthy dark-complexioned

swathe to wrap closely or fully

sybarite one who is fond of luxuries and pleasure

sycophant a flatterer; a parasite

sylvan wooded; pertaining to the forest

symbiosis mutual dependence between two different organisms

symmetrical balanced; well-proportioned

synchronize to happen at the same time

synthesis a combination; a fusion

synthetic not genuine; artificial

TABLEAU – TYRO

---

tableau dramatic scene or picture

taboo forbidden; unacceptable

tabulation a systematic listing by columns or rows

tacit silent; not expressed

taciturn speaking very little

tactics plan; method; strategy

tactile pertaining to sense of touch

taint to infect; to harm a person's reputation

talisman a good luck charm

tally to count; to make a record of

tangent touching

tangible real; capable of being touched

tantalize to tease or torment

tantamount equivalent to

tarn a small lake or pool

tarnish to soil; to discolor; to stain

tarry to linger; to delay

taunt to ridicule; to tease

taurine like a bull

taut tight; tense

tawdry cheap; showy; flashy

tawny yellowish-brown

tedious boring; monotonous

teeming overfilled; pouring out

temerity reckless boldness; rashness

temper (*verb*) to moderate; to soften or tone down

temperate not extreme; moderate

temporal pertaining to time

temporize to be indecisive; to be evasive; to delay an action

tenacious holding on; persistent; stubborn

tendentious biased; favoring a cause

tenet a doctrine; a belief

tensile capable of being stretched; elastic

tentative for the time being; experimental

tenuous slender; flimsy; without substance

tenure the holding or possessing of anything

tepid lukewarm

terminate to put an end to; to conclude

terminus a boundary; a limit

terpsichorean pertaining to dancing

terrestrial earthly; living on land

terse brief; to the point

testy irritable

thanatology the study of death and dying

theocracy government by religious leaders

therapeutic pertaining to the treatment and curing of disease

thermal pertaining to heat

thesaurus a book of synonyms and antonyms; a dictionary

thespian an actor

thrall a slave

threnody a funeral song

throes a violent struggle; pains (*of childbirth*); agony (*of death*)

throng a crowd

thwart to prevent or hinder

timorous fearful; cowardly

tinge a faint color; a trace

tirade a long angry speech; an outburst of bitter denunciation

titanic huge

titillate to tickle; to excite agreeably

titter to laugh in a self-conscious or nervous way

token (*two meanings*) sign or symbol (*noun*); slight or unimportant (*adjective*)

tome large, heavy book

toothsome tasty

topple to overturn; to fall over

torpid inactive; sluggish

torsion twisting; bending

torso the human body excluding the head and limbs

tortuous twisting; winding

torturous causing extreme pain

touchstone standard; a test or criterion for quality

toxic poisonous; harmful

tractable easy to manage

traduce to speak badly of; to slander

trait a characteristic; a quality

tranquil calm; peaceful

transcend to go beyond; to overcome

transcendental supernatural; going beyond ordinary experience or belief

trangression violation of a rule or law

transient temporary; passing

transitory lasting a short time; brief

translucent letting light pass through

transmute to change from one form to another; to transform

transparent easily seen through; clear

transpire to be revealed or become known; to occur

trappings articles of dress; equipment

trauma a shock; an after-effect

travail very hard work; intense pain

travesty an absurd or inadequate imitation

treacherous dangerous; deceptive; disloyal

treatise a book or writing about some particular subject

treble three times as much

tremulous trembling; quivering

trenchant keen or incisive; vigorous; effective

trepidation fear; alarm

trespass to invade; to enter wrongfully

tribulation trouble

tributary a stream flowing into a river

tribute a gift; an acknowledgment to show admiration

trinity group of three

trite worn out; stale; commonplace

trivia matters or things that are very unimportant; trivialities

truckle (*to*) to submit; to yield

truculent savage; brutal; cruel

truism a self-evident, obvious truth

truncate to shorten; to cut off

truncheon a club

tryst a secret meeting

tumid swollen; bulging

tumult great noise and confusion

turbid muddy; unclear

turbulence wild disorder; violent motion

turgid swollen

turmoil confusion

turpitude baseness; shameful behavior

tussle a struggle; a fight

tutelage instruction

twain two

tycoon a wealthy businessman

tyro a beginner

UBIQUITOUS – UXORIOUS

ubiquitous present everywhere

ulcerous infected

ulterior lying beyond; hidden

ultimatum a final demand or proposal

umbrage a feeling of resentment

unanimity agreement; oneness

unassailable unable to be attacked

uncanny weird; strange

unconscionable unreasonable; excessive

uncouth crude; clumsy

unctuous oily; excessively polite

undue inappropriate; unreasonable

undulate to move or sway in wavelike motion

unequivocal clear; definite

unerring accurate; not going astray or missing the mark

unfledged not feathered; immature

unilateral one-sided

unimpeachable above suspicion; unquestionable

uninhibited free; not restricted

unique being the only one of its kind

unison harmony; agreement

universal broad; general; effective everywhere or in all cases

unkempt untidy; sloppy

unmindful unaware

unmitigated absolute; not lessened

unobtrusive inconspicuous; not noticeable

unruly not manageable; disorderly

unsavory unpleasant to taste or smell

unscathed unharmed; uninjured

unseemly not in good taste

untenable unable to be defended or upheld

unwieldy hard to manage because of size or weight

unwitting unintentional; unaware

upbraid to scold; to find fault with

uproarious loud; outrageously funny

urbane refined; suave; citified

urchin a mischievous child

ursine like a bear

usurp to seize illegally

usury excessive amount of money charged as interest

utilitarian useful; practical

utopian perfect; ideal

uxorious overly fond of one's wife

VACILLATE – VULPINE

vacillate to sway back and forth; to hesitate in making a decision

vagabond a wanderer

vagary an odd notion; an unpredictable action

vagrant a homeless person; a wanderer

vain conceited; excessively proud about one's appearance

vainglorious boastfully proud

valedictory saying farewell

valiant courageous; brave

valid true; logical; sound

validate to approve; to confirm

valor courage; bravery

vanguard the front part

vanity excessive pride; conceit

vanquish to defeat

vapid uninteresting; tasteless; tedious

variegated having different colors; diversified

vaunt to brag or boast

veer to change direction

vegetate lead a dull, inactive life

vehement forceful; furious

velocity speed

venal corrupt; able to be bribed

vendetta bitter quarrel or feud

veneer an outward show that misrepresents

venerable worthy of respect

venerate to regard with respect

venial excusable; minor

venomous poisonous; spiteful; malicious

vent to give release to; to be relieved of a feeling

venturesome daring; adventurous; risky

veracious truthful; honest

verbatim word for word

verbiage overabundance of words

verbose wordy

verdant green; flourishing

verisimilitude the appearance of truth

veritable true; actual; genuine

verity truth

vernacular native language; informal speech

vernal pertaining to spring

versatile good at many things; serving many purposes

vertex top; highest point

vertiginous whirling; dizzy; unstable

verve energy; enthusiasm

vestige a trace; visible evidence of something that is no longer present

veteran an experienced person

vex to irritate; to annoy

viable capable of living; workable; practicable

viaduct a bridge

viands various foods

vicarious taking the place of another person or thing; substituted

viceroy a representative; a deputy appointed by a sovereign to rule a province

vicissitudes unpredictable changes; ups and downs

victimize to make a victim of; to swindle or cheat

victuals food

vie to compete

vigilant watchful

vignette a short literary sketch; a decorative design

vilify to speak evil of; to defame

vindicate to clear of guilt or blame

vindictive spiteful; seeking revenge

vintage representative of the best (*especially of wines*)

viper a poisonous snake; a malignant or spiteful person

virago a loud, bad-tempered woman; a shrew

virile masculine; manly

virtuoso an expert; a skilled person

virulent deadly; poisonous; harmful

visage the face; appearance

visceral pertaining to instinctive rather than intellectual motivation

viscous sticky

vista a distant view

vitiate to weaken; to impair

vitreous of or like glass

vitriolic biting; sharp; bitter

vituperate to scold; to criticize

vivify to give life to; to enliven

vixen female fox; ill-tempered woman

vociferous loud; shouting

vogue fashion; style

volant capable of flying

volatile unstable; explosive

volition free will

voluble talkative; fluent

voluminous large; copious

voluptuous sensual; shapely

voracious extremely hungry; greedy

votary loyal follower

vouchsafe to grant; to allow or permit

vulgar showing poor taste or manners

vulnerable defenseless; open to attack

vulpine like a fox; clever

WAIF – ZEST

waif a homeless person

waive to give up (a right)

wallow to indulge oneself; to roll around in

wan pale; weak; tired

wane to gradually decrease in size or intensity

wangle to manipulate; to obtain by scheming or by underhand methods

wanton reckless; immoral

warble to sing melodiously

warp to bend out of shape; to pervert

wary cautious; watchful

wastrel a spendthrift; one who wastes

waver to sway; to be uncertain

wax to grow in size or intensity

weighty   of utmost importance

wend   to direct one's way

wheedle   to coax or to persuade

whet   to stimulate; to make sharp

whimsical   unpredictable; changeable

wield   to handle (*a tool*); to exercise control (*over others*)

willful   contrary; stubborn

wily   tricky; sly

wince   to shrink, as in pain, fear, etc; to flinch

windfall   unexpected good fortune

winsome   pleasing; charming

withal   in spite of all; nevertheless

wizened   withered; shriveled

woe   sorrow; grief

wolfish   ferocious

wont   (*to*) accustomed (*adjective*)

workaday   everyday; ordinary

wraith   a ghost; an apparition

wrangle   to quarrel

wrath   anger; rage

wrench   to twist; to pull

wrest   to take away by force

wroth   angry

wrought   produced or shaped

wry   produced by distorting the face (*a wry grin*); ironic (*wry humor*)

xenophobia   fear of foreigners or strangers

xyloid   pertaining to wood

yen   an intense desire; a longing

yoke   to join together; to link

zany   comical; clownishly crazy

zeal   great enthusiasm

zealot   a fanatic

zenith   the highest point

zephyr   a gentle, mild breeze

zest   hearty enjoyment

100 Tests to Strengthen Your Vocabulary

This vocabulary section consists of 100 vocabulary tests. Each test consists of 10 multiple-choice questions, including SAT-type words. Practically all the words whose meanings you are tested on in these 100 tests are among the 3400 words in the SAT Word List beginning on page 119.

These 100 vocabulary tests provide you with an opportunity of making sure that you really know the meanings of the hundreds of words you are being tested on. Several of these words are likely to appear on your actual SAT test.

We suggest that you use the following procedure while you are taking these 100 tests:

STEP 1. Take Vocabulary Test 1.

STEP 2. Turn to the Answer Keys beginning on page 191.

STEP 3. For each word that you got wrong, jot down the word on a "Special List" of your own.

STEP 4. Make up a sentence using each word that you got wrong on Vocabulary Test 1.

STEP 5. Repeat the above procedure for Vocabulary Tests 2, 3, 4—right on through Vocabulary Test 100.

STEP 6. When you have finished taking the 100 Vocabulary Tests, go back to your "Special List." See whether you really know the meanings of these words by having someone else test you on them. For those words you still have trouble with, look up their meanings in a dictionary. Compose three sentences including each of these "troublemakers."

Gentle reminder: Each correct answer in the Antonym section alone—25 questions—adds approximately 10 additional points to your SAT Verbal score. Moreover, knowing the meanings of many of the words in these 100 tests is likely to raise your score substantially in the other Verbal sections—Analogies, Sentence Completions, and Reading Comprehension.

DIRECTIONS FOR THE 100 VOCABULARY TESTS

Each vocabulary question consists of a word in capital letters, followed by five lettered words or phrases. Choose the word or phrase that is most nearly the *same* in meaning as the word in capital letters. Since some of the questions require you to distinguish fine shades of meaning, consider all choices before deciding which is best.

Vocabulary Test 1

1. FILCH (A) hide (B) swindle (C) drop (D) steal (E) covet

2. URBANE (A) crowded (B) polished (C) rural (D) friendly (E) prominent

3. DECANT (A) bisect (B) speak wildly (C) bequeath (D) pour off (E) abuse verbally

4. ANTITHESIS (A) contrast (B) conclusion (C) resemblance (D) examination (E) dislike

5. HERETICAL (A) heathenish (B) impractical (C) quaint (D) rash (E) unorthodox

6. COALESCE (A) associate (B) combine (C) contact (D) conspire (E) cover

7. CHARLATAN (A) clown (B) philanthropist (C) jester (D) dressmaker (E) quack

8. GAUCHE (A) clumsy (B) stupid (C) feeble-minded (D) impudent (E) foreign

9. REDUNDANT (A) necessary (B) plentiful (C) sufficient (D) diminishing (E) superfluous

10. ATROPHY (A) lose leaves (B) soften (C) waste away (D) grow (E) spread

Vocabulary Test 2

1. RESILIENCE (A) submission (B) elasticity (C) vigor (D) determination (E) recovery

2. ANALOGY (A) similarity (B) transposition (C) variety (D) distinction (E) appropriateness

3. FACETIOUS (A) obscene (B) shrewd (C) impolite (D) complimentary (E) witty

4. DIATRIBE (A) debate (B) monologue (C) oration (D) tirade (E) conversation

5. MALEDICTION (A) curse (B) mispronunciation (C) grammatical error (D) tactless remark (E) epitaph

6. AGGREGATE (A) result (B) difference (C) quotient (D) product (E) sum

7. APLOMB (A) caution (B) timidity (C) self-assurance (D) shortsightedness (E) self-restraint

8. THERAPEUTIC (A) curative (B) restful (C) warm (D) stimulating (E) professional

9. TRANSMUTE (A) remove (B) change (C) duplicate (D) carry (E) explain

10. ATTRITION (A) annihilation (B) encirclement (C) counter attack (D) appeasement (E) wearing down

Vocabulary Test 3

1. TRUNCATE (A) divide equally (B) end swiftly (C) cut off (D) act cruelly (E) cancel

2. OSCILLATE (A) confuse (B) kiss (C) turn (D) vibrate (E) whirl

3. INOCULATE (A) make harmless (B) infect (C) cure (D) overcome (E) darken

4. PERUSAL (A) approval (B) estimate (C) reading (D) translation (E) computation

5. QUERULOUS (A) peculiar (B) fretful (C) inquisitive (D) shivering (E) annoying

6. AUTONOMY (A) tyranny (B) independence (C) plebiscite (D) minority (E) dictatorship

7. MACHINATIONS (A) inventions (B) ideas (C) mysteries (D) plots (E) alliances

8. SCHISM (A) government (B) religion (C) division (D) combination (E) coalition

9. PUSILLANIMOUS (A) cowardly (B) extraordinary (C) ailing (D) evil-intentioned (E) excitable

10. TERMINOLOGY (A) technicality (B) finality (C) formality (D) explanation (E) nomenclature

Vocabulary Test 4

1. STIPEND (A) increment (B) bonus (C) commission (D) gift (E) salary

2. LITIGATION (A) publication (B) argument (C) endeavor (D) lawsuit (E) ceremony

3. FIASCO (A) disappointment (B) turning point (C) loss (D) celebration (E) complete failure

4. VAGARY (A) caprice (B) confusion (C) extravagance (D) loss of memory (E) shiftlessness

5. GRAPHIC (A) serious (B) concise (C) short (D) detailed (E) vivid

6. CONNOTATION (A) implication (B) footnote (C) derivation (D) comment (E) definition

7. TORTUOUS (A) crooked (B) difficult (C) painful (D) impassable (E) slow

8. FULMINATING (A) throbbing (B) pointed (C) wavelike (D) thundering (E) bubbling

9. CIRCUMVENT (A) freshen (B) change (C) control (D) harass (E) frustrate

10. CARTEL (A) rationing plan (B) world government (C) industrial pool (D) skilled craft (E) instrument of credit

Vocabulary Test 5

1. PROLIFIC (A) meager (B) obedient (C) fertile (D) hardy (E) scanty

2. ASSUAGE (A) create (B) ease (C) enlarge (D) prohibit (E) rub out

3. DECORUM (A) wit (B) charm (C) adornment (D) seemliness (E) charity

4. PHLEGMATIC (A) tolerant (B) careless (C) sensitive (D) stolid (E) sick

5. INTREPID (A) quick-witted (B) brutal (C) fearless (D) torrid (E) hearty

6. ACTUATE (A) frighten (B) direct (C) isolate (D) dismay (E) impel

7. MOUNTEBANK (A) trickster (B) courier (C) scholar (D) cashier (E) pawnbroker

8. LACONIC (A) terse (B) informal (C) convincing (D) interesting (E) tedious

9. BOORISH (A) sporting (B) tiresome (C) argumentative (D) monotonous (E) rude

10. ERUDITE (A) modest (B) egotistical (C) learned (D) needless (E) experienced

Vocabulary Test 6

1. ACRIMONIOUS (A) repulsive (B) enchanting (C) stinging (D) snobbish (E) disgusting

2. EMBRYONIC (A) hereditary (B) arrested (C) developed (D) functioning (E) rudimentary

3. INEXORABLE (A) unfavorable (B) permanent (C) crude (D) relentless (E) incomplete

4. PROTRACTED (A) boring (B) condensed (C) prolonged (D) comprehensive (E) measured

5. OBSEQUIOUS (A) courteous (B) fawning (C) respectful (D) overbearing (E) inexperienced

6. LOQUACIOUS (A) queer (B) logical (C) gracious (D) rural (E) voluble

7. PUGNACIOUS (A) bold (B) combative (C) brawny (D) pug-nosed (E) valiant

8. ASTRINGENT (A) bossy (B) musty (C) flexible (D) corrosive (E) contracting

9. ESCARPMENT (A) threat (B) limbo (C) cliff (D) behemoth (E) blight

10. AMENITIES (A) prayers (B) ceremonies (C) pageantries (D) pleasantries (E) social functions

Vocabulary Test 7

1. DEPLORE (A) condone (B) forget (C) forgive (D) deny (E) regret

2. BANAL (A) commonplace (B) flippant (C) pathetic (D) new (E) unexpected

3. ABACUS (A) casserole (B) blackboard (C) slide rule (D) adding device (E) long spear

4. SEISMISM (A) inundation (B) tide (C) volcano (D) earthquake (E) tornado

5. AMELIORATE (A) favor (B) improve (C) interfere (D) learn (E) straddle

6. CHARY (A) burned (B) careful (C) comfortable (D) fascinating (E) gay

7. CORPULENT (A) dead (B) fat (C) full (D) organized (E) similar

8. ENIGMA (A) ambition (B) foreigner (C) instrument (D) officer (E) riddle

9. INEPT (A) awkward (B) intelligent (C) ticklish (D) tawdry (E) uninteresting

10. INVETERATE (A) evil (B) habitual (C) inconsiderate (D) reformed (E) unintentional

Vocabulary Test 8

1. OBEISANCE (A) salary (B) justification (C) conduct (D) deference (E) forethought

2. PEDANTIC (A) stilted (B) odd (C) footworn (D) selfish (E) sincere

3. PETULANT (A) lazy (B) loving (C) patient (D) peevish (E) wary

4. PROCLIVITY (A) backwardness (B) edict (C) rainfall (D) slope (E) tendency

5. TRENCHANT (A) keen (B) good (C) edible (D) light (E) subterranean

6. VAPID (A) carefree (B) crazy (C) insipid (D) spotty (E) speedy

7. PROGNOSTICATE (A) forecast (B) ravish (C) salute (D) scoff (E) succeed

8. PROPRIETY (A) advancement (B) atonement (C) fitness (D) sobriety (E) use

9. PULCHRITUDE (A) beauty (B) character (C) generosity (D) intelligence (E) wickedness

10. SCRUPULOUS (A) drunken (B) ill (C) masterful (D) exact (E) stony

Vocabulary Test 9

1. INVARIABLE (A) diverse (B) eternal (C) fleeting (D) inescapable (E) uniform

2. VORACIOUS (A) excitable (B) honest (C) greedy (D) inclusive (E) circular

3. CONCENTRATE (A) agitate (B) protest (C) debate (D) harden (E) consolidate

4. PLAGIARIZE (A) annoy (B) borrow (C) steal ideas (D) imitate poorly (E) impede

5. CORTEGE (A) advisers (B) official papers (C) slaves (D) retinue (E) personal effects

6. ANTIPATHY (A) sympathy (B) detachment (C) aversion (D) amazement (E) opposition

7. DEMUR (A) object (B) agree (C) murmur (D) discard (E) consider

8. PARAGON (A) dummy (B) lover (C) image (D) model (E) favorite

9. FINITE (A) impure (B) firm (C) minute (D) limited (E) unbounded

10. ANARCHY (A) laissez-faire (B) motor-mindedness (C) pacifism (D) lawless confusion (E) self-sufficiency

Vocabulary Test 10

1. DISCRIMINATION (A) acquittal (B) insight (C) caution (D) indiscretion (E) distortion

2. INVECTIVE (A) richness (B) goal (C) solemn oath (D) praise (E) verbal abuse

3. ADROIT (A) hostile (B) serene (C) pompous (D) skillful (E) allergic

4. DISTRESS (A) injury (B) contortion (C) suffering (D) convulsion (E) aggravation

5. DILETTANTE (A) epicure (B) dabbler (C) procrastinator (D) literary genius (E) playboy

6. PROVISIONAL (A) military (B) tentative (C) absentee (D) democratic (E) appointed

7. CONDIMENT (A) ledger (B) ore (C) telegraph device (D) musical instrument (E) spice

8. RECALCITRANT (A) insincere (B) obstinate (C) crafty (D) conservative (E) reconcilable

9. BON MOT (A) witticism (B) pun (C) praise (D) last word (E) exact meaning

10. ACCOUTREMENTS (A) sealed orders (B) equipment (C) cartons (D) correspondence (E) financial records

Vocabulary Test 11

1. HYPOTHESIS (A) assumption (B) proof (C) estimate (D) random guess (E) established truth

2. ALACRITY (A) slowness (B) indecision (C) caution (D) promptness (E) fearlessness

3. JETTISON (A) throw overboard (B) dismantle (C) scuttle (D) unload cargo (E) camouflage

4. VACILLATE (A) glitter (B) swerve (C) surrender (D) soften (E) waver

5. ASTUTE (A) shrewd (B) futile (C) potent (D) provocative (E) ruthless

6. PROVISO (A) final treaty (B) condition (C) demand (D) official document (E) proclamation

7. MACABRE (A) gruesome (B) meager (C) sordid (D) fantastic (E) cringing

8. AUGMENT (A) curtail (B) change (C) restore (D) conceal (E) increase

9. INTEGRAL (A) useful (B) powerful (C) essential (D) mathematical (E) indestructible

10. IMPUNITY (A) shamelessness (B) power of action (C) self-reliance (D) haughtiness (E) exemption from punishment

Vocabulary Test 12

1. LATENT (A) inherent (B) lazy (C) dormant (D) crushed (E) anticipated

2. OBDURATE (A) patient (B) stupid (C) rude (D) stubborn (E) tolerant

3. BELLICOSE (A) boastful (B) warlike (C) sluggish (D) fantastic (E) oriental

4. ARROYO (A) cliff (B) plain (C) ranch (D) gully (E) cactus

5. AUGUR (A) enrage (B) foretell (C) suggest (D) evaluate (E) minimize

6. CONTRITE (A) infectious (B) worried (C) penitent (D) sympathetic (E) tolerant

7. PETULANT (A) silly (B) gay (C) sarcastic (D) officious (E) quarrelsome

8. PAEAN (A) prize (B) song of praise (C) decoration (D) certificate (E) story of heroism

9. EXOTIC (A) romantic (B) exciting (C) wealthy (D) strange (E) tropical

10. ARCHIPELAGO (A) slender isthmus (B) long, narrow land mass (C) string of lakes (D) high, flat plain (E) group of small islands

Vocabulary Test 13

1. PREVARICATE   (A) hesitate   (B) lie
(C) protest   (D) ramble   (E) remain silent

2. INCREDULOUS   (A) argumentative
(B) imaginative   (C) indifferent   (D) irreligious
(E) skeptical

3. PLACATE   (A) amuse   (B) appease
(C) embroil   (D) pity   (E) reject

4. COGNIZANT   (A) afraid   (B) aware
(C) capable   (D) ignorant   (E) optimistic

5. DISSONANCE   (A) disapproval   (B) disaster
(C) discord   (D) disparity   (E) dissimilarity

6. IMMINENT   (A) declining   (B) distinguished
(C) impending   (D) terrifying   (E) unlikely

7. TORSION   (A) bending   (B) compressing
(C) sliding   (D) stretching   (E) twisting

8. ACCRUED   (A) added   (B) incidental
(C) miscellaneous   (D) special   (E) unearned

9. EFFRONTERY   (A) bad taste   (B) conceit
(C) dishonesty   (D) impudence
(E) snobbishness

10. ACQUIESCENCE   (A) advice   (B) advocacy
(C) compliance   (D) friendliness   (E) opposition

Vocabulary Test 14

1. RETICENT   (A) fidgety   (B) repetitious
(C) reserved   (D) restful   (E) truthful

2. STIPULATE   (A) bargain   (B) instigate
(C) prefer   (D) request   (E) specify

3. PSEUDO   (A) deep   (B) obvious
(C) pretended   (D) provoking   (E) spiritual

4. FLOTSAM   (A) dark sand   (B) fleet   (C) life
preserver   (D) shoreline   (E) wreckage

5. AWRY   (A) askew   (B) deplorable   (C) odd
(D) simple   (E) striking

6. NEFARIOUS   (A) clever   (B) necessary
(C) negligent   (D) short-sighted   (E) wicked

7. GLIB   (A) cheerful   (B) delightful   (C) dull
(D) fluent   (E) gloomy

8. PAUCITY   (A) abundance   (B) ease
(C) hardship   (D) lack   (E) stoppage

9. LUCRATIVE   (A) debasing   (B) fortunate
(C) influential   (D) monetary   (E) profitable

10. INDUBITABLE   (A) doubtful   (B) fraudulent
(C) honorable   (D) safe   (E) undeniable

Vocabulary Test 15

1. CONNIVANCE   (A) approval   (B) collusion
(C) conflict   (D) permission   (E) theft

2. SAVANT   (A) diplomat   (B) inventor
(C) learned man   (D) thrifty person
(E) wiseacre

3. INCIPIENT   (A) beginning   (B) dangerous
(C) hasty   (D) secret   (E) widespread

4. VIRILE   (A) honest   (B) loyal   (C) manly
(D) pugnacious   (E) virtuous

5. ASSIDUOUS   (A) courteous   (B) diligent
(C) discouraged   (D) frank   (E) slow

6. CATACLYSM   (A) blunder   (B) superstition
(C) treachery   (D) triumph   (E) upheaval

7. AUSPICIOUS   (A) condemnatory
(B) conspicuous   (C) favorable
(D) questionable   (E) spicy

8. SATIRE   (A) conversation   (B) criticism
(C) gossip   (D) irony   (E) jesting

9. VERNACULAR   (A) common speech
(B) correct usage   (C) long words   (D) oratory
(E) poetic style

10. EMOLUMENT   (A) capital
(B) compensation   (C) liabilities   (D) loss
(E) output

Vocabulary Test 16

1. TURGID   (A) dusty   (B) muddy   (C) rolling
(D) swollen   (E) tense

2. EXPUNGE   (A) clarify   (B) copy
(C) delete   (D) investigate   (E) underline

3. ETHNOLOGY   (A) causation   (B) morals
(C) social psychology   (D) study of races
(E) word analysis

4. DEDUCE   (A) diminish   (B) infer
(C) outline   (D) persuade   (E) subtract

5. PANORAMIC   (A) brilliant
(B) comprehensive   (C) pretty
(D) fluorescent   (E) unique

6. IGNOMINY   (A) disgrace   (B) isolation
(C) misfortune   (D) sorrow   (E) stupidity

7. RELEVANT   (A) ingenious   (B) inspiring
(C) obvious   (D) pertinent   (E) tentative

8. GAMUT   (A) game   (B) range   (C) risk
(D) organization   (E) plan

9. APPOSITE   (A) appropriate   (B) contrary
(C) different   (D) spontaneous   (E) tricky

10. AMBULATORY   (A) able to walk   (B) confined
to bed   (C) injured   (D) quarantined
(E) suffering from disease

Vocabulary Test 17

1. DISPARAGE   (A) belittle   (B) upgrade   (C) erase   (D) reform   (E) scatter

2. LIMPID   (A) calm   (B) clear   (C) crippled   (D) delightful   (E) opaque

3. DERISIVE   (A) dividing   (B) furnishing   (C) reflecting   (D) expressing ridicule   (E) suggesting

4. DEBILITATE   (A) encourage   (B) insinuate   (C) prepare   (D) turn away   (E) weaken

5. OPULENT   (A) fearful   (B) free   (C) oversized   (D) trustful   (E) wealthy

6. BLANDISHMENT   (A) dislike   (B) flattery   (C) ostentation   (D) praise   (E) rejection

7. CRYPTIC   (A) appealing   (B) arched   (C) deathly   (D) hidden   (E) intricate

8. RAUCOUS   (A) harsh   (B) loud   (C) querulous   (D) rational   (E) violent

9. AVIDITY   (A) friendliness   (B) greediness   (C) resentment   (D) speed   (E) thirst

10. EPITOME   (A) conclusion   (B) effort   (C) letter   (D) summary   (E) summit

Vocabulary Test 18

1. HIATUS   (A) branch   (B) disease   (C) gaiety   (D) insect   (E) break

2. PLENARY   (A) easy   (B) empty   (C) full   (D) rewarding   (E) untrustworthy

3. CAPRICIOUS   (A) active   (B) fickle   (C) opposed   (D) sheeplike   (E) slippery

4. SPECIOUS   (A) frank   (B) particular   (C) deceptive   (D) suspicious   (E) vigorous

5. EXTIRPATE   (A) besmirch   (B) clean   (C) eradicate   (D) favor   (E) subdivide

6. EQUIVOCAL   (A) doubtful   (B) medium   (C) monotonous   (D) musical   (E) well-balanced

7. RECOMPENSE   (A) approval   (B) blessing   (C) gift   (D) prayer   (E) reward

8. BEATIFIC   (A) giving bliss   (B) eager   (C) hesitant   (D) lovely   (E) sad

9. SANGUINE   (A) limp   (B) mechanical   (C) muddy   (D) red   (E) stealthy

10. SURCEASE   (A) end   (B) hope   (C) resignation   (D) sleep   (E) sweetness

Vocabulary Test 19

1. SENTIENT   (A) very emotional   (B) capable of feeling   (C) hostile   (D) sympathetic   (E) wise

2. OBVIATE   (A) grasp   (B) reform   (C) simplify   (D) smooth   (E) make unnecessary

3. PERUSE   (A) endure   (B) perpetuate   (C) read   (D) undertake   (E) urge

4. RANCOR   (A) dignity   (B) fierceness   (C) odor   (D) spite   (E) suspicion

5. TRUNCHEON   (A) baton   (B) canopy   (C) dish   (D) gun   (E) rejected food

6. SEBACEOUS   (A) fatty   (B) fluid   (C) porous   (D) transparent   (E) watery

7. DILATORY   (A) hairy   (B) happy-go-lucky   (C) ruined   (D) tardy   (E) well-to-do

8. EBULLITION   (A) bathing   (B) boiling   (C) refilling   (D) retiring   (E) returning

9. RELEGATE   (A) banish   (B) deprive   (C) designate   (D) report   (E) request

10. RECONDITE   (A) brittle   (B) concealed   (C) explored   (D) exposed   (E) uninformed

Vocabulary Test 20

1. REDOLENT   (A) odorous   (B) quick   (C) refined   (D) repulsive   (E) supple

2. DISSIMULATE   (A) confound   (B) pretend   (C) question   (D) separate   (E) strain

3. SUBLIME   (A) below par   (B) highly praised   (C) extreme   (D) noble   (E) settled

4. VIXEN   (A) fever   (B) quarrelsome woman   (C) sea bird   (D) sedative   (E) squirrel

5. SEDULOUS   (A) deceptive   (B) diligent   (C) grassy   (D) hateful   (E) sweet

6. VITIATE   (A) contaminate   (B) flavor   (C) freshen   (D) illuminate   (E) refer

7. CURVET   (A) come around   (B) follow   (C) leap   (D) restrain   (E) warp

8. ADVENTITIOUS   (A) accidental   (B) courageous   (C) favorable   (D) risk taking   (E) expected

9. ANIMUS   (A) animosity   (B) breath   (C) faith   (D) light   (E) poison

10. DESCRIED   (A) hailed   (B) rebuffed   (C) recalled   (D) regretted   (E) sighted

Vocabulary Test 21

1. ADULATION   (A) approach   (B) echo
(C) flattery   (D) gift   (E) imitation

2. SUBSEQUENTLY   (A) continually
(B) factually   (C) farther   (D) incidentally
(E) later

3. EXPURGATE   (A) amplify   (B) emphasize
(C) offend   (D) purify   (E) renew

4. LIAISON   (A) derivative   (B) liability
(C) link   (D) malice   (E) officer

5. SEDENTARY   (A) careful   (B) inactive
(C) notched   (D) pleasant   (E) uneventful

6. LASSITUDE   (A) childishness   (B) energy
(C) ignorance   (D) languor   (E) seriousness

7. ALTRUISTICALLY   (A) egotistically
(B) harmfully   (C) harshly   (D) highly
(E) unselfishly

8. PERFIDIOUS   (A) ambiguous   (B) flawless
(C) perforated   (D) treacherous   (E) trusting

9. CONSUMMATE   (A) achieve   (B) devour
(C) effuse   (D) ignite   (E) take

10. MUNIFICENTLY   (A) acutely
(B) awkwardly   (C) cruelly   (D) generously
(E) militarily

Vocabulary Test 22

1. LUGUBRIOUS   (A) calm   (B) doleful
(C) tepid   (D) wan   (E) warm

2. DISCONSOLATE   (A) desolate
(B) emotional   (C) incorrigible   (D) gloomy
(E) sad

3. COTERIE   (A) clique   (B) cure-all   (C) expert
judge   (D) forerunner   (E) society girl

4. CONDUIT   (A) doorway   (B) electric
generator   (C) power   (D) screen   (E) tube

5. SHIBBOLETH   (A) friend in need   (B) lonely
home   (C) personal complaint   (D) reason for
action   (E) watchword

6. EVANESCENT   (A) colorful
(B) consecrated   (C) converted   (D) empty
(E) vanishing

7. PARSIMONIOUS   (A) cautious
(B) ecclesiastical   (C) luxurious   (D) stingy
(E) unique

8. MACHIAVELLIAN   (A) cunning
(B) humble   (C) kingly   (D) machine-like
(E) saintly

9. COMPENDIUM   (A) amplification
(B) appendix   (C) expansion   (D) paraphrase
(E) summary

10. MEGALOMANIA   (A) desire for beauty
(B) mania for sympathy   (C) miserliness
(D) passion for grandeur   (E) pity for the poor

Vocabulary Test 23

1. TORPOR   (A) cyclone   (B) frenzy
(C) sluggishness   (D) strain   (E) twisting

2. ESOTERIC   (A) clear   (B) external
(C) popular   (D) secret   (E) uncertain

3. SUPERCILIOUSLY   (A) critically
(B) disdainfully   (C) hypersensitively
(D) naïvely   (E) softly

4. ABSTEMIOUS   (A) blatant   (B) exhilarating
(C) greedy   (D) temperate   (E) wasteful

5. KEN   (A) acceptance   (B) belief   (C) dune
(D) knowledge   (E) woody glen

6. GERMANE   (A) diseased   (B) foreign
(C) infected   (D) pertinent   (E) polished

7. VITUPERATION   (A) abuse
(B) appendectomy   (C) complication
(D) rejuvenation   (E) repeal

8. CHIMERICAL   (A) clever   (B) imaginary
(C) experimental   (D) foreign   (E) provisional

9. DULCIMER   (A) dolly   (B) doublet
(C) duenna   (D) gadget   (E) musical instrument

10. SARTORIAL   (A) disheveled   (B) frozen
(C) satirical   (D) tailored   (E) warm

Vocabulary Test 24

1. VERTIGO   (A) curiosity   (B) dizziness
(C) enlivement   (D) greenness   (E) invigoration

2. DEBACLE   (A) ceremony   (B) collapse
(C) dance   (D) deficit   (E) dispute

3. CONDIGN   (A) deserved   (B) hidden
(C) perplexed   (D) pretended   (E) unworthy

4. EPHEMERALLY   (A) enduringly   (B) lightly
(C) openly   (D) suspiciously   (E) transiently

5. HISTRIONIC   (A) authentic   (B) hysterical
(C) reportorial   (D) sibilant   (E) theatrical

6. URBANITY   (A) aggressiveness
(B) mercenary   (C) municipality   (D) rustic
(E) suavity

7. TRUCULENT   (A) rambling   (B) relenting
(C) savage   (D) tranquil   (E) weary

8. INVEIGH   (A) allure   (B) entice   (C) guide
cautiously   (D) originate   (E) speak bitterly

9. DESULTORY   (A) delaying   (B) disconnected
(C) flagrant   (D) insulting   (E) irritating

10. INGENUOUS   (A) clever   (B) naïve
(C) ignorant   (D) native   (E) unkind

Vocabulary Test 25

1. CUMULATIVE   (A) additive   (B) clumsy
(C) cumbersome   (D) incorrect   (E) secretive

2. EPIGRAM   (A) chemical term
(B) exclamation   (C) outer skin   (D) pithy
saying   (E) tombstone

3. GESTICULATE   (A) dance   (B) digest easily
(C) ridicule   (D) travel   (E) use gestures

4. BEGUILE   (A) benefit   (B) bind
(C) deceive   (D) envy   (E) petition

5. AVID   (A) eager   (B) glowing
(C) indifferent   (D) lax   (E) potent

6. LABYRINTH   (A) laboratory   (B) maze
(C) path   (D) portal   (E) room

7. REGURGITATE   (A) make new investments
(B) obliterate   (C) restore to solvency
(D) slacken   (E) surge back

8. PODIUM   (A) chemical element   (B) dais
(C) foot specialist   (D) magistrate   (E) Roman
infantryman

9. BEREFT   (A) annoyed   (B) awarded
(C) deprived   (D) enraged   (E) insane

10. ELUCIDATE   (A) condense   (B) escape
(C) evade   (D) explain   (E) shine through

Vocabulary Test 26

1. EMOLLIENT   (A) comical   (B) despicable
(C) enthusiastic   (D) raucous   (E) soothing

2. NOSTALGIC   (A) expressive   (B) forgetful
(C) homesick   (D) inconstant   (E) seasick

3. EXPIATE   (A) atone for   (B) die   (C) hasten
(D) imitate   (E) make holy

4. PARADOX   (A) accepted opinion   (B) axiom
(C) contradiction   (D) enigma   (E) pattern

5. ARCHETYPE   (A) bowman   (B) original
model   (C) public records   (D) roguishness
(E) star

6. MUNDANE   (A) deformed   (B) free
(C) rough-shelled   (D) tearful   (E) worldly

7. PALLIATIVE   (A) boring   (B) callous
(C) permanent   (D) softening   (E) unyielding

8. FOMENT   (A) curb   (B) explode
(C) exclude   (D) turn into wine   (E) instigate

9. PREDACIOUS   (A) beautiful
(B) incongruous   (C) peaceful   (D) preying
(E) valuable

10. RESILIENT   (A) thrifty   (B) elastic
(C) timid   (D) fragile   (E) unsociable

Vocabulary Test 27

1. BLATANT   (A) clamorous   (B) conceited
(C) prudish   (D) reticent   (E) unsuited

2. ADVERSITY   (A) advertising   (B) counsel
(C) criticism   (D) misfortune   (E) proficiency

3. CADAVEROUS   (A) cheerful
(B) contemptible   (C) ghastly   (D) hungry
(E) ill-bred

4. WRAITH   (A) anger   (B) apparition
(C) figurine   (D) mannequin   (E) model

5. PERSPICACITY   (A) clearness   (B) dullness
(C) keenness   (D) vastness   (E) wideness

6. EXTRANEOUS   (A) derived   (B) foreign
(C) unsuitable   (D) visible   (E) wasteful

7. PAROXYSM   (A) catastrophe   (B) sudden
outburst   (C) illusion   (D) lack of harmony
(E) loss of all bodily movement

8. SAPIENT   (A) discerning   (B) foolish
(C) mocking   (D) soapy   (E) youthful

9. FLACCID   (A) flabby   (B) golden   (C) hard
(D) strong   (E) wiry

10. IMPECUNIOUS   (A) frugal   (B) guiltless
(C) miserly   (D) monied   (E) poor

Vocabulary Test 28

1. ABDUCT   (A) ruin   (B) aid   (C) fight
(D) abolish   (E) kidnap

2. DEMERIT   (A) outcome   (B) fault
(C) prize   (D) notice   (E) belief

3. MUTINOUS   (A) silent   (B) oceangoing
(C) rebellious   (D) miserable   (E) deaf

4. NEGLIGENT   (A) lax   (B) desperate
(C) cowardly   (D) ambitious   (E) informal

5. CONTEST   (A) disturb   (B) dispute
(C) detain   (D) distrust   (E) contain

6. QUERY   (A) wait   (B) lose   (C) show
(D) ask   (E) demand

7. INSIDIOUS   (A) treacherous   (B) excitable
(C) internal   (D) distracting   (E) secretive

8. PALPITATE   (A) mash   (B) stifle   (C) creak
(D) pace   (E) throb

9. ANIMOSITY   (A) hatred   (B) interest
(C) silliness   (D) amusement   (E) power

10. EGOTISM   (A) sociability   (B) aggressiveness
(C) self-confidence   (D) conceit   (E) willingness

Vocabulary Test 29

1. CALLIGRAPHY (A) weaving
(B) handwriting (C) drafting (D) mapmaking
(E) graph making

2. SYNCHRONIZE (A) happen at the same time
(B) follow immediately in time (C) alternate
between events (D) postpone to a future time
(E) have difficulty in hearing

3. SEMBLANCE (A) surface (B) diplomacy
(C) replacement (D) appearance
(E) confidence

4. WISTFUL (A) winding (B) mutual
(C) exciting (D) rugged (E) yearning

5. CURTAIL (A) threaten (B) strengthen
(C) lessen (D) hasten (E) collide

6. NOXIOUS (A) spicy (B) smelly
(C) foreign (D) noisy (E) harmful

7. PAUCITY (A) fatigue (B) scarcity
(C) nonsense (D) waste (E) motion

8. JEOPARDIZE (A) soothe (B) cleanse
(C) enjoy (D) reward (E) endanger

9. INTREPID (A) exhausted (B) moderate
(C) anxious (D) youthful (E) fearless

10. TREACHEROUS (A) ignorant (B) envious
(C) disloyal (D) cowardly (E) inconsiderate

Vocabulary Test 30

1. UNSAVORY (A) unfriendly (B) joyless
(C) tactless (D) colorless (E) tasteless

2. HEARSAY (A) testimony (B) argument
(C) rumor (D) accusation (E) similarity

3. HAMPER (A) restrain (B) pack
(C) clarify (D) grip (E) err

4. BEDLAM (A) inadequacy (B) confusion
(C) translation (D) courtesy (E) curiosity

5. INFALLIBLE (A) negative (B) unfair
(C) essential (D) certain (E) weary

6. CONTEND (A) solve (B) observe
(C) outwit (D) encourage (E) compete

7. AMOROUS (A) shapeless (B) helpful
(C) familiar (D) loving (E) solemn

8. ALLEVIATE (A) reject (B) ease
(C) imitate (D) consent (E) elevate

9. NEOPHYTE (A) participant (B) officer
(C) beginner (D) winner (E) quarrel

10. SOLACE (A) comfort (B) weariness
(C) direction (D) complaint (E) respect

Vocabulary Test 31

1. ULTIMATUM (A) shrewd plan (B) final
terms (C) first defeat (D) dominant leader
(E) electric motor

2. GIRD (A) surround (B) appeal (C) request
(D) break (E) glance

3. WANGLE (A) moan (B) mutilate
(C) exasperate (D) manipulate (E) triumph

4. PROCUREMENT (A) acquisition
(B) resolution (C) healing (D) importance
(E) miracle

5. CULMINATION (A) rebellion (B) lighting
system (C) climax (D) destruction
(E) mystery

6. INSUPERABLE (A) incomprehensible
(B) elaborate (C) unusual (D) indigestible
(E) unconquerable

7. CLICHÉ (A) summary argument (B) new
information (C) new hat (D) trite phrase
(E) lock device

8. CONCESSION (A) nourishment (B) plea
(C) restoration (D) similarity
(E) acknowledgment

9. INSIPID (A) disrespectful (B) uninteresting
(C) persistent (D) whole (E) stimulating

10. REPRISAL (A) retaliation (B) drawing
(C) capture (D) release (E) suspicion

Vocabulary Test 32

1. DUBIOUS (A) economical (B) well-groomed
(C) boring (D) discouraged (E) uncertain

2. ATROCIOUS (A) brutal (B) innocent
(C) shrunken (D) yellowish (E) unsound

3. PRESTIGE (A) speed (B) influence
(C) omen (D) pride (E) excuse

4. VINDICATE (A) outrage (B) waver
(C) enliven (D) justify (E) fuse

5. EXUDE (A) accuse (B) discharge
(C) inflect (D) appropriate (E) distress

6. FACTION (A) clique (B) judgment
(C) truth (D) type of architecture (E) health

7. INCLEMENT (A) merciful (B) sloping
(C) harsh (D) disastrous (E) personal

8. SPURIOUS (A) concise (B) false
(C) obstinate (D) sarcastic (E) severe

9. SUBSERVIENT (A) existing
(B) obsequious (C) related (D) underlying
(E) useful

10. IMPORTUNE (A) aggrandize (B) carry
(C) exaggerate (D) prolong (E) urge

Vocabulary Test 33

1. CONTROVERSIAL   (A) faultfinding
   (B) pleasant   (C) debatable   (D) ugly
   (E) talkative

2. GHASTLY   (A) hasty   (B) furious
   (C) breathless   (D) deathlike   (E) spiritual

3. BELLIGERENT   (A) worldly   (B) warlike
   (C) loudmouthed   (D) furious   (E) artistic

4. PROFICIENCY   (A) wisdom   (B) oversupply
   (C) expertness   (D) advancement   (E) sincerity

5. COMPASSION   (A) rage   (B) strength of
   character   (C) forcefulness   (D) sympathy
   (E) uniformity

6. DISSENSION   (A) treatise   (B) pretense
   (C) fear   (D) lineage   (E) discord

7. INTIMATE   (A) charm   (B) hint
   (C) disguise   (D) frighten   (E) hum

8. BERATE   (A) classify   (B) scold
   (C) underestimate   (D) take one's time
   (E) evaluate

9. DEARTH   (A) scarcity   (B) width
   (C) affection   (D) wealth   (E) warmth

10. MEDITATE   (A) rest   (B) stare   (C) doze
    (D) make peace   (E) reflect

Vocabulary Test 34

1. STAGNANT   (A) inactive   (B) alert
   (C) selfish   (D) difficult   (E) scornful

2. MANDATORY   (A) insane   (B) obligatory
   (C) evident   (D) strategic   (E) unequaled

3. INFERNAL   (A) immodest   (B) incomplete
   (C) domestic   (D) second-rate   (E) fiendish

4. EXONERATE   (A) free from blame
   (B) warn   (C) drive out   (D) overcharge
   (E) plead

5. ARBITER   (A) friend   (B) judge   (C) drug
   (D) tree surgeon   (E) truant

6. ENMITY   (A) boredom   (B) puzzle
   (C) offensive language   (D) ill will
   (E) entanglement

7. DISCRIMINATE   (A) fail   (B) delay
   (C) accuse   (D) distinguish   (E) reject

8. DERISION   (A) disgust   (B) ridicule
   (C) fear   (D) anger   (E) heredity

9. EXULTANT   (A) essential   (B) elated
   (C) praiseworthy   (D) plentiful   (E) high-priced

10. OSTENSIBLE   (A) vibrating   (B) odd
    (C) apparent   (D) standard   (E) ornate

Vocabulary Test 35

1. ABHOR   (A) hate   (B) admire   (C) taste
   (D) skip   (E) resign

2. DUTIFUL   (A) lasting   (B) sluggish
   (C) required   (D) soothing   (E) obedient

3. ZEALOT   (A) breeze   (B) enthusiast
   (C) vault   (D) wild animal   (E) musical
   instrument

4. MAGNANIMOUS   (A) high-minded
   (B) faithful   (C) concerned   (D) individual
   (E) small

5. CITE   (A) protest   (B) depart   (C) quote
   (D) agitate   (E) perform

6. OBLIVION   (A) hindrance   (B) accident
   (C) courtesy   (D) forgetfulness   (E) old age

7. CARDINAL   (A) independent   (B) well-
   organized   (C) subordinate   (D) dignified
   (E) chief

8. DEPLETE   (A) restrain   (B) corrupt
   (C) despair   (D) exhaust   (E) spread out

9. SUPERSEDE   (A) retire   (B) replace
   (C) overflow   (D) bless   (E) oversee

10. SPORADIC   (A) bad-tempered
    (B) infrequent   (C) radical   (D) reckless
    (E) humble

Vocabulary Test 36

1. NEUTRALIZE   (A) entangle   (B) strengthen
   (C) counteract   (D) combat   (E) converse

2. INSINUATE   (A) destroy   (B) hint   (C) do
   wrong   (D) accuse   (E) release

3. DIMINUTIVE   (A) proud   (B) slow
   (C) small   (D) watery   (E) puzzling

4. PLIGHT   (A) departure   (B) weight
   (C) conspiracy   (D) predicament   (E) stamp

5. ILLICIT   (A) unlawful   (B) overpowering
   (C) ill-advised   (D) small-scale   (E) unreadable

6. BENIGN   (A) contagious   (B) fatal
   (C) ignorant   (D) kindly   (E) decorative

7. REVERIE   (A) abusive language   (B) love
   song   (C) backward step   (D) daydream
   (E) holy man

8. APPREHENSIVE   (A) quiet   (B) firm
   (C) curious   (D) sincere   (E) fearful

9. RECOIL   (A) shrink   (B) attract
   (C) electrify   (D) adjust   (E) enroll

10. GUISE   (A) trickery   (B) request
    (C) innocence   (D) misdeed   (E) appearance

Vocabulary Test 37

1. ACQUIT   (A) increase   (B) harden   (C) clear
(D) sharpen   (E) sentence

2. DEXTERITY   (A) conceit   (B) skill
(C) insistence   (D) embarrassment   (E) guidance

3. ASSIMILATE   (A) absorb   (B) imitate
(C) maintain   (D) outrun   (E) curb

4. DESPONDENCY   (A) relief   (B) gratitude
(C) dejection   (D) hatred   (E) poverty

5. BUOYANT   (A) conceited   (B) cautioning
(C) youthful   (D) musical   (E) cheerful

6. CULINARY   (A) having to do with cooking
(B) pertaining to dressmaking   (C) fond of
eating   (D) loving money   (E) tending to be
secretive

7. CAPRICE   (A) wisdom   (B) ornament
(C) pillar   (D) whim   (E) energy

8. DETERRENT   (A) restraining   (B) cleansing
(C) deciding   (D) concluding   (E) crumbling

9. PUGNACIOUS   (A) sticky   (B) cowardly
(C) precise   (D) vigorous   (E) quarrelsome

10. ABSCOND   (A) detest   (B) reduce
(C) swallow up   (D) dismiss   (E) flee

Vocabulary Test 38

1. BOUNTY   (A) limit   (B) boastfulness
(C) cheerfulness   (D) reward   (E) punishment

2. NOVICE   (A) storyteller   (B) iceberg
(C) adolescent   (D) mythical creature
(E) beginner

3. BOLSTER   (A) contradict   (B) insist
(C) defy   (D) sleep   (E) prop

4. MOBILE   (A) changeable   (B) scornful
(C) mechanical   (D) stylish   (E) solid

5. CREDULITY   (A) prize   (B) feebleness
(C) balance   (D) laziness   (E) belief

6. DOLDRUMS   (A) charity   (B) curing agents
(C) contagious disease   (D) low spirits
(E) places of safety

7. LOATH   (A) idle   (B) worried   (C) unwilling
(D) ready   (E) sad

8. INVENTIVE   (A) aimless   (B) clever
(C) moist   (D) false   (E) nearby

9. LITHE   (A) tough   (B) obstinate
(C) flexible   (D) damp   (E) gay

10. VACILLATE   (A) waver   (B) defeat
(C) favor   (D) endanger   (E) humiliate

Vocabulary Test 39

1. OBNOXIOUS   (A) dreamy   (B) visible
(C) angry   (D) daring   (E) objectionable

2. VERBATIM   (A) word for word   (B) at will
(C) without fail   (D) in secret   (E) in summary

3. ENTICE   (A) inform   (B) observe
(C) permit   (D) attract   (E) disobey

4. ACCLAIM   (A) discharge   (B) excel
(C) applaud   (D) divide   (E) speed

5. TURBULENCE   (A) treachery
(B) commotion   (C) fear   (D) triumph
(E) overflow

6. DEFER   (A) discourage   (B) postpone
(C) empty   (D) minimize   (E) estimate

7. ADAGE   (A) proverb   (B) supplement
(C) tool   (D) youth   (E) hardness

8. ENSUE   (A) compel   (B) remain
(C) absorb   (D) plead   (E) follow

9. ZENITH   (A) lowest point   (B) compass
(C) summit   (D) middle   (E) wind direction

10. HYPOTHETICAL   (A) magical   (B) visual
(C) two-faced   (D) theoretical   (E) excitable

Vocabulary Test 40

1. IMPROMPTU   (A) offhand   (B) laughable
(C) fascinating   (D) rehearsed   (E) deceptive

2. CHIVALROUS   (A) crude   (B) military
(C) handsome   (D) foreign   (E) courteous

3. HAVOC   (A) festival   (B) disease   (C) ruin
(D) sea battle   (E) luggage

4. REJUVENATE   (A) reply   (B) renew
(C) age   (D) judge   (E) reconsider

5. STILTED   (A) stiffly formal   (B) talking
much   (C) secretive   (D) fashionable
(E) senseless

6. SOLILOQUY   (A) figure of speech
(B) historical incident   (C) monologue
(D) isolated position   (E) contradiction

7. AFFABLE   (A) monotonous   (B) affected
(C) wealthy   (D) sociable   (E) selfish

8. NEBULOUS   (A) subdued   (B) eternal
(C) dewy   (D) cloudy   (E) careless

9. STEREOTYPED   (A) lacking originality
(B) illuminating   (C) pictorial   (D) free from
disease   (E) sparkling

10. STUPEFY   (A) lie   (B) talk nonsense
(C) bend   (D) make dull   (E) overeat

Vocabulary Test 41

1. SUPERFICIAL (A) shallow (B) unusually fine (C) proud (D) aged (E) spiritual

2. DISPARAGE (A) separate (B) compare (C) refuse (D) belittle (E) imitate

3. PROTAGONIST (A) prophet (B) explorer (C) talented child (D) convert (E) leading character

4. LUDICROUS (A) profitable (B) excessive (C) disordered (D) ridiculous (E) undesirable

5. INTREPID (A) moist (B) tolerant (C) fearless (D) rude (E) gay

6. SAGE (A) wise man (B) tropical tree (C) tale (D) era (E) fool

7. ADMONISH (A) polish (B) escape (C) worship (D) distribute (E) caution

8. BESET (A) plead (B) perplex (C) pertain to (D) deny (E) deprive of

9. FIGMENT (A) ornamental openwork (B) perfume (C) undeveloped fruit (D) statuette (E) invention

10. GLIB (A) dull (B) thin (C) weak (D) fluent (E) sharp

Vocabulary Test 42

1. FORTITUDE (A) wealth (B) courage (C) honesty (D) loudness (E) luck

2. ABOLITION (A) retirement (B) disgust (C) enslavement (D) unrestricted power (E) complete destruction

3. EPITOME (A) pool (B) summary (C) formula (D) monster (E) song

4. MAIM (A) heal (B) disable (C) outwit (D) murder (E) bury

5. CRESTFALLEN (A) haughty (B) dejected (C) fatigued (D) disfigured (E) impolite

6. CUISINE (A) headdress (B) game of chance (C) leisurely voyage (D) artistry (E) style of cooking

7. CENSURE (A) erase (B) build up (C) criticize adversely (D) charm (E) help

8. DEVIATE (A) destroy (B) lower in value (C) invent (D) stray (E) depress

9. SWARTHY (A) dark-complexioned (B) slender (C) grass-covered (D) springy (E) rotating

10. MERCENARY (A) poisonous (B) unworthy (C) serving only for pay (D) luring by false charms (E) showing pity

Vocabulary Test 43

1. ACUTE (A) keen (B) bitter (C) brisk (D) genuine (E) certain

2. CLIENTELE (A) legal body (B) customers (C) board of directors (D) servants (E) tenants

3. SUCCUMB (A) follow (B) help (C) respond (D) yield (E) overthrow

4. SLOTH (A) selfishness (B) hatred (C) laziness (D) misery (E) slipperiness

5. INFRINGE (A) enrage (B) expand (C) disappoint (D) weaken (E) trespass

6. UNCANNY (A) ill-humored (B) immature (C) weird (D) unrestrained (E) insincere

7. SUBMISSIVE (A) unintelligent (B) underhanded (C) destructive (D) enthusiastic (E) meek

8. PEER (A) ancestor (B) teacher (C) judge (D) equal (E) assistant

9. EULOGIZE (A) kill (B) apologize (C) glorify (D) soften (E) imitate

10. INNOVATION (A) change (B) prayer (C) hint (D) restraint (E) inquiry

Vocabulary Test 44

1. EXHILARATION (A) animation (B) withdrawal (C) payment (D) suffocation (E) despair

2. RASPING (A) irritating (B) scolding (C) fastening (D) sighing (E) plundering

3. PROPONENT (A) spendthrift (B) rival (C) distributor (D) advocate (E) neighbor

4. REDUNDANT (A) flooded (B) dreadful (C) aromatic (D) excessive (E) reclining

5. BEGRUDGING (A) humid (B) envious (C) living in seclusion (D) involving a choice (E) aimless

6. EMPATHIZE (A) cheapen (B) underestimate (C) charm (D) sympathize (E) forgive

7. PRUDENT (A) lighthearted (B) eager (C) cautious (D) insincere (E) fast-moving

8. OMNIVOROUS (A) devouring everything (B) many-sided (C) powerful (D) living on plants (E) all-knowing

9. APPEND (A) rely (B) recognize (C) arrest (D) divide (E) attach

10. STRATAGEM (A) sneak attack (B) military command (C) thin layer (D) deceptive device (E) narrow passage

Vocabulary Test 45

1. COLLABORATE   (A) condense   (B) converse   (C) arrange in order   (D) provide proof   (E) act jointly

2. FUTILITY   (A) uselessness   (B) timelessness   (C) stinginess   (D) happiness   (E) indistinctness

3. INTACT   (A) blunt   (B) fashionable   (C) hidden   (D) uninjured   (E) attentive

4. FERVOR   (A) originality   (B) justice   (C) zeal   (D) productivity   (E) corruption

5. UNERRING   (A) modest   (B) illogical   (C) ghostly   (D) matchless   (E) unfailing

6. REFUTE   (A) polish   (B) disprove   (C) throw away   (D) break up   (E) shut out

7. CONSENSUS   (A) steadfastness of purpose   (B) general agreement   (C) lack of harmony   (D) informal vote   (E) impressive amount

8. COMPLIANT   (A) tangled   (B) grumbling   (C) self-satisfied   (D) treacherous   (E) submissive

9. ACCESS   (A) agreement   (B) rapidity   (C) welcome   (D) approach   (E) surplus

10. PRUDENT   (A) wise   (B) overcritical   (C) famous   (D) dull   (E) early

Vocabulary Test 46

1. APPEASE   (A) attack   (B) soothe   (C) pray for   (D) estimate   (E) confess

2. RUTHLESS   (A) senseless   (B) sinful   (C) ruddy   (D) pitiless   (E) degrading

3. MUSTER   (A) rebel   (B) mask   (C) gather   (D) dampen   (E) grumble

4. EXECRATE   (A) embarrass   (B) desert   (C) omit   (D) curse   (E) resign

5. KNOLL   (A) elf   (B) mound   (C) bell   (D) development   (E) technique

6. IRATE   (A) evil   (B) wandering   (C) repetitious   (D) colorful   (E) angry

7. GRIMACE   (A) peril   (B) subtle suggestion   (C) signal   (D) wry face   (E) impurity

8. ACME   (A) layer   (B) summit   (C) edge   (D) pit   (E) interval

9. COVENANT   (A) solemn agreement   (B) formal invitation   (C) religious ceremony   (D) general pardon   (E) hiding place

10. APPALL   (A) honor   (B) decorate   (C) calm   (D) bore   (E) dismay

Vocabulary Test 47

1. INCUR   (A) take to heart   (B) anticipate   (C) bring down on oneself   (D) impress by repetition   (E) attack

2. CAUSTIC   (A) solemn   (B) puzzling   (C) biting   (D) influential   (E) attentive

3. DILATE   (A) retard   (B) fade   (C) wander   (D) expand   (E) startle

4. APATHY   (A) fixed dislike   (B) skill   (C) sorrow   (D) lack of feeling   (E) discontent

5. ELICIT   (A) draw forth   (B) cross out   (C) run away   (D) lengthen   (E) revise

6. JUDICIOUS   (A) wise   (B) dignified   (C) light-hearted   (D) confused   (E) respectful

7. UNSCATHED   (A) unashamed   (B) uninjured   (C) unskilled   (D) unsuccessful   (E) unconscious

8. CHIDE   (A) misbehave   (B) cool   (C) select   (D) conceal   (E) scold

9. CHARLATAN   (A) scholar   (B) acrobat   (C) quack   (D) faithful servant   (E) fast talker

10. DISBURSE   (A) remove forcibly   (B) twist   (C) amuse   (D) vary slightly   (E) pay out

Vocabulary Test 48

1. PARAMOUNT   (A) equal   (B) supreme   (C) well-known   (D) difficult   (E) ready

2. BROCHURE   (A) heavy shoe   (B) weapon   (C) pamphlet   (D) trite remark   (E) ornament

3. FIDELITY   (A) happiness   (B) bravery   (C) prosperity   (D) hardness   (E) loyalty

4. DIFFUSE   (A) explain   (B) scatter   (C) differ   (D) congeal   (E) dart

5. AGGRESSIVE   (A) disgusting   (B) impulsive   (C) short-sighted   (D) coarse-grained   (E) self-assertive

6. AMASS   (A) accumulate   (B) encourage   (C) comprehend   (D) blend   (E) astonish

7. DIABOLIC   (A) puzzling   (B) uneducated   (C) ornamental   (D) fiendish   (E) spinning

8. FORBEARANCE   (A) rejection   (B) forgetfulness   (C) sensitivity   (D) patience   (E) expectation

9. TAINT   (A) snarl   (B) infect   (C) unite   (D) annoy   (E) list

10. DISGRUNTLED   (A) untidy   (B) rambling   (C) disabled   (D) cheating   (E) displeased

Vocabulary Test 49

1. PLACID   (A) apparent   (B) peaceful
(C) wicked   (D) unusual   (E) absent-minded

2. EVASIVE   (A) emotional   (B) effective
(C) destructive   (D) empty   (E) shifty

3. CHAOS   (A) complete disorder   (B) deep
gorge   (C) challenge   (D) sudden attack
(E) rejoicing

4. DESPICABLE   (A) insulting   (B) ungrateful
(C) contemptible   (D) unbearable   (E) jealous

5. DERIDE   (A) question   (B) ignore
(C) mock   (D) unseat   (E) produce

6. ELUDE   (A) gladden   (B) fascinate
(C) mention   (D) escape   (E) ignore

7. MUTABLE   (A) colorless   (B) harmful
(C) uniform   (D) changeable   (E) invisible

8. INDICATIVE   (A) suggestive   (B) curious
(C) active   (D) angry   (E) certain

9. LEVITY   (A) cleanness   (B) tastiness
(C) deadliness   (D) sluggishness   (E) lightness

10. EXCRUCIATING   (A) disciplinary
(B) screaming   (C) torturing   (D) offensive
(E) outpouring

Vocabulary Test 50

1. PRECEPT   (A) rule   (B) disguise
(C) refinement   (D) hasty decision   (E) delaying
action

2. HOMOGENEOUS   (A) numerous
(B) healthful   (C) similar   (D) assorted
(E) educational

3. ARCHIVES   (A) public records   (B) models
(C) supporting columns   (D) tombs   (E) large
ships

4. INFAMY   (A) anger   (B) truth   (C) disgrace
(D) weakness   (E) excitement

5. IMPINGE   (A) swear   (B) involve   (C) erase
(D) encroach   (E) beg

6. DEPOSE   (A) lay bare   (B) deprive of office
(C) empty   (D) behead   (E) blemish

7. OSTENTATIOUS   (A) unruly   (B) showy
(C) varied   (D) scandalous   (E) probable

8. CONCLAVE   (A) private meeting   (B) covered
passage   (C) solemn vow   (D) curved surface
(E) ornamental vase

9. FRAY   (A) combat   (B) trickery
(C) unreality   (D) madness   (E) freedom

10. OBSESS   (A) fatten   (B) beset   (C) make
dull   (D) exaggerate   (E) interfere

Vocabulary Test 51

1. CHAFE   (A) pretend   (B) joke   (C) drink
deeply   (D) irritate   (E) lose courage

2. MISCONSTRUE   (A) hate   (B) destroy
(C) misbehave   (D) misinterpret   (E) misplace

3. PHILANTHROPIST   (A) student of language
(B) collector of stamps   (C) lover of mankind
(D) seeker of truth   (E) enemy of culture

4. CASTE   (A) feudal system   (B) division of
society   (C) political theory   (D) method of
punishment   (E) monetary system

5. CHASTEN   (A) punish   (B) engrave
(C) attract   (D) trick   (E) laugh at

6. CONDUCIVE   (A) pardonable   (B) identical
(C) incidental   (D) helpful   (E) exceptional

7. SUBORDINATE   (A) hostile   (B) inferior
(C) separate   (D) earlier   (E) adaptable

8. SUPERFLUOUS   (A) inexact   (B) excessive
(C) insincere   (D) excellent   (E) unreal

9. WIELD   (A) protect   (B) handle
(C) postpone   (D) resign   (E) unite

10. GARISH   (A) showy   (B) talkative
(C) sleepy   (D) thin   (E) vine-covered

Vocabulary Test 52

52. MEANDER   (A) grumble   (B) wander
aimlessly   (C) come between   (D) weigh
carefully   (E) sing

2. DESTITUTION   (A) trickery   (B) fate
(C) lack of practice   (D) recovery   (E) extreme
poverty

3. MALIGN   (A) slander   (B) prophesy
(C) entreat   (D) approve   (E) praise

4. IMPOTENT   (A) unwise   (B) lacking strength
(C) free of sin   (D) without shame
(E) commanding

5. SNIVEL   (A) crawl   (B) cut short
(C) whine   (D) doze   (E) giggle

6. SOJOURN   (A) court order   (B) nickname
(C) temporary stay   (D) slip of the tongue
(E) makeshift

7. PLATITUDE   (A) home remedy   (B) trite
remark   (C) balance wheel   (D) rare animal
(E) protective film

8. CONCORD   (A) brevity   (B) blame
(C) kindness   (D) worry   (E) agreement

9. ABOMINABLE   (A) hateful   (B) ridiculous
(C) untamed   (D) mysterious   (E) boastful

10. QUALM   (A) sudden misgiving   (B) irritation
(C) cooling drink   (D) deceit   (E) attention to
detail

Vocabulary Test 53

1. EQUITABLE   (A) charitable   (B) even-tempered   (C) two-faced   (D) undecided   (E) just

2. AFFRONT   (A) quarrel   (B) fright   (C) denial   (D) boast   (E) insult

3. EPOCH   (A) heroic deed   (B) legend   (C) witty saying   (D) period of time   (E) summary

4. RETRIBUTION   (A) donation   (B) jealousy   (C) intense emotion   (D) slow withdrawal   (E) punishment

5. ABASE   (A) forgive   (B) degrade   (C) attach   (D) take leave   (E) cut off

6. CAREEN   (A) celebrate   (B) mourn   (C) ridicule   (D) lurch   (E) beckon

7. CONVIVIAL   (A) formal   (B) gay   (C) rotating   (D) well-informed   (E) insulting

8. RAMPANT   (A) playful   (B) crumbling   (C) roundabout   (D) unchecked   (E) defensive

9. DOCILE   (A) delicate   (B) positive   (C) dreary   (D) obedient   (E) melodious

10. VESTIGE   (A) bone   (B) test   (C) entrance   (D) cloak   (E) trace

Vocabulary Test 54

1. IMPEDIMENT   (A) foundation   (B) conceit   (C) hindrance   (D) luggage   (E) instrument

2. ADHERE   (A) pursue   (B) control   (C) arrive   (D) cling   (E) attend

3. COMPOSURE   (A) sensitiveness   (B) weariness   (C) stylishness   (D) hopefulness   (E) calmness

4. PROVOCATION   (A) sacred vow   (B) formal announcement   (C) cause of irritation   (D) careful management   (E) expression of disgust

5. SAVORY   (A) thrifty   (B) wise   (C) appetizing   (D) warm   (E) uncivilized

6. CANDID   (A) hidden   (B) shining   (C) straightforward   (D) critical   (E) warmhearted

7. ECLIPSE   (A) stretch   (B) obscure   (C) glow   (D) overlook   (E) insert

8. CORRELATE   (A) punish   (B) wrinkle   (C) conspire openly   (D) give additional proof   (E) connect systematically

9. INFIRMITY   (A) disgrace   (B) unhappiness   (C) rigidity   (D) hesitation   (E) weakness

10. PALPITATE   (A) faint   (B) harden   (C) throb   (D) soothe   (E) taste

Vocabulary Test 55

1. DEBRIS   (A) sadness   (B) decay   (C) ruins   (D) landslide   (E) hindrance

2. CONSOLIDATE   (A) show pity   (B) strengthen   (C) restrain   (D) infect   (E) use up

3. STAMINA   (A) flatness   (B) clearness   (C) hesitation   (D) vigor   (E) reliability

4. FACET   (A) phase   (B) humor   (C) story   (D) discharge   (E) assistance

5. INANIMATE   (A) emotional   (B) thoughtless   (C) lifeless   (D) inexact   (E) silly

6. CALLOUS   (A) frantic   (B) misinformed   (C) youthful   (D) impolite   (E) unfeeling

7. ENHANCE   (A) sympathize   (B) act out   (C) weaken   (D) make greater   (E) fascinate

8. DISREPUTABLE   (A) impolite   (B) bewildered   (C) debatable   (D) unavailable   (E) shameful

9. SEDATE   (A) sober   (B) seated   (C) buried   (D) drugged   (E) timid

10. LUCRATIVE   (A) lazy   (B) coarse   (C) profitable   (D) brilliant   (E) amusing

Vocabulary Test 56

1. IMPRUDENT   (A) reckless   (B) unexcitable   (C) poor   (D) domineering   (E) powerless

2. DISSENSION   (A) friction   (B) analysis   (C) swelling   (D) injury   (E) slyness

3. DISCONCERT   (A) separate   (B) cripple   (C) lessen   (D) upset   (E) dismiss

4. RUDIMENTARY   (A) discourteous   (B) brutal   (C) displeasing   (D) elementary   (E) embarrassing

5. AUTONOMOUS   (A) self-governing   (B) self-important   (C) self-educated   (D) self-explanatory   (E) self-conscious

6. ASCERTAIN   (A) hold fast   (B) long for   (C) declare   (D) find out   (E) avoid

7. LITERAL   (A) flowery   (B) matter-of-fact   (C) sidewise   (D) well-educated   (E) firsthand

8. OSCILLATE   (A) please   (B) swing   (C) purify   (D) saturate   (E) harden

9. CONCISE   (A) accurate   (B) brief   (C) sudden   (D) similar   (E) painful

10. CONSTERNATION   (A) restraint   (B) close attention   (C) dismay   (D) self-importance   (E) acknkowledgment

Vocabulary Test 57

1. COLOSSAL   (A) ancient   (B) influential
(C) destructive   (D) dramatic   (E) huge

2. EVICT   (A) summon   (B) excite   (C) force
out   (D) prove   (E) draw off

3. MISCHANCE   (A) omission   (B) ill luck
(C) feeling of doubt   (D) unlawful act
(E) distrust

4. FELON   (A) criminal   (B) fugitive
(C) traitor   (D) coward   (E) loafer

5. CENSURE   (A) empty   (B) criticize
(C) spread out   (D) take an oath   (E) omit

6. IMPLICIT   (A) unquestioning   (B) rude
(C) relentless   (D) sinful   (E) daring

7. SLOVENLY   (A) sleepy   (B) tricky
(C) untidy   (D) moody   (E) cowardly

8. EXTRANEOUS   (A) familiar   (B) unprepared
(C) foreign   (D) proper   (E) utmost

9. IMPASSE   (A) command   (B) stubbornness
(C) crisis   (D) deadlock   (E) failure

10. ABSOLVE   (A) forgive   (B) reduce   (C) mix
(D) deprive   (E) detect

Vocabulary Test 58

1. CUMBERSOME   (A) habitual   (B) clumsy
(C) hasty   (D) blameworthy   (E) uneducated

2. CAPTIVATE   (A) charm   (B) dictate terms
(C) overturn   (D) find fault   (E) hesitate

3. ZEALOUS   (A) serious   (B) speedy
(C) flawless   (D) necessary   (E) enthusiastic

4. AROMATIC   (A) shining   (B) precise
(C) ancient   (D) fragrant   (E) dry

5. RETROSPECT   (A) careful inspection
(B) reversal of form   (C) review of the past
(D) respect for authority   (E) special attention

6. WHET   (A) bleach   (B) exhaust   (C) harden
(D) stimulate   (E) question

7. CONTUSION   (A) puzzle   (B) shrinkage
(C) bruise   (D) uncleanness   (E) fraud

8. COMPATIBLE   (A) eloquent   (B) adequate
(C) overfed   (D) comfortable   (E) harmonious

9. CALLOUS   (A) secretive   (B) unruly
(C) gloomy   (D) unfeeling   (E) hotheaded

10. REPUDIATE   (A) reject   (B) revalue
(C) repay   (D) forget   (E) forgive

Vocabulary Test 59

1. PROLETARIAT   (A) revolutionists
(B) intellectuals   (C) slaves   (D) laboring
classes   (E) landowners

2. REQUISITE   (A) desirable   (B) ridiculous
(C) liberal   (D) necessary   (E) majestic

3. TENACIOUS   (A) violent   (B) given to
arguing   (C) slender   (D) holding fast
(E) menacing

4. SCINTILLATE   (A) whirl   (B) wander
(C) scorch   (D) sharpen   (E) sparkle

5. PROPRIETY   (A) success   (B) cleverness
(C) nearness   (D) security   (E) suitability

6. UNWITTING   (A) undignified
(B) unintentional   (C) slack   (D) obstinate
(E) unaccustomed

7. ATTRIBUTE   (A) quality   (B) tax
(C) desire   (D) law   (E) final sum

8. SCRUPULOUS   (A) scornful   (B) clean
(C) frightening   (D) doubting   (E) conscientious

9. USURP   (A) lend money   (B) replace
(C) murder   (D) surrender   (E) seize by force

10. CESSATION   (A) witnessing   (B) stopping
(C) strain   (D) leave-taking   (E) unwillingness

Vocabulary Test 60

1. RESOLUTE   (A) determined   (B) vibrating
(C) irresistible   (D) elastic   (E) demanding

2. CRYSTALLIZE   (A) glitter   (B) give definite
form to   (C) chill   (D) sweeten   (E) polish
vigorously

3. REGIME   (A) ruler   (B) military unit
(C) form of government   (D) contagion
(E) guardian

4. LACERATED   (A) unconscious   (B) stitched
(C) slender   (D) raveled   (E) mangled

5. AMISS   (A) friendly   (B) faulty   (C) tardy
(D) central   (E) purposeless

6. INDOLENCE   (A) poverty   (B) laziness
(C) danger   (D) truth   (E) attention

7. PRECARIOUS   (A) trustful   (B) early
(C) previous   (D) cautious   (E) uncertain

8. CONNOISSEUR   (A) investigator
(B) government official   (C) pretender
(D) critical judge   (E) portrait artist

9. HILARITY   (A) wittiness   (B) disobedience
(C) mirth   (D) heedlessness   (E) contentment

10. EMIT   (A) overlook   (B) adorn
(C) discharge   (D) encourage   (E) stress

Vocabulary Test 61

1. DYNAMIC   (A) specialized   (B) active
   (C) fragile   (D) magical   (E) comparative

2. ACHILLES' HEEL   (A) source of strength
   (B) critical test   (C) hereditary curse
   (D) vulnerable point   (E) base conduct

3. AD LIB   (A) cheerfully   (B) freely
   (C) carefully   (D) literally   (E) wisely

4. DECRY   (A) baffle   (B) weep   (C) trap
   (D) belittle   (E) imagine

5. RAVAGE   (A) ruin   (B) tangle   (C) delight
   (D) scold   (E) crave

6. RENDEZVOUS   (A) surrender
   (B) appointment   (C) souvenir   (D) hiding
   place   (E) mutual exchange

7. SKULK   (A) trail   (B) shadow   (C) ambush
   (D) lurk   (E) race

8. PLETHORA   (A) formal farewell   (B) exclusive
   group   (C) abundance   (D) conclusive
   argument   (E) good taste

9. NUPTIAL   (A) moonlike   (B) blunted
   (C) ritualistic   (D) matrimonial   (E) blessed

10. BALKED   (A) swindled   (B) thwarted
    (C) enlarged   (D) waved   (E) punished

Vocabulary Test 62

1. AD INFINITUM   (A) to a limit   (B) from
   eternity   (C) occasionally   (D) endlessly
   (E) periodically

2. EXTRICATE   (A) disentangle   (B) die out
   (C) praise   (D) purify   (E) argue with

3. SQUALID   (A) dirty   (B) unresponsive
   (C) wasteful   (D) stormy   (E) congested

4. COERCE   (A) coincide   (B) strengthen
   (C) accompany   (D) compel   (E) seek out

5. INTER   (A) bury   (B) stab   (C) change
   (D) make peace   (E) emphasize

6. CRESCENDO   (A) increasing volume
   (B) decreasing tempo   (C) abrupt ending
   (D) discordant note   (E) musical composition

7. INDISCREET   (A) unpopular
   (B) embarrassing   (C) disloyal   (D) unwise
   (E) greatly upset

8. UNWIELDY   (A) stubborn   (B) unhealthy
   (C) monotonous   (D) shameful   (E) clumsy

9. ENVISAGE   (A) plot   (B) conceal
   (C) wrinkle   (D) contemplate   (E) sneer

10. INTERIM   (A) go-between   (B) meantime
    (C) mixture   (D) hereafter   (E) period of rest

Vocabulary Test 63

1. DISHEARTEN   (A) shame   (B) discourage
   (C) astound   (D) disown   (E) cripple

2. COMPONENT   (A) memorial   (B) pledge
   (C) convenience   (D) ingredient   (E) similarity

3. LURK   (A) stagger   (B) tempt   (C) sneak
   (D) grin   (E) rob

4. GRUDGING   (A) impolite   (B) dirty
   (C) hoarse   (D) alarming   (E) unwilling

5. SEMBLANCE   (A) likeness   (B) noise
   (C) foundation   (D) glance   (E) error

6. NETTLE   (A) irritate   (B) catch   (C) accuse
   (D) make ill   (E) fade away

7. TREMULOUS   (A) slow   (B) high-pitched
   (C) huge   (D) shaking   (E) spirited

8. TERSE   (A) delicate   (B) nervous   (C) mild
   (D) numb   (E) concise

9. AFFINITY   (A) solemn declaration
   (B) indefinite amount   (C) natural attraction
   (D) pain   (E) wealth

10. VOLATILE   (A) disobedient   (B) changeable
    (C) forceful   (D) willing   (E) luxurious

Vocabulary Test 64

1. HOMAGE   (A) welcome   (B) honor
   (C) cosiness   (D) criticism   (E) regret

2. DISPERSE   (A) restore   (B) spread
   (C) grumble   (D) soak   (E) spend

3. RATIONAL   (A) resentful   (B) overjoyed
   (C) sensible   (D) reckless   (E) apologetic

4. RECLUSE   (A) schemer   (B) criminal
   (C) miser   (D) adventurer   (E) hermit

5. COMPLACENCY   (A) tenderness
   (B) admiration   (C) dependence   (D) unity
   (E) self-satisfaction

6. MENACE   (A) kill   (B) threaten   (C) waste
   (D) indicate   (E) tease

7. DUPE   (A) combine   (B) reproduce   (C) fool
   (D) grab   (E) follow

8. ABATE   (A) surprise   (B) desert
   (C) decrease   (D) humiliate   (E) pay for

9. CONGENITAL   (A) existing at birth
   (B) displaying weakness   (C) related by
   marriage   (D) overcrowded   (E) unintelligent

10. INSURGENT   (A) impractical
    (B) unbearable   (C) overhanging
    (D) rebellious   (E) patriotic

Vocabulary Test 65

1. CONJECTURE (A) work (B) joke (C) initiate (D) add (E) guess

2. DAIS (A) platform (B) easy chair (C) waiting room (D) ornamental pin (E) figurehead

3. IMPETUS (A) deadlock (B) collision (C) warning (D) wickedness (E) stimulus

4. INTROSPECTIVE (A) lacking strength (B) practicing self-examination (C) highly critical (D) intrusive (E) lacking confidence

5. DEIFY (A) describe (B) disobey (C) make presentable (D) worship as a god (E) challenge

6. AGGREGATION (A) method (B) irritation (C) prize (D) collection (E) blessing

7. EXALTED (A) honored (B) underhanded (C) funny (D) conceited (E) secondary

8. POTENTATE (A) slave (B) soldier (C) adviser (D) informer (E) ruler

9. INTIMIDATE (A) frighten (B) suggest (C) dare (D) border upon (E) befriend

10. SARDONIC (A) decorative (B) polished (C) strange (D) fashionable (E) sarcastic

Vocabulary Test 66

1. ELECTRIFY (A) punish (B) improve (C) thrill (D) explain (E) investigate

2. DISCRETION (A) special privilege (B) individual judgment (C) unfair treatment (D) disagreement (E) embarrassment

3. GRAPPLE (A) dive (B) wrestle (C) handle (D) fit together (E) fondle

4. LAUDABLE (A) brave (B) comical (C) peaceful (D) praiseworthy (E) conspicuous

5. LONGEVITY (A) wisdom (B) length of life (C) society (D) system of measure (E) loudness

6. BLANCH (A) destroy (B) drink (C) whiten (D) feel (E) mend

7. SHREW (A) moneylender (B) fortuneteller (C) chronic invalid (D) unruly child (E) scolding woman

8. STALWART (A) diseased (B) feeble (C) needy (D) sturdy (E) truthful

9. APOGEE (A) rate of ascent (B) force of gravity (C) measuring device (D) expression of regret (E) highest point

10. BANTER (A) tease playfully (B) strut boldly (C) ruin (D) bend slightly (E) relieve

Vocabulary Test 67

1. REPRESS (A) sharpen (B) restrain (C) repeat (D) disgust (E) grieve

2. BREACH (A) obstruction (B) violation (C) anticipation (D) accusation (E) decoration

3. DILIGENT (A) hesitant (B) prosperous (C) offensive (D) industrious (E) straightforward

4. CONCOCT (A) devise (B) link together (C) harmonize (D) meet privately (E) sweeten

5. FLAMBOYANT (A) scandalous (B) showy (C) nonsensical (D) manly (E) temporary

6. ECCENTRICITY (A) overabundance (B) self-consciousness (C) adaptability (D) publicity (E) oddity

7. VINDICTIVE (A) gloomy (B) cowardly (C) vengeful (D) cheerful (E) boastful

8. GRAPHIC (A) vivid (B) harsh-sounding (C) free from error (D) dignified (E) pliable

9. PLACARD (A) poster (B) souvenir (C) soothing medicine (D) exact reproduction (E) contemptuous remark

10. PUTREFY (A) scour (B) paralyze (C) rot (D) neglect (E) argue

Vocabulary Test 68

1. GRANDIOSE (A) selfish (B) thankful (C) quarrelsome (D) elderly (E) impressive

2. INCONGRUOUS (A) indistinct (B) unsuitable (C) unimportant (D) illegal (E) inconvenient

3. PRONE (A) disposed (B) speechless (C) tardy (D) two-edged (E) quick

4. EMISSARY (A) rival (B) secret agent (C) master of ceremonies (D) refugee (E) clergyman

5. INVALIDATE (A) turn inward (B) deprive of force (C) mistrust (D) support with facts (E) neglect

6. CLEMENCY (A) purity (B) timidity (C) courage (D) simplicity (E) mildness

7. UNSCATHED (A) uninterested (B) unsettled (C) unspoken (D) unharmed (E) unknown

8. RELINQUISH (A) shrink from (B) take pity on (C) yield (D) lessen (E) recall

9. ALLAY (A) offend (B) suffer (C) resemble (D) assign (E) calm

10. ANIMOSITY (A) liveliness (B) worry (C) ill will (D) regret (E) sarcasm

Vocabulary Test 69

1. SOLICIT   (A) request   (B) worry
   (C) command   (D) deny   (E) depend

2. PERTURB   (A) pierce   (B) filter
   (C) calculate   (D) agitate   (E) disregard

3. JAUNTY   (A) bored   (B) envious
   (C) quarrelsome   (D) chatty   (E) lively

4. DRIVEL   (A) shrill laughter   (B) foolish talk
   (C) untidy dress   (D) waste matter   (E) quaint
   humor

5. FRUGAL   (A) sickly   (B) sparing   (C) slow
   (D) chilled   (E) frightened

6. IOTA   (A) first step   (B) sacred picture
   (C) ornamental scroll   (D) crystalline substance
   (E) very small quantity

7. POACH   (A) squander   (B) trespass
   (C) outwit   (D) bully   (E) borrow

8. DEFECTION   (A) delay   (B) slander
   (C) respect   (D) desertion   (E) exemption

9. MASTICATE   (A) chew   (B) slaughter
   (C) ripen   (D) enroll   (E) tangle

10. ANALOGY   (A) imitation   (B) research
    (C) calendar   (D) similarity   (E) disagreement

Vocabulary Test 70

1. DILEMMA   (A) punishment   (B) division in
   ranks   (C) ability to detect   (D) perplexing
   choice   (E) word with two meanings

2. CELESTIAL   (A) musical   (B) heavenly
   (C) stately   (D) unmarried   (E) aged

3. MILITANT   (A) political   (B) mighty
   (C) aggressive   (D) peaceable   (E) illegal

4. EMINENT   (A) noted   (B) moral
   (C) future   (D) low   (E) unwise

5. PERCEIVE   (A) resolve   (B) observe
   (C) organize   (D) stick in   (E) copy down

6. IDIOSYNCRASY   (A) stupidity   (B) virtue
   (C) personal peculiarity   (D) foreign dialect
   (E) similarity

7. EDIFICE   (A) tool   (B) large building
   (C) garden   (D) mushroom   (E) set of books

8. SEEDY   (A) dishonest   (B) helpless
   (C) vague   (D) nervous   (E) shabby

9. SUPPLANT   (A) spend   (B) unite
   (C) recall   (D) replace   (E) purpose

10. DESIST   (A) loiter   (B) stand   (C) hurry
    (D) stumble   (E) stop

Vocabulary Test 71

1. GIRD   (A) stare   (B) thresh   (C) encircle
   (D) complain   (E) perforate

2. BIZARRE   (A) charitable   (B) joyous
   (C) flattering   (D) insane   (E) fantastic

3. PERENNIAL   (A) superior   (B) unceasing
   (C) notable   (D) short-lived   (E) authoritative

4. PROGENITOR   (A) genius   (B) wastrel
   (C) forefather   (D) magician   (E) publisher

5. EMBELLISH   (A) organize   (B) involve
   (C) rob   (D) beautify   (E) correct

6. IMPLEMENT   (A) carry out   (B) fall apart
   (C) give freely   (D) object strongly   (E) praise
   highly

7. INSUBORDINATE   (A) unreal
   (B) disobedient   (C) inferior   (D) unfaithful
   (E) unnecessary

8. ITINERANT   (A) small   (B) intensive
   (C) repetitive   (D) wandering   (E) begging

9. ADVERSITY   (A) misfortune   (B) surprise
   (C) economy   (D) publicity   (E) warning

10. DISSIPATE   (A) explain   (B) puzzle
    (C) rearrange   (D) envy   (E) waste

Vocabulary Test 72

1. VALOR   (A) courage   (B) honesty
   (C) beauty   (D) alertness   (E) modesty

2. DISSUADE   (A) offend   (B) lessen   (C) advise
   against   (D) spread out   (E) separate

3. ERRATIC   (A) unpredictable   (B) upright
   (C) well-informed   (D) self-centered
   (E) artificial

4. COVET   (A) take for granted   (B) keep secret
   (C) disbelieve   (D) steal   (E) long for

5. VERBOSE   (A) forbidden   (B) expanding
   (C) talented   (D) wordy   (E) opinionated

6. FLIPPANT   (A) fishlike   (B) anxious
   (C) frivolous   (D) savage   (E) shy

7. ACCLAMATION   (A) seasoning
   (B) applause   (C) slope   (D) harmony
   (E) collection

8. INCITE   (A) include   (B) destroy
   (C) withdraw   (D) arouse   (E) perceive

9. FINESSE   (A) end   (B) skill   (C) habit
   (D) expense   (E) vanity

10. TANTALIZE   (A) prevent   (B) protect
    (C) rob   (D) predict   (E) torment

Vocabulary Test 73

1. INSOMNIA   (A) boredom   (B) loss of memory   (C) seasickness   (D) sleeplessness   (E) lonesomeness

2. FEASIBLE   (A) enjoyable   (B) juicy   (C) regrettable   (D) responsible   (E) possible

3. BLURT   (A) brag   (B) utter impulsively   (C) challenge   (D) shout angrily   (E) weep noisily

4. ALIENATE   (A) advise   (B) entertain   (C) forgive   (D) sympathize with   (E) make unfriendly

5. STARK   (A) barely   (B) offensively   (C) uselessly   (D) completely   (E) artistically

6. NONCHALANCE   (A) refinement   (B) foresight   (C) air of indifference   (D) lack of knowledge   (E) lack of common sense

7. GRIT   (A) honesty   (B) reverence   (C) trustworthiness   (D) cheerfulness   (E) bravery

8. MEDIATE   (A) make changes   (B) argue earnestly   (C) consider carefully   (D) propose hesitantly   (E) reconcile differences

9. DE FACTO   (A) commercial   (B) economic   (C) in reality   (D) unnecessary   (E) the following

10. IRREVOCABLE   (A) unreliable   (B) disrespectful   (C) unforgivable   (D) unalterable   (E) heartless

Vocabulary Test 74

1. ABYSMAL   (A) bottomless   (B) ill   (C) forgetful   (D) unoccupied   (E) slight

2. PREROGATIVE   (A) forewarning   (B) formal investigation   (C) privilege   (D) reputation   (E) opening speech

3. ILLUSTRIOUS   (A) believable   (B) unrewarding   (C) cynical   (D) decorative   (E) famous

4. INTERMINABLE   (A) scanty   (B) secret   (C) open-faced   (D) endless   (E) stationary

5. FRANCHISE   (A) secrecy   (B) right to vote   (C) imprisonment   (D) free-for-all   (E) avoidable tragedy

6. LINEAGE   (A) brilliance   (B) ancestry   (C) narrowness   (D) straightness   (E) ceremony

7. RECIPROCATE   (A) reconsider   (B) refresh   (C) repay   (D) recall   (E) reclaim

8. REBUFF   (A) send back   (B) make over   (C) snub   (D) defend   (E) remind

9. CLANDESTINE   (A) unfriendly   (B) fateful   (C) unified   (D) secret   (E) argumentative

10. LETHARGY   (A) unnatural drowsiness   (B) excessive caution   (C) lack of consideration   (D) vice   (E) foolishness

Vocabulary Test 75

1. ACCREDITED   (A) obligated   (B) approved   (C) discharged   (D) quickened   (E) confessed

2. ADHERENT   (A) clergyman   (B) critic   (C) executive   (D) supporter   (E) journalist

3. WHEEDLE   (A) mourn   (B) coax   (C) revolve   (D) hesitate   (E) entertain

4. CIRCUITOUS   (A) electrical   (B) watery   (C) roundabout   (D) forbidding   (E) tender

5. DESPOT   (A) murderer   (B) impostor   (C) invader   (D) avenger   (E) tyrant

6. DETER   (A) hinder   (B) mistake   (C) neglect   (D) injure   (E) restore

7. UTILITARIAN   (A) practical   (B) widespread   (C) inexpensive   (D) praiseworthy   (E) fortunate

8. INCREDULITY   (A) forgetfulness   (B) faithlessness   (C) immaturity   (D) disbelief   (E) unreality

9. INTERDICT   (A) lessen   (B) separate   (C) fatigue   (D) permit   (E) forbid

10. TIMOROUS   (A) necessary   (B) expected   (C) afraid   (D) wild   (E) brief

Vocabulary Test 76

1. BRAWN   (A) boldness   (B) muscular strength   (C) rustiness   (D) unruliness   (E) protective covering

2. STALEMATE   (A) athletic contest   (B) complete defeat   (C) deadlock   (D) storm   (E) refusal to fight

3. KINDLE   (A) relate   (B) pass on   (C) pretend   (D) arouse   (E) punish

4. POMP   (A) splendor   (B) illness   (C) hopefulness   (D) apple   (E) posture

5. TINGE   (A) mold   (B) draw forth   (C) color slightly   (D) sketch   (E) create

6. RECOIL   (A) steer   (B) link up   (C) put down   (D) scrape   (E) shrink back

7. QUASH   (A) creep   (B) mix thoroughly   (C) repeat   (D) suppress completely   (E) falsify

8. PALTRY   (A) trivial   (B) sacred   (C) metallic   (D) careless   (E) positive

9. IMPETUOUS   (A) controlled   (B) hasty   (C) vigorous   (D) defamatory   (E) vehement

10. HARANGUE   (A) unintelligible prose   (B) ranting speech   (C) poetic imagery   (D) anonymous letter   (E) heavy overcoat

Vocabulary Test 77

1. APROPOS   (A) witty   (B) forceful   (C) nearly correct   (D) richly decorated   (E) to the point

2. INIMICAL   (A) speechles   (B) unfriendly (C) unnecessarily rude   (D) poor   (E) hopelessly sad

3. SORDID   (A) biting   (B) filthy (C) mysterious   (D) griefstricken   (E) sickly

4. CATACLYSM   (A) severe criticism   (B) gorge (C) launching device   (D) unconsciousness (E) violent upheaval

5. FETTERED   (A) stricken   (B) scolded (C) commanded   (D) confined   (E) loosened

6. VERACITY   (A) endurance   (B) selfishness (C) truthfulness   (D) courtesy (E) thoughtfulness

7. REPLETE   (A) filled   (B) tarnished (C) golden   (D) economical   (E) wrecked

8. TREED   (A) met   (B) cornered (C) followed   (D) searched   (E) scented

9. DERISIVE   (A) hereditary   (B) rebellious (C) fragmentary   (D) scornful   (E) determined

10. TEMPER   (A) decorate   (B) annoy (C) blame   (D) postpone   (E) moderate

Vocabulary Test 78

1. RESIDUE   (A) dwelling   (B) remainder (C) debt   (D) sample   (E) storehouse

2. BUNGLE   (A) complain   (B) approach (C) live in   (D) handle badly   (E) talk boastfully

3. ADVOCATE   (A) flatter   (B) caution (C) recommend   (D) take an oath   (E) charge

4. CALAMITOUS   (A) disastrous (B) inexperienced   (C) hardhearted (D) scheming   (E) slanderous

5. JILT   (A) fill in   (B) cast aside   (C) move about   (D) pick up   (E) help forward

6. FUTILE   (A) violent   (B) one-sided (C) weary   (D) stingy   (E) useless

7. INCESSANT   (A) even   (B) illegal (C) dirty   (D) continuous   (E) loud

8. PRATTLE   (A) sell   (B) storm   (C) babble (D) explain   (E) keep

9. PERVERSE   (A) contrary   (B) rhythmic (C) imaginary   (D) alert   (E) rich

10. QUARRY   (A) dispute   (B) prey   (C) initial (D) request   (E) output

Vocabulary Test 79

1. PATERNAL   (A) generous   (B) aged (C) fatherly   (D) thrifty   (E) narrowminded

2. CALIBER   (A) gaiety   (B) quality   (C) hope (D) similarity   (E) politeness

3. PARADOX   (A) virtuous man   (B) equal rights   (C) seeming contradiction (D) complicated design   (E) geometric figure

4. DISPEL   (A) punish   (B) excite   (C) pay out (D) drive away   (E) misunderstand

5. VERBATIM   (A) out loud   (B) word for word (C) in set phrases   (D) elegantly expressed (E) using too many words

6. GRUELING   (A) exhausting   (B) surprising (C) insulting   (D) embarrassing   (E) boring

7. CREDIBILITY   (A) freedom from prejudice (B) religious doctrine   (C) capacity for belief (D) questioning attitude   (E) good judgment

8. APPROPRIATE   (A) betray   (B) compliment (C) take possession of   (D) give thanks (E) draw near to

9. EXONERATE   (A) overcharge   (B) lengthen (C) leave out   (D) free from blame   (E) serve as a model

10. BLAND   (A) flattering   (B) foolish (C) successful   (D) soothing   (E) sharp

Vocabulary Test 80

1. EFFIGY   (A) representation   (B) shadow (C) parade   (D) ancestor   (E) present

2. ZEST   (A) operation   (B) mood   (C) great dismay   (D) keen enjoyment   (E) false alarm

3. ASTUTE   (A) shrewd   (B) inflammable (C) defiant   (D) out of tune   (E) bitter

4. DISCREPANCY   (A) variance   (B) disbelief (C) feebleness   (D) insult   (E) forcefulness

5. COPIOUS   (A) copyrighted   (B) tricky (C) abundant   (D) complete   (E) sincere

6. ADVENT   (A) approval   (B) opportunity (C) welcome   (D) recommendation   (E) arrival

7. IMMINENT   (A) about to occur   (B) never-ending   (C) up-to-date   (D) inconvenient (E) youthful

8. RANKLE   (A) spread around   (B) seize quickly   (C) crease   (D) search   (E) irritate deeply

9. INJUNCTION   (A) exclamation (B) rebellion   (C) directive   (D) crisis (E) illegality

10. DEFT   (A) critical   (B) conceited (C) lighthearted   (D) skillful   (E) tactful

Vocabulary Test 81

1. HEEDLESS   (A) unfortunate   (B) expensive
(C) careless   (D) happy   (E) weatherbeaten

2. IMPEDIMENT   (A) obstacle   (B) base
(C) spice   (D) mechanism   (E) footstool

3. QUAVER   (A) launch   (B) quicken
(C) sharpen   (D) tremble   (E) forget

4. SHACKLE   (A) hide   (B) glide   (C) anger
(D) quiet   (E) hamper

5. LOWLY   (A) idle   (B) silent   (C) humble
(D) sorrowful   (E) solitary

6. CUBICLE   (A) wedge   (B) puzzle   (C) tiny
amount   (D) unit of measure   (E) small
compartment

7. ARRAIGN   (A) debate   (B) accuse
(C) excite   (D) cancel   (E) protect

8. OBLIVIOUS   (A) unwanted   (B) disorderly
(C) unaware   (D) sickly   (E) evident

9. PROFOUND   (A) plentiful   (B) beneficial
(C) lengthy   (D) religious   (E) deep

10. WAN   (A) pale   (B) humorous   (C) pleasing
(D) watchful   (E) lovesick

Vocabulary Test 82

1. HAUNT   (A) contain   (B) give up
(C) expect   (D) stay around   (E) extend greatly

2. UNMINDFUL   (A) unaware   (B) illogical
(C) unaccustomed   (D) unchanging
(E) inefficient

3. EMANCIPATE   (A) change   (B) overjoy
(C) bring forward   (D) raise up   (E) set free

4. LOLL   (A) find   (B) respect   (C) lounge
(D) steal   (E) trap

5. SUBSEQUENT   (A) later   (B) lower
(C) thick   (D) secret   (E) light

6. CRUCIAL   (A) reverent   (B) decisive
(C) tiresome   (D) dangerous   (E) rude

7. REBUKE   (A) prove   (B) dislike
(C) overwork   (D) swallow   (E) criticize

8. CLOISTERED   (A) uneasy   (B) agreeable
(C) sincere   (D) regretful   (E) confined

9. DRONE   (A) beggar   (B) nightmare   (C) queen
bee   (D) humming sound   (E) delaying action

10. PEDESTRIAN   (A) clumsy   (B) senseless
(C) curious   (D) learned   (E) commonplace

Vocabulary Test 83

1. DAWDLE   (A) hang loosely   (B) waste time
(C) fondle   (D) splash   (E) paint

2. ANGUISH   (A) torment   (B) boredom
(C) resentment   (D) stubbornness
(E) clumsiness

3. IMPARTIAL   (A) unlawful   (B) incomplete
(C) unprejudiced   (D) unfaithful
(E) unimportant

4. FORESTALL   (A) press   (B) preserve
(C) prevent   (D) boil   (E) restore

5. EFFRONTERY   (A) boldness   (B) agitation
(C) brilliance   (D) toil   (E) talkativeness

6. EMBROIL   (A) explain   (B) entangle
(C) swindle   (D) greet   (E) imitate

7. INCANDESCENT   (A) insincere
(B) melodious   (C) electrical   (D) magical
(E) glowing

8. STENTORIAN   (A) extremely careful   (B) little
known   (C) hardly capable   (D) rarely reliable
(E) very loud

9. RENEGADE   (A) retired soldier   (B) public
speaker   (C) complainer   (D) traitor
(E) comedian

10. INTERMITTENT   (A) emphatic   (B) stormy
(C) hopeless   (D) innermost   (E) periodic

Vocabulary Test 84

1. INTERLOPER   (A) thief   (B) intruder
(C) translator   (D) inquirer   (E) representative

2. SCATHING   (A) bitterly severe   (B) hastily
spoken   (C) unnecessary   (D) ill-advised
(E) easiy misunderstood

3. ACRID   (A) abnormal   (B) gifted
(C) insincere   (D) drying   (E) irritating

4. TALISMAN   (A) peddler   (B) mechanic
(C) charm   (D) juryman   (E) metal key

5. DISPATCH   (A) stir up   (B) leave out
(C) glorify   (D) persuade   (E) send away

6. BOOTY   (A) navy   (B) arson   (C) police
(D) voyage   (E) spoils

7. DEMURE   (A) unforgiving   (B) out-of-date
(C) modest   (D) uncooperative
(E) overemotional

8. CRUX   (A) great disappointment
(B) supporting argument   (C) debatable issue
(D) critical point   (E) criminal act

9. AGGRANDIZE   (A) enlarge   (B) condense
(C) astonish   (D) interpret   (E) attack

10. SUMPTUOUS   (A) dictatorial   (B) topmost
(C) radiant   (D) luxurious   (E) additional

Vocabulary Test 85

1. VERSATILE   (A) lonesome   (B) backward   (C) talkative   (D) brave   (E) all-around

2. FORTHRIGHT   (A) frank   (B) joyful   (C) imaginary   (D) conscious   (E) preferred

3. TUSSLE   (A) meet   (B) struggle   (C) confuse   (D) murmur   (E) practice

4. CLARITY   (A) loudness   (B) certainty   (C) clearness   (D) glamour   (E) tenderness

5. ASSESSMENT   (A) appraisal   (B) revision   (C) property   (D) illness   (E) warning

6. CLIQUE   (A) social outcast   (B) ringing sound   (C) headdress   (D) exclusive group   (E) tangled web

7. NEGATE   (A) polish to a bright shine   (B) find quickly   (C) make ineffective   (D) file a protest   (E) take into consideration

8. IMPEL   (A) accuse   (B) force   (C) encourage   (D) prevent   (E) pierce

9. CONSTRAINTS   (A) group processes   (B) new laws   (C) doctrines   (D) current news   (E) limits

10. ORTHODOX   (A) accepted   (B) flawless   (C) contradictory   (D) dignified   (E) extraordinary

Vocabulary Test 86

1. COUNTERPART   (A) hindrance   (B) peace offering   (C) password   (D) balance of power   (E) duplicate

2. LOW-KEY   (A) official   (B) secret   (C) restrained   (D) unheard of   (E) complicated

3. STIPULATION   (A) imitation   (B) signal   (C) excitement   (D) agreement   (E) decoration

4. ANTITHESIS   (A) fixed dislike   (B) musical response   (C) lack of feeling   (D) direct opposite   (E) prior knowledge

5. TRANSITORY   (A) short-lived   (B) delayed   (C) idle   (D) unexpected   (E) clear

6. ENTRENCHED   (A) filled up   (B) bordered by   (C) followed by   (D) kept down   (E) dug in

7. LOT   (A) name   (B) right   (C) folly   (D) fate   (E) oath

8. APPREHENSION   (A) gratitude   (B) requirement   (C) apology   (D) dread   (E) punishment

9. AMENABLE   (A) religious   (B) masculine   (C) proud   (D) brave   (E) agreeable

10. AFFLUENT   (A) neutral   (B) sentimental   (C) wealthy   (D) handsome   (E) evil

Vocabulary Test 87

1. VELOCITY   (A) willingness   (B) swiftness   (C) truthfulness   (D) smoothness   (E) skillfulness

2. ENVOY   (A) messenger   (B) assistant   (C) planner   (D) expert   (E) leader

3. AUXILIARY   (A) reliable   (B) mechanical   (C) sociable   (D) supporting   (E) protective

4. PINNACLE   (A) topmost point   (B) feather   (C) fastener   (D) card game   (E) small boat

5. BOORISH   (A) shy   (B) rude   (C) thieving   (D) cunning   (E) foreign

6. ENCOMPASS   (A) include   (B) measure   (C) attempt   (D) direct   (E) border on

7. LURCH   (A) trap   (B) brake   (C) stagger   (D) waste time   (E) laugh noisily

8. EFFACE   (A) rub out   (B) paint red   (C) build upon   (D) stay in front   (E) bring about

9. ABOUND   (A) do good   (B) store up   (C) run away   (D) stand firm   (E) be plentiful

10. THWART   (A) avoid   (B) accuse   (C) suffer   (D) block   (E) serve

Vocabulary Test 88

1. PRUNE   (A) cut off   (B) expect   (C) put away   (D) lay waste   (E) remind

2. AMIABLE   (A) active   (B) good-natured   (C) religious   (D) changeable   (E) absent-minded

3. IMPROVISE   (A) object loudly   (B) predict   (C) refuse support   (D) prepare offhand   (E) translate

4. CONNIVE   (A) cooperate secretly   (B) enter quickly   (C) pause slightly   (D) push unexpectedly   (E) need greatly

5. GAIT   (A) turning over and over   (B) passing in review   (C) manner of walking   (D) fundamental attitude   (E) crowd of spectators

6. BOTCH   (A) weep   (B) rebel   (C) resent   (D) blunder   (E) complain

7. DEVOID OF   (A) accompanied by   (B) in the care of   (C) without   (D) behind   (E) despite

8. PANG   (A) feeling of indifference   (B) sense of duty   (C) fatal disease   (D) universal remedy   (E) spasm of pain

9. TEDIUM   (A) bad temper   (B) boredom   (C) warmth   (D) abundance   (E) musical form

10. INTIMATE   (A) hospitable   (B) well-behaved   (C) familiar   (D) plainly seen   (E) forgiving

Vocabulary Test 89

1. DELVE   (A) hope for   (B) believe in   (C) set upon   (D) take into account   (E) dig into

2. SHROUDED   (A) found   (B) torn   (C) stoned   (D) wrapped   (E) rewarded

3. EXPLOIT   (A) annoy   (B) join   (C) use   (D) mix up   (E) set free

4. RUT   (A) fixed practice   (B) honest labor   (C) useless regret   (D) happy home   (E) vain hope

5. CONSTITUENTS   (A) tradesmen   (B) students   (C) voters   (D) judges   (E) ministers

6. REPREHENSIBLE   (A) distracting   (B) blameworthy   (C) glowing   (D) frightening   (E) truthful

7. HAZARD   (A) confuse   (B) avoid   (C) resign   (D) chance   (E) overlook

8. ROBUST   (A) bragging   (B) huge   (C) sincere   (D) upright   (E) sturdy

9. PIECEMEAL   (A) on the spur of the moment   (B) bit by bit   (C) over and over   (D) as a matter of course   (E) from first to last

10. INSCRUTABLE   (A) disorderly   (B) shallow   (C) unwritten   (D) painful   (E) mysterious

Vocabulary Test 90

1. NEEDLE   (A) join   (B) prod   (C) discuss   (D) give   (E) command

2. TENTATIVE   (A) forgotten   (B) fabricated   (C) sunny   (D) temporary   (E) absentee

3. HUMDRUM   (A) false   (B) ugly   (C) uninteresting   (D) mournful   (E) disappointing

4. RATIFY   (A) create   (B) revive   (C) deny   (D) confirm   (E) displease

5. HORDE   (A) crowd   (B) framework   (C) nonbeliever   (D) choir   (E) warrior

6. RELENTLESS   (A) unwise   (B) fearless   (C) straightforward   (D) unappetizing   (E) unyielding

7. MUDDLE   (A) saucy remark   (B) confused mess   (C) delaying tactics   (D) simple truth   (E) great outcry

8. ADULTERATE   (A) grow up   (B) push ahead   (C) make impure   (D) send away   (E) die off

9. CONCEDE   (A) gain   (B) join   (C) force   (D) struggle   (E) admit

10. PLIGHT   (A) final decision   (B) spy system   (C) plant disease   (D) bad situation   (E) listening post

Vocabulary Test 91

1. BURLY   (A) useless   (B) wild   (C) strong   (D) easy   (E) medical

2. DEBASE   (A) call to mind   (B) send from home   (C) rely upon   (D) take part in   (E) reduce the value of

3. STANCE   (A) performance   (B) defense   (C) length   (D) posture   (E) concentration

4. EXACT   (A) fall   (B) appeal   (C) strain   (D) loosen   (E) demand

5. DANK   (A) moist   (B) unhealthy   (C) smoky   (D) frozen   (E) cloudy

6. EXPRESSLY   (A) definitely   (B) regularly   (C) quickly   (D) safely   (E) loudly

7. DISCOUNT   (A) discover   (B) disgrace   (C) disregard   (D) dislike   (E) display

8. TOKEN   (A) timely   (B) minimal   (C) stiff   (D) imaginary   (E) enforced

9. DECADENCE   (A) false reasoning   (B) hasty retreat   (C) self-assurance   (D) period of decline   (E) fraud

10. ALACRITY   (A) eagerness   (B) joy   (C) criticism   (D) milkiness   (E) fullness

Vocabulary Test 92

1. CLAMOR   (A) magic spell   (B) loose garment   (C) poisoned arrow   (D) loud noise   (E) deep-sea fisherman

2. CONVENTIONAL   (A) inexperienced   (B) close   (C) foolish   (D) kindly   (E) usual

3. INDISPUTABLE   (A) unjust   (B) undeniable   (C) indelicate   (D) indescribable   (E) unconcerned

4. PUNY   (A) weak   (B) humorous   (C) quarrelsome   (D) studious   (E) innocent

5. FACILITATE   (A) make angry   (B) copy   (C) make easier   (D) joke about   (E) decorate

6. REPULSE   (A) force   (B) disown   (C) restore   (D) repel   (E) indicate

7. CHARISMA   (A) happy feeling   (B) quality of leadership   (C) Greek letter   (D) deep hole   (E) contrary view

8. RIGOR   (A) padding   (B) mold   (C) liner   (D) building   (E) strictness

9. NOXIOUS   (A) harmful   (B) lively   (C) uncertain   (D) unprepared   (E) calming

10. ENLIGHTEN   (A) please   (B) put away   (C) instruct   (D) reduce   (E) criticize

Vocabulary Test 93

1. INTANGIBLE   (A) incomplete
(B) individual   (C) vague   (D) uninjured
(E) careless

2. COMPLIANT   (A) yielding   (B) standing
(C) admiring   (D) trusting   (E) grabbing

3. ERADICATE   (A) exclaim   (B) heat up
(C) break out   (D) plant   (E) eliminate

4. ABYSS   (A) great ignorance   (B) evil man
(C) bottomless pit   (D) wide sea   (E) religious
sign

5. CRITERION   (A) standard   (B) award
(C) achievement   (D) objection   (E) claim

6. IRREVERENT   (A) illogical
(B) unimportant   (C) violent
(D) disrespectful   (E) unafraid

7. SALLOW   (A) temporary   (B) animal-like
(C) stupid   (D) clean   (E) yellowish

8. RENOUNCE   (A) proclaim   (B) approve
(C) give up   (D) guarantee   (E) speak plainly

9. ASSIMILATE   (A) pretend   (B) absorb
(C) poke   (D) copy   (E) expect

10. EXHORT   (A) annoy   (B) deduct   (C) enlarge
quickly   (D) urge strongly   (E) stick out

Vocabulary Test 94

1. JEST   (A) spout   (B) trot   (C) joke
(D) judge   (E) leap

2. MOLEST   (A) disturb   (B) reduce
(C) submit   (D) delight   (E) urge

3. TURMOIL   (A) conclusion   (B) reversal
(C) meanness   (D) confusion   (E) mistake

4. ORDINANCE   (A) trial   (B) law   (C) right
(D) fault   (E) property

5. LATERAL   (A) financial   (B) lingering   (C) of
the past   (D) from the beginning   (E) to the side

6. PIGMENT   (A) light   (B) pillar   (C) dye
(D) weed   (E) book

7. CONCEPT   (A) desire   (B) thought
(C) solution   (D) method   (E) experiment

8. ORNATE   (A) elaborate   (B) original
(C) systematic   (D) unbecoming   (E) obsolete

9. BEGRUDGE   (A) roar mightily   (B) walk
swiftly   (C) give reluctantly   (D) await eagerly
(E) seek desperately

10. REPOSE   (A) task   (B) calm   (C) strain
(D) fact   (E) surprise

Vocabulary Test 95

1. BOLSTER   (A) reinforce   (B) thicken
(C) uncover   (D) quote   (E) bother

2. INFRINGEMENT   (A) old age   (B) added
benefit   (C) protection   (D) violation
(E) fireproofing

3. AGILE   (A) colored   (B) healthy   (C) dull
(D) false   (E) nimble

4. DIVERSIFY   (A) fix   (B) vary   (C) correct
(D) relieve   (E) explain

5. RUSTLE   (A) steal   (B) instruct   (C) strive
(D) bend   (E) tax

6. HAPLESS   (A) optimistic   (B) uncounted
(C) unfortunate   (D) simple   (E) unyielding

7. UNPRETENTIOUS   (A) loyal   (B) virtuous
(C) modest   (D) fair   (E) extravagant

8. BUOY   (A) wet   (B) dry up   (C) rescue
(D) sustain   (E) direct

9. PARAGON   (A) weak pun   (B) even
distribution   (C) geometric figure   (D) moralistic
story   (E) model of excellence

10. INDIGENOUS   (A) confused   (B) native
(C) poor   (D) unconcerned   (E) wrathful

Vocabulary Test 96

1. PROLOGUE   (A) stairway   (B) introduction
(C) conversation   (D) reading   (E) extension

2. ACKNOWLEDGE   (A) propose   (B) strangle
(C) convict   (D) advance   (E) admit

3. INDICTMENT   (A) accusation   (B) publisher
(C) announcer   (D) conviction   (E) trial

4. LACKLUSTER   (A) sparkling   (B) tender
(C) misty   (D) uninspired   (E) disobedient

5. CONDOMINIUM   (A) new type of metal
(B) noisy celebration   (C) individually owned
apartment   (D) important decision   (E) group
meeting

6. INCUMBENT   (A) office holder   (B) lawyer
(C) politician   (D) green vegetable   (E) sacred
honor

7. POLARIZATION   (A) performance in cold
weather   (B) point of view   (C) change in
opinion   (D) division into opposites   (E) cultural
bias

8. GENESIS   (A) wisdom   (B) origin
(C) classification   (D) humor   (E) night

9. DIMINUTION   (A) devotion   (B) difference
(C) difficulty   (D) decision   (E) decrease

10. WARY   (A) sorrowful   (B) lazy
(C) unfriendly   (D) cautious   (E) hopeful

Vocabulary Test 97

1. SLEEK   (A) smooth   (B) moldy   (C) loose   (D) small   (E) delicate

2. SUCCULENT   (A) literal   (B) tardy   (C) yielding   (D) sportsmanlike   (E) juicy

3. LACERATED   (A) bright   (B) gaunt   (C) punishable   (D) torn   (E) tied

4. SUBSIDE   (A) pay in full   (B) become quiet   (C) return soon   (D) rush around   (E) send forth

5. ACQUITTAL   (A) setting free   (B) agreeing with   (C) holding forth   (D) getting up steam   (E) appealing to higher authority

6. APPREHEND   (A) inform   (B) resound   (C) frighten   (D) squeeze   (E) seize

7. IMPERATIVE   (A) unbiased   (B) obscure   (C) repetitious   (D) compulsory   (E) unworthy

8. SUBSTANTIATE   (A) verify   (B) replace   (C) influence   (D) condemn   (E) accept

9. RANCID   (A) illegal   (B) rotten   (C) ashen   (D) flimsy   (E) mean

10. OUST   (A) nag   (B) evict   (C) excel   (D) defy   (E) emerge

Vocabulary Test 98

1. TOPPLE   (A) drink   (B) choose   (C) stray   (D) stumble   (E) overturn

2. PREVAIL   (A) preview   (B) question   (C) relax   (D) triumph   (E) restore

3. CREDENCE   (A) cowardice   (B) size   (C) belief   (D) variety   (E) nobility

4. DIVULGE   (A) send   (B) shrink   (C) despair   (D) separate   (E) reveal

5. MISGIVINGS   (A) cheap gifts   (B) feelings of doubt   (C) added treats   (D) false promises   (E) slips of the tongue

6. ACCLAIM   (A) find   (B) restore   (C) praise   (D) judge   (E) demand

7. HALLOWED   (A) sacred   (B) noisy   (C) deep   (D) permitted   (E) costumed

8. GUISE   (A) ability   (B) direction   (C) guilt   (D) appearance   (E) mistake

9. TUMULT   (A) vacation   (B) reversal   (C) swelling   (D) suffering   (E) commotion

10. REMINISCENT   (A) amazed by   (B) obligated to   (C) suggestive of   (D) under the control of   (E) careless with

Vocabulary Test 99

1. REMIT   (A) promise   (B) injure   (C) send   (D) profit   (E) menace

2. PANDEMONIUM   (A) wild uproar   (B) diseased state   (C) contempt   (D) luxury   (E) gloom

3. EJECT   (A) expose   (B) exceed   (C) extend   (D) expel   (E) excite

4. TALLY   (A) load   (B) record   (C) hunt   (D) play   (E) move

5. DEVASTATE   (A) cough   (B) ruin   (C) chop   (D) point   (E) swell

6. MAUL   (A) trap   (B) cuddle   (C) carve   (D) throw   (E) beat

7. ANIMATION   (A) liveliness   (B) automation   (C) carelessness   (D) dispute   (E) exchange

8. SMOLDER   (A) show suppressed anger   (B) grow up quickly   (C) find easily   (D) report back   (E) become weary

9. PROTRUDE   (A) make a fool of   (B) fall into   (C) put down   (D) thrust out   (E) steer clear of

10. BENEVOLENT   (A) profitable   (B) sociable   (C) wealthy   (D) receptive   (E) charitable

Vocabulary Test 100

1. UNOBTRUSIVE   (A) annoying   (B) unquestionable   (C) inconspicuous   (D) united   (E) healthy

2. SCRUTINY   (A) signal   (B) plot   (C) delay   (D) investigation   (E) announcement

3. HEINOUS   (A) evil   (B) permanent   (C) unreasonable   (D) open   (E) timid

4. GARRULOUS   (A) confused   (B) eager   (C) panting   (D) talkative   (E) informal

5. CONVERSE   (A) junction   (B) poetry   (C) ancestor   (D) follower   (E) opposite

6. MALEFACTOR   (A) fugitive   (B) joker   (C) showoff   (D) evildoer   (E) daydreamer

7. MARTIAL   (A) heavenly   (B) keen   (C) warlike   (D) tremendous   (E) masculine

8. RETORT   (A) answer   (B) jot   (C) retire   (D) recall   (E) decay

9. VIGILANCE   (A) lawlessness   (B) funeral   (C) watchfulness   (D) processional   (E) strength

10. LESION   (A) dream   (B) group   (C) justice   (D) style   (E) injury

ANSWERS TO VOCABULARY TESTS

Test 1	Test 5	Test 9	Test 13	Test 17	Test 21	Test 25	Test 29
1. D	1. C	1. E	1. B	1. A	1. C	1. A	1. B
2. B	2. B	2. C	2. E	2. B	2. E	2. D	2. A
3. D	3. D	3. E	3. B	3. D	3. D	3. E	3. D
4. A	4. D	4. C	4. B	4. E	4. C	4. C	4. E
5. E	5. C	5. D	5. C	5. E	5. B	5. A	5. C
6. B	6. E	6. C	6. C	6. B	6. D	6. B	6. E
7. E	7. A	7. A	7. E	7. D	7. E	7. E	7. B
8. A	8. A	8. D	8. A	8. A	8. D	8. B	8. E
9. E	9. E	9. D	9. D	9. B	9. A	9. C	9. E
10. C	10. C	10. D	10. C	10. D	10. D	10. D	10. C

Test 2	Test 6	Test 10	Test 14	Test 18	Test 22	Test 26	Test 30
1. B	1. C	1. B	1. C	1. E	1. B	1. E	1. E
2. A	2. E	2. E	2. E	2. C	2. D	2. C	2. C
3. E	3. D	3. D	3. C	3. B	3. A	3. A	3. A
4. D	4. C	4. C	4. E	4. C	4. E	4. C	4. B
5. A	5. B	5. B	5. A	5. C	5. E	5. B	5. D
6. E	6. E	6. B	6. E	6. A	6. E	6. E	6. E
7. C	7. B	7. E	7. D	7. E	7. D	7. D	7. D
8. A	8. E	8. B	8. D	8. A	8. A	8. E	8. B
9. B	9. C	9. A	9. E	9. D	9. E	9. D	9. C
10. E	10. D	10. B	10. E	10. A	10. D	10. B	10. A

Test 3	Test 7	Test 11	Test 15	Test 19	Test 23	Test 27	Test 31
1. C	1. E	1. A	1. B	1. B	1. C	1. A	1. B
2. D	2. A	2. D	2. C	2. E	2. D	2. D	2. A
3. B	3. D	3. A	3. A	3. C	3. B	3. C	3. D
4. C	4. D	4. E	4. C	4. D	4. D	4. B	4. A
5. B	5. B	5. A	5. B	5. A	5. D	5. C	5. C
6. B	6. B	6. B	6. E	6. A	6. D	6. B	6. E
7. D	7. B	7. A	7. C	7. D	7. A	7. B	7. D
8. C	8. E	8. E	8. D	8. B	8. B	8. A	8. E
9. A	9. A	9. C	9. A	9. A	9. E	9. A	9. B
10. E	10. B	10. E	10. B	10. B	10. D	10. E	10. A

Test 4	Test 8	Test 12	Test 16	Test 20	Test 24	Test 28	Test 32
1. E	1. D	1. C	1. D	1. A	1. B	1. E	1. E
2. D	2. A	2. D	2. C	2. B	2. B	2. B	2. A
3. E	3. D	3. B	3. D	3. D	3. A	3. C	3. B
4. A	4. E	4. D	4. B	4. B	4. E	4. A	4. D
5. E	5. A	5. B	5. B	5. B	5. E	5. B	5. B
6. A	6. C	6. C	6. A	6. A	6. E	6. D	6. A
7. A	7. A	7. E	7. D	7. C	7. C	7. A	7. C
8. D	8. C	8. B	8. B	8. A	8. E	8. E	8. B
9. E	9. A	9. D	9. A	9. A	9. B	9. A	9. B
10. C	10. D	10. E	10. A	10. E	10. B	10. D	10. E

Test 33	Test 37	Test 41	Test 45	Test 49	Test 53	Test 57	Test 61
1. C	1. C	1. A	1. E	1. B	1. E	1. E	1. B
2. D	2. B	2. D	2. A	2. E	2. E	2. C	2. D
3. B	3. A	3. E	3. D	3. A	3. D	3. B	3. B
4. C	4. C	4. D	4. C	4. C	4. E	4. A	4. D
5. D	5. E	5. C	5. E	5. C	5. B	5. B	5. A
6. E	6. A	6. A	6. B	6. D	6. D	6. A	6. B
7. B	7. D	7. E	7. B	7. D	7. B	7. C	7. D
8. B	8. A	8. B	8. E	8. A	8. D	8. C	8. C
9. A	9. E	9. E	9. D	9. E	9. D	9. D	9. D
10. E	10. E	10. D	10. A	10. C	10. E	10. A	10. B

Test 34	Test 38	Test 42	Test 46	Test 50	Test 54	Test 58	Test 62
1. A	1. D	1. B	1. B	1. A	1. C	1. B	1. D
2. B	2. E	2. E	2. D	2. C	2. D	2. A	2. A
3. E	3. E	3. B	3. C	3. A	3. E	3. E	3. A
4. A	4. A	4. B	4. D	4. C	4. C	4. D	4. D
5. B	5. E	5. B	5. B	5. D	5. C	5. C	5. A
6. D	6. D	6. E	6. E	6. B	6. C	6. D	6. A
7. D	7. C	7. C	7. D	7. B	7. B	7. C	7. D
8. B	8. B	8. D	8. B	8. A	8. E	8. E	8. E
9. B	9. C	9. A	9. A	9. A	9. E	9. D	9. D
10. C	10. A	10. C	10. E	10. B	10. C	10. A	10. B

Test 35	Test 39	Test 43	Test 47	Test 51	Test 55	Test 59	Test 63
1. A	1. E	1. A	1. C	1. D	1. C	1. D	1. B
2. E	2. A	2. B	2. C	2. D	2. B	2. D	2. D
3. B	3. D	3. D	3. D	3. C	3. D	3. D	3. C
4. A	4. C	4. C	4. D	4. B	4. A	4. E	4. E
5. C	5. B	5. E	5. A	5. A	5. C	5. E	5. A
6. D	6. B	6. C	6. A	6. D	6. E	6. B	6. A
7. E	7. A	7. E	7. B	7. B	7. D	7. A	7. D
8. D	8. E	8. D	8. E	8. B	8. E	8. E	8. E
9. B	9. C	9. C	9. C	9. B	9. A	9. E	9. C
10. B	10. D	10. A	10. E	10. A	10. C	10. B	10. B

Test 36	Test 40	Test 44	Test 48	Test 52	Test 56	Test 60	Test 64
1. C	1. A	1. A	1. B	1. B	1. A	1. A	1. B
2. B	2. E	2. A	2. C	2. E	2. A	2. B	2. B
3. C	3. C	3. D	3. E	3. A	3. D	3. C	3. C
4. D	4. B	4. D	4. B	4. B	4. D	4. E	4. E
5. A	5. A	5. B	5. E	5. C	5. A	5. B	5. E
6. D	6. C	6. D	6. A	6. C	6. D	6. B	6. B
7. D	7. D	7. C	7. D	7. B	7. B	7. E	7. C
8. E	8. D	8. A	8. D	8. E	8. B	8. D	8. C
9. A	9. A	9. E	9. B	9. A	9. B	9. C	9. A
10. E	10. D	10. D	10. E	10. A	10. C	10. C	10. D

Test 65	Test 69	Test 73	Test 77	Test 81	Test 85	Test 89	Test 93	Test 97
1. E	1. A	1. D	1. E	1. C	1. E	1. E	1. C	1. A
2. A	2. D	2. E	2. E	2. A	2. A	2. D	2. A	2. E
3. E	3. E	3. B	3. B	3. D	3. B	3. C	3. E	3. D
4. B	4. B	4. E	4. E	4. E	4. C	4. A	4. C	4. B
5. D	5. B	5. D	5. D	5. C	5. A	5. C	5. A	5. A
6. D	6. E	6. C	6. C	6. E	6. D	6. B	6. D	6. E
7. A	7. B	7. E	7. A	7. B	7. C	7. D	7. E	7. D
8. E	8. D	8. E	8. B	8. C	8. B	8. E	8. C	8. A
9. A	9. A	9. C	9. D	9. E	9. E	9. E	9. B	9. B
10. E	10. D	10. D	10. E	10. A	10. A	10. E	10. D	10. B

Test 66	Test 70	Test 74	Test 78	Test 82	Test 86	Test 90	Test 94	Test 98
1. C	1. D	1. A	1. B	1. D	1. E	1. B	1. C	1. E
2. B	2. B	2. C	2. D	2. A	2. C	2. D	2. A	2. D
3. B	3. C	3. E	3. C	3. E	3. D	3. C	3. D	3. C
4. D	4. A	4. D	4. A	4. C	4. D	4. D	4. B	4. E
5. B	5. B	5. B	5. B	5. A	5. A	5. A	5. E	5. B
6. C	6. C	6. B	6. E	6. B	6. E	6. E	6. C	6. C
7. E	7. B	7. C	7. D	7. E	7. D	7. B	7. B	7. A
8. D	8. E	8. C	8. C	8. E	8. C	8. C	8. A	8. D
9. E	9. D	9. D	9. A	9. D	9. E	9. E	9. C	9. E
10. A	10. E	10. A	10. B	10. E	10. C	10. D	10. B	10. C

Test 67	Test 71	Test 75	Test 79	Test 83	Test 87	Test 91	Test 95	Test 99
1. B	1. C	1. B	1. C	1. B	1. B	1. C	1. A	1. C
2. B	2. E	2. D	2. B	2. A	2. A	2. E	2. D	2. A
3. D	3. B	3. B	3. C	3. C	3. D	3. D	3. E	3. D
4. A	4. C	4. C	4. D	4. C	4. A	4. E	4. B	4. B
5. B	5. D	5. E	5. B	5. A	5. B	5. A	5. A	5. B
6. E	6. A	6. A	6. A	6. B	6. A	6. A	6. C	6. E
7. C	7. B	7. A	7. C	7. E	7. C	7. C	7. C	7. A
8. A	8. D	8. D	8. C	8. E	8. A	8. B	8. D	8. A
9. A	9. A	9. E	9. D	9. D	9. E	9. D	9. E	9. D
10. C	10. E	10. C	10. D	10. E	10. D	10. A	10. B	10. E

Test 68	Test 72	Test 76	Test 80	Test 84	Test 88	Test 92	Test 96	Test 100
1. E	1. A	1. B	1. A	1. B	1. A	1. D	1. B	1. C
2. B	2. C	2. C	2. D	2. A	2. B	2. E	2. E	2. D
3. A	3. A	3. D	3. A	3. E	3. D	3. B	3. A	3. A
4. B	4. E	4. A	4. A	4. C	4. A	4. A	4. D	4. D
5. B	5. D	5. C	5. C	5. E	5. C	5. C	5. C	5. E
6. E	6. C	6. E	6. E	6. E	6. E	6. D	6. A	6. D
7. D	7. B	7. D	7. A	7. C	7. C	7. B	7. D	7. C
8. C	8. D	8. A	8. E	8. D	8. E	8. E	8. B	8. A
9. E	9. B	9. E	9. C	9. A	9. B	9. A	9. E	9. C
10. C	10. E	10. B	10. D	10. D	10. C	10. C	10. D	10. E

Word Building with Roots, Prefixes, and Suffixes

According to some linguistic studies, approximately 60% of our English words are derived from Latin and Greek. One reliable study has shown that a selected list of 20 prefixes and 14 root elements pertain to over 100,000 words in an unabridged dictionary. The following entries of Latin and Greek roots, prefixes, and suffixes frequently show up in some of the words in all four SAT Verbal areas—Antonyms, Analogies, Sentence Completions, and Reading Comprehension. Learn these Latin and Greek word parts to increase your vocabulary immensely—and thus score well in the Verbal part of your SAT.

> "The shortest and best way of learning a language is to know the roots of it; that is, those original primitive words from which other words are formed."
>
> —Lord Chesterfield

Lord Chesterfield is, in effect, saying that roots are used as important "building blocks" of many of our English words. As you study the following list of Latin and Greek roots, prefixes, and suffixes, have a dictionary by your side. Look up the meanings of the word examples that are given if you do not know their meanings.

ROOTS

A ROOT IS THE BASIC ELEMENT—FUNDAMENTAL OR ESSENTIAL PART—OF A WORD.

ROOT	MEANING AND EXAMPLE*
ag, act	do, act; as *agent, counteract*
agr	field; as *agriculture, agoraphobia*
alt	high; as *altitude, altar*
alter	other; as *altercation, alternative*
am	friend, love; as *amity, amorous*
anim	feeling, spirit; as *unanimous, animosity*
ann	year; as *annuity; annual*
anthrop	man; as *philanthropy, anthropoid*
aper	open; as *aperture, aperient*
apt	fit; as *adapt, aptitude*
aqu	water; as *aqueous, aquacade*
arch	rule, govern; as *anarchy, matriarch*
aster, astr	star, as *asteroid, disaster, astronomy*
aud	hear; as *audible, audition*
aur	gold; as *auriferous*
bas	low; as *debase, basement*
bell	war; as *bellicose, antebellum*
ben	good, well; as *benevolent, benefactor*
bibl	book; as *biblical, bibliography*
bio	life; as *biology, biopsy*
brev	short; as *brevity, abbreviation*
cad, cas, cid	fall; as *cadence, casualty, incident*
cand	white, shining; as *candid, candidate*
cap, capt	take, hold; as *capable, captive*
capit	head; as *capital, decapitate*
carn	flesh; as *carnal, carnivorous*
ced, cess	yield, go; as *cede, procession*
celer	swift; as *celerity, accelerate*
cent	hundred; as *century, centipede*
chrom	color; as *chromium, chromatic*
chron	time; as *chronology, chronic*
cid, cis	cut, kill; as *suicide, precision*
clin	lean, bend; as *inclination, recline*
clud, clus	close, shut; as *conclude, recluse*
cogn	know; as *incognito, cognizant*
cord	heart; as *cordial, accord*
corp	body; as *corpulent, corpse*

ROOT	MEANING AND EXAMPLE*
cosm	world; as *cosmic, cosmopolitan*
cred	believe; as *incredible, credentials*
curr, curs	run; as *current, cursory*
dec	ten; as *decimal, decade*
dem	people; as *democracy, demographic*
derm	skin; as *epidermis, dermatologist*
di	day; as *diary, sundial*
dic, dict	speak, say; as *indicate, contradict*
dign	worthy; as *dignity, indignant*
domin	lord, master, as *dominate, indomitable*
dorm	sleep; as *dormant, dormitory*
duc, duct	lead; as *induce, ductile*
ego	I; as *egotism, egomaniac*
equ	equal; as *equity, equanimity*
fac, fact, fect, fic	make, do; as *facile, factory, infection, fiction*
fer	bear, carry; as *fertile, confer*
fid	faith, trust; as *confide, infidelity*
fin	end; as *infinite, final*
flect, flex	bend; as *reflect, flexible*
form	shape; as *conform, reformation*
fort	strong; as *fortitude, fortify*
frag, fract	break; as *fragile, fracture*
fug	flee; as *fugitive, refugee*
fus	pour; as *confuse, fusion*
gen	kind, race, birth; as *generate, generic, generation*
gest	carry, bring; as *congestion, gestation*
grad, gress	step, go; as *graduate, digress*
graph	write; as *autograph, graphic*
grat	pleasing; as *gratitude, congratulate*
hydr	water; as *dehydrated, hydrant*
integr	entire, whole; as *integrate, integral*
ject	throw; as *inject, projection*
junct	join; as *conjunction, juncture*
lat	carry; as *translation, dilate*
leg, lig, lect	choose, gather, as *legible, eligible, collect*
liber	free; as *liberate, libertine*

*Refer to a dictionary for word meanings you don't know.

ROOT	MEANING AND EXAMPLE
loc	place; as *dislocate, local*
log	word, study; as *catalogue, psychology*
loqu, locut	speak, talk; as *loquacious, circumlocution*
luc, lum	light; as *translucent, illuminate*
magn	great; as *magnitude, magnificent*
man	hand; as *manufacture, manual*
mar	sea; as *marine, maritime*
mater	mother; as *maternal, matrimony*
mega	large; as *megaton, megaphone*
ment	mind; as *mentality, mentally*
merg	plunge, sink; as *submerge, merger*
meter	measure; as *chronometer, symmetry*
micro	small; as *microscope, microfilm*
migr	wander; as *migrate, immigration*
mir	look; as *admire, mirror*
mit, miss	send; as *admit, submission*
mon	advise, remind; as *admonish, monument*
mort	death; as *immortality, mortal*
mot, mov	move; as *motor, motility, movable*
mult	many; as *multitude, multifarious*
mut	change; as *mutation, transmute, immutable*
nat	born; as *natal, innate*
nav	ship; as *naval, navigate*
neg	deny; as *negate, renege*
nomen	name; as *nominee, nomenclature, cognomen*
nov	new; as *novelty, novice, innovation*
ocul	eye; as *oculist, binocular*
oper	work; as *cooperation, operate*
pater, patri	father; as *paternal, patriot*
ped, pod	foot; as *impede, biped, tripod*
ped	child; as *pediatrics, pedagogue*
pel, puls	drive; as *compel, expulsion*
pend, pens	hang; as *pendant, pension*
pet	seek; as *impetus, petition*
petr	stone, rock; as *petrify*
phil	loving; as *philosophy*
phob	fear; as *claustrophobia*
phon	sound; as *phonic, phonetics*
plic	fold, bend; as *complicate, implicate*
pon, pos	place, put; as *component, compose*
port	carry, bring; as *porter, import*
pot	drink; as *potion, potable*

ROOT	MEANING AND EXAMPLE
poten	powerful; as *potentate, impotent*
prehend, prehens	take, grasp; as *apprehend, comprehension*
prot	first; as *protagonist, prototype*
psych	mind; as *psychological, psychic*
quer, quir, quis, ques	ask, seek; as *query, inquiry, inquisition, quest*
reg, rig, rect	rule, govern; as *regent, rigid, corrective*
rid, ris	laugh; as *ridiculous, risible*
rupt	break; as *rupture, erupt, interruption*
sacr	holy; as *sacred, sacrificial*
sanct	holy; as *sanction, sanctify*
sci, scio	know; as *science, conscious, omniscient*
scop	watch; as *periscope, horoscope*
scrib, script	write; as *describe, prescription*
sec, sect	cut; as *secant, bisect*
sed, sid, sess	sit, seat; as *sedate, reside, session*
sent, sens	feel, think; as *sentiment, sensible*
sequ, secut	follow; as *sequel, consecutive*
serv	keep; as *reserve, conservation*
sist	place, stand; as *assist, resistance*
solv, solu	loosen; as *dissolve, absolution*
somn	sleep; as *somnambulist, insomnia*
soph	wisdom; as *sophisticated, philosophy*
spec, spect, spic	look, appear; as *specimen, prospect, conspicuous*
spir	breathe; as *conspire, respiration*
stat, stab	stand; as *status, stability*
string, strict	bind; as *stringent, stricture*
stru, struct	build; as *construe, destructive*
sum, sumpt	take; as *assume, presumption*
tang, ting, tact, tig	touch; as *tangent, contingency, contact, contiguous*
teg, tect	cover; as *tegument; detect*
tele	distance; as *telescope, teletype*
tempor	time; as *temporary, extemporaneous*
ten, tain	hold; reach; as *tenant, tension, retain*
term	end; as *terminal, terminate*
ter, terr	land, earth; as *inter, terrace*
therm	heat; as *thermometer, thermos*
tort, tors	twist; as *contort, torsion*
tract	draw; as *attract, extract*
trit	rub; as *trite, attrition*
trud, trus	thrust; as *intrude, abstruse*

ROOT	MEANING AND EXAMPLE
umbra	shade; as *umbrella, umbrage*
urb	city; as *suburb, urban*
vac	empty; as *vacate; evacuation*
vad, vas	go; as *evade, evasive*
val, vail	be strong; as *valid, prevail*
ven, vent	come; as *convene, prevention*
ver	true; as *veracity, aver*

ROOT	MEANING AND EXAMPLE
verb	word; as *verbose, verbatim*
vert, vers	turn; as *convert, reverse*
vid, vis	see; as *evident, visible*
vinc, vict	conquer; as *invincible, evict*
viv, vit	live; as *vivacity, vital*
voc, vok	call; as in *vocation, revoke*
volv, volut	roll, turn; as in *involve, revolution*

PREFIXES

> A PREFIX IS PART OF A WORD THAT MAY BE PLACED BEFORE THE BASIC ELEMENT (ROOT) OF A WORD.

PREFIX	MEANING AND EXAMPLE
a, ab, abs	from, away; as *avert, abjure, absent*
ad	to; as *adhere.* By assimilation, *ad* takes the forms of **a, ac, af, al, an, ap, as, at;** as *aspire, accord, affect, allude, annex, appeal, assume, attract*
ambi, amphi	around, both; as *ambidexterous, amphibious*
ante, anti	before; as *antedate, anticipate*
anti	against; as *antidote, antislavery*
arch	first, chief; as *archangel, archenemy*
auto	self; as *autobiography, automatic*
ben	good, well; as *benediction, benefactor*
bi	two; as *bilateral, bisect*
circum	around, as *circumnavigate, circumvent*
com, con, col, cor, co	together; as *commit, concord, collect, correct, co-worker*
contra, contro, counter	against; as *contradict, controvert, counteract*
de	down, away from, about; as *descend, depart, describe*
demi	half; as *demigod, demitasse*
dia	across, through; as *diameter, diastole*
dis, di, dif	apart, not; as *dissension, division, diffident*
equi	equal; as *equinox, equivalent*
ex, e, ef	out of, from; as *extract, eject, efface*
extra	out of, beyond; as *extraordinary, extraterrestrial*
hyper	too much; as *hypercritical, hypersensitive*
hypo	too little, under; as *hypochondriac, hypodermic*
in, il, im, ir	into, in, on; as *invade, illustrate, immerse, irritate*

PREFIX	MEANING AND EXAMPLE
in, il, im, ir	not; as *indistinct, illegal, impossible, irresponsible*
inter, intro	between, among; as *interpose, introduce*
mal	bad; as *maltreat, malevolent*
mono	one, single; as *monotone, monorail*
neo	new; as *neoplasm, neophyte*
non	not; as *nonentity, nonconformist*
ob, of, op	against; as *obviate, offend, oppose*
omni	all; as *omniscient, omnipresent*
ortho	straight; as *orthodox, orthopedic*
pan	all; as *pantheism, Pan-American*
peri	around; as *perimeter, periscope*
poly	many; as *polygon, polygamy*
post	after; as *postpone, post-mortem*
pro	forward, before; as *proceed, provide*
re	back, again; as *recur, recede*
retro	backwards; as *retrogress, retrospect*
se	apart, away; as *seduce, sedition*
semi	half; as *semicircle, semiconscious*
sub	under; as *submarine, subversive*
super	above, beyond; as *superpose, supernatural*
syn, sym	with, at the same time; as *synonymous, sympathetic*
trans	across; as *transcontinental, transmit*
ultra	beyond; as *ultraliberal, ultramodern*
un	not; as *unaware, uninformed*
uni	one; as *unanimous, uniform*
vice	instead of; as *vice-chancellor, viceroy*

SUFFIXES

A SUFFIX IS PART OF A WORD THAT MAY FOLLOW THE BASIC ELEMENT (ROOT) OF A WORD.

SUFFIX	MEANING AND EXAMPLE
able	able; as *pliable, returnable*
acious, cious	having the quality of; as *capacious, meretricious*
age	act, condition; as *courage, foliage*
al	belonging to; as *legal, regal*
ance, ence	state of; as *abundance, indulgence*
ate	one who; as *candidate, advocate*
ary, eer, er	one who, concerning; as *secretary, engineer, mariner*
cy	state, position of; as *adequacy, presidency*
dom	state of; as *freedom, serfdom*
ence	state of; as *presence, credence*
er, or	one who; as *player, actor*
escent	becoming; as *adolescent, putrescent*
fy	make; as *beautify; sanctify*
hood	state of; as *knighthood, childhood*
ic, id	of, like; as *bucolic, acrid*

SUFFIX	MEANING AND EXAMPLE
il, ile	capable of being; as *evil, servile*
ion	act of; as *desperation, perspiration*
ious	characterized by; as *spacious, illustrious*
ish	like; as *boyish, foolish*
ism	belief in or practice of; as *idealism, capitalism*
ist	one who practices or is devoted to; as *anarchist, harpist*
ive	relating to; as *abusive, plaintive*
mony	state of; as *harmony, matrimony*
ness	quality of; as *willingness, shrewdness*
or, er	one who; as *monitor, employer*
ory	a place for; as *factory, depository*
ous, ose	full of; as *ponderous, verbose*
ship	state of, skill; as *friendship, gamesmanship*
some	characteristic of; as *loathsome; fearsome*
tude	state of; as *lassitude, rectitude*
ward	in the direction of; as *windward, backward*
y	full of; as *unruly, showy*

A LIST OF SAT ANTONYM QUESTION STEM WORDS APPEARING MORE THAN ONCE ON ACTUAL SAT EXAMS

We have made a computerized analysis of all the Antonym questions on 47 complete recent SAT exams. (1125 Antonym questions have been examined.) Following is a list of 132 SAT Antonym question stem words appearing <u>more than once</u> on these 47 actual SAT tests.

The definitions of these words have not been included here because we want you to <u>refer to a dictionary</u> to learn the meanings of these words which have been repeated in subsequent SAT Antonym question sections.

Note that, after each word, there is a numeral which indicates the number of times that the word has appeared on the 47 actual SAT exams.

Also note that certain pairs of words have a left-side bracket. The bracket indicates that the words are very closely allied in meaning so that if you learn the meaning of one of the two words in the pair, you will easily arrive at the meaning of the other word of the pair.

Learn the meanings of these words since they have a tendency to be repeated in the Antonym questions of the SAT.

abolish 2	[confide 1	evacuate 2	mitigate 2	ruffle 2
abridge 2	[confidential 1	evanescent 2	mobile 2	rupture 2
abstemious	confound 2	[expedite 1	munificent 2	saccharine 2
[accent 1	congeal 2	[expeditious 1	munificence 1	salubrious 2
[accented 1	[contaminant 1	[expendable 1	myriad 2	somber 4
accolade 2	[contaminate 2	[expenditures 1	nefarious 2	[specify 1
acquiesce 2	converge 2	exclude 2	[obscure 1	[specificity 1
affirmation 2	convivial 2	facilitate 2	[obscurity 1	spurn 2
amass 2	copious 2	fallow 2	[opaque 1	squander 2
[ambivalence 1	corroborate 2	fertile 2	[opacity 1	stymie 2
[ambivalent 1	corrugated 2	[flourish 3	parsimony 2	subtle 2
ambulatory 2	[corrupt 1	[flower 1	paucity 2	summary 2
ameliorate 2	[corruption 1	fraudulent 3	penury 2	summon 3
amity 2	cursory 2	[fruitful 1	[peripheral 2	sumptuous 2
anchor 2	[daunt 3	[fruitless 1	[periphery 2	[surreptitious 1
antediluvian 2	[dauntless 1	garner 2	placate 2	[surreptitiously 1
ascendancy 2	debilitate 2	guile 2	[precise 1	tantamount 2
atrophy 2	deplete 2	hackneyed 2	[precision 1	[tenacious 1
[bane 1	discrepancy 3	hefty 2	premature 2	[tenacity 1
[baneful 1	disentangle 2	hideous 2	premeditated 2	[transience 1
bizarre 2	[disputatious 1	hilarity 2	prevalent 2	[transient 1
blunder 2	[dispute 2	humane 2	proclivity 2	turbulence 3
bungle 2	[distend 1	[hypocrisy 1	[prodigal 1	venturesome 3
burgeon 2	[distention 1	[hypocritical 1	[prodigious 2	viable 2
[capitulate 1	drawback 2	innocuous 2	[profuse 1	[vibrancy 1
[capitulation 1	efface 3	irascible 2	[profusion 2	[vibrant 1
capricious 4	[effervesce 1	jettison 2	[pulverize 1	vilification 2
clemency 2	[effervescent 1	kindle 2	[pulverized 1	[virulence 1
[coalesce 2	enhance 2	[leniency 1	rant 2	[virulent 1
[coalescence 1	enigmatic 2	[lenient 1	recalcitrant 2	whet 2
[cohere 1	ephemeral 3	[levity 1	recant 2	zany 2
[coherent 1	equilibrium 3	[levitate 1	replete 2	
[compress 1	[euphonious 1	listless 2	rescind 2	
[compression 1	[euphony 1	maladroit 2	reserve 2	

SAT MATH REFRESHER

There are many SAT exam-takers whose Math background is not quite up to par—probably because their basic Math skills are "rusty"—or because they never did do well in their Math classes. For these Math-troubled students, this Math Refresher section will be "manna from heaven." The pages that follow constitute a complete basic Math course that will help students greatly in preparing for the Math part of the SAT.

This Math Refresher offers the following:

(1) a systematic review of every Math area covered by the questions in the Math part of the SAT

and

(2) short review tests throughout the Refresher to check whether the student has grasped the math principles that he or she has just studied

The review tests will also provide students with valuable reinforcement so that they will remember how to go about solving math problems they would otherwise have difficulty with on the actual SAT.

Each of the 6 "Sessions" in this Math Refresher has a review test ("Practice Test"). Every review test has 50 questions followed by 50 detailed solutions. All of the solutions for the 6 review tests include a number (or numbers) in parentheses *after each solution.* The number refers to a specific instructional section where the rules and principles involved in the question are explained simply and clearly.

There is another very important purpose that this Math Refresher serves. You will find, after every solution in the Math sections of the 7 SAT Practice Tests in this book, a key to the mathematical principles of this Math Refresher. For example, a solution may direct you to Math Refresher 202, which deals with Distance and Time problems. If you happen to be weak in this mathematical operation, the 202 Math Refresher explanation will immediately clarify for you how to do Distance and Time problems. In other words, for those who are weak in any phase of Basic Math, this invaluable keying system will help you get the right answer to your SAT Math question—and thereby add approximately 10 points to your SAT score.

MATH REFRESHER
SESSION 1

Fractions, Decimals, Percentages, Deviations, Ratios and Proportions, Variations, and Comparison of Fractions

FRACTIONS, DECIMALS, PERCENTAGES

These problems involve the ability to perform numerical operations quickly and correctly. It is essential that you learn the arithmetical procedures outlined in this section.

101. Four different ways to write "a divided by b" are $a \div b$, $\dfrac{a}{b}$, $a : b$, $b \overline{)a}$.

Example: 7 divided by 15 is $7 \div 15 = \dfrac{7}{15} = 7 : 15 = 15 \overline{)7}$.

102. The numerator of a fraction is the upper number and the denominator is the lower number.

Example: In the fraction $\dfrac{8}{13}$, the numerator is 8 and the denominator is 13.

103. Moving a decimal point one place to the right multiplies the value of a number by 10, whereas moving the decimal point one place to the left divides a number by 10. Likewise, moving a decimal point two places to the right multiplies the value of a number by 100, whereas moving the decimal point two places to the left divides a number by 100.

Example: $24.35 \times 10 = 243.5$ (decimal point moved to *right*)
$24.35 \div 10 = 2.435$ (decimal point moved to *left*)

104. To change a fraction to a decimal, divide the numerator of the fraction by its denominator.

Example: Express $\dfrac{5}{6}$ as a decimal. We divide 5 by 6, obtaining 0.83.

$$\tfrac{5}{6} = 5 \div 6 = 0.833\ldots$$

105. To convert a decimal to a fraction, delete the decimal point and divide by whatever unit of 10 the number of decimal places represents.

Example: Convert 0.83 to a fraction. First, delete the decimal point. Second, two decimal places represent hundredths, so divide 83 by 100: $\frac{83}{100}$.

$$0.83 = \frac{83}{100}$$

106. To change a fraction to a percent, find its decimal form, multiply by 100, and add a percent sign.

Example: Express $\frac{3}{8}$ as a percent. To convert $\frac{3}{8}$ to a decimal, divide 3 by 8, which gives us 0.375. Multiplying 0.375 by 100 gives us 37.5%.

$$\frac{3}{8} = 3 \div 8 = .375$$
$$.375 \times 100 = 37.5\%$$

107. To change a percent to a fraction, drop the percent sign and divide the number by 100.

Example: Express 17% as a fraction. Dropping the % sign gives us 17, and dividing by 100 gives us $\frac{17}{100}$.

108. To *reduce* a fraction, divide the numerator and denominator by the largest number that divides them both evenly.

Example: Reduce $\frac{10}{15}$. Dividing both the numerator and denominator by 5 gives us $\frac{2}{3}$.

Example: Reduce $\frac{12}{36}$. The largest number that goes into both 12 and 36 is 12. Reducing the fraction, we have $\frac{\overset{1}{\cancel{12}}}{\underset{3}{\cancel{36}}} = \frac{1}{3}$.

Note: In both examples, the reduced fraction is exactly equal to the original fraction; $\frac{2}{3} = \frac{10}{15}$ and $\frac{12}{36} = \frac{1}{3}$.

109. To add fractions with like denominators, add the numerators of the fractions, keeping the same denominator.

Example: $\frac{1}{7} + \frac{2}{7} + \frac{3}{7} = \frac{6}{7}$.

110. To add fractions with different denominators, you must first change all of the fractions to *equivalent fractions* with the same denominators.

STEP 1. Find the *lowest (or least) common denominator*, the smallest number divisible by all of the denominators.

Example: If the fractions to be added are $\frac{1}{3}$ $\frac{1}{4}$, and $\frac{5}{6}$, then the lowest common denominator is 12, because 12 is the smallest number that is divisible by 3, 4, and 6.

STEP 2. Convert all of the fractions to *equivalent fractions*, each having the lowest common denominator as its denominator. To do this, multiply the numerator of each fraction by the number of times that its denominator goes into the lowest common denominator. The product of this multiplication will be the *new numerator*. The denominator of the equivalent fractions will be the lowest common denominator. (See Step 1 above.)

Example: The lowest common denominator of $\frac{1}{3}$, $\frac{1}{4}$, and $\frac{5}{6}$ is 12. Thus, $\frac{1}{3} = \frac{4}{12}$, because 12 divided by 3 is 4, and 4 times $1 = 4$. $\frac{1}{4} = \frac{3}{12}$, because 12 divided by 4 is 3, and 3 times $1 = 3$. $\frac{5}{6} = \frac{10}{12}$ because 12 divided by 6 is 2, and 2 times $5 = 10$.

STEP 3. Now add all of the equivalent fractions by adding the numerators.

Example: $\frac{4}{12} + \frac{10}{12} + \frac{3}{12} = \frac{17}{12}$

STEP 4. Reduce the fraction if possible, as shown in Section 108.

Example: Add $\frac{4}{5}$, $\frac{2}{3}$ and $\frac{8}{15}$. The lowest common denominator is 15 because 15 is the smallest number that is divisible by 5, 3, and 15. Then, $\frac{4}{5}$ is equivalent to $\frac{12}{15}$; $\frac{2}{3}$ is equivalent to $\frac{10}{15}$; and $\frac{8}{15}$ remains as $\frac{8}{15}$. Adding these numbers gives us $\frac{12}{15} + \frac{10}{15} + \frac{8}{15} = \frac{30}{15}$ Both 30 and 15 are divisible by 15, giving us $\frac{2}{1}$, or 2.

111. To *multiply fractions,* follow this procedure:

STEP 1. To find the numerator of the product, multiply all the numerators of the fractions being multiplied.

STEP 2. To find the denominator of the answer, multiply all of the denominators of the fractions being multiplied.

STEP 3. Reduce the product.

Example: $\frac{5}{7} \times \frac{2}{15} = \frac{5 \times 2}{7 \times 15} = \frac{10}{105}$. Reduce by dividing both the numerator and denominator by 5, the common factor. $\frac{10}{105} = \frac{2}{21}$.

112. To *divide fractions,* follow this procedure:

STEP 1. Invert the divisor. That is, switch the positions of the numerator and denominator in the fraction you are dividing *by.*

STEP 2. Replace the division sign with a multiplication sign.

STEP 3. Carry out the multiplication indicated.

STEP 4. Reduce the product.

Example: Find $\frac{3}{4} \div \frac{7}{8}$. Inverting $\frac{7}{8}$ the divisor, gives us $\frac{8}{7}$. Replacing the division sign with a multiplication sign gives us $\frac{3}{4} \times \frac{8}{7}$. Carrying out the multiplication gives us $\frac{3}{4} \times \frac{8}{7} = \frac{24}{28}$. The fraction $\frac{24}{28}$ may then be reduced to $\frac{6}{7}$ by dividing both the numerator and the denominator by 4.

113. To multiply decimals, follow this procedure:

STEP 1. Disregard the decimal point. Multiply the factors (the numbers being multiplied) as if they were whole numbers.

STEP 2. In each factor, count the number of digits to the *right* of the decimal point. Find the total number of these digits in all the factors. In the product start at the right and count to the left this (total) number of places. Put the decimal point there.

Example: Multiply 3.8×4.01. First, multiply 38 and 401, getting 15,238. There is a total of 3 digits to the right of the decimal points in the factors. Thus, the decimal point in the product is placed 3 units to the left of the digit farthest to the right (8).

$$3.8 \times 4.01 = 15.238$$

Example: 0.025×3.6. First, multiply 25×36, getting 900. In the factors, there is a total of 4 digits to the right of the decimal points; therefore, in the product, we place the decimal point 4 units to the left of the digit farthest to the right in 900. However, there are only 3 digits in the product, so we add a 0 to the left of the 9, getting 0900. This makes it possible to place the decimal point correctly, thus: .0900. From this example, we can make up the rule that in the product we add as many zeros as are needed to provide the proper number of digits to the left of the digit farthest to the right.

114. To find a percent of a given quantity:

STEP 1. Replace the word "of" with a multiplication sign.

STEP 2. Convert the percent to a decimal: drop the percent sign and divide the number by 100. This is done by moving the decimal point two places to the left, adding zeros where necessary.

Examples: $30\% = 0.30$. $2.1\% = 0.021$. $78\% = 0.78$.

STEP 3. Multiply the given quantity by the decimal.

Example: Find 30% of 200.

$$30\% \text{ of } 200 = 30\% \times 200 = 0.30 \times 200 = 60.00$$

DEVIATIONS

Estimation problems arise when dealing with approximations, that is, numbers that are not mathematically precise. The error, or *deviation*, in an approximation is a measure of the closeness of that approximation.

115. *Absolute error,* or *absolute deviation,* is the difference between the estimated value and the real value (or between the approximate value and the exact value).

Example: If the actual value of a measurement is 60.2 and we estimate it as 60, then the absolute deviation (absolute error) is $60.2 - 60 = 0.2$.

116. *Fractional error,* or *fractional deviation,* is the ratio of the absolute error to the exact value of the quantity being measured.

Example: If the exact value is 60.2 and the estimated value is 60, then the fractional error is

$$\frac{60.2 - 60}{60.2} = \frac{0.2}{60.2} = \frac{1}{301}$$

117. *Percent error,* or *percent deviation,* is the fractional error expressed as a percent. (See Section 106 for the method of converting fractions to percents.)

118. Many business problems, including the calculation of loss, profit, interest, and so forth, are treated as deviation problems. Generally, these problems concern the difference between the original value of a quantity and some new value after taxes, after interest, etc. The following chart shows the relationship between business and estimation problems.

BUSINESS PROBLEMS		ESTIMATION PROBLEMS
original value	=	exact value
new value	=	approximate value
net profit net loss net interest	=	absolute error
fractional profit fractional loss fractional interest	=	fractional error
percent profit percent loss percent interest	=	percent error

Example: An item which originally cost $50 is resold for $56. Thus the *net profit* is $56 — $50 = $6. The *fractional profit* is $\dfrac{\$56 - \$50}{\$50} = \dfrac{\$6}{\$50} = \dfrac{3}{25}$. The *percent profit* is equal to the percent equivalent of $\dfrac{3}{25}$, which is 12%.

119. When there are two or more *consecutive changes in value*, remember that the new value of the first change becomes the original value of the second; consequently, successive fractional or percent changes may not be added directly.

Example: Suppose that a $100 item is reduced by 10% and then by 20%. The first reduction puts the price at $90 (10% of $100 = $10; $100 — $10 = $90). Then, reducing the $90 (the new original value) by 20% gives us $72 (20% of $90 = $18; $90 — $18 = $72). Therefore, it is *not* correct to simply add 10% and 20% and then take 30% of $100.

RATIOS AND PROPORTIONS

120. A proportion is an equation stating that two ratios are equal. For example, $3 : 2 = 9 : x$ and $7 : 4 = a : 15$ are proportions. To solve a proportion:

STEP 1. First change the ratios to fractions. To do this, remember that $a : b$ is the same as $\dfrac{a}{b}$, or $1 : 2$ is equivalent to $\dfrac{1}{2}$, or $7 : 4 = a : 15$ is the same as $\dfrac{7}{4} = \dfrac{a}{15}$.

STEP 2. Now cross-multiply. That is, multiply the numerator of the first fraction by the denominator of the second fraction. Also multiply the denominator of the first fraction by the numerator of the second fraction. Set the first product equal to the second. This rule is sometimes stated as "The product of the means equals the product of the extremes."

Example: When cross-multiplying in the equation $\dfrac{3}{2} = \dfrac{9}{y}$, we get $3 \times y = 2 \times 9$, or $3y = 18$.

When we cross-multiply in the equation $\frac{a}{2} = \frac{4}{8}$, we get $8a = 8$.

STEP 3. Solve the resulting equation. This is done algebraically.

Example: Solve for a in the proportion $7 : a = 6 : 18$.

Change the ratios to the fractional relation $\frac{7}{a} = \frac{6}{18}$. Cross-multiply: $7 \times 18 = 6 \times a$, or $126 = 6a$.

Solving for a gives us $a = 21$.

121. In solving proportions that have units of measurement (feet, seconds, miles, etc.), each ratio must have the same units. For example, if we have the ratio 5 inches : 3 feet, we must convert the 3 feet to 36 inches and then set up the ratio 5 inches : 36 inches, or 5 : 36. We might wish to convert inches to feet. Noting that 1 inch $= \frac{1}{12}$ foot, we get 5 inches : 3 feet $= 5\left(\frac{1}{12}\right)$ feet : 3 feet $= 5$ feet : 36 feet, or again, 5 : 36.

Example: On a blueprint, a rectangle measures 6 inches in width and 9 inches in length. If the actual width of the rectangle is 16 inches, how many feet are there in the length?

Solution: We set up the proportions, 6 inches : 9 inches = 16 inches : x feet. Since x feet is equal to $12x$ inches, we substitute this value in the proportion. Thus, 6 inches : 9 inches = 16 inches : $12x$ inches. Since all of the units are now the same, we may work with the numbers alone. In fractional terms we have $\frac{6}{9} = \frac{16}{12x}$. Cross multiplication gives us $72x = 144$ and solving for x gives us $x = 2$. The rectangle is 2 feet long.

VARIATIONS

122. In a variation problem, you are given a relationship between certain variables. The problem is to determine the change in one variable when one or more of the other variables changes.

Example: In the formula $A = bh$, if b doubles and h triples, what happens to the value of A?

STEP 1. Express the new values of the variables in terms of their original values, i.e., $b' = 2b$ and $h' = 3h$.

STEP 2. Substitute these values in the formula and solve for the desired variable: $A' = b'h' = (2b)(3h) = 6bh$.

STEP 3. Express this answer in terms of the original value of the variable, i.e., since the new value of A is $6bh$, and the old value of A was bh, we can express this as $A_{\text{new}} = 6A_{\text{old}}$. The new value of the variable is expressed with a prime mark and the old value of the variable is left as it was. In this problem the new value of A would be expressed as A' and the old value as A. $A' = 6A$.

Example: If $V = e^3$ and e is doubled, what happens to the value of V?

Solution: Replace e with $2e$. The new value of V is $(2e)^3$. Since this is a new value, V becomes V'. Thus $V' = (2e)^3$, or $8e^3$. Remember, from the original statement of the problem, that $V = e^3$. Using this, we may substitute V for e^3 found in the equation $V' = 8e^3$. The new equation is $V' = 8V$. Therefore, the new value of V is 8 times the old value.

COMPARISON OF FRACTIONS

In fraction comparison problems, you are given two or more fractions and you are asked to arrange them in increasing or decreasing order, or to select the larger or the smaller. The following rules and suggestions will be very helpful in determining which of two fractions is greater.

123. If fractions A and B have the same denominators, and A has a larger numerator, then fraction A is larger. (We are assuming here, and for the rest of this Refresher Session, that numerators and denominators are positive.)

Example: $\frac{56}{271}$ is greater than $\frac{53}{271}$ because the numerator of the first fraction is greater than the numerator of the second.

124. If fractions A and B have the same numerator, and A has a larger denominator, then fraction A is smaller.

Example: $\frac{37}{256}$ is smaller than $\frac{37}{254}$.

125. If fraction A has a larger numerator and a smaller denominator than fraction B, then fraction A is larger than B.

Example: $\frac{6}{11}$ is larger than $\frac{4}{13}$. (If this does not seem obvious, compare both fractions with $\frac{6}{13}$.)

126. Another method is to convert all of the fractions to equivalent fractions. To do this follow these steps:

STEP 1. First find the *lowest common denominator* of the fractions. This is the smallest number that is divisible by all of the denominators of the original fractions. See Section 108 for the method of finding lowest common denominators.

STEP 2. The fraction with the greatest numerator is the largest fraction.

127. Still another method is the *conversion to approximating decimals.*

Example: To compare $\frac{5}{9}$ and $\frac{7}{11}$, we might express both as decimals to a few places of accuracy: $\frac{5}{9}$ is approximately equal to 0.555, while $\frac{7}{11}$ is approximately equal to 0.636, so $\frac{7}{11}$ is obviously greater. To express a fraction as a decimal, divide the numerator by the denominator.

128. If all of the fractions being compared are very close in value to some easy-to-work-with number, such as $\frac{1}{2}$ or 5, you may subtract this number from each of the fractions without changing their order.

Example: To compare $\frac{151}{75}$ with $\frac{328}{163}$ we notice that both of these fractions are approximately equal to 2. If we subtract 2 (that is $\frac{150}{75}$ and $\frac{326}{163}$ respectively) from each, we get $\frac{1}{75}$ and $\frac{2}{163}$, respectively. Since $\frac{1}{75}$ (or $\frac{2}{150}$) exceeds $\frac{2}{163}$, we see that $\frac{151}{75}$ must also exceed $\frac{328}{163}$.

Example: Which is larger, $\frac{37}{150}$ or $\frac{49}{202}$?

Solution: We notice that both these numbers are close to $\frac{1}{4}$. If we subtract the equivalent of $\frac{1}{4}$ (that is, $\frac{150}{600}$ and $\frac{101}{404}$ respectively) from the equivalent of each, ($\frac{148}{600} - \frac{150}{600}$ and $\frac{98}{404} - \frac{101}{404}$, respectively) we get $\frac{-2}{600}$ and $\frac{-3}{600}$ respectively. Now $\frac{-2}{600}$ is larger than $\frac{-3}{600}$ because it is *less* negative. Therefore, $\frac{37}{150}$ is larger than $\frac{49}{202}$.

An alternative method of comparing fractions is to change the fractions to their decimal equivalents, then, compare the decimals. (See Section 104.) The student would weigh the relative amount of work and difficulty involved in each method when he faces each problem.

PRACTICE TEST 1

Fractions, Decimals, Percentages, Deviations, Ratios and Proportions, Variations, and Comparison of Fractions

Correct answers and solutions follow each test.

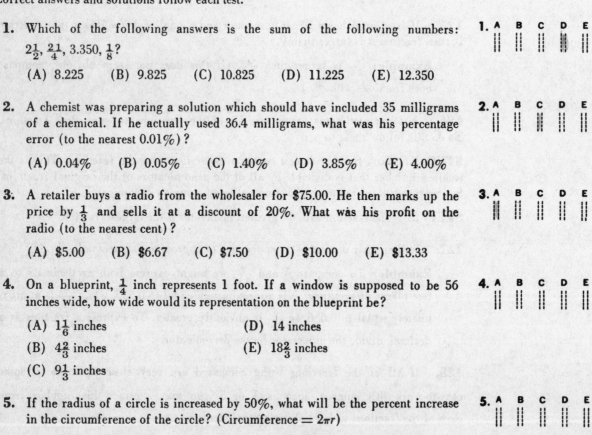

1. Which of the following answers is the sum of the following numbers: $2\frac{1}{2}, \frac{21}{4}, 3.350, \frac{1}{8}$?

   (A) 8.225   (B) 9.825   (C) 10.825   (D) 11.225   (E) 12.350

2. A chemist was preparing a solution which should have included 35 milligrams of a chemical. If he actually used 36.4 milligrams, what was his percentage error (to the nearest 0.01%)?

   (A) 0.04%   (B) 0.05%   (C) 1.40%   (D) 3.85%   (E) 4.00%

3. A retailer buys a radio from the wholesaler for $75.00. He then marks up the price by $\frac{1}{3}$ and sells it at a discount of 20%. What was his profit on the radio (to the nearest cent)?

   (A) $5.00   (B) $6.67   (C) $7.50   (D) $10.00   (E) $13.33

4. On a blueprint, $\frac{1}{4}$ inch represents 1 foot. If a window is supposed to be 56 inches wide, how wide would its representation on the blueprint be?

   (A) $1\frac{1}{6}$ inches   (D) 14 inches

   (B) $4\frac{2}{3}$ inches   (E) $18\frac{2}{3}$ inches

   (C) $9\frac{1}{3}$ inches

5. If the radius of a circle is increased by 50%, what will be the percent increase in the circumference of the circle? (Circumference $= 2\pi r$)

   (A) 25%   (B) 50%   (C) 100%   (D) 150%   (E) 225%

6. A B C D E

6. Which of the following fractions is the greatest?

(A) $\frac{403}{134}$ (B) $\frac{79}{26}$ (C) $\frac{527}{176}$ (D) $\frac{221}{73}$ (E) $\frac{99}{34}$

7. A B C D E

7. A store usually sells a certain item at a 40% profit. One week the store has a sale, during which the item is sold for 10% less than the usual price. During the sale, what is the percent profit the store makes on each of these items?

(A) 4%   (B) 14%   (C) 26%   (D) 30%   (E) 36%

8. A B C D E

8. What is 0.05 percent of 6.5?

(A) 0.00325   (B) 0.013   (C) 0.325   (D) 1.30   (E) 130.0

9. A B C D E

9. What is the value of $\dfrac{3\frac{1}{2} + 3\frac{1}{4} + 3\frac{1}{4} + 3\frac{1}{2}}{4\frac{1}{2}}$?

(A) $1\frac{1}{2}$ (B) $2\frac{1}{4}$ (C) 3   (D) $3\frac{1}{4}$ (E) $3\frac{3}{8}$

10. A B C D E

10. If 8 men can chop down 28 trees in one day, how many trees can 20 men chop down in one day?

(A) 28 trees   (D) 100 trees

(B) 160 trees   (E) 80 trees

(C) 70 trees

11. A B C D E

11. What is the product of the following fractions: $\frac{3}{100}, \frac{15}{49}, \frac{7}{9}$?

(A) $\frac{215}{44,100}$ (B) $\frac{1}{140}$ (C) $\frac{1}{196}$ (D) $\frac{25}{158}$ (E) $\frac{3}{427}$

12. A B C D E

12. In reading a thermometer, Mr. Downs mistakenly observed a temperature of 72° instead of 77°. What was his percentage error (to the nearest hundredth of a percent)?

(A) 6.49%   (B) 6.50%   (C) 6.64%   (D) 6.94%   (E) 6.95%

13. A B C D E

13. A businessman buys 1440 dozen pens at $2.50 a dozen and then sells them at a price of 25¢ apiece. What is his total profit on the lot of pens?

(A) $60.00   (B) $72.00   (C) $720.00   (D) $874.00

(E) $8740.00

14. A B C D E

14. On a map, 1 inch represents 1000 miles. If the area of a country is actually 16 million square miles, what is the area of the country's representation on the map?

(A) 4 square inches   (D) 16,000 square inches

(B) 16 square inches   (E) 4,000,000 square inches

(C) 4000 square inches

15. A B C D E

15. The formula for the volume of a cone is $V = \frac{1}{3}\pi r^2 h$. If the radius (r) is doubled and the height (h) is divided by 3, what will be the ratio of the new volume to the original volume?

(A) 2 : 3   (B) 3 : 2   (C) 4 : 3   (D) 3 : 4

(E) none of these

16. Which of the following fractions has the smallest value:

    (A) $\frac{34.7}{163}$ (B) $\frac{125}{501}$ (C) $\frac{173}{700}$ (D) $\frac{10.9}{42.7}$ (E) $\frac{907}{3715}$

16. A B C D E

17. Mr. Cutler usually makes a 45% profit on every radio he sells. During a sale, he reduces his margin of profit to 40%, while his sales increase by 10%. What is the ratio of his new total profit to the original profit?

    (A) 1 : 1   (B) 9 : 8   (C) 9 : 10   (D) 11 : 10   (E) 44 : 45

17. A B C D E

18. What is 1.3 percent of 0.26?

    (A) 0.00338   (B) 0.00500   (C) 0.200   (D) 0.338   (E) 0.500

18. A B C D E

19. What is the average of the following numbers: 3.2, $\frac{47}{12}$, $\frac{10}{3}$?

    (A) 3.55   (B) $\frac{10}{3}$ (C) $\frac{103}{30}$ (D) $\frac{209}{60}$ (E) $\frac{1254}{120}$

19. A B C D E

20. If it takes 16 faucets 10 hours to fill 8 tubs, how long will it take 12 faucets to fill 9 tubs?

    (A) 10 hours   (D) 14 hours

    (B) 12 hours   (E) 15 hours

    (C) 13 hours

20. A B C D E

21. If the 8% tax on a sale amounts to 96¢, what is the final price (tax included) of the item?

    (A) $1.20   (B) $2.16   (C) $6.36   (D) $12.00   (E) $12.96

21. A B C D E

22. In a certain class, 40% of the students are girls, and 20% of the girls wear glasses. What percent of the children in the class are girls who wear glasses?

    (A) 6%   (B) 8%   (C) 20%   (D) 60%   (E) 80%

22. A B C D E

23. What is 1.2% of 0.5?

    (A) 0.0006   (B) 0.006   (C) 0.06   (D) 0.6   (E) 6.0

23. A B C D E

24. Which of the following quantities is the largest?

    (A) $\frac{275}{369}$ (B) $\frac{134}{179}$ (C) $\frac{107}{144}$ (D) $\frac{355}{476}$ (E) $\frac{265}{352}$

24. A B C D E

25. If the length of a rectangle is increased by 120%, and its width is decreased by 20%, what happens to the area of the rectangle?

    (A) It decreases by 4%.

    (B) It remains the same.

    (C) It increases by 24%.

    (D) It increases by 76%.

    (E) It increases by 100%.

25. A B C D E

26. A merchant buys an old carpet for $25.00. He spends $15.00 to have it restored to good condition and then sells the rug for $50.00. What is the percent profit on his total investment?

    (A) 20%   (B) 25%   (C) 40%   (D) $66\frac{2}{3}$%   (E) 100%

26. A B C D E

27. A B C D E

27. Of the following sets of fractions, which one is arranged in *decreasing* order?

(A) $\frac{5}{9}, \frac{7}{11}, \frac{3}{5}, \frac{2}{3}, \frac{10}{13}$

(D) $\frac{10}{13}, \frac{2}{3}, \frac{7}{11}, \frac{3}{5}, \frac{5}{9}$

(B) $\frac{2}{3}, \frac{3}{5}, \frac{7}{11}, \frac{5}{9}, \frac{10}{13}$

(E) none of these

(C) $\frac{3}{5}, \frac{5}{9}, \frac{7}{11}, \frac{10}{13}, \frac{2}{3}$

28. A B C D E

28. If the diameter of a circle doubles, the circumference of the larger circle is how many times the circumference of the original circle? (Circumference $= \pi d$)

(A) π (B) 2π (C) 1   (D) 2   (E) 4

29. A B C D E

29. The scale on a set of plans is 1 : 8. If a man reads a certain measurement on the plans as 5.6″, instead of 6.0″, what will be the resulting approximate percent error on the full-size model?

(A) 6.7%   (B) 7.1%   (C) 12.5%   (D) 53.6%   (E) 56.8%

30. A B C D E

30. A salesman bought 2 dozen television sets at $300 each. He sold two-thirds of them at a 25% profit, but was forced to take a 30% loss on the rest. What was his total profit (or loss) on the television sets?

(A) a loss of $200

(D) a gain of $20

(B) a loss of $15

(E) a gain of $480

(C) no profit or loss

31. A B C D E

31. The sum of $\frac{1}{2}$, $\frac{1}{3}$, $\frac{1}{8}$, and $\frac{1}{15}$ is:

(A) $\frac{9}{8}$ (B) $\frac{16}{15}$ (C) $\frac{41}{40}$ (D) $\frac{65}{64}$ (E) $\frac{121}{120}$

32. A B C D E

32. What is $\frac{2}{3}$% of 90?

(A) 0.006   (B) 0.06   (C) 0.6   (D) 6.0   (E) 60

33. A B C D E

33. A man borrows $360. If he pays it back in 12 monthly payments of $31.50, what is his interest rate?

(A) 1.5%   (B) 4.5%   (C) 10%   (D) 5%   (E) 7.5%

34. A B C D E

34. A merchant marks a certain lamp up 30% above cost. Then he gives a customer a 15% discount. If the final selling price of the lamp was $86.19, what was the original cost?

(A) $66.30   (B) $73.26   (C) $78.00   (D) $99.12   (E) $101.40

35. A B C D E

35. In a certain recipe, $2\frac{1}{4}$ cups of flour are called for to make a cake that serves 6. If Mrs. Jenkins wants to use the same recipe to make a cake for 8, how many cups of flour must she use?

(A) $2\frac{1}{3}$ cups

(D) $3\frac{3}{8}$ cups

(B) $2\frac{3}{4}$ cups

(E) 4 cups

(C) 3 cups

36. If 10 men can survive for 24 days on 15 cans of rations, how many cans will be needed for 8 men to survive for 36 days?

    (A) 15 cans   (D) 18 cans

    (B) 16 cans   (E) 19 cans

    (C) 17 cans

37. If, on a map, $\frac{1}{2}$ inch represents 1 mile, how long is a border whose representation is $1\frac{1}{15}$ feet long?

    (A) $2\frac{1}{30}$ miles   (D) $25\frac{3}{5}$ miles

    (B) $5\frac{1}{15}$ miles   (E) $51\frac{1}{5}$ miles

    (C) $12\frac{4}{5}$ miles

38. In the formula $e = hf$, if e is doubled and f is halved, what happens to the value of h?

    (A) h remains the same.   (D) h is multiplied by 4.

    (B) h is doubled.   (E) h is halved.

    (C) h is divided by 4.

39. Which of the following expresses the ratio of 3 inches to 2 yards?

    (A) $3:2$ (B) $3:9$ (C) $3:12$ (D) $3:24$ (E) $3:72$

40. If it takes Mark twice as long to earn $6.00 as it takes Carl to earn $4.00, what is the ratio of Mark's pay per hour to Carl's pay per hour?

    (A) $2:1$ (B) $3:1$ (C) $3:2$ (D) $3:4$ (E) $4:3$

41. What is the lowest common denominator of the following set of fractions: $\frac{1}{6}$, $\frac{13}{27}$, $\frac{4}{5}$, $\frac{3}{10}$, $\frac{2}{15}$?

    (A) 27   (D) 270

    (B) 54   (E) none of these

    (C) 135

42. The average grade on a certain examination was 85. Ralph, on the same examination, scored 90. What was Ralph's *percent* deviation from the average score (to the nearest tenth of a percent)?

    (A) 5.0%   (B) 5.4%   (C) 5.5%   (D) 5.8%   (E) 5.9%

43. Successive discounts of 20% and 12% are equivalent to a single discount of:

    (A) 16.0%   (B) 29.6%   (C) 31.4%   (D) 32.0%   (E) 33.7%

44. On a blueprint of a park, 1 foot represents $\frac{1}{2}$ mile. If an error of $\frac{1}{2}$ inch is made in reading the blueprint, what will be the corresponding error on the actual park?

    (A) 110 feet   (D) 440 feet

    (B) 220 feet   (E) none of these

    (C) 330 feet

36. A B C D E
37. A B C D E
38. A B C D E
39. A B C D E
40. A B C D E
41. A B C D E
42. A B C D E
43. A B C D E
44. A B C D E

45. A B C D E

45. If the two sides of a rectangle change in such a manner that the rectangle's area remains constant, and one side increases by 25%, what must happen to the other side?

(A) It decreases by 20%.   (D) It decreases by 50%.

(B) It decreases by 25%.   (E) none of these

(C) It decreases by $33\frac{1}{3}$%.

46. A B C D E

46. Which of the following fractions has the smallest value:

(A) $\frac{6043}{2071}$ (B) $\frac{4290}{1463}$ (C) $\frac{5107}{1772}$ (D) $\frac{8935}{2963}$ (E) $\frac{8016}{2631}$

47. A B C D E

47. A certain company increased its prices by 30% during 1969. Then, in 1970, it was forced to cut back its prices by 20%. What was the net change in price?

(A) A net decrease in prices of more than 10%

(B) A net decrease in prices of 10% or less

(C) No net change in prices

(D) A net increase in prices of 10% or less

(E) A net increase in prices of more than 10%

48. A B C D E

48. What is 0.04%, expressed as a fraction?

(A) $\frac{2}{5}$ (B) $\frac{1}{25}$ (C) $\frac{4}{25}$ (D) $\frac{1}{250}$ (E) $\frac{1}{2500}$

49. A B C D E

49. What is the value of the fraction:

$$\frac{16 + 12 + 88 + 34 + 66 + 21 + 79 + 11 + 89}{25}?$$

(A) 15.04   (D) 16.64

(B) 15.44   (E) none of these

(C) 16.24

50. A B C D E

50. If coconuts are twice as expensive as bananas, and bananas are one-third as expensive as grapefruits, what is the ratio of the price of one coconut to one grapefruit?

(A) 2 : 3   (B) 3 : 2   (C) 6 : 1   (D) 1 : 6   (E) none of these

ANSWER KEY FOR PRACTICE TEST 1

1. D	8. A	15. C	22. B
2. E	9. C	16. A	23. B
3. A	10. C	17. E	24. E
4. A	11. B	18. A	25. D
5. B	12. A	19. D	26. B
6. B	13. C	20. E	27. D
7. C	14. B	21. E	28. D

ANSWER KEY FOR PRACTICE TEST 1 (continued)

29. A	35. C	40. D	46. C
30. E	36. D	41. D	47. D
31. C	37. D	42. E	48. E
32. C	38. D	43. B	49. D
33. D	39. E	44. A	50. A
34. C		45. A	

ANSWERS AND SOLUTIONS FOR PRACTICE TEST 1

1. **(D)** First, convert the fractions to decimals since the final answer must be expressed in decimals: $2.500 + 5.250 + 3.350 + 0.125 = 11.225$. (104, 109)

2. **(E)** This is an estimation problem. Note that the correct value was 35, not 36.4. Thus the *real* value is 35 mg. and the *estimated* value is 36.4 mg. Thus, percent error is equal to $(36.4 - 35) \div 35$, or 0.04, expressed as a percent, which is 4%. (117)

3. **(A)** This is a business problem. First, the retailer marks up the wholesale price by $\frac{1}{3}$, so the marked-up price equals $75(1 + \frac{1}{3})$, or \$100; then it is reduced 20% from the \$100 price, leaving a final price of \$80. Thus, the net profit on the radio was \$5.00. (118)

4. **(A)** Here we have a proportion problem: length on blueprint: actual length = $\frac{1}{4}$ inch : 1 foot. The second ratio is the same as 1 : 48 because 1 foot = 12 inches. In the problem the actual length is 56 inches, so that if the length on the blueprint equals x, we have the proportion $x : 56 = 1 : 48$; $\frac{x}{56} = \frac{1}{48}$. $48x = 56$; so $x = \frac{56}{48}$, or $1\frac{1}{6}$ inches. (120)

5. **(B)** Since $C = 2\pi r$ (where r is the radius of the circle, and C is its circumference), the new value of r, r', is $(1.5)r$ since r is increased by 50%. Using this value of r', we get the new C, $C' = 2\pi r' = 2\pi(1.5)r = (1.5)2\pi r$. Remembering that $C = 2\pi r$, we get that $C' = (1.5)C$. Since the new circumference is 1.5 times the original, there is an increase of 50%. (122)

6. **(B)** In this numerical comparison problem, it is helpful to realize that all of these fractions are approximately equal to 3. If we subtract 3 from each of the fractions, we get $\frac{1}{134}$, $\frac{1}{26}$, $\frac{-1}{176}$, $\frac{2}{73}$, and $\frac{-3}{34}$, respectively. Clearly, the greatest of these is $\frac{1}{26}$, and is therefore the greatest of the five given fractions. Another method of solving this sype of numerical comparison problem is to convert the fractions to decimals by dividing the numerator by the denominator. (127, 128)

7. **(C)** This is another business problem, this time asking for percentage profit. Let the original price be P. Then the marked-up price will be $1.4(P)$. Ten percent is taken off this price, to yield a final price of $(0.90)(1.40)(P)$, or

(1.26) (P). Thus, the fractional increase was 0.26, so the percent increase was 26%. (118)

8. **(A)** Remember that the phrase "percent of" may be replaced by a multiplication sign. Thus, 0.05% × 6.5 = 0.0005 × 6.5, so the answer is 0.00325. (114)

9. **(C)** First, add the fractions in the numerator to obtain $13\frac{1}{2}$. Then divide $13\frac{1}{2}$ by $4\frac{1}{2}$. If you cannot see immediately that the answer is 3, you can convert the halves to decimals and divide, or you can express the fractions in terms of their common denominator, thus: $13\frac{1}{2} = \frac{27}{2}$; $4\frac{1}{2} = \frac{9}{2}$; $\frac{27}{2} \div \frac{9}{2} = \frac{27}{2} \times \frac{2}{9} = \frac{54}{18} = 3$. (110, 112)

10. **(C)** This is a proportion problem. If x is the number of men needed to chop down 20 trees, then we form the proportion: 8 men : 28 trees = 20 men : x trees, or $\frac{8}{28} = \frac{20}{x}$. Solving for x, we get $x = \frac{(28)(20)}{8}$, or $x = 70$. (120)

11. **(B)** $\frac{3}{100} \times \frac{15}{49} \times \frac{7}{9} = \frac{3 \times 15 \times 7}{100 \times 49 \times 9}$. Cancelling 7 out of the numerator and denominator gives us $\frac{3 \times 15}{100 \times 7 \times 9}$. Cancelling 5 out of the numerator and denominator gives us $\frac{3 \times 3}{20 \times 7 \times 9}$. Finally, cancelling 9 out of both numerator and denominator gives us $\frac{1}{20 \times 7}$, or $\frac{1}{140}$. (111)

12. **(A)** Percent error = (absolute error) ÷ (correct measurement) = 5 ÷ 77 = 0.0649 (approximately) × 100 = 6.49%. (117)

13. **(C)** Profit on each dozen pens = selling price − cost = 12(25¢) − $2.50 = $3.00 − $2.50 = 50¢, profit per dozen. Total profit = profit per dozen × number of dozens = 50¢ × 1440 = $720.00. (118)

14. **(B)** If 1 inch represents 1000 miles, then 1 square inch represents 1000 miles squared, or 1,000,000 square miles. Thus, the area would be represented by 16 squares of this size, or 16 square inches. (120)

15. **(C)** Let V' equal the new volume. Then if $r' = 2r$ is the new radius, and $h' = \frac{h}{3}$ is the new height, $V' = \frac{1}{3}\pi(r')^2(h') = \frac{1}{3}\pi(2r)^2\left(\frac{h}{3}\right) = \frac{4}{9}\pi r^2 h = \frac{4}{3}V$, so the ratio $V' : V$ is equal to 4 : 3. (122)

16. **(A)** All of these fractions are approximately equal to $\frac{1}{4}$. Thus, by subtracting $\frac{1}{4}$ from each one we get remainders of, respectively, $\frac{-6.05}{163}$, $\frac{-0.25}{501}$, $\frac{-2}{700}$, $+\frac{0.225}{42.7}$, and $-\frac{21.75}{3715}$. The first of these is the smallest. That is because of all of the negative fractions, it has the largest value without its sign. Therefore, it is the most negative and, consequently, the smallest so that $\frac{34.7}{163}$ is the desired answer. (123–128)

17. **(E)** Let $N =$ the original cost of a radio. Then, original profit $= 45\% \times N$. New profit $= 40\% \times 110\% N = 44\% \times N$. Thus, the ratio of new profit to original profit is 44 : 45. (118)

18. **(A)** $1.3\% \times 0.26 = 0.013 \times 0.26 = 0.00338$ (114)

19. **(D)** Average $= \frac{1}{3}(3.2 + \frac{47}{12} + \frac{10}{3})$. The decimal $3.2 = \frac{320}{100} = \frac{16}{5}$, and the lowest common denominator of the three fractions is 60, then $\frac{16}{5} = \frac{192}{60}$, $\frac{47}{12} = \frac{235}{60}$, and $\frac{10}{3} = \frac{200}{60}$. Then, $\frac{1}{3}(\frac{192}{60} + \frac{235}{60} + \frac{200}{60}) = \frac{1}{3}(\frac{627}{60}) = \frac{209}{60}$

(101, 105, 109)

20. **(E)** If it takes 16 faucets 10 hours to fill 8 tubs, then it takes 1 faucet 160 hours to fill 8 tubs (16 faucets : 1 faucet $= x$ hours : 10 hours; $\frac{16}{1} = \frac{x}{10}$; $x = 160$). If it takes 1 faucet 160 hours to fill 8 tubs, then (dividing by 8) it takes 1 faucet 20 hours to fill 1 tub. If it takes 1 faucet 20 hours to fill 1 tub, then it takes 1 faucet 180 hours (9×20 hours) to fill 9 tubs. If it takes 1 faucet 180 hours to fill 9 tubs, then it takes 12 faucets $\frac{180}{12}$ or 15 hours to fill 9 tubs. (120)

21. **(E)** Let P be the original price. Then $0.08P = 96\text{¢}$, so that $8P = \$96$, or $P = \$12$. Adding the tax, which equals 96¢, we obtain our final price of \$12.96. (118)

22. **(B)** The number of girls who wear glasses is 20% of 40% of the children in the class. Thus, the indicated operation is multiplication; $20\% \times 40\% = 0.20 \times 0.40 = 0.08 = 8\%$. (114)

23. **(B)** $1.2\% \times 0.5 = 0.012 \times 0.5 = 0.006$. (114)

24. **(E)** Here, we can use $\frac{3}{4}$ as an approximate value for all the fractions, Subtracting $\frac{3}{4}$ from each, we get remainders of: $\frac{-1.75}{369}, \frac{-0.25}{179}, \frac{-1.00}{144}, \frac{-2.00}{476}$ and $+\frac{1.00}{352}$. Clearly, the last of these is the greatest (it is the only positive one), so, $\frac{256}{352}$ is the fraction that is the largest. This problem may also be solved by converting the fractions to decimals. (104, 123, 127)

25. **(D)** Area $=$ length $\times$ width. The new area will be equal to the new length (2.20 times the old length) times the new width (0.80 times the old width), giving a product of 1.76 times the original area, an increase of 76%. (122)

26. **(B)** Total cost to merchant $= \$25.00 + \$15.00 = \$40.00$.

Profit $=$ selling price $-$ cost $= \$50 - \$40 = \$10$.
Percent profit $=$ profit $\div$ cost $= \$10 \div \$40 = 25\%$. (118)

27. (D) We can convert the fractions to decimals or to fractions with a lowest common denominator. Inspection will show that all sets of fractions contain the same members; therefore, if we convert one set to decimals or find the lowest common denominator for one set, we can use our results for all sets. Converting a fraction to a decimal involves only one operation—a single division; whereas converting to the lowest common denominator involves a multiplication which must be followed by a division and a multiplication to change each fraction to one with the lowest common denominator. Thus, conversion to decimals is often the simpler method: $\frac{10}{13} = 0.769$; $\frac{2}{3} = 0.666$; $\frac{7}{11} = 0.636$; $\frac{3}{5} = 0.600$; $\frac{5}{9} = 0.555$. (104)

However, in this case there is an even simpler method. Convert two of the fractions to equivalent fractions: $\frac{3}{5} = \frac{6}{10}$ and $\frac{2}{3} = \frac{8}{12}$. We now have $\frac{5}{9}$, $\frac{6}{10}$, $\frac{7}{11}$, $\frac{8}{12}$, and $\frac{10}{13}$. Remember this rule: when the numerator and denominator of a fraction are both positive, adding 1 to both will bring the value of the fraction closer to 1. (For example, $\frac{3}{4} = \frac{2+1}{3+1}$, so $\frac{3}{4}$ is closer to 1 than $\frac{2}{3}$, and is therefore the greater fraction.) Thus we see that $\frac{5}{9}$ is less than $\frac{6}{10}$, which is less than $\frac{7}{11}$, which is less than $\frac{8}{12}$, which is less than $\frac{9}{13}$. $\frac{9}{13}$ is obviously less than $\frac{10}{13}$, so $\frac{10}{13}$ must be the greatest fraction. Thus, in decreasing order the fractions are $\frac{10}{13}$, $\frac{2}{3}$, $\frac{7}{11}$, $\frac{3}{5}$, and $\frac{5}{9}$. This method is a great time-saver once you become accustomed to it.

28. (D) The formula governing this situation is $C = \pi d$, where C = circumference, and d = diameter. Thus, if the new diameter is $d' = 2d$, then the new circumference is $C' = \pi d' = 2\pi d = 2C$. Thus, the new, larger circle has a circumference of twice that of the original circle. (122)

29. (A) The most important feature of this problem is recognizing that the scale does not affect percent (or fractional) error, since it simply results in multiplying the numerator and denominator of a fraction by the same factor. Thus, we need only calculate the original percent error. Although it would not be incorrect to calculate the full-scale percent error, it would be time-consuming, and might result in unnecessary errors.) Absolute error = 0.4″. Actual measurement = 6.0″. Therefore, percent error = (absolute error ÷ actual measurement) × 100% = $\frac{0.4}{6.0}$ × 100%, which equals 6.7% (approximately.) (117)

30. (E) Total cost = number of sets × cost of each = 24 × $300 = $7200.
Revenue = (number sold at 25% profit × price at 25% profit)
+ (number sold at 30% loss × price at 30% loss)
= (16 × $375) + (8 × $210) = $6000 + $1680 = $7680.
Profit = revenue − cost = $7680 − $7200 = $480. (118)

31. (C) $\frac{1}{2} + \frac{1}{3} + \frac{1}{8} + \frac{1}{15} = \frac{60}{120} + \frac{40}{120} + \frac{15}{120} + \frac{8}{120} = \frac{123}{120} = \frac{41}{40}$ (110)

32. (C) $\frac{2}{3}\% \times 90 = \frac{2}{300} \times 90 = \frac{180}{300} = \frac{6}{10} = 0.6$ (114)

33. (D) If the man makes 12 payments of $31.50, he pays back a total of $378.00. Since the loan is for $360.00, his net interest is $18.00. Therefore, his rate of interest is $\dfrac{\$18.00}{\$360.00}$ which can be reduced to 0.05, or 5%. (118)

34. **(C)** Final selling price $= 85\% \times 130\% \times \text{cost} = 110\frac{1}{2}\% \times \text{cost}$. Thus, $86.19 $= 1.105C$, where $C = \text{cost}$. $C = \$86.19 \div 1.105 = \$78.00$ (exactly).   (118)

35. **(C)** If x is the amount of flour needed for 8 people, then we can set up the proportion $2\frac{1}{4}$ cups : 6 people $= x : 8$ people. Solving for x gives us $x = \frac{8}{6} \times 2\frac{1}{4}$ or $\frac{8}{6} \times \frac{9}{4} = 3$ (120)

36. **(D)** If 10 men can survive for 24 days on 15 cans, then 1 man can survive for 240 days on 15 cans. If 1 man can survive for 240 days on 15 cans then 1 man can survive for $\frac{240}{15}$ or 16 days on 1 can. If 1 man can survive for 16 days on 1 can, then 8 men can survive for $\frac{16}{8}$ or 2 days on 1 can. If 8 men can survive for 2 days on 1 can, then for 36 days 8 men need $\frac{36}{2}$ or 18 cans to survive.   (120)

37. **(D)** $1\frac{1}{15}$ feet $= 12\frac{4}{5}$ inches. Thus, we have the proportion: $\frac{1}{2}$ inch : 1 mile $=$ 12.8 inches : x. Solving for x, we have $x = 25.6$ miles $= 25\frac{3}{5}$ miles.   (120)

38. **(D)** If $e = hf$, then $h = \frac{e}{f}$. If e is doubled and f is halved, then the new value of h, $h' = \left(\frac{2e}{\frac{1}{2}f}\right)$. Multiplying the numerator and denominator by 2 gives us $h' = \frac{4e}{f}$. Since $h = \frac{e}{f}$ and $h' = \frac{4e}{f}$ we see that $h' = 4h$. This is the same as saying that h is multiplied by 4.   (122)

39. **(E)** 3 inches : 2 yards $=$ 3 inches : 72 inches $=$ 3 : 72.   (121)

40. **(D)** If Carl and Mark work for the same length of time, then Carl will earn $8.00 for every $6.00 Mark earns (since in the time Mark can earn one $6.00 wage, Carl can earn *two* $4.00 wages). Thus, their hourly wage rates are in the ratio $6.00 (Mark) : $8.00 (Carl) $= 3 : 4$.   (120)

41. **(D)** The lowest common denominator is the smallest number that is divisible by all of the denominators. Thus we are looking for the smallest number that is divisible by 6, 27, 5, 10, and 15. The smallest number that is divisible by 6 and 27 is 54. The smallest number that is divisible by 54 and 5 is 270. Since 270 is divisible by 10 and 15 also, so it is the lowest common denominator.   (110, 126)

42. **(E)** Percent deviation $= \dfrac{\text{absolute deviation}}{\text{average score}} \times 100\%$.

Absolute deviation $=$ Ralph's score $-$ average score $= 90 - 85 = 5$.

Percent deviation $= \frac{5}{85} \times 100\% = 500\% \div 85 = 5.88\%$ (approximately). 5.88% is closer to 5.9% than to 5.8%, so 5.9% is correct.   (117)

43. **(B)** If we discount 20% and then 12%, we are, in effect, taking 88% of 80% of the original price. Since "of" represents multiplication, when we deal with percent we can multiply $88\% \times 80\% = 70.4\%$. This is a deduction of 29.6% from the original price.   (119, 114)

44. (A) This is a simple proportion: $\dfrac{1 \text{ foot}}{\frac{1}{2} \text{ mile}} = \dfrac{\frac{1}{2} \text{ inch}}{x}$. Our first step must be to convert all these measurements to one unit. The most logical unit is the one our answer will take — feet. Thus, $\dfrac{1 \text{ ft.}}{2640 \text{ ft.}} = \dfrac{\frac{1}{24} \text{ ft.}}{x}$. (Recall that 1 mile equals 5280 feet.) Solving for x, we find $x = \frac{2640}{24}$ feet $= 110$ feet. (120, 121)

45. (A) Let the two original sides of the rectangle be a and b, and the new sides be a' and b'. We know that $a' = 1.25a = \dfrac{5a}{4}$, and that $ab = (a')\,(b') = \dfrac{5a(b')}{4}$. Therefore, $b' = \left(\frac{4}{5}\right)b$, a decrease of $\frac{1}{5}$, or 20%. (122)

46. (C) The first thing to notice is that these fractions are all approximately equal to 3. Thus, it will aid our comparison if we subtract 3 from each of the numbers and compare the remainders instead. The five remainders are: $\dfrac{-170}{2071}$, $\dfrac{-99}{1463}$, $\dfrac{-209}{1772}$ $\dfrac{+46}{2963}$, and $\dfrac{+123}{2631}$ respectively. We must find the smallest of these remainders, which is obviously the third one (the fourth and fifth are positive, and the other two are greater than $\frac{-1}{10}$). Thus, the third choice, $\dfrac{5107}{1772}$, is the smallest one. (123–128)

47. (D) The new prices are 80% of 130% of the original prices; multiplying 80% by 130%, we obtain 104%, which is the new price as a percent of the original one. Thus, the increase was 4%. (118)

48. (E) $0.04\% = \dfrac{0.04}{100} = \dfrac{4}{10,000} = \dfrac{1}{2500}$. (107)

49. (D) Before adding you should examine the numbers to be added. They form pairs, like this: $16 + (12 + 88) + (34 + 66) + (21 + 79) + (11 + 89)$ which equals $16 + 100 + 100 + 100 + 100 = 416$. Dividing 416 by 25, we obtain $16\frac{16}{25}$, which equals 16.64. (112)

50. (A) We can set up a proportion as follows:

$\dfrac{1 \text{ coconut}}{1 \text{ banana}} = \dfrac{2}{1}$, $\dfrac{1 \text{ banana}}{1 \text{ grapefruit}} = \dfrac{1}{3}$, so, by multiplying the two equations together $\left(\dfrac{1 \text{ coconut}}{1 \text{ banana}} \times \dfrac{1 \text{ banana}}{1 \text{ grapefruit}} \text{ and } \dfrac{2}{1} \times \dfrac{1}{3}\right)$, and cancelling the bananas and the 1's in the numerators and denominators, we get: $\dfrac{1 \text{ coconut}}{1 \text{ grapefruit}} = \dfrac{2}{3}$. (120)

MATH REFRESHER SESSION 2

Rate Problems: Distance and Time, Work, Mixture, and Cost

200. *Word Problem Set-up.* Some problems require translation of words into algebraic expressions or equations. For example: 8 more than 7 times a number is 22. Find the number. Let $n =$ the number. We have

$$7n + 8 = 22 \qquad 7n = 14 \qquad n = 2$$

Another example: There are 3 times as many boys as girls in a class. What is the ratio of boys to the total number of students?. Let $n =$ number of girls. Then

$$3n = \text{number of boys}$$
$$4n = \text{Total number of students}$$

$$\frac{\text{number of boys}}{\text{Total students}} = \frac{3n}{4n} = \frac{3}{4}$$

201. Rate Problems concern a special type of relationship which is very common: rate $\times$ input $=$ output. This results from the definition of rate as *the ratio between output and input*. In these problems, input may represent any type of "investment," but the most frequent quantities used as inputs are time, work, and money. Output is usually distance traveled, work done, or money spent.

Note that the word *per*, as used in rates, signifies a ratio. Thus a rate of 25 miles per hour signifies the ratio between an output of 25 miles and an input of 1 hour.

Frequently, the word "per" will be represented by the fraction sign, thus: $\dfrac{25 \text{ miles}}{1 \text{ hour}}$.

Example: Peter can walk a mile in 10 minutes. He can travel a mile on his bicycle in 2 minutes. How far away is his uncle's house if Peter can walk there and bicycle back in 1 hour exactly?

To solve a rate problem such as the one above, follow these steps:

STEP 1. Determine the names of the quantities which represent input, output, and rate in the problem you are doing. In the example, Peter's input is *time* and his output is *distance*. His rate will be *distance per unit of time*, which is commonly called *speed*.

STEP 2. Write down the fundamental relationship in terms of the quantities mentioned, making each the heading of a column. In the example, set up the table like this:

$$\text{speed} \quad \times \quad \text{time} \quad = \quad \text{distance}$$

STEP 3. Directly below the name of each quantity, write the unit of measurement in terms of the answer you want. Your choice of unit should be the most convenient one but, remember once you have chosen a unit, you must convert all quantities to that unit.

226

We must select a unit of time. Since a *minute* was the unit used in the problem, it is the most logical choice. Similarly, we will choose a *mile* for our unit of distance. *Speed* (which is the ratio of distance to time) will therefore be expressed in *miles per minute*, usually abbreviated as mi/min. Thus, our chart now looks like this:

speed	×	time	=	distance
mi/min		minutes		miles

STEP 4. The problem will mention various situations in which some quantity of input is used to get a certain quantity of output. Represent each of these situations on a different line of the table, leaving blanks for unknown quantities.

In the sample problem, four situations are mentioned: Peter can walk a mile in 10 minutes; he can bicycle a mile in 2 minutes; he walks to his uncle's house; and he bicycles home. On the diagram, with the appropriate boxes filled, the problem will look like this:

	speed ×	time =	distance
	mi/min	minutes	miles
1. walking		10	1
2. bicycling		2	1
3. walking			
4. bicycling			

STEP 5. From the chart and from the relationship at the top of the chart, quantities for filling some of the empty spaces may become obvious. Fill in these values directly.

In the example, on the first line of the chart, we see that the walking speed times 10 equals 1. Thus, the walking *speed* is 0.1 mi/min (mi/min × 10 = 1 mi; mi/min $= \dfrac{1 \text{ mi}}{10 \text{ min}} = 0.1$). Similarly, on the second we see that the bicycle speed equals 0.5 mi/min. Furthermore, his walking speed shown on line 3 will be 0.1, the same speed as on line 1; and his bicycling speed shown on line 4 will equal the speed (0.05) shown on line 2. Adding this information to our table, we get:

	speed ×	time =	distance
	mi/min	minutes	miles
1. walking	0.1	10	1
2. bicycling	0.5	2	1
3. walking	0.1		
4. bicycling	0.5		

STEP 6. Next, fill in the blanks with algebraic expressions to represent the quantities indicated, being careful to take advantage of simple relationships stated in the problem or appearing in the chart.

Continuing the example, we represent the time spent traveling shown on line 3 by x. According to the fundamental relationship, the distance traveled on this trip must be $(0.1)x$. Similarly, if y represents the time shown on line 4, the distance traveled is $(0.5)y$. Thus our chart now looks like this:

	speed ×	time =	distance
	mi/min	minutes	miles
1. walking	0.1	10	1
2. bicycling	0.5	2	1
3. walking	0.1	x	$(0.1)x$
4. bicycling	0.5	y	$(0.5)y$

STEP 7. Now, from the statement of the problem, you should be able to set up enough equations to solve for all the unknowns. In the example, there are two facts which we have not used yet. First, since Peter is going to his uncle's house and back, it is assumed that the distances covered on the two trips are equal. Thus we get the equation: $(0.1)x = (0.5)y$. We are told that the total time to and from his uncle's house is one hour. Since we are using minutes as our unit of time, we convert the one hour to 60 minutes. Thus we get the equation: $x + y = 60$. Solving these two equations ($0.1x = 0.5y$ and $x + y = 60$) algebraically, we find that $x = 50$ and $y = 10$. (See Section 407 for the solution of simultaneous equations.)

STEP 8. Now that you have all the information necessary, you can calculate the answer required. In the sample problem we are required to determine the distance to the uncle's house which is $(0.1)x$ or $(0.5)y$. Using $x = 50$ or $y = 10$ gives us the distance as 5 miles.

Now that we have shown the fundamental steps in solving a rate problem we shall discuss various types of rate problems.

DISTANCE AND TIME

202. In *distance and time problems* the fundamental relationship that we use is *speed × time = distance*. Speed is the rate, time is the input, and distance is the output. The example in Section 201 was this type of problem.

Example: In a sports car race, David gives Kenny a head start of 10 miles. David's car goes 80 miles per hour and Kenny's car goes 60 miles per hour. How long should it take David to catch up to Kenny if they both leave their starting marks at the same time?

STEP 1. Here the fundamental quantities are *speed, time*, and *distance*.

STEP 2. The fundamental relationship is speed × time = distance. Write this at the top of the chart.

STEP 3. The unit for *distance* in this problem will be a *mile*. The unit for *speed* will be *miles per hour*. Since the speed is in miles per hour, our *time* will be in *hours*. Now our chart looks like this:

speed ×	time =	distance
mi/hr	hours	miles

STEP 4. The problem offers us certain information that we can add to the chart. First we must make two horizontal rows, one for Kenny and one for David. We know that Kenny's speed is 60 miles per hour and that David's speed is 80 miles per hour.

STEP 5. In this case, none of the information in the chart can be used to calculate other information in the chart.

STEP 6. Now we must use algebraic expressions to represent the unknowns. We know that both Kenny and David travel for the same amount of time but we do not know for how much time, so we will place an x in the space for each boy's time. Now from the relationship of speed $\times$ time = distance, we can calculate Kenny's distance as $60x$ and David's distance as $80x$. Now the chart looks like this:

	speed	$\times$ time	= distance
	mi/hr	hours	miles
Kenny	60	x	$60x$
David	80	x	$80x$

STEP 7. From the statement of the problem we know that David gave Kenny a 10-mile head start. In other words, David's distance is 10 more miles than Kenny's distance. This can be stated algebraically as $60x + 10 = 80x$. That is, Kenny's distance + 10 miles = David's distance. Solving for x gives us $x = \frac{1}{2}$.

STEP 8. The question asks how much time is required for David to catch up to Kenny. If we look at the chart, this time is x, and x has already been calculated as $\frac{1}{2}$ so the answer is $\frac{1}{2}$ hour.

WORK

203. In *work problems* the input is time and output is the amount of work done. The rate is the work per unit of time.

Example: Jack can chop down 20 trees in 1 hour, while it takes Ted $1\frac{1}{2}$ hours to chop down 18 trees. If the two of them work together, how long will it take them to chop down 48 trees?

Solution: By the end of Step 5 your chart should look like this:

	rate	$\times$ time	= work
	trees/hr.	hours	trees
1. Jack	20	1	20
2. Ted	12	$1\frac{1}{2}$	18
3. Jack	20		
4. Ted	12		

In Step 6, we represent the time that it takes Jack by x in line 3. Since we have the relationship that rate $\times$ time = work, we see that in line 3 the work is $20x$. Since the two boys work together (therefore, for the same amount of time), the time in line 4 must be x and the work must be $12x$. Now, in Step 7, we see that the total work is 48 trees. From lines 3 and 4, then $20x + 12x = 48$. Solving for x gives us $x = 1\frac{1}{2}$. We are asked to find the number of hours needed by the boys to chop down the 48 trees together, and we see that this time is x, or $1\frac{1}{2}$ hours.

MIXTURE

204. In *mixture problems* you are given a percent or a fractional composition of a substance, and you are asked questions about the weights and compositions of the substances. The basic relationship here is that the percentage of a certain substance in a mixture $\times$ the amount of the mixture = the amount of substance.

Note that it is often better to change percents to decimals because it makes it easier to avoid errors.

Example: A chemist has two quarts of 25% acid solution, and one quart of 40% acid solution. If he mixes these, what will be the concentration of the mixture?

Solution: Let $x = $ concentration of the mixture. At the end of Step 6, our table will look like this:

	rate $\times$	amount of sol $=$	amount of acid
	$\dfrac{\text{qt (acid)}}{\text{qt (sol)}}$	qts (sol)	qts (acid)
25%, solution	0.25	2	0.50
40% solution	0.40	1	0.40
mixture	x	3	$3x$

We now have one additional bit of information: The amount of acid in the mixture must be equal to the total amount of acid in each of the two parts, so $3x = 0.50 + 0.40$. Therefore x is equal to 0.30, which is the same as a 30% concentration of the acid in the mixture.

COST

205. In *cost problems* the rate is the *price per item*, the input is the *number of items*, and the output is the *value* of the items considered. When you are dealing with dollars and cents, you must be very careful to use the decimal point correctly.

Example: Jim has $3.00 in nickels and dimes in his pocket. If he has twice as many nickels as he has dimes, how many coins does he have altogether?

Solution: After Step 6, our chart should look like this (where c is the number of dimes Jim has):

rate	×	number	=	value
	cents/coin	coins	cents
nickels	5	2c	10c
dimes	10	c	10c

Now we recall the additional bit of information that the total value of the nickels and dimes is $3.00, or 300 cents. Thus, $5(2c) + 10c = 300$; $20c = 300$; so $c = 15$, the number of dimes. Jim has twice as many nickels, so $2c = 30$.

The total number of coins is $c + 2c = 3c = 45$.

The following table will serve as review for this Refresher Session.

TYPE OF PROBLEM	FUNDAMENTAL RELATIONSHIP
distance	speed × time = distance
work	rate × time = work done
mixture	concentration × amount of solution = amount of ingredient
cost	rate × number of items = value

PRACTICE TEST 2

Rate Problems:
Distance and Time, Work, Mixture, and Cost

Correct answers and solutions follow each test.

1. A B C D E

1. A man rowed 3 miles upstream in 90 minutes. If the river flowed with a current of 2 miles per hour, how long did the man's return trip take?

(A) 20 minutes (D) 60 minutes

(B) 30 minutes (E) 80 minutes

(C) 45 minutes

2. A B C D E

2. Charles can do a job in 1 hour, Bill can do the same job in 2 hours, and Bob can do the job in 3 hours. How long does it take them to do the job working together?

(A) $\frac{6}{11}$ hours (D) $\frac{1}{3}$ hours

(B) $\frac{1}{2}$ hour (E) $\frac{1}{6}$ hours

(C) 6 hours

3. A B C D E

3. Mr. Smith had $2000 to invest. He invested part of it at 5% per year, and the remainder at 4% per year. After one year, his investment grew to $2095. How much of the original investment was at the 5% rate?

(A) $500 (B) $750 (C) $1000 (D) $1250 (E) $1500

4. A B C D E

4. A man walks down the road for half an hour at an average speed of 3 miles per hour. He waits 10 minutes for a bus, which brings him back to his starting

point at 3:15. If the man began his walk at 2:25 the same afternoon, what was the average speed of the bus?

(A) 1.5 miles per hour

(D) 6 miles per hour

(B) 3 miles per hour

(E) 9 miles per hour

(C) 4.5 miles per hour

5. Faucet A lets water flow into a 5-gallon tub at a rate of 1.5 gallons per minute. Faucet B lets water flow into the same tub at a rate of 1.0 gallons per minute. Faucet A runs alone for 100 seconds; then the two of them together finish filling up the tub. How long does the whole operation take?

(A) 120 seconds

(D) 180 seconds

(B) 150 seconds

(E) 190 seconds

(C) 160 seconds

5. A B C D E

6. Coffee A normally costs 75¢ per pound. It is mixed with Coffee B, which normally costs 80¢ per pound, to form a mixture which costs 78¢ per pound. If there are 10 pounds of the mix, how many pounds of Coffee A were used in the mix?

(A) 3   (B) 4   (C) 4.5   (D) 5   (E) 6

6. A B C D E

7. If a man can run p miles in x minutes, how long would it take him to run q miles at the same rate?

(A) $\dfrac{pq}{x}$ minutes

(D) $\dfrac{qx}{p}$ minutes

(B) $\dfrac{px}{q}$ minutes

(E) $\dfrac{x}{pq}$ minutes

(C) $\dfrac{q}{px}$ minutes

7. A B C D E

8. A train went 300 miles from City X to City Y at an average rate of 80 mph. At what speed did it travel on the way back if its average speed for the whole trip was 100 mph?

(A) 120 mph

(D) $137\frac{1}{2}$ mph

(B) 125 mph

(E) 150 mph

(C) $133\frac{1}{3}$ mph

8. A B C D E

9. A man spent exactly $2.50 on 3¢, 6¢, and 10¢ stamps. If he bought ten 3¢ stamps, and twice as many 6¢ stamps as 10¢ stamps, how many 10¢ stamps did he buy?

(A) 5   (B) 10   (C) 12   (D) 15   (E) 20

9. A B C D E

10. If 6 workers can complete 9 identical jobs in 3 days, how long will it take 4 workers to complete 10 such jobs?

(A) 3 days

(D) 6 days

(B) 4 days

(E) more than 6 days

(C) 5 days

10. A B C D E

11. A B C D E **11.** A barge travels twice as fast when empty as when it is full. If it travels 20 miles north with a cargo, spends 20 minutes unloading, and returns to its original port empty, taking 8 hours to complete the entire trip, what is the speed of the barge when it is empty?

(A) less than 3 mph

(B) less than 4 mph but not less than 3 mph

(C) less than 6 mph but not less than 4 mph

(D) less than 8 mph but not less than 6 mph

(E) 8 mph or more

12. A B C D E **12.** Bill can hammer 20 nails in 6 minutes. Jeff can do the same job in only 5 minutes. How long will it take them to finish if Bill hammers the first 5 nails, then Jeff hammers for 3 minutes, then Bill finishes the job?

(A) 4.6 minutes   (D) 5.8 minutes

(B) 5.0 minutes   (E) 6.0 minutes

(C) 5.4 minutes

13. A B C D E **13.** Jack has two quarts of a 30% acid solution and three pints of a 20% solution. If he mixes them, what will be the concentration (to the nearest percent) of the resulting solution?

(A) 22%   (B) 23%   (C) 24%   (D) 25%   (E) 26%

14. A B C D E **14.** Robert has 12 coins totalling $1.45. None of his coins is larger than a quarter. Which of the following *cannot* be the number of quarters he has?

(A) 1   (B) 2   (C) 3   (D) 4   (E) 5

15. A B C D E **15.** Jim's allowance is $1.20 per week. Stan's is 25¢ per day. How long will they have to save, if they save both their allowances together, before they can get a walkie-talkie set that costs $23.60?

(A) 6 weeks   (D) 13 weeks

(B) 8 weeks   (E) 16 weeks

(C) 10 weeks

16. A B C D E **16.** Chuck can earn money at the following schedule: $2.00 for the first hour, $2.50 an hour for the next two hours, and $3.00 an hour after that. He also has the opportunity of taking a different job that pays $2.75 an hour. He wants to work until he has earned $15.00. Which of the following is true?

(A) The first job will take him longer by 15 minutes or more.

(B) The first job will take him longer by less than 15 minutes.

(C) The two jobs will take the same length of time.

(D) The second job will take him longer by 30 minutes or more.

(E) The second job will take him longer by less than 10 minutes.

17. A B C D E **17.** If Robert can seal 40 envelopes in one minute, and Paul can do the same job in 80 seconds, how many minutes (to the nearest minute) will it take the two of them, working together, to seal 350 envelopes?

(A) 4 minutes   (D) 7 minutes

(B) 5 minutes   (E) 8 minutes

(C) 6 minutes

18. Towns A and B are 400 miles apart. If a train leaves A in the direction of B, at 50 miles per hour, how long will it take before that train meets another train, going from B to A, at a speed of 30 miles per hour?

18. A B C D E

(A) 4 hours   (D) $5\frac{2}{3}$ hours

(B) $4\frac{1}{3}$ hours   (E) $6\frac{2}{3}$ hours

(C) 5 hours

19. A tub is shaped like a rectangular solid, with internal measurements of 2 feet $\times$ 2 feet $\times$ 5 feet. If two faucets, each with an output of 2 cubic feet of water per minute, pour water into the tub simultaneously, how many minutes does it take to fill the tub completely?

19. A B C D E

(A) less than 3 minutes

(B) less than 4 minutes, but not less than 3

(C) less than 5 minutes, but not less than 4

(D) less than 6 minutes, but not less than 5

(E) 6 minutes or more

20. A 30% solution of barium chloride is mixed with 10 grams of water to form a 20% solution. How many grams of the original solution did we start with?

20. A B C D E

(A) 10   (B) 15   (C) 20   (D) 25   (E) 30

21. Mr. Adams had a coin collection including only nickels, dimes, and quarters. He had twice as many dimes as he had nickels, and half as many quarters as he had nickels. If the total face value of his collection was $300.00, how many quarters did the collection contain?

21. A B C D E

(A) 75   (B) 100   (C) 250   (D) 400   (E) 800

22. A storekeeper stocks a high-priced pen and a lower-priced model. If he sells the high-priced pens, which yields a profit of $1.20 per pen sold, he can sell 30 in a month. If he sells the lower-priced pens, making a profit of 15¢ per pen sold, he can sell 250 pens in a month. Which type of pen will yield more profit per month, and by how much?

22. A B C D E

(A) The cheaper pen will yield a greater profit, by $1.50.

(B) The more expensive pen will yield a greater profit, by $1.50.

(C) The cheaper pen will yield a greater profit, by 15¢.

(D) The more expensive pen will yield a greater profit, by 15¢.

(E) Both pens will yield exactly the same profit.

23. At a cost of $2.50 per square yard, what would be the price of carpeting a rectangular floor, $18' \times 24'$?

23. A B C D E

(A) $120   (D) $1000

(B) $360   (E) $1080

(C) $750

24. A B C D E

24. Tom and Bill agreed to race across a 50-foot pool and back again. They started together, but Tom finished 10 feet ahead of Bill. If their rates were constant, and Tom finished the race in 27 seconds, how long did Bill take to finish it?

(A) 28 seconds   (D) 35 seconds

(B) 30 seconds   (E) 37 seconds

(C) $33\frac{1}{3}$ seconds

25. A B C D E

25. If four men need $24.00 worth of food for a three-day camping trip, how much will two men need for a two-week trip?

(A) $12.00   (B) $24.00   (C) $28.00   (C) $42.00   (E) $56.00

26. A B C D E

26. A man walks 15 blocks to work every morning at a rate of 2 miles per hour. If there are 20 blocks in a mile, how long does it take him to walk to work?

(A) $12\frac{1}{2}$ minutes   (D) $37\frac{1}{2}$ minutes

(B) 15 minutes   (E) 45 minutes

(C) $22\frac{1}{2}$ minutes

27. A B C D E

27. A certain river has a current of 3 miles per hour. A boat takes twice as long to travel upstream between two points as it does to travel downstream between the same two points. What is the speed of the boat in still water?

(A) 3 miles per hour

(B) 6 miles per hour

(C) 9 miles per hour

(D) 12 miles per hour

(E) The speed cannot be determined from the given information.

28. A B C D E

28. Stan can run 10 miles per hour, while Jack can run only 8 miles per hour. If they start at the same time from the same point, and run in opposite directions, how far apart (to the nearest mile) will they be after 10 minutes?

(A) 1 mile   (D) 4 miles

(B) 2 miles   (E) 5 miles

(C) 3 miles

29. A B C D E

29. Machine A can produce 40 bolts per minute, while Machine B can produce only 30 per minute. Machine A begins alone to make bolts but it breaks down after $1\frac{1}{2}$ minutes, and Machine B must complete the job. If the job requires 300 bolts, how long does the whole operation take?

(A) $7\frac{1}{2}$ minutes   (D) 9 minutes

(B) 8 minutes   (E) $9\frac{1}{2}$ minutes

(C) $8\frac{1}{2}$ minutes

30. A B C D E

30. Ten pints of 15% salt solution are mixed with 15 pints of 10% salt solution. What is the concentration of the resulting solution?

(A) 10%   (B) 12%   (C) 12.5%   (D) 13%   (E) 15%

31. Jeff makes $5.00 every day, from which he must spend $3.00 for various expenses. Pete makes $10.00 a day, but has to spend $7.00 each day for expenses. If the two of them save together, how long will it take before they can buy a $150 car?

31. A B C D E

    (A) 10 days   (D) 50 days

    (B) 15 days   (E) 75 days

    (C) 30 days

32. Two cities are 800 miles apart. At 3:00 P.M., Plane A leaves one city, traveling toward the other city at a speed of 600 miles per hour. At 4:00 the same afternoon, Plane B leaves the first city, traveling in the same direction at a rate of 800 miles per hour. Which of the following answers represents the actual result?

32. A B C D E

    (A) Plane A arrives first, by an hour or more.

    (B) Plane A arrives first, by less than an hour.

    (C) The two planes arrive at exactly the same time.

    (D) Plane A arrives after Plane B, by less than an hour.

    (E) Plane A arrives after Plane B, by an hour or more.

33. Peter has as many nickels as Charlie has dimes; Charlie has twice as many nickels as Peter has dimes. If together they have $2.50 in nickels and dimes, how many nickels does Peter have?

33. A B C D E

    (A) 1 nickel

    (B) 4 nickels

    (C) 7 nickels

    (D) 10 nickels

    (E) Cannot be determined from the given information.

34. A man can travel 120 miles in either of two ways. He can travel at a constant rate of 40 miles per hour; or he can travel half way at 50 miles per hour, then slow down to 30 miles per hour for the second 60 miles. Which way is faster, and by how much?

34. A B C D E

    (A) The constant rate is faster by 10 minutes or more.

    (B) The constant rate is faster by less than 10 minutes.

    (C) The two ways take exactly the same time.

    (D) The constant rate is slower by less than 10 minutes.

    (E) The constant rate is slower by 10 minutes or more.

35. John walks 10 miles at an average rate of 2 miles per hour, and returns on a bicycle at an average rate of 10 miles per hour. How long (to the nearest hour) does the entire trip take him?

35. A B C D E

    (A) 3 hours   (D) 6 hours

    (B) 4 hours   (E) 7 hours

    (C) 5 hours

36. A B C D E   **36.** If a plane can travel P miles in Q hours, how long will it take to travel R miles?

(A) $\dfrac{PQ}{R}$ hours   (D) $\dfrac{Q}{PR}$ hours

(B) $\dfrac{P}{QR}$ hours   (E) $\dfrac{PR}{Q}$ hours

(C) $\dfrac{QR}{P}$ hours

37. A B C D E   **37.** A boy can swim 75 feet in 12 seconds. What is his rate to the nearest mile per hour?

(A) 1 mph   (B) 2 mph   (C) 3 mph   (D) 4 mph   (E) 5 mph

38. A B C D E   **38.** How many pounds of a $1.20 per pound nut mixture must be mixed with two pounds of a 90¢ per pound mixture to produce a mixture that sells for $1.00 per pound?

(A) 0.5   (B) 1.0   (C) 1.5   (D) 2.0   (E) 2.5

39. A B C D E   **39.** A broken clock is set correctly at 12:00 noon. However, it registers only 20 minutes for each hour. In how many hours will it again register the correct time?

(A) 12   (B) 18   (C) 24   (D) 30   (E) 36

40. A B C D E   **40.** If a man travels p hours at an average rate of q miles per hour, and then r hours at an average rate of s miles per hour, what is his overall average rate of speed?

(A) $\dfrac{pq+rs}{p+r}$ (B) $\dfrac{q+s}{2}$ (C) $\dfrac{q+s}{p+r}$ (D) $\dfrac{p}{q}+\dfrac{r}{s}$ (E) $\dfrac{p}{s}+\dfrac{r}{q}$

41. A B C D E   **41.** If Walt can paint 25 feet of fence in an hour, and Joe can paint 35 feet in an hour, how many minutes will it take them to paint a 150-foot fence, if they work together?

(A) 150   (B) 200   (C) 240   (D) 480   (E) 500

42. A B C D E   **42.** If a man travels for a half hour at a rate of 20 miles per hour, and for another half hour at a rate of 30 miles per hour, what is his average speed?

(A) 24 miles per hour

(B) 25 miles per hour

(C) 26 miles per hour

(D) 26.5 miles per hour

(E) Cannot be determined from the given information.

43. A B C D E   **43.** New York is 3000 miles from Los Angeles. Sol leaves New York aboard a plane heading toward Los Angeles at the same time that Robert leaves Los Angeles aboard a plane heading toward New York. If Sol is moving at 200 miles per hour and Robert is moving at 400 miles per hour, how soon will one plane pass the other?

(A) 2 hours   (D) 4 hours

(B) $22\frac{1}{2}$ hours   (E) 12 hours

(C) 5 hours

44. A man exchanged a dollar bill for change and received 7 coins, none of which were half dollars. How many of these coins were dimes?

(A) 0

(B) 1

(C) 4

(D) 5

(E) Cannot be determined from the information given.

44. A B C D E

45. A man adds two quarts of pure alcohol to a 30% solution of alcohol in water. If the new concentration is 40%, how many quarts of the original solution were there?

(A) 12   (B) 15   (C) 18   (D) 20   (E) 24

45. A B C D E

46. A certain power company charges 8¢ per kilowatt-hour for the first 1000 kilo-watt-hours, and 6¢ per kilowatt-hour after that. If a man uses a 900-watt toaster for 5 hours, a 100-watt lamp for 25 hours, and a 5-watt clock for 400 hours, how much is he charged for the power he uses? (1 kilowatt = 1000 watts)

(A) 56¢   (B) 64¢   (C) 72¢   (D) $560.00   (E) $720.00

46. A B C D E

47. At 30¢ per yard, what is the price of 96 inches of ribbon?

(A) 72¢   (B) 75¢   (C) 80¢   (D) 84¢   (E) 90

47. A B C D E

48. A man travels for 6 hours at a rate of 50 miles per hour. His return trip takes him $7\frac{1}{2}$ hours. What is his average speed for the whole trip?

(A) 44.4 miles per hour   (D) 48.2 miles per hour

(B) 45.0 miles per hour   (E) 50.0 miles per hour

(C) 46.8 miles per hour

48. A B C D E

49. Stanley puts $100 in the bank for two years at 5% interest compounded annually. At the end of the two years, what was his balance?

(A) $100.00   (B) $105.00   (C) $105.25   (D) $110.00
(E) $110.25

49. A B C D E

50. A 12-gallon tub has a faucet that lets water in at a rate of 3 gallons per minute, and a drain that lets water out at a rate of 1.5 gallons per minute. If you start with 3 gallons of water in the tub, how long will it take to fill the tub completely?

(A) 3 minutes   (B) 4 minutes   (C) 6 minutes   (D) 7.5 minutes

(E) 8 minutes

50. A B C D E

ANSWER KEY FOR PRACTICE TEST 2

1. B	14. A	26. C	39. B
2. A	15. B	27. C	40. A
3. E	16. B	28. C	41. A
4. E	17. B	29. E	42. B
5. C	18. C	30. B	43. C
6. B	19. D	31. C	44. E
7. D	20. C	32. B	45. A
8. C	21. D	33. E	46. C
9. B	22. A	34. A	47. C
10. C	23. A	35. D	48. A
11. D	24. B	36. C	49. E
12. C	25. E	37. D	50. C
13. E		38. B	

ANSWERS AND SOLUTIONS FOR PRACTICE TEST 2

1. (B) The fundamental relationship here is: rate $\times$ time = distance. The easiest units to work with are miles per hour for the rate, hours for time, and miles for distance. Note that the word "per" indicates division because when calculating a rate, we *divide* the number of miles (distance units) by the number of hours (time units).

We can set up our chart with the information given. We know that the upstream trip took $1\frac{1}{2}$ hours (90 minutes) and that the distance was 3 miles. Thus the upstream rate was 2 miles per hour. The downstream distance was also 3 miles, but we use t for the time which is unknown. Thus the downstream rate was $\frac{3}{t}$. Our chart looks like this:

	rate $\times$	time =	distance
	mi/hr	hours	miles
upstream	2	$1\frac{1}{2}$	3
downstream	$\frac{3}{t}$	t	3

We use the rest of the information to solve for t. We know that the speed of the current is 2 miles per hour. We assume the boat to be in still water and assign it a speed, s; then the upstream (against the current) speed of the boat is $s - 2$ miles per hour. Since $s - 2 = 2$, $s = 4$.

Now the speed of the boat downstream (with the current) is $s + 2$, or 6 miles per hour. This is equal to $\dfrac{3}{t}$, and we get the equation $\dfrac{3}{t} = 6$, so $t = \dfrac{1}{2}$ hour. We must be careful with our units because the answer must be in minutes. We can convert $\frac{1}{2}$ hour to 30 minutes to get the final answer. (201, 202)

2. **(A)**

rate $\times$ time $=$ work

	job/hr	hours	jobs
Charles	1	1	1
Bill	$\frac{1}{2}$	2	1
Bob	$\frac{1}{3}$	3	1
together	r	t	1

Let $r =$ rate together and $t =$ time together.

Now, $r = 1 + \frac{1}{2} + \frac{1}{3} = \frac{11}{6}$ because *whenever two or more people are work- ing together, their joint rate is the sum of their individual rates.* This is not necessarily true of the time or the work done. In this case, we know that $r \times t = 1$ and $r = \frac{11}{6}$, so $t = \frac{6}{11}$. (201, 203)

3. **(E)**

rate $\times$ principal $=$ interest

	$/$	$	$
5%	0.05	x	$0.05x$
4%	0.04	y	$0.04y$

Let $x =$ part of the $2000 invested at 5%. Let $y =$ part of $2000 invested at 4%. We know that since the whole $2000 was invested, $x + y$ must equal $2000. Furthermore, we know that the sum of the interests on both investments equaled $95, so $0.05x + 0.04x = 95$. Since we have to solve only for x, we can express this as $0.01x + 0.04x + 0.04y = 95$. Then we factor out 0.04. Thus $0.01x + 0.04(x + y) = 95$. Since we know that $x + y = 2000$, we have $0.01x + 0.04(2000) = 95$, $0.01x + 80 = 95$, and $x = 1500$. Thus, $1500 was invested at 5%. (201, 205)

4. **(E)**

rate $\times$ times $=$ distance

	mi/min	min	miles
walk	$\frac{1}{20}$	30	a
wait	0	l	0
bus	r	t	a

Let a = distance the man walks. Since the man walks at 3 miles per hour, he walks at $\dfrac{3 \text{ mi}}{60 \text{ min}}$ or $\dfrac{1 \text{ mi}}{20 \text{ min}}$. From this we can find $a = \dfrac{1 \text{ mi}}{20 \text{ min}} \times 30 \text{ min} = 1\frac{1}{2}$ miles. The total time he spent was 50 minutes (the difference between 3:15 and 2:25), and $30 + 10 + t = 50$, so t must be equal to 10 minutes. This reduces our problem to the simple equation $10r = 1\frac{1}{2}$ (where r = rate of the bus), and, on solving, $r = 0.15$ miles per minute. But the required answer is in miles per hour. In one hour, or 60 minutes, the bus can travel 60 times as far as the 0.15 miles it travels in one minute, so that the bus travels $60 \times 0.15 = 9$ miles per hour. (201, 202)

5. (C)

	rate	×	time	=	water
	gal/min		min		gal
A only	1.5		$\frac{5}{3}$*		2.5
B only	1.0		0		0
A and *B*	2.5		t		x

* $(\frac{5}{3} \text{ min} = 100 \text{ sec})$

Let t = time faucets A and B run together.

Let x = amount of water delivered when A and B run together.

We know that the total number of gallons is 5, and A alone delivers 2.5 gallons (1.5 gal/min $\times \frac{5}{3}$ min = 2.5 gal), so x equals 2.5. This leads us to the simple equation $2.5t = 2.5$, so $t = 1$ minute, or 60 seconds. Thus, the whole operation takes $\frac{5}{3} + t$ minutes, or $100 + 60$ seconds, totalling 160 seconds. (201, 203)

6. (B)

	rate	×	amount	=	cost
	¢/lb		lb		¢
Coffee A	75		x		$75x$
Coffee B	80		y		$80y$
mix	78		10		780

Let x = weight of Coffee A in the mix.

Let y = weight of Coffee B in the mix.

We know that the weight of the mix is equal to the sum of the weights of its components. Thus, $x + y = 10$. Similarly, the cost of the mix is equal to the sum of the costs of the components. Thus, $75x + 80y = 780$. Solving these two equations simultaneously gives us $x = 4$ and $y = 6$, so 4 pounds of Coffee A were used. (201, 204, 407)

7. (D)

rate × time = distance

	mi/min	min	miles
first run	r	x	p
second run	r	t	q

Let r = rate of the man.

Let t = time it takes him to run q miles.

From the first line, we know that $rx = p$, then $r = \dfrac{p}{x}$. Substituting this in the

second line, we get $\left(\dfrac{p}{x}\right) t = q$, so $t = q\left(\dfrac{x}{p}\right)$, or $\dfrac{qx}{p}$ minutes.   (201, 202)

8. (C)

rate × time = distance

	mi/hr	hrs	miles
X to Y	80	t	300
Y to X	r	s	300
whole trip	100	$s + t$	600

Let t = time from city X to city Y.

Let s = time from city Y to city X.

Let n = rate of the train from Y to X.

We know that $80t = 300$, so $t = \frac{300}{80}$, or $\frac{15}{4}$. Also, $100(s + t) = 600$, so $s + t = 6$. This and the last equation lead us to the conclusion that $s = 6 - \frac{15}{4}$, or $\frac{9}{4}$. Now, from the middle line, we have $r\left(\frac{9}{4}\right) = 300$, so $r = \frac{400}{3}$, or $133\frac{1}{3}$ miles per hour. (Note that the reason why we chose the equations in this particular order was that it is easiest to concentrate first on those with the most data already given.)   (201, 202)

9. (B)

rate × number = cost

	¢/stamp	stamps	¢
3¢ stamps	3	10	30
10¢ stamps	10	x	$10x$
6¢ stamps	6	$2x$	$12x$

Let x = the number of 10¢ stamps bought.

We know that the total cost is 250¢, so $30 + 10x + 12x = 250$. This is the same as $22x = 220$ so $x = 10$. Therefore, he bought ten 10¢ stamps.   (201, 205)

10. (C)

	rate	×	time	=	work
	jb/day		days		jobs
6 workers	$6r$		3		9
4 workers	$4r$		t		10

Let r = rate of one worker.

Let t = time for 4 workers to do 10 jobs.

From the first line, we have $18r = 9$, so $r = \frac{1}{2}$. Substituting this in the second line, $4r = 2$, so $2t = 10$. Therefore, $t = 5$. The workers will take 5 days.

(201, 203)

11. (D)

	rate	×	time	=	distance
	mi/hr		hrs		miles
north	r		$\dfrac{20}{r}$		20
unload	0		$\frac{1}{3}$		0
return	$2r$		$\dfrac{10}{r}$		20

Let r = loaded rate; then

$2r$ = empty rate.

Total time $= \dfrac{20}{r} + \dfrac{1}{3} + \dfrac{10}{r} = 8$ hours. Multiplying by $3r$ on both sides, we get $90 = 23r$, so $r = 90 \div 23$, or about 3.9 miles per hour. However, the problem asks for the speed *when empty*, which is $2r$, or 7.8. This is less than 8 mph but not less than 6 mph.

(201, 202)

12. (C)

	rate	×	time	=	work
	nl/min		min		nails
Bill	r		6		20
Jeff	s		5		20
Bill	r		$\dfrac{5}{r}$		5
Jeff	s		3		$3s$
Bill	r		$\dfrac{x}{r}$		x

$r =$ Bill's rate

$s =$ Jeff's rate

$x =$ number of nails left after Jeff takes his turn.

$6r = 20$, so $r = 3\frac{1}{3}$

$5s = 20$, so $s = 4$

Total work $= 5 + 3s + x = 20 = 5 + 12 + x$, so $x = 3$. Thus $\dfrac{x}{r} = 0.9$

Total time $= \dfrac{5}{r} + 3 + \dfrac{x}{r} = 1.5 + 3 + 0.9 = 5.4$.   (201, 203)

13. **(E)**

concentration × volume = amount of acid

	% acid	pts	pts
old sol	30%	4	1.2
	20%	3	0.6
new sol	x%	7	1.8

2 qts $= 4$ pts

Let x% $=$ concentration of new solution.

4 pts of 30% $+$ 3 pts of 20% $=$ 7 pts of x%

1.2 pts $+$ 0.6 pt $= 1.8$ pts

$(x\%)\,(7) = 1.8$, so $x = 180 \div 7 = 25.7$ (approximately), which is closest to 26%.   (201, 204)

14. **(A)**

coin × number = total value

	¢/coin	coins	cents
pennies	1	p	p
nickels	5	n	$5n$
dimes	10	d	$10d$
quarters	25	q	$25q$

Let $p =$ number of pennies

$n =$ number of nickels

$d =$ number of dimes

$q =$ number of quarters

Total number of coins $= p + n + d + q = 12$

Total value $= p + 5n + 10d + 25q = 145$

Now, if $q = 1$, then $p + n + d = 11$, $p + 5n + 10d = 120$. But in this case, the greatest possible value of the other eleven coins would be the value of eleven dimes, or 110 cents, which falls short of the amount necessary to give a total of 145 cents for the twelve coins put together. Therefore, Robert cannot have only one quarter. (201, 205)

15. (B)

	rate	× time	= money
	¢/wk	weeks	cents
Jim	120	w	$120w$
Stan	175	w	$175w$
together	295	w	$295w$

(25¢/day = $1.75/week)

Let $w =$ the number of weeks they save.

Total money $= 295w = 2360$.

Therefore, $w = 2360 \div 295 = 8$.

So, they must save for 8 weeks. (201, 205)

16. (B)

	rate	× time	= pay
	¢/hr	hours	¢
first job	200	1	200
	250	2	500
	300	x	$300x$
second job	275	y	$275y$

Let $x =$ hours at $3.00.

Let $y =$ hours at $2.75.

Total pay first job $= 200 + 500 + 300x = 1500$, so $x = 2\frac{2}{3}$

Total time first job $= 1 + 2 + 2\frac{2}{3} = 5\frac{2}{3}$

Total pay second job $= 275y = 1500$, so $y = 5\frac{5}{11}$

Total time second job $= 5\frac{5}{11}$.

$\frac{2}{3}$ hour $= 40$ minutes

$\frac{5}{11}$ hour $= 27.2727 \ldots$ minutes (less than $\frac{2}{3}$ hour)

Thus, the first job will take him longer by less than 15 minutes.

17. **(B)**

	rate	×	time	=	work
	envelopes/min		min		envelopes
Robert	40		t		$40t$
Paul	30		t		$30t$
both	70		t		$70t$

Let t = time to seal 350 envelopes.

Paul's rate is 30 envelopes/minute, as shown by the proportion:

$$\text{rate} = \frac{40 \text{ envelopes}}{80 \text{ seconds}} = \frac{30 \text{ envelopes}}{60 \text{ seconds}}$$

Total work = $70t = 350$, so $t = 5$ minutes.   (201, 203)

18. **(C)**

	rate	×	time	=	distance
	mi/hr		hr		miles
A to B	50		t		$50t$
B to A	30		t		$30t$

Let t = time to meet

Total distance traveled by two trains together equals
$50t + 30t = 80t = 400$ miles, so $t = 5$ hrs.   (201, 202)

19. **(D)**

	rate	×	time	=	amount of water
	cu. ft/m		min		cu. ft.
2 faucets	4		t		20

Let t = time to fill the tub.

Volume of tub = $2' \times 2' \times 5' = 20$ cu. ft.

Rate = $2 \times$ rate of each faucet = 2×2 cu. ft./min. = 4 cu. ft./min.

Therefore, $t = 5$ minutes.   (201, 203)

20. **(C)**

	concentration	×	weight	=	amount of barium chloride
	%		grams		grams
original	30%		x		$0.30x$
water	0%		10		0
new	20%		$10 + x$		$0.30x$

Let x = number of grams of original solution.

Total weight and amounts of barium chloride may be added by column.

$(20\%) \times (10 + x) = 0.30x$, so $10 + x = 1.50x$, $x = 20$.　　　(201, 204)

21. (D)

	coin	× number	= value
	¢/coin	coins	cents
nickels	5	n	$5n$
dimes	10	$2n$	$20n$
quarters	25	$\dfrac{n}{2}$	$\dfrac{25n}{2}$

Let n = number of nickels.

Total value $= 5n + 20n + \dfrac{25n}{2} = \left(37\dfrac{1}{2}\right) n = 30{,}000$

Thus, $n = 30{,}000 \div 37\dfrac{1}{2} = 800$.

The number of quarters is then $\dfrac{n}{2} = \dfrac{800}{2} = 400$.　　　(201, 205)

22. (A)

	rate	× number	= profit
	¢/pen	pens	cents
high-price	120	30	3600
low-price	15	250	3750

Subtracting 3600¢ from 3750¢, we get 150¢.

Thus, the cheaper pen yields a profit of 150¢, or \$1.50, more per month than the more expensive one.　　　(201, 205)

23. (A)

	price	× area	= cost
	\$/sq yd	sq yd	dollars
	2.50	48	120

Area must be expressed in square yards; $18' = 6$ yds, and $24' = 8$ yds, so $18' \times 24' = 6$ yds $\times 8$ yds $= 48$ sq yds. The cost would then be \$2.50 $\times 48 =$ \$120.00.　　　(201, 205)

24. **(B)**

	ft/sec	sec	feet
Tom	r	27	100
Bill	s	27	90
Bill	s	t	100

rate $\times$ time $=$ distance

Let $r =$ Tom's rate.

Let $s =$ Bill's rate.

Let $t =$ Bill's time to finish the race.

$27r = 100$, so $r = \frac{100}{27}$;

$27s = 90$, so $s = \frac{90}{27} = \frac{10}{3}$;

$st = 100$, and $s = \frac{10}{3}$, so $\frac{10t}{3} = 100$, thus $t = 30$.   (201, 202)

25. **(E)** This is a rate problem in which the fundamental relationship is rate $\times$ time $\times$ number of men $=$ cost. The rate is in dollars/man-days. Thus, our chart looks like this:

rate $\times$ time $\times$ number $=$ cost

	$/man-days	days	men	$
1st trip	r	3	4	$12r$
2nd trip	r	14	2	$28r$

The cost of the first trip is \$24, so $12r = 24$ and $r = 2$.

The cost of the second trip is $28r$, or \$56.   (201, 205)

26. **(C)**

rate $\times$ time $=$ distance

blocks/min.	min	blocks
$\frac{2}{3}$	t	15

Let $t =$ time to walk to work.

2 miles/hr $= 2(20 \text{ blocks})/(60 \text{ min}) = \left(\frac{2}{3}\right)$ blocks/minute

$t = 15 \div \left(\frac{2}{3}\right) = 22\frac{1}{2}$ minutes.   (201, 202)

27. (C)

rate	×	time	=	distance
	mi/hr	**hrs**	**miles**
down	$r + 3$	h	$h(r + 3)$
up	$r - 3$	$2h$	$2h(r - 3)$

Let $h =$ time to travel downstream.

Let $r =$ speed of the boat in still water.

Since the two trips cover the same distance, we can write the equation: $h(r + 3) = 2h(r - 3)$. Dividing by h, $r + 3 = 2r - 6$, so $r = 9$. (201, 202)

28. (C) We could treat this as a regular distance problem, and make up a table that would solve it, but there is an easier way here, if we consider the quantity representing the distance between the boys. This distance starts at zero, and increases at the rate of 18 miles per hour. Thus, in 10 minutes, or $\frac{1}{6}$ hour, they will be 3 miles apart. ($\frac{1}{6}$ hr $\times 18\frac{\text{mi}}{\text{hr}} = 3$ mi). (201, 202)

29. (E)

rate	×	time	=	work
	bolts/min	**min**	**bolts**
A	40	$1\frac{1}{2}$	60
B	30	t	240

Let $t =$ time B works.

Since A produces only 60 out of 300 that must be produced, B must produce 240; then, $30t = 240$, so $t = 8$.

Total time $= t + 1\frac{1}{2} = 8 + 1\frac{1}{2} = 9\frac{1}{2}$. (201, 203)

30. (B)

concentration	×	volume	=	amount of salt
	%	**pints**	**'''pints'' of salt***
15%	15	10	1.5
10%	10	15	1.5
Total	x	25	3.0

*One "pint" of salt actually represents a weight of salt equal to the weight of one pint of water.

Let $x =$ concentration of resulting solution.

$(x\%)(25) = 3.0$, so $x = 300 \div 25 = 12$. (201, 204)

31. (C)

	rate ×	time =	pay (net)
	$/day	days	$
Jeff	2	d	$2d$
Pete	3	d	$3d$
total	5	d	$5d$

(Net pay = pay — expenses.)

Let d = the number of days it takes to save.

Total net pay = $150.00, so $150 = 5d$, thus $d = 30$.

Do not make the mistake of using 5 and 10 as the rates! (201, 205)

32. (B)

	rate ×	time =	distance
	mi/hr	hours	miles
plane A	600	h	800
plane B	0	1	0
plane B	800	t	800

Let h = time for trip at 600 mph — waiting time before second flight.

Let t = time for trip at 800 mph.

Plane A: $600h = 800$, so $h = \frac{800}{600} = 1\frac{1}{3}$ hours = 1 hour, 20 minutes

Plane B: $800t = 800$, so $t = 1$

Total time for plane A = 1 hour, 20 minutes

Total time for plane B = 1 hour + 1 hour = 2 hours

Thus, plane A arrives before plane B by 40 minutes (less than an hour).

(201, 202)

33. (E)

	coin ×	number =	value
	¢/coin	coins	cents
Peter	5	n	$5n$
Peter	10	d	$10d$
Charlie	5	$2d$	$10d$
Charlie	10	n	$10n$

Let n = number of Peter's nickels.

Let d = number of Peter's dimes.

Total value of coins = $5n + 10d + 10d + 10n = 15n + 20d$

Thus, $15n + 20d = 250$. This has many different solutions, each of which is possible (e.g., $n = 2$, $d = 11$, or $n = 6$, $d = 8$, etc.)   (201, 205)

34. (A)

	rate ×	time =	distance
	mi/hr	hours	miles
constant rate	40	h	120
two rates	50	m	60
	30	n	60

Let h = time to travel 120 miles at the constant rate.

Let m = time to travel 60 miles at 50 mi/hr.

Let n = time to travel 60 miles at 30 mi/hr.

Forming the equations for h, m, and n, and solving, we get:

$$40h = 120; \quad h = \frac{120}{40}; \quad h = 3$$

$$50m = 60; \quad m = \frac{60}{50}; \quad m = 1.2$$

$$30n = 60; \quad n = \frac{60}{30}; \quad n = 2$$

Total time with constant rate = $h = 3$ hours.

Total time with changing rate = $m + n = 3.2$ hours.

Thus, the constant rate is faster by 0.2 hours, or 12 minutes.   (201, 202)

35. (D)

	rate ×	time =	distance
	mi/hr	hours	miles
walking	2	h	10
bicycling	10	t	10

Let h = time to walk.

Let t = time to bicycle.

Forming equations: $2h = 10$, so $h = 5$; and $10t = 10$, so $t = 1$.

Total time = $h + t = 5 + 1 = 6$.   (201, 202)

36. (C)

	rate ×	time =	distance
	mi/hr	hours	miles
	x	Q	P
	x	y	R

Let $x =$ rate of traveling Q miles.

Let $y =$ time to travel R miles.

$Qx = P$, so $x = \dfrac{P}{Q}$

$xy = \left(\dfrac{P}{Q}\right)y = R$, so $y = \dfrac{QR}{P}$ hours = time to travel R miles.   (201, 202)

37. (D)

rate	×	time	=	distance
mi/hr		hours		miles
r		$\dfrac{1}{300}$		$\dfrac{75}{5280}$

Let $r =$ rate of swimming.

75 feet $= 75\left(\dfrac{1}{5280}\text{ mile}\right) = \dfrac{75}{5280}$ mile

12 seconds $= 12\left(\dfrac{1}{3600}\text{ hour}\right) = \dfrac{1}{300}$ hour

$r = \dfrac{75}{5280} \div \dfrac{1}{300} = \dfrac{22500}{5280} = 4.3$ (approximately) $=$
4 mi/hr (approximately).   (201, 202)

38. (B)

	price	×	amount	=	value
	¢/lb		lbs.		cents
\$1.20 nuts	120		x		$120x$
\$0.90	90		2		180
mixture	100		$x + 2$		$180 + 120x$

Let $x =$ pounds of \$1.20 mixture.

Total value of mixture $= 100(x + 2) = 180 + 120x$

$100x + 200 = 180 + 120x$, so $x = 1$ pound.   (201, 204)

39. (B)

rate	×	time	=	loss
hr/hr		hrs		hrs
$\dfrac{2}{3}$		t		12

(Loss is the amount by which the
clock time differs from real time.)

Let $t =$ hours to register the correct time.

If the clock registers only 20 minutes each hour, it loses 40 minutes, or $\dfrac{2}{3}$
hour each hour. The clock will register the correct time only if it has lost

some multiple of 12 hours. The first time this can occur is after it has lost 12 hours. $(\frac{2}{3})t = 12$, so $t = 18$ hours. (201)

40. (A)

rate	×	time	=	distance
mi/hr		hrs		miles
q		p		pq
s		r		rs
total x		$p + r$		$pq + rs$

Let x = average speed.

We may add times of travel at the two rates, and also add the distances. Then, $x(p + r) = pq + rs$; thus, $x = \dfrac{pq + rs}{p + r}$. (201, 202)

41. (A)

	rate	×	time	=	work
	ft/hr		hrs		feet
Joe	35		x		$35x$
Walt	25		x		$25x$
Both	60		x		$60x$

Let x = the time the job takes.

Since they are working together, we add their rates and the amount of work they do. Thus, $60x = 150$, so $x = 2.5$ (hours) = 150 minutes. (201, 203)

42. (B)

	rate	×	time	=	distance
	mi/hr		hrs		miles
first $\frac{1}{2}$ hour	20		$\frac{1}{2}$		10
second $\frac{1}{2}$ hour	30		$\frac{1}{2}$		15
total	x		1		25

Let x = average speed.

We add the times and distances; then, using the rate formula, $(x)(1) = 25$, so $x = 25$ mi/hr. (201, 202)

43. (C)

rate	×	time	=	distance
	mi/hr	hours		miles
Sol	200	t		$200t$
Robert	400	t		$400t$

Let x = time from simultaneous departure to meeting.

Sol's time is equal to Robert's time because they leave at the same time and then they meet. Their combined distance is 3000 miles, so $200t + 400t = 3000$, or $t = 5$ hours. (201, 202)

44. (E)

coin	×	number	=	value
	¢/coin	coins		¢
pennies	1	p		p
nickels	5	n		$5n$
dimes	10	d		$10d$
quarters	25	q		$25q$

Let p = number of pennies.

Let n = number of nickels.

Let d = number of dimes.

Let q = number of quarters.

Adding the numbers of coins and their values, we get $p + n + d + q = 7$, and $p + 5n + 10d + 25q = 100$. These equations are satisfied by several values of p, n, d, and q. For example, $p = 0$, $n = 0$, $d = 5$, $q = 2$ satisfies the equation, as does $p = 0$, $n = 3$, $d = 1$, $q = 3$, and other combinations.

Thus, the number of dimes is not determined. (201, 205)

45. (A)

concentration	×	am't of solution	=	amount of alcohol
	%	qts		qts
pure alcohol	100%	2		2
solution	30%	x		$0.30x$
mixture	40%	$2 + x$		$2 + 0.30x$

Let x = qts of original solution.

Amounts of solution and of alcohol may be added.

$(40\%)(2 + x) = 2 + 0.30x$; so $0.8 + 0.4x = 2.0 + 0.30x$; thus, $x = 12$.

(201, 204)

46. (C)

	rate ×	time =	cost
	¢/kwh	kwh	¢
first 1000 kwh	8¢	t	8t

(time expressed in kilowatt-hours, or kwh)

Let t = number of kwh.

This problem must be broken up into two different parts: (1) finding the total power or the total number of kilowatt-hours (kwh) used, and (2) calculating the charge for that amount. (1) Total power used, $t = (900w)(5 \text{ hr}) + (100w)(25 \text{ hr}) + (5w)(400 \text{ hr}) = (4500 + 2500 + 2000)$ watt-hours = 9000 watt-hours. One thousand watt-hours equals one kilowatt-hour. Thus, $t = 9$ kilowatt hours, so that the charge is $(8¢)(9) = 72¢$. (201, 205)

47. (C)

	rate ×	amount =	cost
	¢/in	in	¢
1 yard	r	36	30
96 inches	r	96	96r

Let r = cost per inch of cloth.

From the table, $r \times 36 \text{ in} = 30¢$; $r = \dfrac{30¢}{36 \text{ in}} = \dfrac{5¢}{6 \text{ in}}$
Thus, $96r = 96(\frac{5}{6}) = 80¢$. (201, 205)

48. (A)

	rate ×	time =	distance
	mi/hr	hrs	miles
trip	50	6	300
return	r	$7\frac{1}{2}$	300
total	s	$13\frac{1}{2}$	600

Let r = rate for return.

Let s = average overall rate.

$(13\frac{1}{2})(s) = 600$; thus, $s = 600 \div 13\frac{1}{2} = 44.4$ (approximately). (201, 202)

49. (E)

	rate ×	principal =	interest
	%/year	$	$/year
first year	5	100	5
second year	5	105	5.25

Interest first year equals rate $\times$ principal $= 5\% \times \$100 = \$5$.

New principal $= \$105.00$.

Interest second year $=$ rate $\times$ new principal $= 5\% \times \$105 = \$5.25$.

Final principal $= \$105.00 + \$5.25 = \$110.25$. (201, 205)

50. (C)

	rate	$\times$ time	$=$ amount
	gal/min	min	gallons
in	3	x	$3x$
out	$1\frac{1}{2}$	x	$1\frac{1}{2}x$
net	$1\frac{1}{2}$	x	$1\frac{1}{2}x$

(Net $=$ in $-$ out.)

Let $x =$ time to fill the tub completely.

Since only 9 gallons are needed (there are already 3 in the tub), we have $1\frac{1}{2}x = 9$, so $x = 6$. (201)

MATH REFRESHER SESSION 3

Area, Perimeter, and Volume Problems

301. *Formula Problems.* Here, you are given certain data about one or more geometric figures, and you are asked to supply some missing information. To solve this type of problem, follow this procedure:

STEP 1. If you are not given a diagram, draw your own; this may make the answer readily apparent or it may suggest the best way to solve the problem. You should try to make your diagram as accurate as possible, but *do not waste time perfecting your diagram.*

STEP 2. Determine the formula which relates to the quantities involved in your problem. In many cases it will be helpful to set up tables containing the various data. (See Sections 303–316.)

STEP 3. Substitute the given information for the unknown quantities in your formulas to get the desired answer.

When doing volume, area and perimeter problems, keep this hint in mind: Often the solutions to such problems can be expressed as the sum of the areas *or* volumes *or* perimeters of simpler figures. In such cases do not hesitate to break down your original figure into simpler parts.

In doing problems involving the following figures, these approximations and facts will be useful:

$\sqrt{2}$ is approximately 1.4.

$\sqrt{3}$ is approximately 1.7.

$\sqrt{10}$ is approximately 3.16.

π is approximately $\frac{22}{7}$ or 3.14.

$\sin 30° = \frac{1}{2}$

$\sin 45° = \dfrac{\sqrt{2}}{2}$ which is approximately 0.71.

$\sin 60° = \dfrac{\sqrt{3}}{2}$ which is approximately 0.87.

Example: The figure below contains a square, a right triangle, and a semi-circle. If $ED = CD$ and the length of CD is 1 unit, find the area of the entire figure.

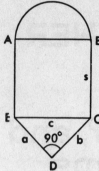

Solution: To calculate the area of the entire figure, we calculate the areas of the triangle, square, and semicircle and then add these together. In a right triangle, the area is $\frac{1}{2}ab$ where a and b are the sides of the triangle. In this case we will call side ED, a and side CD, b. $ED = CD = 1$, so the area of the triangle is $\frac{1}{2}$ (1) (1), or $\frac{1}{2}$.

The area of a square is s^2, where s is a side. We see that the side EC of the square is the hypotenuse of the right triangle. We can calculate this length by using the formula $c^2 = a^2 + b^2$ where $a = b = 1$; then we see that $c = \sqrt{2}$. Thus, in this case, $s = \sqrt{2}$ so the area of the square is $(\sqrt{2})^2 = 2$.

AB is the diameter of the semicircle, so $\frac{1}{2} AB$ is the radius. Since all sides of a square are equal, $AB = \sqrt{2}$, and the radius is $\frac{1}{2}\sqrt{2}$. Further, the area of a semicircle is $\frac{1}{2}\pi r^2$ where r is the radius, so the area of this semicircle is $\frac{1}{2}\pi(\frac{1}{2}\sqrt{2})^2 = \frac{1}{4}\pi$.

The total area of the whole figure is equal to the area of the triangle plus the area of the square plus the area of the semicircle $= \frac{1}{2} + 2 + \frac{1}{4}\pi = 2\frac{1}{2} + \frac{1}{4}\pi$.

Example: If water flows into a rectangular tank with dimensions of 12 inches, 18 inches, and 30 inches at the rate of 0.25 cubic feet per minute, how long will it take to fill the tank?

Solution: This problem is really a combination of a rate problem and a volume problem. First we must calculate the volume, and then we must substitute in a rate equation to get our final answer. The formula for the volume of a rectangular solid is $V = lwh$ where l, w, and h are the length, width, and height respectively. We must multiply the three dimensions of the tank to get the volume. However, if we look ahead to the second part of the problem, we see that we want the volume in cubic *feet*; therefore we convert 12 inches, 18 inches, and 30 inches to 1 foot, 1.5 feet, and 2.5 feet respectively. Multiplying gives us a volume of 3.75 cubic feet. Now substituting in the equation: rate $\times$ time = volume, we get $0.25 \times$ time $= 3.75$; time $= \frac{3.75}{0.25}$; thus, the time is 15 minutes.

302. *Comparison problems.* Here you are asked to identify the largest, or smallest, of a group of figures, or to place them in ascending or descending order of size. The following procedure is the most efficient one:

STEP 1. Always diagram each figure before you come to any conclusions. Whenever possible, try to include two or more of the figures in the same diagram, so that their relative sizes are most readily apparent.

STEP 2. If you have not already determined the correct answer, then (and only then) determine the size of the figures (as you would have done in Section 301), and compare the results. (Note that even if Step 2 is necessary, Step 1 should eliminate most of the possible choices, leaving only a few formula calculations to be done.)

Example: Which of the following is the greatest in length?

(A) The perimeter of a square with a side of 4 inches.

(B) The perimeter of an isosceles right triangle whose equal sides are 8 inches each.

(C) The circumference of a circle with a diameter of $4\sqrt{2}$ inches.

(D) The perimeter of a pentagon whose sides are all equal to 3 inches.

(E) The perimeter of a semicircle with a radius of 5 inches.

Solution: Diagramming the five figures mentioned, we obtain the following illustration:

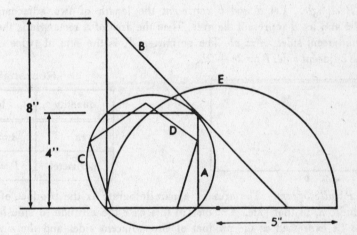

From the diagram, it is apparent that the square and the pentagon are both smaller than the circle. Further observation should show that the circle is smaller than the triangle. Thus we need only to see which is larger—the semicircle or the triangle. The perimeter of the semicircle is found by the formula: $P = 2r + \pi r$ (the sum of the diameter and the semicircular arc, where r, is the radius). Since r in this case is 5 inches the perimeter is approximately $10 + (3.14)5$, or 25.7 inches. The formula for the perimeter of a triangle is the sum of the sides. In this case, two of the sides are 8 inches and the third side can be found by using the relationship $c^2 = a^2 + b^2$, where a and b are the sides of a right triangle, and c is the hypotenuse. Since, in our problem $a = b = 8$ inches, $c = \sqrt{8^2 + 8^2} = \sqrt{128} = \sqrt{2(64)} = 8\sqrt{2}$, which is the third side of the triangle. The perimeter then is $8 + 8 + 8\sqrt{2}$, which is $16 + 8\sqrt{2}$. This is approximately equal to $16 + 8(1.4)$ or 27.2, so the triangle is the largest of the figures.

> ## FORMULAS USED IN AREA, PERIMETER, AND VOLUME PROBLEMS
>
> It is important that you know as many of these formulas as possible. Problems using these formulas appear frequently on tests of all kinds. You should not need to refer to this table when you do problems. Learn these formulas before you go any further.

303. *Square.* The area of a square is the square of one of its sides. Thus, if A represents the area, and s represents the length of a side, $A = s^2$. The area of a square is also one-half of the square of its diagonal, and may be written as $A = \frac{1}{2}d^2$, where d represents the length of a diagonal. The perimeter of a square is 4 times the length of one of its sides, or $4s$.

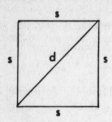

Square

quantity	formula
area	$A = s^2$ $A = \frac{1}{2}d^2$
perimeter	$P = 4s$

304. *Rectangle.* Let a and b represent the length of two adjacent sides of a rectangle, and let A represent the area. Then the area of a rectangle is the product of the two adjacent sides. $A = ab$. The perimeter, P, is the sum of twice one side and twice the adjacent side. $P = 2a + 2b$.

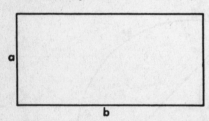

Rectangle

quantity	formula
area	$A = ab$
perimeter	$P = 2a + 2b$

305. *Parallelogram.* The area of a parallelogram is the product of a side and the altitude, h, to that side. $A = bh$ (in this case the altitude to side b). The area can also be expressed as the product of two adjacent sides and the sine of the included angle: $A = ab \sin c$, where c is the angle included between side a and side b. The perimeter is the sum of twice one side and twice the adjacent side. $P = 2a + 2b$. Let a and b represent the length of 2 adjacent sides of a parallelogram. Then, c is the included angle. But A represents its area, P its perimeter, and h the altitude to one of its sides.

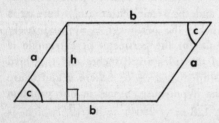

Parallelogram

quantity	formula
area	$A = bh$ $A = ab \sin C$
perimeter	$P = 2a + 2b$

306. *Triangle.* The area of any triangle is one-half of the product of any side and the altitude to that side. $A = \frac{1}{2}bh$, where b is a side, and h the altitude to that side. The area may be written also as one-half of the product of any two adjacent sides and the sine of the included angle. $A = \frac{1}{2}ab \sin C$, where A is the area, a and b are two adjacent sides, and C is the included angle. The perimeter of a triangle is the sum of the sides of the triangle. $P = a + b + c$, where P is the perimeter, and c is the third side.

Triangle

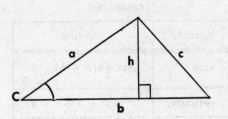

quantity	formula
area	$A = \frac{1}{2}bh$ $A = \frac{1}{2}ab \sin C$
perimeter	$P = a + b + c$

307. *Right triangle.* The area of a right triangle is one-half of the product of the two sides adjacent to the right angle. $A = \frac{1}{2}ab$, where A is the area, and a and b are the adjacent sides. The perimeter is the sum of the sides. $P = a + b + c$, where c is the third side, or hypotenuse.

Right Triangle

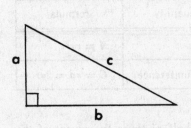

quantity	formula
area	$A = \frac{1}{2}ab$
perimeter	$P = a + b + c$
hypotenuse	$c^2 = a^2 + b^2$

308. *Equilateral triangle.* The area of an equilateral triangle is one-fourth the product of a side squared and $\sqrt{3}$. $A = \frac{1}{4}s^2\sqrt{3}$, where A is the area, and s is one of the equal sides. The perimeter of an equilateral triangle is 3 times one side. $P = 3s$, where P is the perimeter.

Equilateral Triangle

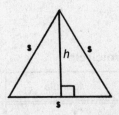

quantity	formula
area	$A = \frac{1}{4}s^2\sqrt{3}$
perimeter	$P = 3s$
altitude	$h = \frac{1}{2}s\sqrt{3}$

NOTE: The equilateral triangle and the right triangle are special cases of the triangle and any law which applies to the triangle applies to both the right triangle and to the equilateral triangle.

309. *Trapezoid.* The area of a trapezoid is one-half of the product of the altitude and the sum of the bases. $A = \frac{1}{2}h(B + b)$, where A is the area, B and b are the bases, and h is their altitude. The perimeter is the sum of the 4 sides. $P = B + b + c + d$, where P is the perimeter, and c and d are the other 2 sides.

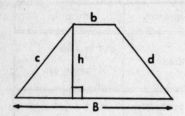

Trapezoid

quantity	formula
area	$A = \frac{1}{2}h(B + b)$
perimeter	$P = B + b + c + d$

310. *Circle.* The area of a circle is π (pi) times the square of the radius. $A = \pi r^2$, where A is the area, and r is the radius. The circumference is pi times the diameter or pi times twice the radius. $C = \pi d = 2\pi r$, where C is the circumference, d the diameter and r the radius.

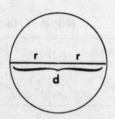

Circle

quantity	formula
area	$A = \pi r^2$
circumference	$C = \pi d = 2\pi r$

311. *Semicircle.* The area of a semicircle is one-half pi times the square of the radius. $A = \frac{1}{2}\pi r^2$, where A is the area and r is the radius. The length of the curved portion of the semicircle is one-half pi times the diameter or pi times the radius. $C = \frac{1}{2}\pi d = \pi r$, where C is the circumference, d is the diameter and r is the radius. The perimeter of a semicircle is equal to the circumference plus the length of the diameter. $P = C + d = \frac{1}{2}\pi d + d$, where P is the perimeter.

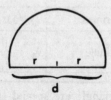

Semicircle

quantity	formula
area	$A = \frac{1}{2}\pi r^2$
length	$L = \frac{1}{2}\pi d = \pi r$
perimeter	$P = d(\frac{1}{2}\pi + 1)$

312. *Rectangular solid.* The volume of a rectangular solid is the product of the length, width, and height. $V = lwh$, where V is the volume, l is the length, w is the width, and h is the height. The volume is also the product of the area of one side and the altitude to that side. $V = Bh$, where B is the area of its base and h the altitude to that side. The surface area is the sum of the area of the six faces. $S = 2wh + 2hl + 2wl$, where S is the surface area.

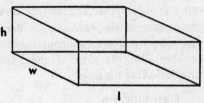

Rectangular Solid

quantity	formula
volume	$V = lwh$ $V = Bh$
surface area	$S = 2wh + 2hl + 2lw$

313. *Cube.* The volume of a cube is its edge cubed. $V = e^3$, where V is the volume and e is an edge. The surface area is the sum of the areas of the six faces. $S = 6e^2$, where S is the surface area.

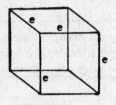

Cube

quantity	formula
volume	$V = e^3$
surface area	$S = 6e^2$

314. *Cylinder.* The volume of a cylinder is the area of the base times the height. $V = Bh$, where V is the volume, B is the area of the base and h is the height. Note that the area of the base is the area of the circle $= \pi r^2$, where r is the radius of a base. The surface area not including the bases is the circumference of the base times the height. $S_1 = Ch = 2\pi rh$, where S_1 is the surface area without the bases, C the circumference, and h the height. The area of the bases $= 2\pi r^2$. Thus, the area of the cylinder, including the bases, $S_2 = 2\pi rh + 2\pi r^2 = 2\pi r(h + r)$.

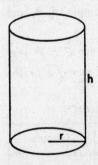

Cylinder

quantity	formula
volume	$V = Bh$ $V = \pi r^2 h$
surface area	$S_1 = 2\pi rh$ (without bases) $S_2 = 2\pi r\,(h + r)$ (with bases)

315. *Sphere.* The volume of a sphere is four-thirds π times the cube of the radius. $V = \frac{4}{3}\pi r^3$, where V is the volume, and r is the radius. The surface area is 4π times the square of the radius. $S = 4\pi r^2$, where S is the surface area.

Sphere

quantity	formula
volume	$V = \frac{4}{3}\pi r^3$
surface area	$S = 4\pi r^2$

316. *Hemisphere.* The volume of a hemisphere is two-thirds π times the cube of the radius. $V = \frac{2}{3}\pi r^3$ where V is the volume, and r is the radius. The surface area not including the area of the base is 2π times the square of the radius. $S_1 = 2\pi r^2$, where S_1 is the surface area without the base. The total surface area, including the base, is equal to the surface area without the base plus the area of the base. $S_2 = 2\pi r^2 + \pi r^2 = 3\pi r^2$, where S_2 is the surface area including the base.

Hemisphere

quantity	formula
volume	$V = \frac{2}{3}\pi r^3$
surface area	$S_1 = 2\pi r^2$ (without bases) $S_2 = 3\pi r^2$ (with bases)

317. *Pythagorean theorem.* The Pythagorean theorem states a very important geometrical relationship. It states that in a right triangle, if c is the hypotenuse (side opposite the right angle), and a and b are the sides adjacent to the right angle, then $c^2 = a^2 + b^2$.

Pythagorean Theorem

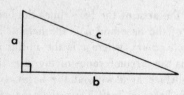

quantity	formula
square of hypotenuse	$c^2 = a^2 + b^2$
length of hypotenuse	$c = \sqrt{a^2 + b^2}$

Examples of right triangles are triangles with sides of 3, 4, and 5 or 5, 12, and 13. Any multiples of these numbers also form right triangles—for example, 6, 8, and 10 or 30, 40, 50.

Using the Pythagorean theorem to find the diagonal of a square we get $d^2 = s^2 + s^2$ or $d^2 = 2s^2$, where d is the diagonal and s is a side. Therefore, $d = s\sqrt{2}$ or the diagonal of a square is $\sqrt{2}$ times the side.

Square

quantity	formula
diagonal	$d = s\sqrt{2}$

318. Another important fact to remember in doing area problems is that areas of two similar (having the same shape) figures are in the same ratio as the squares of corresponding parts of the figures.

Example: Triangles P and Q are similar. Side p of triangle P is 2 inches, the area of triangle P is 3 square inches, and corresponding side q of triangle Q is 4 inches. What is the area of triangle Q.

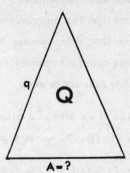

Solution: The square of side p is to the square of side q as the area of P is to the area of Q. If we call x the area of triangle Q, then we get the following relationship: The square of side p is to the square of side q as the area of P is to the area of Q, or

$$\frac{2^2}{4^2} = \frac{3}{x} \text{ or } \frac{4}{16} = \frac{3}{x}$$

Therefore: $x = 12$ square inches.

PRACTICE TEST 3

Area, Perimeter, and Volume Problems

Correct answers and solutions follow each test.

1. Which of the following figures has the largest area?

   (A) a square with a perimeter of 12 inches

   (B) a circle with a radius of 3 inches

   (C) a right triangle with sides of 3, 4, and 5 inches

   (D) a rectangle with a diagonal of 5 inches

   (E) a regular hexagon with a perimeter of 18 inches

2. If the area of the base of a rectangular solid is tripled, what is the percent increase in its volume?

   (A) 200%   (B) 300%   (C) 600%   (D) 800%   (E) 900%

3. How many yards of a carpeting, which is 26 inches wide, will be needed to cover a floor which is 12' by 13'?

   (A) 22 yards   (D) 36 yards

   (B) 24 yards   (E) 46 yards

   (C) 27 yards

4. If water flows into a rectangular tank at the rate of 6 cubic feet per minute, how long will it take to fill the tank, which measures 18″ × 32″ × 27″?

(A) less than one minute

(B) less than two minutes, but not less than one minute

(C) less than three minutes, but not less than two minutes

(D) less than four minutes, but not less than three minutes

(E) four minutes or more

4. A B C D E

5. The ratio of the area of a circle to the radius of the circle is

(A) π (B) 2π (C) π^2 (D) $4\pi^2$ (E) not determinable

5. A B C D E

6. Which of the following figures has the smallest perimeter or circumference?

(A) a circle with a diameter of 2 feet

(B) a square with a diagonal of 2 feet

(C) a rectangle with sides of 6″ and 4 feet

(D) a pentagon with each side equal to 16 inches

(E) a hexagon with each side equal to 14 inches

6. A B C D E

7. In the figure shown DE is parallel to BC. If the area of triangle ADE is half that of trapezoid $DECB$, what is the ratio of AE to AC?

(A) $1:2$ (B) $1:\sqrt{2}$ (C) $1:3$ (D) $1:\sqrt{3}$
(E) $1:\sqrt{3}-1$

7. A B C D E

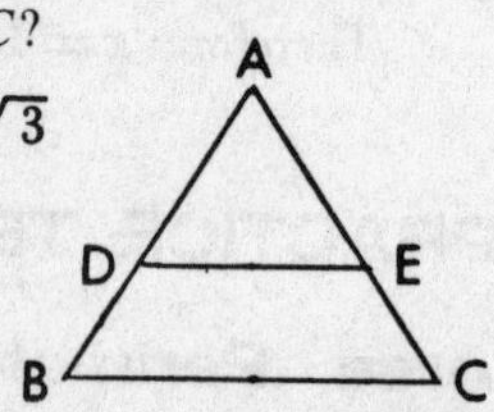

8. At a speed of 22 revolutions per minute, how long will it take a wheel of radius 10″, rolling on its edge, to travel 10 feet? (Assume π equals $\frac{22}{7}$, and express answer to nearest 0.1 second.)

(A) 0.2 seconds
(B) 0.4 seconds
(C) 5.2 seconds
(D) 6.3 seconds
(E) 7.4 seconds

8. A B C D E

9. If the diagonal of a square is 16″ long, what is the area of the square?

(A) 64 square inches
(B) $64\sqrt{2}$ square inches
(C) 128 square inches
(D) $128\sqrt{2}$ square inches
(E) 256 square inches

9. A B C D E

10. In the diagram shown, $ACDF$ is a rectangle, and $GBHE$ is a circle. If $CD = 4$ inches, and $AC = 6$ inches, what is the number of square inches in the shaded area?

10. A B C D E

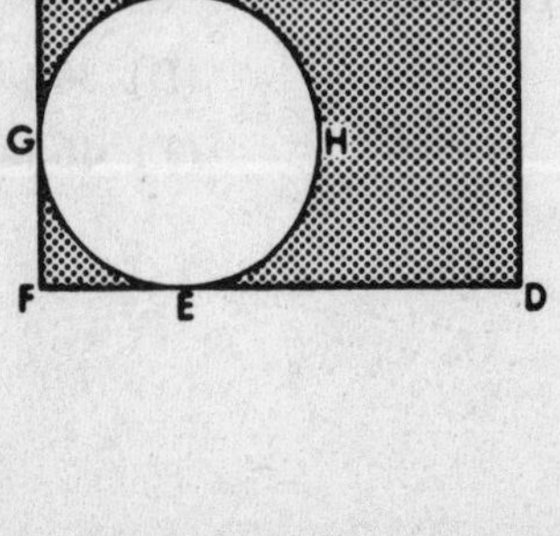

(A) $16 - 4\pi$ square inches

(D) $16 - 2\pi$ square inches

(B) $24 - 4\pi$ square inches

(E) $24 - 2\pi$ square inches

(C) $24 - 16\pi$ square inches

11. A B C D E

11. What is the area of an equilateral triangle with a side of 1 inch?

(A) 1 square inch

(D) $\dfrac{\sqrt{3}}{4}$ square inch

(B) $\dfrac{\sqrt{3}}{2}$ square inch

(E) $\frac{1}{3}$ square inch

(C) $\frac{1}{2}$ square inch

12. A B C D E

12. The measurements of a rectangle are 12 feet by 16 feet. What is the area of the smallest *circle* that can cover this rectangle entirely (so that no part of the rectangle is outside the circle)?

(A) 192 square feet

(B) 384 square feet

(C) 100π square feet

(D) 128π square feet

(E) 400π square feet

13. A B C D E

13. A man wishes to cover his floor with tiles, each one measuring $\frac{3}{4}$ inch by 2 inches. If his room is a rectangle, measuring 12 feet by 18 feet, how many such tiles will he need?

(A) 144   (B) 1152   (C) 1728   (D) 9216   (E) 20,736

14. A B C D E

14. The volume of a sphere is equal to the volume of a cylinder. If the radius of the sphere is 4 miles and the radius of the cylinder is 8 miles, what is the height of the cylinder?

(A) 8 miles

(D) $\frac{16}{3}$ miles

(B) $\frac{4}{3}$ miles

(E) 1 mile

(C) 4 miles

15. A B C D E

15. A wheel travels 33 yards in 15 revolutions. What is its diameter? (Assume $\pi = \frac{22}{7}$.)

(A) 0.35 feet

(D) 1.40 feet

(B) 0.70 feet

(E) 2.10 feet

(C) 1.05 feet

16. A B C D E

16. If a rectangle with a perimeter of 48 inches is equal in area to a right triangle with legs of 12 inches and 24 inches, what is the rectangle's diagonal?

(A) 12 inches

(B) $12\sqrt{2}$ inches

(C) $12\sqrt{3}$ inches

(D) 24 inches

(E) cannot be determined from the given information

17. What is the approximate area that remains after a circle $3\frac{1}{2}''$ in diameter is cut from a square piece of cloth with a side of $8''$? (Use $\pi = \frac{22}{7}$.)

    (A) 25.5 square inches   (D) 142.1 square inches

    (B) 54.4 square inches   (E) 284.2 square inches

    (C) 56.8 square inches

17. A B C D E

18. A container is shaped like a rectangular solid with sides of 3 inches, 3 inches, and 11 inches. What is its approximate capacity, if 1 gallon equals 231 cubic inches?

    (A) 14 ounces   (D) 110 ounces

    (B) 27 ounces   (E) 219 ounces

    (C) 55 ounces

18. A B C D E

19. The 20-inch-diameter wheels of one car travel at a rate of 24 revolutions per minute, while the 30-inch-diameter wheels of another car travel at a rate of 18 revolutions per minute. What is the ratio of the speed of the second car to that of the first?

    (A) $1:1$ (B) $3:2$ (C) $4:3$ (D) $6:5$ (E) $9:8$

19. A B C D E

20. A circular garden twenty feet in diameter is surrounded by a path three feet wide. What is the area of the path?

    (A) 9π square feet   (D) 69π square feet

    (B) 51π square feet   (E) 90π square feet

    (C) 60π square feet

20. A B C D E

21. What is the area of a semicircle with a diameter of 16 inches?

    (A) 32π square inches   (D) 256π square inches

    (B) 64π square inches   (E) 512π square inches

    (C) 128π square inches

21. A B C D E

22. If the edges of a cube add up to 4 feet in length, what is the volume of the cube?

    (A) 64 cubic inches   (D) 512 cubic inches

    (B) 125 cubic inches   (E) none of these

    (C) 216 cubic inches

22. A B C D E

23. The inside of a trough is shaped like a rectangular solid, 25 feet long, 6 inches wide, and filled with water to a depth of 35 inches. If we wish to raise the depth of the water to 38 inches, how much water must be let into the tank?

    (A) $\frac{25}{96}$ cubic foot   (D) 225 cubic feet

    (B) $\frac{25}{8}$ cubic feet   (E) 450 cubic feet

    (C) $\frac{75}{2}$ cubic feet

23. A B C D E

24. If one gallon of water equals 231 cubic inches, approximately how much water will fill a cylindrical vase 7 inches in diameter, and 10 inches high? (Assume $\pi = \frac{22}{7}$.)

    (A) 1.7 gallons   (D) 5.3 gallons

    (B) 2.1 gallons   (E) 6.7 gallons

    (C) 3.3 gallons

24. A B C D E

25. A B C D E

25. Tiles of linoleum, measuring 8 inches × 8 inches, cost 9¢ apiece. At this rate, what will it cost a man to cover a floor with these tiles, if his floor measures 10 feet by 16 feet?

    (A) $22.50   (B) $25.00   (C) $28.00   (D) $32.40   (E) $36.00

26. A B C D E

26. Which of the following figures has the largest area?

    (A) a 3 : 4 : 5 triangle with a hypotenuse of 25 inches

    (B) a circle with a diameter of 20 inches

    (C) a square with a 20-inch diagonal

    (D) a regular hexagon with a side equal to 10 inches

    (E) a rectangle with sides of 10 inches and 30 inches

27. A B C D E

27. If the radius of the base of a cylinder is tripled, and its height is divided by three, what is the ratio of the volume of the new cylinder to the volume of the original cylinder?

    (A) 1 : 9   (B) 1 : 3   (C) 1 : 1   (D) 3 : 1   (E) 9 : 1

28. A B C D E

28. If one cubic foot of water equals 7.5 gallons, how long will it take for a faucet which flows at a rate of 10 gal/min to fill a cube 2 feet on each side (to the nearest minute)?

    (A) 4 minutes   (D) 7 minutes

    (B) 5 minutes   (E) 8 minutes

    (C) 6 minutes

29. A B C D E

29. The ratio of the area of a square to the *square of its diagonal* is which of the following?

    (A) 2 : 1   (B) $\sqrt{2}$: 1   (C) 1 : 1   (D) 1 : $\sqrt{2}$ (E) 1 : 2

30. A B C D E

30. If *ABCD* is a square, with side *AB* = 4 inches, and *AEB* and *CED* are semicircles, what is the area of the shaded portion in the diagram below?

    (A) 8 — π square inches

    (B) 8 — 2π square inches

    (C) 16 — 2π square inches

    (D) 16 — 4π square inches

    (E) 16 — 8π square inches

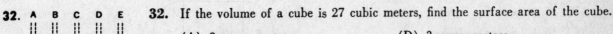

31. A B C D E

31. If the area of a circle is equal to the area of a rectangle, one of whose sides is equal to π, express the other side of the rectangle, *x*, in terms of the radius of the circle, *r*.

    (A) $x = r$ (B) $x = \pi r$ (C) $x = r^2$ (D) $x = \sqrt{r}$ (E) $x = \dfrac{1}{r}$

32. A B C D E

32. If the volume of a cube is 27 cubic meters, find the surface area of the cube.

    (A) 9 square meters   (D) 3 square meters

    (B) 18 square meters   (E) 1 square meter

    (C) 54 square meters

33. What is the area of a regular hexagon one of whose sides is 1 inch?

(A) $\dfrac{3\sqrt{3}}{4}$　　(B) $\sqrt{3}$　(C) $\dfrac{3\sqrt{3}}{2}$　　(D) 3　　(E) 6

34. What is the area of the triangle pictured below?

(A) 18 square units

(B) 32 square units

(C) 24 square units

(D) 12 square units

(E) 124 square units

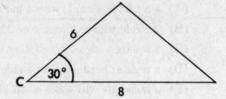

35. If a wheel travels 1 mile in 1 minute, at a rate of 600 revolutions per minute, what is the diameter of the wheel, in feet? (Use $\pi = \frac{22}{7}$.)

(A) 2.2 feet　　(B) 2.4 feet　　(C) 2.6 feet　　(D) 2.8 feet

(E) 3.0 feet

36. Which of the following figures has the largest perimeter?

(A) a square with a diagonal of 5 feet

(B) a rectangle with sides of 3 feet and 4 feet

(C) an equilateral triangle with a side equal to 48 inches

(D) a regular hexagon whose longest diagonal is 6 feet

(E) a parallelogram with sides of 6 inches and 7 feet

37. A man has two containers: the first is a rectangular solid, measuring 3 inches $\times$ 4 inches $\times$ 10 inches; the second is a cylinder having a base with a radius of 2 inches, and a height of 10 inches. If the first container is filled with water, and then this water is poured into the second container, which of the following occurs:

(A) There is room for more water in the second container.

(B) The second container is completely filled, without overflowing.

(C) The second container overflows by less than 1 cubic inch.

(D) The second container overflows by less than 2 (but not less than 1) cubic inches.

(E) The second container overflows by 2 or more cubic inches.

38. If, in this diagram, A represents a square with a side of 4″, and B, C, D, and E are semicircles, what is the area of the entire figure?

(A) $16 + 4\pi$ square inches

(B) $16 + 8\pi$ square inches

(C) $16 + 16\pi$ square inches

(D) $16 + 32\pi$ square inches

(E) $16 + 64\pi$ square inches

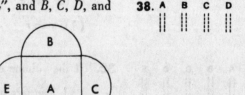

39. A B C D E

39. The area of a square is $81p^2$. What is the length of the square's diagonal?

(A) $9p$ (B) $9p\sqrt{2}$ (C) $18p$ (D) $9p^2$ (E) $18p^2$

40. A B C D E

40. The following diagram represents the floor of a room which is to be covered with carpeting at a price of $2.50 a square yard. What will be the cost of the carpeting?

(A) $70

(B) $125

(C) $480

(D) $630

(E) none of these

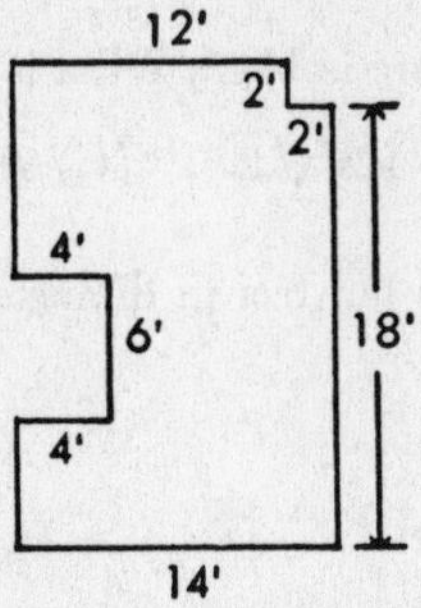

12'
2'
2'
4'
6'   18'
4'
14'

41. A B C D E

41. Which of the following has the largest perimeter?

(A) a square with a diagonal of 10 inches

(B) a 3-4-5 right triangle with a hypotenuse of 15 inches

(C) a pentagon, each of whose sides is 5 inches

(D) a right isosceles triangle with an area of 72 square inches

(E) a regular hexagon with a radius of 5 inches

42. A B C D E

42. If you double the area of the base of a rectangular solid, and also triple the solid's height, what is the ratio of the new volume to the old volume?

(A) 2 : 3   (D) 6 : 1

(B) 3 : 2   (E) none of these

(C) 1 : 6

43. A B C D E

43. A certain type of linoleum costs $1.50 per square yard. If a room measures 27 feet by 14 feet, what will be the cost of covering it with linoleum?

(A) $44.10   (B) $51.60   (C) $63.00   (D) $132.30   (E) $189.00

44. A B C D E

44. How many circles, each with a 4-inch radius, can be cut from a rectangular sheet of paper, measuring 16 inches $\times$ 24 inches?

(A) 6   (B) 7   (C) 8   (D) 12   (E) 24

45. A B C D E

45. The ratio of the area of an equilateral triangle, in square inches, to its perimeter, in inches, is

(A) 3 : 4

(B) 4 : 3

(C) $\sqrt{3}$: 4

(D) 4 : $\sqrt{3}$

(E) cannot be determined from the given information

46. What is the volume of a cylinder whose radius is 4 inches, and whose height is 10 inches? (Assume that $\pi = 3.14$.)

46. A B C D E

(A) 125.6 cubic inches

(D) 201.2 cubic inches

(B) 134.4 cubic inches

(E) 502.4 cubic inches

(C) 144.0 cubic inches

47. The area of a square is $144s^2$. What is the square's diagonal?

47. A B C D E

(A) $12s$ (B) $12s\sqrt{2}$ (C) $24s$ (D) $144s$ (E) $144s^2$

48. A circular pool is ten feet in diameter, and five feet deep. What is its volume, in cubic feet?

48. A B C D E

(A) 50 cubic feet

(D) 250π cubic feet

(B) 50π cubic feet

(E) 500π cubic feet

(C) 125π cubic feet

49. A certain type of carpeting is 30 inches wide. How many yards of this carpet will be needed to cover a floor that measures 20 feet by 24 feet?

49. A B C D E

(A) 48

(D) 192

(B) 64

(E) none of these

(C) 144

50. Two wheels have diameters of 12 inches and 18 inches, respectively. Both wheels roll along parallel straight lines at the same linear speed until the large wheel has revolved 72 times. At this point, how many times has the small wheel revolved?

50. A B C D E

(A) 32   (B) 48   (C) 72   (D) 108   (E) 162

ANSWER KEY FOR PRACTICE TEST 3

1. B	14. B	26. B	39. B
2. A	15. E	27. D	40. A
3. B	16. B	28. C	41. D
4. B	17. B	29. E	42. D
5. E	18. C	30. B	43. C
6. B	19. E	31. C	44. A
7. D	20. D	32. C	45. E
8. C	21. A	33. C	46. E
9. C	22. A	34. D	47. B
10. B	23. B	35. D	48. C
11. D	24. A	36. D	49. B
12. C	25. D	37. A	50. D
13. E		38. B	

ANSWERS AND SOLUTIONS
FOR PRACTICE TEST 3

1. **(B)** This is a fairly difficult comparison problem, but the use of diagrams simplifies it considerably.

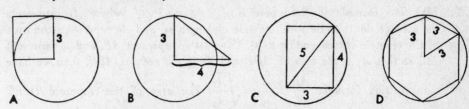

From diagram A it is apparent that the circle is larger than the square. Diagram B shows that the circle is larger than the right triangle. And, since a rectangle with a diagonal of 5 inches is made up of two right triangles, as shown in diagram C, the circle is larger than the rectangle. Finally, as shown in diagram D, the circle is larger than the hexagon. Thus, the circle is the largest of the five figures described. (302)

2. **(A)** This is a formula problem: letting V_o represent the original volume, B_o represent the original area of the base, and h_o represent the original height of the figure, we have the formula $V_o = h_o B_o$. The new volume, V, is equal to $3h_o B_o$. Thus, the new volume is three times the original volume—an *increase* of 200%. (301)

3. **(B)** Here, we must find the length of carpeting needed to cover an area of $12' \times 13'$, or 156 square feet. The formula needed is: $A = lw$, where $l =$ length, and $w =$ width, both expressed in *feet*. Now, since we know that $A = 156$ square feet, and $w = 26$ inches, or $\frac{26}{12}$ feet, we can calculate l as $156 \div \left(\frac{26}{12}\right)$, or 72 feet. But since the answer must be expressed in yards, we express 72 feet as 24 yards. (304)

4. **(B)** First we must calculate the volume of the tank in cubic feet. Converting the dimensions of the box to feet, we get $1\frac{1}{2}$ feet $\times 2\frac{2}{3}$ feet $\times 2\frac{1}{4}$ feet, so the total volume is $\frac{3}{2} \times \frac{8}{3} \times \frac{9}{4}$, or 9, cubic feet. Thus, at a rate of 6 cubic feet per minute, it would take $\frac{9}{6}$, or $1\frac{1}{2}$ minutes to fill the tank. (312, 201)

5. **(E)** Here, we use the formula $A = \pi r^2$, where $A =$ area, and $r =$ radius. Thus, the ratio of A to r is just $\dfrac{A}{r} = \pi r$. Since r is not a constant, the ratio cannot be determined. (310)

6. **(B)** First, we diagram the circle and the square and see that the square has a smaller perimeter. Next, we notice that the circle, which has a larger circumference than the square, has circumference 2π, or about 6.3 feet. But the perimeters of the rectangle (9 feet), of the pentagon (5×16 inches $=$ 80 inches $=$ 6 feet, 8 inches), and of the hexagon (6×14 inches $=$ 84 inches $=$ 7 feet), are all greater than the circumference of the circle, and therefore also greater than the perimeter of the square. Thus, the square has the smallest perimeter. (302)

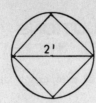

7. (D) The formula involved here is $A_1 : A_2 = s_1{}^2 : s_2{}^2$, where A_1 represents the area of the triangle with one side of length s_1, and A_2 represents the area of the triangle corresponding to s_2. If we let s_1 represent AE, and s_2 represent AC, so that A_1 is the area of ADE and A_2 is the area of ABC, then we have the resulting formula $\dfrac{AE}{AC} = \dfrac{s_1}{s_2} = \sqrt{\dfrac{A_1}{A_2}}$. The area of the trapezoid $DEBC$ is twice the area of ADE, or $2A_1$, so the area of ABC is equal to the sum of the areas of ADE and $DECB$, which equal A_1 and $2A_1$ respectively; thus, the area of ABC is $3A_1$. So, $A_1 : A_2 = 1 : 3$. Thus, $s_1 : s_2 = \sqrt{\tfrac{1}{3}} = 1 : \sqrt{3}$. (318)

8. (C) Since the radius of the circle is 10 inches, its circumference is $2\pi(10$ inches), or $2\left(\tfrac{22}{7}\right)$ (10 inches), which equals $\tfrac{440}{7}$ inches. This is the distance the wheel will travel in one revolution. To travel 10 feet, or 120 inches, it must travel $120 \div \tfrac{440}{7}$, or $\tfrac{21}{11}$ revolutions. At a speed of 22 revolutions per minute, or $\tfrac{11}{30}$ revolution per second, it will take $\tfrac{21}{11} \div \tfrac{11}{30}$ or $\tfrac{630}{121}$ seconds. Carrying the division to the nearest tenth of a second, we get 5.2 seconds. (310)

9. (C) If we let d represent the diagonal of a square, s represent the length of one side, and A represent its area, then we have two formulas: $d = s\sqrt{2}$, and $A = s^2$, relating the three quantities. However, from the first equation, we can see that $s^2 = \dfrac{d^2}{2}$, so we can derive a third formula, $A = \dfrac{d^2}{2}$, relating A and d. We are given that d equals $16''$, so we can calculate the value of A as $\dfrac{(16 \text{ inches})^2}{2}$, or 128 square inches. (303)

10. (B) The area of the shaded figure is equal to the difference between the areas of the rectangle and the circle. The area of the rectangle is defined by the formula $A = bh$, where b and h are the two adjacent sides of the rectangle. In this case, A is equal to 4 inches $\times$ 6 inches, or 24 square inches. The area of the circle is defined by the formula $A = \pi r^2$, where r is the radius. Since BE equals the diameter of the circle and is equal to 4 inches, then the radius must be 2 inches. Thus, the area of the circle is $\pi(2 \text{ inches})^2$, or 4π square inches. Subtracting, we obtain the area of the shaded portion: $24 - 4\pi$ square inches. (304, 310)

11. (D) We use the formula for the area of an equilateral triangle, $\dfrac{\sqrt{3}\,s^2}{4}$, where s is a side. If $s = 1$, then the area of the triangle is $\dfrac{\sqrt{3}}{4}$. (308)

12. (C) An angle, which is inscribed in a circle, whose sides cut off an arc of 180° (that is, intersects the ends of a diameter) is a right angle. According to the Pythagorean theorem, the diameter AC, being the hypotenuse of a triangle with sides of 12 feet and 16 feet, has a length of $\sqrt{12^2 + 16^2} = \sqrt{400} = 20$ feet. Therefore, if we call d the diameter, the area of the circle is

$$A = \pi\left(\frac{d}{2}\right)^2 = \pi\left(\frac{20}{2}\right)^2 = 100\pi \text{ square feet.}$$

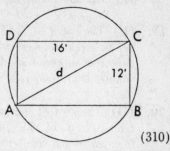

(310)

13. **(E)** The area of the room $= 12$ feet $\times$ 18 feet $= 216$ square feet. The area of one tile $= \frac{3}{4}$ inches $\times$ 2 inches $= \frac{3}{2}$ square inches. The number of tiles $=$ area of the room $\div$ area of one tile $= \dfrac{216 \text{ square feet}}{\frac{3}{2} \text{ square inch}} =$

$$\frac{216 \times 144 \text{ square inches}}{\frac{3}{2} \text{ square inch}} = 216 \times \overset{48}{\cancel{144}} \times \frac{2}{3} = 20{,}736 \text{ tiles.}$$ (304)

14. **(B)** The volume of a sphere is found by using the formula $\frac{4}{3}\pi r^3$ where r is the radius. In this case, the radius is 4 miles, so the volume is $\frac{256}{3}\pi$ cubic miles. This is equal to the volume of a cylinder of radius 8 miles so $\frac{256}{3}\pi = \pi 8^2 h$, since the volume of a cylinder is $\pi r^2 h$, where h is the height, and r is the radius of the base. Solving $\dfrac{256\pi}{3} = \pi 8^2 h$; $\dfrac{256\pi}{3}{}_{\pi 64} = \dfrac{\overset{16}{\cancel{256}}}{3} \times \dfrac{1}{\underset{4}{\cancel{\pi 64}}} = \dfrac{16}{12} = \dfrac{4}{3}$ miles.

(314; 315)

15. **(E)** 33 yards$= 99$ feet $= 15$ revolutions. Thus, 1 revolution $= \frac{99}{15}$ feet $= \frac{33}{5}$ feet $= 6.6$ feet. Since 1 revolution $=$ the circumference of the wheel, the wheel's diameter $=$ circumference $\div \pi$. 6.6 feet $\div \frac{22}{7} = 2.10$ feet. (310)

16. **(B)** The area of the right triangle is equal to $\frac{1}{2}ab$ where a and b are the legs of the triangle. In this case, the area is $\frac{1}{2} \times 12 \times 24$, or 144 square inches. If we call the sides of the rectangle x and y we get $2x + 2y = 48$, or $y = 24 - x$. The area of the rectangle is xy, or $x(24 - x)$. This must be equal to 144, so we get the equation $24x - x^2 = 144$. Rearranging the terms gives us $x^2 - 24x + 144 = 0$, or $(x - 12)^2$. Since $y = 24 - x$, $y = 24 - 12$, or $y = 12$. This is satisfied only by $x = 12$. By the Pythagorean theorem we get: diagonal $= \sqrt{12^2 + 12^2} = \sqrt{144 + 144} = \sqrt{2(144)} = 12\sqrt{2}$.

(304, 306, 317)

17. **(B)** The area of the square is 64 square inches, since $A = s^2$ where s is the length of a side, and A is the area. The area of the circle is $\pi\left(\frac{7}{4}\right)^2 = \frac{22}{7} \times \frac{49}{16} = \frac{77}{8} = 9.625$. Subtracting, $64 - 9.625 = 54.375 = 54.4$ (approximately).

(304, 310)

18. **(C)** The capacity of the volume ($V = lwh$, where l, w, h, are the adjacent sides of the solid) of the container $= (3 \text{ inches})(3 \text{ inches})(11 \text{ inches}) = 99$ cubic inches; since 1 gallon equals 231 cubic inches, 99 cubic inches equal $\frac{99}{231}$ gallons, (the fraction reduces to $\frac{3}{7}$). One gallon equals 128 ounces (1 gallon $=$

4 quarts, 1 quart = 2 pints, 1 pint = 16 ounces), so the container holds $\frac{384}{7}$ ounces = 55 ounces (approximately). (312)

19. **(E)** The speed of the first wheel is equal to its rate of revolution multiplied by its circumference, which equals 24×20 inches $\times \pi = 480\pi$ inches per minute. The speed of the second is 18×30 inches $\times \pi = 540\pi$ inches per minute. Thus, their ratio is $540\pi : 480\pi = 9 : 8$. (310)

20. **(D)** The area of the path is equal to the area of the ring between two concentric circles of radii 10 feet and 13 feet. This area is obtained by subtracting the area of the smaller circle from the area of the larger circle. The area of the larger circle is equal to $\pi \times$ its radius squared $= \pi(13)^2$ feet$^2 = 169\pi$ square feet. By the same process, the area of the smaller circle $= 100\pi$ square feet. The area of the shaded part $= 169\pi - 100\pi = 69\pi$ square feet. (310)

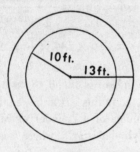

21. **(A)** The diameter = 16 inches, so the radius = 8 inches. Thus, the area of the whole circle $= \pi(8$ inches$)^2 = 64\pi$ square inches. The area of the semicircle is one-half of the area of the whole circle, or 32π square inches. (311)

22. **(A)** A cube has twelve equal edges, so the length of one side of the cube is $\frac{1}{12}$ of 4 feet, or 4 inches. Thus, its volume is 4 inches $\times$ 4 inches $\times$ 4 inches $=$ 64 cubic inches. (313)

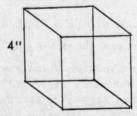

23. **(B)** The additional water will take the shape of a rectangular solid measuring 25 feet $\times$ 6 inches $\times$ 3 inches (3″ = the added depth) $= 25 \times \frac{1}{2} \times \frac{1}{4}$ cubic feet $= \frac{25}{8}$ cubic feet. (312)

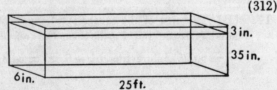

24. **(A)** The volume of the cylinder $= \pi r^2 h = \left(\frac{22}{7}\right)\left(\frac{7}{2}\right)^2 (10)$ cubic inches $=$ 385 cubic inches. 231 cubic inches = 1 gallon, so 385 cubic inches $= \frac{385}{231}$ gallons $= \frac{5}{3}$ gallons = 1.7 gallons (approximately). (314)

25. **(D)** The area of floor = 10 feet × 16 feet = 160 square feet. Area of one tile = 8 inches × 8 inches = 64 square inches = $\frac{64}{144}$ square feet = $\frac{4}{9}$ square feet. Thus, the number of tiles = area of floor ÷ area of tile = 160 ÷ $\frac{4}{9}$ = 360. At 9¢ apiece, the tiles will cost $32.40. (304)

26. **(B)** Looking at the following three diagrams, we can observe that the triangle, square, and hexagon are all smaller than the circle.

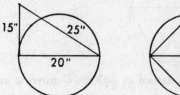

Comparing the areas of the circle and the rectangle, we notice that the area of the circle is $\pi(10 \text{ inches})^2 = 100\pi$ square inches, which is greater than (10 inches) (30 inches) = 300 square inches, the area of the rectangle. (π is approximately 3.14.) (302)

27. **(D)** In a cylinder, $V = \pi r^2 h$, where r is the radius of the base, and h is the height. The new volume, $V' = \pi(3r)^2 \left(\frac{h}{3}\right) = 3\pi r^2 h = 3V$. Thus, the ratio of the new volume to the old volume is 3 : 1. (314)

28. **(C)** A cube 2 feet on each side has a volume of $2 \times 2 \times 2 = 8$ cubic feet. Since 1 cubic foot equals 7.5 gallons, 8 cubic feet equals 60 gallons. If the faucet flows at the rate of 10 gallons/minute it will take 6 minutes to fill the cube. (313)

29. **(E)** Let s = the side of the square. Then, the area of the square is equal to s^2. The diagonal of the square is $s\sqrt{2}$, so the square of the diagonal is $2s^2$. Thus, the ratio of the area of the square to the square of the diagonal is $s^2 : 2s^2$, or 1 : 2. (303)

30. **(B)** The area of the square $ABCD$ is equal to 4 inches × 4 inches = 16 square inches. The two semicircles can be placed together diameter-to-diameter to form a circle with a radius of 2 inches, and thus, an area of 4π. Subtracting the area of the circle from the area of the square, we obtain the combined areas of AED and BEC. But, since the figure is symmetrical, AED and BEC must be equal, so the area of AED is one-half of this remainder, which equals $16 - 4\pi$, or $8 - 2\pi$ square inches. (303, 310)

31. **(C)** The area of the circle is equal to πr^2, and the area of the rectangle is equal to πx. Since these areas are equal, $\pi r^2 = \pi x$, and $x = r^2$. (304, 310)

32. **(C)** The volume of a cube is e^3 where e is the length of an edge. If the volume is 27 cubic meters, then $e^3 = 27$ and $e = 3$ meters. The surface area of a cube is $6e^2$ and if $e = 3$ meters, then the surface area is 54 square meters. (313)

33. **(C)** The area of a regular hexagon, one of whose sides is 1 inch, is equal to the sum of the areas of 6 equilateral triangles, each with a side of 1 inch. The area of an equilateral triangle with a side of 1 inch is equal to $\dfrac{\sqrt{3}}{4}$ square inches. (The formula for the area of an equilateral triangle with a side of s is $A = s^2 \dfrac{\sqrt{3}}{4}$.) The sum of 6 such triangles is $\dfrac{6\sqrt{3}}{4}$, or $\dfrac{3\sqrt{3}}{2}$. \hfill (308)

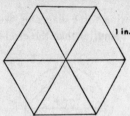

1 in.

34. (D) The area of a triangle can be expressed as $\frac{1}{2}ab \sin C$ where a and b are any two sides and C is the angle between them. In this case $a = 6$, $b = 8$, and $\angle C = 30°$. You should remember that the sine of 30° is $\frac{1}{2}$ so the area is $\frac{1}{2}(6)(8)\left(\frac{1}{2}\right) = 12$. \hfill (307)

35. (D) Since the wheel takes 1 minute to make 600 revolutions and travels 1 mile in that time, we have the relation 1 mile = 5280 feet = 600 revolutions. Thus, 1 revolution = $\frac{5280}{600}$ feet = 8.8 feet = circumference = π(diameter) = $\left(\frac{22}{7}\right)$(diameter). Therefore, the diameter = 8.8 feet ÷ $\left(\frac{22}{7}\right)$ = 2.8 feet. \hfill (310)

36. (D) In this case, it is easiest to calculate the perimeters of the 5 figures. According to the Pythagorean theorem, a square with a diagonal of 5 feet has a side of $\dfrac{5}{\sqrt{2}}$ which is equal to $\dfrac{5\sqrt{2}}{2}$. (This is found by multiplying the numerator and denominator of $\dfrac{5}{\sqrt{2}}$ by $\sqrt{2}$.) If each side of the square is $\dfrac{5\sqrt{2}}{2}$, then the perimeter is $4 \times \dfrac{5\sqrt{2}}{2} = 10\sqrt{2}$ feet. A rectangle with sides of 3 feet and 4 feet has a perimeter of $2(3) + 2(4)$, or 14 feet. An equilateral triangle with a side of 48 inches, or 4 feet, has a perimeter of 12 feet. A regular hexagon whose longest diagonal is 6 feet has a side of 3 feet and, therefore, a perimeter of 18 feet. (See the diagram for Solution 33.) Finally, a parallelogram with sides of 6 inches, or $\frac{1}{2}$ foot, and 7 feet has a perimeter of 15 feet. Therefore, the hexagon has the largest perimeter. \hfill (302, 317)

37. (A) The volume of the first container is equal to 3 inches × 4 inches × 10 inches, or 120 cubic inches. The volume of the second container, the cylinder, is equal to $\pi r^2 h = \pi(2 \text{ inches})^2(10 \text{ inches})$, or 40π cubic inches, which is greater than 120 cubic inches (π is greater than 3). So the second container can hold more than the first. If the first container is filled and the contents poured into the second, there will be room for more water in the second. \hfill (312, 314)

38. (B) The area of the square is 16 square inches. The four semicircles can be added to form two circles, each of radius 2 inches, so the area of each circle is 4π square inches, and the two circles add up to 8π square inches. Thus, the total area is $16 + 8\pi$ square inches. \hfill (303, 311)

39. (B) Since the area of the square is $81p^2$, one side of the square will equal $9p$. According to the Pythagorean theorem, the diagonal will equal $\sqrt{81p^2 + 81p^2}$ $= 9p\sqrt{2}$. (303, 317)

40. (A) We can regard the area as a rectangle, 20 ft $\times$ 14 ft, with two rectangles, measuring 4 ft $\times$ 6 ft and 2 ft $\times$ 2 ft, cut out. Thus, the area is equal to 280 sq ft $-$ 24 sq ft $-$ 4 sq ft $=$ 252 sq ft $= \frac{252}{9}$ sq yd $=$ 28 sq yds. (Remember, 1 square yard equals 9 square feet.) At \$2.50 a square yard, 28 square yards will cost \$70. (304)

41. (D) The perimeter of the square is equal to four times its side; since a side is $\dfrac{1}{\sqrt{2}}$, or $\dfrac{\sqrt{2}}{2}$ times the diagonal, the perimeter of the square in question is $4 \times 5\sqrt{2} = 20\sqrt{2}$, which is approximately equal to 28.28 inches. The perimeter of a right triangle with sides that are in a 3–4–5 ratio, i.e., 9 inches, 12 inches, and 15 inches is $9 + 12 + 15 = 36$ inches. The perimeter of the pentagon is 5×5 inches, or 25 inches. The perimeter of the right isosceles triangle (with sides of 12 inches, 12 inches, and $12\sqrt{2}$ inches is $24 + 12\sqrt{2}$ inches, which is approximately equal to 40.968 inches. The perimeter of the hexagon is 6×5 inches, or 30 inches. Thus, the isosceles right triangle has the largest perimeter of those figures mentioned. You should become familiar with the approximate value of $\sqrt{2}$, which is 1.414. (302)

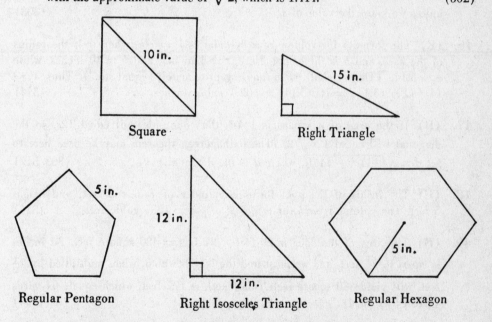

Square   Right Triangle

Regular Pentagon   Right Isosceles Triangle   Regular Hexagon

42. (D) For rectangular solids, the following formula holds:

$V = Ah$, where A is the area of the base, and h is the height.

If we replace A by $2A$, and h by $3h$, we get $V' = (2A)(3h) = 6V$. Thus, $V' : V = 6 : 1$. (312)

43. (C) The area of the room is 27 feet $\times$ 14 feet $=$ 378 square feet. 9 square feet $=$ 1 square yard, so the area of the room is 42 square yards. At \$1.50 per square yard the linoleum to cover the floor will cost \$63.00. (304)

44. (A) A circle with a 4-inch radius has an 8-inch diameter, so there can only be 2 rows of 3 circles each, or 6 circles. (310)

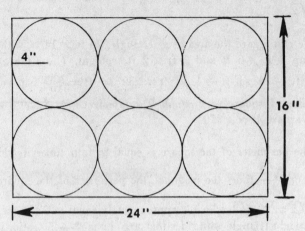

45. (E) Let one side of the triangle be s. Then the area of the triangle is $\dfrac{s^2 \sqrt{3}}{4}$.

(Either memorize this formula or remember that it is derived by drawing an altitude to divide the triangle into two congruent $30° : 60° : 90°$ right triangles.) The perimeter of the equilateral triangle is $3s$, so the ratio of the area to the perimeter is $\dfrac{s^2 \sqrt{3}}{4} : 3s$, or $s : 4\sqrt{3}$, which cannot be determined unless we know the value of s. (308)

46. (E) The formula for volume of a cylinder is $V = r^2 h$, where r is the radius of the base, and h is the height. Here, $r = 4$ inches, and $h = 10$ inches, while $\pi \approx 3.14$. (The symbol $\approx$ means "approximately equal to.") Thus $V \approx (4)^2 (10) (3.14) = 160(3.14) = 502.4$ cubic inches. (314)

47. (B) If the area of a square is $144s^2$, then one side will equal $12s$, so the diagonal will equal $12s \sqrt{2}$. (The Pythagorean theorem may be used here to get $d = \sqrt{144s^2 + 144s^2}$, where d is the diagonal.) (303, 317)

48. (C) The inside of the pool forms a cylinder of radius 5 feet, and height 5 feet. The volume is $\pi r^2 h$, or $\pi \times 5 \times 5 \times 5 = 125\pi$ cubic feet. (314)

49. (B) The area of the floor is 20 feet $\times$ 24 feet $= 480$ square feet. 30 inches is equal to $2\frac{1}{2}$ feet, and we must find the length which, when multiplied by $2\frac{1}{2}$ feet, will yield 480 square feet. This length is 192 feet, which equals 64 yards (3 feet $=$ 1 yard). (304)

50. (D) The circumference of the larger wheel is 18π inches $(C = \pi d)$. After 72 revolutions, the larger wheel will have gone a distance of $72(18\pi)$ inches. Since the smaller wheel moves at the same linear speed, it will also have gone $72(18\pi)$ inches. The circumference of the smaller wheel is 12π inches, and if we call the number of revolutions that the smaller wheel makes, r, then we know that $12\pi r = 72(18\pi)$. Dividing both sides by 12π gives us $r = 6(18)$ or 108 revolutions. Note that in this problem we have used the relation, distance $=$ rate $\times$ time, where the time for both wheels is a fixed quantity. (310)

MATH REFRESHER SESSION 4

Algebra Problems

ALGEBRAIC PROPERTIES

Algebra is the branch of mathematics that applies the laws of arithmetic to symbols which represent unknown quantities. The most commonly used symbols are the letters of the alphabet such as A, B, C, x, y, z, etc. These symbols can be added, subtracted, multiplied, and divided like numbers. For example, $3a + 2a = 5a$, $2x - x = x$, $3(5b) = 15b$, $\dfrac{6x}{3x} = 2$. These symbols can be raised to powers like a^3 or y^2. Remember that raising a number to a power means multiplying the number by itself a number of times. For example, $a^3 = a \cdot a \cdot a$. The power is 3 and a is multiplied by itself 3 times.

Generally, in algebra, a variable (an unknown represented by a symbol) appears in an *equation* (a statement that defines the relationship between certain quantities), and values of the variable that *satisfy* the equation must be found. For example, the equation $6a = 12$ is satisfied when the variable, a, is equal to 2. This section is a discussion on how to solve complicated algebraic equations and other related topics.

Fundamental Laws of our Number System

Below is a list of laws that apply to all the numbers necessary to work with when doing arithmetic and algebra problems. Remember these laws and use them in doing problems.

401. If $x = y$ and $y = z$, then $x = z$. This is called *transitivity*. For example, if $a = 3$ and $b = 3$, then $a = b$.

402. If $x = y$, then $x + z = y + z$, and $x - z = y - z$. This means that the same quantity can be added to or subtracted from both sides of an equation. For example, if $a = b$, then add any number to both sides, say 3, and $a + 3 = b + 3$. Or if $a = b$, then $a - 3 = b - 3$.

403. If $x = y$, then $x \cdot z = y \cdot z$ and $x \div z = y \div z$, unless $z = 0$ (see Section 404). This means both sides of an equation can be multiplied by the same number. For example, if $a = n$, then $5a = 5n$. It also means both sides of an equation can be divided by the same non-zero number. If $a = b$, then $\dfrac{a}{3} = \dfrac{b}{3}$.

404. *Never divide by zero.* This is a very important fact that must be remembered. The quotient of *any* quantity (except zero) divided by zero is infinity.

405. $x + y = y + x$, and $x \cdot y = y \cdot x$. Therefore, $2 + 3 = 3 + 2$, and $2 \cdot 3 = 3 \cdot 2$. Remember this does not work for division and subtraction. $3 \div 2$ does not equal $2 \div 3$; and $3 - 2$ does not equal $2 - 3$. The property described above is called *commutativity*.

EQUATIONS

406. *Linear equation in one unknown.* Equations with one variable are linear equations in one unknown. The variable is always in the first power; *i.e.*, x or y or a, but never in a higher or fractional power, *i.e.*, x^2, y^3, or $a^{1/2}$. Examples of linear equations in one unknown are $x + 5 = 7$, $3a - 2 = 7a + 1$, $2x - 7x = 8 + x$, $8 = -4y$, etc. To solve these equations, follow these steps:

STEP 1. Combine the terms on the left and right sides of the equality. That is, (1) add all of the numerical terms on each side, and (2) add all of the terms with variables on each side. For example, if you have $7 + 2x + 9 = 4x - 3 - 2x + 7 + 6x$, combining terms on the left gives you $16 + 2x$, because $7 + 9 = 16$, and $2x$ is the only variable term on that side. On the right we get $8x + 4$, since $4x - 2x + 6x = 8x$ and $-3 + 7 = 4$. Therefore the new equation is $16 + 2x = 8x + 4$.

STEP 2. Put all of the numerical terms on the right side of the equation and all of the variable terms on the left side. This is done by subtracting the numerical term on the left from both sides of the equation and by subtracting the variable term on the right side from both sides of the equation. In the example $16 + 2x = 8x + 4$, subtract 16 from both sides and obtain $2x = 8x - 12$; then subtracting $8x$ from both sides gives $-6x = -12$.

STEP 3. Divide both sides by the coefficient of the variable. In this case, where $-6x = -12$, dividing by -6 gives 2. This is the final solution to the problem.

Example: Solve for a in the equation $7a + 4 - 2a = 18 + 17a + 10$.

Solution: From Step 1, we combine terms on both sides to get $5a + 4 = 28 + 17a$. As in Step 2, we then subtract 4 and $17a$ from both sides to give $-12a = 24$. By Step 3, we then divide both sides of the equation by the coefficient of a which is -12 to get $a = -2$.

Example: Solve for x in $2x + 6 = 0$.

Solution: Here Step 1 is eliminated because there are no terms to combine on either side. Step 2 requires that 6 be subtracted from both sides to get $2x = -6$. Then dividing by 2 gives $x = -3$.

407. *Simultaneous equations in two unknowns.* These are problems in which two equations, each with two unknowns, are given. These equations must be solved together (simultaneously) in order to arrive at the solution.

STEP 1. Rearrange each equation so that both are in the form that has the x term on the left side and the y term and the constant on the right side. In other words, put the equations in the form $Ax = By + C$ where $A, B,$ and C are numerical constants. For example, if one of the equations is $9x - 10y + 30 = 11y + 3x - 6$, then subtract $-10y$ and 30 from both sides to get $9x = 21y + 3x - 36$. Subtracting $3x$ from both sides gives $6x = 21y - 36$, which is in the form of $Ax = By + C$.

The first equation should be in the form $Ax = By + C$ and the second equation should be in the form $Dx = Ey + F$ where $A, B, C, D, E,$ and F are numerical constants.

STEP 2. Multiply the first equation by the coefficient of x in the second equation (D). Multiply the second equation by the coefficient of x in the first equation (A). Now the equations are in the form $ADx = BDy + CD$ and $ADx = AEy + AF$. For example, in the two equations $2x = 7y - 12$ and $3x = y + 1$, multiply the first by 3 and the second by 2 to get $6x = 21y - 36$ and $6x = 2y + 2$.

STEP 3. Equate the right sides of both equations. This can be done because both sides are equal to ADx. (See Section 401 on transitivity.) Thus, $BDy + CD = AEy + AF$. So $21y - 36$ and $2y + 2$ are both equal to $6x$ and they are equal to each other: $21y - 36 = 2y + 2$.

STEP 4. Solve for y. This is done in the manner outlined in section 406. In the equation $21y - 36 = 2y + 2$, $y = 2$. By this method $y = \dfrac{AF - CD}{BD - AE}$.

STEP 5. Substitute the value of y into either of the original equations and solve for x. In the general equations we would then have either $x = \dfrac{B}{A}\left[\dfrac{AF - CD}{BD - AE}\right] + \dfrac{C}{A}$, or $x = \dfrac{E}{D}\left[\dfrac{AF - CD}{BD - AE}\right] + \dfrac{E}{D}$. In the example, if $y = 2$ is substituted into either $2x = 7y - 12$ or $3x = y + 1$, then $2x = 14 - 12$ or $3x = 3$ can be solved to get $x = 1$.

Example: Solve for a and b in the equation $3a + 4b = 24$ and $2a + b = 11$.

Solution: First note that it makes no difference in these two equations whether the variables are a and b instead of x and y. Subtract $4b$ from the first equation and b from the second equation to get the equations $3a = 24 - 4b$ and $2a = 11 - b$. Multiply the first by 2 and the second by 3. Thus, $6a = 48 - 8b$ and $6a = 33 - 3b$. Equate $48 - 8b$ and $33 - 3b$ to get $48 - 8b = 33 - 3b$. Solving for b in the usual manner gives us $b = 3$. Substituting the value of $b = 3$ into the equation $3a + 4b = 24$ obtains $3a + 12 = 24$. Solving for a gives $a = 4$. Thus the complete solution is $a = 4$ and $b = 3$.

408. *Quadratic Equations.* Quadratic equations are expressed in the form $ax^2 + bx + c = 0$; where $a, b,$ and c are constant numbers (for example, $\frac{1}{2}, 4, -2$, etc.) and x is a variable. An equation of this form may be satisfied by two values of x, one value of x, or no values of x. Actually when there are no values of x that satisfy the equation, there are only *imaginary* solutions. These will not be dealt with. To determine the number of solutions, find the value of the expression $b^2 - 4ac$ where $a, b,$ and c are the constant coefficients of the equation $ax^2 + bx + c = 0$.

> If $b^2 - 4ac$ is *greater* than 0, there are two solutions.
>
> If $b^2 - 4ac$ is *less* than 0, there are no solutions.
>
> If $b^2 - 4ac$ is *equal* to 0, there is one solution.

If solutions exists, they can be found by using the formulas:

$$x = \frac{-b + \sqrt{b^2 - 4ac}}{2a} \text{ and } x = \frac{-b - \sqrt{b^2 - 4ac}}{2a}$$

Note that if $b^2 - 4ac = 0$, the two above solutions will be the same and there will be one solution.

Example: Determine the solutions, if they exist, to the equation $x^2 + 6x + 5 = 0$.

Solution: First, noting $a = 1$, $b = 6$, and $c = 5$, calculate $b^2 - 4ac$, or $6^2 - 4(1)(5)$. Thus, $b^2 - 4ac = 16$. Since this is greater than 0, there are two solutions. They are, from the formulas:

$$x = \frac{-6 + \sqrt{6^2 - 4 \cdot 1 \cdot 5}}{2 \cdot 1} \text{ and } x = \frac{-6 - \sqrt{6^2 - 4 \cdot 1 \cdot 5}}{2 \cdot 1}$$

Simplify these to:

$$x = \frac{-6 + \sqrt{16}}{2} \text{ and } x = \frac{-6 - \sqrt{16}}{2}$$

As $\sqrt{16} = 4$, $x = \frac{-6 + 4}{2} = \frac{-2}{2}$ and $x = \frac{-6 - 4}{2} = \frac{-10}{2}$. Thus, the two solutions are $x = -1$ and $x = -5$.

Another method of solving quadratic equations is to *factor* the $ax^2 + bx + c$ into two expressions. This will be explained in the next section.

409. *Factoring.* Factoring is breaking down an expression into two or more expressions, the product of which is the original expression. For example, 6 can be factored into 2 and 3 because $2 \cdot 3 = 6$. Then, if $x^2 + bx + c$ is factorable, it will be factored into two expressions in the form $(x + d)$ and $(x + e)$. If the expression $(x + d)$ is multiplied by the expression $(x + e)$, their product is $x^2 + (d + e)x + de$. For example, $(x + 3) \cdot (x + 2)$ equals $x^2 + 5x + 6$. To factor an expression such as $x^2 + 6x + 8$, find a d and e such that $d + e = 6$ and $de = 8$. Of the various factors of 8, we find that $d = 4$ and $e = 2$. Thus $x^2 + 6x + 8$ can be factored into the expressions $(x + 4)$ and $(x + 2)$. Below are factored expressions.

$$x^2 + 2x + 1 = (x + 1)(x + 1) \qquad x^2 + 3x + 2 = (x + 2)(x + 1)$$
$$x^2 + 4x + 4 = (x + 2)(x + 2) \qquad x^2 + 5x + 6 = (x + 3)(x + 2)$$
$$x^2 - 4x + 3 = (x - 3)(x - 1) \qquad x^2 - 4x - 5 = (x - 5)(x + 1)$$
$$x^2 + 10x + 16 = (x + 8)(x + 2) \qquad x^2 + 4x - 5 = (x + 5)(x - 1)$$
$$x^2 - 5x + 6 = (x - 2)(x - 3) \qquad x^2 - x - 6 = (x - 3)(x + 2)$$

An important rule to remember in factoring is that $a^2 - b^2 = (a + b)(a - b)$. For example, $x^2 - 9 = (x + 3)(x - 3)$. To apply factoring in solving quadratic equations, factor the quadratic expression into two terms and set each term equal to zero. Then, solve the two resulting equations.

Example: Solve $x^2 - x - 6 = 0$.

Solution: First factor the expression $x^2 - x - 6$ into $x - 3$ and $x + 2$. Setting each of these equal to 0 gives $x - 3 = 0$ and $x + 2 = 0$. Solving these equations gives us $x = 3$ and $x = -2$.

ALGEBRA OF GRAPHS

410. *Coordinate geometry.* These problems deal with the algebra of graphs. A graph consists of a set of points whose position is determined with respect to a set of axes usually labelled the X-axis and the Y-axis and divided into appropriate units. Locate a point on the graph with an "x coordinate" of a units and a "y coordinate" of b units. First move a units along the X axis (either to the left or right depending on whether a is positive or negative. Then move b units along the Y axis (either up or down depending on the sign of b). A point with an x coordinate of a, and a y coordinate of b, is represented by (a, b). The points $(2,3)$, $(-1,4)$, $(-2,-3)$, and $(4,-2)$ are shown on the following graph.

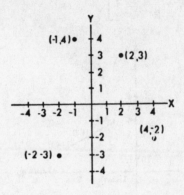

411. *Distance between two points.* If the coordinates of point A are (x_1, y_1) and the coordinates of point B are (x_2, y_2), then the distance on the graph between the two points is $d = \sqrt{(x_2 - x_1)^2 + (y_2 - y_1)^2}$.

Example: Find the distance between the point $(2,-3)$ and the point $(5,1)$.

Solution: In this case $x_1 = 2$, $x_2 = 5$, $y_1 = -3$ and $y_2 = 1$. Substituting into the above formula gives us

$$d = \sqrt{(5-2)^2 + [1-(-3)]^2} = \sqrt{3^2 + 4^2} = \sqrt{25} = 5$$

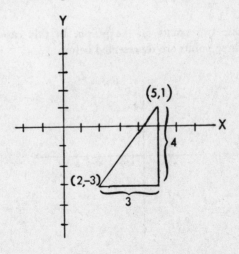

Note: This formula is a consequence of the Pythagorean theorem. Pythagoras, an ancient Greek mathematician, discovered that the square of the length of the hypotenuse (longest side) of a right triangle is equal to the sum of the square of the lengths of the other two sides. See Sections 317 and 509.

412. *Midpoint of the line segment joining two points.* If the coordinates of the first point are (x_1, y_1) and the coordinates of the second point are (x_2, y_2) then the coordinates of the midpoint will be $\left(\dfrac{x_1 + x_2}{2}, \dfrac{y_1 + y_2}{2} \right)$. In other words, each coordinate of the midpoint is equal to the *average* of the corresponding coordinates of the endpoints.

Example: Find the midpoint of the segment connecting the points (2,4) and (6,2).

Solution: The average of 2 and 6 is 4 so the first coordinate is 4. The average of 4 and 2 is 3; thus the second coordinate is 3. The midpoint is (4,3). $\left[\dfrac{2+6}{2} = 4, \dfrac{4+2}{2} = 3 \right]$

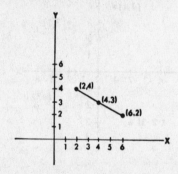

413. *Plotting the graph of a line.* An equation that can be put in the form of $y = mx + b$ where m and b are numerical constants can be represented as a line on a graph. This means that all of the points on the graph that the line passes through will satisfy the equation. Remember that each point has an x and a y value that can be substituted into the equation. To plot a line, follow the steps below:

STEP 1. Select two values of x and two values of y that will satisfy the equation. For example, in the equation $y = 2x + 4$, the point $(x = 1, y = 6)$, will satisfy the equation as will the point $(x = -2, y = 0)$. There are an infinite number of such points on a line.

STEP 2. Plot these two points on the graph. In this case, the two points are (1,6) and (-2,0). These points are represented below.

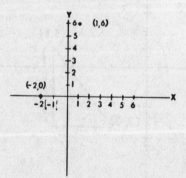

STEP 3. Draw a line connecting the two points. This is the line representing the equation.

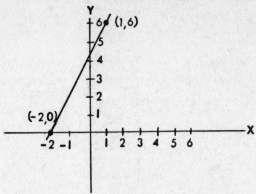

NOTE: A straight line is completely specified by two points.

Example: Graph the equation $2y + 3x = 12$.

Solution: Two points that satisfy this equation are $(2,3)$ and $(0,6)$. Plotting these points and drawing a line between them gives:

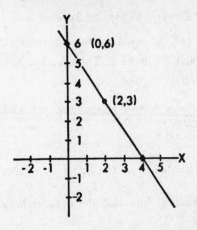

414. *Y-intercept.* The Y-intercept of a line is the point where the line crosses the Y-axis. At any point where a line crosses the Y-axis, $x = 0$. To find the Y-intercept of a line, simply substitute $x = 0$ into the equation of the line and solve for y.

Example: Find the Y-intercept of the equation $2x + 3y = 6$.

Solution: If $x = 0$ is substituted into the equation, it simplifies to $3y = 6$. Solving for y gives $y = 2$. Thus, 2 is the Y-intercept.

If an equation can be put into the form of $y = mx + b$, then b is the Y-intercept.

---

415. *X-intercept.* The point where a line intersects the X-axis is called the X-intercept. At this point $y = 0$. To find the X-intercept of a line, substitute $y = 0$ into the equation and solve for x.

Example: Given the equation $2x + 3y = 6$, find the X-intercept.

Solution: Substitute $y = 0$ into the equation getting $2x = 6$. Solving for x, find $x = 3$. Thus the X-intercept is 3.

In the diagram below, the Y- and X-intercepts of the equation $2x + 3y = 6$ are illustrated.

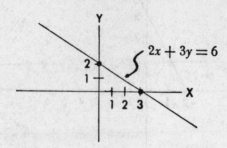

416. *Slope.* The slope of a line is the change in y caused by a 1 unit increase in x. If an equation is in the form of $y = mx + b$, then as x increases 1 unit, y will increase m units. Therefore the slope is m.

Example: Find the slope of the line $2x + 3y = 6$.

Solution: First put the equation into the form of $y = mx + b$. Subtract $2x$ from both sides and divide by 3. The equation becomes $y = -\frac{2}{3}x + 2$. Therefore the slope is $-\frac{2}{3}$.

The slope of the line joining two points, (x_1, y_1) and (x_2, y_2) is given by the expression $m_{12} = \dfrac{y_2 - y_1}{x_2 - x_1}$.

Example: Find the slope of the line joining the points $(3,2)$ and $(4,-1)$.

Solution: Substituting into the above formula gives us $m = \dfrac{-1 - 2}{4 - 3} = \dfrac{-3}{1} = -3$ where $x_1 = 3$, $x_2 = 4$, $y_1 = 2$, $y_2 = -1$.

417. *Graphing Simultaneous Equations.* Recall that simultaneous equations are a pair of equations in two unknowns. Each of these equations is graphed separately; and each is represented by a straight line. The solution of the simultaneous equations (*i.e.*, the pair of values that satisfies *both* at the same time) is represented by the intersection of two lines. Now, for any pair of lines, there are three possible relationships:

1. The lines intersect at one and only one point; in this case, this point represents the unique solution to the pair of equations. This is most often the case. Such lines are called *consistent*.

2. The lines coincide exactly; this represents the case where the two equations are equivalent (just different forms of the same mathematical relation). Any point which satisfies *either* of the two equations automatically satisfies *both*.

3. The lines are parallel and never intersect. In this case the equations are called *inconsistent*, and they have *no* solution at all. Two lines that are parallel will have the same slope.

Example: Solve graphically the equations $4x - y = 5$ and $2x + 4y = 16$.

Solution: Plot the two lines represented by the two equations. (See Section 413.) The graph is shown below.

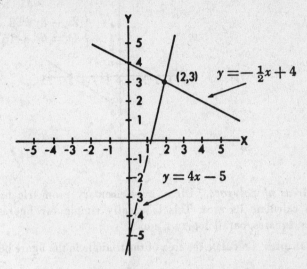

The two lines intersect in the point (2,3) which represents the solution $x = 2$ and $y = 3$. This can be checked by solving the equations as is done in Section 407.

Example: Solve $x + 2y = 6$ and $2x + 4y = 8$.

Solution: Find two points that satisfy each equation. Draw a line connecting these two points. The two graphs will look like this:

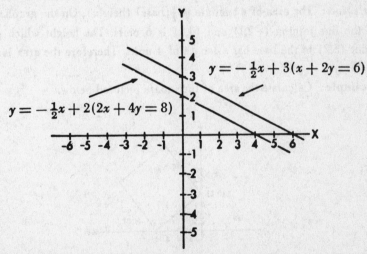

These lines will never intersect and these equations are termed inconsistent. There is no solution.

Remember that two parallel lines have the same slope. This is an easy way to see whether two lines are consistent or inconsistent.

Example: Find the solution to $2x - 3y = 8$ and $4x = 6y + 16$.

Solution: On the graph these two lines are identical. This means that there are an infinite set of points that satisfy both equations.

Identical lines are products of each other and can be reduced to the same equation.

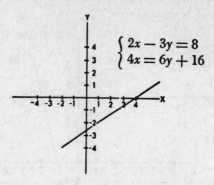

$$\begin{cases} 2x - 3y = 8 \\ 4x = 6y + 16 \end{cases}$$

418. *Areas of polygons.* Often, an elementary geometric figure is placed on a graph to calculate its area. This is usually simple for figures such as triangles, rectangles, squares, parallelograms, etc.

Example: Calculate the area of the triangle in the figure below.

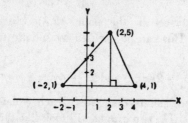

Solution: The area of a triangle is $\frac{1}{2}$(base) (height). On the graph the length of the line joining $(-2,1)$ and $(4,1)$ is 6 units. The height which goes from point $(5,2)$ to the base has a length of 4 units. Therefore the area is $\frac{1}{2}(6)(4)$ = 12.

Example: Calculate the area of the square pictured below.

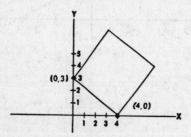

Solution: The area of a square is given by the square of the side. To find this area first find the length of one side. The length of a segment whose endpoints are (x_1, y_1) and (x_2, y_2) is given by the formula $\sqrt{(x_2 - x_1)^2 + (y_2 - y_1)^2}$. Substituting in $(0,3)$ and $(4,0)$ gives a length of 5 units. Thus the length of one side of the square is 5. Using the formula, area = (side)^2, gives an area of 5^2 or 25 square units.

To find the area of more complicated polygons, divide the polygon into simple figures whose areas can be calculated. Add these areas to find the total area.

Example: Find the area of the figure below:

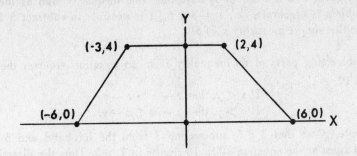

Solution: Divide the figure into two triangles and a rectangle by drawing vertical lines at (−3,4) and (2,4). Thus the polygon is now two triangles and a rectangle.

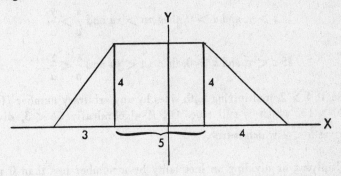

The height of the left triangle is 4 units and the base is 3. Using $A = \frac{1}{2}bh$ gives the area as 6. The height of the right triangle is 4 and the base is 4. The area is 8. The length of one side of the rectangle is 4 and the other side is 5. Using the formula, area = base · height, gives the area as 20. Thus the total area is $6 + 8 + 20 = 34$.

INEQUALITIES

419. *Inequalities.* These problems deal with numbers that are less than, greater than, or equal to other numbers. The following laws apply to all inequalities:

> < means less than, thus $3 < 4$
>
> > means greater than, thus $5 > 2$
>
> ≤ means less than or equal to, thus $3 \leq 4$ and $3 \leq 3$
>
> ≥ means greater than or equal to, thus $5 \geq 2$ and $2 \geq 2$

420. If equal quantities are added to both sides of an inequality, the direction of the inequality does *not* change.

$$\text{If } x < y, \text{ then } x + z < y + z \text{ and } x - z < y - z.$$

$$\text{If } x > y, \text{ then } x + z > y + z \text{ and } x - z > y - z.$$

For example, given the inequality, $4 > 2$, with 1 added to or subtracted from both sides, the results, $5 > 3$ and $3 > 1$, have the same inequality sign as the original. If the problem is algebraic, *i.e.*, $x + 3 < 6$, it is possible to subtract 3 from both sides to get this simple inequality $x < 3$.

421. Subtracting parts of an inequality from an equation *reverses* the order of the inequality.

$$\text{If } x < y, \text{ then } z - x > z - y.$$
$$\text{If } x > y, \text{ then } z - x < z - y.$$

For example, given that $3 < 5$, subtracting 3 from the left-hand and 5 from the right-hand sides of the equation $10 = 10$ results in $7 > 5$. Thus the direction of the inequality is reversed.

422. Multiplying or dividing an inequality by a number greater than zero does not change the order of the inequality.

$$\text{If } x > y, \text{ and } a > 0, \text{ then } xa > ya \text{ and } \frac{x}{a} > \frac{y}{a}.$$

$$\text{If } x < y, \text{ and } a > 0, \text{ then } xa < ya \text{ and } \frac{x}{a} < \frac{y}{a}.$$

For example, if $4 > 2$, multiplying both sides by any arbitrary number (for instance, 5) gives $20 > 10$, which is still true. Or, if algebraically $6h < 3$, dividing both sides by 6 gives $h < \frac{1}{2}$ which is true.

423. Multiplying or dividing an inequality by a number less than 0 reverses the order of the inequality.

$$\text{If } x > y, \text{ and } a < 0, \text{ then } xa < ya \text{ and } \frac{x}{a} < \frac{y}{a}.$$

$$\text{If } x < y, \text{ and } a < 0, \text{ then } xa > ya \text{ and } \frac{x}{a} > \frac{y}{a}.$$

If $-3 < 2$ is multiplied through by -2 it becomes $6 > -4$ and the order of the inequality is reversed.

> Note that negative numbers are always less than positive numbers. Note also that the greater the absolute value of a negative number, the smaller it actually is. Thus, $-10 < -9$, $-8 < -7$, etc.

424. The product of two numbers with like signs is positive.

$$\text{If } x > 0 \text{ and } y > 0, \text{ then } xy > 0.$$

$$\text{If } x < 0 \text{ and } y < 0, \text{ then } xy > 0.$$

For example, -3 times -2 is 6.

425. The product of two numbers with unlike signs is negative.

$$\text{If } x < 0 \text{ and } y > 0 \text{ then } xy < 0.$$

$$\text{If } x > 0 \text{ and } y < 0 \text{ then } xy < 0.$$

For example, -2 times 3 is -6. 8 times -1 is -8, etc.

426. *Linear inequalities in one unknown.* In these problems a first power variable is given in an inequality and this variable must be solved for in terms of the inequality. Examples of linear inequalities in one unknown are: $2x + 7 > 4 + x$, $8y - 3 \leq 2y$, etc.

STEP 1. By ordinary algebraic addition and subtraction (as if it were an equality) get all of the constant terms on one side of the inequality and all of the variable terms on the other side. In the inequality $2x + 4 < 8x + 10$, subtract 4 and $8x$ from both sides and get $-6x < 12$.

STEP 2. Divide both sides by the coefficient of the variable. Important: If the coefficient of the variable is negative, you must reverse the inequality sign. For example, in $-6x < 12$, dividing by -6 gives $x > 2$. (The inequality is reversed.) In $3x < 12$ dividing by 3 gives $x < 4$.

> **Example:** Solve for y in the inequality $4y + 7 \geq 9 - 2y$.
>
> **Solution:** Subtracting $-2y$ and 7 from both sides gives $6y \geq 2$. Dividing both sides by 6 gives $y \geq \frac{1}{3}$.
>
> **Example:** Solve for a in the inequality $10 - 2a < 0$.
>
> **Solution:** Subtracting 10 from both sides gives $-2a < -10$. Dividing both sides by -2 gives $a > \dfrac{-10}{-2}$ or $a > 5$. Note that the inequality sign has been reversed because of the division by a negative number.

427. *Simultaneous linear inequalities in two unknowns.* These are two inequalities, each one in two unknowns. The same two unknowns are to be solved for in each equation. This means the equations must be solved simultaneously.

STEP 1. Plot both inequalities on the same graph. Replace the inequality sign with an equality sign and plot the resulting line. The side of the line which makes the inequality true is then shaded in. For example, graph the inequality $(2x - y > 4)$. First replace the inequality sign getting $2x - y = 4$; then, plot the line. The X-intercept is 2. The Y-intercept is -4.

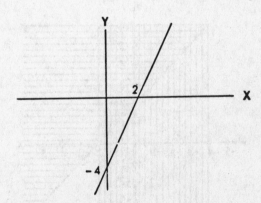

To decide which side of the line satisfies the inequality chose a convenient point on each side and determine which point satisfies the inequality. Shade in that side of the line. In this case, choose the point $(0,0)$. With this point the equation becomes $2(0) - 0 > 4$ or $0 > 4$. This is not true. Thus, shade in the other side of the line.

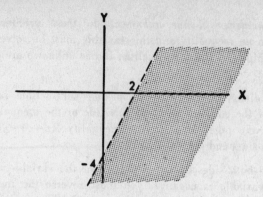

STEP 2. After both inequalities have been solved, the area that is common to both shaded portions is the solution to the problem.

Example: Solve $x + y > 2$ and $3x < 6$.

Solution: First graph $x + y > 2$ by plotting $x + y = 2$ and using the point (4,0) to determine the region where the inequality is satisfied:

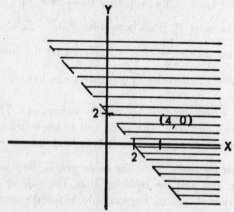

Graph the inequality $3x < 6$ on the same axes and get:

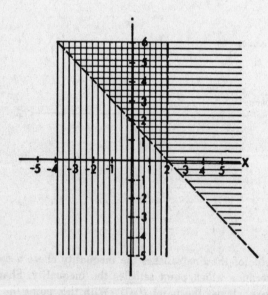

The solution is the double shaded area.

428. *Higher order inequalities in one unknown.* These are inequalities that deal with variables multiplied by themselves. For example, $x^2 + 3 \geq 0$, $(x - 1)(x + 2) < 4$ and $x^3 - 7x > 0$ are such inequalities. The basic rules to remember in doing such problems are:

---

1. The product of any number of positive numbers is positive.

For example, $2 \times 3 \times 4 \times 5 = 120$ which is positive or $\frac{1}{2} \times \frac{1}{2} = \frac{1}{4}$ which is positive.

---

2. The product of an even number of negative numbers is positive.

For example, $(-3)(-2) = 6$ or $(-3)(-1)(-9)(-2) = 54$ which is positive.

---

3. The product of an odd number of negative numbers is negative.

For example, $(-1)(-2)(-3) = -6$ or $(-\frac{1}{2})(-2)(-3)(-6)(-1) = -18$.

---

4. Any number squared or raised to an even power is always positive or zero.

For example, $x^2 \geq 0$ or $a^4 \geq 0$ for all x and for all a.

Often these basic rules will make the solution to an inequality problem obvious.

> **Example:** Which of the following values can x^2 not have?
>
> (A) 5   (B) -2   (C) 0   (D) 144   (E) 9
>
> *Solution:* We know that $x^2 \geq 0$ for all x so x^2 cannot be negative. -2 is negative so x^2 cannot equal -2.

The steps in solving a higher order inequality are:

STEP 1. Bring all of the terms to one side of the inequality making the other side zero. For example, in the inequality $x^2 > 3x - 2$, subtract $3x - 2$ from both sides to get $x^2 - 3x + 2 > 0$.

STEP 2. Factor the resulting expression. To factor a quadratic expression means to write the original expression as the product of two terms in the 1st power, *i.e.*, $x^2 = x \cdot x$. x is a factor of x^2. See Section 409 for a detailed explanation of factoring. The quadratic expression $x^2 - 3x + 2$ when factored is $(x - 2)(x - 1)$. Note that $x \cdot x = x^2$, $-2x - x = -3x$ and $(-1)(-2) = 2$. Most quadratic expressions can easily be factored by taking factors of the last term (in this case 2 and 1) and adding or subtracting them to x. Through trial and error the right combination is found. An important fact to remember when factoring is: $(a + b)(c + d) = ac + ad + bc + bd$. Example: $(x + 4)(x + 2) = x^2 + 4x + 2x + 8 = x^2 + 6x + 8$. Another is that $a^2 - b^2 = (a + b)(a - b)$. Example: $x^2 - 16 = (x + 4)(x - 4)$.

STEP 3. Investigate which terms are positive and which terms are negative. For example, in $(x - 3)(x + 2) > 0$, either $(x - 3)$ and $(x + 2)$ are both positive or $(x - 3)$ and $(x + 2)$ are both negative. If one were positive and the other were negative, the product would be negative and would not satisfy the inequality. If the factors are positive, then $x - 3 > 0$ and $x + 2 > 0$, which yields $x > 3$ and $x > -2$. For x to be greater than 3 and to be greater than -2, it must be greater than 3. If it is greater than 3 it is automatically greater than -2. Thus, with positive factors $x > 3$ is the answer. If the factors are negative, $x - 3 < 0$ and $x + 2 < 0$, or

$x < -2$. For x to be less than 3 and less than -2 it must be less than -2. Thus, with negative factors $x < -2$ is the answer. As both answers are possible from the original equation, the solution to the original problem is $x > 3$ or $x < -2$.

Example: For which values of x is $x^2 + 5 < 6x$?

Solution: First subtract $6x$ from both sides to get $x^2 - 6x + 5 < 0$. The left side factors into $(x - 5)(x - 1) < 0$. Now for this to be true one factor must be positive and one must be negative, *i.e.*, their product is less than zero. Thus, $x - 5 > 0$ and $x - 1 < 0$ or $x - 5 < 0$ and $x - 1 > 0$. If $x - 5 < 0$ and $x - 1 > 0$ then $x < 5$ and $x > 1$, or $1 < x < 5$. If $x - 5 > 0$ and $x - 1 < 0$ then $x > 5$ and $x < 1$, which is impossible because x cannot be less than 1 and greater than 5. Therefore, the solution is $1 < x < 5$.

Example: For what values of x is $x^2 < 4$?

Solution: Subtract 4 from both sides to get $x^2 - 4 < 0$. Remember that $a^2 - b^2 = (a + b)(a - b)$; thus $x^2 - 4 = (x + 2)(x - 2)$. Hence, $(x + 2)(x - 2) < 0$. For this to be true $x + 2 > 0$ and $x - 2 < 0$ or $x + 2 < 0$ and $x - 2 > 0$. In the first case $x > -2$ and $x < +2$ or $-2 < x < 2$. The second case is $x < -2$ and $x > +2$ is impossible because x cannot be less than -2 *and* greater than 2. Thus, the solution is $-2 < x < 2$.

Example 3: When is $(x^2 + 1)(x - 2)^2(x - 3)$ greater than or equal to zero?

Solution: This can be written as $(x^2 + 1)(x - 2)^2(x - 3) \geq 0$. This is already in factors. The individual terms must be investigated. $x^2 + 1$ is always positive because $x^2 \geq 0$ so $x^2 + 1$ must be greater than 0. $(x - 2)^2$ is a number squared so this is always greater than or equal to zero. Therefore, the product of the first two terms is positive or equal to zero for all values of x. The third term $x - 3$ is positive when $x > 3$, and negative when $x < 3$. For the entire expression to be positive, $x - 3$ must be positive, *i.e.*, $x > 3$. For the expression to be equal to zero, $x - 3 = 0$, *i.e.*, $x = 3$, or $(x - 2)^2 = 0$, *i.e.*, $x = 2$. Thus, the entire expression is positive when $x > 3$ and zero when $x = 2$ or $x = 3$.

429. *Exponents.* An exponent is an easy way to express repeated multiplication. For example, $5 \times 5 \times 5 \times 5 = 5^4$. The 4 is the exponent. In the expression $7^3 = 7 \times 7 \times 7$, 3 is the exponent. 7^3 means 7 is multiplied by itself three times. If the exponent is 0, the expression always has a value of 1. Thus, $6^0 = 15^0 = 1$, etc. If the exponent is 1, the value of the expression is the number base. Thus, $4^1 = 4$ and $9^1 = 9$.

In the problem $5^3 \times 5^4$, we can simplify by counting the factors of 5. Thus $5^3 \times 5^4 = 5^{3+4} = 5^7$. When we multiply and the base number is the same, we keep the base number and add the exponents. For example, $7^4 \times 7^8 = 7^{12}$.

For division, we keep the same base number and subtract exponents. Thus, $8^8 \div 8^2 = 8^{8-2} = 8^6$.

A negative exponent indicates the reciprocal of the expression with a positive exponent, thus $3^{-2} = \dfrac{1}{3^2}$.

430. *Roots.* The square root of a number is a number whose square is the original number. For example, $\sqrt{16} = 4$, since $4 \times 4 = 16$. (The $\sqrt{}$ symbol always means a positive number.)

To simplify a square root, we factor the number.

$$\sqrt{32} = \sqrt{16 \cdot 2} = \sqrt{16} \cdot \sqrt{2} = 4\sqrt{2}$$

$$\sqrt{72} = \sqrt{36 \cdot 2} = \sqrt{36} \cdot \sqrt{2} = 6\sqrt{2}$$

$$\sqrt{300} = \sqrt{25 \cdot 12} = \sqrt{25} \cdot \sqrt{12}$$
$$= 5 \cdot \sqrt{12}$$
$$= 5 \cdot \sqrt{4 \cdot 3}$$
$$= 5\sqrt{4}\sqrt{3}$$
$$= 5 \cdot 2\sqrt{3}$$
$$= 10\sqrt{3}$$

We can add expressions with the square roots only if the numbers inside the square root sign are the same. For example,

$$3\sqrt{7} + 2\sqrt{7} = 5\sqrt{7}$$

$$\sqrt{18} + \sqrt{2} = \sqrt{9 \cdot 2} + \sqrt{2} = \sqrt{9}\sqrt{2} + \sqrt{2} = 3\sqrt{2} + \sqrt{2} = 4\sqrt{2}.$$

431. *Evaluation of expressions.* To evaluate an expression means to substitute a value in place of a letter. For example: Evaluate $3a^2 - c^3$; if $a = -2$, $c = -3$.

$$3a^2 - c^3 = 3(-2)^2 - (-3)^3 = 3(4) - (-27) = 12 + 27 = 39$$

Given: $a \bigtriangledown b = ab + b^2$. Find: $-2 \bigtriangledown 3$.
Using the definition, we get

$$-2 \bigtriangledown 3 = (-2)(3) + (3)^2$$
$$= -6 + 9$$
$$-2 \bigtriangledown 3 = 3$$

PRACTICE TEST 4

Algebra Problems

Correct answers and solutions follow each test.

1. For what values of x is the following equation satisfied: $3x + 9 = 21 + 7x$?

   (A) -3 only   (D) no values

   (B) 3 only   (E) an infinite number of values

   (C) 3 or -3 only

2. What values may z have if $2z + 4$ is greater than $z - 6$?

   (A) any values greater than -10 (D) any values less than 10

   (B) any values greater than -2 (E) none of these

   (C) any values less than 2

3. A B C D E   **3.** If $ax^2 + 2x - 3 = 0$ when $x = -3$, what value(s) can a have?

(A) -3 only   (D) -1 and 1 only

(B) -1 only   (E) -3, -1, and 1 only

(C) 1 only

4. A B C D E   **4.** If the coordinates of point P are $(0,8)$, and the coordinates of point Q are $(4,2)$, which of the following points represents the midpoint of PQ?

(A) $(0,2)$ (B) $(2,4)$ (C) $(2,5)$ (D) $(4,8)$ (E) $(4,10)$

5. A B C D E   **5.** In the formula $V = \pi r^2 h$, what is the value of r, in terms of V and h?

(A) $\dfrac{\sqrt{V}}{\pi h}$ (B) $\pi \sqrt{\dfrac{V}{h}}$ (C) $\sqrt{\pi V h}$ (D) $\dfrac{\pi h}{\sqrt{V}}$ (E) $\sqrt{\dfrac{V}{\pi h}}$

6. A B C D E   **6.** Solve the inequality $x^2 - 3x < 0$.

(A) $x < -3$ (D) $0 < x < 3$

(B) $-3 < x < 0$ (E) $3 < x$

(C) $x < 3$

7. A B C D E   **7.** Which of the following lines is parallel to the line represented by $2y = 8x + 32$?

(A) $y = 8x + 32$ (D) $y = 4x + 32$

(B) $y = 8x + 16$ (E) $y = 2x + 16$

(C) $y = 16x + 32$

8. A B C D E   **8.** In the equation $4.04x + 1.01 = 9.09$, what value of x is necessary to make the equation true?

(A) -1.5 (B) 0 (C) 1 (D) 2 (E) 2.5

9. A B C D E   **9.** What values of x satisfy the equation $(x + 1)(x - 2) = 0$?

(A) 1 only   (D) -1 and 2 only

(B) -2 only   (E) any values between -1 and 2

(C) 1 and -2 only

10. A B C D E   **10.** What is the largest possible value of the following expression:

$$(x + 2)(3 - x)(2 + x)^2(2x - 6)(2x + 4)?$$

(A) -576 (D) 12

(B) -24 (E) cannot be determined

(C) 0

11. A B C D E   **11.** For what value(s) of k is the following equation satisfied:

$$2k - 9 - k = 4k + 6 - 3k?$$

(A) -5 only   (D) no values

(B) 0 only   (E) more than one value

(C) $\frac{5}{2}$ only

12. In the equation $p = aq^2 + bq + c$, if $a = 1$, $b = -2$, and $c = 1$, which of the following expresses p in terms of q?

(A) $p = (q - 2)^2$ (B) $p = (q - 1)^2$ (C) $p = q^2$
(D) $p = (q + 1)^2$ (E) $p = (q + 2)^2$

13. If $A + B + C = 10$, $A + B = 7$, and $A - B = 5$, what is the value of C?

(A) 1

(B) 3

(C) 6

(D) 7

(E) cannot be determined from the given information

14. $5x + 15$ is greater than 20, which of the following best describes the possible values of x?

(A) x must be greater than 5 (D) x must be less than 5

(B) x must be greater than 3 (E) x must be less than 1

(C) x must be greater than 1

15. If $\dfrac{t^2 - 1}{t - 1} = 2$, then what value(s) may t have?

(A) 1 only (D) no values

(B) -1 only (E) an infinite number of values

(C) 1 or -1

16. If $4m = 9n$, what is the value of $7m$, in terms of n?

(A) $\dfrac{63n}{4}$ (B) $\dfrac{9n}{28}$ (C) $\dfrac{7n}{9}$ (D) $\dfrac{28n}{9}$ (E) $\dfrac{7n}{4}$

17. The coordinates of a triangle are $(0,2)$, $(2,4)$, and $(1,6)$. What is the area of the triangle, in square units (to the nearest unit)?

(A) 2 square units (D) 5 square units

(B) 3 square units (E) 6 square units

(C) 4 square units

18. In the formula $s = \frac{1}{2}gt^2$, what is the value of t, in terms of s and g?

(A) $\dfrac{2s}{g}$ (B) $2\sqrt{\dfrac{s}{g}}$ (C) $\dfrac{s}{2g}$ (D) $\sqrt{\dfrac{s}{2g}}$ (E) $\sqrt{\dfrac{2s}{g}}$

19. In the triangle ABC, angle A is a $30°$ angle, and angle B is obtuse. If x represents the number of degrees in angle C, which of the following best represents the possible values of x?

(A) $0 < x < 60$ (D) $120 < x < 180$

(B) $0 < x < 150$ (E) $120 < x < 150$

(C) $60 < x < 180$

20. A B C D E

20. Which of the following sets of coordinates does *not* represent the vertices of an isosceles triangle?

(A) (0,2), (0,−2), (2,0)

(B) (1,3), (1,5), (3,4)

(C) (1,3), (1,7), (4,5)

(D) (2,2), (2,0), (1,1)

(E) (2,3), (2,5), (3,3)

21. A B C D E

21. If $2 < a < 5$, and $6 > b > 3$, what are the possible values of $a + b$?

(A) $a + b$ must equal 8.

(B) $a + b$ must be between 2 and 6.

(C) $a + b$ must be between 3 and 5.

(D) $a + b$ must be between 5 and 8.

(E) $a + b$ must be between 5 and 11.

22. A B C D E

22. The area of a square will be doubled if:

(A) The length of the diagonal is divided by 2.

(B) The length of the diagonal is divided by $\sqrt{2}$.

(C) The length of the diagonal is multiplied by 2.

(D) The length of the diagonal is multiplied by $\sqrt{2}$.

(E) none of the above

23. A B C D E

23. Find the value of y that satisfies the equation $8.8y - 4 = 7.7y + 7$.

(A) 1.1   (B) 7.7   (C) 8.0   (D) 10.0   (E) 11.0

24. A B C D E

24. Which of the following is a factor of the expression $2x^2 + 1$?

(A) $x + 2$

(B) $x - 2$

(C) $x + \sqrt{2}$

(D) $x - \sqrt{2}$

(E) none of these

25. A B C D E

25. A businessman has ten employees; his salary is equal to six times the *average* of the employees' salaries. If the eleven of them received a total of $64,000 in one year, what was the businessman's salary that year?

(A) $4000   (B) $6000   (C) $24,000   (D) $40,000   (E) $44,000

26. A B C D E

26. If $6x + 3$ equals 15, what is the value of $12x - 3$?

(A) 21   (B) 24   (C) 28   (D) 33   (E) 36

27. A B C D E

27. If $2p + 7$ is greater than $3p - 5$, which of the following best describes the possible values of p?

(A) p must be greater than 2.

(B) p must be greater than 12.

(C) p must be less than 2.

(D) p must be less than 12.

(E) p must be greater than 2, but less than 12.

28. What is the value of q if $x^2 + qx + 1 = 0$, if $x = 1$?

(A) −2   (B) −1   (C) 0   (D) 1   (E) 2

29. What is the area (to the nearest unit) of the shaded figure in the diagram below, assuming that each of the squares has an area of 1?

(A) 12

(B) 13

(C) 14

(D) 15

(E) 16

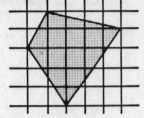

30. Which of the following statements is *false*?

(A) Any two numbers, a and b, have a sum, equal to $a + b$.

(B) Any two numbers, a and b, have a product, equal to $a \cdot b$.

(C) Any two numbers, a and b, have a difference, equal to $a - b$.

(D) Any two numbers, a and b, have a quotient, equal to $\dfrac{a}{b}$.

(E) Any two numbers, a and b, have an average, equal to $\dfrac{(a + b)}{2}$.

31. If $(x - 1)(x - 2)(x^2 - 4) = 0$, what are the possible values of x?

(A) −2 only

(B) +2 only

(C) −1, −2, or −4 only

(D) +1, +2, or +4 only

(E) +1, −2, or +2 only

32. If $P + Q = R$, and $P + R = 2Q$, what is the ratio of P to R?

(A) 1:1   (B) 1:2   (C) 2:1   (D) 1:3   (E) 3:1

33. For what value(s) of r is $\dfrac{r^2 + 5r + 6}{r + 2}$ equal to 0?

(A) −2 only

(B) −3 only

(C) +3 only

(D) −2 or −3

(E) +2 or +3

34. What is the value of $a^2b + 4ab^2 + 4b^3$, if $a = 15$ and $b = 5$?

(A) 1625   (B) 2125   (C) 2425   (D) 2725   (E) 3125

35. If $m + 4n = 2n + 8m$, what is the ratio of n to m?

(A) 1:4   (B) 1:−4   (C) −4:1   (D) 2:7   (E) 7:2

36. If the value of a lies between −5 and +2, and the value of b lies between −7 and +1, what are the possible values for the product, $a \cdot b$?

(A) between −14 and +2

(B) between −35 and +2

(C) between +2 and +35

(D) between −12 and +3

(E) between −14 and +35

37. A B C D E   **37.** What is the area, in square units, of a triangle whose vertices lie on points $(-5, 1)$, $(-5, 4)$, and $(2, 4)$?

(A) 10.5 square units   (D) 20.0 square units

(B) 12.5 square units   (E) 21.0 square units

(C) 15.0 square units

38. A B C D E   **38.** If $A + B = 12$, and $B + C = 16$, what is the value of $A + C$?

(A) -4

(B) -28

(C) $+4$

(D) $+28$

(E) cannot be determined from the given information

39. A B C D E   **39.** What is the solution to the equation $x^2 + x + 1 = 0$?

(A) $-\dfrac{1}{2} + \dfrac{\sqrt{3}}{2}$ and $-\dfrac{1}{2} - \dfrac{\sqrt{3}}{2}$ (D) no real solutions

(B) $-\dfrac{1}{2} + \dfrac{\sqrt{3}}{2}$ only   (E) 0

(C) $-\dfrac{1}{2} - \dfrac{\sqrt{3}}{2}$ only

40. A B C D E   **40.** Which of the following equations will have a vertical line as its graph?

(A) $x + y = 1$ (B) $x - y = 1$ (C) $x = 1$ (D) $y = 1$

(E) $xy = 1$

41. A B C D E   **41.** For what values of x does $x^2 + 3x + 2$ equal zero?

(A) -1 only   (D) 1 or 2 only

(B) $+2$ only   (E) none of these

(C) -1 or -2 only

42. A B C D E   **42.** If $a + b$ equals 12, and $a - b$ equals 6, what is the value of b?

(A) 0   (B) 3   (C) 6   (D) 9

(E) cannot be determined from the given information.

43. A B C D E   **43.** For what values of m is $m^2 + 4$ equal to $4m$?

(A) -2 only   (D) $+4$ only

(B) 0 only   (E) more than one value

(C) $+2$ only

44. A B C D E   **44.** If $x = 0$, and $y = 2$, and $x^2yz + 3xz^2 + y^2z + 3y + 4x = 0$, what is the value of z?

(A) $-\dfrac{4}{3}$

(B) $-\dfrac{3}{2}$

(C) $+\dfrac{3}{4}$

(D) $+\dfrac{4}{3}$

(E) cannot be determined from the given information

45. If $c + 4d = 3c - 2d$, what is the ratio of c to d?

(A) $1:3$ (D) $2:3$
(B) $1:-3$ (E) $2:-3$
(C) $3:1$

46. If $3 < x < 7$, and $6 > x > 2$, which of the following best describes x?

(A) $2 < x < 6$
(B) $2 < x < 7$
(C) $3 < x < 6$
(D) $3 < x < 7$
(E) no value of x can satisfy both of these conditions.

47. What are the coordinates of the midpoint of the line segment whose endpoints are $(4,9)$ and $(5,15)$?

(A) $(4,5)$ (D) $(4.5,12)$
(B) $(5,9)$ (E) $(9,24)$
(C) $(4,15)$

48. If $\dfrac{t^2 + 2t}{2t + 4} = \dfrac{t}{2}$, what does t equal?

(A) -2 only
(B) $+2$ only
(C) any value except $+2$
(D) any value except -2
(E) any value

49. If $x + y = 4$, and $x + z = 9$, what is the value of $(y - z)$?

(A) -5
(B) $+5$
(C) -13
(D) $+13$
(E) cannot be determined from the given information

50. Of the following statements, which are equivalent?

I. $-3 < x < 3$
II. $x^2 < 9$
III. $\dfrac{1}{x} < \dfrac{1}{3}$

(A) I and II only
(B) I and III only
(C) II and III only
(D) I, II, and III
(E) none of the above

ANSWER KEY FOR PRACTICE 4

1. A	14. C	26. A	39. D
2. A	15. D	27. D	40. C
3. C	16. A	28. A	41. C
4. C	17. B	29. B	42. B
5. E	18. E	30. D	43. C
6. D	19. A	31. E	44. B
7. D	20. E	32. D	45. C
8. D	21. E	33. B	46. C
9. D	22. D	34. E	47. D
10. C	23. D	35. E	48. D
11. D	24. E	36. E	49. A
12. B	25. C	37. A	50. A
13. B		38. E	

ANSWERS AND SOLUTIONS FOR PRACTICE TEST 4

1. **(A)** The original equation is $3x + 9 = 21 + 7x$. First subtract 9 and $7x$ from both sides to get: $-4x = 12$. Now divide both sides by the coefficient of x, -4, obtaining the solution, $x = -3$. (406)

2. **(A)** Given $2z + 4 > x - 6$. Subtracting equal quantities from both sides of an inequality does not change the order of the inequality. Therefore, subtracting z and 4 from both sides gives a solution of $z > -10$. (419, 420)

3. **(C)** Substitute -3 for x in the original equation to get the following:

$$a(-3)^2 + 2(-3) - 3 = 0$$
$$9a - 6 - 3 = 0$$
$$9a - 9 = 0$$
$$a = 1$$ (406)

4. **(C)** To find the midpoint of the line segment connecting two points, find the point whose x-coordinate is the average of the two given x-coordinates, and whose y-coordinate is the average of the two given y-coordinates. The midpoint here will be $\left(\dfrac{0+4}{2}, \dfrac{8+2}{2}\right)$, or $(2,5)$. (412)

5. **(E)** Divide both sides of the equation by πh:

$$\frac{V}{\pi h} = r^2$$

Take the square root of both sides:

$$r \text{ equals } \sqrt{\frac{V}{\pi h}}.$$ (408)

6. **(D)** Factor the original expression into $x(x-3) < 0$. In order for the product of two expressions to be less than 0 (negative), one must be positive and the other must be negative. Thus, $x < 0$ and $x - 3 > 0$; or $x > 0$ and $x - 3 < 0$. In the first case, $x < 0$ and $x > 3$. This is impossible because x cannot be less than 0 and greater than 3 at the same time. In the second case $x > 0$ and $x < 3$ which can be rewritten as $0 < x < 3$. (428)

7. **(D)** Divide both sides of the equation $2y = 8x + 32$ by 2 to get $y = 4x + 16$. Now it is in the form of $y = mx + b$, where m is the slope of the line and b is the Y intercept. Thus the slope of the line is 4. Any line parallel to this line must have the same slope. The answer must have a slope of 4. This is the line $y = 4x + 32$. Note that all of the choices are already in the form of $y = mx + b$. (416)

8. **(D)** Subtract 1.01 from both sides to give: $4.04x = 8.08$. Dividing both sides by 4.04 gives a solution of $x = 2$. (406)

9. **(D)** If a product is equal to zero, then one of the factors must equal zero. If $(x + 1)(x - 2) = 0$, either $x + 1 = 0$, or $x - 2 = 0$. Solving these two equations, we see that either $x = -1$; or $x = 2$. (408, 409)

10. **(C)** It is possible, but time-consuming, to examine the various ranges of x, but it will be quicker if you realize that the same factors appear, with numerical multiples, more than once in the expression. Properly factored, the expression becomes:

$$-4(x + 2)^4(3 - x)^2 = (x + 2)(2 + x)^2(2)(x + 2)(3 - x)(-2)(3 - x)$$

Since squares of real numbers can never be negative, the whole product has only one negative term, and is therefore negative, except when one of the terms is zero, in which case the product is also zero. Thus, the product cannot be larger than zero for any x. (428)

11. **(D)** Combine like terms on both sides of the given equations and obtain the equivalent form: $k - 9 = k + 6$. This is true for no values of k. If k is subtracted from both sides, -9 will equal 6 which is impossible. (406)

12. **(B)** Substitute for the given values of a, b, and c and obtain $p = q^2 - 2q + 1$; or rearranging terms, $p = (q - 1)^2$. (409)

13. **(B)** $A + B + C = 10$. Also, $A + B = 7$. Substitute the value 7 for the quantity $(A + B)$ in the first equation and obtain the new equation: $7 + C = 10$ or $C = 3$. $A - B = 5$ could be used with the other two equations to find the values of A and B. (406)

14. **(C)** If $5x + 15 > 20$, then subtract 15 from both sides to get $5x > 5$. Now divide both sides by 5. This does not change the order of the inequality because 5 is a positive number. The solution is $x > 1$. (419, 426)

15. **(D)** Factor $(t^2 - 1)$ to obtain the product $(t + 1)(t - 1)$. For any value of t, except 1, the equation is equivalent to $(t + 1) = 2$, or $t = 1$. One is the only possible value of t. However this value is not possible as $t - 1$ would equal 0, and the quotient $\dfrac{t^2 - 1}{t - 1}$ would not be defined. (404, 409)

16. **(A)** If $4m = 9n$, then $m = \dfrac{9n}{4}$. Multiplying both sides of the equation by

7, we obtain: $7m = \dfrac{63n}{4}$.   (403)

17. **(B)**

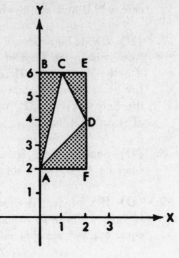

As the diagram shows, the easiest way to calculate the area of this triangle is to start with the area of the enclosing rectangle, and subtract the three shaded triangles.

The area of the rectangle $ABEF = (2)(4) = 8$ square units.

The area of the triangle $ABC = \frac{1}{2}(1)(4) = 2$ square units.

The area of the triangle $CDE = \frac{1}{2}(1)(2) = 1$ square unit.

The area of the triangle $ADF = \frac{1}{2}(2)(2) = 2$ square units.

Thus the area of the triangle $ACD = 8 - 5 = 3$ square units.   (418)

18. **(E)** Since $s = \frac{1}{2}gt^2$ divide both sides of the equation by $\frac{1}{2}g$, to obtain the

form, $\dfrac{2s}{g} = t^2$. Then, after taking the square roots, $t = \sqrt{\dfrac{2s}{g}}$.   (403)

19. **(A)** The sum of the three angles of a triangle must be 180°. Since angle A is 30°, and angle B is between 90° and 180° (it is obtuse) their sum is greater than 120°, and less than 180° (the sum of all three angles is 180°). Their sum subtracted from the total of 180° gives a third angle greater than zero, but less than 60°.   (419)

20. **(E)** An isosceles triangle has two equal sides. To find the length of the sides, we use the distance formula, $\sqrt{(x_2 - x_1)^2 + (y_2 - y_1)^2}$. In the first case the length of the sides are 4, $2\sqrt{2}$ and $2\sqrt{2}$. Thus two sides have the same length and it is an isosceles triangle. The only set of points which is not an isosceles triangle is the last one.   (411)

21. **(E)** The smallest possible value of a is 2, and the smallest possible value of b is 3, so the smallest possible value of $a + b$ must be $2 + 3 = 5$. Similarly, the largest values of a and b are 5 and 6, respectively, so the largest possible of $a + b$ is 11. Thus, the sum must be between 5 and 11.   (419)

22. **(D)** If the sides of the original square are each equal to s, then the area of the square is s^2, and the diagonal is $s\sqrt{2}$. Now, a new square, with an area

of $2s^2$, must have a side of $s\sqrt{2}$. Thus, the diagonal is $2s$, which is $\sqrt{2}$ times the original length of the diagonal. (302, 303)

23. **(D)** First place all of the variable terms on one side and all of the numerical terms on the other side. Subtracting $7.7y$ and adding 4 to both sides of the equation gives $1.1y = 11$. Now divide both sides by 1.1 to solve for $y = 10$. (406)

24. **(E)** To determine whether an expression is a factor of another expression give the variable a specific value in both expressions. An expression divided by its factor will be a whole number. If we give x the value 0, then the expression $2x^2 + 1$ has the value of 1. $x + 2$ then has the value of 2. 1 is not divisible by 2, so the first choice is not a factor. The next choice has the value of -2; also not a factor of 1. Similarly $x + \sqrt{2}$ and $x - \sqrt{2}$ take on the values of $\sqrt{2}$ and $-\sqrt{2}$ respectively when $x = 0$ and are not factors of $2x^2 + 1$. Therefore, the correct choice is (E). (409)

25. **(C)** Let x equal the average salary of the employees. Then the employees receive a total of $10x$ dollars, and the businessman receives six times the average, or $6x$. Together, the eleven of them receive a total of $10x + 6x = 16x$, which equals \$64,000. Thus, x equals \$4,000, and the businessman's salary is $6x$, or \$24,000. (406)

26. **(A)** $6x + 3 = 15$, therefore $6x = 12$ and $x = 2$. Substituting $x = 2$ into the expression $12x - 3$, gives $24 - 3$ which equals 21. (406)

27. **(D)** $2p + 7 > 3p - 5$. To both sides of the equation add 5 and subtract $2p$ obtaining $12 > p$. Thus, p is less than 12. (419, 426)

28. **(A)** Substituting 1 for x in the given equation obtains $1 + q + 1 = 0$, or $q + 2 = 0$. This is solved only for $q = -2$. (406)

29. **(B)**

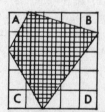

The area of the shaded figure can most easily be found by taking the area of the square surrounding it (25), and subtracting the areas of the four triangles marked A (1), B (2), C (3), and D (6), leaving an area of $25 - (1 + 2 + 3 + 6) = 13$ square units. (418)

30. **(D)** If the number b is equal to zero, the quotient $\dfrac{a}{b}$ is not defined. For all other pairs, all five statements are true. (401–405)

31. **(E)** If a product equals zero, one of the factors must be equal to zero also. Thus, either $x - 1 = 0$, or $x - 2 = 0$, or $x^2 - 4 = 0$. The possible solutions, therefore, are $x = 1$, $x = 2$, and $x = -2$. (408)

32. **(D)** Solve the equation $P + Q = R$, for Q (the variable we wish to eliminate), to get $Q = R - P$. Substituting this for Q in the second equation, yields $P + R = 2(R - P) = 2R - 2P$, or $3P = R$. Therefore, the ratio of P to R is $\dfrac{P}{R}$, or $\dfrac{1}{3}$. (406)

33. **(B)** The fraction in question will equal zero if the numerator equals zero, and the denominator is non-zero. The expression $r^2 + 5r + 6$ can be factored into $(r + 2)(r + 3)$. As long as r is not equal to -2 the equation is defined and $r + 2$ can be cancelled in the original equation to yield $r + 3 = 0$, or $r = -3$. For r equals -2 the denominator is equal to zero and the fraction in the original equation is not defined. (404, 409)

34. **(E)** This problem can be shortened considerably by factoring the expression $a^2 b + 4ab^2 + 4b^3$ into the product $(b)(a + 2b)^2$. Now, since $b = 5$, and $(a + 2b) = 25$, our product equals $5 \times 25 \times 25$, or 3125. (409)

35. **(E)** Subtract $m + 2n$ from both sides of the given equation and obtain the equivalent form, $2n = 7m$. Dividing this equation by $2m$ gives $\dfrac{n}{m} = \dfrac{7}{2}$, the ratio of n to m. (406)

36. **(E)** The product will be positive in the case: a positive and b positive, or a negative and b negative; and negative in the case: a positive and b negative, or a negative and b positive. Thus, the positive products must be $(+2)(+1)$ and $(-5)(-7)$. The largest positive value is $+35$. Similarly, the negative products are $(-5)(+1)$ and $(+2)(-7)$; and the most negative value that can be obtained is -14. Thus, the product falls between -14 and $+35$. (419)

37. **(A)** As can be seen from a diagram, this triangle must be a right triangle, since the line from $(-5,1)$ to $(-5,4)$ is vertical, and the line from $(-5,4)$ to $(2,4)$ is horizontal. The lengths of these two perpendicular sides are 3 and 7, respectively. Since the area of a right triangle is half the product of the perpendicular sides, the area is equal to $\frac{1}{2} \times 3 \times 7$, or 10.5. (410, 418)

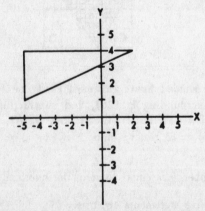

38. **(E)** Solving the first equation for A, gives $A = 12 - B$. Solving the second equation for C gives $C = 16 - B$. Thus, the sum $A + C$ is equal to $28 - 2B$. There is nothing to determine the value of B so the sum of A and C is not determined from the information given. (406)

39. (D) The value of $b^2 - 4ac$ determines the nature of the roots. From the equation substitute $a = 1$, $b = 1$ and $c = 1$ into the expression. $b^2 - 4ac = 1 - 4 = -3$. As $b^2 - 4ac$ is negative, there are no real solutions to the equation. (408)

40. (C) If we graph the five choices we will get:

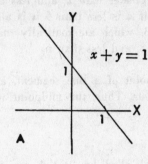

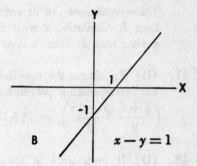

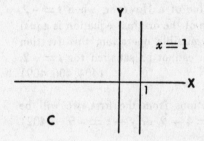

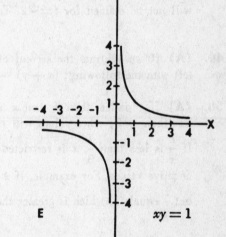

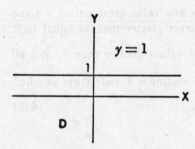

The only choice which is a vertical line is $x = 1$. (413)

41. (C) The factors of $x^2 + 3x + 2$ are $(x + 1)$ and $(x + 2)$. Either $x + 1 = 0$, or $x + 2 = 0$. x may equal either -1 or -2. (408)

42. (B) $a + b = 12$ and $a - b = 6$. Rewrite these equations as $a = 12 - b$ and $a = 6 + b$. $12 - b$ and $6 + b$ are both equal to a. Or, $12 - b = 6 + b$. Thus, $6 = 2b$ and $b = 3$. (407)

43. (C) Let $m^2 + 4 = 4m$. Subtracting $4m$ from both sides yields $m^2 - 4m + 4 = 0$. Factor to get the following equation: $(m - 2)^2 = 0$. Thus, $m = 2$ is the only solution. (408)

44. (B) Substitute for the given values of x and y, obtaining: $(0)^2 (2) (z) + (3)(0)(z)^2 + (2)^2(z) + (3)(2) + (4)(0) = 0$. Perform the indicated multiplications, and combine terms. $0(z) + 0(z^2) + 4z + 6 + 0 = 4z + 6 = 0$. This equation has $z = -\frac{3}{2}$ as its only solution. (406)

45. (C) $c + 4d = 3c - 2d$. Add $2d - c$ to each side and get: $6d = 2c$. (Be especially careful about your signs here.) Dividing by $2d$: $\dfrac{c}{d} = \dfrac{6}{2} = \dfrac{3}{1}$. Thus, $c : d = 3 : 1$. (406)

46. (C) x must be greater than 3, less than 7, greater than 2, and less than 6. These conditions can be reduced as follows: if x is less than 6 it is also less than 7. Similarly, x must be greater than 3, which automatically makes it greater than 2. Thus, x must be greater than 3, and less than 6. (419)

47. (D) To obtain the coordinates of the midpoint of a line segment, average the corresponding coordinates of the endpoints. Thus, the midpoint will be $\left(\dfrac{4 + 5}{2}, \dfrac{9 + 15}{2} \right)$, or $(4.5, 12)$. (412)

48. (D) If both sides of the equation are multiplied by $2t + 4$, we obtain: $t^2 + 2t = t^2 + 2t$, which is true for every value of t. However, when $t = -2$, the denominator of the fraction on the left side of the original equation is equal to zero. Since division by zero is not a permissible operation, this fraction will not be defined for $t = -2$. The equation cannot be satisfied for $t = -2$. (404, 406, 409)

49. (A) If we subtract the second of our equations from the first, we will be left with the following: $(x + y) - (x + z) = 4 - 9$, or $y - z = -5$. (402)

50. (A) If x^2 is less than 9, then x may take on any value greater than -3 and less than $+3$; other values will produce squares greater than or equal to 9. If $\dfrac{1}{x}$ is less than $\dfrac{1}{3}$, x is restricted to positive values greater than 3, and all negative values. For example, if $x = 1$, then conditions I and II are satisfied, but $\dfrac{1}{x}$ equals 1, which is greater than $\dfrac{1}{3}$. (419)

MATH REFRESHER
SESSION 5

Geometry Problems

BASIC DEFINITIONS

500. *Plane geometry* deals with points and lines. A point has no dimensions and is generally represented by a dot (.). A line has no thickness, but it does have length. Lines can be straight or curved but here it will be assumed that a line is straight unless it is otherwise indicated. All lines have infinite length. Part of a line which has a finite length is called a line segment.

Remember the word *distance* always means the perpendicular distance. Thus, the distance between two lines pictured below is line *A* as this is the only perpendicular line. Also, the distance from a line to a point is the perpendicular from the point to the line. Thus, *AB* is the distance from the point *A* to the line segment *CBD*.

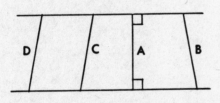
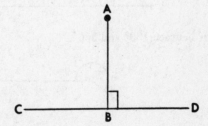

501. *Angles.* An angle is formed when two lines intersect at a point.

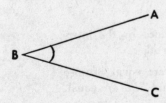

Angle *B*, angle *ABC*, ∠*B*, ∠*ABC* are all possible names for the angle shown.

The measure of the angle is given in degrees. If the sides of the angle form a straight line, then the angle is said to be a straight angle and has 180°. A circle has 360° and a straight angle is a turning through a half circle. All other angles are either greater or less than 180°.

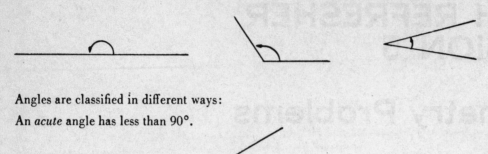

Angles are classified in different ways:

An *acute* angle has less than 90°.

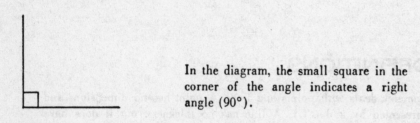

A *right* angle has exactly 90°.

In the diagram, the small square in the corner of the angle indicates a right angle (90°).

An *obtuse* angle has between 90° and 180°.

A *straight* angle has exactly 180°.

A *reflex* angle has between 180° and 360°.

502. Two angles are *complementary* if their sum is 90°. For example, an angle of 30° and an angle of 60° are complementary. Two angles are *supplementary* if their sum is 180°. If one angle is 82°, then its supplement is 98°.

503. ˙ *Vertical angles.* These are pairs of opposite angles formed by the intersection of two straight lines. Vertical angles are always equal to each other.

> **Example:** In the diagram shown, angles *AEC* and *BED* are equal because they are vertical angles. For the same reason, angles *AED* and *BEC* are equal.

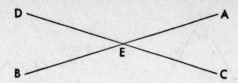

504. When a pair of parallel lines are crossed by a third straight line (called a *transversal*), then all the acute angles formed are equal, and all of the obtuse angles are equal.

Example: In the diagram below, angles 1, 4, 5, and 8 are all equal. Angles 2, 3, 6, and 7 are also equal.

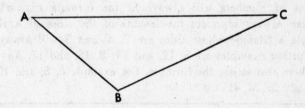

TRIANGLES

505. *Triangles.* A triangle is a closed figure with three sides, each side being a line segment. The sum of the angles of a triangle is *always* 180°.

506. *Scalene triangles* are triangles with no two sides equal. Scalene triangles also have no two angles equal.

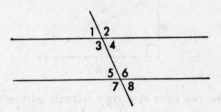

507. *Isosceles triangles* have two equal sides and two equal angles formed by the equal sides and the unequal side. See the figure below.

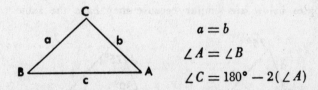

$$a = b$$
$$\angle A = \angle B$$
$$\angle C = 180° - 2(\angle A)$$

508. *Equilateral triangles* have all three sides and all three angles equal. Since the sum of the three angles of a triangle is 180°, each angle of an equilateral triangle is 60°.

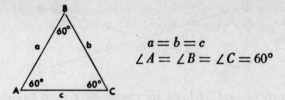

$$a = b = c$$
$$\angle A = \angle B = \angle C = 60°$$

509. A *right triangle* has one angle equal to a right angle (90°). The sum of the other two angles of a right triangle is, therefore, 90°. The most important relationship in a right triangle is the *Pythagorean theorem*. It states that $c^2 = a^2 + b^2$ where c is the length of the side opposite the right angle and a and b are the lengths of the other two sides. Recall that this was discussed in Section 317.

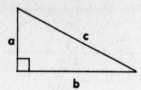

Example: If the two sides of a right triangle adjacent to the right angle are 3 inches and 4 inches respectively, find the length of the side opposite the right angle.

Solution:

Use the Pythagorean theorem, $c^2 = a^2 + b^2$, where $a = 3$ and $b = 4$. Then, $c^2 = 3^2 + 4^2$ or $c^2 = 9 + 16 = 25$. Thus $c = 5$.

Certain sets of numbers will always fit the formula $c^2 = a^2 + b^2$. These numbers can always represent the lengths of the sides of a right triangle. For example a triangle whose sides are 3, 4, and 5 will always be a right triangle. Further examples are 5, 12, and 13; 8, 15, and 17. Any multiples of these numbers also satisfy the formula. For example 6, 8, and 10; 9, 12, and 15; 10, 24, and 26; 24, 45, and 51 etc.

PROPERTIES OF TRIANGLES

510. Two triangles are said to be *similar* (having the same shape) if their corresponding angles are equal. The sides of similar triangles are in the same proportion. The two triangles below are similar because they have the same corresponding angles.

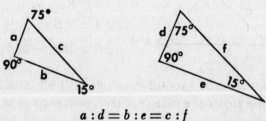

$$a : d = b : e = c : f$$

Example: Two triangles both have angles of 30°, 70° and 80°. If the sides of the triangles are as indicated below, find the length of side *x*.

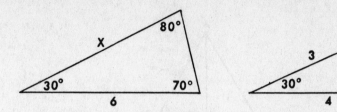

Solution: The two triangles are similar because they have the same corresponding angles. The corresponding sides of similar triangles are in proportion, so $x : 3 = 6 : 4$. This can be rewritten as $\frac{x}{3} = \frac{6}{4}$. Multiplying both sides by 3 gives $x = \frac{18}{4}$, or $x = 4\frac{1}{2}$.

511. Two triangles are *congruent* (*identical* in shape and size) if any one of the following conditions is met:

1. Each side of the first triangle equals the corresponding side of the second triangle.

2. Two sides of the first triangle equal the corresponding sides of the second triangle and their included angles are equal. The included angle is formed by the two sides of the triangle.

3. Two angles of the first triangle equal the corresponding angles of the second triangle, and any pair of corresponding sides are equal.

Example: Triangles *ABC* and *DEF*, in the diagram below, are congruent if any one of the following conditions can be met:

1. The three sides are equal (*sss*) = (*sss*).

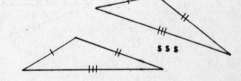

2. Two sides and the included angle are equal (*sas*) = (*sas*).

3. Two angles and any one side are equal (*aas*) = (*aas*) or (*asa*) = (*asa*).

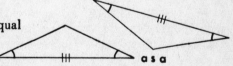

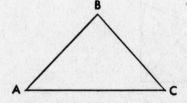
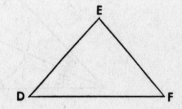

Example: In the equilateral triangle below, line *AD* is perpendicular (forms a right angle) to side *BC*. If the length of *BD* is 5 feet, what is the length of *DC*?

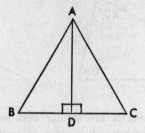

Solution: Since the large triangle is an equilateral triangle, each ∠ is 60°. Therefore ∠*B* is 60° and ∠*C* is 60°. Thus, ∠*B* = ∠*C*. *ADB* and *ADC* are both right angles and are equal. Two angles of each triangle are equal to the corresponding two angles of the other triangle. Side *AD* is shared by both triangles and side *AB* = side *AC*. Thus, according to condition 3 in Section 511, the two triangles are congruent. Then *BD* = *DC* and, since *BD* is 5 feet, *DC* is 5 feet.

512. The *medians* of a triangle are the lines drawn from each vertex to the mid-point of its opposite side. The medians of a triangle cross at a point which divides each median into two parts: one part of one third the length of the median and the other part of two thirds the length.

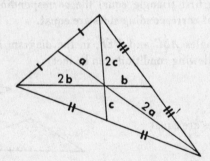

513. The *angle bisectors* of a triangle are the lines that divide each angle of the triangle into two equal parts. These lines meet in a point which is the center of a circle inscribed in the triangle.

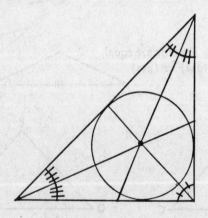

514. The *altitudes* of the triangle are lines drawn from the vertices perpendicular to the opposite sides. The lengths of these lines are useful in calculating the area of the triangle since the area of the triangle is $\frac{1}{2}$(base) (height) and the height is identical to the altitude.

515. The *perpendicular bisectors* of the triangle are the lines which bisect and are perpendicular to each of the three sides. The point where these lines meet is the center of the circumscribed circle.

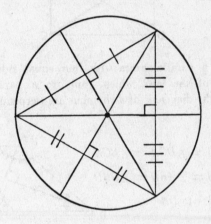

516. The sum of any two sides of a triangle is greater than the third side.

Example: If the three sides of a triangle are 4, 2, and x, then what is known about the value of x?

Solution: Since the sum of two sides of a triangle is always greater than the third side, then $4 + 2 > x$, $4 + x > 2$, and $2 + x > 4$. These three inequalities can be rewritten as $6 > x$, $x > -2$ and $x > 2$. For x to be greater than -2 and 2, it must be greater than 2. Thus, the values of x are $2 < x < 6$.

FOUR-SIDED FIGURES

517. A *parallelogram* is a four-sided figure with each pair of opposite sides parallel.

A parallelogram has the following properties:

1. Each pair of opposite sides are equal. ($AD = BC$, $AB = DC$)

2. The diagonals bisect each other. ($AF = FC$, $DF = FB$)

3. The opposite angles are equal. ($\angle A = \angle C$, $\angle D = \angle B$)

4. One diagonal divides the parallelogram into two congruent triangles. Two diagonals divide the parallelogram into two pairs of congruent triangles.

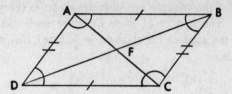

518. A *rectangle* is a parallelogram in which all the angles are right angles. Since a rectangle is a parallelogram, all of the laws which apply to a parallelogram apply to a rectangle. In addition, the diagonals of a rectangle are equal.

$$AC = BD$$

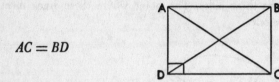

519. A *rhombus* is a parallelogram with four equal sides. Since a rhombus is a parallelogram, all of the laws which apply to a parallelogram, apply to a rhombus. In addition, the diagonals of a rhombus are perpendicular to each other and bisect the vertex angles.

$$\angle DAC = \angle BAC = \angle DCA = \angle BCA$$
$$\angle ADB = \angle CDB = \angle ABD = \angle CBD$$

AC is perpendicular to DB

520. A *square* is a rectangular rhombus. Thus the square has the following properties:

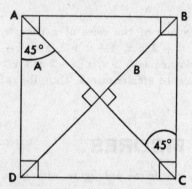

1. All four sides equal. ($AB = BC = CD = DA$)

2. Opposite pairs of sides are parallel. ($AD \parallel BC$, $AB \parallel DC$)

3. Diagonals are equal, perpendicular to each other, and bisect each other.
   ($AC = BD$, $AC \perp BD$, $AE = EC = DE = EB$)

4. All the angles are right angles (90°). ($\angle A = \angle B = \angle C = \angle D = 90°$)

5. Diagonals intersect the vertices at 45°. ($\angle DAC = \angle BAC = 45°$, and similarly for the other 3 vertices)

MANY-SIDED FIGURES

521. A *polygon* is a closed plane figure whose sides are straight lines. The sum of the angles in any polygon is equal to $180(n-2)°$, where n is the number of sides. Thus, in a polygon of 3 sides (a triangle), the sum of the angles is $180(3-2)°$ or $180°$.

522. A *regular polygon* is a polygon all of whose sides are equal and all of whose angles are equal. These polygons have special properties:

1. A regular polygon can be inscribed in a circle and can be circumscribed about another circle. For example, a hexagon is inscribed in a circle in the diagram below.

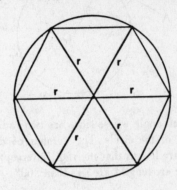

2. Each angle of a polygon is equal to the sum of the angles divided by the number of sides, $\dfrac{180(n-2)°}{n}$. Thus, a square, which is a regular polygon of 4 sides, has each angle equal to $\dfrac{180(4-2)°}{4}$ or $90°$.

523. An important regular polygon is the *hexagon*. The diagonals of a regular hexagon divide it into 6 equilateral triangles, the sides of which are equal to the sides of the hexagon. If a hexagon is inscribed in a circle, the length of each side is equal to the length of the radius of the circle. (See diagram of hexagon.)

CIRCLES

524. A *circle* (also see Section 310) is a set of points equidistant from a given point, the *center*. The distance from the center to the circle is the *radius*. Any line which connects two points on the circle is a *chord*. A chord through the center of the circle is a *diameter*. On the circle below O is the center, line segment OF is a radius, DOE is a diameter, and AC is a chord.

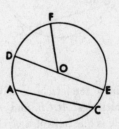

The length of the diameter of a circle is twice the length of the radius. The circumference (length of the curve) is 2π times the length of the radius. π is a constant approximately equal to $\frac{22}{7}$ or 3.14. The formula for the circumference of a circle is, $C = 2\pi r$ where $C =$ circumference and $r =$ radius.

525. A *tangent* to a circle is a line that is perpendicular to a radius and that passes through only one point of the circle. In the diagram AB is a tangent.

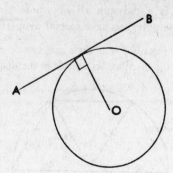

526. A *central angle* is an angle whose sides are two radii of the circle. The vertex of this angle is the center of the circle. The number of degrees in a central angle is equal to the amount of arc length that the radii intercept. As the complete circumference has 360°, any other arc lengths are less than 360°.

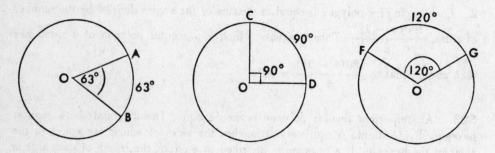

Angles AOB, COD, and FOG are all central angles.

527. An *inscribed angle* of a circle is an angle whose sides are two chords. The vertex of the angle lies on the circumference of the circle. The number of degrees in the inscribed angle is equal to one half the intercepted arc.

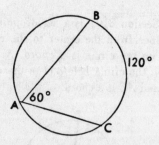

$\angle BAC$ is an inscribed angle.

528. An angle inscribed in a semicircle is always a right angle. $\angle ABC$ and $\angle ADC$ are inscribed in semicircles $AOCB$ and $AOCD$ respectively and are thus right angles. *Note:* A semicircle is one half of a circle.

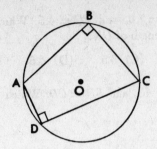

529. Two tangents to a circle from a point outside of the circle are always equal.

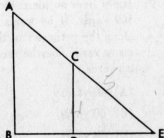

Tangents *AB* and *AD* are equal.

PRACTICE TEST 5

Geometry Problems

Correct answers and solutions follow each test.

1. In the following diagram, angle 1 is equal to 40°, and angle 2 is equal to 150°. What is the number of degrees in angle 3?

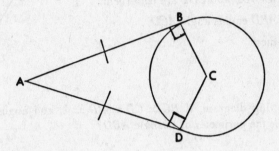

(A) 70°

(B) 90°

(C) 110°

(D) 190°

(E) cannot be determined from the given information

1. A B C D E

2. In this diagram, *AB* and *CD* are both perpendicular to *BE*. If *EC* = 5, and *CD* = 4, what is the ratio of *AB* to *BE*?

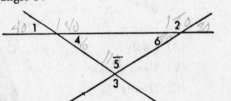

(A) 1 : 1

(B) 4 : 3

(C) 5 : 4

(D) 5 : 3

(E) none of these

2. A B C D E

3.
A B C D E

3. In triangle PQR, $PR = 7.0$, and $PQ = 4.5$. Which of the following cannot possibly represent the length of QR?

(A) 2.0   (B) 3.0   (C) 3.5   (D) 4.5   (E) 5.0

4.
A B C D E

4. In this diagram, $AB = AC$, and $BD = CD$. Which of the following statements is true?

(A) $BE = EC$

(B) AD is perpendicular to BC.

(C) Triangles BDE and CDE are congruent.

(D) Angle ABD equals angle ACD.

(E) All of these

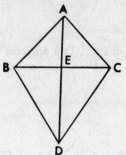

5.
A B C D E

5. In the following diagram, if $BC = CD = BD = 1$, and angle ADC is a right angle, what is the perimeter of triangle ABD?

(A) 3

(B) $2 + \sqrt{2}$

(C) $2 + \sqrt{3}$

(D) $3 + \sqrt{3}$

(E) 4

6.
A B C D E

6. In this diagram, if $PQRS$ is a parallelogram, which of the following can be deduced:

I. $QT + PT = RT + ST$

II. QS is perpendicular to PR

III. The area of the shaded portion is exactly three times the area of triangle QRT.

(A) I only

(B) I and II only

(C) II only

(D) I and III only

(E) I, II, and III

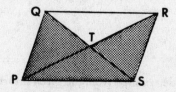

7.
A B C D E

7. James lives on the corner of a rectangular field which measures 120 yards by 160 yards. If he wants to walk to the opposite corner, he can either travel along the perimeter of the field, or cut directly across in a straight line. How many yards does he save by taking the direct route? (Express to the nearest ten yards.)

(A) 40 yards   (D) 100 yards

(B) 60 yards   (E) 110 yards

(C) 80 yards

8. In a square, the perimeter is how many times the length of the diagonal?

(A) $\dfrac{\sqrt{2}}{2}$ (B) $\sqrt{2}$ (C) 2   (D) $2\sqrt{2}$ (E) 4

9. How many degrees are there in the angle formed by two adjacent sides of a regular nonagon (nine-sided polygon)?

(A) 40°   (B) 70°   (C) 105°   (D) 120°   (E) 140°

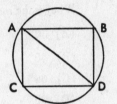

10. In the diagram below, $AB = CD$. From this we can deduce that:

(A) AB is parallel to CD.

(B) AB is perpendicular to BD.

(C) $AC = BD$

(D) Angle ABD equals angle BDC.

(E) Triangle ABD is congruent to triangle ACD.

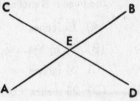

Figure not drawn to scale.

11. If two lines, AB and CD, intersect at a point E, which of the following statements is *not* true?

(A) Angle AEB equals angle CED.

(B) Angles AEC and BEC are complementary.

(C) Angle CED is a straight angle.

(D) Angle AEC equals angle BED.

(E) Angle BED plus angle AED equals 180 degrees.

12. In the following diagram, $AC = CE$ and $BD = DE$. Which of these statements is (are) true?

I. AB is twice as long as CD.

II. AB is parallel to CD.

III. Triangle AEB is similar to triangle CED.

(A) I only

(B) II and III, only

(C) I and III, only

(D) I, II, and III

(E) none of these

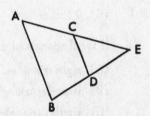

13. In triangle ABC, angle A is obtuse, and angle B equals 30°. Which of the following statements *best* describes angle C?

(A) Angle C must be less than 60°.

(B) Angle C must be less than or equal to 60°.

(C) Angle C must be equal to 60°.

(D) Angle C must be greater than or equal to 60°.

(E) Angle C must be greater than 60°.

14.

14. In this diagram, *ABCD* is a parallelogram, and *BFDE* is a square. If *AB* = 20 and *CF* = 16, what is the perimeter of the parallelogram *ABCD*?

(A) 72

(B) 78

(C) 86

(D) 92

(E) 96

15.

15. The hypotenuse of a right triangle is exactly twice as long as the shorter leg. What is the number of degrees in the smallest angle of the triangle?

(A) 30°

(B) 45°

(C) 60°

(D) 90°

(E) cannot be determined from the given information

16.

16. The legs of an isosceles triangle are equal to 17 inches each. If the altitude to the base is 8 inches long, how long is the base of the triangle?

(A) 15 inches

(B) 20 inches

(C) 24 inches

(D) 25 inches

(E) 30 inches

17.

17. The perimeter of a right triangle is 18 inches. If the midpoints of the three sides are joined by line segments, they form another triangle. What is the perimeter of this new triangle?

(A) 3 inches

(B) 6 inches

(C) 9 inches

(D) 12 inches

(E) cannot be determined from the given information

18.

18. If the diagonals of a square divide it into four triangles, the triangles *cannot* be

(A) right triangles.

(B) isosceles triangles.

(C) similar triangles.

(D) equilateral triangles.

(E) equal in area.

19.

19. In the diagram below, *ABCDEF* is a regular hexagon. How many degrees are there in angle *ADC*?

(A) 45°

(B) 60°

(C) 75°

(D) 90°

(E) none of these

20. This diagram depicts a rectangle inscribed in a circle. If the measurements of the rectangle are 10″ × 14″, what is the area of the circle?

(A) 74π

(B) 92π

(C) 144π

(D) 196π

(E) 296π

21. How many degrees are included between the hands of a clock at 5:00?

(A) 50°   (B) 60°   (C) 75°   (D) 120°   (E) 150°

22. *ABCD* is a square. If the midpoints of the four sides are joined to form a new square, the perimeter of the old square is how many times the perimeter of the new square?

(A) 1   (B) $\sqrt{2}$ (C) 2   (D) $2\sqrt{2}$ (E) 4

23. Angles *A* and *B* of triangle *ABC* are both acute angles. Which of the following *best* describes angle *C*?

(A) Angle *C* is between 0° and 180°.

(B) Angle *C* is between 0° and 90°.

(C) Angle *C* is between 60° and 180°.

(D) Angle *C* is between 60° and 120°.

(E) Angle *C* is between 60° and 90°.

24. The angles of a quadrilateral are in the ratio 1 : 2 : 3 : 4. What is the number of degrees in the largest angle?

(A) 72   (B) 96   (C) 120   (D) 144   (E) 150

25. *ABCD* is a rectangle; the diagonals *AC* and *BD* intersect at *E*. Which of the following statements is *not necessarily true*?

(A) $AE = BE$

(B) Angle *AEB* equals angle *CED*.

(C) *AE* is perpendicular to *BD*.

(D) Triangles *AED* and *AEB* are equal in area.

(E) Angle *BAC* equals angle *BDC*.

26. City A is 200 miles from City B, and City B is 400 miles from City C. Which of the following best describes the distance between City A and City C?
(Note: The cities A, B, C do *not* all lie on a straight line.)

(A) It must be greater than zero.

(B) It must be greater than 200 miles.

(C) It must be less than 600 miles and greater than zero.

(D) It must be less than 600 miles and greater than 200.

(E) It must be exactly 400 miles.

27. A B C D E

27. At 7:30, how many degrees are included between the hands of a clock?

(A) 15°   (B) 30°   (C) 45°   (D) 60°   (E) 75°

28. A B C D E

28. If a ship is sailing in a northerly direction, and then turns to the right until it is sailing in a southwesterly direction, it has gone through a rotation of:

(A) 45°   (B) 90°   (C) 135°   (D) 180°   (E) 225°

29. A B C D E

29. x, y, and z are the angles of a triangle. If $x = 2y$, and $y = z + 30°$, how many degrees are there in angle x?

(A) 22.5°   (B) 37.5°   (C) 52.5°   (D) 90.0°   (E) 105.0°

30. A B C D E

30. In the diagram shown, AB is parallel to CD. Which of the following statements is *not necessarily true*?

(A) $\angle 1 + \angle 2 = 180°$

(B) $\angle 4 = \angle 7$

(C) $\angle 5 + \angle 8 + \angle 2 + \angle 4 = 360°$

(D) $\angle 2 + \angle 3 = 180°$

(E) $\angle 2 = \angle 6$

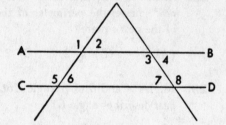

31. A B C D E

31. What is the ratio of the diagonal of a square to the hypotenuse of the isosceles right triangle having the same area?

(A) $1:2$ (B) $1:\sqrt{2}$ (C) $1:1$ (D) $\sqrt{2}:1$ (E) $2:1$

32. A B C D E

32. How many degrees are there between two adjacent sides of a regular ten-sided figure?

(A) 36°   (B) 72°   (C) 120°   (D) 144°   (E) 154°

33. A B C D E

33. Which of the following sets of numbers *cannot* represent the lengths of the sides of a right triangle?

(A) 5, 12, 13

(B) 4.2, 5.6, 7.0

(C) 9, 28, 35

(D) 16, 30, 34

(E) 7.5, 18, 19.5

34. A B C D E

34. How many degrees are there in the angle which is its own supplement?

(A) 30°   (B) 45°   (C) 60°   (D) 90°   (E) 180°

35. A B C D E

35. If a central angle of 45° intersects an arc 6 inches long on the circumference of a circle, what is the radius of the circle?

(A) $\dfrac{24}{\pi}$ inches   (D) 24 inches

(B) $\dfrac{48}{\pi}$ inches   (E) 48 inches

(C) 6π inches

36. What is the length of the line segment connecting the two most distant vertices of a 1-inch cube?

(A) 1 inch
(B) $\sqrt{2}$ inches
(C) $\sqrt{3}$ inches
(D) $\sqrt{5}$ inches
(E) $\sqrt{6}$ inches

36. A B C D E

37. Through how many degrees does the hour hand of a clock move in 70 minutes?

(A) 35° (B) 60° (C) 80° (D) 90° (E) 120°

37. A B C D E

38. In the diagram pictured below, *BA* is tangent to circle *O* at point *A*. *CD* is perpendicular to *OA* at *C*. Which of the following statements is (are) true?

I. Triangles *ODC* and *OBA* are similar.
II. $OA : DC = OB : AB$
III. *AB* is twice as long as *CD*.

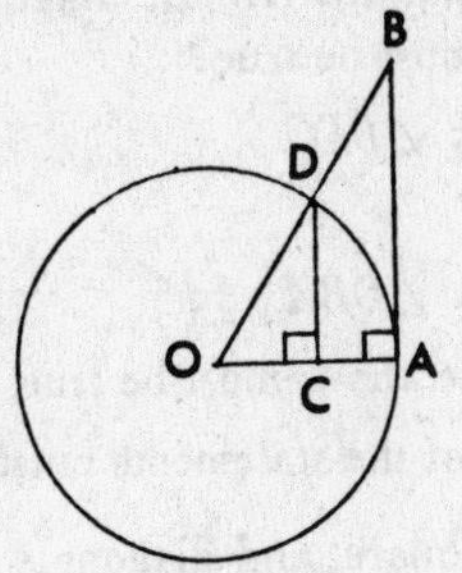

(A) I only
(B) III only
(C) I and II, only
(D) II and III, only
(E) none of the above combinations

38. A B C D E

39. The three angles of triangle *ABC* are in the ratio 1 : 2 : 6. How many degrees are in the largest angle?

(A) 45° (B) 90° (C) 120° (D) 135° (E) 160°

39. A B C D E

40. In this diagram, $AB = AC$, angle $A = 40°$, and *BD* is perpendicular to *AC* at *D*. How many degrees are there in angle *DBC*?

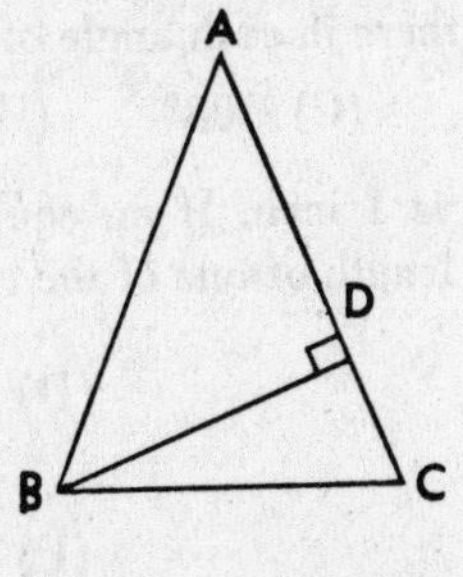

(A) 20°
(B) 40°
(C) 50°
(D) 70°
(E) none of these

40. A B C D E

41. If the line *AB* intersects the line *CD* at point *E*, which of the following pairs of angles need *not* be equal?

(A) $\angle AEB$ and $\angle CED$
(B) $\angle AEC$ and $\angle BED$
(C) $\angle AED$ and $\angle CEA$
(D) $\angle BEC$ and $\angle DEA$
(E) $\angle DEC$ and $\angle BEA$

41. A B C D E

42. All right isosceles triangles must be

(A) similar
(B) congruent
(C) equilateral
(D) equal in area
(E) none of these

42. A B C D E

43. | A | B | C | D | E |

43. What is the area of a triangle whose sides are 10 inches, 13 inches, and 13 inches?

(A) 39 square inches

(B) 52 square inches

(C) 60 square inches

(D) 65 square inches

(E) cannot be determined from the given information

44. | A | B | C | D | E |

44. If each side of an equilateral triangle is 2 inches long, what is the triangle's altitude?

(A) 1 inch

(B) $\sqrt{2}$ inches

(C) $\sqrt{3}$ inches

(D) 2 inches

(E) $\sqrt{5}$ inches

45. | A | B | C | D | E |

45. In the parallelogram $ABCD$, diagonals AC and BD intersect at E. Which of the following must be true?

(A) $\angle AED = \angle BEC$

(B) $AE = EC$

(C) $\angle BDC = \angle DBA$

(D) Two of the above must be true.

(E) All three of the statements must be true.

46. | A | B | C | D | E |

46. If $ABCD$ is a square, and diagonals AC and BD intersect at point E, how many isosceles right triangles are there in the figure?

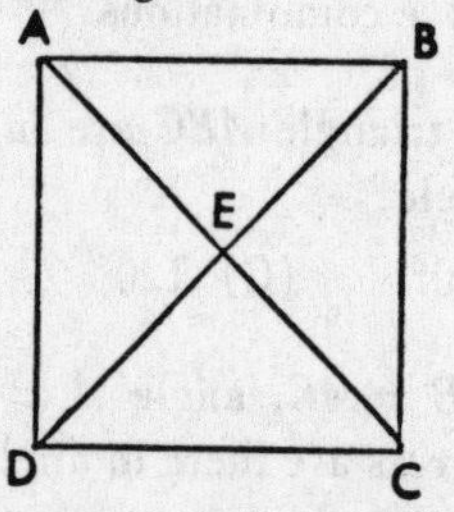

(A) 4

(B) 5

(C) 6

(D) 7

(E) 8

47. | A | B | C | D | E |

47. How many degrees are there in each angle of a regular hexagon?

(A) 60°   (B) 90°   (C) 108°   (D) 120°   (E) 144°

48. | A | B | C | D | E |

48. The radius of a circle is 1 inch. If an equilateral triangle is inscribed in the circle, what will be the length of one of the triangle's sides?

(A) 1 inch

(B) $\dfrac{\sqrt{2}}{2}$ inches

(C) $\sqrt{2}$ inches

(D) $\dfrac{\sqrt{3}}{2}$ inches

(E) $\sqrt{3}$ inches

49. | A | B | C | D | E |

49. If the angles of a triangle are in the ratio $2:3:4$, how many degrees are there in the largest angle?

(A) 20°   (B) 40°   (C) 60°   (D) 80°   (E) 120°

50. | A | B | C | D | E |

50. Which of the following combinations may represent the lengths of the sides of a right triangle?

(A) 4, 6, 8

(B) 12, 16, 20

(C) 7, 17, 23

(D) 9, 20, 27

(E) none of these

ANSWER KEY FOR PRACTICE TEST 5

1. C	14. E	26. D	39. C
2. B	15. A	27. C	40. A
3. A	16. E	28. E	41. C
4. E	17. C	29. E	42. A
5. C	18. D	30. D	43. C
6. D	19. B	31. B	44. C
7. C	20. A	32. D	45. E
8. D	21. E	33. C	46. E
9. E	22. B	34. D	47. D
10. D	23. A	35. A	48. E
11. B	24. D	36. C	49. D
12. D	25. C	37. A	50. B
13. A		38. C	

ANSWERS AND SOLUTIONS
FOR PRACTICE TEST 5

1. **(C)** In the problem it is given that $\angle 1 = 40°$ and $\angle 2 = 150°$. The diagram below makes it apparent that: (1) $\angle 1 = \angle 4$ and $\angle 3 = \angle 5$ (vertical angles); (2) $\angle 6 + \angle 2 = 180°$ (straight angle); (3) $\angle 4 + \angle 5 + \angle 6 = 180°$ (sum of angles in a triangle). To solve the problem, $\angle 3$ must be related through the above information to the known quantities in $\angle 1$ and $\angle 2$. Proceed as follows: $\angle 3 = \angle 5$, but $\angle 5 = 180° - \angle 4 - \angle 6$. $\angle 4 = \angle 1 = 40°$ and $\angle 6 = 180° - \angle 2 = 180° - 150° = 30°$. Therefore, $\angle 3 = 180° - 40° - 30° = 110°$.   (501, 503, 505)

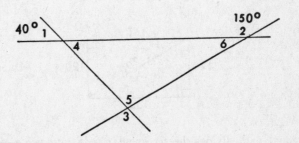

2. **(B)** Since CD is perpendicular to DE, CDE is a right triangle, and using the Pythagorean theorem yields $DE = 3$. Thus, the ratio of CD to DE is $4 : 3$. But triangle ABE is similar to triangle CDE. Therefore $AB : BE = CD : DE = 4 : 3$.   (509, 510)

3. (A) In a triangle, it is impossible for one side to be longer than the sum of the other two (a straight line is the shortest distance between two points). Thus 2.0, 4.5, and 7.0 cannot be three sides of a triangle. (516)

4. (E) $AB = AC$, $BD = CD$, and AD equal to itself is sufficient information (three sides) to prove triangles ABD and ACD congruent. Also, since $AB = AC$, $AE = AE$, and $\angle BAE = \angle CAE$ (by the previous congruence), triangles ABE and ACE are congruent. Since $BD = CD$, $ED = ED$, and angle BDE equals angle CDE (by initial congruence), triangles BDE and CDE are congruent. Through congruence of triangle ABE and triangle ACE, angles BEA and CEA are equal, and their sum is a straight angle (180°). They must both be right angles. Thus, from the given information, we can deduce all the properties given as choices. (511)

5. (C) The perimeter of triangle ABD is $AB + BD + AD$. The length of BD is 1. Since $BC = CD = BD$, triangle BCD is an equilateral triangle. Therefore, angle $C = 60°$ and angle $BDC = 60°$. Angle A + angle $C = 90°$ (the sum of two acute angles in a right triangle is 90°) and angle BDC + angle $BDA = 90°$ (these two angles form a right angle). Since angle C and angle BDC both equal 60°, angle A = angle $BDA = 30°$. Now two angles of triangle ADB are equal. Therefore, triangle ADB is an isosceles triangle with side BD = side AB. Since $BD = 1$ then $AB = 1$. AD is a leg of the right triangle, with side $CD = 1$ and hypotenuse $AC = 2$. ($AC = AB + BC = 1 + 1$.) Using the relationship $c^2 = a^2 + b^2$ gives us the length of AD as $\sqrt{3}$. Thus the perimeter is $1 + 1 + \sqrt{3}$ or $2 + \sqrt{3}$. (505, 507, 509)

6. (D) (I) must be true, since the diagonals of a parallelogram bisect each other, so $QT = ST$, and $PT = RT$. Thus, since the sums of equals are equal, $QT + PT = RT + ST$.

(II) is not necessarily true, and, in fact, can only be true if the parallelogram is also a rhombus (all four sides equal).

(III) is true, since the four small triangles each have the same area. The shaded portion contains three such triangles. This can be seen by noting that the altitudes from point P to the bases of triangles PQT and PTS are identical. We have already seen from part (I) that these bases (QT and TS) are also equal. Therefore, only I and III can be deduced from the given information. (514, 517)

7. (C)

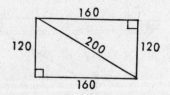

The diagonal path divides the rectangular field into two right triangles. The Pythagorean theorem gives the length of the diagonal as 200 yards. If James takes the route around the perimeter, he will travel $120 + 160$, or 280 yards. Thus, the shorter route saves him 80 yards. (509, 518)

8. (D) Let one side of a square be s. Then the perimeter must be $4s$. The diagonal of a square with side s is equal to $s\sqrt{2}$. Dividing the perimeter by the diagonal produces $2\sqrt{2}$. The perimeter is $2\sqrt{2}$ times the diagonal. (509, 520)

9. **(E)** The sum of the angles of any polygon is equal to $180°(n-2)$, where n is the number of sides. Thus the total number of degrees is a nonagon $= 180°(9-2) = 180° \times 7 = 1260°$. The number of degrees in each angle is $\dfrac{1260°}{n} = \dfrac{1260°}{9} = 140°$. (521, 522)

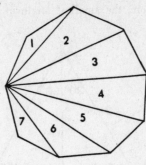

10. **(D)** Since chord AB equals chord CD, it must be true that arc AB equals arc CD. By adding arc AC to arc CD and to arc AB it is apparent that arc ACD is equal to arc CAB. These arcs are intersected by inscribed angles ABD and BDC. Therefore, the two inscribed angles must be equal. If we redraw the figure as shown below, the falseness of statements (A), (B), (C), and (E) becomes readily apparent. (527)

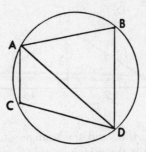

11. **(B)** $\angle AEC + \angle BEC = \angle AEB$, a straight angle (180°). Thus, angles AEC and BEC are *supplementary*. (Complementary means that the two angles add up to a *right* angle, or 90°.) (501, 502)

12. **(D)** Since $AC = CE$ and $BD = DE$, triangles AEB and CED are similar, and AE is twice as long as CE; since by proportionality, $AB : CD = AE : CE = 2 : 1$. From the similarity it is found that angle ABE equals angle CDE, and, therefore, that AB is parallel to CD. Thus, all three statements are true. (504, 510)

13. **(A)** Angle A must be greater than 90°; angle B equals 30°. Thus, the sum of angles A and B must be greater than 120°. Since the sum of the three angles A, B, and C, must be 180°, angle C must be *less than* 60°. (It cannot equal 60°, because then angle A would be a right angle instead of an obtuse angle.) (501, 505)

14. **(E)** CDF is a right triangle with one side of 16 and a hypotenuse of 20. Thus, the third side, DF, equals 12. Since $BFDE$ is a square, BF and ED are also equal to 12. Thus, $BC = 12 + 16 = 28$, and $CD = 20$. $ABCD$ is a parallelogram, so $AB = CD$, $AD = BC$. The perimeter is $28 + 20 + 28 + 20 = 96$. (509, 517, 520)

15. **(A)** Either recognize immediately that the sides of a $30° - 60° - 90°$ triangle are in the proportion $1 : \sqrt{3} : 2$ and the problem is solved. Or, construct an isosceles triangle by placing two of the right triangles so that the unknown sides touch (see diagram). This isosceles triangle is equilateral with angles of $60°$. Therefore, the smallest angle in the right triangle is equal to angle BAC, or $30°$.   (509)

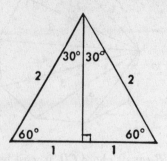

16. **(E)** The altitude to the base of an isosceles triangle divides it into two congruent right triangles, each with one leg of 8 inches, and a hypotenuse of 17 inches. By the Pythagorean theorem, the third side of each right triangle must be 15 inches long. The base of the isosceles triangle is the sum of two such sides, totaling 30 inches.   (507, 509, 514)

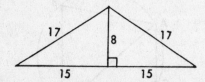

17. **(C)** Call the triangle ABC, and the triangle of midpoints PQR, where P is the midpoint of BC, Q is the midpoint of AC, and R is the midpoint of AB. Then, PQ is equal to half the length of AB, $QR = \frac{1}{2}BC$, and $PR = \frac{1}{2}AC$. This has nothing to do with the fact that ABC is a right triangle. Thus, the perimeter of the small triangle is equal to $PQ + QR + PR = \frac{1}{2}(AB + BC + AC)$. The new perimeter is half the old perimeter, or 9 inches.   (509, 510, 512)

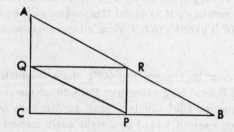

18. **(D)** The diagonals of the square form four right triangles, each of which is isosceles because each has two $45°$ angles. The triangles are all identical in shape and size so they all are similar and have the same area. The only choice left is equilateral, which cannot be true, since then the sum of the angles at the intersection of the diagonals must be $360°$. The sum of four $60°$ angles would be only $240°$.   (520)

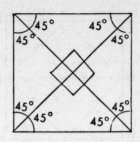

19. (B) First, draw in the lines *CF* and *BE*. These intersect *AD* at its midpoint (also the midpoint of *CF* and *BE*), and divide the hexagon into six equilateral triangles. Since *ADC* is an angle of one of these equilateral triangles, it must be equal to 60°. (Another way to do this problem is to calculate the number of degrees in one angle of a regular hexagon, and divide this by 2.)

(508, 523)

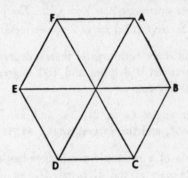

20. (A) The diagonal of an inscribed rectangle is equal to the diameter of the circle. To find this length use the Pythagorean theorem on one of the two triangles formed by two of the sides of the rectangle and the diagonal. Thus, the square of the diagonal is equal to $10^2 + 14^2 = 100 + 196 = 296$. The area of the circle is equal to π times the square of the radius. The square of the radius of the circle is one-fourth of the diameter squared (since $d = 2r$, $d^2 = 4r^2$) or 74. Thus, the area is 74π. (509, 518, 524)

21. (E) Each number on a clock (or hour marking) represents an angle of 30° as 360° divided by 12 is 30°, (a convenient fact to remember for other clock problems). Since the hands of the clock are on the 12 and the 5, there are five hour units between the hands; $5 \times 30° = 150°$. (501, 526)

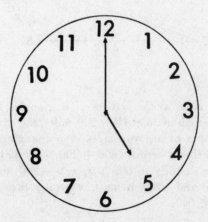

22. (B)

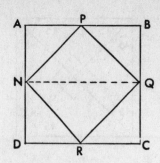

Let S represent the side of the large square. Then the perimeter is $4S$. Let s represent the side of the smaller square. Then the perimeter is $4s$. Line NQ is the diagonal of the smaller square, so the length of NQ is $\sqrt{2}s$. (The diagonal of a square is $\sqrt{2}$ times the side.) Now, NQ is equal to DC, or S, which is the side of the larger square. So now $S = \sqrt{2}s$. The perimeter of the large square equals $4S = 4\sqrt{2}s = \sqrt{2}(4s) = \sqrt{2} \times$ perimeter of the small square. (520)

23. (A) Angles A and B are both greater than 0 degrees and less than 90 degrees, so their sum is between 0 degrees and 180 degrees. Then angle C must be between 0 and 180 degrees. (501, 505)

24. (D) Let the four angles be x, $2x$, $3x$, and $4x$. The sum, $10x$, must equal $360°$. Thus, $x = 36°$, and the largest angle, $4x$, is $144°$. (505)

25. (C) The diagonals of a rectangle are perpendicular only when the rectangle is a square. AE is part of the diagonal AC, so AE will not necessarily be perpendicular to BD. (518)

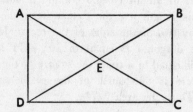

26. (D)

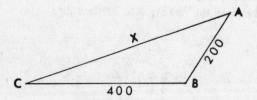

Draw the three cities as the vertices of a triangle. The length of side CB is 400 miles, the length of side AB is 200 miles and x, the length of side AC, is unknown. The sum of any two sides of a triangle is greater than the third side, or in algebraic terms: $400 + 200 > x$, $400 + x > 200$ and $200 + x > 400$. These simplify to $600 > x$, $x > -200$ and $x > 200$. For x to be greater than 200 and -200, it must be greater than 200. Thus, the values of x are $200 < x < 600$. (506, 516)

27. **(C)** At 7:30, the hour hand is *halfway between the 7 and the 8*, and the minute hand is on the 6. Thus, there are one and one-half "hour units," each equal to 30°, so the whole angle is 45°. (501, 526)

28. **(E)** If a ship is facing north, a right turn of 90° will face it eastward. Another 90° turn will face it south, and an additional 45° turn will bring it to south-west. Thus, the total rotation is $90° + 90° + 45° = 225°$. (501)

29. **(E)** Since $y = z + 30°$ and $x = 2y$, then $x = 2(z + 30°) = 2z + 60°$. Thus, $x + y + z$ equals $(2z + 60°) + (z + 30°) + z = 4z + 90°$. This must equal 180° (the sum of the angles of a triangle). So $4z + 90° = 180°$, and the solution is $z = 22\frac{1}{2}°$; $x = 2z + 60° = 45° + 60° = 105°$. (505)

30. **(D)** Since AB is parallel to CD, angle 2 = angle 6, and angle 3 + angle 7 = 180°. If angle 2 + angle 3 equals 180°, then angle 2 = angle 7 = angle 6. However, since there is no evidence that angles 6 and 7 are equal, angle 2 + angle 3 does not necessarily equal 180°. Therefore, the answer is (D). (504)

31. **(B)** Call the side of the square, s. Then, the diagonal of the square is $\sqrt{2}s$ and the area is s^2. The area of an isosceles right triangle with leg r is $\frac{1}{2}r^2$. Now, the area of the triangle is equal to the area of the square so $s^2 = \frac{1}{2}r^2$. Solving for r gives $r = \sqrt{2}s$. The hypotenuse of the triangle is $\sqrt{r^2 + r^2}$. Substituting $r = \sqrt{2}s$, the hypotenuse is $\sqrt{2s^2 + 2s^2} = \sqrt{4s^2} = 2s$. Therefore, the ratio of the diagonal to the hypotenuse is $\sqrt{2}s : 2s$. Since $\sqrt{2}s : 2s$ is $\dfrac{\sqrt{2}s}{2s}$ or $\dfrac{\sqrt{2}}{2}$, multiply by $\dfrac{\sqrt{2}}{\sqrt{2}}$ which has a value of 1. Thus $\dfrac{\sqrt{2}}{2} \cdot \dfrac{\sqrt{2}}{\sqrt{2}} = \dfrac{2}{2\sqrt{2}} = \dfrac{1}{\sqrt{2}}$ or $1 : \sqrt{2}$, which is the final result. (507, 509, 520)

32. **(D)** The formula for the number of degrees in the angles of a polygon is $180(n - 2)$, where n is the number of sides. For a ten-sided figure this is $10(180°) - 360° = (1800 - 360)° = 1440°$. Since the ten angles are equal, they must each equal 144°. (521, 522)

33. **(C)** If three numbers represent the lengths of the sides of a right triangle, they must satisfy the Pythagorean theorem: the squares of the smaller two must equal the square of the largest one. This condition is met in all the sets given except the set 9,28,35. There, $9^2 + 28^2 = 81 + 784 = 865$, but $35^2 = 1225$. (509)

34. **(D)** Let the angle be x. Since x is its own supplement, then $x + x = 180°$, or, since $2x = 180°$, $x = 90°$. (502)

35. **(A)** The length of the arc intersected by a central angle of a circle is proportional to the number of degrees in the angle. Thus, if a 45° angle cuts off a 6-inch arc, a 360° angle intersects an arc eight times as long, or 48 inches. This is equal to the circle's circumference, or 2π times the radius. Thus, to obtain the radius, divide 48 inches by 2π. 48 inches $\div 2\pi = \dfrac{24}{\pi}$ inches.

(524, 526)

36. **(C)** Refer to the diagram pictured below. Calculate the distance from vertex 1 to vertex 2. This is simply the diagonal of a 1 inch square and equal to $\sqrt{2}$ inches. Now, vertices 1, 2, and 3 form a right triangle, with legs of 1 and $\sqrt{2}$. By the Pythagorean theorem, the hypotenuse is $\sqrt{3}$. This is the distance from vertex 1 to vertex 3, the two most distant vertices. (509, 520)

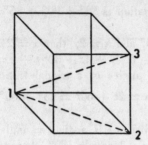

37. **(A)** In one hour, the hour hand of a clock moves through an angle of 30° (one "hour unit"). 70 minutes equals $\frac{7}{6}$ hours so, during that time, the hour hand will move through $\frac{7}{6} \times 30°$, or 35°. (501, 526)

38. **(C)** In order to be similar, two triangles must have corresponding angles equal. This is true of triangles ODC and OBA, since angle O equals itself, and angles OCD and OAB are both right angles. (The third angles of these triangles must be equal, as the sum of the angles of a triangle is always 180°.) Since the triangles are similar, $OD:DC = OB:AB$. But, OD and OA are radii of the same circle and are equal. Therefore, substitute OA for OD in the above proportion. Hence, $OA:DC = OB:AB$. There is, however, no information given on the relative sizes of any of the line segments, so that statement III may or may not be true. (509, 510, 524)

39. **(C)** Let the three angles equal x, $2x$, and $6x$. Then, $x + 2x + 6x = 9x = 180°$. Therefore, $x = 20°$ and $6x = 120°$. (505)

40. **(A)** Since $AB = AC$, angle ABC must equal angle ACB. (Base angles of an isosceles triangle are equal.) As the sum of angles BAC, ABC, and ACB is 180°, and angle BAC equals 40°, angle ABC and angle ACB must each equal 70°. Now, DBC is a right triangle, with angle $BDC = 90°$ and angle $DCB = 70°$. (The three angles must add up to 180°.) Angle DBC must equal 20°. (507, 514)

41. **(C)**

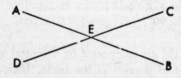

$\angle AEB$ and $\angle CED$ are both straight angles, and are equal; similarly, $\angle DEC$ and $\angle BEA$ are both straight angles. $\angle AEC$ and $\angle BED$ are vertical angles, as are $\angle BEC$ and $\angle DEA$, and are equal. $\angle AED$ and $\angle CEA$ are supplementary, and need not be equal. (501, 502, 503)

42. (A) All right isosceles triangles have angles of 45°, 45°, and 90°. Since all triangles with the same angles are similar, all right isosceles triangles are similar. (507, 509, 510)

43. (C)

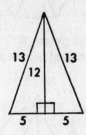

As the diagram shows, the altitude to the base of the isosceles triangle divides it into two congruent right triangles, each with 5-12-13 sides. Thus, the base is 10, height is 12 and the area is $\frac{1}{2}(10)(12) = 60$. (505, 507, 509)

44. (C) The altitude to any side divides the triangle into two congruent 30°-60°-90° right triangles, each with a hypotenuse of 2 inches and a leg of 1 inch. The other leg equals the altitude. By the Pythagorean theorem the altitude is equal to $\sqrt{3}$ inches. (The sides of a 30°-60°-90° right triangle are always in the proportion $1 : \sqrt{3} : 2$. (509, 514)

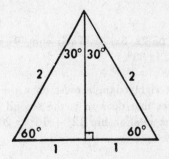

45. (E)

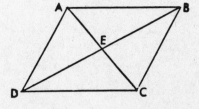

As the diagram illustrates, angles *AED* and *BEC* are vertical and, therefore, equal. *AE = EC*, because the diagonals of a parallelogram bisect each other. Angles *BDC* and *DBA* are equal because they are alternate interior angles of parallel lines (*AB || CD*). (503, 517)

46. (E) There are eight isosceles right triangles: *ABE, BCE, CDE, ADE, ABC, BCD, CDA,* and *ABD*. (520)

47. (D) Recall that a regular hexagon may be broken up into six equilateral triangles.

Since the angles of each triangle are 60°, and two of these angles make up each angle of the hexagon, an angle of the hexagon must be 120°.   (523)

48. (E)

Since the radius equals 1″, AD, the diameter, must be 2″. Now, since AD is a diameter, ACD must be a right triangle, because an angle inscribed in a semicircle is a right angle. Thus, because $\angle DAC = 30°$, it must be a 30°-60°-90° right triangle. The sides will be in the proportion $1 : \sqrt{3} : 2$. As $AD : AC = 2 : \sqrt{3}$, so AC, one of the sides of the equilateral triangle, must be $\sqrt{3}$ inches long.   (508, 524)

49. (D) Let the angles be $2x$, $3x$, $4x$. Their sum, $9x = 180°$ and $x = 20°$. Thus, the largest angle, $4x$, is 80°.   (505)

50. (B) The sides of a right triangle must obey the Pythagorean theorem. The only group of choices that does so is the second : 12, 16, and 20 are in the $3 : 4 : 5$ ratio and the relationship $12^2 + 16^2 = 20^2$ is satisfied.   (509)

MATH REFRESHER
SESSION 6

Miscellaneous Problems Including Averages, Series, Properties of Integers, and Approximations

AVERAGES

601. *Averages.* The average of n numbers is merely their sum, divided by n.

Example: Find the average of: 20, 0, 80 and 12.

Solution: The average is the sum divided by the number of entries, or:

$$\frac{20 + 0 + 80 + 12}{4} = \frac{112}{4} = 28$$

A quick way of obtaining an average of a set of numbers that are close together is the following:

STEP 1. Choose any number which will approximately equal the average.

STEP 2. Subtract this approximate average from each of the numbers (this will give some positive and negative results). Add up the results.

STEP 3. Divide this sum by the number of entries.

STEP 4. Add the result of Step 3 to the approximate average chosen in Step 1. This sum will be the true average.

Example: Find the average of 92, 93, 93, 96 and 97.

Solution: Choose 95 as an approximate average. Subtracting 95 from 92, 93, 93, 96, and 97 gives -3, -2, -2, 1, and 2. The sum is -4. Divide -4

by 5 (the number of entries) to obtain −0.8. Add −0.8 to the original approximation of 95 to get the true average, 95 − 0.8 or 94.2.

SERIES

602.   *Number series or sequences* are progressions of numbers arranged according to some design. By recognizing the type of series from the first four terms, it is possible to know all the terms in the series. Below are given a few different types of number series which appear frequently.

1.   *Arithmetic progressions* are very common. In an arithmetic progression, each term exceeds the previous one by some fixed number.

Example: In the series 3, 5, 7, 9, . . . find the next term.

Solution: Each term in the series is 2 more than the preceding one so that the next term is 9 + 2 or 11.

If the difference in successive terms is negative, then the series decreases.

Example: Find the next term: 100, 93, 86, 79 . . . .

Solution: Each term is 7 less than the previous one, so the next term is 72.

2.   In a *geometric progression* each term equals the previous term multiplied by a fixed number.

Example: What is the next term of the series 2, 6, 18, 54 . . . ?

Solution: Each term is 3 times the previous term so the fifth term is 3 times 54 or 162.

If the multiplying factor is negative, the series will alternate between positive and negative terms.

Example: Find the next term of −2, 4, −8, 16. . . .

Solution: Each term is −2 times the previous term so the next term is −32.

Example: Find the next term in the series 64, −32, 16, −8 . . .

Solution: Each term in this series is $-\frac{1}{2}$ times the previous term so the next term is 4.

3.   In *mixed step progressions* the successive terms can be found by repeating a pattern of add 2, add 3, add 2, add 3; or a pattern of add 1, multiply by 5, add 1, multiply 5, etc. The series is the result of a combination of operations.

Example: Find the next term in the series 1, 3, 9, 11, 33, 35. . . .

Solution: The pattern of successive terms is, add 2, multiply by 3, add 2, multiply by 3, etc. The next step is to multiply 35 by 3 to get 105.

Example: Find the next term in the series 4, 16, 8, 32, 16. . . .

Solution: Here, the pattern is to multiply by 4, divide by 2, multiply by 4, divide by 2, etc. Thus, the next term is 16 times 4 or 64.

4. If no obvious solution presents itself, it may be helpful to calculate the difference between each term and the preceding one. Then if it is possible to determine the next *increment* (the difference between successive terms), add it to the last term to obtain the term in question. Often the series of *increments* is a simpler series than the series of original terms.

Example: Find the next term in the series 3, 9, 19, 33, 51....

Solution: Write out the series of increments: 6, 10, 14, 18 ... (each term is the difference between two terms of the original series). This series is an arithmetic progression whose next term is 22. Adding 22 to the term 51 from the original series produces the next term, 73.

5. If none of the above methods is effective, the series may be a combination of two or three different series. In this case, make a series out of every other term or out of every third term and see whether these terms form a series which can be recognized.

Example: Find the next term in the series 1, 4, 4, 8, 16, 12, 64, 16....

Solution: Divide this series into two series by taking out every other term, yielding: 1, 4, 16, 64 ... and 4, 8, 12, 16 ... These series are easy to recognize as a geometric and arithmetic series but the first series has the needed term. The next term in this series is 4 times 64 or 256.

PROPERTIES OF INTEGERS

603. *Even-Odd.* These are problems that deal with even and odd numbers. An even number is divisible by 2 and an odd number is not divisible by 2. All even numbers end in the digits 0, 2, 4, 6, or 8; while odd numbers end in the digits 1, 3, 5, 7, or 9. For example the numbers 358, 90, 18, 9874, and 46 are even numbers. The numbers 67, 871, 475, and 89 are odd numbers. It is important to remember the following facts:

604. The sum of *two even* numbers is *even*, and the sum of *two odd* numbers is *even*, but the sum of an *odd* number *and* an *even* number is *odd*. For example, $4 + 8 = 12$, $5 + 3 = 8$ and $7 + 2 = 9$.

605. The product of *two odd* numbers is *odd*, but the product of an even number and *any other* number is an *even* number. For example, $3 \times 5 = 15$ (odd); $4 \times 5 = 20$ (even); $4 \times 6 = 24$ (even).

606. Even numbers are expressed in the form $2k$ where k may be any integer. Odd numbers are expressed in the form of $2k + 1$ or $2k - 1$ where k may be any integer. For example, if $k = 17$, then $2k = 34$ and $2k + 1 = 35$. If $k = 6$, then we have $2k = 12$ and $2k + 1 = 13$.

Example: If m is any integer, is the number $6m + 3$ an even or an odd number?

Solution: Rewrite the number $6m + 3$ as $2(3m + 1) + 1$. Since m is an arbitrary number, $3m + 1$ is an arbitrary number. Let $3m + 1$ be called p. Now, the number is in the form of an odd number, $2p + 1$. ($2k + 1$ is odd, where k is any number, so $2p + 1$ is also odd. In both cases, the k and the p are arbitrary.)

607. *Divisibility.* If an integer P is divided by an integer Q, and an integer is obtained as the quotient, then P is said to be divisible by Q. In other words, if P can be expressed as an integral multiple of Q, then P is said to be divisible by Q. For example, dividing 51 by 17 gives 3, an integer. 51 is divisible by 17, or 51 equals 17 times 3. On the other hand, dividing 8 by 3 gives $2\frac{2}{3}$ which is not an integer. 8 is not divisible by 3 and there is no way to express 8 as an integral multiple of 3. There are various tests to see whether an integer is divisible by certain numbers. These tests are listed below:

1. Any integer is divisible *by 2* if the last digit of the number is a 0, 2, 4, 6, or 8.

   Example: The numbers 98, 6534, 70, and 32 are divisible by 2 because they end in 8, 4, 0 and 2 respectively.

2. Any integer is divisible *by 3* if the sum of its digits is divisible by 3.

   Example: Is the number 34,237,023 divisible by 3?

   Solution: Add the digits of the number. $3 + 4 + 2 + 3 + 7 + 0 + 2 + 3 = 24$. Now, 24 is divisible by 3 $(24 \div 3 = 8)$ so the number 34,237,023 is also divisible by 3.

3. Any integer is divisible *by 4* if the last two digits of the number are divisible by 4.

   Example: Which of the following numbers is divisible by 4?
   3456, 6,787,612, 67,408, 7877, 345, 98.

   Solution: Look at the last two digits of the numbers. 56, 12, 08, 77, 45, 98. Only 56, 12, and 08 are divisible by 4 so only the numbers 3456, 6,787,612, and 67,408 are divisible by 4.

4. An integer is divisible *by 5* if the last digit is either a 0 or a 5.

   Example: The numbers 780, 675, 9000, and 15 are divisible by 5, while the numbers 786, 5509, and 87 are not divisible by 5.

5. Any integer is divisible *by 6* if it passes the divisibility tests for both 2 and 3.

   Example: Is the number 12,414 divisible by 6?

   Solution: Test whether 12,414 is divisible by 2 and 3. The last digit is a 4, so it is divisible by 2. Adding the digits yields $1 + 2 + 4 + 1 + 4 = 12$. 12 is divisible by 3 so the number 12,414 is divisible by 3. Since it is divisible by both 2 and 3, it is divisible by 6.

6. Any integer is divisible *by 8* if the last three digits are divisible by 8. (Since 1000 is divisible by 8, you can ignore all multiples of 1000.)

   Example: Is the number 342,169,424 divisible by 8?

   Solution: $424 \div 8 = 53$, so 342,169,424 is divisible by 8.

7. Any integer is divisible *by 9* if the sum of its digits is divisible by 9.

   Example: Is the number 243,091,863 divisible by 9?

Solution: Adding the digits yields $2+4+3+0+9+1+8+6+3=$ 36. 36 is divisible by 9 so the number 243,091,863 is divisible by 9.

8. Any integer is divisible *by 10* if the last digit is a 0.

   Example: The numbers 60, 8900, 5640, and 34,000 are all divisible by 10 because the last digit in each is a 0.

> Note that if a number **P** is divisible by a number **Q**, then **P** is also divisible by all the factors of **Q**. For example, 60 is divisible by 12 so 60 is also divisible by 2, 3, 4, and 6 which are all factors of 12.

608. *Prime numbers.* A prime number is one that is divisible only by 1 and itself. The first few prime numbers are 2, 3, 5, 7, 11, 13, 17, 19, 23, 29, 31, 37.... Note that the number 1 is not considered a prime number. To determine if a number is prime, follow these steps.

STEP 1. Determine a very rough approximate square root of the number. Remember that the square root of a number is that number which when multiplied by itself, gives the original number. For example, the square root of 25 is 5 because $5 \times 5 = 25$.

STEP 2. Divide the number by all of the primes which are less than the approximate square root. If the number is not divisible by any of these primes, then it is prime. If it is divisible by one of the primes, then it is not prime.

   Example: Is the number 97 prime?

   Solution: An approximate square root of 97 is 10. All of the primes less than 10 are 2, 3, 5, and 7. Divide 97 by 2, 3, 5, and 7. No integer results, so 97 is prime.

   Example: Is the number 161 prime?

   Solution: An approximate square root of 161 is 13. The primes less than 13 are 2, 3, 5, 7, and 11. Divide 161 by 2, 3, 5, 7, and 11. 161 is divisible by 7 $(161 \div 7 = 23)$, so 161 is not prime.

APPROXIMATIONS

609. *Rounding off.* A number expressed to a certain number of places is rounded of when it is approximated as a number with fewer places of accuracy. For example, the number 8.987 is expressed more accurately than the number rounded off to 8.99. To round off to *n* places look at the digit that is to the right of the *n*th digit. (The *n*th digit is found by counting *n* places to the right of the decimal point.) If this digit is less than 5 eliminate all of the digits to the right of the *n*th digit. If the digit to the right of the *n*th digit is 5 or more, then add 1 to the *n*th digit and eliminate all of the digits to the right of the *n*th digit.

   Example: Round off 8.73 to the nearest tenth.

   Solution: The digit to the right of the 7 (.7 is seven tenths), is 3. Since this is less than 5 eliminate it and the rounded off answer is 8.7.

   Example: Round off 986 to the nearest tens' place.

Solution: The number to the right of the tens' place is 6. Since this is 5 or more add 1 to the 8 and replace the 6 with a 0 to get 990.

610. *Approximating sums.* When adding a given set of numbers and when the answer must have a given number of places of accuracy, follow the steps below.

STEP 1. Round off each addend (number being added) to one more place than the number of places the answer is to have.

STEP 2. Add the rounded addends.

STEP 3. Round off the sum to the desired number of places of accuracy.

Example: What is the sum of 12.0775, 1.20163, and 121.303 correct to the nearest hundredth?

Solution: Round off the three numbers to the nearest thousandth (one more place than the accuracy of the sum): 12.078, 1.202, and 121.303. The sum of these is 134.583. Rounded off to the nearest hundredth, this is 134.58.

611. *Approximating products.* To multiply certain numbers and have an answer to the desired number of places of accuracy, follow the steps below.

STEP 1. Round off the numbers being multiplied to the number of places of accuracy desired in the answer.

STEP 2. Multiply the rounded off factors (numbers being multiplied).

STEP 3. Round off the product to the desired number of places.

Example: Find the product of 3316 and 1432 to three places.

Solution: First, round off 3316 to 3 places, to obtain 3320. Round off 1432 to 3 places to give 1430. The product of these two numbers is 4,747,600. Rounded off to 3 places this is 4,750,000.

612. *Approximating square roots.* The square root of a number is that number which, when multiplied by itself, gives the original number. For example, 6 is the square root of 36. Often on tests a number with different choices for the square root is given. Follow this procedure to determine which is the best choice.

STEP 1. Square all of the choices given.

STEP 2. Select the closest choice that is too large and the closest choice that is too small (assuming that no choice is the exact square root). Find the average of these two *choices* (not of their squares).

STEP 3. Square this average; if its square is greater than the original number, choose the lower of the two choices; if its square is lower than the original number, choose the higher.

Example: Which of the following is closest to the square root of 86: 9.0, 9.2, 9.4, 9.6 or 9.8?

Solution: The squares of the five numbers are: 81, 84.64, 88.36, 92.16 and 96.04 respectively. (Actually it was not necessary to calculate the last two, since they are greater than the third square which is already greater than 86.) The two closest choices are 9.2 and 9.4; their average is 9.3. The square of 9.3 is 86.49. Therefore, 9.3 is greater than the square root of 86. So, the square root must be closer to 9.2 than to 9.4.

PRACTICE TEST 6

Miscellaneous Problems Including Averages, Series, Properties of Integers, and Approximations

Correct answers and solutions follow each test.

1. If n is the first of five consecutive odd numbers, what is their average?

   (A) n (B) $n+1$ (C) $n+2$ (D) $n+3$ (E) $n+4$

2. What is the average of the following numbers: 35.5, 32.5, 34.0, 35.0, 34.5?

   (A) 33.0   (B) 33.8   (C) 34.0   (D) 34.3   (E) 34.5

3. What is the next number in the following series: 1, 5, 9, 13, ... ?

   (A) 11   (B) 15   (C) 17   (D) 19   (E) 21

4. Which of the following is the next number in the series: 3, 6, 4, 9, 5, 12, 6, ... ?

   (A) 7   (B) 9   (C) 12   (D) 15   (E) 24

5. If P is an even number, and Q and R are both odd, which of the following *must* be true?

   (A) $P \cdot Q$ is an odd number

   (B) $Q - R$ is an even number

   (C) $PQ - PR$ is an odd number

   (D) $Q + R$ cannot equal P

   (E) $P + Q$ cannot equal R

6. If a number is divisible by 102, then it is also divisible by:

   (A) 23   (B) 11   (C) 103   (D) 5   (E) 2

7. Which of the following numbers is divisible by 36?

   (A) 35,924   (B) 64,530   (C) 74,098   (D) 152,640   (E) 192,042

8. How many prime numbers are there between 45 and 72?

   (A) 4   (B) 5   (C) 6   (D) 7   (E) 8

9. Which of the following represents the smallest possible value of $(M - \frac{1}{2})^2$, if M is an integer?

   (A) 0.00   (B) 0.25   (C) 0.50   (D) 0.75   (E) 1.00

10. Which of the following best approximates $\dfrac{7.40096 \times 10.0342}{.2001355}$?

    (A) 0.3700   (B) 3.700   (C) 37.00   (D) 370.0   (E) 3700

    10. A B C D E
‖ ‖ ‖ ‖ ‖

11. A B C D E

11. In a class with six boys and four girls, the students all took the same test. The boys' scores were 74, 82, 84, 84, 88, and 95, while the girls' scores were 80, 82, 86, and 86. Which of the following statements is true?

(A) The boys' average was 0.1 higher than the average for the whole class.

(B) The girls' average was 0.1 lower than the boys' average.

(C) The class average was 1.0 higher than the boys' average.

(D) The boys' average was 1.0 higher than the class average.

(E) The girls' average was 1.0 lower than the boys' average.

12. A B C D E

12. If the following series continues to follow the same pattern, what will be the next number: 2, 6, 3, 9, 6, . . . ?

(A) 3   (B) 6   (C) 12   (D) 14   (E) 18

13. A B C D E

13. Which of the following numbers *must* be odd?

(A) The sum of an odd number and an odd number.

(B) The product of an odd number and an even number.

(C) The sum of an odd number and an even number.

(D) The product of two even numbers.

(E) The sum of two even numbers.

14. A B C D E

14. Which of the following numbers is the best approximation of the length of one side of a square with an area of 12 square inches?

(A) 3.2 inches

(B) 3.3 inches

(C) 3.4 inches

(D) 3.5 inches

(E) 3.6 inches

15. A B C D E

15. If n is an odd number, then which of the following *best* describes the number represented by $n^2 + 2n + 1$?

(A) It can be odd or even.

(B) It must be odd.

(C) It must be divisible by four.

(D) It must be divisible by six.

(E) cannot be determined from the given information

16. A B C D E

16. What is the next number in the series: 2, 5, 7, 8, . . . ?

(A) 8   (B) 9   (C) 10   (D) 11   (E) 12

17. A B C D E

17. What is the average of the following numbers: $3\frac{1}{2}$, $4\frac{1}{4}$, $2\frac{1}{4}$, $3\frac{1}{4}$, 4?

(A) 3.25   (B) 3.35   (C) 3.45   (D) 3.50   (E) 3.60

18. A B C D E

18. Which of the following numbers is divisible by 24?

(A) 76,300   (B) 78,132   (C) 80,424   (D) 81,234   (E) 83,636

19. In order to graduate, a boy needs an average of 65 percent for his five major subjects. His first four grades were 55, 60, 65, and 65. What grade does he need in the fifth subject in order to graduate?

    (A) 65   (B) 70   (C) 75   (D) 80   (E) 85

20. If t is any integer, which of the following represents an odd number?

    (A) $2t$ (B) $2t + 3$ (C) $3t$ (D) $2t + 2$ (E) $t + 1$

21. If the average of five whole numbers is an even number, which of the following statements *is not true*?

    (A) The sum of the five numbers must be divisible by 2.

    (B) The sum of the five numbers must be divisible by 5.

    (C) The sum of the five numbers must be divisible by 10.

    (D) At least one of the five numbers must be even.

    (E) All of the five numbers must be odd.

22. What is the product of 23 and 79 to one place of accuracy?

    (A) 1600   (B) 1817   (C) 1000   (D) 1800   (E) 2000

23. What is the next term in the series: 1, 1, 2, 3, 5, 8, 13 ... ?

    (A) 18   (B) 21   (C) 13   (D) 9   (E) 20

24. What is the next number in the series: 1, 4, 2, 8, 6, ... ?

    (A) 4   (B) 6   (C) 8   (D) 15   (E) 24

25. Which of the following numbers is closest to the square root of $\frac{1}{2}$?

    (A) 0.25   (B) 0.5   (C) 0.6   (D) 0.7   (E) 0.8

26. How many prime numbers are there between 56 and 100?

    (A) 8   (B) 9   (C) 10   (D) 11   (E) none of the above

27. If you multiply one million, two hundred thousand, one hundred seventy-six, by five hundred twenty thousand, two hundred four, and then divide the product by one billion, your result will be closest to:

    (A) 0.6   (B) 6   (C) 600   (D) 6000   (E) 6,000,000

28. The number 89.999 rounded off to the nearest tenth is equal to which of the following?

    (A) 90.0   (B) 89.0   (C) 89.9   (D) 89.99   (E) 89.90

29. a, b, c, d, and e, are integers, M is their average and S is their sum. What is the ratio of S to M?

    (A) 1 : 5   (D) 2 : 1

    (B) 5 : 1   (E) depends on the values of a, b, c, d, and e

    (C) 1 : 1

30. A B C D E

30. What is the next number in the series: 1, 1, 2, 4, 5, 25, . . . ?

(A) 8 (B) 12 (C) 15 (D) 24 (E) 26

31. A B C D E

31. The sum of five odd numbers is always:

(A) even (D) a prime number

(B) divisible by three (E) none of the above

(C) divisible by five

32. A B C D E

32. If E is an even number, and F is divisible by three, then what is the *largest* number by which E^2F^3 *must* be divisible?

(A) 6 (B) 12 (C) 54 (D) 108 (E) 144

33. A B C D E

33. If the average of five consecutive even numbers is 8, which of the following is the smallest of the five numbers?

(A) 4 (D) 8

(B) 5 (E) none of the above

(C) 6

34. A B C D E

34. What is the next number in the sequence: 1, 4, 7, 10, . . . ?

(A) 13 (D) 16

(B) 14 (E) 18

(C) 15

35. A B C D E

35. If a number is divisible by 23, then it is also divisible by which of the following?

(A) 7 (D) 3

(B) 24 (E) none of these

(C) 9

36. A B C D E

36. What is the next term in the series: 3, 6, 2, 7, 1, . . . ?

(A) 0 (B) 1 (C) 3 (D) 6 (E) 8

37. A B C D E

37. What is the average (to the nearest tenth) of the following numbers: 91.4, 91.5, 91.6, 91.7, 91.7, 92.0, 92.1, 92.3, 92.3, 92.4?

(A) 91.9 (D) 92.2

(B) 92.0 (E) 92.3

(C) 92.1

38. A B C D E

38. What is the next term in the following series: 8, 3, 10, 9, 12, 27, . . . ?

(A) 8 (B) 14 (C) 18 (D) 36 (E) 81

39. A B C D E

39. Which of the following numbers is divisible by 11?

(A) 30,217 (D) 60,411

(B) 44,221 (E) none of the above

(C) 59,403

40. What is the next number in the series: 1, 4, 9, 16, ... ?

(A) 22   (B) 23   (C) 24   (D) 34   (E) 25

41. Which of the following is the best approximation of the product (1.005) (20.0025) (0.0102) ?

(A) 0.02   (B) 0.2   (C) 2.0   (D) 20   (E) 200

42. What is the next number in the series: 5, 2, 4, 2, 3, 2, ...?

(A) 1   (B) 2   (C) 3   (D) 4   (E) 5

43. If a, b, and c are all divisible by 8, then their average must be

(A) divisible by 8   (D) an integer
(B) divisible by 4   (E) none of these
(C) divisible by 2

44. Which of the following numbers is divisible by 24?

(A) 13,944   (D) 16,012
(B) 15,746   (E) none of the above
(C) 15,966

45. Which of the following numbers is a prime?

(A) 147   (B) 149   (C) 153   (D) 155   (E) 161

46. What is the next number in the following series: 4, 8, 2, 4, 1, ... ?

(A) 1   (B) 2   (C) 4   (D) 8   (E) 16

47. The sum of four consecutive odd integers must be:

(A) even, but not necessarily divisible by 4
(B) divisible by 4, but not necessarily by 8
(C) divisible by 8, but not necessarily by 16
(D) divisible by 16
(E) none of the above

48. Which of the following is closest to the square root of $\frac{3}{5}$?

(A) $\frac{1}{2}$ (B) $\frac{2}{3}$ (C) $\frac{3}{4}$ (D) $\frac{4}{5}$ (E) 1

49. What is the next term in the series: 9, 8, 6, 3, ...?

(A) 0   (B) −2   (C) 1   (D) −3   (E) −1

50. The sum of an odd and an even number is

(A) a perfect square   (D) odd
(B) negative   (E) none of these
(C) even

ANSWER KEY FOR PRACTICE TEST 6

1. E	14. D	26. B	39. A
2. D	15. C	27. C	40. E
3. C	16. A	28. A	41. B
4. D	17. C	29. B	42. B
5. B	18. C	30. E	43. E
6. E	19. D	31. E	44. A
7. D	20. B	32. D	45. B
8. C	21. E	33. A	46. B
9. B	22. E	34. A	47. C
10. D	23. B	35. E	48. C
11. E	24. E	36. E	49. E
12. E	25. D	37. A	50. D
13. C		38. B	

ANSWERS AND SOLUTIONS
FOR PRACTICE TEST 6

1. **(E)** The five consecutive odd numbers must be n, $n + 2$, $n + 4$, $n + 6$, and $n + 8$. Their average is equal to their sum, $5n + 20$, divided by the number of addends, 5, which yields $n + 4$ as the average. (601)

2. **(D)** Choosing 34 as an approximate average results in the following addends: $+ 1.5$, $- 1.5$, 0, $+ 1.0$, and $+ 0.5$. Their sum is $+ 1.5$. Now, divide by 5, to get $+ 0.3$, and add this to 34 to get 34.3. (To check this add the five original numbers, and divide by 5). (601)

3. **(C)** This is an arithmetic sequence: each term is 4 more than the preceding one. The next term is. $13 + 4$ or 17. (602)

4. **(D)** This series can be divided into two parts: the even-numbered terms: 6, 9, 12,... and the odd-numbered terms: 3, 4, 5, 6,... (Even- and odd-numbered terms refers to the terms' *place* in the series and not if the term itself is even or odd). The next term in the series is even-numbered, so it will be formed by adding 3 to the 12 (the last of the even-numbered terms), to get 15. (602)

5. **(B)** Since Q is an odd number, it may be represented by $2m + 1$ where m is an integer. Similarly, call R, $2n + 1$ where n is an integer. Thus $Q - R$ is equal to $(2m + 1) - (2n + 1)$, $2m - 2n$, or $2(m - n)$. Now, since m and n are integers, $m - n$ will be some integer p. Thus $Q - R = 2p$. Any number in the form of $2p$, where p is any integer, is an even number. Therefore, $Q - R$ *must* be even. (A) and (C) are wrong, because an even number multiplied by an odd is always even. (D) and (E) are only true for specific values of P, Q, and R. (604)

6. **(E)** If a number is divisible by 102 then it must be divisible by all of the factors of 102. The only choice which is a factor of 102 is 2. (607)

7. **(D)** To be divisible by 36, a number must be divisible by both 4 and 9. Only (A) and (D) are divisible by 4. (Recall that only the last two digits must be examined.) Of these, only (D) is divisible by 9. (The sum of the digits of (A) is 23, which is not divisible by 9; the sum of the digits of (D) is 18.) (607)

8. **(C)** The prime numbers between 45 and 72 are 47, 53, 59, 61, 67, and 71. All of the others have factors other than 1 and themselves. (608)

9. **(B)** Since M must be an *integer*, the closest value it can have to $\frac{1}{2}$ is either 1 or 0. In either case, $(M - \frac{1}{2})^2$ is equal to $\frac{1}{4}$, or 0.25. (409)

10. **(D)** Approximate to only one place (this is permissible, because the choices are so far apart; if they had been closer together, two or three places would have been used). After this approximation, the expression is: $\frac{7 \times 10}{0.2}$, which is equal to 350. This is closest to 370. (609)

11. **(E)** The average for the boys alone was $\frac{74 + 82 + 84 + 84 + 88 + 95}{6}$, or

    $507 \div 6 = 84.5$. The girls' average was $\frac{80 + 82 + 86 + 86}{4}$, or $334 \div 4 = 83.5$, which is 1.0 below the boys' average. (601)

12. **(E)** To generate this series start with 2; multiply by 3 to get 6; subtract 3 to get 3; multiply by 3; subtract 3; etc. Thus, the next term will be found by multiplying the previous term, 6, by 3, to get 18. (602)

13. **(C)** The sum of an odd number and an even number can be expressed as $(2n + 1) + (2m)$, where n and m are integers. ($2n + 1$ must be odd, and $2m$ must be even). Their sum is equal to $2n + 2m + 1$, or $2(m + n) + 1$. Since $(m + n)$ is an integer, the quantity $2(m + n) + 1$ *must* represent an odd integer. (604, 605)

14. **(D)** The actual length of one of the sides would be the square root of 12. Square each of the five choices to find the square of 3.4 is 11.56, and the square of 3.5 is 12.25. The square root of 12 must lie between 3.4 and 3.5. Squaring 3.45, (halfway between the two choices) yields 11.9025, which is less than 12. Thus the square root of 12 must be greater than 3.45 and therefore closer to 3.5 than to 3.4. (612)

15. **(C)** Factor $n^2 + 2n + 1$ to $(n + 1)(n + 1)$ or $(n + 1)^2$. Now, since n is an odd number, $n + 1$ must be even (the number after every odd number is even). Thus, representing $n + 1$ as $2k$ where k is an integer, ($2k$ is the standard representation for an even number) yields the expression: $(n + 1)^2 = (2k)^2$ or $4k^2$. Thus, $(n + 1)^2$ is a multiple of 4 and it must be divisible by 4. A number divisible by 4 must also be even, so (C) is the best choice. (604–607)

16. (A) The differences between terms are as follows: 3, 2, and 1. Thus, the next term should be found by adding 0, leaving a result of 8. (602)

17. (C) Convert to decimals. Then calculate the value of:
$$\frac{3.50 + 4.25 + 2.25 + 3.25 + 4.00}{5}.$$ This equals $17.25 \div 5$, or 3.45. (601)

18. (C) If a number is divisible by 24, it must be divisible by 3 and by 8. Of the five choices given, only choice (C) is divisible by 8. Add the digits in 80,424 to get 18. As this is divisible by 3, the number is divisible by 3. The number, therefore, is divisible by 24. (607)

19. (D) If the boy is to average 65 for five subjects, the total of his five grades must be five times 65 or 325. The sum of the first four grades is $55 + 60 + 65 + 65$, or 245. Therefore, the fifth mark must be $325 - 245$, or 80. (601)

20. (B) If t is any integer, then $2t$ is an even number. Adding 3 to an even number always produces an odd number. Thus, $2t + 3$ is always odd. (606)

21. (E) Call the five numbers a, b, c, d, and e. Then the average is
$\frac{(a + b + c + d + e)}{5}$. Since this must be even, $\frac{(a + b + c + d + e)}{5} = 2k$,
where k is an integer. Thus $a + b + c + d + e = 10k$. Therefore, the sum of the 5 numbers is divisible by 10, 2, and 5. Thus the first three choices are eliminated. If the five numbers were 1, 1, 1, 1, and 6 then the average would be 2. Thus, the average is even, but not all of the numbers are even. Thus, choice (D) can be true. If all the numbers were odd the sum would have to be odd. This contradicts the statement that the average is even. Thus, choice (E) is the answer. (601, 607)

22. (E) First, round off 23 and 79 to one place of accuracy. The numbers become 20 and 80. The product of these two numbers is 1600, which rounded off to one place is 2000. (611)

23. (B) Each term in this series is the sum of the two previous terms. Thus the next term is $8 + 13$ or 21. (602)

24. (E) This series can be generated by the following steps: multiply by 4; subtract 2; multiply by 4; subtract 2; etc. Since the term "6" was obtained by subtracting 2, multiply by 4 to obtain $4 \times 6 = 24$, the next term. (602)

25. (D) 0.7 squared is 0.49. Squaring 0.8 yields 0.64. Thus, the square root of $\frac{1}{2}$ must lie between 0.7 and 0.8. Take the number halfway between these two, 0.75, and square it. This number, 0.5625, is more than $\frac{1}{2}$, so the square root must be closer to 0.7 than to 0.8. An easier way to do problems concerning the square roots of 2 and 3, and their multiples is to memorize the values of these two square roots. The square root of 2 is about 1.414 (remember fourteen-fourteen), and the square root of three is about 1.732 (remember that 1732 was the year of George Washington's birth). Apply these as follows: $\frac{1}{2} = \frac{1}{4} \times 2$. Thus, $\sqrt{\frac{1}{2}} = \sqrt{\frac{1}{4}} \times \sqrt{2} = \frac{1}{2} \times 1.414 = 0.707$, which is very close to 0.7. (612)

26. (B) The prime numbers can be found by taking all the odd numbers between 56 and 100 (the even ones cannot be primes), and eliminating all the ones divisible by 3, by 5 and by 7. If a number under 100 is divisible by none of these, it must be prime. Thus, the only primes between 56 and 100 are: 59, 61, 67, 71, 73, 79, 83, 89, and 97. (608)

27. (C) Since all the answer requires is an order-of-ten approximation, do not calculate the exact answer. Approximate the answer in the following manner: $\frac{1,000,000 \times 500,000}{1,000,000,000} = 500$. The only choice on the same order of magnitude is 600. (609)

28. (A) To round off 89.999, look at the number in the hundredths' place. 9 is more than 5, so add 1 to the number in the tenths' place and eliminate all of the digits to the right. Thus, we get 90.0. (609)

29. (B) The average of five numbers is found by dividing their sum by five. Thus, the sum is five times the average, so $S : M = 5 : 1$. (601)

30. (E) The series can be generated by the following steps: to get the second term, square the first term; to get the third, add 1 to the second; to get the fourth, square the third; to get the fifth, add 1 to the fourth; etc. The pattern can be written as: square; add 1; repeat the cycle. Following this pattern, the seventh term is found by adding one to the sixth term. Thus, the seventh term is $1 + 25$, or 26. (602)

31. (E) None of the first four choices is necessarily true. The sum, $5 + 7 + 9 + 13 + 15 = 49$, is neither even, divisible by 3, divisible by 5, nor prime. (604, 607, 608)

32. (D) Any even number can be written as $2m$ and any number divisible by 3 can be written as $3n$, where m and n are integers. Thus, E^2F^3 equals $(2m)^2 (3n)^3 = (4m^2) (27n^3) = 108(m^2n^3)$, and 108 is the largest number by which E^2F^3 must be divisible. (607)

33. (A) The five consecutive even numbers can be represented as n, $n + 2$, $n + 4$, $n + 6$, and $n + 8$. Taking the sum and dividing by five yields an average of $n + 4$. Thus, $n + 4 = 8$, the given average and $n = 4$, the smallest number. (601)

34. (A) To find the next number in this sequence add 3 to the previous number. This is an arithmetic progression. The next term is $10 + 3$, or 13. (602)

35. (E) If a number is divisible by 23, then it is divisible by all of the factors of 23. But 23 is a prime with no factors except 1 and itself. Therefore, the correct choice is (E). (607)

36. (E) The steps generating the successive terms in this series are (to the previous term): add 3; subtract 4; add 5; subtract 6; add 7; etc. The next term is $1 + 7 = 8$. (602)

37. (A) To find the average, it is convenient to choose 92.0 as an approximate average, and then find the average of the differences between the actual numbers and 92.0. Thus, add up: $(-0.6) + (-0.5) + (-0.4) + (-0.3) + (-0.3) +$

$(0.0) + 0.1 + 0.3 + 0.3 + 0.4$, to -1.0; divide this by ten (the number of quantities to be averaged), to obtain -0.1. Finally, add this to the approximate average, 92.0, to obtain a final average of 91.9. (601)

38. (B) This series is a combination of two sub-series: the odd-numbered terms, 3, 9, 27, etc. form a geometric series; the even-numbered terms, 8, 10, 12, 14, etc. form an arithmetic sequence. The next number in the sequence is from the arithmetic sequence and is 14. (Note that in the absence of any other indication, assume a series to be as simple as possible, i.e., arithmetic or geometric.). (602)

39. (A) To determine if a number is divisible by 11, take each of the digits separately, and, beginning with either end, subtract the second from the first, add the following digit, subtract the next one, add the one after that, etc. If this result is divisible by 11, the entire number is. Thus, because $3 - 0 + 2 - 1 + 7 = 11$, we know 30,217 is divisible by 11. Using the same method, we find that the other four choices are not divisible by 11. (607)

40. (E) This is the series of integers squared. $1^2, 2^2, 3^2, 4^2 \ldots$ the next term is 5^2 or 25. (602)

41. (B) This is simply an order-of-ten approximation, so round off the numbers, and work the following problem: $(1.0)(20.0)(0.01) = 0.20$. The actual answer is closest to 0.2. (611)

42. (B) The even-numbered terms of this series form the sub-series: 2, 2, 2, ... The odd-numbered terms form the arithmetic series: 5, 4, 3, 2, ... The next term in the series is a 2. (602)

43. (E) Represent the three numbers as $8p$, $8q$, and $8r$, respectively. Thus, their sum is $8p + 8q + 8r$, and their average is $\dfrac{(8p + 8q + 8r)}{3}$. This need not even be a whole number. For example, the average of 8, 16, and 32 is $\frac{56}{3}$, or $18\frac{2}{3}$. (601, 607)

44. (A) To be divisible by 24, a number must be divisible by both 3 and 8. Only 13,944 and 15,966 are divisible by 3; of these, only 13,944 is divisible by 8. $(13,944 = 24 \times 581)$. (607)

45. (B) The approximate square root of each of these numbers is 13. Merely divide each of these numbers by the primes up to 13, which are 2, 3, 5, 7, and 11. The only number not divisible by any of these primes is 149. (608, 612)

46. (B) The sequence is formed by the following operations: Multiply by 2, divide by 4, multiply by 2, divide by 4, etc. Accordingly, the next number is 1×2, or 2. (602)

47. (C) Call the first odd integer $2k + 1$. (This is the standard representation for a general odd integer.) Thus, the next 3 odd integers are $2k + 3$, $2k + 5$, and $2k + 7$. (Each one is 2 more than the previous one.) The sum of these integers is $(2k + 1) + (2k + 3) + (2k + 5) + (2k + 7) = 8k + 16$. This can be rewritten as $8(k + 2)$ which is divisible by 8, but not necessarily by 16. (606, 607)

48. **(C)** By squaring the five choices, it is evident that the two closest choices are: $\left(\frac{3}{4}\right)^2 = 0.5625$, and $\left(\frac{4}{5}\right)^2 = 0.64$. Squaring the number halfway between $\frac{3}{4}$ and $\frac{4}{5}$ gives $(0.775)^2 = 0.600625$. This is greater than $\frac{3}{5}$ so the square root of $\frac{3}{5}$ must be closer to $\frac{3}{4}$ than to $\frac{4}{5}$. (612)

49. **(E)** The terms decrease by 1, then 2, then 3, so the next term is 4 less than 3, or -1. (602)

50. **(D)** Let the even number be $2k$, where k is an integer, and let the odd number be $2m + 1$, where m is an integer. Thus, the sum is $2k + (2m + 1)$, $2k + 2m + 1$, or $2(k + m) + 1$. Now $k + m$ is an integer since k and m are integers. Call $k + m$ by another name, p. Thus, $2(k + m) + 1$ is $2p + 1$, which is the representation of an odd number. (604, 606)

SIX MORE PRACTICE SCHOLASTIC APTITUDE TESTS

Four Important Reasons for Taking These Practice Tests

Each of the 6 Practice SATs in the final part of this book is modeled very closely after the actual SAT. You will find that each of these Practice Tests has

a) the same level of difficulty as the actual SAT

and

b) the same question formats that the actual SAT questions have.

Accordingly, *taking each of the following tests is like taking the actual SAT.* There are four important reasons for taking each of these Practice SATs:

Reason 1. To find out in which areas of the SAT you are still weak.

Reason 2. To know just where to concentrate your efforts to eliminate these weaknesses.

Reason 3. To reinforce the Critical Thinking Skills—25 Math Strategies and 25 Verbal Strategies—that you learned in Part 2 of this book, "Using Critical Thinking Skills to Score High on the SAT." As we advised you, at the beginning of Part 2, diligent study of these strategies will result in a sharp rise in your SAT Math and Verbal scores.

Reason 4. To strengthen your Basic Math skills that might still be a bit rusty. We hope that Part 4, "SAT Math Refresher," helped you substantially to scrape off some of this rust.

These four reasons, given above, for taking the six Practice Tests in this section of the book, tie up closely with a very important educational principle:

WE LEARN BY DOING!

10 TIPS FOR TAKING THE PRACTICE TESTS

1. Observe the time limits exactly as given.

2. Allow no interruptions.

3. Permit no talking by anyone in the "test area."

4. Use the Answer Sheets provided at the beginning of each Practice Test. Don't make extra marks. Two answers for one question constitute an omitted question.

5. Use scratch paper to figure things out. (On your actual SAT, you are permitted to use the testbook for scratchwork.)

6. Omit a question when you start "struggling" with it. Go back to that question later if you have time to do so.

7. Don't get upset if you can't answer several of the questions. You can still get a high score on the test. Even if only 40 to 60 percent of the questions you answer are correct, you will get an average or above average score.

8. You get the same credit for answering an easy question correctly as you do for answering a tough question correctly.

9. It is advisable to guess if you are sure that some of the question choices are wrong. Don't guess otherwise because about 2½ points are deducted from your score for every wrong answer.

10. *Your SAT score increases by approximately 10 points for every answer you get correct.*

Answer Sheet—Practice Test 2

SECTION 1: VERBAL ABILITY

1 Ⓐ Ⓑ Ⓒ Ⓓ Ⓔ   10 Ⓐ Ⓑ Ⓒ Ⓓ Ⓔ   19 Ⓐ Ⓑ Ⓒ Ⓓ Ⓔ   28 Ⓐ Ⓑ Ⓒ Ⓓ Ⓔ   37 Ⓐ Ⓑ Ⓒ Ⓓ Ⓔ
2 Ⓐ Ⓑ Ⓒ Ⓓ Ⓔ   11 Ⓐ Ⓑ Ⓒ Ⓓ Ⓔ   20 Ⓐ Ⓑ Ⓒ Ⓓ Ⓔ   29 Ⓐ Ⓑ Ⓒ Ⓓ Ⓔ   38 Ⓐ Ⓑ Ⓒ Ⓓ Ⓔ
3 Ⓐ Ⓑ Ⓒ Ⓓ Ⓔ   12 Ⓐ Ⓑ Ⓒ Ⓓ Ⓔ   21 Ⓐ Ⓑ Ⓒ Ⓓ Ⓔ   30 Ⓐ Ⓑ Ⓒ Ⓓ Ⓔ   39 Ⓐ Ⓑ Ⓒ Ⓓ Ⓔ
4 Ⓐ Ⓑ Ⓒ Ⓓ Ⓔ   13 Ⓐ Ⓑ Ⓒ Ⓓ Ⓔ   22 Ⓐ Ⓑ Ⓒ Ⓓ Ⓔ   31 Ⓐ Ⓑ Ⓒ Ⓓ Ⓔ   40 Ⓐ Ⓑ Ⓒ Ⓓ Ⓔ
5 Ⓐ Ⓑ Ⓒ Ⓓ Ⓔ   14 Ⓐ Ⓑ Ⓒ Ⓓ Ⓔ   23 Ⓐ Ⓑ Ⓒ Ⓓ Ⓔ   32 Ⓐ Ⓑ Ⓒ Ⓓ Ⓔ   41 Ⓐ Ⓑ Ⓒ Ⓓ Ⓔ
6 Ⓐ Ⓑ Ⓒ Ⓓ Ⓔ   15 Ⓐ Ⓑ Ⓒ Ⓓ Ⓔ   24 Ⓐ Ⓑ Ⓒ Ⓓ Ⓔ   33 Ⓐ Ⓑ Ⓒ Ⓓ Ⓔ   42 Ⓐ Ⓑ Ⓒ Ⓓ Ⓔ
7 Ⓐ Ⓑ Ⓒ Ⓓ Ⓔ   16 Ⓐ Ⓑ Ⓒ Ⓓ Ⓔ   25 Ⓐ Ⓑ Ⓒ Ⓓ Ⓔ   34 Ⓐ Ⓑ Ⓒ Ⓓ Ⓔ   43 Ⓐ Ⓑ Ⓒ Ⓓ Ⓔ
8 Ⓐ Ⓑ Ⓒ Ⓓ Ⓔ   17 Ⓐ Ⓑ Ⓒ Ⓓ Ⓔ   26 Ⓐ Ⓑ Ⓒ Ⓓ Ⓔ   35 Ⓐ Ⓑ Ⓒ Ⓓ Ⓔ   44 Ⓐ Ⓑ Ⓒ Ⓓ Ⓔ
9 Ⓐ Ⓑ Ⓒ Ⓓ Ⓔ   18 Ⓐ Ⓑ Ⓒ Ⓓ Ⓔ   27 Ⓐ Ⓑ Ⓒ Ⓓ Ⓔ   36 Ⓐ Ⓑ Ⓒ Ⓓ Ⓔ   45 Ⓐ Ⓑ Ⓒ Ⓓ Ⓔ

SECTION 2: MATH ABILITY

1 Ⓐ Ⓑ Ⓒ Ⓓ Ⓔ   6 Ⓐ Ⓑ Ⓒ Ⓓ Ⓔ   11 Ⓐ Ⓑ Ⓒ Ⓓ Ⓔ   16 Ⓐ Ⓑ Ⓒ Ⓓ Ⓔ   21 Ⓐ Ⓑ Ⓒ Ⓓ Ⓔ
2 Ⓐ Ⓑ Ⓒ Ⓓ Ⓔ   7 Ⓐ Ⓑ Ⓒ Ⓓ Ⓔ   12 Ⓐ Ⓑ Ⓒ Ⓓ Ⓔ   17 Ⓐ Ⓑ Ⓒ Ⓓ Ⓔ   22 Ⓐ Ⓑ Ⓒ Ⓓ Ⓔ
3 Ⓐ Ⓑ Ⓒ Ⓓ Ⓔ   8 Ⓐ Ⓑ Ⓒ Ⓓ Ⓔ   13 Ⓐ Ⓑ Ⓒ Ⓓ Ⓔ   18 Ⓐ Ⓑ Ⓒ Ⓓ Ⓔ   23 Ⓐ Ⓑ Ⓒ Ⓓ Ⓔ
4 Ⓐ Ⓑ Ⓒ Ⓓ Ⓔ   9 Ⓐ Ⓑ Ⓒ Ⓓ Ⓔ   14 Ⓐ Ⓑ Ⓒ Ⓓ Ⓔ   19 Ⓐ Ⓑ Ⓒ Ⓓ Ⓔ   24 Ⓐ Ⓑ Ⓒ Ⓓ Ⓔ
5 Ⓐ Ⓑ Ⓒ Ⓓ Ⓔ   10 Ⓐ Ⓑ Ⓒ Ⓓ Ⓔ   15 Ⓐ Ⓑ Ⓒ Ⓓ Ⓔ   20 Ⓐ Ⓑ Ⓒ Ⓓ Ⓔ   25 Ⓐ Ⓑ Ⓒ Ⓓ Ⓔ

SECTION 3: STANDARD WRITTEN ENGLISH

1 Ⓐ Ⓑ Ⓒ Ⓓ Ⓔ   11 Ⓐ Ⓑ Ⓒ Ⓓ Ⓔ   21 Ⓐ Ⓑ Ⓒ Ⓓ Ⓔ   31 Ⓐ Ⓑ Ⓒ Ⓓ Ⓔ   41 Ⓐ Ⓑ Ⓒ Ⓓ Ⓔ
2 Ⓐ Ⓑ Ⓒ Ⓓ Ⓔ   12 Ⓐ Ⓑ Ⓒ Ⓓ Ⓔ   22 Ⓐ Ⓑ Ⓒ Ⓓ Ⓔ   32 Ⓐ Ⓑ Ⓒ Ⓓ Ⓔ   42 Ⓐ Ⓑ Ⓒ Ⓓ Ⓔ
3 Ⓐ Ⓑ Ⓒ Ⓓ Ⓔ   13 Ⓐ Ⓑ Ⓒ Ⓓ Ⓔ   23 Ⓐ Ⓑ Ⓒ Ⓓ Ⓔ   33 Ⓐ Ⓑ Ⓒ Ⓓ Ⓔ   43 Ⓐ Ⓑ Ⓒ Ⓓ Ⓔ
4 Ⓐ Ⓑ Ⓒ Ⓓ Ⓔ   14 Ⓐ Ⓑ Ⓒ Ⓓ Ⓔ   24 Ⓐ Ⓑ Ⓒ Ⓓ Ⓔ   34 Ⓐ Ⓑ Ⓒ Ⓓ Ⓔ   44 Ⓐ Ⓑ Ⓒ Ⓓ Ⓔ
5 Ⓐ Ⓑ Ⓒ Ⓓ Ⓔ   15 Ⓐ Ⓑ Ⓒ Ⓓ Ⓔ   25 Ⓐ Ⓑ Ⓒ Ⓓ Ⓔ   35 Ⓐ Ⓑ Ⓒ Ⓓ Ⓔ   45 Ⓐ Ⓑ Ⓒ Ⓓ Ⓔ
6 Ⓐ Ⓑ Ⓒ Ⓓ Ⓔ   16 Ⓐ Ⓑ Ⓒ Ⓓ Ⓔ   26 Ⓐ Ⓑ Ⓒ Ⓓ Ⓔ   36 Ⓐ Ⓑ Ⓒ Ⓓ Ⓔ   46 Ⓐ Ⓑ Ⓒ Ⓓ Ⓔ
7 Ⓐ Ⓑ Ⓒ Ⓓ Ⓔ   17 Ⓐ Ⓑ Ⓒ Ⓓ Ⓔ   27 Ⓐ Ⓑ Ⓒ Ⓓ Ⓔ   37 Ⓐ Ⓑ Ⓒ Ⓓ Ⓔ   47 Ⓐ Ⓑ Ⓒ Ⓓ Ⓔ
8 Ⓐ Ⓑ Ⓒ Ⓓ Ⓔ   18 Ⓐ Ⓑ Ⓒ Ⓓ Ⓔ   28 Ⓐ Ⓑ Ⓒ Ⓓ Ⓔ   38 Ⓐ Ⓑ Ⓒ Ⓓ Ⓔ   48 Ⓐ Ⓑ Ⓒ Ⓓ Ⓔ
9 Ⓐ Ⓑ Ⓒ Ⓓ Ⓔ   19 Ⓐ Ⓑ Ⓒ Ⓓ Ⓔ   29 Ⓐ Ⓑ Ⓒ Ⓓ Ⓔ   39 Ⓐ Ⓑ Ⓒ Ⓓ Ⓔ   49 Ⓐ Ⓑ Ⓒ Ⓓ Ⓔ
10 Ⓐ Ⓑ Ⓒ Ⓓ Ⓔ   20 Ⓐ Ⓑ Ⓒ Ⓓ Ⓔ   30 Ⓐ Ⓑ Ⓒ Ⓓ Ⓔ   40 Ⓐ Ⓑ Ⓒ Ⓓ Ⓔ   50 Ⓐ Ⓑ Ⓒ Ⓓ Ⓔ

SECTION 4: VERBAL ABILITY

1 Ⓐ Ⓑ Ⓒ Ⓓ Ⓔ   9 Ⓐ Ⓑ Ⓒ Ⓓ Ⓔ   17 Ⓐ Ⓑ Ⓒ Ⓓ Ⓔ   25 Ⓐ Ⓑ Ⓒ Ⓓ Ⓔ   33 Ⓐ Ⓑ Ⓒ Ⓓ Ⓔ

2 Ⓐ Ⓑ Ⓒ Ⓓ Ⓔ   10 Ⓐ Ⓑ Ⓒ Ⓓ Ⓔ   18 Ⓐ Ⓑ Ⓒ Ⓓ Ⓔ   26 Ⓐ Ⓑ Ⓒ Ⓓ Ⓔ   34 Ⓐ Ⓑ Ⓒ Ⓓ Ⓔ

3 Ⓐ Ⓑ Ⓒ Ⓓ Ⓔ   11 Ⓐ Ⓑ Ⓒ Ⓓ Ⓔ   19 Ⓐ Ⓑ Ⓒ Ⓓ Ⓔ   27 Ⓐ Ⓑ Ⓒ Ⓓ Ⓔ   35 Ⓐ Ⓑ Ⓒ Ⓓ Ⓔ

4 Ⓐ Ⓑ Ⓒ Ⓓ Ⓔ   12 Ⓐ Ⓑ Ⓒ Ⓓ Ⓔ   20 Ⓐ Ⓑ Ⓒ Ⓓ Ⓔ   28 Ⓐ Ⓑ Ⓒ Ⓓ Ⓔ   36 Ⓐ Ⓑ Ⓒ Ⓓ Ⓔ

5 Ⓐ Ⓑ Ⓒ Ⓓ Ⓔ   13 Ⓐ Ⓑ Ⓒ Ⓓ Ⓔ   21 Ⓐ Ⓑ Ⓒ Ⓓ Ⓔ   29 Ⓐ Ⓑ Ⓒ Ⓓ Ⓔ   37 Ⓐ Ⓑ Ⓒ Ⓓ Ⓔ

6 Ⓐ Ⓑ Ⓒ Ⓓ Ⓔ   14 Ⓐ Ⓑ Ⓒ Ⓓ Ⓔ   22 Ⓐ Ⓑ Ⓒ Ⓓ Ⓔ   30 Ⓐ Ⓑ Ⓒ Ⓓ Ⓔ   38 Ⓐ Ⓑ Ⓒ Ⓓ Ⓔ

7 Ⓐ Ⓑ Ⓒ Ⓓ Ⓔ   15 Ⓐ Ⓑ Ⓒ Ⓓ Ⓔ   23 Ⓐ Ⓑ Ⓒ Ⓓ Ⓔ   31 Ⓐ Ⓑ Ⓒ Ⓓ Ⓔ   39 Ⓐ Ⓑ Ⓒ Ⓓ Ⓔ

8 Ⓐ Ⓑ Ⓒ Ⓓ Ⓔ   16 Ⓐ Ⓑ Ⓒ Ⓓ Ⓔ   24 Ⓐ Ⓑ Ⓒ Ⓓ Ⓔ   32 Ⓐ Ⓑ Ⓒ Ⓓ Ⓔ   40 Ⓐ Ⓑ Ⓒ Ⓓ Ⓔ

SECTION 5: MATH ABILITY

1 Ⓐ Ⓑ Ⓒ Ⓓ Ⓔ   8 Ⓐ Ⓑ Ⓒ Ⓓ Ⓔ   15 Ⓐ Ⓑ Ⓒ Ⓓ Ⓔ   22 Ⓐ Ⓑ Ⓒ Ⓓ Ⓔ   29 Ⓐ Ⓑ Ⓒ Ⓓ Ⓔ

2 Ⓐ Ⓑ Ⓒ Ⓓ Ⓔ   9 Ⓐ Ⓑ Ⓒ Ⓓ Ⓔ   16 Ⓐ Ⓑ Ⓒ Ⓓ Ⓔ   23 Ⓐ Ⓑ Ⓒ Ⓓ Ⓔ   30 Ⓐ Ⓑ Ⓒ Ⓓ Ⓔ

3 Ⓐ Ⓑ Ⓒ Ⓓ Ⓔ   10 Ⓐ Ⓑ Ⓒ Ⓓ Ⓔ   17 Ⓐ Ⓑ Ⓒ Ⓓ Ⓔ   24 Ⓐ Ⓑ Ⓒ Ⓓ Ⓔ   31 Ⓐ Ⓑ Ⓒ Ⓓ Ⓔ

4 Ⓐ Ⓑ Ⓒ Ⓓ Ⓔ   11 Ⓐ Ⓑ Ⓒ Ⓓ Ⓔ   18 Ⓐ Ⓑ Ⓒ Ⓓ Ⓔ   25 Ⓐ Ⓑ Ⓒ Ⓓ Ⓔ   32 Ⓐ Ⓑ Ⓒ Ⓓ Ⓔ

5 Ⓐ Ⓑ Ⓒ Ⓓ Ⓔ   12 Ⓐ Ⓑ Ⓒ Ⓓ Ⓔ   19 Ⓐ Ⓑ Ⓒ Ⓓ Ⓔ   26 Ⓐ Ⓑ Ⓒ Ⓓ Ⓔ   33 Ⓐ Ⓑ Ⓒ Ⓓ Ⓔ

6 Ⓐ Ⓑ Ⓒ Ⓓ Ⓔ   13 Ⓐ Ⓑ Ⓒ Ⓓ Ⓔ   20 Ⓐ Ⓑ Ⓒ Ⓓ Ⓔ   27 Ⓐ Ⓑ Ⓒ Ⓓ Ⓔ   34 Ⓐ Ⓑ Ⓒ Ⓓ Ⓔ

7 Ⓐ Ⓑ Ⓒ Ⓓ Ⓔ   14 Ⓐ Ⓑ Ⓒ Ⓓ Ⓔ   21 Ⓐ Ⓑ Ⓒ Ⓓ Ⓔ   28 Ⓐ Ⓑ Ⓒ Ⓓ Ⓔ   35 Ⓐ Ⓑ Ⓒ Ⓓ Ⓔ

SECTION 6: MATH ABILITY

1 Ⓐ Ⓑ Ⓒ Ⓓ Ⓔ   8 Ⓐ Ⓑ Ⓒ Ⓓ Ⓔ   15 Ⓐ Ⓑ Ⓒ Ⓓ Ⓔ   22 Ⓐ Ⓑ Ⓒ Ⓓ Ⓔ   29 Ⓐ Ⓑ Ⓒ Ⓓ Ⓔ

2 Ⓐ Ⓑ Ⓒ Ⓓ Ⓔ   9 Ⓐ Ⓑ Ⓒ Ⓓ Ⓔ   16 Ⓐ Ⓑ Ⓒ Ⓓ Ⓔ   23 Ⓐ Ⓑ Ⓒ Ⓓ Ⓔ   30 Ⓐ Ⓑ Ⓒ Ⓓ Ⓔ

3 Ⓐ Ⓑ Ⓒ Ⓓ Ⓔ   10 Ⓐ Ⓑ Ⓒ Ⓓ Ⓔ   17 Ⓐ Ⓑ Ⓒ Ⓓ Ⓔ   24 Ⓐ Ⓑ Ⓒ Ⓓ Ⓔ   31 Ⓐ Ⓑ Ⓒ Ⓓ Ⓔ

4 Ⓐ Ⓑ Ⓒ Ⓓ Ⓔ   11 Ⓐ Ⓑ Ⓒ Ⓓ Ⓔ   18 Ⓐ Ⓑ Ⓒ Ⓓ Ⓔ   25 Ⓐ Ⓑ Ⓒ Ⓓ Ⓔ   32 Ⓐ Ⓑ Ⓒ Ⓓ Ⓔ

5 Ⓐ Ⓑ Ⓒ Ⓓ Ⓔ   12 Ⓐ Ⓑ Ⓒ Ⓓ Ⓔ   19 Ⓐ Ⓑ Ⓒ Ⓓ Ⓔ   26 Ⓐ Ⓑ Ⓒ Ⓓ Ⓔ   33 Ⓐ Ⓑ Ⓒ Ⓓ Ⓔ

6 Ⓐ Ⓑ Ⓒ Ⓓ Ⓔ   13 Ⓐ Ⓑ Ⓒ Ⓓ Ⓔ   20 Ⓐ Ⓑ Ⓒ Ⓓ Ⓔ   27 Ⓐ Ⓑ Ⓒ Ⓓ Ⓔ   34 Ⓐ Ⓑ Ⓒ Ⓓ Ⓔ

7 Ⓐ Ⓑ Ⓒ Ⓓ Ⓔ   14 Ⓐ Ⓑ Ⓒ Ⓓ Ⓔ   21 Ⓐ Ⓑ Ⓒ Ⓓ Ⓔ   28 Ⓐ Ⓑ Ⓒ Ⓓ Ⓔ   35 Ⓐ Ⓑ Ⓒ Ⓓ Ⓔ

SAT Practice Test 2*

SECTION 1 VERBAL ABILITY
30 MINUTES 45 QUESTIONS

For each question in this section, choose the best answer and blacken the corresponding space on the answer sheet.

Each question below consists of a word in capital letters, followed by five lettered words or phrases. Choose the word or phrase that is most nearly *opposite* in meaning to the word in capital letters. Since some of the questions require you to distinguish fine shades of meaning, consider all the choices before deciding which is best.

Example:

> GOOD: (A) sour (B) bad (C) red
> (D) hot (E) ugly
>
> Ⓐ ● Ⓒ Ⓓ Ⓔ

1. GARBLE: (A) enjoy (B) rinse (C) enclose
   (D) clarify (E) accept

2. GALLANT: (A) rude (B) serious
   (C) doubtful (D) neutral (E) ordinary

3. FURTIVE: (A) hopeless (B) shy (C) open
   (D) temporary (E) angelic

4. THERMAL: (A) improving (B) possible
   (C) beginning (D) reduced (E) frigid

5. PERNICIOUS: (A) delicious (B) healing
   (C) swerving (D) precious (E) conservative

6. SLOTHFUL: (A) permanent (B) ambitious
   (C) average (D) truthful (E) plentiful

7. WROTH: (A) surprised (B) enthusiastic
   (C) commonplace (D) foolish (E) pleased

8. FORTITUDE: (A) timidity (B) conservatism
   (C) placidity (D) laxness (E) ambition

9. CONCUR: (A) pertain (B) reveal
   (C) delay (D) oppose (E) anticipate

10. ANATHEMA: (A) obstacle (B) appreciation
    (C) blessing (D) protection (E) reward

11. RIFE: (A) rare (B) sharp (C) complete
    (D) smooth (E) puny

12. CIRCUMSPECT: (A) suspicious
    (B) overbearing (C) listless (D) determined
    (E) careless

13. CONDONE: (A) question (B) disturb
    (C) continue (D) punish (E) commence

14. ITINERANT: (A) fruitful (B) swift
    (C) restful (D) stationary (E) errant

15. FLACCID: (A) bold (B) alert (C) firm
    (D) ugly (E) protective

Each sentence below has one or two blanks, each blank indicating that something has been omitted. Beneath the sentence are five lettered words or sets of words. Choose the word or set of words that *best* fits the meaning of the sentence as a whole.

Example:

> Although its publicity has been ____, the film itself is intelligent, well-acted, handsomely produced, and altogether ____.
>
> (A) tasteless . . . respectable
> (B) extensive . . . moderate
> (C) sophisticated . . . amateur
> (D) risqué . . . crude
> (E) perfect . . . spectacular
>
> ● Ⓑ Ⓒ Ⓓ Ⓔ

16. Though he was a highly skilled computer programmer, he had little or no _____ in designing educational software

    (A) emotion (B) opportunity (C) exposure
    (D) competition (E) creativity

17. Millie craved attention, and in line with this desire for _____, she attended as many social functions as she could.

    (A) solitude (B) pleasure (C) identification
    (D) cooperation (E) understanding

18. He is one of the most _____ professors that I have ever had, with a _____ knowledge of his subject and a thoroughness in his teaching.

    (A) capable . . . limited
    (B) tantamount . . . tremendous
    (C) collegiate . . . remarkable
    (D) scholarly . . . profound
    (E) active . . . carefree

* The Diagnostic SAT Pre-Test at the beginning of this book is considered Practice Test 1.

19. Because the people of India were _____under British rule, many went over to the Japanese side during World War II.

    (A) employed   (B) deported   (C) educated
    (D) abused   (E) satisfied

20. The author told the publisher that the royalty payment specified in the contract was _____because the research costs, including traveling for writing the book, were far more than the royalties projected for a year.

    (A) rational   (B) precarious   (C) payable
    (D) insufficient   (E) incomprehensible

Each passage below is followed by questions based on its content. Answer all questions following a passage on the basis of what is *stated* or *implied* in that passage.

It was at Arles, the small city in the south of France where he stayed from early in 1888 to the spring of 1889, that Vincent van Gogh had his first real bout with madness. After a quarrel with Paul Gauguin, he cut off part of his
5 own ear. Yet Arles was also the scene of an astonishing burst of creativity. Over the short span of 15 months, van Gogh produced some 200 paintings and more than 100 drawings and watercolors, a record that only Picasso has matched in the modern era. Orchards and wheatfields un-
10 der the glowing sun, neighbors and townspeople, interiors of the Yellow House where he lived, were all subjects of his frenetic brush. The Arles canvases, alive with color— vermilion, emerald green, Prussian blue and a particularly brilliant yellow—have intensity of feeling that mark the
15 high point of his career, and deeply affected the work of artists to follow, notably the Fauves and the German Expressionists.

Van Gogh went to Arles after two years in Paris, where his beloved younger brother Theo, who supported him
20 psychologically and financially for most of his adult life, was an art dealer. In Paris, Vincent had met Gauguin, and other important artists—Lautrec, Degas, Pissarro, and Seurat. Like the last two, he worked in the Neo-Impres- sionist or Pointillist style—applying color in tiny dots or
25 strokes that "mixed" in the viewer's eye to create effects of considerable intensity. But he wanted "gayer" colors than Paris provided, the kind of atmosphere evoked by the Japanese prints he so admired. Then, too, the French cap- ital had exhausted him, mentally and physically. He felt
30 that in Arles, not exactly a bustling arts center, he might find serenity, and even establish an artistic tradition.

It was van Gogh's hope of founding a new artists' colony in the south that made him eager to have Gauguin, whose talent van Gogh readily recognized, join him at
35 Arles. The plan, on Vincent's part, was for Gauguin to stay in Arles for maybe a year, working and sharing with him the small living quarters and studio he had found for himself and dubbed the Yellow House. At first, the two men got along well. But they did not at all agree on judg-
40 ments of other artists. Still, Gauguin had an influence on van Gogh. Gaugin began pushing the younger artist to paint from memory rather than actuality.

Before the year was up, whether because of Gauguin's attempts to change van Gogh's style, or what, the two
45 men had apparently begun to get on each other's nerves. Gauguin wrote to Theo that he felt he had to return to

Paris, citing his and Vincent's "temperamental incompat- ibility." A letter from Vincent to Theo followed, noting that Gauguin was "a little out of sorts with the good town of Arles, and especially with me."
50
But then, the two apparently made up—but not for long. Gauguin returned to Paris and never saw van Gogh again, although they later had friendly correspondence.

21. Which of the following is the best title for the passage?

    (A) Where Van Gogh's Art Reached Its Zenith
    (B) An Unfortunate Mismatch Between Two Great Artists
    (C) Another Tale of a Genius Unable to Adjust to Society
    (D) A Prolific Painter Whose Art Will Live On
    (E) Van Gogh's Frustration in His Hope to Found a New Artists' Colony

22. According to the passage, which of the following statements is *not* true?

    (A) Fauvism is a movement in painting typified by vivid colors.
    (B) Gauguin was an older man than Theo.
    (C) Pissarro was a painter associated with the Neo- Impressionist school.
    (D) Van Gogh's work began to deteriorate after Gauguin's departure from Arles.
    (E) Van Gogh's behavior was, at times, quite abnormal.

23. For which of the following reasons did van Gogh decide to leave Paris and go to Arles?

    I. He sought a different environment for the kind of painting he wished to do.
    II. He had hopes of forming a new artists' colony.
    III. He wanted a more peaceful location where there was less stress.

    (A) II only
    (B) III only
    (C) I and II only
    (D) I and III only
    (E) I, II, and III

24. Gauguin's attitude toward van Gogh is best described in the passage as one of

(A) gentle ridicule
(B) unallayed suspicion
(C) tolerant acceptance
(D) open condescension
(E) resentful admiration

25. Aside from his quarrel with Gauguin, we may infer that a major contributory reason for van Gogh's going to the extreme of cutting off part of his ear was his

(A) concern about being able to support himself financially
(B) inability to get along with Gauguin
(C) failure to form an artists' colony in Arles
(D) mental and emotional instability
(E) being upset by Gauguin's attempts to change his style

As in the case of so many words used by the biologist and physiologist, the word acclimatization is hard to define. With increase in knowledge and understanding, meanings of words change. Originally the term acclima-
5　tization was taken to mean only the ability of human beings or animals or plants to accustom themselves to new and strange climatic conditions, primarily altered temperature. A person or a wolf moves to a hot climate and is uncomfortable there, but after a time is better able to withstand
10　the heat. But aside from temperature, there are other aspects of climate. A person or an animal may become adjusted to living at higher altitudes than those it was originally accustomed to. At really high altitudes, such as aviators may be exposed to, the low atmospheric pressure
15　becomes a factor of primary importance. In changing to a new environment, a person may, therefore, meet new conditions of temperature or pressure, and in addition may have to contend with different chemical surroundings. On high mountains, the amount of oxygen in the atmosphere
20　may be relatively small; in crowded cities, a person may become exposed to relatively high concentrations of carbon dioxide or even carbon monoxide, and in various areas may be exposed to conditions in which the water content of the atmosphere is extremely high or extremely low.
25　Thus in the case of humans, animals, and even plants, the concept of acclimatization includes the phenomena of increased toleration of high or low temperature, of altered pressure, and of changes in the chemical environment.
　　Let us define acclimatization, therefore, as the process
30　in which an organism or a part of an organism becomes accustomed or inured to an environment which is normally unsuitable to it or lethal for it. By and large, acclimatization is a relatively slow process. The term should not be taken to include relatively rapid adjustments such as
35　our sense organs are constantly making. This type of adjustment is commonly referred to by physiologists as "adaptation." Thus our touch sense soon becomes accustomed to the pressure of our clothes and we do not feel them; we soon fail to hear the ticking of a clock; obnoxious odors

after a time fail to make much impression on us, and our　40
eyes in strong light rapidly become insensitive.
　　The fundamental fact about acclimatization is that all animals and plants have some capacity to adjust themselves to changes in their environment. This is one of the most remarkable characteristics of living organisms, a　45
characteristic for which it is extremely difficult to find explanations.

26. According to the reading selection, all animals and plants

(A) have an ability for acclimatization.
(B) can adjust to only one change in the environment at a time.
(C) are successful in adjusting themselves to changes in their environments.
(D) can adjust to natural changes in the environment but not to artificially induced changes.
(E) that have once acclimatized themselves to an environmental change can acclimatize themselves more rapidly to subsequent changes.

27. It can be inferred from the reading selection that

(A) every change in the environment requires acclimatization by living things.
(B) plants and animals are more alike than they are different.
(C) biologists and physiologists study essentially the same things.
(D) the explanation of acclimatization is specific to each plant and animal.
(E) as science develops the connotation of terms may change.

28. According to the reading selection, acclimatization

(A) is similar to adaptation.
(B) is more important today than formerly.
(C) involves positive as well as negative adjustment.
(D) may be involved with a part of an organism but not with the whole organism.
(E) is more difficult to explain with the more complex present-day environment than formerly.

29. By inference from the reading selection, which one of the following would *not* require the process of acclimatization?

(A) An ocean fish placed in a lake
(B) A skin diver making a deep dive
(C) An airplane pilot making a high-altitude flight
(D) A person going from daylight into a darkened room
(E) A businessman moving from Denver, Colorado to New Orleans, Louisiana

30. According to the passage, a major distinction between acclimatization and adaptation is that acclimatization

(A) is more important than adaptation
(B) is relatively slow and adaptation is relatively rapid
(C) applies to adjustments while adaptation does not apply to adjustments
(D) applies to terrestrial animals and adaptation to aquatic animals
(E) is applicable to all animals and plants and adaptation only to higher animals and man

Select the words or set of words that *best* completes each of the following sentences.

31. The typist made no effort to be _____; she double-spaced the first and third letter, then single-spaced the second, fourth, and fifth letters.

(A) consistent (B) prompt (C) amicable
(D) courteous (E) considerate

32. As an outstanding publisher, Alfred Knopf was able to make occasional _____, but his bad judgment was tolerated in view of his tremendous _____.

(A) appearances . . . energy
(B) mistakes . . . success
(C) remarks . . . connections
(D) enemies . . . audacity
(E) conferences . . . patience

33. A desire to be applauded by those in attendance, not his sensitivity to the plight of the underprivileged, was the reason for his _____ at the charity affair.

(A) shyness (B) discomfort (C) surprise
(D) arrogance (E) generosity

34. A hundred years ago, the anti-evolutionists _____ Darwin's man's-descent-from-monkey theory; today a new group called Creationists is likewise contesting the same _____.

(A) communicated . . . lesson
(B) studied . . . downfall
(C) favored . . . program
(D) opposed . . . belief
(E) regarded . . . hypothesis

35. Many of the executives were aware that the owner was known not only for his _____ contracts but also for his _____ certain attractive employees.

(A) complex . . . addressing
(B) tricky . . . favoring
(C) simple . . . assisting
(D) wordy . . . disregarding
(E) legal . . . observing

Each question below consists of a related pair of words or phrases, followed by five lettered pairs of words or phrases. Select the lettered pair that *best* expresses a relationship similar to that expressed in the original pair.

Example:

YAWN : BOREDOM : :   (A) dream : sleep
(B) anger : madness   (C) smile : amusement
(D) face : expression   (E) impatience : rebellion
Ⓐ Ⓑ ● Ⓓ Ⓔ

36. CLIENT : ATTORNEY : :

(A) teacher : principal
(B) prisoner : policeman
(C) patient : doctor
(D) shopkeeper : customer
(E) audience : actor

37. CANCEL : SUBSCRIPTION : :

(A) nullify : contract
(B) reprimand : child
(C) ignore : summons
(D) renew : prescription
(E) challenge : adversary

38. HUB : WHEEL : :

(A) spoke : bicycle
(B) link : chain
(C) bullseye : target
(D) earth : universe
(E) noon : morning

39. BOAT : SLIP : :

(A) skate : rink
(B) surfboard : wave
(C) train : schedule
(D) paddle : oar
(E) airplane : hangar

40. PRIDE : LIONS : :

(A) gaggle : geese
(B) nest : birds
(C) slyness : wolves
(D) hospital : nurses
(E) family : children

41. PIONEER : WEST : :

(A) astronaut : moon
(B) pilgrim : shrine
(C) admiral : navy
(D) Indian : reservation
(E) invalid : obstacle

42. QUIVER : ARROW : :

(A) trigger : gun
(B) purse : money
(C) pea : pod
(D) sheath : sword
(E) cabinet : cupboard

43. DISINTERESTED : BIASED : :

(A) pious : gullible
(B) affluent : impecunious
(C) ruthless : vicious
(D) haughty : careless
(E) quixotic : daring

44. ACCOLADE : HERO : :

(A) blame : culprit
(B) laughter : actor
(C) disgust : bully
(D) gratitude : ingrate
(E) anger : monster

45. CLIP : HAIR : :

(A) raze : building
(B) dress : dummy
(C) cross : river
(D) photograph : scene
(E) hew : bough

S T O P

IF YOU FINISH BEFORE TIME IS CALLED, YOU MAY CHECK YOUR WORK ON THIS SECTION ONLY.
DO NOT WORK ON ANY OTHER SECTION IN THE TEST.

SECTION 2   MATH ABILITY

30 MINUTES   25 QUESTIONS

In this section solve each problem, using any available space on the page for scratchwork. Then decide which is the best of the choices given and blacken the corresponding space on the answer sheet.

The following information is for your reference in solving some of the problems.

Circle of radius r: Area = πr^2; Circumference = $2\pi r$
  The number of degrees of arc in a circle is 360.
The measure in degrees of a straight angle is 180.

Definitions of symbols:
  =   is equal to   ≦   is less than or equal to
  ≠   is unequal to   ≧   is greater than or equal to
  <   is less than   ‖   is parallel to
  >   is greater than   ⊥   is perpendicular to

Triangle: The sum of the measure in degrees of the angles of a triangle is 180.
  If ∠ CDA is a right angle, then

(1)   area of $\triangle ABC = \dfrac{AB \times CD}{2}$

(2) $AC^2 = AD^2 + DC^2$

Note: Figures which accompany problems in this test are intended to provide information useful in solving the problems. They are drawn as accurately as possible EXCEPT when it is stated in a specific problem that its figure is not drawn to scale. All figures lie in a plane unless otherwise indicated. All numbers used are real numbers.

1. There are 22 people on an island. A tram can carry at most 4 people at a time. What is the least number of trips that the tram must make to the mainland to get all of the people to the mainland?

   (A) 5   (B) 5.5   (C) 6   (D) 6.5   (E) 7

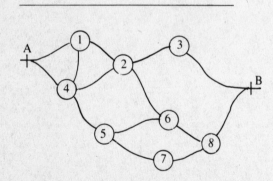

2. The figure above is a piece of fish net. Any path to get from point A to point B goes through points 1, 2, 3, 4, 5, 6, 7 and 8 as shown. Which of the following statements must be true about an ant crawling on the net from Point A to Point B?

   (A) If it goes through 2, it must go through 7.
   (B) If it goes through 3, it must go through 1.
   (C) Its route must go through either 2 or 7.
   (D) If it goes through 4, it must go through 3 or 5.
   (E) If it goes through 8, it must go through 2 or 5.

3. Susan has 3 times as many jellybeans as Mary, and Rose has 18 times as many jellybeans as Mary. What is the ratio

   $\dfrac{\text{Rose's jellybeans}}{\text{Susan's jellybeans}}$?

   (A) $\dfrac{72}{1}$ (B) $\dfrac{6}{1}$ (C) $\dfrac{2}{1}$ (D) $\dfrac{1}{2}$ (E) $\dfrac{1}{6}$

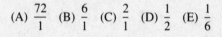

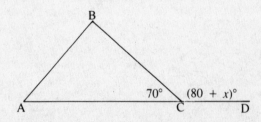

4. If AD is a straight line segment in the figure above, find the value of x.

   (A) 150   (B) 100   (C) 50   (D) 30   (E) 10

5. If 3 is added to a number and this sum is divided by 4 the result is 6. What is the number?

(A) 5   (B) 7   (C) 12   (D) 21   (E) 27

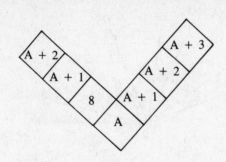

6. If the sum of the four terms in each of the diagonal rows is the same, then A =

(A) 4   (B) 5   (C) 6   (D) 7   (E) 8

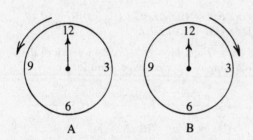

7. The two dials shown above operate simultaneously in the following manner: The hand in A turns counterclockwise while the hand in B turns clockwise. The hand of A moves to 9 at exactly the same moment that the hand of B moves to 3. Then the hand of A moves to 6 at exactly the same moment that the hand of B moves to 6, etc. If each hand starts at 12, where will each hand be at the end of 17 moves?

(A) Both at 12   (B) Both at 9
(C) A at 3 and B at 12   (D) A at 3 and B at 9
(E) A at 9 and B at 3

8. Given that $w = 7r + 6r + 5r + 4r + 3r$. Which of the terms listed below may be added to w so the resulting sum will be divisible by 7 for every positive integer r?

(A) $7r$ (B) $6r$ (C) $5r$ (D) $4r$ (E) $3r$

9. If the perimeter of a square is 20 meters, how many square meters are contained in its area?

(A) 100   (B) 25   (C) 20   (D) 10   (E) 5

10. Given that $80 + a = -32 + b$. Find the value of $b - a$.

(A) −112   (B) −48   (C) 2.5   (D) 48   (E) 112

11. If x is a positive integer, which of the following must be an even integer?

(A) $x + 2$ (B) $2x + 1$ (C) $3x + 1$
(D) $x^2 + x + 1$ (E) $x^2 + x + 2$

12. If $x^2 + 2xy + y^2 = 25$, $x + y > 0$ and $x - y = 1$, then $x =$

(A) 1   (B) 3   (C) 5   (D) 6   (E) 9

13. Given that $\frac{3}{4} < x < \frac{4}{5}$, which of the following is a possible value of x?

(A) $\frac{7}{16}$ (B) $\frac{13}{20}$ (C) $\frac{31}{40}$ (D) $\frac{16}{20}$ (E) $\frac{6}{7}$

14. A painter earns $10 an hour for all hours spent on a job. For a certain job, he worked from 7:00 a.m. until 5:00 p.m. on Monday, Tuesday, and Thursday and from 1:00 p.m. until 7:00 p.m. on Wednesday, Friday, and Saturday. How much did he earn for the whole job?

(A) $420   (B) $450   (C) $480   (D) $510
(E) $540

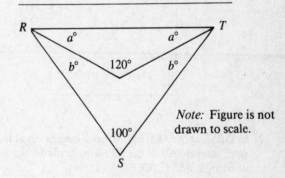

Note: Figure is not drawn to scale.

15. Given △RST above, what is the value of b?

(A) 50   (B) 40   (C) 30   (D) 20   (E) 10

Questions 16–18 refer to the following chart:

	Wins	Losses
Alan	8	2
Edward	6	4
Howard	4	6
Robert	2	8

Alan, Edward, Howard, and Robert are the only participants in a singles tennis tournament. Each individual has played 10 games and has achieved the record shown in the chart above. Each individual has 8 games remaining to play.

16. If Edward wins 6 of his remaining games, how many of his remaining games must Howard win to have 3/4 as many wins as Edward for the tournament?

(A) 3   (B) 4   (C) 5   (D) 6   (E) 7

17. What is the least number of remaining games that Robert must win in order to have more wins than losses for the tournament? (No tie games are possible.)

(A) 9 (B) 8 (C) 7 (D) 6 (E) 5

18. If Alan wins exactly $\frac{1}{2}$ of his remaining 8 games, it is possible for Edward, Howard, and Robert to finish the 18-game tournament with identical records. If no tie games occurred, the records for each of these three individuals would have to be which of the following?

(A) 10 wins and 8 losses
(B) 9 wins and 9 losses
(C) 8 wins and 10 losses
(D) 7 wins and 11 losses
(E) It cannot be determined from the information given.

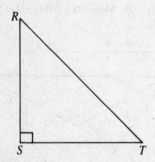

19. In △RST above, RS and ST have lengths equal to the same integer. All of the following could be the area of triangle RST EXCEPT

(A) $\frac{1}{2}$ (B) 2 (C) $4\frac{1}{2}$ (D) $12\frac{1}{2}$ (E) 20

20. A rectangular solid has dimensions of 2 feet × 2 feet × 1 foot. If it is sliced into small cubes, each of edge .1 foot, what is the maximum number of such cubes which can be formed?

(A) 40 (B) 500 (C) 1000 (D) 2000 (E) 4000

21. A circle is inscribed in a square. If the perimeter of the square is 40, what is the area of the circle?

(A) 100π (B) 50π (C) 40π (D) 25π (E) 5π

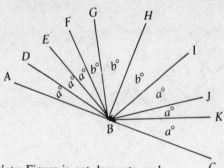

Note: Figure is not drawn to scale.

22. In the figure above, AC is a straight line segment. Line segments are drawn from B to D, E, F, G, H, I, J, and K respectively. Which of the following angles has a degree measure which can be found?

(A) ∠FBG (B) ∠EBG (C) ∠DBG
(D) ∠GBI (E) ∠GBJ

23. If $ax = r$ and $by = r - 1$, then which of the following is a correct expression for x?

(A) $\frac{by + 1}{a}$ (B) $\frac{by - 1}{a}$ (C) $\frac{by + r}{a}$
(D) $by + ar$ (E) $ab + ry$

24. A bag contains exactly 4 blue marbles, 7 green marbles, and 8 yellow marbles. Fred draws marbles at random from the bag without replacement, one by one. If he does not look at the marbles he draws out, how many marbles will he have to draw out before he knows for sure, that on his <u>next</u> draw he will have 1 marble for every color?

(A) 2 (B) 3 (C) 14 (D) 15 (E) 16

25. If 12 is the average (arithmetic mean) of 5 different integers, each integer >0, then the greatest that any one of the integers could be is

(A) 36 (B) 40 (C) 46 (D) 50 (E) 56

S T O P

IF YOU FINISH BEFORE TIME IS CALLED, YOU MAY CHECK YOUR WORK ON THIS SECTION ONLY.
DO NOT WORK ON ANY OTHER SECTION IN THE TEST.

SECTION 3   STANDARD WRITTEN ENGLISH TEST

30 MINUTES   50 QUESTIONS

The questions in this section measure skills that are important to writing well. In particular, they test your ability to recognize and use language that is clear, effective, and correct according to the requirements of standard written English, the kind of English found in most college textbooks.

Directions: The following contain problems in grammar, usage, diction (choice of words), and idiom.

> Some sentences are correct.
> No sentence contains more than one error.

You will find that the error, if there is one, is underlined and lettered. Assume that elements of the sentence that are not underlined are correct and cannot be changed. In choosing answers, follow the requirements of standard written English.

If there is an error, select the *one underlined part* that must be changed to make the sentence correct and blacken the corresponding space on your answer sheet.

If there is no error, blacken answer space Ⓔ .

EXAMPLE:

The region has a climate <u>so severe that</u> plants
                          A

<u>growing there</u> rarely <u>had been</u> more than twelve
      B   C

inches <u>high.</u> <u>No error</u>
        D   E

SAMPLE ANSWER

Ⓐ Ⓑ ● Ⓓ Ⓔ

---

1. When one leaves his car <u>to be repaired,</u> he <u>assumes</u>
   A   B   C

   that the mechanic will repair the car <u>good.</u> <u>No error</u>
                                          D   E

2. Bob could easily <u>have gotten</u> a higher score <u>on his</u>
                       A   B

   college entrance test if he <u>would have read</u> more
                                    C

   <u>in his school career.</u> <u>No error</u>
          D   E

3. Any modern novelist <u>would</u> <u>be thrilled</u> to have <u>his</u>
       A   B   C

   stories compared <u>with Dickens.</u> <u>No error</u>
                         D   E

4. After President Reagan <u>underwent</u> major abdominal
                              A

   <u>surgery for removal</u> of a polyp, his doctors said that
          B

   he had withstood the operation very <u>well.</u> <u>No error</u>
                                          C   D   E

5. Many people in the United States <u>don't scarcely</u>
                                        A

   <u>know about</u> the terrible hardships that the Lebanese
        B

   are experiencing in their <u>war-ravaged</u> country.
          C   D

   <u>No error</u>
       E

6. Cesar Chavez, president of the United Farm Workers
   Union, called for a Congressional investigation of
                  A
   certain California lettuce growers whom, he said,
                                      B
   were giving bribes to a rival union. No error.
      C   D   E

7. The automobile industry is experimenting with a new
                              A
   type of a motor that will consume less gasoline and
      B   C
   cause much less pollution. No error.
      D   E

8. The girl who won the beauty contest is nowhere near
            A   B
   as beautiful as my mother was when she was a bride.
            C   D
   No error.
      E

9. Sitting opposite my sister and me in the subway were
           A   B
   them same men who walked alongside us and tried to
      C   D
   pinch us on Fifth Avenue. No error.
                               E

10. Even if Detroit could provide nonpolluting cars by
       A   B
    the original deadline to meet prescribed Federal
                                 C
    standards for clean air, the effect in big cities would
    be slight because only new cars would be properly
                       D
    equipped. No error.
              E

11. Of the two cars that the Smiths have, the Plymouth
                                     A
    is, without any question, the cheapest to run.
        B   C   D
    No error.
       E

12. Since one of their members was a prisoner of war in
                   A
    Vietnam, the family felt badly when they heard
                             B
    over the radio that the peace talks
       C
    were to be discontinued. No error.
       D   E

13. Man cannot live by bread alone, or can he live
        A   B   C   D
    without bread. No error.
                     E

14. Have you read in the *Columbia Spectator* that Jeff's
       A   B
    leg was broken while playing football? No error.
       C   D   E

15. Having swam two-thirds of the distance across the
       A   B   C
    English Channel, Dixon could not give up now.
                           D
    No error.
       E

16. George Foreman did like he said when he forecast
                       A   B
    that he would knock out Joe Frazier to win the
                   C   D
    world's heavyweight championship. No error.
                                       E

17. In the discussion, one speaker held that, since we
                               A
    live in a money-oriented society, the average
             B
    individual cares little about solving anyone's else
                       C   D
    problems. No error.
              E

18. Due to the meat boycott, the butchers were doing
       A   B
    about half of the business that they were doing
          C
    previous to the boycott. No error.
       D   E

19. We requested the superintendent of the building
to clean up the storage room <u>in</u> the basement <u>so that</u>
　　A　　　　　　　　　　B　　　　　　C
the children <u>had</u> enough space for their bicycles.
　　　　　　D

<u>No error.</u>
　　E

20. <u>Lidocaine's</u> usefulness <u>as</u> a local anesthetic was
　　A　　　　　　　　B
discovered by two Swedish chemists who
<u>repeatedly tested</u> the <u>drug's</u> effects on their bodies.
　　　C　　　　　　　D

<u>No error.</u>
　　E

21. Namath played a <u>real fine game</u> <u>in spite of</u> the fact
　　　　　　　　　　A　　　　　　B
that the Jets lost <u>by</u> a touchdown <u>which</u> the opposing
　　　　　　　　　C　　　　　　　D
team scored in the last minute of play. <u>No error.</u>
　　　　　　　　　　　　　　　　　　E

22. You <u>may not realize</u> it <u>but</u> the weather in Barbados
　　　　A　　　　　　B
<u>during Christmas</u> is <u>like New York</u> in June.
　　C　　　　　　　D

<u>No error.</u>
　　E

23. Stores were <u>jammed</u> with <u>last-minute</u> Christmas
　　　　　　　A　　　　　B
shoppers, but the festive spirit was <u>slightly</u> disrupted
　　　　　　　　　　　　　　C
by homemade bombs that <u>exploded</u> at two
　　　　　　　　　　D
department stores. <u>No error.</u>
　　　　　　　　　E

24. The teacher did not encourage the student <u>any</u> even
　　　　　　　　　　　　　　　　A
though the boy began <u>to weep</u> when he <u>was told</u> that
　　　　　　　　B　　　　　　　C
his poor marks would likely <u>hold up</u> his graduation.
　　　　　　　　　　　　D

<u>No error.</u>
　　E

25. Allen <u>has stated</u> that he <u>has always had</u> a great
　　　　A　　　　　　　　B
<u>interest and admiration</u> for the <u>work</u> of the British
　　C　　　　　　　　　　　D
economist Keynes. <u>No error.</u>
　　　　　　　　E

Directions: In each of the following sentences, some part or all of the sentence is underlined. Below each sentence you will find five ways of phrasing the underlined part. Select the answer that produces the most effective sentence, one that is clear and exact, without awkwardness or ambiguity, and blacken the corresponding space on your answer sheet. In choosing answers, follow the requirements of standard written English. Choose the answer that best expresses the meaning of the original sentence.

Answer (A) is always the same as the underlined part. Choose answer (A) if you think the original sentence needs no revision.

EXAMPLE: SAMPLE ANSWER

Laura Ingalls Wilder published her first book
and she was sixty-five years old then.
(A) and she was sixty-five years old then
(B) when she was sixty-five years old
(C) at age sixty-five years old
(D) upon reaching sixty-five years
(E) at the time when she was sixty-five

---

26. At the top of the hill <u>to the left of the tall oak</u> is where they live.

    (A) to the left of the tall oak
    (B) where the tall oak is to the left of it
    (C) and the tall oak is to the left
    (D) left of the tall oak
    (E) to the tall oak's left

27. Martin pretended to be asleep <u>whenever she came</u> into the room.

    (A) whenever she came
    (B) at the time she comes
    (C) although she came
    (D) since she came
    (E) by the time she came

28. Once a person starts taking addictive drugs <u>it is most likely he will be led to take more.</u>

    (A) it is most likely he will be led to take more
    (B) he will probably take them over and over again
    (C) it is hard to stop him from taking more
    (D) he is likely to continue taking them
    (E) he will have a tendency to continue taking them

29. We have not yet been informed <u>concerning the one who broke the window.</u>

    (A) concerning the one who broke the window
    (B) about the identity of the individual who is responsible for breaking the window
    (C) of the window-breaker
    (D) as to who broke the window
    (E) who broke the window

30. Having the highest marks in his class, <u>the college offered him a scholarship.</u>

    (A) the college offered him a scholarship
    (B) the college offered a scholarship to him
    (C) he was offered a scholarship by the college
    (D) a scholarship was offered him by the college
    (E) a college scholarship was offered to him

31. <u>The government's failing to keep it's pledges</u> will mean disaster.

    (A) The government's failing to keep it's pledges
    (B) The governments failing to keep it's pledges
    (C) The government's failing to keep its pledges
    (D) The government failing to keep its pledges
    (E) The governments failing to keep their pledges

32. Her father <u>along with her mother and sister insist</u> that she stop smoking.

    (A) along with her mother and sister insist
    (B) along with her mother and sister insists
    (C) along with her mother and sister are insisting
    (D) along with her mother and sister were insisting
    (E) as well as her mother and sister insist

33. Most gardeners like to cultivate <u>these kind of flowers</u> in the early spring.

    (A) these kind of flowers
    (B) these kind of flower
    (C) them kinds of flowers
    (D) those kind of flower
    (E) this kind of flowers

34. The doctor informs us that my aunt <u>has not and never will recover</u> from the fall.

(A) has not and never will recover
(B) has not recovered and never will
(C) has not and never would recover
(D) has not recovered and never will recover
(E) had not and never will recover

35. The senator was neither in favor of <u>or opposed to the proposed legislation.</u>

(A) or opposed to the proposed legislation
(B) and was not opposed to the proposed legislation
(C) the proposed legislation or opposed to it
(D) nor opposed to the proposed legislation
(E) the proposed legislation or opposed to the proposed legislation

36. <u>Glory as well as gain is to be his reward.</u>

(A) Glory as well as gain is to be his reward.
(B) As his reward, glory as well as gain is to be his.
(C) He will be rewarded by glory as well as gain.
(D) Glory also gain are to be his reward.
(E) First glory, then gain, will be his reward.

37. She prefers to write poems which describe the slums and <u>study the habits of the underprivileged.</u>

(A) study the habits of the underprivileged
(B) study the underprivileged's habits
(C) studying the habits of the underprivileged
(D) to study the habits of the underprivileged
(E) she prefers to study the habits of the underprivileged

38. <u>By studying during weekends, her grades improved surprisingly.</u>

(A) By studying during weekends, her grades improved surprisingly.
(B) By studying during weekends, she improved her grades surprisingly.
(C) She was surprised to find her grades improved after studying during weekends.
(D) Her grades, by studying during weekends, improved surprisingly.
(E) Surprisingly, by studying during weekends, her grades improved.

39. The streets here are <u>as dirty as any other city,</u> according to recent research studies.

(A) as dirty as any other city
(B) so dirty as any other city
(C) dirty like any other city
(D) as dirty as those of any other city
(E) as those of any city

40. Betty is buxom, <u>with blue eyes, and has a pleasant manner.</u>

(A) with blue eyes, and has a pleasant manner
(B) with eyes of blue, and a pleasant manner
(C) blue-eyed and pleasant
(D) blue eyes as well as pleasant
(E) and has blue eyes as well as a pleasant manner

<u>Note</u>: The remaining questions are like those at the beginning of the section.

<u>Directions</u>: For each sentence in which you find an error, select the one underlined part that must be changed to make the sentence correct and blacken the corresponding space on your answer sheet.

If there is no error, blacken answer space Ⓔ

EXAMPLE:

SAMPLE ANSWER

Ⓐ Ⓑ ● Ⓓ Ⓔ

The region has a climate <u>so severe</u> that plants
                 A

<u>growing</u> there <u>rarely had been</u> more than twelve
  B   C

<u>inches high.</u> <u>No error</u>
   D   E

41. According to the most recent estimates, Greater
    $\underline{\text{A}}$

    Miami has more than 450,000 Spanish-speaking
    $\underline{\qquad}$ $\underline{\qquad}$
    B   C

    residents, of who about 400,000 are Cubans.
    $\underline{\text{D}}$

    No error.
    $\underline{\text{E}}$

42. Sharon planned to pay around a hundred dollars for a
    $\underline{\text{A}}$ $\underline{\text{B}}$

    new spring coat but when she saw a gorgeous coat

    which sold for two hundred dollars, she decided
    $\underline{\text{C}}$

    to buy it. No error.
    $\underline{\text{D}}$ $\underline{\text{E}}$

43. Had Lincoln have been alive during World War II,
    $\underline{\qquad}$
    A

    he would have regarded the racial situation in the
    $\underline{\qquad}$ $\underline{\qquad}$
    B   C

    armed forces as a throwback to pre-Civil War days.
    $\underline{\text{D}}$

    No error.
    $\underline{\text{E}}$

44. Members of the staff of the District Attorney made
    $\underline{\qquad}$
    A

    more than $100,000 from a get-rich-quick scheme in
    $\underline{\qquad}$
    B

    which investors were bilked of about $1-million.
    $\underline{\qquad}$ $\underline{\qquad}$
    C   D

    No error.
    $\underline{\text{E}}$

45. The reason that Roberto Clemente, the great baseball
    $\underline{\text{A}}$

    star, was on the plane that crashed was because he
    $\underline{\qquad}$ $\underline{\qquad}$
    B   C

    was on his way to help the victims of the earthquake.
    $\underline{\text{D}}$

    No error.
    $\underline{\text{E}}$

46. Since oxygen is indispensable to human life,
    $\underline{\qquad}$
    A

    scientists are exploring the possibility of providing
    $\underline{\qquad}$ $\underline{\qquad}$
    B   C

    oxygen for future inhabitants of space stations.
    $\underline{\qquad}$
    D

    No error.
    $\underline{\text{E}}$

47. Its my opinion that learning the correct pronunciation
    $\underline{\text{A}}$ $\underline{\text{B}}$

    should precede any attempt to learn the correct
    $\underline{\qquad}$ $\underline{\qquad}$
    C   D

    spelling of a word. No error.
    $\underline{\qquad}$
    E

48. If I would have known more about the person whom
    $\underline{\qquad}$ $\underline{\qquad}$ $\underline{\qquad}$
    A   B   C

    I was writing to, I would have written a better
    $\underline{\qquad}$
    D

    answer. No error.
    $\underline{\qquad}$
    E

49. If you compare Bill and Joe as far as scholarship
    $\underline{\qquad}$ $\underline{\qquad}$
    A   B

    goes, you will have to conclude that Bill is, without
    $\underline{\qquad}$
    C

    any question, the brightest. No error.
    $\underline{\qquad}$ $\underline{\qquad}$
    D   E

50. In spite of how very poor Ellen had done in the art
    $\underline{\qquad}$ $\underline{\qquad}$ $\underline{\qquad}$
    A   B   C

    competition, she was far from discouraged. No error.
    $\underline{\qquad}$ $\underline{\qquad}$
    D   E

S T O P

**IF YOU FINISH BEFORE TIME IS CALLED, YOU MAY CHECK YOUR WORK ON THIS SECTION ONLY.
DO NOT WORK ON ANY OTHER SECTION IN THE TEST.**

SECTION 4 VERBAL ABILITY

30 MINUTES   40 QUESTIONS

For each question in this section, choose the best answer and blacken the corresponding space on the answer sheet.

Each question below consists of a word in capital letters, followed by five lettered words or phrases. Choose the word or phrase that is most nearly *opposite* in meaning to the word in capital letters. Since some of the questions require you to distinguish fine shades of meaning, consider all the choices before deciding which is best.

Example:

GOOD: (A) sour (B) bad (C) red
(D) hot (E) ugly

(A) ● (C) (D) (E)

1. ROBUST: (A) clumsy (B) quiet
   (C) ridiculous (D) feeble (E) flatchested

2. GARRULOUS: (A) silent (B) brilliant
   (C) capable (D) fabulous (E) skimpy

3. ABHOR: (A) renew (B) join (C) associate
   (D) cancel (E) appreciate

4. PLACATE: (A) cleanse (B) relocate
   (C) ruffle (D) displace (E) complicate

5. FRUGAL: (A) beautiful (B) wasteful
   (C) hardy (D) warm (E) certain

6. BINGE: (A) simple task (B) quick decision
   (C) reluctant person (D) formal affair
   (E) dangerous move

7. LUCID: (A) underlying (B) complex
   (C) luxurious (D) tight (E) general

8. VOUCHSAFE: (A) steal (B) postpone
   (C) refuse (D) injure (E) flee

9. LATITUDE: (A) frenzy (B) attitude
   (C) promptness (D) altitude (E) restriction

10. RECALCITRANT: (A) manageable
    (B) disregarded (C) dynamic (D) unworthy
    (E) monotonous

Each sentence below has one or two blanks, each blank indicating that something has been omitted. Beneath the sentence are five lettered words or sets of words. Choose the word or set of words that *best* fits the meaning of the sentence as a whole.

Example:

Although its publicity has been ____, the film itself is intelligent, well-acted, handsomely produced, and altogether ____.

(A) tasteless . . . respectable
(B) extensive . . . moderate
(C) sophisticated . . . amateur
(D) risqué . . . crude
(E) perfect . . . spectacular

● (B) (C) (D) (E)

11. Maggie was quite _____ about having her husband remove his shoes before he stepped into the living room; yet the rest of the apartment was very _____ whenever I visited them.

(A) indifferent . . . comfortable
(B) perplexed . . . weird
(C) firm . . . disorderly
(D) considerate . . . modern
(E) humorous . . . attractive

12. Those who were invited to Peter's party had to come dressed in _____ clothes, thus convincing all the guests of his _____ inclination.

(A) sonorous . . . imaginative
(B) tawdry . . . humble
(C) raucous . . . peaceloving
(D) tattered . . . nightmarish
(E) oldfashioned . . . nostalgic

13. In large cities, the number of family-owned grocery stores has fallen so sharply that the opportunity to shop in such a place is _____ occasion.

(A) a celebrated (B) an old (C) a fanciful
(D) a rare (E) an avid

14. In view of the company's _____ claims that their scalp treatment would grow hair on bald heads, the newspaper _____ their advertising.

    (A) unproved . . . banned
    (B) interesting . . . canceled
    (C) unreasonable . . . welcomed
    (D) innocent . . . settled
    (E) immune . . . questioned

15. The foreman's leniency, especially in being overfriendly, had its _____ , one of which was _____ workmanship.

    (A) compensations . . . unacceptable
    (B) innuendoes . . . superior
    (C) drawbacks . . . shoddy
    (D) frequencies . . . attractive
    (E) cancellations . . . mediocre

Each question below consists of a related pair of words or phrases, followed by five lettered pairs of words or phrases. Select the lettered pair that *best* expresses a relationship similar to that expressed in the original pair.

Example:

YAWN : BOREDOM : :   (A) dream : sleep
(B) anger : madness   (C) smile : amusement
(D) face : expression   (E) impatience : rebellion

Ⓐ Ⓑ ● Ⓓ Ⓔ

16. DOLPHIN : FLIPPER : :

    (A) insect : antenna
    (B) burglar : mask
    (C) gull : wing
    (D) plane : radar
    (E) man : lung

17. GUILE : INGENUOUS : :

    (A) appetite : voracious
    (B) chivalry : natural
    (C) prudence : demanding
    (D) courage : timorous
    (E) nobility : charming

18. ECOLOGY : ENVIRONMENT : :

    (A) petrology : rocks
    (B) meteorology : heavenly bodies
    (C) botany : animal life
    (D) etymology : insects
    (E) physiology : motion

19. ZEBRA : STRIATED : :

    (A) penguin : flightless
    (B) cat : domesticated
    (C) sluggard : indolent
    (D) monkey : imitative
    (E) leopard : mottled

20. ANIMAL : HIDE : :

    (A) sailor : uniform
    (B) child : blanket
    (C) floor : carpet
    (D) head : hat
    (E) person : skin

21. DEFOLIATE : TREE : :

    (A) molt : snake
    (B) blossom : flower
    (C) melt : glacier
    (D) amputate : limb
    (E) criticize : idea

22. CARAVAN : DESERT : :

    (A) library : books
    (B) safari : jungle
    (C) worship : temple
    (D) casino : betting
    (E) boat : cruise

23. HOBO : HOME : :

    (A) professional : team
    (B) citizen : country
    (C) orphan : parent
    (D) dreamer : hope
    (E) philosopher : follower

24. EMULATE : MODEL : :

    (A) paraphrase : sentence
    (B) provide : alibi
    (C) testify : judge
    (D) worship : icon
    (E) smile : joke

25. PROTEAN : IMMUTABLE : :

    (A) noxious : harmful
    (B) prodigal : reckless
    (C) perfidious : treacherous
    (D) acquired : innate
    (E) antiquated : archaic

Each passage is followed by questions based on its content. Answer all questions following a passage on the basis of what is *stated* or *implied* in that passage.

A successful city neighborhood is a place that keeps sufficiently abreast of its problems so it is not destroyed by them. An unsuccessful neighborhood is a place that is overwhelmed by its defects and problems and is progres-
5 sively more helpless before them. Our cities contain all degrees of success and failure. But on the whole we Americans are poor at handling city neighborhoods, as can be seen by the long accumulations of failures in our great gray belts on the one hand, and by the Turfs of rebuilt
10 city on the other hand.

It is fashionable to suppose that certain touchstones of the good life will create good neighborhoods—schools, parks, clean housing and the like. How easy life would be if this were so! How charming to control a complicated
15 and ornery society by bestowing upon it rather simple physical goodies. In real life, cause and effect are not so simple. Thus a Pittsburgh study, undertaken to show the supposed clear correlation between better housing and improved social conditions, compared delinquency records
20 in still uncleared slums to delinquency records in new housing projects, and came to the embarrassing discovery that the delinquency was higher in the improved housing. Does this mean improved shelter increases delinquency? Not at all. It means other things may be more important
25 than housing, however, and it means also that there is no direct, simple relationship between good housing and good behavior, a fact which the whole tale of the Western world's history, the whole collection of our literature, and the whole fund of observation open to any of us should long
30 since have made evident. Good shelter is a useful good in itself, as shelter. When we try to justify good shelter instead on the pretentious grounds that it will work social or family miracles we fool ourselves. The philosopher Reinhold Niebuhr has called this particular self-deception,
35 "The doctrine of salvation by bricks."

26. The writer would probably agree that

(A) there is little delinquency among rich children because of their superior living quarters
(B) an increase in a family's earning power should reduce delinquency among the children
(C) a successful city neighborhood is one that has no problems
(D) if the people of a neighborhood have good housing, parks, and schools, then their neighborhood will certainly be a good one
(E) Reinhold Niebuhr argues that new housing for the poor will benefit society generally

27. The passage does *not* indicate that

(A) Americans have a poor record in their supervision and improvement of city neighborhoods
(B) the Pittsburgh study shows no connection between good housing and a good neighborhood
(C) the better the housing the more incidents of delinquency
(D) history shows that there is no definite correlation between good housing and good behavior
(E) improved housing should be encouraged regardless of correlation studies.

28. The "gray belts" and the "Turfs" in line 9 refer respectively to

(A) unused parks and newly developed areas with trees
(B) clothing stores and golf courses
(C) a large proportion of older people and an influx of foreigners
(D) rundown sections and territories under gang control
(E) unlit parkways and tall buildings

Within 80 years, some scientists estimate, the world must produce more than eight times the present world food supply. The productiveness of the sea raises our hopes for an adequate food supply in the future. Aided by men of
5 science, we have set forth to plumb that 70 percent of the earth that remains unexplored—the ocean depths. Thus, we may better discover and utilize the sea's bounties for the world's hungry.

It is fish protein concentrate that is sought from the
10 seas. By utilizing the unharvested fish in United States waters alone, enough fish protein concentrate can be obtained to provide supplemental animal protein for one billion people for one year at the cost of less than half a cent per day per person. The malnutrition of children is ap-
15 pallingly tragic. But the crime lies in society's unrestrained procreation, not in its negligence in producing fish powder. But wherever the population projections are contemplated, the answer to the problem is something like this: There are few projects that could do more to raise the nutritional
20 level of mankind than a full-scale scientific effort to develop the resources of the sea. Each year some thirty million tons of food products are taken from the sea, which account for 12 percent of the world's animal proteins. Nations with their swelling populations must push forward
25 into the sea frontiers for food supplies. Private industry must step up its marine research and the federal government must make new attacks on the problem of marine research development. There is a tone of desperateness in all these designs on the sea.

30 But what is most startling is the assumption that the seas are a virgin resource unsullied and unmauled. The fact is that the seas have been, and are being, hurt, directly and indirectly, by the same forces that have abused the

land. In the broad pattern of ecological relationships the
35 seas are not separable from what happens on the land. The
poisons that contaminate the soil and the air bring in mas-
·sive doses into the continental shelf waters. The salt marshes
and estuaries that serve as breeding grounds for the sea
are victims of the same development that pressure of pop-
40 ulation has brought to the inland areas. The filth and pollution that spills from our urban sewers and industrial
outfalls despoil our bays and coastal waters. All the border
seas are already heavily contaminated by the same exploitation drives that have undermined the quality of life
45 on land.

29. According to the passage, which of the following
statements is true?

(A) Though the situation is not urgent, we should
press forward with our marine research.
(B) Nations throughout the world must be provided
fish, fresh or frozen, for needed protein.
(C) There are enough fish in the seas to allow for the
annual protein needs of a quarter of the world's 4
billion people.
(D) The oceans are the major source of the world's
protein supply.
(E) Scientists are at work examining 70 percent of the
ocean areas of the world.

30. The author's primary concern is that

(A) the oceans will help to provide enough food for
the world in the future
(B) we will find a way to stop unethical businessmen
from contaminating our water areas
(C) thirty million tons of food products are taken
from the sea every year
(D) city sewers are pouring forth polluted matter into
bays and coastal waters
(E) a steady increase in population will result in more
hungry mouths to feed.

31. The tone of the passage is one of

(A) patient watchfulness
(B) philosophical resignation
(C) sheer despair
(D) pretended anger
(E) justifiable anxiety

32. The most appropriate title for this passage is

(A) The Role of Science in Fighting Hunger
(B) Water Pollution and How to Avoid It
(C) There's Many a Fish in the Sea
(D) The Sea and Our Future Food Supply
(E) The Importance of Protein in our Diets

The most striking fact about higher learning in America
is the confusion that besets it. The first cause of this confusion is very vulgar; it is the love of money. I do not
mean, of course, that universities do not need money and

that they should not try to get it. I mean only that they 5
should have an educational policy and then try to finance
it, instead of letting financial accidents determine their
educational policy. Undoubtedly the love of money and
that sensitivity to public demands that it creates has a good
deal to do with the service-station conception of a uni- 10
versity. According to this conception a university must
make itself felt in the community; it must be constantly,
currently felt. A state university must help the farmers
look after their cows. An endowed university must help
adults get better jobs by giving them courses in the after- 15
noon and evening.

Even more important than the love of money as a cause
of our confusion is our confused notion of democracy. It
is assumed that a student may stay in public education as
long as he likes, may study what he likes, and may claim 20
any degree. As a result, we again have the conclusion
drawn that education should be immediately responsive to
public opinion. But what really determines the length of
free education for all? Not democratic principles but economic conditions. Under present conditions some kind of 25
educational activity must be provided up to approximately
the twentieth year. This means that the public junior college will become the characteristic educational institution
of the United States. Free education should exist beyond
the sophomore level also, but it should be open only to 30
those who have clearly demonstrated their ability to profit
by it. The only hope of securing a true university in this
country is to see to it that it does not become a finishing
school for students incapable of receiving intellectual training or a mere school for vocational training. A university 35
must be a home of independent intellectual work. It cannot
make its contribution to democracy on any other terms.

Some institutions must be strong enough and clear enough
to stand firm and show our people what the higher learning
is. As education it is the single-minded pursuit of the 40
intellectual virtues. As scholarship it is the single-minded
devotion to the advancement of knowledge. Only if the
colleges and universities can devote themselves to these
objects can we look hopefully to the future of higher learning in America. 45

33. Which statement(s) is(are) stated or implied by the
passage?

I. Some universities must stand firm against
public opinion.
II. The general public has a correct conception
of the nature of higher learning.
III. Universities should not adopt an educational
policy merely because they think they can get
financial support for this policy from the public.
IV. The state universities, as they now function,
are good examples of what a true university
should be.

(A) I and III only
(B) II and IV only
(C) I, II, and III only
(D) II, III, and IV only
(E) I, II, III, and IV

34. It can be inferred from the passage that the author believes

(A) job training should be an important part of the university curriculum
(B) a free university education should be available to all Americans
(C) money matters should be of some concern to university administrators
(D) the future of higher learning is very bleak for our nation's universities
(E) universities should include such courses as how to get along with others and how to succeed in business

35. Which one of the following titles best reflects the main focus of the passage?

(A) Universities Are Becoming Big Business
(B) Democracy and Our Universities
(C) Historical Development of Our University System
(D) How Our Universities Must Change to Survive
(E) Nation's Universities Need An Overhauling

36. The author's approach to his subject is

(A) emotional   (B) analytical   (C) forgiving
(D) statistical   (E) casual

37. According to the passage, which of the following statements is *not* true?

(A) It is the function of a university to encourage students to work with intellectual independence.
(B) Money is an important factor today in determining how much free education a person can get.
(C) The love of money has negative value for a quality program of higher learning.
(D) The author favors state universities' giving afternoon and evening courses for adults to get better jobs.
(E) Higher learning involves the development of characteristics such as sincerity, discipline, and consideration for others.

Violence is alive and well on television. Yet there appears to be a difference in the quality, variety and pervasiveness of today's televised violence. Some observers believe that, as a result of more than three decades of
5 television, viewers have developed a kind of immunity to the horror of violence. By the age of 16, for example, the average young person will have seen some 18,000 murders on television. One extension of this phenomenon may be an appetite for more varied kinds of violence. On the basis of the amount of exposure, certain things that initially 10 would have been beyond the pale have become more readily accepted.

Violence on TV has been more prevalent than in recent years, in large measure because there are fewer situation comedies and more action series. But also because some 15 25 million of the nation's 85 million homes with television now receive one of the pay cable services which routinely show uncut feature films containing graphic violence as early as 8 in the evening.

The evidence is becoming overwhelming that just as 20 witnessing violence in the home may contribute to children learning and acting out violent behavior, violence on TV and in the movies may lead to the same result. Studies have shown that a steady diet of watching graphic violence or sexually violent films such as those shown on cable TV 25 has caused some men to be more willing to accept violence against women such as rape and wife-beating. Not only actual violence, but the kind of violence coming through the television screen is causing concern. One of the principal developments is the increasing sophistication of the 30 weaponry. The simple gunfight of the past has been augmented by high-tech crimes like terrorist bombings. A gunfighter shooting down a sheriff is one thing. When you have terrorist bombs, the potential is there for hundreds to die. Programs in the past used the occasional machine 35 gun, but such weapons as the M-60 machine gun and Uzi semi-automatic have become commonplace today on network shows.

Many people are no longer concerned about televised violence because they feel it is the way of the world. It is 40 high time that broadcasters provide public messages on TV screens that would warn viewers about the potentially harmful effects of viewing televised violence.

38. The title that best summarizes the content of the passage is

(A) TV's Role in the Rising Crime Rate
(B) Violence on TV—Past and Present
(C) TV Won't Let Up on Violence
(D) Violence Raises the TV Ratings
(E) Violence Galore on Cable TV

39. Which of the following types of TV programs would the author be *least* likely to approve of?

(A) A cowboy Western called "Have Gun, Will Travel"

(B) A talk show dealing with teen-age pregnancy caused by a rape

(C) A documentary dealing with Vietnam veterans suffering from the aftereffects of herbicide spraying during the war

(D) A movie showing a bomb exploding in a bus carrying civilians on their way to work

(E) A soap opera in which a jealous husband is shown murdering his wife's lover, then his own wife

40. According to the passage,

(A) television programs are much different today from what they were a generation ago

(B) a very large percentage of the viewers are presently worried about the showing of violence on television

(C) situation comedy programs are more popular on TV now than ever before

(D) broadcasting stations are considering notifying viewers about possible dangers of watching programs that include violence

(E) violence on the television screen is more extreme than it was about 20 years ago

S T O P

IF YOU FINISH BEFORE TIME IS CALLED, YOU MAY CHECK YOUR WORK ON THIS SECTION ONLY.
DO NOT WORK ON ANY OTHER SECTION IN THE TEST.

SECTION 5   MATH ABILITY

30 MINUTES   35 QUESTIONS

In this section solve each problem, using any available space on the page for scratchwork. Then decide which is the best of the choices given and blacken the corresponding space on the answer sheet.

The following information is for your reference in solving some of the problems.

Circle of radius r: Area $= \pi r^2$; Circumference $= 2\pi r$
  The number of degrees of arc in a circle is 360.
The measure in degrees of a straight angle is 180.

Definitions of symbols:

$=$	is equal to	$\leqq$	is less than or equal to
$\neq$	is unequal to	$\geqq$	is greater than or equal to
$<$	is less than	$\parallel$	is parallel to
$>$	is greater than	$\perp$	is perpendicular to

Triangle: The sum of the measure in degrees of the angles of a triangle is 180. If $\angle CDA$ is a right angle, then

(1)   area of $\triangle ABC = \dfrac{AB \times CD}{2}$

(2) $AC^2 = AD^2 + DC^2$

Note: Figures which accompany problems in this test are intended to provide information useful in solving the problems. They are drawn as accurately as possible EXCEPT when it is stated in a specific problem that its figure is not drawn to scale. All figures lie in a plane unless otherwise indicated. All numbers used are real numbers.

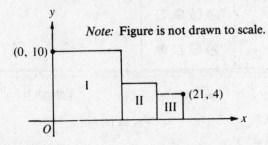

Note: **Figure is not drawn to scale.**

1. In the figure above, squares I, II and III are situated along the x-axis as shown. Find the area of square II.

(A) 16   (B) 25   (C) 49   (D) 100   (E) 121

2. A certain cup holds 100 grams of butter. If a cake requires 75 grams of butter and a pie requires 225 grams of butter, then 4 cups of butter is *not* enough for any of the following *except*

(A) 6 cakes   (B) 2 pies   (C) 3 cakes and 1 pie
(D) 2 cakes and 2 pies   (E) 2 cakes and 1 pie

3. A classroom has 12 seated students, 5 students at the board, and 7 empty seats. If 3 students leave the room, 2 enter, and all sit down, how many empty seats will there be?

(A) None   (B) 1   (C) 2   (D) 3   (E) 4

4. Given that $500w = 3 \times 700$. Find the value of w.

(A) $\dfrac{5}{21}$ (B) 2   (C) $\dfrac{11}{5}$

(D) $\dfrac{21}{5}$ (E) 7

5. If $\dfrac{3 + y}{y} = 7$, then $y =$

(A) 4   (B) 3   (C) 2   (D) 1   (E) $\dfrac{1}{2}$

6. The positive integer x is a multiple of 9 and also a multiple of 12. The smallest possible value of x is

(A) 3   (B) 12   (C) 21   (D) 36   (E) 72

7. Find $(r - s)(t - s) + (s - r)(s - t)$ for all numbers r, s, and t.

(A) 0   (B) 2   (C) $2rt$ (D) $2(s - r)(t - s)$
(E) $2(r - s)(t - s)$

Questions 8-27 each consist of two quantities, one in Column A and one in Column B. You are to compare the two quantities and on the answer sheet blacken space

    A if the quantity in Column A is greater;
    B if the quantity in Column B is greater;
    C if the two quantities are equal;
    D if the relationship cannot be determined from the information given.

Notes: 1. In certain questions, information concerning one or both of the quantities to be compared is centered above the columns.
        2. In a given question, a symbol that appears in both columns represents the same thing in Column A as it does in Column B.
        3. Letters such as x, n, and k stand for real numbers.

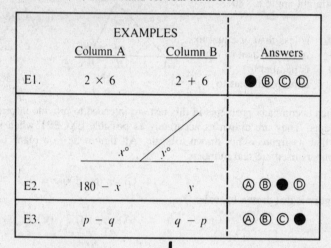

	EXAMPLES		
	Column A	Column B	Answers
E1.	2×6	$2 + 6$	● Ⓑ Ⓒ Ⓓ
E2.	$180 - x$	y	Ⓐ Ⓑ ● Ⓓ
E3.	$p - q$	$q - p$	Ⓐ Ⓑ Ⓒ ●

	Column A	Column B
8.	The remainder when 14 is divided by 5	The remainder when 14 is divided by 3

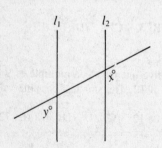

9.

	180	$x + y$

10.	$7^2(6^2 + 1)$	$7^2 \cdot 7^2$

11.	$5x \div 3$	$\dfrac{x}{3} \times 5$

12.	8×8	7×9

	Column A	Column B
13.	y is an integer $y < 0$	
	-1	$\dfrac{1}{y} - 1$

14.
$$\frac{2}{3} + \frac{r}{s} = \frac{5}{3}$$

	r	s

15.

	$a + d$	$b + c$

16.	$x > 0 > y$	
	$y - x$	$x - y$

17.
$w \leqq 60$
$x \leqq 60$

	80	$w + x$

SUMMARY DIRECTIONS FOR COMPARISON QUESTIONS

Answer:
A if the quantity in Column A is greater;
B if the quantity in Column B is greater;
C if the two quantities are equal;
D if the relationship cannot be determined from the information given.

Column A	Column B

18.

$$3y - 2 < 0$$

$3y$	-2

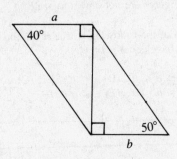

Note: Figure is not drawn to scale.

19. a b

20. y is a positive integer.

y^3 3^y

21. $\dfrac{3}{a} = 2$ and $\dfrac{5}{b} = 2$

a b

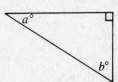

22.

$a + b$ 90

Column A	Column B

23.   Units' digit of the product of the first 7 positive integers   Units' digit of the product $8 \cdot 9 \cdot 10 \cdot 11 \cdot 12 \cdot 13 \cdot 14$

24. x is any non-negative integer.

The minimum value of $4x^2 + 1$ The minimum value of $5x^2 + 1$

25. $\dfrac{4}{a} = \dfrac{b}{4}$

a b

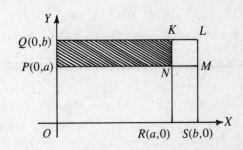

26. $QLMP$ and $RKLS$ are rectangles.

$b(b - a)$ Area of rectangle $QKNP$

27. $xy + 7$ $x(y + 7)$

Solve each of the remaining problems in this section by using any available space for scratchwork. Then decide which is the best of the choices given and blacken the corresponding space on the answer sheet.

28. If $y = r - 6$ and $z = r + 5$, which of the following is an expression representing r in terms of y and z?

(A) $\dfrac{y + z + 1}{2}$ (B) $\dfrac{y + z - 1}{2}$

(C) $y + z - 1$ (D) $y + z$ (E) $y + z + 1$

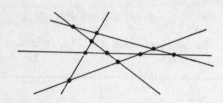

29. The figure above demonstrates that 5 straight lines can have 10 points of intersection. The maximum number of points of intersection of 4 straight lines is

(A) 8   (B) 7   (C) 6   (D) 5   (E) 4

30. A box of candy contains 0.6 of a pound of caramels and 3.6 pounds of coconut. What percent of the contents of the box, by weight, consists of caramels?

(A) 6%   (B) $14\frac{2}{7}$%   (C) $16\frac{2}{3}$%   (D) 25%

(E) $33\frac{1}{3}$%

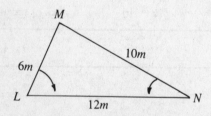

31. In the figure above, if sides LM and NM are cut apart from each other at point M creating 2 free swinging segments and each is folded down to LN in the directions shown by the arrows, what will be the length, in meters, of the overlap of the 2 segments? (Disregard the thickness of the segments.)

(A) 4   (B) 6   (C) 10   (D) 16   (E) 28

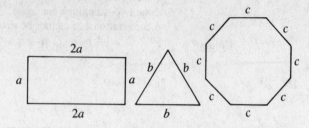

Note: Figures are not drawn to scale.

32. Which of the following is true if the three polygons above have equal perimeters?

(A) $b < a < c$ (B) $a < c < b$ (C) $a < b < c$
(D) $c < b < a$ (E) $c < a < b$

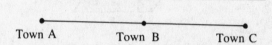

Town A   Town B   Town C

33. A car travels from Town A to Town B in 3 hours. It travels from Town B to Town C in 5 hours. If the distance AB is equal to the distance BC, what is the ratio of the car's average speed between A and B to its average speed for the whole distance AC?

(A) 5 : 3   (B) 4 : 3   (C) 1 : 1   (D) 1 : 3
(E) 1 : 5

34. Given that ax is an integer and bx is an integer, which of the following must also be an integer?

   I. a and b
  II. x
  III. $(a + b)x$

(A) None
(B) I only
(C) III only
(D) II and III only
(E) I, II and III

35. When a racing car travels at 48 laps per hour, it takes exactly 12 hours to finish the race. To the nearest hour, how many hours would it take to finish the same race if the car traveled at 30 laps per hour?

(A) 8   (B) 19   (C) 24   (D) 30   (E) 72

S T O P

IF YOU FINISH BEFORE TIME IS CALLED, YOU MAY CHECK YOUR WORK ON THIS SECTION ONLY.
DO NOT WORK ON ANY OTHER SECTION IN THE TEST.

SECTION 6   MATH ABILITY

30 MINUTES   35 QUESTIONS

In this section solve each problem, using any available space on the page for scratchwork. Then decide which is the best of the choices given and blacken the corresponding space on the answer sheet.

The following information is for your reference in solving some of the problems.

Circle of radius r: Area $= \pi r^2$; Circumference $= 2\pi r$
    The number of degrees of arc in a circle is 360.
The measure in degrees of a straight angle is 180.

Definitions of symbols:
$=$	is equal to	$\leqq$	is less than or equal to
$\neq$	is unequal to	$\geqq$	is greater than or equal to
$<$	is less than	$\parallel$	is parallel to
$>$	is greater than	$\perp$	is perpendicular to

Triangle: The sum of the measure in degrees of the angles of a triangle is 180.
If $\angle CDA$ is a right angle, then

(1)   area of $\triangle ABC = \dfrac{AB \times CD}{2}$

(2) $AC^2 = AD^2 + DC^2$

Note: Figures which accompany problems in this test are intended to provide information useful in solving the problems. They are drawn as accurately as possible EXCEPT when it is stated in a specific problem that its figure is not drawn to scale. All figures lie in a plane unless otherwise indicated. All numbers used are real numbers.

1. A boy planned to buy some chocolate bars at 50 cents each but instead decided to purchase 30 cent chocolate bars. If he originally had enough money to buy 21 of the 50 cent bars, how many of the less expensive ones did he buy?

   (A) 20   (B) 25   (C) 30   (D) 35   (E) 40

2. A certain number is divided by 3 but its value remains the same. What is this number?

   (A) -1 (B) $-\dfrac{1}{2}$ (C) 0   (D) $\dfrac{1}{2}$ (E) 1

3. A man walks a certain distance in the direction 30° south of west, stops, and then turns 35° to his right. In what new direction is he facing?

   (A) 65° north of west   (B) 35° north of west

   (C) $32\dfrac{1}{2}$° north of west   (D) 30° north of west

   (E) 5° north of west

4. What is the value of $\dfrac{1}{5}K$ if $\dfrac{9}{5}K = 18$?

   (A) $\dfrac{1}{9}$ (B) $\dfrac{1}{5}$ (C) 2   (D) 5   (E) 10

5. Let x, y, and z be negative numbers such that $x < y < z$. Which expression is the smallest?

   (A) $(z)(z)$ (B) $(y)(z)$ (C) $(x)(z)$ (D) $(y)(x)$
   (E) $(x)(x)$

6. A sequence of integers is defined as follows: The first term is 2 and every additional term is obtained by subtracting 2 from the previous term and tripling the resulting difference. For example, the second term would be 0. Which of the following is a true statement about this sequence?

   (A) The terms behave as follows: even, even, odd, odd, even, even, odd, odd, . . .
   (B) The terms behave as follows: even, odd, even, odd, even, odd, . . .
   (C) The terms behave as follows: even, even, even, odd, odd, odd, even, even, even, . . .
   (D) All of the terms, except for the first one, are odd.
   (E) All of the terms are even.

7. From the equations $7a = 4$ and $7a + 4b = 12$, one can conclude that b is

   (A) -1 (B) 0   (C) 1   (D) 2   (E) Any integer

<u>Questions 8-27</u> each consist of two quantities, one in Column A and one in Column B. You are to compare the two quantities and on the answer sheet blacken space

A if the quantity in Column A is greater;
B if the quantity in Column B is greater;
C if the two quantities are equal;
D if the relationship cannot be determined from the information given.

Notes: 1. In certain questions, information concerning one or both of the quantities to be compared is centered above the columns.
2. In a given question, a symbol that appears in both columns represents the same thing in Column A as it does in Column B.
3. Letters such as x, n, and k stand for real numbers.

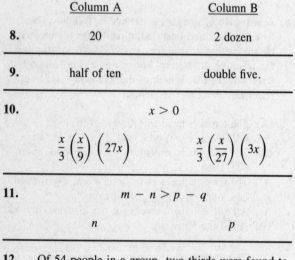

	EXAMPLES		
	Column A	Column B	Answers
E1.	2×6	$2 + 6$	● Ⓑ Ⓒ Ⓓ
E2.	$180 - x$	y	Ⓐ Ⓑ ● Ⓓ
E3.	$p - q$	$q - p$	Ⓐ Ⓑ Ⓒ ●

Column A	Column B
8. 20	2 dozen
9. half of ten	double five.

10. $x > 0$

$$\frac{x}{3}\left(\frac{x}{9}\right)(27x) \qquad \frac{x}{3}\left(\frac{x}{27}\right)(3x)$$

11. $m - n > p - q$

$n \qquad\qquad p$

12. Of 54 people in a group, two-thirds were found to be Democrats while the remaining individuals were Republicans

17   Number of Republicans

Column A   Column B

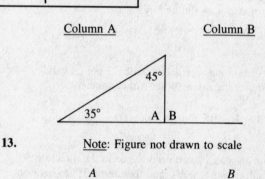

13. <u>Note: Figure not drawn to scale</u>

$A \qquad\qquad B$

14. $.008 + .007 + .006 \qquad 30 \times .007$

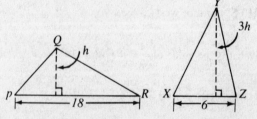

15. <u>Note: Figures not drawn to scale</u>

Area of $\triangle PQR$ Area of $\triangle XYZ$

SUMMARY DIRECTIONS FOR COMPARISON QUESTIONS

<u>Answer:</u> A if the quantity in Column A is greater;
          B if the quantity in Column B is greater;
          C if the two quantities are equal;
          D if the relationship cannot be determined from the information given.

	Column A	Column B
16.	$0 < y < 1$	
	$\dfrac{y^3}{2}$	$\dfrac{y \cdot y \cdot y}{y + y}$
17.	$\dfrac{7k + 8}{7}$	$k + 1$
18.	$(15 \times 68) - 22$	$15 \times (68 - 22)$
19.	$\dfrac{\frac{5}{3}}{\frac{10}{9}}$	$\dfrac{\frac{10}{9}}{\frac{2}{3}}$
20.	$m : n = n : m = 1$	
	1	mn

21. $\square$ is one of the operations $+, -, \times,$ *or* $\div$
$\square$ satisfies $x \,\square\, (-x) = 0$ for all x

	Column A	Column B
	$x \,\square\, y$	$y \,\square\, x$

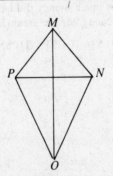

22. Area $\triangle MNP <$ Area $\triangle NOP$
         $MO \perp PN$

	Column A	Column B
	$NO + OP$	$MP + NM$
23.	$x \neq \pm 1$	
	$\dfrac{x^2 - 1}{x - 1}$	$\dfrac{x^2 + 2x + 1}{x + 1}$

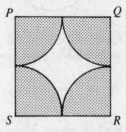

24. *PQRS* is a square and the four
shaded regions are quartercircles.

	Column A	Column B
	$\dfrac{2}{\pi}$	The ratio of the area of the square to the total shaded area

25. Tom has 8 less eggs than Joe, Joe has 6 less eggs than Sue, and Sue has 4 less eggs than Robert.

	Column A	Column B
	13	The least number of eggs that must be exchanged in order that everyone has the same number of eggs
26.	$x \neq 0$	
	x	x^{-1}

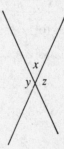

27. $x + 2y + z = 5y$

	Column A	Column B
	$\dfrac{3}{2} z$	x

Solve each of the remaining problems in this section using any available space for scratchwork. Then decide which is the best of the choices given and blacken the corresponding space on the answer sheet.

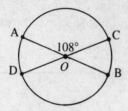

28. O is a circle of diameter 20 and ⦨AOC = 108°. Find the sum of the lengths of minor arcs $\overarc{AC}$ and $\overarc{DB}$

(A) 5π   (B) 8π   (C) 10π   (D) 12π   (E) 15π

29. Let d be the least integer greater than 96,666 such that four of d's digits are identical. Then $d - 96,666$ is

(A) 33   (B) 99   (C) 333   (D) 999   (E) 3333

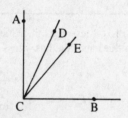

Note: Figure is not drawn to scale.

30. Given that AC ⊥ BC, ⦨DCB = 62° and ⦨ACE = 37°, find ⦨DCE in degrees.

(A) 5°   (B) 9°   (C) 13°   (D) 25°   (E) 27°

31. $2 \times 10^{-5} \times 8 \times 10^2 \times 5 \times 10^2 =$

(A) .00008   (B) .008   (C) .08   (D) 8   (E) 800

32. Over the first few weeks of the baseball season, the league's five leading pitchers had the following won-lost records. (All games ended in a win or loss for that pitcher.)

	Won	Lost
Pitcher A	4	2
Pitcher B	3	2
Pitcher C	4	1
Pitcher D	2	2
Pitcher E	3	1

At the time these statistics were compiled, which pitcher was leading the league in winning percentage? (That is, which pitcher had won the greatest percentage of his games?)

(A) Pitcher A   (B) Pitcher B   (C) Pitcher C
(D) Pitcher D   (E) Pitcher E.

33. Let us define the operation ⊙ as

$$a \odot b = (a + b)^2 - (a - b)^2$$

Then $\sqrt{18} \odot \sqrt{2}$ equals

(A) 1.14   (B) 3.6   (C) 24   (D) 36   (E) 42

34. How many ordered pairs of *integers* (x,y) satisfy $x^2 + y^2 < 9$

(A) 4   (B) 9   (C) 16   (D) 25   (E) 36

35. Johnny spent $\frac{2}{5}$ of his allowance on candy and $\frac{5}{6}$ of the remainder on ice cream. If his allowance is 30 dollars, how much money did he have left after buying the candy and ice cream?

(A) $1   (B) $2   (C) $3   (D) $5   (E) $10

S T O P

IF YOU FINISH BEFORE TIME IS CALLED, YOU MAY CHECK YOUR WORK ON THIS SECTION ONLY.
DO NOT WORK ON ANY OTHER SECTION IN THE TEST.

HOW DID YOU DO ON THIS TEST?

STEP 1. Go to the Answer Key on page 390.

STEP 2. For your "raw score," count your correct answers in each of the test parts of the test you have just taken:

Verbal (Section 1 and 4 combined) _____.

Math (Sections 2, 5, and 6 combined) _____.

Standard Written English (Section 3) _____.

STEP 3. Get your "scaled score" for the test by referring to the Raw Score/ Scaled Score Conversion Tables on pages 64–66.

THERE'S ALWAYS ROOM FOR IMPROVEMENT!

ANSWER KEY FOR PRACTICE TEST 2

Section 1—Verbal

1. D	8. A	15. C	22. D	29. D	36. C	43. B
2. A	9. D	16. E	23. E	30. B	37. A	44. A
3. C	10. C	17. C	24. C	31. A	38. C	45. E
4. E	11. A	18. D	25. D	32. B	39. E	
5. B	12. E	19. D	26. A	33. E	40. A	
6. B	13. D	20. D	27. E	34. D	41. A	
7. E	14. D	21. A	28. A	35. B	42. D	

Section 2—Math

1. C	5. D	9. B	13. C	17. B	21. D	25. D
2. E	6. B	10. E	14. C	18. C	22. C	
3. B	7. E	11. E	15. E	19. E	23. A	
4. D	8. E	12. B	16. C	20. E	24. D	

Section 3—Standard Written English

1. D	9. C	17. D	25. C	33. E	41. D	49. D
2. C	10. E	18. A	26. A	34. D	42. A	50. B
3. D	11. C	19. D	27. A	35. D	43. A	
4. E	12. B	20. E	28. D	36. A	44. E	
5. A	13. C	21. A	29. D	37. D	45. C	
6. B	14. D	22. D	30. C	37. B	46. E	
7. B	15. A	23. E	31. C	39. D	47. A	
8. B	16. A	24. A	32. B	40. C	48. A	

Section 4—Verbal

1. D	7. B	13. D	19. E	25. D	31. E	37. D
2. A	8. C	14. A	20. E	26. B	32. D	38. C
3. E	9. E	15. C	21. A	27. C	33. A	39. D
4. C	10. A	16. C	22. B	28. D	34. C	40. E
5. B	11. C	17. D	23. C	29. C	35. E	
6. D	12. E	18. A	24. D	30. A	36. B	

Section 5—Math

1. C	6. D	11. C	16. B	21. B	26. A	31. A
2. E	7. E	12. A	17. D	22. C	27. D	32. E
3. D	8. A	13. A	18. D	23. C	28. A	33. B
4. D	9. D	14. C	19. A	24. C	29. C	34. C
5. E	10. B	15. A	20. D	25. D	30. B	35. B

Section 6—Math

1. D	6. E	11. D	16. B	21. C	26. D	31. D
2. C	7. D	12. B	17. A	22. A	27. B	32. C
3. E	8. B	13. A	18. A	23. C	28. D	33. C
4. C	9. B	14. B	19. B	24. B	29. C	34. D
5. A	10. A	15. C	20. D	25. A	30. B	35. C

EXPLANATORY ANSWERS FOR PRACTICE TEST 2

Section 1: Verbal Ability

> As you read these Explanatory Answers, you are advised to refer to "Using Critical Thinking Skills in Verbal Questions" (beginning on page 90) whenever a specific Strategy is referred to in the answer. Of particular importance are the following Master Verbal Strategies:
>
> Sentence Completion Master Strategy 1—page 94.
> Sentence Completion Master Strategy 2—page 95.
> Analogies Master Strategy 1—page 90.
> Antonyms Master Strategy 1—page 99.
> Reading Comprehension Master Strategy 2—page 109.

1. **(D)** Choice D is correct. See **Antonym Strategy 3.** *Garble* means *to distort;* to confuse. The opposite of *garble* is *clarify.*

2. **(A)** Choice A is correct. See **Antonym Strategy 3.** *Gallant* means *polite; noble.* The opposite of *gallant* is *rude.*

3. **(C)** Choice C is correct. *Furtive* means *secretive; stealthy.* The opposite of *furtive* is *open.*

4. **(E)** Choice E is correct. See **Antonym Strategy 3.** *Thermal* pertains to *heat.* The opposite of *thermal* is *frigid.*

5. **(B)** Choice B is correct. See **Antonym Strategy 2.** *Pernicious* means *destructive; injurious.* The opposite of *pernicious* is *healing.*

6. **(B)** Choice B is correct. See **Antonym Strategy 3.** *Slothful* means *lazy.* The opposite of *slothful* is *ambitious.*

7. **(E)** Choice E is correct. *Wroth* means *angry.* The opposite of *wroth* is *pleased.*

8. **(A)** Choice A is correct. See **Antonym Strategies 1, 3.** *Fortitude* means *courage.* The opposite of *fortitude* is *timidity.*

9. **(D)** Choice D is correct. See **Antonym Strategy 1.** *Concur* means *to agree.* The opposite of *concur* is *to oppose.*

10. **(C)** Choice C is correct. See **Antonym Strategies 1, 2.** *Anathema* is a *curse.* The opposite of *anathema* is a *blessing.*

11. **(A)** Choice A is correct. *Rife* means *frequently occurring.* The opposite of *rife* is *rare.*

12. **(E)** Choice E is correct. See **Antonym Strategies 1, 3.** *Circumspect* means *cautious; careful.* The opposite of *circumspect* is *careless.*

13. **(D)** Choice D is correct. See **Antonym Strategy 1.** *Condone* means *to forgive.* The opposite of *condone* is *punish.*

14. **(D)** Choice D is correct. See **Antonym Strategy 3.** *Itinerant* means *traveling from place to place.* The opposite of *itinerant* is *stationary.*

15. **(C)** Choice C is correct. *Flaccid* means *flabby.* The opposite of *flaccid* is *firm.*

16. **(E)** Choice E is correct. See **Sentence Completion Strategy 4.** The first word, "Though" is an *opposition indicator.* The beginning of the sentence speaks positively about the computer programmer. We must find a word that gives us a negative idea about him. Choice (E) creativity, is the appropriate word. The other choices are incorrect because their words are not appropriate to give us that opposite feeling.

17. **(C)** Choice C is correct. See **Sentence Completion Strategy 1.** The very fact that Millie craved attention points to her desire for identification (Choice C). None of the other choices makes sense in the sentence.

18. **(D)** Choice D is correct. See **Sentence Completion Strategy 2.** Examine the first word of each choice. Choice (B) tantamount (meaning equivalent to) . . . and Choice (C) collegiate . . . do *not* make sense because we do not speak of a tantamount professor or a collegiate professor. Now consider the other choices. Choice (D) scholarly . . . profound, is the only choice which has a word pair that makes sentence sense.

19. **(D)** Choice D is correct. See **Sentence Completion Strategy 1.** The beginning word "Because" is a *result indicator.* We may expect, then, a reason in the first part of the sentence for the Indian people to escape from British rule and join the Japanese. The word "abused" (Choice D) provides the reason. The words in the other choices do not make good sense in the sentence.

20. **(D)** Choice D is correct. See **Sentence Completion Strategy 1.** The author is obviously not satisfied with the royalty payment specified, since the sentence refers to the high research costs necessary for writing the book. Accordingly, Choices A, B, C, and E are incorrect.

21. **(A)** Choice A is correct. The passage deals mainly with van Gogh's 15-month stay in Arles. It was in this small French town that his art, in fact, did reach its zenith. See lines 5–9: "Yet Arles . . . in the modern era." Although Choices B, C, D, and E have some association with the passage, none of these choices represents the best title for the passage as a whole. Therefore, these choices are incorrect.

22. **(D)** Choice D is *not* stated nor is it implied in the passage. Therefore, it is the correct choice. First see lines 43–47: "Before the year was up . . . had to return to Paris." Note that Gauguin had stayed in Arles *less* than a year. Now see lines 5–9: "Yet Arles was also the scene . . . in the modern era." Choice A is true—therefore an incorrect choice. See lines 12–16: "The Arles canvases, alive with color . . . notably the Fauves." Choice B is true—therefore an incorrect choice. First see lines 18–21: "Van Gogh went to Arles . . . beloved younger brother Theo . . . an art dealer." Now see lines 40–42: "Gauguin had an influence on van Gogh . . . pushing the younger artist . . . than actuality." Choice C is true—therefore an incorrect choice. See lines 21–24: "In Paris . . . Neo-Impressionist . . . style." Choice E is true—therefore incorrect. See lines 1–5: "It was at Arles . . . cut off part of his own ear."

23. **(E)** Choice E is correct. Let us consider each of the three Roman numeral items. Item I is true. See lines 26–28: "But he wanted 'gayer' colors . . . Japanese prints he so admired."

Item II is true. First see lines 29–31: "He felt that in Arles . . . establish an artistic tradition." Now see lines 32–35: "It was van Gogh's hope . . . join him at Arles."

Item III is true. See lines 28–31: "Then, too, the French capital . . . an artistic tradition."

Accordingly, Choice E is the only correct choice.

24. **(C)** Choice C is correct. Gauguin's attitude of tolerant acceptance of van Gogh is indicated in the following lines of the passage. Lines 38–42: "At first . . . rather than actuality." Lines 46–50: "Gauguin wrote to Theo . . . especially with me." Lines 51–53: "But then . . . they later had friendly correspondence."

Choices A, B, D, and E are incorrect because the passage does not give evidence of the attitudes mentioned in these choices.

25. **(D)** Choice D is correct. The passage indicates that there was a buildup of stresses and strains on van Gogh which he was eventually unable to cope with because of his mental and emotional instability. This condition led him to such acts as cutting off a piece of his ear. Finally—though the passage does not include this fact—van Gogh committed suicide in Paris on July 29, 1890 by shooting himself in the chest. The following lines in the passage are related to van Gogh's mental and emotional instability. Lines 1–3: "It was at Arles . . . had his first real bout with madness." Lines 18–21: "Van Gogh went to Arles . . . supported him psychologically and financially . . . art dealer." Lines 46–48: "Gauguin wrote to Theo . . . 'temperamental in compatability'."

Choices B and E are incorrect because these were not the basic reasons for van Gogh's extreme action. The basic reason was van Gogh's mental and emotional instability (Choice A). Choice C is incorrect because the passage mentions nothing about van Gogh's failure to form an artists' colony in Arles.

26. **(A)** Choice A is correct. See lines 42–44: "The fundamental fact . . . in their environment." Choices B, D, and E are incorrect because the passage does not indicate that these statements are true. Choice C is incorrect because it is only partially true. The passage does not state that *all* animals and plants are successful in adjusting themselves to changes in their environments.

27. **(E)** Choice E is correct. See lines 4–7: "Originally the term acclimatization . . . altered temperature." Also see lines 10–13: "But aside from temperature . . . originally accustomed to." Choices A, B, C, and D are incorrect because one *cannot* infer from the passage what any of these choices state.

28. **(A)** Choice A is correct. Acclimatization and adaptation are both forms of adjustment. Accordingly, these two processes are similar. The difference between the two terms, however, is brought out in lines 32–37: "By and large . . . as adaptation." Choice D is incorrect because the passage does not indicate what is expressed in Choice D. See lines 29–32: "Let us define acclimatization . . . lethal for it." Choices B, C, and E are incorrect because the passage does not indicate that any of these choices are true.

29. **(D)** Choice D is correct. A person going from daylight into a darkened room is an example of adaptation—not acclimatization. See lines 32–37: "By and large . . . as 'adaptation'." Choices A, B, C, and E all require the process of acclimatization. Therefore, they are incorrect choices. An ocean fish placed in a lake (Choice A) is a chemical change. Choices B, C, and E are all pressure changes. Acclimatization, by definition, deals with chemical and pressure changes.

30. **(B)** Choice B is correct. See lines 33–37: "The term [acclimatization] should not be taken . . . as 'adaptation'." Choices A, D, and E are incorrect because the passage does not indicate that these choices are true. Choice C is partially correct in that acclimatization does apply to adjustments but the choice is incorrect because adaptation also applies to adjustments. See lines 35–37: "This type of adjustment . . . as 'adaptation'."

31. **(A)** Choice A is correct. See **Sentence Completion Strategy 1.** The typist's inconsistency is obvious in the manner in which she typed the five letters. Choices B, C, D, and E are incorrect because they do not make good sense in the sentence.

32. **(B)** Choice B is correct. See **Sentence Completion Strategy 2.** Let us first examine the first words of each choice. We can then eliminate Choice (C) remarks . . . and Choice (E) conferences . . . because an outstanding publisher being able to make occasional remarks or occasional conferences does not make good sense. Now we go on to the three remaining choices. When you fill in the two blanks of Choice A and of Choice D, the sentence does not make sense. So these two choices are also incorrect. Filling in the two blanks of Choice B makes the sentence meaningful.

33. **(E)** Choice E is correct. See **Sentence Completion Strategy 1.** No other choice makes sense in the sentence. It is clear that the person was primarily interested in being appreciated for his donation.

34. **(D)** Choice D is correct. See **Sentence Completion Strategy 2.** Examine the first words of each choice. We eliminate Choice (A) communicated . . . and Choice (E) regarded, because the first part of the sentence does not make sense when we fill the initial blank with "communicated" or "regarded." Now we consider Choice (B) downfall, and Choice (C) program. These choices are incorrect because Darwin's theory is neither a "downfall" or "a program." Choice (D) opposed . . . belief, makes good sense in the sentence.

35. **(B)** Choice B is correct. See **Sentence Completion Strategy 2.** Examine the first words of each choice. Choice (E) legal, may be immediately eliminated because every contract is supposed to be legal and the executives would not have to be aware about this fact. Choice (B) tricky . . . favoring, is the only choice which makes good sense in the sentence.

36. **(C)** Choice C is the answer. A client seeks the services of an attorney. A patient seeks the services of a doctor.
(Person to Person Association relationship)

37. **(A)** Choice A is correct. One cancels (stops) a subscription and one nullifies (stops) a contract.
(Action to Object relationship)

38. **(C)** Choice C is correct. The hub is the central part of a wheel. The bullseye is the central part of a target.
(Part-Whole and Place relationship)

39. **(E)** Choice E is correct. A slip is a place to keep a boat when it is not being used. A hangar is a place to keep an airplane when it is not being used. Note that the word "slip" is a noun in this analogy question because all of the other first choice words are nouns. "Slip" may also act as a verb meaning to slide suddenly and accidentally—but *not* in this question. See **Analogy Strategy 5.**
(Purpose and Place relationship)

40. **(A)** Choice A is correct. A pride of lions is a group of lions. A gaggle of geese is a group of geese. Note that the word "pride" also has the meaning of "self respect"—but *not* in this analogy. See **Analogy Strategy 5.**
(Whole-Part relationship)

41. **(A)** Choice A is correct. The pioneers made history by being the first white men to live and settle in the West. The American astronauts made history by being the first human beings to land on the moon.
(Association and Place relationship)

42. **(D)** Choice D is correct. A quiver is a case for holding or carrying an arrow. A sheath is a case for holding or carrying a sword. This is a PURPOSE analogy. Choice (B) purse : money is also a purpose analogy. However this choice is incorrect because this choice has a neutral or peaceful implication. The capitalized words and Choice D both have a battle or attack implication. See **Analogy Strategy 4.**
(Purpose relationship)

43. **(B)** Choice B is correct A person who is disinterested is *not* biased. A person who is affluent is *not* impecunious.
(Opposite relationship)

44. **(A)** Choice A is correct. A hero gets approval or an award for his honorable action. A culprit gets blame or a punishment for his dishonorable action.
(Cause and Effect relationship)

45. **(E)** Choice E is correct. When one clips hair from someone else's head or hews a bough from a tree, he is severing or separating a part from the whole in each case. This is an ACTION to OBJECT relationship. Choices A, B, C, and D are also action to object relationships but they do not involve a part from the whole separation. Accordingly, these four choices are incorrect. See **Analogy Strategy 4.**
(Action to Object relationship)

EXPLANATORY ANSWERS FOR
PRACTICE TEST 2 (continued)

Section 2: Math Ability

As you read these solutions, you are advised to do two things if you answered the Math question incorrectly:

1) When a specific Strategy is referred to in the solution, study that strategy, which you will find in "Using Critical Thinking Skills in Math Questions" (beginning on page 69).

2) When the solution directs you to the "Math Refresher" (beginning on page 205)—for example, Math Refresher #305—study the 305 Math principle to get a clear idea of the Math operation that was necessary for you to know in order to answer the question correctly.

---

1. **(C)** Choice C is correct. **(Use Strategy 17: Use the given information effectively.)** If the tram carries its maximum of 4 people then

$$\frac{22 \text{ people}}{\frac{4 \text{ people}}{\text{trip}}} = 5\frac{1}{2} \text{ trips},$$

(Use Strategy 16: The obvious may be tricky!)
There is no such thing as $\frac{1}{2}$ a trip. The $\frac{1}{2}$ arises because the last trip, the <u>6th</u> trip only, takes 2 people.

$$\text{The } \frac{1}{2} \text{ represents } \frac{\frac{2 \text{ people}}{4 \text{ people}}}{\text{trip}} = \frac{1}{2}$$

The are 5 trips at 4 people each = 20 people
1 trip at 2 people = 2 people
TOTAL = 6 trips   totaling   22 people

(Logical Reasoning)

2. **(E)** Choice E is correct. **(Use Strategy 8: When all choices must be tested, start with E and work backwards.)** The only way to solve this question is to test the choices one by one. We start with Choice E and it is correct. **(Logical Reasoning)**

3. **(B)** Choice B is correct. **(Use Strategy 2: Translate from words to algebra.)**

Let M = number of Mary's jellybeans ⬚1

Let S = number of Susan's jellybeans ⬚2

And R = number of Rose's jellybeans ⬚3

We are looking for $\dfrac{\text{Rose's jellybeans}}{\text{Susan's jellybeans}}$ ⬚4

According to the given, S = 3M ⬚5

Also given, R = 18M ⬚6

Dividing ⬚6 by ⬚5, we get

$$\frac{R}{S} = \frac{6}{1}$$

(Math Refresher #200 and #120)

4. **(D)** Choice D is correct.

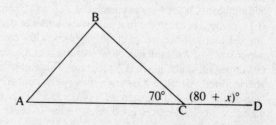

(Use Strategy 3: The whole equals the sum of its parts.)

$$m\angle ACB + m\angle BCD = m\angle ACD \qquad ⬚1$$

We are given that AD is a straight line segment. We know that

$$m\angle ACD = 180 \qquad ⬚2$$

$$\text{Given: } m\angle ACB = 70 \qquad ⬚3$$

$$m\angle BCD = 80 + x \qquad ⬚4$$

We substitute ⬚2, ⬚3 and ⬚4 into ⬚1

Thus, $70 + 80 + x = 180$

$$150 + x = 180$$

$$x = 30$$

Math Refresher #501 and #406)

5. **(D)** Choice D is correct. **(Use Strategy 2: Translate from words to algebra.)**

Let n = the number.

Then $\dfrac{n + 3}{4} = 6$

Multiplying both sides by 4, we have

$$4\left(\dfrac{n + 3}{4}\right) = (6)4$$
$$n + 3 = 24$$
$$n = 21$$

(Math Refresher #200)

6. **(B)** Choice B is correct. **(Use Strategy 2: Translate from words to algebra.)** We are told:

$$A + 8 + A + 1 + A + 2$$
$$= A + A + 1 + A + 2 + A + 3 \quad \boxed{1}$$

(Use Strategy 1: Cancel expressions which appear on both sides of an equation.)

Each side contains and A, $A + 1$ and $A + 2$. Canceling each of these from each side, we get $\cancel{A} + 8 + \cancel{A+1} + \cancel{A+2} = \cancel{A} + \cancel{A+1} + \cancel{A+2} + A + 3$.

Thus, $8 = A + 3$

$$5 = A$$

(Math Refresher #406)

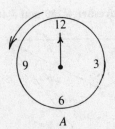 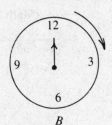

A   B

7. **(E)** Choice E is correct. **(Use Strategy 11: New definitions lead to easy questions.)**

By the definition of a move, every 4 moves brings each hand back to 12

Thus, after 4, 8, 12 and 16 moves, respectively, each hand is at 12.

Hand A, moving counter clockwise, moves to 9 on its 17th move.

Hand B, moving clockwise, moves to 3 on its 17th move. **(Logical Reasoning)**

8. **(E)** Choice E is correct. **(Use Strategy 17: Use the given information effectively.)**

Given: $w = 7r + 6r + 5r + 4r + 3r$

Then, $w = 25r$ \qquad $\boxed{1}$

We are told we must add something to w so that the resulting sum will be divisible by 7 for every positive integer r.

Check the choices. **(Use Strategy 8: Start with Choice E.)** Add $3r$ to $\boxed{1}$

$$25r + 3r = 28r = 7(4r)$$

will always be divisible by 7. Thus, choice E is the correct choice. \qquad **(Math Refresher #431)**

9. **(B)** Choice B is correct. **(Use Strategy 2: Translate from words to algebra)**

Perimeter of a square = $4 \times$ side. \quad $\boxed{1}$

We are given that Perimeter = 20 meters \quad $\boxed{2}$

Substituting $\boxed{2}$ into $\boxed{1}$, we get

20 meters = $4 \times$ side.
5 meters = side \qquad $\boxed{3}$
Area of a square = (side)^2 \quad $\boxed{4}$

Substituting $\boxed{3}$ into $\boxed{4}$, we get

Area of square = $(5 \text{ meter})^2$

Area of square = 25 square meters

(Math Refresher #303)

10. **(E)** Choice E is correct. **(Use Strategy 17: Use the given information effectively.)**

Given: $80 + a = -32 + b$

Subtract a from both sides, getting

$$\begin{array}{rcl} 80 + a & = & -32 + b \\ -a & & -a \\ \hline 80 & = & -32 + b - a \end{array}$$

Add 32 to both sides, giving

$$\begin{array}{rcl} 80 & = & -32 + b - a \\ +32 & & +32 \\ \hline 112 & = & b - a \end{array}$$

(Math Refresher #406)

11. **(E)** Choice E is correct. **(Use Strategy 8: When all choices must be tested start with E and work backwards.)**

Choice E is $x^2 + x + 2$

(Use Strategy 7: Use specific number examples.)

Let $x = 3$ (an odd positive integer)

Then $x^2 + x + 2 =$

$3^2 + 3 + 2 =$

$9 + 3 + 2 =$

$14 \quad = $ (an even result)

Now let $x = 2$ (an even positive integer)

Then $x^2 + x + 2 =$

$2^2 + 2 + 2 =$

$4 + 2 + 2 =$

8 = (an even result)

Whether x is odd or even, Choice E is even.

(Math Refresher #431)

12. **(B)** Choice B is correct. **(Use Strategy 4: Remember classic expressions.)**

$$x^2 + 2xy + y^2 = (x + y)^2 \quad \boxed{1}$$
Given: $x^2 + 2xy + y^2 = 25 \quad \boxed{2}$

Substitute $\boxed{1}$ into $\boxed{2}$, giving

$$(x + y)^2 = 25$$

$$x + y = \pm 5 \quad \boxed{3}$$

Given: $x + y > 0 \quad \boxed{4}$

Using $\boxed{3}$ and $\boxed{4}$ together, we conclude that

$$x + y = +5 \quad \boxed{5}$$

Given: $x - y = 1 \quad \boxed{6}$

(Use Strategy 13: Find an unknown by adding equations.)

Adding $\boxed{5}$ and $\boxed{6}$, we have

$$2x = 6$$

$$x = 3$$

(Math Refresher #409 and #407)

13. **(C)** Choice C is correct. **(Use Strategy 17: Use the given information effectively.)**

Given: $\dfrac{3}{4} < x < \dfrac{4}{5}$

Change both fractions to fractions with the same denominator. Thus,

$$\dfrac{3}{4} < x < \dfrac{4}{5}$$

becomes

$$\dfrac{15}{20} < x < \dfrac{16}{20}$$

(Use Strategy 15: Certain choices may be easily eliminated.)

Choice B $= \dfrac{13}{20}$ can be instantly eliminated.

Choice D $= \dfrac{16}{20}$ can be instantly eliminated.

Change both fractions to 40^{ths} to compare Choice C. Thus,

$$\dfrac{30}{40} < x < \dfrac{32}{40}$$

Choice C $= \dfrac{31}{40}$ is a possible value of x.

(Math Refresher #108 and #419)

14. **(C)** Choice C is correct. **(Use Strategy 2: Translate from words to algebra).**

The number of hours from 7:00 a.m. to 5:00 p.m. is 10.

The number of hours from 1:00 p.m. to 7:00 p.m. is 6.

He worked 10 hours for 3 days and 6 hours for 3 days. Thus,

Total Hours $= 3(10) + 3(6)$

$= 30 + 18$

Total Hours $= 48 \quad \boxed{1}$

Total Earnings $=$ Hours worked $\times$ Hourly rate $\quad \boxed{2}$

Given: He earns $10 per hour $\quad \boxed{3}$

Substituting $\boxed{1}$ and $\boxed{3}$ into $\boxed{2}$, we get

Total Earnings $= 48 \times \$10$
Total Earnings $= \$480$

(Math Refresher #200 and #406)

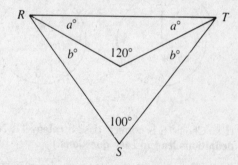

15. **(E)** Choice E is correct. **(Use Strategy 3: The whole equals the sum of its parts.)**

The sum of the angles in a $\triangle = 180$. For the small triangle we have

$$120 + a + a = 180$$

$$120 + 2a = 180$$

$$2a = 60$$

$$a = 30 \quad \boxed{1}$$

For $\triangle RST$, we have

$$100 + m\angle SRT + m\angle STR = 180 \quad \boxed{2}$$
From the diagram, we get

$$m\angle SRT = a + b \qquad \boxed{3}$$

$$m\angle STR = a + b \qquad \boxed{4}$$

Substituting $\boxed{3}$ and $\boxed{4}$ into $\boxed{2}$, we get

$$100 + a + b + a + b = 180$$

$$100 + 2a + 2b = 180$$

$$2a + 2b = 80 \qquad \boxed{5}$$

Substituting $\boxed{1}$ into $\boxed{5}$, we get

$$2(30) + 2b = 80$$

$$60 + 2b = 80$$

$$2b = 20$$

$$b = 10$$

(Math Refresher #505 and #406)

16. **(C)** Choice C is correct. **(Use Strategy 2: Translate from words to algebra.)**

	Wins	Losses
Alan	8	2
Edward	6	4
Howard	4	6
Robert	2	8

If Edward wins 6 more games, he will have
$$6 + 6 = 12 \text{ wins} \qquad \boxed{1}$$

We are told Howard's wins
$$= \frac{3}{4} \text{ (Edward's wins)} \qquad \boxed{2}$$

Substituting $\boxed{1}$ into $\boxed{2}$, we get

$$\text{Howard's wins} = \frac{3}{4}(12) = \frac{3}{\cancel{4}}(3 \times \cancel{4})$$

$$\text{Howard's wins} = 9 \qquad \boxed{3}$$

Howard currently has 4 wins. $\qquad \boxed{4}$

Subtracting $\boxed{4}$ from $\boxed{3}$, we get $9 - 4 = 5$ more games that Howard must win.

(Math Refresher #200 and #406)

17. **(B)** Choice B is correct. **(Use Strategy 2: Translate from words to algebra.)**

Robert's record is 2 wins, 8 losses. $\qquad \boxed{1}$

Let $x = $ # of additional wins $\qquad \boxed{2}$

Let $y = $ # of additional losses $\qquad \boxed{3}$

In order to end up with more wins than losses, we use $\boxed{1}$, $\boxed{2}$ and $\boxed{3}$ and get

WINS		LOSSES	
$2 + x$	$>$	$8 + y$	$\boxed{4}$

We know Robert has 8 games left to play $\qquad \boxed{5}$
Using $\boxed{2}$, $\boxed{3}$ and $\boxed{5}$ we have

$$x + y = 8$$

$$y = 8 - x \qquad \boxed{6}$$

(Use Strategy 6: Know how to solve inequalities.)
Substituting $\boxed{6}$ into $\boxed{4}$, we get

$$2 + x > 8 + 8 - x$$

$$2 + x > 16 - x$$

$$2 + 2x > 16$$

$$2x > 14$$

$$x > 7 \qquad \boxed{7}$$

Since 8 games remain to be played and Robert's number of wins must be greater than 7 (from $\boxed{7}$ above), then Robert must win all 8 remaining games. **(Math Refresher #200 and #426)**

18. **(C)** Choice C is correct.

	Wins	Losses
Alan	8	2
Edward	6	4
Howard	4	6
Robert	2	8

(Use Strategy 2: Translate from words to algebra.) If the 4 individuals each have 8 games remaining to be played, then there are $4(8) = 32$ games remaining. Each game involves 2 people, so there will be 16 wins and 16 losses. $\qquad \boxed{1}$

If Alan wins $\frac{1}{2}$ of his 8 games, he will win $\frac{1}{2}(8)$

$$= 4 \text{ games.} \qquad \boxed{2}$$

Subtracting $\boxed{2}$ from $\boxed{1}$, we have

16 wins $-$ 4 wins $= 12$ wins left to be distributed to the other 3 players. $\qquad \boxed{3}$

(Use Strategy 8: When all choices must be tested, start with E and work backwards.) Choice E cannot be tested, so we start with choice D.

7 wins and 11 losses $\qquad \boxed{4}$

From the chart above

		Needs	
Robert has 2 wins	$+$	5	$= 7$ wins
Howard has 4 wins	$+$	3	$= 7$ wins
Edward has 6 wins	$+$	1	$= 7$ wins
Total wins needed	$=$	9	$\boxed{5}$

$\boxed{5}$ does not use up all the wins available from $\boxed{3}$, 9 versus 12. Thus, Choice D is incorrect.

Try Choice C: 8 wins and 10 losses

<u>Needs</u>

Robert has 2 wins	+	6	= 8 wins
Howard has 4 wins	+	4	= 8 wins
Edward has 6 wins	+	2	= 8 wins
Total wins needed	=	12	

Total wins needed = 12   ⑥

⑥ does use up all 12 wins from ③ Now we check losses.

Since each has 8 games remaining, from ⑥ we get

Robert has 6 wins; therefore, 2 losses more   ⑦
Howard has 4 wins; therefore, 4 losses more   ⑧
Edward has 2 wins; therefore, 6 losses more   ⑨

Using current losses from the chart above, and ⑦, ⑧ and ⑨, we get

Robert's total losses   = 8 + 2 = 10 losses
Howard's total losses   = 6 + 4 = 10 losses
Edward's total losses   = 4 + 6 = 10 losses   ⑩

From ⑥ and ⑩ we see that

Choice C is correct. Each would end up with 8 wins and 10 losses. **(Logical Reasoning)**

19. **(E)** Choice E is correct. **(Use Strategy 17: Use the given information effectively.)**

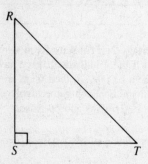

We know that Area of $\triangle = \frac{1}{2} \times$ base $\times$ height   ①

We are given that $RS = ST =$ an integer   ②

Substituting ② into ①, we get

Area $\triangle RST = \frac{1}{2} \times$ (An integer) $\times$ (same integer)

Area $\triangle RST = \frac{1}{2} \times$ (An integer)^2 ③

Multiplying ③ by 2, we have

2(Area $\triangle RST$) = (An integer)^2 ④

(Use Strategy 8: When all choices must be tested, start with E and work backwards.)

Substituting Choice E, 20, into ④, we get

$2(20) =$ (An integer)^2

$40 =$ (An integer)^2 ⑤

⑤ is *not* possible, since

40 isn't the square of an integer.

(Math Refresher #366, #406, and #431)

20. **(E)** Choice E is correct. **(Use Strategy 17: Use the given information effectively.)**

Volume of rectangler solid $= l \times w \times h$ ①

Substituting the given dimensions into ①, we get

Volume of solid $=$ 2 feet $\times$ 2 feet $\times$ 1 foot

Volume of solid $=$ 4 cubic feet   ②

Volume of cube $=$ (edge)^3 ③

Substituting edge $=$ .1 foot into ③, we get

Volume of cube $=$ (.1 foot)^3

Volume of cube $=$ .001 cubic feet   ④

(Use Strategy 3: The whole equals the sum of it parts.) Since the volume of the rectangular solid must equal the sum of the small cubes, we need to know

$$\frac{\text{Volume of rectangular solid}}{\text{Volume of cube}} = \text{Number of cubes} \quad ⑤$$

Substituting ② and ④ into ⑤, we get

$$\frac{\text{Volume of rectangular solid}}{\text{Volume of cube}} = \text{Number of cubes}$$

$$\frac{4 \cancel{\text{ cubic feet}}}{.001 \cancel{\text{ cubic feet}}} = \text{Number of cubes}$$

$$\frac{4}{.001} = \text{Number of cubes}$$

Multiplying numerator and denominator by 1000, we get

$$\frac{4}{.001} \times \frac{1000}{1000} = \text{Number of cubes}$$

$$\frac{4000}{1} = \text{Number of cubes}$$

$$4000 = \text{Number of cubes}$$

(Math Refresher #312 and #313)

21. **(D)** Choice D is correct.(Use Strategy 2: Translate from words to algebra.) (Use Strategy 17: Use the given information effectively.)

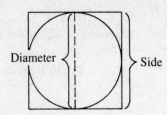

Diameter — Side

Given the perimeter of the square $= 40$

Thus, $4(\text{side}) = 40$

$\text{side} = 10$ $\boxed{1}$

A side of the square $=$ length of diameter of circle.

Thus, diameter $= 10$ from $\boxed{1}$
Since diameter $= 2$ (radius)
$10 = 2$ (radius)
$5 = $ radius $\boxed{2}$

Area of a circle $= \pi r^2$ $\boxed{3}$
Substituting $\boxed{2}$ into $\boxed{3}$, we have

Area of circle $= \pi(5)^2$

Area of circle $= 25\pi$

(Math Refresher #303 and #310)

22. **(C)** Choice C is correct.

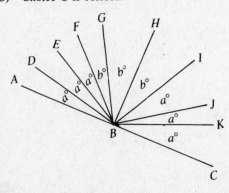

(Use Strategy 3: The whole equals the sum of its parts.) The whole straight angle ABC is equal to the sum of the individual angles.

Thus, $m\angle ABC = a + a + a + b + b +$

$b + a + a + a$ $\boxed{1}$

$m\angle ABC = 6a + 3b$

We know $m\angle ABC = 180$ $\boxed{2}$

Substituting $\boxed{2}$ into $\boxed{1}$, we get

$180° = 6a + 3b$ $\boxed{3}$

(Use Strategy 13: Find an unknown expression by dividing.) Dividing both sides of $\boxed{3}$ by 3, we have

$60° = 2a + b$ $\boxed{4}$

Choice C, $m\angle DBG = 2a + b$, so its measure can be determined. It is $60°$ (from $\boxed{4}$).

(Math Refresher #501 and #406)

23. **(A)** Choice A is correct. **(Use Strategy 17: Use the given information effectively.)**

Given: $ax = r$ $\boxed{1}$

$by = r - 1$ $\boxed{2}$

The quick method is to substitute $\boxed{1}$ into $\boxed{2}$, giving

$by = ax - 1$

$by + 1 = ax$

$\dfrac{by + 1}{a} = x$

(Math Refresher #431 and #406)

24. **(D)** Choice D is correct. **(Use Strategy 17: Use the given information effectively.)**

Given a bag with 4 blue, 7 green, and 8 yellow marbles.

Fred could draw 15 marbles and have only green and yellow marbles ($8 + 7$). On his next pick, however, he would be sure of having one of each color.

(Use Strategy 16: The obvious may be tricky!)

It is his 16th draw that gets Fred one of each color, but the question asks how many Fred would have drawn, so that on his <u>next</u> draw he will have 1 marble of every color.

He will have <u>15</u>. The 16th is the next draw, but not the answer to the question.

15 is the correct answer.

(Logical Reasoning)

25. **(D)** Choice D is correct. $\Big($ **Use Strategy 5:**

Remember average $= \dfrac{\textbf{Sum of Values}}{\textbf{Total Number of Values}}\Big)$

We are told that the average of 5 different integers is 12. Thus,

$\dfrac{x + y + z + w + v}{5} = 12$ $\boxed{1}$

Multiplying $\boxed{1}$ by 5, we get

$\cancel{5}\left(\dfrac{x + y + z + w + v}{\cancel{5}}\right) = 5(12)$

$x + y + z + w + v = 60$ $\boxed{2}$

(Use Strategy 17: Use the given information effectively.)

For one of the integers to be the greatest the other 4 must be as small as possible. Thus,

$$\text{let } x = 1 \qquad \boxed{3}$$

$$\text{let } y = 2 \qquad \boxed{4}$$

$$\text{let } z = 3 \qquad \boxed{5}$$

$$\text{let } w = 4 \qquad \boxed{6}$$

The 4 smallest possible different integers > 0

Substituting $\boxed{3}$, $\boxed{4}$, $\boxed{5}$ and $\boxed{6}$ into $\boxed{2}$ we get

$$1 + 2 + 3 + 4 + v = 60$$

$$10 + v = 60$$

$$v = 50$$

Thus, the greatest possible value for any of the integers is 50.

(Math Refresher #601 and #406)

EXPLANATORY ANSWERS FOR PRACTICE TEST 2 (continued)

Section 3: Standard Written English

> Section 3 does not count toward your SAT score. This Standard Written English section is used only for Freshman English placement when you get to college. However, you are advised to improve yourself in grammar and usage, and also in sentence structure. If you do well in the Standard Written English Test, you will be placed more advantageously in your college Freshman English class.

1. **(D)** "... will repair the car *well*."
The adverb (*well*)—not the adjective (*good*)—is used to modify the verb (*will repair*).

2. **(C)** "... if he *had read* more ..."
The "if" clause of a contrary-to-fact past tense requires the verb *had read*—not *would have read*.

3. **(D)** "... to have his stories *compared with those of Dickens*."
We have an improper ellipsis in the original sentence. The additional words (*those of*) are necessary to complete the meaning of the sentence.

4. **(E)** All underlined parts are correct.

5. **(A)** "Many people in the United States *scarcely know* ..."
Omit the word *don't*. The word *scarcely* is sufficiently negative to express the meaning intended.

6. **(B)** "... *who*, he said, were giving bribes ..."
The subject of the dependent clause must have a nominative case form (*who*)—not an objective case form (*whom*).

7. **(B)** "... with a new *type* of motor ..."
Do not use the article *a* or *an* after *kind of, type of, sort of*, etc.

8. **(B)** "... is not *nearly* as beautiful ..."
Do not use the expression *nowhere near* for *not nearly*.

9. **(C)** "... where *those* same men ..."
The demonstrative pronoun-adjective form (*those*)—not the personal pronoun form (*them*)—must be used to modify the noun *men*.

10. **(E)** All underlined parts are correct.

11. **(C)** "... the *cheaper* to run."
Since we are here comparing two things, we must use the comparative degree—not the superlative degree (*cheapest*).

12. **(B)** "... the family felt *bad* ..."
In this sentence, an adjective (*bad*)—not an adverb (*badly*)—is used after a "sense" verb (*felt*).

13. **(C)** "... *nor* can he live without bread."
The coordinate conjunction *nor* is used when the alternative statement is negative.

14. **(D)** "... Jeff's leg was broken while *he was playing football?*"
We have a dangling elliptical clause in the original sentence. We must make clear that *Jeff was playing football*. Otherwise, the sentence may be understood to mean that *Jeff's leg was playing football*.

15. **(A)** "*Having swum* two-thirds of the distance ..."
The past participle of *swim* is *having swum*.

16. **(A)** "George Foreman did *as* he said ..."
The conjunction (*as*) should be used to introduce the dependent clause (*as he said*)—not the preposition (*like*).

17. **(D)** "... about solving *anyone else's* problems." Say *anyone else's, somebody else's*, etc. Do *not* say *anyone's else, somebody's else*.

18. **(A)** "*Because of* the meat boycott ..."
Do not begin a sentence with the words *due to*. *Due* is an adjective. As an adjective, it must have a noun to modify.

19. **(D)** "... so that the children *would have* enough space ..."
In a clause expressing purpose, the subjunctive form of the verb (*would have*)—not the indicative form (*had*) should be used.

20. **(E)** All underlined parts are correct.

21. **(A)** "Namath played a *really* fine game . . . "
An adverb (*really*)—not an adjective (*real*)—is used to modify the adjective *fine*.

22. **(D)** ". . . is like *that of* New York in June." We have an improper ellipsis here. We must include the words *that of*, meaning *the weather of*.

23. **(E)** All underlined parts are correct.

24. **(A)** "The teacher did not encourage the student *in any way* even though . . ."
We cannot properly use the indefinite pronoun *any* to modify the verb (*did not encourage*). The adverbial phrase *in any way* should be used for this purpose.

25. **(C)** ". . . a great interest *in* and admiration for the work of . . ."
We are not permitted to omit the preposition *in* since it is necessary to introduce the object of the preposition (*work*).

26. **(A)** Choice A is correct. Choice B is awkward. The parenthetical effect of Choice C gives the sentence an ungrammatical structure. The ellipsis of "to the" before the beginning of Choice D, is improper. The possessive use ("oak's") in Choice E results in a bad-sounding sentence.

27. **(A)** Choice A is correct. The present tense in Choice B is incorrect. Choices C, D, and E change the meaning of the original sentence.

28. **(D)** Choices A, B, and E are too wordy. Choice C changes the meaning of the original sentence. Choice D is correct.

29. **(D)** Choice A does not come to the point immediately with the use of the expression "concerning the one." Choice B is too wordy. Choice C is not clear. Choice D is correct. Choice E requires an introductory prepositional compound such as "as to."

30. **(C)** Choices A, B, D, and E are incorrect because of a dangling participle error. In these four choices, the participle "Having" must refer to the subject of the sentence. This subject must follow directly after the participial construction ("Having . . . in his class,"). Accordingly, Choice C is the only correct choice.

31. **(C)** Choice A is incorrect because "its" as a possessive pronoun does not take an apostrophe. Choice B is incorrect because the possessive of "government" ("government's") must be used to modify the gerund "failing." Choice C is correct. Choice D is incorrect for the same reason that Choice B is incorrect. Choice E is incorrect for two reasons: (1) it changes the meaning of the original sentence; (2) even if we change the meaning from singularity to plurality, "governments" must correctly be the possessive form "governments' " to modify the gerund "failing."

32. **(B)** The key to getting the correct answer in this question is knowing this grammatical rule: *When explanatory words intervene between the subject and the verb, the number or person of the real subject is not changed.* Note that the subject "father" of the original sentence is singular. Accordingly, Choices A, C, D, and E (each of which has a singular subject, "father") are incorrect with a plural verb. Moreover, Choice D changes the present time of the original sentence to past time. Choice B is correct.

33. **(E)** The demonstrative adjective ("this," "that," "these," "those,") must agree in number with the noun ("kind") it modifies. Accordingly, Choices A, B, and D are incorrect. Choice C is incorrect because the personal pronoun "them" may not be used as an adjective. Choice E is correct.

34. **(D)** Choices A, B, C, and E are incorrect because they suffer from incomplete verb comparison. This is a form of improper ellipsis. The corrections would be as follows: Choice A—"has not recovered"; Choice B—"never will recover"; Choice C—(two corrections necessary) "has not recovered" and "never will recover" (the subjunctive "would" should not be used here). Choice E—"has not recovered." Note that in Choice E, the past perfect tense should not be used. Choice D is correct.

35. **(D)** It is important to know that "neither-nor" go together as correlative conjunctions. The pairing of "neither" with "or" is incorrect. Therefore, Choices A, C and E are incorrect. Choice B is awkward. Choice D is correct.

36. **(A)** Choice A is correct. Note that "Glory" is the singular subject which takes the singular verb "is." "Reward" is the predicate nominative after the copulative verb "is." The other four choices are incorrect because they are indirect and awkward.

37. **(D)** Choices A, B, and C are incorrect because they lack parallelism. Note that the infinitive phrase "to write poems" should balance with the infinitive phrase "to study the habits." Choice D, which does have the parallelism required, is correct. Choice E is too wordy.

38. **(B)** This question is concerned with the correct position of the gerund phrase "By studying." Choice A is incorrect because "grades" have been doing the "studying" with such sentence structure. Choices C, D, and E are incorrect for the same reason. Choice B is correct since "she" is obviously the one who is doing the "studying."

39. **(D)** Choice A is incorrect because of the improper omission of the demonstrative pronoun "those." Choices B and C are incorrect for the same reason. Choice D is correct. Choice E is incorrect because we must bring out the comparison with *another* city.

40. **(C)** Parallelism is the important consideration here. Choice C is correct as the only choice that fulfills the requirements of parallel structure.

41. **(D)** ". . . of *whom* about . . ."
The object of the preposition must take the objective form (*whom*)—not the nominative form (*who*).

42. **(A)** "Sharon planned to pay *about* . . ."
About means *approximately;* around means *on all sides*.

43. **(A)** "Had Lincoln *been* alive . . ."
In a past contrary to fact situation, the "if clause" verb should take the form *had been*—not *had have been*.

44. **(E)** All underlined parts are correct.

45. **(C)** ". . . was *that* he was on his way . . ."

Do not use the expression *reason is (was) because*—it is always incorrect. Say the *reason is (was) that*.

46. **(E)** All underlined parts are correct.

47. **(A)** "*It's* my opinion . . ."
We need the contraction here (*It's* meaning *It is*).

48. **(A)** "If I *had known* more . . ."
The "if clause" of the past contrary-to-fact conditional statement requires the *had known* form—not the *would have known* form.

49. **(D)** "If you compare Bill and Joe . . . Bill is, without any question, the *brighter*."
In comparing two individuals, we use the comparative form (*brighter*)—not the superlative form (*brightest*).

50. **(B)** "In spite of how *poorly* Ellen had done . . ."
The adverb (*poorly*)—not the adjective (*poor*)—must be used to modify the verb (*had done*).

EXPLANATORY ANSWERS FOR
PRACTICE TEST 2 (continued)

Section 4: Verbal Ability

1. **(D)** Choice D is correct. *Robust* means *strong; vigorous; hardy.* The opposite of *robust* is *feeble.*

2. **(A)** Choice A is correct. *Garrulous* means *talkative.* The opposite of *garrulous* is *silent.*

3. **(E)** Choice E is correct. See **Antonym Strategies 1, 2.** *Abhor* means *to hate; to detest.* The opposite of *abhor* is *appreciate.*

4. **(C)** Choice C is correct. See **Antonym Strategy 3.** *Placate* means *to soothe; to calm.* The opposite of *placate* is *ruffle.*

5. **(B)** Choice B is correct. *Frugal* means *economical; thrifty.* The opposite of *frugal* is *wasteful.*

6. **(D)** Choice D is correct. A *binge* is a *wild party.* The opposite of *binge* is *formal affair.*

7. **(B)** Choice B is correct. See **Antonym Strategy 3.** *Lucid* means *clear; easily understood.* The opposite of *lucid* is *complex.*

8. **(C)** Choice C is correct. See **Antonym Strategy 3.** *Vouchsafe* means *to grant; to allow.* The opposite of *vouchsafe* is *refuse.*

9. **(E)** Choice E is correct. See **Antonym Strategy 3.** *Latitude* means *freedom from restriction.* The opposite of *latitude* is *restriction.* [*Latitude* has another meaning: The distance north and south of the equator.]

10. **(A)** Choice A is correct. *Recalcitrant* means *disobedient; hard to manage.* The opposite of *recalcitrant* is *manageable.*

11. **(C)** Choice C is correct. See **Sentence Completion Strategy 2.** The first step is to examine the first words of each choice. We eliminate Choice (B) perplexed, and Choice (D) considerate, because the first part of the sentence makes no sense with these choices. Now we go to the remaining choices. Choice A and Choice E do *not* make sense in the sentence and are therefore incorrect. Choice C *does* make sense in the sentence.

12. **(E)** Choice E is correct. See **Sentence Completion Strategy 2.** The first step is to examine the first words of each choice. We eliminate Choice A and Choice C because there is no such thing as "sonorous clothes" or "raucous clothes." Now we go on to the remaining choices. Choice (B) tawdry . . . humble, and Choice (D) tattered . . . nightmarish, do *not* make sense in the sen-

tence. Choice (E) oldfashioned . . . nostalgic *does* make sense in the sentence.

13. **(D)** Choice D is correct. See **Sentence Completion Strategy 1.** A rare occasion is one that you seldom have the opportunity to participate in. Shopping in a grocery store today is, indeed, a rare occasion.

14. **(A)** Choice A is correct. See **Sentence Completion Strategy 2.** The first step is to examine the first words of each choice. We eliminate Choice (D) innocent . . . and Choice (E) immune . . . because "claims" are not innocent or immune. Now we go on to the remaining choices. When you fill in the two blanks of Choice B and of Choice C, the sentence does *not* make sense. So these two choices are also incorrect. Filling in the two blanks of Choice A makes the sentence meaningful.

15. **(C)** Choice C is correct. See **Sentence Completion Strategy 2.** The first step is to examine the first words of each choice. We eliminate Choice (B) innuendoes, Choice (D) frequencies, and Choice (E) cancellations, because the the foreman's leniency did not have innuendoes or frequencies or cancellations. Now we go to the remaining choices. Choice (A) compensations . . . unacceptable, does *not* make sense in the sentence. Choice (C) drawbacks . . . shoddy, makes the sentence meaningful.

16. **(C)** Choice C is correct. A dolphin uses his flippers for mobility in the water. A gull uses his wings for mobility in the air. Choices A, B, D, and E also have a PURPOSE relationship but not for the purpose of mobility. So these four choices are incorrect. See **Analogy Strategy 4.** **(Purpose relationship)**

17. **(D)** Choice D is correct. A person who has guile is *not* ingenuous. A person who has courage is *not* timorous. **(Opposite relationship)**

18. **(A)** Choice A is correct. Ecology is the study of environment. Petrology is the study of rocks. **(Association relationship)**

19. **(E)** Choice E is correct. A zebra's body is striated (marked with stripes). A leopard's body is mottled (spotted). We have here a CHARACTERISTIC relationship. Choice A, B, C, and D also have characteristic relationships. However, these four choices do not deal with a color pattern on the body. Accordingly, these four choices are incorrect. See **Analogy Strategy 4.** **(Characteristic relationship)**

20. **(E)** Choice E is correct. The natural covering of an animal is his hide. The natural covering of a person is his skin. We have here a PURPOSE relationship. The coverings referred to in the second word of Choices A, B, C, and E also show a purpose. However, the coverings in each of these four choices are *not* natural coverings. So these choices are incorrect. See **Analogy Strategy 4.** **(Purpose relationship)**

21. **(A)** Choice A is correct. A tree defoliates (loses leaves which are replaced by other leaves). A snake molts (loses his skin which is replaced by other skin).
(Action to Object relationship)

22. **(B)** Choice B is correct. A caravan is a group of travelers that journey through a desert. A safari is a group of hunters that hunt usually in a jungle.
(People-Place relationship)

23. **(C)** Choice C is correct. A hobo does *not* have a home. An orphan does *not* have a parent.
(Opposite relationship)

24. **(D)** Choice D is correct. Many people emulate (imitate) a model. Many people worship an icon (a picture or an image). The word "model" in this analogy means a standard or an example for imitation. The word has other meanings—for example, a person that poses for an artist or photographer—but not in this analogy. See **Analogy Strategy 5. (Action to Object relationship)**

25. **(D)** Choice D is correct. Protean means changeable and immutable means unchangeable. Something that is acquired is gotten after one is born and something that is innate is gotten (by way of genes) before one is born. **(Opposite and Association relationship)**

26. **(B)** Choice B is correct. See lines 24–25: "It means other things may be more important than housing . . ." Money, for instance. It is reasonable that delinquency may be caused, in part, by economic deprivation—seldom by economic advantages. Choice A is incorrect because the author indicates that good housing does not necessarily lead to a decrease in delinquency. See lines 17–22: "Thus a Pittsburgh study . . . the delinquency was higher in the improved housing." Choice C is incorrect. Hardly any neighborhood has *no* problems. See lines 1–2: "A successful city neighborhood . . . keeps sufficiently abreast of its problems . . ." Choice D is incorrect. See lines 14–17: "How charming to control . . . cause and effect are not so simple." Choice E is incorrect because the author implies agreement with Reinhold Niebuhr. See lines 31–35: "When we try . . . salvation by bricks."

27. **(C)** Choice C is not true—therefore correct since the passage states the opposite to that which the choice states. See lines 23–24: "Does this mean improved shelter increases delinquency? Not at all." Choice A is true—therefore incorrect. See lines 6–8: "But on the whole we Americans are poor at handling city neigh-borhoods . . . accumulations of failures . . ." Choice B is true—therefore incorrect. See lines 17–22: "Thus a Pittsburgh study . . . delinquency was higher in the improved housing." Choice D is true—therefore incorrect because history *does* indicate there is "no direct, simple relationship between good housing and good behavior." (See lines 25–27.) Choice E is true—therefore incorrect because the passage does encourage improved housing. See lines 30–31: "Good shelter is a useful good in itself, as shelter."

28. **(D)** Choice D is correct. The adjective "gray" is probably used by the author to mean dull in mood or outlook. The word, no doubt, has a derogatory connotation in the passage. The term "turf" is commonly used in run-down sections to refer to a neighborhood that "belongs"—that is "taken over" by young hoodlums who operate in gangs. There is no basis to accept Choice A or B or C or E as meanings of "gray belts" and "Turfs." Accordingly, these choices are incorrect.

29. **(C)** Choice C is correct. See lines 10–14: "By utilizing . . . per day per person." A quarter of four billion people equals one billion people. Choice A is incorrect. The situation *is* urgent. See lines 25–29: "Private industry must step up . . . desperateness in all these designs on the sea." Choice B is incorrect. The nations need fish protein concentrate—not fish, fresh or frozen. See lines 6–10: "Thus we may better discover . . . sought from the seas." Choice D is incorrect. The oceans are an important source—but not the *major* source. See lines 21–23: "Each year . . . 12 percent of the world's animal proteins." Choice E is incorrect. Scientists are at work examining *70% of the earth that remains explored*—not 70% of the ocean areas of the world. This means that scientists are examining *all* of the ocean depths.

30. **(A)** Choice A is correct. The passage from beginning to end shows that the author is primarily concerned about the water areas of the world being able to provide food for the world's future population. For example, see lines 3–4: "The productiveness of the sea . . . food supply in the future." His concern is shown right on to the very end of the passage. Choices B, D, and E are also of definite concern to the author. But they do not represent a *primary* concern. His primary concern is that the sea will provide us with an adequate food supply in the future. Therefore, Choices B, D, and E are incorrect. Choice C is incorrect. The author is, no doubt, happy about Choice C. It is, therefore, not a primary concern, so choice C is incorrect.

31. **(E)** Choice C is correct. Throughout the passage, the author expresses uneasiness and apprehension about what will happen to the world's future food supply if we cannot utilize the nutritional potential of the sea. For example, see lines 28–29: "There is a tone of desperateness in all these designs on the sea." Choices A, B, C, and D express tones that are not evident in the passage. Therefore, these choices are incorrect.

32. **(D)** Choice D is correct. This title succinctly covers what the passage is about. Choices A, B, and E are referred to in the passage but they do not include the two vital elements discussed in the passage—namely the *sea* and the *future food supply*. Therefore, these choices are incorrect. Choice C, though true, is not relevant. Therefore, it is incorrect.

33. **(A)** Choice A is correct. See lines 38–40: "Some institutions . . . show our people what the higher learning is." These lines confirm Item I. Now see lines 8–11: "Undoubtedly the love of money . . . service-station conception of a university." These lines confirm Item III. Choice B is incorrect. See lines 38–40 again. These lines contradict Item II. Now see lines 13–16: "A state university . . . afternoon and evening." Also, see lines 32–35: "The only hope of securing a true university . . . for vocational training." These two sets of lines contradict Item IV. Choice C is incorrect because lines 38–40 contradict Item II. Choice D is incorrect because lines 38–40 contradict Item II and lines 13–16 together with lines 32–35 contradict Item IV. Choice E is incorrect because, as we have shown above, specific lines in the passage contradict Item II and Item IV.

34. **(C)** Choice C is correct. See lines 3–8: "I do not mean . . . determine their educational policy." We must infer from this statement that money matters should be of concern to university administrators. Choice A is incorrect. The author is opposed to the service-station conception of a university. See lines 8–16: ". . . the love of money . . . afternoon and evening." Choice B is incorrect. See lines 29–32: "Free education should exist . . . profit by it." Choice D is incorrect. See lines 42–45: "Only if the colleges . . . in America." The author is *not* saying that the future holds little hope for our nation's universities. Choice E is incorrect. See lines 32–35: "The only hope . . . vocational training."

35. **(E)** Choice E is correct. Throughout the passage the author is giving his views about what is wrong with our universities—"the service-station conception" (line 10), "must help the farmers look after their cows" (lines 13–14), "a finishing school" (lines 33–34), etc. Also, refer to the final paragraph. Choice A is incorrect because, true as it may be, it does not express the main idea of the passage. Choice B is incorrect. Although the author refers to democratic principles as applied to education in lines 23–25, the matter of democracy is not the main focus of the passage. Choice C is incorrect because the passage does not present a historical comparison. Choice D is incorrect. Although the passage strongly suggests changes, the need for the university system *to survive* is not discussed.

36. **(B)** Choice B is correct because throughout the passage the author gives evidence that he has analyzed the university situation as a result of which he proposes changes. Choice A is incorrect. The term "emotional" implies a strong feeling arising subjectively rather than through conscious mental effort. The author has clearly shown the latter. Choice C is incorrect. The word "forgiving" means "excusing" or "condoning." The author is certainly not excusing or allowing what is going on in the university system. Choice D is incorrect because statistics are not being used in the passage. Choice E is incorrect because the author is far from casual—unconcerned, without specific purpose—in this approach.

37. **(D)** Choice D is false—therefore a correct choice. See lines 11–16: "According to this [service-station] conception . . . in the afternoon and evening." Choice A is true—therefore a wrong choice. See lines 35–37: "A university . . . on any other terms." Choice B is true—therefore a wrong choice. See lines 23–25: "But what really determines . . . but economic conditions." Choice C is true—therefore a wrong choice. See lines 8–11: "Undoubtedly the love of money . . . of a university." Choice E is true—therefore a wrong choice. See lines 38–41: "Some institutions . . . a pursuit of the intellectual virtues." Sincerity, discipline, and consideration for others are certainly intellectual virtues.

38. **(C)** Choice C is correct. Throughout the passage, the author is bringing out the fact that violence is widely shown and well received on television. For example: Line 1: "Violence is alive and well on television." Lines 4–6: ". . . as a result of . . . the horror of violence." Lines 13–14: "Violence on TV . . . in recent years." Although Choices A, B, D, and E are discussed or implied in the passage, none of these choices summarizes the content of the passage as a whole. Therefore, these choices are incorrect.

39. **(D)** Choice D is correct. See lines 31–35: "The simple gunfight . . . for hundreds to die." Accordingly, Choice A is incorrect. Choices B and C are incorrect because there is no violence shown on the screen in these choices. Choice E is incorrect because the violence of a double murder by a jealous husband hardly compares in intensity with the violence of a bomb exploding in a bus carrying a busload of innocent civilians.

40. **(E)** Choice E is correct. See lines 31–35: "The simple gunfight of the past . . . for hundreds to die." Choice A is incorrect because, though the statement may be true, the passage nowhere indicates that TV programs generally are different today from what they were a generation ago. Choice B is incorrect. See lines 39–40: "Many people . . . the way of the world." Choice C is incorrect. See lines 13–15: "Violence on TV . . . and more action series." Choice D is incorrect. See lines 40–43: "It is high time . . . viewing televised violence." No mention is made in the passage that broadcasting stations are doing any warning or notifying about the dangers of showing violence on TV.

EXPLANATORY ANSWERS FOR PRACTICE TEST 2 (continued)

Section 5: Math Ability

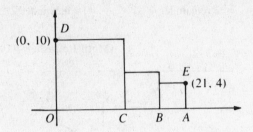

1. **(C)** Choice C is correct.

We want to find the area of the middle square, which is $(CB)^2$. **(Use Strategy 3: The whole equals the sum of its parts.)**

$$OA = OC + CB + BA \qquad \boxed{1}$$

From the diagram, we get

$$OA = 21 \qquad \boxed{2}$$
$$AE = 4 \qquad \boxed{3}$$
$$OD = 10 \qquad \boxed{4}$$

Since each figure is a square, we get

$$BA = AE \qquad \boxed{5}$$
$$OC = OD \qquad \boxed{6}$$

Substituting $\boxed{5}$ into $\boxed{3}$, we get

$$AE = BA = 4 \qquad \boxed{7}$$

Substituting $\boxed{6}$ into $\boxed{4}$, we get

$$OD = OC = 10 \qquad \boxed{8}$$

Substituting $\boxed{2}$, $\boxed{7}$ and $\boxed{8}$ into $\boxed{1}$, we get

$$21 = 10 + CB + 4$$
$$21 = 14 + CB$$
$$7 = CB \qquad \boxed{9}$$

Area of square II $= (CB)^2$
Area of square II $= 7^2$ (From $\boxed{9}$)
Area of square II $= 49$

(Math Refresher #410 and #303)

2. **(E)** Choice E is correct.

Given:
$$\begin{array}{lll} 1 \text{ cup} & = 100 \text{ grams} & \boxed{1} \\ 1 \text{ cake} & = 75 \text{ grams} & \boxed{2} \\ 1 \text{ pie} & = 225 \text{ grams} & \boxed{3} \end{array}$$

Using $\boxed{1}$, we get

$$4 \text{ cups} = 4 \,(100 \text{ grams})$$
$$4 \text{ cups} = 400 \text{ grams} \qquad \boxed{4}$$

(Uses Strategy 8: When all choices must be tested, start with E and work backwards.)

2 cakes and 1 pie is Choice E. $\qquad \boxed{5}$
Substituting $\boxed{2}$ and $\boxed{3}$ in $\boxed{5}$, we get

$$2\,(75 \text{ grams}) + 225 \text{ grams} =$$
$$150 \text{ grams} + 225 \text{ grams} =$$
$$375 \text{ grams} \qquad \boxed{6}$$

Since $\boxed{6}$ is less than $\boxed{4}$, there <u>is enough</u> in 4 cups. So choice E is correct.

(Math Refresher #121 and #431)

3. **(D)** Choice D is correct. **(Use Strategy 2: Translate from words to algebra.)**

Given: 12 seated students, 5 students at board

This translates to $12 + 5 = 17$ students in all. $\quad \boxed{1}$

Given: 12 seated students, 7 empty seats

This translates to $12 + 7 = 19$ seats in all. $\quad \boxed{2}$

Subtracting $\boxed{1}$ from $\boxed{2}$ gives

$19 - 17 = 2$ vacant seats when all are seated $\quad \boxed{3}$

Given: 3 leave and 2 enter

This translates to $-3 + 2$
$\qquad\qquad = -1$, or a net loss of 1 student. $\quad \boxed{4}$

Combining $\boxed{4}$ and $\boxed{3}$, we have

$2 + 1 = 3$ vacant seats.

(Math Refresher #200 and Logical Reasoning)

4. **(D)** Choice D is correct.

$$\text{Given that } 500w = 3 \times 700 \qquad \boxed{1}$$

(Use Strategy 13: Find an unknown by dividing.)

Divide $\boxed{1}$ by 500, giving

$$\frac{\cancel{500}w}{\cancel{500}} = \frac{3 \times 700}{500}$$

(Use Strategy 19: Factor and reduce first. Then multiply.)

$$w = \frac{3 \times 7 \times \cancel{100}}{5 \times \cancel{100}}$$
$$w = \frac{21}{5}$$

(Math Refresher #406)

5. **(E)**   Choice E is correct.

$$Given: \frac{3 + y}{y} = 7 \qquad \boxed{1}$$

(Use Strategy 13: Find an unknown by multiplying.)

Multiply $\boxed{1}$ by y, to get

$$\not{y}\left(\frac{3 + y}{\not{y}}\right) = (7)y$$
$$3 + y = 7y$$
$$3 = 6y$$
$$\frac{3}{6} = y$$
$$\frac{1}{2} = y$$

(Math Refresher #406)

6. **(D)**   Choice D is correct. **(Use Strategy 2: Translate from words to algebra.)**

x is a multiple of 9, gives

$$x \; \varepsilon \; \{9, 18, 27, 36, 45, 54, \ldots \ldots\} \qquad \boxed{1}$$

x is a multiple of 12, gives

$$x \; \varepsilon \; \{12, 24, 36, 48, 60, 72, \ldots \ldots\} \qquad \boxed{2}$$

The smallest value that appears in both sets $\boxed{1}$ and $\boxed{2}$ is 36.

(Logical Reasoning)

7. **(E)**   Choice E is correct.

$$Method \; 1: \quad Given: (r - s)(t - s)$$
$$+ \quad (s - r)(s - t) \qquad \boxed{1}$$

(Use Strategy 17: Use the given information effectively.)

$$Recognizing \; that \; (s - r) = -1(r - s) \qquad \boxed{2}$$
$$(s - t) = -1(t - s) \qquad \boxed{3}$$

Substituting $\boxed{2}$ and $\boxed{3}$ into $\boxed{1}$, we get

$$(r - s)(t - s) + [-1(r - s)][-1(t - s)] =$$
$$(r - s)(t - s) + (r - s)(t - s) =$$
$$2(r - s)(t - s)$$

$Method \; 2$:

$$Given: (r - s)(t - s) + (s - r)(s - t) \qquad \boxed{1}$$

Multiply both pairs of quantities from $\boxed{1}$, giving

$$rt - rs - st + s^2 + s^2 - st - rs + rt =$$
$$2rt - 2rs - 2st + 2s^2 =$$
$$2(rt - rs - st + s^2) =$$
$$2[r(t - s) - s(t - s)] =$$
$$2(r - s)(t - s)$$

(Math Refresher #409)

8. **(A)**   Choice A is correct.

Column A	Column B
The remainder when 14 is divided by 5	The remainder when 14 is divided by 3
$\dfrac{14}{5} = 2$ remainder 4	$\dfrac{14}{3} = 4$ remainder 2

(Math Refresher #101)

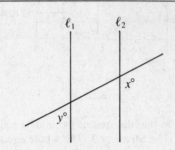

9. **(D)**   Choice D is correct.

(Use Strategy C: Use numerical examples when it appears that a comparison cannot be determined.)

*We are given no information about the relationship between l_1, l_2 and the third line.

Choose x and y so that $x + y > 180$.

If $x = 120$ and $y = 50$, then $x + y = 170$ $\boxed{1}$
If $x = 130$ and $y = 70$, then $x + y = 200$ $\boxed{2}$

Since two different results are possible, we cannot determine which is the correct answer.

* (The temptation to make $l_1 \parallel l_2$ is great but incorrect. Parallelism may not be assumed.)

(Math Refresher #504 and #501)

10. **(B)**   Choice B is correct.

Column A	Column B
$7^2(6^2 + 1)$	$7^2 \cdot 7^2$

(Use Strategy B: Cancel like positive quantities by division.) We can divide both sides by 7^2, and get

$\dfrac{\not{7^2}(6^2 + 1)}{\not{7^2}}$	$\dfrac{7^2 \cdot 7^2}{\not{7^2}}$
$(6^2 + 1) =$	$7^2 =$
$36 + 1 =$	7^2
37	49

(Math Refresher #429)

11. **(C)** Choice C is correct.

Column A	Column B
$5x \div 3 =$	$\dfrac{x}{3} \times 5 =$
$\dfrac{5x}{3}$	$\dfrac{5x}{3}$

The answer is clearly C. **(Division)**

12. **(A)** Choice A is correct. This problem is easily solved by evaluating both columns directly.

Column A	Column B
$8 \times 8 = 64$	$7 \times 9 = 63$

(Multiplication)

13. **(A)** Choice A is correct. **(Use Strategy 17: Use the given information effectively.)**

Given: y is an integer
$y < 0$

Therefore, $\dfrac{1}{y} < 0$ ☐1

(Use Strategy 6: Know how to work with inequalities.)

Adding -1 to both sides of ☐1, we get

$\dfrac{1}{y} - 1 < -1$

(Math Refresher #420)

14. **(C)** Choice C is correct. **(Use Strategy 17: Use the given information effectively.)**

Given: $\dfrac{2}{3} + \dfrac{r}{s} = \dfrac{5}{3}$ ☐1

Subtract $\dfrac{2}{3}$ from both sides of ☐1, giving

$\dfrac{r}{s} = \dfrac{3}{3}$

$\dfrac{r}{s} = 1$

Thus, $r = s$.

(Math Refresher #406)

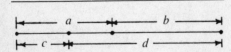

15. **(A)** Choice A is correct.

From the diagram we see that

$a > c$ ☐1
$d > b$ ☐2

(Use Strategy 6: Know how to add inequalities.)

Adding ☐1 and ☐2, we get $a + d > b + c$

(Math Refresher #420)

16. **(B)** Choice B is correct. **(Use Strategy D: Add a quantity to both columns to get rid of minus signs.)**

	Column A	Column B
		$x > 0 > y$
	$y - x$	$x - y$
Add x:	$y - x + x$	$x - y + x$
	y	$2x - y$
Add y:	$y + y$	$2x - y + y$
	$2y$	$2x$
Divide by 2:	y	x

Since $x > 0 > y$, $x > y$

(Math Refresher #421)

17. **(D)** Choice D is correct.

Given: $w \leqq 60$
$x \leqq 60$

(Use Strategy C: Use numerical examples when it appears that a comparison cannot be determined.)

First: Let $w = 50$
$x = 50$

Then $w + x = 100$ ☐1
which is > 80

Second: $w = 30$
$x = 20$

Then $w + x = 50$ ☐2
which is < 80

From ☐1 and ☐2 we see that two different answers are possible. Therefore, we cannot determine the correct answer. **(Math Refresher #122)**

18. **(D)** Choice D is correct.
(Use Strategy 6: Know how to work with inequalities.)

Given: $3y - 2 < 0$ ☐1
Add 2 to both sides of ☐1. We get $3y < 2$ ☐2

Now look at the two columns.
(Use Strategy C: Use number examples when it appears that a comparison cannot be determined.)

$3y$ could $= 1$ ☐3
This satisfies ☐2
$3y$ could $= -3$ ☐4
This satisfies ☐2
From ☐3, $1 > -2$ ☐5
From ☐4, $-3 < -2$ ☐6

Since there are 2 possible relations, we cannot determine a definite relationship for the columns.

(Math Refresher #419 and #431)

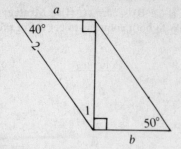

19. (A) Choice A is correct.

(Use Strategy 18: Remember right triangle facts.)

In a right triangle, the sum of the 2 acute $\angle$ s is 90° 〔1〕

In the left hand triangle, using 〔1〕, we have

$$40 + \angle 1 = 90$$
$$\angle 1 = 50 \quad 〔2〕$$

In the righthand triangle, using 〔2〕, we have

$$50 + \angle 2 = 90$$
$$\angle 2 = 40 \quad 〔3〕$$

From 〔1〕, 〔2〕 and 〔3〕 we see that each triangle has a 40°, 50°, and 90° angle.

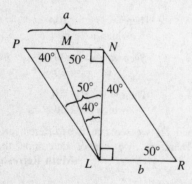

(Use Strategy 14: Draw lines to make the problem easier.) Draw LM, making a 50° angle with a.

$$\triangle\ MNL \cong \triangle\ RLN \text{ by Angle–Side–Angle}$$
$$\text{Therefore, } MN \cong LR$$
$$MN = b \quad 〔4〕$$

From the diagram, we know that

$$PN = a \quad 〔5〕$$

It is obvious that $PN > MN$, 〔6〕

Substituting 〔4〕 and 〔5〕 into 〔6〕, we get

$$a > b$$

(Math Refresher #501 and #511)

20. (D) Choice D is correct. **(Use Strategy C: Use numerical examples when it appears that a comparison cannot be determined.)**

$$\text{Let } y = 1, \text{ then}$$
$$Y^3 = 1^3 = 1 \qquad\qquad 3^y = 3^1 = 3$$
$$1 < 3$$
$$\text{Let } Y = 3, \text{ then}$$
$$Y^3 = 3^3 = 27 \qquad\qquad 3^3 = 27$$
$$27 = 27$$

There are two different possibilities, so you cannot determine which is the correct answer.

(Math Refresher #431)

21. (B) Choice B is correct.

$$\text{Given: } \frac{3}{a} = 2 \quad 〔1〕$$
$$\frac{5}{b} = 2 \quad 〔2〕$$

(Use Strategy 13: Find an unknown by multiplication.)

Multiplying 〔1〕 by a, we get

$$a\left(\frac{3}{a}\right) = a(2)$$
$$3 = 2a$$
$$\frac{3}{2} = a \quad 〔3〕$$

Multiplying 〔2〕 by b, we get

$$b\left(\frac{5}{b}\right) = b(2)$$
$$5 = 2b$$
$$\frac{5}{2} = b \quad 〔4〕$$

Comparing 〔3〕 and 〔4〕 we get
$b > a$

(Math Refresher #406)

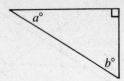

22. (C) Choice C is correct.

(Use Strategy 3: The whole equals the sum of its parts.)

The sum of the 3 angles of a triangle $= 180$ ☐1

Substituting from the diagram into ☐1, we get

$$a + b + 90 = 180 \qquad ☐2$$

(Use Strategy 13: Find an unknown expression by subtracting.)

Subtracting 90 from both sides of ☐2, we get

$$a + b = 90$$

(Math Refresher #505)

23. (C) Choice C is correct.

Column A	Column B
Translates to the units' digit of $1 \cdot 2 \cdot 3 \cdot 4 \cdot 5 \cdot 6 \cdot 7$	The units' digit of $8 \cdot 9 \cdot 10 \cdot 11 \cdot 12 \cdot 13 \cdot 14$

(Use Strategy 17: Use the given information effectively.)

Seeing in Column A that $4 \cdot 5 = 20$, we know that any product of integers with 20 will have a units' digit of 0.   ☐1

Seeing in Column B that 10 is one of the factors, we know that any product of integers with 10 will have a units' digit of 0.   ☐2

Since ☐1 and ☐2, we know that choice C is correct.

(Use Strategy 12: Do not make tedious calculations.) No tedious calculations were necessary!

(Math Refresher #200)

24. (C) Choice C is correct.

Given: x is any non-negative integer, gives

$$x \in \{0,1,2,3,4,5,6, \ldots \ldots \}$$

(Use Strategy C: Use number examples when it appears that a comparison cannot be determined.)

Column A	Column B
The minimum value of $4x^2 + 1$	The minimum value of $5x^2 + 1$

Let $x = 0$, we have

$4(0)^2 + 1$	$5(0)^2 + 1$
$0 + 1$	$0 + 1$
$1 \qquad =$	1

(Math Refresher #431)

25. (D) Choice D is correct.

Given: $\dfrac{4}{a} = \dfrac{b}{4}$

Multiplying means and extremes (cross multiplying), we get

$$ab = 16 \qquad\qquad ☐1$$

(Use Strategy C: Use numerical examples when it appears that a comparison cannot be determined.)

If $a = 16$ and $b = 1$, then $ab = 16$ as in ☐1

If $b = 16$ and $a = 1$, then $ab = 16$ as in ☐1

$a > b$ or $b > a$

Since there are two possible answers, we cannot determine which is the correct answer.

(Math Refresher #120 and #431)

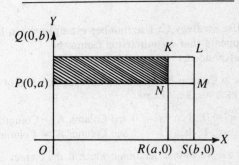

26. (A) Choice A is correct.

From the diagram above, we see that:

$$QP = b - a \qquad ☐1$$
$$QK = a \qquad\quad ☐2$$
$$b > a \qquad\quad\;\; ☐3$$

Area of rectangle $= l \times w$ ☐4

Substituting ☐1 and ☐2 into ☐4, we get Area of rectangle $QKNP = a(b - a)$ ☐5

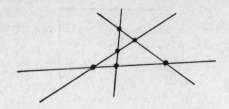

Column A   Column B

Given: $b(b - a)$ $a(b - a)$:From ⑤

(Use Strategy B: Cancel positive quantities from both sides by dividing.)

From ③ we have that $b - a > 0$ or $b - a$ is positive

Thus, we can divide both columns by $b - a$, giving

$$\frac{b(\cancel{b - a})}{\cancel{b - a}} \qquad \frac{a(\cancel{b - a})}{\cancel{b - a}}$$

$$b \qquad\qquad a$$

From ③ we know that $b > a$
Thus, Column A > Column B

(Math Refresher #410 and #304)

27. **(D)** Choice D is correct.

Column A   Column B

Given: $xy + 7$ $x(y + 7)$

Distribute in Column B, to get

$$xy + 7 \qquad\qquad xy + 7x$$

(Use Strategy A: Cancel equal quantities from both sides by subtracting.)

Subtract xy from both sides.
We then have

$$7 \qquad\qquad 7x$$

(Use Strategy C: Use number examples when it appears that a comparison cannot be determined.)

$7x$ in Column B depends on the specific value of x, which we don't know.

If $x = 0$, then $7x = 0$ and Column A > Column B
If $x = 1$, then $7x = 7$ and Column A = Column B

Thus, we cannot determine which is the correct answer.

(Math Refresher #431)

28. **(A)** Choice A is correct.

Given: $y = r - 6$ ①
          $z = r + 5$ ②

(Use Strategy 13: Find unknown expressions by addition of equations.)

Adding ① and ②, we get

$$y + z = 2r - 1$$
$$y + z + 1 = 2r$$
$$\frac{y + z + 1}{2} = r$$

(Math Refresher #407)

29. **(C)** Choice C is correct.

Method 1: The figure above shows 4 straight lines intersecting in 6 points. 6 is the maximum number of points of intersection of 4 straight lines.

Method 2: There is a formula for finding the maximum number of points of intersection of n straight line segments. It is $\dfrac{n(n - 1)}{2}$ ①

Substituting 4 into ①, we get

$$\frac{4(4 - 1)}{2} = \frac{4(3)}{2} =$$

$$\frac{12}{2} = 6$$

(Logical Reasoning)

30. **(B)** Choice B is correct.

(Use Strategy 2: Know the definition of percent.)

$$\text{Percent of Caramels} = \frac{\text{Weight of Caramels}}{\text{Total Weight}} \times 100 \quad ①$$

Given: ②
Weight of Caramels = 0.6 pound   ③
Weight of Coconuts = 3.6 pounds

Adding ② and ③, we get

Total Weight = 0.6 pounds + 3.6 pounds
Total Weight = 4.2 pounds   ④

Substituting ② and ④ into ①, we have

$$\text{Percent of Caramels} = \frac{0.6 \cancel{\text{ pounds}}}{4.2 \cancel{\text{ pounds}}} \times 100$$

$$= \frac{.6}{4.2} \times 100$$

$$= \frac{6}{42} \times 100$$

$$= \frac{600}{42} = \frac{300}{21} =$$

$$\text{Percent of Caramels} = 14\frac{2}{7}$$

(Math Refresher #106 and #107)

31. **(A)** Choice A is correct.
Method 1: **(Use Strategy 17: Use the given information effectively.)**

Remembering that the sum of 2 sides of a triangle is greater than third, we know that

$$LM + MN > LN$$
or
$$6 + 10 > 12$$
$$16 > 12$$

The difference between 16 and 12: $16 - 12 = 4$ is the amount of overlap.

Method 2: **(Use Strategy 14: Draw lines when appropriate.)**

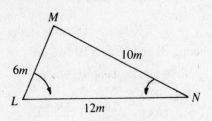

In the figure above, the segments have been redrawn so the result can be easily discovered.

In ②, the distance $LM = 12 - 10 = 2$ ④

Subtracting ④ from the distance LM in ③, we get $6 - 2 = 4m$ overlap.

(Math Refresher #419)

32. **(E)** Choice E is correct. **(Use Strategy 2: Translate from words to algebra.)**

Given: The 3 polygons have equal perimeters, gives us

$$6a = 3b \qquad ①$$
$$8c = 6a \qquad ②$$

Dividing ① by 6, we get

$$a = \frac{3}{6}b = \frac{1}{2}b \qquad ③$$

Thus, $a < b$

Dividing ② by 8, we get

$$c = \frac{6}{8}a = \frac{3}{4}a \qquad ④$$

Thus, $c < a$

(Use Strategy 6: Know how to use inequalities.)

Using the Transitive Property of Inequality with ③ and ④ We have, $c < a < b$.

(Math Refresher #304, 306, and #406)

33. **(B)** Choice B is correct. **(Use Strategy 9: Know the formula for rate, time and distance.)**

$$\text{Rate} \times \text{Time} = \text{Distance} \qquad ①$$

Given: Time from A to B = 3 hours   ②
Time from B to C = 5 hours   ③
Distance from A to B =
Distance from B to C ④

Using ④, let Distance from A to B =
Distance from B to C = D ⑤

Substituting ② and ⑤ into ①, we get

$$\text{Rate}_{AB} \times 3 = D$$
$$\text{Rate}_{AB} = \frac{D}{3} \qquad ⑥$$

Substituting ③ and ⑤ into ①, we get

$$\text{Rate}_{BC} \times 5 = D$$
$$\text{Rate}_{BC} = \frac{D}{5} \qquad ⑦$$

From ⑤ we get whole distance from A to C = $2D$ ⑧

From ② and ③ we get time for whole trip = $3 + 5 = 8$ ⑨

Substituting ⑧ and ⑨ into ①, we get

$$\text{Rate}_{AC} \times 8 = 2D$$
$$\text{Rate}_{AC} = \frac{2D}{8}$$
$$\text{Rate}_{AC} = \frac{D}{4} \qquad ⑩$$

We are asked to find the ratio

$$\frac{\text{Average Speed from } A \text{ to } B}{\text{Average Speed from } A \text{ to } C} \qquad ⑪$$

Substituting ⑥ and ⑩ into ⑪, we have

$$\frac{\text{Average Speed from } A \text{ to } B}{\text{Average Speed from } A \text{ to } C} =$$

$$\frac{\dfrac{D}{3}}{\dfrac{D}{4}} =$$

$$\frac{D}{3} \div \frac{D}{4} =$$

$$\frac{\not{D}}{3} \times \frac{4}{\not{D}} =$$

$$\frac{4}{3} = 4 : 3$$

(Math Refresher #201, #202, and #120)

34. **(C)** Choice C is correct. **(Use Strategy 7: Use number examples.)**

$$\text{If } a = \frac{2}{3}, b = \frac{4}{3} \text{ and } x = \frac{3}{2} \qquad \boxed{1}$$

Then, substituting from $\boxed{1}$, we get

$$ax = \frac{2}{3}\left(\frac{3}{2}\right) \qquad\qquad bx = \frac{4}{3}\left(\frac{3}{2}\right) = \frac{4}{2}$$

$$ax = 1 \qquad\qquad\qquad bx = 2$$

Neither a nor b nor x are integers, but both ax and bx are integers.

Thus, Choices B, D, and E are eliminated,

(Use Strategy 13: Find unknown expressions by addition of equations.)

$$\text{Adding } ax \text{ to } bx, \text{ we get}$$
$$ax + bx =$$
$$(a + b)x \qquad \boxed{2}$$

Since ax and bx are integers, $\boxed{2}$ is an integer. Thus, Choice C is correct result.

(Math Refresher #431)

35. **(B)** Choice B is correct.

(Use Strategy 9: Know the formula for rate, time and distance.)

$$\text{Rate} \times \text{Time} = \text{Distance} \qquad \boxed{1}$$

$$\text{Given:} \quad \text{Initial rate} = \frac{48 \text{ laps}}{\text{hour}} \qquad \boxed{2}$$
$$\text{Initial time} = 12 \text{ hours} \qquad \boxed{3}$$
$$\text{Second rate} = \frac{30 \text{ laps}}{\text{hour}} \qquad \boxed{4}$$

Substituting $\boxed{2}$ and $\boxed{3}$ into $\boxed{1}$, we have

$$\frac{48 \text{ laps}}{\text{hour}} \times 12 \text{ hours} = \text{Distance}$$

$$576 \text{ laps} = \text{Distance} \qquad \boxed{5}$$

Substituting $\boxed{4}$ and $\boxed{5}$ into $\boxed{1}$, we get

$$\frac{30 \text{ laps}}{\text{hour}} \times \text{Time} = 576 \text{ laps}$$

$$\text{Time} = \frac{576 \text{ laps}}{30 \frac{\text{laps}}{\text{hour}}}$$

$$= \frac{576 \text{ hours}}{30}$$

$$= 19\frac{1}{5} \text{ hours}$$

$19\frac{1}{5}$ hours, to the nearest hour, equals 19 hours.

(Math Refresher #201 and #202)

EXPLANATORY ANSWERS FOR PRACTICE TEST 2 (continued)

Section 6: Math Ability

1. **(D)** Choice D is correct. **(Use Strategy 2: Translate from words to algebra)** The boy originally had enough money to buy 21 bars at 50¢ per bar. Thus, he had $21 \times 50 = 1050$ cents = \$10.50. Therefore,

Number of 30¢ bars he bought

$$= \frac{\text{Total amount he had}}{\text{Price of each bar}}$$
$$= \frac{\$10.50}{\$\ .30}$$
$$= 35 \text{ bars (Answer)}$$

(Math Refresher #200 and #406)

2. **(C)** Choice C is correct. **(Use Strategy 2: Translate from words to algebra)** Let n = the number. We are told

$$\frac{n}{3} = n \qquad \boxed{1}$$

Subtracting $\frac{n}{3}$ from both sides of $\boxed{1}$,

$$n - \frac{n}{3} = 0 \qquad \boxed{2}$$

Multiplying $\boxed{2}$ by 3 we get

$$3\left(n - \frac{n}{3}\right) = 0$$
$$3n - n = 0$$
$$2n = 0$$
$$n = 0$$

(Math Refresher #200 and #406)

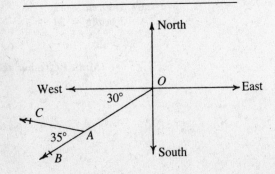

3. **(E)** Choice E is correct.

Originally, the man is facing in the direction of OA.

After he turns, he is facing in the direction of $\overrightarrow{AC}$, where $m \sphericalangle CAB = 35$. We want to find out the direction of $\overrightarrow{AC}$ with respect to the North–South–East–West axes. In other words, when we redraw the above diagram with $\overleftrightarrow{l} \parallel W\text{-}E$ axis, and $\overleftrightarrow{m} \parallel N\text{-}S$ axis, then $\overrightarrow{AC}$ is $x°$ north of west $\boxed{1}$

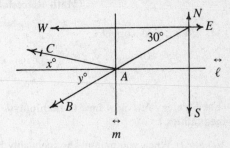

Since $m \sphericalangle CAB = 35$, then

$$x + y = 35 \qquad \boxed{2}$$

Since $\overleftrightarrow{l} \parallel W\text{-}E$ axis, then

$$y = 30° \qquad \boxed{3}$$

Subtracting $\boxed{3}$ from $\boxed{2}$,

$$x = 5° \qquad \boxed{4}$$

Thus, using $\boxed{4}$ and $\boxed{1}$, $\overrightarrow{AC}$ is 5° north of west.

(Math Refresher #504 and #501)

4. **(C)** Choice C is correct.

Short Method: Given $\frac{9}{5} K = 18 \qquad \boxed{1}$

(Use Strategy 13: Find unknowns by division) Dividing $\boxed{1}$ by 9, we have

$$\left(\frac{1}{\cancel{9}}\right) \frac{\cancel{9}}{5} K = \overset{2}{\cancel{18}} \left(\frac{1}{\cancel{9}}\right)$$

$$\frac{1}{5} K = 2 \text{ (Answer)}$$

Long Method: Given $\frac{9}{5} K = 18 \qquad \boxed{1}$

Multiply $\boxed{1}$ by $\dfrac{5}{9}$, getting

$$\left(\frac{\cancel{5}}{\cancel{9}}\right)\frac{\cancel{9}}{\cancel{5}}K = \overset{2}{\cancel{18}}\left(\frac{5}{\cancel{9}}\right)$$

Giving $K = 10$ $\qquad\boxed{2}$

Multiplying $\boxed{2}$ by $\dfrac{1}{5}$ gives

$$\frac{1}{5}K = \overset{2}{\cancel{10}}\left(\frac{1}{\cancel{5}}\right)$$

$$\frac{1}{5}K = 2 \text{ (Answer)}$$

(Math Refresher #406)

5. **(A)** Choice A is correct.

$$\begin{array}{ll} \textit{Given: } x, y, z < 0 & \boxed{1} \\ x < y & \boxed{2} \\ y < z & \boxed{3} \end{array}$$

(Use Strategy 6: Know how to manipulate inequalities.)

Method 1: When you multiply an inequality by a negative number, you must reverse the inequality. For example, multiplying $\boxed{2}$ and $\boxed{3}$ by x, we get

$$\begin{array}{ll} x^2 > xy & \boxed{4} \\ xy > xz & \boxed{5} \end{array}$$

multiplying $\boxed{2}$ and $\boxed{3}$ by z, we get

$$\begin{array}{ll} xz > yz & \boxed{6} \\ yz > z^2 & \boxed{7} \end{array}$$

Comparing $\boxed{4}$, $\boxed{5}$, $\boxed{6}$, and $\boxed{7}$, we have

$$x^2 > xy > xz > yz > z^2$$

Thus, choice A is correct.

(Use Strategy 7: Use numerics to help.)

Method 2: Choose specific numeric values for x, y, z satisfying $\boxed{1}$, $\boxed{2}$, and $\boxed{3}$.

For example, let $x = -3, y = -2, z = -1$
The choices become
   (A) 1   (B) 2   (C) 3   (D) 6   (E) 9
Choice A is correct.

(Math Refresher #419, #423, and #431)

6. **(E)** Choice E is the correct answer. **(Use Strategy 11: Use new definitions carefully. These problems are generally easy.)** The first few terms of the sequence are found as follows:

Given: Term 1 = 2

$$\begin{aligned} \text{By definition, Term 2} &= (\text{Term 1} - 2)3 \\ &= (2 - 2)3 \\ &= (0)3 \\ \text{Term 2} &= 0 \end{aligned}$$

$$\begin{aligned} \text{Term 3} &= (\text{Term 2} - 2)3 \\ &= (0 - 2)3 \\ &= (-2)3 \\ &= -6 \end{aligned}$$

$$\begin{aligned} \text{Term 4} &= (\text{Term 3} - 2)3 \\ &= (-6 - 2)3 \\ &= (-8)3 \\ &= -24 \end{aligned}$$

and so on.

$2, 0, -6, -24$ are all even, so Choices A, B, C and D can be eliminated.

(Math Refresher #431)

7. **(D)** Choice D is correct. **(Use Strategy 17: Use the given information effectively.)**
Given:

$$\begin{array}{ll} 7a = 4 & \boxed{1} \\ 7a + 4b = 12 & \boxed{2} \end{array}$$

Substituting $\boxed{1}$ into $\boxed{2}$,

$$\begin{array}{ll} & 4 + 4b = 12 \\ \text{or} & 4b = 8 \\ \text{or} & b = 2 \end{array}$$

(Math Refresher #460)

8. **(B)** Choice B is correct. **(Use Strategy 10: Know how to use units.)**

$$\begin{array}{ll} \text{We know} & 1 \text{ dozen} = 12 \\ \text{Thus,} & 2 \text{ dozen} = 24 \end{array}$$

$$24 > 20$$

(Math Refresher #121)

9. **(B)** Choice B is correct. We want to compare

Column A	Column B
half of ten = 5	double five = 10

and the answer is clear. **(Logical Reasoning)**

10. **(A)** Choice A is correct.

Column A	Column B

$$\frac{x}{3}\left(\frac{x}{9}\right)(27x) = \left(\frac{x}{3}\right)\left(\frac{x}{27}\right)(3x) =$$

$$x^3 \qquad\qquad \frac{x^3}{27}$$

Since $x > 0$, we have

$$x^3 > \frac{x^3}{27}$$

(Math Refresher #431 and #428)

11. **(D)** Choice D is correct. **(Use Strategy C: When a comparison is difficult, use numbers instead of variables.)**

$$Given\ m - n > p - q \qquad \boxed{1}$$

Choose specific values of m, n, p, q that satisfy $\boxed{1}$.

EXAMPLE 1

$$m = 0, n = -1, p = 0, q = 0$$

The columns become

Column A	Column B
−1	0

and the quantity in Column B is greater.

EXAMPLE 2

$$m = 3, n = 0, p = 0, q = 1$$

The columns become

Column A	Column B
0	0

and the two quantities are equal. Thus, the answer depends on specific values of m, n, p, and q.

(Math Refresher #431)

12. **(B)** Choice B is correct. **(Use Strategy 2: Translate from words to algebra.)**

Given: $\frac{2}{3} \times 54$ = number of Democrats

$$\frac{2}{\cancel{3}} \times \frac{18 \times \cancel{3}}{1} =$$

$$36 = \text{number of Democrats}$$

Thus, $54 - 36 = 18$ Republicans

$$18 > 17$$

(Math Refresher #200)

13. **(A)** Choice A is correct. **(Use Strategy 3: The whole equals the sum of the parts.)** The sum of the measures of the angles of a triangle is 180. Thus,

$$35° + 45° + A = 180°$$
$$or \qquad 80° + A = 180°$$
$$or \qquad A = 100° \qquad \boxed{1}$$

From the diagram, we see that

$$A + B = 180° \qquad \boxed{2}$$

Substituting $\boxed{1}$ into $\boxed{2}$

$$100° + B = 180°$$
$$or \qquad B = 80° \qquad \boxed{3}$$

From $\boxed{3}$ and $\boxed{1}$, we have

$$A > B$$

(Math Refresher #505 and #406)

14. **(B)** Choice B is correct. **(Use Strategy 17: Use the given information effectively.)**

METHOD 1:
$$.008 + .007 + .006 = (.007 + .001) + .007 + (.007 - .001)$$
$$= .007 + .007 + .007$$
$$= 3\ (.007)$$

Thus, we want to compare

Column A	Column B
3 (.007)	30 (.007)

and the answer is clear. Notice that neither quantity was actually calculated.

METHOD 2:

Column A	Column B
.008 + .007 + .006 = .021	.007 × 30 = .21

Clearly, Column B is greater.

(Math Refresher: Addition of decimals and #113)

15. **(C)** Choice C is correct. **(Use Strategy F: For straightforward calculations, try Choice C.)** Area of a triangle = $\frac{1}{2}$(base)(height)

Thus,

$$Area\ of\ \triangle PQR = \frac{1}{2}(18)(h)$$
$$= 9h \qquad \boxed{1}$$

$$Area\ of\ \triangle XYZ = \frac{1}{2}(6)(3h)$$
$$= 9h \qquad \boxed{2}$$

From $\boxed{1}$ and $\boxed{2}$, we see that
Area of $\triangle PQR$ = Area of $\triangle XYZ$

(Math Refresher #306 and #431)

16. **(B)**   Choice B is correct.

Column A	Column B
$\dfrac{y^3}{2}$	$\dfrac{y^3}{2y}$

(Use Strategy B: Cancel equal positive quantities from both sides by division.) Since y^3 is a positive quantity in both columns, we divide both columns by y^3, giving

Column A	Column B
$\dfrac{1}{2}$	$\dfrac{1}{2y}$

(Use Strategy 6: Know how to manipulate inequalities.) Since we are given that $y < 1$, we know

$$\frac{1}{y} > 1 \qquad \boxed{1}$$

(Use Strategy 13: Find unknown expressions by multiplication.) Multiply $\boxed{1}$ by $\dfrac{1}{2}$, we get

$$\frac{1}{2y} > \frac{1}{2}$$

and Column B is larger.

(Math Refresher #108 and #422)

17. **(A)**   Choice A is correct.

Column A	Column B
$\dfrac{7K + 8}{7} =$	$K + 1$
$\dfrac{7K}{7} + \dfrac{8}{7} =$	$K + 1$
$K + 1\dfrac{1}{7}$	$K + 1$

(Use Strategy A: Cancel equal quantities from both sides by subtracting.) Subtract K from both columns, giving

$1\dfrac{1}{7}$	1

Clearly Choice A is correct.

(Math Refresher #108)

18. **(A)**   Choice A is correct.

Try not to actually calculate each quantity. Notice that

$$15 \times (68 - 22) = (15 \times 68) - (15 \times 22)$$

Thus, we want to compare

Column A	Column B
$(15 \times 68) - 22$	$(15 \times 68) - (15 \times 22)$

(Use Strategy A: Cancel equal quantitiies from both sides by subtracting.)

Since 15×68 appears in both columns, it will not change the answer. Thus, we really want to compare

Column A	Column B
-22	$-(15 \times 22)$

Clearly, $-22 > -15 \times 22$

(Logical Reasoning)

19. **(B)**   Choice B is correct.

Column A	Column B
$\dfrac{\dfrac{5}{3}}{\dfrac{10}{9}} =$	$\dfrac{\dfrac{10}{9}}{\dfrac{2}{3}} =$
$\dfrac{5}{3} \div \dfrac{10}{9} =$	$\dfrac{10}{9} \div \dfrac{2}{3} =$
$\dfrac{5}{3} \times \dfrac{9}{10} =$	$\dfrac{10}{9} \times \dfrac{3}{2} =$
$\dfrac{\cancel{5}}{\cancel{3}} \times \dfrac{\cancel{3} \times 3}{\cancel{5} \times 2} =$	$\dfrac{5 \times \cancel{2}}{3 \times \cancel{3}} \times \dfrac{\cancel{3}}{\cancel{2}} =$
$\dfrac{3}{2} =$	$\dfrac{5}{3} =$
$1\dfrac{1}{2}$ $\qquad < \qquad$	$1\dfrac{2}{3}$

Thus, Choice B is correct.

(Math Refresher #112)

20. **(D)** Choice D is correct.

Given: $m:n = n:m = 1$

or $\dfrac{m}{n} = \dfrac{n}{m} = 1$

or $m = n$ 1

so that $mn = m^2 = n^2$ 2

Method 1: Clearly, from 2, it should be clear that

$mn > 1, \quad mn = 1, \quad mn < 1$

can all be true. Thus the answer cannot be determined

(Use Strategy C: Try numerics if it appears like it can't be determined.)

Method 2: If you don't see this, take some numeric examples which satisfy 1.

EXAMPLE 1

$m = 1 \qquad n = 1$

The columns become

Column A	Column B
1	1

and the 2 quantities are equal.

EXAMPLE 2

$m = 2, \quad n = 2$ The columns become

Column A	Column B
1	4

and the quantity in column B is greater. Thus, the answer cannot be determined.

(Math Refresher #431)

21. **(C)** Choice C is correct.

(Use Strategy 11: Use new definitions carefully.)

Given: $x \,\square\, (-x) = 0$ for all x 1

where $\square$ is one of $+$, $-$, $\times$, or $\div$

Clearly, $\square$ cannot be $-$, $\times$, or $\div$ because

$$x - (-x) = 2x \neq 0$$
$$x \times (-x) = -x^2 \neq 0$$
$$x \div (-x) = -1 \neq 0$$

and 1 is not satisfied.

But notice that

$$x + (-x) = 0$$

so that $\square$ is the same as $+$. Thus, we want to compare

Column A	Column B
$x + y$	$y + x$

and the two quantities are equal.

(Math Refresher #431)

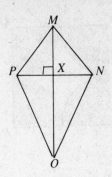

22. **(A)** Choice A is correct.

1 *Given*: Area $\triangle MNP <$ Area $\triangle NOP$ 1

2 Area of $\triangle MNP = \dfrac{1}{2}(PN)(MX)$ 2

3 Areas of $\triangle NOP = \dfrac{1}{2}(PN)(OX)$ 3

Substituting 2 and 3 into 1 gives

$$\frac{1}{2}(PN)(MX) < \frac{1}{2}(PN)(OX)$$

(Use Strategy 13: Find unknown by division.)

Dividing both sides by $\dfrac{1}{2}PN$ we get

$$MX < OX$$

This translates to: Point O is farther from PN than point M is.

From this it is obvious that $PO > PM$ and $NO > NM$ 4

(Use Strategy 13: Find unknowns by addition.)

Adding the 2 parts of 4 yields

$$PO + NO > PM + NM.$$

(Math Refresher #306 and #422)

23. **(C)** Choice C is correct.

(Use Strategy 4: Remember classic expressions.)

Remember the factorization,

$$x^2 - 1 = (x - 1)(x + 1)$$
$$x^2 + 2x + 1 = (x + 1)(x + 1)$$

where $x^2 \neq 1$ (or $x \neq 1$ and $x \neq -1$) Thus, we want to compare

Column A	Column B
$\dfrac{(x - 1)(x + 1)}{x - 1}$	$\dfrac{(x + 1)(x + 1)}{x + 1}$
$\dfrac{(x - 1)(x + 1)}{x - 1} = x + 1$	$\dfrac{(x + 1)(x + 1)}{x + 1} = x + 1$

and the two quantities are equal.

(Math Refresher #409)

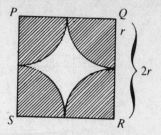

24. (B) Choice B is correct.

Since the diagram shows 4 quartercircles, the radius of each quartercircle is r, and each side of the square has length $2r$. We know that

$$\text{Area of circle} = \pi \, (\text{radius})^2$$

$$\text{Area of quartercircle} = \frac{1}{4} \, \pi \, (\text{radius})^2$$

(Use Strategy 3: The whole equals the sum of its parts.)

$$\text{Area of shaded region} = \text{the sum of the areas of the four quartercircles}$$

$$= 4 \left(\frac{1}{4}\right) \pi r^2$$

$$= \pi r^2$$

$$\text{Area of square} = (\text{side})^2$$

$$= (2r)^2$$

$$= 4r^2$$

Thus, ratio of the area of the square to that of the shaded region $= \dfrac{4r^2}{\pi r^2} = \dfrac{4}{\pi}$

and $\dfrac{4}{\pi} > \dfrac{2}{\pi}$

(Math Refresher #310 and #303)

25. (A) Choice A is correct.

(Use Strategy 2: Translate from words to algebra.)

$$\text{Let } r = \text{number of Robert's eggs} \quad \boxed{1}$$
$$\text{Then: } r - 4 = \text{number of Sue's eggs} \quad \boxed{2}$$
$$r - 4 - 6 = \text{number of Joe's eggs} \quad \boxed{3}$$
$$r - 4 - 6 - 8 = \text{number of Tom's eggs} \quad \boxed{4}$$

(Use Strategy 13: Find unknown expressions by addition.)

Adding $\boxed{1}$, $\boxed{2}$, $\boxed{3}$ and $\boxed{4}$ we get

$$\text{Total number of eggs} = 4r - 32 \quad \boxed{5}$$

If everyone is to have the same number of eggs, then

$$\text{number of eggs per person} = \frac{\text{Total number of eggs}}{4}$$

$$\boxed{6}$$

Substitute $\boxed{5}$ into $\boxed{6}$. We get

$$\text{number of eggs per person} = \frac{4r - 32}{4}$$

$$= r - 8$$

Thus, we can make the following chart:

$$\begin{array}{c} \text{number of eggs} \\ \text{each has to} \\ \text{gain or lose} \end{array} = \begin{array}{c} \text{number of eggs} \\ \text{each originally had} \end{array} - \begin{array}{c} \text{number of eggs} \\ \text{each is to have} \end{array}$$

Person	Number of eggs he (she) originally had	Number of eggs each is to have	Number of eggs each has to gain or lose
Tom	$r - 18$	$r - 8$	gain 10
Joe	$r - 10$	$r - 8$	gain 2
Sue	$r - 4$	$r - 8$	lose 4
Robert	r	$r - 8$	lose 8

From the chart above, we see that Tom and Joe together must gain 12 eggs, and Sue and Robert together must lose 12 eggs. Thus, the least number of eggs that must be exchanged in order that everyone has the same number of eggs

$$= 12$$

To answer the question, note that

$$13 > 12$$

(Math Refresher #200 and Logical Reasoning)

26. (D) Choice D is correct.

(Use Strategy C: Try numerics if it appears that it can't be determined.)

Choose numeric values of x.

EXAMPLE 1

$$x = 1$$

The columns then become

Column A	Column B
1	1

and the two quantities are equal.

EXAMPLE 2

$$x = 2$$

The columns then become

Column A	Column B
2	$\dfrac{1}{2}$

and the quantity in Column A is greater.
Thus, a definite comparison cannot be made.

(Math Refresher #431)

27. **(B)** Choice B is correct.

Given: $x + 2y + z = 5y$ ☐1

From the diagram and basic geometry,

$y = z$ ☐2

(Remember vertical angles?)
Substituting ☐2 into ☐1,

$$x + 2z + z = 5z$$
$$\text{or} \quad x = 2z \quad ☐3$$

Using ☐3, the columns become

Column A	Column B
$\frac{3}{2}z$	$2z$

and the answer is clear.

(Math Refresher #503 and #406)

28. **(D)** Choice D is correct.

Since vertical angles are equal, then
$m \angle AOC = m \angle DOB = 108$ ☐1
Thus, from ☐1, we get length of
minor $\overset{\frown}{AC}$ = length of minor $\overset{\frown}{DB}$ ☐2

From geometry we know

length of minor $\overset{\frown}{AC} = \dfrac{108}{360} \times$ circumference of circle

$= \dfrac{108}{360} \times \pi(\text{diameter})$

$= \dfrac{108}{360} \times \pi(20)$

(Use Strategy 19: Factor and reduce.)

length of minor $\overset{\frown}{AC} = \dfrac{\cancel{18} \times 6}{\cancel{18} \times 20} \times \pi(\cancel{20})$

length of minor $\overset{\frown}{AC} = 6\pi$ ☐3

Length $\overset{\frown}{AC}$ + Length $\overset{\frown}{DB}$ can be found using ☐2
and ☐3
Length $\overset{\frown}{AC}$ + Length $\overset{\frown}{DB} = 6\pi + 6\pi$
Length $\overset{\frown}{AC}$ + Length $\overset{\frown}{DB} = 12\pi$

(Math Refresher #503 and #310)

29. **(C)** Choice C is correct.

(Use Strategy 16: The obvious may be tricky!)
From the problem, we see that

$$d = 96,999; \; not \; 97,777$$

Thus, $d - 96,666 = 333$

(Logical Reasoning)

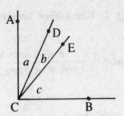

30. **(B)** Choice B is correct.

Label angles as above with a, b, c.

You are given that

$$a + b + c = 90 \quad ☐1$$
$$b + c = 62 \quad ☐2$$
$$a + b = 37 \quad ☐3$$

You want to find $\angle DCE = b$

(Use Strategy 13: Find unknown expressions by adding or subtracting.)

First add ☐2 and ☐3:
We get:

$$a + 2b + c = 62 + 37 = 99 \quad ☐4$$

Now subtract ☐1 from ☐4:

$$\begin{array}{r} a + 2b + c = 99 \\ a + b + c = 90 \\ \hline b \quad\quad = 9 \quad (Answer) \end{array}$$

(Math Refresher #509 and Angle Addition)

31. **(D)** Choice D is correct.

(Use Strategy 17: Use the given information effectively.)

$2 \times 10^{-5} \times 8 \times 10^2 \times 5 \times 10^2$
$= 2 \times 8 \times 5 \times 10^{-5} \times 10^2 \times 10^2$
$= 8 \times 10^0$
$= 8 \times 1$
$= 8$

(Math Refresher #429)

32. **(C)** Choice C is correct.

(Use Strategy 2: Remember how to calculate percent.)

$$\text{Winning percentage} = \frac{\text{\# of games won}}{\text{Total \# of games played}} \times 100$$

For example,

$$\text{Winning \% for pitcher A} = \frac{4}{4+2} \times 100 = \frac{4}{6} \times 100$$

$$= \frac{2 \times 2}{2 \times 3} \times 100$$

$$= \frac{200}{3} = 66\frac{2}{3}\%$$

For each pitcher, we have

Pitcher	Winning Percentage
A	$66\frac{2}{3}\%$
B	60%
C	80%
D	50%
E	75%

Pitcher C has the highest winning percentage.

(Math Refresher #106)

33. **(C)** Choice C is correct.

Method 1: **(Use Strategy 4: Remember classic expressions.)**

$$(a + b)^2 = a^2 + 2ab + b^2 \quad \boxed{1}$$
$$(a - b)^2 = a^2 - 2ab + b^2 \quad \boxed{2}$$

(Use Strategy 11: Use new definitions carefully. These problems are generally easy.)

Using $\boxed{1}$ and $\boxed{2}$, we have

$$a \odot b = (a + b)^2 - (a - b^2)$$
$$= a^2 + 2ab + b^2 - (a^2 - 2ab + b^2)$$
$$= 4ab \quad \boxed{3}$$

When, we use $\boxed{3}$, we get

$$\sqrt{18} \odot \sqrt{2} = 4(\sqrt{18})(\sqrt{2})$$
$$= 4\sqrt{36}$$
$$= 4(6)$$
$$= 24$$

Method 2: $a \odot b = (a + b)^2 - (a - b)^2$

$$\sqrt{18} \odot \sqrt{2}$$
$$= (\sqrt{18} + \sqrt{2})^2 - (\sqrt{18} - \sqrt{2})^2$$
$$= 18 + 2\sqrt{36} + 2 - (18 - 2\sqrt{36} + 2)$$
$$= 18 + 12 + 2 - 18 + 12 - 2$$
$$= 24$$

The calculations in Method 2 are much more complex!

(Math Refresher #409 and #431)

34. **(D)** Choice D is correct.

If you have patience, it is not too hard to list all ordered pairs of integers (x, y) such that
$$x^2 + y^2 < 9$$

(Use Strategy 17: Use the given information effectively.)

Another way to do this problem is to note that $x^2 + y^2 = 9$ is the equation of a circle of radius 3 whose center is at $(0, 0)$.

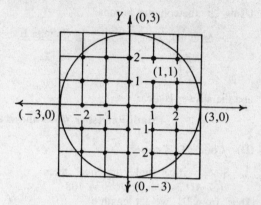

Thus, $x^2 + y^2 < 9$ is the region inside the circle. We want to find the number of ordered pairs of integers (x, y) inside the circle. As we can count from the picture above, there are 25 such ordered pairs.

(Math Refresher #410 and #431)

35. **(C)** Choice C is correct.

(Use Strategy 2: Translate from words to algebra.)

$$\text{Allowance} = \$30$$

$$\text{Amount spent on candy} = \frac{2}{5} \times \$30 = \$12$$

$$\begin{array}{c}\text{Amount left after}\\\text{Johnny bought candy}\end{array} = \$30 - \$12 = \$18$$

$$\text{Amount spent on ice cream} = \frac{5}{6} \times \$18 = \$15$$

$$\begin{array}{c}\text{Amount left after buying}\\\text{candy and ice cream}\end{array} = \$18 - \$15$$
$$= \$3$$

(Math Refresher #200)

ANSWER KEY FOR PRACTICE TEST 3

SECTION 1: VERBAL ABILITY

1 Ⓐ Ⓑ Ⓒ Ⓓ Ⓔ   10 Ⓐ Ⓑ Ⓒ Ⓓ Ⓔ   19 Ⓐ Ⓑ Ⓒ Ⓓ Ⓔ   28 Ⓐ Ⓑ Ⓒ Ⓓ Ⓔ   37 Ⓐ Ⓑ Ⓒ Ⓓ Ⓔ
2 Ⓐ Ⓑ Ⓒ Ⓓ Ⓔ   11 Ⓐ Ⓑ Ⓒ Ⓓ Ⓔ   20 Ⓐ Ⓑ Ⓒ Ⓓ Ⓔ   29 Ⓐ Ⓑ Ⓒ Ⓓ Ⓔ   38 Ⓐ Ⓑ Ⓒ Ⓓ Ⓔ
3 Ⓐ Ⓑ Ⓒ Ⓓ Ⓔ   12 Ⓐ Ⓑ Ⓒ Ⓓ Ⓔ   21 Ⓐ Ⓑ Ⓒ Ⓓ Ⓔ   30 Ⓐ Ⓑ Ⓒ Ⓓ Ⓔ   39 Ⓐ Ⓑ Ⓒ Ⓓ Ⓔ
4 Ⓐ Ⓑ Ⓒ Ⓓ Ⓔ   13 Ⓐ Ⓑ Ⓒ Ⓓ Ⓔ   22 Ⓐ Ⓑ Ⓒ Ⓓ Ⓔ   31 Ⓐ Ⓑ Ⓒ Ⓓ Ⓔ   40 Ⓐ Ⓑ Ⓒ Ⓓ Ⓔ
5 Ⓐ Ⓑ Ⓒ Ⓓ Ⓔ   14 Ⓐ Ⓑ Ⓒ Ⓓ Ⓔ   23 Ⓐ Ⓑ Ⓒ Ⓓ Ⓔ   32 Ⓐ Ⓑ Ⓒ Ⓓ Ⓔ   41 Ⓐ Ⓑ Ⓒ Ⓓ Ⓔ
6 Ⓐ Ⓑ Ⓒ Ⓓ Ⓔ   15 Ⓐ Ⓑ Ⓒ Ⓓ Ⓔ   24 Ⓐ Ⓑ Ⓒ Ⓓ Ⓔ   33 Ⓐ Ⓑ Ⓒ Ⓓ Ⓔ   42 Ⓐ Ⓑ Ⓒ Ⓓ Ⓔ
7 Ⓐ Ⓑ Ⓒ Ⓓ Ⓔ   16 Ⓐ Ⓑ Ⓒ Ⓓ Ⓔ   25 Ⓐ Ⓑ Ⓒ Ⓓ Ⓔ   34 Ⓐ Ⓑ Ⓒ Ⓓ Ⓔ   43 Ⓐ Ⓑ Ⓒ Ⓓ Ⓔ
8 Ⓐ Ⓑ Ⓒ Ⓓ Ⓔ   17 Ⓐ Ⓑ Ⓒ Ⓓ Ⓔ   26 Ⓐ Ⓑ Ⓒ Ⓓ Ⓔ   35 Ⓐ Ⓑ Ⓒ Ⓓ Ⓔ   44 Ⓐ Ⓑ Ⓒ Ⓓ Ⓔ
9 Ⓐ Ⓑ Ⓒ Ⓓ Ⓔ   18 Ⓐ Ⓑ Ⓒ Ⓓ Ⓔ   27 Ⓐ Ⓑ Ⓒ Ⓓ Ⓔ   36 Ⓐ Ⓑ Ⓒ Ⓓ Ⓔ   45 Ⓐ Ⓑ Ⓒ Ⓓ Ⓔ

SECTION 2: MATH ABILITY

1 Ⓐ Ⓑ Ⓒ Ⓓ Ⓔ   6 Ⓐ Ⓑ Ⓒ Ⓓ Ⓔ   11 Ⓐ Ⓑ Ⓒ Ⓓ Ⓔ   16 Ⓐ Ⓑ Ⓒ Ⓓ Ⓔ   21 Ⓐ Ⓑ Ⓒ Ⓓ Ⓔ
2 Ⓐ Ⓑ Ⓒ Ⓓ Ⓔ   7 Ⓐ Ⓑ Ⓒ Ⓓ Ⓔ   12 Ⓐ Ⓑ Ⓒ Ⓓ Ⓔ   17 Ⓐ Ⓑ Ⓒ Ⓓ Ⓔ   22 Ⓐ Ⓑ Ⓒ Ⓓ Ⓔ
3 Ⓐ Ⓑ Ⓒ Ⓓ Ⓔ   8 Ⓐ Ⓑ Ⓒ Ⓓ Ⓔ   13 Ⓐ Ⓑ Ⓒ Ⓓ Ⓔ   18 Ⓐ Ⓑ Ⓒ Ⓓ Ⓔ   23 Ⓐ Ⓑ Ⓒ Ⓓ Ⓔ
4 Ⓐ Ⓑ Ⓒ Ⓓ Ⓔ   9 Ⓐ Ⓑ Ⓒ Ⓓ Ⓔ   14 Ⓐ Ⓑ Ⓒ Ⓓ Ⓔ   19 Ⓐ Ⓑ Ⓒ Ⓓ Ⓔ   24 Ⓐ Ⓑ Ⓒ Ⓓ Ⓔ
5 Ⓐ Ⓑ Ⓒ Ⓓ Ⓔ   10 Ⓐ Ⓑ Ⓒ Ⓓ Ⓔ   15 Ⓐ Ⓑ Ⓒ Ⓓ Ⓔ   20 Ⓐ Ⓑ Ⓒ Ⓓ Ⓔ   25 Ⓐ Ⓑ Ⓒ Ⓓ Ⓔ

SECTION 3: STANDARD WRITTEN ENGLISH

1 Ⓐ Ⓑ Ⓒ Ⓓ Ⓔ   11 Ⓐ Ⓑ Ⓒ Ⓓ Ⓔ   21 Ⓐ Ⓑ Ⓒ Ⓓ Ⓔ   31 Ⓐ Ⓑ Ⓒ Ⓓ Ⓔ   41 Ⓐ Ⓑ Ⓒ Ⓓ Ⓔ
2 Ⓐ Ⓑ Ⓒ Ⓓ Ⓔ   12 Ⓐ Ⓑ Ⓒ Ⓓ Ⓔ   22 Ⓐ Ⓑ Ⓒ Ⓓ Ⓔ   32 Ⓐ Ⓑ Ⓒ Ⓓ Ⓔ   42 Ⓐ Ⓑ Ⓒ Ⓓ Ⓔ
3 Ⓐ Ⓑ Ⓒ Ⓓ Ⓔ   13 Ⓐ Ⓑ Ⓒ Ⓓ Ⓔ   23 Ⓐ Ⓑ Ⓒ Ⓓ Ⓔ   33 Ⓐ Ⓑ Ⓒ Ⓓ Ⓔ   43 Ⓐ Ⓑ Ⓒ Ⓓ Ⓔ
4 Ⓐ Ⓑ Ⓒ Ⓓ Ⓔ   14 Ⓐ Ⓑ Ⓒ Ⓓ Ⓔ   24 Ⓐ Ⓑ Ⓒ Ⓓ Ⓔ   34 Ⓐ Ⓑ Ⓒ Ⓓ Ⓔ   44 Ⓐ Ⓑ Ⓒ Ⓓ Ⓔ
5 Ⓐ Ⓑ Ⓒ Ⓓ Ⓔ   15 Ⓐ Ⓑ Ⓒ Ⓓ Ⓔ   25 Ⓐ Ⓑ Ⓒ Ⓓ Ⓔ   35 Ⓐ Ⓑ Ⓒ Ⓓ Ⓔ   45 Ⓐ Ⓑ Ⓒ Ⓓ Ⓔ
6 Ⓐ Ⓑ Ⓒ Ⓓ Ⓔ   16 Ⓐ Ⓑ Ⓒ Ⓓ Ⓔ   26 Ⓐ Ⓑ Ⓒ Ⓓ Ⓔ   36 Ⓐ Ⓑ Ⓒ Ⓓ Ⓔ   46 Ⓐ Ⓑ Ⓒ Ⓓ Ⓔ
7 Ⓐ Ⓑ Ⓒ Ⓓ Ⓔ   17 Ⓐ Ⓑ Ⓒ Ⓓ Ⓔ   27 Ⓐ Ⓑ Ⓒ Ⓓ Ⓔ   37 Ⓐ Ⓑ Ⓒ Ⓓ Ⓔ   47 Ⓐ Ⓑ Ⓒ Ⓓ Ⓔ
8 Ⓐ Ⓑ Ⓒ Ⓓ Ⓔ   18 Ⓐ Ⓑ Ⓒ Ⓓ Ⓔ   28 Ⓐ Ⓑ Ⓒ Ⓓ Ⓔ   38 Ⓐ Ⓑ Ⓒ Ⓓ Ⓔ   48 Ⓐ Ⓑ Ⓒ Ⓓ Ⓔ
9 Ⓐ Ⓑ Ⓒ Ⓓ Ⓔ   19 Ⓐ Ⓑ Ⓒ Ⓓ Ⓔ   29 Ⓐ Ⓑ Ⓒ Ⓓ Ⓔ   39 Ⓐ Ⓑ Ⓒ Ⓓ Ⓔ   49 Ⓐ Ⓑ Ⓒ Ⓓ Ⓔ
10 Ⓐ Ⓑ Ⓒ Ⓓ Ⓔ   20 Ⓐ Ⓑ Ⓒ Ⓓ Ⓔ   30 Ⓐ Ⓑ Ⓒ Ⓓ Ⓔ   40 Ⓐ Ⓑ Ⓒ Ⓓ Ⓔ   50 Ⓐ Ⓑ Ⓒ Ⓓ Ⓔ

SECTION 4: VERBAL ABILITY

1 Ⓐ Ⓑ Ⓒ Ⓓ Ⓔ   9 Ⓐ Ⓑ Ⓒ Ⓓ Ⓔ   17 Ⓐ Ⓑ Ⓒ Ⓓ Ⓔ   25 Ⓐ Ⓑ Ⓒ Ⓓ Ⓔ   33 Ⓐ Ⓑ Ⓒ Ⓓ Ⓔ
2 Ⓐ Ⓑ Ⓒ Ⓓ Ⓔ   10 Ⓐ Ⓑ Ⓒ Ⓓ Ⓔ   18 Ⓐ Ⓑ Ⓒ Ⓓ Ⓔ   26 Ⓐ Ⓑ Ⓒ Ⓓ Ⓔ   34 Ⓐ Ⓑ Ⓒ Ⓓ Ⓔ
3 Ⓐ Ⓑ Ⓒ Ⓓ Ⓔ   11 Ⓐ Ⓑ Ⓒ Ⓓ Ⓔ   19 Ⓐ Ⓑ Ⓒ Ⓓ Ⓔ   27 Ⓐ Ⓑ Ⓒ Ⓓ Ⓔ   35 Ⓐ Ⓑ Ⓒ Ⓓ Ⓔ
4 Ⓐ Ⓑ Ⓒ Ⓓ Ⓔ   12 Ⓐ Ⓑ Ⓒ Ⓓ Ⓔ   20 Ⓐ Ⓑ Ⓒ Ⓓ Ⓔ   28 Ⓐ Ⓑ Ⓒ Ⓓ Ⓔ   36 Ⓐ Ⓑ Ⓒ Ⓓ Ⓔ
5 Ⓐ Ⓑ Ⓒ Ⓓ Ⓔ   13 Ⓐ Ⓑ Ⓒ Ⓓ Ⓔ   21 Ⓐ Ⓑ Ⓒ Ⓓ Ⓔ   29 Ⓐ Ⓑ Ⓒ Ⓓ Ⓔ   37 Ⓐ Ⓑ Ⓒ Ⓓ Ⓔ
6 Ⓐ Ⓑ Ⓒ Ⓓ Ⓔ   14 Ⓐ Ⓑ Ⓒ Ⓓ Ⓔ   22 Ⓐ Ⓑ Ⓒ Ⓓ Ⓔ   30 Ⓐ Ⓑ Ⓒ Ⓓ Ⓔ   38 Ⓐ Ⓑ Ⓒ Ⓓ Ⓔ
7 Ⓐ Ⓑ Ⓒ Ⓓ Ⓔ   15 Ⓐ Ⓑ Ⓒ Ⓓ Ⓔ   23 Ⓐ Ⓑ Ⓒ Ⓓ Ⓔ   31 Ⓐ Ⓑ Ⓒ Ⓓ Ⓔ   39 Ⓐ Ⓑ Ⓒ Ⓓ Ⓔ
8 Ⓐ Ⓑ Ⓒ Ⓓ Ⓔ   16 Ⓐ Ⓑ Ⓒ Ⓓ Ⓔ   24 Ⓐ Ⓑ Ⓒ Ⓓ Ⓔ   32 Ⓐ Ⓑ Ⓒ Ⓓ Ⓔ   40 Ⓐ Ⓑ Ⓒ Ⓓ Ⓔ

SECTION 5: MATH ABILITY

1 Ⓐ Ⓑ Ⓒ Ⓓ Ⓔ   8 Ⓐ Ⓑ Ⓒ Ⓓ Ⓔ   15 Ⓐ Ⓑ Ⓒ Ⓓ Ⓔ   22 Ⓐ Ⓑ Ⓒ Ⓓ Ⓔ   29 Ⓐ Ⓑ Ⓒ Ⓓ Ⓔ
2 Ⓐ Ⓑ Ⓒ Ⓓ Ⓔ   9 Ⓐ Ⓑ Ⓒ Ⓓ Ⓔ   16 Ⓐ Ⓑ Ⓒ Ⓓ Ⓔ   23 Ⓐ Ⓑ Ⓒ Ⓓ Ⓔ   30 Ⓐ Ⓑ Ⓒ Ⓓ Ⓔ
3 Ⓐ Ⓑ Ⓒ Ⓓ Ⓔ   10 Ⓐ Ⓑ Ⓒ Ⓓ Ⓔ   17 Ⓐ Ⓑ Ⓒ Ⓓ Ⓔ   24 Ⓐ Ⓑ Ⓒ Ⓓ Ⓔ   31 Ⓐ Ⓑ Ⓒ Ⓓ Ⓔ
4 Ⓐ Ⓑ Ⓒ Ⓓ Ⓔ   11 Ⓐ Ⓑ Ⓒ Ⓓ Ⓔ   18 Ⓐ Ⓑ Ⓒ Ⓓ Ⓔ   25 Ⓐ Ⓑ Ⓒ Ⓓ Ⓔ   32 Ⓐ Ⓑ Ⓒ Ⓓ Ⓔ
5 Ⓐ Ⓑ Ⓒ Ⓓ Ⓔ   12 Ⓐ Ⓑ Ⓒ Ⓓ Ⓔ   19 Ⓐ Ⓑ Ⓒ Ⓓ Ⓔ   26 Ⓐ Ⓑ Ⓒ Ⓓ Ⓔ   33 Ⓐ Ⓑ Ⓒ Ⓓ Ⓔ
6 Ⓐ Ⓑ Ⓒ Ⓓ Ⓔ   13 Ⓐ Ⓑ Ⓒ Ⓓ Ⓔ   20 Ⓐ Ⓑ Ⓒ Ⓓ Ⓔ   27 Ⓐ Ⓑ Ⓒ Ⓓ Ⓔ   34 Ⓐ Ⓑ Ⓒ Ⓓ Ⓔ
7 Ⓐ Ⓑ Ⓒ Ⓓ Ⓔ   14 Ⓐ Ⓑ Ⓒ Ⓓ Ⓔ   21 Ⓐ Ⓑ Ⓒ Ⓓ Ⓔ   28 Ⓐ Ⓑ Ⓒ Ⓓ Ⓔ   35 Ⓐ Ⓑ Ⓒ Ⓓ Ⓔ

SECTION 6: MATH ABILITY

1 Ⓐ Ⓑ Ⓒ Ⓓ Ⓔ   6 Ⓐ Ⓑ Ⓒ Ⓓ Ⓔ   11 Ⓐ Ⓑ Ⓒ Ⓓ Ⓔ   16 Ⓐ Ⓑ Ⓒ Ⓓ Ⓔ   21 Ⓐ Ⓑ Ⓒ Ⓓ Ⓔ
2 Ⓐ Ⓑ Ⓒ Ⓓ Ⓔ   7 Ⓐ Ⓑ Ⓒ Ⓓ Ⓔ   12 Ⓐ Ⓑ Ⓒ Ⓓ Ⓔ   17 Ⓐ Ⓑ Ⓒ Ⓓ Ⓔ   22 Ⓐ Ⓑ Ⓒ Ⓓ Ⓔ
3 Ⓐ Ⓑ Ⓒ Ⓓ Ⓔ   8 Ⓐ Ⓑ Ⓒ Ⓓ Ⓔ   13 Ⓐ Ⓑ Ⓒ Ⓓ Ⓔ   18 Ⓐ Ⓑ Ⓒ Ⓓ Ⓔ   23 Ⓐ Ⓑ Ⓒ Ⓓ Ⓔ
4 Ⓐ Ⓑ Ⓒ Ⓓ Ⓔ   9 Ⓐ Ⓑ Ⓒ Ⓓ Ⓔ   14 Ⓐ Ⓑ Ⓒ Ⓓ Ⓔ   19 Ⓐ Ⓑ Ⓒ Ⓓ Ⓔ   24 Ⓐ Ⓑ Ⓒ Ⓓ Ⓔ
5 Ⓐ Ⓑ Ⓒ Ⓓ Ⓔ   10 Ⓐ Ⓑ Ⓒ Ⓓ Ⓔ   15 Ⓐ Ⓑ Ⓒ Ⓓ Ⓔ   20 Ⓐ Ⓑ Ⓒ Ⓓ Ⓔ   25 Ⓐ Ⓑ Ⓒ Ⓓ Ⓔ

SAT Practice Test 3

SECTION 1 VERBAL ABILITY
30 MINUTES 45 QUESTIONS

For each question in this section, choose the best answer and blacken the corresponding space on the answer sheet.

Each question below consists of a word in capital letters, followed by five lettered words or phrases. Choose the word or phrase that is most nearly *opposite* in meaning to the word in capital letters. Since some of the questions require you to distinguish fine shades of meaning, consider all the choices before deciding which is best.

Example:

> GOOD: (A) sour (B) bad (C) red
> (D) hot (E) ugly
>
> Ⓐ ● Ⓒ Ⓓ Ⓔ

1. JOCOSE: (A) cautious (B) realistic
   (C) provident (D) serious (E) dramatic

2. RAVAGE: (A) build (B) escape (C) purify
   (D) disregard (E) move slowly

3. ABORTIVE: (A) deteriorated (B) passive
   (C) supportive (D) wide-awake (E) successful

4. SAGACITY: (A) wildness (B) foolishness
   (C) innocence (D) hopelessness (E) poverty

5. ABSTRUSE: (A) adjacent (B) vague
   (C) understandable (D) colorful (E) reducible

6. INDIGENT: (A) lighthearted (B) liberating
   (C) provident (D) inflated (E) prosperous

7. NOXIOUS: (A) curative (B) spirited
   (C) feeble (D) illuminated (E) advantageous

8. CASTIGATE: (A) cleanse (B) relieve
   (C) reward (D) unravel (E) liberate

9. ACUMEN: (A) reimbursement (B) revenge
   (C) placidity (D) dullness (E) laziness

10. ODIOUS: (A) ardent (B) pertinent
    (C) possible (D) biting (E) agreeable

11. DIVERGENT: (A) similar (B) benign
    (C) limitless (D) attached (E) plentiful

12. ELICIT: (A) endorse (B) excite
    (C) hold back (D) refine (E) list

13. SATURNINE: (A) heavenly (B) hopeful
    (C) rabid (D) eloquent (E) timid

14. PHLEGMATIC: (A) creative (B) active
    (C) secretive (D) fairy-like (E) automatic

15. OBSEQUIOUS: (A) optimistic (B) searching
    (C) inconclusive (D) uncooperative (E) sectional

Each sentence below has one or two blanks, each blank indicating that something has been omitted. Beneath the sentence are five lettered words or sets of words. Choose the word or set of words that *best* fits the meaning of the sentence as a whole.

Example:

> Although its publicity has been ____, the film itself is intelligent, well-acted, handsomely produced, and altogether ____.
>
> (A) tasteless . . . respectable
> (B) extensive . . . moderate
> (C) sophisticated . . . amateur
> (D) risqué . . . crude
> (E) perfect . . . spectacular
>
> ● Ⓑ Ⓒ Ⓓ Ⓔ

16. Although the physical setup of the high school's lunchroom seems rundown in many respects, it was enlarged and _____ quite recently.

    (A) visited (B) examined (C) occupied
    (D) renovated (E) criticized

17. The activities that interested Jack were those that provided him with _____ pleasure, like dancing, feasting, and partying.

    (A) questionable (B) distant (C) immediate
    (D) limited (E) delayed

18. His current inability to complete his assignments in a timely and efficient manner has resulted in a feeling of _____ even in his most _____ backers.

    (A) urgency . . . lackadaisical
    (B) flexibility . . . hostile
    (C) expectancy . . . cautious
    (D) dizziness . . . visible
    (E) disappointment . . . fervent

19. The two performers taking the parts of shy, romantic teenagers were quite _____ in their roles even though they were actually man and wife.

    (A) convincing (B) flippant (C) amateurish
    (D) comfortable (E) boring

20. He was _____ about a rise in the value of the stocks he had recently purchased, and was eager to make a change in his investment portfolio.

    (A) fearful (B) unconcerned (C) hesitant
    (D) amused (E) dubious

Each passage below is followed by questions based on its content. Answer all questions following a passage on the basis of what is *stated* or *implied* in that passage.

The special quality which makes an artist of any worth might be defined, indeed, as an extraordinary capacity for irritation, a pathological sensitiveness to environmental pricks and stings. He differs from the rest of us mainly
5 because he reacts sharply and in an uncommon manner to phenomena which leave the rest of us unmoved, or, at most, merely annoy us vaguely. He is, in brief, a more delicate fellow than we are, and hence less fitted to prosper and enjoy himself under the conditions of life which he
10 and we must face alike. Therefore, he takes to artistic endeavor, which is at once a criticism of life and an attempt to escape from life.

So much for the theory of it. The more the facts are studied, the more they bear it out. In those fields of art,
15 at all events, which concern themselves with ideas as well as with sensations it is almost impossible to find any trace of an artist who was not actively hostile to his environment, and thus an indifferent patriot. From Dante to Tolstoy and from Shakespeare to Mark Twain the story is ever the
20 same. Names suggest themselves instantly: Goethe, Heine, Shelley, Byron, Thackeray, Balzac, Rabelais, Cervantes, Swift, Dostoevsky, Carlyle, Molière, Pope—all bitter critics of their time and nation, most of them piously hated by the contemporary 100 percenters, some of them actually
25 fugitives from rage and reprisal.

Dante put all of the patriotic Italians of his day into Hell, and showed them boiling, roasting and writhing on hooks. Cervantes drew such a devastating picture of the Spain that he lived in that it ruined the Spaniards. Shake-
30 speare made his heroes foreigners and his clowns Englishmen. Goethe was in favor of Napoleon. Rabelais, a citizen of Christendom rather than of France, raised a cackle against it that Christendom is still trying in vain to suppress. Swift, having finished the Irish and then the English, proceeded
35 to finish the whole human race. The exceptions are few and far between, and not many of them will bear examination. So far as I know, the only eminent writer in English history who was also a 100% Englishman, absolutely beyond suspicion, was Samuel Johnson. But was Johnson
40 actually an artist? If he was, then a kazoo-player is a musician. He employed the materials of one of the arts, to wit, words, but his use of them was mechanical, not artistic. If Johnson were alive today, he would be a United States Senator, or a university president. He left such wounds
45 upon English prose that it was a century recovering from them.

21. Which of the following quotations is related most closely to the principal idea of the passage?

(A) "All nature is but art unknown to thee,
    All chance, direction which thou canst not see."
(B) "When to her share some human errors fall,
    Look on her face and you'll forget them all."
(C) "All human things are subject to decay,
    "And, when fate summons, monarchs must
    obey."
(D) "A little learning is a dangerous thing;
    "Drink deep or taste not the Pierian spring."
(E) "Great wits are sure to madness near allied,
    And thin partitions do their bounds divide."

22. The author seems to regard the artist as

(A) the best representative of his time
(B) an unnecessary threat to the social order
(C) one who creates out of discontent
(D) one who truly knows how to enjoy life
(E) one who is touched with genius

23. It can be inferred that the author believes that United States Senators and university presidents

(A) must be treated with respect because of their position
(B) are to be held in low esteem
(C) are generally appreciative of the great literary classics
(D) have native writing ability
(E) have the qualities of the artist

24. All of the following ideas about artists are mentioned in the passage *except* that

(A) they are irritated by their surroundings
(B) they are escapists from reality
(C) they are lovers of beauty
(D) they are hated by their contemporaries
(E) they are critical of their times

25. Which of the following best describes the author's attitude toward artists?

(A) Sharply critical
(B) Sincerely sympathetic
(C) Deeply resentful
(D) Mildly annoyed
(E) Completely delighted

Neoplasia, or the development of tumors, is the abnormal biological process in which some intrinsic cellular change within a group of normal cells produces a group of cells which no longer respond to the mechanisms which
5 regulate normal cells. As a result, this group of cells increases in number but fails to achieve the specialized characteristics associated with normal cells. The degree to which neoplastic cells resemble their normal counterpart cells, both in appearance and behavior, allows us to classify
10 tumors as either benign or malignant. Benign tumors look and behave like their normal tissue of origin, are usually slow-growing, are rarely fatal and remain localized. Malignant tumors, on the other hand, look very little like their tissue of origin and behave in such a manner that the animal
15 which bears the tumor frequently succumbs.

The characteristic which most strikingly separates malignant tumors from benign tumors is the ability of malignant cells to become widely disseminated and to establish secondary sites of tumor far distant from the original tu-
20 mor. This process of widespread dissemination, which is called metastasis, is not well understood; however, some of the features of the process have been ascertained. Before metastasis can occur, the malignant cells must invade the surrounding normal tissue. Initial attempts to invade are
25 inhibited by the normal tissue. With time, the neoplastic cells undergo changes which allow them to overcome this inhibition, and tumor cells leave the primary mass of tumor. The entire process of inhibition by normal tissue and the eventual breakdown of inhibition is undoubtedly com-
30 plex.

Malignant cells are characteristically less adhesive, one to another, than are normal cells. The outer membrane of the malignant cells contains less calcium than the membrane of normal cells. The malignant cell also acquires a
35 greater negative electrical charge. After malignant cells have invaded the surrounding normal tissue, they ultimately enter the bloodstream where most of the cells die. Those cells which survive will form a metastasis at a distant site only if they can adhere to the wall of a small
40 blood vessel. The factors which govern this adherence include the size of the malignant cell or a clump of these cells, the diameter of the blood vessel and the stickiness of the blood vessel wall. Stickiness of the blood vessel wall is at least partially due to the status of bloodclotting
45 components in the blood. In addition to these mechanical considerations, some patterns of metastasis are explicable only on the basis of a receptive chemical environment or "soil" in which the malignant cell can grow. Finally, although a number of the characteristics of malignant neo-
50 plastic cells have been elucidated as described above, it still must be stated that many aspects of their behavior remain a mystery.

26. The main topic of this passage is

(A) the meaning of neoplasia
(B) the inhibition of tumor metastasis by normal tissue
(C) the transformation of benign tumors into malignant tumors
(D) the manner in which malignant tumors behave in the body
(E) the fate of malignant cells after they enter the bloodstream

27. Before malignant cells can be disseminated to widespread parts of the body, they must first

(A) acquire new outer membrane characteristics
(B) inhibit the lethal effects of components of the blood
(C) penetrate the surrounding normal tissue
(D) locate the proper chemical environment in which to grow
(E) achieve sufficient size to become lodged in a blood vessel

28. According to the passage, the property of a malignant cell which most greatly enhances its metastatic potential is

(A) its ability to choose the proper "soil"
(B) its ability to invade the surrounding tissue
(C) the amount of calcium in the outer membrane of the cell
(D) the extent of deviation from the appearance of a normal cell
(E) its ability to attach itself to the wall of a small blood vessel

29. It can be concluded from the passage that

(A) benign tumors usually progress to malignant tumors
(B) malignant cells reach distant tissues by routes yet to be ascertained
(C) if the wall of a blood vessel is "sticky," a tumor metastasis has a better chance to develop
(D) the outer membrane of malignant cells is the same as that of normal cells
(E) the pattern of metastasis of a particular tumor is predictable with considerable accuracy

30. According to this passage, characteristics which distinguish malignant neoplastic cells from normal cells include all of the following *except*

(A) their growth rate
(B) their physical appearance
(C) their outer membrane characteristics
(D) their normal tissue of origin
(E) their ability to invade surrounding tissue and metastasize

Select the word or set of words that *best* completes each of the following sentences.

31. Nature's brute strength is never more _____ than during a major earthquake when the earth shifts with a sickening sway.

    (A) frightening   (B) effective   (C) replaceable
    (D) placating   (E) complete

32. Instead of providing available funds to education and thus _____ the incidence of crime, the Mayor is _____ the funds to the building of more prisons.

    (A) disdain . . . denying
    (B) revoke . . . assigning
    (C) abolish . . . confining
    (D) reduce . . . diverting
    (E) nourish . . . planning

33. The dancer excelled neither in grace nor technique but the _____ musical accompaniment gives the performance a(n) _____ of excellence.

    (A) gradual . . . sensation
    (B) soothing . . . mandate
    (C) well-rehearsed . . . diction
    (D) superb . . . aura
    (E) chronic . . . effervescence

34. Her fine reputation as a celebrated actress was _____ by her appearance in a TV soap opera.

    (A) enhanced   (B) blemished   (C) appreciated
    (D) concluded   (E) intensified

35. The dictator's slow, easy manner and his air of gentility _____ his firm intention to insure no opposition to his planned _____ policies.

    (A) revealed . . . eager
    (B) accepted . . . professional
    (C) belied . . . drastic
    (D) disregarded . . . inane
    (E) animated . . . crude

Each question below consists of a related pair of words or phrases, followed by five lettered pairs of words or phrases. Select the lettered pair that *best* expresses a relationship similar to that expressed in the original pair.

Example:

YAWN : BOREDOM : :   (A) dream : sleep
(B) anger : madness   (C) smile : amusement
(D) face : expression   (E) impatience : rebellion
                    Ⓐ Ⓑ ● Ⓓ Ⓔ

36. PEEL : ORANGE : :

    (A) fur : coat   (B) cover : page
    (C) petal : stem   (D) rind : melon   (E) crest : wave

37. TERMITE : WOOD : :

    (A) mold : bread   (B) pearl : oyster
    (C) weevil : cotton   (D) wasp : nest
    (E) barnacle : ship

38. TEST : KEY : :

    (A) weight : scale   (B) puzzle : solution
    (C) anagram : word   (D) guide : tour
    (E) lock : door

39. GORGE : NIBBLE : :

    (A) laugh : guffaw   (B) quaff : sip
    (C) hurry : amble   (D) scrutinize : examine
    (E) spend : counterfeit

40. TIDAL WAVE : FLOOD : :

    (A) earthquake : tremors   (B) avalanche : snow
    (C) gale : wind   (D) sunspot : activity
    (E) lava : eruption

41. BLEAT : SHEEP : :

    (A) shear : lamb   (B) flight : plane
    (C) honk : goose   (D) laughter : comedy
    (E) sting : bee

42. LOBSTER : SHELL : :

    (A) cattle : herb   (B) kangaroo : pouch
    (C) mammal : whale   (D) insect : wing
    (E) wool : sheep

43. CANDID : FURTIVE : :

    (A) miserly : scanty   (B) transparent : opaque
    (C) romantic : idealistic   (D) amicable : unfriendly
    (E) closed : ajar

44. RUN : STOCKING : :

(A) pattern : flaw   (B) painting : image
(C) blemish : skin   (D) thread : fabric
(E) race : finish

45. SPEAKER : DAIS : :

(A) policeman : car   (B) actor : stage
(C) physician : medicine   (D) owner : property
(E) salesman : briefcase

SECTION 2   MATH ABILITY
30 MINUTES   25 QUESTIONS

In this section solve each problem, using any available space on the page for scratchwork. Then decide which is the best of the choices given and blacken the corresponding space on the answer sheet.

The following information is for your reference in solving some of the problems.

Circle of radius r: Area $= \pi r^2$; Circumference $= 2\pi r$
   The number of degrees of arc in a circle is 360.
The measure in degrees of a straight angle is 180.

Definitions of symbols:
   $=$ is equal to $\leqq$ is less than or equal to
   $\neq$ is unequal to $\geqq$ is greater than or equal to
   $<$ is less than $\parallel$ is parallel to
   $>$ is greater than $\perp$ is perpendicular to

Triangle: The sum of the measure in degrees of the angles of a triangle is 180.
   If $\angle CDA$ is a right angle, then

(1)   area of $\triangle ABC = \dfrac{AB \times CD}{2}$

(2) $AC^2 = AD^2 + DC^2$

Note: Figures which accompany problems in this test are intended to provide information useful in solving the problems. They are drawn as accurately as possible EXCEPT when it is stated in a specific problem that its figure is not drawn to scale. All figures lie in a plane unless otherwise indicated. All numbers used are real numbers.

1. Mr. Howard spent $40 for a new jacket. The amount of money he has left is equal to three times the $40 jacket price. What amount of money did he have just prior to buying the jacket?

(A) $40   (B) $80   (C) $140   (D) $160   (E) $200

$$\begin{array}{r} N\ 5 \\ \underline{L\ M} \\ 3\ 8\ 5 \\ \underline{3\ 8\ 5} \\ 4{,}2\ 3\ 5 \end{array}$$

2. In the multiplication problem above, L, M, and N each represent one of the digits 0 through 9. If the problem is computed correctly, find N.

(A) 8   (B) 7   (C) 5   (D) 3   (E) 2

3. Find 3×3^b, if $9^b = 81$

(A) 3   (B) 9   (C) 27   (D) 36   (E) 81

4. If 54 students out of a class of 60 students passed all their exams, then what percent passed all their exams?

(A) 94%   (B) 90%   (C) 84%   (D) 10%   (E) 6%

5. If $2y + 4y + 6y = 2 + 4 + 6$, then $y =$

(A) -2 (B) 0   (C) $\dfrac{1}{12}$ (D) 1   (E) 12

6. Three times the sum of 50 and a certain number is equal to the product of 4, 5 and 9. Find the number.

(A) 4   (B) 10   (C) 20   (D) 50   (E) 110

Dial Y   Dial Z

7. In the figure above, the hand of dial Z moves in a clockwise direction. When its hand makes one complete revolution, it causes the hand of dial Y to move 1 number in the counterclockwise direction. How many complete revolutions of the hand of dial Z are needed to move the hand of dial Y 3 complete revolutions?

(A) 2   (B) 7   (C) 8   (D) 21   (E) 24

8. If $\dfrac{5r}{w} = \dfrac{15s}{x}$, $r = s \neq 0$, $w \neq 0$, $x \neq 0$, then find an expression for x in terms of w.

(A) $\dfrac{w}{3}$ (B) w (C) $3w$ (D) $5w$ (E) $15w$

9. The allowable weight of an elevator plus passengers is 2300 pounds. The empty weight of the elevator is 1340 pounds. How many additional pounds would be allowed, if the average weight of its six passengers is 140 pounds?

(A) 120   (B) 160   (C) 1200   (D) 1480   (E) 2160

10. If *r* and *s* are negative numbers, then all of the following must be positive *except*

(A) $\frac{r}{s}$ (B) rs (C) $(rs)^2$ (D) $r + s$

(E) $-r - s$

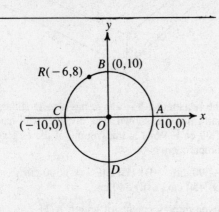

11. In the figure above, *S* is a point (not shown) such that segment *RS* divides the area of circle *O* into two equal parts. What are the coordinates of *S*?

(A) $(6, -8)$ (B) $(6, 8)$ (C) $(8, -6)$
(D) $(-6, -8)$ (E) $(8, 6)$

12. To make enough paste to hang 6 rolls of wallpaper, a $\frac{1}{4}$-pound package of powder is mixed with $2\frac{1}{2}$ quarts of water. How many pounds of powder are needed to make enough of the same mixture of paste to hang 21 rolls of paper?

(A) $\frac{3}{4}$ (B) $\frac{7}{8}$ (C) 1   (D) $2\frac{1}{2}$ (E) $8\frac{3}{4}$

	First Place (6 points)	Second place (4 points)	Third Place (2 points)
Game 1			
Game 2		Bob	
Game 3			Bob

13. The figure above is a partially filled in score card for a video game contest. Alan, Bob, and Carl each played in all of the three games. There were no ties. What is the *minimum* possible score for Carl in this tournament?

(A) 2   (B) 6   (C) 8   (D) 12   (E) It cannot be determined from the information given.

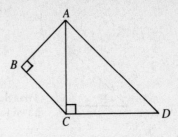

14. In the figure above, $AB = BC$ and $AC = CD$. How many of the angles have a measure of 45 degrees?

(A) None   (B) Two   (C) Three   (D) Four
(E) Five

15. Which of the rectangles below has a length of $\frac{4}{3}$, if each has an area of 4? (Rectangles not drawn to scale.)

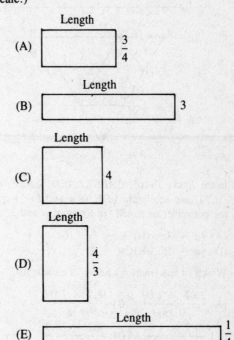

Note: Figures are not drawn to scale.

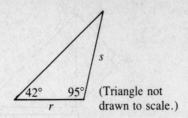

(Triangle not drawn to scale.)

16. In the triangle above, which of the following is *always* true?

(A) *r* is less than *s*
(B) *r* is greater than *s*
(C) *r* is equal to *s*
(D) *r* = 43
(E) It cannot be determined from the information given.

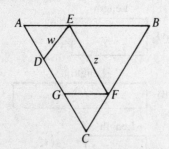

17. In the figure above, △*ABC*, △*AED*, △*BEF*, and △*CFG* are equilateral. *DE* = *w* and *EF* = *z*. Find the perimeter of △*ABC* in terms of *w* and *z*.

(A) 3*w* + 3*z*   (B) 3*z* − 3*w*   (C) 4*w* + 2*z*
(D) 4*w* − 2*z*   (E) 2*w* + 2*z*

18. Which of the fractions below is closest to 7?

(A) $\dfrac{3.82 \times 7.09}{0.38}$ (B) $\dfrac{38.2 \times 7.09}{0.38}$

(C) $\dfrac{38.2 \times 7.09}{3.8}$ (D) $\dfrac{.382 \times 70.9}{3.8}$

(E) $\dfrac{38.2 \times 70.9}{38}$

19. If $\dfrac{a}{3} = b$ and $3b + b = 0$, find the value of *a*.

(A) 0   (B) 1   (C) 2   (D) 4   (E) It cannot be determined from the information given.

20. In the country of Gorx, the Pink Tree Festival is always celebrated on the third Friday in April. The earliest day in April that the festival could occur is

(A) April 14   (B) April 15   (C) April 16
(D) April 21   (E) April 22

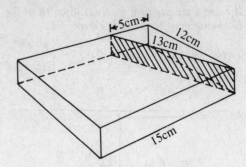

21. The rectangular box above has a rectangular dividing wall inside, as shown. The dividing wall has an area of 39 cm². What is the volume of the larger compartment?

(A) 90 cm³   (B) 180 cm³   (C) 360 cm³
(D) 450 cm³   (E) 540 cm³

22. Given three segments of length *x*, 11 − *x*, and *x* − 4, respectively. Which of the following indicates the set of all numbers *x* such that the 3 segments could be the lengths of the sides of a triangle?

(A) *x* > 4   (B) *x* < 11   (C) 0 < *x* < 7
(D) 5 < *x* < 15   (E) 5 < *x* < 7

23. A unicycle has one wheel of radius .3 of a yard. If it is pedaled 2000 yards in one hour, then how many revolutions per *minute* does the wheel make?

(A) $\dfrac{500\pi}{9}$ (B) $\dfrac{500}{9\pi}$

(C) $\dfrac{50}{9\pi}$ (D) $\dfrac{5\pi}{9}$ (E) $\dfrac{10}{\pi}$

24. For all integers *r* and *s*, let *r* ◊ *s* = 4*r* − 3*s*. Which of the following must be true?

 I. 4 ◊ 3 = 7
 II. (1 ◊ 0) ◊ 2 = 1 ◊ (0 ◊ 2)
 III. *r* ◊ *s* = *s* ◊ *r*

(A) I only
(B) II only
(C) III only
(D) II and III only
(E) I, II and III

25. Points A, B, and C lie on a straight line. B is 5 miles from C. B is 2 miles from A. What is the distance, in miles, between A and C?

(A) 3   (B) 5   (C) 7   (D) $\sqrt{29}$
(E) It cannot be determined from the information given.

S T O P

IF YOU FINISH BEFORE TIME IS CALLED, YOU MAY CHECK YOUR WORK ON THIS SECTION ONLY.
DO NOT WORK ON ANY OTHER SECTION IN THE TEST.

SECTION 3   STANDARD WRITTEN ENGLISH TEST

30 MINUTES   50 QUESTIONS

The questions in this section measure skills that are important to writing well. In particular, they test your ability to recognize and use language that is clear, effective, and correct according to the requirements of standard written English, the kind of English found in most college textbooks.

Directions: The following contain problems in grammar, usage, diction (choice of words), and idiom.

Some sentences are correct.
No sentence contains more than one error.

You will find that the error, if there is one, is underlined and lettered. Assume that elements of the sentence that are not underlined are correct and cannot be changed. In choosing answers, follow the requirements of standard written English.

If there is an error, select the *one underlined part* that must be changed to make the sentence correct and blacken the corresponding space on your answer sheet.

If there is no error, blacken answer space Ⓔ .

EXAMPLE: SAMPLE ANSWER

Ⓐ Ⓑ ● Ⓓ Ⓔ

The region has a climate so severe that plants
                           A

growing there rarely had been more than twelve
      B   C

inches high. No error
      D   E

---

1. Besides my job as a legal secretary I also have a job
   A

   as a condominium manager which requires me to
   B   C

   solve a large amount of problems. No error
                D   E

2. Who's to decide that certain terminally-ill patients
   A   B

   should be taken off life-support systems while others
                    C   D

   should remain dependent upon machines? No error
                                            E

3. When the results of the polls were published in the
                                A

   paper, my brother, who was a candidate for mayor,
                               B

   was not discouraged any because he was among the
                     C   D

   top four candidates. No error
                        E

4. Being that a senator was aboard the shuttle *Discovery*
   A   B

   on its most recent flight, many private citizens now
            C

   hope that in the near future they will have a chance
                                   D

   to join the astronauts. No error
                           E

5. A mother <u>along with</u> her five children <u>were rescued</u>
   <u> A </u> <u> B </u>

   from the burning apartment building by a postal

   worker <u>who</u> was making his daily deliveries earlier
   <u>C</u>

   than usual. <u>No error.</u>
   <u>D</u> <u>E</u>

6. <u>At</u> the age of 44, Pete Rose, <u>player-manager</u> of the
   <u>A</u> <u>B</u>

   Cincinnati Reds, <u>passed</u> Ty <u>Cobb's</u> career hit total of
   <u>C</u> <u>D</u>

   4,191. <u>No error.</u>
   <u>E</u>

7. My partner in the computer class <u>worked on the</u>
   <u>A</u>

   same programs as <u>I</u>, but his method of solving the
   <u>B</u>

   problems was <u>quite</u> <u>different than</u> mine. <u>No error.</u>
   <u>C</u> <u>D</u> <u>E</u>

8. The school board members did <u>like</u> <u>they</u>
   <u>A</u> <u>B</u>

   were expected to do when they decided to increase
   <u>C</u>

   the length of the school day <u>rather than</u> the length of
   <u>D</u>

   the school year. <u>No error.</u>
   <u>E</u>

9. <u>Because of</u> the bomb threat everyone <u>was asked to</u>
   <u>A</u> <u>B</u>

   evacuate the bank <u>but</u> a security guard, a fireman,
   <u>C</u>

   and <u>I</u>. <u>No error.</u>
   <u>D</u> <u>E</u>

10. <u>Having drank</u> almost all the lemonade <u>which</u> his wife
    <u>A</u> <u>B</u>

    <u>had made</u> for the picnic, Dick <u>could</u> not face her.
    <u>C</u> <u>D</u>

    <u>No error.</u>
    <u>E</u>

11. The wealthy socialite decided that her fortune

    <u>would be left</u> to <u>whomever</u> of her relatives
    <u>A</u> <u>B</u>

    <u>could present</u> her with the best plan for dispensing
    <u>C</u>

    part of the money to <u>deserving</u> charities. <u>No error.</u>
    <u>D</u> <u>E</u>

12. Shortly after <u>arriving</u> at the amusement park with the
    <u>A</u>

    eager third-graders, the parents <u>realized</u> that they had
    <u>B</u>

    brought <u>nowhere near</u> the <u>number</u> of chaperones
    <u>C</u> <u>D</u>

    required to control the children. <u>No error.</u>
    <u>E</u>

13. The board members <u>along with</u> the chairman
    <u>A</u>

    <u>were planning</u> a <u>series</u> of speakers to lecture on
    <u>B</u> <u>C</u>

    different dividend plans for <u>their</u> employees.
    <u>D</u>

    <u>No error.</u>
    <u>E</u>

14. <u>Due to</u> <u>his</u> not studying and not attending review
    <u>A</u> <u>B</u>

    sessions, Paul <u>got</u> a failing mark in his bar exam,
    <u>C</u>

    <u>resulting in</u> a retraction of the job offer from the law
    <u>D</u>

    firm. <u>No error.</u>
    <u>E</u>

15. When I <u>was</u> in high school, I worked <u>hard</u> to buy the
    <u>A</u> <u>B</u>

    kind <u>of a car</u> that <u>most of</u> my friends were also
    <u>C</u> <u>D</u>

    driving. <u>No error.</u>
    <u>E</u>

16. The literature professor <u>has complained</u> that many
    <u>A</u>

    student poets are <u>so conceited</u> that they compare <u>their</u>
    <u>B</u> <u>C</u>

    poems <u>with</u> Robert Frost. <u>No error.</u>
    <u>D</u> <u>E</u>

17. I appreciate <u>you</u> offering <u>to help</u> me with my
           A   B

    research project, but the honor system <u>prevents</u>
                                           C

    students from giving and receiving <u>assistance</u>.
                                              D

    <u>No error.</u>
     E

18. In the final heat of the mile race, <u>only two runners</u>
                                          A

    finished the race, but even the <u>slowest of the two</u>
                                       B

    <u>was able</u> to break the school record that <u>had been set</u>
      C   D

    a decade earlier. <u>No error.</u>
                 E

19. <u>Since</u> we first started high school, <u>there has been</u>
     A   B

    great competition for grades <u>between</u> him and <u>I</u>.
                          C   D

    <u>No error.</u>
     E

20. Many people in the suburbs <u>scarcely</u> know <u>about</u> the
                              A   B

    transportation problems <u>that</u> city dwellers experience
                           C

    every day. <u>No error.</u>
      D   E

21. The subject of the evening editorial was <u>us</u>
                                         A

    instructors <u>who</u> <u>have</u> refused to cross the picket lines
              B   C

    of the <u>striking</u> food service workers. <u>No error.</u>
          D   E

22. After the contestants <u>had completed</u> their speeches, I
                          A

    knew that the prize would go to <u>he</u> <u>whom</u> the
                               B   C

    audience had given a <u>standing</u> ovation. <u>No error.</u>
                       D   E

23. Falsely accused of a <u>triple-murder</u> and <u>imprisoned</u> for
                        A   B

    19 years, Ruben (Hurricane) Carter, a former boxer,

    was <u>freed</u> when a Federal judge declared <u>him</u>
        C   D

    guiltless. <u>No error.</u>
            E

24. Your math instructor would have been <u>happy</u> to give
                                   A

    you a makeup examination if you <u>would have gone</u>
                                   B

    to him and <u>explained</u> that your parents were
                   C

    hospitalized. <u>No error.</u>
       D   E

25. The child <u>asking</u> a difficult question was perhaps
        A   B

    more shocking to the speaker <u>than</u> to the <u>child's</u>
                             C   D

    parents. <u>No error.</u>
           E

Directions: In each of the following sentences, some part or all of the sentence is underlined. Below each sentence you will find five ways of phrasing the underlined part. Select the answer that produces the most effective sentence, one that is clear and exact, without awkwardness or ambiguity, and blacken the corresponding space on your answer sheet. In choosing answers, follow the requirements of standard written English. Choose the answer that best expresses the meaning of the original sentence.

Answer (A) is always the same as the underlined part. Choose answer (A) if you think the original sentence needs no revision.

EXAMPLE:

Laura Ingalls Wilder published her first book <u>and she was sixty-five years old then</u>.
(A) and she was sixty-five years old then
(B) when she was sixty-five years old
(C) at age sixty-five years old
(D) upon reaching sixty-five years
(E) at the time when she was sixty-five

SAMPLE ANSWER

---

26. Further acquaintance with the memoirs of Elizabeth Barrett Browning and Robert Browning enables us to appreciate the depth of influence that two people <u>of talent can have on one another</u>.

    (A) of talent can have on one another
    (B) of talent can exert on one another
    (C) with talent can have one for the other
    (D) of talent can have on each other
    (E) who are talented can have

27. <u>If you saw the amount of pancakes he consumed</u> at breakfast this morning, you would understand why he is so overweight.

    (A) If you saw the amount of pancakes he consumed
    (B) If you would see the amount of pancakes he consumed
    (C) When you see the amount of pancakes he consumed
    (D) If you saw the number of pancakes he consumed
    (E) If you had seen the number of pancakes he consumed

28. <u>The debutante went to the concert with her fiancé wearing a sheer blouse.</u>

    (A) The debutante went to the concert with her fiancé wearing a sheer blouse.
    (B) The debutante went to the concert, wearing a sheer blouse, with her fiancé.
    (C) The debutante, wearing a sheer blouse, went to the concert with her fiancé.
    (D) With her fiancé, wearing a sheer blouse, the debutante went to the concert.
    (E) To the concert, wearing a sheer blouse, went the debutante with her fiancé.

29. Briefly the functions of a military staff are to advise the commander, transmit his instructions, <u>and the supervision of the execution of his decisions.</u>

    (A) and the supervision of the execution of his decisions
    (B) also the supervision of the execution of his decisions
    (C) and supervising the execution of his decisions
    (D) and supervise the execution of his decisions
    (E) and have supervision of the execution of his decisions

30. <u>The 15-round decision that Frazier was given over Ali</u> was not popular with all of the boxing fans.

    (A) The 15-round decision that Frazier was given over Ali
    (B) Frazier's 15-round decision over Ali
    (C) The Frazier 15-round decision over Ali
    (D) The decision of 15 rounds that Frazier was given over Ali
    (E) Ali's 15-round decision that Frazier was given over him

31. Although I know this house and this neighborhood as well as I know myself, <u>and although my friend here seems not hardly to know them at all</u>, nevertheless he has lived here longer than I.

    (A) and although my friend here seems not hardly to know them at all.
    (B) and even though my friend here seems hardly to know them at all
    (C) and in spite of the fact that my friend doesn't hardly seem to know them at all
    (D) and because my friend here hardly seems to know them at all
    (E) my friend here seems hardly to know them at all

32. So I leave it with all of you: Which came out of the open door—the lady or the tiger.

    (A) the lady or the tiger.
    (B) the lady or the Tiger!
    (C) the Tiger or the lady.
    (D) the Lady or the tiger.
    (E) the lady or the tiger?

33. The machine is not easy to fool, it isn't altogether foolproof either.

    (A) it isn't altogether foolproof either
    (B) or is it foolproof
    (C) and it isn't completely fooled by anyone
    (D) nor is it entirely foolproof
    (E) so it isn't altogether foolproof

34. The police and agents of the F.B.I. arrested the owner of a Madison Avenue art gallery yesterday and charged him with receiving paintings stolen last November.

    (A) arrested the owner of a Madison Avenue art gallery yesterday
    (B) yesterday arrested the owner of a Madison Avenue art gallery
    (C) arrested the owner yesterday of a Madison Avenue art gallery
    (D) had the owner of a Madison Avenue art gallery yesterday arrested
    (E) arranged the arrest yesterday of a Madison Avenue art gallery owner

35. At the end of the play about women's liberation, the leading lady cautioned the audience not to judge womanhood by the way she dresses.

    (A) she dresses   (B) she dressed   (C) they dress
    (D) they dressed   (E) it dresses

36. Go where he may, he is the life of the party

    (A) Go where he may,
    (B) Where he may go,
    (C) Wherever he goes,
    (D) Wherever he may happen to go,
    (E) Whatever he does,

37. At first we were willing to support him, afterwards it occurred to us that he ought to provide for himself.

    (A) afterwards it occurred to us that
    (B) that wasn't the thing to do since
    (C) but we came to realize that
    (D) we came to the conclusion, however, that
    (E) then we decided that

38. The statistics were checked and the report was filed.

    (A) The statistics were checked and the report was filed.
    (B) The statistics and the report were checked and filed.
    (C) The statistics were checked and the report filed.
    (D) The statistics and the report were checked and filed respectively.
    (E) Only after the statistics were checked was the report filed.

39. Dick was awarded a medal for bravery on account he risked his life to save the drowning child.

    (A) on account he risked his life
    (B) being that he risked his life
    (C) when he risked his life
    (D) the reason being on account of his risking his life
    (E) since he had risked his life

40. The teacher asked the newly-admitted student which was the country that she came from.

    (A) which was the country that she came from
    (B) from which country she had come from
    (C) the origin of the country she had come from
    (D) which country have you come from?
    (E) which country she was from

Note: The remaining questions are like those at the beginning of the section.

Directions: For each sentence in which you find an error, select the one underlined part that must be changed to make the sentence correct and blacken the corresponding space on your answer sheet.

If there is no error, blacken answer space Ⓔ

EXAMPLE:

The region has a climate so severe that plants
                     A

growing there rarely had been more than twelve
      B   C

inches high. No error
     D   E

SAMPLE ANSWER

Ⓐ Ⓑ ● Ⓓ Ⓔ

---

41. Now that the pressure of selling the house and
    A   B

packing our belongings is over, we can
              C

look forward to moving to our new home in
    D

California. No error.
      E

42. My grandmother leads a more active life than many
           A   B

other retirees who are younger than her. No error.
       C   D   E

43. I appreciate your offering to change my flat tire, but
       A   B

I would rather have you drive me to my meeting
      C

so that I will be on time. No error.
   D   E

44. After he won the marathon relatively easily, he
      A   B

decided to continue his training program and

even to enter more races. No error.
    D   E

45. Learning by doing, long a guiding principal of many
      A   B   C

educators, has been somewhat neglected during the
            D

current back-to-basics boom. No error.
          E

46. The Pirates lost the game against the Dodgers
       A

because Smith hit a home run with the bases full and
        B   C

played beautiful in the outfield. No error.
    D   E

47. The Watergate scandal may be a thing of the past but
           A   B

the Republicans will feel it's effects for a long time
          C D

to come. No error.
      E

48. If we had began our vacation a day earlier, we
     A   B

wouldn't have had so much trouble getting a plane
     C   D

reservation. No error.
      E

49. We're <u>sure</u> that Chris Evert and Tracy Austin are
        A

<u>both</u> great tennis players but <u>who's</u> to judge which
 B   C

one is the <u>best</u> of the two? <u>No error.</u>
         D   E

50. All of the class <u>presidents</u> but Jerry, Alice, and <u>I</u>
            A   B

were <u>at the meeting</u> to select the delegates for next
      C

month's convention. <u>No error.</u>
   D   E

S T O P

**IF YOU FINISH BEFORE TIME IS CALLED, YOU MAY CHECK YOUR WORK ON THIS SECTION ONLY.
DO NOT WORK ON ANY OTHER SECTION IN THE TEST.**

SECTION 4   VERBAL ABILITY
30 MINUTES   40 QUESTIONS

For each question in this section, choose the best answer and blacken the corresponding space on the answer sheet.

Each question below consists of a word in capital letters, followed by five lettered words or phrases. Choose the word or phrase that is most nearly *opposite* in meaning to the word in capital letters. Since some of the questions require you to distinguish fine shades of meaning, consider all the choices before deciding which is best.

Example:

```
GOOD:  (A) sour  (B) bad  (C) red
(D) hot  (E) ugly
                              Ⓐ ● Ⓒ Ⓓ Ⓔ
```

1. JUBILATION: (A) disturbance
   (B) correctness (C) sorrow (D) arrogance
   (E) denunciation

2. OBESE: (A) severe (B) slender (C) stingy
   (D) backward (E) lightheaded

3. INNOCUOUS: (A) ornate (B) insecure
   (C) technical (D) injurious (E) nocturnal

4. REMISS: (A) confused (B) haughty
   (C) sophisticated (D) accurate (E) cautious

5. CANDOR: (A) tolerance (B) splendor
   (C) deceitfulness (D) cowardice (E) darkness

6. CHASTE: (A) defiled (B) immature
   (C) scattered (D) stationary (E) curious

7. SUCCULENT: (A) ordinary (B) fruitless
   (C) inexpensive (D) invigorating (E) tasteless

8. OCCULT: (A) exposed (B) industrious
   (C) adept (D) cultured (E) conventional

9. INTRANSIGENT: (A) conclusive
   (B) workable (C) recognizable (D) amenable
   (E) improved

10. RECUMBENT: (A) restrained (B) dominant
    (C) upright (D) comfortable (E) ignorant

Each sentence below has one or two blanks, each blank indicating that something has been omitted. Beneath the sentence are five lettered words or sets of words. Choose the word or set of words that *best* fits the meaning of the sentence as a whole.

Example:

```
Although its publicity has been ____, the film itself is
intelligent, well-acted, handsomely produced, and
altogether ____.

(A) tasteless . . . respectable
(B) extensive . . . moderate
(C) sophisticated . . . amateur
(D) risqué . . . crude
(E) perfect . . . spectacular        ● Ⓑ Ⓒ Ⓓ Ⓔ
```

11. As a general dealing with subordinates, he was like
    two sides of a coin: _____ yet known for his
    severity, _____ yet a man of few words.

    (A) agreeable . . . talkative
    (B) brilliant . . . handsome
    (C) fair . . . candid
    (D) understanding . . . outgoing
    (E) harsh . . . pleasant

12. The profession of a major league baseball player
    involves more than _____ in these times when
    astronomical salaries and _____ contract
    bargaining are commonplace.

    (A) skill . . . astute
    (B) agitation . . . traditional
    (C) practice . . . minimal
    (D) enthusiasm . . . whimsical
    (E) intellect . . . mystical

13. Her question was not so innocent as it seemed. She
    _____ asked John whom he was taking to the
    Senior Prom because she thought he might suggest
    taking her.

    (A) flatteringly (B) nervously (C) abruptly
    (D) deliberately (E) rapidly

14. Internal dissension in this Congressional committee can _____ affirmative action for months and increase the chances of racial _____ .

    (A) encourage . . . regard
    (B) complicate . . . agreement
    (C) induce . . . movement
    (D) apply . . . validity
    (E) delay . . . upheaval

15. Although there was considerable _____ among the members of the panel as to the qualities essential for a champion, Sugar Ray Robinson was _____ voted the greatest fighter of all time.

    (A) suspicion . . . quietly
    (B) disagreement . . . overwhelmingly
    (C) discussion . . . incidentally
    (D) sacrifice . . . happily
    (E) research . . . irrelevantly

Each question below consists of a related pair of words or phrases, followed by five lettered pairs of words or phrases. Select the lettered pair that *best* expresses a relationship similar to that expressed in the original pair.

Example:

YAWN : BOREDOM : :   (A) dream : sleep
(B) anger : madness   (C) smile : amusement
(D) face : expression   (E) impatience : rebellion
Ⓐ Ⓑ ● Ⓓ Ⓔ

16. IMITATION : INDIVIDUALITY : :

    (A) veneration : deference
    (B) determination : success
    (C) recklessness : courage
    (D) vanity : conformity
    (E) debauchery : morality

17. ODORIFEROUS : SMELL : :

    (A) rancid : taste
    (B) myopic : vision
    (C) euphonious : sound
    (D) decrepit : age
    (E) disoriented : thought

18. BLAND : PIQUANT : :

    (A) pacific : grateful
    (B) terse : serious
    (C) slavish : servile
    (D) naive : genuine
    (E) inane : relevant

19. HORSE : COLT : :

    (A) bird : eaglet
    (B) child : adult
    (C) seed : fruit
    (D) pig : sow
    (E) sheep : lamb

20. WALK : STUMBLE : :

    (A) trot : race
    (B) look : ogle
    (C) hear : ignore
    (D) build : destroy
    (E) speak : stammer

21. RUN : BASEBALL : :

    (A) goal : soccer
    (B) education : school
    (C) puck : hockey
    (D) down : football
    (E) award : actress

22. SHARPEN : PENCIL : :

    (A) hone : blade
    (B) ice : cake
    (C) wrap : package
    (D) polish : furniture
    (E) stretch : canvas

23. BACKLOG : MERCHANDISE : :

    (A) jam : traffic
    (B) intermission : play
    (C) deficit : money
    (D) bonus : worker
    (E) prey : hunter

24. ORCHESTRA : MUSICIAN : :

    (A) museum : statue
    (B) school : desk
    (C) team : owner
    (D) army : soldier
    (E) novel : author

25. SAND : DUNE : :

    (A) rain : sleet
    (B) beach : strand
    (C) snow : bank
    (D) sun : mist
    (E) drift : ocean

Each passage below is followed by questions based on its content. Answer all questions following a passage on the basis of what is *stated* or *implied* in that passage.

Biography is the molding of the disparate and the unshapely facts of an actual life into a coherent form. Writing a biography is an enormously demanding undertaking and the lengthy process of gathering information is only the
5　beginning. The sleuthing must be followed by the incorporation of widely diverse materials into an intelligible and interesting picture—a task that calls for the combined skills of historian, psychologist, and novelist, and for a sense of the multiple contexts within which an individual
10　life enfolds.

Biographers nowadays are much more interested in the minor characters—because people do not evolve in isolation. The counter picture brings the main character to life. But although all biographers acknowledge the im-
15　portance of minor characters, and of the small, revealing detail, they seem to be unanimous in their recoil from the "laundry-list" biography, which progresses by massive accumulation of chronological data.

Attending to the revealing detail, or to the minor char-
20　acters, does not mean that biographers eschew the more traditional themes of public power and the relationship between important individuals and an era. While there are many different kinds of power—the power of intellect, of literature, the power within relationships—a choice of bi-
25　ographical subjects is usually governed by the desire to show a figure who is a key for her or his generation.

26. Which of these titles best suits the passage?

(A) The Use of Minor Characters in Biography
(B) Current Trends in Biography
(C) Stressing the Main Character in a Biography
(D) The Complex Demands of Writing Biography
(E) Getting the Facts Prior to Writing a Biography

27. According to the passage, which of the following statements is true?

(A) An historian is better equipped than a novelist to write a biography.
(B) A biographer may alter the facts in order to make his book more interesting.
(C) It is proper for a biographer to express freely his own opinions about his main character.
(D) Minor characters are generally as important as the main character in a biography.
(E) A duty of a biographer to the reader is to present his materials clearly and interestingly.

28. In the passage, a "laundry list" refers to a list of

(A) all the events that a biographer should consider for inclusion in his book
(B) the unwholesome experiences or actions of some of the characters that are included in the biography
(C) the day-to-day happenings in the lives of the main character of a biography
(D) the various places that the situations described in a biography have taken place
(E) the unshapely facts that the biographer reveals in his book

Slums and their population are the victims (and the perpetuators) of seemingly endless troubles that reinforce each other. Slums operate as vicious circles. In time, these vicious circles enmesh the whole operations of cities. Spreading slums require ever greater amounts of public　5
money—and not simply more money for publicly financed improvement or to stay even, but more money to cope with ever widening retreat and regression. As needs grow greater, the wherewithal grows less.

Our present urban renewal laws are an attempt to break　10
this particular linkage in the vicious circles by forthrightly wiping away slums and their populations, and replacing them with projects intended to produce higher tax yields, or to lure back easier populations with less expensive public requirements. The method fails. At best, it merely shifts　15
slums from here to there, adding its own tincture of extra hardship and disruption. At worst, it destroys neighborhoods where constructive and improving communities exist and where the situation calls for encouragement rather than destruction.　20

Like Fight Blight and Conservation campaigns in neighborhoods declining into slums, slum shifting fails because it tries to overcome causes of trouble by diddling with symptoms. Sometimes even the very symptoms that preoccupy the slum shifters are, in the main, vestiges of former　25
troubles rather than significant indications of current or future ills.

Conventional planning approaches to slums and slum dwellers are thoroughly paternalistic. The trouble with paternalists is that they want to make impossibly profound　30
changes, and they choose impossibly superficial means for doing so. To overcome slums, we must regard slum dwellers as people capable of understanding and acting upon their own self-interests, which they certainly are. We need to discern, respect and build upon the forces for regen-　35
eration that exist in slums themselves, and that demonstrably work in real cities. This is far from trying to patronize people into a better life, and it is far from what is done today.

29. According to this passage,

(A) present urban renewal laws are effectively eliminating slums
(B) the problems of slum neighborhoods eventually affect the entire city
(C) slum dwellers require a paternalistic approach to their problems
(D) conventional planning approaches to slums involve the cooperation of the slum dwellers
(E) slum shifters are interested in remedying problems that presently exist

30. The author feels that a successful neighborhood improvement program depends upon

(A) public assistance given in a fatherly manner
(B) Fight Blight and Conservation campaigns
(C) an increase in the number of projects intended to produce higher tax yields
(D) the recognition and promotion of the positive aspects of the neighborhood
(E) the merging of different types of neighborhoods

31. Apt examples of slum shifting as it is currently practiced by the government are all of the following *except*

(A) removing old buildings and replacing them with new high-rise, low-cost apartments
(B) encouraging middle-class tenants of various nationalities to move into a slum neighborhood
(C) allowing the slum-dwellers to spend government funds as they themselves see fit
(D) institute "clean up your neighborhood" campaigns
(E) making the slum-dweller feel that the government is a parent caring for them

32. The author's attitude toward the government's handling of slum rehabilitation is one of

(A) unalloyed annoyance
(B) cheerful acceptance
(C) gentle sarcasm
(D) willing compromise
(E) patient neutrality

Flashes of X-rays lasting only billionths of a second are giving scientists their first highly detailed looks at individual human cells. The images, obtained with a new technique called contact X-ray microscopy, can show in-
5 ternal structures as well as surface structures. Although electron microscopes can reveal finer detail than is possible with X-ray microscopes, they cannot make images that capture an instant of life. For viewing under the electron microscope, subjects must be housed in a vacuum chamber
10 and therefore cannot ordinarily be pictured while they are still alive. The new technique kills the specimen but since the flash lasts only 100 billionths of a second, the image is formed before the destructive effects occur.

Blood platelets, crucial to the healing of wounds, were the first subjects for this new kind of microscopy, but skin 15 cells are already under study and a wide variety of other living cells and components will be examined soon. While the latest report on the X-ray technique describes research on platelets, the technique is considered applicable to many kinds of human cells and to the study of many important 20 functions of life. Platelets are pancake-shaped structures, about half the size of red blood cells, that serve a vital thumb-in-the-dike function in the human circulatory system. They circulate in the blood in an inactive state until breakage or injury occurs. They become activated when 25 they encounter a break or damage in a blood vessel. Their role in wound healing is that of clumping together quickly to stop blood flow through breaks in the injured vessels. This stoppage comes before the actual formation of a durable blood clot. It is an early stage of wound healing. As 30 a key part in their function in halting bleeding, activated platelets send out projections called pseudopods and evidently tangle with each other and adhere to the blood vessel to block off blood flow. Just how the pseudopods form is still unknown, but the new X-ray microscopy shows clearly 35 that the pseudopods are not just exterior projections but have roots deep inside.

33. The passage is primarily concerned with

(A) science research and new techniques
(B) pseudopods and blood vessels
(C) human cells and blood clotting
(D) the circulatory system and red blood cells
(E) the X-ray microscope and platelets

34. The closest meaning of "thumb-in-the-dike" (line 23) as it is used in the passage is

(A) releasing   (B) enforcing   (C) blocking
(D) washing   (E) removing

35. According to the passage, which is the correct choice?

(A) Because of its roots, the platelet is able to grow and expand
(B) The electronic microscope is able to provide a clearer image than the X-ray microscope
(C) The shape of a red blood cell is thin and flat.
(D) A cell dies at exactly the same time that the X-ray flash occurs.
(E) Pseudopods operate separately from the platelets.

The literature of an oppressed people is the conscience of man, and nowhere is this seen with more intense clarity than in the literature of Afroamerica. An essential element of Afroamerican literature is that the literature as a whole—not the work of occasional authors—is a movement against 5 concrete wickedness. In Afroamerican literature, accordingly, there is a grief rarely to be found elsewhere in American literature, and frequently a rage rarely to be found in American letters: a rage different in quality, pro-

10 founder, more towering, more intense—the rage of the oppressed. Whenever an Afroamerican artist picks up pen or horn, his target is likely to be American racism, his subject the suffering of his people, and the core element his own grief and the grief of his people. Almost all of
15 Afroamerican literature carries the burden of this protest.

The cry for freedom and the protest against injustice indicate a desire for the birth of the New Man, a testament to the New Unknown World to be discovered, to be created by man. Afroamerican literature is, as a body, a declaration
20 that despite the perversion and cruelty that cling like swamproots to the flesh of man's feet, man has options for freedom, for cleanliness, for wholeness, for human harmony, for goodness: for a human world. Like the spirituals that are a part of it, Afroamerican literature is a
25 passionate assertion that man will win freedom. Thus, Afroamerican literature rejects despair and cynicism; it is a literature of realistic hope and life-affirmation. This is not to say that no Afroamerican literary work reflects cynicism or despair, but rather that the basic theme of Af-
30 roamerican literature is that man's goodness will prevail.

Afroamerican literature is a statement against death, a statement as to what life should be: life should be vivacious, exuberant, wholesomely uninhibited, sensual, sensuous, constructively antirespectable, life should abound
35 and flourish and laugh, life should be passionately lived and man should be loving: life should be not a sedate waltz or foxtrot but a vigorous breakdance; thus, when the Afroamerican writer criticizes America for its cruelty, the criticism implies that America is drawn to death and re-
40 pelled by what should be the human style of life, the human way of living.

Black literature in America is, then, a setting-forth of man's identity and destiny; an investigation of man's iniquity and a statement of belief in his potential godliness;
45 a prodding of man toward exploring and finding deep joy in his humanity.

36. The author states or implies that

(A) a separate but equal doctrine is the answer to American racism
(B) Afroamerican literature is superior to American literature
(C) hopelessness and lack of trust are the keynotes of Afroamerican literature
(D) standing up for one's rights and protesting about unfairness are vital
(E) traditional forms of American-type dancing should be engaged in

37. When the author, in referring to Afroamerican literature, states that "life should be . . . constructively antirespectable (lines 32–34)," it can be inferred that people ought to

(A) do their own thing provided what they do is worthwhile
(B) show disrespect for others when they have the desire to do so
(C) be passionate in public whenever the urge is there
(D) shun a person because he is of another race or color
(E) be enraged if their ancestors have been unjustly treated

38. With reference to the passage, which of the following statements is true about Afroamerican literature?

I. It expresses the need for nonviolent opposition to antiracism.
II. It urges a person to have respect for himself and for others.
III. It voices the need for an active, productive, and satisfying life.

(A) I only
(B) II only
(C) I and III only
(D) II and III only
(E) I, II, and III

39. The tone of the passage is one of

(A) anger and vindictiveness
(B) hope and affirmation
(C) forgiveness and charity
(D) doubt and despair
(E) grief and cruelty

40. The author would most probably be a strong admirer of

(A) George Washington
(B) Muhammad Ali
(C) Robert E. Lee
(D) Ronald Reagan
(E) Martin Luther King

S T O P

IF YOU FINISH BEFORE TIME IS CALLED, YOU MAY CHECK YOUR WORK ON THIS SECTION ONLY.
DO NOT WORK ON ANY OTHER SECTION IN THE TEST.

SECTION 5   MATH ABILITY
30 MINUTES   35 QUESTIONS

In this section solve each problem, using any available space on the page for scratchwork. Then decide which is the best of the choices given and blacken the corresponding space on the answer sheet.

The following information is for your reference in solving some of the problems.

Circle of radius r: Area $= \pi r^2$; Circumference $= 2\pi r$
    The number of degrees of arc in a circle is 360.
The measure in degrees of a straight angle is 180.

Definitions of symbols:

$=$	is equal to	$\leq$	is less than or equal to
$\neq$	is unequal to	$\geq$	is greater than or equal to
$<$	is less than	$\parallel$	is parallel to
$>$	is greater than	$\perp$	is perpendicular to

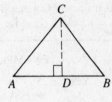

Triangle: The sum of the measure in degrees of the angles of a triangle is 180.
If $\angle CDA$ is a right angle, then

(1) area of $\triangle ABC = \dfrac{AB \times CD}{2}$

(2) $AC^2 = AD^2 + DC^2$

Note: Figures which accompany problems in this test are intended to provide information useful in solving the problems. They are drawn as accurately as possible EXCEPT when it is stated in a specific problem that its figure is not drawn to scale. All figures lie in a plane unless otherwise indicated. All numbers used are real numbers.

1. If -7 is the average of -13, -7, -9, -2 and w, then $w =$

    (A) -50 (B) -7 (C) -4 (D) 4 (E) 8

2. If $A = 2 + \dfrac{2}{3} + \dfrac{2}{5} + \dfrac{2}{7} + \dfrac{2}{9}$ and

    $B = 2 + \dfrac{2}{3} + \dfrac{2}{5} + \dfrac{2}{7}$ then find the value of $A - B$.

    (A) $-\dfrac{1}{24}$ (B) $-\dfrac{2}{9}$ (C) $\dfrac{1}{24}$ (D) $\dfrac{2}{9}$ (E) $\dfrac{1026}{315}$

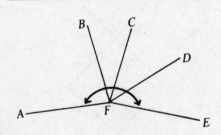

Note: Figure is not drawn to scale.

3. In the figure above $\angle CFE = 60°$, $\angle BFD = 50°$, $\angle AFB = 80°$ and $\angle CFD = 20°$. What is the measure, in degrees, of the marked $\angle AFE$?

    (A) $100°$ (B) $110°$ (C) $170°$ (D) $190°$ (E) $210°$

4. Which of the products below is (are) *NOT* equal to 1?

    I. $\dfrac{3}{4} \times \dfrac{4}{3} \times \dfrac{3}{4} \times \dfrac{4}{3} \times \dfrac{3}{4}$

    II. $\dfrac{3}{4} \times \dfrac{4}{3} \times \dfrac{3}{4} \times \dfrac{4}{3} \times \dfrac{3}{4} \times \dfrac{4}{3}$

    III. $\dfrac{3}{4} \times \dfrac{4}{3} \times \dfrac{3}{4} \times \dfrac{4}{3} \times \dfrac{3}{4} \times \dfrac{4}{3} \times \dfrac{3}{4}$

    (A) I only
    (B) II only
    (C) I and III only
    (D) II and III only
    (E) I, II and III

5. $\dfrac{4^2 + 4^2 + 4^2}{3^3 + 3^3 + 3^3} =$

    (A) $\dfrac{16}{27}$ (B) $\dfrac{8}{9}$ (C) $\dfrac{4}{3}$ (D) $\dfrac{64}{27}$ (E) $\dfrac{512}{81}$

6. If $\widehat{a}\,\widehat{b} = \dfrac{a + 1}{b - 1}$ where a and b are positive integers and $b > 1$, which of the following is largest?

    (A) $\widehat{2}\,\widehat{3}$ (B) $\widehat{3}\,\widehat{3}$ (C) $\widehat{3}\,\widehat{5}$ (D) $\widehat{4}\,\widehat{5}$
    (E) $\widehat{5}\,\widehat{3}$

7. The length of a rectangle is four times its width. Let w represent the width. Find an expression for the perimeter of the rectangle in terms of w.

    (A) $5w$ (B) $\dfrac{5}{4}w$ (C) $10w$ (D) $4w + 2$ (E) $4w^2$

Questions 8-27 each consist of two quantities, one in Column A and one in Column B. You are to compare the two quantities and on the answer sheet blacken space

A if the quantity in Column A is greater;
B if the quantity in Column B is greater;
C if the two quantities are equal;
D if the relationship cannot be determined from the information given.

Notes: 1. In certain questions, information concerning one or both of the quantities to be compared is centered above the columns.
2. In a given question, a symbol that appears in both columns represents the same thing in Column A as it does in Column B.
3. Letters such as x, n, and k stand for real numbers.

	EXAMPLES		
	Column A	Column B	Answers
E1.	2×6	$2 + 6$	● Ⓑ Ⓒ Ⓓ
E2.	$180 - x$	y	Ⓐ Ⓑ ● Ⓓ
E3.	$p - q$	$q - p$	Ⓐ Ⓑ Ⓒ ●

In E2, an angle diagram shows $x°$ and $y°$ formed by a line crossing another line.

Column A   **Column B**

8.
$$\frac{a}{18} = \frac{2}{9}$$
$$\frac{b}{28} = \frac{1}{7}$$

| a | b |

9. $\dfrac{5}{4} + \dfrac{5}{7}$ $5\left(\dfrac{1}{4} + \dfrac{1}{7}\right)$

10. $Y = \sqrt{64} + \sqrt{225}$

Y 17

11. Darrin is older than Stephanie and Jimmy is older than Stephanie.

Darrin's age   Jimmy's age

12. 0.32 0.0467

13. The number of positive integer factors of 11   The number of positive integer factors of 23

14. $1^8 + 3^8$ 4^8

Column A   **Column B**

15.
x is an odd integer and y is an even integer.

The probability that x^2 is odd   The probability that y^2 is odd

16. $9 \cdot 8 \cdot 7 \cdot 6$ $54 \cdot 56$

17.
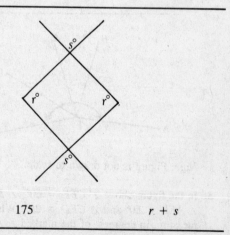

175 $r + s$

18. $y = (x - 3)(x + 4)$

-3 The smallest value of x for which $y = 0$

SUMMARY DIRECTIONS FOR COMPARISON QUESTIONS

Answer: A if the quantity in Column A is greater;
B if the quantity in Column B is greater;
C if the two quantities are equal;
D if the relationship cannot be determined from the information given.

Column A	Column B

19. 1   The total surface area of a cube having edge 0.4

20.

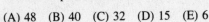

21   3p

21. $a + b + 2c = 10$ and $b = 2c$

b   5

22. $\dfrac{7}{8}$ $\dfrac{8}{9}$

23. Let Ⓐ be defined by the equation $x \, Ⓐ \, y = y^4$

7 Ⓐ a   5 Ⓐ a

Column A	Column B

24. $\sqrt{x^4 + 6x^2 + 9}$ $x^2 + 3x + 3$

25. On a particular map, 1 inch represents 3 miles.

The area represented by 17 square inches on this map   153 square miles

26. Area of parallelogram with a diagonal of length 6   Area of a square with a diagonal of length 6

27.

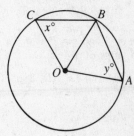

O is the center of the circle and $x < y$

Segment CB   Segment BA

Solve each of the remaining problems in this section using any available space for scratchwork. Then decide which is the best of the choices given and blacken the corresponding space on the sheet.

28. Plane A starts from Z and travels at an average rate of 500 kilometers per hour. Plane B starts from Z 8 hours later and travels the same route at an average rate of 600 kilometers per hour. Exactly how many hours after plane B leaves Z will it overtake plane A?

(A) 48   (B) 40   (C) 32   (D) 15   (E) 6

29. A woman gave $\dfrac{5}{12}$ of her money to her son and $\dfrac{1}{36}$ to each of her 6 daughters. Another $\dfrac{1}{18}$ was divided equally among her 6 nephews. She gave the remainder of her money to charity. What part of her money did she give to charity?

(A) $\dfrac{1}{12}$ (B) $\dfrac{1}{3}$ (C) $\dfrac{13}{36}$ (D) $\dfrac{23}{36}$ (E) $\dfrac{11}{12}$

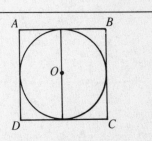

30. In the figure above, ABCD is a square with each of its four sides touching the circle with center O. If the radius of the circle is w, what is the perimeter of ABCD in terms of w?

(A) $4w^2$ (B) $2w^2$ (C) $16w$ (D) $12w$ (E) $8w$

31. Which of the following designs *can* be formed by combining rectangles with size and shading the same as that shown above if overlap is not permitted.?

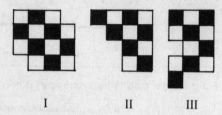

I   II   III

(A) I only   (B) II only   (C) III only   (D) I and II only   (E) II and III only

32. If *A* is the least positive 5-digit integer with *nonzero* digits, none of which is repeated, and *B* is the greatest of such positive integers, then $B - A =$

(A) 2,468   (B) 66,666   (C) 86,420
(D) 86,424   (E) 89,999

33. Given that $r \neq 0$ and $r = 5w = 7a$. Find the value of $r - w$ in terms of *a*.

(A) $\dfrac{1a}{7}$ (B) $\dfrac{7a}{5}$ (C) $3a$ (D) $\dfrac{28a}{5}$ (E) $28a$

34. On a mathematics test, the average score for a certain class was 90. If 40 percent of the class scored 100 and 10 percent scored 80, what was the average score for the remainder of the class?

(A) 78   (B) 80   (C) 82   (D) 84   (E) 86

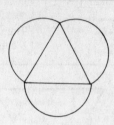

35. The figure above consists of equal semi-circles each touching the other at the ends of their diameters. If the radius of each circle is 2, what is the *total enclosed* area?

(A) $\dfrac{\sqrt{3}}{4} + \pi$ (B) $\sqrt{3} + 2\pi$

(C) $4\sqrt{3} + 6\pi$ (D) 6π

(E) $\dfrac{\sqrt{2}}{4} + 4\pi$

S T O P

IF YOU FINISH BEFORE TIME IS CALLED, YOU MAY CHECK YOUR WORK ON THIS SECTION ONLY.
DO NOT WORK ON ANY OTHER SECTION IN THE TEST.

SECTION 6   MATH ABILITY
30 MINUTES   25 QUESTIONS

In this section solve each problem, using any available space on the page for scratchwork. Then decide which is the best of the choices given and blacken the corresponding space on the answer sheet.

The following information is for your reference in solving some of the problems.

Circle of radius r: Area $= \pi r^2$; Circumference $= 2\pi r$
   The number of degrees of arc in a circle is 360.
The measure in degrees of a straight angle is 180.

Definitions of symbols:
   $=$ is equal to $\leqq$ is less than or equal to
   $\neq$ is unequal to $\geqq$ is greater than or equal to
   $<$ is less than $\parallel$ is parallel to
   $>$ is greater than $\perp$ is perpendicular to

Triangle: The sum of the measure in degrees of the angles of a triangle is 180.
   If $\angle CDA$ is a right angle, then

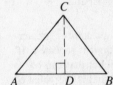

   (1)   area of $\triangle ABC = \dfrac{AB \times CD}{2}$

   (2) $AC^2 = AD^2 + DC^2$

Note: Figures which accompany problems in this test are intended to provide information useful in solving the problems. They are drawn as accurately as possible EXCEPT when it is stated in a specific problem that its figure is not drawn to scale. All figures lie in a plane unless otherwise indicated. All numbers used are real numbers.

1. If $\dfrac{81 \times y}{27} = 21$, then $y =$

   (A) $\dfrac{1}{21}$ (B) $\dfrac{1}{7}$ (C) 3   (D) 7   (E) 21

2. Which of the following computations represents the greatest value less than 120?

   (A) $3 \times 4 \times 5$ (B) $3 \times 4 \times 7$
   (C) $2 \times 5 \times 13$
   (D) $3 \times 4 \times 9$ (E) $3 \times 5 \times 9$

3. Suppose w, x, y, and z are positive integers such that $w + z = x + y$. Which of the following *must* be true?

   (A) $w + z < y$ (B) $x + y < z$ (C) $w = x$
   (D) $z < y$ (E) $w - x = y - z$

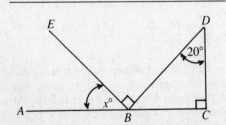

4. In the figure above $DC \perp AC$, $EB \perp DB$ and AC is a line segment. What is the value of x?

   (A) 15   (B) 20   (C) 30   (D) 80   (E) 160

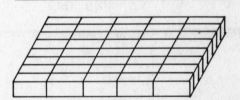

5. This figure above represents a layer of bricks, where each brick has a volume of 40 cubic inches. If all bricks are stacked in layers as shown, and the final pile of bricks occupies 8000 cubic inches, how many layers are there in the final pile of bricks?

   (A) 4   (B) 5   (C) 20   (D) 200   (E) 240

6. If a,b are odd numbers, and c is even, which of the following is an even number?

   (A) $ab + c$ (B) $a(b + c)$
   (C) $(a + b) + (b + c)$ (D) $(a + b) - c$
   (E) $a + bc$

7. In the addition problem shown below, if $\square$ is a constant, what must $\square$ equal in order for the answer to be correct?

$$
\begin{array}{r}
\square\,6\,\square\,1 \\
8\,\square\,6\,\square \\
\square\,8\,\square\,9 \\
\hline
1\ 7\,9\,5\,\square
\end{array}
$$

   (A) 3   (B) 4   (C) 5   (D) 6   (E) 7

8. At a certain distance from an island, a 60 foot lighthouse appears to be only 5 inches tall. How tall is a flagpole which appears to be $1\frac{2}{3}$ inches tall at the same distance?

(A) 20 feet   (B) 12 feet   (C) $\frac{25}{3}$ feet

(D) 6 feet   (E) 5 feet

9. If $a = 10b$ and $b = 2c$, what is c in terms of a?

(A) $\frac{a}{20}$ (B) $\frac{a}{10}$ (C) $\frac{a}{2}$ (D) $5a$ (E) $20a$

10. Let x be the smallest possible 3-digit number greater than or equal to 100 in which no digit is repeated. If y is the largest positive 3-digit number that can be made using all of the digits of x, what is the value of $y - x$?

(A) 9   (B) 99   (C) 108   (D) 198   (E) 199

11. If $x = \frac{1}{4}$, then $16x^2 - .8x + 1 =$

(A) $-\frac{1}{2}$ (B) 0   (C) $\frac{1}{4}$ (D) $\frac{1}{2}$ (E) 4

12. How many real values of x satisfy

$$\frac{5}{6}x^2 - \frac{10}{12}x^2 = 0$$

(A) 0   (B) 1   (C) 2   (D) more than 2 but finitely many   (E) infinitely many

13. Which of the following squares not necessarily drawn to scale, has a perimeter equal to the circumference of a circle of radius r?

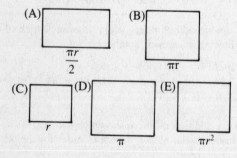

14. In the figure above, ABC is a line segment. What is the value of x?

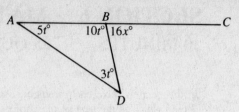

(A) 5   (B) 10   (C) 20   (D) 80
(E) 100

Questions 15-16

Let "δ" be defined as: $a \, \delta \, b = a^2 + 2ab$
For example, $5 \, \delta \, 3 = 5^2 + 2 \cdot 5 \cdot 3 = 55$.

15. Find $\frac{1}{4} \, \delta \, 6$

(A) $\frac{25}{8}$ (B) $\frac{7}{2}$ (C) $\frac{49}{16}$ (D) $\frac{97}{16}$ (E) $\frac{5}{16}$

16. If $3 \, \delta \, x = 25$, then $x =$

(A) $\frac{4}{3}$ (B) $\frac{19}{6}$ (C) 4   (D) $\frac{8}{3}$ (E) $\frac{3}{8}$

17. A horizontal line has a length of 100 yards. A vertical line is drawn at one of its ends. If lines are drawn every ten yards thereafter, until the other end is reached, how many vertical lines are finally drawn?

(A) 9   (B) 10   (C) 11   (D) 12   (E) 100

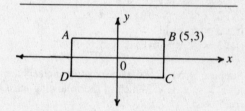

18. In the figure above, the sides of rectangle $ABCD$ are parallel to the y-axis and x-axis as shown. If the rectangle is rotated clockwise about the origin through 90°, what are the new coordinates of B?

(A) $(3, -5)$ (B) $(-3, 5)$ (C) $(-3, -5)$
(D) $(5, -3)$ (E) $(-5, 3)$

19. The half-life of a certain radioactive substance is 6 hours. In other words, if you start with 8 grams of the substance, 6 hours later you will have 4 grams. If a sample of this substance contains x grams, how many grams remain after 24 hours?

(A) $\frac{x}{32}$ (B) $\frac{x}{16}$ (C) $\frac{x}{8}$ (D) $2x$ (E) $4x$

20. Bobby had b marbles and Charlie had c marbles. After Bobby gave 6 marbles to Charlie, Bobby still had 18 more marbles than Charlie. Find $c - b$.

(A) 30   (B) 12   (C) 3   (D) -12 (E) -30

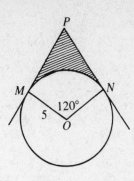

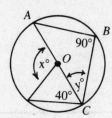

21. In the circle above with center O, diameter AC, and $AB = BC$, $x + y =$

(A) 200   (B) 125   (C) 100   (D) 75   (E) 60

22. In a certain class containing 60 students, the average (arithmetic mean) age is 20. In another class containing 20 students, the average age is 40. The average age of all 80 students is

(A) 23   (B) 23.5   (C) 24   (D) 24.5   (E) 25

23. If $ab^2c > 0$ which of the following must be true:

I. $ab^2 > 0$
II. $ac > 0$
III. $abc > 0$

(A) I only
(B) II only
(C) III only
(D) I and II only
(E) II and III only

24. $\overline{PM}$ and $\overline{PN}$ are tangent to circle O at M and N respectively; $m \angle MON = 120°$ and $OM = ON = 5$. Find the perimeter of the shaded region.

(A) $10 + 10\pi$ (B) $5\sqrt{3} + 10\pi$

(C) $5\sqrt{3} + \dfrac{10}{3}\pi$ (D) $10\sqrt{3} + \dfrac{10\pi}{3}$

(E) $10\sqrt{3} + 10\pi$

25. When Stanley received $10x$ tapes, he then had $5y + 1$ times as many tapes as he had originally. In terms of x and y, how many tapes did Stanley have originally?

(A) $10x(5y + 1)$ (B) $\dfrac{5y + 1}{10x}$ (C) $\dfrac{2x}{y}$

(D) $\dfrac{10x}{5y + 1}$ (E) None of the above

S T O P

IF YOU FINISH BEFORE TIME IS CALLED, YOU MAY CHECK YOUR WORK ON THIS SECTION ONLY.
DO NOT WORK ON ANY OTHER SECTION IN THE TEST.

HOW DID YOU DO ON THIS TEST?

STEP 1. Go to the Answer Key on page 453.

STEP 2. For your "raw score," count your correct answers in each of the test parts of the test you have just taken:

Verbal (Section 1 and 4 combined) _____.

Math (Sections 2, 5, and 6 combined) _____.

Standard Written English (Section 3) _____.

STEP 3. Get your "scaled score" for the test by referring to the Raw Score/ Scaled Score Conversion Tables on pages 64–66.

THERE'S ALWAYS ROOM FOR IMPROVEMENT!

ANSWER KEY FOR PRACTICE TEST 3

Section 1—Verbal

1. D	8. C	15. D	22. C	29. C	36. D	43. D
2. A	9. D	16. D	23. B	30. D	37. C	44. C
3. E	10. E	17. C	24. C	31. A	38. B	45. B
4. B	11. A	18. E	25. B	32. D	39. B	
5. C	12. C	19. A	26. D	33. D	40. A	
6. E	13. B	20. E	27. C	34. B	41. C	
7. A	14. B	21. E	28. E	35. C	42. B	

Section 2—Math

1. D	5. D	9. A	13. C	17. A	21. D	25. E
2. C	6. B	10. D	14. D	18. D	22. E	
3. C	7. E	11. A	15. B	19. A	23. B	
4. B	8. C	12. B	16. B	20. B	24. A	

Section 3—Standard Written English

1. D	9. D	17. A	25. A	33. D	41. E	49. D
2. E	10. A	18. B	26. D	34. B	42. D	50. B
3. C	11. B	19. D	27. E	35. E	43. E	
4. A	12. C	20. E	28. C	36. C	44. A	
5. B	13. E	21. A	29. D	37. C	45. C	
6. E	14. A	22. B	30. A	38. A	46. D	
7. D	15. C	23. E	31. B	39. E	47. C	
8. A	16. D	24. B	32. E	40. E	48. A	

Section 4—Verbal

1. C	7. E	13. D	19. E	25. C	31. C	37. A
2. B	8. A	14. E	20. E	26. D	32. A	38. D
3. D	9. D	15. B	21. A	27. E	33. E	39. B
4. E	10. C	16. E	22. A	28. A	34. C	40. E
5. C	11. C	17. C	23. A	29. B	35. B	
6. A	12. A	18. E	24. D	30. D	36. D	

Section 5—Math

1. C	6. E	11. D	16. C	21. D	26. D	31. C
2. D	7. C	12. A	17. B	22. B	27. A	32. C
3. C	8. C	13. C	18. A	23. C	28. B	33. D
4. C	9. C	14. B	19. A	24. D	29. C	34. D
5. A	10. A	15. A	20. C	25. C	30. E	35. C

Section 6—Math

1. D	6. D	11. B	16. D	21. B
2. D	7. B	12. E	17. C	22. E
3. E	8. A	13. A	18. A	23. B
4. B	9. A	14. A	19. B	24. D
5. B	10. C	15. C	20. E	25. C

EXPLANATORY ANSWERS FOR PRACTICE TEST 3

Section I: Verbal Ability

As you read these Explanatory Answers, you are advised to refer to "Using Critical Thinking Skills in Verbal Questions" (beginning on page 90) whenever a specific Strategy is referred to in the answer. Of particular importance are the following Master Verbal Strategies:

Sentence Completion Master Strategy 1—page 94.
Sentence Completion Master Strategy 2—page 95.
Analogies Master Strategy 1—page 90.
Antonyms Master Strategy 1—page 99.
Reading Comprehension Master Strategy 2—page 109.

1. **(D)** Choice D is correct. See **Antonym Strategy 3.** *Jocose* means *joking; humorous.* The opposite of *jocose* is *serious.*

2. **(A)** Choice A is correct. *Ravage* means *to destroy; to ruin.* The opposite of *ravage* is *to build.*

3. **(E)** Choice E is correct. See **Antonym Strategy 1.** *Abortive* means *unsuccessful; failing to succeed.* The opposite of *abortive* is *successful.*

4. **(B)** Choice B is correct. See **Antonym Strategy 3.** *Sagacity* means *wisdom.* The opposite of *sagacity* is *foolishness.*

5. **(C)** Choice C is correct. See **Antonym Strategy 2.** *Abstruse* means *hard to understand; concealed.* The opposite of *abstruse* is *understandable.*

6. **(E)** Choice E is correct. *Indigent* means *extremely poor.* The opposite of *indigent* is *prosperous.*

7. **(A)** Choice A is correct. See **Antonym Strategy 2.** *Noxious* means *harmful; injurious.* The opposite of *noxious* is *curative.*

8. **(C)** Choice C is correct. *Castigate* means *to punish.* The opposite of *castigate* is *to reward.*

9. **(D)** Choice D is correct. See **Antonym Strategy 3.** *Acumen* means *shrewdness; mental keenness.* The opposite of *acumen* is *dullness.*

10. **(E)** Choice E is correct. See **Antonym Strategy 3.** *Odious* means *disgusting; hateful.* The opposite of *odious* is *agreeable.*

11. **(A)** Choice A is correct. See **Antonym Strategy 3.** *Divergent* means *different; varying.* The opposite of *divergent* is *similar.*

12. **(C)** Choice C is correct. *Elicit* means *to draw forth.* The opposite of *elicit* is to *hold back.*

13. **(B)** Choice B is correct. See **Antonym Strategy 3.** *Saturnine* means *gloomy.* The opposite of *saturnine* is *hopeful.*

14. **(B)** Choice B is correct. *Phlegmatic* means *slow-moving; sluggish.* The opposite of *phlegmatic* is *active.*

15. **(D)** Choice D is correct. *Obsequious* means *overly attentive and submissive.* The opposite of *obsequious* is *uncooperative.*

16. **(D)** Choice D is correct. See **Sentence Completion Strategy 4.** The word "Although" at the beginning of the sentence is an opposition indicator. As a contrast to the rundown condition of the school, the word "renovated" is the acceptable choice.

17. **(C)** Choice C is correct. The word "immediate" is the only one that makes sense in the blank. See **Sentence Completion Strategy 1.**

18. **(E)** Choice E is correct. See **Sentence Completion Strategy 2.** The first words of Choice B (flexibility) and Choice D (dizziness) do not make sense in the first part of the sentence. Therefore, we eliminate these two choices. When we try the two words in each of the remaining choices, only Choice E (disappointment . . . fervent) makes good sense in the sentence as a whole.

19. **(A)** Choice A is correct. See **Sentence Completion Strategy 4.** The opposition indicator "even though" should lead us to the correct Choice A with the fill-in word "convincing."

20. **(E)** Choice E is correct. The fact that the investor was eager to make an investment change points to his being "dubious" about his current investment—the stocks he had recently purchased. See **Sentence Completion Strategy 1.**

21. **(E)** Choice E is correct. The author is stressing the point that the true artist—the person with rare creative ability and keen perception, or high intelligence—fails to communicate well with those about him—"differs from the rest of us." (Line 4) He is likely to be considered a "nut" by many whom he comes in contact with. "Great wits" in the Choice E quotation refer to the true artist. The quotation states, in effect, that there is a thin line between the true artist and the "nut." Choices A, B, C, and D are incorrect because they have little, if anything, to do with the main idea of the passage.

[Note: Choices C and E were composed by John Dryden (1631–1700) and Choices A, B, and D by Alexander Pope (1688–1744).]

22. **(C)** Choice C is correct. See lines 8–10. The artist creates because he is "less fitted to prosper and enjoy himself under the conditions of life which he and we must face alike." Choices A and E are incorrect. Although they may be true, they are never mentioned in the passage. Choice B is incorrect because, although the artist may be a threat to the social order, he is by no means an unnecessary one. The author, throughout the passage, is siding with the artist against the social order. Choice D is incorrect. See lines 10–12: "Therefore he takes . . . attempt to escape from life." A person who is attempting to escape from life hardly knows how to enjoy his life.

23. **(B)** Choice B is correct. The author ridicules Samuel Johnson, saying that that he is as much a true artist as a kazoo-player is a musician. He then says that if Johnson were alive today, he would be a Senator or a university president. The author thus implies that these positions do not merit high respect. Choice A is the opposite of Choice B. Therefore, Choice A is incorrect. Choice C is incorrect because, although the statement may be true, the author neither states nor implies that senators and university presidents are generally appreciative of the great literary classics. Choice D is incorrect. The fact that the author lumps Johnson, senators, and university presidents together as non-artistic people indicates that senators and university presidents do not have native writing ability. Choice E is incorrect for this reason: The author believes that Johnson lacked the qualities of an artist. Johnson, if alive today, would be a Senator or University president. We may conclude, then, that Senators and university presidents lack the qualities of an artist.

24. **(C)** Choice C is correct. Although a love of beauty is a quality we usually associate with artists, that idea about artists is never mentioned in the passage. All of the other characteristics are expressly mentioned in the first two paragraphs of the passage.

25. **(B)** Choice B is correct. The author's sincere sympathy is shown toward artists in lines 18–25: "From Dante to Tolstoy . . . actually fugitives from range and reprisal." There is no evidence in the passage to indicate that the author's attitude toward artists is Choice A, C, D or E. Therefore, these choices are incorrect.

26. **(D)** Choice D is correct. Beginning with line 12 ("Malignant tumors on the other hand . . ."), the passage is primarily concerned with the manner in which malignant tumors behave in the body. Choice A is incorrect because the definition of neoplasia is confined only to the first sentence: "Neoplasia . . . normal cells." Choice B is incorrect because the inhibition of tumor metastasis is discussed only in lines 22–30. Choice C does not occur and is not discussed in the passage. Therefore, Choice C is incorrect. Choice E is not discussed until line 35: "After malignant cells . . . most of the cells die." Therefore, Choice E is not correct.

27. **(C)** Choice C is correct. See lines 22–24: "Before metastasis can occur . . . surrounding normal tissue." Choice A is incorrect because the passage does not indicate that malignant cells shed their original membrane in order to acquire a new membrane. The passage simply states in lines 32–34: "The outer membrane . . . of normal cells." Choice B is incorrect because the passage nowhere states that malignant cells inhibit the lethal effects of the components of the blood." Choices D and E are incorrect because the passage does not indicate in any way what these two choices state.

28. **(E)** Choice E is correct. See lines 38–40: "Those cells which survive . . . small blood vessel." Although the passage does refer to Choices A, B, C, and D, none of these choices represents a characteristic of a malignant cell which most greatly enhances its metastatic potential. Therefore, these four choices are all incorrect.

29. **(C)** Choice C is correct. See lines 38–43: "The cells which survive . . . stickiness of the blood vessel wall." Choice A is incorrect because the passage does not indicate that benign tumors become malignant tumors. Choice B is incorrect. See lines 20–22: "This process . . . have been ascertained." Choice D is incorrect. See lines 32–34: "The outer membrane . . . of normal cells." Choice E is incorrect. See lines 50–52: ". . . it still must be stated . . . a mystery."

30. **(D)** Choice D is correct. First see lines 10–11: "Benign tumors . . . tissue of origin." Now see lines 12–14: "Malignant tumors . . . tissue of origin." Choice A is incorrect. See lines 10–12: "Benign tumors . . . are usually slow growing." We infer, therefore, that malignant cells are fast-growing. Choice B is incorrect. See lines 12–14: "Malignant tumors . . . tissue of origin . . ." Choice C is incorrect. See lines 32–34: "The outer membrane . . . of normal cells." Choice E is incorrect. See lines 16–20: "The characteristic . . . the original tumor."

31. **(A)** Choice A is correct. See **Sentence Completion Strategy 4.** The word "when" is a support indicator in this sentence. As we try each choice in the sentence we find that "frightening" is the only word that fits in this sentence. The fact that "the earth shifts with a sickening sway" reinforces the initial idea that "nature's brute strength is never more frightening."

32. **(D)** Choice D is correct. See **Sentence Completion Strategy 2.** Consider the first word of each choice. We can thus eliminate Choice (A) disdain because one doesn't "disdain" the incidence of crime—and we can eliminate Choice (B) revoke because one doesn't "revoke" the incidence of crime. Now consider the other three choices. Choice D with its two fill-in words "reduce" and "diverting" is the only choice that makes sense in the sentence.

33. **(D)** Choice D is correct. See **Sentence Completion Strategy 2.** Consider the first word of each choice. We can first eliminate Choice (A) gradual because the "gradual" musical accompaniment does not make sense—and we can eliminate Choice (E) chronic because the "chronic" musical accompaniment does not make sense. Now consider the other three choices. Choice D with its two fill-in words "superb" and "aura" is the only choice that makes sense in the sentence.

34. **(B)** Choice B is correct. See **Sentence Completion Strategy 4.** The first part of the sentence about her fine reputation as a celebrated actress is obviously in opposition to her appearance in a TV soap opera. Accordingly, the word "blemish" is the only possible choice.

35. **(C)** Choice C is correct. See **Sentence Completion Strategy 2.** First, let us examine the first words in each choice. We eliminate Choice B because one's manner does not "accept" his intention. We eliminate Choice D because one's manner does not "disregard" his intention. We eliminate Choice E because one's manner does not "animate" his intention. This leaves us with Choice A (revealed . . . eager) which does *not* make good sense, and Choice C (belied . . . drastic) which *does* make good sense.

36. **(D)** Choice D is correct. The peel is the outer covering of an orange. The rind is the outer covering of a melon. Also see **Analogy Strategy 5.** The word peel may be a noun or a verb. It is a noun in this analogy.
(**Part-Whole relationship**)

37. **(C)** Choice C is correct. A termite is an insect that feeds on wood in a destructive way. A weevil is a beetle (also an insect) that feeds on cotton in a destructive way. Note that, in Choice A, mold is a fungus growth that is destructive to bread. However, mold is not an insect. So Choice A is incorrect. See **Analogy Strategy 4.**
(**Action to Object relationship**)

38. **(B)** Choice B is correct. A key provides the answers for a test. A solution provides the answers for a puzzle. Note that "key" has a special meaning here as something that provides answers. See **Analogy Strategy 5.**
(**Purpose relationship**)

39. **(B)** Choice B is correct. To gorge means to eat greedily; to nibble means to eat slightly—that is, in small pieces. To quaff is to drink heartily; to sip is to drink bit by bit. We have here a Degree relationship. Choice (A) laugh : guffaw, would be correct if the two words were reversed. See **Analogy Strategy 3.**
(**Degree relationship**)

40. **(A)** Choice A is correct. A tidal wave may cause a flood. An earthquake may cause tremors.
(**Cause and Effect relationship**)

41. **(C)** Choice C is correct. The cry of a sheep is a bleat. The cry of a goose is a honk.
(**Association relationship**)

42. **(B)** Choice B is correct. A lobster has a shell. A kangaroo has a pouch. Choice (D) insect : wing is wrong because not all insects have wings. See **Analogy Strategy 4.** Choice (E) wool : sheep would be correct if the words were reversed. See **Analogy Strategy 3.**
(**Whole-Part relationship**)

43. **(D)** Choice D is correct. A person who is candid is *not* furtive. A person who is amicable is *not* unfriendly. We have an opposite relationship here. Choice (B) transparent : opaque and Choice (E) closed : ajar also express an opposite relationship. However, these two choices are incorrect because they do *not* refer to people. The capitalized words and the words of Choice D *do* refer to people. See **Analogy Strategy 4.**
(**Opposite relationship**)

44. **(C)** Choice C is correct. A run is a defect or damage in a stocking. A blemish is a defect or flaw on the skin—such as a pimple or blackhead. Also see **Analogy Strategy 5.** The word "run" may be a noun or a verb. It is a noun in this analogy. You might have selected Choice (D) thread : fabric which is a Part-Whole relationship just as RUN : STOCKING is. However we must include the idea of a defect or damage in the correct choice. Therefore, Choice D is incorrect.
(**Action to Object relationship** and **Part-Whole relationship**)

45. **(B)** Choice B is correct. A speaker uses a dais—which is on a higher level—so that he may be seen by the audience. An actor uses a stage—which is on a higher level—so that he may be seen by the audience.
(**Purpose relationship**)

EXPLANATORY ANSWERS FOR PRACTICE
TEST 3 (continued)

Section 2: Math Ability

> As you read these solutions, you are advised to do two things if you answered the Math question incorrectly:
>
> 1) When a specific Strategy is referred to in the solution, study that strategy, which you will find in "Using Critical Thinking Skills in Math Questions" (beginning on page 69).
>
> 2) When the solution directs you to the "Math Refresher" (beginning on page 205)—for example, Math Refresher #305—study the 305 Math principle to get a clear idea of the Math operation that was necessary for you to know in order to answer the question correctly.

1. **(D)** Choice D is correct. **(Use Strategy 2: Translate from words to algebra.)** Let $x = $ The amount of money Mr. Howard started with.

   Then
   $$x - 40 = 3(40)$$
   $$x - 40 = 120$$
   $$x = 160$$

   (Math Refresher #200 and #406)

2. **(C)** Choice C is correct.

   $$\begin{array}{r} N5 \\ \underline{LM} \\ 385 \\ \underline{385} \\ 4235 \end{array}$$

   (Use Strategy 17: Use the given information effectively.) From the given problem we see that

   $$N5 \times M = 385$$
   (Use Strategy 8: When all choices must be tested, start with E.)

   $$25 \times M = 385$$

   M must be greater than 10, which is incorrect.

   Try Choice D: $N = 3$

   $$35 \times M = 385$$

   M must be greater than 10, which is incorrect.

   Try Choice C: $N = 5$

   $$55 \times M = 385. \text{ Thus, } M = 7$$

   Therefore, L can be equal to 7 to give:

   $$\begin{array}{r} 55 \\ \times\ 77 \\ \hline 385 \\ \underline{385} \\ 4235 \end{array}$$

   Thus, Choice C is correct.

   (Logical Reasoning)

3. **(C)** Choice C is correct. **(Use Strategy 17: Use the given information effectively.)**

   $$\begin{array}{ll} \text{Given:} & 9^b = 81 \\ & (3^2)^b = (3)^4 \\ & 3^{2b} = 3^4 \\ & b = 2 \qquad \boxed{1} \end{array}$$

   We need: 3×3^b $\boxed{2}$

   Substituting $\boxed{1}$ into $\boxed{2}$, we get

   $$\begin{array}{l} 3 \times 3^2 = \\ 3 \times 9 = \\ 27 \end{array}$$

   (Math Refresher #429 and #431)

4. **(B)** Choice B is correct. **(Use Strategy 2: Know the definition of percent.)**

   $$\frac{54}{60} = \frac{P}{100}$$
   $$60P = 54 \times 100$$
   $$P = \frac{54 \times 100}{60}$$

(Use Strategy 19: Factor and reduce.)

$$P = \frac{\cancel{6} \times 9 \times \cancel{10} \times 10}{\cancel{6} \times \cancel{10}}$$
$$P = 90$$

(Math Refresher #120)

5. **(D)** Choice D is correct.

METHOD 1

Given: $2y + 4y + 6y = 2 + 4 + 6$
$$12y = 12$$
$$y = 1$$

METHOD 2

(Use Strategy 19: Factor and reduce.)

$$2y + 4y + 6y = 2 + 4 + 6$$
$$y(2 + 4 + 6) = 2 + 4 + 6$$
$$y = 1$$

(Math Refresher #406)

6. **(B)** Choice B is correct. **(Use Strategy 2: Translate from words to algebra.)** Let x = the number.

We are given: $3(50 + x) = 4 \times 5 \times 9$ ☐1

Divide ☐1 by 3. We get

$$\frac{\cancel{3}(50 + x)}{\cancel{3}} = \frac{4 \times 5 \times \cancel{3} \times \cancel{3}}{3}$$
$$50 + x = 60$$
$$x = 10$$

(Math Refresher #200 and #406)

7. **(E)** Choice E is correct. **(Use Strategy 11: Use new definitions carefully.)**

By definition, the hand of dial Y moves one number for each complete revolution of the hand of dial Z. ☐1

The hand of Dial Y must move 8 numbers to complete one of its own revolutions. Therefore it must move 24 numbers to complete 3 of its revolutions.

From ☐1 above, 24 numbers on dial Y correspond to 24 complete revolutions on dial Z.

(Logical Reasoning)

8. **(C)** Choice C is correct.

Given: $\dfrac{5r}{w} = \dfrac{15s}{x}$ ☐1

$$r = s$$ ☐2

(Use Strategy 13: Find unknown by multiplication.) Multiply ☐1 by wx. We get

$$\cancel{w}x\left(\frac{5r}{\cancel{w}}\right) = wx\left(\frac{15s}{x}\right)$$
$$5rx = 15s.$$ ☐3

Substitute ☐2 into ☐3. We get

$$5sx = 15sw$$ ☐4

(Use Strategy 13: Find unknowns by division)

Divide ☐4 by $5s$, we get

$$\frac{\cancel{5s}x}{\cancel{5s}} = \frac{15\cancel{s}w}{5\cancel{s}}$$
$$x = 3w$$

(Math Refresher #406)

9. **(A)** Choice A is correct. **(Use Strategy 2: Translate from words to algebra.)** Let x = additional pounds the elevator can hold.   ☐1

Given: Maximum total weight of elevator

plus passengers = 2300 pounds   ☐2
Empty weight of elevator = 1340 pounds   ☐3
Average weight of each of 6
passengers = 140 pounds   ☐4

From ☐4, we get
Total weight of 6 passengers = 6×140
pounds = 840 pounds   ☐5

(Use Strategy 3: The whole equals the sum of its parts.) We know:
Maximum total weight of elevator plus passengers =
Empty weight of elevator + weight of passengers + additional weight the elevator can hold   ☐6

Substituting ☐1, ☐2, ☐3 and ☐5 into ☐6, we get

$$2300 = 1340 + 840 + x$$
$$2300 = 2180 + x$$
$$120 \text{ pounds} = x$$

(Math Refresher #200 and #406)

10. **(D)** Choice D is correct.

Method 1:
By inspection, Choice D is the sum of two negatives which must be negative.

Method 2: **(Use Strategy 7: Try numerics to help find the answer.)**

Let $r = -1, s = -2$

(Use Strategy 8: When all choices must be tested, start with E.)

Choice E is $-r - s = -(-1) - (-2)$
$$= 1 + 2$$
$$= 3$$

Choice D is $r + s = -1 + -2 = -3$
Thus D is negative and the answer.

(Math Refresher #431)

11. **(A)** Choice A is correct. **(Use Strategy 17: Use the given information effectively.)** A segment that divides the area of a circle into two equal parts must be a diameter. Thus, segment RS must go through point O.

Since ROS is a diameter, then $RO = OS$, each segment being a radius.

Since R is the 2nd quadrant, S must be in the 4th quadrant.

The coordinates of S must each be the negative of the coordinates of R.

Thus, $S = (-1(-6), -1(8))$
$\qquad S = (6, -8)$

(Math Refresher #524 and #410)

12. **(B)** Choice B is correct. **(Use Strategy 17: Use the given information effectively.)**

Given: 6 rolls uses $\frac{1}{4}$ pound of powder $\qquad$ ①

$\qquad$ 6 rolls uses $2\frac{1}{2}$ quarts of water $\qquad$ ②

Number ② is not necessary to solve the problem!

We need to know how much powder is needed for the same mixture for 21 rolls. Let $x =$ number of pounds for 21 rolls. We set up a proportion:

$$\frac{6 \text{ rolls}}{\frac{1}{4} \text{ pound}} = \frac{21 \text{ rolls}}{x}$$

(Use Strategy 10: Know how to use units.)

$$(6 \text{ rolls})x = (21 \text{ rolls}) \times \left(\frac{1}{4} \text{ pound}\right)$$

$$6x = 21 \times \frac{1}{4} \text{ pound} \qquad ③$$

(Use Strategy 13: Find unknowns by multiplication.) Multiply ③ by $\frac{1}{6}$. We get

$$\frac{1}{6}(6x) = \frac{1}{6}\left(21 \times \frac{1}{4} \text{ pound}\right)$$

$$x = \frac{1}{6} \times 21 \times \frac{1}{4} \text{ pound}$$

$$x = \frac{21}{24} \text{ pound}$$

$$x = \frac{7}{8} \text{ of a pound.}$$

(Math Refresher #200, #120, and #406)

	First Place (6 points)	Second place (4 points)	Third Place (2 points)
Game 1			
Game 2		Bob	
Game 3			Bob

13. **(C)** Choice C is correct.

(Use Strategy 17: Use the given information effectively.) Carl can attain the *minimum* possible score by placing third in Game 1 and Game 2 and second in Game 3.

From the chart he would have 2, 2, and 4 points for each of these finishes.

Thus, minimum score $= 2 + 2 + 4$
$\qquad$ minimum score $= 8$ points

(Logical Reasoning)

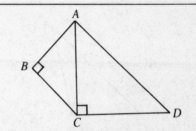

14. **(D)** Choice D is correct. **(Use Strategy 18: Remember the isosceles right triangle.)**

$\qquad$ *Given:* $\quad AB = BC \qquad$ ①
$\qquad\qquad\qquad\quad AC = CD \qquad$ ②

From ① we get that $\triangle ABC$ is an isosceles right triangle. Therefore, $\angle BAC$ and $\angle BCA$ are each 45 degree angles.

From ② we get that $\triangle ACD$ is an isosceles right triangle. Therefore, $\angle CAD$ and $\angle CDA$ are each 45 degree angles.

Thus, there are four 45 degree angles.

(Math Refresher #505 and #509)

15. **(B)** Choice B is correct. **(Use Strategy 2: Translate from words to algebra.)**

We know that:

$$\text{Area of rectangle} = \text{length} \times \text{width} \quad \boxed{1}$$

We are given: $\text{Area} = 4 \quad \boxed{2}$

$$\text{length} = \frac{4}{3} \quad \boxed{3}$$

Substituting $\boxed{2}$ and $\boxed{3}$ into $\boxed{1}$, we get

$$4 = \frac{4}{3} \times \text{width} \quad \boxed{4}$$

(Use Strategy 13: Find unknowns by multiplication.)

Multiply $\boxed{4}$ by $\frac{3}{4}$. We get

$$\frac{3(4)}{4} = \frac{3}{4}\left(\frac{4}{3} \times \text{width}\right)$$

$$3 = \text{width}$$

(Math Refresher #304 and #406)

_____

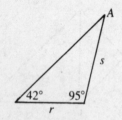

16. **(B)** Choice B is correct.

(Use Strategy 3: The whole equals the sum of its parts.)

We know that the sum of the angles of a triangle is $180°$.

Using the given triangle and substituting in $\boxed{1}$, we get

$$42 + 95 + A = 180$$
$$137 + A = 180$$
$$A = 43 \quad \boxed{2}$$

(Use Strategy 18: Know triangle inequality facts.)
We know that in a triangle, the larger side is opposite the larger angle. $\quad \boxed{3}$

Using $\boxed{2}$ and the given triangle, we apply $\boxed{3}$ and get $r > s$

(Math Refresher #406 and #505)

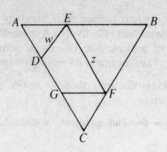

17. **(A)** Choice A is correct.

Since $\triangle ADE$ is equilateral, $AE = w$. $\quad \boxed{1}$
Since $\triangle EFB$ is equilateral, $EB = z$. $\quad \boxed{2}$

(Use Strategy 3: The whole equals the sum of its parts.)

Segment $AB = AE + EB \quad \boxed{3}$
Substituting $\boxed{1}$ and $\boxed{2}$ into $\boxed{3}$, we have
$$AB = w + z \quad \boxed{4}$$
Since $\triangle ABC$ is equilateral, $AB = BC = CA$. $\quad \boxed{5}$
Substitute $\boxed{4}$ into $\boxed{5}$. We have
$$AB = w + z; BC = w + z; CA = w + z. \quad \boxed{6}$$

(Use Strategy 13: Find unknowns by addition.)

Adding together all parts of $\boxed{6}$, we get
Perimeter of $\triangle ABC = AB + BC + CA =$
$w + z + w + z + w + z = 3w + 3z$

(Math Refresher #508)

18. **(D)** Choice D is correct. **(Use Strategy 8: When all choices must be tested, start with E.) (Use Strategy 12: Try not to make tedious calculations.)**

$$\text{Choice E is: } \frac{38.2 \times 70.9}{38}$$

38.2 is nearly equal to 38. We divide them out as if they were equal. The approximate value is 70.9. Definitely *not* close to 7.

$$\text{Choice D is: } \frac{.382 \times 70.9}{3.8} \quad \boxed{1}$$

$$3.8 = .38 \times 10 \quad \boxed{2}$$

Substitute $\boxed{2}$ into $\boxed{1}$. We get

$$\frac{.382 \times 70.9}{.38 \times 10} =$$

$$\frac{7.09 \times 10}{10} =$$

$$7 \approx$$

(Math Refresher #609 and #113)

19. **(A)** Choice A is correct.

$$Given: 3b + b = 0 \qquad \boxed{1}$$
$$\frac{a}{3} = b \qquad \boxed{2}$$

(Use Strategy 17: Use the information that is most useful.)

Solve $\boxed{1}$: $\quad 3b + b = 0$
$$4b = 0$$
$$b = 0 \qquad \boxed{3}$$

Substitute $\boxed{3}$ into $\boxed{2}$. We get

$$\frac{a}{3} = 0$$
$$a = 0$$

(Math Refresher #406)

20. **(B)** Choice B is correct. **(Use Strategy 17: Use the given information effectively.)** In order that the third Friday occur as early as possible, the first of the month must be on a Friday.

Thus, the Fridays will be the first, eighth, fifteenth, twenty-second, and twenty-ninth.

The third Friday is the fifteenth.

(Logical Reasoning)

21. **(D)** Choice D is correct. **(Use Strategy 3: The whole equals the sum of its parts.)**

$$\text{Volume of rectangular solid}$$
$$= \text{Volume of small compartment}$$
$$+ \text{Volume of larger compartment} \qquad \boxed{1}$$
$$\text{Area of rectangular dividing wall}$$
$$= l \times w$$
$$39\text{cm}^2 = 13\text{cm} \times w$$
$$3\text{cm} = w \qquad \boxed{2}$$

$\boxed{2}$ is the height of the rectangular solid as well.

$$\text{Volume of rectangular solid} = l \times w \times h$$
$$= 15\text{cm} \times 12\text{cm} \times h \qquad \boxed{3}$$

Substituting $\boxed{2}$ into $\boxed{3}$, we get

$$\text{Volume of rectangular solid} = 15\text{cm} \times 12\text{cm} \times 3\text{cm}$$
$$\text{Volume of rectangular solid} = 540\text{cm}^3 \qquad \boxed{4}$$

$$\text{Volume of small compartment}$$
$$= \text{Area of base} \times \text{height}$$
$$= \frac{1}{2} \times 12\text{cm} \times 5\text{cm} \times 3\text{cm} \qquad \boxed{5}$$
$$\text{Volume of small compartment} = 90\text{cm}^3$$

Substitute $\boxed{4}$ and $\boxed{5}$ into $\boxed{1}$. We get

$$540\text{cm}^3 = 90\text{cm}^3 + \text{Volume of larger compartment}$$
$$450\text{cm}^3 = \text{Volume of larger compartment}$$

(Math Refresher #312 and #306)

22. **(E)** Choice E is correct. **(Use Strategy 17: Use the given information effectively.)**

$$Given: x \qquad \boxed{1}$$
$$11 - x \qquad \boxed{2}$$
$$x - 4 \qquad \boxed{3}$$

as the lengths of the three sides of a triangle.

We know that the sum of any two sides of a triangle is greater than the third $\qquad \boxed{4}$

First, we use $\boxed{1} + \boxed{2} > \boxed{3}$. We have

$$x + 11 - x > x - 4$$
$$11 > x - 4$$
$$15 > x \qquad \boxed{5}$$

Next, we use $\boxed{2} + \boxed{3} > \boxed{1}$. We have

$$11 - x + x - 4 > x$$
$$7 > x \qquad \boxed{6}$$

To satisfy $\boxed{6}$ and $\boxed{5}$, we choose $\boxed{6}$.

$$7 > x, \text{ or, } x < 7 \text{ satisfies both} \qquad \boxed{7}$$

Finally, we use $\boxed{1} + \boxed{3} > \boxed{2}$. We have

$$x + x - 4 > 11 - x$$
$$2x - 4 > 11 - x$$
$$3x > 15$$
$$x > 5, \text{ or, } 5 < x \qquad \boxed{8}$$

(Use Strategy 6: Know how to manipulate inequalities.) Combining $\boxed{7}$ and $\boxed{8}$, we get

$$5 < x < 7$$

(Math Refresher #516, #419, and #420)

23. **(B)** Choice B is correct. **(Use Strategy 10: Know how to use units.)**

Given: radius of wheel $= .3$ of a yard ⬜1
Distance pedaled $= 2000$ yards ⬜2
Time of pedaling $= 1$ hour ⬜3

We now that:

1 complete revolution $=$ length of circumference of the wheel ⬜4

Circumference $= 2 \times \pi \times r$ ⬜5
Substituting ⬜1 into ⬜5, we get

$$C = 2 \times \pi \times .3 \text{ yard}$$
$$C = .6\pi \text{ yards}$$ ⬜6

Substituting ⬜6 into ⬜4, we have

$$1 \text{ revolution} = .6\pi \text{ yards}$$ ⬜7

We know that:

Number of revolutions per hour

$$= \frac{\text{Total distance traveled}}{\text{Length of 1 revolution}}$$ ⬜8

Substituting ⬜2 and ⬜7 into ⬜8, we get

Number of revolutions per hour $= \dfrac{2000 \text{ yards}}{.6\pi \text{ yards}}$ ⬜9

We need number of revolutions per minute.

Multiply ⬜9 by $\dfrac{1 \text{ hour}}{60 \text{ minutes}}$. We get

Number of revolutions per minute

$$= \left(\frac{2000}{.6\pi} \frac{\text{revolutions}}{\text{hour}}\right)\left(\frac{1 \text{ hour}}{60 \text{ minutes}}\right)$$
$$= \frac{2000 \text{ revolutions}}{.6\pi \times 60 \text{ minutes}}$$

(Use Strategy 19: Factor and reduce)

$$= \frac{2 \times 100 \times 10 \text{ revolutions}}{.6\pi \times 2 \times 3 \times 10 \text{ minute}}$$
$$= \frac{100 \text{ revolutions}}{1.8\pi \text{ minute}}$$ ⬜10

Multiply ⬜10 by $\dfrac{10}{10}$. We get

$$= \frac{1000 \text{ revolutions}}{18\pi \text{ minute}}$$
$$= \frac{500 \text{ revolutions}}{9\pi \text{ minute}}$$

(Math Refresher #310, #431 and #121)

24. **(A)** Choice A is correct. **(Use Strategy 11: Use new definitions carefully.)**

Given: $r \Diamond s = 4r - 3s$ ⬜1
Choice I: $4 \Diamond 3 = 7$ ⬜2

Using ⬜1 to evaluate ⬜2, we have

$$4 \Diamond 3 = 4(4) - 3(3)$$
$$= 16 - 9$$
$$= 7$$

Choice I is true.

Choice II: $(1 \Diamond 0) \Diamond 2 = 1 \Diamond (0 \Diamond 2)$ ⬜3
Using ⬜1 to evalue ⬜3, we have

$$(1 \Diamond 0) = 4(1) - 3(0) = 4 - 0 = 4$$ ⬜4
$$(0 \Diamond 2) = 4(0) - 3(2) = 0 - 6 = -6$$ ⬜5

Substitute ⬜4 and ⬜5 into ⬜3. We get
$$4 \Diamond 2 = 1 \Diamond -6$$ ⬜6
Using ⬜1 to evaluate both parts of ⬜6, we get

$$4 \Diamond 2 = 4(4) - 3(2) = \quad 16 - 6 = 10$$ ⬜7
$$1 \Diamond -6 = 4(1) - 3(-6) = 4 + 18 = 22$$ ⬜8

Since ⬜7 does not equal ⬜8, choice II is not true.

Choice III: $r \Diamond s = s \Diamond r$ ⬜9
Using ⬜1 to evaluate ⬜9, we have

$$r \Diamond s = 4r - 3s$$ ⬜10
$$s \Diamond r = 4s - 3r$$ ⬜11

(Use Strategy 7: Use numerics to help find the answer.)

Let $r = 1$, $s = 2$ ⬜12
Substitute ⬜12 into ⬜10 and ⬜11. We get ⬜13
$$r \Diamond s = 4(1) - 3(2) = 4 - 6 = -2$$
$$s \Diamond r = 4(2) - 3(1) = 8 - 3 = 5$$ ⬜14

Since ⬜13 does not equal ⬜14, ⬜9 is not always true. Thus, Choice III is not true.

From all of the above, only Choice I is true. Thus, Choice A is correct.

(Math Refresher #431)

25. **(E)** Choice E is correct.
(Use Strategy 14: Draw lines to help.)

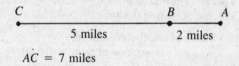

$AC = 7$ miles

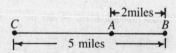

$AC = 5 - 2 = 3$ miles

Since both of the above diagrams meet the given conditions, there are two possible answers. Therefore, it cannot be determined from the information given.

(Logical Reasoning)

EXPLANATORY ANSWERS FOR PRACTICE TEST 3 (continued)

SECTION 3: STANDARD WRITTEN ENGLISH

> Section 3 does not count toward your SAT score. This Standard Written English section is used only for Freshman English placement when you get to college. However, you are advised to improve yourself in grammar and usage, and also in sentence structure. If you do well in the Standard Written English Test, you will be placed more advantageously in your college Freshman English class.

1. **(D)** ". . . requires me to solve a large *number* of problems." *Amount* is used to refer to things in bulk. *Number* is used to refer to things or people that can be counted.

2. **(E)** All underlined parts are correct.

3. **(C)** ". . . my brother . . . was not discouraged *in any way* . . ."
We cannot properly use the indefinite pronoun *any* to modify the adjective (*discouraged*). The adverbial phrase *in any way* should be used for this purpose.

4. **(A)** "*Since* a senator was aboard . . ."
Being that is always incorrect for *since* or *because*.

5. **(B)** "A mother . . . was rescued . . ."
The singular subject (*mother*) requires a singular subject (*was rescued*—not *were rescued*).

6. **(E)** All underlined parts are correct.

7. **(D)** ". . . his method was quite *different from* mine."
Different from is always the correct form; *different than* is always incorrect.

8. **(A)** "The school board members did *as* they were expected . . ."
The conjunction (*as*) should be used to introduce the dependent clause (*as they were expected to*)—not the preposition (*like*).

9. **(D)** ". . . but a security guard, a fireman, and *me*."
The preposition *but* is understood before *me*. Since *me* is the object of the preposition *but,* it has an objective form (*me*)—not a nominative form (*I*).

10. **(A)** "Having drunk . . . the lemonade . . ."
The past participle of *drink* is *having drunk*.

11. **(B)** ". . . to *whoever* . . . could present her . . ."
The subject of the dependent clause must have a nominative case form (*whoever*)—not an objective case form (*whomever*).

12. **(C)** ". . . they had brought *not nearly* the number . . ."
Do not use the expression *nowhere near* for *not nearly*.

13. **(E)** All underlined parts are correct.

14. **(A)** "*Because of* his not studying . . ."
Do not begin a sentence with the words *due to*. *Due* is an adjective. As an adjective, it must have a noun to modify.

15. **(C)** ". . . to buy the *kind of* car . . ."
Do not use the article *a* or *an* after *kind of, type of, sort of,* etc.

16. **(D)** ". . . compare their poems *with those of Robert Frost.*"
We have an improper ellipsis in the original sentence. The additional words (*those of*) are necessary to complete the meaning of the sentence.

17. **(A)** "I appreciate *your* offering . . ."
The subject of a gerund is in the possessive case. We, therefore, say *your offering*—not *you offering*.

18. **(B)** ". . . the *slower* of the two . . ."
Since we are here comparing two runners, we must use the comparative degree (*slower*)—not the superlative degree (*slowest*).

19. **(D)** ". . . between *him* and *me*."
The object of the preposition *between* must be an objective case form (*me*—not *I*).

20. **(E)** All underlined parts are correct.

21. **(A)** "The subject . . . was *we* . . ."
The predicate nominative form is *we*—not *us*.

22. **(B)** ". . . the prize would go to him . . ."
The object of the preposition *to* must be an objective case form (*him*—not *he*).

23. **(E)** All underlined parts are correct.

24. **(B)** ". . . if you *had gone* to *him* . . ."
In the "if clause" of a past contrary-to-fact condition, one must use the past perfect subjunctive form *had gone*—not the future perfect subjunctive form *would have gone*.

25. **(A)** The *child's* asking . . ."
The subject of a gerund is in the possessive case. We, therefore, say *child's asking*—not *child asking*.

26. **(D)** The expression "one another" refers to three or more; "each other" refers to two only. Therefore, Choices A and B are incorrect and Choice D is correct. Choice C is awkward. Choice E changes the meaning of the original sentence.

27. **(E)** The past contrary-to-fact conditional form is "had seen." Therefore, Choices A, B, C, and D are all incorrect. Choice E is correct. Moreover, Choice C has the wrong tense and the wrong tense sequence.

28. **(C)** A misplaced modifier may create a very embarrassing situation—so we can observe in the original sentence. We certainly don't want the fiancé wearing a sheer blouse. Such a blouse clearly belongs on the female. Choices A and D are, therefore, incorrect. Choice B is incorrect because it may appear that the concert is wearing the sheer blouse. Choice C is, of course, correct. Choice E is not acceptable because (1) the phrase "wearing a sheer blouse" is a "squinting" modifier, and (2) the sentence would be inappropriately poetic.

29. **(D)** We are looking for *balanced construction* in this question. Note that the correct Choice D gives us a balanced infinitive construction: "to advise," "(to) transmit", and "(to) supervise." None of the other choices offers this balanced construction.

30. **(A)** Choice A is correct. Choices B and C are incorrect because Frazier did not "own" the decision—it was rendered by the judges and the referee. Choice D is too roundabout. Choice E changes the meaning of the original sentence—and it is too roundabout.

31. **(B)** Avoid the double negative. Choices A and C suffer from the double negative fault. Choice B is correct. Choice D changes the meaning of the original sentence. Choice E creates a run-on sentence.

32. **(E)** The original sentence is interrogative. Accordingly, the sentence must end with a question mark. Choice E is correct.

33. **(D)** Choice A is incorrect because it creates a run-on sentence. Choice B fails to include the all-inclusive ("altogether," "completely," "entirely") idea of the original sentence. Choice C changes the meaning of the original sentence. Choice D is correct. Choice E changes the meaning of the original sentence.

34. **(B)** The adverb "yesterday" should, in this sentence, be placed before the modified verb ("arrested"). Therefore, Choices A and C are incorrect and Choice B is correct. Choices D and E are too roundabout.

35. **(E)** The singular historical present tense should be used here. Reasons: (1) a general truth is being expressed—this requires the present tense; (2) "womanhood" is singular. Also, the personal pronoun "it" must be used since its antecedent is "womanhood"—an abstract noun. Therefore Choice E is correct and all the other choices are incorrect.

36. **(C)** Choice A is out-of-date. Choice B does not give the meaning intended in the original sentence. Choice C is correct. Choice D is too wordy. Choice E changes the meaning of the original sentence.

37. **(C)** Choices A, B, D, and E are incorrect because each choice begins its own new sentence. Each of these choices, therefore, creates a run-on sentence. Choice C is correct.

38. **(A)** Choice A is correct. Choices B and E change the meaning of the original sentence. Choice C is incorrect grammatically because the verb ellipsis is improper— "the report *was* filed." Choice D is too involved.

39. **(E)** The expression "on account" in Choice A cannot be used as a subordinate conjunction. The expression "being that" in Choice B is always incorrect. Choice C changes the meaning of the original sentence. Choice D is too wordy. Choice E is correct.

40. **(E)** Choice A is too wordy. The double use of the preposition "from" in Choice B is incorrect. Choice C is too wordy. Choice D, as direct discourse, would be correct with the proper punctuation: . . . student, "Which country have you come from?" Choice E is correct.

41. **(E)** All underlined parts are correct.

42. **(D)** ". . . who are younger than *she*."
The nominative case (*she*—not *her*) must be used after the conjunction *than* when the pronoun is the subject of an elliptical clause ("than she is").

43. **(E)** All underlined parts are correct.

44. **(A)** "After he *had won* the marathon . . . he decided . . ."
The past perfect tense (*had won*)—not the past tense (*won*) is necessary when an action in the past has taken place *before* another action in the past.

45. **(C)** ". . . long a guiding *principle* of many educators . . ." *Principal* applies to a chief or the chief part of something. *Principle* applies to a basic law.

46. **(D)** ". . . played *beautifully* in the outfield."
The adverb (*beautifully*)—not the adjective (*beautiful*)—must be used to modify the verb (*played*).

47. **(C)** ". . . the Republicans will feel *its* effects . . ."
The possessive pronoun-adjective *its* does not have an apostrophe. There is another word *it's* which means *it is*.

48. **(A)** "If we *had begun* our vacation . . ."
The past perfect tense of *to begin* is *had begun*—not *had began*.

49. **(D)** ". . . which one is the *better* of the two?"
In comparing two persons or things, we use the comparative degree (*better*)—not the superlative degree (*best*).

50. **(B)** "All of the class presidents but Jerry, Alice, and *me* . . ."
The preposition (*but*) must take an object form (*me*)—not a subject form (*I*).

EXPLANATORY ANSWERS FOR PRACTICE TEST 3 (continued)

Section 4: Verbal Ability

1. **(C)** Choice C is correct. See **Antonym Strategy 3.** *Jubilation* means *rejoicing.* The opposite of *jubilation* is *sorrow.*

2. **(B)** Choice B is correct. *Obese* means *very fat.* The opposite of *obese* is *slender.*

3. **(D)** Choice D is correct. *Innocuous* means *harmless.* The opposite of *innocuous* is *injurious.*

4. **(E)** Choice E is correct. See **Antonym Strategies 1, 3.** *Remiss* means *negligent.* The opposite of *remiss* is *cautious.*

5. **(C)** Choice C is correct. *Candor* means *openness; frankness.* The opposite of *candor* is *deceitfulness.*

6. **(A)** Choice A is correct. *Chaste* means *clean; pure.* The opposite of *chaste* is *defiled.*

7. **(E)** Choice E is correct. See **Antonym Strategy 3.** *Succulent* means *juicy.* The opposite of *succulent* is *tasteless.*

8. **(A)** Choice A is correct. See **Antonym Strategy 3.** *Occult* means *hidden; secret; mysterious.* The opposite of *occult* is *exposed.*

9. **(D)** Choice D is correct. See **Antonym Strategies 1, 3.** *Intransigent* means *stubborn.* The opposite of *intransigent* is *amenable.*

10. **(C)** Choice C is correct. See **Antonym Strategies 1, 3.** *Recumbent* means *lying down.* The opposite of *recumbent* is *upright.*

11. **(C)** Choice C is correct. See **Sentence Completion Strategy 4.** Since the general "was like two sides of a coin," we have an Opposition indicator to guide us. It is not ordinary for a man who is fair to be a man of severity. Nor is it ordinary for a man who is candid to be a man of few words.

12. **(A)** Choice A is correct. See **Sentence Completion Strategy 2.**

    STEP 1 [ELIMINATION]
    We have eliminated Choices B and E because "agitation" and "intellect" do not make sense in the first blank.
    STEP 2 [REMAINING CHOICES]
    This leaves us with the remaining choices to be considered. The sentence *does not* make sense with the second word "minimal" of Choice C and the second word "whimsical" of Choice D. The sentence *does* make

sense with the words "skill" and "astute" (meaning "cunning") of Choice A.

13. **(D)** Choice D is correct. See **Sentence Completion Strategy 4.** The fact that her question was not so innocent as it seemed, gives us the idea that she is going to do something that is not innocent. This Opposition indicator leads us to Choice D: "She *deliberately* asked John . . ." because she had the ulterior motive of wanting to be asked by John to go to the Senior Prom with him.

14. **(E)** Choice E is correct. See **Sentence Completion Strategy 4.** "Internal dissension" is likely to have a negative effect on "affirmative action." We, accordingly, have an Opposition indicator. Therefore, we eliminate Choice (A) encourage, Choice (C) induce, and Choice (D) apply. This leaves us with Choice (B) complicate and Choice (E) delay. Choice (B) complicate . . . agreement, *does not* make sense. Choice (E) delay . . . upheaval, *does* make sense.

15. **(B)** Choice B is correct. See **Sentence Completion Strategy 2.** We can first eliminate Choice (A) suspicion . . . and Choice (D) sacrifice . . . because these first blank words do not make sense in the sentence. This leaves us with Choice (B) disagreement, Choice (C) discussion, and Choice (E) research. However, Choice (C) discussion . . . incidentally, and Choice (E) research . . . irrelevantly, *do not* make sense. Choice (B) disagreement . . . overwhelmingly, *does* make sense.

16. **(E)** Choice E is correct. A person who is characterized by imitation shows *no* individuality. A person who is characterized by debauchery shows *no* morality.
    (Association relationship and Opposite relationship)

17. **(C)** Choice C is correct. Odoriferous refers to a pleasant smell. Euphonious refers to a pleasant sound. Note that odoriferous and euphonious have positive connotations. Choices A, B, D, and E are incorrect because they have negative connotations. See **Analogy Strategy 4.**　　**(Association and Result relationship)**

18. **(E)** Choice E is correct. Something that is bland is *not* piquant. Something that is inane is *not* relevant.
    (Opposite relationship)

19. **(E)** Choice E is correct. A colt is a young horse. A lamb is a young sheep. Choice (A) bird: eaglet, is incorrect because *not* all young birds are eaglets. See **Analogy Strategy 4.** Choice (B) child: adult, would be correct if the words were reversed. See **Analogy Strategy 3.**　　**(Part-Whole relationship)**

20. **(E)** Choice E is correct. To stumble is to walk defectively. To stammer is to speak defectively. Note that, in Choice B, ogle is to look in a certain manner—but not defectively. So Choice B is incorrect. **(Action-Result relationship)**

21. **(A)** Choice A is correct. In baseball, a player scores a run. In soccer, a player scores a goal. The scores are made in order to win the game. You will note that in Choice (D) down : football, a player *makes* (not *scores*) a down. So Choice D is incorrect. See **Analogy Strategy 4.** **(Purpose relationship)**

22. **(A)** Choice A is correct. One sharpens a pencil for better use of the pencil. One hones a blade for better use of the blade. Note, however, that the better use comes about by *taking away* part of the pencil and the blade. Choice (C) wrap : package, Choice (D) polish : furniture, and Choice (E) stretch : canvas, also involve a better use. However, nothing is taken away from the package, the furniture, or the canvas in bringing about a better use of these items. See **Analogy Strategy 4.** **(Action to Object relationship)**

23. **(A)** Choice A is correct. A backlog holds up the flow of merchandise. A jam holds up the flow of traffic. We have here a Cause and Effect relationship. Choice (B) intermission : play, also indicates cause and effect but it does not have the *negative* quality of the cause and effect relationship of the pair of capitalized words and the Choice A words. So Choice B is incorrect. See **Analogy Strategy 4.** **(Cause and Effect relationship)**

24. **(D)** Choice D is correct. A musician is an individual member of an orchestra. A soldier is an individual member of an army. We have here a Whole-Part relationship. Note that Choice (A) museum : statue, and Choice (B) school : desk, are also whole-part relationships but these two choices involve inanimate objects while a musician and a soldier are human beings. See **Analogy Strategy 4.** **(Whole-Part relationship)**

25. **(C)** Choice C is correct. Sand, as a result of the wind, may form a dune. Snow, as a result of the wind, may form a bank. **(Action to Object and Part-Whole relationship)**

26. **(D)** The first paragraph indicates how many different elements go into the preparation and writing of a biography. Especially see lines 2–5: "Writing a biography . . . is only the beginning." The rest of the passage indicates how these elements are used by the biographer. Therefore, Choice D is correct. Choice A in incorrect because the use of minor characters is only one of the important points discussed in the passage. Choice B is incorrect because the passage does not discuss current trends as opposed to previous approaches, in writing a biography. Choice C is incorrect. It is obvious that a biographer should stress the main character, but such stress is not the main idea of the passage. Choice E is incorrect because getting the facts is not the central idea of the passage.

27. **(E)** Choice E is correct. See lines 5–7: "The sleuthing . . . interesting picture." Choice A is incorrect because there is no evidence in the passage to indicate that this statement is true. Choice B is incorrect. Giving the reader an imaginative or fictional version of events in the life of a person is not accepted in a work that is supposed to be biographical. Choice C is correct. An author who damages the reputation of another person merely on the basis of the author's opinion, may be sued for libel. Choice D is incorrect. See lines 24–26: ". . . a choice of biographical subjects . . . key for her or his generation."

28. **(A)** Choice A is correct. See lines 16–18: ". . . they (biographers) seem to be unanimous . . . massive accumulation of chronological data." A laundry list literally means a long list of several items that are to be washed. In this passage, a laundry list is meant to mean a list of several bits of information. Choice C is incorrect because it is not complete. Happenings in the lives of minor characters may also tie up with the behavior and actions of the main character. Choices B, D, and E are incorrect because the passage does not indicate that biographers recoil—that is, shrink back as in alarm—only from that which is expressed in each of these choices.

29. **(B)** Choice B is correct. See lines 1–4: "Slums and their population . . . whole operations of cities." Choice A is incorrect. See lines 10–15: "Our present urban renewal laws . . . method fails." Choice C is incorrect. See lines 28–32: "Conventional planning . . . impossibly superficial methods for doing so." Choice D is incorrect. See lines 32–39: "To overcome slums . . . far from what is done today." Choice E is incorrect. See lines 24–27: "Sometimes even . . . current or future ills."

30. **(D)** Choice D is correct. See lines 32–39: "To overcome slums . . . far from what is done today." Choice A is incorrect. See lines 28–32: "Conventional planning . . . for doing so." Choice B is incorrect. See lines 21–24: "Like Fight Blight . . . diddling with symptoms." Choice C is incorrect. See lines 10–15: "Our present urban renewal laws . . . method fails." Choice E is incorrect. See lines 12–15: ". . . wiping away slums . . . to lure back easier populations . . . The method fails."

31. **(C)** Choice C is *not* true according to the passage. Therefore it is a correct choice. See lines 32–39: "To overcome slums . . . far from what is done today." Choices A and B are true according to the passage—therefore, incorrect. See lines 10–15: "Our present urban renewal laws . . . method fails." Choice D is true according to the passage—therefore, incorrect. See lines 21–24: "Like Fight Blight . . . diddling with symptoms." Choice E is true according to the passage—therefore, incorrect. See lines 28–32: "Conventional planning . . . superficial means for doing so."

32. **(A)** Choice A is correct. Throughout the passage, the author is showing his disagreement in no uncertain terms with the manner in which the government is going about to improve the slum situation. For example:
Lines 10–15: "Our present urban renewal laws . . . this method fails."
Lines 21–24: "Like Fight Blight . . . diddling with symptoms."
Lines 28–32: "Conventional planning . . . impossible superficial means for doing so."
Lines 34–39: "We need to discern . . . far from what is done today."
Choices B, C, D, and E are incorrect because they do not correctly express the author's attitude.

33. **(E)** Choice E is correct. The first paragraph of the passage features the advantages of the new X-ray microscope. The second (final) paragraph discusses, for the most part, the function of platelets. Choices A, B, C, and D are all referred to in the passage but the passage is not primarily concerned with what each choice includes. Therefore, these choices are incorrect.

34. **(C)** Choice C is the correct answer. A dike is a bank or levee designed to prevent flooding. A famous poem, "The Leak in the Dike," a poem by Phoebe Cary, tells the story of a Dutch boy who saved his town from a disastrous flood by keeping his thumb, for several hours until help arrived, in a hole in the dike. See lines 21–28: "Platelets are . . . breaks in the injured vessels."

35. **(B)** Choice B is correct. See lines 5–8: "Although electron microscopes . . . capture an instant life." Choice A is incorrect. The platelet itself has no roots. It is the pseudopod projection of the platelet that has roots. Moreover, the passage does not tell what makes the platelet grow and expand. See lines 31–37: ". . . activated platelets send out projections . . . have roots deep inside." Choice C is incorrect. See lines 21–22: "Platelets are pancake-shaped . . . red blood cells." The platelets, then, are thin and flat. Nothing in the passage states that the red blood cells are thin and flat. Choice D is incorrect. See lines 11–13: "The new technique . . . before the destructive effects occur." Choice

E is incorrect. see lines 31–34: ". . . activated platelets . . . to block off blood flow." Accordingly, pseudopods, as projections, remain an organic part of the platelets.

36. **(D)** Choice D is correct. See lines 16–17: "The cry for freedom . . . birth of the New Man." Choice A is incorrect. Although the author may agree to what the choice says, he does not actually state or imply such. Choice B is incorrect because nowhere in the passage is Choice B stated or implied. Choice C is incorrect. See lines 26–27: "Afroamerican literature rejects the despair and cynicism; it is a literature of realistic hope and life-affirmation. Choice E is incorrect. See lines 36–37: ". . . life should not be a sedate waltz or foxtrot . . ."

37. **(A)** Choice A is correct. See lines 32–36: ". . . life should be vivacious, exuberant, wholesomely uninhibited . . . and man should be loving." Choice B is incorrect because nowhere does the passage indicate that Choice B is true. Choice C is incorrect. Although lines 35–36 state that "life should be passionately lived and man should be loving," these lines do not mean that people should demonstrate their passions in public whenever the urge is there. Choice D is incorrect. Nowhere does the passage recommend Choice D. Choice E is incorrect. Although lines 6–11 state "In Afroamerican literature . . . the rage of the oppressed," the passage does not state or imply that the ancestors of those who have been oppressed should be enraged.

38. **(D)** Choice D is correct. Let us consider each item.
Item I is incorrect because the passage nowhere expresses the need for *nonviolent* opposition to racism.
Item II is correct. See lines 42–46: "Black literature in America (Afroamerican literature) is . . . finding deep joy in humanity."
Item III is correct. See lines 31–36: "Afroamerican literature is a statement . . . and man should be loving."
Accordingly, only Choices II and III are correct. Therefore, Choice D is correct and Choices A, B, C, and E are incorrect.

39. **(B)** Choice B is correct. See lines 23–27: "Like the spirituals . . . realistic hope and life-affirmation." Choice A is incorrect. See lines 6–15: "In Afroamerican literature . . . the burden of protest." Although an indication of anger is present in the passage, it is not dominant. Moreover, nowhere in the passage is there evidence of vindictiveness. Choice C is incorrect because forgiveness and charity are not referred to in the passage. Choice D is incorrect. See lines 23–30: "Like the spirituals . . . goodness will prevail." Choice E is incorrect. Although the passage refers to *grief* in line 14 and also *cruelty* in line 38, grief and cruelty do not represent the tone of the passage.

40. **(E)** Choice E is correct. Many of the principles and ideas expressed in the passage were shared by Martin Luther King. For examples: Line 12: " . . . his target . . . American racism." Lines 16–18: "The cry for freedom . . . the New Unknown World." Lines 24–25: ". . . a passionate assertion that man will win his freedom." Choices A and B are incorrect. Washington would have some appeal to the author on the basis that Washington did seek and help to get freedom for the American colonies. Muhammad Ali also would have some appeal to the author because Ali did disagree with the government in regard to the draft issue on the basis of his religious belief. Also, Ali—a Black man—did get the respect of the entire world as the greatest pugilist. Yet the appeal of Martin Luther King included many more elements than the appeal of either Washington or Ali to the author.

Choices C and D are clearly incorrect. General Lee was obviously anti-Black since he headed the Confederate forces in the Civil War. President Reagan's policies are known to have been opposed by Black leaders generally.

EXPLANATORY ANSWERS FOR PRACTICE
TEST 3 (continued)

Section 5: Math Ability

1. **(C)** Choice C is correct.

$\left(\right.$**Use Strategy 5:**

$$\text{Average} = \frac{\text{Sum of values}}{\text{Total number of values}}.\left.\right)$$

Given: Average = -7 $\boxed{1}$
Values = $-13, -7, -9, -2, w$ $\boxed{2}$

Using $\boxed{1}$ and $\boxed{2}$, we get

$$-7 = \frac{-13 - 7 - 9 - 2 + w}{5} \qquad \boxed{3}$$

(Use Strategy 13: Find unknowns by multiplication.)

Multiply both sides of $\boxed{3}$ by 5. We have

$$5(-7) = \cancel{5}\left(\frac{-13 - 7 - 9 - 2 + w}{\cancel{5}}\right)$$
$$-35 = -13 - 7 - 9 - 2 + w$$
$$-35 = -31 + w$$
$$-4 = w$$

(Math Refresher #601 and #406)

2. **(D)** Choice D is correct.
(Use Strategy 12: Try not to make tedious calculations.)

Do *not* calculate the value of A and B individually.

(Use Strategy 13: Find unknowns by subtracting.)

Given: $A = 2 + \dfrac{2}{3} + \dfrac{2}{5} + \dfrac{2}{7} + \dfrac{2}{9}$ $\boxed{1}$

$B = 2 + \dfrac{2}{3} + \dfrac{2}{5} + \dfrac{2}{7}$ $\boxed{2}$

Subtract $\boxed{2}$ from $\boxed{1}$. We get

$$A - B = 2 + \frac{2}{3} + \frac{2}{5} + \frac{2}{7} + \frac{2}{9} - \left(2 + \frac{2}{3} + \frac{2}{5} + \frac{2}{7}\right)$$

$$A - B = \cancel{2} + \cancel{\frac{2}{3}} + \cancel{\frac{2}{5}} + \cancel{\frac{2}{7}} + \frac{2}{9} - \cancel{2} - \cancel{\frac{2}{3}} - \cancel{\frac{2}{5}} - \cancel{\frac{2}{7}}$$

$$A - B = \frac{2}{9}$$

(Math Refresher #109)

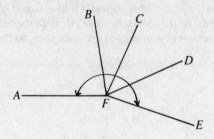

3. **(C)** Choice C is correct.

(Use Strategy 3: The whole equals the sum of its parts.)

We know:

$$\angle AFE = \angle AFB + \angle BFD + \angle DFE \qquad \boxed{1}$$

Given: $\angle CFE = 60°$ $\boxed{2}$
$\angle BFD = 50°$ $\boxed{3}$
$\angle AFB = 80°$ $\boxed{4}$
$\angle CFD = 20°$ $\boxed{5}$

We know: $\angle CFE = \angle CFD + \angle DFE$ $\boxed{6}$

Substituting $\boxed{2}$ and $\boxed{5}$ into $\boxed{6}$, we get
$$60° = 20° + \angle DFE$$
$$40° = \angle DFE \qquad \boxed{7}$$

Substituting $\boxed{3}$, $\boxed{4}$ and $\boxed{7}$ into $\boxed{1}$, we get
$$\angle AFE = 80° + 50° + 40°$$
$$\angle AFE = 170°$$

(Math Refresher #501 and #431)

4. **(C)** Choice C is correct.

(Use Strategy 17: Use the given information effectively.)

The only factors in choices I, II and III are $\dfrac{3}{4}$ and $\dfrac{4}{3}$.

$$\text{The product of } \frac{3}{4} \text{ and } \frac{4}{3} = 1$$

$$\text{Choice I} = \underbrace{\frac{3}{4} \times \frac{4}{3}}_{1} \times \underbrace{\frac{3}{4} \times \frac{4}{3}}_{1} \times \underbrace{\frac{3}{4}}_{\frac{3}{4}} =$$

$$\text{Choice I} = \frac{3}{4}$$

$$\text{Choice II} = \underbrace{\frac{3}{4} \times \frac{4}{3}}_{1} \times \underbrace{\frac{3}{4} \times \frac{4}{3}}_{1} \times \underbrace{\frac{3}{4} \times \frac{4}{3}}_{1} =$$

$$\text{Choice II} = 1$$

$$\text{Choice III} = \underbrace{\frac{3}{4} \times \frac{4}{3}}_{1} \times \underbrace{\frac{3}{4} \times \frac{4}{3}}_{1} \times \underbrace{\frac{3}{4} \times \frac{4}{3}}_{1} \times \underbrace{\frac{3}{4}}_{\frac{3}{4}} =$$

$$\text{Choice III} = \frac{3}{4}$$

(Math Refresher #111)

5. **(A)** Choice A is correct.

(Use Strategy 17: Use the given information effectively.)

(Use Strategy 19: Factor and reduce.)

$$\frac{4^2 + 4^2 + 4^2}{3^3 + 3^3 + 3^3} =$$

$$\frac{\cancel{3}(4^2)}{\cancel{3}(3^3)} =$$

$$\frac{16}{27}$$

(Math Refresher #429 and #431)

6. **(E)** Choice E is correct.

(Use Strategy 11: Use new definitions carefully.)

(Use Strategy 8: When all choices must be tested, start with E.)

$$\textit{Given:} \quad \textcircled{a}\,\textcircled{b} \quad = \frac{a + 1}{b - 1}$$

$$\text{Choice E:} \quad \textcircled{5}\,\textcircled{3} \quad = \frac{5 + 1}{3 - 1} = \frac{6}{2} = 3$$

Choice E is the only choice with $a > b$.

Therefore, it must be the largest.
The remaining choices are shown below.

$$\text{Choice D:} \quad \textcircled{4}\,\textcircled{5} \quad = \frac{4 + 1}{5 - 1} = \frac{5}{4} = 1\frac{1}{4}$$

$$\text{Choice C:} \quad \textcircled{3}\,\textcircled{5} \quad = \frac{3 + 1}{5 - 1} = \frac{4}{4} = 1$$

$$\text{Choice B:} \quad \textcircled{3}\,\textcircled{3} \quad = \frac{3 + 1}{3 - 1} = \frac{4}{2} = 2$$

$$\text{Choice A:} \quad \textcircled{2}\,\textcircled{3} \quad = \frac{2 + 1}{3 - 1} = \frac{3}{2} = 1\frac{1}{2}$$

(Math Refresher #431)

7. **(C)** Choice C is correct.

(Use Strategy 2: Translate from words to algebra.)

$$\textit{Given:} \quad \text{width} = w \qquad \boxed{1}$$
$$\text{length} = 4w \qquad \boxed{2}$$

Perimeter $= 2 \times \text{length} + 2 \times \text{width} \qquad \boxed{3}$

Substituting $\boxed{1}$ and $\boxed{2}$ into $\boxed{3}$, we get

Perimeter $= 2(4w) + 2(w)$
$= 8w + 2w$
Perimeter $= 10w$

(Math Refresher #304)

8. **(C)**   Choice C is correct.

$$Given: \quad \frac{a}{18} = \frac{2}{9} \qquad \boxed{1}$$

$$\frac{b}{28} = \frac{1}{7} \qquad \boxed{2}$$

(Use Strategy 13: Find unknowns by multiplication.)
Multiply $\boxed{1}$ by 18. We get

$$\cancel{18}\left(\frac{a}{\cancel{18}}\right) = 18\left(\frac{2}{9}\right)$$
$$a = 4$$

Multiply $\boxed{2}$ by 28. We get

$$\cancel{28}\left(\frac{b}{\cancel{28}}\right) = 28\left(\frac{1}{7}\right)$$
$$b = 4$$

(Math Refresher #406)

9. **(C)**   Choice C is correct.

Column A	Column B
$\frac{5}{4} + \frac{5}{7}$	$5\left(\frac{1}{4} + \frac{1}{7}\right) =$
	$\frac{5}{4} + \frac{5}{7}$

(Math Refresher #111)

10. **(A)**   Choice A is correct.

$$Given: \quad Y = \sqrt{64} + \sqrt{225}$$
$$Y = 8 + 15$$
$$Y = 23$$

(Math Refresher #431)

11. **(D)**   Choice D is correct.

Given: Darrin is older than Stephanie. $\boxed{1}$
Jimmy is older than Stephanie. $\boxed{2}$

(Use Strategy C: Use numerics if it appears that the answer cannot be determined.)

Let Darrin = 15, Jimmy = 13, Stephanie = 10
Darrin's age is greater than Jimmy's age.

Now, let Darrin = 15, Jimmy = 17, Stephanie = 10
Darrin's age is less than Jimmy's age.

Since two different results are possible, the answer cannot be determined.

(Math Refresher #431 and Logical Reasoning)

12. **(A)**   Choice A is correct.

By inspection, Choice A is the correct response.

(Place Value in Decimals)

13. **(C)**   Choice C is correct.

Column A	Column B
The number of positive integer factors of 11.	The number of positive integer factors of 23.

(Use Strategy 17: Use the given information effectively.)

Since both 11 and 23 are prime, they each have only 2 positive integer factors: 1 and themselves.

(Math Refresher #608)

14. **(B)**   Choice B is correct.

Method 1:   By inspection, it would appear that Column B is larger.

Method 2:

Column A	Column B
$1^8 + 3^8 =$	$4^8 =$
$1^8 + 3^8 =$	$(1 + 3)^8 =$
$1^8 + 3^8$	1^8 + positive middle terms + 3^8

(Use Strategy A: Cancel common terms from both columns.)

Obviously, Column B is larger.

(Math Refresher #429)

15. **(A)**   Choice A is correct.

$$Given: \quad x \text{ is an odd integer} \qquad \boxed{1}$$
$$y \text{ is an even integer} \qquad \boxed{2}$$

From $\boxed{1}$ we know that x^2 is odd $\boxed{3}$
From $\boxed{2}$ we know that y^2 is even $\boxed{4}$

Column A	Column B
The probability that x^2 is odd	The probability that y^2 is odd
From $\boxed{3}$, we see that Column A = 1	From $\boxed{4}$, we see that Column B = 0

(Math Refresher #603 and #605)

16. **(C)**   Choice C is correct.

Column A	Column B
$9 \cdot 8 \cdot 7 \cdot 6$	$54 \cdot 56$

(Use Strategy 19: Factor.)

$9 \cdot 8 \cdot 7 \cdot 6$	$9 \cdot 6 \cdot 7 \cdot 8$

Both columns contain identical factors!

(Factors of Multiplication)

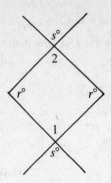

17. (B) Choice B is correct.

We know $\angle 1 = s°$ and $\angle 2 = s°$ because they are each pairs of vertical angles. ☐1

(Use Strategy 3: The whole equals the sum of its parts.)

We know: $360° = \angle 1 + r° + \angle 2 + r°$ ☐2

Substituting ☐1 into ☐2, we get

$$360° = s° + r° + s° + r°$$
$$360° = 2s° + 2r°$$ ☐3

(Use Strategy 13: Find unknowns by division.)

Divide ☐3 by 2. We get.

$$\frac{360°}{2} = \frac{2s° + 2r°}{2}$$
$$180 = s + r$$

Thus, the columns become:

Column A	Column B
175	180

(Math Refresher #503, #521, and #406)

18. (A) Choice A is correct.

Given: $y = (x - 3)(x + 4)$ ☐1

Column A	Column B
−3	The smallest value of ☐2
	x for which $y = 0$.

Substitute ☐2 into ☐1. We get

$$0 = (x - 3)(x + 4)$$
$$x = 3 \text{ or } x = -4$$

The columns become:

−3	−4

(Use Strategy 16: The obvious may be tricky!)

Column A is larger. With negative numbers the smaller the digit, the larger the value. −3 is larger than −4.

(Math Refresher #408)

19. (A) Choice A is correct.
(Use Strategy 2: Translate from words to algebra.)

Column A	Column B
1	The total surface area
	of a cube having edge
	0.4 ☐1

We know: Total surface area of cube = 6 (edge)² ☐2

Substituting ☐1 into ☐2, we get

1	Total surface area = $6(0.4)^2$
1	= 6(0.16)
1	= 0.96

(Math Refresher #313)

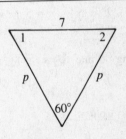

20. (C) Choice C is correct.

(Use Strategy 18: Know the equilateral and isosceles triangles.)

Since the triangle has 2 equal sides, the angles opposite these sides are equal. Thus,
$$\angle 1 = \angle 2$$ ☐1

(Use Strategy 3: The whole equals the sum of its parts.)
We know that the sum of the angles of a triangle = 180°

Thus, $\angle 1 + \angle 2 + 60° = 180°$ ☐2

Substituting ☐1 into ☐2, we get

$$\angle 1 + \angle 1 + 60° = 180°$$
$$2(\angle 1) + 60 = 180°$$
$$2(\angle 1) = 120°$$
$$\angle 1 = 60°$$ ☐3

Substituting ☐3 into ☐1, we have
$$\angle 1 = \angle 2 = 60°$$

Thus, all three angles each = 60° and the triangle is equilateral.
Therefore all three sides are equal. ☐4

From ☐4 and the diagram, we get $p = 7$. ☐5

Column A	Column B
21	3p ☐6

Substituting ☐5 into ☐6, we get

21	$3p =$
	$3(7) =$
21	21

(Math Refresher #507, #508, and #505)

21. **(D)** Choice D is correct.

$$a + b + 2c = 10 \quad \boxed{1}$$
$$b = 2c \quad \boxed{2}$$

Substituting $\boxed{2}$ into $\boxed{1}$, we get

$$a + b + b = 10$$
$$a + 2b = 10$$
$$2b = 10 - a$$
$$b = 5 - \frac{a}{2} \quad \boxed{3}$$

(Use Strategy C: Try numerics if it appears that the answer cannot be determined.)

Let $a = 2$. $\quad \boxed{4}$
Substituting $\boxed{4}$ into $\boxed{3}$, we get

$$b = 5 - \frac{2}{2} = 5 - 1 = 4$$

Let $a = 0$. $\quad \boxed{5}$
Substituting $\boxed{5}$ into $\boxed{3}$, we get

$$b = 5 - \frac{0}{2} = 5 - 0 = 5$$

Column A	Column B
b	5

Since two different answers are possible, the answer cannot be determined.

(Math Refresher #406 and #431)

22. **(B)** Choice B is correct.

Column A	Column B
$\dfrac{7}{8}$	$\dfrac{8}{9}$

(Use Strategy D: Compare the fractions by multiplying by a positive quantity.)

Multiply both columns by 72, which is the product of both denominators.

$$72\left(\frac{7}{8}\right) = \qquad\qquad 72\left(\frac{8}{9}\right) =$$
$$63 \qquad\qquad\qquad 64$$

(Math Refresher #126)

23. **(C)** Choice C is correct.

(Use Strategy 11: Use new definitions carefully.)

Given: $x \triangle y = y^4 \quad \boxed{1}$

Column A	Column B
$7 \triangle a$	$5 \triangle a$

Using $\boxed{1}$, we get

$$7 \triangle a = a^4 \qquad\qquad 5 \triangle = a^4$$

(Math Refresher #431)

24. **(D)** Choice D is correct.

Column A	Column B
$\sqrt{x^4 + 6x^2 + 9} =$	$x^2 + 3x + 3$
$\sqrt{(x^2 + 3)^2} =$	
$x^2 + 3$	$x^2 + 3x + 3$

(Use Strategy A: Cancel equal things from both columns by subtracting.)

Subtract $(x^2 + 3)$ from both columns. They become

$$0 \qquad\qquad\qquad 3x$$

(Use Strategy C: Use numerics if it appears that the answer cannot be determined.)

Let $x = -1$. The columns become
$$0 \qquad\qquad 3(-1) = -3 \quad \boxed{1}$$
Let $x = 1$. The columns become
$$0 \qquad\qquad 3(1) = 3 \quad \boxed{2}$$

From $\boxed{1}$ and $\boxed{2}$ we see that two different relationships are possible. Thus, the answer cannot be determined.

(Math Refresher #430 and #409)

25. **(C)** Choice C is correct.

(Use Strategy 10: Know how to use units.)

Given: 1 inch = 3 miles $\quad \boxed{1}$
Squaring $\boxed{1}$, we get
$$1 \text{ square inch} = 9 \text{ square miles} \quad \boxed{2}$$

(Use Strategy 13: Find unknowns by multiplication.)

Multiply $\boxed{2}$ by 17. We get

$$17 (1 \text{ square inch}) = 17(9 \text{ square miles})$$
$$17 \text{ square inches} = 153 \text{ square miles} \quad \boxed{3}$$

Column A	Column B
The area represented by 17 square inches on this map	153 square miles

From $\boxed{3}$, we see that the columns are equal.

(Math Refresher #121)

26. **(D)** Choice D is correct.

Column A	Column B
Area of parallelogram with a diagonal of length 6.	Area of square with a diagonal of length 6.

(Use Strategy 14: Draw lines to help solve the problem.)

Below is a square with a diagonal of length 6.

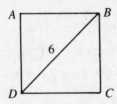

Below is a parallelogram *BEDF* with a diagonal of length 6, inside the square from above. □1

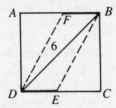

Below is square *ABCD* inside parallelogram *BEDF*, with a diagonal of length 6. □2

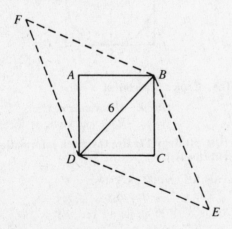

From □1 it must be true that

$$\left.\begin{array}{l}\text{Area of parallelogram}\\ \textit{BEDF} \text{ with diagonal}\\ \text{of length 6}\end{array}\right\} < \left\{\begin{array}{l}\text{Area of square}\\ \textit{ABCD} \text{ with a}\\ \text{diagonal of length 6.}\end{array}\right.$$

From □2 it must be true that

$$\left.\begin{array}{l}\text{Area of square } \textit{ABCD}\\ \text{with a diagonal of}\\ \text{length 6}\end{array}\right\} < \left\{\begin{array}{l}\text{Area of parallelogram}\\ \textit{BEDF} \text{ with a diagonal}\\ \text{of length 6.}\end{array}\right.$$

Since two different relationships between the columns are possible, the answer cannot be determined.

(Math Refresher #305 and #303)

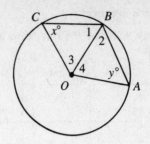

27. **(A)** Choice A is correct.

$$\text{Given:} \quad O \text{ is the center of the circle} \quad \boxed{1}$$
$$x < y \quad \boxed{2}$$

From □1 we know that *OC*, *OB* and *OA* are radii and $OC = OB = OA$ □3

(Use Strategy 18: Remember the isosceles triangle.)

From □3 we know:

$$\text{In } \triangle COB, \angle 1 = x° \quad \boxed{4}$$
$$\text{In } \triangle BOA, \angle 2 = y° \quad \boxed{5}$$

(Use Strategy 3: The whole equals the sum of its parts.)

We know that the sum of angles of a triangle = 180°. □6

Using □6 in $\triangle COB$, we get

$$\angle 1 + x° + \angle 3 = 180° \quad \boxed{7}$$

Substituting □4 into □7, we get

$$x° + x° + \angle 3 = 180°$$
$$2x° + \angle 3 = 180°$$
$$\angle 3 = 180° - 2x° \quad \boxed{8}$$

Using □6 in $\triangle BOA$, we get

$$\angle 2 + y° + \angle 4 = 180° \quad \boxed{9}$$

Substituting □5 into □9, we get

$$y° + y° + \angle 4 = 180°$$
$$2y° + \angle 4 = 180°$$
$$\angle 4 = 180° - 2y° \quad \boxed{10}$$

Multiply □2 by 2. We get $2x < 2y$ □11

(Use Strategy 6: Know how to manipulate inequalities.)

From □11, we know that

$$180 - 2x > 180 - 2y \quad \boxed{12}$$

Substituting □8 and □10 into □12, we get $\angle 3 > \angle 4$ □13

Using □1 and □13, we know that
$$\text{Segment } CB > \text{Segment } BA$$

(Math Refresher #524, #507, #505, and #420)

28. (B) Choice B is correct.

(Use Strategy 9: Know the rate, time and distance relationship.)

We know:

	Rate ×	Time =	Distance
Plane A			
Plane B			

Given: A's rate $= 500$ km/h ☐1
B's rate $= 600$ km/h ☐2
Let A's time $= T$ ☐3
Then B's time $= T - 8$ ☐4

Substituting ☐1, ☐2, ☐3 and ☐4 into the chart we get

	Rate ×	Time =	Distance	
Plane A	500	T	500 T	☐5
Plane B	600	T − 8	600(T − 8)	☐6

Since both planes cover the same distance we know the distances from ☐5 and ☐6 are equal.

Thus, $500T = 600 (T - 8)$
$$500T = 600T - 4800$$
$$-100T = -4800$$
$$T = 48 \qquad ☐7$$

(Use Strategy 16: The obvious may be tricky!)

Choice A is 48, but this is *not correct*!

The question asks for the number of hours plane B travels.

Using ☐7 and ☐4, we have

$$B\text{'s Time} = T - 8$$
$$= 48 - 8$$
$$= 40$$

(Math Refresher #201, #202, and #406)

29. (C) Choice C is correct.

(Use Strategy 2: Translate from words to algebra.)

Let x
$=$ amount of money the woman started with ☐1
Then:
$\frac{5}{12}x =$ amount of money her son received ☐2

$\frac{1}{36}x =$ amount of money each of her 6 daughters received ☐3

$\frac{1}{18}x =$ amount of money divided among her 6 nephews ☐4

Let
C $=$ amount remaining for charity ☐5

(Use Strategy 3: The whole equals the sum of its parts.)

Using ☐1, ☐2, ☐3, ☐4 and ☐5, we have

$$x = \frac{5}{12}x + 6\left(\frac{1}{36}x\right) + \frac{1}{18}x + C$$
$$x = \frac{5}{12}x + \frac{1}{6}x + \frac{1}{18}x + C \qquad ☐6$$

(Use Strategy 13: Find unknowns by multiplication.)

Multiply ☐6 by 36. We get

$$36(x) = 36\left(\frac{5}{12}x\right) + 36\left(\frac{1}{6}x\right) + 36\left(\frac{1}{18}x\right) + 36C$$
$$36x = 15x + 6x + 2x + 36C$$
$$36x = 23x + 36C$$
$$13x = 36C$$
$$\frac{13}{36}x = C$$

Thus charity receives $\frac{13}{36}$ of the woman's original amount of money.

(Math Refresher #200 and #406)

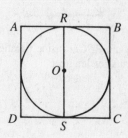

30. (E) Choice E is correct.

Given: O is center of circle ☐1
Radius of circle $= w$ ☐2

(Use Strategy 17: Use the given information effectively.)

From ☐1 and ☐2 we know:

$$OR = w, OS = w \qquad ☐3$$
From ☐3 we get $RS = 2w$ ☐4

Since $ABCD$ is a square, we know that
$$AB = BC = CD = DA \qquad ☐5$$

From the given and the diagram we know that
$$RS = BC = AD \qquad ☐6$$

Using ☐4, ☐5 and ☐6, we get
$$AB = BC = CD = DA = 2w \qquad ☐7$$

We know that Perimeter of a square $=$ sum of all four sides ☐8

Substituting ☐7 and ☐8, we get

$$\text{Perimeter of } ABCD = 2w + 2w + 2w + 2w$$
$$\text{Perimeter of } ABCD = 8w$$

(Math Refresher #303 and #524)

31. **(C)** Choice C is correct.

(Use Strategy 17: Use the given information effectively.)

Given: 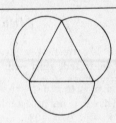 ⓵

In order for a given figure to have been formed from ⓵, it must have the same number of shaded and unshaded squares.

Choice I has 8 unshaded and 6 shaded squares. Thus, it could <u>not</u> be formed from ⓵.

Choice II has 5 unshaded and 6 shaded squares. Thus, it could <u>not</u> be formed from ⓵.

Looking at Choices A through E, it must be Choice C: III only. **(Logical Reasoning)**

32. **(C)** Choice C is correct.

(Use Strategy 11: Use new definitions carefully.)

By definition, $A = 12345$ ⓵
$B = 98765$ ⓶

(Use Strategy 13: Find unknowns by subtracting.)

Subtracting ⓵ from ⓶, we get

$B - A = 98765 - 12345$
$B - A = 86420$ **(Logical Reasoning)**

33. **(D)** Choice D is correct.

Given: $r = 7a$ ⓵
$5w = 7a$ ⓶

From ⓶ we get $w = \dfrac{7a}{5}$ ⓷

(Use Strategy 13: Find unknowns by subtracting.)

Subtract ⓷ from ⓵. We get

$r - w = 7a - \dfrac{7}{5}a$

$= \dfrac{35a}{5} - \dfrac{7}{5}a$

$r - w = \dfrac{28a}{5}$

(Math Refresher #406)

34. **(D)** Choice D is correct.

$\Bigg($ **Use Strategy 5:**

$$\textbf{Average} = \frac{\textbf{Sum of the values}}{\textbf{Total number of values}}\Bigg)$$

Let x = Total number of students ⓵
Then ⓶
$.40x$ = Number of students scoring 100 ⓷
$.10x$ = Number of students scoring 80 ⓸
y = Average score of remaining students

We know the whole class is 100%. ⓹

From ⓶ and ⓷ we know: 40% + 10% = 50% have been accounted for. ⓺

(Use Strategy 3: The whole equals the sum of its parts.)

Subtracting ⓺ from ⓹, we get
remaining students represent 50% of the class. ⓻
Using ⓻ and ⓵, we get
Number of remaining students = $.5x$ ⓼
We know

$$\text{Average} = \frac{\text{Sum of the values}}{\text{Total number of values}}$$ ⓽

Given: Average = 90 ⓾

Substituting ⓵, ⓶, ⓷, ⓸, ⓼ and ⓾ into ⓽, we get

$$90 = \frac{.40x(100) + .10x(80) + .5x(y)}{x}$$ ⑪

Multiply ⑪ by x. We get

$90x = 40x + 8x + .5xy$
$90x = 48x + .5xy$
$42x = .5xy$
$42 = .5y$
$84 = y$

(Math Refresher # 601, #114, and #406)

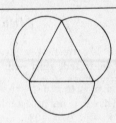

35. **(C)** Choice C is correct.

(Use Strategy 3: The whole equals the sum of its parts.)

Total area = Area of triangle + 3(area of semicircle) ⓵
Given: Radius of each semicircle = 2 ⓶
From ⓶ we know each diameter = 4
Thus, the triangle has three equal sides of length 4 and is equilateral ⓷

We know: Area of equilateral triangle = $\dfrac{S^2\sqrt{3}}{4}$ ⓸

Area of semicircle = $\dfrac{\pi r^2}{2}$ ⓹

Substituting ⓸ and ⓹ into ⓵, we get

$$\text{Total area} = \frac{S^2\sqrt{3}}{4} + 3\left(\frac{\pi r^2}{2}\right)$$ ⓺

Substituting ⓶ and ⓷ into ⓺, we get

$$\text{Total area} = \frac{4^2\sqrt{3}}{4} + 3\left(\frac{\pi(2)^2}{2}\right)$$

$$= \frac{16\sqrt{3}}{4} + 3\left(\frac{4\pi}{2}\right)$$

$$\text{Total area} = 4\sqrt{3} + 6\pi$$

(Math Refresher #308, #310, and #311)

EXPLANATORY ANSWERS FOR
PRACTICE TEST 3 (continued)

Section 6: Math Ability

1. **(D)** Choice D is correct.

$$\text{Given: } \frac{81 \times y}{27} = 21$$

Multiply both sides by 27 to get
$81 \times y = 21 \times 27$

$$y = \frac{27 \times 21}{81}$$

(Use Strategy 19: Factor and reduce.)

$$y = \frac{3 \cdot 7 \times 3 \cdot \cancel{9}}{9 \cdot \cancel{9}}$$

$$= \frac{\cancel{3} \cdot 7 \times \cancel{3}}{\cancel{3} \cdot \cancel{3}}$$

$$y = 7$$

(Math Refresher #406)

2. **(D)** Choice D is correct. **(Use Strategy 8: When all choices must be tested, start with E.)**

Choice E, $3 \times 5 \times 9 = 135$
$135 > 120$. Thus E is not acceptable
Choice D, $3 \times 4 \times 9 = 108$
(Use Strategy 15: Know how to eliminate certain choices.) Choices A and B are easily eliminated, since $3 \times 4 \times 5$ and $3 \times 4 \times 7$ each have 2 identical elements to D, but their 3rd element is less.

Choice C, $2 \times 5 \times 13 = 130$
$130 > 120$

Thus, Choice D is correct.

(Math Refresher #431)

3. **(E)** Choice E is correct. We are told

$$w + z = x + y \qquad \boxed{1}$$

(Use Strategy 13: Find unknowns by subtracting.)

Subtracting x from both sides of $\boxed{1}$

$$w + z - x = y \qquad \boxed{2}$$

Subtracting z from both sides of $\boxed{2}$

$$w - x = y - z$$

Thus, Choice E is the correct answer.

(Math Refresher #406)

4. **(B)** Choice B is correct. Since $DC \perp AC$, $\angle DCB$ is a right angle and has a measure of 90°. **(Use Strategy 3: The whole equals the sum of its parts.)** Since the sum of the angles of a $\triangle$ is 180° we have

$$\angle DBC + 90 + 20 = 180$$
$$\angle DBC = 70 \qquad \boxed{1}$$

Since $EB \perp BD$, $\angle DBE$ is a right angle and has a measure of 90° $\qquad \boxed{2}$
(Use Strategy 3: The whole equals the sum of its parts.) The whole straight $\angle ABC$ is $=$ to the sum of its parts. Thus

$$\angle DBC + \angle DBE + x = 180 \qquad \boxed{3}$$

Substituting $\boxed{1}$ and $\boxed{2}$ into $\boxed{3}$ we have

$$70 + 90 + x = 180$$
$$x = 20$$

(Math Refresher #501, #505, #406, and #431)

5. **(B)** Choice B is correct. We are given that

Volume of 1 brick = 40 cubic inches $\qquad \boxed{1}$
Volume of the final pile
  of bricks = 8000 cubic inches $\qquad \boxed{2}$

(Use Strategy 3: The whole equals the sum of its parts.) Logically, we know the number of layers in the final pile of bricks

$$= \frac{\text{Volume of the final pile of bricks}}{\text{Volume of each layer of bricks}} \qquad \boxed{3}$$

From the diagram in the question, we see that

1 layer of bricks = 40 bricks $\qquad \boxed{4}$

Thus, by using $\boxed{1}$ and $\boxed{4}$, we know that the volume of each layer of bricks

$=$ volume of 1 brick
  $\times$ number of bricks in 1 layer
$=$ 40 cubic inches $\times$ 40
$=$ 1600 cubic inches $\qquad \boxed{5}$

Substituting $\boxed{2}$ and $\boxed{5}$ into $\boxed{3}$,
the number of layers in the final pile of bricks

$$= \frac{8000 \text{ cubic inches}}{1600 \text{ cubic inches}}$$

(Use Strategy 19: Factor and reduce.)

$$= \frac{8 \times 1000}{16 \times 100}$$

$$= \frac{\cancel{8} \times 10 \times \cancel{100}}{\cancel{8} \times 2 \times \cancel{100}}$$

$$= \frac{10}{2} = 5$$

(Math Refresher #200 and #601)

6. **(D)** Choice D is correct.
Method 1: Remember that
1. The sum of two odd numbers is even.
2. The sum, difference, and product of two even numbers is even.
3. The product of two odd number is odd.

   Given: a is odd, b is odd, c is even. Therefore, $a + b$ is even.

$$(a + b) - c \text{ is even.}$$

Method 2: Choose a numerical example.
(Use Strategy 7: Use number examples.)
Let $a = 3$, $b = 5$, and $c = 4$
(Use Strategy 8: When all choices must be tested, start with choice E.)
Then choice E $(a + bc) = 23$
Therefore, choice E is odd.
Choice D $(a + b) - c = 4$
Therefore, choice D is even.

(Math Refresher #603, #604, #605, and #431)

7. **(B)** Choice B is correct. By trial and error, it is easily seen that Choice B is correct.

(Math Refresher #431)

8. **(A)** Choice A is correct. **(Use Strategy 2: Translate from words to algebra.)**
Let x = actual height of the flagpole (in feet)
Since both the lighthouse and the flagpole are seen from the same distance, then

$$\frac{\text{Actual height of the lighthouse}}{\text{Apparent height of the lighthouse}} =$$

$$\frac{\text{Actual height of the flagpole}}{\text{Apparent height of the flagpole}}$$

$$\frac{60 \text{ feet}}{5 \text{ inches}} = \frac{x}{1\frac{2}{3} \text{ inches}}$$

(Use Strategy 10: Know how to use units of distance.)

$$\frac{60 \text{ feet}}{5 \text{ inches}} = \frac{x}{\frac{5}{3} \text{ inches}}$$

$$60 \text{ feet} \times \frac{5}{3} = 5x$$

(Use Strategy 19: Factor and reduce.)

$$(20 \times 3) \text{ feet} \times \frac{5}{3} = 5x$$

$$\frac{20 \text{ feet} \times 5}{5} = \frac{5x}{5}$$

$$20 \text{ feet} = x$$

(Math Refresher #200, #120 and #121)

9. **(A)** Choice A is correct. **(Use Strategy 17: Use the given information effectively.)**

$$\text{Given: } a = 10b \qquad \boxed{1}$$
$$b = 2c \qquad \boxed{2}$$

Substituting $\boxed{2}$ into $\boxed{1}$

$$a = 20c$$

$$\text{or } \frac{a}{20} = c \ (\textit{Answer})$$

(Math Refresher #406)

10. **(C)** Choice C is correct. **(Use Strategy 11: Use new definitions carefully.)**

The first few 3-digit numbers are 100, 101, 102, 103, 104, etc.

Clearly, the smallest possible 3-digit number in which no digit is repeated is $x = 102$

From the definition of y, y must be $y = 210$

Thus, $y - x =$

$$210 - 102 =$$
$$108$$

(Logical Reasoning)

11. **(B)** Choice B is correct. **(Use Strategy 4: Remember the classic expressions.)**

Method 1:
Remember $(a - b)^2 = a^2 - 2ab + b^2$

$$\text{Given: } 16x^2 - 8x + 1 =$$
$$(4x - 1)^2 \qquad \boxed{1}$$

Substitute $x = \frac{1}{4}$ into $\boxed{1}$. We get

$$\left(4\left(\frac{1}{4}\right) - 1\right)^2 = (1 - 1)^2 = 0$$

(Use Strategy 17: Use the given information effectively.)

Method 2:

$$\text{Given: } 16x^2 - 8x + 1 \qquad \boxed{1}$$

Substitute $x = \frac{1}{4}$ into $\boxed{1}$. We get

$$16\left(\frac{1}{4}\right)^2 - 8\left(\frac{1}{4}\right) + 1 =$$

$$16\left(\frac{1}{16}\right) - 8\left(\frac{1}{4}\right) + 1 =$$

$$1 - 2 + 1 = 0$$

(Math Refresher #409 and #431)

12. **(E)** Choice E is correct.

Method 1:

$$\text{Given: } \frac{5}{6}x^2 - \frac{10}{12}x^2 = 0$$

(Use Strategy 13: Find unknowns by multiplying.)

Multiply both sides by $\frac{6}{5}$,

$$x^2 - x^2 = 0$$

Clearly this is true for all values of x. **(Use Strategy 17: Use the given information effectively.)**

Method 2:

$$\text{Given: } \frac{5}{6}x^2 - \frac{10}{12}x^2 = 0$$

Reduce $\frac{10}{12}$ to $\frac{5}{6}$

$$\frac{5}{6}x^2 - \frac{5}{6}x^2 = 0$$

$$0 = 0$$

All real values are solutions

Method 3:

$$\text{Given } \frac{5}{6}x^2 - \frac{10}{12}x^2 = 0$$

(Use Strategy 13: Find unknowns by multiplying.)
Multiply both sides by 12 (the common denominator)

$$10x^2 - 10x^2 = 0$$

$$0 = 0$$

All real values are solutions.

(Math Refresher #406)

13. **(A)** Choice A is correct. **(Use Strategy 17: Use the given information effectively.)** The circumference of a circle of radius r is $2\pi r$.

Perimeter of a square = 4 × length of a side $\boxed{1}$

Using $\boxed{1}$ for choice A,

$$P = 4\left(\frac{\pi r}{2}\right)$$

$$P = 2\pi r$$

Thus, choice A is correct.

(Math Refresher #310 and #303)

14. **(A)** Choice A is correct. **(Use Strategy 3: The whole equals the sum of its parts.)** The sum of the angles in a triangle = 180°,

$$\text{Therefore } 3t° + 5t° + 10t° = 180$$

$$18t = 180$$

$$t = 10 \qquad \boxed{1}$$

Since ABC is a line segment,
straight angle $ABC = 180°$ $\boxed{2}$

(Use Strategy 3: The whole equals the sum of its parts.)

$$\angle ABC = \angle ABD + \angle DBC \qquad \boxed{3}$$

Substituting the given and $\boxed{2}$ in $\boxed{3}$ gives

$$180 = 10t + 16x \qquad \boxed{4}$$

Substituting $\boxed{1}$ in $\boxed{4}$ we have

$$180 = 10(10) + 16x$$

$$180 = 100 + 16x$$

$$80 = 16x$$

$$5 = x$$

(Math Refresher #505, #406, and #501)

15. **(C)** Choice C is correct. **(Use Strategy 11: Use new definitions carefully.)** Using the given definition of

$$a \,\delta\, b = a^2 + 2ab \qquad \boxed{1}$$

Substituting $\frac{1}{4}$ and 6 in $\boxed{1}$ gives

$$\frac{1}{4} \,\delta\, 6 = \left(\frac{1}{4}\right)^2 + 2\left(\frac{1}{4}\right)\left(6\right)$$

$$= \frac{1}{16} + \frac{12}{4}$$

$$= \frac{1}{16} + 3$$

$$= 3\frac{1}{16}$$

Looking at the answer choices we note that all are in fraction form!

We change $3\frac{1}{16}$ to $\frac{49}{16}$

(Math Refresher #431)

16. **(D)** Choice D is correct. **(Use Strategy 11: Use new definitions carefully.)** We are given that

$$3\delta x = 25 \qquad \boxed{1}$$

From the definition of

$$a \,\delta\, b = a^2 + 2ab \qquad \boxed{2}$$

We substitute from $\boxed{1}$ into $\boxed{2}$ and get

$$3\delta x = 3^2 + 2(3)(x)$$

$$25 = 9 + 6x$$

$$\frac{16}{6} = x$$

$$\frac{8}{3} = x$$

(Math Refresher #431 and #406)

17. **(C)** Choice C is correct. Since lines are drawn every 10 yards after the first one, $\dfrac{100}{10}$ lines or 10 additional lines are drawn. **(Use Strategy 2: Translate from words to algebra.)** The total number of lines on the field = the original line + the number of additional lines

$$= 1 + 10 = 11$$

(Math Refresher #200 and Logical Reasoning)

18. **(A)** Choice A is correct. Before the rotation, we have

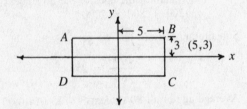

After the rotation, we have

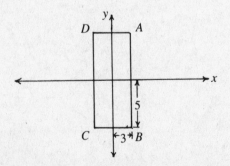

Note that the new y-coordinate of B is negative because B is below the x-axis. Since B is to the right of the y-axis, its x-coordinate is positive. By looking at the second diagram, we see that the coordinates of B are

$$(3, -5)$$

(Math Refresher #410 and Logical Reasoning)

19. **(B)** Choice B is correct. **(Use Strategy 11: Use new definitions carefully.)**

After 6 hours, $\dfrac{x}{2}$ grams remain.

After 12 hours, $\dfrac{1}{2}\left(\dfrac{x}{2}\right)$ grams remain.

After 18 hours, $\dfrac{1}{2}\left(\dfrac{1}{2}\right)\left(\dfrac{x}{2}\right)$ grams remain.

After 24 hours, $\dfrac{1}{2}\left(\dfrac{1}{2}\right)\left(\dfrac{1}{2}\right)\left(\dfrac{x}{2}\right) = \dfrac{x}{16}$ grams remain.

(Math Refresher #431)

20. **(E)** Choice E is correct. **(Use Strategy 2: Translate from words to algebra.)** From what we are told in the problem, notice that

$b - 6 =$ the number of Bobby's marbles after Bobby gave 6 away

$c + 6 =$ the number of Charlie's marbles after Bobby gave 6 away

We are told

$$b - 6 = c + 6 + 18$$
$$\text{or } b - 6 = c + 24 \qquad \boxed{1}$$

(Use Strategy 13: Find unknowns by adding equations or expressions.) Adding $-b - 24$ to both sides of $\boxed{1}$, we get

$$c - b = -30$$

(Math Refresher #200 and #406)

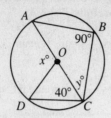

21. **(B)** Choice B is correct.
(Use Strategy 18: Remember the isosceles triangle.)
Since $AB = BC$ in $\triangle ABC$, it is isosceles, and the opposite angles are equal. So

$$m\angle A = \angle y. \qquad \boxed{1}$$

(Use Strategy 3: The whole equals the sum of its parts.) The sum of the angles in a triangle is 180°, so

$$m\angle A + y + 90 = 180$$

Subtracting 90 from both sides gives

$$m\angle A + y = 90 \qquad \boxed{2}$$

From $\boxed{1}$, the angles are =, so substituting y for $\angle A$ in $\boxed{2}$ gives

$$y + y = 90$$
$$\frac{2y}{2} = \frac{90}{2}$$
$$y = 45° \qquad \boxed{3}$$

Since OD and OC are radii of the circle, they are equal. $\triangle DOC$ is isosceles and $\angle D = \angle OCD$ (see $\boxed{1}$ above.)

$$\text{Thus, } \angle D = 40° \qquad \boxed{4}$$

(Use Strategy 3: The whole equals the sum of its parts.) The sum of angles of $\triangle DOC = 180°$.

Therefore, $\angle D + \angle OCD + \angle DOC + 180 \qquad \boxed{5}$
Substituting from $\boxed{4}$ and the given into $\boxed{5}$, we have

$$40 + 40 + \angle DOC = 180$$
$$\angle DOC = 100 \qquad \boxed{6}$$

Since AC is a diameter, it is a straight line segment and $\angle AOC$ is a straight angle.
Thus, $\angle AOC = 180 \qquad \boxed{7}$

(Use Strategy 3: The whole equals the sum of its parts.)

$$\angle AOC = \angle AOD + \angle DOC \qquad \boxed{8}$$

Substituting $\boxed{6}$ and $\boxed{7}$ into $\boxed{8}$, we get

$$180 = \angle AOD + 100$$
$$80 = \angle AOD \qquad \boxed{9}$$

We need $x + y$, so substituting $\boxed{9}$ and $\boxed{3}$ here gives

$$80 + 45 = 125$$

(Math Refresher #507, #505, and #406)

22. **(E)** Choice E is correct.
(Use Strategy 5:

$$\textbf{Average} = \frac{\textbf{sum of values}}{\textbf{total number of values}} \Bigg)$$

Average age of students in a class

$$= \frac{\text{sum of the ages of students in the class}}{\text{number of students in the class}} \qquad \boxed{1}$$

Thus,
Average age of all 80 students

$$= \frac{\text{sum of the ages of the 80 students}}{80} \qquad \boxed{2}$$

Using $\boxed{1}$, we know that

$$20 = \frac{\text{sum of the ages of the 60 students}}{60}$$

$$\text{and } 40 = \frac{\text{sum of the ages of the 20 students}}{20}$$

Thus,
sum of the ages of the 60 students

$$= (60)(20) = 1200$$

and the sum of the ages of the 20 students

$$= (40)(20) = 800$$

Hence, the sum of the ages of the 80 students

$$= \text{sum of the ages of the 60 students}$$
$$+ \text{sum of the ages of the 20 students}$$
$$= 1200 + 800 = 2000 \qquad \boxed{3}$$

Substituting $\boxed{3}$ into $\boxed{2}$, we get

$$\frac{2000}{80} = 25$$

Average age of all 80 students $= 25$ *(Answer)*

(Math Refresher #601 and #406)

23. **(B)** Choice B is correct.

$$\text{Given: } ab^2c > 0 \qquad \boxed{1}$$

(Use Strategy 7: Use numeric examples to prove or disprove your guess.)

Method 1: Choose numeric values of *a*, *b* and *c* that satisfy $\boxed{1}$.

$$\text{Let } a = -1, b = -1, c = -1$$
$$\text{Thus, for Item I, } ab^2 = -1 < 0$$
$$\text{for Item II, } ac = 1 > 0$$
$$\text{for Item III, } abc = -1 < 0$$

Only Item II is true.

(Use Strategy 6: Know how to use inequalities.)

Method 2: It is always true that

$$b^2 \geq 0 \qquad \boxed{2}$$

From $\boxed{1}$ and $\boxed{2}$ together,

$$b^2 > 0 \qquad \boxed{3}$$

For Item I: $ab^2 > 0$ if, and only if, $a > 0$, since $\boxed{3}$ is true. Thus, Item I is not always true. (We are not told that $a > 0$.

For Item II: $ab^2c = (ac)(b^2) > 0 \qquad \boxed{4}$

[We get this by using $\boxed{1}$]

Since we know $\boxed{3}$, then it is true that $ac > 0 \qquad \boxed{5}$

Thus, Item II is true.

For Item III: $abc = (ac)(b) > 0$ if, and only if, $b > 0$, since $\boxed{5}$ is true. Thus Item III is not always true, since we are not told that $b > 0$. Only Item II is true.

(Math Refresher #431 and #428)

24. **(D)** Choice D is correct. **(Use Strategy 3: The whole equals the sum of its parts.)** The perimeter of the shaded region

$$= PM + PN + \text{length of } \overset{\frown}{MN} \qquad \boxed{1}$$

From basic geometry, we know that

$$PM = PN \qquad m \angle PMO = 90 \qquad \boxed{2}$$

and that $\overset{\leftrightarrow}{OP}$ bisects $\angle MON$ **(Use Strategy 14: Draw additional lines.)** Thus, we can redraw the diagram:

(Use Strategy 18: Remember standard right triangles.)

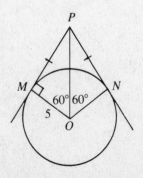

$\triangle PMO$ is similar to one of the standard triangles previously discussed.

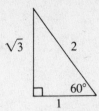

Corresponding sides of similar triangles are *in proportion*, so that

$$\frac{\sqrt{3}}{1} = \frac{PM}{5}$$
$$\text{or } PM = 5\sqrt{3} = PN \qquad \boxed{3}$$

It is always true that length of $\overset{\frown}{MN}$

$$= \frac{m \angle MON}{360} \times \text{circumference of the circle}$$
$$= \frac{m \angle MON}{360} \times 2\pi(5)$$
$$= \frac{120}{360} \times 2\pi(5)$$

(Use Strategy 19: Factor and reduce.)

$$= \frac{12 \times \cancel{10}}{36 \times \cancel{10}} \times 2\pi(5)$$
$$= \frac{\cancel{12}}{\cancel{12} \times 3} \times 2\pi(5)$$
$$= \frac{10\pi}{3} \qquad \boxed{4}$$

Substituting $\boxed{4}$ and $\boxed{3}$ into $\boxed{1}$, we get the

$$\text{perimeter of shaded region} = 10\sqrt{3} + \frac{10\pi}{3}$$

(Math Refresher #310, #509, #510, and #529)

25. **(C)** Choice C is correct. **(Use Strategy 2: Translate from words to algebra.)** Let $s =$ the number of tapes Stanley originally had.

Thus, $s + 10x =$ the number of tapes Stanley had after receiving $10x$ tapes

We are told

$$s + 10x = (5y + 1)s$$
$$\text{or} \qquad s + 10x = 5ys + s$$
$$\text{or} \qquad 10x = 5ys$$
$$\text{or} \qquad s = \frac{10x}{5y}$$
$$s = \frac{2x}{y}$$

(Math Refresher #200)

Answer Sheet—Practice Test 4

SECTION 1: VERBAL ABILITY

1 Ⓐ Ⓑ Ⓒ Ⓓ Ⓔ   10 Ⓐ Ⓑ Ⓒ Ⓓ Ⓔ   19 Ⓐ Ⓑ Ⓒ Ⓓ Ⓔ   28 Ⓐ Ⓑ Ⓒ Ⓓ Ⓔ   37 Ⓐ Ⓑ Ⓒ Ⓓ Ⓔ
2 Ⓐ Ⓑ Ⓒ Ⓓ Ⓔ   11 Ⓐ Ⓑ Ⓒ Ⓓ Ⓔ   20 Ⓐ Ⓑ Ⓒ Ⓓ Ⓔ   29 Ⓐ Ⓑ Ⓒ Ⓓ Ⓔ   38 Ⓐ Ⓑ Ⓒ Ⓓ Ⓔ
3 Ⓐ Ⓑ Ⓒ Ⓓ Ⓔ   12 Ⓐ Ⓑ Ⓒ Ⓓ Ⓔ   21 Ⓐ Ⓑ Ⓒ Ⓓ Ⓔ   30 Ⓐ Ⓑ Ⓒ Ⓓ Ⓔ   39 Ⓐ Ⓑ Ⓒ Ⓓ Ⓔ
4 Ⓐ Ⓑ Ⓒ Ⓓ Ⓔ   13 Ⓐ Ⓑ Ⓒ Ⓓ Ⓔ   22 Ⓐ Ⓑ Ⓒ Ⓓ Ⓔ   31 Ⓐ Ⓑ Ⓒ Ⓓ Ⓔ   40 Ⓐ Ⓑ Ⓒ Ⓓ Ⓔ
5 Ⓐ Ⓑ Ⓒ Ⓓ Ⓔ   14 Ⓐ Ⓑ Ⓒ Ⓓ Ⓔ   23 Ⓐ Ⓑ Ⓒ Ⓓ Ⓔ   32 Ⓐ Ⓑ Ⓒ Ⓓ Ⓔ   41 Ⓐ Ⓑ Ⓒ Ⓓ Ⓔ
6 Ⓐ Ⓑ Ⓒ Ⓓ Ⓔ   15 Ⓐ Ⓑ Ⓒ Ⓓ Ⓔ   24 Ⓐ Ⓑ Ⓒ Ⓓ Ⓔ   33 Ⓐ Ⓑ Ⓒ Ⓓ Ⓔ   42 Ⓐ Ⓑ Ⓒ Ⓓ Ⓔ
7 Ⓐ Ⓑ Ⓒ Ⓓ Ⓔ   16 Ⓐ Ⓑ Ⓒ Ⓓ Ⓔ   25 Ⓐ Ⓑ Ⓒ Ⓓ Ⓔ   34 Ⓐ Ⓑ Ⓒ Ⓓ Ⓔ   43 Ⓐ Ⓑ Ⓒ Ⓓ Ⓔ
8 Ⓐ Ⓑ Ⓒ Ⓓ Ⓔ   17 Ⓐ Ⓑ Ⓒ Ⓓ Ⓔ   26 Ⓐ Ⓑ Ⓒ Ⓓ Ⓔ   35 Ⓐ Ⓑ Ⓒ Ⓓ Ⓔ   44 Ⓐ Ⓑ Ⓒ Ⓓ Ⓔ
9 Ⓐ Ⓑ Ⓒ Ⓓ Ⓔ   18 Ⓐ Ⓑ Ⓒ Ⓓ Ⓔ   27 Ⓐ Ⓑ Ⓒ Ⓓ Ⓔ   36 Ⓐ Ⓑ Ⓒ Ⓓ Ⓔ   45 Ⓐ Ⓑ Ⓒ Ⓓ Ⓔ

SECTION 2: MATH ABILITY

1 Ⓐ Ⓑ Ⓒ Ⓓ Ⓔ   6 Ⓐ Ⓑ Ⓒ Ⓓ Ⓔ   11 Ⓐ Ⓑ Ⓒ Ⓓ Ⓔ   16 Ⓐ Ⓑ Ⓒ Ⓓ Ⓔ   21 Ⓐ Ⓑ Ⓒ Ⓓ Ⓔ
2 Ⓐ Ⓑ Ⓒ Ⓓ Ⓔ   7 Ⓐ Ⓑ Ⓒ Ⓓ Ⓔ   12 Ⓐ Ⓑ Ⓒ Ⓓ Ⓔ   17 Ⓐ Ⓑ Ⓒ Ⓓ Ⓔ   22 Ⓐ Ⓑ Ⓒ Ⓓ Ⓔ
3 Ⓐ Ⓑ Ⓒ Ⓓ Ⓔ   8 Ⓐ Ⓑ Ⓒ Ⓓ Ⓔ   13 Ⓐ Ⓑ Ⓒ Ⓓ Ⓔ   18 Ⓐ Ⓑ Ⓒ Ⓓ Ⓔ   23 Ⓐ Ⓑ Ⓒ Ⓓ Ⓔ
4 Ⓐ Ⓑ Ⓒ Ⓓ Ⓔ   9 Ⓐ Ⓑ Ⓒ Ⓓ Ⓔ   14 Ⓐ Ⓑ Ⓒ Ⓓ Ⓔ   19 Ⓐ Ⓑ Ⓒ Ⓓ Ⓔ   24 Ⓐ Ⓑ Ⓒ Ⓓ Ⓔ
5 Ⓐ Ⓑ Ⓒ Ⓓ Ⓔ   10 Ⓐ Ⓑ Ⓒ Ⓓ Ⓔ   15 Ⓐ Ⓑ Ⓒ Ⓓ Ⓔ   20 Ⓐ Ⓑ Ⓒ Ⓓ Ⓔ   25 Ⓐ Ⓑ Ⓒ Ⓓ Ⓔ

SECTION 3: STANDARD WRITTEN ENGLISH

1 Ⓐ Ⓑ Ⓒ Ⓓ Ⓔ   11 Ⓐ Ⓑ Ⓒ Ⓓ Ⓔ   21 Ⓐ Ⓑ Ⓒ Ⓓ Ⓔ   31 Ⓐ Ⓑ Ⓒ Ⓓ Ⓔ   41 Ⓐ Ⓑ Ⓒ Ⓓ Ⓔ
2 Ⓐ Ⓑ Ⓒ Ⓓ Ⓔ   12 Ⓐ Ⓑ Ⓒ Ⓓ Ⓔ   22 Ⓐ Ⓑ Ⓒ Ⓓ Ⓔ   32 Ⓐ Ⓑ Ⓒ Ⓓ Ⓔ   42 Ⓐ Ⓑ Ⓒ Ⓓ Ⓔ
3 Ⓐ Ⓑ Ⓒ Ⓓ Ⓔ   13 Ⓐ Ⓑ Ⓒ Ⓓ Ⓔ   23 Ⓐ Ⓑ Ⓒ Ⓓ Ⓔ   33 Ⓐ Ⓑ Ⓒ Ⓓ Ⓔ   43 Ⓐ Ⓑ Ⓒ Ⓓ Ⓔ
4 Ⓐ Ⓑ Ⓒ Ⓓ Ⓔ   14 Ⓐ Ⓑ Ⓒ Ⓓ Ⓔ   24 Ⓐ Ⓑ Ⓒ Ⓓ Ⓔ   34 Ⓐ Ⓑ Ⓒ Ⓓ Ⓔ   44 Ⓐ Ⓑ Ⓒ Ⓓ Ⓔ
5 Ⓐ Ⓑ Ⓒ Ⓓ Ⓔ   15 Ⓐ Ⓑ Ⓒ Ⓓ Ⓔ   25 Ⓐ Ⓑ Ⓒ Ⓓ Ⓔ   35 Ⓐ Ⓑ Ⓒ Ⓓ Ⓔ   45 Ⓐ Ⓑ Ⓒ Ⓓ Ⓔ
6 Ⓐ Ⓑ Ⓒ Ⓓ Ⓔ   16 Ⓐ Ⓑ Ⓒ Ⓓ Ⓔ   26 Ⓐ Ⓑ Ⓒ Ⓓ Ⓔ   36 Ⓐ Ⓑ Ⓒ Ⓓ Ⓔ   46 Ⓐ Ⓑ Ⓒ Ⓓ Ⓔ
7 Ⓐ Ⓑ Ⓒ Ⓓ Ⓔ   17 Ⓐ Ⓑ Ⓒ Ⓓ Ⓔ   27 Ⓐ Ⓑ Ⓒ Ⓓ Ⓔ   37 Ⓐ Ⓑ Ⓒ Ⓓ Ⓔ   47 Ⓐ Ⓑ Ⓒ Ⓓ Ⓔ
8 Ⓐ Ⓑ Ⓒ Ⓓ Ⓔ   18 Ⓐ Ⓑ Ⓒ Ⓓ Ⓔ   28 Ⓐ Ⓑ Ⓒ Ⓓ Ⓔ   38 Ⓐ Ⓑ Ⓒ Ⓓ Ⓔ   48 Ⓐ Ⓑ Ⓒ Ⓓ Ⓔ
9 Ⓐ Ⓑ Ⓒ Ⓓ Ⓔ   19 Ⓐ Ⓑ Ⓒ Ⓓ Ⓔ   29 Ⓐ Ⓑ Ⓒ Ⓓ Ⓔ   39 Ⓐ Ⓑ Ⓒ Ⓓ Ⓔ   49 Ⓐ Ⓑ Ⓒ Ⓓ Ⓔ
10 Ⓐ Ⓑ Ⓒ Ⓓ Ⓔ   20 Ⓐ Ⓑ Ⓒ Ⓓ Ⓔ   30 Ⓐ Ⓑ Ⓒ Ⓓ Ⓔ   40 Ⓐ Ⓑ Ⓒ Ⓓ Ⓔ   50 Ⓐ Ⓑ Ⓒ Ⓓ Ⓔ

SECTION 4: VERBAL ABILITY

1 Ⓐ Ⓑ Ⓒ Ⓓ Ⓔ	9 Ⓐ Ⓑ Ⓒ Ⓓ Ⓔ	17 Ⓐ Ⓑ Ⓒ Ⓓ Ⓔ	25 Ⓐ Ⓑ Ⓒ Ⓓ Ⓔ	33 Ⓐ Ⓑ Ⓒ Ⓓ Ⓔ
2 Ⓐ Ⓑ Ⓒ Ⓓ Ⓔ	10 Ⓐ Ⓑ Ⓒ Ⓓ Ⓔ	18 Ⓐ Ⓑ Ⓒ Ⓓ Ⓔ	26 Ⓐ Ⓑ Ⓒ Ⓓ Ⓔ	34 Ⓐ Ⓑ Ⓒ Ⓓ Ⓔ
3 Ⓐ Ⓑ Ⓒ Ⓓ Ⓔ	11 Ⓐ Ⓑ Ⓒ Ⓓ Ⓔ	19 Ⓐ Ⓑ Ⓒ Ⓓ Ⓔ	27 Ⓐ Ⓑ Ⓒ Ⓓ Ⓔ	35 Ⓐ Ⓑ Ⓒ Ⓓ Ⓔ
4 Ⓐ Ⓑ Ⓒ Ⓓ Ⓔ	12 Ⓐ Ⓑ Ⓒ Ⓓ Ⓔ	20 Ⓐ Ⓑ Ⓒ Ⓓ Ⓔ	28 Ⓐ Ⓑ Ⓒ Ⓓ Ⓔ	36 Ⓐ Ⓑ Ⓒ Ⓓ Ⓔ
5 Ⓐ Ⓑ Ⓒ Ⓓ Ⓔ	13 Ⓐ Ⓑ Ⓒ Ⓓ Ⓔ	21 Ⓐ Ⓑ Ⓒ Ⓓ Ⓔ	29 Ⓐ Ⓑ Ⓒ Ⓓ Ⓔ	37 Ⓐ Ⓑ Ⓒ Ⓓ Ⓔ
6 Ⓐ Ⓑ Ⓒ Ⓓ Ⓔ	14 Ⓐ Ⓑ Ⓒ Ⓓ Ⓔ	22 Ⓐ Ⓑ Ⓒ Ⓓ Ⓔ	30 Ⓐ Ⓑ Ⓒ Ⓓ Ⓔ	38 Ⓐ Ⓑ Ⓒ Ⓓ Ⓔ
7 Ⓐ Ⓑ Ⓒ Ⓓ Ⓔ	15 Ⓐ Ⓑ Ⓒ Ⓓ Ⓔ	23 Ⓐ Ⓑ Ⓒ Ⓓ Ⓔ	31 Ⓐ Ⓑ Ⓒ Ⓓ Ⓔ	39 Ⓐ Ⓑ Ⓒ Ⓓ Ⓔ
8 Ⓐ Ⓑ Ⓒ Ⓓ Ⓔ	16 Ⓐ Ⓑ Ⓒ Ⓓ Ⓔ	24 Ⓐ Ⓑ Ⓒ Ⓓ Ⓔ	32 Ⓐ Ⓑ Ⓒ Ⓓ Ⓔ	40 Ⓐ Ⓑ Ⓒ Ⓓ Ⓔ

SECTION 5: MATH ABILITY

1 Ⓐ Ⓑ Ⓒ Ⓓ Ⓔ	8 Ⓐ Ⓑ Ⓒ Ⓓ Ⓔ	15 Ⓐ Ⓑ Ⓒ Ⓓ Ⓔ	22 Ⓐ Ⓑ Ⓒ Ⓓ Ⓔ	29 Ⓐ Ⓑ Ⓒ Ⓓ Ⓔ
2 Ⓐ Ⓑ Ⓒ Ⓓ Ⓔ	9 Ⓐ Ⓑ Ⓒ Ⓓ Ⓔ	16 Ⓐ Ⓑ Ⓒ Ⓓ Ⓔ	23 Ⓐ Ⓑ Ⓒ Ⓓ Ⓔ	30 Ⓐ Ⓑ Ⓒ Ⓓ Ⓔ
3 Ⓐ Ⓑ Ⓒ Ⓓ Ⓔ	10 Ⓐ Ⓑ Ⓒ Ⓓ Ⓔ	17 Ⓐ Ⓑ Ⓒ Ⓓ Ⓔ	24 Ⓐ Ⓑ Ⓒ Ⓓ Ⓔ	31 Ⓐ Ⓑ Ⓒ Ⓓ Ⓔ
4 Ⓐ Ⓑ Ⓒ Ⓓ Ⓔ	11 Ⓐ Ⓑ Ⓒ Ⓓ Ⓔ	18 Ⓐ Ⓑ Ⓒ Ⓓ Ⓔ	25 Ⓐ Ⓑ Ⓒ Ⓓ Ⓔ	32 Ⓐ Ⓑ Ⓒ Ⓓ Ⓔ
5 Ⓐ Ⓑ Ⓒ Ⓓ Ⓔ	12 Ⓐ Ⓑ Ⓒ Ⓓ Ⓔ	19 Ⓐ Ⓑ Ⓒ Ⓓ Ⓔ	26 Ⓐ Ⓑ Ⓒ Ⓓ Ⓔ	33 Ⓐ Ⓑ Ⓒ Ⓓ Ⓔ
6 Ⓐ Ⓑ Ⓒ Ⓓ Ⓔ	13 Ⓐ Ⓑ Ⓒ Ⓓ Ⓔ	20 Ⓐ Ⓑ Ⓒ Ⓓ Ⓔ	27 Ⓐ Ⓑ Ⓒ Ⓓ Ⓔ	34 Ⓐ Ⓑ Ⓒ Ⓓ Ⓔ
7 Ⓐ Ⓑ Ⓒ Ⓓ Ⓔ	14 Ⓐ Ⓑ Ⓒ Ⓓ Ⓔ	21 Ⓐ Ⓑ Ⓒ Ⓓ Ⓔ	28 Ⓐ Ⓑ Ⓒ Ⓓ Ⓔ	35 Ⓐ Ⓑ Ⓒ Ⓓ Ⓔ

SECTION 6: MATH ABILITY

1 Ⓐ Ⓑ Ⓒ Ⓓ Ⓔ	8 Ⓐ Ⓑ Ⓒ Ⓓ Ⓔ	15 Ⓐ Ⓑ Ⓒ Ⓓ Ⓔ	22 Ⓐ Ⓑ Ⓒ Ⓓ Ⓔ	29 Ⓐ Ⓑ Ⓒ Ⓓ Ⓔ
2 Ⓐ Ⓑ Ⓒ Ⓓ Ⓔ	9 Ⓐ Ⓑ Ⓒ Ⓓ Ⓔ	16 Ⓐ Ⓑ Ⓒ Ⓓ Ⓔ	23 Ⓐ Ⓑ Ⓒ Ⓓ Ⓔ	30 Ⓐ Ⓑ Ⓒ Ⓓ Ⓔ
3 Ⓐ Ⓑ Ⓒ Ⓓ Ⓔ	10 Ⓐ Ⓑ Ⓒ Ⓓ Ⓔ	17 Ⓐ Ⓑ Ⓒ Ⓓ Ⓔ	24 Ⓐ Ⓑ Ⓒ Ⓓ Ⓔ	31 Ⓐ Ⓑ Ⓒ Ⓓ Ⓔ
4 Ⓐ Ⓑ Ⓒ Ⓓ Ⓔ	11 Ⓐ Ⓑ Ⓒ Ⓓ Ⓔ	18 Ⓐ Ⓑ Ⓒ Ⓓ Ⓔ	25 Ⓐ Ⓑ Ⓒ Ⓓ Ⓔ	32 Ⓐ Ⓑ Ⓒ Ⓓ Ⓔ
5 Ⓐ Ⓑ Ⓒ Ⓓ Ⓔ	12 Ⓐ Ⓑ Ⓒ Ⓓ Ⓔ	19 Ⓐ Ⓑ Ⓒ Ⓓ Ⓔ	26 Ⓐ Ⓑ Ⓒ Ⓓ Ⓔ	33 Ⓐ Ⓑ Ⓒ Ⓓ Ⓔ
6 Ⓐ Ⓑ Ⓒ Ⓓ Ⓔ	13 Ⓐ Ⓑ Ⓒ Ⓓ Ⓔ	20 Ⓐ Ⓑ Ⓒ Ⓓ Ⓔ	27 Ⓐ Ⓑ Ⓒ Ⓓ Ⓔ	34 Ⓐ Ⓑ Ⓒ Ⓓ Ⓔ
7 Ⓐ Ⓑ Ⓒ Ⓓ Ⓔ	14 Ⓐ Ⓑ Ⓒ Ⓓ Ⓔ	21 Ⓐ Ⓑ Ⓒ Ⓓ Ⓔ	28 Ⓐ Ⓑ Ⓒ Ⓓ Ⓔ	35 Ⓐ Ⓑ Ⓒ Ⓓ Ⓔ

SAT Practice Test 4

SECTION 1   VERBAL ABILITY
30 MINUTES   45 QUESTIONS

For each question in this section, choose the best answer and blacken the corresponding space on the answer sheet.

Each question below consists of a word in capital letters, followed by five lettered words or phrases. Choose the word or phrase that is most nearly *opposite* in meaning to the word in capital letters. Since some of the questions require you to distinguish fine shades of meaning, consider all the choices before deciding which is best.

Example:

GOOD: (A) sour   (B) bad   (C) red
(D) hot   (E) ugly

Ⓐ ● Ⓒ Ⓓ Ⓔ

1. TANTALIZE: (A) lengthen   (B) respect
(C) bring together   (D) comfort   (E) classify

2. CHIDE: (A) reconcile   (B) praise
(C) moisten   (D) construct   (E) mix

3. NEBULOUS: (A) certain   (B) possible
(C) entangled   (D) responsive   (E) glaring

4. BLATANT: (A) definite   (B) amicable
(C) concealed   (D) ragged   (E) punctual

5. SULLY: (A) rise   (B) mock   (C) appreciate
(D) admire   (E) cleanse

6. CARNAL: (A) flippant   (B) gay
(C) spiritual   (D) healthful   (E) mature

7. TACIT: (A) dislodged   (B) modern
(C) unaware   (D) forgiving   (E) expressed

8. EXTRANEOUS: (A) unknown   (B) related
(C) apt   (D) solitary   (E) miscellaneous

9. OPULENT: (A) harsh   (B) needy
(C) unpolished   (D) pushy   (E) discreet

10. QUEASY: (A) comfortable   (B) replaceable
(C) awkward   (D) difficult   (E) steady

11. REFRACTORY: (A) busy   (B) inferior
(C) inventive   (D) manageable   (E) constructive

12. EBULLIENT: (A) unmoved   (B) vague
(C) inferior   (D) tame   (E) pompous

13. OMNIVOROUS: (A) inadequate   (B) solitary
(C) empty   (D) uniform   (E) selective

14. NADIR: (A) relative   (B) cleverness
(C) poverty   (D) tolerance   (E) peak

15. DISPASSIONATE: (A) partial
(B) combined   (C) developed   (D) displeased
(E) angry

Each sentence below has one or two blanks, each blank indicating that something has been omitted. Beneath the sentence are five lettered words or sets of words. Choose the word or set of words that *best* fits the meaning of the sentence as a whole.

Example:

Although its publicity has been ____, the film itself is intelligent, well-acted, handsomely produced, and altogether ____.

(A) tasteless . . . respectable
(B) extensive . . . moderate
(C) sophisticated . . . amateur
(D) risqué . . . crude
(E) perfect . . . spectacular   A Ⓑ Ⓒ Ⓓ Ⓔ

16. The Police Commissioner insisted on severity in dealing with the demonstrators rather than the _____ approach that his advisers suggested.

(A) arrogant   (B) defeatist   (C) violent
(D) conciliatory   (E) retaliatory

17. Just as the person who is kind brings happiness to others, so does he bring _____ to himself.

(A) wisdom   (B) guidance   (C) satisfaction
(D) stinginess   (E) insecurity

18. The renowned behaviorist B.F. Skinner believes that those colleges set up to train teachers should _____ change their training philosophy, or else be _____.

(A) inconsistently . . . supervised
(B) drastically . . . abolished
(C) haphazardly . . . refined
(D) secretly . . . dedicated
(E) doubtlessly . . . destroyed

19. There are some individuals who thrive on action and, accordingly, cannot tolerate a _____ life style.

(A) passive   (B) chaotic   (C) brazen
(D) grandiose   (E) vibrant

20. The girl's extreme state of _____ aroused in him a feeling of pity.

(A) disapproval   (B) exultation
(C) enthusiasm   (D) degradation   (E) jubilation

Each passage below is followed by questions based on its content. Answer all questions following a passage on the basis of what is *stated* or *implied* in that passage.

The most striking feature of medical care is its rapid and continuing evolution. From its origin, as an aspect of primitive religion, exorcising the forces of evil, medical care has ascended to a modern day system using scientific
5   skills for the benefit of humanity. This metamorphosis has been particularly marked and striking in the past half century.

Consider the familiar portrait of the family doctor at the turn of the century pondering at a child's bedside what,
10 if anything, he can do about the pathology his stethoscope has detected. Contrast this with the highly complex scene of a team of surgeons, cardiologists, anesthesiologists, nurses, and technicians as they prepare to perform open heart surgery.

15 Between these two scenes lie tremendous technological advances. The contents of the "little black bag" and the single guiding hand of the family doctor are being supplanted by the technical capacity of the modern hospital and the skills of many specialists. Coincident with these
20 changes have come problems of complexity and rising costs; problems in achieving accessibility to and continuity in services; problems of fragmentation and depersonalization in patient care.

The specialization and increased technical capacity which
25 characterizes medical care is a reflection of changing health needs and changing patterns in the organization and financing of personal health services. Our population is living longer; it is surviving the formerly deadly childhood diseases, and is increasingly encountering the degenerative
30 diseases and chronic disabilities. Mortality rates have declined generally, and the leading causes of death have changed since 1900. Heart disease and cancer are now the major killers, instead of diarrhea, pneumonia, and tuberculosis.

35 Industrialization, urbanization, and higher standards of living contribute to increased capacities for providing and using services. The population explosion, higher levels of educational attainment, and increasing population mobility also influence rising demand for health services and create
40 a need for new and flexible patterns in their delivery.

To combat today's killers, to prevent untimely death, to diagnose and cure disease, and to control and manage chronic disability, we depend upon the people who are trained to provide health services. Here, too, we observe
45 remarkable changes. The ratio of physicians to population has remained fairly constant over the past 20 years. The number of dentists in relation to the population has declined markedly during these years. In the same period, however, nursing personnel and the newer types of aux-
50 iliary personnel, such as technicians and physical and occupational therapists, have grown in numbers proportion-

ately higher than the population generally. Changes have occurred within each health profession as well. For instance, more than half of all physicians are now specialists, whereas thirty years ago only 15 percent were specialists.   55

21. According to the passage, which one of the following statements is *false*?

(A) The percentage of physicians in the general population has increased.
(B) The percentage of dentists in the general population has decreased.
(C) The total number of physicians has increased.
(D) The percentage of nurses and therapists in the general population has increased.
(E) ·The percentage of specialists within the medical profession has increased.

22. The author's main purpose in outlining the changes which medicine has gone through during the past half-century is to

(A) point out the dangers of increased specialization
(B) describe the loss of personal care with the development of sophisticated technology
(C) give an idea of the scope and pace of the change in health care
(D) point out the inadequacy of the health care available 50 years ago, as compared with today
(E) give some explanation for the dramatic rise in the cost of health care

23. In his or her relationship to the medical profession, the author is best described as a(n)

(A) apologist   (B) reformer   (C) critic
(D) watchdog   (E) observer

24. According to the passage, which of the following statements is true?

(A) Degenerative and chronic ailments are the diseases of a century ago.
(B) Diarrhea, pneumonia and tuberculosis are no longer health problems today.
(C) A physician at the turn of the century was unable to treat most of the illnesses with which people came to him.
(D) Heart disease and cancer were responsible for most deaths by illness in 1900.
(E) The "little black bag" symbolized confidence which the patient had in the family doctor.

25. Which one of the following statements is the author *not* likely to agree with?

(A) A patient today is likely to find his illness divided into separate diseases, treated by different doctors.
(B) The exorcising of demons may be considered religious, but it has nothing to do with medicine.
(C) All communities do not have the same health needs.
(D) A better-educated community will use more health services.
(E) The "little black bag" is becoming a thing of the past.

In 1575—over 400 years ago!—the French scholar Louis Le Roy published a learned book in which he voiced despair over the upheavals caused by the social and technological innovations of his time, what we now call the
5 Renaissance. "All is pell-mell, confounded, nothing goes as it should." We, also, feel that our times are out of joint; we even have reason to believe that our descendants will be worse off than we are.

The earth will soon be overcrowded and its resources
10 exhausted. Pollution will ruin the environment, upset the climate, damage human health. The gap in living standards between the rich and the poor will widen and lead the angry, hungry people of the world to acts of desperation including the use of nuclear weapons as blackmail. Such
15 are the inevitable consequences of population and technological growth *if* present trends continue. But what a big *if* this is!

The future is never a projection of the past. Animals probably have no chance to escape from the tyranny of
20 biological evolution, but human beings are blessed with the freedom of social evolution. For us, trend is not destiny. The escape from existing trends is now facilitated by the fact that societies anticipate future dangers and take preventive steps against expected upheavals.

25 Despite the widespread belief that the world has become too complex for comprehension by the human brain, modern societies have often responded effectively to critical situations.

The decrease in birth rates, the partial banning of pesticides,
30 the rethinking of technologies for the production and use of energy are but a few examples illustrating a sudden reversal of trends caused not by political upsets or scientific breakthroughs, but by public awareness of consequences.

35 Even more striking are the situations in which social attitudes concerning future difficulties undergo rapid changes before the problems have come to pass—witness the heated controversies about the ethics of behavior control and of genetic engineering even though there is as yet no proof
40 that effective methods can be developed to manipulate behavior and genes on a population scale.

One of the characteristics of our times is thus the rapidity with which steps can be taken to change the orientation of certain trends and even to reverse them. Such
45 changes usually emerge from grassroot movements rather than from official directives.

26. In the first paragraph of the selection, the mood expressed is one of

(A) blatant despair
(B) guarded optimism
(C) poignant nostalgia
(D) muted pessimism
(E) unbridled idealism

27. According to the reading selection, if present trends continue, which one of the following situations will *not* occur?

(A) New sources of energy from vast coal deposits will be substituted for the soon-to-be-exhausted resources of oil and natural gas.
(B) The rich will become richer and the poor will become poorer.
(C) An overpopulated earth will be unable to sustain its inhabitants.
(D) Nuclear weapons will play a more prominent role in dealings among peoples.
(E) The ravages of pollution will render the earth and its atmosphere a menace to mankind.

28. Which of the following is the best illustration of the meaning of "trend is not destiny" in lines 21-22?

(A) Urban agglomerations are in a state of crisis.
(B) Human beings are blessed with the freedom of social evolution.
(C) The world has become too complex for comprehension by the human brain.
(D) Critical processes can overshoot and cause catastrophes.
(E) The earth will soon be overcrowded and its resources exhausted.

29. According to the passage, evidences of the insight of the public into the dangers which surround us can be found in all of the following *except*

(A) an increase in the military budget by the president
(B) a declining birth rate
(C) picketing against expansion of nuclear plants
(D) opposition to the use of pesticides
(E) public meetings to complain about dumping chemicals

30. The author's attitude is one of

(A) willing resignation
(B) definite optimism
(C) thinly veiled cynicism
(D) carefree abandon
(E) angry impatience

Select the word or set of words that *best* completes each of the following sentences.

31. Although our team was aware that the Raiders' attack power was _____ as compared with that of our players, we were stupid to be so _____.

(A) calculated . . . alert
(B) sluggish . . . easygoing
(C) acceptable . . . serious
(D) determined . . . detailed
(E) premeditated . . . willing

32. The _____ prime minister caused the downfall of the once _____ country.

(A) heroic . . . important
(B) respected . . . rich
(C) incompetent . . . powerful
(D) vacillating . . . confidential
(E) insightful . . . unconquerable

33. The main character in the novel was dignified and _____, a man of great reserve.

(A) garrulous   (B) aloof   (C) boring
(D) hypocritical   (E) interesting

34. The nonsmoker's blood contains _____ amounts of carbon monoxide; on the other hand, the smoker's blood contains _____ amounts.

(A) frequent . . . extensive
(B) heavy . . . adequate
(C) minute . . . excessive
(D) definite . . . puzzling
(E) bland . . . moderate

35. As a truly objective person, Mr. Jones allows neither _____ attempts to please him nor open _____ on the part of his students to influence his marks.

(A) unearned . . . respect
(B) condescending . . . humor
(C) sincere . . . reliance
(D) backward . . . offense
(E) hypocritical . . . defiance

Each question below consists of a related pair of words or phrases, followed by five lettered pairs of words or phrases. Select the lettered pair that *best* expresses a relationship similar to that expressed in the original pair.

Example:

YAWN : BOREDOM : :   (A) dream : sleep
(B) anger : madness   (C) smile : amusement
(D) face : expression   (E) impatience : rebellion

Ⓐ Ⓑ ● Ⓓ Ⓔ

36. SEW : TEAR : :

(A) settle : dispute
(B) caulk : leak
(C) alleviate : pain
(D) open : door
(E) research : dictionary

37. INFINITE : END : :

(A) spontaneous : occur
(B) isolated : envision
(C) buoyant : sink
(D) parallel : align
(E) condoned : excuse

38. COERCE : COAX : :

(A) avenge : reform
(B) suggest : demand
(C) declaim : argue
(D) diminish : expunge
(E) shove : nudge

39. REJUVENATE : YOUTH : :

(A) recuperate : disease
(B) re-elect : president
(C) reiterate : item
(D) review : play
(E) reimburse : money

40. SNEER : CONTEMPT : :

(A) stalk : prey
(B) applaud : approval
(C) cringe : fear
(D) cough : throat
(E) grimace : pain

41. UNPRETENTIOUS : OSTENTATION : :

(A) puerile : fact
(B) inconsequential : importance
(C) conventional : routine
(D) priceless : value
(E) lenient : humility

42. ENIGMATIC : CLEAR : :

    (A) copious : scarce
    (B) academic : masterful
    (C) lucrative : monetary
    (D) slanderous : illegal
    (E) adroit : effective

43. EMBARKATION : JOURNEY : :

    (A) inception : project
    (B) self-reliance : rebellion
    (C) sanction : permission
    (D) skepticism : failure
    (E) suspicion : perjury

44. EPICURE : PLEASURE : :

    (A) student : classes
    (B) hermit : society
    (C) critic : acceptance
    (D) miser : wealth
    (E) guardian : child

45. TOUCH : INTANGIBLE : :

    (A) question : unreliable
    (B) learn : ignorant
    (C) convict : innocent
    (D) fix : irreparable
    (E) examine : vague

S T O P

IF YOU FINISH BEFORE TIME IS CALLED, YOU MAY CHECK YOUR WORK ON THIS SECTION ONLY.
DO NOT WORK ON ANY OTHER SECTION SAT THE TEST.

SECTION 2   MATH ABILITY

30 MINUTES   25 QUESTIONS

In this section solve each problem, using any available space on the page for scratchwork. Then decide which is the best of the choices given and blacken the corresponding space on the answer sheet.

The following information is for your reference in solving some of the problems.

Circle of radius r: Area $= \pi r^2$; Circumference $= 2\pi r$
  The number of degrees of arc in a circle is 360.
The measure in degrees of a straight angle is 180.

Definitions of symbols:

$=$	is equal to	$\leqq$	is less than or equal to
$\neq$	is unequal to	$\geqq$	is greater than or equal to
$<$	is less than	$\parallel$	is parallel to
$>$	is greater than	$\perp$	is perpendicular to

Triangle: The sum of the measure in degrees of the angles of a triangle is 180.
If $\angle CDA$ is a right angle, then

(1) area of $\triangle ABC = \dfrac{AB \times CD}{2}$

(2) $AC^2 = AD^2 + DC^2$

Note: Figures which accompany problems in this test are intended to provide information useful in solving the problems. They are drawn as accurately as possible EXCEPT when it is stated in a specific problem that its figure is not drawn to scale. All figures lie in a plane unless otherwise indicated. All numbers used are real numbers.

1. If the last digit and the first digit are interchanged in each of the numbers below, which will result in the number with the *largest* value?

   (A) 2,534 (B) 4,235 (C) 5,243 (D) 4,352
   (E) 2,345

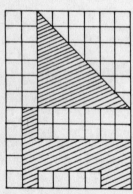

2. If each square in the grid above has a side of length 1, find the sum of the areas of the shaded regions.

   (A) 55 (B) 46 (C) 37 (D) 30 (E) 24

3. Given $\dfrac{4^3 + 4^3 + 4^3 + 4^3}{4^y} = 4$. Find y.

   (A) 3 (B) 4 (C) 8 (D) 12 (E) 64

Game		Darrin	Tom
1		69	43
2		59	60
3		72	55
4		70	68
5		78	73
Totals		348	299

4. Darrin and Tom played five games of darts. The table above lists the scores for each of the games. By how many points was Tom behind Darrin at the end of the first four games?

   (A) 8 (B) 10 (C) 42 (D) 44 (E) 48

5. Find w if $(4 + 3)(w + 2) = 28$

   (A) 1 (B) 2 (C) 3 (D) 4 (E) 6

6. Find the value of $\dfrac{y^2 - 7y + 10}{y - 2}$ rounded to the nearest whole number if $y = 8.000001$

   (A) 2 (B) 3 (C) 5 (D) 6 (E) 16

7. Given an isosceles triangle with two sides of length 9 and 16. Find the length of the third side.

   (A) 8 (B) 9 (C) 14 (D) 16 (E) It cannot be determined from the information given.

8. If $ab = 40$, $\dfrac{a}{b} = \dfrac{5}{2}$ and a and b are positive numbers, find the value of a.

(A) 5   (B) 6   (C) 10   (D) 12   (E) 20

Item	Value
1	P
2	$P \times 3$
3	$(P \times 3) \div 2$
4	$[(P \times 3) \div 2] + 12$
5	$[(P \times 3) \div 2] + 12 - 1$

9. According to the table above, which item has the greatest value when $P = 12$?

(A) 1   (B) 2   (C) 3   (D) 4   (E) 5

10. If $\dfrac{3x}{4} = 9$, find $6x$.

(A) 12   (B) 18   (C) 27   (D) 36   (E) 72

11. If 8 people share a winning lottery ticket and divide the cash prize equally, what percent of the prize do 2 of them together receive?

(A) 8%   (B) 10%   (C) 20%   (D) 25%   (E) 40%

12. Given $8r + 3s = 12$ and $7r + 2s = 9$. Find the value of $5(r + s)$.

(A) 5   (B) 10   (C) 15   (D) 20   (E) 25

13. Paul's average (arithmetic mean) for 3 tests was 85. The average of his scores for the first 2 tests was also 85. What was his score for the third test?

(A) 80   (B) 85   (C) 90   (D) 95   (E) It cannot be determined from the information given.

14. Stephanie earned $\$x$ while working 10 hours. Evelyn earned $\$y$ while working 20 hours. If they both earn the same hourly wage and $x + y = 60$, how many dollars did Stephanie earn?

(A) 10   (B) 20   (C) 30   (D) 40   (E) 60

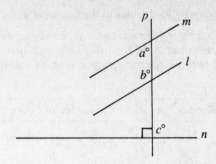

15. In the figure above, m is parallel to l and p is perpendicular to n. Find the value of $a + b + c$.

(A) 180   (B) 210   (C) 245   (D) 270   (E) 310

16. The operation $\boxdot$ is defined for all numbers x and y by the following: $x \boxdot y = 3 + xy$. For example, $2 \boxdot 7 = 3 + 2(7) = 17$. If $y \ne 0$ and x is a number such that $x \boxdot y = 3$, then find x.

(A) 0   (B) $-\dfrac{3}{y}$ (C) $-y + 3$

(D) $\dfrac{3}{y}$ (E) $y + 3$

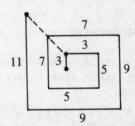

Note: Figure not drawn to scale.

17. In the figure above, each pair of intersecting segments are perpendicular with lengths as shown. Find the length of the dashed line segment.

(A) 7   (B) $6\sqrt{3}$ (C) $4\sqrt{2}$

(D) $\sqrt{46}$ (E) $\sqrt{59}$

18. For how many two-digit positive numbers will tripling the tens' digit give us a two-digit number which is triple the original number?

(A) None   (B) One   (C) Two   (D) Three   (E) Four

19. The difference of the areas of two circles is 21π. If their radii are $r + 3$ and r, find the radius of the *larger* circle.

(A) 2   (B) 3   (C) 4   (D) 5   (E) 9

Questions 20–21 refer to the following game.

A computer generates numbers. Points are assigned as described in the following table each time any of the four number pairs given appears in a number.

Number Pair	Number of Points
"33"	11
"34"	6
"43"	4
"44"	3

20. As an example, the number 4347 is assigned 4 points for "43" and 6 points more for "34," giving a total of 10 points. Which of the following numbers would be assigned the most points?

(A) 934432 (B) 464457 (C) 834415
(D) 437934 (E) 336283

21. If a certain number has 13 points assigned to it, which of the following statements must be true?

    I. 33 is not in the number.
    II. 34 and 43 are both in the number.
    III. 43 is in the number.

(A) I only (B) II only (C) III only (D) I and III only (E) I, II, and III

22. Given the volume of a cube is 8 cubic meters. Find the distance from any vertex to the center point inside the cube.

(A) 1 m (B) $\sqrt{2}\ m$ (C) $2\sqrt{2}\ m$
(D) $2\sqrt{3}\ m$ (E) $\sqrt{3}\ m$

23. The ratio of Sue's age to Bob's age is 3 to 7. The ratio of Sue's age to Joe's age is 4 to 9. The ratio of Bob's age to Joe's is

(A) 28 to 27 (B) 7 to 9 (C) 27 to 28
(D) 10 to 13 (E) 13 to 10

24. The sum of r consecutive positive integers will always be divisible by 2 if r is a multiple of

(A) 6 (B) 5 (C) 4 (D) 3 (E) 2

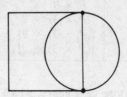

25. The square in the figure above has two sides tangent to the circle. If the area of the circle is $9a^2\pi^2$, find the area of the square.

(A) $12a^2\pi^2$ (B) $36a^2\pi$ (C) $36a^2\pi^2$
(D) $18a^4\pi^2$ (E) It cannot be determined from the information given.

S T O P

IF YOU FINISH BEFORE TIME IS CALLED, YOU MAY CHECK YOUR WORK ON THIS SECTION ONLY.
DO NOT WORK ON ANY OTHER SECTION IN THE TEST.

SECTION 3   STANDARD WRITTEN ENGLISH TEST

30 MINUTES   50 QUESTIONS

The questions in this section measure skills that are important to writing well. In particular, they test your ability to recognize and use language that is clear, effective, and correct according to the requirements of standard written English, the kind of English found in most college textbooks.

Directions: The following contain problems in grammar, usage, diction (choice of words), and idiom.

Some sentences are correct.
No sentence contains more than one error.

You will find that the error, if there is one, is underlined and lettered. Assume that elements of the sentence that are not underlined are correct and cannot be changed. In choosing answers, follow the requirements of standard written English.

If there is an error, select the *one underlined part* that must be changed to make the sentence correct and blacken the corresponding space on your answer sheet.

If there is no error, blacken answer space Ⓔ

EXAMPLE: SAMPLE ANSWER

The region has a climate so severe that plants
                               A

growing there rarely had been more than twelve
       B   C

inches high. No error
        D   E

Ⓐ Ⓑ ● Ⓓ Ⓔ

---

1. Everyone who attends a concert at the sports arena
        A   B

   knows that they will be searched for drugs before
                C

   entering. No error
     D   E

2. Our professor assigned us to write a short story, but I
                           A   B

   found I could not write one quick. No error
                         C   D   E

3. One of the key suspects in the killing of a
            A   B

   United States drug agent were captured early today
        C   D

   by the police. No error
               E

4. The Toronto Blue Jays sent every Canadian
                          A

   soaring into ecstasy by winning the American League
        B   C

   East championship for the first time in their nine-year
                                              D

   history. No error
              E

5. A woman perished on Sunday when the hot air
      A

   balloon in which she had rode caught fire as it
                            B   C

   touched down. No error
     D   E

6. From every community <u>comes</u> reports <u>that</u> there
          A   B

   <u>has been</u> an increase in vandalism by <u>teenagers</u>.
    C   D

   <u>No error.</u>
    E

7. When the hurricane <u>struck</u>, the people who <u>had gone</u>
         A   B

   to the shelter found that there <u>wasn't</u> scarcely enough
             C

   food for <u>everyone</u>. <u>No error.</u>
      D   E

8. By the time I <u>graduate</u> <u>from</u> law school, my sister
        A   B

   <u>will have been practicing</u> law <u>for three years</u>.
       C   D

   <u>No error.</u>
    E

9. I had to borrow a book <u>off of</u> my English instructor
           A

   since the campus bookstore <u>had sold</u> <u>all</u> the copies of
    B   C D

   the required text. <u>No error.</u>
          E

10. Neither the school board members <u>or</u> the city <u>council</u>
               A   B

    wanted <u>to change</u> the school boundaries <u>in order to</u>
       C   D

    reduce the overenrollment. <u>No error.</u>
              E

11. When my neighbor, <u>who cannot</u> <u>swim</u>, was a
           A   B

    teenager, he <u>had rescued</u> a <u>drowning</u> swimmer by
         C   D

    pulling him into his rowboat. <u>No error.</u>
              E

12. <u>As an incentive</u> <u>to attend</u> the local college, our father
     A   B

    told my brother and <u>I</u> that we could use his
           C

    company car <u>for</u> transportation. <u>No error.</u>
         D   E

13. Passing the <u>written test</u> <u>that</u> is required for a driver's
        A   B

    license is usually <u>easier</u> than <u>to pass</u> the driving test.
          C   D

    <u>No error.</u>
     E

14. All the <u>aspiring</u> young writers submitted their <u>stories</u>,
       A   B

    each <u>hoping</u> that <u>they</u> would win first prize. <u>No error.</u>
      C   D   E

15. Her answer <u>to</u> the essay question on the test was
        A

    <u>all together</u> incorrect, but because it was very
     B

    <u>well written</u> she received <u>partial</u> credit for her work.
     C   D

    <u>No error.</u>
     E

16. When I introduced Scott and Wilma, <u>they</u> acted <u>as if</u>
               A   B

    they never <u>met</u> before <u>even though</u> they had gone to
        C   D

    the same high school. <u>No error.</u>
            E

17. The realtor felt <u>badly</u> about not <u>being able</u> to sell
         A   B

    their house because they were in a big hurry
     C

    to move to their condominium. <u>No error.</u>
     D   E

18. The president of the newly-formed nation <u>took steps</u>
                 A

    to <u>encourage</u> <u>several thousands</u> of people to
     B   C

    <u>immigrate into</u> the country. <u>No error.</u>
     D   E

19. The Governor asked the attorney <u>to head</u> the
              A

    committee because <u>he</u> <u>was convinced</u> <u>that</u> the
         B   C   D

    committee needed to start work immediately.

    <u>No error.</u>
     E

20. $\underline{\text{Both}}_{A}$ my sisters $\underline{\text{participate}}_{B}$ in sports, but my $\underline{\text{older}}_{C}$

sister is the $\underline{\text{better}}_{D}$ athlete. $\underline{\text{No error.}}_{E}$

21. The box of books, $\underline{\text{together with}}_{A}$ the dishes and $\underline{\text{all of}}_{B}$

the silverware, $\underline{\text{were}}_{C}$ put on a truck that $\underline{\text{was headed}}_{D}$

for the wrong city. $\underline{\text{No error.}}_{E}$

22. A seamstress $\underline{\text{repaired}}_{A}$ the drum major's uniform

$\underline{\text{as soon as}}_{B}$ possible because she $\underline{\text{knew that}}_{C}$ he needed

$\underline{\text{it}}_{D}$ for the parade the next day. $\underline{\text{No error.}}_{E}$

23. At the police lineup, my neighbor had $\underline{\text{to identify}}_{A}$ the

young man $\underline{\text{which}}_{B}$ she $\underline{\text{had seen}}_{C}$ $\underline{\text{walking}}_{D}$ up and down

the street the other night. $\underline{\text{No error.}}_{E}$

24. $\underline{\text{Both}}_{A}$ my brother and my sister gave me a list of

items to bring to them at camp, but $\underline{\text{that of my}}_{B}$

brother $\underline{\text{was}}_{C}$ the $\underline{\text{shortest.}}_{D}$ $\underline{\text{No error.}}_{E}$

25. The wreck $\underline{\text{laid}}_{A}$ in twenty $\underline{\text{feet}}_{B}$ of water, but the divers

were unable to remove $\underline{\text{any}}_{C}$ of the cargo from the

ship $\underline{\text{because}}_{D}$ of the storm. $\underline{\text{No error.}}_{E}$

Directions: In each of the following sentences, some part or all of the sentence is underlined. Below each sentence you will find five ways of phrasing the underlined part. Select the answer that produces the most effective sentence, one that is clear and exact, without awkwardness or ambiguity, and blacken the corresponding space on your answer sheet. In choosing answers, follow the requirements of standard written English. Choose the answer that best expresses the meaning of the original sentence.

Answer (A) is always the same as the underlined part. Choose answer (A) if you think the original sentence needs no revision.

EXAMPLE: SAMPLE ANSWER

Laura Ingalls Wilder published her first book
and she was sixty-five years old then.
(A) and she was sixty-five years old then
(B) when she was sixty-five years old
(C) at age sixty-five years old
(D) upon reaching sixty-five years
(E) at the time when she was sixty-five

---

26. If Jack $\underline{\text{would have listened to his wife,}}$ he would not have bought those worthless stocks.

(A) would have listened to his wife
(B) would listen to his wife
(C) had listened to his wife
(D) listened to what his wife had said
(E) would have listened to his wife's advice

27. The bank robber approached the teller quietly, cautiously, $\underline{\text{and in an unpretentious manner.}}$

(A) and in an unpretentious manner
(B) and with no pretense
(C) and by acting unpretentious
(D) and by acting unpretentiously
(E) and unpretentiously

28. The conduct of the judge <u>with the accused</u> seemed very unfair to the jury.

   (A) with the accused
   (B) toward the accused
   (C) as to the man who was accused
   (D) and the accused
   (E) as far as the accused was concerned

29. Every typist in the office <u>except she</u> was out sick at least one day during the past month.

   (A) except she (B) except her (C) excepting she (D) but not her (E) outside of her

30. Sam is a professor of theoretical physics, <u>while his brothers are architects</u> with outstanding reputations.

   (A) while his brothers are architects
   (B) also his brothers are architects
   (C) his brothers architects
   (D) as his brothers are architects
   (E) and his brothers are architects

31. A reward was offered <u>to whoever would return the dog to its owner.</u>

   (A) to whoever would return the dog to its owner.
   (B) to whomever would return the dog to its owner.
   (C) to whosoever would return the dog to its owner.
   (D) to whomsoever would return the dog to its owner.
   (E) to whichever person would return the dog to its owner.

32. <u>Irregardless of the outcome of the battle,</u> neither side will be able to claim a decisive victory.

   (A) Irregardless of the outcome of the battle,
   (B) Irregardless of how the battle ends,
   (C) Regardless of the outcome of the battle,
   (D) Despite the outcome of the battle,
   (E) Irregardless of the battle,

33. One of the finest examples of early Greek sculpture <u>are to be found in the British Museum</u> in London.

   (A) are to be found in the British Museum
   (B) were to be found in the British Museum
   (C) are found in the British Museum
   (D) is to be found in the British Museum
   (E) are in the British Museum

34. <u>We were surprised at him canceling the order without giving any previous indication of his intentions.</u>

   (A) We were surprised at him canceling the order without giving any previous indication of his intentions.
   (B) We were surprised that he canceled the order and didn't tell anyone.
   (C) His canceling the order surprised us all.
   (D) We were surprised at his canceling the order without giving any previous indication of his intentions.
   (E) We were surprised at him canceling the order and not letting anyone know about it.

35. When going for an interview, <u>a high school graduate should be prepared to answer the questions that will be asked of him without hesitation.</u>

   (A) a high school graduate should be prepared to answer the questions that will be asked of him without hesitation.
   (B) a high school graduate should without hesitation be prepared to answer the questions that will be asked of him.
   (C) a high school graduate should be prepared without hesitation to answer the questions that will be asked of him.
   (D) a high school graduate should be prepared to answer without hesitation the questions that will be asked of him.
   (E) a high school graduate should be prepared to answer the questions without hesitation that will be asked of him.

36. The most primitive boat of all is the dugout canoe, <u>being carved from a tree trunk.</u>

   (A) being carved from a tree trunk
   (B) carving from a tree trunk
   (C) carved from a tree trunk
   (D) having been carved from a tree trunk
   (E) its being carved from a tree trunk

37. <u>Whether you can find a place to park your car</u> is probably the hardest part of the day's outing.

   (A) Whether you can find a place to park your car
   (B) Finding a place to park your car
   (C) To park your car in a place
   (D) Taking your car to a place where you can park it
   (E) Finding a car parking place near you

38. The trustee resigned <u>in protest from the town board against its approval</u> of the rent control law.

   (A) in protest from the town board against its approval
   (B) protesting against the approval by the town board
   (C) from the town board in protest against its approval
   (D) against the town board, protesting its approval
   (E) in protest from the town board, protesting its approval

39. In the summer, the number of injuries <u>from ladder falls</u> soars.

   (A) from ladder falls
   (B) coming from people falling off their ladders
   (C) because of falls from ladders
   (D) caused by falls from ladders
   (E) which come from the result of falls from ladders

40. Thousands of people are blind <u>because their glaucoma</u> has reached an advanced stage.

   (A) because their glaucoma
   (B) due to their glaucoma
   (C) since they have their glaucoma and it
   (D) having their glaucoma
   (E) from their glaucoma

Note: The remaining questions are like those at the beginning of the section.

Directions: For each sentence in which you find an error, select the one underlined part that must be changed to make the sentence correct and blacken the corresponding space on your answer sheet.

If there is no error, blacken answer space   E .

EXAMPLE:

The region has a climate <u>so severe that</u> plants
                  A

<u>growing</u> there rarely <u>had been</u> more than twelve
   B   C

<u>inches high</u>. <u>No error</u>
   D   E

SAMPLE ANSWER

---

41. The novelists <u>who</u> readers <u>choose</u> as <u>their</u> favorites
           A   B   C
are not always the <u>most skilled</u> writers. <u>No error</u>.
          D   E

42. The problem of <u>how to deal with</u> all the <u>mosquitoes</u>
          A   B
<u>disturb</u> many <u>residents</u> of the Tropics. <u>No error</u>.
  C   D   E

43. The family's only son <u>could of</u> <u>gone</u> to college, but
        A   B   C
he decided to join the army after he graduated <u>from</u>
                                  D
high school. <u>No error</u>.
        E

44. Yesterday at the race track many <u>persons</u> <u>were</u>
         A   B
<u>fearful</u> of betting on the horse <u>who</u> had fallen in the
   C   D
last race. <u>No error</u>.
       E

45. If someone wants to buy <u>all</u> the antiques <u>that</u> I have
                 A   B
for the rummage sale, <u>then</u> <u>they</u> should make me a
                C   D
reasonable offer. <u>No error</u>.
          E

46. The man <u>who</u> Mexican authorities believe <u>to be</u> the
       A   B
country's number 1 drug <u>trafficker</u> <u>has been</u> arrested
                C   D
in a Pacific resort area. <u>No error</u>.
             E

47. When the Los Angeles voters reelected Tom Bradley
  _____ A _____ B
to the largest popular victory in his mayoral career,
         C
they did like we expected them to do. No error.
        D   E

48. William Schroeder became the first person to live
                        A
outside a hospital with an artificial heart when he
  B
moved to a specially equipped apartment across the
  C   D
street. No error.
        E

49. While her mother was inside the house talking on the
         A   B
phone, the child fell off of the unscreened porch.
                       C   D
No error.
  E

50. The racehorse ran swifter in today's race than he ran
                    A   B   C
in his practice sessions last week. No error.
                         D   E

S T O P

**IF YOU FINISH BEFORE TIME IS CALLED, YOU MAY CHECK YOUR WORK ON THIS SECTION ONLY.
DO NOT WORK ON ANY OTHER SECTION IN THE TEST.**

SECTION 4   VERBAL ABILITY
30 MINUTES   40 QUESTIONS

For each question in this section, choose the best answer and blacken the corresponding space on the answer sheet.

Each question below consists of a word in capital letters, followed by five lettered words or phrases. Choose the word or phrase that is most nearly *opposite* in meaning to the word in capital letters. Since some of the questions require you to distinguish fine shades of meaning, consider all the choices before deciding which is best.

Example:

```
GOOD:   (A) sour   (B) bad   (C) red
(D) hot   (E) ugly
                         Ⓐ ● Ⓒ Ⓓ Ⓔ
```

1. MALIGN: (A) defend   (B) separate
   (C) repair   (D) dry   (E) clarify

2. LITHE: (A) loose   (B) honest   (C) coherent
   (D) clumsy   (E) ignorant

3. BOUNTIFUL: (A) disappointing
   (B) inexpensive   (C) scarce   (D) plain
   (E) repulsive

4. HAGGARD: (A) astute   (B) delighted   (C) blown
   up   (D) refreshed   (E) smooth

5. IRASCIBLE: (A) responsible   (B) moral
   (C) possible   (D) detailed   (E) calm

6. BURGEON: (A) fall down   (B) retire   (C) scurry
   about   (D) deceive   (E) waste away

7. GRATUITOUS: (A) noticeable   (B) useful
   (C) costly   (D) original   (E) selfish

8. EMOLUMENT: (A) claim   (B) beginning
   (C) criticism   (D) loss   (E) annoyance

9. MERETRICIOUS: (A) simple   (B) inferior
   (C) unrewarding   (D) amateurish   (E) young

10. VAPID: (A) reasonable   (B) interesting
    (C) disagreeable   (D) flighty   (E) helpful

Each sentence below has one or two blanks, each blank indicating that something has been omitted. Beneath the sentence are five lettered words or sets of words. Choose the word or set of words that *best* fits the meaning of the sentence as a whole.

Example:

```
Although its publicity has been ____, the film itself is
intelligent, well-acted, handsomely produced, and
altogether ____.

(A) tasteless . . . respectable
(B) extensive . . . moderate
(C) sophisticated . . . amateur
(D) risqué . . . crude
(E) perfect . . . spectacular      ● Ⓑ Ⓒ Ⓓ Ⓔ
```

11. In a rising tide of _____ in public education, Miss Anderson was an example of an informed and _____ teacher—a blessing to children and an asset to the nation.

    (A) compromise . . . inept
    (B) pacifism . . . inspiring
    (C) ambiguity . . . average
    (D) mediocrity . . . dedicated
    (E) oblivion . . . typical

12. It is _____ that primitive man considered eclipses to be _____ .

    (A) foretold . . . spectacular
    (B) impossible . . . ominous
    (C) understandable . . . magical
    (D) true . . . rational
    (E) glaring . . . desirable

13. By _____ the conversation, the girl had once again proved that she had overcome her shyness.

    (A) appreciating   (B) recognizing   (C) hearing
    (D) initiating   (E) considering

14. The outbreak of World War II _____ the faith of the world and its leaders.

   (A) shattered   (B) questioned   (C) upheld
   (D) pacified   (E) solidified

15. Only an authority in that area would be able to _____ such highly _____ subject matter included in the book.

   (A) understand . . . general
   (B) confuse . . . simple   (C) read . . . useless
   (D) comprehend . . . complex
   (E) misconstrue . . . sophisticated

Each question below consists of a related pair of words or phrases, followed by five lettered pairs of words or phrases. Select the lettered pair that *best* expresses a relationship similar to that expressed in the original pair.

Example:

YAWN : BOREDOM : :   (A) dream : sleep
(B) anger : madness   (C) smile : amusement
(D) face : expression   (E) impatience : rebellion
                                    Ⓐ Ⓑ ● Ⓓ Ⓔ

16. PORTHOLE : SHIP : :

   (A) stem : flower
   (B) pupil : eye
   (C) blister : skin
   (D) score : music
   (E) antenna : insect

17. PROCRASTINATOR : DELAY : :

   (A) flatterer : undermine
   (B) genius : creativity
   (C) tyrant : influence
   (D) general : salute
   (E) historian : prediction

18. WATERTIGHT : MOISTURE : :

   (A) hermetic : air
   (B) claustrophobic : closeness
   (C) combatant : strife
   (D) somnolent : boredom
   (E) ocean : shore

19. DRIZZLE : CLOUDBURST : :

   (A) grass : dew
   (B) wind : air
   (C) shore : waves
   (D) flurry : blizzard
   (E) dune : sand

20. APIARY : BEE : :

   (A) mountain : skier
   (B) airport : flight
   (C) schedule : event
   (D) theatre : ticket
   (E) stable : horse

21. FOREMAN : JURY : :

   (A) doctor : nurse
   (B) fish : school
   (C) policeman : law
   (D) captain : team
   (E) dancer : chorus

22. GENEALOGY : FAMILY : :

   (A) pseudonym : author
   (B) etymology : word
   (C) password : entry
   (D) royalty : king
   (E) boundary : limit

23. CRASS : REFINEMENT

   (A) frivolous : continuity
   (B) fallow : emphasis
   (C) indifferent : pretense
   (D) orthodox : conviction
   (E) craven : bravery

24. APPLE : CORE : :

   (A) disease : virus
   (B) flower : petal
   (C) year : spring
   (D) cell : nucleus
   (E) potato : root

25. CATCHER : MASK : :

   (A) artist : palette
   (B) owner : insurance
   (C) butcher : apron
   (D) prisoner : sentence
   (E) driver : visor

Each passage below is followed by questions based on its content. Answer all questions following a passage on the basis of what is *stated* or *implied* in that passage.

They say America is parched by a climate of hatred and they don't know what they're talking about, but they're right anyhow.

The *real* hatred in America is the hatred between the
5 desk-diner, who distinctly ordered the cheeseburger with ketchup, not mustard, and the mumbling delivery boy who doesn't give a damn. Or between the man who needs change for a phone call and the merchant who not only refuses but refuses with a deliberation that suggests he's
10 waited years for precisely this opportunity.

Ponder the relationship between the man waiting outside a pay phone booth and the man snuggled up inside. The dialogue is silent but savage.

If you like gratitude in unexpected spurts, try opening
15 the door of the phone booth when it's yours, smiling at the person waiting, and saying "I'll just be another minute," or "This call may take a while. Sorry to make you wait." The impact is as galvanic as if the Vietcong were to wake a sleeping GI patrol and say, "Fellows, we've
20 just got our radio working. Would you like to come over and listen to the Superbowl?"

Americans used to ask themselves, "How nice can I be without seeming ridiculous?" Now we ask, "How rude can I be and still get away with it?"

25 People don't accept apologies anymore. They simply enjoy the sweet sting of hostility. If you want to spread some happiness, try hailing the next off-duty cab driver, whether you want him or not. That Cossack brush-off he waves you doesn't betoken apology or regret. It's pure
30 thrill.

People crave triumph, and if they can't get it through personal victory, they'll get it through personal viciousness. Most people have never known any triumph higher than looking out the window of an express train as it zips
35 past a local.

26. Some of the people that the author speaks about are

    (A) commonplace and boring
    (B) uneasy and frightened
    (C) inconsiderate and spiteful
    (D) helpful and sincere
    (E) pleasant and secure

27. When the author uses the expression "the sweet sting of hostility" in line 26, he refers to a person who

    (A) curses when the waiter spills soup on his
        recently cleaned suit
    (B) gets pleasure seeing his favorite football team
        thrash the opposing team on television
    (C) becomes irate and spanks his child for refusing
        to go to bed
    (D) remains silent and poker-faced instead of
        greeting a person with "Good morning."
    (E) enjoys making another person unhappy or
        uncomfortable

28. The tone of the passage is one of

    (A) justified anger   (B) moderate sympathy
    (C) critical analysis   (D) subtle humor
    (E) impatient disdain

The old Middle West is gone. However, it still lives in song and story. Give most children the choice of visiting Valley Forge or Dodge City . . . Dodge City wins. It is more glamorous in their imagination than Valley Forge.
5 The old Middle West developed a strong, compassionate people out of the hardships and suffering of the destructive blizzards of earlier generations—"northers" that swept over it with white clouds of blinding snow and ice—and southern winds that brought the black blizzards of dust storms.

10 The Middle West is realistic about the nation's domestic and international affairs. It views both with intense interest and anxiety, for it knows that—although stubborn resistance to change can lead to catastrophe—change often does have unforeseen ramifications. This caution is still—es-
15 pecially on political major questions—present in the modern Middle West and is its particular contribution to our national relationships. I think the Middle West's strength is in its customary cautious approach to the day of reckoning in our complex industrial structure and what should
20 be put forward for its solution. That solution will take time, for slapdash approaches never work.

There is still a noticeable difference between the atmosphere in the Middle West and that of the Eastern states. It is more free and easy. The parallel factor is the desire
25 on the part of many heads of families in many lines of activity to change from the tensions and insecurity of life in the big cities to the pleasure and comfort that come from the security of living in smaller towns. In the Middle West, it has increasingly taken the form of people re-
30 maining in the smaller cities and giving them new life and intelligence. This has strengthened smaller communities and offset the flow of Middle Westerners to the big cities. There are, however, signs that cities in general are no longer content to be corrupt. There is pragmatic awakening
35 that can mean a new leadership—with a growing understanding of their problems and responsibilities. This newly awakened urban leadership, joining the Midwest and small city leadership in the quest for stability, may just possibly be the salvation of the big cities.

29. The author would agree that the "Old Middle West" remains

    (A) intact in only a few areas
    (B) only in tales that are told
    (C) unchanged in many small towns
    (D) in spirit but is lost in practice
    (E) a reality only to children who view it on
        television

30. The author feels that the strength of the Middle West lies in its

    (A) tolerance of differences of opinion
    (B) worldliness
    (C) cautiousness
    (D) free and easy atmosphere
    (E) ability to recover from strife

31. A current trend which the author finds encouraging is

    (A) a gradual reduction in inflation
    (B) the increasing complexity of the national industrial structure
    (C) realism in domestic and international affairs
    (D) people staying in the smaller towns and cities
    (E) a growing sense of national identity

32. The character of the old Middle West was formed by

        I. weather hardships
       II. the Gold Rush of 1849
      III. the Civil War

    (A) I only
    (B) II only
    (C) III only
    (D) I and II only
    (E) I and III only

The shedding of tears as an accompaniment of emotional distress has been attributed to other animals, but the fact is that psychic weeping is not known to occur in any animal other than man.

5   As is well known, human infants do not usually cry with tears until they are about 6 weeks of age. Weeping, then, would appear to be a trait acquired not with, but some time after the birth of a human being.

    The length of the dependency period of the human child 10 suggests itself as a responsible factor in the appearance of weeping. During the earlier part of his dependency period the human infant's principal means of attracting the attention of others when he is in distress is by crying. Even a fairly short session of tearless crying in a young infant has 15 a drying effect upon the mucous membranes of his nasopharynx.

    It is the mucous membrane of the nose that constitutes the most immediate contact of the respiratory system with the external world. The nasal mucous membrane must 20 withstand the impact of respired air laden with bacteria, dust, particles, and gases. Tear ducts, called lacrimal ducts, begin at the inner corner of each eye. Discharges from the eye which have entered by the lacrimal ducts trickle down over the nasal mucous membrane. If drying is produced 25 in the mucous membrane, the little hairs, called cilia, die and a gelatinous mass of mucus is found. This mass constitutes a most hospitable culture medium for bacteria, which may then in large numbers easily pass through the nasal mucosa. The consequences of this are not infre- 30 quently lethal. The hypothesis is advanced that natural selection favored those infants who could produce tears. In this way, the function became established in man.

33. The main topic of this passage is

    (A) the psychological relation of animal and man
    (B) the infant's respiratory system
    (C) the importance of infant crying
    (D) weeping and survival in humans
    (E) the structure and function of the nasal mucous membrane

34. Which of the following statements is *not* correct according to the passage?

    (A) One should try to keep the mucous membrane of his nose dry.
    (B) Breathing in certain particles and gases may be harmful.
    (C) Mucus may sometimes invite germs that can be deadly.
    (D) Being able to cry with tears is a natural blessing.
    (E) A lacrimal duct is located somewhere in the head.

35. According to the passage,

    (A) animals other than man have been found to cry because of psychological reasons
    (B) a new-born baby cries with tears because of respiratory problems
    (C) the mucous membrane in the nose forms a defense against outside bacteria
    (D) crying on the part of a 2-year old child often causes drying up of his nasal mucous membrane
    (E) a woman commonly resorts to crying in order to get attention

Siddhartha was now pleased with himself. He could have dwelt for a long time yet in that soft, well-upholstered hell, if this had not happened, this moment of complete hopelessness and despair and the tense moment when he 5 was ready to commit suicide. Was it not his Self, his small, fearful and proud Self, with which he had wrestled for many years, which had always conquered him again and again, which robbed him of happiness and filled him with fear?

10   Siddhartha now realized why he had struggled in vain with this Self when he was a Brahmin and an ascetic. Too much knowledge had hindered him; too many holy verses, too many sacrificial rites, too much mortification of the flesh, too much doing and striving. He had been full of 15 arrogance; he had always been the cleverest, the most eager—always a step ahead of the others, always the learned and intellectual one, always the priest or the sage. His Self had crawled into his priesthood, into this arrogance, into this intellectuality. It sat there tightly and grew, while 20 he thought he was destroying it by fasting and penitence. Now he understood it and realized that the inward voice had been right, that no teacher could have brought him salvation. That was why he had to go into the world, to lose himself in power, women and money; that was why 25 he had to be a merchant, a dice player, a drinker and a man of property, until the priest and Samana in him were dead. That was why he had to undergo those horrible years, suffer nausea, learn the lesson of the madness of an empty,

futile life till the end, till he reached bitter despair, so that
30 Siddhartha the pleasure-monger and Siddhartha the man
of property could die. He had died and a new Siddhartha
had awakened from his sleep. He also would grow old
and die. Siddhartha was transitory, all forms were transitory, but today he was young, he was a child—the new
35 Siddhartha—and he was very happy.

These thoughts passed through his mind. Smiling, he
listened thankfully to a humming bee. Happily he looked
into the flowing river. Never had a river attracted him as
much as this one. Never had he found the voice and ap-
40 pearance of flowing water so beautiful. It seemed to him
as if the river had something special to tell him, something
which he did not know, something which still awaited
him. The new Siddhartha felt a deep love for this flowing
water and decided that he would not leave it again so
45 quickly.

36. The "soft well-upholstered hell" (lines 2–3) is a
reference by the speaker to

(A) an attractive yet uncomfortable dwelling where he
resided
(B) his lifestyle which made him an unhappy person
(C) a place to which he went when he wished to be
completely by himself
(D) his abode in a previous life not referred to in the
passage
(E) a figment of his imagination that used to haunt
him

37. Which of the following best describes the relation
between the second and third paragraphs.

(A) Paragraph 3 shows how much happier one can be
by living alone than in living with others, as
brought out in paragraph 2
(B) Paragraph 3 discusses the advantages of a simple
life as opposed to the more complicated lifestyle
discussed in paragraph 2
(C) Paragraph 3 contrasts the life of a person without
wealth and a formal religion with a person who
has wealth and a formal religion, as in paragraph
2
(D) Paragraph 3 demonstrates the happiness that can
come as a result of giving up the power and the
worldly pleasures referred to in paragraph 2.
(E) Paragraph 3 generalizes about the specific points
made in paragraph 2.

38. Which of the following questions does the passage
answer?

(A) What is the meaning of a Brahmin?
(B) Why did Siddhartha decide to commit suicide?
(C) Where did Siddhartha own property?
(D) For how many years was Siddhartha a member of
the priesthood?
(E) Where did Siddhartha go to school?

39. Which statement best expresses the main idea of this
passage?

(A) Arrogance constitutes a great hindrance for one
who seeks to lead a peaceful life.
(B) One has to discipline himself so that he will
refrain from seeking pleasures that will prove
harmful later.
(C) The quest for knowledge is commendable
provided that search has its limitations.
(D) There is a voice within a person that can advise
him how to attain contentment.
(E) Peace and quiet are more important than wealth
and power in bringing happiness.

40. What is the meaning of "Self" as it is referred to in
the passage?

(A) one's love of nature
(B) one's own life style
(C) one's inner voice
(D) one's remembrances
(E) one's own interests

S T O P

IF YOU FINISH BEFORE TIME IS CALLED, YOU MAY CHECK YOUR WORK ON THIS SECTION ONLY.
DO NOT WORK ON ANY OTHER SECTION IN THE TEST.

SECTION 5   MATH ABILITY
30 MINUTES   35 QUESTIONS

In this section solve each problem, using any available space on the page for scratchwork. Then decide which is the best of the choices given and blacken the corresponding space on the answer sheet.

The following information is for your reference in solving some of the problems.

Circle of radius r: Area $= \pi r^2$; Circumference $= 2\pi r$
  The number of degrees of arc in a circle is 360.
The measure in degrees of a straight angle is 180.

Definitions of symbols:
  $=$ is equal to $\leqq$ is less than or equal to
  $\neq$ is unequal to $\geqq$ is greater than or equal to
  $<$ is less than $\parallel$ is parallel to
  $>$ is greater than $\perp$ is perpendicular to

Triangle: The sum of the measure in degrees of the angles of a triangle is 180.
If $\angle CDA$ is a right angle, then

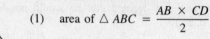

(1) area of $\triangle ABC = \dfrac{AB \times CD}{2}$

(2) $AC^2 = AD^2 + DC^2$

Note: Figures which accompany problems in this test are intended to provide information useful in solving the problems. They are drawn as accurately as possible EXCEPT when it is stated in a specific problem that its figure is not drawn to scale. All figures lie in a plane unless otherwise indicated. All numbers used are real numbers.

1. Janie is older than Tammy, but she is younger than Lori. Let j, t, and l be the ages in years of Janie, Tammy and Lori, respectively. Which of the following is true?

(A) $j < t < l$ (B) $t < j < l$ (C) $t < l < j$
(D) $l < j < t$ (E) $l < t < j$

2. The closest approximation to $\dfrac{(201.2)(.498)}{1.99}$ is

(A) 2500   (B) 100   (C) 50   (D) 25   (E) 5

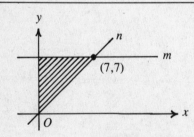

3. In the figure above, m is parallel to the x-axis. All of the following points lie in the shaded area EXCEPT

(A) (4,3)   (B) (1,2)   (C) (5,6)   (D) (4,5)
(E) (2,5)

4. It will be 7:45 in three hours. What time was it $\dfrac{1}{2}$ hour ago?

(A) 1:15   (B) 3:15   (C) 3:45   (D) 4:15   (E) 7:45

5. A certain number increased by 6 equals four times the number. Find the number.

(A) 2   (B) 3   (C) 4   (D) 5   (E) 6

6. A box contains 17 slips of paper. Each is labeled with a different integer from 1 to 17 inclusive. If 5 even numbered slips of paper are removed, what fraction of the remaining slips of paper are even numbered?

(A) $\dfrac{3}{17}$ (B) $\dfrac{3}{8}$ (C) $\dfrac{5}{12}$ (D) $\dfrac{1}{4}$ (E) $\dfrac{1}{6}$

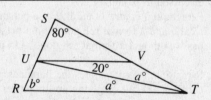

Note: Figure not drawn to scale.

7. In $\triangle RST$ above $UV \parallel RT$. Find b.

(A) 10   (B) 20   (C) 30   (D) 40   (E) 60

Questions 8-27 each consist of two quantities, one in Column A and one in Column B. You are to compare the two quantities and on the answer sheet blacken space

A if the quantity in Column A is greater;
B if the quantity in Column B is greater;
C if the two quantities are equal;
D if the relationship cannot be determined from the information given.

Notes: 1. In certain questions, information concerning one or both of the quantities to be compared is centered above the columns.
2. In a given question, a symbol that appears in both columns represents the same thing in Column A as it does in Column B.
3. Letters such as x, n, and k stand for real numbers.

	EXAMPLES		
	Column A	Column B	Answers
E1.	2×6	$2 + 6$	● Ⓑ Ⓒ Ⓓ
E2.	$180 - x$	y	Ⓐ Ⓑ ● Ⓓ
E3.	$p - q$	$q - p$	Ⓐ Ⓑ Ⓒ ●

For E2: $x°$ $y°$

Column A **Column B**

8. r is an even integer and $5 < r < 8$

$r + 1$ | 7

---

9. The number of hours in w days | v hours

---

10. $\sqrt{48} + \sqrt{80}$ | $7 + 9$

---

11. One face of a solid cube is striped and the other faces are solid red.

The number of faces of the cube that are red | 5

---

12. $8 = 36 - 7w$

w | 7

---

13. $r > 3$

The average rate when r words are typed in 3 hours | The average rate when 3 words are typed in r hours

---

Column A **Column B**

14. $w > 0$

$\dfrac{w + 3}{4}$ | $\dfrac{w + 6}{8}$

15.

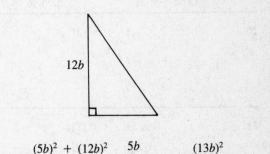

$12b$

$(5b)^2 + (12b)^2$ $5b$ | $(13b)^2$

---

16. 50×150 | 100×100

SUMMARY DIRECTIONS FOR COMPARISON QUESTIONS

Answer: A if the quantity in Column A is greater;
B if the quantity in Column B is greater;
C if the two quantities are equal;
D if the relationship cannot be determined from the information given.

Column A	Column B

17.

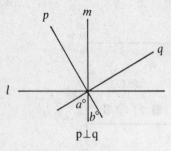

$p \perp q$

$a + b$	90

18. m is an integer > 0
$0 < y < 1$

$\dfrac{m}{y}$	m

19.

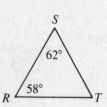

Length of ST	Length of RT

20. $-\dfrac{1}{3}y = \dfrac{1}{3}y$

$-y$	$\dfrac{-2}{3}$

21.   For all $x < 0, \textcircled{x} = 2x^2$
For all $x > 0, \textcircled{x} = \dfrac{x}{4}$

$\textcircled{-3}$	$\textcircled{72}$

22.   Given $\triangle RST$, $RS = 4$ and $ST = 9$

Area $\triangle RST$	18

Column A	Column B

23. r, s and $t > 0$

$t + s + r$	$\dfrac{1}{t + s + r}$

24.

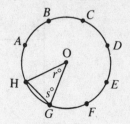

All the points A,B,C,D,E,F,G, and H are equally spaced on the circumference of the circle with center O.

$r°$	$s°$

25.   For a class of 100 students, exactly 80 percent take Calculus, exactly 60 percent take Physics and exactly 50 percent take German.

The number of students who take both Physics and German.	50

26. a,b,c,d and e are all integers > 0.
$a < b < c < d < e$
$a \times b = 7$ and $d \times e = 90$

c	8

27.   The average (arithmetic mean) of a and b is 8.
$a - b + 4 = 0$

a	6

Solve each of the remaining problems in this section using any available space for scratchwork. Then decide which is the best of the choices given and blacken the corresponding space on the answer sheet.

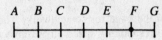

28. AG is divided into six equal segments in the figure above. A circle, not visible, with center F and radius $\frac{1}{5}$ the length of AG, will intersect AG between

(A) F and G (B) E and F (C) D and E
(D) C and D (E) A and B

29. Rose has earned $44 in 8 days. If she continues to earn at the same daily rate, in how many <u>more</u> days will her total earnings be $99?

(A) 22   (B) 16   (C) 14   (D) 12   (E) 10

30. If $x < 0$ and $y < 0$, which of the following must always be positive?

     I. $x \cdot y$
    II. $x + y$
   III. $x - y$

(A) I only
(B) I and II only
(C) I and III only
(D) II and III only
(E) I, II, and III

31. Given that $a + 3b = 11$ and a and b are positive integers. What is the largest possible value of a?

(A) 4   (B) 6   (C) 7   (D) 8   (E) 10

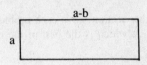

32. The figure above is a rectangle having width a and length $a - b$. Find its perimeter in terms of a and b.

(A) $a^2 - ab$ (B) $4a - 2b$ (C) $4a - b$
(D) $2a - 2b$ (E) $2a - b$

$$
\begin{array}{r}
AB \\
+ \ BA \\
\hline
CDC
\end{array}
$$

33. If each of the four letters in the sum above represents a different digit, which of the following *cannot* be a value of A?

(A) 6   (B) 5   (C) 4   (D) 3   (E) 2

34. $\dfrac{1}{11^{20}} - \dfrac{1}{11^{21}} =$

(A) $\dfrac{1}{11}$ (B) $\dfrac{10}{11^{21}}$ (C) $\dfrac{1}{11^{21}}$ (D) $-\dfrac{10}{11^{21}}$ (E) $-\dfrac{1}{11}$

35. Given three integers a, b and 4. If their average (arithmetic mean) is 6, which of the following could *not* be the value of the product ab?

(A) 13   (B) 14   (C) 40   (D) 48   (E) 49

S T O P

IF YOU FINISH BEFORE TIME IS CALLED, YOU MAY CHECK YOUR WORK ON THIS SECTION ONLY.
DO NOT WORK ON ANY OTHER SECTION IN THE TEST.

SECTION 6   MATH ABILITY
30 MINUTES   35 QUESTIONS

In this section solve each problem, using any available space on the page for scratchwork. Then decide which is the best of the choices given and blacken the corresponding space on the answer sheet.

The following information is for your reference in solving some of the problems.

Circle of radius r: Area = πr^2; Circumference = $2\pi r$
    The number of degrees of arc in a circle is 360.
The measure in degrees of a straight angle is 180.

Definitions of symbols:
=	is equal to	$\leqq$	is less than or equal to
$\neq$	is unequal to	$\geqq$	is greater than or equal to
$<$	is less than	$\parallel$	is parallel to
$>$	is greater than	$\perp$	is perpendicular to

Triangle: The sum of the measure in degrees of the angles of a triangle is 180.
If $\angle\,CDA$ is a right angle, then

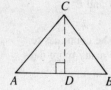

(1)   area of $\triangle\,ABC = \dfrac{AB \times CD}{2}$

(2) $AC^2 = AD^2 + DC^2$

Note: Figures which accompany problems in this test are intended to provide information useful in solving the problems. They are drawn as accurately as possible EXCEPT when it is stated in a specific problem that its figure is not drawn to scale. All figures lie in a plane unless otherwise indicated. All numbers used are real numbers.

1. If $0.25 + 0.50 + x = 1.25$, then $x =$

(A) $\dfrac{1}{2}$ (B) $\dfrac{3}{4}$ (C) 25 (D) 50 (E) 70

2. Which statement(s) is(are) true?

   I. $6^2 = 36$
   II. $6^4 = 2^2 \cdot 3^4$
   III. $6^6 > 216$

(A) I only
(B) II only
(C) III only
(D) I and III only
(E) I, II, and III

3. If 4 out of 20 marbles in a bag are blue, what fraction of the marbles are blue?

(A) $\dfrac{1}{80}$ (B) $\dfrac{1}{24}$ (C) $\dfrac{1}{16}$ (D) $\dfrac{1}{6}$ (E) $\dfrac{1}{5}$

4. Which of the following even numbers is a prime number?

(A) 2 (B) 4 (C) 14 (D) 32 (E) 50

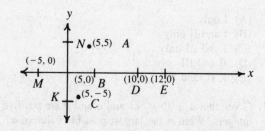

5. $\overleftrightarrow{NK}$ is the perpendicular bisector of $\overline{MP}$. (P is *not* shown.) Then P is the same as which of the following points?

(A) A (B) B (C) C (D) D (E) E

6. In how many different arrangements can 3 unlike books be placed on a shelf?

(A) 3 (B) 4 (C) 6 (D) 9 (E) 12

7. The areas of triangles I, II, III, IV, V, VI, VII, VIII, IX, X, XI, XII are the same. If the region outlined by the heavy line has area = 256 and the area of square *ABCD* is 128, determine the shaded area.

(A) 16   (B) 32   (C) 48   (D) 100   (E) 160

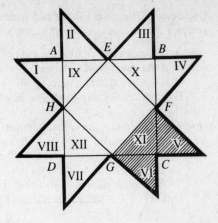

Questions 8-27 each consist of two quantities, one in Column A and one in Column B. You are to compare the two quantities and on the answer sheet blacken space

A if the quantity in Column A is greater;
B if the quantity in Column B is greater;
C if the two quantities are equal;
D if the relationship cannot be determined from the information given.

Notes: 1. In certain questions, information concerning one or both of the quantities to be compared is centered above the columns.
2. In a given question, a symbol that appears in both columns represents the same thing in Column A as it does in Column B.
3. Letters such as x, n, and k stand for real numbers.

	EXAMPLES		
	Column A	Column B	Answers
E1.	2×6	$2 + 6$	● Ⓑ Ⓒ Ⓓ
E2.	$180 - x$	y	Ⓐ Ⓑ ● Ⓓ
E3.	$p - q$	$q - p$	Ⓐ Ⓑ Ⓒ ●

For E2, the figure shows angles $x°$ and $y°$ on a line.

	Column A	Column B
8.	$256 \div 4$	16×4
9.	$\dfrac{24x - 72}{24}$	$x - 4$

10.

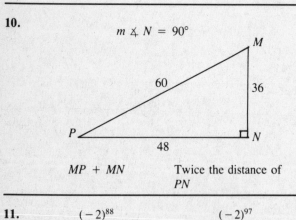

$$m \angle N = 90°$$

	Column A	Column B
	$MP + MN$	Twice the distance of PN
11.	$(-2)^{88}$	$(-2)^{97}$

	Column A	Column B
12.	$-5 < y < 5$	
	$-y$	6

13.

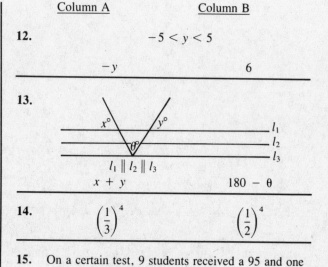

$$l_1 \parallel l_2 \parallel l_3$$

	Column A	Column B
	$x + y$	$180 - \theta$
14.	$\left(\dfrac{1}{3}\right)^4$	$\left(\dfrac{1}{2}\right)^4$

15. On a certain test, 9 students received a 95 and one student received less than a 95.

	average (arithmetic mean) of test scores	95

SUMMARY DIRECTIONS FOR COMPARISON QUESTIONS

<u>Answer:</u> A if the quantity in Column A is greater;
B if the quantity in Column B is greater;
C if the two quantities are equal;
D if the relationship cannot be determined from the information given.

<u>Column A</u>	<u>Column B</u>

16. $x = -y, x > 0$

xy $\qquad\qquad$ y^2

17. $1 < \dfrac{1}{6}x < 2$

x $\qquad\qquad$ 10

18. $a + b < 0$

$c(a + b) + d(a + b)$ $\qquad$ $c(a + b) + (d + 1)(a + b)$

19. $3x = 4y$
$x > 0$

x $\qquad\qquad$ y

20. A drawing is made of a cube.

Using a scale that measures 2 inches = 3 ft., the length of a side of the cube	Using a scale that measures 2 inches = 4 ft., the length of a side of the cube

21. $(x + a)(x + b) = 24$
$x + a > 0$

a $\qquad\qquad$ b

22.

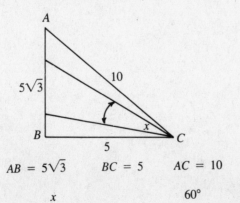

$AB = 5\sqrt{3}$ $\quad$ $BC = 5$ $\quad$ $AC = 10$

x $\qquad\qquad$ $60°$

<u>Column A</u>	<u>Column B</u>

23. On consecutive days a man earns \$5 one day and loses \$5 the next day, then earns \$5, then loses \$5, and so on.

The sum of his money earned from working 2 consecutive days	The product of his money earned from working 2 consecutive days

24. The volume of a cone is $\dfrac{1}{3}\pi r^2 h$ where r is the radius of the base and h is the height of the cone.

Volume of a cone with radius r and height h	Volume of a cone with radius $3h$ and height $\dfrac{r}{3}$

25. $n > 0$

24% of n $\qquad\qquad$ $\dfrac{6n}{25}$

26.

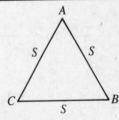

The area of $\triangle ABC$ $\qquad\qquad$ $\dfrac{1}{2}S^2$

27.   is the greatest integer less than or equal to x

 $\qquad\qquad$ X Y

Solve each of the remaining problems in this section using any available space for scratchwork. Then decide which is the best of the choices given and blacken the corresponding space on the answer sheet.

28. Since one gross = 12 dozen, what fraction of a gross of eggs is 3 eggs?

(A) $\frac{1}{144}$ (B) $\frac{1}{72}$ (C) $\frac{1}{48}$ (D) $\frac{1}{12}$ (E) $\frac{1}{4}$

	FIRST PLACE	SECOND PLACE	THIRD PLACE
	(8 points)	(4 points)	(2 points)
EVENT ①	TEAM A	TEAM B	TEAM C
EVENT ②	TEAM B	TEAM A	TEAM C

29. The results of two games involving 3 teams are shown above. Thus, we have the following standings: A and B both have 12 points and C has 4 points. Assuming no ties, what is the least number of additional games that Team C will have to play in order to have the highest total score?

(A) 1 (B) 2 (C) 3 (D) 4 (E) 5

30. If x is the average of k numbers and y is the average of j numbers, then find the average of the $k + j$ numbers.

(A) $\frac{x + y + k + j}{k + j}$ (B) $\frac{ky + jx}{k + j}$

(C) $\frac{kx + jy}{k + j}$ (D) $x + y$

(E) $\frac{(k + j)(x + y)}{kj}$

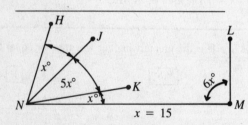

Note: Figure not drawn to scale.

31. If the figure above were drawn to scale and all line segments were extended indefinitely in *both directions*, how many intersection points would there be in addition to N and M?

(A) 0 (B) 1 (C) 2 (D) 3 (E) 4

32. Two sailors start to swim at the same time from opposite ends of a pool which is 120 meters long. If one of the sailors swims at a rate of 2 meters per second, and the other at a rate of 3 meters per second, how many more meters must the former swim after the latter has finished?

(A) 1 (B) 20 (C) 30 (D) 40 (E) 80

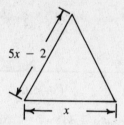

33. The figure above is an equilateral triangle. What is its perimeter?

(A) $\frac{1}{4}$ (B) $\frac{1}{2}$ (C) $1\frac{1}{2}$ (D) $3\frac{1}{2}$

(E) Cannot be determined from the information given.

34. If w waves pass through a certain point in s seconds, how many waves would pass through that point in t seconds?

(A) wst (B) $\frac{t}{s}$ (C) $\frac{ws}{t}$ (D) $\frac{ts}{w}$ (E) $\frac{tw}{s}$

35. If a is 10 percent greater than b, and ac is 32 percent greater than bd, then c is what percent greater than d?

(A) 10 (B) 20 (C) 32 (D) 50 (E) 320

S T O P

IF YOU FINISH BEFORE TIME IS CALLED, YOU MAY CHECK YOUR WORK ON THIS SECTION ONLY.
DO NOT WORK ON ANY OTHER SECTION IN THE TEST.

HOW DID YOU DO ON THIS TEST?

STEP 1. Go to the Answer Key on page 516.

STEP 2. For your "raw score," count your correct answers in each of the test parts of the test you have just taken:

Verbal (Section 1 and 4 combined) _____.

Math (Sections 2, 5, and 6 combined) _____.

Standard Written English (Section 3) _____.

STEP 3. Get your "scaled score" for the test by referring to the Raw Score/ Scaled Score Conversion Tables on pages 64–66.

THERE'S ALWAYS ROOM FOR IMPROVEMENT!

ANSWER KEY FOR PRACTICE TEST 4

Section 1—Verbal

1. D	8. B	15. A	22. C	29. A	36. B	43. A
2. B	9. B	16. D	23. E	30. B	37. C	44. D
3. A	10. A	17. C	24. E	31. B	38. E	45. D
4. C	11. D	18. B	25. B	32. C	39. E	
5. E	12. A	19. A	26. D	33. B	40. E	
6. C	13. E	20. D	27. A	34. C	41. B	
7. E	14. E	21. A	28. B	35. E	42. A	

Section 2—Math

1. E	5. B	9. B	13. B	17. C	21. D	25. B
2. C	6. B	10. E	14. B	18. D	22. E	
3. A	7. E	11. D	15. D	19. D	23. A	
4. D	8. C	12. C	16. A	20. A	24. C	

Section 3—Standard Written English

1. C	9. A	17. A	25. A	33. D	41. A	49. C
2. D	10. A	18. E	26. C	34. D	42. C	50. A
3. D	11. C	19. B	27. E	35. D	43. B	
4. E	12. C	20. E	28. B	36. C	44. D	
5. B	13. D	21. C	29. B	37. B	45. D	
6. A	14. D	22. E	30. E	38. C	46. A	
7. C	15. B	23. B	31. A	39. D	47. D	
8. E	16. C	24. D	32. C	40. A	48. E	

Section 4—Verbal

1. A	7. C	13. D	19. D	25. E	31. D	37. D
2. D	8. D	14. A	20. E	26. C	32. A	38. B
3. C	9. A	15. D	21. D	27. E	33. E	39. E
4. D	10. B	16. B	22. B	28. D	34. A	40. E
5. E	11. D	17. B	23. E	29. B	35. C	
6. E	12. C	18. A	24. D	30. C	36. B	

Section 5—Math

1. B	6. D	11. C	16. B	21. C	26. C	31. D
2. C	7. E	12. B	17. C	22. D	27. C	32. B
3. A	8. C	13. A	18. A	23. D	28. C	33. E
4. D	9. D	14. A	19. B	24. B	29. E	34. B
5. A	10. B	15. C	20. A	25. D	30. A	35. B

Section 6—Math

1. A	6. C	11. A	16. B	21. D	26. B	31. C
2. D	7. C	12. B	17. D	22. B	27. D	32. D
3. E	8. C	13. C	18. A	23. A	28. C	33. C
4. A	9. A	14. B	19. A	24. D	29. B	34. E
5. B	10. C	15. B	20. A	25. C	30. C	35. B

EXPLANATORY ANSWERS FOR PRACTICE TEST 4

Section 1: Verbal Ability

As you read these Explanatory Answers, you are advised to refer to "Using Critical Thinking Skills in Verbal Questions" (beginning on page 90) whenever a specific Strategy is referred to in the answer. Of particular importance are the following Master Verbal Strategies:

Sentence Completion Master Strategy 1—page 94.
Sentence Completion Master Strategy 2—page 95.
Analogies Master Strategy 1—page 90.
Antonyms Master Strategy 1—page 99.
Reading Comprehension Master Strategy 2—page 109.

1. **(D)** Choice D is correct. *Tantalize* means *tease; torment*. The opposite of *tantalize* is *to comfort*.

2. **(B)** Choice B is correct. *Chide* means *to scold*. The opposite of *chide* to *to praise*.

3. **(A)** Choice A is correct. See **Antonym Strategy 3**. *Nebulous* means *hazy; vague; uncertain*. The opposite of *nebulous* is *certain*.

4. **(C)** Choice C is correct. *Blatant* means *obvious; conspicuous*. The opposite of *blatant* is *concealed*.

5. **(E)** Choice E is correct. *Sully* means to *soil* or *dirty*. The opposite of *sully* is to *cleanse*.

6. **(C)** Choice C is correct. See **Antonym Strategy 3**. *Carnal* means *sensual; sexual*. The opposite of *carnal* is *spiritual*.

7. **(E)** Choice E is correct. See **Antonym Strategy 3**. *Tacit* means *silent; not expressed*. The opposite of *tacit* is *expressed*.

8. **(B)** Choice B is correct. See **Antonym Strategy 3**. *Extraneous* means *unrelated; not essential*. The opposite of *extraneous* is *related*.

9. **(B)** Choice B is correct. See **Antonym Strategy 2**. *Opulent* means *rich; luxurious*. The opposite of *opulent* is *needy*.

10. **(A)** Choice A is correct. See **Antonym Strategy 2**. *Queasy* means *nauseated; uneasy*. The opposite of *queasy* is *comfortable*.

11. **(D)** Choice D is correct. *Refractory* means *stubborn*. The opposite of *refractory* is *manageable*.

12. **(A)** Choice A is correct. See **Antonym Strategy 2**. *Ebullient* means *enthusiastic*. The opposite of *ebullient* is *unmoved*.

13. **(E)** Choice E is correct. See **Antonym Strategy 1**. *Omnivorous* means *eating any kind of food*. The opposite of *omnivorous* is *selective*.

14. **(E)** Choice E is correct. *Nadir* means the *lowest point*. The opposite of *nadir* is *peak*.

15. **(A)** Choice A is correct. See **Antonym Strategies 1, 3**. *Dispassionate* means *impartial; calm*. The opposite of *dispassionate* is *partial*.

16. **(D)** Choice D is correct. See **Sentence Completion Strategies 3 and 4**. The key words "rather than" tell us that a word which is *opposite* to "severity" is needed to fill the blank space. If you used the strategy of trying to complete the sentence *before* looking at the five choices, you might have chosen for your blank fill-in one of these appropriate words: easy, friendly, diplomatic, pleasing, soothing. Each of these words has a meaning much like that of the word "conciliatory." The words of the other four choices are *not* appropriate in the sentence. Therefore, these choices are incorrect.

17. **(C)** Choice C is correct. **See Sentence Completion Strategy 4**. The key word "so" indicates, in this case, a result that is similar to what takes place at the beginning of the sentence. "Happiness" for others balances with satisfaction for himself.

18. **(B)** Choice B is correct. See **Sentence Completion Strategy 2**. We can first eliminate Choice (A) inconsistently, Choice (C) haphazardly, and Choice (D) secretly because these first blank words do *not* make sense in the sentence. This leaves us with Choice (B) drastically and Choice (E) doubtlessly. But Choice (E) doubtlessly . . . destroyed, does *not* make sense. Choice (B) drastically . . . abolished, *does* make sense.

19. **(A)** Choice A is correct. The word "passive" means submissive, not participating, accepting without objection. See **Sentence Completion Strategy 1**. A person who loves action certainly cannot tolerate a passive life style. Choices B, C, D, and E are incorrect because an action-loving person may, indeed, tolerate a chaotic or brazen or grandiose or vibrant life style.

20. **(D)** Choice D is correct. The word "degradation" means deterioration, a lowering of position. The sight of a person in such a state would generally bring about a feeling of pity. Choices A, B, C, and E do *not* make good sense in the sentence. Therefore, these choices are incorrect. See **Sentence Completion Strategy 1**.

21. **(A)** Choice A is a false statement—therefore, the correct choice. See lines 45–46: "The ratio of physicians to population has remained fairly constant over the past 20 years." Accordingly, the percentage of physicians in the general population has not increased. Choice B is a true statement—therefore, an incorrect choice. See lines 46–48: "The number of dentists . . . during these years." Choice C is a true statement even though the passage does not state Choice C directly. See the reference to a "population explosion." This indicates that there are more doctors today even though "The ratio of physicians to population has remained fairly constant." (Lines 45–46) Therefore, Choice C is an incorrect choice. Likewise, the following are true statements—therefore, incorrect choices: Choice D (lines 48–52): "In the same period . . . population generally." Choice E (lines 54–55): ". . . more than half . . . were specialists."

22. **(C)** The correct choice is C. The passage begins, "The most striking feature of medical care is its rapid and continuing evolution." The rest of the passage is an illustration of this point by example. Though the passage does discuss the negative effects of increased specialization when it speaks of "problems of complexity . . . depersonalization of patient care" (lines 20–23) in part as the result of technological advances, neither Choice A nor B can be considered to be the main point of the passage. Therefore, these choices are incorrect. Although Choices D and E are brought out in the passage, neither choice constitutes the main purpose of the author's message. Therefore, Choices D and E are incorrect.

23. **(E)** The correct choice is E. This question is probably best answered through elimination. The author cannot be described as an apologist, reformer, critic, or watchdog. He discusses both advantageous and deleterious effects of changes which have taken place in the medical field, but the tone remains neutral. No positions or stands are taken. The word "observer" means one who watches and indicates a person who takes no definite position or stand on a subject.

24. **(E)** The correct choice is E. See lines 15–17: "The contents . . . family doctor." Choice A is incorrect. According to the passage, the population is "increasingly encountering the degenerative diseases and chronic disabilities." (lines 29–30). These are the health problems of today, not of a century ago. Choice B is incorrect. Diarrhea, pneumonia and tuberculosis are no longer the major killers, as they were in 1900 (see lines 32–34), but the passage does not say that they are no longer health problems. Choice C is incorrect. Lines 8–11 describe a family doctor at the turn of the century, unsure whether he will be able to cure a heart disorder his stethoscope has detected, but this is neither a statement nor a suggestion that the 19th century doctor was unable to treat most of the illnesses of his day. Choice D is incorrect. Heart disease and cancer are responsible for most deaths by illness today. In 1900, it was diarrhea, pneumonia, and tuberculosis (lines 32–34).

25. **(B)** The correct choice is B. See lines 2–4, "From its origin, as an aspect of primitive religion, exorcising the forces of evil, medical care has ascended to a modern day system . . ." Since the author places the origin of medicine in such practices as exorcisms, he clearly does not believe these practices have nothing to do with medicine. The other statements all follow from the passage: Choices A and E follow from the author's observation that medical care is becoming increasingly specialized and impersonal. The replacement of the "little black bag" with sophisticated hospital equipment is discussed in lines 8–14. The author mentions that our health needs have changed as our society has changed (lines 24–34), so he is likely to agree that different communities will have different health needs (Choice C). Lines 37–38 refer to "higher levels of educational attainment" among the factors contributing to an increased demand for services. Therefore, the author would apparently agree that a better-educated community will use more health services (Choice D).

26. **(D)** Choice A is incorrect because the author stops short of outright despair in the last sentence of the first paragraph by tempering the outbursts of the Renaissance scholar with the milder "our times are out of joint." Choices B and E are incorrect because there is no positive feeling expressed in the first paragraph. Choice C is incorrect because there is no feeling of attraction toward an earlier age. Choice D is correct because the negative feeling is not quite full-bodied.

27. **(A)** There is no mention of energy sources at any point in the selection. Therefore this answer is correct. Choices B, C, D, and E are mentioned in paragraph 2.

28. **(B)** The positive outlook of the words, "trend is not destiny" is best exemplified by Choice B which implies that man can improve his situation. The other statements are negative or pessimistic pronouncements.

29. **(A)** The author cites Choices B, C, D, and E in paragraph 5 as examples of renewed public awareness. The reference to the president's increase in the military budget does not indicate evidence of the public's insight regarding a danger.

30. **(B)** Choices A and C are incorrect because the author is consistently expressing optimism in man's ability to learn from past mistakes. Choice B is the correct answer. Accordingly, Choice D contradicts the realistic tone of the essay. Choice E is not at all characteristic of the writer's attitude.

31. **(B)** Choice B is correct. See **Sentence Completion Strategy 4.** The key word "although" in this sentence indicates that there is opposition or difference between the first part of the sentence and the last part. Since our team knew that the opponents (the Raiders) were "sluggish," we were stupid—we should have pushed hard instead of being so "easygoing." The other four choices are incorrect because their word pairs do not make sense in the sentence.

32. **(C)** Choice C is correct. See **Sentence Completion Strategy 2.**

    STEP 1

    We first examine the first word of each choice. We then eliminate Choice (A) heroic, Choice (B) respected, and Choice (E) insightful because a prime minister with any of these positive qualities would hardly be expected to cause a downfall of his country. So Choices A, B, and E are incorrect.

    STEP 2

    We now consider the remaining choices. Choice (D) vacillating . . . confidential, does not make sense in the sentence because we cannot refer to a country as confidential. Therefore, Choice D is also incorrect. Choice (C) incompetent . . . powerful, makes sense and *is* the correct choice.

33. **(B)** Choice B is correct. See **Sentence Completion Strategy 1.** The word "aloof" means withdrawn, distant, uninvolved. A character who is dignified and who is a man of reserve is likely to be aloof.

34. **(C)** Choice C is correct. See **Sentence Completion Strategy 2.**

    STEP 1

    Let us first examine the first words of each choice. We can then eliminate Choice (A) frequent, Choice (B) heavy, and Choice (E) bland because saying that blood contains frequent or heavy or bland amounts does not make sense. So Choices A, B, and E are incorrect.

    STEP 2

    We now consider the remaining choices. Choice (D) definite . . . puzzling, does *not* make sense because blood does not contain puzzling amounts. Therefore, Choice D is also incorrect. Choice (C) minute (pronounced "mine-yute"—meaning exceptionally small) . . . excessive, makes sense and *is* the correct choice.

35. **(E)** Choice E is correct. See **Sentence Completion Strategy 2.**

    STEP 1

    Let us first examine the first word of each choice. We can then eliminate Choice (A) unearned and Choice (D) backward because saying unearned attempts to please or backward attempts to please *does not* make sense. So Choices A and D are incorrect.

    STEP 2

    Let us now consider the remaining choices. The second words of Choice (B) . . . humor, and Choice (C) . . . reliance, *do not* make sense in the sentence. Choice (E) hypocritical . . . defiance, makes sense and is the correct choice.

36. **(B)** Choice B is correct. One sews in order to fix a tear. One caulks in order to fix a leak (in a boat). Note that "tear" as it is spelled has another meaning—a "drop"—but not is this analogy. See **Analogy Strategy 5.** **(Purpose relationship)**

37. **(C)** Choice C is correct. That which is infinite does not end. That which is buoyant does not sink. **(Opposite relationship)**

38. **(E)** Choice E is correct. To coerce is to coax forcefully. To shove is to nudge forcefully. We have here a degree relationship. Choice (C) declaim : argue, also has a degree relationship but the two words would have to be reversed for the choice to be correct. See **Analogy Strategy 3.** **(Degree relationship)**

39. **(E)** Choice E is correct. To rejuvenate is to give back youth. To reimburse is to give back money. **(Result relationship)**

40. **(E)** Choice E is correct. One sneers in order to express contempt. One grimaces in order to express pain. We have here a Purpose relationship. Choices B and C are also purpose relationships but they do not have the facial quality that the capitalized words and the Choice E words have. Therefore, Choice B and C are incorrect. See **Analogy Strategy 4.** **(Purpose relationship)**

41. **(B)** Choice B is correct. Something that is unpretentious lacks ostentation. Something that is inconsequential lacks importance. **(Characteristic and opposite relationship)**

42. **(A)** Choice A is correct. Something that is enigmatic is not clear. Something that is copious is not scarce. **(Opposite relationship)**

43. **(A)** Choice A is correct. An embarkation is the beginning of a journey. An inception is the beginning of a project. **(Part-Whole relationship)**

44. **(D)** Choice D is correct. An epicure is a person for whom pleasure is his main goal. A miser is a person for whom wealth is his main goal.
(Purpose relationship)

45. **(D)** Choice D is correct. You can't touch something that is intangible. You can't fix something that is irreparable. Consider Choice (C) convict : innocent. It is possible that a court *can* convict someone who is innocent. Therefore Choice C is incorrect. See **Analogy Strategy 4.**
(Result and Opposite relationship)

EXPLANATORY ANSWERS FOR
PRACTICE TEST 4 (continued)

Section 2: Math Ability

As you read these solutions, you are advised to do two things if you answered the Math question incorrectly:

1) When a specific Strategy is referred to in the solution, study that strategy, which you will find in "Using Critical Thinking Skills in Math Questions" (beginning on page 69).

2) When the solution directs you to the "Math Refresher" (beginning on page 205)—for example, Math Refresher #305—study the 305 Math principle to get a clear idea of the Math operation that was necessary for you to know in order to answer the question correctly.

1. **(E)** Choice E is correct.
(Use Strategy 17: Use the given information effectively.)

The number with the largest last digit will become the largest number after interchanging. ☐1

(Use Strategy 15: Certain choices are easily eliminated.)

Using ☐1, we see that Choices B and E each end in 5. All others end in digits less than 5 and may be eliminated.

(Use Strategy 8: When all choices must be tested, start with E.)

Choice E, 2345, becomes 5342. ☐2
Choice B, 4235, becomes 5234. ☐3
☐2 is larger than ☐3.

(Logical Reasoning)

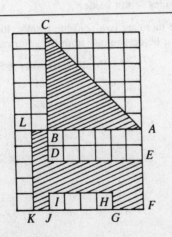

Given: length of side of square = 1. ☐1
Using ☐1, we get $AB = 6, BC = 6$ ☐2

We know that Area of triangle $= \frac{1}{2}$(base)(height) ☐3

Substituting ☐2 into ☐3, we get

Area of Shaded Triangle $ABC = \frac{1}{2}(6)(6)$
$= 18$ ☐4
We know that Area of square $= $ (side)^2 ☐5

Substituting ☐1 into ☐5, we have

Area of each square $= (1)^2 = 1$ ☐6

Counting the number of squares in the other shaded figure ($BDEFGHIJKL$), we find 19. ☐7

Multiplying ☐6 by ☐7, we have

Area of $BDEFGHIJKL = 19 \times 1 = 19$ ☐8

(Use Strategy 3: The whole equals the sum of its parts.)

We know: Total Shaded Area
$= $ Area of $ABC +$
Area of $BDEFGHIJKL$ ☐9

Substituting ☐4 and ☐8 into ☐9, we get

Total Shaded Area $= 18 + 19$
$= 37$

(Math Refresher #303 and #307)

2. **(C)** Choice C is correct.

3. **(A)**   Choice A is correct.
   (Use Strategy 17: Use the given information effectively.)

   Given: $\dfrac{4^3 + 4^3 + 4^3 + 4^3}{4^y} = 4$

   $$\dfrac{4(4^3)}{4^y} = 4$$

   $$\dfrac{4^4}{4^y} = 4$$

   $$4^{4-y} = 4^1 \qquad \boxed{1}$$

   In $\boxed{1}$ each expression has base 4. Since the expressions are equal the exponents must also be equal. Thus,

   $$4 - y = 1$$
   $$-y = -3$$
   $$y = 3$$

   (Math Refresher #429 and #406)

4. **(D)**   Choice D is correct.
   (Use Strategy 17: Use the given information effectively.)

Game	Darrin	Tom
1	69	43
2	59	60
3	72	55
4	70	68
5	78	73
Totals	348	299

   We need the scores at the end of the first four games. We have been given the totals for all five games.

   (Use Strategy 13: Find unknowns by subtraction.)

   $$\text{Darrin's Total} = 348 \qquad \boxed{1}$$
   $$\text{Darrin's Game 5} = 78 \qquad \boxed{2}$$
   $$\text{Tom's Total} = 299 \qquad \boxed{3}$$
   $$\text{Tom's Game 5} = 73 \qquad \boxed{4}$$

   Subtract $\boxed{2}$ from $\boxed{1}$. We get
   Darrin's Total for 1st four games = 348 – 78
   $$= 270 \qquad \boxed{5}$$

   Subtract $\boxed{4}$ from $\boxed{3}$. We get
   Tom's total for 1st four games = 299 – 73
   $$= 226 \qquad \boxed{6}$$

   Subtracting $\boxed{6}$ from $\boxed{5}$, we have

   Number of points Tom was
   behind Darrin after the first four games = 270 – 226
   $$= 44$$

   (Subtraction and Logical Reasoning)

5. **(B)**   Choice B is correct.

   Given: $(4 + 3)(w + 2) = 28$
   $$7(w + 2) = 28 \qquad \boxed{1}$$

   (Use Strategy 13: Find unknowns by division.)
   Divide $\boxed{1}$ by 7. We get

   $$\dfrac{7(w + 2)}{7} = \dfrac{28}{7}$$
   $$w + 2 = 4$$
   $$w = 2$$

   (Math Refresher #406)

6. **(B)**   Choice B is correct.

   $Given:$ $\dfrac{y^2 - 7y + 10}{y - 2} \qquad \boxed{1}$

   (Use Strategy 19: Factor and reduce.)
   Factor the numerator of $\boxed{1}$. We get

   $$\dfrac{(y - 5)(y - 2)}{y - 2} =$$
   $$y - 5 \qquad \boxed{2}$$

   Substitute 8.000001 in $\boxed{2}$. We have

   $$8.000001 - 5 =$$
   $$3.000001 \approx 3$$

   (Math Refresher #409 and #431)

7. **(E)**   Choice E is correct.

   Given: Isosceles triangle with two sides of length 9 and 16.

   (Use Strategy 18: Know the isosceles triangle.)
   An isosceles triangle has two equal sides.

   (Use Strategy 7: Use numerics to help find the answer.)

   It could have sides of 9, 9 and 16 or 9, 16 and 16.

   Each is an acceptable triangle since the sum of any two sides > third side.

   Since there are two possible results, the answer cannot be determined from the information given.

   (Math Refresher #507 and #516)

8. **(C)** Choice C is correct.

$$Given: \quad ab = 40 \qquad \boxed{1}$$
$$\frac{a}{b} = \frac{5}{2} \qquad \boxed{2}$$

(Use Strategy 13: Find unknowns by multiplication.)

Multiplying $\boxed{2}$ by $2b$, we get

$$2b\left(\frac{a}{b}\right) = \left(\frac{5}{2}\right)2b$$
$$2a = 5b$$
$$\frac{2a}{5} = b \qquad \boxed{3}$$

Substitute $\boxed{3}$ into $\boxed{1}$. We have

$$ab = 40$$
$$a\left(\frac{2a}{5}\right) = 40$$
$$\frac{2a^2}{5} = 40 \qquad \boxed{4}$$

Multiplying $\boxed{1}$ by $\frac{5}{2}$, we get

$$\frac{5}{2}\left(\frac{2a^2}{5}\right) = (40)\frac{5}{2}$$
$$a^2 = 100$$
$$\sqrt{a^2} = \sqrt{100}$$
$$a = \pm\, 10$$

Since we were given that a is positive, we have
$a = 10$

(Math Refresher #406, #429, and #430)

9. **(B)** Choice B is correct.

12 must be substituted for P in each of the five expressions and the results evaluated.

Item 1:	$P = 12$	12
Item 2:	$P \times 3 = 12 \times 3 =$	36
Item 3:	$(P \times 3) \div 2 = (12 \times 3) \div 2 =$	18
Item 4:	$[P \times 3 \div 2] + 12 =$	
	$[12 \times 3) \div 2] + 12 =$	30
Item 5:	$[(P \times 3) \div 2] + 12 - 1 =$	
	$[(12 \times 3) \div 2] + 12 - 1 =$	29

Item 2 is greatest in value.

(Math Refresher #431)

10. **(E)** Choice E is correct.

$$Given: \quad \frac{3x}{4} = 9 \qquad \boxed{1}$$

(Use Strategy 13: Find unknowns by multiplication.)

Multiplying $\boxed{1}$ by 4, we get

$$4\left(\frac{3x}{4}\right) = (9)4$$
$$3x = 36 \qquad \boxed{2}$$

Multiply $\boxed{2}$ by 2. We have

$$2(3x) = (36)2$$
$$6x = 72$$

(Math Refresher #406)

11. **(D)** Choice D is correct.

$$Given: \quad \text{8 people divide a cash prize equally} \qquad \boxed{1}$$

(Use Strategy 2: Translate from words to algebra.)

From $\boxed{1}$ we get:

Each person receives $\frac{1}{8}$ of the total prize $\qquad \boxed{2}$

2 people receive $\frac{2}{8} = \frac{1}{4}$ of the prize $\qquad \boxed{3}$

To change $\boxed{3}$ to a percent we multiply by 100.

$$100\left(\frac{1}{4}\right) = \frac{100}{4}$$
$$= 25\%$$

(Math Refresher #200 and #106)

12. **(C)** Choice C is correct.

$$Given: \quad 8r + 3s = 12 \qquad \boxed{1}$$
$$7r + 2s = 9 \qquad \boxed{2}$$

(Use Strategy 13: Find unknowns by subtracting.)

Subtracting $\boxed{2}$ from $\boxed{1}$, we get

$$r + s = 3 \qquad \boxed{3}$$

Multiplying $\boxed{3}$ by 5, we get

$$5(r + s) = (3)5$$
$$5(r + s) = 15$$

(Math Refresher #406 and #407)

13. (B) Choice B is correct.

Given: Paul's average on 3 tests = 85   ①
Paul's average on first 2 tests = 85   ②

$\Bigg($ **Use Strategy 5:**

$$\text{Average} = \frac{\text{Sum of values}}{\text{Total number of values}}\Bigg)$$

We know $\text{Average} = \dfrac{\text{Sum of values}}{\text{Total number of values}}$ ③

Let x be the first test score   ④
y be the second test score   ⑤
z be the third test score   ⑥

Substituting ①, ④, ⑤ and ⑥ into ③, we have

$$85 = \frac{x + y + z}{3} \qquad ⑦$$

(Use Strategy 13: Find unknowns by multiplication.)

Multiply ⑦ by 3. We get

$$3(85) = \left(\frac{x + y + z}{3}\right)3$$
$$255 = x + y + z \qquad ⑧$$

Substituting ②, ④ and ⑤ into ③, we have

$$85 = \frac{x + y}{2} \qquad ⑨$$

Multiply ⑨ by 2, we get

$$2(85) = \left(\frac{x + y}{2}\right)2$$
$$170 = x + y \qquad ⑩$$

Substituting ⑩ into ⑧, we get

$$255 = 170 + z$$
$$85 = z$$

(Math Refresher #601, #431 and #406)

14. (B) Choice B is correct.

(Use Strategy 2: Translate from words to algebra.)

Given: Stephanie's earnings = x ①
Stephanie's time = 10 hours   ②
Evelyn's earnings = y ③
Evelyn's time = 20 hours   ④
$x + y$ = 60   ⑤

We know that hourly wage = $\dfrac{\text{Total Earnings}}{\text{Total Hours}}$ ⑥

Substituting ① and ② into ⑥, we get

Stephanie's hourly wage = $\dfrac{\$x}{10 \text{ hours}}$ ⑦

Substituting ③ and ④ into ⑥, we get

Evelyn's hourly wage = $\dfrac{\$y}{20 \text{ hours}}$ ⑧

We are told they have the same hourly wage. Using ⑦ and ⑧, we have

$$\frac{\$x}{10 \text{ hours}} = \frac{\$y}{20 \text{ hours}}$$
$$\frac{x}{10} = \frac{y}{20} \qquad ⑨$$
$$\overset{2}{20}\left(\frac{x}{10}\right) = \left(\frac{y}{20}\right)20$$
$$2x = y \qquad ⑩$$

Substituting ⑩ into ⑤, we get

$$x + 2x = 60$$
$$3x = 60$$
$$x = 20$$

(Math Refresher #200, #201, and #406)

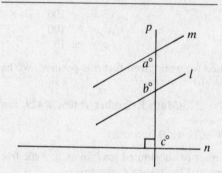

15. (D) Choice D is correct.

Given: $m \parallel l$ ①
$p \perp n$ ②

From ① we get that $a + b = 180$,   ③
because when 2 lines are parallel, the interior angles on the same side of the transversal are supplementary.

From ② we get that $c = 90$ ④
because perpendicular lines form right angles.

(Use Strategy 13: Find unknowns by addition.)

Add ③ and ④. We have

$$a + b + c = 180 + 90$$
$$= 270$$

(Math Refresher #504 #501, and #511)

16. **(A)** Choice A is correct.

(Use Strategy 11: Use new definitions carefully.)

$$\text{Given:} \quad x \boxdot y = 3 + xy \qquad \boxed{1}$$
$$y \neq 0 \qquad \boxed{2}$$
$$x \boxdot y = 3 \qquad \boxed{3}$$

Substituting $\boxed{3}$ into $\boxed{1}$, we get

$$3 = 3 + xy$$
$$0 = xy \qquad \boxed{4}$$

Noting $\boxed{2}$, we divide $\boxed{4}$ by y

$$\frac{0}{y} = \frac{xy}{y}$$
$$0 = x$$

(Math Refresher #431 and #406)

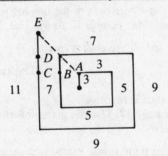

17. **(C)** Choice C is correct.

From the diagram we find that

$$AB = 2 \qquad \boxed{1}$$
$$BC = 2 \qquad \boxed{2}$$
$$CD = 2 \qquad \boxed{3}$$
$$DE = 2 \qquad \boxed{4}$$

(Use Strategy 3: The whole equals the sum of its parts.)

$$\text{We know } AB + BC = AC \qquad \boxed{5}$$

Substituting $\boxed{1}$ and $\boxed{2}$ into $\boxed{5}$, we get

$$2 + 2 = AC$$
$$4 = AC \qquad \boxed{6}$$
$$\text{We know } CD + DE = CE \qquad \boxed{7}$$

Substituting $\boxed{3}$ and $\boxed{4}$ into $\boxed{7}$, we get

$$2 + 2 = CE$$
$$4 = CE \qquad \boxed{8}$$

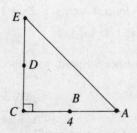

Filling $\boxed{6}$ and $\boxed{8}$ into the diagram and using the fact that all the segments drawn were perpendicular, we have $\triangle ECA$ is an isosceles right triangle.

(Use Strategy 18: Remember the isosceles right triangle.)

In the isosceles right triangle, the
$$\text{hypotenuse} = \text{leg}(\sqrt{2}) \qquad \boxed{9}$$

Substituting $\boxed{6}$ or $\boxed{8}$ into $\boxed{9}$, we get

$$EA = 4\sqrt{2}. \qquad \boxed{6}$$

(Math Refresher #507 and #509)

18. **(D)** Choice D is correct.
(Use Strategy 11: Use new definitions carefully.)

Two-digit numbers which have a units-digit $= 0$ that can be tripled in value when the tens-digit is tripled are the following:

Original number	Tripled tens digit number
10	30
20	60
30	90

The above number are the only numbers which result in a two-digit number as defined in the problem. Thus, 3 is the correct answer.

(Logical Reasoning)

19. **(D)** Choice D is correct.

We know Area of circle $= \pi(\text{radius})^2$ ☐1

Given: radius of larger circle $= r + 3$ ☐2
radius of small circle $= r$ ☐3

Substitute ☐2 into ☐1. We have

Area of larger circle $= \pi(r + 3)^2$ ☐4

(Use Strategy 4: Remember classic expressions.)

$(r + 3)^2 = r^2 + 6r + 9$ ☐5

Substitute ☐5 into ☐4. We have

Area of larger circle $= \pi(r^2 + 6r + 9)$ ☐6

Substituting ☐3 into ☐1, we get

Area of small circle $= \pi r^2$ ☐7

(Use Strategy 13: Find unknowns by subtraction.)

Subtract ☐7 from ☐6. We have

Difference of areas
$= \pi(r^2 + 6r + 9) - \pi r^2$ ☐8

Given: Difference of areas $= 21\pi$ ☐9

Substitute ☐9 into ☐8. We have

$21\pi = \pi(r^2 + 6r + 9) - \pi r^2$ ☐10

(Use Strategy 13: Find unknowns by division.)

$$\frac{21\cancel{\pi}}{\cancel{\pi}} = \frac{\cancel{\pi}(r^2 + 6r + 9)}{\cancel{\pi}} - \frac{\cancel{\pi}r^2}{\cancel{\pi}}$$
$$21 = \cancel{r^2} + 6r + 9 - \cancel{r^2}$$
$$21 = 6r + 9$$
$$12 = 6r$$
$$2 = r \quad ☐11$$

Substitute ☐11 into ☐2. We get

radius of larger circle $= 2 + 3$
$= 5$

(Math Refresher #409, #310, and #406)

20. **(A)** Choice A is correct.
(Use Strategy 11: Use new definitions carefully.)

All choices must be evaluated using the definition.

Choice A, 934432, would be assigned $6 + 3 + 4 = 13$

points, while the other choices all receive fewer than 13 points.

(Logical Reasoning)

Number Pair	Number of Points
"33"	11
"34"	6
"43"	4
"44"	3

21. **(D)** Choice D is correct.

Given: A certain number has 13 points.

(Use Strategy 11: Use new definitions carefully.)

From the chart, the only ways to accumulate 13 points are:

$6 + 4 + 3$ ☐1
$3 + 3 + 3 + 4$ ☐2

I. 33 is not in the number is always true.
II. 34 and 43 are both in the number is *not* true in ☐2
III. 43 is in the number is always true.

Thus, I and III are always true.

(Logical Reasoning)

22. **(E)** Choice E is correct.
(Use Strategy 17: Use the given information effectively.)

The center point inside a cube is the midpoint of an inner diagonal of the cube. Thus, the distance from any vertex to this center point is $\frac{1}{2}$ length of the inner diagonal. ☐1

We know length of inner diagonal of a cube
$$= \sqrt{(\text{edge})^2 + (\text{edge})^2 + (\text{edge})^2}$$
inner diagonal $= \sqrt{3(\text{edge})^2}$
inner diagonal $= \text{edge} \sqrt{3}$ ☐2

Given: Volume $= 8$ cubic meters ☐3

We know volume of a cube $= (\text{edge})^3$ ☐4

Substituting ☐3 into ☐4, we get

8 cubic meters $= (\text{edge})^3$

$\sqrt[3]{8 \text{ cubic meters}} = \sqrt[3]{(\text{edge})^3}$

2 meters $= \text{edge}$ ☐5

Substituting ☐5 into ☐2, we get

inner diagonal $= (2)\sqrt{3}$
inner diagonal $= 2\sqrt{3}$ meters ☐6

Using ☐1 and ☐6 we find

distance we need $= \frac{1}{2}(\text{inner diagonal})$

$= \frac{1}{2}(2\sqrt{3} \text{ meters})$

$= \sqrt{3}$ meters

Distances we need $= \sqrt{3}\ m$

(Math Refresher #313, #430, and #406)

23. **(A)** Choice A is correct.

(Use Strategy 2: Translate from words to algebra.)

The ratio of Sue's age to Bob's age is 3 to 7, becomes

$$\frac{\text{Sue's age } (S)}{\text{Bob's age } (B)} = \frac{3}{7}$$

$$\text{or} \qquad \frac{S}{B} = \frac{3}{7} \qquad \boxed{1}$$

The ratio of Sue's age to Joe's age is 4 to 9, becomes

$$\frac{S}{J} = \frac{4}{9} \qquad \boxed{2}$$

Cross multiplying $\boxed{1}$, we have $7S = 3B$

$$\text{or} \qquad \frac{7S}{3} = B \qquad \boxed{3}$$

Cross multiplying $\boxed{2}$, we have $9S = 4J$

$$\text{or} \qquad \frac{9S}{4} = J \qquad \boxed{4}$$

We need the ratio of Bob's age to Joe's age. $\boxed{5}$

Substituting $\boxed{3}$ and $\boxed{4}$ into $\boxed{5}$, we get

$$\frac{\text{Bob's age}}{\text{Joe's age}} = \frac{\dfrac{7S}{3}}{\dfrac{9S}{4}}$$

$$= \frac{7S}{3} \div \frac{9S}{4}$$

$$= \frac{7S}{3} \times \frac{4}{9S}$$

$$\frac{\text{Bob's age}}{\text{Joe's age}} = \frac{28}{27}$$

(Math Refresher #200, 120, and #112)

24. **(C)** Choice C is correct.

(Use Strategy 2: Translate from words to algebra.)

Let a = a positive integer
Then $a + 1, a + 2, a + 3, a + 4$, etc., are the next positive integers.

(Use Strategy 13: Find unknowns by addition.)

Add the first 2 positive integers. We get
Sum of first 2 positive integers =
$a + a + 1 = 2a + 1$ $\boxed{1}$

$\boxed{1}$ is not divisible by 2.

Now add the third positive integer, $a + 2$, to $\boxed{1}$. We get

Sum of first 3 positive
integers = $2a + 1 + a + 2 = 3a + 3$ $\boxed{2}$

$\boxed{2}$ is not divisible by 2.

Now add the fourth positive integer, $a + 3$, to $\boxed{2}$. We have

Sum of first 4 positive
integers = $3a + 3 + a + 3$
$= 4a + 6$ $\boxed{3}$

Since $\boxed{3}$ can be written as $2(2a + 3)$, it is divisible by 2.

Thus, if r is a multiple of 4, the sum of r consecutive positive integers will be divisible by 2.

(Math Refresher #200 and #607)

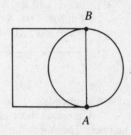

25. **(B)** Choice B is correct.

(Use Strategy 17: Use the given information effectively.)

Given: Area of circle = $9a^2\pi^2$ $\boxed{1}$
Two sides of square are
tangent to the circle $\boxed{2}$

We know that area of a circle = $\pi(\text{radius})^2$ $\boxed{3}$

Substituting $\boxed{1}$ into $\boxed{3}$, we have

$$9a^2\pi^2 = \pi(\text{radius})^2 \qquad \boxed{4}$$

(Use Strategy 13: Find unknowns by division.)

Divide $\boxed{4}$ by π. We get

$$\frac{9a^2\pi^2}{\pi} = \frac{\pi}{\pi}(\text{radius})^2$$

$$9a^2\pi = (\text{radius})^2$$

$$\sqrt{9a^2\pi} = \sqrt{(\text{radius})^2}$$

$$3a\sqrt{\pi} = \text{radius} \qquad \boxed{5}$$

Using $\boxed{2}$ we know that AB is a diameter of the circle $\boxed{6}$

We know diameter = 2(radius) $\boxed{7}$

Using $\boxed{5}$, $\boxed{6}$ and $\boxed{7}$ we get

$$AB = 2(3a\sqrt{\pi}) = 6a\sqrt{\pi} \qquad \boxed{8}$$

We know that Area of a square = $(\text{side})^2$ $\boxed{9}$

Substituting $\boxed{8}$ into $\boxed{9}$, we have

$$\text{Area of square} = (6a\sqrt{\pi})^2$$
$$= 36a^2\pi$$

(Math Refresher #303, #310, #430, and #406)

EXPLANATORY ANSWERS FOR PRACTICE TEST 4 (continued)

Section 3: Standard Written English

> Section 3 does not count toward your SAT score. This Standard Written English section is used only for Freshman English placement when you get to college. However, you are advised to improve yourself in grammar and usage, and also in sentence structure. If you do well in the Standard Written English Test, you will be placed more advantageously in your college Freshman English class.

1. **(C)** "Everyone who attends. . . . knows that *he* will be searched . . ." A pronoun must agree with its antecedent in number. Therefore, the singular pronoun *he*—not *they*—must be used because the antecedent of the pronoun is singular (*everyone*).

2. **(D)** ". . . write one *quickly.*" The adverb form is needed to modify the verb *could write.*

3. **(D)** "One of the key suspects . . . *was captured* . . ." *One* is the singular subject of the sentence. The verb, therefore, must be singular (*was captured*). The plural verb (*were captured*) is incorrect.

4. **(E)** All underlined parts are correct.

5. **(B)** ". . . in which she *had ridden* . . ." The past perfect tense of *to ride* is *had ridden*—not *had rode.*

6. **(A)** "From every community *come* reports . . ." The plural form of the verb (*come*) must be used to agree with the plural subject *reports.* "From every community" is an introductory prepositional phrase.

7. **(C)** ". . . there *was* scarcely enough food . . ." The word *scarcely* is considered a negative. Using *scarcely* with the word *not* (a double negative) is to be avoided.

8. **(E)** All underlined parts are correct.

9. **(A)** ". . . to borrow a book *from* . . ." One borrows *from* someone. The phrase *off of* is always incorrect.

10. **(A)** "Neither the school board members *nor* the city council . . ." Correlative conjunctions are always used in pairs. The correlative conjunction pair is *neither . . . nor*—not *neither . . . or.*

11. **(C)** We must preserve sequence of tenses. When two different parts of a sentence refer to the same period of time, the same tense must be used in each case. In this sentence, when the neither *was* (past tense) a teenager, he *rescued* (past tense) a swimmer.

12. **(C)** ". . . our father told my brother and *me* . . ." The indirect object of a clause or sentence must be in the objective case and, accordingly, must take the objective form (*me*—not *I*).

13. **(D)** ". . . is usually easier than passing the driving test." This sentence requires parallelism: *Passing* the driving test" should parallel "*Passing* the written test . . ."

14. **(D)** ". . . each hoping that *he* would win . . ." A pronoun should be in the same number as the noun or pronoun to which it refers. In the sentence, *he* refers to *each* which is a singular pronoun.

15. **(B)** "Her answer . . . was *altogether* incorrect . . ." *Altogether* means *entirely, wholly. All together* means *as a group.*

16. **(C)** ". . . they acted as if they never *had met* before . . ." We must use the past perfect tense (*had met*) to indicate an action taking place before another past action (*acted*).

17. **(A)** "The realtor felt *bad* . . ." After the copulative verb (*felt*), the word referring to the subject should be a predicate adjective (*bad*)—not an adverb (*badly*).

18. **(E)** All underlined parts are correct.

19. **(B)** The pronoun *he* has an indefinite antecedent. We cannot tell whether *he* refers to the Governor or the attorney. Accordingly, we must be specific by using either *the Governor* or *the attorney.*

20. **(E)** All underlined parts are correct.

21. **(C)** The box of books . . . *was* . . ."
The subject of the sentence (*box*) is singular. Therefore, the verb must be singular (*was*). The other nouns that precede the verb (*books, dishes, silverware*) function as objects of prepositions.

22. **(E)** All underlined parts are correct.

23. **(B)** ". . . the young man *whom* . . ."
The word *which* should be used only to refer to things. When we refer to people, we should use *who* or *whom*. In this sentence the objective case (*whom*) is needed to function as the direct object of the verb (*had seen*).

24. **(D)** ". . . was the *shorter*."
In a comparison of two things (such as two lists), we use the comparative degree (*shorter*)—not the superlative degree (*shortest*).

25. **(A)** "The wreck *lay* . . ."
The past tense of the verb *lie* is *lay*—not *laid*.

26. **(C)** Sequence of tenses in contrary-to-fact past situations requires the "had listened" form of the verb. Choice C is therefore correct and all the other choices are incorrect. Moreover, in Choice E, there is no need to use the word "advice" since the rest of the choice implies that advice has been given.

27. **(E)** Choice E is the only correct choice since the other choices lack parallelism. Choice D is incorrect for an additional reason—the predicate adjective "unpretentious" (not the adverb "unpretentiously") should be used after the copulative verbal "acting".

28. **(B)** Choice A is incorrect because it is unidiomatic. Choice B is correct. Choices C and E are incorrect because they are too wordy. Choice D improperly omits "conduct of the (accused)."

29. **(B)** The object form of the pronoun must be used for the object of any preposition. Therefore, Choices A and C are incorrect and Choice B is correct. Choice D is incorrect because we need the nominative form of the personal pronoun ("she") as the subject ("but not she"). Choice E is incorrect because it is too informal for the context.

30. **(E)** Choice A is incorrect because "while" pertains to time and should not be substituted loosely for "and." Choice B is incorrect because it does not tie up grammatically with the rest of the sentence. Choice C is incorrect for the same reason. Choice D is incorrect because the subordinate conjunction "as" does not make sense here. Choice E is correct.

31. **(A)** Choice A is correct. Choice B wrongly substitutes the objective case "whomever" for the nominative "whoever," the subject of the verb "would return." Choice C uses the form "whosoever," which while correct, is legalistic and not needed here. Choice D again uses the objective case. Choice E is awkward.

32. **(C)** There is no such word as "irregardless." Therefore Choices A, B, and E cannot be right. "Despite" in Choice D does not give the same meaning as "regardless." Choice C is the correct one.

33. **(D)** Choice A wrongly uses the plural verb "are to be found" after the subject of the sentence, "One." (The plural word "examples" is not the subject of the prepositional phrase "of the finest examples.") Choice B simply uses the same plural verb in the past tense instead of the present. Choice C does not correct the error. Choice D does, by using the singular verb "is." Choice E is incorrect because of the use of the plural verb "are."

34. **(D)** Choice A fails to use the possessive case of the pronoun that governs a gerund. Choice B changes the meaning of the sentence. Choice C corrects the error but omits a necessary part of the meaning. Choice D is correct. Choice E retains the error of Choice A and, in addition, distorts the meaning of the sentence.

35. **(D)** Choices A, B, C, and E should place the adverbial phrase "without hesitation" after the infinitive it modifies, "to answer." Since the meaning is to "answer without hesitation," the phrase "without hesitation" should be placed right after the infinitive "to answer." This is done in Choice D.

36. **(C)** Choices A and B are incorrect uses of the present participle form to modify the noun *canoe*. Choice C is the correct use of the past participle. Choice D is incorrect because, in this sentence, it is an awkward use of the past participle. Choice E is an incorrect use of the present participle preceded by the inappropriate possessive pronoun *its*.

37. **(B)** What we are looking for here is a group of words to be used as a subject. Choice A is incorrect because the clause beginning with *whether* conveys an uncertainty, which is not the meaning of the sentence. Choice B is correct as a positive statement. It is a gerund phrase followed by an infinitive phrase. Choices C, D, and E are incorrect because they are awkward and vague.

38. **(C)** Choice A is incorrect because the phrases are misplaced, resulting in an unclear statement. Choices B and D are incorrect. They are awkwardly constructed and omit the fact that the trustee resigned from the town board. Choice C is correct. Choice E is incorrect because it is repetitious and awkward.

39. **(D)** Choice A is incorrect because the meaning of the phrase is unclear. Choice B is incorrect because the use of the participial form *coming* is awkward. Choice C is incorrect because it is too vague. Choice D is correct. Choice E is incorrect because it is too wordy.

40. **(A)** Choice A is correct. Choice B is incorrect. The use of *due to* calls for a participle, *having reached*, while the sentence contains a finite verb *has reached*. Choice E is incorrect also because the structure of the phrase calls for the use of a participle. Choice C is incorrect because it is awkward and wordy. Choice D is incorrect because it makes the sentence ungrammatical.

41. **(A)** "The novelists *whom* readers choose . . ." The direct object of the verb (choose) must be the objective case form (*whom*—not *who*).

42. **(C)** "The problem . . . disturbs . . ." The subject (*problem*) is singular. Therefore the verb (*disturbs*) must be singular.

43. **(B)** ". . . son *could have* gone . . ." The phrase *could of* is always considered substandard. Do not use *of* for *have*.

44. **(D)** ". . . the horse *which* had fallen . . ." The pronoun *which* should be used to refer to animals and things; *who* should be used to refer only to people.

45. **(D)** ". . . then *he* should make . . ." A pronoun must agree with its antecedent (*someone*) in number. Since *someone* is singular, the pronoun must be singular (*he*—not *they*).

46. **(A)** "The man *whom* Mexican authorities believe to be . . ." The subject of an infinitive must be in the objective case. The pronoun "whom" in the objective case—not "who" in the nominative case—is the subject of the verbal infinitive "to be."

47. **(D)** ". . . they did *as* we expected them to do." The preposition "like" should not be used for the subordinate conjunction "as" to introduce a clause.

48. **(E)** All underlined parts are correct.

49. **(C)** ". . . the child fell *off* the unscreened porch." The correct preposition is simply "off"—not "off of"—to introduce a noun or pronoun.

50. **(A)** ". . . ran *more swiftly* . . ." We must use an adverb—not an adjective—to modify a verb. Therefore, we use the adverbial comparative construction "more swiftly" instead of the comparative adjective "swifter" to modify the verb "ran."

EXPLANATORY ANSWERS FOR
PRACTICE TEST 4 (continued)

Section 4: Verbal Ability

1. **(A)** Choice A is correct.   See **Antonym Strategy 1.** *Malign* means *to speak badly of.*   The opposite of *malign* is *to defend.*

2. **(D)** Choice D is correct. *Lithe* means *graceful; flexible.* The opposite of *lithe* is *clumsy.*

3. **(C)** Choice C is correct. See **Antonym Strategy 3.** *Bountiful* means *plentiful; abundant.* The opposite of *bountiful* is *scarce.*

4. **(D)** Choice D is correct. See **Antonym Strategy 2.** *Haggard* means *worn out.* The opposite of *haggard* is *refreshed.*

5. **(E)** Choice E is correct. See **Antonym Strategy 2.** *Irascible* means *easily angered.* The opposite of *irascible* is *calm.*

6. **(E)** Choice E is correct. *Burgeon* means *to flourish; to grow rapidly.* The opposite of *burgeon* is *to waste away.*

7. **(C)** Choice C is correct. See **Antonym Strategy 3.** *Gratuitous* means *free of cost.* (Another meaning is *unnecessary.*) The opposite of *gratuitous* is *costly.*

8. **(D)** Choice D is correct. See **Antonym Strategy 2.** *Emolument* means *profit; gain.* The opposite of *emolument* is *loss.*

9. **(A)** Choice A is correct. See **Antonym Strategy 2.** *Meretricious* means *gaudy; showy.* The opposite of *meretricious* is *simple.*

10. **(B)** Choice B is correct. *Vapid* means *tasteless; uninteresting.* The opposite of *vapid* is *interesting.*

11. **(D)**   Choice D is correct. See **Sentence Completion Strategy 2.** Examine the first word of each choice. Choice (B) pacifism and Choice (E) oblivion are incorrect choices because a rising tide of pacifism or oblivion in public education does *not* make good sense. Now consider the other choices. Choice (A) compromise . . . inept and Choice (C) ambiguity . . . average do *not* make good sense in the sentence. Choice (D) mediocrity . . . dedicated *does* make good sense.

12. **(C)**   Choice C is correct. See **Sentence Completion Strategy 2.** First we eliminate Choice (A) foretold, Choice (B) impossible, and Choice (E) glaring. Reason: These choices do not make sense in the sentence up to the word "eclipses." We further eliminate Choice (D) true . . . rational, because it does not make sense for anyone to consider an eclipse rational. Only Choice (C) understandable . . . magical, makes sense.

13. **(D)**   Choice D is correct. The fact that the girl had become more self-confident indicates that she would be more active in participating in a conversation. If you used **Sentence Completion Strategy 3**—trying to complete the sentence *before* looking at the five choices—you might have come up with any of the following appropriate words:

> starting   beginning
>
> launching   originating

The other choices are, therefore, incorrect.

14. **(A)**   Choice A is correct. See **Sentence Completion Strategy 3.** If you used this strategy of trying to complete the sentence *before* looking at the five choices, you might have come up with any of the following words that have the negative meaning of "to lessen in degree":

> reduced   diminished
>
> destroyed   lessened

These words all come close to the meaning of the correct Choice (A) shattered. Therefore, Choices B, C, D, and E are incorrect.

15. **(D)**   Choice D is correct. See **Sentence Completion Strategy 2.**

STEP 1

Let us first examine the first words of each choice. We can then eliminate Choice (B) confuse and Choice (E) misconstrue because it does *not* make sense to say that an authority would be able to "confuse" or "misconstrue" something in a book. So Choices B and E are incorrect.

STEP 2

Let us now consider the remaining choices. Choice (A) understand . . . simple and Choice (C) read . . . useless, do *not* make sense in the sentence. Therefore, these choices are incorrect. Choice (D) comprehend . . . complex, *does* make sense.

16. **(B)**   Choice B is correct. A porthole is an opening that lets light into a ship. A pupil is an opening in the iris of the eye that lets light pass to the retina of the eye.
   (Part-Whole and Purpose relationship)

17. **(B)**   Choice B is correct. A procrastinator and delay are closely associated. A genius and creativity are closely associated.   **(Association relationship)**

18. **(A)** Choice A is correct. Something that is watertight does not allow water to enter. Something that is hermetic does not allow air to enter.
(Result relationship)

19. **(D)** Choice D is correct. A drizzle is a light rainfall while a cloudburst is a heavy rainfall. A flurry is a light snowfall while a blizzard is a heavy snowfall.
(Degree relationship)

20. **(E)** Choice E is correct. An apiary houses bees. A stable houses horses. **(Purpose relationship)**

21. **(D)** Choice D is correct. A foreman holds a position both of leadership and membership of a jury. A captain holds a position both of leadership and membership of a group. We have here a Part-Whole relationship. Choices B and E also express a Part : Whole relationship but they do not include the leadership quality of the capitalized words and the Choice D words. Therefore, Choices B and E are incorrect. See **Analogy Strategy 4.** **Part-Whole relationship)**

22. **(B)** Choice B is correct. The geneology of a family is the study of its history and origin. The etymology of a word is the study of its history and origin.
(Action-Object and Association relationship)

23. **(E)** Choice E is correct. Someone who is crass lacks refinement. Someone who is craven lacks bravery. We have here an Opposite relationship. Note Choice (A) frivolous : continuity. Someone who is frivolous does lack the ability to finish a job. However, we would not say that such a person lacks continuity. Therefore, Choice A is incorrect. See **Analogy Strategy 4.**
(Opposite relationship)

24. **(D)** An apple always has a core as its center. A cell almost always has a nucleus as an essential element.
(Part-Whole relationship)

25. **(E)** A catcher on a baseball team uses a mask to protect his face from being hit by the ball. A driver of car uses the visor above the windshield to protect his eyes from direct sunlight or glare.
(Purpose relationship)

26. **(C)** Choice C is correct. For example, see the following lines:
Lines 7–10: ". . . the man who needs change . . . he's waited years for precisely this opportunity."
Lines 11–13: "Ponder the relationship . . . silent but savage."
Lines 27–30: ". . . try hailing the next off-duty cab driver . . . pure thrill."
Choices A, B, D, and E are incorrect because none of these choices fits the description of the people whom the author speaks about.

27. **(E)** Choice E is correct. See lines 25–30: "People don't accept apologies . . . pure thrill." Choices A, B, C, and D are incorrect. The actions of people expressed in these choices are not comparable to the behavior of the cab driver who is thrilled by the fact that he's made the disappointed cab seeker unhappy and uncomfortable.

28. **(D)** Choice D is correct. Throughout the passage, the author relates incidents involving various people. He does so quite humorously, but in a subtle way. The word "subtle" means "not immediately obvious." For example:
Lines 4–7: "The real hatred in America . . . doesn't give a damn."
Lines 11–13: "Ponder the relationship . . . dialogue is silent but savage."
Choices A, B, C, and E are incorrect because they do not represent the tone of the passage.

29. **(B)** Choice B is correct. See line 1: "The old Middle West is gone. However, it still lives in song and story." Choices A, C, D, and E are incorrect because the passage makes no reference to what these choices state.

30. **(C)** Choice C is correct. See lines 17–18: "I think the Middle West's strength is in its customary cautious approach . . ." Choice D (line 24) is incorrect because it is not cited as the strength of the Middle West. Choices A, B, and E may be true but they are not indicated in the passage.

31. **(D)** Choice D is correct. See lines 28–31: "In the Middle West it has . . . taken the form of people remaining in the smaller cities and giving them new life and intelligence. This has strengthened smaller communities . . ." Choices A, B, C, and E are incorrect because the passage does not indicate these choices as current trends.

32. **(A)** Choice A is correct. See lines 5–9: "The old Middle West developed . . . out of destructive blizzards . . . and . . . dust storms." Therefore, Item I is true. Items II and III cannot be accepted because the passage says nothing about the Gold Rush of 1849 and the Civil War as factors in the formation of the Middle West. Accordingly, Choices B, C, D, and E are incorrect.

33. **(E)** Choice E is correct. The main topic—the structure and function of the nasal mucous membrane—is discussed beginning with line 17 right on to the end of the passage. Choice A is incorrect. The only animal-man comparison is in the first sentence. Choice B is incorrect because the only reference in the passage to the human respiratory system—not necessarily the infant's—is in lines 17–21: "It is the mucous membrane . . . particles, and gases." Choice C is incorrect because the importance of infant crying is discussed only in lines 5–16: "As is well known . . . of his naso-pharynx." Choice D is incorrect because weeping and survival in humans is discussed only in lines 5–16 and in lines 30–32: "The hypothesis . . . established in man."

34. **(A)** Choice A is false—therefore a correct choice. See lines 24–30: "If drying is produced . . . not infrequently lethal." Choice B is true—therefore a wrong choice. See lines 19–21: "The nasal mucous membrane . . . and gases." Choice C is true—therefore a wrong choice. See lines 26–30: "This [gelatinous] mass [of mucous] constitutes . . . not infrequently lethal." Choice D is true—therefore an incorrect choice. See lines 30–32: "The hypothesis . . . became established in man." Choice E is true—therefore an incorrect choice. See lines 22–24: "Discharges from the eye . . . nasal mucous membrane." A duct which leads from the eye to the nose is obviously somewhere in the head.

35. **(C)** Choice C is correct. See lines 19–20: "The nasal mucous membrane . . . laden with bacteria." Choice A is incorrect. See lines 2–4: ". . . the fact is that psychic weeping . . . other than man." Choice B is incorrect. First of all, see lines 5–6: "As is well known . . . 6 weeks of age." Secondly, there is nothing in the passage about anybody crying with tears because of respiratory problems. Choice D is incorrect. See lines 13–16: "Even a fairly short session of tearless crying in a young infant . . . his naso-pharynx." Only a *young infant* is referred to. Choice E is incorrect because the passage nowhere refers to a crying woman.

36. **(B)** Choice B is correct. See lines 23–31: "That was why . . . until he reached bitter despair . . . the man of property could die." The "well-upholstered hell" constituted the life style that almost caused him to commit suicide. The passage shows no justification for Choices A, C, D, and E. Accordingly, these are incorrect choices.

37. **(D)** Choice D is correct. Throughout paragraph 3 we see the evidences of the speaker's happiness as a result of his renouncing the "power, women and money" (line 24) as well as the arrogance and intellectuality referred to in lines 18–19. Choices A, B, and C are incorrect because, though the passage discusses these choices, they do not really *pinpoint* the relation between the third and fourth paragraphs. Choice E is incorrect because paragraph 3 does not generalize about the specific points made in paragraph 2.

38. **(B)** Choice B is correct. His "complete hopelessness and despair" (lines 3–4) led to Siddhartha's decision to commit suicide. The passage does not answer the questions expressed in Choices A, C, D, and E. Therefore, these choices are incorrect.

39. **(E)** Choice E is correct. The unhappiness that may result from wealth and power are brought out clearly throughout the second paragraph. In contrast, peace and quiet are likely to assure a happy life. The last paragraph demonstrates this conclusively. Although Choices A, B, C, and D are vital points, none of the choices is sufficiently inclusive to be considered the *main* idea of the passage. References to these choices follow. Choice A—lines 14–23: "He had been full of arrogance . . . brought him salvation." Choice B—lines 5–9: "Was it not his Self . . . filled him with fear?" Choice C—lines 11–12: "Too much knowledge had hindered him." Choice D—lines 21–23: "Now he understood . . . brought him salvation."

40. **(E)** Choice E is correct. The word "Self" as it is used in this passage means one's own interests, welfare, or advantage; self-love. By an extension of these definitions, "Self" may be considered selfishness. See lines 5–9: "Was it not his Self . . . filled him with fear." Accordingly, Choices A, B, C, and D are incorrect.

EXPLANATORY ANSWERS FOR PRACTICE TEST 4 (continued)

Section 5: Math Ability

1. **(B)** Choice B is correct. **(Use Strategy 2: Translate from words to algebra.)** Janie is older than Tammy but she is younger than Lori, translates to:

| Janie's age $>$ Tammy's age | [1] |
| Janie's age $<$ Lori's age | [2] |

Given:	Janie's Age $= j$	[3]
	Tammy's age $= t$	[4]
	Lori's age $= l$	[5]

Substituting [3], [4] and [5] into [1] and [2], we get

| $j > t$ | [6] |
| $j < l$ | [7] |

(Use Strategy 6: Know how to manipulate inequalities). Reversing [6], we get

| $t < j$ | [8] |

Combining [8] and [7], we get

$$t < j < l$$

(Math Refresher #200 and #419)

2. **(C)** Choice C is correct.

| *Given*: | $\dfrac{(201.2)(.498)}{1.99}$ | [1] |

Since we need an approximation we do the following:

$201.2 \approx 200$	[2]
$.498 \approx .5$	[3]
$1.99 \approx 2$	[4]

Substituting [2], [3] and [4] into [1], we have

$$\frac{(200)(.5)}{2} =$$

(Use Strategy 19: Factor and reduce.)

$$\frac{(\cancel{2} \times 100)(.5)}{\cancel{2}} =$$
$$(100)(.5) = 50$$

(Math Refresher #609 and #108)

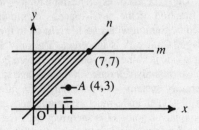

3. **(A)** Choice A is correct.

(Use Strategy 17: Use the given information effectively.) Since n goes through point O, the origin, whose coordinates are (0,0), and through (7,7), all of the points on n have the same x and y coordinates.

Choice A, (4,3), is 4 units to the right of O but only 3 units up. It is below n and not in the shaded area.

(Math Refresher #410)

4. **(D)** Choice D is correct. **(Use Strategy 17: Use the given information effectively.)** If it will be 7:45 in three hours, then right now it is $7:45 - 3 = 4:45$.

Since $\dfrac{1}{2}$ hour $= 30$ minutes, $\dfrac{1}{2}$ hour ago it was $4:45 - 30 = 4:15$

(Logical Reasoning)

5. **(A)** Choice A is correct. **(Use Strategy 2: Translate from words to algebra.)**
Let $n =$ the number.

A certain number increased by 6 equals four times the number, translates to:

$$n + 6 = 4n$$
$$6 = 3n$$
$$2 = n$$

(Math Refresher #200 and #406)

6. **(D)** Choice D is correct. **(Use Strategy 17: Use the given information effectively.)**

The 17 slips, numbered from 1 to 17, consists of ☐1
8 even numbers (2,4,6, . . . 16) and ☐2
9 odd numbers (1,3,5, . . . 17). ☐3

Subtracting 5 even numbered slips from ☐2, leaves
8 − 5 = 3 even numbered slips. ☐4

Adding ☐3 and ☐4 we have
$$9 + 3 = 12 \text{ slips remaining} \quad \boxed{5}$$

We need $\dfrac{\text{even numbered slips}}{\text{Total numbered slips}}$ ☐6

Substituting ☐4 and ☐5 into ☐6, we have

$$\frac{3}{12} = \frac{1}{4}$$

(Math Refresher #603 and Logical Reasoning)

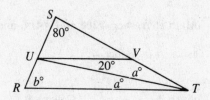

7. **(E)** Choice E is correct.

Given: $UV \parallel RT$ ☐1

From ☐1 we get $a = 20$, since alternate interior angles are equal ☐2

(Use Strategy 3: The whole equals the sum of its parts.) From the diagram we see that

$$\angle STR = a + a \quad \boxed{3}$$

Substituting ☐2 into ☐3, we have

$$\angle STR = 20 + 20 = 40 \quad \boxed{4}$$

We know that the sum of the angles of a triangle = 180, thus

$$\angle R + \angle S + \angle STR = 180 \quad \boxed{5}$$

We are given, in the diagram, that

$$\angle R = b \quad \boxed{6}$$
$$\angle S = 80 \quad \boxed{7}$$

Substituting ☐6, ☐7 and ☐4 into ☐5, we get

$$b + 80 + 40 = 180$$
$$b + 120 = 180$$
$$b = 60$$

(Math Refresher #504, #505 and #406)

8. **(C)** Choice C is correct.

Given: r is an even integer ☐1
$5 < r < 8$ ☐2

(Use Strategy 6: Know how to manipulate inequalities.) Using ☐1 and ☐2 together, the only even integer value of r between 5 and 8 is $r = 6$ ☐3

Column A	Column B	
$r + 1$	7	☐4

Substituting ☐3 into ☐4, the columns become

$6 + 1 = 7$	7

(Math Refresher #603 and #419)

9. **(D)** Choice D is correct.

Column A	Column B
The number of hours in w days	v hours

(Use Strategy C: Use numerics if it appears that the answer cannot be determined.) Let $w = 1$ and $v = 30$, the columns become

The number of hours in 1 day = 24 hours	30 hours

Column B is larger.

Now, let $w = 1$ and $v = 1$, the columns become

The number of hours in 1 day = 24 hours	1 hour

Column A is larger.

Since two different answers are possible, the answer cannot be determined from the information given.

(Math Refresher #431)

10. **(B)** Choice B is correct.

Column A	Column B	
$\sqrt{48} + \sqrt{80}$	$7 + 9$	☐1

We know $\sqrt{48} < \sqrt{49}$
$$\sqrt{48} < 7 \quad \boxed{2}$$
We know $\sqrt{80} < \sqrt{81}$
$$\sqrt{80} < 9 \quad \boxed{3}$$

(Use Strategy 6: Know how to manipulate inequalities.) Adding ☐2 and ☐3, we have

$$\sqrt{48} + \sqrt{80} < 7 + 9$$

(Math Refresher #430 and #419)

11. **(C)** Choice C is correct.

We know that a cube has 6 faces ☐1

Given: Number of striped faces = 1 ☐2
Rest of faces are red. ☐3

(Use Strategy 13: Find unknowns by subtraction.)
Subtract ☐2 from ☐1. We get
$$6 - 1 = 5$$
Thus ☐3, Number of red faces, = 5 ☐4

Column A	Column B	
The number of faces of the cube that are red	5	☐5

Substituting ☐4 into ☐5, we have

5	5

(Math Refresher #313)

12. **(B)** Choice B is correct.

Given:
$$8 = 36 - 7w$$
$$-28 = -7w$$
$$4 = w \quad ☐1$$

Column A	Column B	
w	7	☐2

Substituting ☐1 into ☐2, we get

4	7

Column B is larger.

(Math Refresher #406)

13. **(A)** Choice A is correct.

$$r > 3 \quad ☐1$$

Column A	Column B
The average rate when r words are typed in 3 hours	The average rate when 3 words are typed in r hours

(Use Strategy 2: Translate from words to algebra.) The columns become

$\dfrac{r \text{ words}}{3 \text{ hours}} =$	$\dfrac{3 \text{ words}}{r \text{ hours}} =$	
$\dfrac{r}{3}$ words/hour	$\dfrac{3}{r}$ words/hour	☐2

(Use Strategy 6: Know how to manipulate inequalities.) Divide ☐1 by r. We get

$$\frac{r}{r} > \frac{3}{r}$$
$$1 > \frac{3}{r} \quad ☐3$$

Divide ☐1 by 3. We get

$$\frac{r}{3} > \frac{3}{3}$$
$$\frac{r}{3} > 1 \quad ☐4$$

Combining ☐4 and ☐3, we get

$$\frac{r}{3} > \frac{3}{r} \quad ☐5$$

Substituting ☐2 into ☐5, the columns are

$$\frac{r}{3} \text{ words/hour} > \frac{3}{r} \text{ words/hour.}$$

(Math Refresher #200 and #419, and #422)

14. **(A)** Choice A is correct.

$$w > 0 \quad ☐1$$

Column A	Column B	
$\dfrac{w + 3}{4}$	$\dfrac{w + 6}{8}$	☐2

(Use Strategy D: Compare fractions by multiplying both columns by a positive number.)
Multiply ☐2 by 8. The columns become

$\overset{2}{8}\left(\dfrac{w + 3}{4}\right)$	$8\left(\dfrac{w + 6}{8}\right)$	
$2w + 6$	$w + 6$	☐3

(Use Strategy A: Cancel like quantities from both columns by subtraction.) Subtract 6 from ☐3. The columns become

$2w$	w

Taking note of ☐1, we know

$$2w > w$$

(Math Refresher #406)

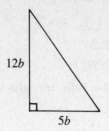

12b

5b

15. **(C)** Choice C is correct.

Column A	Column B
$(5b)^2 + (12b)^2$	$(13b)^2$

(Use Strategy 18: Remember right triangle facts.)
The given triangle is one of the special right
triangles (5,12,13). Its hypotenuse is $13b$ ☐1

The Pythagorean theorem for right triangles is:

$$(leg)^2 + (leg)^2 = (hypotenuse)^2$$ ☐2

Using the diagram and ☐1 and substituting in ☐2 ,
we get

$$(5b)^2 + (12b)^2 = (13b)^2$$

Thus, the columns are equal.

(Math Refresher #509)

16. **(B)** Choice B is correct.

Column A	Column B
50×150	100×100

By direct calculation the columns become

7500	10000

(Multiplication)

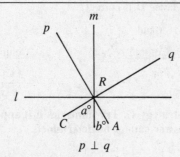

$p \perp q$

17. **(C)** Choice C is correct.

Given: $p \perp q$ ☐1

From ☐1 we know that $\angle ARC = 90$ ☐2
**(Use Strategy 3: The whole equals the sum of its
parts.)**
From the diagram we see that

$$\angle ARC = a + b$$ ☐3

Substituting ☐3 into ☐2 , the columns become

Column A	Column B
$a + b$	
90	90

(Math Refresher #501 and #511)

18. **(A)** Choice A is correct.

METHOD 1

Given: m is an integer > 0 ☐1
              $0 < y < 1$ ☐2

Column A	Column B
$\dfrac{m}{y}$	m

**(Use Strategy 6: Know how to manipulate
inequalities.)** From ☐2 , since $y < 1$, we know that

$$\frac{1}{y} > 1$$ ☐3

**(Use Strategy 13: Find unknowns by
multiplication.) (Use Strategy E: Try to get the
columns and given to look similar.)** Multiply ☐3
by m, remembering, from ☐1 , that $m > 0$. We get

$$m\left(\frac{1}{y}\right) > (1)m$$

$$\frac{m}{y} > m$$

METHOD 2

$$m > 0$$
$$0 < y < 1$$

Column A	Column B
$\dfrac{m}{y}$	m

(Use Strategy B: Cancel numbers by division.)
Cancel m and we get

Column A	Column B
$\dfrac{1}{y}$	1

(Use Strategy D: Multiply both columns by y.) We
get

Column A	Column B
1	y

From the given, $y < 1$. Therefore, Column A >
Column B.

(Math Refresher #419 and #422)

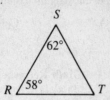

19. (B) Choice B is correct.

Column A	Column B
Length ST	Length RT

(Use Strategy 18: Remember triangle facts.) We know that in a triangle, the side opposite the larger angle is the larger side. Thus, $RT > ST$.

(Triangle inequalities)

20. (A) Choice A is correct.

Given: $\qquad -\dfrac{1}{3}y = \dfrac{1}{3}y$ $\qquad$ ⬚1

(Use Strategy 13: Find unknowns by multiplication.) Multiply ⬚1 by 3. We get

$$3\left(-\frac{1}{3}y\right) = \left(\frac{1}{3}y\right)3$$
$$-y = y$$
$$0 = 2y$$
$$0 = y \qquad ⬚2$$

Column A	Column B
$-y$	$-\dfrac{2}{3}$ ⬚3

Substituting ⬚2 in ⬚3, the columns become

$$-(0) = \qquad\qquad -\frac{2}{3}$$
$$0$$

(Math Refresher #406)

21. (C) Choice C is correct.

Given: $\qquad$ For all $x < 0, \boxed{x} = 2x^2$ $\qquad$ ⬚1

$\qquad\qquad\qquad$ For all $x > 0, \boxed{x} = \dfrac{x}{4}$ $\qquad$ ⬚2

Column A	Column B
$\boxed{-3}$	$\boxed{72}$

(Use Strategy 11: Use new definitions carefully.)
Using ⬚1, column A becomes

$$\boxed{-3} = 2(-3)^2 =$$
$$2(9) =$$
$$18 \qquad ⬚4$$

Using ⬚2, column B becomes

$$\boxed{72} = \frac{72}{4} =$$
$$18 \qquad ⬚5$$

From ⬚4 and ⬚5, we see that the columns are equal.
(Math Refresher #431 and #429)

22. (D) Choice D is correct.

Given: $\triangle RST$, $RS = 4$ and $ST = 9$

Column A	Column B
Area $\triangle RST$	18

(Use Strategy 14: Draw triangles to help find the answers.)

Let $RS \perp ST$, we have

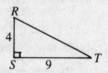

We know area of $\triangle RST = \dfrac{1}{2}b(h) = \dfrac{1}{2}(9)(4) = 18$

The columns are equal.
Now let RST be an acute $\angle$. We have

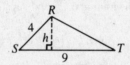

$h < 4$ (shortest distance from a point to a line is the length of the $\perp$ segment)

Thus, $\dfrac{1}{2}(h)(9) < 18$.

Area of $\triangle RST < 18$.
The columns are unequal.

Since two different results are possible, the answer cannot be determined from the information given.
(Math Refresher #306 and #514)

23. (D) Choice D is correct.

Given: r, s and $t > 0$

Column A	Column B
$r + s + t$	$\dfrac{1}{r + s + t}$

(Use Strategy C: Try numerics if it appears that the answer cannot be determined.)

Let $r = \dfrac{1}{4}$, $s = \dfrac{1}{4}$, $t = \dfrac{1}{4}$. The columns become

$$\frac{1}{4} + \frac{1}{4} + \frac{1}{4} = \qquad \frac{1}{\dfrac{1}{4} + \dfrac{1}{4} + \dfrac{1}{4}} = \frac{1}{\dfrac{3}{4}} =$$

$$\frac{3}{4} \qquad\qquad < \qquad\qquad \frac{4}{3}$$

Now let $r = 1$, $s = 2$, $t = 3$. The columns become

$$1 + 2 + 3 = \qquad \frac{1}{1 + 2 + 3} =$$

$$6 \qquad > \qquad \frac{1}{6}$$

Since two different relationships are possible, the answer cannot be determined from the information given.

(Math Refresher #109, #431, and #419)

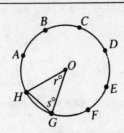

24. **(B)** Choice B is correct.

Given: All points, A through H, are equally spaced. ☐1

We know a whole circle = 360°. Using ☐1, we get

$$\overset{\frown}{HG} = \frac{360}{8} = 45° \qquad ☐2$$

We know a central angle = intercepted arc ☐3
Substituting from the diagram and using ☐2 and ☐3, we get

$$r = \overset{\frown}{HG}$$
$$r = 45 \qquad ☐4$$

We know that $OH = OG$ since all radii of a circle are equal. Thus, $\triangle HOG$ is isosceles ☐5

(Use Strategy 18: Remember triangle facts.)
From ☐5, we get that $\angle OHG = \angle OGH$ ☐6
(Use Strategy 3: The whole equals the sum of its parts.)
We know that the sum of the angles of a $\triangle = 180$ ☐7

Using the diagram and ☐7, we have

$$\angle OHG + \angle OGH + r = 180$$
$$\angle OHG + \quad s \quad + r = 180 \qquad ☐8$$

Substituting ☐4 and ☐6 into ☐8, we get

$$s + s + 45 = 180$$
$$2s + 45 = 180$$
$$2s = 135$$
$$s = 67\frac{1}{2} \qquad ☐9$$

Column A	Column B
r	s

Substituting ☐4 and ☐9 into ☐10, the columns become

45	$67\frac{1}{2}$

(Math Refresher #507, #524, #526, and #406)

25. **(D)** Choice D is correct.

Given: Total students = 100 ☐1
Exactly 80% take Calculus ☐2
Exactly 60% take Physics ☐3
Exactly 50% take German ☐4

(Use Strategy 2: Translate from words to algebra.)

From ☐3, we get

Number of students
taking Physics = .60 × 100
= 60 ☐5

From ☐4, we get

Number of students
taking German = .50 × 100
= 50 ☐6

(Use Strategy C: Try numerics if it appears that the answer cannot be determined.)

All 50 students taking German could also be taking Physics.

Only 49 students taking German could also be taking Physics.

Since there are two possible values for Column A, one equal to Column B and one less than Column B, the answer cannot be determined from the information given.

(Math Refresher #114)

26. **(C)** Choice C is correct.

Given: a, b, c, d and e are all integers > 0. ☐1
$a < b < c < d < e$ ☐2
$a \times b = 7$ ☐3
$d \times e = 90$ ☐4

(Use Strategy 17: Use the given information effectively.)

From ☐1, ☐2 and ☐3, we get

$$a = 1 \text{ and } b = 7 \qquad ☐5$$

Using ☐5, ☐1, ☐2 and ☐4, we get

$$d = 9 \text{ and } e = 10 \qquad ☐6$$

Using ☐1, ☐2, ☐5 and ☐6, we get

$$c = 8 \qquad ☐7$$

Using ☐7, the columns become

Column A	Column B
$c = 8$	8

(Math Refresher #419 and Logical Reasoning)

27. (C) Choice C is correct.

Given:

The average (arithmetic mean) of a and b is 8. $\boxed{1}$

$a - b + 4 = 0$ $\boxed{2}$

Column A	Column B
a	6

$\left(\text{Use Strategy 5:} \right.$

$\left. \text{Average} = \dfrac{\text{Sum of values}}{\text{Total number of values}} \right)$

From $\boxed{1}$, we get

$$\frac{a + b}{2} = 8 \qquad \boxed{3}$$

Multiply $\boxed{3}$ by 2. We get

$$\not{2}\left(\frac{a + b}{\not{2}}\right) = (8)2$$

$$a + b = 16 \qquad \boxed{4}$$

From $\boxed{2}$, $a - b + 4 = 0$, we get

$$a - b = -4 \qquad \boxed{5}$$

(Use Strategy 13: Find unknowns by addition.)

Adding $\boxed{4}$ and $\boxed{5}$, we have

$$2a = 12$$

$$a = 6 \qquad \boxed{6}$$

Using $\boxed{6}$, the columns become

Column A	Column B
$a = 6$	6

(Math Refresher #601, #406, and #407)

$$A \quad B \quad C \quad D \quad E \quad F \quad G$$

28. (C) Choice C is correct.

Given:

AG is divided into 6 equal segments $\boxed{1}$

Radius of circle, centered at $F = \dfrac{1}{5}AG$ $\boxed{2}$

(Use Strategy 2: Translate from words to algebra.)

From $\boxed{1}$ we get

$$DE = EF = FG = \frac{1}{6}AG \qquad \boxed{3}$$

Using $\boxed{2}$ and $\boxed{3}$, we have

$$\frac{1}{5}AG > \frac{1}{6}AG$$

Thus, Radius of circle $> FG$ and $\boxed{4}$

Radius of circle $> EF$ $\boxed{5}$

Using $\boxed{3}$, we get

$$DE + EF = \frac{1}{6}AG + \frac{1}{6}AG$$

$$= \frac{2}{6}AG$$

$$DE + EF = \frac{1}{3}AG \qquad \boxed{6}$$

(Use Strategy 3: The whole equals the sum of its parts.)

From the diagram we have

$$DF = DE + EF \qquad \boxed{7}$$

Substituting $\boxed{6}$ into $\boxed{7}$, we have

$$DF = \frac{1}{3}AG \qquad \boxed{8}$$

We know $\dfrac{1}{5}AG < \dfrac{1}{3}AG$ $\boxed{9}$

Substituting $\boxed{2}$ and $\boxed{8}$ into $\boxed{9}$, we have

$$\text{Radius of circle} < DF \qquad \boxed{10}$$

(Use Strategy 6: Know how to manipulate inequalities.)

Using $\boxed{5}$ and $\boxed{10}$, we get

$$EF < \text{Radius of circle} < DF \qquad \boxed{11}$$

Using $\boxed{11}$ and the diagram, we see that the circle will cross the line segment between D and E.

(Math Refresher #200, #419 and #524)

29. (E) Choice E is correct.

(Use Strategy 2: Translate from words to algebra.)

Given: Rose's earnings = \$44 $\boxed{1}$

Rose's time worked = 8 days $\boxed{2}$

(Use Strategy 13: Find unknowns by division.)

Dividing ① by ②, we have

$$\text{Rose's daily rate} = \frac{\$44}{8 \text{ days}}$$

$$\text{Rose's daily rate} = \frac{\$11}{2 \text{ day}} \qquad ③$$

Given: Total earnings to equal \$99 ④

Substituting ① from ④, we get

Amount left to be earned = \$55 ⑤
We know
(daily rate)(days worked) = money earned ⑥

Substituting ③ and ⑤ into ⑥, we get

$$\left(\frac{\$11}{2 \text{ days}}\right)(\text{days worked}) = \$55 \qquad ⑦$$

Multiplying ⑦ by $\frac{2}{11}$ days, we have

$$\frac{2 \text{ days}}{11}\left(\frac{11}{2 \text{ days}}\right)(\text{days worked}) = (55)\frac{2}{11}\text{ days}$$

$$\text{days worked} = 10 \text{ days}$$

(Math Refresher #200, #406 and #121)

30. **(A)** Choice A is correct.

$$\text{Given:} \quad x < 0 \qquad ①$$
$$y < 0 \qquad ②$$

(Use Strategy 6: Know how to manipulate inequalities.)

Multiply ① by ②, we get

$$x \cdot y > 0 \qquad ③$$

Thus I. is always positive

Adding ① and ② we get

$$x + y < 0 \qquad ④$$

Thus II. is not positive

(Use Strategy 7: Use numerics to help find the answer.)

$$\text{Let } x = -2, y = -3$$
$$\text{III. becomes } x - y = -2 - (-3)$$
$$= -2 + 3$$
$$= 1 \qquad ⑤$$

$$\text{Now let } x = -3, y = -2$$

$$\text{Now let } x = -3, y = -2$$
$$\text{III. becomes } x - y = -3 - (-2)$$
$$= -3 + 2$$
$$= -1 \qquad ⑥$$

From ⑤ and ⑥ we see that III. is not always
positive ⑦

Using ③, ④ and ⑦, we find that only Choice A, I
only, is correct.

(Math Refresher #419, #425, and #431)

31. **(D)** Choice D is correct.

$$\text{Given:} \quad a + 3b = 11 \qquad ①$$
$$a \text{ and } b \text{ are positive integers} \qquad ②$$

(Use Strategy 17: Use the given information effectively.)

From ①, we get

$$a = 11 - 3b \qquad ③$$

From ③ we see that a will be largest when b is
smallest. Using ②, we get

$$b = 1 \text{ is its smallest value} \qquad ④$$

Substituting ④ into ③, we have

$$a = 11 - 3(1)$$
$$a = 11 - 3$$
$$a = 8$$

(Math Refresher #406 and Logical Reasoning)

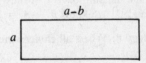

32. **(B)** Choice B is correct.

(Use Strategy 2: Translate from words to algebra.)

Perimeter of a rectangle

$$= 2(\text{length}) + 2(\text{width}) \qquad ①$$

Substituting from the diagram into ①, we have

$$\text{Perimeter} = 2(a - b) + 2(a)$$
$$= 2a - 2b + 2a$$
$$\text{Perimeter} = 4a - 2b$$

(Math Refresher #200, #304, and #431)

33. **(E)** Choice E is correct.

$$
\begin{array}{r}
AB \\
+\ BA \\
\hline
CDC
\end{array}
$$

Given: A, B, C and D are different digits. ☐1

The largest possible AB is 98. Thus,

$$
\begin{array}{r}
98 \\
+\ 89 \\
\hline
187
\end{array}
$$

Thus, the only possible value for C is 1 ☐2

(It cannot be greater than 1 since we used the largest value of AB.)

Using ☐2, the problem becomes

$$
\begin{array}{r}
AB \\
BA \\
\hline
1D1
\end{array}
$$ ☐3

We know that the sum of $B + A$ must end in a 1. ☐4
Using ☐4 and ☐1 we know $B + A = 11$ ☐5

(Use Strategy 8: When all choices must be tested, start with E.)

Use Choice E.

Let $A = 2$. ☐6

Substituting ☐6 in ☐5, we have

$$
B + 2 = 11
$$
$$
B = 9
$$ ☐7

Using ☐6 and ☐7, the problem becomes

$$
\begin{array}{r}
29 \\
+\ 92 \\
\hline
121
\end{array}
$$ ☐8

This cannot be, since in ☐1, we are told A, B, C and D are different digits. We have $D = A$.

Thus, A cannot equal 2.

(Math Refresher #431 and Logical Reasoning)

34. **(B)** Choice B is correct.

Given: $\dfrac{1}{11^{20}} - \dfrac{1}{11^{21}}$ ☐1

(Use Strategy 12: Don't make tedious calculations. Do it the easy way.)

Rewrite ☐1 as $\dfrac{1}{11^{20}} - \dfrac{1}{11^{20} \cdot 11} =$

$$
\frac{1}{11^{20}}(1) - \frac{1}{11^{20}}\left(\frac{1}{11}\right) =
$$

$$
\frac{1}{11^{20}}\left(1 - \frac{1}{11}\right) =
$$

$$
\frac{1}{11^{20}}\left(\frac{11}{11} - \frac{1}{11}\right) =
$$

$$
\frac{1}{11^{20}}\left(\frac{10}{11}\right) =
$$

$$
\frac{10}{11^{21}} =
$$

(Math Refresher #429, #409 and Subtracting Fractions)

35. **(B)** Choice B is correct.

Given: a, b are integers
Average of a, b and 4 is 6

$\left(\right.$**Use Strategy 5: Average**

$$
= \frac{\textbf{Sum of values}}{\textbf{Total number of values}}\left.\right)
$$

Using ☐2, we have

$$
\frac{a + b + 4}{3} = 6
$$ ☐3

(Use Strategy 13: Find unknowns by multiplication.)
Multiply ☐3 by 3. We get

$$
\cancel{3}\left(\frac{a + b + 4}{\cancel{3}}\right) = (6)3
$$
$$
a + b + 4 = 18
$$
$$
a + b = 14
$$ ☐4

Using ☐1 and ☐4, the possiblities are:

$a + b$	ab	
1 + 13	13	Choice A
2 + 12	24	
3 + 11	33	
4 + 10	40	Choice C
5 + 9	45	
6 + 8	48	Choice D
7 + 7	49	Choice E

Checking all the choices, we find only Choice B, 14, is not a possible value of ab.

(Math Refresher #601, #406, and Logical Reasoning)

EXPLANATORY ANSWERS FOR
PRACTICE TEST 4 (continued)

Section 6: Math Ability

1. **(A)** Choice A is correct.

$$\text{Given:} \quad 0.25 + 0.50 + x = 1.25$$
$$.75 + x = 1.25$$
$$x = .50$$
$$.50 = \frac{1}{2}$$

(Math Refresher #406)

2. **(D)** Choice D is correct.

Item I is clearly true.
Item II is not true. Since $6 = 2 \cdot 3$,
   then $6^4 = (2 \cdot 3)^4 = 2^4 \cdot 3^4$ and not $2^2 \cdot 3^4$
Item III is true. Since $6^3 = 216$, then $6^6 > 216$

(Math Refresher #429 and #431)

3. **(E)** Choice E is correct.

(Use Strategy 2: Translate from words to algebra.)

Blue marbles expressed as a fraction of all marbles

$$= \frac{\text{Number of blue marbles}}{\text{Total number of marbles}}$$
$$= \frac{4}{20} = \frac{1}{5}$$

(Math Refresher #200)

4. **(A)** Choice A is correct.

The only even number that is prime is the number 2. The reason for this is that "2" can be divisible only by itself or by 1.

(Math Refresher #608)

5. **(B)** Choice B is correct.

We want $\overleftrightarrow{NK}$ to bisect $\overline{MP}$. Clearly, $P = B$ since $\overleftrightarrow{NK}$ divides $\overline{MB}$ into two equal segments, each of length 5.

(Math Refresher #410 and #515)

6. **(C)** Choice C is correct.

Method 1: Any of the 3 books can be first, with either of the remaining two books being second and the last book being third.

$$3 \cdot 2 \cdot 1 = 6 \text{ possible arrangements}$$

Method 2: Call the books A, B and C, and list all the possible arrangements.

$$\left.\begin{array}{l} ABC \\ ACB \\ BAC \\ BCA \\ CAB \\ CBA \end{array}\right\} \text{ 6 in all.}$$

(Logical Reasoning)

7. **(C)** Choice C is correct.

Given: Areas of all 12 triangles are the same   ①
   Area of outlined region = 256   ②
   Area of square $ABCD$ = 128   ③

(Use Strategy 3: The whole equals the the sum of the parts.)

By looking at the diagram, we observe

Area of 8 triangles (I, II, ... ,VIII) = Area of Outlined Region − Area of Square $ABCD$
Substituting ② and ③ into the above, we get

Area of 8 triangles (I, ... ,VIII)
= 256 − 128
= 128   ④

Using ①, we get
Area of each of the 12 triangles =
$$\frac{\text{Area of 8 triangles}}{8}$$
Substituting ④ into the above, we get

Area of each of the 12 triangles = $\dfrac{128}{8}$

Area of each of the 12 triangles = 16   ⑤

(Use Strategy 3: The whole equals the sum of its parts.)

Shaded Area = Area $\triangle$V + Area $\triangle$VI + Area $\triangle$XI   ⑥

Substituting ① and ⑤ into ⑥, we get

Shaded Area = 16 + 16 + 16 = 48

(Logical Reasoning)

8. **(C)** Choice C is correct.

(Use Strategy F: Try Choice C when straightforward computations must be made.)

The easiest thing to do is to calculate the two quantities. Thus, the columns become

Column A	Column B
64	64

(Division and Multiplication)

9. **(A)** Choice A is correct.

We rewrite the following:

$$\frac{24x - 72}{24} = \frac{24(x - 3)}{24} = x - 3$$

$$x - 4 = \quad x - 3 - 1$$

Thus, the columns become

Column A	Column B
$x - 3$	$x - 3 - 1$

(Use Strategy A: Cancel equal things from both sides by subtracting.)

Subtracting $x - 3$ from both columns, we get

Column A	Column B
0	-1

and the answer is clear.

(Math Refresher #409)

10. **(C)** Choice C is correct.

(Use Strategy F: For straightforward calculations, try Choice C.)

Given: $MP = 60$, $MN = 36$ and $PN = 48$

The columns become:

Column A	Column B
$60 + 36 =$	$2 \times 48 =$
96	96

(Math Refresher #431)

11. **(A)** Choice A is correct.

Method 1: $(-2)^{88}$ is a positive number [a negative number raised to an even power is always positive]
$(-2)^{97}$ is a negative number [a negative number raised to an odd power is always negative]
Any positive is larger than any negative. Thus, $(-2)^{88}$ is larger than $(-2)^{97}$

Method 2: $(-2)^{97} = (-2)^{88}(-2)^9$
Thus, the columns become

Column A	Column B
$(-2)^{88}$	$(-2)^{88}(-2)^9$

(Use Strategy B: Cancel equal, positive things from both sides by division.)

Dividing both columns by $(-2)^{88}$, we get

Column A	Column B
1	$(-2)^9 =$ negative

Thus, Column A is larger.

(Math Refresher #428 and #429)

12. **(B)** Choice B is correct.

(Use Strategy 6: Know how to manipulate inequalities.)

We are told

$$-5 < y \qquad \boxed{1}$$
$$y < 5 \qquad \boxed{2}$$

Multiplying $\boxed{1}$ by -1,

$$5 > -y \qquad \boxed{3}$$

It is always true that $6 > 5$ $\qquad \boxed{4}$

Comparing $\boxed{3}$ and $\boxed{4}$, we have

$$6 > -y$$

(Math Refresher #423)

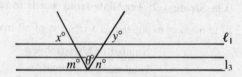

13. **(C)** Choice C is correct.

Know the properties of parallel lines!

In the diagram above, we have

$$x = m \qquad \boxed{1}$$
$$y = n \qquad \boxed{2}$$

(Use Strategy 13: Find unknown expressions by addition.)

Thus, adding $\boxed{1}$ and $\boxed{2}$

$$x + y = m + n \qquad \boxed{3}$$

(Use Strategy 3: The whole equals the sum of its parts.)

Since ℓ_3 is a straight line, then

$$m + n + \theta = 180$$
$$\text{or} \quad m + n \quad = 180 - \theta \qquad \boxed{4}$$

Substituting $\boxed{3}$ into $\boxed{4}$

$$x + y = 180 - \theta$$

(Math Refresher #504 and #406)

14. **(B)** Choice B is correct.

Column A	Column B
$\left(\dfrac{1}{3}\right)^4 = \dfrac{1}{81}$	$\left(\dfrac{1}{2}\right)^4 = \dfrac{1}{16}$

Clearly, B is larger.

(Math Refresher #429)

15. **(B)** Choice B is correct.

$$\left(\text{Use Strategy 5: Average} = \frac{\textbf{Sum of values}}{\textbf{Total number of values}}\right)$$

If all 10 students received a 95, then the average would be 95. Since one student received a grade less than 95, the average of the ten test scores is less than 95.

Column A	Column B
Some number less than 95	95

So the answer is clear.

(Math Refresher #601)

16. **(B)** Choice B is correct.

$$\textit{Given:} \quad x = -y \qquad \boxed{1}$$
$$x > 0 \qquad \boxed{2}$$

Substituting $\boxed{1}$ into $\boxed{2}$,

$$-y > 0$$
$$y < 0 \qquad \boxed{3}$$

(Use Strategy 6: Know how to manipulate inequalities.)

From $\boxed{2}$ and $\boxed{3}$ together, we have

$$xy < 0 \qquad \boxed{4}$$

It is always true that

$$y^2 \geq 0 \qquad \boxed{5}$$

Comparing $\boxed{4}$ and $\boxed{5}$

$$xy < y^2$$

(Math Refresher #423 and 428)

17. **(D)** Choice D is correct.

(Use Strategy 6: Know how to manipulate inequalities.)

$$1 < \frac{1}{6}x \qquad \boxed{1}$$
$$\frac{1}{6}x < 2 \qquad \boxed{2}$$

Method 1: Multiplying $\boxed{1}$ and $\boxed{2}$ by 6, we get

$$6 < x \qquad \boxed{3}$$
$$x < 12 \qquad \boxed{4}$$
$$\text{or} \quad 6 < x < 12 \qquad \boxed{5}$$

Since $\boxed{5}$ is the only restriction on x, we see that x may be greater than, less than, or equal to 10.

(Use Strategy C: When a comparison of the two columns is difficult, use numbers in place of variables.)

Method 2: Choose a value of x which satisfies $\boxed{1}$ and $\boxed{2}$.

Example 1: $x = 7$. Thus $x < 10$.

Example 2: $x = 11$. Thus $x > 10$.

Thus, a definite comparison cannot be made.

(Math Refresher #422 and #431)

18. **(A)** Choice A is correct.

Column A	Column B
$c(a + b) +$	$c(a + b) +$
$d(a + b)$	$(d + 1)(a + b) =$
$= (a + b)(c + d)$	$(a + b)$
	$[c + (d + 1)] =$
	$(a + b)$
	$(c + d + 1) =$
	$(a + b)$
	$[(c + d) + 1] =$
	$(a + b)(c + d) +$
	$a + b$

(Use Strategy A: Cancel equal quantities from both sides by subtracting.)

Subtract $(a + b)(c + d)$ from both sides. We get

Column A	Column B
0	$a + b$

Given: $a + b < 0$

Thus, Column A is larger.

(Algebraic Multiplication)

19. **(A)** Choice A is correct.

Given: $3x = 4y, x > 0$

or $\frac{3}{4}x = y$

Since x is positive, multiplying by $\frac{3}{4}$ (a positive number less than one) gives a smaller result. Thus,

$\frac{3}{4}x$ is less than x

Therefore, y is less than x.

(Math Refresher #406)

20. **(A)** Choice A is correct.

Method 1: Let x = length of a side of the cube

For Column A, the scale is 2 inches = 3 feet

or $\frac{2}{3}$ inch = 1 foot $\boxed{1}$

Multiplying $\boxed{1}$ by x, we get

x feet = $\frac{2}{3} x$ inches $\boxed{2}$

For Column B, the scale is 2 inches = 4 feet

or $\frac{1}{2}$ inch = 1 foot

or x feet = $\frac{1}{2}x$ inches

Thus, we have

Column A	Column B
$\frac{2}{3}x$ inches	$\frac{1}{2}x$ inches

and the answer is clear.

(Use Strategy 7: Use numericals to prove or disprove your guess.)

Method 2: Use a number for the length of a side— say 24 ft.

Column A	Column B
If 2 inches = 3 ft	If 2 inches = 4 ft
then $\frac{24 \text{ ft}}{3 \text{ ft}} = 8$	then $\frac{24 \text{ ft}}{4 \text{ ft}} = 6$
Thus,	Thus,
8×2 inches = 16 inches	6×2 inches = 12 inches
Thus, A is larger.	

(Math Refresher #201, #121, and #431)

21. **(D)** Choice D is correct.

Given: $(x + a)(x + b) = 24$ $\boxed{1}$
$x + a > 0$ $\boxed{2}$

(Use Strategy C: When a comparison of two columns is difficult, use numbers in place of variables.)

Choose numeric values of x, a, and b that satisfy $\boxed{1}$ and $\boxed{2}$

Example 1: $x = 3, a = 1, b = 3$
Here, $a < b$

Example 2: $x = 3, a = 5, b = 0$
Here, $a > b$

Thus, we cannot determine the answer.

(Math Refresher #431)

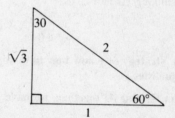

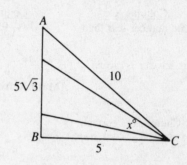

22. **(B)** Choice B is correct.

(Use Strategy B: Know special right triangles.)

The given triangle is similar to one of the standard triangles.

The corresponding sides of the two triangles are proportional. Thus, $m \angle ACB = 60°$ $\boxed{1}$

From the diagram, we see $x < m \angle ACB$ $\boxed{2}$

Comparing, $\boxed{1}$ and $\boxed{2}$, $x < 60°$

(Math Refresher #510 and #509)

23. **(A)** Choice A is correct.

(Use Strategy 2: Translate from words to algebra.)

The sum of his money earned on 2 consecutive days =
$$+5 + (-5) = 0$$
or
$$(-5) + (+5) = 0$$

The product of his money earned on 2 consecutive days =
$$(+5)(-5) = -25$$
or
$$(-5)(+5) = -25$$

$$\frac{A}{0} \qquad\qquad \frac{B}{-25}$$

Clearly, A is larger.

(Math Refresher #200 and Logical Reasoning)

24. **(D)** Choice D is correct.
Since volume
$= \frac{1}{3} \pi \text{ (radius)}^2\text{(height)}$, then the columns become

Column A	Column B
$\frac{1}{3} \pi r^2 h$	$\frac{1}{3} \pi (3h)^2 \left(\frac{r}{3}\right) = \pi h^2 r$

(Use Strategy C: When a comparison of the two columns is difficult, use numbers in place of variables.)

The answer to this question depends on specific values of r and h.

Example 1: $r = 3, h = 2$.
The columns become

Column A	Column B
6π	12π

and the quantity in Column B is greater.

Example 2: $r = 9, h = 2$.
The columns become

Column A	Column B
54π	36π

and the quantity in Column A is greater. Thus, a definite comparison cannot be made.

(Math Refresher #431)

25. **(C)** Choice C is correct.
(Use Strategy 2: Remember the definition of percent.)

$$24\% = \frac{24}{100} = \frac{4 \times 6}{4 \times 25} = \frac{6}{25}$$

Thus 24% of $n = \frac{6}{25}n$

Column A	Column B
$\frac{6}{25}n$	$\frac{6}{25}n$

They are equal.

(Math Refresher #114)

26. **(B)** Choice B is correct.

From basic geometry, we know that the area of $\triangle ABC$
$$= \frac{S^2\sqrt{3}}{4}$$

since $\triangle ABC$ is equilateral.

Thus, we want to compare

Column A	Column B
$\frac{S^2\sqrt{3}}{4} = \frac{S^2}{2} \cdot \frac{\sqrt{3}}{2}$	$\frac{1}{2}S^2 = \frac{S^2}{2}$

(Use Strategy B: Cancel positive quantities from both sides by division.)

Since $\frac{S^2}{2}$ is a positive quantity appearing in both columns, it will not change the answer. Thus, we really want to compare

Column A	Column B
$\frac{\sqrt{3}}{2}$	1

Since $\sqrt{3} \approx 1.732$, then $\frac{\sqrt{3}}{2} < 1$.

(Math Refresher #308)

27. **(D)** Choice D is correct.

(Use Strategy 11: Use new definitions carefully.)

(Use Strategy C: When a comparison of the two columns is difficult, use numbers instead of variables.)

Choose values for x and y.

Example 1: $x = 1, y = 2$
   Thus, $\boxed{x} = 1$, $\boxed{y} = 2$

The columns become

Column A	Column B
2	2

Example 2: $x = \dfrac{3}{2}, y = 2$
   Thus, $\boxed{x} = 1$, $\boxed{y} = 2$

The columns become

Column A	Column B
3	2

Since 2 different answers are possible, the answer cannot be determined.

(Math Refresher #431)

28. **(C)** Choice C is correct.

(Use Strategy 2: Translate from words to algebra.)

Given: We know that   1 gross = 12 dozen
                                    1 dozen = 12 (eggs)

Thus,
   1 gross of eggs = (12 ~~dozens~~)(12 egg/~~dozen~~)
   = 144 eggs

3 eggs, expressed as a fraction of a gross $= \dfrac{3}{144}$

$= \dfrac{1}{48}$

(Math Refresher #200 and #121)

29. **(B)** Choice B is correct.

(Use Strategy 17: Use the given information effectively.)

The most favorable conditions for Team C would be the following:

EVENT	FIRST PLACE (8 points)	SECOND PLACE (4 points)	THIRD PLACE (2 points)
3	Team C	Team A	Team B
4	Team C	Team B	Team A

Thus, Team C has a total of $4 + 8 + 8 = 20$ points after 2 more games. Team A has $12 + 4 + 2 = 18$ points. Team B has $12 + 2 + 4 = 18$ points. Thus, Team C will have to play at least 2 more games.

(Logical Reasoning)

30. **(C)** Choice C is correct.

$\left(\text{Use Strategy 5: Average} = \dfrac{\textbf{Sum of values}}{\textbf{Total number of values}} \right)$

Thus,

$x = \dfrac{\text{Sum of the } k \text{ numbers}}{k}$ $\boxed{1}$

$y = \dfrac{\text{Sum of the } j \text{ numbers}}{j}$ $\boxed{2}$

Average of $k + j$ numbers =

$\dfrac{\text{Sum of the } k + j \text{ numbers}}{k + j}$ $\boxed{3}$

From $\boxed{1}$ and $\boxed{2}$, we have

Sum of the k numbers $= kx$ $\boxed{4}$
Sum of the j numbers $= jy$ $\boxed{5}$

It is always true that

sum of the k and j numbers
= Sum of the k numbers + Sum of the j numbers
= $kx + jy$ $\boxed{6}$

Substituting $\boxed{6}$ into $\boxed{3}$, we get

$\dfrac{\text{Average of}}{k \text{ and } j \text{ numbers}} = \dfrac{kx + jy}{k + j}$

(Math Refresher #601)

31. **(C)** Choice C is correct.

(Use Strategy 17: Use the given information effectively.)

Since $x = 15$, then

$$m \angle LMN = 90$$
$$m \angle JNK = 75$$
$$m \angle KNM = 15$$
$$m \angle JNM = 90$$

Thus, the figure, with dashed line extensions, follows:

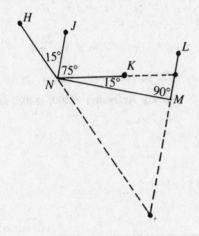

Clearly $\overleftrightarrow{JN} \parallel \overleftrightarrow{ML}$ and $\overleftrightarrow{JN}$ will not intersect $\overleftrightarrow{ML}$. $\overleftrightarrow{NK}$ and $\overleftrightarrow{NH}$ will each intersect $\overleftrightarrow{ML}$ exactly once. Thus, there will be exactly 2 more additional points of intersection.

(Math Refresher #504 and Logical Reasoning)

32. **(D)** Choice D is correct.

(Use Strategy 9: Remember Rate × Time = Distance.)

The time required for the second swimmer to swim the length of the pool

$$= \frac{120 \text{ meters}}{3 \text{ meters per second}} = 40 \text{ seconds}$$

During this time, the distance covered by the first swimmer

$$= (2 \text{ meters per second})(40 \text{ seconds})$$
$$= 80 \text{ meters}$$

The first swimmer must still swim
$$120 - 80 \text{ meters} = 40 \text{ meters}$$

(Math Refresher #201 and #202)

33. **(C)** Choice C is correct.

(Use Strategy 17: Use the given information effectively.)

Since the triangle is equilateral, all of its sides are equal. Thus,

$$5x - 2 = x$$
$$4x = 2$$
$$x = \frac{1}{2}$$

$$\text{Perimeter} = \text{Sum of 3 sides} = \frac{1}{2} + \frac{1}{2} + \frac{1}{2}$$
$$= 1\frac{1}{2}$$

(Math Refresher #508 and #406)

34. **(E)** Choice E is correct.

(Use Strategy 10: Know how to use units of time, distance, area.)

The number of waves that pass through a certain point in t seconds

$$= \frac{w \text{ waves}}{s \text{ seconds}} (t \text{ seconds})$$
$$= \frac{wt}{s} \text{ waves}$$

(Math Refresher #121)

35. **(B)** Choice B is correct.

(**Use Strategy 2: Translate English words into mathematical expressions.**)

We are told that

$$a = b + \frac{10}{100}b = \frac{11}{10}b \qquad \boxed{1}$$

$$ac = bd + \frac{32}{100}bd = \frac{33}{25}bd \qquad \boxed{2}$$

(**Use Strategy 13: Find unknowns by division.**)

We divide $\boxed{2}$ by a

$$c = \frac{33}{25}\left(\frac{b}{a}\right)d \qquad \boxed{3}$$

(**Use Strategy 13: Find unknowns by multiplication.**)

Multiply $\boxed{1}$ by $\frac{1}{b}$, giving

$$\frac{a}{b} = \frac{11}{10}$$

$$\text{or} \quad \frac{b}{a} = \frac{10}{11} \qquad \boxed{4}$$

Substituting $\boxed{4}$ into $\boxed{3}$, we get

$$c = \frac{6}{5}d$$

$$\text{or} \quad c = d + \frac{1}{5}d$$

$$\text{or} \quad c = d + \frac{20}{100}d$$

Thus, c is 20 percent greater than d.

(**Math Refresher #200, #406, and #431**)

Answer Sheet—Practice Test 5

SECTION 1: VERBAL ABILITY

1 Ⓐ Ⓑ Ⓒ Ⓓ Ⓔ   10 Ⓐ Ⓑ Ⓒ Ⓓ Ⓔ   19 Ⓐ Ⓑ Ⓒ Ⓓ Ⓔ   28 Ⓐ Ⓑ Ⓒ Ⓓ Ⓔ   37 Ⓐ Ⓑ Ⓒ Ⓓ Ⓔ
2 Ⓐ Ⓑ Ⓒ Ⓓ Ⓔ   11 Ⓐ Ⓑ Ⓒ Ⓓ Ⓔ   20 Ⓐ Ⓑ Ⓒ Ⓓ Ⓔ   29 Ⓐ Ⓑ Ⓒ Ⓓ Ⓔ   38 Ⓐ Ⓑ Ⓒ Ⓓ Ⓔ
3 Ⓐ Ⓑ Ⓒ Ⓓ Ⓔ   12 Ⓐ Ⓑ Ⓒ Ⓓ Ⓔ   21 Ⓐ Ⓑ Ⓒ Ⓓ Ⓔ   30 Ⓐ Ⓑ Ⓒ Ⓓ Ⓔ   39 Ⓐ Ⓑ Ⓒ Ⓓ Ⓔ
4 Ⓐ Ⓑ Ⓒ Ⓓ Ⓔ   13 Ⓐ Ⓑ Ⓒ Ⓓ Ⓔ   22 Ⓐ Ⓑ Ⓒ Ⓓ Ⓔ   31 Ⓐ Ⓑ Ⓒ Ⓓ Ⓔ   40 Ⓐ Ⓑ Ⓒ Ⓓ Ⓔ
5 Ⓐ Ⓑ Ⓒ Ⓓ Ⓔ   14 Ⓐ Ⓑ Ⓒ Ⓓ Ⓔ   23 Ⓐ Ⓑ Ⓒ Ⓓ Ⓔ   32 Ⓐ Ⓑ Ⓒ Ⓓ Ⓔ   41 Ⓐ Ⓑ Ⓒ Ⓓ Ⓔ
6 Ⓐ Ⓑ Ⓒ Ⓓ Ⓔ   15 Ⓐ Ⓑ Ⓒ Ⓓ Ⓔ   24 Ⓐ Ⓑ Ⓒ Ⓓ Ⓔ   33 Ⓐ Ⓑ Ⓒ Ⓓ Ⓔ   42 Ⓐ Ⓑ Ⓒ Ⓓ Ⓔ
7 Ⓐ Ⓑ Ⓒ Ⓓ Ⓔ   16 Ⓐ Ⓑ Ⓒ Ⓓ Ⓔ   25 Ⓐ Ⓑ Ⓒ Ⓓ Ⓔ   34 Ⓐ Ⓑ Ⓒ Ⓓ Ⓔ   43 Ⓐ Ⓑ Ⓒ Ⓓ Ⓔ
8 Ⓐ Ⓑ Ⓒ Ⓓ Ⓔ   17 Ⓐ Ⓑ Ⓒ Ⓓ Ⓔ   26 Ⓐ Ⓑ Ⓒ Ⓓ Ⓔ   35 Ⓐ Ⓑ Ⓒ Ⓓ Ⓔ   44 Ⓐ Ⓑ Ⓒ Ⓓ Ⓔ
9 Ⓐ Ⓑ Ⓒ Ⓓ Ⓔ   18 Ⓐ Ⓑ Ⓒ Ⓓ Ⓔ   27 Ⓐ Ⓑ Ⓒ Ⓓ Ⓔ   36 Ⓐ Ⓑ Ⓒ Ⓓ Ⓔ   45 Ⓐ Ⓑ Ⓒ Ⓓ Ⓔ

SECTION 2: MATH ABILITY

1 Ⓐ Ⓑ Ⓒ Ⓓ Ⓔ   6 Ⓐ Ⓑ Ⓒ Ⓓ Ⓔ   11 Ⓐ Ⓑ Ⓒ Ⓓ Ⓔ   16 Ⓐ Ⓑ Ⓒ Ⓓ Ⓔ   21 Ⓐ Ⓑ Ⓒ Ⓓ Ⓔ
2 Ⓐ Ⓑ Ⓒ Ⓓ Ⓔ   7 Ⓐ Ⓑ Ⓒ Ⓓ Ⓔ   12 Ⓐ Ⓑ Ⓒ Ⓓ Ⓔ   17 Ⓐ Ⓑ Ⓒ Ⓓ Ⓔ   22 Ⓐ Ⓑ Ⓒ Ⓓ Ⓔ
3 Ⓐ Ⓑ Ⓒ Ⓓ Ⓔ   8 Ⓐ Ⓑ Ⓒ Ⓓ Ⓔ   13 Ⓐ Ⓑ Ⓒ Ⓓ Ⓔ   18 Ⓐ Ⓑ Ⓒ Ⓓ Ⓔ   23 Ⓐ Ⓑ Ⓒ Ⓓ Ⓔ
4 Ⓐ Ⓑ Ⓒ Ⓓ Ⓔ   9 Ⓐ Ⓑ Ⓒ Ⓓ Ⓔ   14 Ⓐ Ⓑ Ⓒ Ⓓ Ⓔ   19 Ⓐ Ⓑ Ⓒ Ⓓ Ⓔ   24 Ⓐ Ⓑ Ⓒ Ⓓ Ⓔ
5 Ⓐ Ⓑ Ⓒ Ⓓ Ⓔ   10 Ⓐ Ⓑ Ⓒ Ⓓ Ⓔ   15 Ⓐ Ⓑ Ⓒ Ⓓ Ⓔ   20 Ⓐ Ⓑ Ⓒ Ⓓ Ⓔ   25 Ⓐ Ⓑ Ⓒ Ⓓ Ⓔ

SECTION 3: STANDARD WRITTEN ENGLISH

1 Ⓐ Ⓑ Ⓒ Ⓓ Ⓔ   11 Ⓐ Ⓑ Ⓒ Ⓓ Ⓔ   21 Ⓐ Ⓑ Ⓒ Ⓓ Ⓔ   31 Ⓐ Ⓑ Ⓒ Ⓓ Ⓔ   41 Ⓐ Ⓑ Ⓒ Ⓓ Ⓔ
2 Ⓐ Ⓑ Ⓒ Ⓓ Ⓔ   12 Ⓐ Ⓑ Ⓒ Ⓓ Ⓔ   22 Ⓐ Ⓑ Ⓒ Ⓓ Ⓔ   32 Ⓐ Ⓑ Ⓒ Ⓓ Ⓔ   42 Ⓐ Ⓑ Ⓒ Ⓓ Ⓔ
3 Ⓐ Ⓑ Ⓒ Ⓓ Ⓔ   13 Ⓐ Ⓑ Ⓒ Ⓓ Ⓔ   23 Ⓐ Ⓑ Ⓒ Ⓓ Ⓔ   33 Ⓐ Ⓑ Ⓒ Ⓓ Ⓔ   43 Ⓐ Ⓑ Ⓒ Ⓓ Ⓔ
4 Ⓐ Ⓑ Ⓒ Ⓓ Ⓔ   14 Ⓐ Ⓑ Ⓒ Ⓓ Ⓔ   24 Ⓐ Ⓑ Ⓒ Ⓓ Ⓔ   34 Ⓐ Ⓑ Ⓒ Ⓓ Ⓔ   44 Ⓐ Ⓑ Ⓒ Ⓓ Ⓔ
5 Ⓐ Ⓑ Ⓒ Ⓓ Ⓔ   15 Ⓐ Ⓑ Ⓒ Ⓓ Ⓔ   25 Ⓐ Ⓑ Ⓒ Ⓓ Ⓔ   35 Ⓐ Ⓑ Ⓒ Ⓓ Ⓔ   45 Ⓐ Ⓑ Ⓒ Ⓓ Ⓔ
6 Ⓐ Ⓑ Ⓒ Ⓓ Ⓔ   16 Ⓐ Ⓑ Ⓒ Ⓓ Ⓔ   26 Ⓐ Ⓑ Ⓒ Ⓓ Ⓔ   36 Ⓐ Ⓑ Ⓒ Ⓓ Ⓔ   46 Ⓐ Ⓑ Ⓒ Ⓓ Ⓔ
7 Ⓐ Ⓑ Ⓒ Ⓓ Ⓔ   17 Ⓐ Ⓑ Ⓒ Ⓓ Ⓔ   27 Ⓐ Ⓑ Ⓒ Ⓓ Ⓔ   37 Ⓐ Ⓑ Ⓒ Ⓓ Ⓔ   47 Ⓐ Ⓑ Ⓒ Ⓓ Ⓔ
8 Ⓐ Ⓑ Ⓒ Ⓓ Ⓔ   18 Ⓐ Ⓑ Ⓒ Ⓓ Ⓔ   28 Ⓐ Ⓑ Ⓒ Ⓓ Ⓔ   38 Ⓐ Ⓑ Ⓒ Ⓓ Ⓔ   48 Ⓐ Ⓑ Ⓒ Ⓓ Ⓔ
9 Ⓐ Ⓑ Ⓒ Ⓓ Ⓔ   19 Ⓐ Ⓑ Ⓒ Ⓓ Ⓔ   29 Ⓐ Ⓑ Ⓒ Ⓓ Ⓔ   39 Ⓐ Ⓑ Ⓒ Ⓓ Ⓔ   49 Ⓐ Ⓑ Ⓒ Ⓓ Ⓔ
10 Ⓐ Ⓑ Ⓒ Ⓓ Ⓔ   20 Ⓐ Ⓑ Ⓒ Ⓓ Ⓔ   30 Ⓐ Ⓑ Ⓒ Ⓓ Ⓔ   40 Ⓐ Ⓑ Ⓒ Ⓓ Ⓔ   50 Ⓐ Ⓑ Ⓒ Ⓓ Ⓔ

SECTION 4: VERBAL ABILITY

1 Ⓐ Ⓑ Ⓒ Ⓓ Ⓔ   9 Ⓐ Ⓑ Ⓒ Ⓓ Ⓔ   17 Ⓐ Ⓑ Ⓒ Ⓓ Ⓔ   25 Ⓐ Ⓑ Ⓒ Ⓓ Ⓔ   33 Ⓐ Ⓑ Ⓒ Ⓓ Ⓔ
2 Ⓐ Ⓑ Ⓒ Ⓓ Ⓔ   10 Ⓐ Ⓑ Ⓒ Ⓓ Ⓔ   18 Ⓐ Ⓑ Ⓒ Ⓓ Ⓔ   26 Ⓐ Ⓑ Ⓒ Ⓓ Ⓔ   34 Ⓐ Ⓑ Ⓒ Ⓓ Ⓔ
3 Ⓐ Ⓑ Ⓒ Ⓓ Ⓔ   11 Ⓐ Ⓑ Ⓒ Ⓓ Ⓔ   19 Ⓐ Ⓑ Ⓒ Ⓓ Ⓔ   27 Ⓐ Ⓑ Ⓒ Ⓓ Ⓔ   35 Ⓐ Ⓑ Ⓒ Ⓓ Ⓔ
4 Ⓐ Ⓑ Ⓒ Ⓓ Ⓔ   12 Ⓐ Ⓑ Ⓒ Ⓓ Ⓔ   20 Ⓐ Ⓑ Ⓒ Ⓓ Ⓔ   28 Ⓐ Ⓑ Ⓒ Ⓓ Ⓔ   36 Ⓐ Ⓑ Ⓒ Ⓓ Ⓔ
5 Ⓐ Ⓑ Ⓒ Ⓓ Ⓔ   13 Ⓐ Ⓑ Ⓒ Ⓓ Ⓔ   21 Ⓐ Ⓑ Ⓒ Ⓓ Ⓔ   29 Ⓐ Ⓑ Ⓒ Ⓓ Ⓔ   37 Ⓐ Ⓑ Ⓒ Ⓓ Ⓔ
6 Ⓐ Ⓑ Ⓒ Ⓓ Ⓔ   14 Ⓐ Ⓑ Ⓒ Ⓓ Ⓔ   22 Ⓐ Ⓑ Ⓒ Ⓓ Ⓔ   30 Ⓐ Ⓑ Ⓒ Ⓓ Ⓔ   38 Ⓐ Ⓑ Ⓒ Ⓓ Ⓔ
7 Ⓐ Ⓑ Ⓒ Ⓓ Ⓔ   15 Ⓐ Ⓑ Ⓒ Ⓓ Ⓔ   23 Ⓐ Ⓑ Ⓒ Ⓓ Ⓔ   31 Ⓐ Ⓑ Ⓒ Ⓓ Ⓔ   39 Ⓐ Ⓑ Ⓒ Ⓓ Ⓔ
8 Ⓐ Ⓑ Ⓒ Ⓓ Ⓔ   16 Ⓐ Ⓑ Ⓒ Ⓓ Ⓔ   24 Ⓐ Ⓑ Ⓒ Ⓓ Ⓔ   32 Ⓐ Ⓑ Ⓒ Ⓓ Ⓔ   40 Ⓐ Ⓑ Ⓒ Ⓓ Ⓔ

SECTION 5: MATH ABILITY

1 Ⓐ Ⓑ Ⓒ Ⓓ Ⓔ   8 Ⓐ Ⓑ Ⓒ Ⓓ Ⓔ   15 Ⓐ Ⓑ Ⓒ Ⓓ Ⓔ   22 Ⓐ Ⓑ Ⓒ Ⓓ Ⓔ   29 Ⓐ Ⓑ Ⓒ Ⓓ Ⓔ
2 Ⓐ Ⓑ Ⓒ Ⓓ Ⓔ   9 Ⓐ Ⓑ Ⓒ Ⓓ Ⓔ   16 Ⓐ Ⓑ Ⓒ Ⓓ Ⓔ   23 Ⓐ Ⓑ Ⓒ Ⓓ Ⓔ   30 Ⓐ Ⓑ Ⓒ Ⓓ Ⓔ
3 Ⓐ Ⓑ Ⓒ Ⓓ Ⓔ   10 Ⓐ Ⓑ Ⓒ Ⓓ Ⓔ   17 Ⓐ Ⓑ Ⓒ Ⓓ Ⓔ   24 Ⓐ Ⓑ Ⓒ Ⓓ Ⓔ   31 Ⓐ Ⓑ Ⓒ Ⓓ Ⓔ
4 Ⓐ Ⓑ Ⓒ Ⓓ Ⓔ   11 Ⓐ Ⓑ Ⓒ Ⓓ Ⓔ   18 Ⓐ Ⓑ Ⓒ Ⓓ Ⓔ   25 Ⓐ Ⓑ Ⓒ Ⓓ Ⓔ   32 Ⓐ Ⓑ Ⓒ Ⓓ Ⓔ
5 Ⓐ Ⓑ Ⓒ Ⓓ Ⓔ   12 Ⓐ Ⓑ Ⓒ Ⓓ Ⓔ   19 Ⓐ Ⓑ Ⓒ Ⓓ Ⓔ   26 Ⓐ Ⓑ Ⓒ Ⓓ Ⓔ   33 Ⓐ Ⓑ Ⓒ Ⓓ Ⓔ
6 Ⓐ Ⓑ Ⓒ Ⓓ Ⓔ   13 Ⓐ Ⓑ Ⓒ Ⓓ Ⓔ   20 Ⓐ Ⓑ Ⓒ Ⓓ Ⓔ   27 Ⓐ Ⓑ Ⓒ Ⓓ Ⓔ   34 Ⓐ Ⓑ Ⓒ Ⓓ Ⓔ
7 Ⓐ Ⓑ Ⓒ Ⓓ Ⓔ   14 Ⓐ Ⓑ Ⓒ Ⓓ Ⓔ   21 Ⓐ Ⓑ Ⓒ Ⓓ Ⓔ   28 Ⓐ Ⓑ Ⓒ Ⓓ Ⓔ   35 Ⓐ Ⓑ Ⓒ Ⓓ Ⓔ

SECTION 6: MATH ABILITY

1 Ⓐ Ⓑ Ⓒ Ⓓ Ⓔ   6 Ⓐ Ⓑ Ⓒ Ⓓ Ⓔ   11 Ⓐ Ⓑ Ⓒ Ⓓ Ⓔ   16 Ⓐ Ⓑ Ⓒ Ⓓ Ⓔ   21 Ⓐ Ⓑ Ⓒ Ⓓ Ⓔ
2 Ⓐ Ⓑ Ⓒ Ⓓ Ⓔ   7 Ⓐ Ⓑ Ⓒ Ⓓ Ⓔ   12 Ⓐ Ⓑ Ⓒ Ⓓ Ⓔ   17 Ⓐ Ⓑ Ⓒ Ⓓ Ⓔ   22 Ⓐ Ⓑ Ⓒ Ⓓ Ⓔ
3 Ⓐ Ⓑ Ⓒ Ⓓ Ⓔ   8 Ⓐ Ⓑ Ⓒ Ⓓ Ⓔ   13 Ⓐ Ⓑ Ⓒ Ⓓ Ⓔ   18 Ⓐ Ⓑ Ⓒ Ⓓ Ⓔ   23 Ⓐ Ⓑ Ⓒ Ⓓ Ⓔ
4 Ⓐ Ⓑ Ⓒ Ⓓ Ⓔ   9 Ⓐ Ⓑ Ⓒ Ⓓ Ⓔ   14 Ⓐ Ⓑ Ⓒ Ⓓ Ⓔ   19 Ⓐ Ⓑ Ⓒ Ⓓ Ⓔ   24 Ⓐ Ⓑ Ⓒ Ⓓ Ⓔ
5 Ⓐ Ⓑ Ⓒ Ⓓ Ⓔ   10 Ⓐ Ⓑ Ⓒ Ⓓ Ⓔ   15 Ⓐ Ⓑ Ⓒ Ⓓ Ⓔ   20 Ⓐ Ⓑ Ⓒ Ⓓ Ⓔ   25 Ⓐ Ⓑ Ⓒ Ⓓ Ⓔ

SAT Practice Test 5

SECTION 1 VERBAL ABILITY
30 MINUTES 45 QUESTIONS

For each question in this section, choose the best answer and blacken the corresponding space on the answer sheet.

Each question below consists of a word in capital letters, followed by five lettered words or phrases. Choose the word or phrase that is most nearly *opposite* in meaning to the word in capital letters. Since some of the questions require you to distinguish fine shades of meaning, consider all the choices before deciding which is best.

Example:

> GOOD: (A) sour (B) bad (C) red
> (D) hot (E) ugly
>
> Ⓐ ● Ⓒ Ⓓ Ⓔ

1. CAJOLE: (A) reject (B) shorten
   (C) postpone (D) invade (E) discourage

2. ARDUOUS: (A) formal (B) easy
   (C) pacified (D) fit (E) regulated

3. WHET: (A) regain (B) dry (C) grind
   (D) dull (E) attack

4. PULCHRITUDE: (A) ugliness
   (B) similarity (C) crudity (D) solitude
   (E) prosperity

5. GNARLED: (A) stabilized (B) loosened
   (C) straightened (D) reformed (E) squeezed.

6. SCRUTINIZE: (A) glance at (B) pass by
   (C) escape from (D) tighten up (E) see through

7. CRASS: (A) clothed (B) glistening
   (C) greedy (D) refined (E) rebuilt

8. PURLOIN: (A) offer (B) accept
   (C) pardon (D) antagonize (E) whip

9. SUAVE: (A) irksome (B) inflexible
   (C) rough (D) methodical (E) faulty

10. FORBEARANCE: (A) promptness
    (B) disappearance (C) clearance
    (D) impatience (E) posterity

11. LUGUBRIOUS: (A) lovely (B) subtle
    (C) respected (D) inspired (E) joyful

12. COMMODIOUS: (A) complicated
    (B) ancient (C) unsatisfied (D) confined
    (E) tragic

13. ENCUMBRANCE: (A) renewal (B) utility
    (C) forgetfulness (D) reduction
    (E) desire

14. TORTUOUS: (A) pleasing (B) difficult
    (C) direct (D) immoderate (E) crafty

15. BANAL: (A) solid (B) fulfilling
    (C) haphazard (D) harmless (E) extraordinary

Each sentence below has one or two blanks, each blank indicating that something has been omitted. Beneath the sentence are five lettered words or sets of words. Choose the word or set of words that *best* fits the meaning of the sentence as a whole.

Example:

> Although its publicity has been ____, the film itself is intelligent, well-acted, handsomely produced, and altogether ____.
>
> (A) tasteless . . . respectable
> (B) extensive . . . moderate
> (C) sophisticated . . . amateur
> (D) risqué . . . crude
> (E) perfect . . . spectacular ● Ⓑ Ⓒ Ⓓ Ⓔ

16. Because the subject matter was so technical, the instructor made every effort to use _____ terms to describe it.

    (A) candid (B) simplified (C) discreet
    (D) specialized (E) involved

17. Violent crime has become so _____ in our cities that hardly a day goes by when we are not made aware of some _____ act on our local news broadcasts.

    (A) scarce . . . momentous
    (B) pervasive . . . benign
    (C) conclusive . . . serious
    (D) common . . . heinous
    (E) ridiculous . . . unacceptable

18. Although they are _____ by intense police patrols, burglars _____ to prowl the subways.

   (A) incited . . . decline
   (B) enlivened . . . attempt
   (C) hindered . . . cease
   (D) persuaded . . . refuse
   (E) impeded . . . continue

19. Britain's seizure of American ships and _____ our sailors to serve in the British Navy were two major causes of the War of 1812.

   (A) compelling   (B) recruiting   (C) bribing
   (D) enlisting   (E) deriding

20. Since he had not worked very hard on his project, the student was quite _____ upon learning that he had won the contest.

   (A) composed   (B) apathetic   (C) rebuffed
   (D) dismayed   (E) enraptured

Each passage below is followed by questions based on its content. Answer all questions following a passage on the basis of what is *stated* or *implied* in that passage.

According to the new school of scientists, technology is an overlooked force in expanding the horizons of scientific knowledge. Science moves forward, they say, not so much through the insights of great men of genius as
5 because of more mundane things like improved techniques and tools. "In short," a leader of the new school contends, "the scientific revolution, as we call it, was largely the improvement and invention and use of a series of instruments of revelation that expanded the reach of science in
10 innumerable directions."

The new school is controversial because it is totally at odds with long-held views of how science works. The conventional wisdom holds that thoughts and the men thinking them are all-important to progress. In the standard
15 view, laboratory instruments are simply passive tools. Further, such technologies are seen not only as unimportant to progress but also as dependent on pure science for their creation. The conventional wisdom sees advances such as Maxwell's discovery of the laws of electromag-
20 netism as the source of oscilloscopes and other modern-day laboratory tools. Thus, great men and science beget technology.

Over the years, tools and technology themselves as a source of fundamental innovation—rather than the other
25 way around—have largely been ignored by historians and philosophers of science. The modern school that hails technology argues that such masters as Galileo, Newton, Maxwell, Einstein, and inventors such as Edison set great store by, and derived great benefit from, miscellaneous craft
30 information and technological devices that were usable in scientific experiments.

The centerpiece of the argument of a technology-yes, genius-no advocate was an analysis of Galileo's role at the start of the scientific revolution. The wisdom of the
35 day was derived from Ptolemy, an astronomer of the second century, whose elaborate celestial system put Earth at the center of all heavenly motions. Galileo's crowning glory was that in 1609 he was the first person to turn the newly invented telescope on the heavens to prove that the
40 planets revolve around the sun rather than around the Earth.

But the real hero of the story, according to the new school scientist, was the long evolution in the improvement of machinery for making eyeglasses. A key development was the invention of the glass lathe in the late 16th century,
45 which made it possible to produce powerful concave lenses. Two of these were soon combined to produce crude telescopes. "Galileo just happened along at the right time."

Federal policy is necessarily involved in the technology vs. genius dispute. Whether the Government should in-
50 crease the financing of pure science at the expense of technology or vice versa often turns on the issue of which is seen as the driving force.

21. Which of the following is the most appropriate title for this passage?

   (A) Who Is the Greatest Scientist of All Time?
   (B) Does Genius or Technology Rule Science?
   (C) Whom Should the Government Favor with Grants—Technologists or the Science Wizard?
   (D) What's Wrong with Science Education?
   (E) Did Galileo Receive the Credit That He Deserved?

22. The position taken by the new school scientists, as expressed in this passage, is strengthened by the fact that

   (A) the Federal government is much interested in improving the teaching of science in the nation's schools
   (B) a widespread desire to have a nuclear freeze has been voiced by many Americans
   (C) the Nobel Prize is regularly awarded for research in Biology, Chemistry, and Physics
   (D) the American Association for the Advancement of Science is a highly respected organization
   (E) computers are able to do all kinds of new calculations and handle fantastic amounts of data

23. In the passage, the author seems

 (A) to give preference to the new school point of view
 (B) to give preference to the conventional point of view
 (C) to give no preference to either side
 (D) to indicate a friendly relationship between the new school advocates and the conventional group
 (E) to be a member of one of the two groups

24. A scientist opposing the new school philosophy would probably agree with which one of the following statements?

 (A) Many great advances in science have been based on measurements and new techniques.
 (B) We are now much less prone to think in terms which subordinate technology to pure science.
 (C) Physicists are likely to be lined up at a new atom smasher.
 (D) Human insight and pure research have always been of primary importance.
 (E) Instruments can help us to find out things not able to be deduced by mere brain power.

25. Which is a correct statement according to the passage?

 (A) Galileo and Ptolemy exchanged ideas for their mutual benefit.
 (B) Maxwell, Edison, and Newton were inventors of renown.
 (C) Galileo was a person of royal birth.
 (D) Einstein avoided the use of technological devices in his calculations.
 (E) The Government takes an active interest in technology as well as in pure science.

The funeral procession begins at the poet's house, where the corpse was lying in state attended by his widow and sisters. The wake is held in the middle of a muddy, flooded room that was once his library. Books and documents are
5 floating in the mud along with furniture. The day before, a stream was diverted into the house by the military, who smashed everything in sight with their rifle butts and left the house flooded.

The coffin has been removed and is being carried by
10 some friends of the poet. Only a few people are present accompanying the widow and sisters, and the Mexican ambassador.

Someone inquires and is told "Pablo Neruda." "What?" "Yes, sir, Pablo Neruda." And quietly the word spreads,
15 and the name opens doors and windows, it begins to appear at half-closed shops, it descends from telephone poles with the workers who worked on them, it stops buses and it empties them, brings out people running from the distant streets, people who arrive already crying, still hoping it
20 is not true. The name keeps emerging like a miracle of anger, in hundreds and hundreds of people—men,

women, children, almost all poor, almost all people of the shantytowns of Santiago—each of them becoming Pablo Neruda.

Then we hear a sound; shy, half-choked, prayed in 25 secret—"Pablo Neruda"—and we hear an answer of someone who is saying, "Don't tell that I said it. Here, now and forever."

A voice shouts, "Pablo Neruda!" and there, already in anger. "Here!"—already throwing a hat, stepping firmly 30 and facing the military who are approaching and surrounding the crowd.

And here begins some kind of giant litany for who knows how many dead. Who knows how many more murdered people this litany is for? A remote shrill voice howls 35 in a bestial, heartbreaking way, "Pablo Neruda!" And a choir watched by millions of assassins, by millions of informers, sings, "Here, with us, now and forever!"

There, farther, on the right, on the left, at the end of the marching column, a column of three thousand, the 40 Chilean cries rise up: "Pablo Neruda!" "Pablo Neruda!" "Here!" "Here!" "Here, with us, now and forever!" "Chilean people, they are stepping on you, they are assassinating you, they are torturing you!" "Chilean people, don't give up, the revolution is awaiting us, we'll fight until we 45 finish with the henchmen!"

Swirls of crying, swearing, threats, wailings, of darkness at noon, of voices choking with anger. Hellish vocabulary, crazy heavenly words. Three thousand overwhelmingly defeated people are howling. 50

And suddenly, howling powerfully, a woman begins to sing Neruda's verses. Her voice grows suddenly alone, "I have been reborn many times from the depths / of defeated stars. . ." And all shout, they shout from their memories, ". . . reconstructing the threads / of eternities 55 that I populated with my hands."

26. For whom is the funeral procession which is described in this passage?

 (A) a friend of Pablo Neruda
 (B) a poor old man from Santiago
 (C) a Chilean poet
 (D) a much admired politician
 (E) a Mexican ambassador

27. Which words best describe the mood of the crowd?

 (A) happy throughout
 (B) fearful throughout
 (C) at first fearful, then later happy
 (D) at first happy, then later fearful
 (E) at first fearful, then later defiant

28. What occurred shortly before the funeral procession?

 (A) a large pre-election rally
 (B) a closely contested election
 (C) a strike by a union
 (D) a massacre by the military
 (E) an attempt to overthrow the government

29. What does the pronoun "it," mentioned several times in the third paragraph, refer to?

(A) the impending revolution
(B) the name of the person in the coffin
(C) an approaching storm
(D) the miracle of a corpse returning to life
(E) a force that will bring salvation

30. According to the passage, Pablo Neruda seemed to be all of the following *except*

(A) hopeful   (B) married   (C) admired
(D) intellectual   (E) lonely

Select the word or set of words that *best* completes each of the following sentences.

31. The professor displayed extreme stubbornness; not only did he _____ the logic of the student's argument, but he _____ to acknowledge that the textbook conclusion was correct.

(A) amplify . . . hesitated
(B) reject . . . refused
(C) clarify . . . consented
(D) justify . . . expected
(E) ridicule . . . proposed

32. The _____ of the explorers was reflected in their refusal to give up.

(A) tenacity   (B) degradation   (C) greed
(D) harassment   (E) sociability

33. Ironically, the protest held in order to strengthen the labor movement served to_____ it.

(A) justify   (B) coddle   (C) weaken
(D) invigorate   (E) appease

34. Governor Edwards combined _____ politics with administrative skills to dominate the state; in addition to these assets, he was also _____ .

(A) corrupt . . . glum
(B) inept . . . civil
(C) incriminating . . . sincere
(D) astute . . . dapper
(E) trivial . . . lavish

35. In spite of David's tremendous intelligence, he was frequently _____ when confronted with practical matters.

(A) coherent   (B) baffled   (C) cautious
(D) philosophical   (E) pensive

Each question below consists of a related pair of words or phrases, followed by five lettered pairs of words or phrases. Select the lettered pair that *best* expresses a relationship similar to that expressed in the original pair.

Example:

YAWN : BOREDOM : :   (A) dream : sleep
(B) anger : madness   (C) smile : amusement
(D) face : expression   (E) impatience : rebellion
Ⓐ Ⓑ ● Ⓓ Ⓔ

36. DROUGHT : RAIN : :

(A) smog : pollution
(B) insolvency : funds
(C) depression : normalcy
(D) profusion : activity
(E) indolence : ambition

37. RECESS : SCHOOL : :

(A) parole : convict
(B) session : government
(C) work : vacation
(D) intermission : theatre
(E) convention : delegation

38. CLOTH : THREADBARE : :

(A) mosaic : colorful
(B) expression : hackneyed
(C) performance : dynamic
(D) beauty : superficial
(E) smell : piquant

39. INTREPID : FEARFUL : :

(A) infallible : meaningful
(B) impotent : powerful
(C) wealthy : unscrupulous
(D) unemployed : slothful
(E) callow : unwise

40. LOAFER : SHOE : :

(A) leather : hide
(B) cuff : shirt
(C) slicker : coat
(D) play : tragedy
(E) fireman : uniform

41. PEDANTIC : KNOWLEDGE : :

(A) truthful : innocence
(B) grandiloquent : speech
(C) virtuous : reward
(D) pungent : taste
(E) assertive : egotism

42. GELID : COOL : :

    (A) abortive : normal
    (B) sultry : warm
    (C) dismal : transparent
    (D) tepid : moderate
    (E) thermal : frigid

43. MISNOMER : NAME : :

    (A) malapropism : word
    (B) faith : heresy
    (C) rationalization : excuse
    (D) autocracy : crime
    (E) hypocrisy : follower

44. EMANCIPATE : SLAVERY : :

    (A) erase : document
    (B) inveigle : agreement
    (C) exonerate : blame
    (D) ratify : contract
    (E) supplant : favor

45. CAST : ACTOR : :

    (A) integrity : barrister
    (B) molecule : space
    (C) corporation : firm
    (D) harem : shiek
    (E) clientele : customer

S T O P

IF YOU FINISH BEFORE TIME IS CALLED, YOU MAY CHECK YOUR WORK ON THIS SECTION ONLY.
DO NOT WORK ON ANY OTHER SECTION IN THE TEST.

SECTION 2   MATH ABILITY
30 MINUTES   25 QUESTIONS

In this section solve each problem, using any available space on the page for scratchwork. Then decide which is the best of the choices given and blacken the corresponding space on the answer sheet.

The following information is for your reference in solving some of the problems.

Circle of radius r: Area $= \pi r^2$; Circumference $= 2\pi r$
   The number of degrees of arc in a circle is 360.
The measure in degrees of a straight angle is 180.

Definitions of symbols:

$=$	is equal to	$\leqq$	is less than or equal to
$\neq$	is unequal to	$\geqq$	is greater than or equal to
$<$	is less than	$\parallel$	is parallel to
$>$	is greater than	$\perp$	is perpendicular to

Triangle: The sum of the measure in degrees of the angles of a triangle is 180.
If $\angle CDA$ is a right angle, then

(1)   area of $\triangle ABC = \dfrac{AB \times CD}{2}$

(2) $AC^2 = AD^2 + DC^2$

Note: Figures which accompany problems in this test are intended to provide information useful in solving the problems. They are drawn as accurately as possible EXCEPT when it is stated in a specific problem that its figure is not drawn to scale. All figures lie in a plane unless otherwise indicated. All numbers used are real numbers.

1. If n is a multiple of 4, which of the following is also a multiple of 4?

(A) $n - 3$ (B) $n + 2$
(C) $4n + 10$ (D) $5n + 30$ (E) $6n + 8$

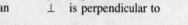

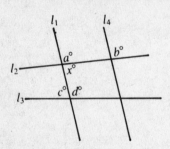

2. In the figure above, l_1, is parallel to l_4. Which of the following has the same value as x?

(A) a (B) b (C) c
(D) d (E) It cannot be determined from the information given.

3. If $x \rightarrow y$ means that $\dfrac{x^2}{y^2} < 1$, then which of the following relations is true?

(A) $4 \rightarrow \dfrac{1}{4}$ (B) $3 \rightarrow 1$ (C) $-2 \rightarrow 2$

(D) $\dfrac{1}{3} \rightarrow \dfrac{1}{9}$ (E) $\dfrac{1}{4} \rightarrow \dfrac{1}{2}$

4. If $\dfrac{5}{8}$ of x is 40, then $\dfrac{3}{8}$ of x is

(A) 5   (B) 8   (C) 15   (D) 24   (E) 25

5. If $\dfrac{3x + x - 3x}{4} = \dfrac{3}{4}$, then $x =$

(A) $\dfrac{1}{4}$ (B) $\dfrac{3}{4}$ (C) 1   (D) $\dfrac{3}{2}$ (E) 3

6. If the average (arithmetic mean) of three numbers is 7, and if one of the numbers is 5, then what is the average (arithmetic mean) of the other two numbers?

(A) 6   (B) 8   (C) 24   (D) 28   (E) It cannot be determined from the information given.

7. If the perimeter of $\triangle MNP$ is 70 units, side NP is twice the length of side MN, and if MP is the longest side of the triangle, what is the length of side MN?

(A) 12   (B) 13   (C) 14   (D) 24   (E) It cannot be determined from the information given.

8. $2^6 \cdot 2^3 =$

(A) 2^3 (B) 2^9 (C) 2^{18} (D) 4^9 (E) 4^{18}

ABA	BBB	CBA	BBA
ACC	CBC	CCC	ACA
BAC	ABC	BCA	CAB
CBB	BCA	AAB	ACC

9. In the triple arrangement of letters above, a triple has a value of 1 if exactly 2 of the letters in the triple are the same. Any other combination has a value of 0. The value of the entire arrangement is the sum of the values of each of the triples. What is the value of the above arrangement?

(A) 2   (B) 5   (C) 7   (D) 8   (E) 10

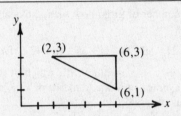

10. In the figure above, the area of the triangle is

(A) 4   (B) 6   (C) 8   (D) 9   (E) 18

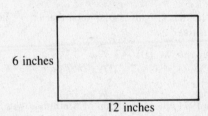

11. How many squares 2 inches on an edge can be placed, without overlapping, into the rectangle shown above?

(A) 288   (B) 144   (C) 72   (D) 36   (E) 18

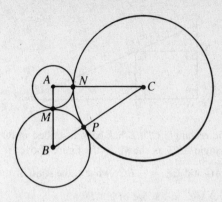

12. The circles having their centers at A, B, and C have radii of 1, 2, and 3 respectively. The circles are tangent at points M, N, and P as shown above. What is the product of the lengths of the sides of the triangle?

(A) 6   (B) 12   (C) 30   (D) 60   (E) 120

13. If the average (arithmetic mean) of 4 numbers is 8000 and the average (arithmetic mean) of 3 of the 4 numbers is 7500, then the fourth number must be?

(A) 500   (B) 1500   (C) 2000   (D) 9500
(E) 15500

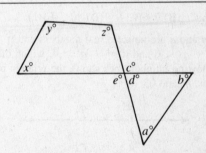

14. Five line segments intersect to form the figure above. What is the value of $x + y + z$ if $c = 100$?

(A) 80   (B) 100   (C) 260   (D) 280
(E) None of the above.

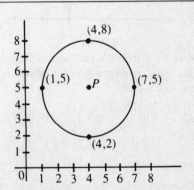

15. Given the circle, above, with center P, what is the length of its radius?

(A) 7   (B) 6   (C) 5   (D) 4   (E) 3

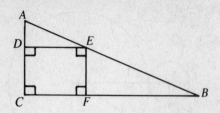

16. The rectangle *CDEF* has been inscribed in the right triangle *ABC* as shown in the figure above. If $CD = \frac{3}{4} AC$ and $CF = \frac{2}{7} BC$, what is the ratio of the area of $\triangle ABC$ to the are of $\Box CDEF$?

(A) $\frac{14}{3}$ (B) $\frac{7}{3}$ (C) $\frac{7}{6}$ (D) $\frac{1}{6}$

(E) It cannot be determined from the information given.

17. A piece of wire is bent to form a circle of radius 3 feet. How many pieces of wire, each 2 feet long can be made from the wire?

(A) 2   (B) 3   (C) 6   (D) 9   (E) 12

18. Dick spent $7 in order to buy baseballs and tennis balls. If baseballs are 70¢ each and tennis balls are 60¢ each, what is the greatest possible number of tennis balls that Dick could have bought?

(A) 4   (B) 7   (C) 9   (D) 10   (E) 11

19. If *p* and *q* are nonzero real numbers and if $p^2 + q^3 < 0$ and if $p^3 + q^5 > 0$, which of the following number lines shows the relative positions of *p*, *q*, and 0?

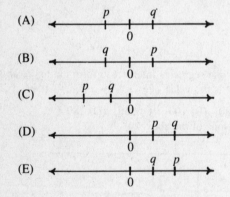

20. There are 3 feet in a yard and 12 inches in a foot. How many yards are there altogether in 1 yard, 1 foot, and 1 inch?

(A) $1\frac{1}{3}$ (B) $1\frac{13}{36}$ (C) $1\frac{11}{18}$ (D) $2\frac{5}{12}$ (E) $4\frac{1}{12}$

21. Ross wants to make up nonsense words. He wants each word to have exactly 3 of the following letters: *A*, *B*, *C*, and *D*. No letter can be used more than once in a nonsense word. For example, "*AAB*" is not a nonsense word. What is the maximum number of (distinct) nonsense words that Ross can make up? (The order of the letters must be considered. Example: "*ABC*" and "*CBA*" are two distinct nonsense words.)

(A) 6   (B) 9   (C) 24   (D) 27   (E) 64

22. The number of boys in a certain class exceed the number of girls by 7. If the number of boys is $\frac{5}{4}$ of the number of girls, how many boys are there in the class?

(A) 21   (B) 28   (C) 35   (D) 42   (E) 63

23. If $x + y + z = 3(a + b)$, which of the following is the average (arithmetic mean) of *x*, *y*, *z*, *a*, and *b* in terms of *a* and *b*?

(A) $\frac{a + b}{5}$ (B) $\frac{4(a + b)}{15}$ (C) $\frac{a + b}{2}$

(D) $\frac{4(a + b)}{5}$ (E) $a + b$

24. What are all values of *x* such that $(x - 7)(x + 3)$ is positive?

(A) $x > 7$ (B) $-7 < x < 3$
(C) $-3 < x < 7$ (D) $x > 7$ or $x < -3$
(E) $x > 3$ or $x < -7$

25. In 1971, the population of Smithdale was 900. Every year, the population of Smithdale had a net increase of 100. For example, in 1972, the population of Smithdale was 1000. In which of the following periods was the percent increase in population of Smithdale the greatest?

(A) 1971–1972   (B) 1972–1973
(C) 1973–1974   (D) 1974–1975   (E) It cannot be determined from the information given.

S T O P

IF YOU FINISH BEFORE TIME IS CALLED, YOU MAY CHECK YOUR WORK ON THIS SECTION ONLY.
DO NOT WORK ON ANY OTHER SECTION IN THE TEST.

SECTION 3   STANDARD WRITTEN ENGLISH TEST

30 MINUTES   50 QUESTIONS

The questions in this section measure skills that are important to writing well. In particular, they test your ability to recognize and use language that is clear, effective, and correct according to the requirements of standard written English, the kind of English found in most college textbooks.

Directions: The following contain problems in grammar, usage, diction (choice of words), and idiom.

> Some sentences are correct.
> No sentence contains more than one error.

You will find that the error, if there is one, is underlined and lettered. Assume that elements of the sentence that are not underlined are correct and cannot be changed. In choosing answers, follow the requirements of standard written English.

If there is an error, select the *one underlined part* that must be changed to make the sentence correct and blacken the corresponding space on your answer sheet.

If there is no error, blacken answer space Ⓔ.

EXAMPLE: SAMPLE ANSWER

The region has a climate <u>so severe that</u> plants
                          A

<u>growing there</u> rarely <u>had been</u> more than twelve
       B   C

inches <u>high.</u> <u>No error</u>
        D   E

Ⓐ Ⓑ ● Ⓓ Ⓔ

---

1. The <u>union</u> delegates who <u>are going</u> to the convention
        A   B

   in <u>Miami Beach</u> are Thompson, Steinmetz, and <u>me.</u>
            C   D

   <u>No error.</u>
       E

2. After being wheeled <u>into</u> the <u>infirmary,</u> the <u>nurse</u> at
                         A   B   C

   the desk asked me <u>several questions.</u> <u>No error.</u>
                          D   E

3. <u>Us</u> boys insist on <u>your</u> giving them <u>what is theirs</u> and
      A   B   C

   us what is <u>ours.</u> <u>No error.</u>
                 D   E

4. We hear <u>dissent</u> from a young man who, we <u>firmly</u>
              A   B

   believe, is not about <u>to pay</u> compliments to our
                            C

   political leaders <u>or</u> to the local draft board. <u>No error.</u>
                        D   E

5. She <u>wore</u> a dress <u>to the party</u> that was far <u>more</u>
          A   B   C

   attractive than <u>the other</u> girls. <u>No error.</u>
                        D   E

6. Controversial matters <u>involving</u> the two groups
                             A

   <u>were discussed;</u> nevertheless, <u>most</u> of the
           B   C

   <u>representatives remained calm.</u> <u>No error.</u>
                 D   E

7. If he had laid quietly under the tree as he
        A   B

   had been instructed to do, we would have found him.
       C   D

   No error.
     E

8. If one reads a great many articles in *Elementary*
                 A

   English, you will become familiar with the problems
         B   C

   of the beginning teacher of reading. No error.
        D   E

9. Down the field came the students of South High
       A

   School: members of the newly organized, somewhat
                       B

   incompetent band; drum majorettes in white,

   spangled skirts; and the team, muddy and wretched.
     C   D

   No error.
     E

10. If I would have been there, I certainly would have
    A   B

    taken care of the problem in a hurry. No error.
      C   D   E

11. Between you and I, I am convinced that this painting
           A   B

    by Dali shows greater artistry than that of Picasso.
                  C   D

    No error.
      E

12. He believes in witchcraft, but he doubts that they
         A   B   C

    ride on broomsticks. No error.
      D   E

13. Being that you are interested in the outcome of the
      A   B

    election, let us wait until the final tally
            C

    has been made. No error.
        D   E

14. The retreat of the enemy soldiers into caves and
        A

    tunnels are deceiving the oncoming infantrymen.
          B   C   D

    No error.
      E

15. The millennium will have arrived when parents give
        A   B

    appropriate responsibilities to we teenagers. No error.
      C   D   E

16. In contrast to Arnold's intellectual prowess was his
      A   B   C

    slovenly appearance and his nervous demeanor.
      D

    No error.
      E

17. The crisis in the Middle East is one of the topics that
        A   B

    has been discussed at our weekly forums. No error.
      C   D   E

18. I wouldn't be interested in buying this here farm
      A   B

    even if you were to offer it to me for a hundred
         C   D

    dollars. No error.
          E

19. The trouble with a good many people in our country
          A

    is that they have vested interests—that is, they are
             B   C

    concerned with theirselves first and foremost.
            D

    No error.
      E

20. There is no sense in getting angry with them radicals
              A   B

    just because they disagree with you. No error.
      C   D   E

21. There seem nowadays to be little of the optimism
        A   B

    that imbued our ancestors with courage and hope.
      C   D

    No error.
      E

22. The high school graduate, if he is eighteen or
       $\overline{}$
                                A

nineteen, has these alternatives: attending college,
         $\overline{\text{B}}$ $\overline{\text{C}}$

finding a job, or the army. No error.
      $\overline{}$ D $\overline{\text{E}}$

23. Since it was an unusually warm day, the dog laid
                    $\overline{\text{A}}$ $\overline{\text{B}}$

under the tree all afternoon without barking at
                $\overline{\text{C}}$

passersby—something he usually does. No error.
$\overline{\text{D}}$ $\overline{\text{E}}$

24. There was only an apple and three pears
           $\overline{\text{A}}$

in the refrigerator when we came home after a
   $\overline{\text{B}}$ $\overline{\text{C}}$

weekend in the country. No error.
$\overline{\text{D}}$ $\overline{\text{E}}$

25. The Chairman of the Board of Directors made it
                        $\overline{\text{A}}$

clear at the meeting that he will not step down from
$\overline{\text{B}}$ $\overline{\text{C}}$

his position as chairman. No error.
      $\overline{\text{D}}$ $\overline{\text{E}}$

Directions: In each of the following sentences, some part or all of the sentence is underlined. Below each sentence you will find five ways of phrasing the underlined part. Select the answer that produces the most effective sentence, one that is clear and exact, without awkwardness or ambiguity, and blacken the corresponding space on your answer sheet. In choosing answers, follow the requirements of standard written English. Choose the answer that best expresses the meaning of the original sentence.

Answer (A) is always the same as the underlined part. Choose answer (A) if you think the original sentence needs no revision.

> EXAMPLE:
>
> Laura Ingalls Wilder published her first book
> and she was sixty-five years old then.
> (A) and she was sixty-five years old then
> (B) when she was sixty-five years old
> (C) at age sixty-five years old
> (D) upon reaching sixty-five years
> (E) at the time when she was sixty-five
>
> SAMPLE ANSWER
> Ⓐ ● Ⓒ Ⓓ Ⓔ

26. Driving a racing car on a speedway is in some ways like when you are riding a horse on a bridle path.

(A) is in some ways like when you are riding
(B) in some ways is in the same class as riding
(C) is in some ways similar to when you are riding
(D) is in some ways similar to riding
(E) is like a ride in some ways of

27. Seeing their father, the cigarettes were immediately concealed by the children.

(A) Seeing their father, the cigarettes were immediately concealed by the children.
(B) Their father being seen by them, the children immediately concealed the cigarettes.
(C) The children having seen their father, the cigarettes were concealed immediately.
(D) When the children saw their father, they immediately concealed the cigarettes.
(E) When their father was seen, the children immediately concealed the cigarettes.

28. Barrymore had many wives, Garrick one, but each is
    remembered not for his women but for his talent.

    (A) Barrymore had many wives, Garrick one
    (B) Barrymore had many wives, Garrick having one
    (C) Barrymore having many wives, Garrick just one
    (D) Barrymore has had many wives, but Garrick only
        one
    (E) Barrymore had many wives, Garrick had only one
        wife

29. Biologists often say that it is not chemists or

    physicists but that they have the answer to the

    improvement of life on earth.

    (A) it is not chemists or physicists but that they have
    (B) it is not chemists or physicists but they have
    (C) they, and not chemists or physicists have
    (D) it is not chemists or physicists but it is they who
        have
    (E) it is they, not chemists or physicists, who have

30. The underprivileged student is getting a better

    education, there are better teachers for them and

    better facilities.

    (A) education, there are better teachers for them
    (B) education; he has better teachers
    (C) education; they have better teachers
    (D) education, he has better teachers
    (E) education; because he has better teachers

31. When the university administration changed its role

    from that of a judge and prosecutor to that of an

    adviser and friend, not only did the students stop

    their demonstrations but they also sided with the

    administration against the outsiders.

    (A) When the university administration changed its
        role from that of a judge and prosecutor to that of
        an adviser and friend
    (B) When the university administration changed its
        role from that of a judge and prosecutor to an
        adviser and friend
    (C) When the university administration changed its
        role from that of a judge and prosecutor to one of
        an adviser and friend
    (D) As a result of the administration's changing its
        role from judge and prosecutor to that of adviser
        and friend
    (E) As to the university administration, in changing
        its role from that of a judge and prosecutor to that
        of an adviser and friend

32. The Soviet Union has reorganized and modernized its
    intelligence network in the Western Hemisphere
    toward the goal of diminishing and to possibly
    replace United States influence.

    (A) to possibly replace
    (B) possibly to replace
    (C) possibly replacing
    (D) to replace possibly
    (E) for replacement of

33. In the next booklet, the sales manager and personnel
    director will tell you something about his work.

    (A) the sales manager and personnel director will tell
        you something about his work
    (B) the sales manager who is also director of
        personnel will tell you something about their
        work
    (C) the sales manager who is also personnel director
        will tell you something
    (D) the sales manager and personnel director will tell
        you something as it applies to his work
    (E) the sales manager and the personnel director will
        tell you something about what his work is

34. I have enjoyed the study of the Spanish language not
    only because of its beauty but also to make use of it
    in business.

    (A) to make use of it in business
    (B) because of its use in business
    (C) on account it is useful in business
    (D) one needs it in business
    (E) since all business people use it

35. Known to every man, woman, and child in the town,
    friends were never lacking to my grandfather.

    (A) friends were never lacking to my grandfather
    (B) my grandfather was not lacking to his friends
    (C) friends never lacked my grandfather
    (D) my grandfather never lacked no friends
    (E) my grandfather never lacked friends

36. No sooner had he entered the room when the lights
    went out and everyone began to scream.

    (A) when the lights went out
    (B) than the lights went out
    (C) and the lights went out
    (D) but the lights went out
    (E) the lights went out

37. John, whose mother is a teacher, <u>is not so good a student as many other friends</u> I have with no academic background in their families.

   (A) is not so good a student as many other friends
   (B) is not as good a student like many other friends
   (C) is not quite the student as are other friends
   (D) as a student is not a good as many other friends
   (E) does not have the studious qualities of many other friends

38. After our waiting in line for three hours, <u>much to our disgust, the tickets had been sold out</u> when we reached the window.

   (A) much to our disgust, the tickets had been sold out
   (B) the tickets had been, much to our disgust, sold out
   (C) the tickets had been sold out, much to our disgust,
   (D) the sold-out tickets had, much to our disgust, been disposed of
   (E) and much to our disgust, the tickets had been sold out

39. When the members of the committee are at odds, <u>and when also, in addition, they are in the process</u> of offering their resignations, problems become indissoluble.

   (A) and when also, in addition, they are in the process
   (B) and also when they are in the process
   (C) and when, in addition, they are in the process
   (D) they are in the process
   (E) and when the members of the committee are in the process

40. <u>There is no objection to him joining the party</u> if he is willing to fit in with the plans of the group.

   (A) There is no objection to him joining the party
   (B) There is no objection on him joining the party
   (C) There is no objection to his joining the party
   (D) No objection will be raised upon him joining the party
   (E) If he decides to join the party, there will be no objection

<u>Note:</u> The remaining questions are like those at the beginning of the section.

<u>Directions:</u> For each sentence in which you find an error, select the one underlined part that must be changed to make the sentence correct and blacken the corresponding space on your answer sheet.

If there is no error, blacken answer space Ⓔ.

EXAMPLE:

The region has a climate <u>so severe that</u> plants
                A

<u>growing</u> there rarely <u>had been</u> more than twelve
  B   C

inches <u>high.</u> <u>No error</u>
      D   E

SAMPLE ANSWER

Ⓐ Ⓑ ● Ⓓ Ⓔ

41. Although Hank was the captain of our high school

track team, and <u>was hailed</u> as the fastest man on the
           A

team, I have <u>no doubt about</u> <u>my being able</u> to run
         B   C

faster than <u>him</u> today. <u>No error.</u>
       D   E

42. <u>These kind</u> of people who have little education, who
   A

have no desire for cultural pursuits, and whose sole

purpose <u>is acquiring</u> wealth, are not the <u>type</u> I wish
       B   C

<u>to associate with.</u> <u>No error.</u>
      D   E

43. Even in chess, a game in which every great player
    A

was once a child prodigy, few champions have swept
          B   C

to the top as swiftly or relentlessly as Gary
          D

Kasparov. No error.
          E

44. Neither Sam Atkins nor Henry Miller, sales
            A

representatives for the company, presented their
                               B

summaries of sales before the deadline for doing so.
          C   D

No error.
  E

45. A recent poll has indicated that Harold, who is a
           A

senior at South Palmetto High School, is considered

brighter than any student in the senior class at that
    B   C   D

school. No error.
      E

46. I must have read scores of novels, but this here book
        A   B   C

is the most interesting I have ever read. No error.
          D   E

47. Being that he is still in high school, he needs several
    A   B   C

more years of education before he will be ready for
                         D

any profession. No error.
       E

48. If any man among the hundreds attending this
             A

convention does not agree with me, they should
                     B

set forth another plan for bettering the conditions
    C

under which these people live. No error.
   D   E

49. The study of grammar can be an exciting experience
                    A

for all of us—you and I included—when the proper
      B   C

technique of instruction is used. No error.
           D   E

50. If you are tired when you arrive home each day from
      A   B

work, you should lay down for a short time
          C

before dinner. No error.
    D   E

S T O P

IF YOU FINISH BEFORE TIME IS CALLED, YOU MAY CHECK YOUR WORK ON THIS SECTION ONLY.
DO NOT WORK ON ANY OTHER SECTION IN THE TEST.

SECTION 4 VERBAL ABILITY
30 MINUTES 40 QUESTIONS

For each question in this section, choose the best answer and blacken the corresponding space on the answer sheet.

Each question below consists of a word in capital letters, followed by five lettered words or phrases. Choose the word or phrase that is most nearly *opposite* in meaning to the word in capital letters. Since some of the questions require you to distinguish fine shades of meaning, consider all the choices before deciding which is best.

Example:

GOOD: (A) sour (B) bad (C) red (D) hot (E) ugly

Ⓐ ● Ⓒ Ⓓ Ⓔ

1. FUTILE: (A) revealing (B) casual (C) worthwhile (D) usual (E) fertile

2. STEADFAST: (A) wobbly (B) formless (C) tentative (D) effortless (E) picturesque

3. LATENT: (A) narrow (B) closed (C) proud (D) obvious (E) secure

4. DIVULGE: (A) combine (B) increase (C) recover (D) accomplish (E) conceal

5. TENUOUS: (A) cordial (B) substantial (C) relaxed (D) wholesome (E) insensitive

6. SCRUPULOUS: (A) wasteful (B) flippant (C) changeable (D) sloppy (E) shady

7. ACCOLADE: (A) rejection (B) separation (C) negligence (D) descent (E) snub

8. LICENTIOUS: (A) healthful (B) sweet (C) graceful (D) lawful (E) sensible

9. FESTER: (A) delay (B) stretch (C) comply (D) thrive (E) soothe

10. TEMERITY: (A) foolhardiness (B) negligence (C) timidity (D) care (E) compliance

Each sentence below has one or two blanks, each blank indicating that something has been omitted. Beneath the sentence are five lettered words or sets of words. Choose the word or set of words that *best* fits the meaning of the sentence as a whole.

Example:

Although its publicity has been ____, the film itself is intelligent, well-acted, handsomely produced, and altogether ____.

(A) tasteless . . . respectable
(B) extensive . . . moderate
(C) sophisticated . . . amateur
(D) risqué . . . crude
(E) perfect . . . spectacular

● Ⓑ Ⓒ Ⓓ Ⓔ

11. After four years of _____ curbs designed to protect the American auto industry, the President cleared the way for Japan to _____ more cars to the United States.

(A) profitable . . . . drive
(B) flexible . . . produce
(C) motor . . . direct
(D) import . . . ship
(E) reciprocal . . . sell

12. Illegally parked vehicles block hydrants and crosswalks, _____ the flow of traffic when double-parked, and _____ the law.

(A) stem . . . enforce
(B) expedite . . . violate
(C) reduce . . . resist
(D) drench . . . challenge
(E) impede . . . flout

13. The photographs of Ethiopia's starving children demonstrate the _____ of drought, poor land use, and overpopulation.

(A) consequences (B) prejudices
(C) inequities (D) indications (E) mortalities

14. There is a yearning for an end to _____ with the Soviet Union, but little evidence exists that nuclear-arms agreements have contributed to our _____.

(A) treaties . . . silence
(B) advantages . . . relations
(C) differences . . . amity
(D) tensions . . . security
(E) commerce . . . decision

15. With the film rental business _____ , the video cassette recorder is changing the way millions of Americans use their _____ time.

(A) advertising . . . canceled
(B) suffering . . . valuable
(C) stabilizing . . . extra
(D) recording . . . unused
(E) booming . . . leisure

Each question below consists of a related pair of words or phrases, followed by five lettered pairs of words or phrases. Select the lettered pair that *best* expresses a relationship similar to that expressed in the original pair.

Example:

YAWN : BOREDOM : :   (A) dream : sleep
(B) anger : madness   (C) smile : amusement
(D) face : expression   (E) impatience : rebellion

Ⓐ Ⓑ ● Ⓓ Ⓔ

16. PLAYWRIGHT : SCRIPT : :

(A) composer : score
(B) physician : diagnosis
(C) verse : poet
(D) king : parliament
(E) day dreamer : fantasy

17. WANE : SIZE : :

(A) contort : shape
(B) abet : crime
(C) decelerate : speed
(D) exacerbate : annoyance
(E) amass : wealth

18. LICENTIOUS : MORALITY : :

(A) ludicrous : wittiness
(B) pugnacious : amiability
(C) stolid : ridicule
(D) nebulous : favoritism
(E) indelible : error

19. SEAMSTRESS : PATTERN : :

(A) teacher : classroom
(B) architect : blueprint
(C) army : maneuver
(D) novelist : typewriter
(E) cook : recipe

20. ARCHIPELAGO : ISLANDS : :

(A) universe : stars
(B) chorus : voices
(C) chaos : rules
(D) ocean : ships
(E) conspiracy : allies

21. AMPLIFY : SOUND : :

(A) overthrow : dictator
(B) enlarge : photograph
(C) remediate : reader
(D) reflect : image
(E) alleviate : pain

22. NUGATORY : WORTH : :

(A) resonant : sound
(B) garbled : speech
(C) desultory : continuity
(D) circumspect : validity
(E) malleable : substance

23. ENERVATE : STRENGTH : :

(A) encourage : motivation
(B) conserve : excitement
(C) persecute : indulgence
(D) abase : destruction
(E) incarcerate : freedom

24. LOOT : BOOTY : :

(A) shout : attention
(B) travel : map
(C) rob : bank
(D) lace : shoe
(E) suckle : milk

25. PICK : BANJO

(A) string : violin
(B) compose : album
(C) strum : guitar
(D) pound : piano
(E) play : organ

Each passage below is followed by questions based on its content. Answer all questions following a passage on the basis of what is *stated* or *implied* in that passage.

Botanists exploring the ocean floor have recently discovered an abundant form of plant life growing deeper and in less light than any previously known. As a result of this discovery, some scientists are anticipating a change
5 in the understanding of basic elements of marine life, such as the nature of the food chain, ocean productivity, and reef building. Perhaps of greatest importance is that the finding indicates that plant life exists in far greater quantity on the ocean floor than had been supposed.
10 The discovery of this previously unknown plant species, a purple coral-like algae of the seaweed family, was made at a depth of 884 feet. It has long been standard textbook wisdom that marine plants cannot grow at a depth greater than 700 feet because so little sunlight penetrates
15 beyond this depth. Plants depend on sunlight for photosynthesis, the production of nutrients, chiefly sugars, from carbon dioxide and water. It had been widely recognized that marine plants needed at least 1 percent of the peak irradiance of sunlight at the surface to survive on the ocean
20 floor. However, the new species of plant life discovered needed only about .0005 percent of the peak surface sunlight.
The great abundance of this plant at previously unknown depths means that we will have to rethink the role
25 that such plants play in the total productivity of the oceans, the marine food chains, the sediment-forming process, and the way reefs are built. Algae on the oceans' floor play vital roles in the earth's geology and its web of life. They provide food for many fish, snails, and sea urchins, pro-
30 duce limestone with their calcified shells that contribute most of the beach sand of the Caribbean, and create deep-sea reefs similar to the ones build by the coral animals at higher levels.

26. The primary purpose of this passage is to

(A) show how important marine plants are in providing food for fish and sand for beaches
(B) indicate that there is far more plant life growing on the ocean floor than had been previously assumed
(C) describe the process of photosynthesis in the sea algae which needs much less of the sunlight beamed for the surface
(D) tell about a new species of algae discovered at record depths in the ocean
(E) reevaluate the importance of sea algae in regard to the total productivity of the oceans

27. Which of the following statements are supported by the passage?

I. Sea algae are responsible for much of the sand that we find on our beaches.
II. Fish benefit from the fact that sea algae are exposed to peak surface sunlight.
III. The sea algae described in this passage are one-celled plants.

(A) I only
(B) II only
(C) III only
(D) I and II only
(E) II and III only

28. What are the main purposes of the second and third paragraphs?

(A) Paragraph 2 describes the life style of sea algae while paragraph 3 indicates how food chains and reefs are produced by them.
(B) Paragraph 2 refers to previous incorrect beliefs about sea algae while paragraph 3 speaks positively about their benefits.
(C) Paragraph 2 tells where algae live while paragraph 3 refers to the algae's neighbors.
(D) Paragraph 2 explains how the sun penetrates the ocean depths while paragraph 3 indicates places where the algae grow.
(E) Paragraph 2 talks about the food that the algae consume while paragraph 3 brings out the algae's function on land as well as in the sea.

The art we call Baroque was a popular art. The art of the Renaissance had appealed through intellectual means—geometry, perspective, knowledge of antiquity—to a small group of humanists. The Baroque appealed through the emotions to the widest possible audience. The subjects
5 were often obscure, thought out by some theologian; but the means of communication were popular, and even remind one of the films. Caravaggio, the earliest and, on the whole, the greatest Italian painter of the period, experimented with the kind of lighting fashionable in high-
10 brow films of the 1920s, and gained thereby a new dramatic impact.
Later Baroque artists delighted in emotive close-ups with open lips and glistening tears. The huge scale, the restless movement, the shifting lights and dissolves—all
15 these devices were to be rediscovered in the movies. The extraordinary thing is that the Baroque artists did it in bronze and marble, not on celluloid. In a way it is a frivolous comparison, because however much one admires the films, one must admit that they are often commercial
20 and short-lived, whereas the work of Bernini is ideal and eternal. He was a very great artist, and although his work may seem to lack the awe-inspiring seriousness and concentration of Michelangelo, it was in its century even more

25 pervasive and influential. He not only gave Baroque Rome its character, but he was the chief source of an international style that spread all over Europe, as Gothic had done, and the Renaissance style never did.

Bernini was dazzlingly precocious. At sixteen one of
30 his carvings was bought by the Borghese family, and by the time he was twenty he was already commissioned to do a portrait of the Borghese Pope, Paul V. In the next three years he became more skillful in the carving of marble than any sculptor has ever been, before or since. His
35 *David,* in contrast with the static *David* of Michelangelo, catches the sudden twist of action; and the vehement expression of the head is almost overdone—actually it is a self-portrait of the young Bernini, who made a face in a mirror, a mirror said to have been held for him by his
40 patron, the Cardinal Scipione Borghese. The *Apollo and Daphne* is an even more extraordinary example of how marble can be made into something fluid and fleeting, because it represents the moment when Daphne, crying for help to her father, is changed into a laurel tree. Her
45 fingers are becoming leaves already. It is just beginning to dawn on Apollo that he has lost her forever.

29. The author's primary purpose in the last paragraph is to

(A) compare Bernini to Michelangelo
(B) demonstrate Bernini's value as an artist
(C) mention Bernini's relation to the Borghese family
(D) refer to specific works by Bernini
(E) describe Bernini's artistic career

30. It can be inferred that the author regards popular art as

(A) inferior to intellectual art
(B) appealing only to the masses
(C) appealing to the emotions rather than the intellect
(D) appealing to a relatively small number of art critics
(E) being more beneficial to society than intellectual art

31. The author refers to films in lines 7–22 in order to show that they

(A) share similarities with Baroque art
(B) were influenced by Baroque art
(C) are commercial and short-lived
(D) can never be as good as painting or sculpture
(E) were artistic only in the 1920s

Nobody should suppose that good writing—the kind that says what it means while being pleasant to read—has ever been easy; or that once upon a time, in the golden
5 age, every one who could write wrote well. Yet I think it true that ordinary writing today is radically worse than it has ever been in the past; that it most often fails of its purpose, which is communication; and that it rarely affords pleasure.

The reasons for this falling off are many. Poor school-
10 ing is not alone responsible. The modern school only reflects and concentrates in its misdirected efforts the ideas and attitudes prevailing in society. In short, the cause of our bad writing is cultural first and only secondarily instructional. Teachers and parents do no more than transmit
15 the bad habits and bad intentions they share and pursue in the workaday world.

One proof of this conclusion is that the objectionable features of modern prose are not found in one language or one country only. It is not American English that is
20 ailing in isolation, but English English and also French, German, Italian, and the rest of the western languages. About the Orient I am not qualified to speak, but I should be surprised if the blight did not affect it now or later.

For if these bad habits and bad intentions had to be
25 summed up in a phrase, one could say that they derive from assembly-line thinking. Leaving out poetry and some prose fiction, contemporary writing is made up of prefabricated parts—not words denoting things which one can see, hear, smell, or touch, but ready-made expressions and
30 clichés pointing vaguely to human experience by way of abstraction and metaphor. For example:

—a successful young person relating a decisive encounter: "It had a terrific impact on my growth potential."

—a congresswoman explaining why she will not seek
35 re-election: "It is for reasons predicated totally on my internal compass."

—a reviewer describing a new art book: "The visual nucleus is refined by the contribution of a personal and expressive text—a coalition of invisible energies required
40 for the creation of any art work."

This kind of prose greets us daily, hourly, in our reading casual or serious. It is the stuff of all but a negligible portion of what gets into print. We have learned to "understand" it. Having done so, we think naturally in these
45 jigsaw forms, and when we write we re-assemble them each time in slightly different patterns, like an automated factory, not like a mind.

32. What is the person trying to say in his statement: "It had a terrific impact on my growth potential." [line 33]

(A) "It made me more experienced about growing things."
(B) "It really retarded my ability to grow."
(C) "It made me realize my latent power."
(D) "It had a great effect in helping me to improve myself."
(E) "It gave me important ideas about my physical development."

33. The manner in which the three people who are quoted in the passage, expressed themselves indicates that

(A) they were sophisticated individuals who used words effectively
(B) there was a conscious desire to conceal their real thoughts
(C) they failed to take advantage of instruction offered in their English clases
(D) they were using a style that was required in their social or business surroundings
(E) there was a lack of directness in their communication

34. The tone of the passage is

(A) mildly complaining
(B) reasonably permissive
(C) highly critical
(D) obviously one-sided
(E) sharply argumentative

35. It can be inferred from the context of the passage that "assembly-line thinking" mentioned in line 26 is done by

(A) executives who tolerate no disagreement on the part of their employees with company policy
(B) speakers who use expressions that are trite and overused
(C) teachers who insist that their students do several hours of homework
(D) book reviewers who judge books according to their own personal likes and dislikes
(E) politicians who express opinions that will appeal primarily to an influential segment of our society

36. All of the following ideas are expressed in the passage *except* that

(A) the primary reason for our poor writing habits is that students get inadequate instruction in school
(B) a common characteristic of bad writing is the use of fancy words when simple words will do
(C) we may associate much of the writing we encounter today with puzzles
(D) the kind of writing that is simple, direct, and understandable is generally difficult to do
(E) it is reasonable to assume that parents bear a share of responsibility for the bad writing habits of their children

People need housing and they want forests.

These same people want the nearly 5,000 products that are derived basically from wood fiber. They can have both products and forests, but only if they recognize that trees are living things that, like people, grow with proper care and nutrition, mature, and eventually die and return to the earth. Trees in commercial forests that have stopped growing should be harvested and used so they will not be wasted. Highly productive lands can then be made available to grow healthy new forests. 5 ... 10

While a forest is growing it provides many basic environmental benefits. Growing trees manufacture oxygen and absorb carbon dioxide; they feed and shelter wildlife; they protect and expand soil and watershed values, and they afford unlimited oportunities for a variety of outdoor recreational experiences from camping and hunting through picnicking and berry picking. 15

When forests grow old, however, like people, they decline. Left to themselves, without care or protection, forests fall victim to old age, fire, insect infestation, storm and disease. They lose their beauty and they cease to provide their multiple benefits for other living things. 20

Old forests absorb as much oxygen as they produce, through decay; game and birds flee their oppressive shade since nutritious ground cover disappears; recreation values diminish except for the hardy and wealthy few who can penetrate a remote, roadless wilderness. 25

The public benefits of a so-called "preserved" forest are available to only the exceptional citizen. And, most seriously, both the standing timber on such forests and the land potential for growing dynamic new forests are wasted. 30

The areas of national forest designated as "commercial timberlands" are a classic case in point. Because of well-meaning, but ill-conceived public pressures to "preserve" forests, the publicly owned stockpile of mature timber is being surrendered to fire, pestilence, disease and senility. 35

37. The author is in favor of

(A) chopping trees down only in times of timber scarcity
(B) chopping trees down only for firewood
(C) preventing trees from being chopped down at any time
(D) chopping down only young trees
(E) chopping down a tree at a non-growing stage of its life

38. Which of the following are characteristics of growing forests.

I. They take in carbon dioxide and produce oxygen.
II. They provide a food source for animals.
III. They attract insects, thereby freeing populated areas from insect infestation.

(A) I only
(B) II only
(C) III only
(D) I and II only
(E) I, II and III

39. The author explains that old forests

    (A) absorb more carbon dioxide than the amount of oxygen they produce
    (B) provide good shelter for wildlife
    (C) have little recreational value
    (D) should be preserved as national monuments
    (E) offer good insight into geology

40. The author views public pressure to preserve forests as being

    (A) instigated by students and radicals
    (B) aimed at undermining the government's Forest Service
    (C) honestly motivated but not well thought out
    (D) backed by the timber industry
    (E) encouraged by selfish individuals

S T O P

IF YOU FINISH BEFORE TIME IS CALLED, YOU MAY CHECK YOUR WORK ON THIS SECTION ONLY.
DO NOT WORK ON ANY OTHER SECTION IN THE TEST.

SECTION 5 MATH ABILITY
30 MINUTES 35 QUESTIONS

In this section solve each problem, using any available space on the page for scratchwork. Then decide which is the best of the choices given and blacken the corresponding space on the answer sheet.

The following information is for your reference in solving some of the problems.

Circle of radius r: Area $= \pi r^2$; Circumference $= 2\pi r$
  The number of degrees of arc in a circle is 360.
The measure in degrees of a straight angle is 180.

Definitions of symbols:
  $=$ is equal to $\leqq$ is less than or equal to
  $\neq$ is unequal to $\geqq$ is greater than or equal to
  $<$ is less than $\parallel$ is parallel to
  $>$ is greater than $\perp$ is perpendicular to

Triangle: The sum of the measure in degrees of the angles of a triangle is 180.
If $\angle CDA$ is a right angle, then

(1) area of $\triangle ABC = \dfrac{AB \times CD}{2}$

(2) $AC^2 = AD^2 + DC^2$

Note: Figures which accompany problems in this test are intended to provide information useful in solving the problems. They are drawn as accurately as possible EXCEPT when it is stated in a specific problem that its figure is not drawn to scale. All figures lie in a plane unless otherwise indicated. All numbers used are real numbers.

1. $\left(\dfrac{1}{2} - \dfrac{1}{3}\right) + \left(\dfrac{1}{3} - \dfrac{1}{4}\right) + \left(\dfrac{1}{4} - \dfrac{1}{5}\right) +$

   $\left(\dfrac{1}{5} - \dfrac{1}{6}\right) + \left(\dfrac{1}{6} - \dfrac{1}{7}\right) + \left(\dfrac{1}{7} - \dfrac{1}{8}\right) +$

   $\left(\dfrac{1}{8} - \dfrac{1}{9}\right) =$

   (A) $\dfrac{1}{72}$ (B) $\dfrac{3}{8}$ (C) $\dfrac{9}{22}$ (D) $\dfrac{2}{5}$ (E) $\dfrac{7}{18}$

2. In a certain year, May 3rd is a Monday. In that same year, what day of the week is August 3rd?

   (A) Monday (B) Tuesday (C) Wednesday
   (D) Friday (E) Saturday

3. If the first two elements of a number series are 1 and 2, and if each succeeding term is found by multiplying the two terms immediately preceding it, what is the fifth element of the series?

   (A) 5 (B) 8 (C) 16 (D) 32 (E) 120

4. If p is $\dfrac{3}{5}$ of m and if q is $\dfrac{9}{10}$ of m, then, when $q \neq$

   0, the ratio $\dfrac{p}{q} =$

   (A) $\dfrac{1}{3}$ (B) $\dfrac{2}{5}$ (C) $\dfrac{1}{2}$ (D) $\dfrac{2}{3}$ (E) 2

5. If $m = 94$ and $n = 6$, then $23m + 23n =$

   (A) 123 (B) 230 (C) 1230 (D) 2162 (E) 2300

6. If the average (arithmetic mean) of 40, 40, 40, and z is 45, then $z =$

   (A) 50 (B) 55 (C) 60 (D) 65 (E) 70

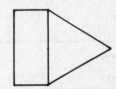

7. In the figure above, the perimeter of the equilateral triangle is 39 and the area of the rectangle is 65. What is the perimeter of the rectangle?

   (A) 25 (B) 29 (C) 36 (D) 52 (E) 88

Each passage below is followed by questions based on its content. Answer all questions following a passage on the basis of what is *stated* or *implied* in that passage.

Questions 8-27 each consist of two quantities, one in Column A and one in Column B. You are to compare the two quantities and on the answer sheet blacken space

A if the quantity in Column A is greater;
B if the quantity in Column B is greater;
C if the two quantities are equal;
D if the relationship cannot be determined from the information given.

Notes: 1. In certain questions, information concerning one or both of the quantities to be compared is centered above the columns.
2. In a given question, a symbol that appears in both columns represents the same thing in Column A as it does in Column B.
3. Letters such as x, n, and k stand for real numbers.

EXAMPLES		
	Column A	Column B	Answers
E1.	2×6	$2 + 6$	● Ⓑ Ⓒ Ⓓ
	$x°$ $y°$		
E2.	$180 - x$	y	Ⓐ Ⓑ ● Ⓓ
E3.	$p - q$	$q - p$	Ⓐ Ⓑ Ⓒ ●

	Column A	Column B

8.
$$7x + 21 = 35$$

| $4x + 12$ | 21 |

9. $\dfrac{298,376}{10,000}$ | 30

10.
$$a - b = 5$$
$$a + b = -1$$

| a | b |

11. 5.7 milliliters of water are poured into a graduated cylinder which already contains 11.5 milliliters of water.

| The total number of milliliters of water in the graduated cylinder after the water has been poured in | 16.2 |

12.
$$b > y$$
$$y > a$$

| a | b |

	Column A	Column B

13. Rock sample A has a volume of 33 cubic centimeters. Rock sample B has a volume of 12 cubic centimeters.

$$\left(\text{Density} = \frac{\text{Mass}}{\text{Volume}} \right)$$

| The mass of rock A if its density is 3 grams per cubic centimeter | The mass of rock B if its density is 8 grams per cubic centimeter |

14. Rectangle I has an area of 60.
Rectangle II has an area of 72.

| perimeter of rectangle I | perimeter of rectangle II |

15.
$$n > 0$$

| The number of positive, integral divisors of $3n$ | The number of positive, integral divisors of $6n$ |

SUMMARY DIRECTIONS FOR COMPARISON QUESTIONS

<u>Answer:</u> A   if the quantity in Column A is greater;
B   if the quantity in Column B is greater;
C   if the two quantities are equal;
D   if the relationship cannot be determined from the information given.

<u>Column A</u>	<u>Column B</u>

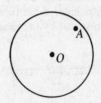

Row 1 ——————>
Row 2 —————>
Row 3 ————>
⋮   ⋮
Row 9 —————————>

16. Each row has two more boxes than the one above it.

The total number of boxes in Row 9	18

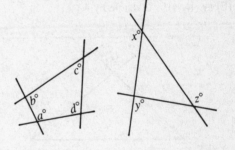

(circle with center *O*, point *A* inside, labeled *A* and *O*)

17. *A* is a point inside the circle with center *O*.
P is a point, not shown, on the circumference of the circle with center *O*.

OA	*OP*

18. $8 + 4x - x = 5 + 3x + 3$

x	3

19. In a certain grocery store, pears are 20¢ each, tangerines are 30¢ each, apples are 70¢ each, and peaches are 90¢ each.

The minimum number of pieces of the above fruits that can be bought with exactly $2.60	4

20. John is now 10 years older than David was 4 years ago. 4 years ago, David was *J* years old.

John's age (in years) two years from now	David's age (in years) eight years from now

<u>Column A</u>	<u>Column B</u>

21. | $\dfrac{.65}{3}$ | $\dfrac{1}{3} \times \dfrac{5}{8}$ |
| --- | --- |

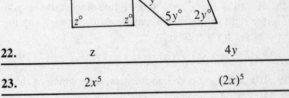

(figures showing a square with angles $z°$ at each corner, and a quadrilateral with angles $4y°$, $y°$, $5y°$, $2y°$)

22. | z | $4y$ |
| --- | --- |

23. | $2x^5$ | $(2x)^5$ |
| --- | --- |

24.
$$x < 1$$
$$x \neq 0$$

x	x^3

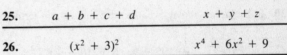

(figures with angles $a°$, $b°$, $c°$, $d°$ and $x°$, $y°$, $z°$)

25. | $a + b + c + d$ | $x + y + z$ |
| --- | --- |

26. | $(x^2 + 3)^2$ | $x^4 + 6x^2 + 9$ |
| --- | --- |

27. Bag A has 9 blue and *x* green marbles. The green marbles are 70% of all the marbles in Bag A. Bag B has 15 red and *y* purple marbles. The purple marbles are 50% of all the marbles in Bag B.

x	y

In this section solve each problem, using any available space on the page for scratchwork. Then decide which is the best of the choices given and blacken the corresponding space on the answer sheet.

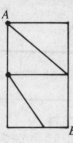

28. A rat can move only to the right, diagonally down to the right or down. How many different ways can the rat get from A to B?

(A) 6 (B) 5 (C) 4 (D) 3 (E) 2

29. If x and y are both odd integers, then which of the following statements is *not* always true?

(A) xy is odd.
(B) $x + y$ is even.
(C) $x^2 + y^2$ is even.
(D) $x^2 + y^2$ is divisible by 4.
(E) $(x + y)^2$ is divisible by 4.

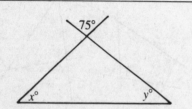

30. In the figure above, what is the value of y in terms of x?

(A) $75 + x$ (B) $105 - x$ (C) $210 - 2x$
(D) $255 - x$ (E) $285 - 2x$

31. If $a < b$ and $b < c$, which of the following is also true? (You may assume that $d > 0$.)

  I. $a < c$
  II. $ad < cd$
  III. $a < bc$

(A) I only
(B) II only
(C) I and II only
(D) II and III only
(E) III only

32. The sum of 3 positive, consecutive even integers is w. In terms of w, represent the smallest of these integers.

(A) $\dfrac{w}{3} - 6$ (B) $w - 6$

(C) $\dfrac{w + 6}{3}$ (D) $\dfrac{w}{3}$ (E) $\dfrac{w - 6}{3}$

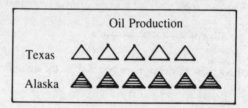

33. In the chart above, the amount represented by each shaded triangle is three times that represented by each unshaded triangle. What fraction of the total production represented by the chart was produced in Alaska?

(A) $\dfrac{6}{11}$ (B) $\dfrac{18}{5}$ (C) $\dfrac{18}{23}$ (D) $\dfrac{12}{17}$ (E) $\dfrac{23}{17}$

34. A car wash cleans x cars per hour, for y hours at z dollars per car. How much money in *cents* did the car wash receive?

(A) $\dfrac{xy}{100z}$ (B) $\dfrac{xyz}{100}$

(C) $100xyz$ (D) $\dfrac{100x}{yz}$

(E) $\dfrac{yz}{100x}$

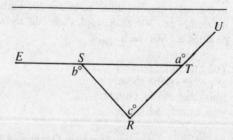

35. In the figure above, *EST* is a line segment and *RTU* is a line segment. If b is 30 less than twice c, find $a + c$.

(A) 150 (B) 180 (C) 200 (D) 210 (E) 240

S T O P

IF YOU FINISH BEFORE TIME IS CALLED, YOU MAY CHECK YOUR WORK ON THIS SECTION ONLY. DO NOT WORK ON ANY OTHER SECTION IN THE TEST.

SECTION 6   MATH ABILITY
30 MINUTES   25 QUESTIONS

In this section solve each problem, using any available space on the page for scratchwork. Then decide which is the best of the choices given and blacken the corresponding space on the answer sheet.

The following information is for your reference in solving some of the problems.

Circle of radius r: Area $= \pi r^2$; Circumference $= 2\pi r$
    The number of degrees of arc in a circle is 360.
The measure in degrees of a straight angle is 180.

Definitions of symbols:

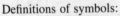

$=$	is equal to	$\leqq$	is less than or equal to
$\neq$	is unequal to	$\geqq$	is greater than or equal to
$<$	is less than	$\parallel$	is parallel to
$>$	is greater than	$\perp$	is perpendicular to

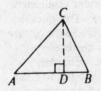

Triangle: The sum of the measure in degrees of the angles of a triangle is 180.
If $\angle CDA$ is a right angle, then

(1)   area of $\triangle ABC = \dfrac{AB \times CD}{2}$

(2) $AC^2 = AD^2 + DC^2$

<u>Note</u>: Figures which accompany problems in this test are intended to provide information useful in solving the problems. They are drawn as accurately as possible EXCEPT when it is stated in a specific problem that its figure is not drawn to scale. All figures lie in a plane unless otherwise indicated. All numbers used are real numbers.

1. If $x + 7 = 20$, then $x + 5 =$

(A) 5   (B) 7   (C) 13   (D) 18   (E) 20

2. Johnny buys a frying pan and two coffee mugs for $27. Joanna buys the same-priced frying pan and one of the same-priced coffee mugs for $23. How much does one of those frying pans cost?

(A) $4   (B) $7   (C) $19   (D) $20   (E) 21

3. Stanley will be m years of age 8 years from now. In terms of m, how old was Stanley 8 years ago?

(A) $m - 16$ (B) $m - 8$ (C) $m + 8$
(D) $8m$ (E) $\dfrac{m}{8}$

4. At Lincoln County High School, 36 students are taking either calculus or physics or both, and 10 students are taking both calculus and physics. If there are 31 students in the calculus class, how many students are in the physics class?

(A) 14   (B) 15   (C) 16   (D) 17   (E) 18

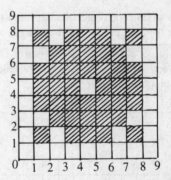

5. What is the area of the shaded region in the figure above?

(A) 36   (B) 40   (C) 41   (D) 49   (E) 64

6. If $a^2 - b^2 = 64$, what is the value of $a - b$?

(A) 0   (B) 2   (C) 8   (D) 16   (E) There is not enough information to determine the answer.

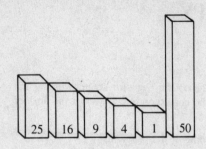

7. Six containers, whose capacities in cubic centimeters are shown, appear in the figure above. The 25-cubic centimeter container is filled with flour and the rest are empty. The contents of the 25-cubic centimeter container are used to fill the 16-cubic centimeter container and the excess is dumped into the 50-cubic centimeter container. Then the 16-cubic centimeter container is used to fill the 9-cubic centimeter container and the excess is dumped into the 50-cubic centimeter container. The process is repeated until all containers, except the 1-cubic centimeter and the 50-cubic centimeter containers, are empty. What percent of the 50-cubic centimeter container is *empty*?

(A) 24%   (CB) 48%   (C) 50%   (D) 52%
(E) 76%

8. If the sum of the digits of a two-digit number is even, then the product of those digits is

(A) always even   (B) always odd   (C) sometimes even and sometimes odd   (D) divisible by 4
(E) none of the above

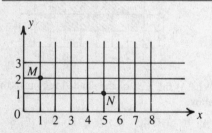

9. If a rectangle is drawn on the grid above with $\overline{MN}$ as one of its diagonals, which of the following could be the coordinates of another vertex of the rectangle?

(A) (1,0)   (B) (2,0)   (C) (3,3)   (D) (4,3)
(E) (5,2)

10. If $\sqrt{x}$ is an odd integer, which of the following MUST be even?

(A) x (B) $3\sqrt{x}$ (C) $\sqrt{2x}$ (D) $2\sqrt{x}$ (E) x^2

11. The degree measures of the four angles of a quadrilateral are w, x, y, and z respectively. If w is the average (arithmetic mean) of x, y, and z, then $x + y + z =$

(A) 45°   (B) 90°   (C) 120°   (D) 180°   (E) 270°

Questions 12-13 refer to the figure above where W, X, Y, and Z are four distinct digits from 0 to 9, inclusive, and $W + X + Y = 5Z$

12. In the figure above, what is the value of Z?

(A) 3   (B) 5   (C) 8   (D) 10   (E) 15

13. Under the given conditions, all of the following could be values of Z except

(A) 1   (B) 2   (C) 3   (D) 4   (E) 5

14. If p and q are positive integers, x and y are negative integers, and if $p > q$ and $x > y$, which of the following must be less than zero?

    I. $q - p$
    II. qy
    III. $p + x$

(A) I only
(B) III only
(C) I and II only
(D) II and III only
(E) I, II, and III

15. A lawn covers 108.6 square feet. Russ mowed all of the lawn in three evenings. He mowed $\frac{2}{9}$ of the lawn during the first evening. He mowed twice that amount on the second evening. On the third and final evening he mowed the remaining lawn. How many square feet were mowed the third evening?

(A) 18.1   (B) 36.2   (C) 39.2   (D) 54.3   (E) 72.4

16. If N is a positive integer, which of the following does *not* have to be a divisor of the sum of N, $6N$ and $9N$?

(A) 1   (B) 2   (C) 4   (D) 9   (E) 16

17. If $x = 3a - 18$ and $5y = 3a + 7$, then find $5y - x$.

(A) -11 (B) 11   (C) 18   (D) 25   (E) $6a - 11$

18. If 9 people are standing in a straight line, what is the *smallest* number of people who must move so that all 9 will be standing on the circumference of a circle?

(A) 5   (B) 6   (C) 7   (D) 8   (E) 9

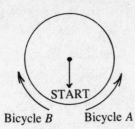

START

Bicycle *B*   Bicycle *A*

19. In the figure above, two bicycles are being pedaled in opposite directions around a circular race track of circumference = 120 feet. Bicycle *A* is traveling a 5 feet/second in the counterclockwise direction and Bicycle *B* is traveling at 8 feet/second in the clockwise direction. When Bicycle *B* has completed exactly 600 revolutions, how many complete revolutions will Bicycle *A* have made.?

(A) 180   (B) 375   (C) 475   (D) 960   (E)It cannot be determined from the given information.

20. *A* is the set of 11 consecutive integers whose sum is 0. *B* is the set of 5 consecutive integers whose sum is 5. How many members of *A* are *NOT* in *B*?

(A) 0   (B) 2   (C) 4   (D) 6   (E) 8

21. If there are 100 people in a room, $\frac{4}{5}$ of them are male and $\frac{1}{4}$ of them are blonde. The *LEAST* number of men who are blonde is

(A) 5   (B) 10   (C) 15   (D) 20   (E) 25

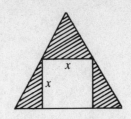

22. A square of side x is inscribed inside an equilateral triangle of area $x^2\sqrt{3}$. If a rectangle with width x has the same area as the shaded region shown in the figure above, what is the length of the rectangle in terms of x?

(A) $\sqrt{3}\,x - 1$ (B) $x\sqrt{3}$ (C) $\sqrt{3} - x$

(D) $x(\sqrt{3} - 1)$ (E) $x^2\sqrt{3} - x^2$

23. If p is the average of x and y, and if q is the average of y and z, and if r is the average of x and z, then what is the average of x, y, and z?

(A) $\dfrac{p + q + r}{3}$ (B) $\dfrac{p + q + r}{2}$

(C) $\dfrac{2}{3}(p + q + r)$ (D) $p + q + r$

(E) $\dfrac{3}{2}(p + q + r)$

24. Let $f(x)$ be defined for all x by the equation $f(x) = 12x + 8$. Thus, $f(2) = 32$. If $f(x) \div f(0) = 2x$, then $x =$

(A) $\dfrac{1}{2}$ (B) $\dfrac{2}{3}$ (C) 1   (D) $\dfrac{3}{2}$ (E) 2

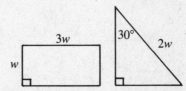

25. The length and width of a rectangle are $3w$ and w respectively. The length of the hypotenuse of a right triangle, one of whose acute angles is 30°, is $2w$. What is the ratio of the area of the rectangle to that of the triangle?

(A) $2\sqrt{3} : 1$ (B) $\sqrt{3} : 1$ (C) $1 : \sqrt{3}$

(D) $1 : 2\sqrt{3}$ (E) $1 : 6$

S T O P

IF YOU FINISH BEFORE TIME IS CALLED, YOU MAY CHECK YOUR WORK ON THIS SECTION ONLY.
DO NOT WORK ON ANY OTHER SECTION IN THE TEST.

HOW DID YOU DO ON THIS TEST?

<u>STEP 1.</u> Go to the Answer Key on page 581.

<u>STEP 2.</u> For your "raw score," count your correct answers in each of the test parts of the test you have just taken:

Verbal (Section 1 and 4 combined) _____.

Math (Sections 2, 5, and 6 combined) _____.

Standard Written English (Section 3) _____.

<u>STEP 3.</u> Get your "scaled score" for the test by referring to the Raw Score/ Scaled Score Conversion Tables on pages 64–66.

THERE'S ALWAYS ROOM FOR IMPROVEMENT!

ANSWER KEY FOR PRACTICE TEST 5

Section 1—Verbal

1. E	8. A	15. E	22. E	29. B	36. B	43. A
2. B	9. C	16. B	23. A	30. E	37. D	44. C
3. D	10. D	17. D	24. D	31. B	38. B	45. E
4. A	11. E	18. E	25. E	32. A	39. B	
5. C	12. D	19. A	26. C	33. C	40. C	
6. A	13. B	20. E	27. E	34. D	41. B	
7. D	14. C	21. B	28. D	35. B	42. B	

Section 2—Math

1. E	5. E	9. D	13. D	17. D	21. C	25. A
2. E	6. B	10. A	14. D	18. B	22. C	
3. E	7. E	11. E	15. E	19. B	23. D	
4. D	8. B	12. D	16. B	20. B	24. D	

Section 3—Standard Written English

1. D	9. E	17. E	25. C	33. A	41. D	49. C
2. C	10. B	18. B	26. D	34. B	42. A	50. C
3. A	11. A	19. D	27. D	35. E	43. E	
4. E	12. C	20. B	28. A	36. B	44. B	
5. D	13. A	21. A	29. E	37. A	45. C	
6. E	14. B	22. D	30. B	38. C	46. C	
7. A	15. D	23. B	31. A	39. C	47. A	
8. B	16. C	24. A	32. C	40. C	48. B	

Section 4—Verbal

1. C	7. A	13. A	19. E	25. C	31. A	37. E
2. A	8. D	14. D	20. B	26. D	32. D	38. D
3. D	9. D	15. E	21. B	27. B	33. E	39. C
4. E	10. C	16. A	22. C	28. B	34. C	40. C
5. B	11. D	17. C	23. E	29. B	35. B	
6. E	12. E	18. B	24. E	30. C	36. A	

Section 5—Math

1. E	6. C	11. A	16. A	21. A	26. C	31. C
2. B	7. C	12. B	17. B	22. B	27. A	32. E
3. B	8. B	13. A	18. D	23. D	28. B	33. C
4. D	9. B	14. D	19. C	24. D	29. D	34. C
5. E	10. A	15. B	20. C	25. C	30. B	35. D

Section 6—Math

1. D	5. B	9. E	13. E	17. D	21. A	25. A
2. C	6. E	10. D	14. C	18. C	22. D	
3. A	7. D	11. E	15. B	19. B	23. A	
4. B	8. C	12. A	16. D	20. D	24. E	

EXPLANATORY ANSWERS FOR PRACTICE TEST 5

Section 1: Verbal Ability

> As you read these Explanatory Answers, you are advised to refer to "Using Critical Thinking Skills in Verbal Questions" (beginning on page 90) whenever a specific Strategy is referred to in the answer. Of particular importance are the following Master Verbal Strategies:
>
> Sentence Completion Master Strategy 1—page 94.
> Sentence Completion Master Strategy 2—page 95.
> Analogies Master Strategy 1—page 90.
> Antonyms Master Strategy 1—page 99.
> Reading Comprehension Master Strategy 2—page 109.

1. **(E)** Choice E is correct. *Cajole* means *to coax; to persuade.* The opposite of *cajole* is *discourage.*

2. **(B)** Choice B is correct. See **Antonym Strategy 2.** *Arduous* means *difficult; strenuous.* The opposite of *arduous* is *easy.*

3. **(D)** Choice D is correct. *Whet* means *to stimulate; to sharpen.* The opposite of *whet* is *dull.*

4. **(A)** Choice A is correct. *Pulchritude* means *beauty.* The opposite of *pulchritude* is *ugliness.*

5. **(C)** Choice C is correct. See **Antonym Strategy 2.** *Gnarled* means *twisted; knotty; roughened.* The opposite of *gnarled* is *straightened.*

6. **(A)** Choice A is correct. *Scrutinize* means *to examine closely.* The opposite of *scrutinize* is *glance at.*

7. **(D)** Choice D is correct. See **Antonym Strategy 2.** *Crass* means *stupid; unrefined.* The opposite of *crass* is *refined.*

8. **(A)** Choice A is correct. *Purloin* means *to steal.* The opposite of *purloin* is *offer.*

9. **(C)** Choice C is correct. *Suave* means *polished; sophisticated.* The opposite of *suave* is *rough.*

10. **(D)** Choice D is correct. See **Antonym Strategy 3.** *Forbearance* means *patience; restraint.* The opposite of *forbearance* is *impatience.*

11. **(E)** Choice E is correct. See **Antonym Strategy 2.** *Lugubrious* means *sad; mournful.* The opposite of *lugubrious* is *joyful.*

12. **(D)** Choice D is correct. See **Antonym Strategy 3.** *Commodious* means *roomy; spacious.* The opposite of *commodious* is *confined.*

13. **(B)** Choice B is correct. See **Antonym Strategies 1, 3.** *Encumbrance* means *hindrance; obstruction.* The opposite of *encumbrance* is *utility.*

14. **(C)** Choice C is correct. See **Antonym Strategy 2.** *Tortuous* means *twisting; winding; indirect.* The opposite of *tortuous* is *direct.*

15. **(E)** Choice E is correct. *Banal* means *common; ordinary.* The opposite of *banal* is *extraordinary.*

16. **(B)** Choice B is correct. See **Sentence Completion Strategy 3.** If you used this strategy of trying to complete the sentence *before* looking at the five choices, you might have come up with any one of the following words:

simple	ordinary
understandable	common
easy-to-understand	

    These words all mean about the same as the correct Choice (B) simplified. Therefore, Choices A, C, D, and E are incorrect.

17. **(D)** Choice D is correct. See **Sentence Completion Strategy 2.** We first examine the first words of each choice. We can then eliminate Choice (C) conclusive . . . and Choice (E) ridiculous . . . because violent crime does not become conclusive or ridiculous. Now we go on to the three remaining choices. When you fill in the two blanks of Choice A and of Choice B, the sentence does not make sense. So these two choices are also incorrect. Filling in the two blanks of Choice D makes the sentence acceptable.

18. **(E)** Choice E is correct. See **Sentence Completion Strategy 4.** We have an Opposition indicator here with the first word "Although." We can now assume that the opening clause of the sentence—"Although . . . patrols"—will contradict the thought expressed in the rest of the sentence. Choice (E) impeded . . . continue, fills in the blanks so that the sentence makes sense. The other choices are incorrect because their word-pairs do not make sense.

19. **(A)** Choice A is correct. See **Sentence Completion Strategy 3.** This strategy suggests that you try to complete the sentence *before* looking at the five choices. Doing this, you might have come up with any of the following words that indicate an additional type of force or injury besides "seizure":

    coercing   forcing   pressuring

    These words all come close to the meaning of the correct Choice (A) compelling. Therefore, Choices B, C, D, and E are incorrect.

20. **(E)** Choice E is correct. See **Sentence Completion Strategy 4.** We have an Opposition indicator here—the student's not working hard and his winning the contest. We, therefore, look for a definitely positive word as our choice to contrast with the negative thought embodied in his not working hard. That positive word is "enraptured" (Choice E), which means delighted beyond measure. Accordingly Choices A, B, C, and D are incorrect.

21. **(B)** The passage is devoted to a debate as to which is more important for the advancement of science—technology or the individual outstanding scientist. Therefore, Choice B is correct. Choices A and D are not discussed in the passage. Therefore they are incorrect. Choice C is discussed only in the last paragraph so this choice does not merit consideration as the title for the passage. Choice C is, accordingly, incorrect. Galileo is discussed in the paragraph but there is no mention about his getting credit that he deserves. Therefore, Choice E is incorrect.

22. **(E)** The stand taken in the passage by the new school scientists is that technology is more important than genius for the advancement of science. Since calculations and data collecting are very important for the science technologists, Choice E is correct. Choices A, B, C, and D are not directly related to what will help the science technologist. Therefore, these choices are incorrect.

23. **(A)** Although the author shows no obvious bias to indicate that he favors one or the other school of thought, he does devote substantially more discussion to the new school. In fact, the first, third, and fourth paragraphs all give favorable treatment to the new school position. Therefore, the best choice is Choice A. It follows that Choices B and C are incorrect. Choice D is incorrect because there is no indication in the passage of a friendly relationship between the new school advocates and the conventional group. Choice E is incorrect because there is no inkling in the passage that the author is a member of one of the two groups.

24. **(D)** A scientist opposing the new school philosophy would necessarily favor the conventional view. A conventional view scientist would definitely believe that human insight and pure research—rather than technology—have always been of primary importance. Therefore, Choice D is correct. The new school scientist believes that technology in its various forms—measurements, atom smashers, instruments, for example—are far more important than the brain power of the individual scientist. Accordingly, Choices A, B, C, and E are incorrect.

25. **(E)** The last paragraph of the passage states: "Federal policy is necessarily involved in the technology vs. genius dispute." Therefore, Choice E is correct. Choice A is incorrect because Ptolemy lived many centuries before Galileo, so they could not have exchanged ideas. Choice B is incorrect because the passage indicates that only Edison among the three scientists was an inventor. Choice C is incorrect because the passage nowhere shows that Galileo was of royal birth, although the passage refers figuratively to his "crowning glory." Choice D is incorrect because Einstein had to depend on technological devices to do his calculations and to get his data.

26. **(C)** Choice C is correct. First of all, we learn that the dead man is a poet. See lines 8–9: "The coffin . . . of the poet." Secondly, we know that he is a Chilean by references to the Chilean people who mourn his death in lines 41–48: ". . . the Chilean cries rise up . . . finish with the henchmen!" Choice A is incorrect because lines 13–14 indicate that the dead man is Pablo Neruda himself: "Someone inquires . . . Pablo Neruda." Choices B, C, and E are incorrect because nowhere in the passage is the dead man identified as a poor man from Santiago, a publisher, or an ambassador.

27. **(E)** First, see lines 25–28: "Then we hear a sound . . . now and forever." This is a fearful response. Now see lines 29–32: "A voice shouts . . . surrounding the crowd." This shows a defiant attitude. So Choice E is correct. Accordingly, Choices A, B, C, and D are incorrect.

28. **(D)** Choice D is correct. See lines 5–8: "The day before . . . left the house flooded." Also, see lines 42–44: "Chilean people . . . they are torturing you." The passage does not indicate in any way that the events expressed in Choices A, B, C, or E occurred shortly before the funeral procession. Therefore, these four choices are incorrect.

29. **(B)** Clearly, the person in the coffin is Pablo Neruda according to lines 13–14: "Someone inquires . . . Pablo Neruda." Also see lines 20–24: "The name . . . each of them becoming Pablo Neruda." Therefore, Choice B is correct. It follows that Choices A, C, D, and E are incorrect.

30. **(E)** Choice E is correct because the passage neither states nor implies that Pablo Neruda was a lonely man. He was hopeful (Choice A) as indicated by his verse in lines 53–56: "I have been reborn . . . populated with my hands." He was married (Choice B) because he left a widow (line 2). He was admired (Choice C). See lines 36–38: "Pablo Neruda . . . now and forever!" He was intellectual (Choice D) since he was a respected poet whose verses were quoted widely. See lines 51–56: ". . . a woman begins to sing . . . populated with my hands." Accordingly, Choices A, B, C, and D are incorrect.

31. **(B)** Choice B is correct. See **Sentence Completion Strategy 4.** The words "not only" constitute a Support indicator. The second part of the sentence is, therefore, expected to reinforce the first part of the sentence. Choice (B) reject . . . refused, supplies the two words that provide a sentence that makes sense. Choices A, C, D, and E are incorrect because their word pairs do not produce sentences that make sense.

32. **(A)** Choice A is correct. See **Sentence Completion Strategy 3.** If you used this strategy of trying to complete the sentence *before* looking at the five choices, you might have come up with any of the following appropriate words:

   persistence   perseverance
   steadfastness   indefatigability

These words all mean the same as Choice (A) tenacity. Accordingly, Choices B, C, D, and E are incorrect.

33. **(C)** Choice C is correct. See **Sentence Completion Strategy 4.** The adverb "Ironically" means in a manner so that the opposite of what is expected takes place. So we have an Opposition indicator here. Choice (C) weaken is, of course, the opposite of strengthen. Accordingly, Choices A, B, D, and E are incorrect.

34. **(D)** Choice D is correct. See **Sentence Completion Strategy 4.** The words "in addition to" constitute a Support indicator. We can then expect an additional favorable word to complete the sentence. That word is dapper (Choice D) meaning "neatly dressed." Choices A, B, C, and E are incorrect because they do not make good sense in the sentence.

35. **(B)** Choice B is correct. See **Sentence Completion Strategy 4.** The words "in spite of" constitute an Opposition indicator. We can then expect an opposing idea to complete the sentence. The word "baffled" means "puzzled" or "unable to comprehend." Choice (B) baffled gives us the word that brings out the opposition thought we expect in the sentence. Choices A, C, D, and E do not give us a sentence that makes sense.

36. **(B)** Choice B is correct. Drought is the lack or absence of rain. Insolvency is the lack of funds. Choice (E) indolence : ambition, also shows a Result relationship in a negative way. However, the second capitalized word (RAIN) and the second Choice B word (funds) are *concrete* nouns, whereas the second Choice E word (ambition) is an *abstract* noun. Therefore, Choice E is incorrect. See **Analogy Strategy 4.**
   (Result relationship)

37. **(D)** Choice D is correct. A recess is a break or pause in a school for relaxation. An intermission is a break or pause in a theater for relaxation. Choice (C) work : vacation, also indicates a break or pause at a place or in an activity. However, the two words of Choice C would have to be reversed to be considered as a correct choice. Therefore, Choice C, as it stands, is an incorrect choice. See **Analogy Strategy 3.**
   (Purpose relationship)

38. **(B)** Choice B is correct. Cloth that is worn (overused) becomes threadbare. An expression that is overused becomes hackneyed.
   (Action to Object and Result relationship)

39. **(B)** Choice B is correct. One who is intrepid is *not* fearful. One who is impotent is *not* powerful.
   (Opposite relationship)

40. **(C)** Choice C is correct. A loafer is a specific type of shoe—a slip-on shoe for casual wear. A slicker is a specific type of coat—a long, loose oilskin raincoat. Choice (D) play : tragedy would be considered correct if the order of words were reversed. See **Analogy Strategy 3.** **(Part-Whole relationship)**

41. **(B)** Choice B is correct. One who is pedantic shows off his knowledge. One who is grandiloquent shows off his speech. **(Characteristic relationship)**

42. **(B)** Choice B is correct. Gelid is extemely cool. Sultry is extremely warm. **(Degree relationship)**

43. **(A)** Choice A is correct. A misnomer is an error in naming a person or thing. A malapropism is an error in the use of a word.
(Action to Object and Opposite relationship)

44. **(C)** Choice C is correct. When one is emancipated, he is freed from slavery. When one is exonerated, he is freed from blame. **(Result relationship)**

45. **(E)** Choice E is correct. All the actors together make up the cast for a play. All the customers together make up the clientele for a business.
(Whole-Part relationship)

EXPLANATORY ANSWERS FOR PRACTICE TEST 5 (continued)

Section 2: Math Ability

> As you read these solutions, you are advised to do two things if you answered the Math question incorrectly:
>
> 1) When a specific Strategy is referred to in the solution, study that strategy, which you will find in "Using Critical Thinking Skills in Math Questions" (beginning on page 69).
>
> 2) When the solution directs you to the "Math Refresher" (beginning on page 205)—for example, Math Refresher #305—study the 305 Math principle to get a clear idea of the Math operation that was necessary for you to know in order to answer the question correctly.

1. **(E)** Choice E is correct. **(Use Strategy 2: Translate from words to algebra.)**
Method 1: Since n is a multiple of 4, then

$$n = 4z \qquad \boxed{1}$$

must be true for some integer z. For example, 12 is a multiple of 4 because $12 = 4 \times 3$ where 3 is an integer. **(Use Strategy 8: When all choices must be tested, start with E.)** Using $\boxed{1}$, rewrite Choice E as

$$\begin{aligned} 6n + 8 &= 6(4z) + 8 \\ &= 4(6z) + 8 \\ &= 4[6z + 2] \qquad \boxed{2} \end{aligned}$$

where $6z + 2$ is clearly integral. Comparing $\boxed{1}$ and $\boxed{2}$, we see that $6n + 8$ is a multiple of 4. None of the other choices can be rewritten in the form of $\boxed{1}$. In choice A, for example, using $\boxed{1}$, we write

$$\begin{aligned} n - 3 &= 4z - 3 \\ &= 4\left(z - \frac{3}{4}\right) \end{aligned}$$

but $z - \frac{3}{4}$ is not an integer. Thus, Choice A cannot be rewritten in the form of $\boxed{1}$ and neither can Choices B, C, or D.

You could also choose values for n satisfying $\boxed{1}$, and see which of the choices is a multiple of 4. Since you must check all of the choices, you should start with Choice E.

Method 2: **(Use Strategy 7: Use numerics to help find the answer.)** Let $n = $ any multiple of 4—for example, 8. **(Use Strategy 8: When all choices must be tested, start with E.)**

$$\begin{aligned} \text{Choice E} = 6n + 8 &= 6(8) + 8 \\ &= 48 + 8 = 56 = 4(14). \end{aligned}$$

Clearly, Choice E is the correct choice. The other choices serve for demonstration:

Choice D =
$$5n + 30 = 5(8) + 30 = 40 + 70 = 4\left(17\frac{1}{2}\right)$$

Choice C =
$$4n + 10 = 4(8) + 10 = 32 + 10 = 42 = 4\left(10\frac{1}{2}\right)$$

$$\text{Choice B} = n + 2 = 8 + 2 = 10 = 4\left(2\frac{1}{2}\right)$$

$$\text{Choice A} = n - 3 = 8 - 3 = 5 = 4\left(1\frac{1}{4}\right)$$

(Math Refresher #200, #431, and #406)

2. **(E)** Choice E is correct. Know the properties of parallel lines! We are given

$$l_1 \parallel l_4 \qquad \boxed{1}$$

From $\boxed{1}$, we can write

$$a = b \qquad \boxed{2}$$
$$a + x = 180 \qquad \boxed{3}$$

However, this is not enough information to answer the question. We need to know how l_2 and l_3 have been drawn with respect to l_1 and l_4.

(Math Refresher #504)

3. **(E)** Choice E is correct. **(Use Strategy 11: Use new definitions correctly.)**

$$\textit{Given:} \qquad x \rightarrow y \text{ means that } \frac{x^2}{y^2} < 1 \qquad \boxed{1}$$

(Use Strategy 8: When all choices must be tested, start with E.) Clearly, Choice E is true because

$$\frac{\left(\frac{1}{4}\right)^2}{\left(\frac{1}{2}\right)^2} = \frac{\frac{1}{16}}{\frac{1}{4}} = \frac{1}{16} \times 4 = \frac{1}{4} \qquad \boxed{2}$$

$$\text{and } \frac{1}{4} < 1 \qquad \boxed{3}$$

Thus, from $\boxed{1}$, $\boxed{2}$, and $\boxed{3}$ we have

$$\frac{1}{4} \rightarrow \frac{1}{2} \qquad \text{is true.}$$

(Math Refresher #429 and #431)

4. **(D)** Choice D is correct. **(Use Strategy 2: Translate from words to algebra.)**

$$\textit{Given:} \qquad \frac{5}{8} \text{ of } x \text{ is } 40$$
$$\downarrow \quad \downarrow \quad \downarrow \quad \downarrow \quad \downarrow$$
$$\frac{5}{8} \times x = 40 \qquad \boxed{1}$$

(Use Strategy 13: Find unknowns by multiplication.)

Fast Method: Multiply $\boxed{1}$ by $\frac{3}{5}$ to get

$$\frac{3}{5}\left(\frac{5}{8}x\right) = \frac{3}{5}(40)$$

$$\frac{3}{8}x = \frac{3}{5} \times 5 \times 8$$

$$\frac{3}{8}x = 24 \qquad \textit{(Answer)}$$

Slow Method: Solve $\boxed{1}$ for x by multiplying $\boxed{1}$ by $\frac{8}{5}$:

$$x = 64 \qquad \boxed{2}$$

Now substitute $\boxed{2}$ into the unknown expression:

$$\frac{3}{8}x = \frac{3}{8}(64)$$

$$= \frac{3}{8} \times 8 \times 8$$

$$= 24 \qquad \textit{(Answer)}$$

(Math Refresher #200 and #406)

5. **(E)** Choice E is correct.

$$\textit{Given:} \qquad \frac{3x + x - 3x}{4} = \frac{3}{4} \qquad \boxed{1}$$

Simplifying, the numerator on the left side of $\boxed{1}$ becomes

$$\frac{x}{4} = \frac{3}{4} \qquad \boxed{2}$$

Multiply both sides of $\boxed{2}$ by 4 to get
$$x = 3 \qquad \textit{(Answer)}$$

(Math Refresher #406)

6. **(B)** Choice B is correct.
(Use Strategy 5:

$$\text{Average} = \left(\frac{\text{Sum of values}}{\text{Total number of values}}\right)$$

Let w, x, y = the three numbers.

Given: $\dfrac{w + x + y}{3} = 7$

It does not matter which of the three variables has a value of 5. So we will let $w = 5$. Thus,

$$\frac{5 + x + y}{3} = 7 \qquad \boxed{1}$$

Find $\qquad \dfrac{x + y}{2} \qquad \boxed{2}$

(Use Strategy 13: Find unknowns by multiplication and subtraction.)
Multiply $\boxed{1}$ by 3,

$$5 + x + y = 21 \qquad \boxed{3}$$

Subtract 5 from $\boxed{3}$,

$$x + y = 16 \qquad \boxed{4}$$

Substitute $\boxed{4}$ into $\boxed{2}$ to get

$$\frac{x + y}{2} = \frac{16}{2} = 8 \qquad (Answer)$$

(Math Refresher #601, #431, and #406)

7. **(E)** Choice E is correct. **(Use Strategy 7: Use numerics to help find the answer.)** Let $x = MP$, $y = NP$, $z = MN$.

Method 1: Choose numeric values of x, y, and z that satisfy the given requirements:

EXAMPLE 1
If $x = 34$, $y = 24$, $z = 12$, the requirements are satisfied.

EXAMPLE 2
If $x = 31$, $y = 26$, $z = 13$, the requirements are satisfied.

Clearly, MN has at least two possible values.

(Use Strategy 2: Translate from words to algebra.)

Method 2: We are given that

$$x + y + z = 70 \qquad \boxed{1}$$
$$y = 2z \qquad \boxed{2}$$
$$x > y \qquad \boxed{3}$$
$$x > z \qquad \boxed{4}$$

Substitute $\boxed{2}$ into $\boxed{3}$:

$$x > 2z \qquad \boxed{5}$$

Substitute $\boxed{2}$ into $\boxed{1}$:

$$x + 3z = 70 \qquad \boxed{6}$$

Using $\boxed{5}$, it is clear that

$$x + 3z > 2z + 3z$$
$$\text{or } x + 3z > 5z \qquad \boxed{7}$$

Substitute $\boxed{6}$ into $\boxed{7}$

$$70 > 5z \qquad \boxed{8}$$
$$\text{or } z < 14$$

Thus, $z = MN$ can have any value less than 14, and it cannot be exactly determined.
(Math Refresher #200, #431, and #419)

8. **(B)** Choice B is correct.

$$2^6 \cdot 2^3 = 2^{6+3}$$
$$= 2^9$$

(Math Refresher #429)

9. **(D)** Choice D is correct. **(Use Strategy 11: Use new definitions carefully.)**
In the given letter columns, only 8 triples have the property that exactly 2 of the letters in the triple are the same. Thus, 8 triples have a value of 1, and all the other triples have a value of 0. Hence, the value of the entire group of letter columns is 8.
(Logical Reasoning)

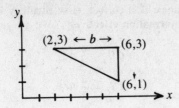

10. (A) Choice A is correct. **(Use Strategy 17: Use the given information effectively.)**

It is clear from the diagram above that the triangle is a right triangle whose area is

$$A = \frac{1}{2} bh \qquad \boxed{1}$$

From the given coordinates, we can also say that

$$b = 6 - 2 = 4 \qquad \boxed{2}$$
$$h = 3 - 1 = 2 \qquad \boxed{3}$$

Substituting $\boxed{2}$ and $\boxed{3}$ into $\boxed{1}$,

$$A = \frac{1}{2} (4)(2)$$
$$A = 4$$

(Math Refresher #306 and #410)

11. (E) Choice E is correct. **(Use Strategy 17: Use the given information effectively.)**

The area of a rectangle is length × width. The number of squares that can be packed into the rectangle

$$= \frac{\text{Area of entire rectangle}}{\text{Area of each square}}$$
$$= \frac{6 \times 12}{2 \times 2}$$
$$= \frac{72}{4}$$
$$= \frac{\cancel{4} \times 18}{\cancel{4}}$$
$$= 18 \qquad (Answer)$$

(Math Refresher #304 and #431)

12. (D) Choice D is correct. Since we are given the radii of the circles, we have

$$AN = AM = 1 \qquad \boxed{1}$$
$$BM = BP = 2 \qquad \boxed{2}$$
$$CN = CP = 3 \qquad \boxed{3}$$

We want to find

$$(AB)(BC)(AC) \qquad \boxed{4}$$

(Use Strategy 3: The whole equals the sum of its parts.) From the diagram, we see that

$$AB = AM + BM \qquad \boxed{5}$$
$$BC = BP + CP \qquad \boxed{6}$$
$$AC = AN + CN \qquad \boxed{7}$$

Substituting $\boxed{1}$, $\boxed{2}$, $\boxed{3}$ into $\boxed{5}$, $\boxed{6}$, $\boxed{7}$, we have

$$AB = 3$$
$$BC = 5$$
$$AC = 4$$

Thus,

$$(AB)(BC)(AC) = (3)(5)(4)$$
$$= 60 \qquad (Answer)$$

(Math Refresher #524)

13. (D) Choice D is correct.

$$\left(\text{Use Strategy 5:} \right.$$
$$\left. \text{Average} = \frac{\text{Sum of values}}{\text{Total number of values}} \right)$$

We are given:

$$\frac{x + y + z + w}{4} = 8000 \qquad \boxed{1}$$

(Use Strategy 13: Find unknowns by multiplication.) Multiplying $\boxed{1}$ by 4, we get

$$x + y + z + w = 32000 \qquad \boxed{2}$$

We are given any 3 have an average of 7500, so using x, y and z as the 3, we get

$$\frac{x + y + z}{3} = 7500 \qquad \boxed{3}$$

Multiplying $\boxed{3}$ by 3, we get

$$x + y + z = 22500 \qquad \boxed{4}$$

Substituting $\boxed{4}$ into $\boxed{2}$, we get

$$22500 + w = 32000$$
$$\text{or} \qquad w = 9500 \qquad (Answer)$$

(Math Refresher #601 and #406)

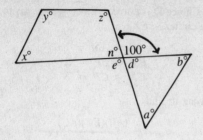

14. (D) Choice D is correct.

(Use Strategy 17: Use the given information effectively.)

From the diagram, $n = d$ (vertical angles) $\boxed{1}$
We know $x + y + z + n = 360$ $\boxed{2}$
Substituting $\boxed{1}$ into $\boxed{2}$, we get
$$x + y + z + d = 360 \quad \boxed{3}$$

Subtracting d from $\boxed{3}$, we have
$$x + y + z = 360 - d \quad \boxed{4}$$

We know that $100 + d = 180$ from the diagram
So, $d = 180 - 100 = 80$ $\boxed{5}$

Substituting $\boxed{5}$ into $\boxed{4}$, we get
$$x + y + z = 360 - 80$$
$$x + y + z = 280$$

(Math Refresher #521, #503, and #406)

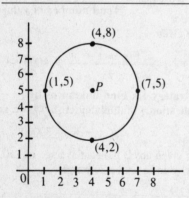

15. (E) Choice E is correct.

The coordinates of the center P are $(4,5)$

By definition, the length of a radius is the distance from the center to any point on the circle. Therefore,

radius = distance from $(7,5)$ to $(4,5)$ =
$$= 7 - 4$$
radius = 3

(Math Refresher #410 and #524)

16. (B) Choice B is correct. **(Use Strategy 17: Use the given information effectively.)** We are given

$$CD = \frac{3}{4} AC \quad \boxed{1}$$

$$CF = \frac{2}{7} BC \quad \boxed{2}$$

We want to find

$$\frac{\text{Area of } \triangle ABC}{\text{Area of Rectangle } CDEF}$$

We know that the Area of rectangle $CDEF$
$$= (CD)(CF) \quad \boxed{3}$$
and Area of $\triangle ABC$

$$= \frac{1}{2}(AC)(BC) \quad \boxed{4}$$

Substituting $\boxed{1}$ and $\boxed{2}$ into $\boxed{3}$,
Area of rectangle $CDEF$

$$= \left(\frac{3}{4}AC\right)\left(\frac{2}{7}BC\right) = \frac{3}{14}(AC)(BC) \quad \boxed{5}$$

Substituting $\boxed{4}$ anf $\boxed{5}$ into the unknown expression,

$$\frac{\text{Area of } \triangle ABC}{\text{Area of rectangle } CDEF} =$$

$$\frac{\frac{1}{2}(AC)(BC)}{\frac{3}{14}(AC)(BC)}$$

$$= \frac{1}{2} \times \frac{14}{3} = \frac{14}{6} = \frac{7}{3} \text{ (Answer)}$$

(Math Refresher #304, #306, #431, and #120)

17. (D) Choice D is correct. **(Use Strategy 2: Translate from words to algebra.)** We are given the wire is bent to form a circle of radius 3 feet. This means its length is equal to the circumference of the circle.

Thus, Length of wire $= 2\pi r = 2\pi(3)$ feet
$$= 6\pi \text{ feet}$$
$$\approx 6(3.14) \text{ feet}$$
Length of wire ≈ 18.84 feet $\boxed{1}$

(Use Strategy 3: Know how to find unknown quantities.)

$$\frac{\text{Number of pieces}}{2 \text{ feet long}} = \frac{\text{Total length}}{2 \text{ feet}} \quad \boxed{2}$$

Substituting $\boxed{1}$ into $\boxed{2}$, we have

$$\frac{\text{Number of pieces}}{2 \text{ feet long}} \approx \frac{18.84 \text{ feet}}{2 \text{ feet}}$$

$$\approx 9.42$$
$$\approx 9 \text{ complete pieces}$$

(Math Refresher #310)

18. **(B)** Choice B is correct. **(Use Strategy 2: Translate from words to algebra.)**

Let b = number of baseballs that Dick bought
 t = number of tennis balls that Dick bought
.70b = amount spent on baseballs
.60t = amount spent on tennis balls

Thus, we are told

$$.70b + .60t = 7.00 \qquad \boxed{1}$$

Multiply $\boxed{1}$ by 10,

$$7b + 6t = 70 \qquad \boxed{2}$$

Solve $\boxed{2}$ for t,

$$t = \frac{70 - 7b}{6} \qquad \boxed{3}$$

(Use Strategy 17: Use the given information effectively.) From $\boxed{3}$, we see that the maximum value of t occurs at the minimum value of b. Since b and t are numbers of balls, b and t must be nonnegative integers. Thus, the minimum value of b is 0. When $b = 0$, $t = \dfrac{70}{6}$ which is not integral. For t to be an integer, $\boxed{3}$ tells us that $(10 - b)$ is a multiple of 6. The smallest value of b which makes $(10 - b)$ a multiple of 6 is $b = 4$. Thus, $t = 7$ is the maximum value of t, which must be the answer.

(Math Refresher #200, #406, #431, and Logical Reasoning.)

19. **(B)** Choice B is correct.

Method 1: Given: $p^2 + q^3 < 0$ $\qquad \boxed{1}$
 $p^3 + q^5 > 0$ $\qquad \boxed{2}$

(Use Strategy 6: Know how to manipulate inequalities.) Subtracting p^2 from $\boxed{1}$ and q^5 from $\boxed{2}$, we have

$$q^3 < -p^2 \qquad \boxed{3}$$
$$p^3 > -q^5 \qquad \boxed{4}$$

By transitivity of $\boxed{3}$ and $\boxed{6}$,

Multiplying $\boxed{5}$ by -1, $-p^2 \le 0$ $\qquad \boxed{6}$

By transitivity of $\boxed{3}$ and $\boxed{6}$,

$$q^3 < 0 \qquad \boxed{7}$$

Thus, $q < 0$ $\qquad \boxed{8}$

From $\boxed{8}$, we can say $q^5 < 0$ or $-q^5 > 0$ $\qquad \boxed{9}$

By transitivity of $\boxed{4}$ and $\boxed{9}$, $p^3 > 0$ or $p > 0$ $\qquad \boxed{10}$

Using $\boxed{8}$ and $\boxed{10}$, it is easily seen that Choice B is correct.

Method 2: **(Use Strategy 6: Know how to interpret inequalities.)**

Given: $p^2 + q^3 < 0$ $\qquad \boxed{1}$
 $p^3 + q^5 > 0$ $\qquad \boxed{2}$

Since p^2 is always > 0, using this with $\boxed{1}$, we know that $q^3 < 0$ and, therefore, $q < 0$ $\qquad \boxed{3}$
If $q^3 < 0$ then $q^5 < 0$. $\qquad \boxed{4}$

Using $\boxed{4}$ and $\boxed{2}$ we know that
$p^3 > 0$, and therefore $p > 0$ $\qquad \boxed{5}$

Using $\boxed{3}$ and $\boxed{5}$, only Choice B is correct.

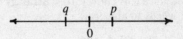

(Math Refresher #419, #420, and #421)

20. **(B)** Choice B is correct. **(Use Strategy 10: Know how to work with units.)**

Given: 3 feet = 1 yard
 12 inches = 1 foot

Thus,

$$1 \text{ yard} + 1 \text{ foot} + 1 \text{ inch} =$$

$$1 \text{ yard} + 1 \text{ foot} \left(\frac{1 \text{ yard}}{3 \text{ feet}} \right) +$$

$$1 \text{ inch} \left(\frac{1 \text{ foot}}{12 \text{ inches}} \right) \left(\frac{1 \text{ yard}}{3 \text{ feet}} \right) =$$

$$1 + \frac{1}{3} + \frac{1}{36} \text{ yards} =$$

$$1 + \frac{12}{36} + \frac{1}{36} \text{ yards} =$$

$$1 \frac{13}{36} \text{ yards}$$

(Math Refresher #121)

21. **(C)** Choice C is correct. There are 4 choices for the first letter of the nonsense word. Since each letter cannot be used more than once in a nonsense word, there are only 3 choices for the second letter and only 2 choices for the third letter of the nonsense word. Thus, the maximum number of distinct nonsense words that Ross can make up is

$$= 4 \cdot 3 \cdot 2$$
$$= 24 \quad \text{(Answer)}$$

(Logical Reasoning)

22. **(C)** Choice C is correct. **(Use Strategy 2: Translate from words to algebra.)**

Let b = number of boys
g = number of girls

We are given

$$b = g + 7 \qquad \boxed{1}$$

$$b = \frac{5}{4} g \qquad \boxed{2}$$

(Use Strategy 13: Find unknowns by multiplication.) Multiplying $\boxed{2}$ by $\frac{4}{5}$,

$$\frac{4}{5} b = g \qquad \boxed{3}$$

Substituting $\boxed{3}$ into $\boxed{1}$,

$$b = \frac{4}{5} b + 7 \qquad \boxed{4}$$

Multiplying $\boxed{4}$ by 5,

$$5b = 4b + 35$$
$$\text{or} \qquad b = 35$$

(Math Refresher #200 and #406)

23. **(D)** Choice D is correct.

$\left(\right.$**Use Strategy 5:**

$\text{Average} = \dfrac{\textbf{Sum of values}}{\textbf{Total number of values}}\left.\right)$

We want to find

$$\frac{x + y + z + a + b}{5} \qquad \boxed{1}$$

We are given

$$x + y + z = 3(a + b) \qquad \boxed{2}$$

By substituting $\boxed{2}$ into $\boxed{1}$, the unknown expression becomes

$$\frac{3(a + b) + a + b}{5}$$

$$= \frac{3a + 3b + a + b}{5}$$

$$= \frac{4a + 4b}{5}$$

$$= \frac{4(a + b)}{5}$$

(Math Refresher #601 and #431)

24. **(D)** Choice D is correct. **(Use Strategy 6: Know how to manipulate inequalities.)**

$$(x - 7)(x + 3) > 0 \text{ when}$$

$$x - 7 > 0 \text{ and } x + 3 > 0 \qquad \boxed{1}$$
$$\text{or} \quad x - 7 < 0 \text{ and } x + 3 < 0 \qquad \boxed{2}$$

From $\boxed{1}$ we have $x > 7$ and $x > -3 \qquad \boxed{3}$
when $x > 7 \qquad \boxed{4}$
then $\boxed{3}$ and $\boxed{1}$ are always satisfied.

From $\boxed{2}$, we have $x < 7$ and $x < -3 \qquad \boxed{5}$
when $x < -3 \qquad \boxed{6}$
then $\boxed{5}$ and $\boxed{2}$ are always satisfied.

Thus, $\boxed{4}$ and $\boxed{6}$ together represent the entire solution.

(Math Refresher #428)

25. **(A)** Choice A is correct. **(Use Strategy 2: Remember how to find percent increase.)**

$$\text{Percent increase} = \frac{\text{Amount of increase}}{\text{Original amount}} \qquad \boxed{1}$$

Amount of increase is given as 100 per year $\qquad \boxed{2}$

Substituting $\boxed{2}$ into $\boxed{1}$, we get

$$\% \text{ increase} = \frac{100}{\text{Original amount}} \qquad \boxed{3}$$

(Use Strategy 12: Try not to make tedious calculations.) The greatest % increase will occur when the original amount is least.

Since the population is increasing by 100 every year, it is least at the beginning, in 1971.

Thus $\boxed{3}$ will be greatest from 1971–1972.

(Math Refresher #114 and #118)

EXPLANATORY ANSWERS FOR
PRACTICE TEST 5 (continued)

Section 3: Standard Written English

> Section 3 does not count toward your SAT score. This Standard Written English section is used only for Freshman English placement when you get to college. However, you are advised to improve yourself in grammar and usage, and also in sentence structure. If you do well in the Standard Written English Test, you will be placed more advantageously in your college Freshman English class.

1. **(D)** "... are Thompson, Steinmetz, and *I*."
The predicate nominative form is *I* (not *me*).

2. **(C)** "... into the infirmary, *I* was asked several questions by the nurse at the desk."
It is *I* who was being wheeled—not the *nurse*. The participial construction should modify the subject. In the original sentence, the subject is *nurse*.

3. **(A)** "*We* boys insist ..."
The pronoun-adjective which modifies a subject (*boys* in this case) must take the subject form *we* (not *us*).

4. **(E)** All underlined parts are correct.

5. **(D)** "... than *those* of the other girls."
We have an improper ellipsis here. The dress that the girl wore was more attractive than the dresses of the other girls—not more attractive than the other girls.

6. **(E)** All underlined parts are correct.

7. **(A)** "If he *had lain* ..."
The past perfect tense form of *to lie* is *had lain* (not *had laid*). The past perfect tense form of *to lay*—meaning to place or to put—is *had laid*.

8. **(B)** "... *one* will become ..."
Do not shift the number or person of a noun if the noun represents another noun which precedes in the sentence. In the original sentence, *one* and *you* refer to the same person. Since *one* is third person and *you* is second person, we have a shift error.

9. **(E)** All underlined parts are correct.

10. **(B)** "If I *had been* there ..."
In a contrary-to-fact conditional construction in past time, sequence of tenses requires the past perfect subjunctive form (*had been*) in the "if" clause instead of the future perfect subjunctive form (*would have been*).

11. **(A)** "Between you and *me* ..."
The object of the preposition *between* must be an objective case form (*me*—not *I*).

12. **(C)** "... that *witches* ride on broomsticks."
The pronoun *they* must have an antecedent, which is obviously *witchcraft*. But since witchcraft is a singular abstract noun, the plural personal pronoun *they* cannot be used here. Accordingly, we must substitute a noun, such as *witches*, for the pronoun. The word *witches*, of course, has no antecedent because it is a noun. Only pronouns have antecedents.

13. **(A)** "*Since* you are interested ..."
Being that is unacceptable for *since* or *because*.

14. **(B)** "... into caves and tunnels is *deceiving*..."
Since the subject (*retreat*) is singular, the verb must be singular (*is* deceiving—not *are* deceiving).

15. **(D)** "... to *us* teenagers."
The pronoun-adjective modifying the object of the preposition must be objective in form. *Teenagers* is the object of the preposition *to*. The pronoun-adjective modifying teenagers must, therefore, be the object form (*us*—not *we*).

16. **(C)** "... *were* his slovenly appearance and his nervous demeanor."
The two subjects (*appearance* and *demeanor*) constitute plurality. We must, accordingly, have a plural verb (*were*—not *was*).

17. **(E)** All underlined parts are correct.

18. **(B)** "... in buying *this farm* ..."
The expression *this here* is unacceptable for *this*.

19. **(D)** "... are concerned with *themselves* ..."
The correct form of the reflexive pronoun is *themselves*—not *theirselves*.

20. **(B)** ". . . angry with *those* radicals . . ."
The adjective-pronoun *those* must be used to modify the noun *radicals*. The pronoun *them* cannot be used to modify a noun.

21. **(A)** "There *seems* nowadays to be little of the optimism . . ."
The subject of the sentence (*little*) is singular and it therefore takes a singular verb (*seems*—not *seem*).

22. **(D)** ". . . attending college, finding a job, or—*joining the army*."
The need for parallelism requires *joining the army*, in order to have a balanced construction with the preceding gerund phrases (*attending college* and *finding a job*).

23. **(B)** ". . . the dog *lay* under the tree . . ."
The past tense of the verb *lie* is *lay*—not *laid*.

24. **(A)** "There *were* only an apple and three pears . . ."
The subject of the sentence is plural (*an apple and three pears*). Therefore the verb must be plural (*were*—not *was*). Incidentally, the word *there* is not the subject—it is an expletive.

25. **(C)** ". . . that he *would* not step down . . ." Since the verb of the main clause (*made*) is in the past tense, the verb of the subordinate clause must also be in the past tense (*would speak*). Incidentally, *would speak* is a past subjunctive.

26. **(D)** Choice A is incorrect because "like when" is ungrammatical. Choice B is incorrect because it is too indirect. Choice C is incorrect because "similar to when" is ungrammatical. Choice D is correct. Choice E is incorrect because it is awkwardly expressed.

27. **(D)** Choice A is incorrect because the present participle "Seeing" is incorrectly modifying "the cigarettes." Choices B, C, and E are too roundabout. Choice D is correct.

28. **(A)** Choice A is correct. Choice B is incorrect because the nominative absolute construction "Garrick having one" throws the sentence out of balance. Choice C is incorrect because we need a finite verb ("had"), not the participle "having". Choice D is incorrect because the present perfect tense ("has had") should be replaced by the past tense ("had"). Choice E is too wordy.

29. **(E)** Choice A is incorrect because it is awkward and because the pronoun "they" has an indefinite antecedent. Choice B is incorrect for the same reason. Choice C is incorrect—it would be correct if changed to "they, not chemists and physicists, have." Choice D is too wordy. Choice E is correct.

30. **(B)** Choice A is incorrect because we have a run-on sentence. The comma should be replaced by a semicolon or a period. Choice A is incorrect for another reason: the singular pronoun "him" (not "them") should be used because the antecedent ("student") of the pronoun is singular. Choice B is correct. Choice C is incorrect because the pronoun "they" should be singular. Choice D is incorrect because it creates a run-on sentence. Choice E is incorrect—the semicolon should be eliminated.

31. **(A)** Choice A is correct. Choice B is incorrect because of the improper ellipsis of the words "that of" which should precede "an adviser and friend." Choice C is incorrect, because the word "one" should be replaced by the words "that of." Choices D and E are incorrect because they are too indirect. Moreover, in Choice D, right after the words "its role" we should place the words "that of."

32. **(C)** Choice A is incorrect because we should have a gerund ("replacing") to balance with the previous gerund "diminishing." Moreover, there is no need to split the infinitive ("to . . . replace"). Choice B is incorrect also because of lack of gerund balance. Choice C is correct. Choice D is incorrect because of lack of gerund balance and because of awkwardness. Choice E is incorrect because of awkwardness.

33. **(A)** Choice A is correct. If you are questioning the singularity of the possessive pronoun-adjective "his," it is correct. The subject of the sentence consists of a singular compound subject, "the sales manager and personnel director." If we wanted to indicate plurality here, we would have to insert the article "the" before the second member ("personnel director") of the compound subject. Choice B is incorrect because "their" must refer to a plural antecedent. Choice C is incorrect because it changes the meaning of the original sentence. Choice D is awkward. Choice E is too wordy.

34. **(B)** Choice A is incorrect because it does not parallel the structure of "not only because of its beauty." Choice B is correct. Choices C, D, and E are incorrect for the same reason that Choice A is incorrect—the lack of parallel structure. Moreover, Choice C is incorrect because "on account" cannot be used as a subordinate conjunction.

35. **(E)** The past participle "known" must modify the subject of the sentence. Choices A and C are, therefore, incorrect because the subject must be "grandfather"—he is the one (not "friends") that is "known to every man, woman, and child in the town." Choice B changes the meaning of the original sentence. Choice D has a double negative ("never . . . no . . ."). Choice E is correct.

36. **(B)** Choice A is incorrect since the correct expression is "no sooner . . . than . . ." Choice B is correct. Choices C, D, and E are incorrect because we must have the "no sooner . . . than" construction.

37. **(A)** Choice A is correct. Choice B is incorrect for two reasons: (1) We use the adverb "so" instead of "as" in a negative comparison; (2) "like" may not be used instead of "as" in this type of comparison. Choice C is awkward. Choice D is roundabout. Choice E changes the meaning of the original sentence.

38. **(C)** The problem in this question is the correct placement of the modifier. The prepositional phrase "much to our disgust" is an adverbial phrase showing result. The phrase, therefore modifies the verb "had been sold out." Accordingly, the phrase should, in this sentence, follow right after the verb it modifies. Choice C, therefore, is correct and the other choices are incorrect. Choice D, incidentally, is incorrect for another reason—it is illogical: the sold-out tickets are obviously disposed of when they are sold out.

39. **(C)** Choice A is incorrect because in this sentence "also" means the same as "in addition." Choice B is awkward. Choice C is correct as a subordinate clause which parallels the preceding subordinate clause. Choice D creates a run-on sentence. Choice E is too wordy.

40. **(C)** Choices A, B, and D are incorrect because of the use of "him joining." The word "joining" is a gerund in this sentence. Its possessive pronoun-adjective must be "his"—not "him." Choice B, moreover, has the unidiomatic expression "objection on." Choice C is correct. Choice E changes the meaning of the original sentence.

41. **(D)** ". . . no doubt about my being able to run faster than *he* today." The nominative case (*he*—not *him*) must be used after the conjunction *than* when the pronoun is the subject of an elliptical clause ("than he can run today").

42. **(A)** "*These kinds* of people . . ."
A plural pronoun-adjective (*These*—not *this*) must be used to modify a plural noun (*kinds*).

43. **(E)** All underlined parts are correct.

44. **(B)** ". . . presented *his* summaries of sales . . ."
Singular antecedents (*Atkins* and *Miller*) which are joined by *or* or *nor* are referred to by singular pronouns (*his*, in this case—not *their*).

45. **(C)** ". . . brighter than *any other* student . . ."
As the original sentence stands, Harold is brighter than himself. In a comparative construction, we must be sure that, if A and B are compared, A is not included as part of B.

46. **(C)** ". . . but *this book* is . . ."
The word *here* is redundant (unnecessary).

47. **(A)** "*Since* he is still in high school . . ."
The expression *Being that* is always incorrect. Use instead *Since* or *Because*.

48. **(B)** "If any man . . . does not agree with me, *he* should set forth . . ."
The subject (*any man*) is singular. This subject is the antecedent of the pronoun *he*. A pronoun must agree with its antecedent in number. Accordingly, we must use *he*—not *they*.

49. **(C)** ". . . for all of us—you and *me* included . . ."
The object of a preposition must take an objective form. The pronoun *me* is the object of the preposition *for* (just as *all* and *you* are the objects of *for*).

50. **(C)** ". . . you should *lie* down . . ."
In this case, the word *should* means *ought to*. Since the meaning we wish to convey here is *you ought to rest*, we must use the infinitive of *to lie* (which means *to rest*). The infinitive *to lay* means *to place* or *to put*.

EXPLANATORY ANSWERS FOR
PRACTICE TEST 5 (continued)

Section 4: Verbal Ability

1. **(C)** Choice C is correct. *Futile* means *useless; hopeless.* The opposite of *futile* is *worthwhile.*

2. **(A)** Choice A is correct. See **Antonym Strategy 3.** *Steadfast* means *firmly fixed.* The opposite of *steadfast* is *wobbly.*

3. **(D)** Choice D is correct. See **Antonym Strategy 3.** *Latent* means *hidden.* The opposite of *latent* is *obvious.*

4. **(E)** Choice E is correct. *Divulge* means *to reveal.* The opposite of *divulge* is *conceal.*

5. **(B)** Choice B is correct. *Tenuous* means *flimsy; without substance.* The opposite of *tenuous* is *substantial.*

6. **(E)** Choice E is correct. *Scrupulous* means *honest; ethical.* The opposite of *scrupulous* is *shady.*

7. **(A)** Choice A is correct. *Accolade* means *honor; award; approval.* The opposite of *accolade* is *rejection.*

8. **(D)** Choice D is correct. See **Antonym Strategy 3.** *Licentious* means *lawless; lewd.* The opposite of *licentious* is *lawful.*

9. **(D)** Choice D is correct. *Fester* means *to rot.* The opposite of *fester* is *thrive.*

10. **(C)** Choice C is correct. See **Antonym Strategy 3.** *Temerity* means *rashness; boldness.* The opposite of *temerity* is *timidity.*

11. **(D)** Choice D is correct. See **Sentence Completion Strategy 2.** Examine the first word of each choice. We eliminate Choice (C) motor and Choice (E) reciprocal because motor curbs and reciprocal curbs do not make good sense in the opening clause of the sentence. Now we consider Choice (A) profitable . . . drive, which does not make sentence sense; Choice (B) flexible . . . produce, which also does *not* make sentence sense; and Choice (D) export . . . ship, which *does* make sentence sense.

12. **(E)** Choice E is correct. See **Sentence Completion Strategy 2.** Examine the first words of each choice. We eliminate Choice (B) expedite (meaning "to speed up") and Choice (D) drench (which means "to wet through and through") because the parked vehicles do not expedite or drench the flow of traffic. Now we consider Choices A, C, and E. The only word pair that makes good sentence sense is Choice (E) impede . . . flout. The word "impede" means "to block up or obstruct" and the word "flout" means "to mock or ridicule."

13. **(A)** Choice A is correct. See **Sentence Completion Strategy 1.** Photographs of starving children demonstrate something. The logical choice among all the choices constitutes the results or consequences of drought, poor land, and overpopulation. The other choices are incorrect because they do not make sense in the sentence.

14. **(D)** Choice D is correct. See **Sentence Completion Strategy 2.** Examine the first words of each choice. We can eliminate Choice (B) advantages . . . because it doesn't make sense in the sentence. The first words of the other four choices *do* make sense, so let us proceed to fill the two spaces for each of these remaining choices. Only Choice (D) tension . . . security, makes good sentence sense.

15. **(E)** Choice E is correct. See **Sentence Completion Strategy 2.** Examine the first words of each choice. We eliminate Choice (D) recording because the film rental business is not recording. Now we consider the four remaining word pairs. The only choice that makes sense in the sentence is Choice (E) booming . . . leisure.

16. **(A)** Choice A is correct. A playwright writes a script for a play. A composer writes a score for a musical performance. In Choice (C) verse : poet, there is also an Action to Object relationship since a poet does write verses in creating poetry. However, the words in Choice C would have to be reversed in order to make Choice C correct. See **Analogy Strategy 3.**

    (Action to Object relationship)

17. **(C)** Choice C is correct. To wane is to decrease in size. To decelerate is to decrease in speed.

    (Result relationship)

18. **(B)** Choice B is correct. One who is licentious lacks morality. One who is pugnacious lacks amiability.

    (Opposite relationship)

19. **(E)** Choice E is correct. A seamstress follows a pattern to make clothing. A cook follows a recipe to make a meal. Consider also Choice (B) architect : blueprint. An architect *makes* a blueprint for someone else to follow. Therefore, Choice B is incorrect because it does not have the same relationship as the capitalized words and the Choice E words. See **Analogy Strategy 4.**

    (Action to Object and Result relationship)

20. **(B)** Choice B is correct. An archipelago consists of many islands. A chorus consists of many voices. Consider Choice (A) universe : stars. The stars do *not* make up the entire universe. Some of the space of the universe consists of other matter. But the islands *do* make up the entire archipelago and the voices *do* make up the entire chorus. So Choice A is incorrect. See **Analogy Strategy 4.**   (Whole-Part relationship)

21. **(B)** Choice B is correct. One amplifies sound to make it more noticeable. One enlarges a picture to make it more noticeable.

    (Action to Object and Purpose relationship)

22. **(C)** Choice C is correct. Something that is nugatory has no worth. Something that is desultory has no continuity.   **(Opposite relationship)**

23. **(E)** Choice E is correct. To enervate is to deprive of strength. To incarcerate is to deprive of freedom.

    (Result relationship)

24. **(E)** Choice E is correct. A person may loot in order to get booty. A child may suckle in order to get milk. We have here a Purpose relationship. Choice (A) shout : attention, also shows a purpose. However, attention is not a material thing such as booty and milk. Therefore, Choice A is incorrect. See **Analogy Strategy 4.**   **(Purpose relationship)**

25. **(C)** In this question, PICK is a verb meaning to play an instrument by pulling at the strings of the instrument either with the fingers or with a plectrum. Just as one picks a banjo, one strums a guitar. We have here an action-object relationship. (The word pick may also be a verb meaning to choose. The same word pick may also be a noun meaning a plectrum which is a small, thin piece of metal or plastic.) See **Strategy 5.**

    (Action to Object relationship)

26. **(D)** Choice D is the correct answer. Throughout the passage, the author gives important information about the new species of algae. For example: Lines 10–12: "The discovery . . . made at a depth of 884 feet." Lines 17–22: "It had been widely recognized . . . peak surface sunlight." Lines 27–33: "Algae on the ocean's floor . . . coral animals at higher levels." Choices A, B, C, and E give pertinent and interesting information about the new species of algae. However, each of these choices is too narrow to be considered the primary purpose of the passage. Therefore, these four choices are incorrect.

27. **(B)** Choice B is correct. Let us consider each of the Roman numeral items.

    Item I is *not* true. See lines 28–31: "They [algae] . . . contribute most of the beach sand of the Caribbean." Algae, according to the paragraph, do *not* contribute beach sand on *our beaches*.

Item II *is* true. First see lines 15–17: "Plants [including algae] depend on sunlight . . . carbon dioxide and water. Now see lines 28–29: "They [algae] provide food for many fish." Accordingly, if it weren't for the sunlight, the algae would not grow to be eaten by the fish.

Item III is *not* true. The passage does not specifically say whether sea algae are unicellular or multicellular. But the passage does tell us that these new algae are part of the seaweed family in lines 10–11: "The discovery . . . algae of the seaweed family."

By definition, algae are chlorophyll-containing plants ranging from unicellular, usually microscopic, forms to multicellular forms sometimes 100 feet or more in length. Since the algae described in the passage are seaweed in form, we may safely assume that they are *not* one-celled plants.

28. **(B)** Choice B is correct. Paragraph 2 refers to two incorrect beliefs—the first about the depth of the water where algae may survive (lines 10–15); the second incorrect belief concerning the percent of surface sunlight that the algae require (lines 15–22). Choices A, C, and D are true but they do not bring out the *main* purpose of paragraphs 2 and 3. Therefore, these choices are incorrect. Choice E is incorrect because paragraph 2 does *not* talk about the food that the algae consume and paragraph 3 does not bring out the algae's function on land as well as in the sea.

29. **(B)** Choice B is correct. Although all of the other choices are mentioned in the passage, the author is using all of them in order to show us Bernini's artistic gifts. Choices A, C and D are incorrect because the passage does more than just favorably compare Bernini to Michelangelo, or mention his relation to a powerful family, or refer to specific works of art. All these things exemplify his artistic talent. Choice E is incorrect because the passage mentions only the early part of Bernini's career.

30. **(C)** Choice C is correct. In line 1 the author calls Baroque "a popular art," and in lines 4–5 he says it "appealed through the emotions." Choices A, B and D are incorrect because they are highly unfavorable to popular art, whereas the author is very favorable throughout the passage to the popular art of Baroque, going so far as to call the work of the popular artist Bernini "ideal and eternal" (lines 21–22). Choice E is incorrect because at no point does the author say he thinks either popular or intellectual art is superior; he merely acknowledges that they are different.

31. **(A)** Choice A is correct. The author states that the devices used by Baroque artists to appeal to the emotions "were to be rediscovered in the movies." (line 16). Choice B is incorrect because the author uses the word "rediscovered." It was a coincidence that Baroque art and the movies used the same devices, not a matter of influence. Choice C is incorrect because, although the author does say the movies are "often commercial and short-lived" (lines 20–21), the purpose of the passage is not to examine the shortcomings of the movies but to compare them to another form of art. Choice D is incorrect because the author says "often commercial and short-lived," not "always commercial and short-lived." The author's opinion of the overall artistic qualities of the movies is not stated. Choice E is incorrect because he is not comparing the movies of the 1920s to any other movies.

32. **(D)** Choice D is correct. The words "terrific impact" may be translated into "great effect." The words "growth potential" may be translated into "one's capacity to improve himself." Choices A, B, C, and E are incorrect because their meanings are much different from the correct *translation* for "terrific impact" and "growth potential."

33. **(E)** Choice E is correct. Each of the three individuals could have expressed what they had to say in a much simpler and more direct manner. For example, see Question 32 and its explanatory answer (above). Accordingly, Choice A is incorrect. Choices B, C, and D are incorrect because there is no evidence in the passage that these choices are true.

34. **(C)** Choice C is correct. Throughout the passage, the author is quite severe in his criticism of the way people are writing today. For example, see lines 5–8: ". . . writing today . . . rarely affords pleasure." Also see lines 24–26: "For if these bad habits . . . assembly-line thinking." Accordingly, Choices A and B are incorrect. Choice B is incorrect because there is no indication in the passage that the author is biased. He bases his criticism on fact. Choice E is incorrect because the passage does not indicate that an argument is going on.

35. **(B)** Choice B is correct. See lines 24–31: "For if these bad habits . . . of abstraction and metaphor." Choices A, C, D, and E are incorrect because they do not fit in with what the author describes as "assembly-line thinking."

36. **(A)** Choice A is *not* true according to the passage. Therefore, it is a correct choice. See lines 12–14: ". . . the cause of our bad writing is cultural *first* and only *secondarily* instructional." Choice B is true. Therefore it is incorrect. See lines 31–40: "For example . . . of any art work." Choice C is true. Therefore, it is incorrect. See lines 41–46: "This kind of prose . . . different patterns." Choice D is true. Therefore, it is incorrect. See lines 1–3: "Nobody should suppose . . . has ever been easy." Choice E is true. Therefore, it is incorrect. See lines 14–16: "Teachers and parents . . . in the workaday world."

37. **(E)** Choice E is the correct answer. See lines 7–8: "Trees in commercial forests . . . not be wasted." Choices A, B, C, and D are incorrect because the author does not recommend any of the procedures expressed in these choices.

38. **(D)** Choice D is correct. Let us consider the Roman numeral items. Item I is true and Item II is true according to lines 12–13: "Growing trees manufacture oxygen and absorb carbon dioxide; [Item I] they feed and shelter wild life." [Item II] Item III is *not* true according to lines 18–20 which apply to *old* (non-growing) trees: "When forests grow old . . . insect infestation." Since Items I and II are characteristics of growing forests—but not Item III—Choice D is the only correct choice.

39. **(C)** Choice C is correct. See lines 25–27: ". . . recreation values (of old forests) diminish . . . roadless wilderness." Choice A is incorrect. See lines 23–24: "Old forests absorb . . . as they produce, through decay." Choice B is incorrect. See lines 21–22: "They lose their beauty . . . other living things." Choice D is incorrect. See lines 28–31: "The public benefits . . . are wasted." Choice E is incorrect. The passage nowhere states that old forests offer good insight into geology.

40. **(C)** Choice C is correct. See lines 33–36: "Because of well-meaning . . . disease and senility." Choices A, B, D, and E are incorrect because the passage nowhere makes mention of these choices.

EXPLANATORY ANSWERS FOR
PRACTICE TEST 5 (continued)

Section 5: Math Ability

1. **(E)** Choice E is correct.
   (Use Strategy 12: Try not to make tedious calculations.)

$$\left(\frac{1}{2} - \frac{1}{3}\right) + \left(\frac{1}{3} - \frac{1}{4}\right) + \left(\frac{1}{4} - \frac{1}{5}\right) +$$

$$\left(\frac{1}{5} - \frac{1}{6}\right) + \left(\frac{1}{6} - \frac{1}{7}\right) + \left(\frac{1}{7} - \frac{1}{8}\right) +$$

$$\left(\frac{1}{8} - \frac{1}{9}\right) =$$

$$\frac{1}{2} + \left(-\frac{1}{3} + \frac{1}{3}\right) + \left(-\frac{1}{4} + \frac{1}{4}\right) +$$

$$\left(-\frac{1}{5} + \frac{1}{5}\right) + \left(-\frac{1}{6} + \frac{1}{6}\right) + \left(-\frac{1}{7} + \frac{1}{7}\right) +$$

$$\left(-\frac{1}{8} + \frac{1}{8}\right) - \frac{1}{9} =$$

$$\frac{1}{2} + 0 + 0 + 0 + 0 + 0 + 0 - \frac{1}{9} =$$

$$\frac{1}{2} - \frac{1}{9} =$$

$$\frac{9}{18} - \frac{2}{18} =$$

$$\frac{7}{18} \quad (Answer)$$

(Math Refresher #110 and Logical Reasoning)

2. **(B)** Choice B is correct. **(Use Strategy 17: Use the given information effectively.)**

If all months were 28 days (4 weeks × 7 days/week), then the third day of all the months would be on the same day (Monday as given). It is the days over 28 that disturb this pattern.

May has 31 days or 28 + <u>3</u>
June has 30 days or 28 + <u>2</u>
July has 31 days or 28 + <u>3</u>

Adding the *extra* days we get

$$3 + 2 + 3 = 8 \text{ extra days}$$

7 of them are a full week and do not disturb the pattern, so

$$8 - 7 = 1 \text{ extra days exists.}$$

Given that May 3rd is a Monday, the 1 extra day makes August 3rd a Tuesday.

(Logical Reasoning)

3. **(B)** Choice B is correct.
   (Use Strategy 11: Use new definitions carefully.)

The first five elements of the series, calculated by the definition, are

$$1, 2, 2, 4, 8$$

(Logical Reasoning)

4. **(D)** Choice D is correct.
   (Use Strategy 2: Translate from words to algebra.)

$$P = \frac{3}{5}m \qquad \boxed{1}$$

$$q = \frac{9}{10}m \qquad \boxed{2}$$

(Use Strategy 13: Find unknowns by division of equations.)

Thus, $\quad \dfrac{p}{q} = \dfrac{\dfrac{3}{5}m}{\dfrac{9}{10}m}$

$$= \frac{\dfrac{3}{5}}{\dfrac{9}{10}}$$

$$= \frac{3}{5} \times \frac{10}{9} = \frac{3}{5} \times \frac{5 \times 2}{3 \times 3}$$

$$\frac{p}{q} = \frac{2}{3} \quad (Answer)$$

(Math Refresher #200 and #112)

5. **(E)** Choice E is correct.
   (Use Strategy 12: Try not to make tedious calculations.)

$$23m + 23n = 23(m + n)$$
$$= 23(94 + 6)$$
$$= 23(100)$$
$$= 2300$$

Multiplying 23(94) and
     23(6) and adding would be time consuming.

(Math Refresher #431)

6. **(C)** Choice C is correct.

$$\left(\text{Use Strategy 2:} \atop \text{Average} = \frac{\text{sum of values}}{\text{total number of values}}\right)$$

Given: $\dfrac{40 + 40 + 40 + z}{4} = 45$ ☐1

Multiplying ☐1 by 4,

$$40 + 40 + 40 + z = 180$$
$$120 + z = 180$$
$$z = 60$$

(Math Refresher #601 and #406)

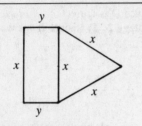

7. **(C)** Choice C is correct.
(Use Strategy 2: Translate from words to algebra.)

When the given diagram has been labeled as above, then we know

$$3x = 39 \quad\quad ☐1$$
$$xy = 65 \quad\quad ☐2$$

From ☐1 we have

$$x = 13 \quad\quad ☐3$$

Substituting ☐3 into ☐2, we have

$$13y = 65$$
$$\text{or} \quad y = 5 \quad\quad ☐4$$

The perimeter of the rectangle

$$= 2x + 2y$$
$$= 2(13) + 2(5)$$
$$= 36$$

(Math Refresher #200, #304, #308, and #431)

8. **(B)** Choice B is correct.
(Use Strategy 13: Find unknowns by multiplication.)

Method 1: $7x + 21 = 35$ ☐1

Multiplying ☐1 by $\dfrac{4}{7}$,

$$4x + 12 = 20$$

Thus, the columns become

Column A	Column B
20	21

and the answer is clear.

Method 2:

Given: $7x + 21 = 35$

Solve to get x:

$$7x = 14$$
$$x = 2 \quad\quad ☐1$$

Substitute ☐1 into $4x + 12$

$$4(2) + 12 = 8 + 12$$
$$= 20$$

Clearly $20 < 21$.

(Math Refresher #406 and #431)

9. **(B)** Choice B is correct.

Method 1: $\dfrac{298,376}{10,000} = 29.8376$

and $29.8376 < 30$ is always true.

(Use Strategy D: To compare fractions, multiply both columns by a positive quantity.)

Method 2: Multiply both columns by 10,000

Column A	Column B
298,376	300,000

and the answer is clear.

(Division and Multiplication)

10. **(A)** Choice A is correct.

Given: $\quad a - b = 5 \quad\quad ☐1$
$\quad\quad\quad\quad a + b = -1 \quad\quad ☐2$

(Use Strategy 17: Use the given information effectively.)

Fast Method: Add b to both sides of ☐1,

$$a = b + 5 \quad\quad ☐3$$

From ☐3, we can say right away that

$$a > b$$

Slow method: Substitute ☐3 into ☐2,

$$b + 5 + b = -1$$
$$\text{or} \quad 2b + 5 = -1$$
$$\text{or} \quad 2b = -6$$
$$\text{or} \quad b = -3 \quad\quad ☐4$$

Substituting ☐4 into ☐3,

$$a = 2 \quad\quad ☐5$$

Comparing ☐4 and ☐5, we see that

$$a > b$$

(Math Refresher #406 and #407)

11. **(A)** Choice A is correct.

By using the given information, we can write the columns as

Column A	Column B
$11.5 + 5.7 = 17.2$	16.2

and the answer is clear.

(Addition of decimals)

12. **(B)** Choice B is correct.
(Use Strategy 6: Know how to manipulate inequalities.)

Given:

$$b > y \qquad \boxed{1}$$
$$y > a \qquad \boxed{2}$$

The transitive property of inequality gives

$$b > a$$

(Math Refresher #419)

13. **(A)** Choice A is correct.
(Use Strategy 2: Translate from words to algebra.)

We are given

Volume of rock A = 33 cubic cm.	$\boxed{1}$
Volume of rock B = 12 cubic cm.	$\boxed{2}$

By definition

$$\text{Density} = \frac{\text{Mass}}{\text{Volume}}$$

or $\qquad$ Mass = Density × Volume $\qquad \boxed{3}$

We are also given

Density of rock A = 3 grams per cubic cm.	$\boxed{4}$
Density of rock B = 8 grams per cubic cm.	$\boxed{5}$

By substituting $\boxed{4}$, $\boxed{5}$, $\boxed{1}$, and $\boxed{2}$ into $\boxed{3}$, we can calculate the quantities in both columns:

Column A	Column B
99	96

The answer is clear.

(Math Refresher #200 and #431)

14. **(D)** Choice D is correct.

Given:	Area of rectangle I = 60	$\boxed{1}$
	Area of rectangle II = 72	$\boxed{2}$

It is always true that the perimeter of any rectangle

$$= 2 \times \text{length} + 2 \times \text{width} \qquad \boxed{3}$$

(Use Strategy C: Use numbers in place of variables when a comparison is difficult.)

To answer this question, choose specific rectangles which satisfy $\boxed{1}$ and $\boxed{2}$, and which use $\boxed{3}$ to calculate the perimeters.

EXAMPLE 1

Rectangle I has length = 20 and width = 3.

Rectangle II has length = 12 and width = 6.

Thus, the columns become

Column A	Column B
46	36

and the quantity in Column A is greater.

EXAMPLE 2

Rectangle I has length = 12 and width = 5.

Rectangle II has length = 9 and width = 8.

Thus the columns become

Column A	Column B
34	34

and both quantities are equal.

Clearly, the answer to this question depends on specific examples.

(Math Refresher #304 and #431)

15. **(B)** Choice B is correct.
(Use Strategy 17: Use the given information effectively.)

Note that $3n$ is a divisor of $6n$ because $6n = 2 \times 3n$. So, every divisor of $3n$ is also a divisor of $6n$.

Thus, the number of divisors of $6n$

$$\geq \text{the number of divisors of } 3n \qquad \boxed{1}$$

Clearly, there is a divisor of $6n$—namely, itself—which divides $6n$ and not $3n$. Accordingly, the divisors of $6n$ include all the divisors of $3n$ and the number $6n$. $\qquad \boxed{2}$
Hence, it is clear that $\qquad \boxed{3}$

the number of divisors of $6n$

$$> \text{the number of divisors of } 3n$$

(Math Refresher #607 and Logical Reasoning)

16. **(A)** Choice A is correct.
(Use Strategy 11: Use new definitions carefully.)

In Row 1, there are 3 boxes.
In Row 2, there are 5 boxes.
In Row 3, there are 7 boxes.
Thus, in Row n, there are $2n + 1$ boxes, so that in Row 9, there are $2(9) + 1 = 19$ boxes.

You may also keep adding 2 for each new row:

Row	Number of Boxes
3	7
4	9
5	11
6	13
7	15
8	17
9	19

(Math Refresher #406 and #431)

17. **(B)** Choice B is correct.
(Use Strategy 17: Use the given information effectively.)

By definition of a circle, all points on the circumference are the same distance from the center.

Any point inside the circle is closer to the center. Thus,

$$OA < OP$$

(Math Refresher #524 and Logical Reasoning)

18. **(D)** Choice D is correct.

Given: $8 + 4x - x = 5 + 3x + 3$

Simplifying both sides we get

$$8 + 3x = 8 + 3x$$

which is true for all values of x.

(Math Refresher #406)

19. **(C)** Choice C is correct.
(Use Strategy 2: Translate from words to algebra.)

Let p = the number of pears bought
t = the number of tangerines bought
a = the number of apples bought
h = the number of peaches bought

Thus, we are told

$$20p + 30t + 70a + 90h = 260 \qquad \boxed{1}$$

We want to minimize the value of

$$p + t + a + h \qquad \boxed{2}$$

When $t = 1$, $a = 2$, and $h = 1$, $\boxed{1}$ is satisfied and

$$p + t + a + h = 4.$$

If you are convinced that 4 is the minimum value of $\boxed{2}$, then you have finished. If not, then read on.

We want to show that when $\boxed{1}$ is satisfied, the minimum value of $\boxed{2}$ is 4. To show this, we will indicate that when the value of $\boxed{2}$ is less than 4 (1, 2, 3), $\boxed{1}$ is not satisfied. We will consider the quantity

$$20p + 30t + 70a + 90h = \qquad \boxed{3}$$

amount spent in grocery store

When

$$p + t + a + h = 1,$$
$$20p + 30t + 70a + 90h = 20 \text{ or } 30 \text{ or } 70 \text{ or } 90$$

but *not* 260. Thus, $\boxed{1}$ is not satisfied. When $p + t + a + h = 2$, the maximum value of $\boxed{3}$ occurs when $h = 2$.

We get $20p + 30t + 70a + 90h = 180$. This result is less than 260. Thus, $\boxed{1}$ is not satisfied.

When $p + t + a + h = 3$,
$20p + 30t + 70a + 90h = 270$ or 250 or values less than 250.

Thus, $\boxed{1}$ is still not satisfied.

Hence, when the value of $\boxed{2}$ is less than 4, $\boxed{1}$ is not satisfied, thus, when $\boxed{1}$ is satisfied, the minimum value of $\boxed{2}$ is 4.

(Use Strategy F: Use the Choice C method when straightforward computations must be made.)

(Math Refresher #200 and #431)

20. **(C)** Choice C is correct.
(Use Strategy 2: Translate from words to algebra.)

	4 years ago	Now
John		
David	J	

Given above, we get

	4 years ago	Now
John		
David	J	$J + 4$

Since John is now 10 years older than David was 4 years ago, we have.

	4 years ago	Now
John		$J + 10$
David	J	$J + 4$

Column A	Column B
John's age 2 years from now	David's age 8 years from now
$J + 10 + 2$	$J + 4 + 8$
$J + 12$	$J + 12$

(Math Refresher #200 and #431)

21. **(A)** Choice A is correct.

Method 1: Try to get both quantities to look similar. Try not to do the actual arithmetic.

For example, $\dfrac{.65}{3} = \dfrac{1}{3} \times .65$

Thus, we want to compare

Column A	Column B
$\dfrac{1}{3} \times .65$	$\dfrac{1}{3} \times \dfrac{5}{8}$

(Use Strategy B: Cancel positive quantities from both sides by division.)

Since $\dfrac{1}{3}$ is positive and since $\dfrac{1}{3}$ appears in both columns, dividing each column by $\dfrac{1}{3}$ does *not* change the answer to this question. Thus, we really want to compare

Column A	Column B
$.65$	$\dfrac{5}{8}$

Remembering that
$\dfrac{5}{8} = .625$, we can rewrite the columns

Column A	Column B
$.65$	$.625$

and the answer is clear.

(Use Strategy D: Compare fractions by multiplying both columns by a positive quantity.)

Method 2: Multiply both columns by 24, giving

Column A	Column B
$8(.65)$ $= 5.20$	$\dfrac{1}{3} \times 15$ $= 5$

The answer is clear.

(Multiplication)

22. **(B)** Choice B is correct.
(Use Strategy 3: The whole equals the sum of its parts.)

The sum of the measures of the angles of any quadrilateral is 360. Thus, for the first quadrilateral,

$$z + z + z + z = 360$$
or $\qquad\qquad 4z = 360$
or $\qquad\qquad\quad z = 90 \qquad \boxed{1}$

For the second quadrilateral,

$$y + 4y + 2y + 5y = 360$$
or $\qquad\qquad\quad 12y = 360$
or $\qquad\qquad\qquad y = 30$
or $\qquad\qquad\quad 4y = 120 \qquad \boxed{2}$

We are asked to compare $\boxed{1}$ and $\boxed{2}$. The answer is clear.

(Math Refresher #521 and #406)

23. **(D)** Choice D is correct.
(Use Strategy C: Use numbers in place of variables when a comparison of the two columns is difficult.)

EXAMPLE 1
$x = 1$

The columns become

Column A	Column B
2	$2^5 = 32$

and the quantity in Column B is greater.

EXAMPLE 2
$x = -1$

Column A	Column B
-2	$-2^5 = -32$

and the quantity in Column A is greater.

Clearly, the answer depends on specific values of x.

(Math Refresher #429 and #431)

24. **(D)** Choice D is correct.

Given: $x < 1$ $\boxed{1}$
          $x \neq 0$ $\boxed{2}$

(Use Strategy C: Use numbers in place of variables, when a comparison is difficult.)

Choose specific values of x that satisfy $\boxed{1}$ and $\boxed{2}$.

EXAMPLE 1
$x = -1$

The columns become

Column A	Column B
-1	-1

and both quantities are equal.

EXAMPLE 2
$x = -2$

The columns become

Column A	Column B
-2	-8

The quantity of Column A is greater.

Thus, the answer depends on specific values of x.

(Math Refresher #431)

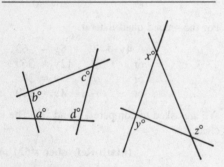

25. **(C)** Choice C is correct.
(Use Strategy 3: The whole equals the sum of its parts.)

$a + b + c + d = 360$
(the sum of the external angles in a
quadrilateral = 360) $\boxed{1}$

(Use Strategy 18: Know and use facts about triangles.)

$x + y + z = 360$
(the sum of the angles of a triangle = 360) $\boxed{2}$

Since $\boxed{1} = \boxed{2}$, Choice C is correct.

(Math Refresher #521)

26. **(C)** Choice C is correct.

Column A	Column B
$(x^2 + 3)^2$	$(x^4 + 6x^2 + 9)$

(Use Strategy 4: Remember classic expressions.)

$x^4 + 6x^2 + 9$ $x^4 + 6x^2 + 9$

They are equal.

(Math Refresher #409)

27. **(A)** Choice A is correct.
(Use Strategy 2: Translate from words to algebra.)

Let $9 + x = $ total marbles in Bag A,
where $x = $ green marbles, then

$$\frac{x}{9 + x} = \frac{70}{100} = \frac{7}{10}$$

$$10x = 7(9 + x)$$

$$10x = 63 + 7x$$

$$3x = 63$$

$$x = 21$$

For Bag B, we have $15 + y = $ Total marbles. Then

$$\frac{y}{15 + y} = \frac{50}{100} = \frac{1}{2}$$

$$2y = 15 + y$$

$$y = 15$$

Clearly, $y < x$.

(Math Refresher #200 and #406)

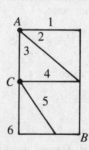

28. **(B)** Choice B is correct.
(Use Strategy 17: Use the given information effectively.)

There are 3 distinct paths leaving A: (Paths 1, 2 and 3)

1 and 2 go directly to B with no other possibilities.

Path 3 has 3 choices at point C: (Paths 4, 5, 6)

The possible paths are: 1, 2, 3–4, 3–5, 3–6.

Accordingly, there are five possible paths.

(Logical Reasoning)

29. **(D)** Choice D is correct.
(Use Strategy 7: Use numerical examples to help to prove or disprove your guess.)

Choose specific values of x and y.

EXAMPLE 1

$$x = 3 \qquad\qquad y = 5$$

$xy = 15$ is odd.
$x + y = 8$ is even.
$x^2 + y^2 = 34$ is even
$(x + y)^2 = 64$ is divisible by 4.

But $x^2 + y^2 = 34$ is *not* divisible by 4.

So it seems that Choice D is the answer.

EXAMPLE 2

$$x = 1 \qquad\qquad y = 7$$

$x^2 + y^2 = 50$ is *not* divisible by 4. Thus, Choice D is the answer.

(Math Refresher #431, #605 and #607)

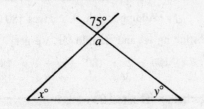

30. **(B)** Choice B is correct.

From the diagram we know that $a = 75$ ☐1

Use Strategy 3: The whole equals the sum of its parts.)

The sum of the angles of a triangle $= 180$ ☐2
Using ☐2 we have
$$x + y + a = 180 \qquad ☐3$$
Substituting ☐1 into ☐3 we get
$$x + y + 75 = 180 \qquad ☐4$$

(Use Strategy 13: Find unknowns by subtraction.)
Subtract $x + 75$ from both sides of ☐4. We get
$$y = 105 - x$$

(Math Refresher #503 and #505)

31. **(C)** Choice C is correct.
(Use Strategy 6: Know how to manipulate inequalities.)

$$\text{Given } a < b, \, b < c \qquad ☐1$$
$$d > 0 \qquad ☐2$$

Using both parts of ☐1, the transitive property gives

$$a < c \text{ and I is true} \qquad ☐3$$

Multiply ☐1 by d and noting ☐2, we have
$$ad < cd \text{ and II is true} \qquad ☐4$$

Only Choice C can now be correct.

(Math Refresher #419 and #422)

32. **(E)** Choice E is correct.
(Use Strategy 2: Translate from words to algebra.)

Let x, $x + 2$ and $x + 4$ represent the 3 positive, consecutive even integers.

We are given

$$x + x + 2 + x + 4 = w$$
$$3x + 6 = w$$

(Use Strategy 13: Know how to find unknown expressions by adding, subtracting, multiplying, or dividing equations.)

$$\text{Then} \qquad 3x = w - 6$$
$$x = \frac{w - 6}{3}$$

and the answer is clear.

(Math Refresher #200 and #406)

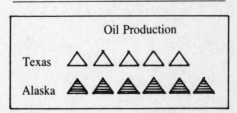

Oil Production

33. **(C)** Choice C is correct.

(Use Strategy 2: Translate from words to algebra.)

We are told $\blacktriangle = 3\triangle$

(Use Strategy 17: Use the given information effectively.)

Texas total $= 5$
Alaska total $= 3(6) = 18$

(Use Strategy 3: Know how to find unknown quantities from known quantities.)

$$\frac{\text{Alaska production}}{\text{Total production}} = \frac{18}{5 + 18} =$$
$$\frac{18}{23} = \text{required ratio}$$

(Math Refresher #200 and 431)

34. **(C)** Choice C is correct.
    (Use Strategy 10: Know how to use units.)

$$\left(\frac{x\,\text{cars}}{\text{hour}}\right)(y\,\text{hours})\left(\frac{z\,\text{dollars}}{\text{car}}\right) =$$
$$xyz\,\text{dollars} \qquad \boxed{1}$$

Multiply $\boxed{1}$ by 100. We get

$100xyz$ cents.

(Math Refresher #121)

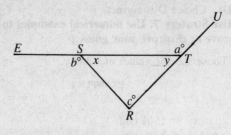

35. **(D)** Choice D is correct.
    (Use Strategy 2: Translate from words to algebra.)

From the diagram, we have

$$b + x = 180 \qquad \boxed{1}$$
$$a + y = 180 \qquad \boxed{2}$$

$\boxed{1}$ and $\boxed{2}$ become

$$x = 180 - b \qquad \boxed{3}$$
$$y = 180 - a \qquad \boxed{4}$$
$$\text{We are given:} \quad b = 2c - 30 \qquad \boxed{5}$$

(Use Strategy 3: The whole equals the sum of its parts.)

$$\text{Adding } x + y + c \text{ gives } 180 \qquad \boxed{6}$$

Substituting $\boxed{3}$ and $\boxed{4}$ into $\boxed{6}$, we get

$$180 - b + 180 - a + c = 180$$
$$360 - b - a + c = 180 \qquad \boxed{7}$$

Substituting $\boxed{5}$ into $\boxed{7}$, we get

$$360 - (2c - 30) - a + c = 180$$
$$360 - 2c + 30 - a + c = 180$$
$$390 - c - a = 180$$
$$210 - c - a = 0$$
$$210 = a + c$$

(Math Refresher #200 and #505)

EXPLANATORY ANSWERS FOR
PRACTICE TEST 5 (continued)

Section 6: Math Ability

1. **(D)** Choice D is correct. **(Use Strategy 1: Cancel numbers on both sides of an equation.)**

Fast Method:
Given: $x + 7 = 20$. Thus, $x + 5 + 2 = 20$. Subtract 2 from both sides of the equation to get $x + 5 = 18$ (*Answer*)

Slow Method:
Given: $x + 7 = 20$
Solve for x by subtracting 7 from both sides of the equation to get

$$x = 13$$

Thus, $x + 5 = 13 + 5 = 18$ (*Answer*)

The key to this problem is to solve for the quantity $x + 5$ in *one* step. This can save a great deal of time in problems involving large numbers.
(Math Refresher #406)

2. **(C)** Choice C is correct. **(Use Strategy 2: Translate from words to algebra.)** The key is to be able to translate English sentences into mathematical equations.
Let p = price of one frying pan
  m = price of one coffee mug
  We are given

$$p + 2m = \$27 \qquad \boxed{1}$$
$$p + m = \$23 \qquad \boxed{2}$$

Subtract equation $\boxed{2}$ from equation $\boxed{1}$ to get
$$m = \$4 \qquad \boxed{3}$$
Substitute equation $\boxed{3}$ into equation $\boxed{2}$
$$p + \$4 = \$23$$
Subtract \$4 from both sides of the above equation
$$p = \$19 \text{ (\textit{Answer})}$$
(Math Refresher #200, #407, and #406)

3. **(A)** Choice A is correct. **(Use Strategy 2: Translate from words to algebra.)** Be able to translate English sentences into mathematical expressions.
Let s = Stanley's age now.
Thus, $s - 8$ = Stanley's age 8 years ago. $\boxed{1}$
  $s + 8$ = Stanley's age 8 year from now.

We are given that
m = Stanley's age 8 years from now.
Thus, $s + 8 = m$
Subtracting 8 from both sides of the above equation, we get
$$s = m - 8 \qquad \boxed{2}$$
We can find expression $\boxed{1}$ in terms of m by substituting $\boxed{2}$ into $\boxed{1}$:
$$s - 8 = (m - 8) - 8 = m - 16 \text{ (\textit{Answer})}$$
(Math Refresher #200 and #406)

4. **(B)** Choice B is correct. **(Use Strategy 2: Tanslate from words to algebra.)** This problem tests the concepts of set union and set intersection. We can solve these types of problems with a diagram. Let

  c = set of all calculus students
  p = set of all physics students

Thus, draw the diagram:

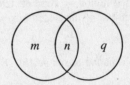

Where

  m = number of students taking *only* calculus
  q = number of students taking *only* physics
  n = number of students taking *both* calculus and physics

Thus,

  $m + n$ = number of students in calculus class
  $n + q$ = number of students in physics class
  $m + n + q$ = number of students taking either calculus or physics or both

We are given that

$$m + n + q = 36 \qquad \boxed{1}$$
$$n = 10 \qquad \boxed{2}$$
$$m + n = 31 \qquad \boxed{3}$$

We want to find

$$n + q \qquad \boxed{4}$$

(Use Strategy 13: Find unknowns by subtracting equations.) Subtract equation $\boxed{2}$ from equation $\boxed{3}$ to get

$$m = 21 \qquad \boxed{5}$$

Now subtract equation $\boxed{5}$ from equation $\boxed{1}$ to get

$$n + q = 15 \text{ (\textit{Answer})}$$
(Math Refresher #406 and Logical Reasoning)

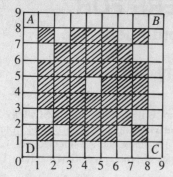

5. (B) Choice B is correct.
Method 1: (Use Strategy 3: the whole equals the sum of its parts.)
Area of shaded region = Area of *ABCD*
minus the number of ulnshaded boxes in *ABCD* [1]

Area of *ABCD* = $7 \times 7 = 49$ [2]

Number of unshaded boxes in *ABCD* = 9 [3]

Substitute [2] and [3] in [1]. We get
Area of shaded region = $49 - 9 = 40$

Method 2:
Count the number of shaded boxes. It takes a little longer, but you get 40 as the answer.
(Math Refresher #303)

6. (E) Choice E is correct.
Method 1: (Use Strategy 4: Remember classic expressions.)
Remember the factorization:

$$a^2 - b^2 = (a - b)(a + b)$$

We are given $(a - b)(a + b) = 64$ [1]

There are many values of a and b satisfying equation [1]. Thus, you can see that the value of $a - b$ cannot be determined.
(Use Strategy 7: Use specific numerical examples to prove or disprove your guess.)

Method 2: Choose values of a and b satifying equation [1], but which have different values of $a - b$.

EXAMPLE 1

$a = 10$ and $b = 6$ Thus,
$a^2 - b^2 = 64$, but $a - b = 4$.

EXAMPLE 2

$a = 17$ and $b = 15$ Thus, $a^2 - b^2 = 64$,
but $a - b = 2$.
Accordingly, Choice E must be the answer.
(Math Refresher #409 and #431)

7. (D) Choice D is correct.
The procedure, as described, can be summarized in the following table:

Given Container	–	Receiving Container	=	Excess to 50 cc Container
25cc	–	16cc	=	9cc
16cc	–	9cc	=	7cc
9cc	–	4cc	=	5cc
4cc	–	1cc	=	3cc
		Total	=	24cc

(Use Strategy 2: Remember the definition of percent.)
Thus, $\dfrac{24cc}{50cc} \times 100 = 48\%$ of the 50cc container is full.
(Use Strategy 3: The whole equals the sum of its parts.)
So, $100\% - 48\% = 52\%$ of the 50 cc container is empty.
(Math Refresher #107 and Logical Reasoning)

8. (C) Choice C is correct. **(Use Strategy 7: Use numerics to help decide the answer.)**
Choose some numerical examples.

EXAMPLE 1

Consider the number 42.
$$4 + 2 = 6$$
which is *even* as required, but
$$4 \times 2 = 8 \text{ is also even.}$$

EXAMPLE 2

Consider the number 35.
$$3 + 5 = 8$$
which is *even* as required, but
$$3 \times 5 = 15 \text{ is odd.}$$
Thus Choice C must be the answer.
(Math Refresher #431)

9. (E) Choice E is correct. **(Use Strategy 8: When all choices must be tested, start with Choice E.)**
Since we must check all the choices, we should start with Choice E. Clearly, if x is the point whose coordinates are (5,2), then $m \angle MXN = 90°$ and Choice E must be correct.
(Math Refresher #410)

10. **(D)** Choice D is correct.
Method 1: **(Use Strategy 8: When all choices must be tested, start with Choice E.)**

Since $\sqrt{x}$ is odd, then x is odd. [1]
Let us start with solution E.

Choice E: If x is odd (from [1] above) then x^2 is odd.

Choice D: If $\sqrt{x}$ is odd, $2\sqrt{x}$ is *even*, and the solution is found.

(Use Strategy 7: Use numerics to help you get the answer.)

Method 2: Choose an odd number for $\sqrt{x}$—for example,

$$\sqrt{x} = 3$$

Then $x = 9$

Choice E $\qquad x^2 = 81$ (odd)

Choice D $\qquad 2\sqrt{x} = 2(3) = 6$ (even)

The answer is clearly Choice D.

(Math Refresher #430 and #431, and #603)

11. **(E)** Choice E is correct. **(Use Strategy 2: Translate from words to algebra.)** The sum of the degree measures of the 4 angles of any quadrilateral is always 360. Therefore,

$$w + x + y + z = 360° \qquad [1]$$

(Use Strategy 5: Average =

$$\frac{\text{Sum of values}}{\text{Total number of values}})$$

If w is the average (arithmetic mean) of x, y, and z, then

$$w = \frac{x + y + z}{3}$$

Multiplying both sides of the above equation by 3, we have

$$3w = x + y + z \qquad [2]$$

Substituting equation [2] into equation [1], we get

$$w + 3w = 360°$$
$$\text{or} \qquad 4w = 360°$$
$$\text{or} \qquad w = 90°$$

From equation [2], we conclude that
$x + y + z = 3w = 3(90) = 270°$
(Math Refresher #521, #601, and #406)

12. **(A)** Choice A is correct. **(Use Strategy 11: Use new definitions carefully.)**
From the definition we get

$$2 + 6 + 7 = 5Z$$
$$15 = 5Z$$
$$3 = Z$$

(Math Refresher #431)

13. **(E)** Choice E is correct. **(Use Strategy 11: Use new definitions carefully.)**
Since W, X, Y, and Z are distinct digits from 0 to 9, the largest possible sum of $W + X + Y = 7 + 8 + 9 = 24$ [1]

By definiton, $W + X + Y = 5Z$ [2]
Substituting [1] into [2], we get

largest value of $5Z = 24$

(Use Strategy 8: When all choices must be tested, start with Choice E.) Look at the choices, starting with Choice E. If $Z = 5$ then $5Z = 25$ which is larger than 24. Thus, Choice E is correct.
(Math Refresher #431 and Logical Reasoning)

14. **(C)** Choice C is correct. **(Use Strategy 2: Translate from words to algebra.)** We are given

$$p > 0 \qquad [1]$$
$$q > 0 \qquad [2]$$
$$x < 0 \qquad [3]$$
$$y < 0 \qquad [4]$$

(Use Strategy 6: Know how to manipulate inequalities.)

$$p > q \text{ or } q < p \qquad [5]$$
$$x > y \text{ or } y < x \qquad [6]$$

For I: Add $-p$ to both sides of inequality [5]:
$$q - p < 0$$
Thus, I is less than zero.

For II: From inequalities [2] and [4], $qy < 0$ and II is less than zero.

For III: The value of p and x depends on specific values of p and x:
(Use Strategy 7: Use numerics to help decide the answer.)

EXAMPLE 1
$$p = 3 \text{ and } x = -5$$
Thus, $\qquad p + x < 0$
EXAMPLE 2
$$p = 5 \text{ and } x = -3$$
Thus, $\qquad p + x > 0$
Thus, II is not always less than zero. Choice C is correct.

(Math Refresher #420, #421, and #431)

15. **(B)** Choice B is correct. **(Use Strategy 2: Translate from words to algebra.)**

Fraction mowed during evening 1 = $\frac{2}{9}$ ①

Fraction mowed during evening 2 = $2\left(\frac{2}{9}\right) = \frac{4}{9}$ ②

Adding ① and ②, we get

Total fraction mowed during

first two evenings = $\frac{2}{9} + \frac{4}{9}$

$= \frac{6}{9}$

Total fraction mowed during

first two evenings = $\frac{2}{3}$

(Use Strategy 3: The whole equals the sum of its parts.)

Amount left for evening 3 =

1 whole lawn $- \frac{2}{3}$ already mowed   ③

Amount left for evening 3 = $\frac{1}{3}$ ④

Given: Lawn area = 108.6 square feet

Multiplying ③ by ④, we get

Amount left for eveing 3 = $\frac{1}{3} \times 108.6$ square feet

Amount left for evening 3 = 36.2 square feet

(Math Refresher #200 and #109)

16. **(D)** Choice D is correct. **(Use Strategy 2: Translate from words to algebra.)**

$$N + 6N + 9N = 16N$$

Any divisor of 16 or of N will divide $16N$.

(Use Strategy 8: When all choices must be tested, start with Choice E.) Starting with Choice E, we see 16 divides $16N$ evenly. Choice D, however, does *not* divide $16N$ evenly. Thus we have found the answer.

(Math Refresher #200 and #431)

17. **(D)** Choice D is correct.

We are given: $x = 3a - 18$ ①

$5y = 3a + 7$ ②

We need $5y - x$.   ③

(Use Strategy 13: Find unknown expressions by subtracting equations.) Subtracting ① from ②, we get

$$5y - x = 3a + 7 - (3a - 18)$$
$$= 3a + 7 - 3a + 18$$
$$5y - x = 25 \text{ (Answer)}$$

(Math Refresher #406)

18. **(C)** Choice C is correct. A line and a circle in the same plane can intersect either in no points, in one point (as a tangent), or in two points.

So any two people can remain, representing the intersection of the straight line between them and the circumference of the circle. All others must move. Therefore, $9 - 2 = 7$ must move.

(Logical Reasoning)

19. **(B)** Choice B is correct. **(Use Strategy 2: Translate from words to algebra.)** Each complete revolution is one circumference.

one circumference = 120 feet

B completed 600 revolutions.

Total distance =

(600 revolutions)(120 feet/revolution)

Total distance = 600×120 feet

(Use Strategy 9: Know the rate, time and distance relationship.)

Time for B = $\dfrac{\text{Total distance}}{\text{Rate}}$ =

$\dfrac{600 \times 120 \text{ feet}}{8 \text{ feet/second}}$

(Use Strategy 19: Factor and reduce.)

$\dfrac{600 \times \cancel{8} \times 15 \text{ feet}}{\cancel{8} \text{ feet/second}}$

Time for B = 9,000 seconds

A traveled at 5 feet/second
A's total distance is

5 feet/second $\times$ 9,000 seconds
= 45,000 feet

Dividing by the circumference of 120 feet, we have

number of revolutions = $\dfrac{45,000 \text{ feet}}{120 \text{ feet/revolution}}$

(Use Strategy 19: Factor and reduce.)

$\dfrac{\cancel{3} \times 15 \times \cancel{10} \times 25 \times \cancel{4}}{\cancel{3} \times \cancel{4} \times \cancel{10}}$

375 revolutions (*Answer*)
(Math Refresher #200, #201, and #202)

20. **(D)** Choice D is correct. **(Use Strategy 2: Translate from words to algebra.)** If the sum of consecutive integers is 0, then for every positive, we need a matching negative. Thus, the 11 members are A are:

$$-5 -4 -3 -2 -1 +0 +1 +2 +3 +4 +5 = 0 \quad \boxed{1}$$

Five consecutive integers in B whose sum is 5 are:

$$-1 +0 +1 +2 +3 = 5 \quad \boxed{2}$$

All of B's members are in A. What is left is $-5\ -4\ -3\ -2\ +4\ +5$. Thus, 6 members of A are *not* in B.

(Math Refresher #200 and Logical Reasoning)

21. **(A)** Choice A is correct. **(Use Strategy 2: Translate from words to algebra.)**

Given $\dfrac{4}{5} \times 100$ are male $=$

$$\dfrac{4}{5} \times 5 \times 20 = 80 \text{ males} \quad \boxed{1}$$

Given $\dfrac{1}{4} \times 100$ are Blonde $=$

$$\dfrac{1}{4} \times 4 \times 25 = 25 \text{ Blondes} \quad \boxed{2}$$

(Use Strategy 17: Use the given information effectively.) Adding $\boxed{1}$ and $\boxed{2}$ together $= 105$
But there are only 100 people.
So there must be at least $105 - 100 = 5$ Blonde males at minimum.

(Math Refresher #200 and Logical Reasoning)

22. **(D)** Choice D is correct. The key to this problem is to find the area of the shaded region in terms of known quantities.
(Use Strategy 3: The whole equals the sum of its parts.) Area of shaded region and also the area of the rectangle

$$= \text{Area of triangle } - \text{ Area of square}$$
$$= x^2\sqrt{3} - x^2$$
$$= x^2(\sqrt{3} - 1)$$

We are given that an unknown rectangle
has width $= x$ $\qquad\qquad\boxed{1}$
and area $= x^2(\sqrt{3} - 1)$ $\qquad\boxed{2}$

Since length $\times$ width $=$ area,
length $=$ area $\div$ width $\qquad\boxed{3}$
Substituting $\boxed{1}$ and $\boxed{2}$ into $\boxed{3}$, we have

$$\text{length of rectangle} = \dfrac{x^2(\sqrt{3} - 1)}{x}$$

$$\text{length of rectangle} = x(\sqrt{3} - 1)$$

(Math Refresher #303, #304, and #306)

23. **(A)** Choice A is correct.

(Use Strategy 5: Average
$$= \dfrac{\text{Sum of values}}{\text{Total number of values}})$$

$$p = \dfrac{x + y}{2} \quad \boxed{1}$$

$$q = \dfrac{y + z}{2} \quad \boxed{2}$$

$$r = \dfrac{x + z}{2} \quad \boxed{3}$$

(Use Strategy 13: Find unknown expressions by adding equations.) Adding $\boxed{1}$, $\boxed{2}$ and $\boxed{3}$ we get

$$p + q + r = \dfrac{x + y}{2} + \dfrac{y + z}{2} + \dfrac{x + z}{2}$$

$$= \dfrac{2x + 2y + 2z}{2}$$

$$p + q + r = x + y + z \quad \boxed{4}$$

The average of x, y and $z = \dfrac{x + y + z}{3} \quad \boxed{5}$

Substitute $\boxed{4}$ into $\boxed{5}$. We have

The average of x, y and $z = \dfrac{p + q + r}{3}$ *(Answer)*

(Math Refresher #601 and #109)

24. **(E)** Choice E is correct. **(Use Strategy 11: Use new definitions carefully.)**

Given:

$$f(x) = 12x + 8 \quad \boxed{1}$$
$$\text{and } f(x) \div f(0) = 2x \quad \boxed{2}$$

Calculate $f(0)$:

$$f(0) = 12(0) + 8 = 8 \quad \boxed{3}$$

Substitute $\boxed{1}$ and $\boxed{3}$ into $\boxed{2}$:

$$\dfrac{12x + 8}{8} = 2x \quad \boxed{4}$$

Multiply both sides by $\boxed{4}$ by 8:

$$12x + 8 = 16x$$
or $\qquad 8 = 4x$
or $\qquad x = 2$ *(Answer)*

(Math Refresher #431 and #406)

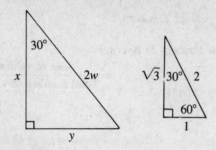

25. **(A)** Choice A is correct. **(Use Strategy 18: Remember special right triangles.)** The triangle at left (given) is similar to the triangle at right, which is one of the standard triangles.
Corresponding sides of similar triangles are proportional. Thus,

$$\frac{2w}{2} = \frac{y}{1} \text{ and } \frac{2w}{2} = \frac{x}{\sqrt{3}}$$

or $\qquad y = w \text{ and } x = w\sqrt{3}$

$$\text{Area of triangle} = \frac{1}{2}\,(\text{base})(\text{height})$$

$$= \frac{1}{2}\,(y)(x)$$

$$= \frac{1}{2}\,(w)(w\sqrt{3})$$

$$\text{Area of triangle} = \frac{\sqrt{3}}{2}\,w^2 \qquad \boxed{1}$$

$$\text{Area of rectangle} = (3w)(w) = 3w^2 \qquad \boxed{2}$$

Using $\boxed{1}$ and $\boxed{2}$, we have

$$\frac{\text{Area of rectangle}}{\text{Area of triangle}} = \frac{3w^2}{\dfrac{\sqrt{3}}{2}\,w^2}$$

$$= \frac{3}{\dfrac{\sqrt{3}}{2}} = 3 \times \frac{2}{\sqrt{3}}$$

$$= \frac{6}{\sqrt{3}} = \frac{6\sqrt{3}}{3} = 2\sqrt{3}$$

or $2\sqrt{3} : 1$ *(Answer)*

(Math Refresher #510, #509, #306, and #304)

Answer Sheet—Practice Test 6

SECTION 1: VERBAL ABILITY

1 Ⓐ Ⓑ Ⓒ Ⓓ Ⓔ   10 Ⓐ Ⓑ Ⓒ Ⓓ Ⓔ   19 Ⓐ Ⓑ Ⓒ Ⓓ Ⓔ   28 Ⓐ Ⓑ Ⓒ Ⓓ Ⓔ   37 Ⓐ Ⓑ Ⓒ Ⓓ Ⓔ
2 Ⓐ Ⓑ Ⓒ Ⓓ Ⓔ   11 Ⓐ Ⓑ Ⓒ Ⓓ Ⓔ   20 Ⓐ Ⓑ Ⓒ Ⓓ Ⓔ   29 Ⓐ Ⓑ Ⓒ Ⓓ Ⓔ   38 Ⓐ Ⓑ Ⓒ Ⓓ Ⓔ
3 Ⓐ Ⓑ Ⓒ Ⓓ Ⓔ   12 Ⓐ Ⓑ Ⓒ Ⓓ Ⓔ   21 Ⓐ Ⓑ Ⓒ Ⓓ Ⓔ   30 Ⓐ Ⓑ Ⓒ Ⓓ Ⓔ   39 Ⓐ Ⓑ Ⓒ Ⓓ Ⓔ
4 Ⓐ Ⓑ Ⓒ Ⓓ Ⓔ   13 Ⓐ Ⓑ Ⓒ Ⓓ Ⓔ   22 Ⓐ Ⓑ Ⓒ Ⓓ Ⓔ   31 Ⓐ Ⓑ Ⓒ Ⓓ Ⓔ   40 Ⓐ Ⓑ Ⓒ Ⓓ Ⓔ
5 Ⓐ Ⓑ Ⓒ Ⓓ Ⓔ   14 Ⓐ Ⓑ Ⓒ Ⓓ Ⓔ   23 Ⓐ Ⓑ Ⓒ Ⓓ Ⓔ   32 Ⓐ Ⓑ Ⓒ Ⓓ Ⓔ   41 Ⓐ Ⓑ Ⓒ Ⓓ Ⓔ
6 Ⓐ Ⓑ Ⓒ Ⓓ Ⓔ   15 Ⓐ Ⓑ Ⓒ Ⓓ Ⓔ   24 Ⓐ Ⓑ Ⓒ Ⓓ Ⓔ   33 Ⓐ Ⓑ Ⓒ Ⓓ Ⓔ   42 Ⓐ Ⓑ Ⓒ Ⓓ Ⓔ
7 Ⓐ Ⓑ Ⓒ Ⓓ Ⓔ   16 Ⓐ Ⓑ Ⓒ Ⓓ Ⓔ   25 Ⓐ Ⓑ Ⓒ Ⓓ Ⓔ   34 Ⓐ Ⓑ Ⓒ Ⓓ Ⓔ   43 Ⓐ Ⓑ Ⓒ Ⓓ Ⓔ
8 Ⓐ Ⓑ Ⓒ Ⓓ Ⓔ   17 Ⓐ Ⓑ Ⓒ Ⓓ Ⓔ   26 Ⓐ Ⓑ Ⓒ Ⓓ Ⓔ   35 Ⓐ Ⓑ Ⓒ Ⓓ Ⓔ   44 Ⓐ Ⓑ Ⓒ Ⓓ Ⓔ
9 Ⓐ Ⓑ Ⓒ Ⓓ Ⓔ   18 Ⓐ Ⓑ Ⓒ Ⓓ Ⓔ   27 Ⓐ Ⓑ Ⓒ Ⓓ Ⓔ   36 Ⓐ Ⓑ Ⓒ Ⓓ Ⓔ   45 Ⓐ Ⓑ Ⓒ Ⓓ Ⓔ

SECTION 2: MATH ABILITY

1 Ⓐ Ⓑ Ⓒ Ⓓ Ⓔ   6 Ⓐ Ⓑ Ⓒ Ⓓ Ⓔ   11 Ⓐ Ⓑ Ⓒ Ⓓ Ⓔ   16 Ⓐ Ⓑ Ⓒ Ⓓ Ⓔ   21 Ⓐ Ⓑ Ⓒ Ⓓ Ⓔ
2 Ⓐ Ⓑ Ⓒ Ⓓ Ⓔ   7 Ⓐ Ⓑ Ⓒ Ⓓ Ⓔ   12 Ⓐ Ⓑ Ⓒ Ⓓ Ⓔ   17 Ⓐ Ⓑ Ⓒ Ⓓ Ⓔ   22 Ⓐ Ⓑ Ⓒ Ⓓ Ⓔ
3 Ⓐ Ⓑ Ⓒ Ⓓ Ⓔ   8 Ⓐ Ⓑ Ⓒ Ⓓ Ⓔ   13 Ⓐ Ⓑ Ⓒ Ⓓ Ⓔ   18 Ⓐ Ⓑ Ⓒ Ⓓ Ⓔ   23 Ⓐ Ⓑ Ⓒ Ⓓ Ⓔ
4 Ⓐ Ⓑ Ⓒ Ⓓ Ⓔ   9 Ⓐ Ⓑ Ⓒ Ⓓ Ⓔ   14 Ⓐ Ⓑ Ⓒ Ⓓ Ⓔ   19 Ⓐ Ⓑ Ⓒ Ⓓ Ⓔ   24 Ⓐ Ⓑ Ⓒ Ⓓ Ⓔ
5 Ⓐ Ⓑ Ⓒ Ⓓ Ⓔ   10 Ⓐ Ⓑ Ⓒ Ⓓ Ⓔ   15 Ⓐ Ⓑ Ⓒ Ⓓ Ⓔ   20 Ⓐ Ⓑ Ⓒ Ⓓ Ⓔ   25 Ⓐ Ⓑ Ⓒ Ⓓ Ⓔ

SECTION 3: STANDARD WRITTEN ENGLISH

1 Ⓐ Ⓑ Ⓒ Ⓓ Ⓔ   11 Ⓐ Ⓑ Ⓒ Ⓓ Ⓔ   21 Ⓐ Ⓑ Ⓒ Ⓓ Ⓔ   31 Ⓐ Ⓑ Ⓒ Ⓓ Ⓔ   41 Ⓐ Ⓑ Ⓒ Ⓓ Ⓔ
2 Ⓐ Ⓑ Ⓒ Ⓓ Ⓔ   12 Ⓐ Ⓑ Ⓒ Ⓓ Ⓔ   22 Ⓐ Ⓑ Ⓒ Ⓓ Ⓔ   32 Ⓐ Ⓑ Ⓒ Ⓓ Ⓔ   42 Ⓐ Ⓑ Ⓒ Ⓓ Ⓔ
3 Ⓐ Ⓑ Ⓒ Ⓓ Ⓔ   13 Ⓐ Ⓑ Ⓒ Ⓓ Ⓔ   23 Ⓐ Ⓑ Ⓒ Ⓓ Ⓔ   33 Ⓐ Ⓑ Ⓒ Ⓓ Ⓔ   43 Ⓐ Ⓑ Ⓒ Ⓓ Ⓔ
4 Ⓐ Ⓑ Ⓒ Ⓓ Ⓔ   14 Ⓐ Ⓑ Ⓒ Ⓓ Ⓔ   24 Ⓐ Ⓑ Ⓒ Ⓓ Ⓔ   34 Ⓐ Ⓑ Ⓒ Ⓓ Ⓔ   44 Ⓐ Ⓑ Ⓒ Ⓓ Ⓔ
5 Ⓐ Ⓑ Ⓒ Ⓓ Ⓔ   15 Ⓐ Ⓑ Ⓒ Ⓓ Ⓔ   25 Ⓐ Ⓑ Ⓒ Ⓓ Ⓔ   35 Ⓐ Ⓑ Ⓒ Ⓓ Ⓔ   45 Ⓐ Ⓑ Ⓒ Ⓓ Ⓔ
6 Ⓐ Ⓑ Ⓒ Ⓓ Ⓔ   16 Ⓐ Ⓑ Ⓒ Ⓓ Ⓔ   26 Ⓐ Ⓑ Ⓒ Ⓓ Ⓔ   36 Ⓐ Ⓑ Ⓒ Ⓓ Ⓔ   46 Ⓐ Ⓑ Ⓒ Ⓓ Ⓔ
7 Ⓐ Ⓑ Ⓒ Ⓓ Ⓔ   17 Ⓐ Ⓑ Ⓒ Ⓓ Ⓔ   27 Ⓐ Ⓑ Ⓒ Ⓓ Ⓔ   37 Ⓐ Ⓑ Ⓒ Ⓓ Ⓔ   47 Ⓐ Ⓑ Ⓒ Ⓓ Ⓔ
8 Ⓐ Ⓑ Ⓒ Ⓓ Ⓔ   18 Ⓐ Ⓑ Ⓒ Ⓓ Ⓔ   28 Ⓐ Ⓑ Ⓒ Ⓓ Ⓔ   38 Ⓐ Ⓑ Ⓒ Ⓓ Ⓔ   48 Ⓐ Ⓑ Ⓒ Ⓓ Ⓔ
9 Ⓐ Ⓑ Ⓒ Ⓓ Ⓔ   19 Ⓐ Ⓑ Ⓒ Ⓓ Ⓔ   29 Ⓐ Ⓑ Ⓒ Ⓓ Ⓔ   39 Ⓐ Ⓑ Ⓒ Ⓓ Ⓔ   49 Ⓐ Ⓑ Ⓒ Ⓓ Ⓔ
10 Ⓐ Ⓑ Ⓒ Ⓓ Ⓔ   20 Ⓐ Ⓑ Ⓒ Ⓓ Ⓔ   30 Ⓐ Ⓑ Ⓒ Ⓓ Ⓔ   40 Ⓐ Ⓑ Ⓒ Ⓓ Ⓔ   50 Ⓐ Ⓑ Ⓒ Ⓓ Ⓔ

SECTION 4: VERBAL ABILITY

1 Ⓐ Ⓑ Ⓒ Ⓓ Ⓔ   9 Ⓐ Ⓑ Ⓒ Ⓓ Ⓔ   17 Ⓐ Ⓑ Ⓒ Ⓓ Ⓔ   25 Ⓐ Ⓑ Ⓒ Ⓓ Ⓔ   33 Ⓐ Ⓑ Ⓒ Ⓓ Ⓔ
2 Ⓐ Ⓑ Ⓒ Ⓓ Ⓔ   10 Ⓐ Ⓑ Ⓒ Ⓓ Ⓔ   18 Ⓐ Ⓑ Ⓒ Ⓓ Ⓔ   26 Ⓐ Ⓑ Ⓒ Ⓓ Ⓔ   34 Ⓐ Ⓑ Ⓒ Ⓓ Ⓔ
3 Ⓐ Ⓑ Ⓒ Ⓓ Ⓔ   11 Ⓐ Ⓑ Ⓒ Ⓓ Ⓔ   19 Ⓐ Ⓑ Ⓒ Ⓓ Ⓔ   27 Ⓐ Ⓑ Ⓒ Ⓓ Ⓔ   35 Ⓐ Ⓑ Ⓒ Ⓓ Ⓔ
4 Ⓐ Ⓑ Ⓒ Ⓓ Ⓔ   12 Ⓐ Ⓑ Ⓒ Ⓓ Ⓔ   20 Ⓐ Ⓑ Ⓒ Ⓓ Ⓔ   28 Ⓐ Ⓑ Ⓒ Ⓓ Ⓔ   36 Ⓐ Ⓑ Ⓒ Ⓓ Ⓔ
5 Ⓐ Ⓑ Ⓒ Ⓓ Ⓔ   13 Ⓐ Ⓑ Ⓒ Ⓓ Ⓔ   21 Ⓐ Ⓑ Ⓒ Ⓓ Ⓔ   29 Ⓐ Ⓑ Ⓒ Ⓓ Ⓔ   37 Ⓐ Ⓑ Ⓒ Ⓓ Ⓔ
6 Ⓐ Ⓑ Ⓒ Ⓓ Ⓔ   14 Ⓐ Ⓑ Ⓒ Ⓓ Ⓔ   22 Ⓐ Ⓑ Ⓒ Ⓓ Ⓔ   30 Ⓐ Ⓑ Ⓒ Ⓓ Ⓔ   38 Ⓐ Ⓑ Ⓒ Ⓓ Ⓔ
7 Ⓐ Ⓑ Ⓒ Ⓓ Ⓔ   15 Ⓐ Ⓑ Ⓒ Ⓓ Ⓔ   23 Ⓐ Ⓑ Ⓒ Ⓓ Ⓔ   31 Ⓐ Ⓑ Ⓒ Ⓓ Ⓔ   39 Ⓐ Ⓑ Ⓒ Ⓓ Ⓔ
8 Ⓐ Ⓑ Ⓒ Ⓓ Ⓔ   16 Ⓐ Ⓑ Ⓒ Ⓓ Ⓔ   24 Ⓐ Ⓑ Ⓒ Ⓓ Ⓔ   32 Ⓐ Ⓑ Ⓒ Ⓓ Ⓔ   40 Ⓐ Ⓑ Ⓒ Ⓓ Ⓔ

SECTION 5: MATH ABILITY

1 Ⓐ Ⓑ Ⓒ Ⓓ Ⓔ   8 Ⓐ Ⓑ Ⓒ Ⓓ Ⓔ   15 Ⓐ Ⓑ Ⓒ Ⓓ Ⓔ   22 Ⓐ Ⓑ Ⓒ Ⓓ Ⓔ   29 Ⓐ Ⓑ Ⓒ Ⓓ Ⓔ
2 Ⓐ Ⓑ Ⓒ Ⓓ Ⓔ   9 Ⓐ Ⓑ Ⓒ Ⓓ Ⓔ   16 Ⓐ Ⓑ Ⓒ Ⓓ Ⓔ   23 Ⓐ Ⓑ Ⓒ Ⓓ Ⓔ   30 Ⓐ Ⓑ Ⓒ Ⓓ Ⓔ
3 Ⓐ Ⓑ Ⓒ Ⓓ Ⓔ   10 Ⓐ Ⓑ Ⓒ Ⓓ Ⓔ   17 Ⓐ Ⓑ Ⓒ Ⓓ Ⓔ   24 Ⓐ Ⓑ Ⓒ Ⓓ Ⓔ   31 Ⓐ Ⓑ Ⓒ Ⓓ Ⓔ
4 Ⓐ Ⓑ Ⓒ Ⓓ Ⓔ   11 Ⓐ Ⓑ Ⓒ Ⓓ Ⓔ   18 Ⓐ Ⓑ Ⓒ Ⓓ Ⓔ   25 Ⓐ Ⓑ Ⓒ Ⓓ Ⓔ   32 Ⓐ Ⓑ Ⓒ Ⓓ Ⓔ
5 Ⓐ Ⓑ Ⓒ Ⓓ Ⓔ   12 Ⓐ Ⓑ Ⓒ Ⓓ Ⓔ   19 Ⓐ Ⓑ Ⓒ Ⓓ Ⓔ   26 Ⓐ Ⓑ Ⓒ Ⓓ Ⓔ   33 Ⓐ Ⓑ Ⓒ Ⓓ Ⓔ
6 Ⓐ Ⓑ Ⓒ Ⓓ Ⓔ   13 Ⓐ Ⓑ Ⓒ Ⓓ Ⓔ   20 Ⓐ Ⓑ Ⓒ Ⓓ Ⓔ   27 Ⓐ Ⓑ Ⓒ Ⓓ Ⓔ   34 Ⓐ Ⓑ Ⓒ Ⓓ Ⓔ
7 Ⓐ Ⓑ Ⓒ Ⓓ Ⓔ   14 Ⓐ Ⓑ Ⓒ Ⓓ Ⓔ   21 Ⓐ Ⓑ Ⓒ Ⓓ Ⓔ   28 Ⓐ Ⓑ Ⓒ Ⓓ Ⓔ   35 Ⓐ Ⓑ Ⓒ Ⓓ Ⓔ

SECTION 6: MATH ABILITY

1 Ⓐ Ⓑ Ⓒ Ⓓ Ⓔ   8 Ⓐ Ⓑ Ⓒ Ⓓ Ⓔ   15 Ⓐ Ⓑ Ⓒ Ⓓ Ⓔ   22 Ⓐ Ⓑ Ⓒ Ⓓ Ⓔ   29 Ⓐ Ⓑ Ⓒ Ⓓ Ⓔ
2 Ⓐ Ⓑ Ⓒ Ⓓ Ⓔ   9 Ⓐ Ⓑ Ⓒ Ⓓ Ⓔ   16 Ⓐ Ⓑ Ⓒ Ⓓ Ⓔ   23 Ⓐ Ⓑ Ⓒ Ⓓ Ⓔ   30 Ⓐ Ⓑ Ⓒ Ⓓ Ⓔ
3 Ⓐ Ⓑ Ⓒ Ⓓ Ⓔ   10 Ⓐ Ⓑ Ⓒ Ⓓ Ⓔ   17 Ⓐ Ⓑ Ⓒ Ⓓ Ⓔ   24 Ⓐ Ⓑ Ⓒ Ⓓ Ⓔ   31 Ⓐ Ⓑ Ⓒ Ⓓ Ⓔ
4 Ⓐ Ⓑ Ⓒ Ⓓ Ⓔ   11 Ⓐ Ⓑ Ⓒ Ⓓ Ⓔ   18 Ⓐ Ⓑ Ⓒ Ⓓ Ⓔ   25 Ⓐ Ⓑ Ⓒ Ⓓ Ⓔ   32 Ⓐ Ⓑ Ⓒ Ⓓ Ⓔ
5 Ⓐ Ⓑ Ⓒ Ⓓ Ⓔ   12 Ⓐ Ⓑ Ⓒ Ⓓ Ⓔ   19 Ⓐ Ⓑ Ⓒ Ⓓ Ⓔ   26 Ⓐ Ⓑ Ⓒ Ⓓ Ⓔ   33 Ⓐ Ⓑ Ⓒ Ⓓ Ⓔ
6 Ⓐ Ⓑ Ⓒ Ⓓ Ⓔ   13 Ⓐ Ⓑ Ⓒ Ⓓ Ⓔ   20 Ⓐ Ⓑ Ⓒ Ⓓ Ⓔ   27 Ⓐ Ⓑ Ⓒ Ⓓ Ⓔ   34 Ⓐ Ⓑ Ⓒ Ⓓ Ⓔ
7 Ⓐ Ⓑ Ⓒ Ⓓ Ⓔ   14 Ⓐ Ⓑ Ⓒ Ⓓ Ⓔ   21 Ⓐ Ⓑ Ⓒ Ⓓ Ⓔ   28 Ⓐ Ⓑ Ⓒ Ⓓ Ⓔ   35 Ⓐ Ⓑ Ⓒ Ⓓ Ⓔ

SAT Practice Test 6

SECTION 1 VERBAL ABILITY
30 MINUTES 45 QUESTIONS

For each question in this section, choose the best answer and blacken the corresponding space on the answer sheet.

Each question below consists of a word in capital letters, followed by five lettered words or phrases. Choose the word or phrase that is most nearly *opposite* in meaning to the word in capital letters. Since some of the questions require you to distinguish fine shades of meaning, consider all the choices before deciding which is best.

Example:

GOOD: (A) sour (B) bad (C) red
(D) hot (E) ugly

Ⓐ ● Ⓒ Ⓓ Ⓔ

1. PROPAGATE: (A) acknowledge (B) amass
(C) limit (D) question (E) suspect

2. NAIVE: (A) competitive (B) alert
(C) disruptive (D) celebrated (E) complex

3. ACME: (A) shrewd move (B) sharp advance
(C) selfish proposal (D) lowest point
(E) unexpected event

4. KINDLE: (A) overcook (B) reconsider
(C) damage (D) resist (E) relax

5. UPBRAID: (A) compliment (B) volunteer
(C) isolate (D) clarify (E) downgrade

6. BURLY: (A) downcast (B) delicate
(C) tumultuous (D) appreciative
(E) conservative

7. HILARITY: (A) willingness (B) sadness
(C) silence (D) clarity (E) feebleness

8. DELECTABLE: (A) disagreeable
(B) retarded (C) disruptive (D) flexible
(E) uncollectible

9. SPURIOUS: (A) watchful (B) downhearted
(C) humorous (D) superficial (E) genuine

10. ANTIPATHY: (A) quick response
(B) vulnerability (C) rapidity (D) attraction
(E) vain effort

11. CORPULENT: (A) insecure (B) curious
(C) logical (D) crooked (E) slender

12. MOLLIFY: (A) change (B) alienate
(C) excite (D) misuse (E) renew

13. DIFFIDENCE: (A) aggressiveness
(B) outrage (C) agreement (D) dignity
(E) slander

14. PERFIDIOUS: (A) curious (B) imperfect
(C) religious (D) faithful (E) advisable

15. CIRCUITOUS: (A) modified (B) direct
(C) clearheaded (D) indefinite (E) irregular

Each sentence below has one or two blanks, each blank indicating that something has been omitted. Beneath the sentence are five lettered words or sets of words. Choose the word or set of words that *best* fits the meaning of the sentence as a whole.

Example:

Although its publicity has been ____, the film itself is intelligent, well-acted, handsomely produced, and altogether ____.

(A) tasteless . . . respectable
(B) extensive . . . moderate
(C) sophisticated . . . amateur
(D) risqué . . . crude
(E) perfect . . . spectacular

● Ⓑ Ⓒ Ⓓ Ⓔ

16. The union struck shortly after midnight after its negotiating committee _____ a company offer of a 20% raise.

(A) applauded (B) rejected (C) considered
(D) postponed (E) accepted

17. The shape and horsepower of auto manufacturers' _____ products are among Detroit's most closely _____ secrets.

(A) union . . . watched
(B) guaranteed . . . dealt
(C) future . . . guarded
(D) labor . . . resolved
(E) reliable . . . financed

18. The report indicates that the crime rate in the United States remains _____ and that one in every three households _____ some form of major crime in any year.

(A) incredible . . . visualizes
(B) astronomical . . . experiences
(C) simultaneous . . . welcomes
(D) unsuccessful . . . initiates
(E) constant . . . anticipates

19. The scientist averred that a nuclear war could
_____ enough smoke and dust to blot out the sun
and freeze the earth.

(A) pervert
(B) extinguish
(C) generate
(D) evaluate
(E) perpetrate

20. The Bank of America sued six employees, charging
them with gross _____ that resulted in huge losses
for the bank.

(A) negligence (B) handling (C) management
(D) attentiveness (E) expenses

Each passage below is followed by questions based on its content. Answer all questions following
a passage on the basis of what is *stated* or *implied* in that passage.

When we use a word in speech and writing, its most
obvious purpose is to point to some thing or relation or
property. This is the word's "meaning." We see a small
four-footed animal on the road and call it a "dog," indi-
5 cating that it is a member of the class of four-footed animals we call dogs. The word "dog" as we have used it
there has a plain, straightforward, "objective" meaning.
We have in no way gone beyond the requirements of exact
scientific description.

10 Let us suppose also that one grandparent of the dog
was a collie, another was an Irish terrier, another a fox
terrier, and the fourth a bulldog. We can express these
facts equally scientifically and objectively by saying that
he is a dog of mixed breed. Still we have in no way gone
15 beyond the requirements of exact scientific description.

Suppose, however, that we had called that same animal
a "mongrel." The matter is more complicated. We have
used a word which objectively means the same as "dog
of mixed breed," but which also arouses in our hearers an
20 emotional attitude of disapproval toward that particular
dog. A word, therefore, can not only indicate an object,
but can also suggest an emotional attitude toward it. Such
suggestion of an emotional attitude does go beyond exact
and scientific discussion because our approvals and dis-
25 approvals are individual—they belong to ourselves and not
to the objects we approve or disapprove of. An animal
which to the mind of its master is a faithful and noble dog
of mixed ancestry may be a "mongrel" to his neighbor
whose chickens are chased by it.

30 Once we are on the lookout for this difference between
"objective" and "emotional" meanings, we shall notice that
words which carry more or less strong suggestions of emotional attitudes are very common and are ordinarily used
in the discussion of such controversial questions as those
35 of politics, morals, and religion. This is one reason why
such controversies cannot yet be settled.

When, during World War II, thoughts were dominated
by emotions, the newspapers contrasted the *heroism* of our
troops with the enemy's *ruthlessness*. Now, with the more
40 objective attitude that has been brought by the lapse of
time, we can look back and see that *heroism* and *ruthlessness* are objectively the same thing, only one word has
an emotional meaning of approval, the other of disapproval. A soldier going forward under shellfire to probable
45 death is doing the same thing whether he is a German or
an American. Applying the word *ruthlessness* to the action
of one and *heroism* to that of the other is to distort reality
by using words to make an emotional distinction between
two actions which are objectively identical.

21. According to the passage,

(A) there is no real difference between calling a dog a
mongrel and calling it a dog of mixed breed
(B) "a dog of mixed breed" is an emotional term
(C) "mongrel" is an objective term
(D) words may suggest emotional attitudes as well as
objective meanings
(E) dogs should be treated with consideration

22. The author maintains that in discussing

(A) scientific subjects, emotional words are often used
to make meanings clearer
(B) controversial questions, objective terms are
generally used to help clarify meanings
(C) scientific subjects, objective terms are generally
used in order to avoid controversy
(D) any question, one should at no time use obscene
language
(E) controversial questions, emotional terms are used
very often

23. The author believes that people have disagreements
on many subjects because

(A) people have not yet learned how to get along with
each other without conflict and argument
(B) words used in discussing those subjects carry
emotional overtones which tend to antagonize
people
(C) words with objective meanings mean different
things to different persons, and must be used
carefully
(D) politics, morals, and religion cause controversies
that cannot yet be settled
(E) different languages are used by various nations
throughout the world

24. The passage indicates that in World War II

    (A) our men showed spirit and heroism, while the Germans displayed ruthlessness and savagery

    (B) although our men acted heroically, there were occasions when they were almost as ruthless as the Germans

    (C) there was no difference at all between the actions of the Americans and those of the Germans

    (D) most people thought that both sides had fought equally bravely, but with the passage of time they began to realize how ruthless the Germans had really been

    (E) the German soldiers were, by nature, much crueler and much less civilized generally than the American soldiers

25. The tone of the passage is that of

    (A) controlled emotion
    (B) cautious neutrality
    (C) guarded partiality
    (D) reasonable compromise
    (E) studied objectivity

Many of the unfavorable changes in the climatic factors in a city can be mitigated or reversed by growing plants, and by installing trees and green belts. Trees have a material effect on the dust content of the city's atmosphere.
5 Comparative measurements taken in thoroughfares lined with trees and those free from trees show that with a comparable traffic flow the dust content in the road lined with trees is about 70% less. The reason for this is mainly that the dust adheres to the surface of the leaves and branches
10 or settles more easily between the trees because of reduced wind pressure.
    The reduction in the dust content of the air naturally has an influence on other climatic elements dependent on the dust. As dust is responsible both for the haze canopy
15 (and the consequent reduction in hours of sunshine and of ultra-violet irradiation) and for the increase in fog (due to the condensation of water vapor), a reduction in dust by trees can have a favorable effect on the frequency and density of the haze canopy and fog.
20   A second important characteristic of trees in city precincts is the influence they exert on temperature and wind movement. Compared with country districts, the temperature in cities is higher. In the hot season of the year, in which the higher temperatures in cities can prove partic-
25 ularly unpleasant, trees can help to ameliorate the climate. In the summer, trees provide areas of shade, which because of the difference in temperature distribution sets up special air currents, which lead, in turn, to a pleasant, gentle wind movement.

Apart from these physically measurable positive characteristics, trees and green belts in cities also have an esthetic and psychological function. They make a vital contribution to the beauty of a city and furnish identification points. A public opinion poll in big cities on the question "What appeals to you most about this city?" elicited the reply in most cases that verdure in the city was the prime attraction. Appreciation of this often unconscious attitude of city dwellers toward green belts accounts for the sharp reactions, from representative institutions, to the plans of municipal authorities to cut down fine trees to make way for new buildings or to widen streets. As the city dweller is usually able to visit country districts for recreational purposes only on holidays and weekends, trees and parks represent a vital opportunity to install at least a tiny fragment of nature in the city.

26. The most appropriate title for this passage would be

    (A) Pollution and City Weather
    (B) Trees Go to Town
    (C) Can Weather Be Controlled?
    (D) Trees: Regulators of City Climate
    (E) Trees and the Well-Being of Cities

27. Which of the following general differences between city and country climates are stated or implied in the passage?

    I. Cities have higher temperatures than the surrounding country areas.
    II. Cities have less fog than the surrounding country areas.
    III. Cities receive more solar radiation than the surrounding country areas.

    (A) I only
    (B) III only
    (C) I and II
    (D) II and III
    (E) I, II, and III

28. According to the passage, with what feeling would city dwellers most likely react if the government decided to remove trees in order to widen the streets?

    (A) strong criticism
    (B) obvious indifference
    (C) civic pride
    (D) questioning curiosity
    (E) mild surprise

29. With which of the following statements would the author most likely agree?

 (A) Trees are useful and should be planted in cities.
 (B) Cars causing pollution should be banned from cities.
 (C) Parks in cities waste vital space.
 (D) Shade trees cause excess air movement.
 (E) Lining streets with trees will result in a minor reduction in airborne dust.

30. For what purpose are the two parenthetical statements in the second paragraph used?

 (A) To express a cause—then an effect
 (B) To express an effect—then a cause
 (C) To express two effects
 (D) To express two causes
 (E) To express neither a cause nor an effect

Select the word or set of words that *best* completes each of the following sentences.

31. Some researchers believe that fat people _____ carbohydrates and gobble down snacks because these foods act on the brain to improve their _____ .

 (A) crave . . . moods
 (B) fancy . . . figures
 (C) study . . . physiques
 (D) enjoy . . . diets
 (E) avoid . . . senses

32. Britain's coal miners called off their _____ strike today, almost a year after it began, and will _____ their jobs at once.

 (A) experimental . . . fill
 (B) shameful . . . demand
 (C) unpopular . . . expect
 (D) querulous . . . seek
 (E) turbulent . . . resume

33. Hunger has reached epidemic proportions nationwide, leaving up to 20 million people _____ to illness and fear.

 (A) agreeable   (B) vulnerable   (C) obvious
 (D) acclimated   (E) sensitive

34. The _____ of thousands of bicycles along city streets make many Japanese regard bikes as _____ , creating serious traffic problems.

 (A) sight . . . a relief
 (B) noise . . . an aftermath
 (C) sprawl . . . a menace
 (D) pollution . . . a necessity
 (E) carelessness . . . an oddity

35. Consumption of red meat has _____ because its fat content has become a worrisome and _____ issue.

 (A) yielded . . . debated
 (B) skyrocketed . . . interesting
 (C) abounded . . . serious
 (D) stabilized . . . newsworthy
 (E) decreased . . . controversial

Each question below consists of a related pair of words or phrases, followed by five lettered pairs of words or phrases. Select the lettered pair that *best* expresses a relationship similar to that expressed in the original pair.

Example:

YAWN : BOREDOM : :   (A) dream : sleep
(B) anger : madness   (C) smile : amusement
(D) face : expression   (E) impatience : rebellion
         Ⓐ Ⓑ ● Ⓓ Ⓔ

36. CONTRITE : CAREFREE : :

 (A) commonplace : obvious
 (B) accidental : injurious
 (C) descriptive : informational
 (D) contrary : doubtful
 (E) dignified : informal

37. TAUNT : VILIFY : :

 (A) favor : assist
 (B) promote : discourage
 (C) chuckle : guffaw
 (D) remark : imply
 (E) flaunt : display

38. MINT : MONEY : :

 (A) pound : gold
 (B) mail : stamp
 (C) inform : notice
 (D) obliterate : movement
 (E) publish : literature

39. CYNIC : GULLIBLE : :

 (A) artist : creative
 (B) pacifist : pugnacious
 (C) teacher : instructive
 (D) lion : timid
 (E) violinist : orchestral

40. FURNITURE : CHAIR : :

(A) general : colonel
(B) newspaper : magazine :
(C) drizzle : raindrop
(D) food : bread
(E) sedan : automobile

41. OVERHEAR : EAVESDROP : :

(A) tremble : frighten
(B) underplay : exaggerate
(C) speak : inform
(D) observe : overlook
(E) amble : prowl

42. WHEEL : BICYCLE : :

(A) propeller : jet
(B) runner : sled
(C) incentive : success
(D) hand : clock
(E) highway : automobile

43. SHARD : GLASS : :

(A) wool : sheep
(B) crumb : cookie
(C) pound : weight
(D) rung : ladder
(E) slice : meat

44. SLUR : SPEECH : :

(A) scribble : writing
(B) crack : pottery
(C) chirp : bird
(D) fester : wound
(E) refresh : sleep

45. PUNCTURE : TIRE : :

(A) pierce : ear
(B) retract : statement
(C) inflate : balloon
(D) catch : fish
(D) owe : favor

S T O P

IF YOU FINISH BEFORE TIME IS CALLED, YOU MAY CHECK YOUR WORK ON THIS SECTION ONLY.
DO NOT WORK ON ANY OTHER SECTION IN THE TEST.

SECTION 2   MATH ABILITY
30 MINUTES   25 QUESTIONS

In this section solve each problem, using any available space on the page for scratchwork. Then decide which is the best of the choices given and blacken the corresponding space on the answer sheet.

The following information is for your reference in solving some of the problems.

Circle of radius r: Area = πr^2; Circumference = $2\pi r$
   The number of degrees of arc in a circle is 360.
The measure in degrees of a straight angle is 180.

Definitions of symbols:

=	is equal to		$\leqq$	is less than or equal to
$\neq$	is unequal to		$\geqq$	is greater than or equal to
<	is less than		$\parallel$	is parallel to
>	is greater than		$\perp$	is perpendicular to

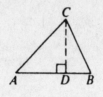

Triangle: The sum of the measure in degrees of the angles of a triangle is 180.
If $\angle CDA$ is a right angle, then

(1)   area of $\triangle ABC = \dfrac{AB \times CD}{2}$

(2) $AC^2 = AD^2 + DC^2$

Note: Figures which accompany problems in this test are intended to provide information useful in solving the problems. They are drawn as accurately as possible EXCEPT when it is stated in a specific problem that its figure is not drawn to scale. All figures lie in a plane unless otherwise indicated. All numbers used are real numbers.

1. What is another expression for 8 less than the quotient of x and 3?

   (A) $\dfrac{x - 8}{3}$ (B) $\dfrac{x}{3} - 8$ (C) $8 - 3x$

   (D) $3x - 8$ (E) $3(8 - x)$

2. Each of Phil's buckets have a capacity of 11 gallons. Each of Mark's buckets can hold 8 gallons. How much more water, in gallons, can 7 of Phil's buckets hold than 7 of Mark's buckets?

   (A) 3   (B) 7   (C) 21   (D) 24   (E) 56

3. Which of the following is *not* equal to a whole number?

   (A) $\dfrac{66 - 36}{3}$ (B) $\dfrac{66 + 36}{6}$ (C) $\dfrac{66 + 36}{12}$

   (D) $\dfrac{66 - 36}{15}$ (E) $\dfrac{66 + 36}{17}$

4. Dick has $15.25 and spent $7.50 at the sporting goods store. How much money does he have left?

   (A) $0.25   (B) $1.75   (C) $6.75   (D) $7.75
   (E) $8.25

5. $(.67)^2 - 2(.62)(.67) + (.62)^2 =$

   (A) 25.0000   (B) 2.5000   (C) 0.2500
   (D) 0.0250   (E) 0.0025

6. If $6 \times 7 \times 8 \times 9 = \dfrac{12 \times 14 \times 18}{x}$, then $x =$

   (A) $\dfrac{1}{2}$ (B) 1   (C) 4   (D) 8   (E) 12

7. If $5x = 3$, then $(5x + 3)^2 =$

   (A) 0   (B) 9   (C) 25   (D) 36   (E) 64

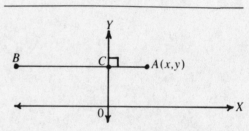

8. If $3AC = BC$ in the figure above, what are the coordinates of B?

   (A) $(x, 3y)$ (B) $(-x, 3y)$
   (C) $(3x, y)$ (D) $(-3x, y)$ (E) $(-3x, + 3y)$

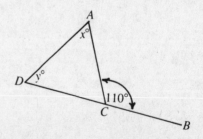

9. In the figure above, $m\angle ACB = 110°$ and $AC = CD$. What is the value of $2y$?

   (A) 45   (B) 70   (C) 90   (D) 110   (E) 140

10. If $(x + y)^2 = 9$, what is $x + y$?

(A) 0 (B) 3 (C) 9 (D) 27 (E) It cannot be determined from the information given.

11. The average (arithmetic mean) of five numbers is 34. If three of the numbers are 28, 30, and 32, what is the sum of the other two?

(A) 40 (B) 50 (C) 60 (D) 70 (E) 80

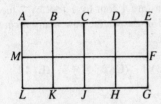

12. In the figure above, rectangle $AEGL$ has been divided into 8 congruent squares. If the perimeter of one of these squares is 16, what is the value of $AE + MF + LG + AL + BK + CJ + DH + EG$?

(A) 32 (B) 44 (C) 88 (D) 128 (E) 176

13. For any positive integer x, $\textcircled{x} = \dfrac{x^2}{3}$ and $\boxed{x} = \dfrac{9}{x}$. What is an expression for $\textcircled{x} \times \boxed{x}$?

(A) $3x$ (B) x (C) 1 (D) $\dfrac{x^3}{64}$ (E) $27x^3$

14. If each of the 3 distinct points A, B and C are the same distance from point D, which of the following could be true?

  I. A, B, C and D are the four vertices of a square.
  II. A, B, C and D lie on the circumference of a circle.
  III. A, B and C lie on the circumference of the circle whose center is D.

(A) I only (B) II only (C) III only
(D) II and III only (E) I, II and III

15. If $x + by = 3x + y = 5$ and $y = 2$, then $b =$

(A) 0 (B) 1 (C) 2 (D) 3 (E) 4

16. There are 2 boys and 3 girls in the class. The ratio of boys to girls in the class is equal to all of the following except

(A) 4:6 (B) 9:12 (C) 6:9 (D) 12:18 (E) 18:27

17. At a certain small town, p gallons of gasoline are needed per month for each car in town. At this rate, if there are r cars in town, how long, in months, will q gallons last?

(A) $\dfrac{pq}{r}$ (B) $\dfrac{qr}{p}$ (C) $\dfrac{r}{pq}$

(D) $\dfrac{q}{pr}$ (E) pqr

18. What fraction of 1 week is 24 min?

(A) $\dfrac{1}{60}$ (B) $\dfrac{1}{168}$ (C) $\dfrac{1}{420}$ (D) $\dfrac{1}{1440}$ (E) $\dfrac{1}{10080}$

Questions 19–20

The next two questions refer to the following definition:
  The l-length of the segment from point A to point B is $B - A$.

19. What is the l-length from -3 to 3?

(A) -6 (B) -3 (C) 0 (D) 3 (E) 6

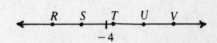

20. Of all segments beginning at -4 and ending at one of the integers indicated above on the number line, which segment has the *least* l-length?

(A) R (B) S (C) T (D) U (E) V

21. If the sum of 5 consecutive positive integers is w, in terms of w, which of the following represents the sum of the next 5 consecutive positive integers?

(A) $w + 5$ (B) $5w + 5$
(C) $5w + 25$ (D) $w + 25$ (E) $w^2 + 25$

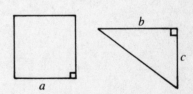

22. If the area of the square is twice the area of the triangle and $bc = 100$, then find a^2.

(A) 400 (B) 200 (C) 100 (D) 50 (E) 25

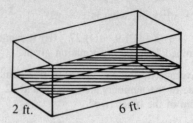

2 ft.   6 ft.

23. In the figure above, $\overline{AB}$ and $\overline{CD}$ are diameters of the circle whose center is O. If the radius of the circle is 2 inches and the sum of the lengths of arcs $\overset{\frown}{AD}$ and $\overset{\frown}{BC}$ is 3π inches, then $y =$

(A) 45 (B) 90 (C) 120 (D) 135 (E) 180

24. Five years ago, Ross was N times as old as Amanda was. If Amanda is now 19 years old, how old is Ross now in terms of N?

(A) $14N - 5$ (B) $14N + 5$ (C) $19N + 5$
(D) $15N + 5$ (E) $19N - 5$

25. The figure above shows water in a tank whose base is 2 feet by 6 feet. If a rectangular solid whose dimensions are 1 foot by 1 foot by 2 feet is totally immersed in the water, how many *inches* will the water rise?

(A) $\dfrac{1}{6}$ (B) 1 (C) 2 (D) 3 (E) 12

S T O P

IF YOU FINISH BEFORE TIME IS CALLED, YOU MAY CHECK YOUR WORK ON THIS SECTION ONLY.
DO NOT WORK ON ANY OTHER SECTION IN THE TEST.

SECTION 3   STANDARD WRITTEN ENGLISH TEST

30 MINUTES   50 QUESTIONS

The questions in this section measure skills that are important to writing well. In particular, they test your ability to recognize and use language that is clear, effective, and correct according to the requirements of standard written English, the kind of English found in most college textbooks.

Directions: The following contain problems in grammar, usage, diction (choice of words), and idiom.

> Some sentences are correct.
> No sentence contains more than one error.

You will find that the error, if there is one, is underlined and lettered. Assume that elements of the sentence that are not underlined are correct and cannot be changed. In choosing answers, follow the requirements of standard written English.

If there is an error, select the *one underlined part* that must be changed to make the sentence correct and blacken the corresponding space on your answer sheet.

If there is no error, blacken answer space Ⓔ

EXAMPLE: SAMPLE ANSWER

Ⓐ Ⓑ ● Ⓓ Ⓔ

The region has a climate so severe that plants
                              A

growing there rarely had been more than twelve
        B   C

inches high. No error.
        D   E

---

1. The reason her and her cousin decided to take the
                  A   B

   train instead of the plane was that there was a
                                     C

   forecast over the radio about an impending storm.
                                    D

   No error.
   E

2. Though Seaver pitched real well, the Orioles scored
       A   B   C

   four runs in the ninth inning as a result of two Met
                                 D

   errors. No error.
           E

3. Jim and him, after spending several hours trying to
            A

   ascertain the whereabouts of the missing children,
                    B

   finally discovered them in their aunt's house.
   C   D

   No error.
   E

4. After the critics see the two plays, they will, as a
       A   B

   result of their experience and background, be able to
              C

   judge which is the most effective and moving.
                          D

   No error.
   E

5. Each of the <u>hotel's 500 rooms</u> <u>were equipped</u> with
           A   B

<u>high</u> quality <u>air conditioning</u> and television. <u>No error.</u>
  C   D   E

6. A textbook <u>used</u> in a college class <u>usually always</u>
           A   B

<u>contains</u> an introduction, a glossary, and
  C

<u>an annotated</u> bibliography. <u>No error.</u>
  D   E

7. On any <u>given</u> weekend—especially holiday
  A   B

<u>weekends</u>—the number of highway deaths <u>is</u>
  C   D

predictable. <u>No error.</u>
          E

8. The <u>youth</u> of today are <u>seemingly</u> more sophisticated
     A   B

than were <u>they're</u> parents <u>at</u> the corresponding age.
          C   D

<u>No error.</u>
  E

9. The sun <u>hadn't hardly</u> set when the mosquitoes began
         A

<u>to sting</u> so <u>annoyingly</u> that we had to <u>run off</u> from
  B   C   D

the picnic grounds. <u>No error.</u>
               E

10. The lilacs in my <u>Uncle Joe's</u> garden smell <u>sweetly</u> <u>at</u>
           A   B   C

<u>this time</u> of the year. <u>No error.</u>
      D   E

11. A wise <u>and</u> experienced administrator <u>will assign</u> a
        A   B

job to <u>whomever</u> is <u>best qualified.</u> <u>No error.</u>
     C   D   E

12. <u>Being that</u> the United States has a food surplus, it is
    A

hard to see why <u>anyone</u> in our country <u>should go</u>
    B   C   D

hungry. <u>No error.</u>
        E

13. Unless <u>there can be some assurance</u> of increased pay,
      A

factory <u>morale</u>, <u>all ready</u> low, will collapse
      B   C

<u>completely.</u> <u>No error.</u>
  D   E

14. A series of debates <u>between</u> the major candidates
      A   B

<u>were</u> scheduled for the Labor Day
  C

<u>weekend.</u> <u>No error.</u>
  D   E

15. As she was small, <u>her</u> huge eyes and her <u>long black</u>
          A   B

<u>hair were</u> neither outstanding <u>or</u> attractive. <u>No error.</u>
  C   D   E

16. We did the job as <u>good</u> as we <u>could</u>; however, it did
     A   B   C

<u>not turn out</u> to be satisfactory. <u>No error.</u>
  D   E

17. If we <u>are given</u> the opportunity to <u>stage</u> a play,
        A   B

<u>whose</u> to decide which play we <u>shall produce?</u>
  C   D

<u>No error.</u>
  E

18. If I <u>would have had</u> more time, I <u>would have written</u>
         A   B

a much <u>more interesting</u> and a <u>far</u> more thorough
       C   D

report. <u>No error.</u>
       E

19. More leisure, <u>as well as</u> an <u>abundance</u> of goods, <u>are</u>
           A   B   C

attainable <u>through</u> automation. <u>No error.</u>
      D   E

20. Morphine and other <u>narcotic drugs</u> are valuable
                 A

<u>medically</u>; if misused, however, <u>it</u> can cause
  B   C

<u>irreparable</u> damage. <u>No error.</u>
  D   E

SAT PRACTICE TEST SIX • 625

21. An old miser who picked up yellow <u>pieces</u> of gold
                                       A

had <u>something</u> of the <u>simple ardor</u> of a child who
       B   C

<u>picks out</u> yellow flowers. <u>No error.</u>
  D   E

22. If we here in America <u>cannot live</u> <u>peaceably</u> and
                       A   B

happily <u>together</u>, we cannot hope that nations which
      C

have different living conditions—different economic

standards, different aspirations, different mores,

different interests—<u>to live</u> peaceably with us.
                    D

<u>No error.</u>
 E

23. Although Marilyn <u>was not invited</u> <u>to the wedding,</u>
                A   B

she would <u>very much</u> have liked
         C

<u>to have gone.</u> <u>No error.</u>
  D   E

24. Every man, woman, and child <u>in this community</u> <u>are</u>
                            A   B

now aware of the <u>terrible consequences</u> <u>of the habit</u>
                C   D

of smoking. <u>No error.</u>
          E

25. The inexperienced teacher had difficulty in

controlling the students <u>whom</u> she <u>was escorting</u> on a
                 A   B

visit to the chemical factory, because it

<u>stunk</u> <u>so.</u> <u>No error.</u>
  C   D   E

Directions: In each of the following sentences, some part or all of the sentence is underlined. Below each sentence you will find five ways of phrasing the underlined part. Select the answer that produces the most effective sentence, one that is clear and exact, without awkwardness or ambiguity, and blacken the corresponding space on your answer sheet. In choosing answers, follow the requirements of standard written English. Choose the answer that best expresses the meaning of the original sentence.

Answer (A) is always the same as the underlined part. Choose answer (A) if you think the original sentence needs no revision.

EXAMPLE:

Laura Ingalls Wilder published her first book <u>and she was sixty-five years old then</u>.
(A) and she was sixty-five years old then
(B) when she was sixty-five years old
(C) at age sixty-five years old
(D) upon reaching sixty-five years
(E) at the time when she was sixty-five

SAMPLE ANSWER

---

26. <u>Tricia Nixon was just engaged and was born on St. Patrick's Day.</u>

    (A) Tricia Nixon was just engaged and was born on St. Patrick's Day.
    (B) Tricia Nixon was just engaged, she was born on St. Patrick's Day.
    (C) On St. Patrick's Day Tricia Nixon was born, she was just engaged.
    (D) Tricia Nixon, born on St. Patrick's Day, was just engaged.
    (E) Tricia Nixon was engaged and she was born on St. Patrick's Day.

27. As no one knows the truth <u>as fully as him, no one but him</u> can provide the testimony needed to clear the accused of the very serious charges.

    (A) as fully as him, no one but him
    (B) as fully as he, no one but him
    (C) as fully as he, no one but he
    (D) as fully as he does, no one but he
    (E) as fully as he does, no one but he alone

28. <u>After the defendant charged him with being prejudiced,</u> the judge withdrew from the case.

    (A) After the defendant charged him with being prejudiced
    (B) On account of the defendant charged him with being prejudiced
    (C) Charging the defendant with being prejudiced
    (D) Upon the defendant charging him with being prejudiced
    (E) The defendant charged him with being prejudiced

29. <u>Although the mourners differed in color and in dress,</u> they all sat silently together for an hour to honor Whitney M. Young, Jr.

    (A) Although the mourners differed in color and in dress
    (B) Because the mourners differed in color and in dress
    (C) The mourners having differed in color and in dress
    (D) When the mourners differed in color and in dress
    (E) The mourners differed in color and in dress

30. <u>To avoid the hot sun, our plans were that we would travel at night.</u>

    (A) To avoid the hot sun, our plans were that we would travel at night.
    (B) To try to avoid the hot sun, our plans were for travel at night.
    (C) Our plans were night travel so that we could avoid the hot sun.
    (D) We planned to travel at night, that's how we would avoid the hot sun.
    (E) To avoid the hot sun, we made plans to travel at night.

31. <u>Whatever she had any thoughts about,</u> they were interrupted as the hotel lobby door opened.

    (A) Whatever she had any thoughts about
    (B) Whatever her thoughts
    (C) Whatever be her thoughts
    (D) What her thoughts were
    (E) What thoughts

32. The use of radar, as well as the two-way radio, <u>make it possible</u> for state troopers to intercept most speeders.

   (A) make it possible
   (B) makes it possible
   (C) allows the possibility
   (D) makes possible
   (E) make it a possibility

33. <u>Irregardless what reasons or excuses are offered,</u> there is only one word for his behavior: cowardice.

   (A) Irregardless what reasons or excuses are offered
   (B) Regardless about what reasons or excuses he may offer
   (C) Since he offered reasons and excuses
   (D) Nevertheless he offered reasons and excuses
   (E) No matter what reasons and excuses are offered

34. <u>What a man cannot state, he does not perfectly know.</u>

   (A) What a man cannot state, he does not perfectly know.
   (B) A man cannot state if he does not perfectly know.
   (C) A man cannot perfectly know if he does not state.
   (D) That which a man cannot state is that which he cannot perfectly know.
   (E) What a man cannot state is the reason he does not perfectly know.

35. Professional writers realize that <u>they cannot hope to effect</u> the reader precisely as they wish without care and practice in the use of words.

   (A) they cannot hope to effect
   (B) they cannot hope to have an effect on
   (C) they cannot hope to affect
   (D) they cannot hope effecting
   (E) they cannot try to affect

36. I've met two men <u>whom, I believe,</u> were policemen.

   (A) whom, I believe,
   (B) who, I believe
   (C) each, I believe,
   (D) and I believe they
   (E) who

37. Such people <u>never have and never will be trusted.</u>

   (A) never have and never will be trusted
   (B) never have and will be trusted
   (C) never have trusted and never will trust
   (D) never have been trusted and never will be trusted
   (E) never have had anyone trust them and never will have anyone trust them

38. Your employer would have been inclined to favor your request <u>if you would have waited for an occasion</u> when he was less busy.

   (A) if you would have waited for an occasion
   (B) if you would only have waited for an occasion
   (C) if you were to have waited for an occasion
   (D) if you waited for an occasion
   (E) if you had waited for an occasion

39. <u>I find Henry James' prose style more difficult to read than James Joyce.</u>

   (A) I find Henry James' prose style more difficult to read than James Joyce.
   (B) I find Henry Jame's prose style more difficult to read than James Joyce'.
   (C) I find Henry James's prose style more difficult to read than James Joyce's.
   (D) I find the prose style of Henry James more difficult to read than James Joyce.
   (E) Henry James' prose style I find more difficult to read than I find James Joyce.

40. <u>Neither Dr. Conant nor his followers knows what to do about the problem.</u>

   (A) Neither Dr. Conant nor his followers knows what to do about the problem.
   (B) Neither Dr. Conant or his followers knows what to do about the problem.
   (C) Neither Dr. Conant nor his followers know what to do about the problem.
   (D) Neither Dr. Conant nor his followers knows what to do as far as the problem goes.
   (E) As to the problem, neither Dr. Conant nor his followers know what to do.

Note: The remaining questions are like those at the beginning of the section.

Directions: For each sentence in which you find an error, select the one underlined part that must be changed to make the sentence correct and blacken the corresponding space on your answer sheet.

If there is no error, blacken answer space Ⓔ

EXAMPLE:

SAMPLE ANSWER

Ⓐ Ⓑ ● Ⓓ Ⓔ

The region has a climate so severe that plants
                          A

growing there rarely had been more than twelve
        B   C

inches high. No error.
        D   E

---

41. The question arises as to who should go out this
                    A   B   C

morning in this below-zero weather to clean the snow

from the garage entrance, you or me. No error.
                          D   E

42. Since I loved her very much when she was alive, I
                A

prize my mother's-in-law picture and I wouldn't sell
            B   C

it for all the money in the world. No error.
        D   E

43. Had I have been in my brother's position, I would
        A   B

have hung up the phone in the middle of the
        C   D

conversation. No error.
                E

44. Lie detectors measure physiological changes
        A   B

in respiration, perspiration, blood pressure, and
            C   D

muscular grip. No error.
                E

45. The company is planning a series of lectures for their
                            A   B

executives so that they may be aware of how to deal
        C

with racial problems that may occur

from time to time. No error.
        D   E

46. In order to calculate the percentage of gain on an
        A   B

investment, we need to know the principal and the
                C   D

amount of profit. No error.
                E

47. Classroom routines are an important factor in keeping
                            A

children constructively busy, in encouraging self-
            B

discipline, and above all, to facilitate learning.
                    C   D

No error.
E

48. Although we were <u>all ready</u> to <u>continue</u> on our trip,
               A   B

our host at the hotel still <u>expressed</u> doubts about the
                      C

ability of the guide we <u>had chose</u>. <u>No error</u>.
                D   E

49. Television, <u>along with</u> other means of
           A

communication, <u>help</u> us to <u>keep</u> informed <u>about</u>
            B   C   D

contemporary affairs. <u>No error</u>.
                E

50. Because of his lack of <u>marketable</u> skills, the high
       A   B

school dropout <u>finds</u> it difficult <u>on succeeding</u> to get
          C   D

employment. <u>No error</u>.
          E

S T O P

**IF YOU FINISH BEFORE TIME IS CALLED, YOU MAY CHECK YOUR WORK ON THIS SECTION ONLY.
DO NOT WORK ON ANY OTHER SECTION IN THE TEST.**

SECTION 4 VERBAL ABILITY
30 MINUTES   40 QUESTIONS

For each question in this section, choose the best answer and blacken the corresponding space on the answer sheet.

Each question below consists of a word in capital letters, followed by five lettered words or phrases. Choose the word or phrase that is most nearly *opposite* in meaning to the word in capital letters. Since some of the questions require you to distinguish fine shades of meaning, consider all the choices before deciding which is best.

Example:

> GOOD: (A) sour (B) bad (C) red
> (D) hot (E) ugly
>
> Ⓐ ● Ⓒ Ⓓ Ⓔ

1. COMPATIBLE: (A) brief (B) inharmonious
   (C) recognizable (D) unavoidable (E) vital

2. REFUTE: (A) befriend (B) calculate
   (C) accompany (D) hasten (E) confirm

3. CULPABLE: (A) innocent (B) unpretentious
   (C) industrious (D) sympathetic (E) capable

4. PORTLY: (A) tidy (B) unimportant
   (C) slim (D) glamorous (E) tolerable

5. DEFECTION: (A) protection
   (B) responsibility (C) loyalty (D) vitality
   (E) reliability

6. UNCANNY: (A) productive (B) likeable
   (C) cheerful (D) usual (E) modest

7. ALTRUSIM: (A) lowliness (B) stinginess
   (C) deception (D) unconcern (E) selfishness

8. DEFT: (A) unfriendly (B) awkward
   (C) shabby (D) plain (E) brawny

9. FETTER: (A) assist (B) purify (C) engulf
   (D) gratify (E) lead

10. MENDACIOUS: (A) decisive
    (B) progressive (C) precious (D) honorable
    (E) irreparable

Each sentence below has one or two blanks, each blank indicating that something has been omitted. Beneath the sentence are five lettered words or sets of words. Choose the word or set of words that *best* fits the meaning of the sentence as a whole.

Example:

> Although its publicity has been ____, the film itself is intelligent, well-acted, handsomely produced, and altogether ____.
>
> (A) tasteless . . . respectable
> (B) extensive . . . moderate
> (C) sophisticated . . . amateur
> (D) risqué . . . crude
> (E) perfect . . . spectacular   ● Ⓑ Ⓒ Ⓓ Ⓔ

11. Some illnesses, such as malaria, which have been virtually eliminated in the United States, are still _____ in many places abroad.

    (A) discussed (B) prevalent (C) scarce
    (D) unknown (E) hospitalized

12. With lack of _____, almost anyone can develop the disease we call alcoholism, just as any of us can contract pneumonia by _____ exposing ourselves to its causes.

    (A) advice . . . carefully
    (B) control . . . foolishly
    (C) opportunity . . . knowingly
    (D) sympathy . . . fortunately
    (E) conscience . . . happily

13. The discouragement and _____ that so often plague perfectionists can lead to decreases in _____ and production.

    (A) pressure . . . creativity
    (B) uplift . . . motivation
    (C) enthusiasm . . . efficiency
    (D) boredom . . . idleness
    (E) involvement . . . laziness

14. The Bavarians consider beer their national beverage, yet at the same time they do not view it as a drink but rather as _____ bread—a staple food.

(A) fresh (B) liquid (C) stale (D) bitter
(E) costly

15. The Forest Service warned that the spring forest fire season was in full swing and urged that _____ caution be exercised in wooded areas.

(A) moderate (B) scant (C) customary
(D) extreme (E) reasonable

Each question below consists of a related pair of words or phrases, followed by five lettered pairs of words or phrases. Select the lettered pair that *best* expresses a relationship similar to that expressed in the original pair.

Example:

YAWN : BOREDOM : : (A) dream : sleep
(B) anger : madness (C) smile : amusement
(D) face : expression (E) impatience : rebellion

16. PRESERVE : ANIMALS : :

(A) lighthouse : signals
(B) reservation : wigwams
(C) orphanage : institution
(D) vault : money
(E) penitentiary : warden

17. TEPID : HOT : :

(A) cool : frigid
(B) spotless : clean
(C) warm : comfortable
(D) humorous : mature
(E) curious : coy

18. ADVOCATE : CHANGE : :

(A) bypass : road
(B) endorse : candidate
(C) raze : building
(D) provoke : anger
(E) eradicate : mistake

19. FARE : PASSENGER : :

(A) magazine : subscriber
(B) parking : ticket
(C) tuition : student
(D) bond : premium
(E) usury : interest

20. BARBER : RAZOR : :

(A) nurse : patient
(B) plumber : sink
(C) gardener : weed
(D) chef : knife
(E) telescope : astronomer

21. KENNEL : DOG : :

(A) trap : rat
(B) dock : ship
(C) barn : cow
(D) ape : jungle
(E) school : children

22. PIG : SNOUT : :

(A) elephant : trunk
(B) bill : bird
(C) hide : horse
(D) scorpion : sting
(E) lion : den

23. STAPLE : SHEETS : :

(A) balance : scales
(B) nail : boards
(C) grind : kernels
(D) mold : clay
(E) type : memos

24. SUSPECT : CONVICT : :

(A) agony : prolong
(B) president : impeach
(C) student : expel
(D) enemy : condemn
(E) slave : fetter

25. SANDPAPER : ABRASIVE : :

(A) emollient : soothing
(B) anger : justified
(C) analgesic : irritating
(D) revenge : sweet
(E) remedy : prescribed

Each passage below is followed by questions based on its content. Answer all questions following a passage on the basis of what is *stated* or *implied* in that passage.

Science, like everything else that man has created, exists, of course, to gratify certain human needs and desires. The fact that it has been steadily pursued for so many centuries, that it has attracted an ever-wider extent of at-
5 tention, and that it is now the dominant intellectual interest of mankind, shows that it appeals to a very powerful and persistent group of appetites. It is not difficult to say what these appetites are, at least in their main divisions. Science is valued for its practical advantages, it is valued because
10 it gratifies curiosity, and it is valued because it provides the imagination with objects of great aesthetic charm. This last consideration is of the least importance, so far as the layman is concerned, although it is probably the most important consideration of all to scientific men. It is quite
15 obvious, on the other hand, that the bulk of mankind value science chiefly for the practical advantages it brings with it.

This conclusion is borne out by everything we know about the origin of science. Science seems to have come
20 into existence merely for its bearings on practical life.

More than two thousand years before the beginning of the Christian era both the Babylonians and the Egyptians were in possession of systematic methods of measuring space and time. They had a rudimentary geometry and a
25 rudimentary astronomy. This rudimentary science arose to meet the practical needs of an agricultural population. Their geometry resulted from the measurements made necessary by the problems of land surveying. The cultivation of crops, dependent on the seasons, made a calendar almost
30 a necessity. The day, as a unit of time, was, of course, imposed by nature. The movement of the moon conveniently provided another unit, the month, which was reckoned from one new moon to the next. Twelve of these months were taken to constitute a year, and the necessary
35 adjustments were made from time to time by putting in extra months.

26. The main idea of the passage is that

(A) science originated and developed because of the practical advantages it offers
(B) the Egyptians and the Babylonians used scientific methods to meet the practical needs of feeding their people
(C) the use of geometry and astronomy are very important for agricultural development
(D) science has a different value for scientists than it does for the rest of the population
(E) science is valued not only for its practical contributions to mankind but also for its potential to stir the imagination

27. According to the passage,

(A) the Babylonians and the Egyptians were the first to use scientific methods
(B) the Christians were the first to have a calendar
(C) a 12-month calendar was first used by the Egyptians or Babylonians
(D) the Christians preceded the Babylonians and Egyptians
(E) scientists are probably more attracted to the charm of science than to its practical benefits

28. The author implies that scientists are generally

(A) sociable   (B) imaginative   (C) practical
(D) philosophical   (E) arrogant

A spectacular sunset lit the marble obelisk with the words WILLIAM HAZARD carved in its base. George uncovered his eyes, gave a last adjustment to the black wreath he had laid, and rose.

He dusted his knees as his mother approached. She had
5 come with him to the graveyard in the hard, bright light of the winter afternoon. But she had remained several yards away while he silently said his farewell.

They walked down a precipitous path toward the waiting carriage. George had been home only a few hours, but
10 Maude Hazard was already bubbling with plans for the wedding.

"It's a tragedy your father couldn't have lived long enough to meet Constance," she said.

"Do you think he would have approved of her?"
15 Maude sighed. "Probably not. But we'll make her welcome. I promise."

"Will everyone make her welcome?" His tone expressed skepticism.

"George"—she faced him—"you already know that some
20 will hate you for the step you've taken. The Irish are a despised lot, though I don't quite understand why. You, however, are obviously very realistic, and I admire that. I admire you for your willingness to face up to the hate you may encounter."
25 "I hadn't thought of it in those terms, Mother. I love Constance."

"I know, but there is still a great deal of un-Christian hate in the world. Love will somehow defeat it. It will and, if we're all to survive, it must."
30 He thought of certain members of the family, and his own sister. He could believe in *must*. But *will?* He had great doubts about that.

29. The "step" that George has taken (line 21) is

(A) leaving his home and family
(B) coming back home to visit his father's grave
(C) making the decision to marry Constance
(D) failing to communicate with his family while away
(E) refusing to see his own sister

30. According to the passage, Constance was probably

(A) George's sweetheart when they were schoolchildren
(B) of a different religion from George's family
(C) a maid in the Hazard household
(D) a friend of George's sister
(E) a distant cousin of George's

31. George's attitude in regard to what may happen in the future was one of

(A) great confidence
(B) mild confusion
(C) utter despair
(D) troubled uncertainty
(E) philosophical acceptance

32. "He could believe in *must*. But *will*? He had great doubts about that." (See lines 32–33) These words mean that George is not sure whether his family

(A) will learn to love Constance
(B) will attend the wedding
(C) will ever forgive him for leaving home
(D) will take care of his mother if George leaves home again
(E) will remain together or drift apart

A man in his early 40's in the quiet New England town of Framingham, Massachusetts stands one chance in eight of developing heart disease within 14 years. For a man in his late 40's, the risk is one in six. And for a man in his
5   early 50's, one in five. But nowhere in this country would the prospects be any better. Framingham is just like any other city in America where, according to the World Health Organization, the greatest epidemic mankind has faced continues to cut off millions of men prematurely, at the
10 peak of their productive lives.
     The Framingham Heart Study, which initially included half the middle-aged men and women living there, is the longest-running and most comprehensive project of its kind in medical history. The project has generated facts that
15 have already been used to save millions of lives. By revealing the roles that high blood cholesterol, high blood pressure, cigarette smoking, obesity, high blood sugar, lack of exercise, stress, electrocardiographic abnormalities and other factors play in cardiovascular diseases, they say
20 they have demonstrated that heart disease is not an inevitable consequence of age but rather is largely the result of how people live.

Moreover, the study shows it is possible to predict years ahead who is mostly likely to get sick or die suddenly from heart and blood vessel diseases. Although only mea-   25
surement, not direct treatment, of risk factors has been Framingham's mission, its findings indicate that early disease and death can often be avoided if people reduce their risk, for example by stopping smoking or controlling high blood pressure. These conclusions emerged from moun-   30
tains of data collected through the years from the 5,209 participants, aged 30 to 62 and nearly all healthy when the study began.

33. Which statement is true according to the passage?

(A) Heart disease is second to cancer as a major cause of death in our nation.
(B) The directors of the Framingham Heart Study were successful in their treatment of heart disease patients.
(C) Doctors are unable to foresee who will or will not get a heart attack.
(D) The Framingham Heart Study project is now complete.
(E) The heart disease rate in Framingham was about the same as it was in other parts of the country.

34. One may infer from the passage that

(A) women are less prone to heart disease than men
(B) the businessman who has many worries in and out of the office is a likely candidate for heart disease
(C) low blood pressure is a common cause of heart disease
(D) every country in the world considers heart disease the greatest epidemic mankind has faced
(E) a 50-year-old man in Framingham has a 20% chance of getting heart disease before he is 70 years old

35. Which quotation is most appropriate in describing the author's attitude?

(A) "Thanks to the human heart by which we live."
(B) "There is a disease called money."
(C) "Concerning the tastes of men there is no disputing."
(D) "An ounce of prevention is worth tons of cure."
(E) "Death be not proud, though some have called thee mighty."

We have always been a lawless and a violent people. Thus, our almost unbroken record of violence against the Indians and all others who got in our way—the Spaniards in the Floridas, the Mexicans in Texas; the violence of the vigilantes on a hundred frontiers; the pervasive violence of slavery (a "perpetual exercise," Jefferson called it, "of the most boisterous passions"); the lawlessness of the Ku Klux Klan during Reconstruction and after; and of scores of race riots from those of New Orleans in the 1960s to those of Chicago in 1919. Yet, all this violence, shocking as it doubtless was, no more threatened the fabric of our society or the integrity of the Union than did the lawlessness of Prohibition back in the Twenties. The explanation for this is to be found in the embarrassing fact that most of it was official, quasi-official, or countenanced by public opinion: exterminating the Indian; flogging the slave; lynching the outlaw; exploiting women and children in textile mills and sweatshops; hiring Pinkertons to shoot down strikers; condemning immigrants to fetid ghettos; punishing Negroes who tried to exercise their civil or political rights. Most of this was socially acceptable—or at least not wholly unacceptable—just as so much of our current violence is socially acceptable: the many thousands of automobile deaths every year; the mortality rate for Negro babies twice that for white; the deaths from cancer induced by cigarettes or by air pollution; the sadism of our penal system and the horrors of our prisons; the violence of some police against the so-called "dangerous classes of society."

What we have now is the emergence of violence that is not acceptable either to the Establishment, which is frightened and alarmed, or to the victims of the Establishment, who are no longer submissive and who are numerous and powerful. This is the now familiar "crime in the streets," or it is the revolt of the young against the economy, the politics, and the wars of the established order, or it is the convulsive reaction of the blacks to a century of injustice. But now, too, official violence is no longer acceptable to its victims—or to their ever more numerous sympathizers: the violence of great corporations and of government itself against the natural resources of the nation; the long drawn-out violence of the white majority against Negroes and other minorities; the violence of the police and the National Guard against the young; the massive and never-ending violence of the military against the peoples of Vietnam and Cambodia. These acts can no longer be absorbed by large segments of our society. It is this new polarization that threatens the body politic and the social fabric much as religious dissent threatened them in the Europe of the sixteenth and seventeenth centuries.

36. As an illustration of current "socially acceptable" violence the author would probably include

   (A) National Guard violence at Kent, Ohio
   (B) the Vietnam War
   (C) the cruelties of our prison system
   (D) the police behavior in Chicago
   (E) "crime in the streets"

37. It can be inferred that the author's definition of violence

   (A) includes the social infliction of harm
   (B) is limited to nongovernmental acts of force
   (C) is confined to governmental acts of illegal force
   (D) is synonymous with illegal conduct by either government or citizen
   (E) is shared by the F.B.I.

38. The author describes current violence as

   I. acceptable neither to the authorities nor to the victims
   II. carried out primarily by corporations
   III. increasingly of a vigilante nature

   (A) I only
   (B) II only
   (C) III only
   (D) I and II only
   (E) II and III only

39. The author mentions all of the following forms of violence in the nineteenth century except

   (A) the activities of the Klan during Reconstruction
   (B) wiping out the Indians
   (C) the New York City draft riots of the 1860's
   (D) the Annexation of Texas and Florida
   (E) the practice of slavery

40. Which action or activity would the author be most likely to disapprove of?

   (A) trying to prevent a mugging
   (B) reading a science fiction story
   (C) watching a rock music TV performance
   (D) attending a Super Bowl football game
   (E) participating in a country square dance

S T O P

IF YOU FINISH BEFORE TIME IS CALLED, YOU MAY CHECK YOUR WORK ON THIS SECTION ONLY.
DO NOT WORK ON ANY OTHER SECTION IN THE TEST.

SECTION 5 MATH ABILITY
30 MINUTES   35 QUESTIONS

In this section solve each problem, using any available space on the page for scratchwork. Then decide which is the best of the choices given and blacken the corresponding space on the answer sheet.

The following information is for your reference in solving some of the problems.

Circle of radius r: Area $= \pi r^2$; Circumference $= 2\pi r$
  The number of degrees of arc in a circle is 360.
The measure in degrees of a straight angle is 180.

Definitions of symbols:

$=$	is equal to		$\leq$	is less than or equal to
$\neq$	is unequal to		$\geq$	is greater than or equal to
$<$	is less than		$\parallel$	is parallel to
$>$	is greater than		$\perp$	is perpendicular to

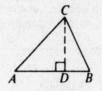

Triangle: The sum of the measure in degrees of the angles of a triangle is 180.
If $\angle CDA$ is a right angle, then

(1) area of $\triangle ABC = \dfrac{AB \times CD}{2}$

(2) $AC^2 = AD^2 + DC^2$

Note: Figures which accompany problems in this test are intended to provide information useful in solving the problems. They are drawn as accurately as possible EXCEPT when it is stated in a specific problem that its figure is not drawn to scale. All figures lie in a plane unless otherwise indicated. All numbers used are real numbers.

1. Tommy and Bobby like to watch their school's baseball team play. Tommy watched $\frac{2}{3}$ of all the games the team played last season. Bobby watched 28 games. If Tommy watched more games than Bobby did last season, which of the following could be the number of games the team played last season?

(A) 33   (B) 36   (C) 39   (D) 42   (E) 45

2. $3x(4x + 2y) =$

(A) $7x + 5xy$ (B) $12x + 6xy$
(C) $12x^2 + 2y$ (D) $12x^2 + 6xy$ (E) $12x^2 + 6x$

Box Number	Height of Box (in millimeters)
A	1700
B	2450
C	2735
D	1928
E	2130

3. Exactly how many of the boxes listed in the table above are more than 20 decimeters high?
(1 decimeter = 100 millimeters)

(A) Zero   (B) One   (C) Two   (D) Three   (E) Four

4. If $a - 3 = 7$, then $2a - 14 =$

(A) -6 (B) -4 (C) 2   (D) 4   (E) 6

5. An athlete runs 90 laps in 6 hours. This is the same as how many laps per minute?

(A) $\dfrac{1}{15}$ (B) $\dfrac{1}{9}$ (C) $\dfrac{1}{4}$ (D) $\dfrac{1}{2}$ (E) 1

6. $\dfrac{7}{10} + \dfrac{7}{100} + \dfrac{77}{1000} =$

(A) .0091   (B) .7777   (C) .784   (D) .847
(E) .854

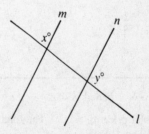

7. Parallel lines m and n are intersected by line l as shown. Find the value of $x + y$

(A) 180   (B) 150   (C) 120   (D) 90
(E) It cannot be determined from the information given.

Questions 8-27 each consist of two quantities, one in Column A and one in Column B. You are to compare the two quantities and on the answer sheet blacken space

    A if the quantity in Column A is greater;
    B if the quantity in Column B is greater;
    C if the two quantities are equal;
    D if the relationship cannot be determined from the information given.

Notes: 1. In certain questions, information concerning one or both of the quantities to be compared is centered above the columns.
        2. In a given question, a symbol that appears in both columns represents the same thing in Column A as it does in Column B.
        3. Letters such as x, n, and k stand for real numbers.

EXAMPLES

	Column A	Column B	Answers
E1.	2×6	$2 + 6$	● Ⓑ Ⓒ Ⓓ
E2.	$180 - x$	y	Ⓐ Ⓑ ● Ⓓ
E3.	$p - q$	$q - p$	Ⓐ Ⓑ Ⓒ ●

(E2 figure: angles $x°$ and $y°$ on a straight line)

Column A	Column B

8. a and b are positive integers

$$ab = 13$$

a	b

9. $\dfrac{1}{\dfrac{3}{4}}$ 1.25

10. The price of 1 pencil is 48¢

The total price of 1 pencil and 1 pen   The total price of 2 pens

11. $2^3 + 2^2 + 2 + 1$ 2^4

Column A	Column B

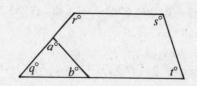

12. $r + s + t$ $a + b + 180$

13. $x - y < 0$

x y

14. An athlete pedals his bicycle 48 miles in $1\dfrac{1}{2}$ hours.

The average speed that the athlete pedaled at (in miles per hour)   36 miles per hour

SUMMARY DIRECTIONS FOR COMPARISON QUESTIONS

Answer: A if the quantity in Column A is greater;
            B if the quantity in Column B is greater;
            C if the two quantities are equal;
            D if the relationship cannot be determined from the information given.

Column A	Column B

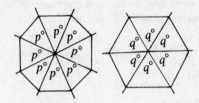

15. p q

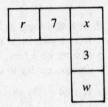

16. The sum of the numbers in the horizontal row is equal to the sum of the numbers in the vertical column.

      r w

17. $\triangle RST$ is scalene.

Length of altitude to side RT Length of side SR

18. $p < -2$

$(p - 2)^3 \, (p + 2)^3$ 0

19. The population of Jonesville was 12,200,000 last year. This year the population was 10 percent higher than last year.

The population of Jonesville this year   13,500,000

20. x is a multiple of 7 and $40 < x < 50$

      x 47

Column A	Column B

21. A wheel of radius r rolls, without slipping along a straight line, a distance of 24 centimeters in 3 seconds. The wheel makes one revolution per second.

      r 1 cm

22.
$$2a + 2b = 14$$
$$3x + 3y = 24$$

The average (arithmetic mean) of a and b The average (arithmetic mean) of x and y

23. p and q are positive integers

$\dfrac{p}{q}$ $\dfrac{p + q}{q + q}$

24. Let $x \,\square\, y = x^2 y$ for all real numbers x and y

$r \,\square\, s$ $-r \,\square\, s$

25. Area of the triangular region bounded by the X-axis, Y-axis, and the graph of the line $4x + 4y = 20$ 12.5

26.
$$3x - y = 8$$
$$2x - 4y = 7$$

$x - y$ 3

27. The sum of two different prime numbers, each between 10 and 20   The sum of two even integers, each between 10 and 20

Solve each of the remaining problems in this section using any available space for scratchwork. Then decide which is the best of the choices given and blacken the corresponding space on the answer sheet.

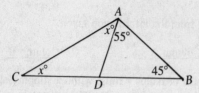

28. In the figure above what is the value of *x*?

(A) 30   (B) 40   (C) 50   (D) 80   (E) 100

29. A pile of 400 bricks of uniform thickness is 32 meters high. What is the thickness, in meters, of 1 brick?

(a) .8   (B) .12   (C) .08   (D) .012   (E) .008

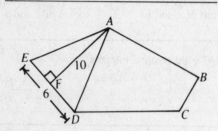

Note: Not drawn to scale.

30. In the figure above, pentagon *ABCDE* has an area of 120. What is the area of quadrilateral *ABCD*?

(A) 30   (B) 45   (C) 60   (D) 90
(E) It cannot be determined from the information given.

31. If the symbol ☆ can represent either the minus (−) arithmetic operation or the division (÷) arithmetic operation, which of the following could be the value of 12☆ (8 ☆ 4)? (The second ☆ in the foregoing expression may or may not represent the same arithmetic operation as the first ☆)

   I. 6
  II. 8
 III. 10

(A) I only
(B) II only
(C) I and II only
(D) II and III only
(E) I, II, and III

32. A rectangular floor 8 feet long and 6 feet wide is to be completely covered with tiles. Each tile is a square with a perimeter of 2 feet. What is the least number of such tiles necessary to cover the floor?

(A) 7   (B) 12   (C) 24   (D) 48   (E) 192

33. At a certain college, the number of freshmen is three times the number of seniors. If $\frac{1}{4}$ of the freshmen and $\frac{1}{3}$ of the seniors attend a football game, what fraction of the total number of freshmen and seniors attend the game?

(A) $\frac{5}{24}$ (B) $\frac{13}{48}$ (C) $\frac{17}{48}$ (D) $\frac{11}{24}$ (E) $\frac{23}{48}$

34. At Jones College, there are a total of 100 students. If 30 of the students have cars on campus, and 50 have bicycles, and 20 have both cars and bicycles, then how many students have neither a car nor a bicycle on campus?

(A) 80   (B) 60   (C) 40   (D) 20   (E) 0

35. If 9 and 12 each divide *Q* without remainder, which of the following must *Q* divide without remainder?

(A) 1   (B) 3   (C) 36   (D) 72
(E) It cannot be determined from the given information.

S T O P

IF YOU FINISH BEFORE TIME IS CALLED, YOU MAY CHECK YOUR WORK ON THIS SECTION ONLY.
DO NOT WORK ON ANY OTHER SECTION IN THE TEST.

SECTION 6   MATH ABILITY
30 MINUTES   35 QUESTIONS

In this section solve each problem, using any available space on the page for scratchwork. Then decide which is the best of the choices given and blacken the corresponding space on the answer sheet.

The following information is for your reference in solving some of the problems.

Circle of radius r: Area $= \pi r^2$; Circumference $= 2\pi r$
    The number of degrees of arc in a circle is 360.
The measure in degrees of a straight angle is 180.

Definitions of symbols:
$=$	is equal to	$\leqq$	is less than or equal to
$\neq$	is unequal to	$\geqq$	is greater than or equal to
$<$	is less than	$\parallel$	is parallel to
$>$	is greater than	$\perp$	is perpendicular to

Triangle: The sum of the measure in degrees of the angles of a triangle is 180.
If $\angle CDA$ is a right angle, then

(1)   area of $\triangle ABC = \dfrac{AB \times CD}{2}$

(2) $AC^2 = AD^2 + DC^2$

<u>Note:</u> Figures which accompany problems in this test are intended to provide information useful in solving the problems. They are drawn as accurately as possible EXCEPT when it is stated in a specific problem that its figure is not drawn to scale. All figures lie in a plane unless otherwise indicated. All numbers used are real numbers.

1. After giving $5 to Greg, David has $25. Greg now has $\dfrac{1}{5}$ as much as David does. How much did Greg start with?

    (A) $0   (B) $5   (C) $7   (D) $10   (E) $15

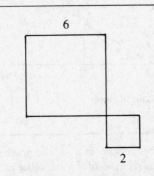

2. The figure above shows two squares with sides as shown. What is the ratio of the perimeter of the larger square to that of the smaller?

    (A) 3 : 2   (B) 2 : 1   (C) 3 : 1   (D) 6 : 1   (E) 9 : 1

3. A car travels 1056 feet in 12 seconds. In feet per second, what is the average speed of the car?

    (A) 98.0   (B) 78.8   (C) 85.8   (D) 84.0   (E) 88.0

4. If $2z + 1 + 2 + 2z + 3 + 2z = 3 + 1 + 2$ then $z + 4 =$

    (A) 1   (B) 4   (C) 5   (D) 6   (E) 10

5. If $mn \neq 0$, then $\dfrac{1}{n^2} \left(\dfrac{m^5 \, n^3}{m^3} \right)^2 =$

    (A) mn^4 (B) m^4n^2 (C) m^4n^3 (D) m^4n^4 (E) m^4n^5

6. $2(w)(x)(-y) - 2(-w)(-x)(y) =$

    (A) 0   (B) $-4wxy$ (C) $4wxy$ (D) $-4w^2x^2y^2$
    (E) $2w^2x^2y^2$

7. What is an expression for 5 times the sum of the square of x and the square of y?

    (A) $5(x^2 + y^2)$ (B) $5x^2 + y^2$ (C) $5(x + y)^2$
    (D) $5x^2 + y$ (E) $5(2x + 2y)$

<u>Questions 8-27</u> each consist of two quantities, one in Column A and one in Column B. You are to compare the two quantities and on the answer sheet blacken space

A if the quantity in Column A is greater;
B if the quantity in Column B is greater;
C if the two quantities are equal;
D if the relationship cannot be determined from the information given.

Notes: 1. In certain questions, information concerning one or both of the quantities to be compared is centered above the columns.
2. In a given question, a symbol that appears in both columns represents the same thing in Column A as it does in Column B.
3. Letters such as x, n, and k stand for real numbers.

	EXAMPLES		
	Column A	Column B	Answers
E1.	2×6	$2 + 6$	● Ⓑ Ⓒ Ⓓ
E2.	$180 - x$	y	Ⓐ Ⓑ ● Ⓓ
E3.	$p - q$	$q - p$	Ⓐ Ⓑ Ⓒ ●

In E2, the figure shows angles $x°$ and $y°$.

Column A	Column B

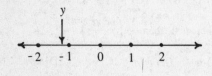

8. y^5 | y^2

9. $.06 \times 1000$ | $.6 \times 100$

10. Twenty million copies of a certain album were sold in 1985.

| The number of copies of the album sold between January 1, 1985 and January 31, 1985 | The number of copies of the album sold between January 1, 1985 and April 30, 1985 |

11. $(2 \times 3 + 4(5 - 6))$ | $(6 \times 5 + 4(3 - 2))$

12.
$$5 + m > 12$$
$$5 + n > 12$$

m | n

Column A	Column B

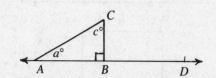

$\overline{AD}$ is a straight line.

13. 0 | $90 - (a + c)$

14. The number of girls in a group of 60 if 10% of the group are girls | The number of boys in another group of 80 people if 5% of the group are boys

15. $y \neq 0$

$\dfrac{y + y + y}{y}$ | y

16. Craig bought a football and a basketball for $9. Chris bought the same-priced football and two of the same-priced basketballs for $m. Ben bought two of the same-priced footballs and one of the same-priced basketballs for $n.

$m + n$ | 18

SUMMARY DIRECTIONS FOR COMPARISON QUESTIONS

<u>Answer:</u> A if the quantity in Column A is greater;
B if the quantity in Column B is greater;
C if the two quantities are equal;
D if the relationship cannot be determined from the information given.

<u>Column A</u>	<u>Column B</u>

17. A square and a regular octagon are inscribed in circles having the same radius

Area of the square	Area of the regular octagon

18. $10^3 + 10^2$ | $10^3 \times 10^2$

Group I	Group II	Group III
0 1 2 3 4 5	0 1 2 3 4 5	0 1 2 3 4 5

19. If a and b are positive integers less than 6, $a \triangle b$ is defined as the number in the figure above that is located by starting at a in Group I, and moving b spaces to the right, continuously, until you end up in Group III. For example $2 \triangle 5 = 0$ since starting at 2 in group I and moving 5 to the right puts you at 1 in group II and moving 5 to the right again puts you at 0 in group III.

$3 \triangle 4$ | 5

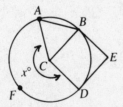

20. Equilateral triangle ABC and square $BCDE$ have side $\overline{BC}$ in common. C is the center of the circle.

x | 200

<u>Column A</u>	<u>Column B</u>

21. n is a positive integer greater than 1.

$\left(-\dfrac{1}{2}\right)^{n} (57)^{n-1}$ | $\left(-\dfrac{1}{2}\right)^{n-1} (57)^{n-1}$

22. $x - 2, 2x - 4, 3x - 6, 4x - 8, \ldots nx - 2n$ is a sequence of numbers where $n > 10$.

The sum of the first 10 elements of the sequence above, when $x = 2$ | 10

23. The average (arithmetic mean) of 90, 90, and 100 | The average (arithmetic mean) of 90, 100, and 100

24. Let $\bigcirc{y}$ denote the decimal part of y. For example $\bigcirc{7.3} = .3$ and $\bigcirc{8} = 0$
x and y are positive numbers

$\bigcirc{x} + \bigcirc{y}$ | 2

25. $a + b = 3$
$b + c = 4$

$a + b + c$ | 7

Note: Figure not drawn to scale.

26. $0 < a < 1$

a | ab

27. City A is 5 miles from City B and 12 miles from City C.

The distance in miles of City B from City C | 18

Solve each of the remaining problems in this section using any available space for scratchwork. Then decide which is the best of the choices given and blacken the corresponding space on the answer sheet.

28. If $p + pq$ is 4 times $p - pq$, which of the following has exactly one value? $(pq \neq 0)$

(A) p (B) q (C) pq (D) $p + pq$ (E) $p - pq$

29. If $2 + \dfrac{1}{z} = 0$, then what is the value of $9 + 9z$?

(A) $-\dfrac{9}{2}$ (B) $-\dfrac{1}{2}$ (C) 0 (D) $\dfrac{9}{2}$

(E) It cannot be determined from the information given.

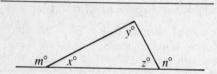

30. In the figure above, $m + n =$

(A) 90 (B) 180 (C) $180 + y$
(D) $90 + x + y + z$ (E) $2(x + y + z)$

31. Let $wx = y$, where $wxy \neq 0$.

If both x and y are multiplied by 6, then w is

(A) multiplied by $\dfrac{1}{36}$

(B) multiplied by $\dfrac{1}{6}$

(C) multiplied by 1
(D) multiplied by 6
(E) multiplied by 36

32. The volume of a cube is less than 25 and the length of one of its edges is a positive integer. What is the largest possible value for the total area of the six faces?

(A) 1 (B) 6 (C) 24 (D) 54 (E) 150

33. The ratio of smokers to nonsmokers on a particular flight was 2 : 3. Smoking passengers represented five more than $\dfrac{1}{3}$ of all the passengers aboard. How many passengers were on that flight?

(A) 15 (B) 25 (C) 30 (D) 45 (E) 75

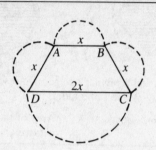

34. The quadrilateral $ABCD$ is a trapezoid with $x = 4$. The diameter of each semicircle is a side of the trapezoid. What is the sum of the lengths of the 4 dotted semicircles?

(A) 8π (B) 10π (C) 12π (D) 14π (E) 20π

35. $\dfrac{7x}{144}$ yards and $\dfrac{5y}{12}$ feet together equal how many inches?

(A) $\dfrac{7x}{12} + \dfrac{5y}{4}$

(B) $\dfrac{7x}{12} + 5y$

(C) $\dfrac{7x}{4} + 5y$

(D) $\dfrac{7x}{4} + 60y$

(E) $7x + \dfrac{5}{4}y$

S T O P

IF YOU FINISH BEFORE TIME IS CALLED, YOU MAY CHECK YOUR WORK ON THIS SECTION ONLY.
DO NOT WORK ON ANY OTHER SECTION IN THE TEST.

HOW DID YOU DO ON THIS TEST?

STEP 1. Go to the Answer Key on page 644.

STEP 2. For your "raw score," count your correct answers in each of the test parts of the test you have just taken:

Verbal (Section 1 and 4 combined) _____.

Math (Sections 2, 5, and 6 combined) _____.

Standard Written English (Section 3) _____.

STEP 3. Get your "scaled score" for the test by referring to the Raw Score/ Scaled Score Conversion Tables on pages 64–66.

THERE'S ALWAYS ROOM FOR IMPROVEMENT!

ANSWER KEY FOR PRACTICE TEST 6

Section 1—Verbal

1. C	8. A	15. B	22. E	29. A	36. E	43. B
2. E	9. E	16. B	23. B	30. B	37. C	44. A
3. D	10. D	17. C	24. C	31. A	38. E	45. A
4. E	11. E	18. B	25. E	32. E	39. B	
5. A	12. C	19. C	26. E	33. B	40. D	
6. B	13. A	20. A	27. A	34. C	41. E	
7. B	14. D	21. D	28. A	35. E	42. B	

Section 2—Math

1. B	5. E	9. D	13. A	17. D	21. D	25. C
2. C	6. B	10. E	14. C	18. C	22. C	
3. C	7. D	11. E	15. C	19. E	23. A	
4. D	8. D	12. C	16. B	20. A	24. B	

Section 3—Standard Written English

1. A	9. A	17. C	25. C	33. E	41. D	49. B
2. B	10. B	18. A	26. D	34. A	42. B	50. D
3. A	11. C	19. C	27. B	35. C	43. A	
4. D	12. A	20. C	28. A	36. B	44. E	
5. B	13. C	21. E	29. A	37. D	45. B	
6. B	14. C	22. D	30. E	38. E	46. E	
7. E	15. D	23. D	31. B	39. C	47. D	
8. C	16. B	24. B	32. B	40. C	48. D	

Section 4—Verbal

1. B	7. E	13. A	19. C	25. A	31. D	37. A
2. E	8. B	14. B	20. D	26. A	32. A	38. A
3. A	9. A	15. D	21. C	27. E	33. E	39. C
4. C	10. D	16. D	22. A	28. B	34. B	40. D
5. C	11. B	17. A	23. B	29. C	35. D	
6. D	12. B	18. B	24. C	30. B	36. C	

Section 5—Math

1. E	6. D	11. B	16. B	21. A	26. C	31. E
2. D	7. A	12. C	17. B	22. B	27. D	32. E
3. D	8. D	13. B	18. A	23. D	28. B	33. B
4. E	9. A	14. B	19. B	24. C	29. C	34. C
5. C	10. D	15. B	20. D	25. C	30. D	35. E

Section 6—Math

1. A	6. B	11. B	16. A	21. D	26. A	31. C
2. C	7. A	12. D	17. B	22. B	27. B	32. C
3. E	8. B	13. C	18. B	23. B	28. B	33. E
4. B	9. C	14. A	19. B	24. B	29. D	34. B
5. D	10. D	15. D	20. A	25. D	30. C	35. C

EXPLANATORY ANSWERS FOR PRACTICE TEST 6

Section 1: Verbal Ability

As you read these Explanatory Answers, you are advised to refer to "Using Critical Thinking Skills in Verbal Questions" (beginning on page 90) whenever a specific Strategy is referred to in the answer. Of particular importance are the following Master Verbal Strategies:

Sentence Completion Master Strategy 1—page 94.
Sentence Completion Master Strategy 2—page 95.
Analogies Master Strategy 1—page 90.
Antonyms Master Strategy 1—page 99.
Reading Comprehension Master Strategy 2—page 109.

1. **(C)** Choice C is correct. See **Antonym Strategy 1**. *Propagate* means *to spread; to multiply*. The opposite of *propagate* is *limit*.

2. **(E)** Choice E is correct. *Naive* means *simple; unsophisticated*. The opposite of *naive* is *complex*.

3. **(D)** Choice D is correct. See **Antonym Strategy 3**. *Acme* means *highest point; peak*. The opposite of *acme* is *lowest point*.

4. **(E)** Choice E is correct. See **Antonym Strategy 3**. *Kindle* means *to excite; to set on fire*. The opposite of *kindle* is *relax*.

5. **(A)** Choice A is correct. *Upbraid* means to *scold*. The opposite of *upbraid* is *compliment*.

6. **(B)** Choice B is correct. *Burly* means *muscular; husky*. The opposite of *burly* is *delicate*.

7. **(B)** Choice B is correct. See **Antonym Strategy 3**. *Hilarity* means *joy; gaiety*. The opposite of *hilarity* is *sadness*.

8. **(A)** Choice A is correct. See **Antonym Strategy 3**. *Delectable* means *delicious; quite pleasing*. The opposite of *delectable* is *disagreeable*.

9. **(E)** Choice E is correct. *Spurious* means *not genuine; counterfeit*. The opposite of *spurious* is *genuine*.

10. **(D)** Choice D is correct. See **Antonym Strategies 1, 3**. *Antipathy* means *intense dislike*. The opposite of *antipathy* is *attraction*.

11. **(E)** Choice E is correct. See **Antonym Strategy 3**. *Corpulent* means *fat; fleshy*. The opposite of *corpulent* is *slender*.

12. **(C)** Choice C is correct. *Mollify* means *to calm*. The opposite of *mollify* is *excite*.

13. **(A)** Choice A is correct. See **Antonym Strategies 1, 3**. *Diffidence* means *shyness; timidity*. The opposite of *diffidence* is *aggressiveness*.

14. **(D)** Choice D is correct. See **Antonym Strategy 2**. *Perfidious* means *deceitful; treacherous*. The opposite of *perfidious* is *faithful*.

15. **(B)** Choice B is correct. See **Antonym Strategy 3**. *Circuitous* means *indirect; roundabout*. The opposite of *circuitous* is *direct*.

16. **(B)** Choice B is correct. If you used **Sentence Completion Strategy 3**, you might have come up with any of the following words:

refused   repudiated   shunned

These words all mean about the same as the correct Choice (B) rejected.

17. **(C)** Choice C is correct. See **Sentence Completion Strategy 2**. Examine the first words of each choice. Eliminate Choice (D) labor because we don't speak of an automobile manufacturer's labor product. Now we consider the word pairs of the other choices. The only word pair that makes sense in the sentence is Choice (C) future . . . guarded.

18. **(B)** Choice B is correct. See **Sentence Completion Strategy 2**. Examine the first word of each choice. We eliminate Choice (C) simultaneous and Choice (D) unsuccessful because it does not make sense to say the crime rate remains simultaneous or successful. Now we consider Choice (A) which does *not* make sense in the sentence; Choice B *does* make sense; and Choice E does *not* make sense.

19. **(C)** Choice C is correct. See **Sentence Completion Strategy 1.** The word "generate" (meaning *"to produce"*) completes the sentence so that it makes good sense. The other choices don't do that.

20. **(A)** Choice A is correct. See **Sentence Completion Strategy 1.** The word "negligence" (meaning "neglect"; "failure to be careful") completes the sentence so that is makes good sense. The other choices don't do that.

21. **(D)** Choice D is correct. Throughout the passage the author is showing that words may suggest both emotional attitudes as well as objective meanings. Following are examples from the passage.

Lines 10–15: "Let us suppose . . . exact scientific description."
Lines 16–22: "Suppose, however . . . emotional attitude toward it."
Lines 46–49: "By applying . . . objectively identical."

Choice A is incorrect. See lines 16–21: "Suppose, however, that we had called the same animal a mongrel . . . emotional attitude of disapproval for that particular dog." Choice B is incorrect. See lines 12–14: "We can express . . . of mixed breed." Choice C is incorrect. See lines 16–22: "Suppose however . . . emotional attitude toward it." Choice E is incorrect. The passage neither states nor implies that dogs should be treated with consideration.

22. **(E)** Choice E is correct. See lines 30–36: "Once we are on the lookout . . . controversies cannot be settled." Choices B and C are incorrect. Lines 30–36 will also indicate why these two choices are incorrect. Choice A is incorrect. See lines 21–25: "A word, therefore . . . our approvals and disapprovals are individual." Choice D is incorrect because the passage nowhere indicates that one should never use obscene language.

23. **(B)** Choice B is correct. First see lines 30–36: "Once we are on the lookout . . . why such controversies cannot be settled." Now see lines 37–42: "When, during World War II . . . objectively the same thing." Finally, see lines 46–49: "By applying . . . objectively identical." Choice A is incorrect. The author does not state that disagreements arise because people have not yet learned how to get along with each other. He is saying that the use of words with emotional meanings often causes disagreements among people. Choice C is incorrect. The author is saying that words with emotional meanings (not objective meanings) mean different things to different persons. Choice D is incorrect. The author

does not state that politics or morals or religion as such cause controversies—it is the use of words with emotional meanings in discussions that very often cause the disagreements. See lines 30–36. Choice E is incorrect. The author in no way indicates that different languages used by various nations cause the disagreements.

24. **(C)** Choice C is correct. See lines 46–49: "By applying the word ruthlessness . . . objectively identical." Accordingly, Choice A is incorrect. Choice B and Choice E are incorrect because there is no indication in the passage that these choices are true. Choice D is incorrect. See lines 39–42: "Now with the more objective attitude . . . the same thing."

25. **(E)** Choice E is correct. The participial adjective *studied*, as the word implies, means carefully considered or prepared. The noun *objectivity* means the quality of being factual, impersonal, and fair, without favoring either side for emotional reasons. Throughout the passage, the author is showing how important it is to be objective. He has given carefully researched illustrations dealing with various subjects such as dogs, politics, morals, religion and war. Choices A, B, C, and D are incorrect because the passage is not marked by controlled emotion or cautious neutrality or guarded partiality or reasonable compromise.

26. **(E)** Choice E is correct. All of the titles listed suggest elements from the passage. One must look for the title which most completely and accurately reflects the central theme of the passage. In the passage, the author is concerned with the beneficial effects of trees on city dwellers as well as the beneficial effects of trees and other vegetation on city weather. The term "well-being" can include both physical and psychological aspects. Thus, the best answer is Choice E. Choice B is incorrect because it is flippant in tone but the passage is not. Choices A, C, and D can be eliminated because they deal only with city climate.

27. **(A)** Choice A is correct. Item I is true. See lines 22–23: "Compared with country districts . . . temperature in cities is higher." Item II is false. See lines 14–19: "As dust is responsible . . . haze canopy and fog." Item III is false. See lines 14–16: ". . . dust is responsible . . . ultra-violet irradiation." Accordingly, Choice A alone is correct.

28. **(A)** Choice A is correct. See lines 34–37: "A public opinion poll . . . verdure in the city was the prime attraction." Also see lines 37–41: "Appreciation of this . . . or to widen streets." There is no evidence in the passage that Choices B, C, D, and E are true. Therefore, these choices are incorrect.

29. **(A)** Choice A is correct. The author speaks favorably of the effects of trees and green belts. See lines (1–3): "Many of. . . . green belts." See also lines (30–34): "Apart from. . . . identification points." Thus, it is likely that he would recommend planting trees. Choice B is incorrect because the passage does not deal with the subject matter of Choice B at all even though the statement may be true. Choice C is incorrect. The central point of the passage is that plants modify the city's climate in a beneficial way. Green belts then cannot be considered a waste of space. Choice D is incorrect. According to the passage, tree shade causes "pleasant gentle wind movements" (lines 28–29). These can hardly be characterized as excessive. Choice E is incorrect. Lines 5–19 indicate that lining thoroughfares with trees results in a 70% reduction in dust. This is not minor. Therefore, Choice E is incorrect.

30. **(B)** Choice B is correct because the parenthetical statement in lines 15–16 gives the result of the statement which immediately precedes it. The parenthetical statement in lines 16–17 states the cause of the statement which precedes it. Accordingly Choices A, C, D, and E are incorrect.

31. **(A)** Choice A is correct. See **Sentence Completion Strategy 2.** Examine the first word of each choice. We eliminate Choice (B) fancy and Choice (C) study because fat people are not likely to fancy or to study carbohydrates and gobble down snacks. We now consider Choice (D) enjoy . . . diets, and Choice (E) avoid . . . senses, neither of which makes sense in the sentence. Choice (A) crave . . . moods, *does* make sense in the sentence.

32. **(E)** Choice E is correct. See **Sentence Completion Strategy 2.** Examine the first word of each choice. We eliminate Choice (A) experimental . . . and Choice (D) querulous (meaning complaining) . . . because coal miners do not call off an experimental or a complaining strike. Now we consider (B) shameful . . . demand, and Choice (C) unpopular . . . expect, neither of which makes sentence sense. Choice (E) turbulent (meaning violent) . . . resume, *does* make sentence sense.

33. **(B)** Choice B is correct. See **Sentence Completion Strategy 3.** You might have come up with any of the following words:

    susceptible (to)   open (to)
         unprotected (from)

    These words all mean about the same as the correct Choice (B) vulnerable.

34. **(C)** Choice C is correct. See **Sentence Completion Strategy 2.** Examine the first word of each choice. We eliminate Choice (B) noise and Choice (D) pollution because we do not associate bicycles with either noise or pollution. Now let us consider the other choices.

Choice (A) sight . . . a relief, does *not* make sentence sense. Choice (C) sprawl (meaning spreading out or wandering off) . . . a menace, *does* make sentence sense. Choice (E) carelessness . . . an oddity, does *not* make sentence sense.

35. **(E)** Choice E is correct. See **Sentence Completion Strategy 2.** Examine the first word of each choice. Choice (A) yielded and Choice (C) abounded don't make sense because consumption of meat neither yields nor abounds. Now consider the other choices. Choice (B) skyrocketed . . . interesting; and Choice (D) stabilized . . . newsworthy, do *not* make good sentence sense. Choice (E) decreased . . . controversial *does* make good sentence sense.

36. **(E)** Choice E is correct. A person who is contrite is not carefree. A person who is dignified is not informal. **(Opposite relationship)**

37. **(C)** Choice C is correct. To taunt is to ridicule or mock while vilify is to defame or slander. To chuckle is to laugh softly while to guffaw is to laugh loudly and boisterously. **(Degree relationship)**

38. **(E)** Choice E is correct. In this question the word MINT means to coin money—as when the government mints money by stamping metal. (The word mint may also refer to a special type of plant whose leaves are used for flavoring and in medicine—but not in this question). Just as money is minted for general circulation to the public, literature is published for the public to read. We have here an Action/Object as well as a Purpose analogy. See **Analogy Strategy 5.** **(Purpose relationship)**

39. **(B)** Choice B is correct. A cynic is a person who does not trust others. A gullible person trusts just about anybody and is easily deceived. A pacifist is peaceful and opposed to violence. A pugnacious person is warlike and in favor of violence. We have here an Opposite relationship. Choice (D) lion : timid is also an Opposite relationship since a lion is courageous and certainly not timid. However, note that a cynic and a pacifist are both persons. A lion is an animal. So Choice D is incorrect. See **Analogy Strategy 4.** **(Association relationship)**

40. **(D)** Choice D is correct. A chair is a specific type of furniture. A bread is a specific type of food. We have here a Whole–Part relationship. Note the position of the words in Choice (E) sedan : automobile. In order to follow through with the FURNITURE : CHAIR position, we would have to change Choice E to automobile : sedan. See **Analogy Strategy 3.** **(Whole–Part relationship)**

41. **(E)** Choice E is correct. To overhear is to listen without any previous intention to get information while to eavesdrop is to listen secretly with a previous intention to get information. To amble is to walk at an easy pace while to prowl is to go about stealthily to find out about something.   **(Degree and Purpose relationship)**

42. **(B)** Choice B is correct. The wheels on a bicycle give it mobility. The runners on a sled give it mobility.
    (Purpose relationship)

43. **(B)** Choice B is correct. A shard is a small, broken off piece of glass. A crumb is a small broken off piece of cookie. The analogy is a Part–Whole type. Choices A, D, and E are also Part–Whole analogies but, in each case, the first word is *not* a small broken off piece of the second word. See **Analogy Strategy 4.**
    (Part–Whole relationship)

44. **(A)** Choice A is correct. To slur is to speak carelessly or hastily. To scribble is to write carelessly or hastily.
    (Action to Situation relationship)

45. **(A)** Choice A is correct. When a tire is punctured, it results in a hole in the tire. A pierced ear results in a hole in the ear.   **(Result relationship)**

EXPLANATORY ANSWERS FOR PRACTICE TEST 6 (continued)

Section 2: Math Ability

As you read these solutions, you are advised to do two things if you answered the Math question incorrectly:

1) When a specific Strategy is referred to in the solution, study that strategy, which you will find in "Using Critical Thinking Skills in Math Questions" (beginning on page 69).

2) When the solution directs you to the "Math Refresher" (beginning on page 205)—for example, Math Refresher #305—study the 305 Math principle to get a clear idea of the Math operation that was necessary for you to know in order to answer the question correctly.

1. **(B)**   Choice B is correct.

(Use Strategy 2: Translate from words to algebra.)

The quotient of x and 3

$\dfrac{x}{3}$

$\left.\dfrac{x}{3} - 8\right\}$ = 8 less than the quotient

and is the required answer.

(Math Refresher #200)

2. **(C)**   Choice C is correct.
(Use Strategy 2: Translate from words to algebra.)

7 of Phil's buckets − 7 of Mark's buckets =
7 × 11 gallons − 7 × 8 gallons =
77 gallons − 56 gallons =
21 gallons (*Answer*)

(Math Refresher #200)

3. **(C)**   Choice C is correct.

Method 1: Do the calculation of each of the answers until you find a solution which is not a whole number.

Method 2: Rewrite each choice as follows:

(A) $\dfrac{66}{3} - \dfrac{36}{3} = 22 - 12 = 10$

(B) $\dfrac{66}{6} + \dfrac{36}{6} = 11 + 6 = 17$

(C) $\dfrac{66}{12} + \dfrac{36}{12} = \dfrac{11}{2} + 3 = 5\dfrac{1}{2} + 3 = 8\dfrac{1}{2}$

Therefore, Choice C is correct.

(Math Refresher #431)

4. **(D)**   Choice D is correct.
(Use Strategy 3: The whole equals the sum of its parts.)

Amount left = Original amount − Amount spent
= \$15.25 − \$7.50
= \$ 7.75 (*Answer*)

(Subtracting Decimals)

5. **(E)**   Choice E is correct.
(Use Strategy 4: Remember classic expressions.)

Remember the factorization.

$$x^2 - 2xy + y^2 = (x - y)^2$$
Let $x = .67$ and $y = .62$
So, $(.67)^2 - 2(.62)(.67) + (.62)^2 =$
$(.67 - .62)^2 =$
$(0.05)^2 =$
0.0025 (*Answer*)

(Math Refresher #409 and #431)

6. **(B)** Choice B is correct.

Given: $6 \times 7 \times 8 \times 9 = \dfrac{12 \times 14 \times 18}{x}$ ☐1

so that $x = \dfrac{12 \times 14 \times 18}{6 \times 7 \times 8 \times 9}$ ☐2

(Use Strategy 12: Try not to make tedious calculations.)

Do *not* multiply the numbers out in the numerator and denominator of ☐2! It is too much work! Rewrite ☐2.

(Use Strategy 19: Factor and reduce.)

$x =$

$\dfrac{12 \times 14 \times 18}{6 \times 7 \times 8 \times 9} = \dfrac{2 \times \cancel{6} \times 2 \times \cancel{7} \times 2 \times \cancel{9}}{\cancel{6} \times \cancel{7} \times 8 \times \cancel{9}}$

$= \dfrac{2 \times 2 \times 2}{8} = \dfrac{\cancel{8}}{\cancel{8}} = 1$

(Answer)

(Math Refresher #108)

7. **(D)** Choice D is correct.

Given:

$$5x = 3 \qquad ☐1$$

(Use Strategy 12: Try not to make tedious calculations.)

Method 1: Add 3 to both sides of ☐1

$$5x + 3 = 6 \qquad ☐2$$

(Use Strategy 13: Find unknown expressions by multiplication.)

Square both sides of ☐2

$$(5x + 3)^2 = 36 \qquad \text{(Answer)} \qquad ☐3$$

This method involves simpler arithmetic (no fractions) than the next method.

Method 2: This method is a bit slower. Solve ☐1 for x to get

$$x = \dfrac{3}{5} \qquad ☐4$$

Using ☐4, calculate the unknown expression.

$$(5x + 3)^2 =$$
$$\left[5\left(\dfrac{3}{5}\right) + 3 \right]^2 =$$
$$(3 + 3)^2 =$$
$$6^2 = 36 \qquad \text{(Answer)}$$

(Math Refresher #406 and #431)

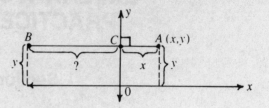

8. **(D)** Choice D is correct.

As shown in the diagram above, the y-coordinates of A and B must be the same because they both lie along the same horizontal line. Since B lies to the left of the y-axis, its x-coordinate must be negative. Since $3AC = BC$, then the x-coordinate of B is

$$-3x$$

and we already know that the y-coordinate is y.

Thus, $(-3x, y)$ is the answer.

(Math Refresher #410)

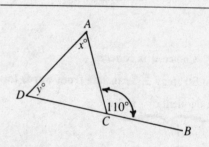

9. **(D)** Choice D is correct.

(Use Strategy 18: Remember isosceles triangle facts.)

Since $AC = CD$, we know that

$$x = y \qquad ☐1$$

We also know that

$$m \angle ACB = m \angle D + m \angle A \qquad ☐2$$

Substituting the given into ☐2, we have

$$110 = y + x \qquad ☐3$$

Substituting ☐1 into ☐3, we get

$$110 = y + y$$
$$110 = 2y \qquad \text{(Answer)}$$

(Math Refresher #507 and #406)

10. **(E)** Choice E is correct.
(Use Strategy 16: The obvious may be tricky!)

Given: $(x + y)^2 = 9$
So that $x + y = 3 \text{ or } -3$

From the information given, we cannot determine whether $x + y$ equals 3 or -3

(Logical Reasoning)

11. **(E)** Choice E is correct.

$$\left(\text{Use Strategy 5: } \quad \text{Average} = \frac{\text{sum of values}}{\text{total number of values}}\right)$$

Let x, y = two unknown numbers.

Thus, $\dfrac{28 + 30 + 32 + x + y}{5} = 34$ ☐1

Multiplying ☐1 by 5,

$$28 + 30 + 32 + x + y = 170$$
or $\qquad 90 + x + y = 170$
or $\qquad\qquad x + y = 80$ *(Answer)*

(Math Refresher #601 and #406)

12. **(C)** Choice C is correct.

(Use Strategy 2: Translate from words to algebra.)

Let x = side of one of the eight squares.

Thus, we are given

$$4x = 16$$
or $\quad x = 4$ ☐1

From what we are told in the problem, we conclude that

$$AE = MF = LG = 4x \qquad ☐2$$
and $\quad AL = BK = CJ = DH = EG = 2x \qquad ☐3$

(Use Strategy 3: The whole equals the sum of its parts.)

Thus,

$AE + MF + LG + AL + BK + CJ + DH + EG =$
$4x + 4x + 4x + 2x + 2x + 2x + 2x + 2x =$
$22x = 88$ *(Answer)*

using ☐1, ☐2, and ☐3.

(Math Refresher #200, # 303, and #304)

13. **(A)** Choice A is correct.

(Use Strategy 11: Use new definitions carefully.)

Given: $\qquad \otimes = \dfrac{x^2}{3}$ and $\boxtimes = \dfrac{9}{x}$

Thus, $\quad \otimes \times \boxtimes = \dfrac{x^2}{3} \times \dfrac{9}{x} = 3x$ *(Answer)*

(Math Refresher #431)

14. **(C)** Choice C is correct.

(Use Strategy 17: Use the given information effectively.)

For I, we have:

Clearly $DB > DA$. So I could not be true.

Clearly D can be the same distance from 2 points (A and B), but not from 3, so II does not apply.

Only Choice C, III only, is now possible.

Choice III is demonstrated below, although it was not necessary for us to examine it.

By definition, all points on the circle are the same distance from the center. So $DA = DB = DC$.

(Math Refresher #303 and #310)

15. **(C)** Choice C is correct.

(Use Strategy 17: Use the given information effectively.)

Given: $\qquad x + by = 5 \qquad ☐1$
$\qquad\qquad 3x + y = 5 \qquad ☐2$
$\qquad\qquad\qquad y = 2 \qquad ☐3$

We want to find b.

Substituting ☐3 into ☐2, we get

$$3x + 2 = 5$$
or $\qquad x = 1$ ☐4

Substituting ☐3 and ☐4 into ☐1, we have

$$1 + 2b = 5$$
or $\qquad 2b = 4$
or $\qquad b = 2$ *(Answer)*

(Math Refresher #406 and #431)

16. **(B)** Choice B is correct.

The ratio of boys to girls in the class is 2:3. Choice C is the answer because 9:12 = 3:4 which does not equal 2:3

(Math Refresher #108)

17. **(D)** Choice D is correct.

(Use Strategy 10: Know how to use units.)

$$\left(\frac{p \text{ gallons}}{\text{car}}\right) \times (r \text{ cars}) = pr \text{ gallons for each month}$$

$$\frac{q \text{ gallons}}{\dfrac{pr \text{ gallons}}{\text{month}}} = \frac{q}{pr} \text{ months}$$

(Math Refresher #121)

18. **(C)** Choice C is correct.
(Use Strategy 10: Know how to use units.)

Since 7 days = 1 week, 24 hours = 1 day, and 60 minutes = 1 hour, then

$$1 \text{ week} = (1 \text{ week})\left(\frac{7 \text{ days}}{\text{week}}\right)\left(\frac{24 \text{ hours}}{\text{day}}\right)\left(\frac{60 \text{ minutes}}{\text{hour}}\right)$$
$$= (7)(24)(60) \text{ minutes}$$

Thus,

$$\frac{24 \text{ minutes}}{1 \text{ week}} = \frac{24 \text{ minutes}}{(7)(24)(60) \text{ minutes}} = \frac{1}{420} \quad (Answer)$$

(Math Refresher #121)

19. **(E)** Choice E is correct.
(Use Strategy 11: Use new definitions carefully.)

By definition, the l-length from -3 to $3 =$

$$3 - (-3) =$$
$$3 + 3 =$$
$$6 \qquad (Answer)$$

(Math Refresher #431)

20. **(A)** Choice A is correct.

By definition, the l-length from -4 to each of the other points follow:

$$R - (-4) = R + 4 \qquad \boxed{1}$$
$$S - (-4) = S + 4 \qquad \boxed{2}$$
$$T - (-4) = T + 4 \qquad \boxed{3}$$
$$U - (-4) = U + 4 \qquad \boxed{4}$$
$$V - (-4) = V + 4 \qquad \boxed{5}$$

From their position on the number line we know that:

$$R < S < T < U < V \qquad \boxed{6}$$

(Use Strategy 6: Know how to manipulate inequalities.)

Adding 4 to each term of $\boxed{6}$, we get

$$R + 4 < S + 4 < T + 4$$
$$< U + 4 < V + 4 \quad \boxed{7}$$

It is obvious, from $\boxed{7}$ that $R + 4$ is smallest.

Thus, $\boxed{1}$ above, point R, has the least l-length from -4.

(Logical Reasoning)

21. **(D)** Choice D is correct.

(Use Strategy 2: Translate from words to algebra.)

Let $x, x + 1, x + 2, x + 3, x + 4$ represent the 5 consecutive integers.

Then, $x + x + 1 + x + 2 + x + 3 + x + 4 = w$
$$5x + 10 = w \qquad \boxed{1}$$

The next 5 consecutive positive integers will be:

$$x + 5, x + 6, x + 7, x + 8, x + 9$$

Their sum will be:

$$x + 5 + x + 6 + x + 7 + x + 8 + x + 9 =$$
$$5x + 35 \qquad \boxed{2}$$

We can write $\boxed{2}$ as $5x + 35$
$$= 5x + 10 + 25 \qquad \boxed{3}$$

Substituting $\boxed{1}$ into $\boxed{3}$, we get

$$5x + 10 + 25 = w + 25 \qquad (Answer)$$

(Math Refresher #200 and #406)

22. **(C)** Choice C is correct.
(Use Strategy 2: Translate from words to algebra.)

We are told that area of the square is twice area of triangle.
This translates to:

$$a^2 = 2\left(\frac{1}{2} \times b \times c\right)$$
$$a^2 = bc \qquad \boxed{1}$$

We are given that $bc = 100$ $\qquad \boxed{2}$

Substituting $\boxed{2}$ into $\boxed{1}$, we get

$$a^2 = 100 \qquad (Answer)$$

(Math Refresher #200, #303, and #306)

23. **(A)** Choice A is correct.

Given
that the radius of the circle $= 2$, we have
Circumference $= 2\pi(\text{radius}) = 2\pi(2)$
$$= 4\pi \text{ inches} \qquad \boxed{1}$$
We are given that $\overarc{AD} + \overarc{BC} = 3\pi$ inches $\qquad \boxed{2}$

(Use Strategy 3: The whole equals the sum of its parts.)

We know that $\overarc{AD} + \overarc{BC} + \overarc{AC} + \overarc{DB} =$ circumference of circle $\qquad \boxed{3}$

Substituting $\boxed{1}$ and $\boxed{2}$ into $\boxed{3}$, we have

$$3\pi \text{ inches} + \overarc{AC} + \overarc{DB} = 4\pi \text{ inches}$$
$$\overarc{AC} + \overarc{DB} = \pi \text{ inches} \qquad \boxed{4}$$

We know that the measure of an arc can be found by:

$$\text{measure of arc} = \left(\frac{\text{length of arc}}{\text{circumference of circle}}\right) \times 360 \qquad \boxed{5}$$

Substituting $\boxed{1}$ and $\boxed{4}$ into $\boxed{5}$, we get

measure of $AC + DB$
$$= \left(\frac{\pi \text{ inches}}{4\pi \text{ inches}}\right) \times 360 = \frac{\cancel{4} \times 90}{\cancel{4}} = 90 \qquad \boxed{6}$$

(Use Strategy 19: Factor and reduce.)

From the diagram $m \angle AOC = m \angle DOB = y$
Therefore, $m\overarc{AC} = m\overarc{DB} = y \qquad \boxed{7}$

Substituting $\boxed{7}$ into $\boxed{6}$, we get

$$y + y = 90 \quad \text{or} \quad 2y = 90$$
$$\text{or} \quad y = 45 \ (Answer)$$

(Math Refresher #310 and #524)

24. **(B)** Choice B is correct.
(Use Strategy 2: Translate from words to algebra.)

Let $r =$ Ross's age now.
$19 =$ Amanda's age now.
Thus, $r - 5 =$ Ross's age five years ago. $\qquad \boxed{1}$
$19 - 5 = 14 =$ Amanda's age five years ago. $\qquad \boxed{2}$

We are given: Five years ago, Ross was N times as old as Amanda was.

Substituting $\boxed{1}$ and $\boxed{2}$ into $\boxed{3}$, we have

$$r - 5 = N(14)$$
$$r = 14N + 5 \qquad (Answer)$$

25. **(C)** Choice C is correct.

The volume of the rectangular solid to be immersed is:

$$V = (1 \text{ ft})(1 \text{ ft})(2 \text{ ft}) = 2 \text{ cu. ft} \qquad \boxed{1}$$

When the solid is immersed, the volume of the displaced water will be:

$$(2 \text{ ft.})(6 \text{ ft.})(x \text{ ft.}) = 12x \text{ cu. ft.} \qquad \boxed{2}$$

where x represents the height of the displaced water. $\boxed{1}$ and $\boxed{2}$ must be equal. So

$$2 \text{ cu. ft.} = 12x \text{ cu. ft.}$$
$$\frac{1}{6} \text{ ft.} = x$$

(Use Strategy 10: Know how to use units.)

$$\left(\frac{1}{6} \text{ ft}\right)\left(\frac{12 \text{ inches}}{\text{foot}}\right) =$$

$$\frac{12}{6} = 2 \text{ inches that the displaced water will rise.}$$

(Math Refresher #312 and #121)

EXPLANATORY ANSWERS FOR PRACTICE TEST 6 (continued)

Section 3: Standard Written English

> Section 3 does not count toward your SAT score. This Standard Written English section is used only for Freshman English placement when you get to college. However, you are advised to improve yourself in grammar and usage, and also in sentence structure. If you do well in the Standard Written English Test, you will be placed more advantageously in your college Freshman English class.

1. **(A)** "The reason *she* and her cousin . . ."
The subject form of the personal pronoun is *she*—not *her*.

2. **(B)** "Though Seaver pitched *really* well . . ."
The adverb *well* must be modified by another adverb such as *really*—not by an adjective such as *real*.

3. **(A)** "Jim and *he* . . . finally discovered . . ."
Jim and *he* are the compound subjects of the verb *discovered*. The subject form of the pronoun is *he*—not *him*.

4. **(D)** ". . . the *more* effective and moving."
In a comparison of two things (such as two plays), we use the comparative degree (*more*)—not the superlative degree (*most*).

5. **(B)** "Each of the hotel's 500 rooms *was* equipped . . ."
The singular subject (*Each*) requires a singular verb (*was equipped*—not *were equipped*).

6. **(B)** "A textbook . . . usually contains . . ."
One cannot use the two words *usually* and *always* together because one word contradicts the other. *Usually* means almost all the time; *always* means all the time.

7. **(E)** All underlined parts are correct.

8. **(C)** ". . . than were *their* parents . . ."
The possessive adjective *their* modifies the noun *parents*. The contraction *they're* means *they are*.

9. **(A)** "The sun *had hardly* set . . ."
The expression *hadn't hardly* is always incorrect.

10. **(B)** "The lilacs . . . smell *sweet* . . ."
We use the predicate adjective (*sweet*) after the copulative verb (*smell*). The use of the adverb *sweetly* is incorrect in this case.

11. **(C)** ". . . to *whoever* is best qualified."
Since the underlined word is the subject of the subordinate clause, *whoever* (the nominative form) must be used. *Whomever* is the objective form.

12. **(A)** "*Since* the United States has a food surplus . . ."
Being that is always incorrect for *since* or *because*.

13. **(C)** ". . . factory morale, *already* low . . ."
All ready means everybody (is) ready. The adverb *already* modifying the adjective *low* is correct here.

14. **(C)** "A series of debates . . . *was* scheduled . . ."
Series is a collective noun with a feeling of singularity. As a singular subject, it takes a singular verb (*was scheduled*).

15. **(D)** ". . . neither outstanding *nor* attractive."
The correlative conjunctions are *neither . . . nor*—not *neither . . . or*.

16. **(B)** "We did the job as *well* as we could . . ."
The adverb *well* must be used to modify the verb *did*. The adjective *good* is incorrect for such modification.

17. **(C)** ". . . *who's* to decide . . .
The interrogative pronoun-adjective *whose* should not be used here. We mean: *who is* (*who's*).

18. **(A)** "If I *had had* more time . . ."
In a contrary to fact condition in the past, the "if clause" must have a past perfect subjunctive form (*had had*).

19. **(C)** "More leisure . . . *is* attainable . . ."
Since the subject (*leisure*) is singular, the verb must be singular (*is attainable*).

20. **(C)** "*. . . they* can cause irreparable damage."
We have a plural subject: *Morphine* and *drugs*. Accordingly, the pronoun which occurs later in the sentence must be plural *(they)* since a pronoun must agree with its antecedent in number.

The verb in this past conditional situation should be *had been*—not *had have been*. Another way of correctly starting the sentence would be "If I had been . . ."

21. **(E)** All underlined parts are correct.

22. **(D)** ". . . we cannot hope that nations . . . *will live* peaceably with us."
The clause beginning with *that nations . . .* requires a finite verb *(will live)*—not an infinitive *(to live)*.

23. **(D)** ". . . she would very much have liked *to go*." A present infinitive *(to go)*—not a past infinitive *(to have gone)* is used after a verb which is in the perfect tense *(would have liked)*.

24. **(B)** ". . . *is* now aware of . . ."
A compound subject *(man, woman, and child)* which is introduced by *every* must have a singular verb *(is now aware*—not *are* now aware).

25. **(C)** ". . . because it *stank* so."
The past tense of the verb *stink* is *stank*—not *stunk*. The present perfect tense, however, is *has stunk*.

26. **(D)** The important thing is that Tricia Nixon had (finally) become engaged. Choice D, alone, brings out the primary importance of the engagement and the secondary importance of her being born on St. Patrick's Day. Moreover, Choices B and C are run-on sentences.

27. **(B)** Choice A is incorrect because the nominative form ("he") is required: "as fully as him" is wrong. Choice B is correct. Choices C, D, and E are incorrect because the object of the preposition must have an objective case form—the preposition "but" must be followed by the object case form "him."

28. **(A)** Choice A is correct. Choice B is incorrect because "on account" may not be used as a subordinate conjunction. Choice C is incorrect because it gives the meaning that the judge is doing the charging. Choice D is incorrect because the possessive noun ("defendant") modifying the gerund ("charging") must take the form "defendant's." Choice E creates a run-on sentence.

29. **(A)** Choice A is correct. Choices B, C, and D are incorrect because they change the meaning of the original sentence. Choice E creates a run-on sentence.

30. **(E)** Choices A and B are incorrect because they give the idea that the plans are trying to avoid the hot sun. Choice C is awkward. Choice D is a run-on sentence. Choice E is correct.

31. **(B)** Choice A is too wordy. Choice B is correct. Choice C is incorrect because it changes the tense of the original sentence—"Whatever (may) be her thoughts" is in the present tense. Choice D does not retain the meaning of the original sentence. Choice E makes no sense.

32. **(B)** Choices A and E are incorrect because the subject word "use" requires a singular verb ("makes"). Choice B is correct. Choices C and D are awkward.

33. **(E)** "Irregardless" (Choice A) is incorrect. "Regardless about" (Choice B) is unidiomatic. Choices C and D change the meaning of the original sentence. Moreover, Choice D makes the sentence ungrammatical. Choice E is correct.

34. **(A)** Choice A is correct. Choices B, C, and E change the meaning of the original sentence. Choice D is too wordy.

35. **(C)** The infinitive "to effect" means "to bring about"—this is not the meaning intended in the original sentence. Therefore, Choices A, B, and D are incorrect. Choice C is correct. Choice E changes the meaning of the original sentence.

36. **(B)** In the original sentence, "who" should replace "whom" as the subject of the subordinate clause ("who were policemen"). "I believe" is simply a parenthetical expression. Therefore, Choice A is incorrect and Choice B is correct. Choice C creates a run-on sentence. Choice D improperly changes the sentence from a complex type to a compound type. Choice E does not retain the meaning of the original sentence.

37. **(D)** Choices A and B suffer from improper ellipsis. Choice C changes the meaning of the original sentence. Choice D is correct. Choice E is too wordy.

38. **(E)** Sequence of tenses in a past contrary-to-fact condition requires the "had waited" form in the "if" clause. Therefore Choices A, B, C, and D are incorrect and Choice E is correct.

39. **(C)** We are concerned here with the apostrophe use with a singular name ending in "s." We are also concerned with improper ellipsis. In Choice A, "James'" is correct but we must either say "to read than *the prose style* of James Joyce" or "to read than James Joyce's." In Choice B, "Jame's" is incorrect—his name is not "Jame." Choice C is correct. Choices D and E are incorrect for the same reason that Choice A is incorrect—improper ellipsis.

40. **(C)** Choice A is incorrect because in a "neither . . . nor" construction, the number of the verb is determined by the "nor" subject noun ("followers"). Since "followers" is plural, the verb must be plural ("know"). Choices B, D, and E are incorrect for the same reason. Moreover, Choice B is incorrect for another reason: the correlative form is "neither . . . nor"—not "neither . . . or". Choice C is correct.

41. **(D)** "... you or *I*."
A pronoun which is an appositive of a subject must, like the subject, be in the nominative case. The word *who* is the subject of the clause "who should go out ..." The subject of a clause or a sentence is in the nominative case. The pronouns which act as appositives to the subject must, accordingly, have nominative case forms (*you and I*—not *you and me*).

42. **(B)** "I prize my *mother-in-law's* picture ..." When you form the possessive of a compound word, you must add the *apostrophe* and *s* only to the last word in the compound.

43. **(A)** "Had I *been* in my brother's position ..." The past contrary-to-fact verb form *had been* should be used in the subordinate clause of the sentence, the action of which has occurred in the past.

44. **(E)** All underlined parts are correct.

45. **(B)** "The company is planning a series of lectures for *its* executives ..."
A singular pronoun-adjective (*its*—not *their*) must be used to refer to a collective noun (*company*) when the members of the collective noun are considered as a unit.

46. **(E)** All underlined parts are correct.

47. **(D)** "... and, above all, *in facilitating* learning."
Parallelism requires consistency of grammatical usage. Since we have two preceding gerunds (*keeping* and *encouraging*), we must follow through with another gerund (*facilitating*)—not an infinitive (*to facilitate*).

48. **(D)** "... of the guide we *had chosen*."
The past perfect of *to choose* is *had chosen*.

49. **(B)** "Television ... *helps* us ..."
The subject of the sentence is singular (*Television*). It follows that the verb must be singular (*helps*).

50. **(D)** "... difficult to *succeed*."
The correct expression is *difficult to succeed*—not *difficult on succeeding*.

EXPLANATORY ANSWERS FOR
PRACTICE TEST 6 (continued)
Section 4: Verbal Ability

1. **(B)** Choice B is correct. *Compatible* means *agreeable; harmonious*. The opposite of *compatible* is *inharmonious*.

2. **(E)** Choice E is correct. *Refute* means *to prove wrong*. The opposite of *refute* is *confirm*.

3. **(A)** Choice A is correct. *Culpable* means *blameworthy*. The opposite of *culpable* is *innocent*.

4. **(C)** Choice C is correct. See **Antonym Strategy 3.** *Portly* means *stout; large*. The opposite of *portly* is *slim*.

5. **(C)** Choice C is correct. See **Antonym Strategies 1, 3.** *Defection* means *desertion*. The opposite of *defection* is *loyalty*.

6. **(D)** Choice D is correct. *Uncanny* means *weird; strange*. The opposite of *uncanny* is *usual*.

7. **(E)** Choice E is correct. *Altruism* means *concern for others; unselfishness*. The opposite of *altruism* is *selfishness*.

8. **(B)** Choice B is correct. *Deft* means *skillful*. The opposite of *deft* is *awkward*.

9. **(A)** Choice A is correct. *Fetter* means *to shackle; to confine; to restrain*. The opposite of *fetter* is *assist*.

10. **(D)** Choice D is correct. *Mendacious* means *lying; false*. The opposite of *mendacious* is *honorable*.

11. **(B)** Choice B is correct. See **Sentence Completion Strategy 1.** The word "prevalent" (meaning widely or commonly occurring) completed the sentence so that it makes good sense. The other choices don't do that.

12. **(B)** Choice B is correct. Since this question has the two-blank choices, let us use **Sentence Completion Strategy 2.** When we use Step 1 of Strategy 2, we find a very unusual situation in this question—the first words in all five choices make sense: "With lack of" *advice* or *control* or *opportunity* or *sympathy* or *conscience*, "anyone can develop the disease of alcoholism . . ." Accordingly, we must go to Step 2 of Strategy 2 and consider *both* words of each choice. When we do so, we find that only Choice (B) *control . . . foolishly*, makes good sentence sense.

13. **(A)** Choice A is correct. See **Sentence Completion Strategy 2.** Examine the first word of each choice. Choice (B) uplift and Choice (C) enthusiasm do not make sense because "uplift" and "enthusiasm" are not likely to plague any person. Now consider the other choices. Choice (D) boredom . . . idleness, and Choice (E) involvement . . . laziness, do *not* make sense in the sentence as a whole. Choice (A) pressure . . . creativity, *does* make sense.

14. **(B)** Choice B is correct. See **Sentence Completion Strategy 1.** Something staple, such as bread, is in constant supply and demand. Beer, then, is considered as a liquid bread by the Bavarians. Choices A, C, D, and E do not make good sense in the sentence.

15. **(D)** Choice D is correct. See **Sentence Completion Strategy 1.** The word "extreme" is the most appropriate among the five choices because the forest fire season is in *full swing*. The other choices are, therefore, not appropriate.

16. **(D)** Choice D is correct. A preserve is a place which protects animals. A vault is a place which protects money. Note that the word "preserve" in this analogy is a noun. This word may also be used as a verb—but not in this analogy. See **Analogy Strategy 5.**
(Purpose relationship)

17. **(A)** Choice A is correct. The word tepid means moderately warm. When something is very, very warm, it is hot. The word cool means moderately cold. When something is very, very cold, it is frigid. We have here a Degree relationship. Note the position of the words in Choice (B) spotless: clean. Spotless means perfectly clean. We have here a Degree relationship also. But in order to follow through with the TEPID: HOT position of words, we would have to change Choice B to clean: spotless. See **Analogy Strategy 3.**
(Degree relationship)

18. **(B)** Choice B is correct. To advocate a change is to encourage its acceptance. To endorse a candidate is to encourage his/her acceptance.
(Action to Object relationship)

19. **(C)** Choice C is correct. A fare is paid by a passenger. Tuition is paid by a student. **(Purpose relationship)**

20. **(D)** Choice D is correct. A barber uses a razor to do his job. A chef uses a knife to do his job. We have here a Purpose relationship. Choice (E) telescope: astronomer does *not* have the proper word order necessary to be the correct answer. A telescope does not use an astronomer to do its job. If this choice were reversed to read astronomer: telescope, it would have the proper word order for the correct answer since an astronomer *does* use a telescope to do his job. See **Analogy Strategy 3.** **(Association and Purpose relationship)**

21. **(C)** Choice C is correct. A kennel is a place that provides shelter for a dog. A barn is a place that provides shelter for a cow. We have here a purpose analogy. Choices A, B, and E are also purpose analogies but they do not express the same purpose as the capitalized words and Choice C do. See **Analogy Strategy 4.** **(Purpose relationship)**

22. **(A)** Choice A is correct. A pig's nose is called a snout. An elephant's "nose" is called a trunk. **(Association relationship)**

23. **(B)** Choice B is correct. One staples sheets to hold them together. One nails boards to hold them together. **(Purpose relationship)**

24. **(C)** Choice C is correct. A suspect may be convicted if wrongdoing has been shown. A student may be expelled if wrongdoing has been shown. Choice C may seem correct but it is not. A president is impeached simply because he is accused. Wrongdoing has not been decided at the time of impeachment. See **Analogy Strategy 4.** **(Result relationship)**

25. **(A)** Choice A is correct. The purpose of sandpaper is to be abrasive. The purpose of an emollient is to be soothing. **(Purpose relationship)**

26. **(A)** Choice A is correct. The main idea of the passage is expressed in lines 19–20: "Science seems to have come into existence merely for its bearings on practical life." This main idea is also expressed in other parts of the passage. For example—Lines 1–2: "Science, like everything else . . . needs and desires." Also lines 15–17: ". . . the bulk of mankind . . . advantages it brings with it." Finally, all through the last paragraph of the passage we learn how the Babylonians and the Egyptians reaped practical benefits with the help of science.
Choices B, C, D, and E are true but they are too confining to be considered the main idea of the passage. Therefore, these choices are incorrect.

27. **(E)** Choice E is correct. See lines 8–14: "Science is valued . . . most important consideration of all to scientific men." Choice A is incorrect. The passage does not indicate that this choice is true. Furthermore, others *before* the Babylonians and the Egyptians also used scientific methods. Choice B is incorrect. See lines 28–30: "The cultivation of crops . . . made a calendar almost a necessity (for the Babylonians and Egyptians)." Choice C is incorrect. First see lines 21–24: "More than two thousand years before . . . measuring space and time." Now see lines 33–36: "Twelve of these months . . . putting in extra months." Choice D is incorrect. See lines 21–24 again.

28. **(B)** Choice B is correct. See lines 8–14: "Science is valued . . . provides the imagination . . . most important consideration of all to scientific men." Choices A, C, D, and E are incorrect because the author does not imply in any way that scientists are sociable, practical, philosophical, or arrogant people.

29. **(C)** Choice C is correct. The passage brings out clearly that George's family will not welcome Constance. When George asks: "Will everyone make her welcome?"— his mother replies: "Probably not." Choices A, B, D, and E are incorrect because there is no indication in the passage that any one of these choices is related to the mother's saying "you already know that some will hate you for the step you've taken."

30. **(B)** Choice B is correct. See lines 21–22 in which George's mother says: "The Irish are a despised lot, though I don't understand why." It is very likely that George's family are Protestants and that Constance is Catholic. Choice A is incorrect. Constance is probably a newcomer as indicated by lines 13–14: "It's a tragedy your father couldn't have lived long enough to meet Constance." Therefore, Constance could not have been George's school sweetheart. Choices C and E are incorrect because there is no indication of these choices in the passage. Choice D is incorrect because Constance has just come to George's home town for the first time and probably has not even met George's sister.

31. **(D)** George was certainly much concerned about how his future wife Constance was going to be dealt with by his family. The passage indicates that there will likely be hostility shown to Constance. George must wonder whether Constance will be able to take that hostility. Accordingly, Choice D is correct. It follows that George's attitude toward what the future has in store is not one of great confidence nor utter despair nor mild confusion nor philosophical acceptance. Therefore, Choices A, B, C, and E are incorrect.

32. **(A)** The auxiliary verb *must* refers to something that ought to happen or is supposed to happen. Example: You *must* do your homework." The auxiliary verb *will* refers to something that will definitely happen or will most probably happen. Example: "You *will* do your homework." The latter part of the passage refers to the attitude that George's family may take toward his forthcoming marriage to Constance. George's mother reassures him by telling him that "... there is still a great deal of un-Christian hate in the world. Love will somehow defeat it. It will and, if we're all to survive, it must." Therefore, Choice A is correct. The passage does not indicate or imply Choices B, C, D, or E. Therefore, these are incorrect choices.

33. **(E)** Choice E is correct. See lines 5–7: "But nowhere in this country . . . any other city in America." Choice A is incorrect. See lines 8–10: "... the greatest epidemic . . . peak of their productive lives." The epidemic referred to is, of course, heart disease. Cancer is not mentioned. Choice B is incorrect. See lines 25–27: "Although only measurement . . . Framingham's mission." Choice C is incorrect. See lines 23–25: "Moreover, the study shows . . . blood vessel diseases." Choice D is incorrect because the passage does not indicate that the Framingham project is now complete.

34. **(B)** Choice B is correct. See lines 15–22: "By revealing . . . stress . . . how people live." Having worries and having stress are strongly connected. Choice A is incorrect because the passage gives no statistics or facts about the risk women run in the matter of getting heart disease. Choice C is incorrect. See lines 27–30: "... its (the Framingham project) findings indicate . . . controlling high blood pressure." Low blood pressure is not referred to. Choice D is not correct. See lines 6–8: "Framingham is just like . . . mankind has faced." Only cities in America are referred to. Choice E is incorrect. See lines 4–5: "And for a man in his early 50's, one in five [chances of getting heart disease within 14 years]." The 50-year-old man would be 64 years old—not 70 years old—after 14 years.

35. **(D)** Choice D is correct. The passage throughout stresses the importance of avoiding certain things and taking certain steps in order to prevent the occurrence of heart disease. For example, see lines 15–22: "By revealing the roles . . . how people live." The other choices consist of quotations that are not as appropriate in describing the author's attitude, as Choice D is. Accordingly, Choices A, B, C, and E are incorrect.

36. **(C)** The cruelties of our prison system are referred to in lines 22–29: "... just as so much of our current violence is socially acceptable . . . classes of society." The horrors of our prisons were current at the time the author wrote this article and they are current today. The violence spoken about in Choices A, B, and D were socially acceptable at the time they occurred in the past. The question asks for an illustration of *current* "socially acceptable" violence. Accordingly, Choices A, B, and D are incorrect. Choice E, though it refers to current violence, is *not* socially acceptable. See lines 30–35: "What we have now . . . familiar 'crime in the streets'." Therefore, Choice E is incorrect.

37. **(A)** Choice A is correct. The author's definition of violence is extremely broad—including not only acts of force but also the social infliction of harm as in "exploiting women and children in textile mills and sweatshops." (Lines 17–18). The passage refers to acts of violence other than those expressed in Choices B and C. Therefore, these choices are incorrect. One could easily cite illegal conduct on the part of the government or a citizen that would *not* be of a violent nature. Therefore, Choice D is incorrect. The F.B.I. could conceivably commit an act of violence. The author would not condone this. See lines 38–40: "But now, too, official violence . . . numerous sympathizers." Therefore, Choice E is incorrect.

38. **(A)** The author describes current violence as "acceptable neither to the authorities nor to the victims" [Item I]. Item II and Item III are not indicated anywhere in the passage. Therefore, only Choice A is correct.

39. **(C)** Choice C is the only form of violence which is *not* mentioned in the passage. Therefore, Choice C is correct. The following line references are given to indicate that Choices A, B, D, and E represent forms of violence that *are* mentioned in the passage. Choice A—See lines 7–8: "... the lawlessness . . . during Reconstruction and after." Choice B—See lines 2–3: "... our almost . . . against the Indians." Choice D—See lines 3–4: "... and all the others . . . Mexicans in Texas." Choice E—See lines 5–6: "... the pervasive violence of slavery."

40. **(D)** The author, throughout the passage, expresses opposition to any type of violence—whether one engages in violence or tolerates it. Therefore, Choice D is correct because the author would not approve of the violence practiced by football players. Accordingly, Choices A, B, C, and E are incorrect. Although Choice A involves violence, a person who tries to prevent a mugging is obviously opposed to the violence of the mugger.

EXPLANATORY ANSWERS FOR PRACTICE TEST 6 (continued)

Section 5: Math Ability

1. **(E)** Choice E is correct.
   (Use Strategy 2: Translate from words to algebra.)

   Let g = number of games the team played
   28 = number of games Bobby watched
   $\frac{2}{3}g$ = number of games Tommy watched

   We are given

   $$\frac{2}{3}g > 28 \qquad \boxed{1}$$

   Multiplying $\boxed{1}$ by $\frac{3}{2}$, we get

   $$\left(\frac{3}{2}\right)\frac{2}{3}g > 28\left(\frac{3}{2}\right)$$
   $$g > 42$$

   Only Choice E satisfies this relationship.

   (Math Refresher #200, #422 and #426)

2. **(D)** Choice D is correct.

   Using the distributive property, we get
   $3x(4x + 2y) = 12x^2 + 6xy$

   (Math Refresher #409)

3. **(D)** Choice D is correct.

   We are told that 1 decimeter = 100 millimeters

   (Use Strategy 17: Use the given information effectively.)

   Dividing each height from the table, we get:

   (A) $\frac{1700}{100} = 17$

   (B) $\frac{2450}{100} = 24.5$

   (C) $\frac{2735}{100} = 27.35$

   (D) $\frac{1928}{100} = 19.28$

   (E) $\frac{2130}{100} = 21.3$

   Note that choices B, C, and E are greater than 20.

   (Math Refresher #121 and Division)

4. **(E)** Choice E is correct.

   Given: $\qquad a - 3 = 7 \qquad \boxed{1}$

   (Use Strategy 13: Find unknowns by addition, subtraction and multiplication.)

   Fast Method: From $\boxed{1}$, we can subtract 7 from both sides, and then add 3 to both sides to get

   $$a - 7 = 3 \qquad \boxed{2}$$

   Multiplying $\boxed{2}$ by 2,

   $$2a - 14 = 6 \qquad \text{(Answer)}$$

   Slow Method: Solve $\boxed{1}$ to get

   $$a = 10 \qquad \boxed{3}$$

   Now substitute $\boxed{3}$:

   $$2a - 14 = 2(10) - 14 = 6 \qquad \text{(Answer)}$$

   (Math Refresher #406 and #431)

5. **(C)** Choice C is correct.
   (Use Strategy 10: Know how to use units.)

   We are given his rate is $\frac{90 \text{ laps}}{6 \text{ hours}}$

   $$\frac{90 \text{ laps}}{6 \text{ hours}} \times \frac{1 \text{ hour}}{60 \text{ minutes}} =$$

   (Use Strategy 19: Factor and reduce.)

   $$\frac{\cancel{3} \times \cancel{3} \times \cancel{10} \text{ laps}}{\cancel{3} \times 2 \times \cancel{3} \times 2 \times \cancel{10} \text{ minutes}} =$$

   $\frac{1}{4}$ lap per minute (*Answer*)

   (Math Refresher #121)

6. **(D)** Choice D is correct.
   Use Strategy 17: Use the given information effectively.)

   Change all fractions to decimal form:

   $$\frac{7}{10} = .7$$
   $$\frac{7}{100} = .07$$
   $$\frac{77}{1000} = .077$$

   Adding these we get .847 (*Answer*)

   (Math Refresher #104)

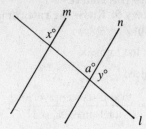

7. (A) Choice A is correct.

Know the properties of parallel lines. If 2 parallel lines are crossed by a transversal, the pairs of corresponding angles are equal. Thus,

$$x = a \qquad \boxed{1}$$

From the diagram, $a + y = 180 \qquad \boxed{2}$

Substituting $\boxed{1}$ into $\boxed{2}$, we get

$$x + y = 180 \qquad (Answer)$$

(Math Refresher #504)

8. (D) Choice D is correct.
(Use Strategy C: Use numbers in place of variables when a comparison is difficult.)

Choose specific values of a and b satisfying the requirements

EXAMPLE 1

$$a = 13 \quad \text{and} \quad b = 1$$

Thus, $a > b$

EXAMPLE 2

$$a = 1 \quad \text{and} \quad b = 13$$

Thus, $a < b$
So Choice D is the answer.

(Math Refresher #431)

9. (A) Choice A is correct.

Since $\dfrac{\frac{1}{3}}{\frac{3}{4}} = \dfrac{4}{3} = 1\frac{1}{3}$ and $1.25 = 1 + \dfrac{1}{4}$,

the columns become

Column A	Column B
$1\frac{1}{3}$	$1\frac{1}{4}$

and the quantity in Column A is greater.

You could also use **Strategy D,** and multiply both columns by $\dfrac{3}{4}$.

Column A	Column B
$\dfrac{4}{3}$	$\dfrac{5}{4}$
$\left(\dfrac{3}{4}\right)\dfrac{4}{3}$	$\left(\dfrac{3}{4}\right)\left(\dfrac{5}{4}\right)$
$1 \qquad >$	$\dfrac{15}{16}$

(Math Refresher #111 and #112)

10. (D) Choice D is correct.
(Use Strategy 2: Translate from words to algebra.)

We are given the price of 1 pencil $= 48¢$
Let $p =$ price of 1 pen

Column A	Column B
$p + 48¢$	$2p$

(Use Strategy C: Use numbers in place of variables when a comparison is difficult.)

Obviously, each result depends on the value of p.

If $p = 48$ then both columns are $=$

$$48 + 48 \quad = \quad 2(48)$$

If $p = 40$, then A is larger.

$$40 + 48 > 2(40)$$
$$88 > 80$$

Since 2 different results are possible, no determination can be made and Choice D is correct.

(Math Refresher #200 and #431)

11. **(B)** Choice B is correct.

The easiest way to do this problem is simply to calculate the given quantities:

Column A		Column B
$2^3 + 2^2 + 2 + 1 =$		$2^4 =$
$8 + 4 + 2 + 1 =$		
15	$<$	16

(**Math Refresher #431**)

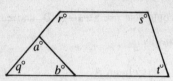

12. **(C)** Choice C is correct.
(**Use Strategy 3: The whole equals the sum of its parts.**)

The sum of the angles of a triangle $= 180$

So, $a + b + q = 180$ ☐1

We know that the sum of the angles of a quadrilateral $= 360$

Therefore, $q + r + s + t = 360$ ☐2

(**Use Strategy 13: Find unknowns by subtracting equations.**)

Subtracting ☐1 from ☐2, we get

$q + r + s + t - (a + b + q)$
$= 360 - 180$
$q + r + s + t - a - b - q = 180$
$r + s + t - a - b = 180$ ☐3

(**Use Strategy 13: Find unknowns by addition.**)

Adding $a + b$ to both sides of ☐3, we get

$r + s + t = a + b + 180$

and the answer is clear.

(**Math Refresher #505 and #406**)

13. **(B)** Choice B is correct.
(**Use Strategy 6: Know how to manipulate inequalities.**)

We are given that $x - y < 0$ ☐1

Adding y to both sides of ☐1, we get $x < y$

(**Math Refresher #420**)

14. **(B)** Choice B is correct.
(**Use Strategy 9: Know the rate, time and distance relationship.**)

Remember the formula:

Average speed

$$= \frac{\text{total distance traveled}}{\text{total time elapsed}}$$

$$= \frac{48 \text{ miles}}{1\frac{1}{2} \text{ hours}}$$

$$= \frac{48}{\frac{3}{2}} = 48 \times \frac{2}{3} = 16 \times 3 \times \frac{2}{3}$$

$$= 32 \text{ miles per hour}$$

(**Math Refresher #201 and #202**)

15. **(B)** Choice B is correct.
(**Use Strategy 3: The whole equals the sum of its parts.**)

From the diagram we see that

$8p = 360$ and $6q = 360$
$p = 45$ $q = 60$

Thus, $p < q$

(**Math Refresher #526 and #406**)

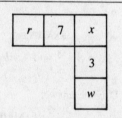

16. **(B)** Choice B is correct.
(**Use Strategy 2: Translate from words to algebra.**)

We are *given:*

$r + 7 + x = w + 3 + x$ ☐1

(**Use Strategy 1: Cancel expressions from both sides of an equation.**)

Subtracting x from both sides ☐1, we get

$r + 7 = w + 3$ ☐2

Subtracting 7 from both sides of ☐2, we get

$r = w - 4$

This translates to r is 4 less than w, so

$r < w$

(**Math Refresher #200 and #406**)

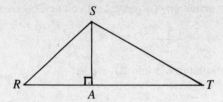

17. **(B)** Choice B is correct.
(Use Strategy 18: Remember triangle facts.)
SA is the altitude to side *RT*.
By definition, $SA \perp RT$.

The shortest distance from a point to a line is the length of $\perp$ segment from the point to the line. Thus, *SA* is the shortest distance from *S* to *RT*.
Thus,

$$SA < SR$$

(Math Refresher #514)

18. **(A)** Choice A is correct.

(Use Strategy 6: Know how to manipulate inequalities.)

We are given $p < -2$ ⃞1

Subtracting 2 from both sides of ⃞1, we get
$p - 2 < -4$

Since $p - 2$ is negative, $(p - 2)^3$ is negative ⃞2

Adding 2 to both sides of ⃞1, we get

$\qquad p + 2 < 0$
Since $p + 2$ is negative, $(p + 2)^3$ is negative ⃞3

Column A
$(p - 2)^3(p + 2)^3$ ⃞4

Using ⃞2 and ⃞3 in ⃞4 we know that
Column A is positive (the product of two negatives is a positive).

Since column A is positive, it is > 0 ⃞5

Column A > 0
Column B $= 0$
Therefore, Choice A is greater.

(Math Refresher #420 and #421)

19. **(B)** Choice B is correct.

(Use Strategy 2: Remember how to find a percent of a number.)

$$10\% \text{ of } 12{,}200{,}000 = \frac{10}{100} \times \frac{12200000}{1}$$

$$= \frac{\cancel{10}}{\cancel{10} \times \cancel{10}} \times \frac{1220000 \times \cancel{10}}{1}$$

$$= 1{,}220{,}000$$

The population of Jonesville this year

$$= 12{,}200{,}000 + 1{,}220{,}000$$
$$= 13{,}420{,}000$$

Column A		Column B
13,420,000	$<$	13,500,000

(Math Refresher #114)

20. **(D)** Choice D is correct.

(Use Strategy 2: Translate from words to algebra.)

The multiples of 7, that satisfy the given condition, $40 < x < 50$, are 42 and 49

Column A	Column B
42 or 49	47

$$42 < 47$$
$$\text{and}$$
$$49 > 47$$

Therefore, Choice D is correct.

(Math Refresher #200 and Logical Reasoning)

21. **(A)** Choice A is correct.
(Use Strategy 9: Know the rate, time and distance relationship.)

We are given the wheel goes 24 cm in 3 sec.

$$\text{Using Rate} = \frac{\text{Distance}}{\text{Time}}, \text{ we have}$$

$$\text{Rate} = \frac{24 \text{ cm}}{3 \text{ sec}} = 8 \text{ cm/sec} \quad \boxed{1}$$

(Use Strategy 10: Know how to use units.)

We are told the wheel makes one revolution per second.

One revolution
$$= \text{the circumference of the wheel} \quad \boxed{2}$$
$$= 2\pi r \text{ cm}$$

From $\boxed{1}$ we know 8 cm are covered in one second.

So, $\boxed{1} = \boxed{2}$. Thus,

$$8 \text{ cm} = 2\pi r \text{ cm}$$

Dividing both sides by 2π, we have

$$\frac{8 \text{ cm/sec}}{2\pi \text{ cm}} = \frac{2\pi r \text{ cm}}{2\pi \text{ cm}}$$

$$\frac{4}{\pi} = r$$

$$\frac{4}{3.14} \approx r$$

$$1.2 \approx r$$

$$r > 1$$

(Math Refresher #201, #202, and #310)

22. **(B)** Choice B is correct.
(Use Strategy 13: Find unknowns by division.)

We are given:
$$2a + 2b = 14 \qquad 3x + 3y = 24$$
$$2(a + b) = 14 \qquad 3(x + y) = 24$$
Dividing by 2, we get   Dividing by 3, we get
$$a + b = 7 \qquad\qquad x + y = 8 \qquad \boxed{1}$$

Column A	Column B
The average of a and b	The average of x and y

$\left(\begin{array}{c}\text{Use Strategy 5: Average} = \\[4pt] \dfrac{\text{Sum of values}}{\text{Total number of values}}\end{array}\right.$

By definition of average, the columns become

$$\frac{a + b}{2} \qquad\qquad \frac{x + y}{2} \qquad \boxed{2}$$

Substituting $\boxed{1}$ into $\boxed{2}$, we get

$$\frac{7}{2} = \qquad\qquad \frac{8}{2} =$$

$$3\frac{1}{2} \qquad < \qquad 4$$

(Math Refresher #601 and #406)

23. **(D)** Choice D is correct.
(Use Strategy C: Use numbers in place of variables when a comparison is difficult.)

Method 1: Choose specific values for p and q:

EXAMPLE 1
$$p = 3 \text{ and } q = 5$$

The columns become

Column A	Column B
$\dfrac{3}{5}$	$\dfrac{8}{10} = \dfrac{4}{5}$

The quantity in Column B is greater.

EXAMPLE 2
$$p = 7 \text{ and } q = 3$$

The columns become

Column A	Column B
$\dfrac{7}{3}$	$\dfrac{10}{6} = \dfrac{5}{3}$

The quantity in Column A is greater.

Method 2: Try to get the expressions in both columns to look similar.

For example,

$$\frac{p}{q} = \frac{p}{2q} + \frac{p}{2q} \text{ and } \frac{p + q}{q + q} = \frac{p + q}{2q} = \frac{p}{2q} + \frac{q}{2q},$$

Thus, the columns become

Column A	Column B
$\dfrac{p}{2q} + \dfrac{p}{2q}$	$\dfrac{p}{2q} + \dfrac{q}{2q}$

Clearly, the answer to this question depends on specific values of p and q.

(Math Refresher #431, #109, and #110)

24. **(C)** Choice C is correct.

(Use Strategy 11: Use new definitions carefully.)

Column A	Column B
$r \square s$	$-r \square s$

By the given definition, we have

$$r \square s = r^2 y \qquad -r \square s = (-r)^2 y$$
$$= r^2 y$$

The columns are equal.

(Math Refresher #431)

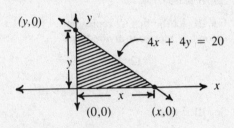

25. **(C)** Choice C is correct.

The triangular region has been drawn above. Clearly, as labeled in the diagram, the area of the triangular region A is

$$A = \frac{1}{2}xy \qquad \boxed{1}$$

where x and y are the x-intercept and y-intercept, respectively. To find the x-intercept, let $y = 0$, and solve for x in the equation of the line in the drawing.

$$4x + 4y = 20$$
$$4x + 4(0) = 20$$
$$4x = 20$$
$$x = 5 \qquad \boxed{2}$$

To find the y-intercept, let $x = 0$, and solve for y in the equation of the line in the drawing.

$$4x + 4y = 20$$
$$4(0) + 4y = 20$$
$$4y = 20$$
$$y = 5 \qquad \boxed{3}$$

Substituting $\boxed{2}$ and $\boxed{3}$ into $\boxed{1}$,

$$A = \frac{1}{2}(5)(5) = 12.5$$

Thus, the columns become

Column A	Column B
12.5	12.5

and the quantities are equal.

(Math Refresher #306, #307, #406 and #410)

26. **(C)** Choice C is correct.

(Use Strategy 13: Find unknowns by addition of equations.)

We are *given:*
$$3x - y = 8 \qquad \boxed{1}$$
$$2x - 4y = 7 \qquad \boxed{2}$$

Adding $\boxed{1}$ and $\boxed{2}$ together, we get

$$5x - 5y = 15 \qquad \boxed{3}$$

Dividing $\boxed{3}$ by 5, we get

$$x - y = 3$$

(Math Refresher #407 and #406)

27. **(D)** Choice D is correct.
(Use Strategy 2: Translate from words to algebra.)

Column A	Column B
All the primes between 10 and 20 are: 11, 13, 17, 19	All the evens between 10 and 20 are: 12, 14, 16, 18
The minimum sum of two primes is $\boxed{1}$ $11 + 13 = 24$	The minimum sum of two even integers is $12 + 14 = 26$
The maximum sum of two primes is $\boxed{2}$ $17 + 19 = 36$	The maximum sum of two even integers is $16 + 18 = 34$

The value from A could be less than or greater than the value from B. (See $\boxed{1}$ and $\boxed{2}$)

Thus, we cannot tell and Choice D is correct.

(Math Refresher #603, #604, and #608)

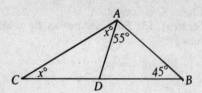

28. **(B)** Choice B is correct.
(Use Strategy 18: Remember triangle facts.)
∠ADB is an exterior angle of △ACD, so
$$m\angle ADB = x + x = 2x \qquad \boxed{1}$$

(Use Strategy 3: The whole equals the sum of its parts.)

In △ADB, the sum of its angles = 180, so

$$m\angle ADB + 55 + 45 = 180$$
or $\qquad m\angle ADB + 100 = 180$
or $\qquad\qquad m\angle ADB = 80 \qquad \boxed{2}$

Equating $\boxed{1}$ and $\boxed{2}$ we have

$$2x = 80$$
$$x = 40 \qquad (Answer)$$

(Math Refresher #505 and #406)

29. **(C)** Choice C is correct.
(Use Strategy 10: Know how to use units.)

$\qquad$ *Given:* $\quad$ 400 bricks = 32 meters $\quad \boxed{1}$

Divide $\boxed{1}$ by 400, giving

$$1 \text{ brick} = \frac{32}{400}$$
$$= \frac{4 \times 8}{4 \times 100}$$
$$= \frac{8}{100}$$
$$= .08 \qquad (Answer)$$

(Math Refresher #121)

30. **(D)** Choice D is correct.
(Use Strategy 3: The whole equals the sum of its parts.)

Find the unknown area from the known areas.

The area of △ADE =
$$\frac{1}{2}(\text{base})(\text{height}) =$$
$$\frac{1}{2}(6)(10) = 30 \qquad \boxed{1}$$

Using $\boxed{1}$, we calculate the unknown area:

Area of quadrilateral ABCD =
Area of pentagon ABCDE − Area of △ADE =
$$120 - 30 = 90 \ (Answer)$$

(Math Refresher #306)

31. **(E)** Choice E is correct.
(Use Strategy 11: Use new definitions carefully.)

For I, let both ☆s represent divided by (÷).

$$12 \ ☆ \ (8 \ ☆ \ 4) =$$
$$12 \div (8 \div 4) =$$
$$12 \div 2 = 6$$

So, I is true.

For II, let both ☆s represent minus (−).

$$12 \ ☆ \ (8 \ ☆ \ 4) =$$
$$12 - (8 - 4) =$$
$$12 - 4 = 8$$

So, II is true.

For III, let the first ☆ represent (−) and let the second ☆ represent divided by (÷).

$$12 \ ☆ \ (8 \ ☆ \ 4) =$$
$$12 - (8 \div 4) =$$
$$12 - 2 = 10$$

So, III is true.

Thus, Choice E is correct.

(Math Refresher #431 and Logical Reasoning)

32. **(E)** Choice E is correct.
(Use Strategy 2: Translate from words to algebra.)

Each tile is a square with perimeter = 2 feet
Each side of the tile is $\frac{1}{4}(2 \text{ feet}) = \frac{1}{2}$ foot $\quad \boxed{1}$

The area of each tile is (Side).²
Using $\boxed{1}$, we get area of each tile

$$= \left(\frac{1}{2}\right)^2 = \frac{1}{4} \text{ square foot} \qquad \boxed{2}$$

The area of the floor is $b \times h =$
$$8 \text{ feet} \times 6 \text{ feet} =$$
$$48 \text{ square feet} \qquad \boxed{3}$$

(Use Strategy 17: Use the given information effectively.)

The number of tiles necessary, at minimum, to cover the floor

$$= \frac{\text{Area of floor}}{\text{Area of 1 tile}} \qquad \boxed{4}$$

Substituting $\boxed{2}$ and $\boxed{3}$ into $\boxed{4}$ we get:
The number of tiles necessary, at minimum, to cover the floor

$$= \frac{48}{\frac{1}{4}} = 48 \times \frac{4}{1}$$

The number of tiles necessary, at minimum, to cover the floor

$$= 192 \qquad (Answer)$$

(Math Refresher #200 and #303)

33. **(B)** Choice B is correct.
(Use Strategy 2: Translate from words to algebra.)

Let f = Number of freshman
s = Number of seniors

We are given $f = 3s$ ☐1

$\frac{1}{4}$ of the freshman = $\frac{1}{4}f$ ☐2

$\frac{1}{3}$ of the seniors = $\frac{1}{3}s$ ☐3

Total number of freshman
and seniors = $f + s$ ☐4

(Use Strategy 17: Use the given information effectively.)

The desired fraction, uses ☐2, ☐3 and ☐4 as follows:

$$\frac{\frac{1}{4}f + \frac{1}{3}s}{f + s}$$ ☐5

Substituting ☐1 in ☐5, we get

$$\frac{\frac{1}{4}(3s) + \frac{1}{3}s}{3s + s} = \frac{\frac{3}{4}s + \frac{1}{3}s}{4s}$$ ☐6

Multiplying ☐6, numerator and denominator, by 12 we get:

$$\left(\frac{12}{12}\right)\frac{\frac{3}{4}s + \frac{1}{3}s}{4s} =$$

$$\frac{9s + 4s}{48s} =$$

$$\frac{13s}{48s} =$$

$$\frac{13}{48} \qquad (Answer)$$

(Math Refresher #200, #402 and #108)

34. **(C)** Choice C is correct.
(Use Strategy 2: Translate from words to algebra.)
Set up a Venn diagram:

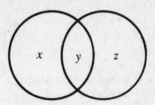

x = number of students with *only* a car
z = number of students with *only* a bicycle
y = number of students having a car and a bicycle

Total students = 100 ☐1
We are given: $x + y = 30$ ☐2
$z + y = 50$ ☐3
$y = 20$ ☐4

Substituting ☐4 into ☐2 and into ☐3, we get

$$x = 10, z = 30$$ ☐5

Using ☐4 and ☐5, we have:

The sum of $x + y + z =$
$10 + 20 + 30 = 60$ ☐6

This is the number of students who have either a car, a bicycle, or both.

Using ☐1 and ☐6, we get $100 - 60 = 40$ as the number who have neither a car nor a bicycle nor both.

(Math Refresher #200 and #406)

35. **(E)** Choice E is correct.
The only restriction is that 9 and 12 must each divide Q without a remainder. ☐1

(Use Strategy 7: Use numerics to help find the answer.)

Choose specific values for Q that satisfy ☐1.

EXAMPLE 1
$Q = 36$

Then, Q will divide 36 and 72.

EXAMPLE 2
$Q = 108$

Then, Q will divide neither 36 nor 72.

Clearly, the answer to this question depends on the specific value of Q

(Math Refresher #431)

EXPLANATORY ANSWERS FOR PRACTICE TEST 6 (continued)

Section 6: Math Ability

1. (A) Choice A is correct. **(Use Strategy 2: Translate from words to algebra.)**
Let x = Amount that Greg had to start.
Then $x + 5$ = Amount that Greg has after receiving $5 from David. $\boxed{1}$

$$\$25 = \text{Amount David has.} \quad \boxed{2}$$

We are told that Greg now has $\frac{1}{5}$ as much as David does.
This translate to:

$$\text{Greg} = \frac{1}{5}(\text{David}) \quad \boxed{3}$$

Substituting $\boxed{1}$ and $\boxed{2}$ into $\boxed{3}$, we get

$$x + 5 = \frac{1}{5}(25)$$
$$x + 5 = \frac{1}{5} \times 5 \times 5$$
$$x + 5 = 5$$
$$x = 0$$

(Math Refresher #200 and #406)

2. (C) Choice C is correct.
The ratio of the perimeter of the larger square to that of the smaller is

$$\frac{6+6+6+6}{2+2+2+2} = \frac{24}{8} = \frac{3}{1} \text{ or } 3:1$$

One can arrive at this result directly if one remembers that the ratio of the perimeters of two squares is the same as the ratio of the lengths of the sides of the two squares.

(Math Refresher #303)

3. (E) Choice E is correct. **(Use Strategy 9: Remember the rate, time, and distance relationship.)**
Remember that rate × time = distance

or   average rate = $\dfrac{\text{total distance}}{\text{total time}}$

or   average rate = $\dfrac{1056 \text{ feet}}{12 \text{ seconds}}$

= 88 feet/second (*Answer*)

(Math Refresher #201 and #202)

4. (B) Choice B is correct.
Given: $2z + 1 + 2 + 2z + 3 + 2z = 3 + 1 + 2$
(Use Strategy 1: Cancel numbers from both sides of an equation.)
We can immediately cancel the $+1$, $+2$ and $+3$ from each side.

We get $2z + 2z + 2z = 0$
$$6z = 0$$
$$z = 0$$

Thus, $z + 4 = 0 + 4 = 4$
(Math Refresher #406 and #431)

5. (D) Choice D is correct. **(Use Strategy 17: Use the given information effectively.)**
$$\frac{1}{n^2}\left(\frac{m^5 n^3}{m^3}\right)^2 = \frac{1}{n^2}(m^2 n^3)^2 = \frac{m^4 n^6}{n^2} = m^4 n^4 \text{ (Answer)}$$

(Math Refresher #429)

6. (B) Choice B is correct.
$$2(w)(x)(-y) - 2(-w)(-x)(y) =$$
$$-2wxy - 2wxy =$$
$$-4wxy \text{ (Answer)}$$

(Direct Calculation)

7. (A) Choice A is correct. **(Use Strategy 2: Translate from words to algebra.)**
The sum of the square of x and the square of y
$$x^2 \quad + \quad y^2$$

So, five times that quantity is
$$5(x^2 + y^2)$$

(Math Refresher #200)

8. (B) Choice B is correct. **(Use Strategy 6: Know the properties of inequality relationships.)**

Since $y < 0$, $(y)^5 < 0$ $\boxed{1}$
$(y)^2 > 0$ $\boxed{2}$

Therefore, $\boxed{2} > \boxed{1}$

(Math Refresher #428)

9. **(C)** Choice C is correct.

Column A	Column B
$.06 \times 1000 =$	$.6 \times 100$

Method 1:

$$\frac{6}{\cancel{100}} \times \frac{\cancel{100} \times 10}{1} = \frac{6}{\cancel{10}} \times \frac{\cancel{10} \times 10}{1}$$

$$60 \qquad\qquad 60$$

Method 2: Knowing the results of multiplying by powers of 10:

Column A	Column B
$.06 \times 1000 =$	$.6 \times 100 =$
$.06 \times 10^3 =$	$.6 \times 10^2 =$
60	60

(Math Refresher #113)

10. **(D)** Choice D is correct.

There is not enough information given to determine whether most of the albums were sold in January or whether most were sold at some other time during the year. (Perhaps no albums were sold in January.)

(Logical Reasoning)

11. **(B)** Choice B is correct. **(Use Strategy 17: Use the given information effectively.)**

Column A	Column B
$(2 \times 3 + 4(5 - 6))$	$(6 \times 5 + 4(3 - 2))$
$(6 + 4(-1))$	$(30 + 4(1))$
$6 - 4$	$30 + 4$
2	34

(Direct Calculation)

12. **(D)** Choice D is correct.

Method 1: We are given that

$$5 + m > 12 \text{ or } m > 7 \qquad \boxed{1}$$
$$5 + n > 12 \text{ or } n > 7 \qquad \boxed{2}$$

However, there is no equation relating m and n.

Method 2: **(Use Strategy C: Use numbers in place of variables when a comparison of the two columns is difficult.)** Choose specific values of m and n that satify $\boxed{1}$ and $\boxed{2}$.

EXAMPLE

$$m = 9 \text{ and } n = 8$$

Thus, $m > n$.

Hence, no conclusion can be drawn.

(Math Refresher #431)

13. **(C)** Choice C is correct. **(Use Strategy 3: The whole equals the sum of its parts.)**

The sum of the angles of a triangle $= 180$ $\qquad \boxed{1}$

Thus, $a + c + 90 = 180$ $\qquad \boxed{2}$

(Use Strategy 13: Find unknown expressions by subtraction.) Subtract $(a + c) + 90$ from both sides of $\boxed{2}$. We get

$$0 = 90 - (a + c)$$

Therefore, the two columns are equal.

(Math Refresher #505 and #406)

14. **(A)** Choice A is correct. **(Use Strategy 2: Know how to find percent of a number.)**

Column A	Column B
10% of $60 =$	5% of $80 =$
$\dfrac{10}{100} \times 60 =$	$\dfrac{5}{100} \times 80 =$
$\dfrac{\cancel{10}}{\cancel{10} \times \cancel{10}} \times \dfrac{6 \times \cancel{10}}{1} =$	$\dfrac{5}{10 \times \cancel{10}} \times \dfrac{8 \times \cancel{10}}{1} =$
6	$\dfrac{\cancel{5}}{\cancel{5} \times 2} \times \dfrac{2 \times 4}{1} =$
	4

(Math Refresher #114)

15. **(D)** Choice D is correct.

Note that $\dfrac{y + y + y}{y} = \dfrac{3y}{y} = 3$, but we don't know whether or not y is greater than 3.

(Math Refresher #431 and Logical Reasoning)

16. **(A)** Choice A is correct. **(Use Strategy 2: Translate from words to algebra.)**

Let $f =$ price of one football

$b =$ price of one basketball

We are given

$$f + b = 9 \qquad \boxed{1}$$
$$f + 2b = m \qquad \boxed{2}$$
$$2f + b = n \qquad \boxed{3}$$

(Use Strategy 13: Find unknown expressions by addition of equations.) Adding $\boxed{2}$ and $\boxed{3}$, we get

$$3f + 3b = m + n$$
$$\text{or} \quad 3(f + b) = m + n \qquad \boxed{4}$$

Substitute $\boxed{1}$ into $\boxed{4}$,

$$3(9) = m + n$$
$$\text{or} \quad m + n = 27 > 18$$

(Math Refresher #200 and #431)

17. **(B)** Choice B is correct. **(Use Strategy 12: Try not to make tedious calculations!)** Whatever you do, do not calculate the areas of the polygons (in terms of, say, the radius of the circle). That would be very time consuming. In this problem it is much faster to use logic. **(Use Strategy 14: Draw lines when appropriate.)** Since the circles in both cases have the same radius, we can superimpose the two pictures.

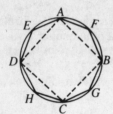

Clearly, the square (*ABCD*) is completely covered by the octagon (*AFBGCHDE*). The octagon has the greater area.

(Logical Reasoning)

18. **(B)** Choice B is correct. **(Use Strategy 17: Use the given information effectively.)**

Column A	Column B
$10^3 + 10^2 =$	$10^3 \times 10^2 =$
$1000 + 100 =$	$10^5 =$
1100	100000

Clearly, Column B is larger.

(Math Refresher #430)

19. **(B)** Choice B is correct. **(Use Strategy 11: Use new definitions carefully.)**

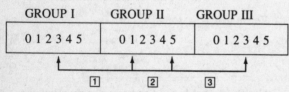

$3 \triangle 4$, using the definition, start at 3 in group I and move 4 to the right, ending up at 1 in group II. ☐1

Move 4 to the right again. We end up at 5 in group II. ☐2

Move 4 to the right again. We end up at 3 in group III. ☐3

Column A	Column B
3	5

(Logical Reasoning)

20. **(A)** Choice A is correct. **(Use Strategy 3: The whole equals the sum of its parts.)** Each angle in an equilateral triangle has a measure of 60°. Each one in a square has a measure of 90°. Thus, $m \angle ACD = 60 + 90 = 150$. Hence, $x = 360 - 150 = 210$ and $210 > 200$.

(Math Refresher #508, #520, and #526)

21. **(D)** Choice D is correct. **(Use Strategy B: Cancel positive quantities from both sides by division.)** Notice that $(57)^{n-1}$ appears in both columns. Since 57 is positive, than $(57)^{n-1}$ is also positive. Since $(57)^{n-1}$ is a positive quantity appearing in both columns, it will not change the answer to this question. Thus, we can rewite the columns:

Column A	Column B
$\left(-\dfrac{1}{2}\right)^n = -\dfrac{1}{2}\left(-\dfrac{1}{2}\right)^{n-1}$	$\left(-\dfrac{1}{2}\right)^{n-1}$

Method 1: Note that the quantity in Column A is $\left(-\dfrac{1}{2}\right)$ times the quantity in Column B. Thus, the two quantities are of opposite sign.
If we know the sign of one quantity, we know the sign of the other. The answer to the question is the quantity whose sign is positive. However, since we don't know n, we don't know the sign of either quantity. (Notice that, since $\left(-\dfrac{1}{2}\right)^{n-1}$ can be either positive or negative, we cannot cancel $\left(-\dfrac{1}{2}\right)^{n-1}$ from both sides of the above columns.)

Method 2: **(Use Strategy 7: Use specific numeric examples to prove or disprove your guess.)** Choose specific values for n.

EXAMPLE 1

$$n = 2$$

Column A	Column B
$\dfrac{1}{4}$	$-\dfrac{1}{2}$

and Column A is greater.

EXAMPLE 2

$$n = 3$$

The columns become

Column A	Column B
$-\dfrac{1}{8}$	$\dfrac{1}{4}$

and Column B is greater.

(Math Refresher #429, #428, and #431)

22. **(B)** Choice B is correct. **(Use Strategy 11: Use new definitions carefully.)** The terms of the sequence are

$$x - 2, 2(x - 2), 3(x - 2), 4(x - 2), \ldots n(x - 2)$$

for $x = 2$, the terms are

$$0, 2(0), 3(0), 4(0), \ldots n(0)$$

Each term is 0.
The sum of the first ten elements is
$$10(0) = 0$$
Clearly, Column B is larger.

(Math Refresher #431)

23. **(B)** Choice B is correct.

$\left(\text{**Use Strategy 5: Average =}} \dfrac{\textbf{Sum of values}}{\textbf{Total number of values}}\right)$

Long Method: We calculate and find that

$$\frac{90 + 90 + 100}{3} = 93\frac{1}{3} \qquad \boxed{1}$$

$$\frac{90 + 100 + 100}{3} = 96\frac{2}{3} \qquad \boxed{2}$$

This can be a tedious method, especially if the numbers are large. **(Remember Strategy 12: Try not to make tedious calculations.)**

Short Method: Without adding, it is obvious that

$$90 + 90 + 100 < 90 + 100 + 100 \qquad \boxed{3}$$

Now divide $\boxed{3}$ by 3:

$$\frac{90 + 90 + 100}{3} < \frac{90 + 100 + 100}{3}$$

(Use Strategy 6: Know how to use inequalities)
(Math Refresher #601 and #422)

24. **(B)** Choice B is correct. **(Use Strategy 11: Use new definitions carefully.)** Since $\textcircled{y}$ denotes the decimal part of y, it follows that

$$\textcircled{y} < 1 \qquad \boxed{1}$$
$$\textcircled{x} < 1 \qquad \boxed{2}$$

(Use Strategy 6: Know how to manipulate inequalities.) Adding $\boxed{1}$ and $\boxed{2}$ above, we have

$$\textcircled{x} + \textcircled{y} < 2$$

Therefore, Choice B is greater.
(Math Refresher #420 and Logical Reasoning)

25. **(D)** Choice D is correct. **(Use Strategy C: Use numbers in place of variables when a comparison is difficult.)** Choose specific numeric values for a, b, and c that satisfy the given equations.

EXAMPLE 1
$$a = 2, b = 1, \text{ and } c = 3$$
$$a + b + c = 6 < 7$$

EXAMPLE 2
$$a = 4, b = 1, \text{ and } c = 5$$
$$a + b + c = 8 > 7$$

Thus, $a + b + c$ does not have a unique value.
(Math Refresher #431)

26. **(A)** Choice A is correct.
(Use Strategy 18: Remember isosceles triangle relationships.) Since both acute angles are 45°, the sides opposite are equal.
Thus, $a = b$ $\qquad \boxed{1}$
(Use Strategy 6: Know how to manipulate inequalities.)
We are *given* $a < 1$ $\qquad \boxed{2}$
Multiply both sides of $\boxed{2}$ by a. We get

$$a(a) < a(1)$$
$$a(a) < a \qquad \boxed{3}$$

Substituting $\boxed{1}$ into $\boxed{3}$, we get

$$a(b) < a$$
$$ab < a$$

Now the answer is clear.
(Math Refresher #507, #509 and #422)

27. **(B)** Choice B is correct. The distance between City B and City C is indeterminate, but must be in the range of $12 - 5 = 7$ to $12 + 5 = 17$ miles. Thus, the quantity in Column B must be greater.
(Logical Reasoning)

28. **(B)** Choice B is correct.
(Use Strategy 2: Translate from words to algebra.)

Given:
$$p + pq = 4(p - pq) \qquad \boxed{1}$$

(Use Strategy 13: Find unknown expressions by division.) Since $pq \neq 0$, divide $\boxed{1}$ by p.

$$\begin{aligned} 1 + q &= 4(1 - q) \qquad \boxed{2} \\ \text{or} \quad 1 + q &= 4 - 4q \\ \text{or} \quad 5q &= 3 \\ \text{or} \quad q &= \frac{3}{5} \end{aligned}$$

Thus, q has exactly one value.
Since p cannot be determined from equation $\boxed{1}$, none of the other choices is correct.
(Math Refresher #406)

29. (D) Choice D is correct. **(Use Strategy 17: Use the given information effectively.)**

Since $2 + \dfrac{1}{z} = 0$, we have

$$\dfrac{1}{z} = -2$$

$$z = -\dfrac{1}{2} \qquad \boxed{1}$$

We need $9 + 9z$ $\qquad \boxed{2}$

Substituting $\boxed{1}$ into $\boxed{2}$, we get

$$9 + 9\left(-\dfrac{1}{2}\right) = 9 - 4\dfrac{1}{2} = 4\dfrac{1}{2} = \dfrac{9}{2} \ (Answer)$$

(Math Refresher #406 and #431)

30. (C) Choice C is correct. **(Use Strategy 3: The whole equals the sum of its parts.)** From the diagram, we see that each straight angle is equal to the sum of two smaller angles. Thus,

$$m = 180 - x \qquad \boxed{1}$$
$$n = 180 - z \qquad \boxed{2}$$

(Use Strategy 13: Find unknown by addition of equations.) Adding $\boxed{1}$ and $\boxed{2}$ we have

$$m + n = 180 + 180 - x - z \qquad \boxed{3}$$

We know that the sum of the angles of a triangle = 180

Therefore, $y + x + z = 180$

or $y = 180 - x - z$ $\qquad \boxed{4}$

Substituting $\boxed{4}$ into $\boxed{3}$, we have
$$m + n = 180 + y$$

Accordingly, Choice C is the correct choice.

(Math Refresher #406, #505, and #501)

31. (C) Choice C is correct.

We are given: $wx = y$ $\qquad \boxed{1}$

or $w = \dfrac{y}{x}$ $\qquad \boxed{2}$

(Use Strategy 2: Translate from words to algebra.)

If x and y are multiplied by 6, in $\boxed{1}$, we have

$$w(6)(x) = (6)(y)$$
$$wx = y$$
$$w = \dfrac{y}{x} \qquad \boxed{3}$$

$\boxed{2}$ and $\boxed{3}$ are the same.

Therefore $\dfrac{y}{x} = 1\left(\dfrac{y}{x}\right)$

The answer is now clear.

(Math Refresher #200 and #406)

32. (C) Choice C is correct. **(Use Strategy 2: Translate from words to algebra.)**

We know that the volume of a cube $= e^3$

We are told that $e^3 < 25$

(Use Strategy 17: Use the given information effectively.)

Since e is a positive integer (which was given),

$$e \text{ can be: } 1 \rightarrow 1^3 = 1$$
$$2 \rightarrow 2^3 = 8$$
$$3 \rightarrow 3^3 = 27$$
$$\text{etc.}$$

For $e = 2$, the volume is 8 which is < 25

Any larger e, will have a volume > 25

Thus, area of one face $= e^2 = 2^2 = 4$

Total area $= 6(4) = 24 \ (Answer)$

(Math Refresher #202 and #313)

33. (E) Choice E is correct. **(Use Strategy 2: Translate from words to algebra.)**

Let s = number of smokers

n = number of non-smokers

Then $s + n$ = Total number of passengers.

We are given: $\dfrac{s}{n} = \dfrac{2}{3}$ or $s = \dfrac{2}{3}n$ $\qquad \boxed{1}$

and: $s = \dfrac{1}{3}(s + n) + 5$ $\qquad \boxed{2}$

Substituting $\boxed{1}$ into $\boxed{2}$, we have

$$\dfrac{2}{3}n = \dfrac{1}{3}\left(\dfrac{2}{3}n + n\right) + 5$$

$$\dfrac{2}{3}n = \dfrac{1}{3}\left(\dfrac{2}{3}n + \dfrac{3}{3}n\right) + 5$$

$$\dfrac{2}{3}n = \dfrac{1}{3}\left(\dfrac{5}{3}n\right) + 5$$

$$\dfrac{2}{3}n = \dfrac{5}{9}n + 5 \qquad \boxed{3}$$

Multiplying both sides of $\boxed{3}$ by 9, we get

$$9\left(\dfrac{2}{3}n\right) = 9\left(\dfrac{5}{9}n + 5\right)$$

$$\dfrac{18}{3}n = 5n + 45$$

$$6n = 5n + 45$$

$$n = 45$$

$$s = \dfrac{2}{3}(45) = 30$$

$$s + n = 75 \ (Answer)$$

(Math Refresher #200 and #406)

34. **(B)** Choice B is correct. **(Use Strategy 3: The whole equals the sum of its parts.)** The path is made up of 4 semicircles, three of diameter 4 and one of diameter 8.

[Remember circumference is $2\pi r$. Thus, $\frac{1}{2}$ circumference $= \frac{1}{2}(2\pi r)$.]

Therefore, the length of the path is

$$\frac{1}{2}(2\pi)\left(\frac{4}{2}\right) + \frac{1}{2}(2\pi)\left(\frac{4}{2}\right) + \frac{1}{2}(2\pi)\left(\frac{4}{2}\right)$$

$$+ \frac{1}{2}(2\pi)\left(\frac{8}{2}\right)$$

$$= 10\pi \ (Answer)$$

(Math Refresher #310 and #311)

35. **(C)** Choice C is correct. **(Use Strategy 10: Know how to use units.)**

$$\frac{7x}{144} \text{ yards} = \left(\frac{7x}{144} \text{ yards}\right)\left(\frac{36 \text{ inches}}{\text{yards}}\right) =$$

(Use Strategy 19: Factor and reduce.)

$$= \frac{7x}{\cancel{12} \times 12} \times \cancel{12} \times 3 \text{ inches}$$

$$= \frac{7x}{\cancel{3} \times 4} \times \cancel{3} \text{ inches}$$

$$\frac{7x}{144} \text{ yards} = \frac{7x}{4} \text{ inches} \qquad \boxed{1}$$

$$\frac{5y}{12} \text{ feet} = \left(\frac{5y}{\cancel{12}} \text{ feet}\right)\left(\cancel{12} \frac{\text{inches}}{\text{foot}}\right) =$$

$$\frac{5y}{12} \text{ feet} = 5y \text{ inches} \qquad \boxed{2}$$

(Use Strategy 13: Find unknown expressions by addition of equations.) Adding $\boxed{1}$ and $\boxed{2}$, we have

$$\frac{7x}{144} \text{ yards} + \frac{5y}{12} \text{ feet}$$

$$= \left(\frac{7x}{4} + 5y\right) \text{ inches} \ (Answer)$$

(Math Refresher #121 and #431)

Answer Sheet—Practice Test 7
(SAT Post-Test)

SECTION 1: VERBAL ABILITY

1 Ⓐ Ⓑ Ⓒ Ⓓ Ⓔ   10 Ⓐ Ⓑ Ⓒ Ⓓ Ⓔ   19 Ⓐ Ⓑ Ⓒ Ⓓ Ⓔ   28 Ⓐ Ⓑ Ⓒ Ⓓ Ⓔ   37 Ⓐ Ⓑ Ⓒ Ⓓ Ⓔ
2 Ⓐ Ⓑ Ⓒ Ⓓ Ⓔ   11 Ⓐ Ⓑ Ⓒ Ⓓ Ⓔ   20 Ⓐ Ⓑ Ⓒ Ⓓ Ⓔ   29 Ⓐ Ⓑ Ⓒ Ⓓ Ⓔ   38 Ⓐ Ⓑ Ⓒ Ⓓ Ⓔ
3 Ⓐ Ⓑ Ⓒ Ⓓ Ⓔ   12 Ⓐ Ⓑ Ⓒ Ⓓ Ⓔ   21 Ⓐ Ⓑ Ⓒ Ⓓ Ⓔ   30 Ⓐ Ⓑ Ⓒ Ⓓ Ⓔ   39 Ⓐ Ⓑ Ⓒ Ⓓ Ⓔ
4 Ⓐ Ⓑ Ⓒ Ⓓ Ⓔ   13 Ⓐ Ⓑ Ⓒ Ⓓ Ⓔ   22 Ⓐ Ⓑ Ⓒ Ⓓ Ⓔ   31 Ⓐ Ⓑ Ⓒ Ⓓ Ⓔ   40 Ⓐ Ⓑ Ⓒ Ⓓ Ⓔ
5 Ⓐ Ⓑ Ⓒ Ⓓ Ⓔ   14 Ⓐ Ⓑ Ⓒ Ⓓ Ⓔ   23 Ⓐ Ⓑ Ⓒ Ⓓ Ⓔ   32 Ⓐ Ⓑ Ⓒ Ⓓ Ⓔ   41 Ⓐ Ⓑ Ⓒ Ⓓ Ⓔ
6 Ⓐ Ⓑ Ⓒ Ⓓ Ⓔ   15 Ⓐ Ⓑ Ⓒ Ⓓ Ⓔ   24 Ⓐ Ⓑ Ⓒ Ⓓ Ⓔ   33 Ⓐ Ⓑ Ⓒ Ⓓ Ⓔ   42 Ⓐ Ⓑ Ⓒ Ⓓ Ⓔ
7 Ⓐ Ⓑ Ⓒ Ⓓ Ⓔ   16 Ⓐ Ⓑ Ⓒ Ⓓ Ⓔ   25 Ⓐ Ⓑ Ⓒ Ⓓ Ⓔ   34 Ⓐ Ⓑ Ⓒ Ⓓ Ⓔ   43 Ⓐ Ⓑ Ⓒ Ⓓ Ⓔ
8 Ⓐ Ⓑ Ⓒ Ⓓ Ⓔ   17 Ⓐ Ⓑ Ⓒ Ⓓ Ⓔ   26 Ⓐ Ⓑ Ⓒ Ⓓ Ⓔ   35 Ⓐ Ⓑ Ⓒ Ⓓ Ⓔ   44 Ⓐ Ⓑ Ⓒ Ⓓ Ⓔ
9 Ⓐ Ⓑ Ⓒ Ⓓ Ⓔ   18 Ⓐ Ⓑ Ⓒ Ⓓ Ⓔ   27 Ⓐ Ⓑ Ⓒ Ⓓ Ⓔ   36 Ⓐ Ⓑ Ⓒ Ⓓ Ⓔ   45 Ⓐ Ⓑ Ⓒ Ⓓ Ⓔ

SECTION 2: MATH ABILITY

1 Ⓐ Ⓑ Ⓒ Ⓓ Ⓔ   6 Ⓐ Ⓑ Ⓒ Ⓓ Ⓔ   11 Ⓐ Ⓑ Ⓒ Ⓓ Ⓔ   16 Ⓐ Ⓑ Ⓒ Ⓓ Ⓔ   21 Ⓐ Ⓑ Ⓒ Ⓓ Ⓔ
2 Ⓐ Ⓑ Ⓒ Ⓓ Ⓔ   7 Ⓐ Ⓑ Ⓒ Ⓓ Ⓔ   12 Ⓐ Ⓑ Ⓒ Ⓓ Ⓔ   17 Ⓐ Ⓑ Ⓒ Ⓓ Ⓔ   22 Ⓐ Ⓑ Ⓒ Ⓓ Ⓔ
3 Ⓐ Ⓑ Ⓒ Ⓓ Ⓔ   8 Ⓐ Ⓑ Ⓒ Ⓓ Ⓔ   13 Ⓐ Ⓑ Ⓒ Ⓓ Ⓔ   18 Ⓐ Ⓑ Ⓒ Ⓓ Ⓔ   23 Ⓐ Ⓑ Ⓒ Ⓓ Ⓔ
4 Ⓐ Ⓑ Ⓒ Ⓓ Ⓔ   9 Ⓐ Ⓑ Ⓒ Ⓓ Ⓔ   14 Ⓐ Ⓑ Ⓒ Ⓓ Ⓔ   19 Ⓐ Ⓑ Ⓒ Ⓓ Ⓔ   24 Ⓐ Ⓑ Ⓒ Ⓓ Ⓔ
5 Ⓐ Ⓑ Ⓒ Ⓓ Ⓔ   10 Ⓐ Ⓑ Ⓒ Ⓓ Ⓔ   15 Ⓐ Ⓑ Ⓒ Ⓓ Ⓔ   20 Ⓐ Ⓑ Ⓒ Ⓓ Ⓔ   25 Ⓐ Ⓑ Ⓒ Ⓓ Ⓔ

SECTION 3: STANDARD WRITTEN ENGLISH

1 Ⓐ Ⓑ Ⓒ Ⓓ Ⓔ   11 Ⓐ Ⓑ Ⓒ Ⓓ Ⓔ   21 Ⓐ Ⓑ Ⓒ Ⓓ Ⓔ   31 Ⓐ Ⓑ Ⓒ Ⓓ Ⓔ   41 Ⓐ Ⓑ Ⓒ Ⓓ Ⓔ
2 Ⓐ Ⓑ Ⓒ Ⓓ Ⓔ   12 Ⓐ Ⓑ Ⓒ Ⓓ Ⓔ   22 Ⓐ Ⓑ Ⓒ Ⓓ Ⓔ   32 Ⓐ Ⓑ Ⓒ Ⓓ Ⓔ   42 Ⓐ Ⓑ Ⓒ Ⓓ Ⓔ
3 Ⓐ Ⓑ Ⓒ Ⓓ Ⓔ   13 Ⓐ Ⓑ Ⓒ Ⓓ Ⓔ   23 Ⓐ Ⓑ Ⓒ Ⓓ Ⓔ   33 Ⓐ Ⓑ Ⓒ Ⓓ Ⓔ   43 Ⓐ Ⓑ Ⓒ Ⓓ Ⓔ
4 Ⓐ Ⓑ Ⓒ Ⓓ Ⓔ   14 Ⓐ Ⓑ Ⓒ Ⓓ Ⓔ   24 Ⓐ Ⓑ Ⓒ Ⓓ Ⓔ   34 Ⓐ Ⓑ Ⓒ Ⓓ Ⓔ   44 Ⓐ Ⓑ Ⓒ Ⓓ Ⓔ
5 Ⓐ Ⓑ Ⓒ Ⓓ Ⓔ   15 Ⓐ Ⓑ Ⓒ Ⓓ Ⓔ   25 Ⓐ Ⓑ Ⓒ Ⓓ Ⓔ   35 Ⓐ Ⓑ Ⓒ Ⓓ Ⓔ   45 Ⓐ Ⓑ Ⓒ Ⓓ Ⓔ
6 Ⓐ Ⓑ Ⓒ Ⓓ Ⓔ   16 Ⓐ Ⓑ Ⓒ Ⓓ Ⓔ   26 Ⓐ Ⓑ Ⓒ Ⓓ Ⓔ   36 Ⓐ Ⓑ Ⓒ Ⓓ Ⓔ   46 Ⓐ Ⓑ Ⓒ Ⓓ Ⓔ
7 Ⓐ Ⓑ Ⓒ Ⓓ Ⓔ   17 Ⓐ Ⓑ Ⓒ Ⓓ Ⓔ   27 Ⓐ Ⓑ Ⓒ Ⓓ Ⓔ   37 Ⓐ Ⓑ Ⓒ Ⓓ Ⓔ   47 Ⓐ Ⓑ Ⓒ Ⓓ Ⓔ
8 Ⓐ Ⓑ Ⓒ Ⓓ Ⓔ   18 Ⓐ Ⓑ Ⓒ Ⓓ Ⓔ   28 Ⓐ Ⓑ Ⓒ Ⓓ Ⓔ   38 Ⓐ Ⓑ Ⓒ Ⓓ Ⓔ   48 Ⓐ Ⓑ Ⓒ Ⓓ Ⓔ
9 Ⓐ Ⓑ Ⓒ Ⓓ Ⓔ   19 Ⓐ Ⓑ Ⓒ Ⓓ Ⓔ   29 Ⓐ Ⓑ Ⓒ Ⓓ Ⓔ   39 Ⓐ Ⓑ Ⓒ Ⓓ Ⓔ   49 Ⓐ Ⓑ Ⓒ Ⓓ Ⓔ
10 Ⓐ Ⓑ Ⓒ Ⓓ Ⓔ   20 Ⓐ Ⓑ Ⓒ Ⓓ Ⓔ   30 Ⓐ Ⓑ Ⓒ Ⓓ Ⓔ   40 Ⓐ Ⓑ Ⓒ Ⓓ Ⓔ   50 Ⓐ Ⓑ Ⓒ Ⓓ Ⓔ

SECTION 4: VERBAL ABILITY

1 Ⓐ Ⓑ Ⓒ Ⓓ Ⓔ   9 Ⓐ Ⓑ Ⓒ Ⓓ Ⓔ   17 Ⓐ Ⓑ Ⓒ Ⓓ Ⓔ   25 Ⓐ Ⓑ Ⓒ Ⓓ Ⓔ   33 Ⓐ Ⓑ Ⓒ Ⓓ Ⓔ
2 Ⓐ Ⓑ Ⓒ Ⓓ Ⓔ   10 Ⓐ Ⓑ Ⓒ Ⓓ Ⓔ   18 Ⓐ Ⓑ Ⓒ Ⓓ Ⓔ   26 Ⓐ Ⓑ Ⓒ Ⓓ Ⓔ   34 Ⓐ Ⓑ Ⓒ Ⓓ Ⓔ
3 Ⓐ Ⓑ Ⓒ Ⓓ Ⓔ   11 Ⓐ Ⓑ Ⓒ Ⓓ Ⓔ   19 Ⓐ Ⓑ Ⓒ Ⓓ Ⓔ   27 Ⓐ Ⓑ Ⓒ Ⓓ Ⓔ   35 Ⓐ Ⓑ Ⓒ Ⓓ Ⓔ
4 Ⓐ Ⓑ Ⓒ Ⓓ Ⓔ   12 Ⓐ Ⓑ Ⓒ Ⓓ Ⓔ   20 Ⓐ Ⓑ Ⓒ Ⓓ Ⓔ   28 Ⓐ Ⓑ Ⓒ Ⓓ Ⓔ   36 Ⓐ Ⓑ Ⓒ Ⓓ Ⓔ
5 Ⓐ Ⓑ Ⓒ Ⓓ Ⓔ   13 Ⓐ Ⓑ Ⓒ Ⓓ Ⓔ   21 Ⓐ Ⓑ Ⓒ Ⓓ Ⓔ   29 Ⓐ Ⓑ Ⓒ Ⓓ Ⓔ   37 Ⓐ Ⓑ Ⓒ Ⓓ Ⓔ
6 Ⓐ Ⓑ Ⓒ Ⓓ Ⓔ   14 Ⓐ Ⓑ Ⓒ Ⓓ Ⓔ   22 Ⓐ Ⓑ Ⓒ Ⓓ Ⓔ   30 Ⓐ Ⓑ Ⓒ Ⓓ Ⓔ   38 Ⓐ Ⓑ Ⓒ Ⓓ Ⓔ
7 Ⓐ Ⓑ Ⓒ Ⓓ Ⓔ   15 Ⓐ Ⓑ Ⓒ Ⓓ Ⓔ   23 Ⓐ Ⓑ Ⓒ Ⓓ Ⓔ   31 Ⓐ Ⓑ Ⓒ Ⓓ Ⓔ   39 Ⓐ Ⓑ Ⓒ Ⓓ Ⓔ
8 Ⓐ Ⓑ Ⓒ Ⓓ Ⓔ   16 Ⓐ Ⓑ Ⓒ Ⓓ Ⓔ   24 Ⓐ Ⓑ Ⓒ Ⓓ Ⓔ   32 Ⓐ Ⓑ Ⓒ Ⓓ Ⓔ   40 Ⓐ Ⓑ Ⓒ Ⓓ Ⓔ

SECTION 5: MATH ABILITY

1 Ⓐ Ⓑ Ⓒ Ⓓ Ⓔ   8 Ⓐ Ⓑ Ⓒ Ⓓ Ⓔ   15 Ⓐ Ⓑ Ⓒ Ⓓ Ⓔ   22 Ⓐ Ⓑ Ⓒ Ⓓ Ⓔ   29 Ⓐ Ⓑ Ⓒ Ⓓ Ⓔ
2 Ⓐ Ⓑ Ⓒ Ⓓ Ⓔ   9 Ⓐ Ⓑ Ⓒ Ⓓ Ⓔ   16 Ⓐ Ⓑ Ⓒ Ⓓ Ⓔ   23 Ⓐ Ⓑ Ⓒ Ⓓ Ⓔ   30 Ⓐ Ⓑ Ⓒ Ⓓ Ⓔ
3 Ⓐ Ⓑ Ⓒ Ⓓ Ⓔ   10 Ⓐ Ⓑ Ⓒ Ⓓ Ⓔ   17 Ⓐ Ⓑ Ⓒ Ⓓ Ⓔ   24 Ⓐ Ⓑ Ⓒ Ⓓ Ⓔ   31 Ⓐ Ⓑ Ⓒ Ⓓ Ⓔ
4 Ⓐ Ⓑ Ⓒ Ⓓ Ⓔ   11 Ⓐ Ⓑ Ⓒ Ⓓ Ⓔ   18 Ⓐ Ⓑ Ⓒ Ⓓ Ⓔ   25 Ⓐ Ⓑ Ⓒ Ⓓ Ⓔ   32 Ⓐ Ⓑ Ⓒ Ⓓ Ⓔ
5 Ⓐ Ⓑ Ⓒ Ⓓ Ⓔ   12 Ⓐ Ⓑ Ⓒ Ⓓ Ⓔ   19 Ⓐ Ⓑ Ⓒ Ⓓ Ⓔ   26 Ⓐ Ⓑ Ⓒ Ⓓ Ⓔ   33 Ⓐ Ⓑ Ⓒ Ⓓ Ⓔ
6 Ⓐ Ⓑ Ⓒ Ⓓ Ⓔ   13 Ⓐ Ⓑ Ⓒ Ⓓ Ⓔ   20 Ⓐ Ⓑ Ⓒ Ⓓ Ⓔ   27 Ⓐ Ⓑ Ⓒ Ⓓ Ⓔ   34 Ⓐ Ⓑ Ⓒ Ⓓ Ⓔ
7 Ⓐ Ⓑ Ⓒ Ⓓ Ⓔ   14 Ⓐ Ⓑ Ⓒ Ⓓ Ⓔ   21 Ⓐ Ⓑ Ⓒ Ⓓ Ⓔ   28 Ⓐ Ⓑ Ⓒ Ⓓ Ⓔ   35 Ⓐ Ⓑ Ⓒ Ⓓ Ⓔ

SECTION 6: MATH ABILITY

1 Ⓐ Ⓑ Ⓒ Ⓓ Ⓔ   6 Ⓐ Ⓑ Ⓒ Ⓓ Ⓔ   11 Ⓐ Ⓑ Ⓒ Ⓓ Ⓔ   16 Ⓐ Ⓑ Ⓒ Ⓓ Ⓔ   21 Ⓐ Ⓑ Ⓒ Ⓓ Ⓔ
2 Ⓐ Ⓑ Ⓒ Ⓓ Ⓔ   7 Ⓐ Ⓑ Ⓒ Ⓓ Ⓔ   12 Ⓐ Ⓑ Ⓒ Ⓓ Ⓔ   17 Ⓐ Ⓑ Ⓒ Ⓓ Ⓔ   22 Ⓐ Ⓑ Ⓒ Ⓓ Ⓔ
3 Ⓐ Ⓑ Ⓒ Ⓓ Ⓔ   8 Ⓐ Ⓑ Ⓒ Ⓓ Ⓔ   13 Ⓐ Ⓑ Ⓒ Ⓓ Ⓔ   18 Ⓐ Ⓑ Ⓒ Ⓓ Ⓔ   23 Ⓐ Ⓑ Ⓒ Ⓓ Ⓔ
4 Ⓐ Ⓑ Ⓒ Ⓓ Ⓔ   9 Ⓐ Ⓑ Ⓒ Ⓓ Ⓔ   14 Ⓐ Ⓑ Ⓒ Ⓓ Ⓔ   19 Ⓐ Ⓑ Ⓒ Ⓓ Ⓔ   24 Ⓐ Ⓑ Ⓒ Ⓓ Ⓔ
5 Ⓐ Ⓑ Ⓒ Ⓓ Ⓔ   10 Ⓐ Ⓑ Ⓒ Ⓓ Ⓔ   15 Ⓐ Ⓑ Ⓒ Ⓓ Ⓔ   20 Ⓐ Ⓑ Ⓒ Ⓓ Ⓔ   25 Ⓐ Ⓑ Ⓒ Ⓓ Ⓔ

SAT Practice Test 7

SECTION 1 VERBAL ABILITY
30 MINUTES 45 QUESTIONS

For each question in this section, choose the best answer and blacken the corresponding space on the answer sheet.

Each question below consists of a word in capital letters, followed by five lettered words or phrases. Choose the word or phrase that is most nearly *opposite* in meaning to the word in capital letters. Since some of the questions require you to distinguish fine shades of meaning, consider all the choices before deciding which is best.

Example:

GOOD: (A) sour (B) bad (C) red
(D) hot (E) ugly

Ⓐ ● Ⓒ Ⓓ Ⓔ

1. PLIANT: (A) malicious (B) watchful
   (C) hardworking (D) progressive (E) rigid

2. IMPETUOUS: (A) sticky (B) controlled
   (C) incredible (D) generous (E) cooperative

3. CALLOUS: (A) yielding (B) jealous
   (C) shining (D) perceiving (E) theoretical

4. SEDATE: (A) occupied (B) lonely
   (C) incompetent (D) passionate (E) tense

5. LOQUACIOUS: (A) incapable (B) prying
   (C) silent (D) unpopular (E) voluptuous

6. TURBID: (A) acceptable (B) undisturbed
   (C) clear (D) picturesque (E) identical

7. RUTHLESS: (A) considerate (B) complete
   (C) widowed (D) staunch (E) indecisive

8. FLAMBOYANT: (A) extinguished
   (B) modest (C) sinking (D) experienced
   (E) abnormal

9. ACCOST: (A) persecute (B) overprice
   (C) disconnect (D) spurn (E) deprive

10. BAWDY: (A) alluring (B) essential
    (C) youthful (D) antisocial (E) decent

11. RESOLUTE: (A) indifferent (B) wavering
    (C) predictable (D) incompetent (E) effervescent

12. ELICIT: (A) hold back (B) use correctly
    (C) move forward (D) regard lightly
    (E) see clearly

13. URBANE: (A) lifeless (B) nonpoisonous
    (C) exaggerated (D) dangerous (E) discourteous

14. VERVE: (A) audacity (B) simplicity
    (C) fatigue (D) doubt (E) scarcity

15. SUPERCILIOUS: (A) inferior
    (B) subordinate (C) durable (D) humble
    (E) elementary

Each sentence below has one or two blanks, each blank indicating that something has been omitted. Beneath the sentence are five lettered words or sets of words. Choose the word or set of words that *best* fits the meaning of the sentence as a whole.

Example:

Although its publicity has been ____, the film itself is intelligent, well-acted, handsomely produced, and altogether ____.

(A) tasteless . . . respectable
(B) extensive . . . moderate
(C) sophisticated . . . amateur
(D) risqué . . . crude
(E) perfect . . . spectacular

● Ⓑ Ⓒ Ⓓ Ⓔ

16. The Classical age of Greek art ended with the defeat of Athens by Sparta; the _____ effect of the long war was the weakening and _____ of the Greek spirit.

    (A) cumulative . . . corrosion
    (B) immediate . . . storing
    (C) imagined . . . cooperation
    (D) delayed . . . rebuilding
    (E) intuitive . . . cancellation

17. Mary, bored by even the briefest periods of idleness, was _____ switching from one activity to another.

    (A) hesitantly (B) lazily (C) slowly
    (D) surprisingly (E) continually

18. The bee _____ the nectar from the different flowers and then _____ the liquid into honey.

    (A) consumes . . . conforms
    (B) observes . . . pours
    (C) rejects . . . solidifies
    (D) crushes . . . injects
    (E) extracts . . . converts

19. Joining _____ momentum for reform in intercollegiate sports, university presidents have called for swift steps to correct imbalances between classwork and _____.

(A) a maximum . . . studies
(B) a rational . . . awards
(C) an increasing . . . athletics
(D) an exceptional . . . professors
(E) a futile . . . contests

20. Although Grete Waitz is the most celebrated female marathon runner, she is noted for her _____.

(A) vigor   (B) indecision   (C) modesty
(D) speed   (E) endurance

Each passage below is followed by questions based on its content. Answer all questions following a passage on the basis of what is *stated* or *implied* in that passage.

Most adolescents, who ought to be treated as individuals, are herded into high schools with more than a thousand others, often 2000 or more in big cities. There they "cover" a succession of topics each day, without any apparent cohesion. To work at all, such schools must control their courses tightly. Under such conditions, significant changes in procedure are vetoed on practical grounds; it disturbs too many things. Yet the existing system is seriously flawed. Students are forced to accept what is given them instead of being expected to educate themselves. Reformers call for "four years of English for all students," but who knows what four years of English entails?

The torrent of facts poured over students is overwhelming and the only way teachers can keep up with the flow is to lecture—and to feed students knowledge rather than expect them to forage on their own. All of the currently discussed reforms will fail unless fundamental changes are made. High schools must set for themselves shorter, simple, better defined goals, and get rid of others. For example, driver education may have to give way to English. Chemistry may have to be dropped so that biology and physics may be taught better. Students entering high school with deficiencies in reading, writing, and figuring would have to concentrate exclusively on those subjects until they mastered them. Skills of reasoning, imagining, and analyzing must be made the core of high school work but they can be learned only through confrontation and dialogue. This calls for different formats of teaching and fewer students per teacher.

The central goal of schooling ought to be for students to teach themselves. But this is impossible as long as the frenzied quality of many high schools cuts the day into snippets of time. We should have large blocks of time and less standardized instruction. Let us pay more attention to what students learn, or could learn, outside of school.

The teacher is of vital importance in improving our educational system. If the schools are to respond properly to the different ways students learn, teachers must have control over schedules and programs. Good teachers value their autonomy. They are not pawns on a chessboard. If their independence is taken away from them, they do mediocre work or get out of teaching altogether. Under current standardization, every teacher, once licensed, is considered equal to every other teacher, an interchangeable part in a machine. This simplifies administration, but stands in the way of educational change and reform. The success of today's reform movement depends on a rebuilding of the system to make it serve the needs of adolescents and to harness the capacities of good teachers.

21. Which is the most appropriate title for this passage dealing with education in the high schools?

(A) Outstanding and Mediocre Teachers
(B) Crowded Schools With Little Taught
(C) Students are Getting a Raw Deal
(D) The Need for Reform in Our Schools
(E) The Courses That Should Be Offered and Those That Shouldn't

22. According to the passage, a primary concern of the author is

(A) the number of students in the high schools of the large cities
(B) the need for more driver education courses
(C) the size of many high school classes
(D) the low salary scale of high school teachers
(E) the infrequency of periods of relaxation for teachers during the school day

23. The author is in favor of all of the following educational practices in the high schools *except*

(A) arranging for special recognition for those teachers who are outstanding
(B) limiting the lecture method wherever possible
(C) encouraging students to think for themselves
(D) giving a greater opportunity to teachers in decision-making
(E) including students who have reading difficulties in regular English classes

24. The author's attitude toward principals and supervisors is likely one of

(A) respect for their efforts in trying to improve the educational system.
(B) disapproval toward their bureaucratic policies and procedures
(C) tolerance because of the difficulty of their tasks.
(D) annoyance because of their leniency toward unruly students
(E) sympathy in view of the reform and status quo supporters who challenge them

25. When the author asks ". . . but who knows what four years of English entails?" (line 12), he is probably referring to

(A) the level of difficulty of the work in English
(B) the various ways in which the instruction will be given
(C) the willingness of the students to take four years of English
(D) the amount of money required if all students get four years of English
(E) the types of literature that the reformers may require to be taught

Despite the fact that cigarette smoking is a colossal threat to personal health, a third of American adults persist in puffing away on about 600 billion cigarettes a year. Four out of five of these smokers say that they want
5 to quit but, after numerous attempts, most find that they cannot.
Recent research into the psychology and pharmacology of nicotine is beginning to explain the remarkable persistence of smoking behavior. The addictive drug appears to
10 have unique properties that make it "perfect" for coping with the vicissitudes of life. The tenacity of nicotine dependence stems from the wide variety of effects it exerts on the nervous system. There is evidence that cigarettes improve memory and the ability to think and concentrate;
15 reduce anxiety; increase tolerance of pain; and reduce hunger as well as the desire for sweet-tasting and high caloric food.
Nicotine produces these temporary improvements in a remarkable two-step process. Studies show that short, quick
20 puffs—low doses—tend to stimulate or arouse brain function and behavior. Deep, full drags—high doses—create the more sedative, relaxing effects of smoking. This may mean that different personality types use smoking to reinforce preferred behavior patterns. Type A people (com-
25 petitive, impatient, hostile) might take shorter puffs to enhance arousal. Type B personalities (relaxed, less concerned with achievement) might take longer puffs to promote relaxation.
While smoking seems to bestow powerful psycho-
30 pharmacological benefits, it carries such highly lethal risks that many nonsmokers find it difficult to understand why anyone continues to smoke. Cigarette smoking is considered the most widespread form of addiction in the world—

even worse than heroin. Smoking kills seven times more people each year than automobile accidents. The Envi- 35
ronmental Protection Agency now lists tobacco smoke as the most dangerous carcinogen. That cigarettes damage heart, lung, and other vital tissues is widely acknowledged by medical authorities and researchers.
Several laboratories are searching for substances that 40
chemically and selectively block nicotine's effects on the nervous system. But ultimately, any treatment will have to include behavior modification techniques that help former smokers cope with signals from the environment that are associated with smoking. The reason that smoking is 45
so insidious is that it affects many different brain regulatory systems simultaneously. And as it affects many moods and types of performance, it is adopted into the performance of an enormous variety of daily tasks. It becomes a crutch, capturing the normal adaptive regulatory systems of the 50
human brain. There is no single explanation for smoking and there is no easy cure. Not is it likely that there will ever be a safe cigarette.

26. Which one of the following statements about cigarette smoking does *not* necessarily involve *psychological* research?

(A) Avoiding withdrawal from nicotine is a major reason why some smokers cannot break the habit.
(B) There is some evidence that nicotine from smoking improves long-term memory.
(C) Virtually all physicians know chest surgeons who remain hopelessly addicted to cigarettes.
(D) Tobacco smoke is the most dangerous airborne carcinogen.
(E) Studies of both humans and animals show nicotine has a direct anxiety-relieving effect.

27. Which of the following best describes the relation between the third and fourth paragraphs in the passage?

(A) The fourth paragraph gives specific examples of general statements made in the third paragraph.
(B) The fourth paragraph disagrees with some of the opinions expressed in the third paragraph.
(C) The fourth paragraph questions the accuracy of certain statements made in the third paragraph.
(D) The fourth paragraph reinforces the arguments made in the third paragraph.
(E) The fourth paragraph indicates that the disadvantages far outweigh the advantages described in the third paragraph.

28. "Several laboratories are searching for substances that chemically and selectively block nicotine's effects on the nervous system (lines 40–42)." Why?

(A) to avoid brain damage
(B) to promote relaxation
(C) to prevent addiction
(D) to arouse brain function
(E) to help one to cope with the vicissitudes of life

29. The author's attitude in regard to the use of nicotine in such a way that it will cause no damage, is one of

    (A) caution   (B) pessimism   (C) curiosity
    (D) patience   (E) indifference

30. The most appropriate title for this passage would be

    (A) An Addiction With Many Lures
    (B) Blow the Man Down
    (C) Nothing Is Stronger Than Habit
    (D) What Fools These Mortals Be
    (E) Cigarettes Are Coffin Nails

Select the word or set of words that *best* completes each of the following sentences.

31. Thinking nothing can be done, many victims of arthritis ignore or delay _____ countermeasures, thus aggravating the problem.

    (A) tardy   (B) injurious   (C) characteristic
    (D) weird   (E) effective

32. Periodically an important government official finds himself pinned and wriggling in the national spotlight, watching his personal _____ exposed on the evening news threatening his _____.

    (A) interests . . . family
    (B) friends . . . life
    (C) misdeeds . . . career
    (D) ambitions . . . conduct
    (E) thoughts . . . position

33. Some animals that hibernate, like the bear, the frog, and the snail, pass the winter in _____ or sleeping state.

    (A) a merry   (B) a productive   (C) an inactive
    (D) an insecure   (E) a creative

34. For years a vocalist of Negro spirituals, Marian Anderson was finally recognized as _____ singer when the Metropolitan Opera House engaged her.

    (A) a versatile   (B) an unusual
    (C) an attractive   (D) a cooperative
    (E) a mediocre

35. Leonardo da Vinci _____ the Law of Gravity two centuries before Newton and also made the first complete _____ charts of the human body.

    (A) examined . . . colorful
    (B) anticipated . . . anatomical
    (C) avoided . . . meaningful
    (D) realized . . . explanatory
    (E) suspected . . . mural

Each question below consists of a related pair of words or phrases, followed by five lettered pairs of words or phrases. Select the lettered pair that *best* expresses a relationship similar to that expressed in the original pair.

Example:

YAWN : BOREDOM : :   (A) dream : sleep
(B) anger : madness   (C) smile : amusement
(D) face : expression   (E) impatience : rebellion
                         (A) (B) ● (D) (E)

36. DRAFTED : ARMY : :

    (A) seduced : felony
    (B) subpoenaed : court
    (C) engaged : ring
    (D) denied : access
    (E) corrupted : society

37. SACCHARINE : SINCERE : :

    (A) unscrupulous : conscientious
    (B) proud : noble
    (C) blithe : aboveboard
    (D) rustic : simple
    (E) insidious : venal

38. BONE : BRITTLE : :

    (A) battle : bloody
    (B) odor : fragrant
    (C) song : melodious
    (D) glass : fragile
    (E) diet : stringent

39. UMPIRE : BASEBALL : :

    (A) matador : bullfighter
    (B) defendant : prosecutor
    (C) father : friends
    (D) judge : law
    (E) conqueror : battle

40. INTRACTABLE : CONTROL : :

    (A) judicious : decide
    (B) pacific : instill
    (C) indicted : arrest
    (D) nullified : forget
    (E) cryptic : decipher

41. PIPE : SEWER : :

    (A) train : schedule
    (B) spine : body
    (C) tunnel : river
    (D) messenger : sender
    (E) artery : heart

42. HECKLER : PERFORMER : :

   (A) foghorn : boat
   (B) audience : stage
   (C) hunter : rifle
   (D) tick : cat
   (E) pest : nuisance

43. AMNESIA : MEMORY : :

   (A) anarchy : citizenry
   (B) incompetence : interest
   (C) aphasia : speech
   (D) torsion : twine
   (E) levity : humor

44. GLANCE : CURSORY : :

   (A) scurry : relaxed
   (B) delve : thorough
   (C) insinuate : damaging
   (D) mandate : conforming
   (E) waive : restrictive

45. OBESE : HEAVY : :

   (A) sad : devastated
   (B) unique : ornate
   (C) quarrelsome : positive
   (D) emaciated : thin
   (E) resonant : vibrant

S T O P

IF YOU FINISH BEFORE TIME IS CALLED, YOU MAY CHECK YOUR WORK ON THIS SECTION ONLY.
DO NOT WORK ON ANY OTHER SECTION IN THE TEST.

SECTION 2   MATH ABILITY
30 MINUTES   25 QUESTIONS

In this section solve each problem, using any available space on the page for scratchwork. Then decide which is the best of the choices given and blacken the corresponding space on the answer sheet.

The following information is for your reference in solving some of the problems.

Circle of radius r: Area $= \pi r^2$; Circumference $= 2\pi r$
The number of degrees of arc in a circle is 360.
The measure in degrees of a straight angle is 180.

Definitions of symbols:
$=$	is equal to	$\leqq$	is less than or equal to
$\neq$	is unequal to	$\geqq$	is greater than or equal to
$<$	is less than	$\parallel$	is parallel to
$>$	is greater than	$\perp$	is perpendicular to

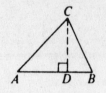

Triangle: The sum of the measure in degrees of the angles of a triangle is 180.
If $\angle CDA$ is a right angle, then

(1)   area of $\triangle ABC = \dfrac{AB \times CD}{2}$

(2) $AC^2 = AD^2 + DC^2$

Note: Figures which accompany problems in this test are intended to provide information useful in solving the problems. They are drawn as accurately as possible EXCEPT when it is stated in a specific problem that its figure is not drawn to scale. All figures lie in a plane unless otherwise indicated. All numbers used are real numbers.

1. Find the value of
$$\frac{(20 + 30) + (10 + 40) + (25 + 25)}{3}$$

   (A) 20   (B) 30   (C) 40   (D) 50   (E) 60

2. A piece of rope is lying on a number line. One of its ends is at coordinate -4 and the other is at coordinate 7. What is the length of the rope?

   (A) 3   (B) 5   (C) 7   (D) 9   (E) 11

3. A long jumper has jumps of 8.4 meters, 8.1 meters, and 9.3 meters. What is the average (arithmetic mean) of these jumps?

   (A) 8.5   (B) 8.6   (C) 8.7   (D) 8.8   (E) 8.9

4. If $x + 9 = -11 - x$, then $x =$
   (A) -10 (B) -2 (C) 2   (D) 10   (E) 20

5. If $3y = 12$ and $\dfrac{10}{x} = 5$, then

   $$\frac{y + 11}{x + 15} =$$

   (A) $\dfrac{7}{10}$ (B) $\dfrac{3}{4}$ (C) $\dfrac{15}{17}$ (D) 1   (E) $\dfrac{17}{15}$

6. Johnny deposited $50 in a savings bank at the beginning of the year. Johnny's money earns him interest at the rate of 8 percent of the amount deposited, for each year that Johnny leaves his money in the bank. If Johnny leaves his $50 in the bank for exactly one year and then decides to withdraw all of his money, how much money (including interest) can he withdraw? (The interest is not compounded.)

   (A) $50.04   (B) $50.08   (C) $54.00
   (D) $54.08   (E) $58.00

7. If $(x + 6)^2 = 12x + 72$, then $x =$
   (A) 0   (B) ± 1 (C) ± 3 (D) ± 6 (E) ± 12

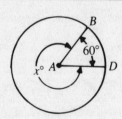

Note: Figure is not drawn to scale.

8. In the circle above, A is the center of the circle. Find the value of $x - 60$.

   (A) 60   (B) 120   (C) 240   (D) 300   (E) 360

9. To the nearest hundred, how many minutes are there in a week?

   (A) 1,000   (B) 1,100   (C) 10,000
   (D) 10,100   (E) 11,000

10. If $\boxed{x}$ is defined by the equation $\boxed{x} = \dfrac{x^3}{4}$ for real numbers x, which of the following equals 16?

(A) $\boxed{2}$ (B) $\boxed{4}$ (C) $\boxed{8}$ (D) $\boxed{16}$ (E) $\boxed{64}$

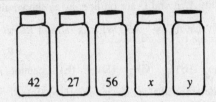

11. 200 pieces of candy have been randomly put into five jars. The number of pieces of candy in three of the five jars is shown in the figure above. What is the maximum possible value of x? (x is the number of pieces of candy in the fourth jar.)

(A) 69   (B) 75   (C) 102   (D) 144   (E) 200

12. There are 16 pages in a book. Last night, Ron read $\dfrac{1}{4}$ of the book. This morning, Ron read $\dfrac{1}{4}$ of the remaining pages. How many pages does Ron still have left to read?

(A) 7   (B) 8   (C) 9   (D) 10   (E) 11

13. A sphere is inscribed in a cube whose volume is 64. What is the diameter of the sphere?

(A) 2   (B) $2\sqrt{2}$ (C) 8   (D) $4\sqrt{2}$ (E) 4

14. The ratio of girls to boys in a class is 8 : 7. The number of students in the class could be any of the following *except*

(A) 15   (B) 45   (C) 50   (D) 60   (E) 90

15. If $\dfrac{m}{n} = \dfrac{x}{m}$, then $x =$

(A) $\dfrac{m^2}{n}$ (B) $\dfrac{m}{n}$ (C) $\dfrac{n}{m^2}$ (D) $\dfrac{1}{n}$ (E) n

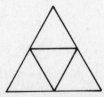

16. The above figure is an equilateral triangle divided into four congruent, smaller, equilateral triangles. If the perimeter of a smaller triangle is 1, then the perimeter of the whole large triangle is

(A) 2   (B) 4   (C) 6   (D) 8   (E) 16

17. A different candle was lit at noon each day between December 9 and December 21, inclusive. How many candles were lit during this period?

(A) 10   (B) 11   (C) 12   (D) 13   (E) 14

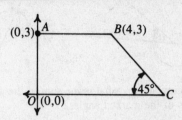

18. What is the area of quadrilateral $ABCO$ in the figure above?

(A) 10.5   (B) 14.5   (C) 16.5   (D) 21.0
(E) It cannot be determined from the information given.

19. The difference between the sum of two numbers and the difference of the two numbers is 6. Find the larger of the two numbers if their product is 15.

(A) 3   (B) 5   (C) 17   (D) 20   (E) 23

20. If $\dfrac{1}{a} + \dfrac{1}{b} = 10$, what is the value of $a + b$?

(A) $\dfrac{1}{10}$ (B) $\dfrac{2}{5}$ (C) 1   (D) 10
(E) It cannot be determined from the information given.

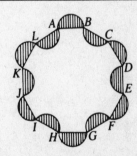

21. In the figure above, $ABCDEFGHIJKL$ is a regular dodecagon (a regular twelve-sided polygon). The curved path is made up of 12 semicircles, each of whose diameters is a side of the dodecagon. If the perimeter of the dodecagon is 24, find the area of the shaded region.

(A) 6π (B) 12π (C) 24π (D) 36π (E) 48π

22. If $x > 0$ and $y > 0$ and $x^9 = 4$ and $x^7 = \dfrac{9}{y^2}$, which of the following is an expression for the value of x in terms of y?

(A) $\dfrac{4}{9}y$ (B) $\dfrac{2}{3}y$ (C) $\dfrac{3}{2}y^2$ (D) $6y$ (E) $36y^2$

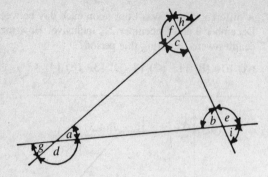

23. In the figure above, what is the sum of the degree measures of the marked angles?

(A) 360° (B) 720° (C) 900° (D) 1080° (E) It cannot be determined from the information given.

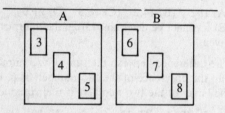

24. Box A contains 3 cards, numbered 3, 4 and 5. Box B contains 3 cards, numbered 6, 7 and 8. If one card is drawn from each box and their sum is calculated, how many different sums are possible?

(A) Eight (B) Seven (C) Six (D) Five (E) Four

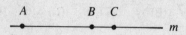

25. Points *A*, *B* and *C* are on line *m*, as shown above, such that $AC = \frac{4}{3}AB$. What is ratio of *BC* to *AB*?

(A) $\frac{1}{4}$ (B) $\frac{1}{3}$ (C) $\frac{1}{2}$ (D) $\frac{2}{3}$ (E) It cannot be determined from the given information.

S T O P

IF YOU FINISH BEFORE TIME IS CALLED, YOU MAY CHECK YOUR WORK ON THIS SECTION ONLY.
DO NOT WORK ON ANY OTHER SECTION IN THE TEST.

SECTION 3   STANDARD WRITTEN ENGLISH TEST

30 MINUTES   50 QUESTIONS

The questions in this section measure skills that are important to writing well. In particular, they test your ability to recognize and use language that is clear, effective, and correct according to the requirements of standard written English, the kind of English found in most college textbooks.

Directions: The following contain problems in grammar, usage, diction (choice of words), and idiom.

Some sentences are correct.
No sentence contains more than one error.

You will find that the error, if there is one, is underlined and lettered. Assume that elements of the sentence that are not underlined are correct and cannot be changed. In choosing answers, follow the requirements of standard written English.

If there is an error, select the *one underlined part* that must be changed to make the sentence correct and blacken the corresponding space on your answer sheet.

If there is no error, blacken answer space Ⓔ .

EXAMPLE: SAMPLE ANSWER
                                                 Ⓐ Ⓑ ● Ⓓ Ⓔ

The region has a climate so severe that plants
                          A

growing there rarely had been more than twelve
     B   C

inches high. No error
     D   E

---

1. We were terrified by sounds: the screaming of the
        A   B

   wind; the restless rustling of leaves in the trees; and the
                        C

   sudden, overwhelming explosions of thunder.
                        D

   No error.
   E

2. His dog having barked a warning, the watchman
              A

   who had been assigned to guard the valuable
        B

   truckload of chemicals pulled out his gun quick and
                                            C

   proceeded to search out a possible intruder. No error.
           D   E

3. Your employer would have been inclined to favor
                                 A

   your request if you would have waited for an
                        B

   occasion when he was less busy with other
                        C

   more important matters. No error.
           D   E

4. Popular impressions about slang are often erroneous:
                          A

   their is no necessary connection, for example,
   B   C

   between what is slang and what is ungrammatical.
           D

   No error.
   E

5. After all the performers had finished their
   <u>   </u>
                                      A

   performances, I knew the winner to be <u>he</u> <u>whom</u> I
                                              B   C

   had singled out <u>the moment</u> I had met him.
                          D

   <u>No error.</u>
      E

6. <u>Nor has</u> the writer even the satisfaction of calling his
    A

   reader a fool for misunderstanding him, since he

   seldom hears <u>of</u> it; it is the reader who calls the
              B

   writer a fool <u>for</u> not being able to express <u>hisself</u>.
               C   D

   <u>No error.</u>
      E

7. Struggling <u>hard</u> against almost <u>insuperable</u> odds, he
            A   B

   was unable <u>to effect</u> even a small change in the
                C

   course of the vehicle. <u>No error.</u>
     D   E

8. I appreciate <u>you</u> helping me <u>to do</u> the dishes, but I
                A   B

   wish you would <u>lay</u> them down on the table more
                 C

   carefully. <u>No error.</u>
     D   E

9. Looking through the <u>main gate</u> at the southwest
                       A

   corner of the park where the bridle path <u>emerges</u>
                                               B

   from the wood, <u>the blooming lilac</u> can be seen in
                         C

   <u>great sprays</u> of purple, lavender, and white.
       D

   <u>No error.</u>
      E

10. No sooner had he <u>begun</u> to speak <u>when</u> an ominous
    <u>   </u>
       A   B   C

    muttering <u>arose</u> from the audience. <u>No error.</u>
             D   E

11. Separate vacations by husband and wife are

    <u>much esteemed</u> in certain circles, but if such holidays
            A

    last more than a year <u>or so</u>, even the most liberal
       B   C

    raise <u>there</u> eyebrows. <u>No error.</u>
        D   E

12. Proud of his skill <u>in serving</u> liquor, he <u>poured</u> some
                    A   B

    of the wine into his own glass first so that he

    <u>would get</u> the cork <u>and not the lady.</u> <u>No error.</u>
      C   D   E

13. The captain of the squad was a sophomore, one of

    last <u>year's</u> <u>freshman</u> team, a player of great
         A   B

    intelligence, and, <u>above all</u>, <u>endurance</u>. <u>No error.</u>
                   C   D   E

14. Everyone <u>is expected</u> <u>to attend</u> the afternoon session
              A   B

    but the field supervisor, the sales manager, and <u>I.</u>
    <u>   </u>
     C   D

    <u>No error.</u>
      E

15. No one who <u>has seen</u> him work in the laboratory
                 A

    can deny that Williams has an <u>interest and an</u>
      B   C

    <u>aptitude</u> for chemical experimentation. <u>No error.</u>
      D   E

16. Manslaughter <u>is where</u> a person is <u>killed</u> <u>unlawfully</u>
                   A   B   C

    but without premeditation. <u>No error.</u>
       D   E

17. The reason teenagers <u>tend</u> to follow the trend while
                     A

    <u>openly declaring</u> <u>themselves</u> nonconformists is
      B   C

    <u>because</u> they are really insecure. <u>No error.</u>
      D   E

18. <u>Its</u> not generally <u>known</u> that the word "buxom"
     A   B

    originally came from the <u>Old English</u> verb meaning
       C   D

    "to bend." <u>No error.</u>
             E

19. A great many educators firmly believe that English is
    A   B
one of the poorest taught subjects in high school
                   C
today. No error.
  D   E

20. Developed by the research engineers of Dupont,
                     A
the government considers the new explosive a sure
              B   C
deterrent to war. No error.
         D   E

21. Baseball, football, and soccer have all been approved
                                        A
as extracurricular activities. From either of them a
   B   C
coach can earn several hundreds of dollars each
                        D
season. No error.
        E

22. After I listened to the violinist and cellist, and
          A
enjoyed their interpretations, I hurried home
       B   C
to practice. No error.
    D   E

23. Most of the citizens have no doubt that the
                          A
Mayor taking a firm stand in the matter
      B
of clamping down on drug peddlers will bear
             C
immediate results in ridding the city of these vermin.
                            D
No error.
  E

24. Having sat the bag of dirty clothes on a bench in the
       A   B
apartment building laundry room, Mrs. Williams
chatted with a neighbor until a washing machine was
   C   D
available. No error.
           E

25. None of the crew members who flew with me over
                                A   B
Hanoi is happy today about the destruction caused in
                       C   D
that bombing mission. No error.
                        E

<u>Directions:</u> In each of the following sentences, some part or all of the sentence is underlined. Below each sentence you will find five ways of phrasing the underlined part. Select the answer that produces the most effective sentence, one that is clear and exact, without awkwardness or ambiguity, and blacken the corresponding space on your answer sheet. In choosing answers, follow the requirements of standard written English. Choose the answer that best expresses the meaning of the original sentence.

Answer (A) is always the same as the underlined part. Choose answer (A) if you think the original sentence needs no revision.

EXAMPLE:

Laura Ingalls Wilder published her first book <u>and she was sixty-five years old then</u>.
(A) and she was sixty-five years old then
(B) when she was sixty-five years old
(C) at age sixty-five years old
(D) upon reaching sixty-five years
(E) at the time when she was sixty-five

SAMPLE ANSWER

Ⓐ ● Ⓒ Ⓓ Ⓔ

---

26. <u>The students requested a meeting with the chancellor</u> since they desired a greater voice in university policy.

(A) The students requested a meeting with the chancellor
(B) A meeting with the chancellor was requested by the students
(C) It occurred to the students to request a meeting with the chancellor
(D) The chancellor was the one with whom the students requested a meeting
(E) The students insisted upon a meeting with the chancellor

27. Three American scientists were jointly awarded the Nobel Prize in Medicine <u>for their study of viruses which led to discoveries.</u>

(A) for their study of viruses which led to discoveries
(B) for their discoveries concerning viruses
(C) as a prize for their discoveries about viruses
(D) the discovery into viruses being the reason
(E) for their virus discoveries

28. <u>You must convince me of promptness in returning the money</u> before I can agree to lend you $100.

(A) You must convince me of promptness in returning the money
(B) The loan of the money must be returned promptly
(C) You must understand that you will have to assure me of a prompt money return
(D) You will have to convince me that you will return the money promptly
(E) You will return the money promptly

29. Because Bob was an outstanding athlete in high school, <u>in addition to a fine scholastic record,</u> he was awarded a scholarship at Harvard.

(A) in addition to a fine scholastic record,
(B) also a student of excellence,
(C) and had amassed an excellent scholastic record,
(D) his scholastic record was also outstanding,
(E) as well as a superior student,

30. Although pre-season odds against the Mets had been 100 to 1, <u>the Orioles were trounced by them in the World Series.</u>

(A) the Orioles were trounced by them in the World Series
(B) the World Series victors were the Mets who trounced the Orioles
(C) they won the World Series by trouncing the Orioles
(D) which is hard to believe since the Orioles were trounced in the World Series
(E) it was the Mets who trounced the Orioles in the World Series

31. Before you can make a fresh fruit salad, <u>you must buy oranges, bananas, pineapples and peaches are necessary.</u>

(A) you must buy oranges, bananas, pineapples and peaches are necessary.
(B) you must buy oranges and bananas and pineapples and peaches.
(C) you must buy oranges and bananas. And other fruit such as pineapples and peaches.
(D) you must buy oranges and bananas and other fruit. Such as pineapples and peaches.
(E) you must buy oranges, bananas, pineapples, and peaches

32. The physical education department of the school offers instruction to learn how to swim, how to play tennis, and how to defend oneself.

    (A) to learn how to swim, how to play tennis, and how to defend oneself
    (B) in swimming, playing tennis, and protecting oneself
    (C) in regard to how to swim, how to play tennis, and how to protect oneself
    (D) for the purpose of swimming, playing tennis, and protecting oneself
    (E) in swimming, playing tennis, and to protect oneself

33. Joe couldn't wait for his return to his home after being in the army for two years.

    (A) Joe couldn't wait for his return to his home
    (B) There was a strong desire on Joe's part to return home
    (C) Joe was eager to return home
    (D) Joe wanted home badly
    (E) Joe arranged to return home

34. Trash, filth, and muck are clogging the streets of the city and that's not all, the sidewalks are full of garbage.

    (A) that's not all, the sidewalks are full of garbage.
    (B) another thing: garbage is all over the sidewalks
    (C) the garbage cans haven't been emptied for days
    (D) in addition, garbage is lying all over the sidewalks
    (E) what's more, the sidewalks have garbage that is lying all over them

35. Tired and discouraged by the problems of the day, Myra decided to have a good dinner, and then lie down for an hour, and then go dancing.

    (A) Myra decided to have a good dinner, and then lie down for an hour, and then go dancing.
    (B) Myra decided to have a good dinner, lying down for an hour, and then dancing.
    (C) Myra decided to have a good dinner, lie down for an hour, and then dancing.
    (D) Myra decided to have a good dinner, lay down for an hour, and then dance.
    (E) Myra decided to have a good dinner, lie down for an hour, and then go dancing.

36. I am not certain in respect to which courses to take.

    (A) in respect to which courses
    (B) about which courses
    (C) which courses
    (D) as to the choice of which courses
    (E) for which courses I am

37. The people of the besieged village had no doubt that the end was drawing near.

    (A) that the end was drawing near
    (B) about the nearness of the end
    (C) it was clear that the end was near
    (D) concerning the end's being near
    (E) that all would die

38. There isn't a single man among us who is skilled in the art of administering first-aid.

    (A) who is skilled in the art of administering first-aid
    (B) who knows how to administer first-aid
    (C) who knows the administration of first-aid
    (D) who is a first-aid man
    (E) who administers first-aid

39. This is the hole that was squeezed through by the mouse.

    (A) that was squeezed through by the mouse
    (B) that the mouse was seen to squeeze through
    (C) the mouse squeezed through it
    (D) that the mouse squeezed through
    (E) like what the mouse squeezed through

40. She soundly fell asleep after having finished the novel.

    (A) She soundly fell asleep
    (B) She decided to sleep
    (C) She went on to her sleep
    (D) She fell to sleep
    (E) She fell fast asleep

Note: The remaining questions are like those at the beginning of the section.

Directions: For each sentence in which you find an error, select the one underlined part that must be changed to make the sentence correct and blacken the corresponding space on your answer sheet.

If there is no error, blacken answer space Ⓔ .

EXAMPLE:

The region has a climate <u>so severe that</u> plants
                              A

<u>growing</u> there rarely <u>had been</u> more than twelve
   B   C

inches <u>high</u>. <u>No error</u>
         D   E

SAMPLE ANSWER

Ⓐ Ⓑ ● Ⓓ Ⓔ

---

41. It was our <u>neighbor's</u> opinion that if Kennedy <u>was</u>
                  A   B

    alive today, the country <u>would have fewer problems</u>
                                         C

    <u>than</u> it has now. <u>No error</u>.
      D   E

42. We, <u>as</u> parents who are interested in the welfare of
          A

    our son, are <u>strongly</u> opposed to <u>him</u> associating with
                     B   C

    individuals who <u>do not seem to have</u> moral scruples.
                            D

    <u>No error</u>.
      E

43. If anyone in the audience <u>has</u> anything <u>to add to</u>
                                  A   B

    <u>what</u> the speaker has already said, let <u>them</u> speak up.
      C   D

    <u>No error</u>.
      E

44. <u>It</u> was very nice of the <u>Rodriguezes</u> to invite my
      A   B

    husband, my mother, and <u>I</u> to their New <u>Year's</u> Eve
                               C   D

    party. <u>No error</u>.
              E

45. Neither rain <u>nor</u> snow nor sleet <u>keep</u> the postman
                   A   B

    from delivering our letters which we so much
         C

    <u>look forward to receiving</u>. <u>No error</u>.
               D   E

46. The <u>tallest</u> of the twins <u>accompanied</u> the detectives
            A   B

    during the search for the missing jewels, a picture

    <u>of which</u> you saw in this <u>morning's</u> newspaper.
         C   D

    <u>No error</u>.
      E

47. Anyone with the <u>necessary</u> equipment can
                        A

    manufacture <u>their</u> own outdoor furniture; however,
                    B

    a certain degree of patience and skill <u>is also required</u>
                  C   D

    <u>No error</u>.
      E

48. Before this bold explorer <u>lay</u> the vast waters of Lake
                                 A   B

    Superior—a lake <u>who's</u> natural beauty is
                        C

    <u>unsurpassed</u>. <u>No error</u>.
          D   E

49. Each of the campers in the senior group is expected

to make his own bed and to take care of the younger
   $\overline{\text{A}}$

campers, who on occasion, cannot take care of
   $\overline{\text{B}}$ $\overline{\text{C}}$

theirselves. No error.
 $\overline{\text{D}}$ $\overline{\text{E}}$

50. We didn't hardly sleep all night because of the
   $\overline{\text{A}}$ $\overline{\text{B}}$

chirping of the crickets and the hooting of the owls.
 $\overline{\text{C}}$ $\overline{\text{D}}$

No error.
 $\overline{\text{E}}$

S T O P

**IF YOU FINISH BEFORE TIME IS CALLED, YOU MAY CHECK YOUR WORK ON THIS SECTION ONLY.
DO NOT WORK ON ANY OTHER SECTION IN THE TEST.**

SECTION 4   VERBAL ABILITY
30 MINUTES   40 QUESTIONS

For each question in this section, choose the best answer and blacken the corresponding space on the answer sheet.

Each question below consists of a word in capital letters, followed by five lettered words or phrases. Choose the word or phrase that is most nearly *opposite* in meaning to the word in capital letters. Since some of the questions require you to distinguish fine shades of meaning, consider all the choices before deciding which is best.

Example:

> GOOD: (A) sour   (B) bad   (C) red
> (D) hot   (E) ugly
>   (A) ● (C) (D) (E)

1. TAUT: (A) formal   (B) loose   (C) quick
   (D) polite   (E) ignorant

2. AFFRONT: (A) assistance   (B) hypocrisy
   (C) diligence   (D) tardiness   (E) compliment

3. DESIST: (A) illuminate   (B) lengthen
   (C) regulate   (D) continue   (E) resist

4. RAUCOUS: (A) melodious
   (B) well-arranged   (C) domesticated   (D) final
   (E) usable

5. NETTLE: (A) animate   (B) unravel
   (C) soothe   (D) combine   (E) prefer

6. PALPABLE: (A) inaudible   (B) permanent
   (C) convincing   (D) graceful   (E) puzzling

7. DEBILITATE: (A) pursue   (B) roughen
   (C) popularize   (D) strengthen   (E) interest

8. METICULOUS: (A) mysterious   (B) healthful
   (C) careless   (D) unproductive   (E) aloof

9. PAUCITY: (A) abundance   (B) freedom
   (C) monotony   (D) complexity   (E) bluntness

10. EMOLLIENT: (A) treatment   (B) irritant
    (C) insult   (D) solution   (E) deprivation

Each sentence below has one or two blanks, each blank indicating that something has been omitted. Beneath the sentence are five lettered words or sets of words. Choose the word or set of words that *best* fits the meaning of the sentence as a whole.

Example:

> Although its publicity has been ____, the film itself is intelligent, well-acted, handsomely produced, and altogether ____.
>
> (A) tasteless . . . respectable
> (B) extensive . . . moderate
> (C) sophisticated . . . amateur
> (D) risqué . . . crude
> (E) perfect . . . spectacular   ● (B) (C) (D) (E)

11. Athens was ruled not by kings and emperors as was common among other _____ at the time, but by a citizenry, which _____ fully in the affairs of the city.

    (A) committees . . . cooperated
    (B) tribes . . . engaged
    (C) cities . . . revolutionized
    (D) populations . . . applied
    (E) societies . . . participated

12. Fossils are _____ in rock formations which were once soft and have _____ with the passage of time.

    (A) abolished . . . corresponded
    (B) interactive . . . communicated
    (C) preserved . . . hardened
    (D) created . . . revived
    (E) discounted . . . deteriorated

13. According to our best historical evidence, the Hebrews were a Semitic people who _____ somewhere in the Arabian peninsula.

    (A) organized   (B) disappeared
    (C) calculated   (D) originated   (E) elevated

14. The social-cultural trends of the 1960's _____ not only the relative affluence of the post-war period, but also the coming to maturity of a generation that was a product of that _____.

   (A) dominated . . . movement
   (B) reflected . . . prosperity
   (C) accentuated . . . depression
   (D) cautioned . . . decade
   (E) accepted . . . revolution

15. Rotation of crops helps to _____ soil fertility and soil usefulness for a long period of time.

   (A) conserve   (B) disperse   (C) employ
   (D) research   (E) shorten

Select the word or set of words that *best* completes each of the following sentences.

Each question below consists of a related pair of words or phrases, followed by five lettered pairs of words or phrases. Select the lettered pair that *best* expresses a relationship similar to that expressed in the original pair.

Example:

```
YAWN : BOREDOM : :   (A) dream : sleep
(B) anger : madness   (C) smile : amusement
(D) face : expression   (E) impatience : rebellion
                            Ⓐ Ⓑ ● Ⓓ Ⓔ
```

16. NOD : HEAD : :

   (A) clap : hands
   (B) bend : legs
   (C) rub : eyes
   (D) limp : feet
   (E) swing : arms

17. ADDENDUM : BOOK : :

   (A) finale : music
   (B) letter : envelope
   (C) epilogue : play
   (D) telegram : communication
   (E) salad : appetizer

18. SURFACE : SUBMERGE : :

   (A) sail : navigate
   (B) conceal : reveal
   (C) mount : ascend
   (D) sink : swim
   (E) emerge : withdraw

19. XENOPHOBIA : ACQUAINTANCE : :

   (A) psychosis : therapy
   (B) hydrophobia : obsession
   (C) jubilation : grief
   (D) agoraphobia : enclosure
   (E) kleptomania : law

20. TREATY : NATIONS : :

   (A) secession : unions
   (B) reneging : deals
   (C) acceptance : differences
   (D) reconciliation : spouses
   (E) hostility : aggression

21. RUTHLESS : MERCY : :

   (A) toothsome : food
   (B) garrulous : literacy
   (C) matchless : power
   (D) inveterate : experience
   (E) immaculate : stain

22. IDIOSYNCRASY : BEHAVIOR : :

   (A) candor : villainy
   (B) reluctance : action
   (C) drivel : bragging
   (D) spectacle : theatre
   (E) vagary : thought

23. LOYALTY : TREASON : :

   (A) honor : traitor
   (B) bravery : nobility
   (C) funds : embezzlement
   (D) danger : coward
   (E) kindness : hostility

24. POTABLE : WATER : :

   (A) flappable : calm
   (B) invincible : battle
   (C) palatable : food
   (D) flammable : torch
   (E) insatiable : thirst

25. FOMENT : INSURGENT : :

   (A) abnegate : king
   (B) dishearten : loser
   (C) slander : victim
   (D) rebel : iconoclast
   (E) applaud : spectator

Each passage below is followed by questions based on its content. Answer all questions following a passage on the basis of what is *stated* or *implied* in that passage.

There probably isn't a grammar school graduate alive who doesn't know something about Custer's last stand—doesn't know, at the very least, that on June 25th, 1876, "old yeller hair" led his Seventh Cavalry troops into the
5 valley of the Little Bighorn, encountered a large force of bellicose Sioux and Cheyenne warriors camped along the bank of the river and charged into what one historian once referred to as a secure, if somewhat controversial place in American history. Hundreds of books have been written
10 in an attempt to explain George Armstrong Custer's legendary mistake. Hundreds of writers have tried to unravel the mystery of why a man about to engage in such dubious battle would divide his meager command into three parts, send them off in different directions and proceed to attack
15 2,000 furious Indians with a personal escort of 210 men; and why, upon surveying the numerical odds against him from the hillside where he was soon to die, he would gleefully shout, "Hurrah boys, we've got them."

The controversy has never been over *what* happened,
20 but *why?* Was Custer mad? Was he misled by his scouts? Was he betrayed? Was he suicidal? There are no definitive answers. One may meticulously sort through all the possibilities, culling the distortions, half-truths and fabrications from the verifiable evidence, and arrive at the same
25 conclusion most Custer researchers have reached—only the General himself will ever know what he had in mind when he tried to bring down Goliath with a peashooter. But it is the durability of the Custer legend, and the fact that this single skirmish seems to loom larger than any
30 other battle in American history except perhaps Gettysburg, that still fascinates us.

26. The most appropriate title for this passage is

    (A) An Immortal and Foolhardy General
    (B) Into the Valley of Death Rode Custer
    (C) A Super Hero of American History
    (D) A Modern Day Samson Who Failed
    (E) Unmatched Courage in Spite of the Odds

27. The attitude of the writer is one of

    (A) obvious indifference
    (B) mild mockery
    (C) lavish praise
    (D) guarded admiration
    (E) friendly tolerance

28. The words "Goliath with a peashooter" in line 27 are a reference to

    (A) a military password
    (B) a sacred book
    (C) a boy's sport
    (D) an Indian chief
    (E) an expression of disappointment

In this age of radical romanticism a certain denigration of science is probably inevitable. An electronic rock musician rates ahead of a physicist, rationalism is equated with insensitivity and science is blamed for all the sour
5 products of materialism, instead of materialism being blamed for the misuses of science. Yet to all who want to right the wrongs supposedly fostered by science, particularly to those who want to clean the air, water and earth of this planet, it should be plain that there has never been greater
10 need of the scientist, the engineer and the technician or less sense in their being unemployed for so much as an hour.

We need them, to start with a modest example, to develop more efficient machinery for recycling waste. Here would be a triple boon to society: It would dispose cleanly
15 of the rubbish that threatens to bury *whole* populations alive; it would yield materials better than many ores now being mined to the detriment of the earth above them, and it would preserve those same resources against the day when they might be desperately in demand.
20

We need scientists, engineers and technicians to develop fuels that can generate more electric power without fouling earth, sea and sky in the process. But why more electric power? Indeed, why not cut back on power and return to a simpler, less demanding, way of life? If only
25 waffle irons and electric toothbrushes were at stake, the argument would be unanswerable.

But the fact is, we need more power to do the very recycling of waste that is so desirable. We need it to operate the vastly expanded sewage treatment plants that
30 a growing population demands. We need it for that immeasurably developed system of mass transportation that our metropolitan areas must have if the automobile is not to make the human lung outmoded. We need it for the herculean clean-up of the nation's lakes and rivers. And,
35 not least, we need it if all who are just emerging from dire poverty are to enjoy a standard of living we have so come to take for granted that many now hold it in scorn (or pretend to). Those who have yet to enjoy it understandably prefer not to knock it till they've tried it.
40

To achieve these ends—and we are concerned here with keeping the planet livable—we are going to require sources of power that do not themselves add to the world's pollution. And here is opportunity for all the technique we can muster.
45

29. The author's attitude toward youth is

    (A) critical   (B) enthusiastic   (C) neutral
    (D) ambiguous   (E) tolerant

30. The author views unemployment of professionals in scientific fields as

(A) a justifiable prejudice against interests that have abused our natural resources
(B) a waste of potential pollution controllers
(C) due to the cutback on space projects
(D) a reflection of the U.S. unemployment crisis
(E) the inevitable denigration of science in a romantic age

31. The article states that the recycling of waste

(A) has potential for replacing the mining of ores
(B) will result in a society dependent upon garbage production
(C) is a project to which U.S. scientists are uncommitted
(D) demands greater expenditures than benefits
(E) will not be possible for another thirty years

32. The author states that we need more electricity because

(A) coal is too dirty to continue using
(B) we must continue to increase our Gross National Product
(C) we need power to recycle waste
(D) we need to rebuild the national resource structure
(E) pollution can be eliminated thereby

Libel, simply put, is damage to a person's reputation in print, writing, pictures or signs. Libel can take many forms. Generally, it is an accusation that tends to hold people up to ridicule, contempt, shame or disgrace; causes
5 "right-thinking persons" to think evil of the subject, diminishes the person's respectability or discredits him or causes him to be shunned or avoided.

A lesson taught to every beginning reporter is that there is only one unconditional defense to a charge of libel: that
10 the facts are provably true.

Another defense is the privilege of immunity from libel charges for true and fair publication of reports of judicial, legislative, public and official proceedings. These proceedings are privileged on the theory that the interests of
15 society require such events to be the subject of public discussion. So are the contents of most public records.

A landmark case in libel law was the Supreme Court's 1964 ruling that a public official cannot recover damages for a report related to his official duties unless he proves
20 malice. The Court linked malice to knowledge that a statement "was false" and to the publishing of an article "with reckless disregard of whether it was false or not."

33. Which situation can likely result in a libel case?

(A) A husband uses obscene language in an argument with his wife, then leaves her for good.
(B) A newspaper prints an article telling about the discovery of a corpse of a convicted criminal in the trunk of his car.
(C) After a trial in which a defendant has been judged guilty of grand larceny, a spectator shouts out: "You crook!"
(D) A television station broadcasts a news clip showing a prominent judge at a banquet shaking hands with a widely known Mafia boss.
(E) A magazine photographer, after taking a picture of a model, changes the negative so that the published picture shows her nude.

34. A Congressman is able to win a damage claim if a newspaper columnist

(A) points out his lack of experience as a lawmaker
(B) holds him up to ridicule
(C) suggests that his colleagues look into his personal business dealings
(D) states an untruth about his Congressional activities
(E) attacks his Congressional voting record

35. Which of the following is the best title for the passage?

(A) The Difference between Slander and Libel
(B) Sometimes It's Libel—Sometimes It's Not
(C) A Landmark Case in Libel
(D) What to Do If Someone Libels You
(E) Some People Are Always Out to Hurt Others

Hundreds of bits of information filed in dossiers on millions of individual Americans today constitute a massive assault on privacy whose ramifications are just beginning to be realized. Most adults have at some time
5 sought credit (or a credit card) and bought insurance. If you have done these things, there are probably at least two dossiers with your name on them.

When you seek to borrow money, your creditor receives a file from the credit bureau to establish your "credit rating."
10 This dossier contains all the personal facts the credit bureau can assemble—your job, salary, length of time on the present job, marital status, a list of present and past debts and their payment history, any criminal record, any lawsuits of any kind, and any real estate you may own. The
15 dossier may include your employer's opinion of your job performance or even your IQ rating from a high school test. By the time the creditor has finished talking to the

credit bureau, he is likely to know more about your personal life than your mother-in-law does. When you try to
20 buy life insurance, a file of even more intimate information about you is compiled by the "inspection agency." The insurance company finds out not only about your health but also about your drinking habits (how often, how much, with others or alone, and even what beverage), your net
25 worth, salary, debts, domestic troubles, reputation, associates, manner of living, and standing in the community. The investigator is also asked to inquire of your neighbors and associates whether there is "any criticism of character or morals," and he must state whether he recommends that
30 the insurance be declined.

Credit bureaus and inspection agencies are the major sources of information about individuals. But government, schools, employers, and banks are also collectors, and sometimes suppliers, of information. Anyone possessing
35 an individual's bank records—now extensively recorded on computers—can reconstruct his associations, movements, habits, and life-style. The Foreign Bank Secrecy Act can be used to require every FDIC-insured bank to make a reproduction of each check you draw on it and
40 keep those reproductions for up to six years. The purpose is to ensure records of large quantities of money going out of the country so as to prevent tax evasions through use of secret Swiss bank accounts. But the act contains no protection for the depositor by limiting in any way the
45 banks' use of these records. Conceivably, a bank could sell them to a credit bureau or an investigation agency. There are millions of files in credit bureaus that give information about bank accounts all over the country.

It is the rare American who does not live in the shadow
50 of his dossier. The "dossier industry" is a huge and growing business. These economic interests have almost total control over the information they collect and sell. They are not accountable to anyone except those who seek to purchase information.

36. The author emphasizes that "invasion of privacy" today affects

   (A) public figures
   (B) candidates for political office
   (C) millions of Americans
   (D) men rather than women
   (E) those with questionable backgrounds

37. The article states that dossiers are filed for the majority of adults having

   I.   unpaid debts
   II. credit cards
   III. drinking or drug problems

   (A) I only
   (B) II only
   (C) III only
   (D) I and II only
   (E) II and III only

38. The article indicates that insurance investigators conduct evaluations of "morals and character" which

   (A) fail to give objective information
   (B) are from sources recommended by the client
   (C) are reasonably reliable
   (D) deliberately attempt to discredit
   (E) are guaranteed to be accurate by the Secrecy Act

39. According to the article, the Foreign Bank Secrecy Act

   (A) encourages the use of Swiss Bank accounts
   (B) fastidiously protects the privacy of depositors in foreign banks
   (C) applies only to FDIC—insured banks
   (D) prevents banks from selling information to investigation agencies
   (E) was designed to control the influx of foreign capital

40. The author would have us believe that a criticism of one's character and morals would best be

   (A) left to neighbors and associates
   (B) left to relatives and friends
   (C) arrived at from the objective view of the investigator
   (D) solicited from the clergy
   (E) omitted from dossiers

S T O P

IF YOU FINISH BEFORE TIME IS CALLED, YOU MAY CHECK YOUR WORK ON THIS SECTION ONLY.
DO NOT WORK ON ANY OTHER SECTION IN THE TEST.

SECTION 5 MATH ABILITY
30 MINUTES   35 QUESTIONS

In this section solve each problem, using any available space on the page for scratchwork. Then decide which is the best of the choices given and blacken the corresponding space on the answer sheet.

The following information is for your reference in solving some of the problems.

Circle of radius r: Area $= \pi r^2$; Circumference $= 2\pi r$
   The number of degrees of arc in a circle is 360.
The measure in degrees of a straight angle is 180.

Definitions of symbols:
   $=$ is equal to
   $\neq$ is unequal to
   $<$ is less than
   $>$ is greater than

   $\leqq$ is less than or equal to
   $\geqq$ is greater than or equal to
   $\parallel$ is parallel to
   $\perp$ is perpendicular to

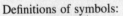

Triangle: The sum of the measure in degrees of the angles of a triangle is 180.
   If $\angle CDA$ is a right angle, then

   (1)   area of $\triangle ABC = \dfrac{AB \times CD}{2}$

   (2) $AC^2 = AD^2 + DC^2$

Note: Figures which accompany problems in this test are intended to provide information useful in solving the problems. They are drawn as accurately as possible EXCEPT when it is stated in a specific problem that its figure is not drawn to scale. All figures lie in a plane unless otherwise indicated. All numbers used are real numbers.

1. If x and y are positive integers such that $x^2 - y^2 = 11$ and $x > y$, then $x + y =$

   (A) 1   (B) 5   (C) 6   (D) 8   (E) 11

2. Each member of a tennis team bought 3 tennis balls at a rate of 50¢ per tennis ball. Together, the entire team spent $15 which included $1.50 in tax. How many members are there on the team?

   (A) 9   (B) 10   (C) 11   (D) 12   (E) 13

3. Which of the following numbers is divisible by 5 and 9, but not by 2?

   (A) 625   (B) 639   (C) 650   (D) 655   (E) 675

4. Eric originally had 9 gallons of wine. After drinking 1.5 gallons of the wine, Eric put the rest of his wine into a 12-gallon container. How much of the container, in gallons, is empty?

   (A) 3.5   (B) 4.5   (C) 5.5   (D) 6.5   (E) 7.5

5. If $\dfrac{5}{8}$ of a number is 3 less than $\dfrac{3}{4}$ of the number, what is the number?

   (A) 3   (B) 4   (C) 8   (D) 24   (E) 32

6. An oddly shaped rock having uniform density and weighing 64 grams is broken into two pieces. One of the two pieces weighs 48 grams and has a volume of 33 cubic centimeters. What was the volume, in cubic centimeters, of the original rock?

   (A) 11   (B) 22   (C) 33   (D) 44   (E) 66

7. If the length of one of the sides of a rectangular field is 35, then the perimeter of the field could be

   I. 60
   II. 70
   III. 80
   (A) I only
   (B) II only
   (C) III only
   (D) I and II
   (E) II and III

<u>Questions 8-27</u> each consist of two quantities, one in Column A and one in Column B. You are to compare the two quantities and on the answer sheet blacken space

A if the quantity in Column A is greater;
B if the quantity in Column B is greater;
C if the two quantities are equal;
D if the relationship cannot be determined from the information given.

<u>Notes:</u>
1. In certain questions, information concerning one or both of the quantities to be compared is centered above the columns.
2. In a given question, a symbol that appears in both columns represents the same thing in Column A as it does in Column B.
3. Letters such as x, n, and k stand for real numbers.

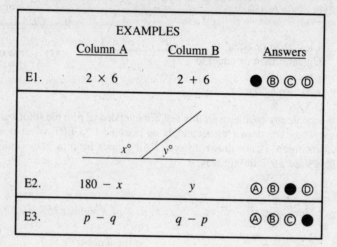

	EXAMPLES		
	Column A	Column B	Answers
E1.	2×6	$2 + 6$	● Ⓑ Ⓒ Ⓓ
E2.	$180 - x$	y	Ⓐ Ⓑ ● Ⓓ
E3.	$p - q$	$q - p$	Ⓐ Ⓑ Ⓒ ●

Column A / Column B

8.

$$x = \frac{1}{6}$$
$$y = \frac{1}{36}$$

Column A	Column B
$\dfrac{y}{x}$	x

9.

$$R = \{7, 8, 9, 10, 11\}$$
$$S = \{6, 7, 8, 9, 10\}$$

Column A	Column B
The number that is a member of set S but not of set R	A number that is a member of both sets R and S

10. z is a positive integer.

Column A	Column B
$(-z)^4$	$-z - z - z - z$

Column A / Column B

11.

Column A	Column B
$\dfrac{1}{4} + \dfrac{1}{8}$	$\dfrac{3}{8}$

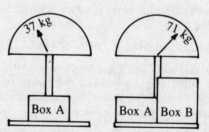

12. The mass of Box A and that of box A and box B are shown on ths scales above.

Column A	Column B
mass of box B	44

13.

Column A	Column B
Average (arithmetic mean) of 3, 7, 11 and 15	Average (arithmetic mean) of 2, 6, 12, 16

n is an integer.

14.

Column A	Column B
The remainder when n is divided by 4	The remainder when n is divided by 8

SUMMARY DIRECTIONS FOR COMPARISON QUESTIONS

<u>Answer:</u> A if the quantity in Column A is greater;
B if the quantity in Column B is greater;
C if the two quantities are equal;
D if the relationship cannot be determined from the information given.

<u>Column A</u>	<u>Column B</u>

15. The number of edges of a rectangular solid | The number of faces of a rectangular solid

---

16. $x - y = 4$

$x + 4$ | y

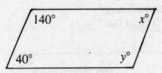

Note: Figure is not drawn to scale.

17. x | y

---

18. $-12 < x < -9$
$-14 < y < -10$

x and y are integers.
y is even.

x | y

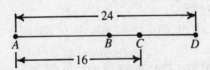

19. Length of BD | 8

---

20. Ten cards numbered 1 through 10, each having the same size and shape, are thoroughly mixed. One card is randomly picked out and then put back. The cards are mixed thoroughly again. Another card is randomly picked out.

The probability of getting a 7 on the first card and a 2 on the second card | The probability of getting a 7 on both the first and second cards

---

<u>Column A</u>	<u>Column B</u>

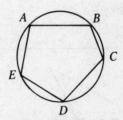

21. The diameter of the circle is 2.
A, B, C, D, and E are on the circumference of the circle.

Perimeter of pentagon *ABCDE* | 7

---

22. $x = 600$
$y = 300$

$(x + y)(x - y)$ | 900×301

---

23. $\dfrac{9}{\sqrt{3}}$ | $3\sqrt{3}$

---

24. m, n, p are positive

Average (arithmetic mean) of m, n, and p | Average (arithmetic mean) of m^3, n^3 and p^3

---

25. $9x(x + y)$ | $9x^2 + 4xy$

26. x | 8

---

27. Let A_n and A_{n+1} be two consecutive terms of the sequence:
$$-1, 1, -1, 1, -1, 1, \text{ etc.}$$

$A_n + A_{n+1}$ | $A_n - A_{n+1}$

In this section solve each problem, using any available space on the page for scratchwork. Then decide which is the best of the choices given and blacken the corresponding space on the answer sheet.

28. If $x = 1 + \dfrac{1}{3} + \dfrac{1}{9} + \dfrac{1}{27} + \dfrac{1}{81} + \dfrac{1}{243}$ and $y = 3x - 3$, then x exceeds y by

(A) $\dfrac{1}{9}$ (B) $\dfrac{1}{27}$ (C) $\dfrac{1}{81}$

(D) $\dfrac{1}{243}$ (E) $\dfrac{1}{729}$

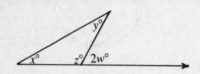

29. In the figure above, one side of a triangle has been extended. What is the value of $w + x + y$?

(A) $3w$ (B) $3z$ (C) $2x + y$ (D) $2x + 2y$
(E) $2w + z$

30. If 16 grams of pure sugar are mixed with 24 grams of pure salt, what percent by mass of the resulting mixture is sugar?

(A) 20% (B) 25% (C) 40% (D) 60% (E) $66\dfrac{2}{3}$%

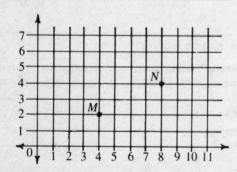

31. Which of the following points, when plotted on the grid above, will be three times as far from $M(4,2)$ as from $N(8,4)$?

(A) (2,1) (B) (4,4) (C) (6,3) (D) (7,1)
(E) (10,5)

32. Let $\otimes$ be defined for all positive x and y by
$$x \otimes y = \frac{x^3 + y^3}{x + y}.$$

Which of the following must be true for positive x and y?

 I. $x \otimes x = x^2$
 II. $x \otimes y = y \otimes x$
 III. $x \otimes (x \otimes x) = (x \otimes x) \otimes x$

(A) I only
(B) III only
(C) I and II only
(D) I and III only
(E) I, II, and III

33. In the figure above, there are two squares. The length of a side of the smaller square is $\dfrac{1}{2}$ the length of a side of the larger square. What is the ratio of the area of the shaded region to the area of the larger square?

(A) 1 : 4 (B) 1 : 3 (C) 1 : 2 (D) 2 : 3 (E) 3 : 4

Questions 34–35
The next two questions refer to the following definition:
For positive integers x,

$$\text{let } \boxed{x} = \begin{cases} \dfrac{1}{2}x & \text{if } x \text{ is even} \\[2mm] x - 1 & \text{if } x \text{ is odd} \end{cases}$$

34. If y is a positive integer, not divisible by 2, then $\boxed{y} =$

(A) $\dfrac{1}{2}y$ (B) $\dfrac{1}{2}y - 1$ (C) $\dfrac{1}{2}(y - 1)$

(D) $y - 1$ (E) $2y$

35. $\boxed{4} + \boxed{7} =$

(A) $\boxed{4}$ (B) $\boxed{9}$ (C) $\boxed{10}$ (D) $\boxed{11}$ (E) $\boxed{18}$

S T O P

IF YOU FINISH BEFORE TIME IS CALLED, YOU MAY CHECK YOUR WORK ON THIS SECTION ONLY.
DO NOT WORK ON ANY OTHER SECTION IN THE TEST.

SECTION 6 MATH ABILITY
30 MINUTES 25 QUESTIONS

In this section solve each problem, using any available space on the page for scratchwork. Then decide which is the best of the choices given and blacken the corresponding space on the answer sheet.

The following information is for your reference in solving some of the problems.

Circle of radius r: Area $= \pi r^2$; Circumference $= 2\pi r$
    The number of degrees of arc in a circle is 360.
The measure in degrees of a straight angle is 180.

Definitions of symbols:

$=$	is equal to	$\leqq$	is less than or equal to
$\neq$	is unequal to	$\geqq$	is greater than or equal to
$<$	is less than	$\parallel$	is parallel to
$>$	is greater than	$\perp$	is perpendicular to

Triangle: The sum of the measure in degrees of the angles of a triangle is 180.
If $\angle CDA$ is a right angle, then

(1)   area of $\triangle ABC = \dfrac{AB \times CD}{2}$

(2) $AC^2 = AD^2 + DC^2$

Note: Figures which accompany problems in this test are intended to provide information useful in solving the problems. They are drawn as accurately as possible EXCEPT when it is stated in a specific problem that its figure is not drawn to scale. All figures lie in a plane unless otherwise indicated. All numbers used are real numbers.

---

1. Find y if $y + 4 = -7$

(A) 11   (B) 3   (C) -3 (D) -9 (E) -11

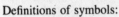

$$\begin{array}{r} 59\triangle \\ -\ 293 \\ \hline \square 97 \end{array}$$

2. In the subtraction problem above, what digit is represented by the $\square$?

(A) 0   (B) 1   (C) 2   (D) 3   (E) 4

3. How many integers are between, but not including, 1 and 1000?

(A) 990   (B) 998   (C) 999   (D) 1000   (E) 1001

4. If $\dfrac{a - b}{b} = \dfrac{1}{2}$, find $\dfrac{a}{b}$.

(A) $\dfrac{9}{2}$ (B) $\dfrac{7}{2}$ (C) $\dfrac{5}{2}$ (D) $\dfrac{1}{2}$ (E) $\dfrac{3}{2}$

Number of pounds of force	Height object is raised
3	6 feet
6	12 feet
9	18 feet

5. In a certain pulley system, the height an object is raised is equal to a constant c times the number of pounds of force exerted. The table above shows some pounds of force and the corresponding height raised. If a particular object is raised 15 feet, how many pounds of force were exerted?

(A) $3\dfrac{3}{4}$ (B) 7   (C) $7\dfrac{1}{2}$ (D) 8   (E) 11

6. If $a = 1$, $b = -2$ and $c = -2$, find the value of $\dfrac{b^2 c}{(a - c)^2}$

(A) $-\dfrac{8}{9}$ (B) $-\dfrac{2}{3}$ (C) $\dfrac{8}{9}$ (D) 8   (E) 9

7. If $\dfrac{y}{3}$, $\dfrac{y}{4}$ and $\dfrac{y}{7}$ represent integers, then y could be

(A) 42   (B) 56   (C) 70   (D) 84   (E) 126

8. The above line is marked with 12 points. The distance between any 2 adjacent points is 3 units. Find the total number of points that are more than 19 units away from point P.

   (A) 2   (B) 3   (C) 4   (D) 5   (E) 6

9. If $y = 28j$, where j is any integer, then $\frac{y}{2}$ will always be

   (A) even   (B) odd   (C) positive   (D) negative
   (E) less than $\frac{y}{3}$

10. Given $(a + 2, a - 2) = [a]$ for all integers a.
    $(6, 2) =$

    (A) [3]   (B) [4]   (C) [5]   (D) [6]   (E) [8]

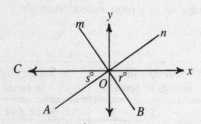

Note: Figure not drawn to scale.

11. If $m \perp n$ in the figure above and COx is a straight line, find the value of $r + s$.

    (A) 180   (B) 135   (C) 110   (D) 90   (E) It cannot be determined from the information given.

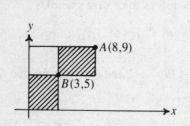

12. Points A and B have coordinates as shown in the figure above. Find the combined area of the two shaded rectangles.

    (A) 20   (B) 26   (C) 32   (D) 35   (E) 87

13. One out of 4 students at Ridge High School studies German. If there are 2800 students at the school, how many students do *not* study German?

    (A) 2500   (B) 2100   (C) 1800   (D) 1000   (E) 700

14. The cost of a drive-in movie is $\$y$ per vehicle. A group of friends in a van shared the admission cost by paying $0.40 each. If 6 more friends had gone along, everyone would have paid only $0.25 each. What is the value of $\$y$?

    (A) $4   (B) $6   (C) $8   (D) $10   (E) $12

15. $8(679) + 679 =$

    (A) $5(679) + 3(679)$ (B) $6(679) + 2(679)$
    (C) $5(679) + 6(679)$ (D) $7(679) + 4(679)$
    (E) $6(679) + 3(679)$

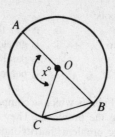

16. If AB is a diameter of circle O in the figure above, and $CB = OB$, then $\frac{x}{6} =$

    (A) 60   (B) 30   (C) 20   (D) 10   (E) 5

17. A certain store is selling an $80 radio for $64. If a different radio had a list price of $200 and was discounted at $1\frac{1}{2}$ times the percent discount on the $80 model, what would its selling price be?

    (A) $90   (B) $105   (C) $120   (D) $140   (E) $160

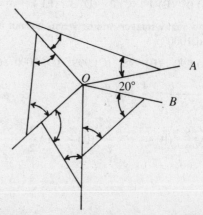

18. If $\angle AOB = 20°$ in the figure above and O is a common vertex of the four triangles, find the sum of the measures of the marked angles in the triangles.

    (A) 380   (B) 560   (C) 740   (D) 760   (E) 920

19. If $3a + 4b = 4a - 4b = 21$, find the value of a.

    (A) 3   (B) 6   (C) 21   (D) 42   (E) It cannot be determined from the information given.

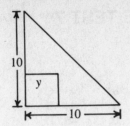

20. In the figure above, the area of the square is equal to $\frac{1}{5}$ the area of the triangle. Find the value of y.

(A) 2   (B) 4   (C) 5   (D) $2\sqrt{5}$ (E) $\sqrt{10}$

21. A certain computer can print at the rate of 80 characters per second and there is an average (arithmetic mean) of 2400 characters per page. If the computer continued to print at this rate, how many *minutes* would it take to print an M–page report?

(A) $\frac{M}{30}$ (B) $\frac{M}{60}$ (C) $\frac{M}{2}$ (D) $\frac{2}{M}$ (E) $\frac{60}{M}$

22. A certain satellite passed over Washington, D.C. at midnight on Friday. If the satellite completes an orbit every 5 hours, when is the next day that it will pass over Washington, D.C. at midnight?

(A) Monday   (B) Wednesday   (C) Friday
(D) Saturday   (E) Sunday

23. The price of a car is reduced by 30 percent. The resulting price is reduced 40 percent. The two reductions are equal to one reduction of

(A) 28%   (B) 42%   (C) 50%   (D) 58%   (E) 70%

24. Find the difference between $\frac{2}{3}$ and the repeating decimal 0.393939. . . .

(A) $\frac{2}{11}$ (B) $\frac{3}{11}$ (C) $\frac{5}{9}$ (D) $\frac{7}{9}$ (E) $\frac{12}{13}$

25. In the figure above, the circle is inscribed in the equilateral triangle. If the diameter of the circle is 2, find the sum of the shaded areas.

(A) $3\sqrt{3} - \pi$

(B) $3\sqrt{3} - 4\pi$

(C) $3\sqrt{3} - \frac{3\pi}{2}$

(D) $6\sqrt{3} - \frac{3\pi}{2}$

(E) $108 - \pi$

S T O P

IF YOU FINISH BEFORE TIME IS CALLED, YOU MAY CHECK YOUR WORK ON THIS SECTION ONLY.
DO NOT WORK ON ANY OTHER SECTION IN THE TEST.

HOW DID YOU DO ON THIS TEST?

STEP 1. Go to the Answer Key on page 704.

STEP 2. For your "raw score," count your correct answers in each of the test parts of the test you have just taken:

Verbal (Section 1 and 4 combined) _____ .
Math (Sections 2, 5, and 6 combined) _____ .
Standard Written English (Section 3) _____ .

STEP 3. Get your "scaled score" for the test by referring to the Raw Score/ Scaled Score Conversion Tables on pages 64–66.

THERE'S ALWAYS ROOM FOR IMPROVEMENT!

ANSWER KEY FOR PRACTICE TEST 7

Section 1—Verbal

1. E	8. B	15. D	22. C	29. B	36. B	43. C
2. B	9. D	16. A	23. E	30. A	37. A	44. B
3. A	10. E	17. E	24. B	31. E	38. D	45. D
4. D	11. B	18. E	25. B	32. C	39. D	
5. C	12. A	19. C	26. D	33. C	40. E	
6. C	13. E	20. C	27. E	34. A	41. E	
7. A	14. C	21. D	28. C	35. B	42. D	

Section 2—Math

1. D	5. C	9. D	13. E	17. D	21. A	25. B
2. E	6. C	10. B	14. C	18. C	22. B	
3. B	7. D	11. B	15. A	19. B	23. B	
4. A	8. C	12. C	16. A	20. E	24. D	

Section 3—Standard Written English

1. E	9. C	17. D	25. E	33. C	41. B	49. D
2. C	10. C	18. A	26. A	34. D	42. C	50. A
3. B	11. D	19. C	27. B	35. E	43. D	
4. B	12. D	20. B	28. D	36. B	44. C	
5. B	13. E	21. C	29. E	37. A	45. B	
6. D	14. D	22. A	30. C	38. B	46. A	
7. E	15. C	23. B	31. E	39. D	47. B	
8. A	16. A	24. A	32. B	40. E	48. C	

Section 4—Verbal

1. B	7. D	13. D	19. D	25. D	31. A	37. B
2. E	8. C	14. B	20. D	26. A	32. C	38. A
3. D	9. A	15. A	21. E	27. D	33. E	39. C
4. A	10. B	16. A	22. E	28. B	34. D	40. E
5. C	11. E	17. C	23. E	29. A	35. B	
6. E	12. C	18. E	24. C	30. B	36. C	

Section 5—Math

1. E	6. D	11. C	16. A	21. B	26. A	31. E
2. A	7. C	12. B	17. D	22. B	27. D	32. E
3. E	8. C	13. C	18. A	23. C	28. D	33. E
4. B	9. B	14. D	19. A	24. D	29. A	34. D
5. D	10. A	15. A	20. C	25. D	30. C	35. B

Section 6—Math

1. E	5. C	9. A	13. B	17. D	21. C	25. A
2. C	6. A	10. B	14. A	18. A	22. B	
3. B	7. D	11. D	15. E	19. B	23. D	
4. E	8. D	12. D	16. C	20. E	24. B	

EXPLANATORY ANSWERS FOR
PRACTICE TEST 7
Section 1: Verbal Ability

As you read these Explanatory Answers, you are advised to refer to "Using Critical Thinking Skills in Verbal Questions" (beginning on page 90) whenever a specific Strategy is referred to in the answer. Of particular importance are the following Master Verbal Strategies:

Sentence Completion Master Strategy 1—page 94.
Sentence Completion Master Strategy 2—page 95.
Analogies Master Strategy 1—page 90.
Antonyms Master Strategy 1—page 99.
Reading Comprehension Master Strategy 2—page 109.

1. **(E)** Choice E is correct. *Pliant* means *easily bent; adaptable*. The opposite of *pliant* is *rigid*.

2. **(B)** Choice B is correct. *Impetuous* means *impulsive; acting without thought*. The opposite of *impetuous* is *controlled*.

3. **(A)** Choice A is correct. *Callous* means *unyielding; insensitive*. The opposite of *callous* is *yielding*.

4. **(D)** Choice D is correct. See **Antonym Strategy 3.** *Sedate* means *quiet; calm; serious*. The opposite of *sedate* is *passionate*.

5. **(C)** Choice C is correct. *Loquacious* means *talkative*. The opposite of *loquacious* is *silent*.

6. **(C)** Choice C is correct. *Turbid* means *muddy; unclear*. The opposite of *turbid* is *clear*.

7. **(A)** Choice A is correct. *Ruthless* means *cruel; merciless*. The opposite of *ruthless* is *considerate*.

8. **(B)** Choice B is correct. See **Antonym Strategy 2.** *Flamboyant* means *showy; conspicuous*. The opposite of *flamboyant* is *modest*.

9. **(D)** Choice D is correct. *Accost* means *to approach; to speak to*. The opposite of *accost* is *spurn*.

10. **(E)** Choice E is correct. *Bawdy* means *indecent; obscene; coarse*. The opposite of *bawdy* is *decent*.

11. **(B)** Choice B is correct. See **Antonym Strategy 3.** *Resolute* means *very determined*. The opposite of *resolute* is *wavering*.

12. **(A)** Choice A is correct. *Elicit* means *to draw forth*. The opposite of *elicit* is *hold back*.

13. **(E)** choice E is correct. See **Antonym Strategy 3.** *Urbane* means *refined*. The opposite of *urbane* is *discourteous*.

14. **(C)** Choice C is correct. *Verve* means *energy; enthusiasm*. The opposite of *verve* is *fatigue*.

15. **(D)** Choice D is correct. *Supercilious* means *proud; haughty*. The opposite of *supercilious* is *humble*.

16. **(A)** Choice A is correct. See **Sentence Completion Strategy 2.** Examine the first words of each choice. We eliminate Choice (C) imagined and Choice (E) intuitive. Reason: The effect of the long war was *not* imagined or intuitive (meaning knowing by a hidden sense). Now we consider Choice (B) immediate . . . staring, and Choice (D) delayed . . . rebuilding. Neither word pair makes sense in the sentence. Choice (A) cumulative . . . corrosion, *does* make sense in the sentence.

17. **(E)** Choice E is correct. See **Sentence Completion Strategy 3.** If you had tried to complete the sentence *before* looking at the five choices, you might have come up with any of the following words meaning "continually" or "regularly":

constantly	always
perpetually	persistently
habitually	

The other choices are, therefore, incorrect.

18. **(E)** Choice E is correct. See **Sentence Completion Strategy 2.** Examine the first word of each choice. Choice (D) crushes is eliminated because it is not likely that the bee will crush the nectar from different flowers. Now consider each pair of words in the other choices. We find that Choice (E) extracts . . . converts, has the only word pair that makes sense in the sentence.

19. **(C)** Choice C is correct. See **Sentence Completion Strategy 2.** Examine the first word of each choice. Choice (E) a futile does *not* make good sense because we do not refer to momentum as futile. Now consider the other choices. Choice (C) an increasing . . . athletics, is the only choice which has a word pair which makes sentence sense.

20. **(C)** Choice C is correct. See **Sentence Completion Strategy 4.** The beginning word "Although" constitutes an *opposition indicator*. We can then expect the second part of the sentence to indicate an idea that is opposite to what is said in the first part of the sentence. Choice (C) modesty provides the word that gives us that opposite idea. The words in the other choices do *not* give us that opposite idea.

21. **(D)** Choice D is correct. Throughout the passage, the need for reform is indicated. For example,
Lines 9–10: "Students are forced . . . to educate themselves."
Lines 16–18: "All of the currently . . . changes are made."
Lines 19–22: "For example . . . may be taught better."
Lines 42–46: "Under current . . . change and reform."
Lines 46–49: "The success . . . of good teachers."
Choices A, B, C, and E do refer to the passage but their coverage is insufficient for any of these titles to be considered the most appropriate. Accordingly, these choices are incorrect.

22. **(C)** Choice C is correct. See lines 28–29: "This calls for . . . fewer students per teacher." The passage indicates no concern on the part of the author for what is expressed in Choices A, D, and E. Therefore, these choices are incorrect. Choice B is incorrect because the passage states just the opposite of what this choice says. See lines 19–20: "For example . . . give way to English. So Choice B is incorrect.

23. **(E)** Choice E is not true according to the passage. Therefore, it is a correct choice. See lines 22–25: "Students entering . . . until they mastered them." Choice A is true—therefore, incorrect. See lines 42–46: "Under current standardization . . . educational change and reform." Choice B is true—therefore, incorrect. See lines 13–16: "The torrent of facts . . . forage on their own." Choice C is true—therefore, incorrect. See lines 9–10: "Students are forced . . . to educate themselves." Choice D is true—therefore, incorrect. See lines 39–42: "Good teachers . . . get out of teaching altogether."

24. **(B)** Choice B is correct. See lines 42–46: "Under current standardization . . . stands in the way of educational change and reform." There is no indication in the passage that the author's attitude toward principals and supervisors is Choice A or C or D or E. Therefore, these choices are incorrect.

25. **(B)** Choice B is correct. The author is implying that just because the reformers are insisting that all students get four years of English, the important thing is *not* that they are sitting in an English class for 45 minutes five days a week for four years. What *is* important is the kind of instruction these students will be getting in their English course; the types of books they will be using; the extent to which the four years of English will benefit them. This is what the passage is all about. For example, see lines 8–10: "Yet the existing . . . to educate themselves." Another example—see lines 14–16: ". . . the only way . . . on their own." Choices A, C, D, and E are incorrect because the passage does *not* indicate that these choices are what the author means when he asks ". . . but who knows what four years of English entails?"

26. **(D)** Choice D is the correct choice because it involves chemical and biological research—not psychological research. Choices A, B, C, and E are incorrect choices because they all involve psychological research.

27. **(E)** Choice E is correct. Several advantages of smoking are described in third paragraph. Here are some examples:
Lines 19–21: "Studies show . . . function and behavior."
Lines 21–22: "Deep, full drags . . . relaxing effects of smoking."
Lines 24–26: "Type A people . . . to enhance arousal."
Several disadvantages of smoking are described in the fourth paragraph which obviously outweigh the advantages. Here are some examples:
Lines 30–32: ". . . it (smoking) carries . . . why anyone continues smoking."
Lines 32–34: "Cigarette smoking . . . worse than heroin."
Lines 35–37: "The Environmental Protection Agency . . . most dangerous carcinogen."

28. **(C)** Choice C is correct. See lines 9–13: "The addictive drug . . . on the nervous system." There is no evidence in the passage that the laboratories are doing their investigations for any of the purposes mentioned in Choices A, B, D, or E. Therefore, these choices are incorrect.

29. **(B)** Choice B is correct. See lines 51–53: "There is no single explanation . . . ever be a safe cigarette."

30. **(A)** Choice A is correct. The main idea of the passage is that smoking is an addiction that is very difficult to throw off because it is "perfect for coping with the vicissitudes of life." (lines 10–11) Choice A brings out this situation neatly. The other choices refer, by implication, to what is stated in the passage. However, none of these choices has sufficiently wide coverage to be considered as the most appropriate title for the passage. Therefore, Choices B, C, D, and E are incorrect.

31. **(E)**   Choice E is correct. See **Sentence Completion Strategy 1.** The word "effective" (meaning "serving the purpose" or "producing a result") makes good sense in the sentence. The other choices don't do that.

32. **(C)**   Choice C is correct. See **Sentence Completion Strategy 2.** Examine the first words of each choice. We eliminate Choice (D) ambitions and Choice (E) thoughts because the official would not be watching his personal ambitions or his personal thoughts exposed on the evening news. This does *not* make sense. Now we consider Choice (A) interests . . . family, and Choice (B) friends . . . life, which do *not* make sentence sense. Choice (C) misdeeds . . . career, *does* make sentence sense.

33. **(C)**   Choice C is correct. See **Sentence Completion Strategy 1.** The word "hibernate" means to pass the winter in a dormant (sleepy or inactive) state. Obviously Choice (C) an inactive is the only correct choice.

34. **(A)**   Choice A is correct. See **Sentence Completion Strategy 1.** The word "versatile" means capable of turning competently from one task or occupation to another. Clearly, Choice (A) versatile is the only correct choice.

35. **(B)**   Choice B is correct. See **Sentence Completion Strategy 2.** Examine the first words of each choice. We eliminate Choice (C) avoided and Choice (D) realized because it does not make sense to see that da Vinci realized or avoided the Law of Gravity. Now we consider Choice (A) examined . . . colorful, and Choice (E) suspected . . . mural, neither of which makes sentence sense. Choice (B) anticipated . . . anatomical, is the only choice which makes sentence sense.

36. **(B)**   Choice B is correct. When one is drafted, he is ordered into the army. When one is subpoenaed, he is ordered into court.   **(Purpose relationship)**

37. **(A)**   Choice A is correct. A saccharine person is not sincere. An unscrupulous person is not conscientious.
(Opposite relationship)

38. **(D)**   Choice D is correct. A bone that is brittle is easily broken. A glass that is fragile is easily broken.
(Result relationship)

39. **(D)**   Choice D is correct. An umpire makes decisions in matters dealing with baseball. A judge makes decisions in matters dealing wih the law.
(Action in Situation relationship)

40. **(E)**   Choice E is correct. A person who is intractable is difficult to control. Something that is cryptic is difficult to understand.   **(Association relationship)**

41. **(E)**   Choice E is correct. A pipe carries waste to the sewer. An artery carries blood to the heart.
(Purpose relationship)

42. **(D)**   Choice D is correct. A heckler annoys a performer. A tick, which is a blood-sucking arachnid, annoys animals like cats and dogs. Note that the word "tick" has other meanings. See **Analogy Strategy 5.**
(Action to Object relationship.)

43. **(C)**   Choice C is correct. Amnesia is the loss of memory. Aphasia is the loss of speech.
(Cause and Effect relationship)

44. **(B)**   Choice B is correct. To glance at something is to give it cursory treatment. To delve into something is to give it thorough treatment.
(Association relationship)

45. **(D)**   Choice D is correct. Obese is extremely heavy. Emaciated is extremely thin.   **(Degree relationship)**

EXPLANATORY ANSWERS FOR
PRACTICE TEST 7 (continued)

Section 2: Math Ability

> As you read these solutions, you are advised to do two things if you answered the Math question incorrectly:
>
> 1) When a specific Strategy is referred to in the solution, study that strategy, which you will find in "Using Critical Thinking Skills in Math Questions" (beginning on page 69).
>
> 2) When the solution directs you to the "Math Refresher" (beginning on page 205)—for example, Math Refresher #305—study the 305 Math principle to get a clear idea of the Math operation that was necessary for you to know in order to answer the question correctly.

1. **(D)** Choice D is correct.
(Use Strategy 17: Use the given information effectively.)

The most straightforward way to do this problem is to do the calculation. A second way, which may be faster, is to note that

$$(20 + 30) = (10 + 40) = (25 + 25) = 50.$$

Thus,

$$\frac{(20 + 30) + (10 + 40) + (25 + 25)}{3}$$
$$= \frac{\cancel{3}(50)}{\cancel{3}} = 50 \quad (Answer)$$

(Math Refresher #431)

2. **(E)** Choice E is correct.

The distance between points on a number line is found by:

$$|a - b| = |-4 - (7)| =$$
$$|-4 - 7| = |-11| = 11 \quad (Answer)$$

(Math Refresher #431)

3. **(B)** Choice B is correct.

$$\left(\text{Use Strategy 5: Average} = \frac{\textbf{Total of values}}{\textbf{Total number of values}}\right)$$

The average is found by $\dfrac{8.4 + 8.1 + 9.3}{3} =$

$$\frac{25.8}{3} =$$
$$8.6 \quad (Answer)$$

(Math Refresher #601)

4. **(A)** Choice A is correct.
$$Given: \qquad x + 9 = -11 - x \qquad \boxed{1}$$
Adding $x - 9$ to both sides of $\boxed{1}$,

$$2x = -20$$
$$\text{or } x = -10 \qquad (Answer)$$

(Math Refresher #406)

5. **(C)** Choice C is correct.

$$Given: \qquad 3y = 12 \text{ and } \frac{10}{x} = 5 \qquad \boxed{1}$$

Solving $\boxed{1}$ for x and y:

$$y = 4 \text{ and } x = 2 \qquad \boxed{2}$$

Substitute equations $\boxed{2}$ into unknown expression.

$$\frac{y + 11}{x + 15} = \frac{4 + 11}{2 + 15} \qquad (Answer)$$
$$= \frac{15}{17}$$

(Math Refresher #406 and #431)

6. **(C)** Choice C is correct.
(Use Strategy 10: Know how to use units.)

Interest = rate × time × amount deposited

$$= \frac{8\%}{year} \times 1 \text{ year} \times \$50$$

$$= .08 \times 1 \times \$50$$

$$= \$4$$

(Use Strategy 3: The whole equals the sum of its parts.)

Total amount = Deposit + Interest
= $50 + $4
= $54

(Math Refresher #113, #114, and #121)

7. **(D)** Choice D is correct.

Given: $(x + 6)^2 = 12x + 72$ $\boxed{1}$

(Use Strategy 17: Use the given information effectively.)

Complete the squaring operation on the left side of the equation:

$$(x + 6)^2 = x^2 + 12x + 36$$

Continue the equation with $\boxed{1}$

$$x^2 + 12x + 36 = 12x + 72 \qquad \boxed{2}$$

(Use Strategy 1: Cancel numbers and expressions which appear on both sides of an equation.)

We get $x^2 + 36 = 72$
Therefore, $x^2 = 36$
$$x = \pm 6 \qquad (Answer)$$

(Math Refresher #409)

8. **(C)** Choice C is correct.
(Use Strategy 3: The whole equals the sum of its parts.)

From the diagram, we see that

$$x + 60 = 360 \qquad \boxed{1}$$

Subtracting 60 from both sides of $\boxed{1}$, we get

$$x = 300 \qquad \boxed{2}$$

Subtracting 60 from both sides of $\boxed{2}$ we get

$$x - 60 = 240 \qquad (Answer)$$

(Math Refresher #526 and #406)

9. **(D)** Choice D is correct.
(Use Strategy 10: Know how to use units.)

Since 60 min = 1 hour, 24 hours = 1 day, and 7 days = 1 week, we have

$$\left(\frac{60 \text{ min}}{\text{hour}}\right)\left(\frac{24 \text{ hours}}{\text{day}}\right)\left(\frac{7 \text{ days}}{\text{week}}\right) = 10,080$$

or 1 week = 10,080 minutes. To the nearest hundred, 1 week ≈ 10,100 minutes

(Math Refresher #121)

10. **(B)** Choice B is correct.
(Use Strategy 11: Use new definitions carefully.)

Method 1:   By definition $\sqrt{x} = \dfrac{x^3}{4}$

We are looking for

$$\frac{x^3}{4} = 16 \qquad \boxed{1}$$

(Use Strategy 13: Find unknowns by multiplication.)
Multiply $\boxed{1}$ by 4 we have

$$x^3 = 64$$
$$x = 4$$

Method 2:   Calculate each of the choices, A through E until you find the one whose value is 16.

(Math Refresher #429 and #431)

11. **(B)** Choice B is correct.
(Use Strategy 2: Translate from words to algebra.)

Be able to translate English sentences into mathematical equations.

We are given:

$$42 + 27 + 56 + x + y = 200$$
or $\qquad 125 + x + y = 200$
or $\qquad x + y = 75$
or $\qquad x = 75 - y \qquad \boxed{1}$

(Use Strategy 17: Use the given information effectively.)

From $\boxed{1}$, it is clear that x is a maximum when y is a minimum. Since y is the number of pieces of candy in a jar, its minimum value is

$$y = 0 \qquad \boxed{2}$$

Substituting $\boxed{2}$ into $\boxed{1}$,

$$x = 75 \qquad (Answer)$$

(Math Refresher #200, #426, and #431)

12. **(C)** Choice C is correct.
(Use Strategy 2: Translate from words to algebra.)

Number of pages Ron read last night
$$= \frac{1}{4} \times 16 = 4$$

(Use Strategy 3: The whole equals the sum of its parts.)

Number of pages remaining immediately after Ron finished reading last night $= 16 - 4 = 12$

Number of pages read this morning $= \frac{1}{4} \times 12 = 3$

Pages still not read
$$= \text{Remaining pages} - \text{pages read this morning}$$
$$= 12 - 3$$
Pages still not read $= 9$ *(Answer)*

(Math Refresher #200 and Logical Reasoning)

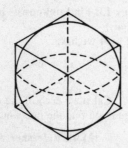

13. **(E)** Choice E is correct.

(Use Strategy 17: Use the given information effectively.)

Clearly, we can see from the picture above that the diameter of the sphere has the same length as a side of the cube. We know

     Volume of cube $= (\text{length of side})^3$ ☐1
We are given
     Volume of cube $= 64$ ☐2
Substituting ☐2 into ☐1, $64 = (\text{length of side})^3$
Thus,
length of side $= 4 =$ diameter of sphere   *(Answer)*

(Math Refresher #313 and #315)

14. **(C)** Choice C is correct.
(Use Strategy 2: Translate from words to algebra.)

     Let $8n =$ number of boys   ☐1
         $7n =$ number of girls   ☐2

The ratio of $\dfrac{\text{boys}}{\text{girls}} = \dfrac{8n}{7n} = \dfrac{8}{7}$ and

the given condition is satisfied.

(Use Strategy 3: The whole equals the sum of its parts.)

Total number of students $=$ Boys plus Girls   ☐3

Substitute ☐1 and ☐2 into ☐3. We get

Total number of students $= 8n + 7n = 15n$ ☐4

☐4 is a multiple of 15
Choices *A, B, D* and *E* are multiples of 15:

     Ⓐ $15 = 15 \times 1$
     Ⓑ $45 = 15 \times 3$
     Ⓓ $60 = 15 \times 4$
     Ⓔ $90 = 15 \times 6$

Only Choice C, 50, is NOT a multiple of 15.

(Math Refresher #200 and #431)

15. **(A)** Choice A is correct.

     Given: $\dfrac{m}{n} = \dfrac{x}{m}$ ☐1

(Use Strategy 13: Find unknowns by multiplication.)

Multiplying ☐1 by m, we have

$$m\left(\frac{m}{n}\right) = \left(\frac{x}{\not{m}}\right)\not{m}$$
$$\frac{m^2}{n} = x \quad \textit{(Answer)}$$

(Math Refresher #406)

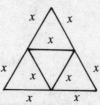

16. **(A)** Choice A is correct.
(Use Strategy 2: Translate from words to algebra.)

     Let $x =$ side of smaller triangles
Thus, $3x =$ perimeter of each smaller triangle
       $6x =$ perimeter of largest triangle

We are told

$$3x = 1$$
$$x = \frac{1}{3} \qquad ☐1$$

(Use Strategy 13: Find unknowns by multiplication.)

Multiply ☐1 by 6, we get

     $6x = 2 =$ perimeter of largest triangle

(Math Refresher #200 and #306)

17. **(D)**   Choice D is correct.

(Use Strategy 16: Watch out for questions which can be tricky.)

Number of candles lit = Number of days between December 9 and 21, *inclusive* = 13

Not $21 - 9 = 12$

(Logical Reasoning)

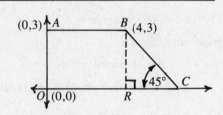

18. **(C)**   Choice C is correct.

Method 1:   **(Use Strategy 17: Use the given information effectively.)**
The above figure has AB parallel to the x-axis. (Both A and B have y-coordinate of 3). Thus, the figure is a trapezoid.

Its height (OA) is 3 $\boxed{1}$
Its top base is 4 $\boxed{2}$

(Use Strategy 14: Draw lines when appropriate.)

Draw BR perpendicular to the x-axis.
$$BR = OA = 3 \text{ and } AB = OR = 4$$

(Use Strategy 18: Remember isosceles triangle facts.)

Triangle BRC is an isosceles right triangle.
Thus, $BR = RC = 3$

The bottom base of the trapezoid $\boxed{3}$
$= OC = OR + RC = 4 + 3 = 7$ $\boxed{4}$
The area of a trapezoid

$$= \frac{1}{2} h (\text{base 1} + \text{base 2})$$

Substituting $\boxed{1}$, $\boxed{2}$ and $\boxed{3}$ into $\boxed{4}$, we have

$$\text{Area of trapezoid} = \frac{1}{2}(3)(4 + 7) = \frac{1}{2}(3)(11)$$
$$= 16.5 \quad (\textit{Answer})$$

Method 2:   **(Use Strategy 14: Draw lines when appropriate.)**

Draw BR perpendicular to the x-axis.

$ABRO$ is a rectangle and BRC is an isosceles triangle.

$$\text{Area } ABRO = (\text{base}) \times (\text{height})$$
$$= 4 \times 3$$
$$= 12 \qquad \boxed{1}$$

$$\text{Area } BRC = \frac{1}{2} \times (\text{base}) \times (\text{height})$$
$$= \frac{1}{2} \times 3 \times 3$$
$$= 4.5 \qquad \boxed{2}$$

(Use Strategy 3: The whole equals the sum of its parts.)

Total Area of figure $ABCO$
$= \text{Area of } ABRO + \text{Area of } BRC$
$= 12 + 4.5$
$= 16.5 \quad (\textit{Answer})$

(Math Refresher #410, #304, #306, #309, and #431)

19. **(B)**   Choice B is correct.
(Use Strategy 2: Translate from words to algebra.)

Let $x + y$ = sum of the 2 numbers $\boxed{1}$
$x - y$ = difference of the 2 numbers $\boxed{2}$
xy = product of the 2 numbers $\boxed{3}$

We are told that the difference between their sum and their difference is 6. $\boxed{4}$

Substituting $\boxed{1}$ asnd $\boxed{2}$ into $\boxed{4}$, we have

$$x + y - (x - y) = 6$$
$$x + y - x + y = 6$$
$$2y = 6$$
$$y = 3 \qquad \boxed{5}$$

Substituting $\boxed{5}$ into $\boxed{3}$, we get

$$x(3) = 15$$
$$x = 5$$

Clearly, 5 is the larger number.

(Math Refresher #200 and #406)

20. **(E)** Choice E is correct.

Given:

$$\frac{1}{a} + \frac{1}{b} = 10 \qquad \boxed{1}$$

Method 1: You should suspect that $a + b$ does not have a unique value because $\boxed{1}$ is one equation in two variables, and thus a and b are not uniquely determined. To prove that $a + b$ is not uniquely determined, you can use the next method.

(Use Strategy 7: Use numerics to help find the answer.)

Method 2: Choose values of a and b

Satisfying $\boxed{1}$, and calculate $a + b$.

EXAMPLE 1

$$a = \frac{1}{4} \quad b = \frac{1}{6}$$

$$a + b = \frac{5}{12}$$

EXAMPLE 2

$$a = -1 \quad b = \frac{1}{11}$$

$$a + b = \frac{-10}{11}$$

Thus, $a + b$ has at least two different values.

(Math Refresher #431 and #110)

21. **(A)** Choice A is correct.

(Use Strategy 3: The whole equals the sum of its parts.)

The area between the curved path and the dodecagon is simply the sum of the areas of the 12 semicircles.

Since   area of circle $= \pi r^2$

then   area of semicircle $= \frac{1}{2}\pi r^2$

where r is radius of circle.

Thus, area of shaded region $= 12\left(\frac{1}{2}\pi r^2\right)$

$$= 6\pi r^2 \qquad \boxed{1}$$

We are told diameter of semicircle = side of dodecagon. $\qquad \boxed{2}$

Since each side of a regular dodecagon has the same length, then

length of a side of dodecagon $=$

$$\frac{\text{perimeter of dodecagon}}{12} =$$

$$\frac{24}{12} = 2$$

From $\boxed{2}$, we know that

diameter of semicircle $= 2$

Thus, radius of semicircle $= 1$ · $\qquad \boxed{3}$

Substituting $\boxed{3}$ into $\boxed{1}$,

area of shaded region $= 6\pi$ (*Answer*)

(Math Refresher #310, #311, and #522)

22. **(B)** Choice B is correct.

Given: $x^9 = 4 \qquad \boxed{1}$

$$x^7 = \frac{9}{y^2} \qquad \boxed{2}$$

$x > 0$ and $y > 0$

(Use Strategy 13: Find unknown by division of equations.)

Divide $\boxed{1}$ by $\boxed{2}$. We get

$$\frac{x^9}{x^7} = \frac{4}{\frac{9}{y^2}}$$

$$x^2 = 4 \times \frac{y^2}{9}$$

$$x^2 = \frac{4}{9}y^2$$

$$\sqrt{x^2} = \sqrt{\frac{4}{9}y^2}$$

$$x = \frac{2}{3}y$$

(*Note:* This is the only solution because $x > 0$ and $y > 0$)

(Math Refresher #431 and #430)

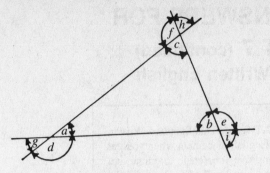

23. (B) Choice B is correct.

From the diagram, we get

$$a + d = 180 \qquad \boxed{1}$$
$$b + e = 180 \qquad \boxed{2}$$
$$c + f = 180 \qquad \boxed{3}$$

(Use Strategy 13: Find unknowns by addition of equations.)

Adding $\boxed{1}$ + $\boxed{2}$ + $\boxed{3}$, we get

$$a + b + c + d + e + f = 540 \qquad \boxed{4}$$

(Use Strategy 3: The whole equals the sum of its parts.)

The sum of the angles of a $\triangle = 180$

$$\text{Thus, } a + b + c = 180 \qquad \boxed{5}$$

From the diagram (vertical angles), we have

$$a = g, \, b = i, \, c = h \qquad \boxed{6}$$

Substituting $\boxed{6}$ into $\boxed{5}$, we get

$$g + i + h = 180 \qquad \boxed{7}$$

Adding $\boxed{4}$ + $\boxed{7}$, we get

$$a + b + c + d + f + g + i + h = 720$$

(Math Refresher #501, #505, and #406)

24. (D) Choice D is correct.

(Use Strategy 11: Use new definitions carefully.)

The smallest sum occurs when we choose 3 from A and 6 from B.

Therefore, the minimum sum = $3 + 6 = 9$

The largest sum occurs when we choose 5 from A and 8 from B.

Therefore, the maximum sum = $5 + 8 = 13$

All numbers from 9 to 13 inclusive can be sums.

Thus, there are 5 different sums possible.

(Math Refresher #431 and Logical Reasoning)

25. (B) Choice B is correct.

$$\text{Given: } AC = \frac{4}{3}(AB) \qquad \boxed{1}$$

(Use Strategy 13: Find unknowns by multiplication.)

Multiply $\boxed{1}$ by 3. We get

$$3(AC) = 4(AB) \qquad \boxed{2}$$

(Use Strategy 3: The whole equals the sum of its parts.)

From the diagram, we see that

$$AC = AB + BC \qquad \boxed{3}$$

Substituting $\boxed{3}$ into $\boxed{2}$, we have

$$3(AB + BC) = 4(AB)$$
$$3AB + 3BC = 4AB$$
$$3BC = 1AB \qquad \boxed{4}$$

(Use Strategy 13: Find unknowns by division.)

Dividing $\boxed{4}$ by $3AB$, we get

$$\frac{3BC}{3AB} = \frac{1\cancel{AB}}{3\cancel{AB}}$$

$$\frac{BC}{AB} = \frac{1}{3} \qquad \text{(Answer)}$$

(Math Refresher #406 and #403)

EXPLANATORY ANSWERS FOR
PRACTICE TEST 7 (continued)
Section 3: Standard Written English

> Section 3 does not count toward your SAT score. This Standard Written English section is used only for Freshman English placement when you get to college. However, you are advised to improve yourself in grammar and usage, and also in sentence structure. If you do well in the Standard Written English Test, you will be placed more advantageously in your college Freshman English class.

1. **(E)** All underlined parts are correct.

2. **(C)** ". . . pulled out his gun *quickly* . . ."
The adverb *quickly*—not the adjective *quick*—should be used to modify the verb *pulled out*.

3. **(B)** ". . . if you *had waited* for an occasion . . ."
In the "if clause" of a past contrary-to-fact condition, one must use the past perfect subjunctive form *had waited*—not the future perfect subjunctive form *would have waited*.

4. **(B)** ". . . *there* is no necessary connection . . ."
We have the expletive use of *there* in this sentence—not the possessive pronoun-adjective *their*.

5. **(B)** ". . . I knew the winner to be *him* . . ."
Since *winner* is the subject of the infinitive *to be, winner* is in the objective case. (The subject of an infinitive is always in the objective case.) The predicate noun or pronoun must be in the same case as the subject. Therefore, the predicate pronoun, in this particular case, must have an objective form *(him).*

6. **(D)** ". . . to express *himself.*"
The objective form of the reflexive pronoun is *himself*—not *hisself.*

7. **(E)** All underlined parts are correct.

8. **(A)** "I appreciate *your* helping me . . ."
The subject of a gerund is in the possessive case. We, therefore, say *your helping*—not *you helping.*

9. **(C)** ". . . from the wood, *we* can see the blooming lilac . . ."
The participle *looking* must modify the subject (which comes right after the comma). It is not the *lilac* that is looking—it is *we* or *one*—that is, a person or persons doing the looking.

10. **(C)** "No sooner had he begun to speak *than* . . ."
The correct expression is *no sooner . . . than*—not *no sooner . . . when.*

11. **(D)** ". . . raise *their* eyebrows."
The possessive pronoun-adjective is *their*—not *there.*

12. **(D)** ". . . so that he, *not the lady,* would get the cork."
The *lady* is misplaced in the original sentence. As you see, the correct (or incorrect placement) may make quite a difference in the meaning of the sentence.

13. **(E)** All underlined parts are correct.

14. **(D)** ". . . but the field supervisor, the sales manager, and *me.*"
The preposition *but* is understood before *me.* Since *me* is the object of the preposition *but,* it has an object form *(me)*—not a nominative form *(I).*

15. **(C)** ". . . that Williams has an interest *in* and an aptitude for . . ."
The preposition *in* must be included after *interest* in order to introduce the object of the preposition *(chemical experimentation).*

16. **(A)** "Manslaughter *occurs when* a person . . ."
Avoid using *where* to introduce a definition unless the definition pertains to place or location.

17. **(D)** "The reason . . . is *that* they are really insecure."
We say *the reason is that*—not *the reason is because.*

18. **(A)** "*It's* not generally known . . ."
We need here the contraction *It's* (meaning *It is*).

19. **(C)** ". . . is one of the *most poorly* taught subjects . . ."
The participle *taught* must be modified by an adverb *(poorly*—the superlative form of which is *most poorly)*—not by an adjective *(poorest).*

20. **(B)** "Developed by the research engineers of Dupont, the new explosive is considered by the government to be . . ."
The participle *(Developed)* is not supposed to modify *the government*—it must modify *the new explosive.* That is the reason we have to rearrange the sentence.

21. **(C)** "From *any one* of them . . ."
The word *either* refers to one of two. Since we are dealing here with three things (baseball, football, and soccer), we cannot say *either*.

22. **(A)** "After I *had listened* . . ."
We must use the past perfect tense (*had listened*) to indicate an action taking place before another past action (*hurried*).

23. **(B)** ". . . that the *Mayor's taking* . . ."
The possesive form (*Mayor's*) must be used for the noun which modifies the gerund *taking*).

24. **(A)** "Having *set* the bag . . ."
The verb *to set* means *to place*. The past participle of *to set* is *having set*. The verb *to sit* means *to rest*. The past participle of *to sit* is *having sat*. This sentence requires the use of the transitive verb *to set*—not the intransitive verb *to sit*.

25. **(E)** All underlined parts are correct.

26. **(A)** Choice A is correct. Choice B's passive verb ("was requested") interferes with the flow of the sentence. "It occurred" in Choice C is unnecessary. Choice D is too wordy for what has to be expressed. Choice E changes the meaning of the original sentence—the students did not "insist."

27. **(B)** Choice A is indirect. Choice B is correct. In Choice C, "as a prize" repeats unnecessarily the "Nobel Prize." Choice D is much too awkward, Choice E is incorrect— the scientists did not discover viruses.

28. **(D)** The important thing is not "promptness"; accordingly, Choice A is wrong. Choice B is incorrect because it is not the "loan" that must be returned. In Choice C, "You must understand" is unnecessary. Choice D is correct. Choice E changes the meaning of the original sentence.

29. **(E)** Choice A, as a phrase, hangs without clearly modifying anything else in the sentence. Choice B would be correct if it were preceded and followed by a dash in order to set the choice off from what goes before and after. Choice C is wrong because one does not "amass a scholastic record." Choice D is a complete sentence within a sentence, thus creating a run-on sentence situation. Choice E is correct.

30. **(C)** In Choice A, the use of the passive verb ("were trounced") reduces the effectiveness of expression. Choice B is indirect. Choice C is correct. In Choice D, "which is hard to believe" is unnecessary. Choice E is indirect.

31. **(E)** In Choice A, "are necessary" is not only not necessary, but the expression makes the sentence ungrammatical with the additional complete predicate ("are necessary").
There are too many "ands" in Choice B. Some grammarians call this an "Andy" sentence.
In Choice C, "And other fruit . . . peaches" is an incomplete sentence—also called a sentence fragment. Choice D also suffers from sentence fragmentation: "Such as pineapples and peaches." Choice E is correct.

32. **(B)** In Choice A, it is unidiomatic to say "instruction to learn." Choice B is correct. Choice C is too wordy. Choice D is not as direct as Choice B. Choice E suffers from lack of parallelism.

33. **(C)** Choice A is awkward and wordy. Choice B is indirect. Choice C is correct. Choice D is unacceptable idiomatically even though the meaning intended is there. Choice E changes the meaning of the original sentence.

34. **(D)** Choice A has incorrect punctuation. A dash (not a comma) is required after "that's not all." In Choice B, the expression "another thing" is too general. Choice C changes the meaning of the original sentence. Choice D is correct. Choice E is too indirectly expressed.

35. **(E)** Choice A suffers from too many "ands" (and-itis). Choices B and C are incorrect because they lack parallel construction. In Choice D, the correct form of the infinitive meaning "to rest" is "(to) lie"— not "(to) lay." Choice E is correct.

36. **(B)** Choice A is awkward. Choice B is correct. Choice C is ungrammatical—"courses" cannot act as a direct object after the copulative construction "am not certain." Choice D is too wordy. Choice E does not make sense.

37. **(A)** Choice A is correct. Choice B is too indirectly stated. Choice C is verbose—since the people "had no doubt," there is no need to use the expression "it was clear." Choice D is indirect and awkward. Choice E changes the meaning of the original sentence.

38. **(B)** Choice A is too wordy. Choice B is correct. Choice C is indirectly stated. Choices D and E change the meaning of the original sentence.

39. **(D)** Choice A is indirectly stated. Choice B deviates from the original statement. Choice C makes the whole sentence run-on. Choice D is correct. Choice E changes the meaning of the original sentence.

40. **(E)** Choice A is awkward. Choice B has a meaning which differs from that of the original sentence. Choices C and D are unidiomatic. Choice E is correct.

41. **(B)** ". . . that if Kennedy were alive today . . ."
The verb in a condition contrary to fact is *were* for all persons—never *was*.

42. **(C)** ". . . are strongly opposed to *his* associating with . . ."
A pronoun in the possessive case (*his*)—not in the objective case (*him*)—should be used to modify a gerund (*associating*) when that pronoun indicates the person who is performing the action of the gerund.

43. **(D)** ". . . let *him* speak up."
An indefinite antecedent (*anyone*) must be referred to by a singular pronoun (*him*—not *them*).

44. **(C)** ". . . to invite my husband, my mother and *me* . . ."
All of the words of a compound object must be in the objective case. Note that the words *husband, mother,* and *me* are all direct objects of the infinitive *to invite*.

45. **(B)** Neither rain nor snow nor sleet *keeps* the postman . . ."
When subjects are connected by *neither . . . nor*, the verb must agree with the subject which is closest to the verb—*sleet* is the closest subject to the verb (*keeps*) in the sentence. Since *sleet* is singular, the verb (*keeps*) must be singular.

46. **(A)** " the *taller* of the twins . . ."
The comparative degree (*taller*)—and not the superlative degree (*tallest*)—is used when we compare two persons or things.

47. **(B)** "Anyone . . . can manufacture *his* own . . ."
Since the antecedent (*Anyone*) of the possessive pronoun-adjective is singular, the pronoun-adjective itself must have a singular form (*his*—not *their*).

48. **(C)** ". . . a lake *whose* natural beauty is unsurpassed."
The contraction *who's* stands for *who is*. What we want in this sentence is the possessive pronoun-adjective *whose*.

49. **(D)** ". . . cannot take care of *themselves*."
The reflexive pronoun is *themselves*. There is no such word as *theirselves*.

50. **(A)** "We *hardly* slept all night . . ."
The word *hardly*, when used with a negative, has the effect of a double negative. Therefore, avoid any other negative with *hardly*.

EXPLANATORY ANSWERS FOR
PRACTICE TEST 7 (continued)
Section 4: Verbal Ability

1. **(B)** Choice B is correct. *Taut* means *tight; tense.* The opposite of *taut* is *loose.*

2. **(E)** Choice E is correct. See **Antonym Strategy 3.** An *affront* is an *insult.* The opposite of *affront* is a *compliment.*

3. **(D)** Choice D is correct. See **Antonym Strategies 1, 3.** *Desist* means *to cease or stop.* The opposite of *desist* is *continue.*

4. **(A)** Choice A is correct. See **Antonym Strategy 2.** *Raucous* means *harsh in sound.* The opposite of *raucous* is *melodious.*

5. **(C)** Choice C is correct. *Nettle* means *to irritate; to annoy.* The opposite of *nettle* is *soothe.*

6. **(E)** Choice E is correct. *Palpable* means *obvious; evident.* The opposite of *palpable* is *puzzling.*

7. **(D)** Choice D is correct. See **Antonym Strategies 1, 2.** *Debilitate* means *to weaken.* The opposite of *debilitate* is *strengthen.*

8. **(C)** Choice C is correct. *Meticulous* means *very careful; finicky.* The opposite of *meticulous* is *careless.*

9. **(A)** Choice A is correct. *Paucity* means *scarcity; a lack of something.* The opposite of *paucity* is *abundance.*

10. **(B)** Choice B is correct. See **Antonym Strategy 3.** *Emollient* means something that *soothes* or *softens.* The opposite of *emollient* is *irritant.*

11. **(E)** Choice E is correct. See **Sentence Completion Strategy 2.** Examine the first word of each choice. Choice (A) committees and Choice (B) tribes are incorrect because it is clear that committees and tribes cannot be equated with cities such as Athens. Now consider the other choices. Choice (E) societies . . . participated, is the only choice which has a word pair that makes sentence sense.

12. **(C)** Choice C is correct. See **Sentence Completion Strategy 2.** Examine the first word of each choice. Choice (A) abolished and Choice (E) discounted do not make sense because we cannot say that fossils are abolished or discounted in rock formations. Now consider the other choices. Choice (C) preserved . . . hardened, is the only choice which has a word pair which makes sentence sense.

13. **(D)** Choice D is correct. See **Sentence Completion Strategy 1.** The word "originate" (meaning "to come into being") completes the sentence so that it makes good sense. The other choices don't do that.

14. **(B)** Choice B is correct. See **Sentence Completion Strategy 2.** Examine the first word of each choice. We eliminate Choice (A) dominated and Choice (D) cautioned because the trends do *not* dominate or caution affluence. Now we consider the other choices. Choice (C) accentuated . . . depression, and Choice (E) accepted . . . revolution, do *not* make sentence sense. Choice (B) reflected . . . prosperity *does* make sentence sense.

15. **(A)** Choice A is correct. See **Sentence Completion Strategy 1.** The word "conserve" (meaning to "protect from loss") completes the sentence so that it makes good sense. The other choices don't do that.

16. **(A)** Choice A is correct. One nods his head to show approval. One claps his hands to show approval.
    (Purpose relationship)

17. **(C)** Choice C is correct. An addendum is attached to the end of a book. An epilogue is attached to the end of a play. You might have considered Choice A as correct. But a finale is *not* added; it is part of the original musical score. See **Analogy Strategy 4.**
    (Action to Object relationship)

18. **(E)** Choice E is correct. To surface is the opposite of to submerge. Emerge is the opposite of to withdraw. The relationship is opposite in each case. In Choice B, conceal is the opposite of reveal, but the order of the words is a reverse of the order of the capitalized words and the Choice E words. See **Analogy Strategy 3.**
    (Opposite relationship)

19. **(D)** Choice D is correct. This "phobia" analogy-type appeared on a recent SAT exam. The Greek root "phobia" means fear. The Greek root "xeno" means stranger or foreigner. So xenophobia is a fear of a stranger. "Agora"—also a Greek root—means open space. So agoraphobia is a fear of open space. Acquaintance is the opposite of stranger and enclosure is the opposite of open space.
    (Opposite relationship)

20. **(D)** Choice D is correct. A treaty brings nations more closely together. A reconciliation brings spouses more closely together.
    (Purpose and Result relationship)

21. **(E)** Choice E is correct. To be ruthless is to be without mercy. To be immaculate is to be without stain.
(Opposite relationship)

22. **(E)** Choice E is correct. An idiosyncrasy is a peculiarity of behavior. A vagary is a peculiarity of thought.
(Part-Whole relationship)

23. **(E)** Choice E is correct. Loyalty is a feeling of attachment to some person. Treason is disloyalty or a betrayal of some person or cause. Kindness is an attitude of sympathy toward a person. Hostility is an attitude of antagonism toward a person. We have here an opposite relationship. Choice (A) honor : traitor is also an opposite relationship. However, honor is a feeling while traitor is a *person*. Therefore, Choice A does not follow the non-person relationships of the capitalized words and the correct Choice E. See **Analogy Strategy 4.**
(Opposite relationship)

24. **(C)** Choice C is correct. Water that is good to drink is potable. Food that is good to eat is palatable.
(Characteristic relationship)

25. **(D)** Choice D is correct. To foment is the act of an insurgent. To rebel is the act of an iconoclast. To applaud is also the act of a spectator (Choice E). However, the capitalized pair of words and the word pair in Choice D both indicate opposition, while the Choice E word pair indicates approval. See **Analogy Strategy 4.**
(Association and Opposition relationship)

26. **(A)** Choice A is correct. The title gives the essence of the passage. General Custer was unwise and rash to fight to the death against tremendous odds. None of the other choices bring out the most important points in the passage. Therefore, Choices B, C, D, and E are incorrect.

27. **(D)** Choice D is correct. First, there is admiration on the part of the author. For example, see lines 1–2: "There probably isn't a grammar school graduate alive who doesn't know something about Custer's last stand." Secondly, the author holds back on his admiration. For example, see lines 9–11: "Hundreds of books . . . legendary mistake." Choices A, B, C, and E are incorrect because these choices do not accurately describe the writer's attitude. The student may consider Choice C as the author's attitude but the author is certainly not lavish (unrestrained) in his praise as indicated by questions raised in lines 20–21: "Was Custer mad? . . . Was he suicidal?"

28. **(B)** Choice B is correct. The words are a reference to the Bible. The Old Testament tells about Goliath, the giant warrior of the Philistines, whom David killed with a stone from a sling. The author substitutes the peashooter for the sling probably because it is more relevant to the shooting done by Custer and his men in his fight with the Indians. Choices A, C, D, and E are incorrect because they have no connection with the quoted words.

29. **(A)** Choice A is correct. See lines 2–6: "An electronic rock musician rates ahead of a physicist . . . materialism being blamed for the misuses of science." Since one associates an electronic rock musician with young people, the author's criticism is obviously directed against youth. Accordingly, Choices B, C, D, and E are incorrect since the author shows no enthusiasm, neutrality, ambiguity, or tolerance toward youth elsewhere in the passage.

30. **(B)** Choice B is correct. See lines 7–12: ". . . to those who want to clean the air . . . so much as an hour." Choices A, C, D, and E are incorrect because nowhere does the passage show that unemployment of professionals in scientific fields ties up with any of these choices.

31. **(A)** Choice A is correct. See lines 14–18: ". . . recycling of waste . . . would yield materials . . . better than many ores now being mined . . ." The passage does not indicate the truth of Choices B, C, D, or E. Therefore, these choices are incorrect.

32. **(C)** Choice C is correct. See lines 28–29: "We need more power . . . is so desirable." There is no reference, direct or indirect, in the passage to Choices A, B, D, or E. Therefore, these choices are incorrect.

33. **(E)** Choice E is correct. The situation described in Choice E is clearly libel since the photographer "diminished" the model's respectability (lines 5–6:) in altering the photograph as he did. Therefore, Choice E is correct. Choice A is incorrect because it does not result in actual damage to the wife's reputation. Choices B, C, and D are incorrect because the facts in each case are "provably true." (line 10)

34. **(D)** Choice D is correct. See lines 17–20: "A landmark case in the libel law was the Supreme Court's 1964 ruling that a public official cannot recover damages for a report related to his official duties unless he proves malice." Choice D constitutes malice. Therefore, Choice D is correct. Accordingly, Choices A, B, C, and E are incorrect because these choices are not considered as having malicious intent.

35. **(B)** Choice B is correct. The article is devoted to explaining when an action is libel and when it is not. Choice A is incorrect. Slander is defined as damage to a person's reputation by spoken words or by gestures. The article does not refer to slander at all. Choices C and D are incorrect because they are dealt with in only part of the article. Neither choice, therefore, merits use as the title of the article. Choice E is incorrect. Nowhere in the article does the author indicate that "some people are always out to hurt others."

36. **(C)** Choice C is correct. See lines 1–3: ". . . information filed in dossiers . . . assault on privacy." Although Choices A, B, and E are, no doubt, affected by an "invasion of privacy" today, the author does not emphasize this in the passage. Choice D is incorrect because the author does not single out men rather than women as being affected by an invasion of privacy.

37. **(B)** Choice B is correct. See lines 4–7: "Most adults . . . with your name on them." It is certainly true that dossiers are filed for *many* adults having unpaid debts (Item I) and drinking or drug problems (Item III), but the author does not say that dossiers are filed for the *majority* of such adults. Therefore, Choices A, C, D, and E are incorrect.

38. **(A)** Choice A is correct. See lines 27–30: "The investigator . . . that the insurance be declined." These lines indicate that the investigator may fail to give *objective* information. The passage does *not* indicate that insurance investigators conduct evaluations of "morals and character" in line with what is expressed in Choices B, C, D, and E. Therefore, these choices are incorrect.

39. **(C)** Choice C is correct. See lines 37–40: "The Foreign Bank Secrecy Act . . . six years." There is nothing in the passage to indicate the truth of Choices A, B, D, or E. Therefore, these choices are incorrect.

40. **(E)** Choice E is correct because this is the implication of the entire article. Lines 1–4 set the tone for the passage: "Hundreds of bits . . . beginning to be realized." Nowhere in the passage does the author indicate that he would have us believe that a criticism of one's character and morals would best be made by the actions of Choices A, B, C, and D. Therefore, these choices are incorrect.

EXPLANATORY ANSWERS FOR
PRACTICE TEST 7 (continued)

Section 5: Math Ability

1. **(E)** Choice E is correct. **(Use Strategy 4: Remember classic expressions.)**

   Method 1:
   Since x and y are integers, $x + y$ and $x - y$ are integers   1

   Using the factorization,

   $$x^2 - y^2 = (x - y)(x + y)$$

   the given statement
   $$x^2 - y^2 = 11$$
   becomes
   $$(x - y)(x + y) = 11 \qquad \boxed{2}$$

   with $x + y$ and $x - y$ as integers. Since we are given that $x > y$ and that x and y are both greater than zero, then $x + y$ and $x - y$ are positive integers. Since 11 is a prime number, the only positive integral solutions of 2 are with

   $$x - y = 1$$
   $$\text{and } x + y = 11$$

   Method 2:
   (Use Strategy 7: Use numerics to help find the answer.) List the squares of the integers, starting with 1, and search to find two values which differ by 11.

   $$1^2 = 1$$
   $$2^2 = 4$$
   $$3^2 = 9$$
   $$4^2 = 16$$
   $$5^2 = 25$$
   $$6^2 = 36$$
   $$36 - 25 = 11$$

   Thus, $x + y = 5 + 6 = 11$ *(Answer)*
   (Math Refresher #409, #431, #430, #608)

2. **(A)** Choice A is correct. **(Use Strategy 2: Translate from words to algebra.)** Since each member bought 3 tennis balls at a rate of 50¢ per ball, each member spent $1.50.
   (Use Strategy 3: The whole equals the sum of its parts.) We know that: Amount spent on tennis balls by all members = Total amount − Tax spent

   $$= \$15.00 - \$1.50$$
   $$= \$13.50$$

   Thus, Number of members =

   $$\frac{\text{Amount spent by all members on tennis balls}}{\text{Amount spent by each member}}$$

   $$= \frac{\$13.50}{\$1.50}$$
   $$= 9 \qquad \textit{(Answer)}$$
   (Math Refresher #200 and #205)

3. **(E)** Choice E is correct. Clearly, a number is divisible by 5 if, and only if, its last digit is either 0 or 5.
   A number is also divisible by 2 if, and only if, its last digit is divisible by 2.
   (Use Strategy 15: Certain choices are easily eliminated.) Thus we can eliminate Choices B and C.

   Method 1: To eliminate some more choices, remember that a number is divisible by 9 if, and only if, the sum of its digits is divisible by 9.
   Thus, Choice E is the only correct answer.
   (Use Strategy 8: When all choices must be tested, start with Choice E.)

   Method 2: If you did not know the test for divisibility by 9, divide the numbers in Choice A, D, and E by 9 to find the answer.

   (Math Refresher #607)

4. **(B)** Choice B is correct. **(Use Strategy 3: The whole equals the sum of its parts.)** We know that

   $$9 \text{ gallons} = \text{initial amount of wine}$$
   $$9 - 1.5 \text{ gallons} = 7.5 \text{ gal} = \text{amount of wine}$$

   after Eric has finished drinking. All of this must be put into a 12-gallon container.
   Thus, $12 - 7.5$ gal $= 4.5$ gallons $=$ amount of container that is empty. *(Answer)*
   (Subtracting Decimals)

5. **(D)** Choice D is correct. **(Use Strategy 2: Translate from words to algebra.)**
Let n = the number
We are given:

$$\frac{5}{8}n = \frac{3}{4}n - 3 \qquad \boxed{1}$$

(Use Strategy 13: Find unknowns by multiplication.) Multiply $\boxed{1}$ by 8. We get

$$8\left(\frac{5}{8}n\right) = 8\left(\frac{3}{4}n - 3\right)$$

$$5n = \frac{24}{4}n - 24$$

$$5n = 6n - 24$$

$$24 = n \qquad (Answer)$$

(Math Refresher #200 and #406)

6. **(D)** Choice D is correct. **(Use Strategy 17: Use the given information effectively.)**

$$64 \text{ grams} = \text{Total weight}$$

$$48 \text{ grams} = \text{Weight of piece}$$

$$33 \text{ cubic cm.} = \text{Volume of piece}$$

Since the uniform density, weight, and volume are proportional, then

$$\frac{48 \text{ grams}}{33 \text{ cubic cm.}} = \frac{64 \text{ grams}}{x}$$

$$(48 \text{ grams})x = (33 \text{ cubic cm.})(64 \text{ grams})$$

$$x = \frac{(33)(64)(\text{cubic cm.})}{48}$$

(Use Strategy 19: Fractor and reduce.)

$$x = \frac{33 \times \cancel{16} \times 4 \,(\text{cubic cm.})}{\cancel{16} \times 3}$$

$$x = \frac{\cancel{3} \times 11 \times 4 \,(\text{cubic cm.})}{\cancel{3}}$$

$$x = 44 \text{ cubic cm.} \qquad (Answer)$$

(Math Refresher #120 and #121)

7. **(C)** Choice C is correct. **(Use Strategy 2: Translate from words to algebra.)**

Let l = length of rectangle
w = width of rectangle

Thus, the perimeter of the rectangle p is

$$p = 2l + 2w \qquad \boxed{1}$$

We are given

$$l = 35 \qquad \boxed{2}$$

with $w > 0$ since w is the width. Substituting $\boxed{2}$ into $\boxed{1}$,

$$p = 70 + 2w$$

with $w > 0$. Thus,

$$p > 70$$

must be true. III is the only possible value for p.

(Math Refresher #200 and #304)

8. **(C)** Choice C is correct.

Method 1: Given: $x = \dfrac{1}{6}$ $\qquad \boxed{1}$

$$y = \frac{1}{36} \qquad \boxed{2}$$

(Use Strategy 13: Find unknowns by division of equations.) Divide $\boxed{2}$ by $\boxed{1}$. We get

$$\frac{y}{x} = \frac{\frac{1}{36}}{\frac{1}{6}} = \frac{1}{36} \times \frac{6}{1} = \frac{6}{36} = \frac{1}{6} \qquad \boxed{3}$$

Now comparison is easy.

Column A	Column B
$\dfrac{y}{x} = \dfrac{1}{6}$	$x = \dfrac{1}{6}$

Method 2: **(Use Strategy D: Compare fractions by multiplying both columns by a positive quantity.)**
Since $x > 0$, we multiply both columns by x. We get

Column A	Column B
$\cancel{x}\left(\dfrac{y}{\cancel{x}}\right) =$ y	$x(x) =$ x^2

Given: $x = \dfrac{1}{6}$, $y = \dfrac{1}{36}$
The columns become

Column A	Column B
$\dfrac{1}{36}$	$\left(\dfrac{1}{6}\right)^2 = \dfrac{1}{36}$

(Math Refresher #430, #431, and #112)

9. **(B)** Choice B is correct. **(Use Strategy 17: Use the given information effectively.)**

$$R = \{7, 8, 9, 10, 11\}$$
$$S = \{6, 7, 8, 9, 10\}$$

Column A	Column B
The number that is a member of set S but not of set R is clearly 6	A number that is a member of both sets R and S is 7, 8, 9 or 10

Clearly, Column B is larger in any case.

(Logical Reasoning)

10. **(A)** Choice A is correct. **(Use Strategy 17: Use the given information effectively.)**

Since z is a positive integer, $-z$ is a negative integer.

Column A	Column B
$(-z)^4$ is positive since a negative number raised to an even power is positive. Therefore, $(-z)^4$ is positive.	$-z - z - z - z = -4(z)$ which is negative, since a positive times a negative is negative. Therefore, $-4z$ is negative.

Clearly, A is greater since any positive number is larger than any negative number.

(Math Refresher #430 and #431)

11. **(C)** Choice C is correct.
Method 1:

Clearly, $\dfrac{1}{4} + \dfrac{1}{8} = \dfrac{2}{8} + \dfrac{1}{8} = \dfrac{3}{8}$

Method 2:
(Use Strategy D: Make a comparison of fractions by multiplying by a positive quantity.)

Multiply both columns by 8. We get

Column A	Column B
$8\left(\dfrac{1}{4} + \dfrac{1}{8}\right) =$ $2 + 1 =$ 3	$8\left(\dfrac{3}{8}\right) =$ 3

Method 3:
(Use Strategy F: For straightforward computations, use the Choice C method.)

(Math Refresher #109)

12. **(B)** Choice B is correct.
(Use Strategy 3: The whole equals the sum of its parts.)

Mass of Box B = mass of boxes A and B together minus mass of Box A

$$= 71 - 37$$
$$= 34 \text{ kg.}$$

Thus the quantity in Column B is greater.

(Logical Reasoning)

13. **(C)** Choice C is correct.

Method 1:

$\Bigg($ **Use Strategy 5: Average**

$$= \frac{\textbf{Sum of values}}{\textbf{Total number of values}} \Bigg)$$

Column A	Column B
Average $= \dfrac{3 + 7 + 11 + 15}{4}$ $= \dfrac{36}{4}$ $= 9$	Average $= \dfrac{2 + 6 + 12 + 16}{4}$ $= \dfrac{36}{4}$ $= 9$

Method 2:
(Use Strategy F: For straightforward calculations, use the Choice C method.)

(Math Refresher #601)

14. **(D)** Choice D is correct.
(Use Strategy 17: Use the given information effectively.)

Method 1: The remainder, when n is divided by 4, could be any integer between 0 and 3, inclusive. The remainder when n is divided by 8 could be any integer between 0 and 7, inclusive.

They could be 0, or one could be 2 and the other could be 6. We do not have enough information. The answer cannot be determined.

Method 2: **(Use Strategy C: Use numbers in place of variables when a comparison is difficult.)**

Let $n = 30$. The columns become

Column A	Column B
$\dfrac{30}{4} = 7$ remainder 2	$\dfrac{30}{8} = 3$ remainder 6

Now let $n = 19$. The columns become

Column A	Column B
$\dfrac{19}{4} = 4$ remainder 3	$\dfrac{19}{8} = 2$ remainder 3

Since two different results are possible, the answer cannot be determined.

(Math Refresher #431 and Logical Reasoning)

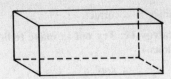

15. (A) Choice A is correct.

A rectangular solid, above, has all of its 6 faces as rectangles. There are 12 edges and 6 faces.

(Math Refresher #312)

16. (A) Choice A is correct.

Given:

$$x - y = 4 \qquad \boxed{1}$$

(Use Strategy 13: Find unknowns by addition.)

Adding y to both sides of $\boxed{1}$ gives

$$x = y + 4 \qquad \boxed{2}$$

Adding 4 to both sides of $\boxed{2}$ gives

$$x + 4 = y + 8 \qquad \boxed{3}$$

(Use Strategy 6: Know how to use inequalities.)

From $\boxed{3}$, it follows that

$$x + 4 > y$$

(Math Refresher #406 and #419)

Label the given diagram as follows:

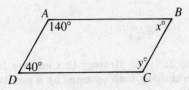

17. (D) Choice D is correct.
(Use Strategy 17: Use the given information effectively.)

(Use Strategy 16: Watch out for tricky questions.)

Study the properties of parallel lines. Since $140 + 40 = 180$, $\overline{AB} \parallel \overline{CD}$ is true. However, we are not told how $\overline{BC}$ has been drawn. In the given diagram, $\overline{BC}$ appears to be parallel to $\overline{AD}$, but it does not have to be. The following diagrams could also have been drawn to satisfy the given requirement:

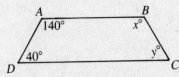

in which $x > y$ appears to be true, and

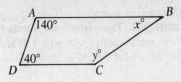

in which $x < y$ appears to be true. Thus, there is no conclusion.

(Math Refresher #504)

18. (A) Choice A is correct.

(Use Strategy 6: Know how to manipulate inequalities.)

$$\begin{array}{ll} \textit{Given:} & -12 < x < -9 \qquad \boxed{1} \\ & -14 < y < -10 \qquad \boxed{2} \\ & x \text{ and } y \text{ are integers.} \quad \boxed{3} \\ & y \text{ is even} \qquad \boxed{4} \end{array}$$

Using $\boxed{2}$, $\boxed{3}$ and $\boxed{4}$ together, we get

$$y = -12 \qquad \boxed{5}$$

Using $\boxed{1}$ and $\boxed{3}$ together, we get

$$x = -10 \text{ or } x = -11 \qquad \boxed{6}$$

Comparing $\boxed{5}$ with either value of $\boxed{6}$, we have

$$x > y$$

(Math Refresher #419 and #603)

19. (A) Choice A is correct.

(Use Strategy 3: Know how to find unknown quantities from known quantities.)

From the diagram,

$$\begin{array}{ll} AC + CD = AD & \boxed{1} \\ \textit{Given:} \quad AC = 16, \ AD = 24 & \boxed{2} \end{array}$$

Substituting $\boxed{2}$ into $\boxed{1}$, we have

$$\begin{array}{ll} 16 + CD = 24 & \\ CD = 8 & \boxed{3} \end{array}$$

From the diagram, $BD > CD \qquad \boxed{4}$

Substituting $\boxed{3}$ into $\boxed{4}$, we get

$$BD > 8$$

(Math Refresher #431 and Logical Reasoning)

20. **(C)** Choice C is correct.

(Use Strategy 2: Translate from words to algebra.)
Since there are 10 cards, each with a different number, we know the probability of getting a 7

$$= \text{Probability of getting a 2} = \frac{1}{10} \qquad \boxed{1}$$

Column A	Column B
$\frac{1}{10} \times \frac{1}{10}$	$\frac{1}{10} \times \frac{1}{10}$

using $\boxed{1}$.

(Math Refresher #200 and Logical Reasoning)

21. **(B)** Choice B is correct.

(Use Strategy 17: Use the given information effectively.)

From the diagram, it is clear that
the perimeter of $ABCDE$ < Circumference
of the circle. $\qquad \boxed{1}$

Since the diameter of the circle $= 2$,

$$\text{its radius} = 1$$
$$\text{Circumference} = 2\pi r = 2(\pi)(1)$$
$$\text{Circumference} = 2\pi$$
$$\approx 2(3.14)$$
$$\approx 6.28 \qquad \boxed{2}$$
$$\text{Clearly, Circumference} < 7$$

(Use Strategy 6: Know how to manipulate inequalities.)

Combining $\boxed{1}$ and $\boxed{2}$, we have

$$\text{Perimeter } ABCD < \text{Circumference of circle} < 7$$
$$\text{Perimeter } ABCD < 7$$

(Math Refresher #310 and 419)

22. **(B)** Choice B is correct.

(Use Strategy 12: Try not to make tedious calculations.)

Given: $\quad x = 600, y = 300$
Substitute the given into Column A. We get

Column A	Column B
$(x + y)(x - y) =$	
$(600 + 300)(600 - 300) =$	900×301
$(900)(300)$	

(Use Strategy B: Cancel positive quantities from both sides by division.)

Divide both columns by 900. We get

Column A	Column B
$\dfrac{(900)(300)}{900}$	$\dfrac{900 \times 301}{900}$
300	301

(Math Refresher #431)

23. **(C)** Choice C is correct.

Method 1: Rationalize the denominator of Column A.

Column A	Column B
$\dfrac{9}{\sqrt{3}}\left(\dfrac{\sqrt{3}}{\sqrt{3}}\right) =$	$3\sqrt{3}$
$\dfrac{9\sqrt{3}}{3} =$	
$3\sqrt{3}$	

Method 2: **(Use Strategy D: Compare fractions by multiplying both columns by a positive quantity.)**

Multiply both columns by $\sqrt{3}$, a positive number.

Column A	Column B
$\sqrt{3}\left(\dfrac{9}{\sqrt{3}}\right) =$	$\sqrt{3}(3\sqrt{3}) =$
	$3(3) =$
9	9

(Math Refresher #430)

24. **(D)** Choice D is correct.

$$\left(\text{Use Strategy 5: Average} = \frac{\text{Sum of values}}{\text{Total number of values}}\right)$$

Since we know the definition of arithmetic mean, we are really trying to compare:

Column A	Column B
$\dfrac{m + n + p}{3}$	$\dfrac{m^3 + n^3 + p^3}{3}$

(Use Strategy C: Use numbers in place of variables when a comparison is difficult.)

Choose specific values of m, n, and p.

EXAMPLE 1

When $m = 1$, $n = 1$, and $p = 1$, the columns become

Column A	Column B
1	1

The two quantities are equal in this example.

EXAMPLE 2

When $m = 2$, $n = 2$, and $p = 2$, the columns become

Column A	Column B
4	8

The quantity in Column B is greater. Hence, the answer to this question depends on specific values of m, n, and p.

(Math Refresher #601, #431, and #429)

25. **(D)** Choice D is correct.
(Use Strategy C: Use numbers in place of variables when a comparison is difficult.)

Method 1: Choose numerical values for x and y.

EXAMPLE 1

$$x = 1 \quad \text{and} \quad y = 1$$

The columns become

Column A	Column B
18	13

and the quantity in Column A is greater.

EXAMPLE 2

$$x = -1 \quad \text{and} \quad y = 1$$

The columns become

Column A	Column B
0	5

and the quantity in column B is greater.

(Use Strategy A: Cancel numbers or expressions common to both columns by addition or subtraction.)

Method 2: Since

$$9x(x + y) =$$
$$9x^2 + 9xy =$$
$$9x^2 + 4xy + 5xy,$$

the columns become

Column A	Column B
$9x^2 + 4xy + 5xy$	$9x^2 + 4xy$

Since $9x^2 + 4xy$ appears in both columns, we are really trying to compare

Column A	Column B
$5xy$	0

The answer, clearly, depends on specific values of x and y.

(Math Refresher #431 and #409)

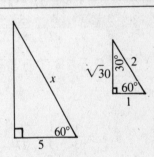

26. **(A)** Choice A is correct.

(Use Strategy 18: Remember special right triangles.)

The given triangle, at the left, is similar to the standard 30–60–90 triangle, at right. Thus, corresponding sides are in proportion.

$$\frac{x}{2} = \frac{5}{1}$$
$$x = 2 \times 5$$
$$x = 10$$

Clearly, 10 is greater than 8.

(Math Refresher #509 and #510)

27. **(D)**   Choice D is correct.

    (Use Strategy 2: Translate from words to algebra.)

    $$A_n + A_{n+1} = -1 + 1 \text{ or } 1 - 1$$
    $$A_n + A_{n+1} = 0 \text{ in either case} \qquad \boxed{1}$$
    $$A_n - A_{n+1} = 1 - (-1) = 2 \qquad \boxed{2}$$
    $$\text{or}$$
    $$A_n - A_{n+1} = -1 - 1 = -2 \qquad \boxed{3}$$

    Since $\boxed{1} < \boxed{2}$ and $\boxed{1} > \boxed{3}$, there are two different possible results. Thus, the answer cannot be determined.

    (Math Refresher #200 and #431)

28. **(D)**   Choice D is correct.

    Given: $x = 1 + \dfrac{1}{3} + \dfrac{1}{9} + \dfrac{1}{27} + \dfrac{1}{81} + \dfrac{1}{243}$ $\boxed{1}$
    Find: $x - y$

    (Use Strategy 12: Try not to make tedious calculations.)

    Try not to calculate the numerical value of x. Use x in the given form.

    (Use Strategy 13: Find unknowns by multiplication.)

    $$3x = 3\left(1 + \frac{1}{3} + \frac{1}{9} + \frac{1}{27} + \frac{1}{81} + \frac{1}{243}\right)$$
    $$= 3 + \frac{3}{3} + \frac{3}{9} + \frac{3}{27} + \frac{3}{81} + \frac{3}{243}$$
    $$= 3 + 1 + \frac{1}{3} + \frac{1}{9} + \frac{1}{27} + \frac{1}{81} \qquad \boxed{2}$$

    Hence, using $\boxed{2}$,

    $$y = 3x - 3$$
    $$= 3 + 1 + \frac{1}{3} + \frac{1}{9} + \frac{1}{27} + \frac{1}{81} - 3$$
    $$= 1 + \frac{1}{3} + \frac{1}{9} + \frac{1}{22} + \frac{1}{81} \qquad \boxed{3}$$

    Using $\boxed{1}$ and $\boxed{3}$, we have

    $$x - y =$$
    $$1 + \frac{1}{3} + \frac{1}{9} + \frac{1}{27} + \frac{1}{81} + \frac{1}{243} -$$
    $$\left(1 + \frac{1}{3} + \frac{1}{9} + \frac{1}{27} + \frac{1}{81}\right) = \frac{1}{243}$$

    (Math Refresher #110, #111, and #406)

29. **(A)**   Choice A is correct.
    (Use Strategy 3: The whole equals the sum of its parts.)

    From the given diagram, it is clear that

    $$z + 2w = 180 \qquad \boxed{1}$$

    Since the sum of the measures of the angles of a triangle is 180, then

    $$x + y + z = 180 \qquad \boxed{2}$$

    (Use Strategy 13: Find unknowns by subtracting equations.)

    Subtracting $\boxed{2}$ from $\boxed{1}$,

    $$2w - (x + y) = 0$$
    $$\text{or} \qquad 2w = x + y \qquad \boxed{3}$$

    Using $\boxed{3}$, we calculate the unknown expression,

    $$w + x + y = w + 2w$$
    $$= 3w$$

    (Math Refresher #501, #505, and #406)

30. **(C)**   Choice C is correct.
    (Use Strategy 2: Know the definition of percent.)

    $$\% \text{ sugar} = \frac{\text{amount of sugar}}{\text{total amount of mixture}} \times 100$$
    $$= \frac{16 \text{ grams}}{16 \text{ grams} + 24 \text{ grams}} \times 100$$
    $$= \frac{16}{40} \times 100$$

    (Use Strategy 19: Factor and reduce.)

    $$\frac{16}{40} \times 100 =$$
    $$\frac{4 \times \cancel{4}}{\cancel{4} \times \cancel{10}} \times \cancel{10} \times 10 =$$
    $$40 \qquad (\textit{Answer})$$

    (Math Refresher #114)

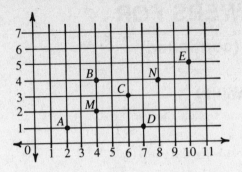

31. **(E)** Choice E is correct.

(Use Strategy 8: When all choices must be tested, start with E.)

In the diagram above, we have plotted each of the points given in the choices. From the diagram, it is clear that

$$MC = CN = NE$$

Thus, since $ME = MC + CN + NE$, then
$$3NE = ME$$

as required, so that point E is the answer.

(Math Refresher #410)

32. **(E)** Choice E is correct.

(Use Strategy 11: Use new definitions carefully.)

$$\text{I: } \quad x \otimes x = \frac{x^3 + x^3}{x + x}$$

$$= \frac{2x^3}{2x} = x^2 \qquad \boxed{1}$$

Thus, I is true.

$$\text{II.} \quad x \otimes y = \frac{x^3 + y^3}{x + y} \qquad \boxed{2}$$

$$y \otimes x = \frac{y^3 + x^3}{y + x} \qquad \boxed{3}$$

Clearly $\boxed{2} = \boxed{3}$, Thus, II is true.

III. $x \otimes (x \otimes x)$ Substituting $\boxed{1}$, we have

$$x \otimes x^2 = \frac{x^3 + x^6}{x + x^2} \qquad \boxed{4}$$

$(x \otimes x) \otimes x$ Substituting $\boxed{1}$, we have

$$x^2 \otimes x = \frac{x^6 + x^3}{x^2 + x} \qquad \boxed{5}$$

Clearly $\boxed{4} = \boxed{5}$. Thus III is true.

(Math Refresher #431)

33. **(E)** Choice E is correct.

(Use Strategy 2: Translate from words to algebra.)

Method 1: Let s = side of smaller square.
Then $2s$ = side of larger square.

(Use Strategy 3: The whole equals the sum of its parts.)

Shaded area = Larger area − Smaller area

$$= (2s)^2 - (s)^2$$

$$= 4s^2 - s^2$$

Shaded area = $3s^2$

$$\frac{\text{Shaded area}}{\text{Larger area}} = \frac{3s^2}{4s^2} = \frac{3}{4}$$

Method 2: **(Use Strategy 7: Use specific numerical examples to prove or disprove your guess.)**

Let Smaller side = 1
Then, Larger side = 2
  Larger area = $2^2 = 4$ $\boxed{1}$
  Smaller area = $1^2 = 1$ $\boxed{2}$

(Use Strategy 3: The whole equals the sum of its parts.)

Shaded area = Larger − Smaller
$$= 4 - 1$$
Shaded area = 3 $\boxed{3}$

Using $\boxed{3}$ and $\boxed{1}$ we have

$$\frac{\text{Shaded area}}{\text{Larger area}} = \frac{3}{4} \qquad (Answer)$$

(Math Refresher #200, #303, and #431)

34. **(D)** Choice D is correct.

(Use Strategy 11: Use new definitions carefully.)

Since y is not divisible by 2, y is odd.

Therefore $\boxed{y} = y - 1$ by definition.

Accordingly, Choice D is correct.

(Math Refresher #607)

35. **(B)** Choice B is correct.

(Use Strategy 11: Use new definitions carefully.)

From the given definition,

$\boxed{4} = 2$ and $\boxed{7} = 6$

Thus, $\boxed{4} + \boxed{7} = 8$ which is the same as $\boxed{9} = 8$

Accordingly, Choice B is correct.

(Math Refresher #431)

EXPLANATORY ANSWERS FOR
PRACTICE TEST 7 (continued)

Section 6: Math Ability

1. (E) Choice E is correct.

(Use Strategy 13: Find unknowns by subtraction.)

$$Given: \quad y + 4 = -7 \quad \boxed{1}$$

Add -4 to both sides of $\boxed{1}$. We get

$$
\begin{array}{rl}
y + \cancel{4} &= -7 \\
-\cancel{4} & \underline{\quad -4} \\
y &= -11 \qquad (Answer)
\end{array}
$$

(Math Refresher #406)

2. (C) Choice C is correct.

$$
Given: \quad
\begin{array}{r}
59\triangle \\
-\ 293 \\
\hline
\square 97
\end{array} \quad \boxed{1}
$$

(Use Strategy 17: Use the given information effectively.)

From $\boxed{1}$ we see that $\triangle - 3 = 7$ $\quad\boxed{2}$
From $\boxed{2}$ we get $\triangle = 10$ $\quad\boxed{3}$

From $\boxed{1}$ and $\boxed{3}$ we get $\triangle = 0$ in $\boxed{1}$ and we had to borrow to get 10. Thus, we have

$$
\begin{array}{r}
8 \\
5\cancel{9}0 \\
-\ 293 \\
\hline
\square 97
\end{array} \quad \boxed{4}
$$

Calculating $\boxed{4}$, we get

$$
\begin{array}{r}
8 \\
5\cancel{9}0 \\
-\ 293 \\
\hline
297
\end{array}
$$

We see that the digit represented by the $\square$ is 2.

(Answer)

(Logical Reasoning and Subtraction)

3. (B) Choice B is correct.

(Use Strategy 16: The obvious may be tricky!)

$1000 - 1 = 999$ is *not* correct.
Neither 1 nor 1000 is to be included.
Thus there are $1000 - 2 = 998$ integers between 1 and 1000.

(Logical Reasoning)

4. (E) Choice E is correct.

$$Given: \quad \frac{a - b}{b} = \frac{1}{2} \quad \boxed{1}$$

(Use Strategy 13: Find unknowns by multiplication.)

Multiply $\boxed{1}$ by $2b$. We have

$$2\cancel{b}\left(\frac{a-b}{\cancel{b}}\right) = \left(\frac{1}{\cancel{2}}\right)\cancel{2}b$$
$$2(a - b) = b$$
$$2a - 2b = b$$
$$2a = 3b \quad \boxed{2}$$

(Use Strategy 13: Find unknowns by division.)

Dividing $\boxed{2}$ by $2b$, we get

$$\frac{\cancel{2}a}{\cancel{2}b} = \frac{3\cancel{b}}{2\cancel{b}}$$
$$\frac{a}{b} = \frac{3}{2} \qquad (Answer)$$

(Math Refresher #406)

5. (C) Choice C is correct.

Number of pounds of force	Height object is raised
3	6 feet
6	12 feet
9	18 feet

$\boxed{1}$

(Use Strategy 2: Translate from words to algebra.)

We are given that:

height raised $= c$ (force exerted) $\quad\boxed{2}$

Substituting $\boxed{1}$ into $\boxed{2}$, we get

$$6 = c(3)$$
$$2 = c \quad \boxed{3}$$

Given: Height object is raised $= 15$ feet $\quad\boxed{4}$
Substituting $\boxed{3}$ and $\boxed{4}$ into $\boxed{2}$, we have

$$15 = 2 \text{ (force exerted)}$$
$$7\frac{1}{2} = \text{force exerted} \qquad (Answer)$$

(Math Refresher #200 and #406)

6. **(A)**   Choice A is correct.

Given: $a = 1, b = -2, c = -2$ ☐1

$$\frac{b^2 c}{(a - c)^2}$$ ☐2

Substitute ☐1 into ☐2. We get

$$\frac{(-2)^2(-2)}{(1 - (-2))^2} =$$

$$\frac{4(-2)}{(3)^2} =$$

$$\frac{-8}{9}$$ *(Answer)*

(Math Refresher #429 and #431)

7. **(D)**   Choice D is correct.

Given: $\frac{y}{3}, \frac{y}{4}, \frac{y}{7}$ are integers.   ☐1

(Use Strategy 17: Use the given information effectively.)

If all items in ☐1 are integers, then 3, 4 and 7 divide *y* evenly (zero remainder). *y* must be a common multiple of 3, 4 and 7. Multiplying 3, 4, and 7 we get 84.   *(Answer)*

(Math Refresher #607)

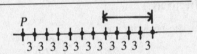

8. **(D)**   Choice D is correct.

(Use Strategy 11: Use new definitions carefully.)

We are told that the points are each 3 units apart, as indicated above. We are looking for all those points which are more than 19 units away from point *P*. By checking the diagram we find 5 such points (marked with arrow in diagram).

(Logical Reasoning)

9. **(A)**   Choice A is correct.

Given: $y = 28j$ ☐1
j is any integer   ☐2

(Use Strategy 13: Find unknowns by division.)

Divide ☐1 by 2. We have

$$\frac{y}{2} = \frac{28j}{2}$$

$$\frac{y}{2} = 14j$$ ☐3

(Use Strategy 19: Factor.)

Factor the 14 in ☐3. We get

$$\frac{y}{2} = (2)(7)(j)$$ ☐4

Using ☐2 and ☐4 we see that $\frac{y}{2}$ is an integer with a factor of 2.

Thus, $\frac{y}{2}$ is even.   *(Answer)*

(Math Refresher #603 and #605)

10. **(B)**   Choice B is correct.

Given: ☐1
$(a + 2, a - 2) = [a]$ for all integers a.   ☐2
We need to find (6,2)

(Use Strategy 11: Use new definitions carefully.)
Using ☐1 and ☐2 we have

$a + 2 = 6$ and $a - 2 = 2$
$a = 4$ $a = 4$ ☐3

Using ☐1, ☐2 and ☐3, we get

$(6,2) = [4]$ *(Answer)*

(Math Refresher #431 and #406)

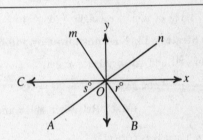

11. **(D)**   Choice D is correct.

Given: $m \perp n$ ☐1

From ☐1 we know that $\angle AOB$ is a right angle.
Thus $\angle AOB = 90°$ ☐2

From the diagram, we see that $\angle COx$ is a straight angle.
Thus $\angle COx = 180°$ ☐3

(Use Strategy 3: The whole equals the sum of its parts.)

We know that $\angle COA + \angle AOB + \angle BOx = \angle COx$ ☐4

Given: $\angle COA = s°$ ☐5
$\angle BOx = r°$ ☐6

Substituting ☐2, ☐3, ☐5 and ☐6 into ☐4, we get

$s + 90 + r = 180$
$s + r = 90$
$r + s = 90$ *(Answer)*

(Math Refresher #501, #511 and #406)

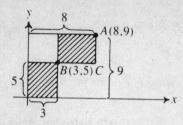

12. **(D)**   Choice D is correct.

(Use Strategy 17: Use the given information effectively.)

From the given coordinates, we can find certain distances, as marked above.

Using these distances we find:

$$BC = 8 - 3 = 5 \quad \boxed{1}$$
$$AC = 9 - 5 = 4 \quad \boxed{2}$$

We know that Area of a rectangle = length × width $\boxed{3}$

Using the diagram and $\boxed{3}$ we have

Area of lower rectangle = $5 \times 3 = 15$ $\boxed{4}$

Substituting $\boxed{1}$ and $\boxed{2}$ into $\boxed{3}$, we get

Area of upper rectangle = $5 \times 4 = 20$ $\boxed{5}$

(Use Strategy 13: Find unknowns by addition.)

Adding $\boxed{4}$ and $\boxed{5}$ together, we get

Total area = $15 + 20 = 35$ (*Answer*)

(Math Refresher #410 and #304)

13. **(B)**   Choice B is correct.

Given: Total number of students = 2800 $\boxed{1}$

(Use Strategy 2: Translate from words to algebra.)

Number of German students = $\dfrac{1}{4} \times 2800$

$$= \dfrac{2800}{4}$$

$$= 700 \quad \boxed{2}$$

(Use Strategy 13: Find unknown by subtraction.)

Subtracting $\boxed{2}$ from $\boxed{1}$ we get

Number of students
not studying German =
$2800 - 700 =$ (*Answer*)
2100

(Math Refresher #200 and #111)

14. **(A)**   Choice A is correct.

(Use Strategy 2: Translate from words to algebra.)

Given:
cost per vehicle = $\$y$ $\boxed{1}$
Let x = number of students paying 0.40 $\boxed{2}$
Then $x + 6$ = number of students paying 0.25 $\boxed{3}$

Using $\boxed{1}$, $\boxed{2}$ and $\boxed{3}$,

We are told that: $x(\$0.40) = \$y$ $\boxed{4}$
$(x + 6)(\$0.25) = \$y$ $\boxed{5}$

From $\boxed{4}$ and $\boxed{5}$ we get

$$x(\$0.40) = (x + 6)(\$0.25)$$
$$.40x = .25x + 1.50$$
$$.15x = 1.50$$
$$x = 10 \quad \boxed{6}$$

Substitute $\boxed{6}$ into $\boxed{4}$. We have

$$10(\$0.40) = \$y$$
$$\$4.00 = y$$
$$\$4 = y \quad (\textit{Answer})$$

(Math Refresher #200, #406, and #431)

15. **(E)**   Choice E is correct.

Given: $8(679) + 679$ $\boxed{1}$

(Use Strategy 17: Use the given information effectively.)

$\boxed{1}$ can be written as:

$$8(679) + 1(679) =$$
$$9(679) \quad \boxed{2}$$

We need to check all the choices.

(Use Strategy 8: When all choices must be tested start with E.)

Choice E = $7(679) + 4(679) =$
$11(679)$

This is not equal to $\boxed{2}$.

Choice D = $6(679) + 3(679) =$
$9(679)$

This does equal $\boxed{2}$.

(Common Factors)

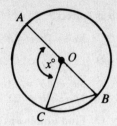

16. **(C)** Choice C is correct.

Given: AB is a diameter   ☐1
O is the center of the circle   ☐2
CB = OB   ☐3

Using ☐2, we know that OB and OC are radii   ☐4

From ☐4 we get that OB = OC.   ☐5

Using ☐3 and ☐5 together, we have

$$OB = OC = CB \qquad ☐6$$

(Use Strategy 18: Remember the equilateral triangle.)

From ☐6, we have △OBC is equilateral   ☐7

From ☐7, we get that ∠B = ∠C =
∠COB = 60°   ☐8

From ☐1, we get ∠AOB is straight angle.   ☐9

From ☐9, we have ∠AOB = 180°   ☐10

(Use Strategy 3: The whole equals the sum of its parts.)

From the diagram we see that:

$$∠AOC + ∠COB = ∠AOB \qquad ☐11$$

Given: ∠AOC = x°   ☐12

Substituting ☐8, ☐10 and ☐12 into ☐11, we get

$$x + 60 = 180$$
$$x = 120 \qquad ☐13$$

(Use Strategy 13: Find unknowns by division.)

Divide by ☐13 by 6. We have

$$\frac{x}{6} = \frac{120}{6}$$

$$\frac{x}{6} = 20 \qquad (Answer)$$

(Math Refresher #501, #508, #524, and 406)

17. **(D)** Choice D is correct.

Given: Selling price of radio = $64   ☐1
Regular price of radio = $80   ☐2

(Use Strategy 2: Remember how to find percent discount.)

$$Percent\ discount = \frac{Amount\ off}{original\ price} \times 100 \qquad ☐3$$

Subtracting ☐1 from ☐2, we get

Amount off = $80 − 64 = $16   ☐4

Substituting ☐2 and ☐4 into ☐3, we have

$$Percent\ discount = \frac{\$16}{\$80} \times 100$$

$$= \frac{\$16 \times 100}{\$80} \qquad ☐5$$

(Use Strategy 19: Factor and reduce.)

$$Percent\ discount = \frac{\cancel{\$16} \times \cancel{\$} \times 20}{\cancel{\$16} \times \cancel{\$}}$$

Percent discount = 20   ☐6

Given: Regular price of different radio = $200   ☐7

New percent discount

$$= 1\frac{1}{2} \times Other\ radio's\ percent\ discount \qquad ☐8$$

Using ☐6 and ☐8, we have

$$New\ percent\ discount = 1\frac{1}{2} \times 20 =$$

$$= \frac{3}{2} \times 20$$

$$= 30 \qquad ☐9$$

(Use Strategy 2: Remember how to find percent of a number.)

We know percent of a number =
percent × number.   ☐10

Substituting ☐7 and ☐9 into ☐10, we have

$$Amount\ of\ discount = 30\% \times \$200$$

$$= \frac{30}{100} \times \$200$$

Amount of discount = $60   ☐11

(Use Strategy 13: Find unknowns by subtraction.)

Subtracting ☐11 from ☐7, we have

Selling price of different radio
= $200 − $60
= $140   *(Answer)*

(Math Refresher #200 and #114)

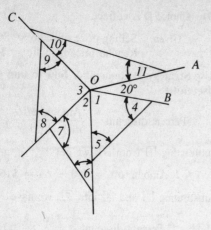

18. (A) Choice A is correct.

> *Given:* $\angle AOB = 20°$ $\boxed{1}$

(Use Strategy 3: The whole equals the sum of its parts.)

We know that the sum of the angles
of a triangle $= 180°$ $\boxed{2}$

For each of the four triangles, applying $\boxed{2}$ yields:

$$\angle 8 + \angle 9 + \angle 3 = 180 \quad \boxed{3}$$
$$\angle 6 + \angle 7 + \angle 2 = 180 \quad \boxed{4}$$
$$\angle 4 + \angle 5 + \angle 1 = 180 \quad \boxed{5}$$
$$\angle 10 + \angle 11 + \angle COA = 180 \quad \boxed{6}$$

We know that the sum of all the angles
about a point $= 360°$ $\boxed{7}$

Applying $\boxed{7}$ to point O, we have

$$\angle 1 + \angle 2 + \angle 3 + \angle COA$$
$$+ \angle AOB = 360° \quad \boxed{8}$$

Substituting $\boxed{1}$ into $\boxed{8}$, we get

$$\angle 1 + \angle 2 + \angle 3 + \angle COA + 20 = 360$$
$$\angle 1 + \angle 2 + \angle 3 + \angle COA = 340 \quad \boxed{9}$$

(Use Strategy 13: Find unknowns by addition.)

Adding $\boxed{3}$, $\boxed{4}$, $\boxed{5}$ and $\boxed{6}$, we have

$$\angle 4 + \angle 5 + \angle 6 + \angle 7 + \angle 8 + \angle 9 + \angle 10 +$$
$$\angle 11 + \angle 1 + \angle 2 + \angle 3 + \angle COA = 720° \quad \boxed{10}$$

(Use Strategy 13: Find unknowns by subtraction.)

Subtracting $\boxed{9}$ from $\boxed{10}$, we get

$$\angle 4 + \angle 5 + \angle 6 + \angle 7 + \angle 8$$
$$+ \angle 9 + \angle 10 + \angle 11 = 380° \quad \boxed{11}$$

Thus, the sum of the marked angles $= 380°$

(Answer)

(Math Refresher #505 and #406)

19. (B) Choice B is correct.

> *Given:* $3a + 4b = 4a - 4b = 21$ $\boxed{1}$

From $\boxed{1}$, we get

$$3a + 4b = 21 \quad \boxed{2}$$
$$4a - 4b = 21 \quad \boxed{3}$$

(Use Strategy 13: Find unknowns by addition.)

Add $\boxed{2}$ and $\boxed{3}$ together. We get

$$3a + \cancel{4b} = 21$$
$$+ \ \underline{4a - \cancel{4b} = 21}$$
$$7a \qquad = 42$$
$$a \qquad = 6 \qquad \textit{(Answer)}$$

(Math Refresher #407)

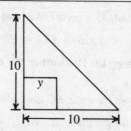

20. (E) Choice E is correct.

We know that area of a triangle

$$= \frac{1}{2} \times \text{base} \times \text{height} \quad \boxed{1}$$

Use the diagram, and substituting into $\boxed{1}$, we get

$$\text{Area of triangle} = \frac{1}{2} \times 10 \times 10$$
$$= 50 \quad \boxed{2}$$

(Use Strategy 2: Translate from words to algebra.)

We are told:

$$\text{Area of square} = \frac{1}{5} \times \text{area of triangle} \quad \boxed{3}$$

We know that
area of a square $= (\text{side})^2$ $\boxed{4}$

Using the diagram, and substituting into $\boxed{4}$, we get

$$\text{Area of square} = y^2 \quad \boxed{5}$$

Substituting $\boxed{2}$ and $\boxed{5}$ into $\boxed{3}$, we have

$$y^2 = \frac{1}{5} \times 50$$
$$y^2 = 10 \quad \boxed{6}$$

Take the square root of both sides of $\boxed{6}$. We get

$$y = \sqrt{10} \qquad \textit{(Answer)}$$

(Math Refresher #200, #303, #307, and #430)

21. **(C)**   Choice C is correct.

$$Given: \quad Print\ rate = \frac{80\ characters}{second} \quad \boxed{1}$$

$$\frac{Number\ of\ characters}{Page} = 2400 \quad \boxed{2}$$

(Use Strategy 13: Find unknowns by division.)

Dividing $\boxed{2}$ by $\boxed{1}$, we have

$$\frac{2400\ characters}{page} \div \frac{80\ characters}{second} =$$

$$\frac{2400\ characters}{page} \times \frac{second}{80\ characters} =$$

$$\frac{2400\ second}{80\ page}$$

$$= \frac{30\ seconds}{page} \quad \boxed{3}$$

The time for an M-page report will be

$$\frac{30\ seconds}{page} \times M\ pages =$$

Time for M–page report $= 30\,M$ seconds $\boxed{4}$

(Use Strategy 10: Know how to use units.)

To change time from seconds to minutes we multiply

$$by \frac{1\ minute}{60\ seconds}. \quad \boxed{5}$$

Applying $\boxed{5}$ to $\boxed{4}$, we get

Time for M page report, in minutes $= 30M$ seconds $\times \dfrac{1\ minute}{60\ seconds}$

$$= \frac{30\,M\ minutes}{60}$$

$$= \frac{M}{2}\ minutes \qquad (Answer)$$

(Math Refresher #201 and #121)

22. **(B)**   Choice B is correct.

Given: On Friday, the satellite passed over Washington, D.C. at midnight $\boxed{1}$
Complete orbit = 5 hours $\boxed{2}$

(Use Strategy 17: Use the given information effectively.)

Using $\boxed{2}$, we see that five complete orbits $= 5 \times 5 = 25$ hours $= 1$ day $+ 1$ hour $\boxed{3}$

From $\boxed{1}$ and $\boxed{2}$ we know that

DAY	TIME PASSING OVER D.C.	
Friday	7:00 PM, Midnight	$\boxed{4}$

Applying $\boxed{3}$ to $\boxed{4}$, and continuing this chart, we have

Saturday	8:00 PM, 1:00 AM
Sunday	9:00 PM, 2:00 AM
Monday	10:00 PM, 3:00 AM
Tuesday	11:00 PM, 4:00 AM
Wednesday	Midnight, 5:00 AM

(Logical Reasoning)

23. **(D)**   Choice D is correct.

(Use Strategy 2: Know how to find percent of a number.)

Let x = price of car $\boxed{1}$
Given: 1st reduction = 30% $\boxed{2}$
2nd reduction = 40% $\boxed{3}$

We know amount of discount

$$= percent \times price \quad \boxed{4}$$

Using $\boxed{1}$, $\boxed{2}$, and $\boxed{4}$, we get

Amount of 1st discount $= 30\% \times x$
$= .30x$ $\boxed{5}$

(Use Strategy 13: Find unknowns by subtraction.)
Subtracting $\boxed{5}$ from $\boxed{1}$, we have

Reduced price $= x - .30x$
$= .70x$ $\boxed{6}$

Using $\boxed{3}$, $\boxed{6}$ and $\boxed{4}$, we get

Amount of 2nd discount $= 40\% \times .70x$
$= .40 \times .70x$
$= .28x$ $\boxed{7}$

Subtracting $\boxed{7}$ from $\boxed{6}$, we have

Price after 2nd reduction $= .70x - .28x$
$= .42x$ $\boxed{8}$

(Use Strategy 16: The obvious may be tricky!)

Since $\boxed{8} = .42x$, it is 42% of the original price of x. This is *not* the answer to the question.

Since $\boxed{8}$ is 42% of the original it is the result of a 58% discount.

The answer is 58%.

(Math Refresher #200 and #114)

24. **(B)** Choice B is correct.

Let $x = 0.393939....$ ☐1

(Use Strategy 13: Find unknowns by multiplication.)

Multiply ☐1 by 100. We get

$100x = 39.393939....$ ☐2

(Use Strategy 13: Find unknowns by subtraction.)

Subtract ☐1 from ☐2. We get

$$99x = 39$$

$$x = \frac{39}{99}$$

$$x = \frac{13}{33} \qquad ☐3$$

To find the difference between $\frac{2}{3}$ and ☐1,

we need $\frac{2}{3} - \frac{13}{33} =$

$$\frac{22}{33} - \frac{13}{33} =$$

$$\frac{9}{33} = \frac{3}{11} \qquad (Answer)$$

(Math Refresher #602)

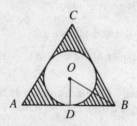

25. **(A)** Choice A is correct.

Given: Diameter of circle $= 2$ ☐1

(Use Strategy 14: Draw lines to help find the answer.)

Draw radius OD, with D the point of tangency and OB as shown above. ☐2

(Use Strategy 18: Remember the equilateral triangle.)

Given: Triangle ACB is equilateral ☐3

From ☐2 we get $OD \perp AB$, since radius $\perp$ tangent at point of tangency. ☐4

From ☐4, we get $\angle ODB = 90°$ ☐5

From ☐3, we get $\angle ABC = 60°$ ☐6

From the geometry of regular polygons, we know that OB bisects $\angle ABC$. ☐7

From ☐6 and ☐7 we get $\angle DBO = 30°$ ☐8

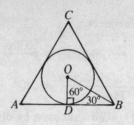

From ☐5 and ☐8 we have

$\triangle ODB$ is a 30–60–90 triangle

From ☐1, we get $OD = 1$ ☐9

(Use Strategy 18: Remember the special right triangles.)

Using ☐9 and the properties of the 30–60–90 right triangle, we get $OB = 2$, $DB = 1\sqrt{3} = \sqrt{3}$ ☐10

We know $AB = 2 \times DB$ ☐11

Substituting ☐10 into ☐11, we have

$$AB = 2\sqrt{3} \qquad ☐12$$

We know the area of an equilateral triangle $= \dfrac{(\text{side})^2 \sqrt{3}}{4}$ ☐13

Substituting ☐12 into ☐13, we get

$$\text{Area of } \triangle ABC = \frac{(2\sqrt{3})^2\sqrt{3}}{4}$$

$$= \frac{12\sqrt{3}}{4}$$

$$= 3\sqrt{3} \qquad ☐14$$

We know the area of a circle $= \pi(\text{radius})^2$ ☐15

Substituting ☐9 into ☐15, we get

$$\text{Area of circle O} = \pi(1)^2$$

$$= \pi \qquad ☐16$$

(Use Strategy 13: Find unknowns by subtraction.)

Subtracting ☐16 from ☐14, we get

Shaded area $= 3\sqrt{3} - \pi$ *(Answer)*

(Math Refresher #308, #310, #508, #524, #525, and #509)

A COMPLETE PSAT PRACTICE TEST

If You Plan to Take the PSAT, Take This PSAT Practice Test Now!

The following PSAT Practice Test is modeled very closely after the actual PSAT. You will find that this PSAT Practice Test has:

a) The same level of difficulty as the actual PSAT

and

b) The same question formats that the actual PSAT questions have.

Accordingly, *taking the following PSAT Practice Test is like taking the actual PSAT.*

There are four important reasons for taking this PSAT Practice Test:

Reason 1. To find out in which areas of the PSAT you are weak.

Reason 2. To know just where to concentrate your efforts to eliminate these weaknesses.

Reason 3. To reinforce the Critical Thinking Skills—25 Math Strategies and 25 Verbal Strategies—that you learned in Part 2 of this book, "Using Critical Thinking Skills to Score High on the SAT." Diligent study of these strategies will result in a sharp rise in your SAT and PSAT Math and Verbal scores.

Reason 4. To strengthen your Basic Math skills that might still be a bit rusty. Part 4, "SAT Math Refresher," will help you substantially to scrape off some of this rust.

These four reasons, given above, for taking the following PSAT Practice Test, tie up closely with a very important educational principle:

WE LEARN BY DOING!

Now refer to Page 357: "10 TIPS FOR TAKING THE PRACTICE TESTS." Although they apply to the 7 SAT Practice Tests in this book, these valuable tips also apply generally to the PSAT Practice Test that you are about to take.

Answer Sheet
for PSAT Practice Test

SECTION 1: VERBAL ABILITY

1 Ⓐ Ⓑ Ⓒ Ⓓ Ⓔ   14 Ⓐ Ⓑ Ⓒ Ⓓ Ⓔ   27 Ⓐ Ⓑ Ⓒ Ⓓ Ⓔ   40 Ⓐ Ⓑ Ⓒ Ⓓ Ⓔ   53 Ⓐ Ⓑ Ⓒ Ⓓ Ⓔ

2 Ⓐ Ⓑ Ⓒ Ⓓ Ⓔ   15 Ⓐ Ⓑ Ⓒ Ⓓ Ⓔ   28 Ⓐ Ⓑ Ⓒ Ⓓ Ⓔ   41 Ⓐ Ⓑ Ⓒ Ⓓ Ⓔ   54 Ⓐ Ⓑ Ⓒ Ⓓ Ⓔ

3 Ⓐ Ⓑ Ⓒ Ⓓ Ⓔ   16 Ⓐ Ⓑ Ⓒ Ⓓ Ⓔ   29 Ⓐ Ⓑ Ⓒ Ⓓ Ⓔ   42 Ⓐ Ⓑ Ⓒ Ⓓ Ⓔ   55 Ⓐ Ⓑ Ⓒ Ⓓ Ⓔ

4 Ⓐ Ⓑ Ⓒ Ⓓ Ⓔ   17 Ⓐ Ⓑ Ⓒ Ⓓ Ⓔ   30 Ⓐ Ⓑ Ⓒ Ⓓ Ⓔ   43 Ⓐ Ⓑ Ⓒ Ⓓ Ⓔ   56 Ⓐ Ⓑ Ⓒ Ⓓ Ⓔ

5 Ⓐ Ⓑ Ⓒ Ⓓ Ⓔ   18 Ⓐ Ⓑ Ⓒ Ⓓ Ⓔ   31 Ⓐ Ⓑ Ⓒ Ⓓ Ⓔ   44 Ⓐ Ⓑ Ⓒ Ⓓ Ⓔ   57 Ⓐ Ⓑ Ⓒ Ⓓ Ⓔ

6 Ⓐ Ⓑ Ⓒ Ⓓ Ⓔ   19 Ⓐ Ⓑ Ⓒ Ⓓ Ⓔ   32 Ⓐ Ⓑ Ⓒ Ⓓ Ⓔ   45 Ⓐ Ⓑ Ⓒ Ⓓ Ⓔ   58 Ⓐ Ⓑ Ⓒ Ⓓ Ⓔ

7 Ⓐ Ⓑ Ⓒ Ⓓ Ⓔ   20 Ⓐ Ⓑ Ⓒ Ⓓ Ⓔ   33 Ⓐ Ⓑ Ⓒ Ⓓ Ⓔ   46 Ⓐ Ⓑ Ⓒ Ⓓ Ⓔ   59 Ⓐ Ⓑ Ⓒ Ⓓ Ⓔ

8 Ⓐ Ⓑ Ⓒ Ⓓ Ⓔ   21 Ⓐ Ⓑ Ⓒ Ⓓ Ⓔ   34 Ⓐ Ⓑ Ⓒ Ⓓ Ⓔ   47 Ⓐ Ⓑ Ⓒ Ⓓ Ⓔ   60 Ⓐ Ⓑ Ⓒ Ⓓ Ⓔ

9 Ⓐ Ⓑ Ⓒ Ⓓ Ⓔ   22 Ⓐ Ⓑ Ⓒ Ⓓ Ⓔ   35 Ⓐ Ⓑ Ⓒ Ⓓ Ⓔ   48 Ⓐ Ⓑ Ⓒ Ⓓ Ⓔ   61 Ⓐ Ⓑ Ⓒ Ⓓ Ⓔ

10 Ⓐ Ⓑ Ⓒ Ⓓ Ⓔ   23 Ⓐ Ⓑ Ⓒ Ⓓ Ⓔ   36 Ⓐ Ⓑ Ⓒ Ⓓ Ⓔ   49 Ⓐ Ⓑ Ⓒ Ⓓ Ⓔ   62 Ⓐ Ⓑ Ⓒ Ⓓ Ⓔ

11 Ⓐ Ⓑ Ⓒ Ⓓ Ⓔ   24 Ⓐ Ⓑ Ⓒ Ⓓ Ⓔ   37 Ⓐ Ⓑ Ⓒ Ⓓ Ⓔ   50 Ⓐ Ⓑ Ⓒ Ⓓ Ⓔ   63 Ⓐ Ⓑ Ⓒ Ⓓ Ⓔ

12 Ⓐ Ⓑ Ⓒ Ⓓ Ⓔ   25 Ⓐ Ⓑ Ⓒ Ⓓ Ⓔ   38 Ⓐ Ⓑ Ⓒ Ⓓ Ⓔ   51 Ⓐ Ⓑ Ⓒ Ⓓ Ⓔ   64 Ⓐ Ⓑ Ⓒ Ⓓ Ⓔ

13 Ⓐ Ⓑ Ⓒ Ⓓ Ⓔ   26 Ⓐ Ⓑ Ⓒ Ⓓ Ⓔ   39 Ⓐ Ⓑ Ⓒ Ⓓ Ⓔ   52 Ⓐ Ⓑ Ⓒ Ⓓ Ⓔ   65 Ⓐ Ⓑ Ⓒ Ⓓ Ⓔ

SECTION 2: MATH ABILITY

1 Ⓐ Ⓑ Ⓒ Ⓓ Ⓔ   11 Ⓐ Ⓑ Ⓒ Ⓓ Ⓔ   21 Ⓐ Ⓑ Ⓒ Ⓓ Ⓔ   31 Ⓐ Ⓑ Ⓒ Ⓓ Ⓔ   41 Ⓐ Ⓑ Ⓒ Ⓓ Ⓔ

2 Ⓐ Ⓑ Ⓒ Ⓓ Ⓔ   12 Ⓐ Ⓑ Ⓒ Ⓓ Ⓔ   22 Ⓐ Ⓑ Ⓒ Ⓓ Ⓔ   32 Ⓐ Ⓑ Ⓒ Ⓓ Ⓔ   42 Ⓐ Ⓑ Ⓒ Ⓓ Ⓔ

3 Ⓐ Ⓑ Ⓒ Ⓓ Ⓔ   13 Ⓐ Ⓑ Ⓒ Ⓓ Ⓔ   23 Ⓐ Ⓑ Ⓒ Ⓓ Ⓔ   33 Ⓐ Ⓑ Ⓒ Ⓓ Ⓔ   43 Ⓐ Ⓑ Ⓒ Ⓓ Ⓔ

4 Ⓐ Ⓑ Ⓒ Ⓓ Ⓔ   14 Ⓐ Ⓑ Ⓒ Ⓓ Ⓔ   24 Ⓐ Ⓑ Ⓒ Ⓓ Ⓔ   34 Ⓐ Ⓑ Ⓒ Ⓓ Ⓔ   44 Ⓐ Ⓑ Ⓒ Ⓓ Ⓔ

5 Ⓐ Ⓑ Ⓒ Ⓓ Ⓔ   15 Ⓐ Ⓑ Ⓒ Ⓓ Ⓔ   25 Ⓐ Ⓑ Ⓒ Ⓓ Ⓔ   35 Ⓐ Ⓑ Ⓒ Ⓓ Ⓔ   45 Ⓐ Ⓑ Ⓒ Ⓓ Ⓔ

6 Ⓐ Ⓑ Ⓒ Ⓓ Ⓔ   16 Ⓐ Ⓑ Ⓒ Ⓓ Ⓔ   26 Ⓐ Ⓑ Ⓒ Ⓓ Ⓔ   36 Ⓐ Ⓑ Ⓒ Ⓓ Ⓔ   46 Ⓐ Ⓑ Ⓒ Ⓓ Ⓔ

7 Ⓐ Ⓑ Ⓒ Ⓓ Ⓔ   17 Ⓐ Ⓑ Ⓒ Ⓓ Ⓔ   27 Ⓐ Ⓑ Ⓒ Ⓓ Ⓔ   37 Ⓐ Ⓑ Ⓒ Ⓓ Ⓔ   47 Ⓐ Ⓑ Ⓒ Ⓓ Ⓔ

8 Ⓐ Ⓑ Ⓒ Ⓓ Ⓔ   18 Ⓐ Ⓑ Ⓒ Ⓓ Ⓔ   28 Ⓐ Ⓑ Ⓒ Ⓓ Ⓔ   38 Ⓐ Ⓑ Ⓒ Ⓓ Ⓔ   48 Ⓐ Ⓑ Ⓒ Ⓓ Ⓔ

9 Ⓐ Ⓑ Ⓒ Ⓓ Ⓔ   19 Ⓐ Ⓑ Ⓒ Ⓓ Ⓔ   29 Ⓐ Ⓑ Ⓒ Ⓓ Ⓔ   39 Ⓐ Ⓑ Ⓒ Ⓓ Ⓔ   49 Ⓐ Ⓑ Ⓒ Ⓓ Ⓔ

10 Ⓐ Ⓑ Ⓒ Ⓓ Ⓔ   20 Ⓐ Ⓑ Ⓒ Ⓓ Ⓔ   30 Ⓐ Ⓑ Ⓒ Ⓓ Ⓔ   40 Ⓐ Ⓑ Ⓒ Ⓓ Ⓔ   50 Ⓐ Ⓑ Ⓒ Ⓓ Ⓔ

PSAT Practice Test

SECTION 1   VERBAL ABILITY
50 MINUTES   65 QUESTIONS

For each question in this section, choose the best answer and blacken the corresponding space on the answer sheet.

Each question below consists of a word in capital letters, followed by five lettered words or phrases. Choose the word or phrase that is most nearly *opposite* in meaning to the word in capital letters. Since some of the questions require you to distinguish fine shades of meaning, consider all the choices before deciding which is best.

Example:

> GOOD: (A) sour (B) bad (C) red
> (D) hot (E) ugly
>
>   (A) ● (C) (D) (E)

1. CAPRICIOUS: (A) cautious (B) limp (C) worthless (D) steady (E) topless

2. ABSTEMIOUS: (A) reasonable (B) greedy (C) flowery (D) empty (E) soiled

3. CORROBORATE: (A) ripen (B) steal (C) remove (D) satisfy (E) undermine

4. DISPUTATIOUS: (A) agreeable (B) frank (C) spontaneous (D) flirtatious (E) distressed

5. DAUNT: (A) imitate (B) care (C) encourage (D) escape (E) display

6. EFFACE: (A) escape (B) change (C) rebuild (D) abandon (E) involve

7. EPHEMERAL: (A) proud (B) modern (C) realistic (D) masculine (E) permanent

8. FALLOW: (A) pure (B) seeded (C) familiar (D) advanced (E) misty

9. FRAUDULENT: (A) honest (B) sweet-smelling (C) exaggerated (D) childlike (E) timeless

10. RECALCITRANT: (A) commonly done (B) recently replaced (C) very dangerous (D) easily managed (E) completely relaxed

11. VILIFICATION: (A) generosity (B) success (C) heroism (D) repetition (E) praise

12. HILARITY: (A) immaturity (B) sadness (C) reliability (D) bravery (E) familiarity

13. IRASCIBLE: (A) even-tempered (B) ridiculous (C) convenient (D) old-fashioned (E) replaceable

14. PAUCITY: (A) dignity (B) urgency (C) abundance (D) preference (E) tenacity

15. PENURY: (A) loneliness (B) popularity (C) freedom (D) scholarship (E) wealth

16. RESCIND: (A) correct (B) enlighten (C) renew (D) move into (E) prepare for

17. SPURN: (A) accept (B) exceed (C) purify (D) solve (E) control

18. SUMPTUOUS: (A) selfish (B) annoying (C) cooperative (D) shoddy (E) loyal

19. TURBULENCE: (A) comfort (B) harmony (C) respect (D) cowardice (E) mildness

20. MITIGATE: (A) appear clear (B) continue uninterrupted (C) act less troublesome (D) make more severe (E) reduce tension

Each sentence in Questions 21–30 has one or two blanks, each blank indicating that something has been omitted. Beneath the sentence are five lettered words or sets of words. Choose the word or set of words that *best* fits the meaning of the sentence as a whole.

Example:

> Although its publicity has been ____, the film itself is intelligent, well-acted, handsomely produced, and altogether ____.
>
> (A) tasteless . . . respectable
> (B) extensive . . . moderate
> (C) sophisticated . . . amateur
> (D) risqué . . . crude
> (E) perfect . . . spectacular
>
> ● (B) (C) (D) (E)

21. The Prime Minister stated that Spain would ____ to its decision to bar United States jet fighters from Spanish soil, despite strong pressure from allies in behalf of our nation.

    (A) yield   (B) return   (C) refer
    (D) succumb   (E) adhere

22. Most of Hitler's actions have aroused ____ and condemnation, but few were as ____ as his policies of mass murder.

    (A) panic . . . sympathetic   (B) solitude . . . cruel   (C) relaxation . . . comforting
    (D) criticism . . . considerate   (E) disgust . . . abominable

23. Steffi Graf, the West German teenager, ____ her hold on the Number 1 ranking, indicating that she was considered the world's best female tennis player.

    (A) confined   (B) solidified   (C) gladdened
    (D) appreciated   (E) forfeited

24. The average income of physicians rose to $120,000 annually but consumer ____ called for more government controls on doctors' earnings.

    (A) advocates   (B) designers   (C) specialists
    (D) radiologists   (E) observers

25. After seven hours of listening to his ____ story-telling, we finally escaped from the ____ old man.

    (A) interminable . . . garrulous   (B) enchanting . . . boring   (C) glaring . . . forgetful
    (D) anticipatory . . . handsome   (E) documented . . . superstitious

26. Even though our math instructor is very ____, he has shown us that he is ____ in our getting a good grade.

    (A) polite . . . gradual   (B) tentative . . . bored
    (C) unfriendly . . . interested   (D) scarce . . . sincere   (E) convincing . . . conciliatory

27. An unarmed man was arrested by secret service officers after he ____ a White House fence and ran to the West Wing, where the President's office is situated.

    (A) painted   (B) spotted   (C) avoided
    (D) scaled   (E) measured

28. Volkswagen, the first foreign automobile company to build cars in the United States, has announced that because of ____ sales, it has decided to close several of its plants in the United States.

    (A) exclusive   (B) indescribable
    (C) astounding   (D) interesting   (E) sluggish

29. Van Gogh's painting "Irises," which was recently auctioned off for $53 million, failed to create ____ among several art critics when it was first shown in Paris a hundred years ago.

    (A) animosity   (B) disagreement
    (C) enthusiasm   (D) ambiguity
    (E) indifference

30. All of the efforts of the teachers will bring about no ____ changes in the scores of the students because the books and other ____ educational materials are not available.

    (A) impartial . . . worthwhile   (B) unique . . . reflected   (C) spiritual . . . inspiring
    (D) markéd . . . necessary   (E) effective . . . interrupted

Each question below consists of a related pair of words or phrases, followed by five lettered pairs of words or phrases. Select the lettered pair that *best* expresses a relationship similar to that expressed in the original pair.

Example:

YAWN : BOREDOM : :   (A) dream : sleep
(B) anger : madness   (C) smile : amusement
(D) face : expression   (E) impatience : rebellion

Ⓐ Ⓑ ● Ⓓ Ⓔ

31. SPILL : STAIN : :   (A) injure : scar   (B) retard : speed   (C) fall : water   (D) flee : persecution
    (E) win : reward

32. STAR : GALAXY : :   (A) sea : ocean   (B) planet : satellite   (C) sunshine : moonbeam   (D) shark : fish   (E) island : archipelago

33. MEAL : TASTELESS : :   (A) movie : exciting
    (B) view : pleasant   (C) job : frustrating
    (D) lesson : beneficial   (E) trip : interesting

34. IRRITATED : FURIOUS : :   (A) defeated : victorious   (B) rescued : regained   (C) saddened : discouraged   (D) damaged : destroyed
    (E) implicated : complicated

35. AMBITIOUS : INDOLENT : :   (A) active : successful   (B) reticent : outspoken   (C) amusing : laughable   (D) hesitant : wavering   (E) unwise : scattered

36. SLUGGISH : FATIGUE : :   (A) unhappy : wealth   (B) reasonable : fairness   (C) honored : bravery   (D) faithful : divorce   (E) delicate : tact

37. GOAL : OBSTACLE : :   (A) sport : race
    (B) attention : distraction   (C) football : hockey
    (D) ambition : failure   (E) winter : icicle

38. SPRINTER : SPEED : : (A) contest : winner
(B) track : field (C) leap : hurdler
(D) champion : challenger (E) weightlifter :
strength

39. EGG : SHELL : : (A) sardine : can (B) sword :
sheath (C) chicken : fish (D) seed : pod
(E) vegetable : animal

40. PIG : PORK : : (A) deer : venison (B) pen :
cage (C) tiger : stripe (D) cow : milk (E) whale
: blubber

41. INTERPRETER : TRANSLATE : : (A) native :
visit (B) foreigner : understand (C) language :
clarify (D) attorney : defend (E) arbitrator :
reconcile

42. TIGER : LION : : (A) horse : elephant
(B) rabbit : mouse (C) shark : whale
(D) hunting : jungle (E) orange : apple

43. MISER : CHARITY : : (A) pioneer : adventure
(B) miner : underground (C) explorer :
discovery (D) dictator : kindness (E) fisherman
: skill

44. APPROPRIATE : TAKE : : (A) cheer : exclaim
(B) refuse : accept (C) embrace : agree
(D) demand : request (E) excite : enjoy

45. SCHOLAR : RESEARCH : : (A) daydreamer :
fantasy (B) teacher : pupil (C) musician :
concert (D) businessman : travel (E) education :
accomplishment

Each passage below is followed by questions based on its content. Answer all questions following a
passage on the basis of what is *stated* or *implied* in that passage.

My father worked for a newspaper so we often heard
the big news before it was on the radio or in the papers.
There were two calls in a single year from my father in his
office that I remember most—the first on April 12,
5 1945, which brought about my mother's crying because
FDR was dead. How could we manage without him?
There was another call in late October of that year.
This time there was no crying. If FDR had been "our
president," then the Brooklyn Dodgers were "our team,"
10 and they had just done a momentous thing: They had
signed a Negro, as we said in those days, and his name
was Jackie Robinson.
We were a white family in an all-white neighborhood
in Long Island. My father brought home rumors that
15 some Dodgers did not want to play on the same team
with Robinson. It was seven years before the Supreme
Court ordered the schools integrated, years before black
people could share restaurants, buses, and depots with
whites, years before Martin Luther King, Jr., marched
20 and dreamed. On that chilly day, Jack Roosevelt
Robinson was marching alone.
Jackie Robinson became the first—the first black
ballplayer in the major leagues. For the first time in the
history of organized baseball a black received a chance
25 to make good—and he converted his opportunity into a
brilliant personal triumph as one of the greatest baseball
players of all time. He was not one of those people who
had a lot of rage. But his anger could be provoked if he
thought that there was an injustice. It was a struggle for
30 him every day. He frequently heard insults shouted
across the field. Some of his own teammates refused to
talk to him. Opposing players flung racial barbs at him.
He was educated, articulate, and intelligent. A man of
character! When Robinson shed the meek role that he
35 had demonstrated in his rookie season, even when he
began to be pictured as a "troublemaker" for complaining about segregation, he was respected more and more.
It may well be that Jackie Robinson, a baseball player,
did more to win equal treatment for black people in this
40 country than anyone else.

46. The expression "our president" (lines 8–9) has
quotation marks because the author

(A) felt that FDR was, in a sense, helping the
author's family
(B) and his family were loyal to their country
(C) and his parents had probably met or spoken
to FDR
(D) was following the custom of referring to an
elected official with the use of the possessive
"our"
(E) people in other parts of the world would
probably read the article

47. The primary focus of the passage is on

(A) the continued willingness of a member of a
minority group to accept segregation
(B) the discouraging effect that racial bias has on
most talented black people
(C) the tremendous importance of the courage
and ability of one person in bringing about a
better life for millions of people
(D) the deserved punishment that people who are
undemocratic and unfair are bound to suffer
(E) the assistance of white persons in helping a
great black baseball player to achieve success

48. Robinson was "marching alone" (line 21) because
he was

(A) practicing for a parade in which he would
participate
(B) disliked by some of his teammates
(C) inclined to be a loner with very few friends
(D) opposed to the principles that Martin Luther
King, Jr., stood for
(E) in the habit of taking brisk walks early in the
morning

On the basis of their relation to man, insects may be classified into two general groups, beneficial and injurious. Many insects may be considered neutral because their numbers are so small or their habits are such that
5 no direct effects are felt by man.

Man benefits from insects in many ways; without them, human society could not exist in its present form. Without the pollinating services of bees and other insects, we would have few vegetables, few fruits, little or
10 no clover and much less beef and wool, no coffee, no tobacco, few flowers—in fact, we would not have a great many of the things that are an integral part of our domestic economy and civilization. Insects provide us with a great many other useful products. Many species are par-
15 asitic or predatory and are important in keeping the pest species under control; others help in the control of noxious weeds; and still others clean up refuse and make the world a little more pleasant. Insects are the sole or major item of food of many birds, fish, and other animals (in-
20 cluding man in some parts of the world). Some species have been used in the treatment of certain diseases. The study of insects has helped scientists solve many problems in heredity, evolution, sociology, stream pollution, and other fields. Insects also have aesthetic value; art-
25 ists, milliners, and designers have made use of their beauty, and many people derive a great deal of pleasure from the study of insects as a hobby.

On the other hand, many insects are obnoxious or destructive. They attack various growing plants, including
30 plants of value to man, and feed on them, injure or kill them, or introduce disease into them. They attack man's possessions, including his home, his clothing, and his food stores, and destroy, damage, or contaminate them. They attack man and animals and are annoying because
35 of their presence, odors, bites, or stings, and many are agents in the transmission of some of the most serious diseases that beset man and animals.

Most people are much more aware of the injurious insects and their effects than they are of the beneficial in-
40 sects, and the injurious species are probably better known than the beneficial ones. In spite of the excessive attention paid to injurious insects by the public in general and entomologists in particular, we believe that the good done by the beneficial insects outweighs the harm
45 done by the injurious ones.

49. Which of the following would be the most appropriate title for the passage?

(A) Insects Are Good to Eat
(B) If You Don't Like Insects, Avoid Them
(C) Some People Behave Like Insects
(D) Human Beings Need Insects
(E) The Relation of Insects to Man

50. The author's attitude to insects generally is

(A) favorable
(B) fearful
(C) negative
(D) impartial
(E) uncertain

51. The author believes that scientists who specialize in insect life

(A) should choose another scientific field that will benefit humanity more
(B) are more interested in winged insects than those which crawl
(C) spend too much of their time studying the harmful effects of insects
(D) are able to find out about human behavior by watching insects
(E) are likely to make better physicians than those doctors who have not worked with insects

52. It can be inferred from the passage that

(A) spraying chemicals on fruit to kill insects is inadvisable
(B) very few people are interested in insect life
(C) some artists draw only insects
(D) some people enjoy eating insects
(E) it is possible to estimate the financial value of insects to man

There has never been a just war, never an honorable one—on the part of the instigator of the war. I can see a million years ahead, and this rule will never change in so many as a half dozen instances. The loud little handful—as usual—will shout for the war. The pulpit 5 will—warily and cautiously—object—at first; the great, big, dull bulk of the nation will rub its sleepy eyes and try to make out why there should be a war, and will say, earnestly and indignantly, "It is unjust and dishonorable, and there is no necessity for it." Then the handful will 10 shout louder. A few fair men on the other side will argue and reason against the war with speech and pen, and at first will have a hearing and be applauded; but it will not last long; those others will outshout them, and presently the anti-war audiences will thin out and lose popularity. 15 Before long you will see this curious thing: the speakers stoned from the platform, and free speech strangled by hordes of furious men who in their secret hearts are still at one with those stoned speakers—as earlier—but do not dare to say so. And now the whole nation—pulpit 20 and all—will take up the war-cry, and shout itself hoarse, and mob any honest man who ventures to open his mouth; and presently such mouths will cease to open. Next the statesmen will invent cheap lies, putting the blame upon the nation that is attacked, and every man 25 will be glad of these conscience-soothing falsities, and will diligently study them, and refuse to examine any refutations of them; and thus he will by and by convince himself that the war is just and will thank God for the better sleep he enjoys after this process of grotesque 30 self-deception.

—Mark Twain

53. The author suggests that pro-war people prevail because of their ability to

(A) reason persuasively
(B) attract financial support
(C) appeal to emotions
(D) drown out the opposition
(E) pray fervently

54. The passage implies that anti-war speakers are "stoned from the platform" (line 17) because they

(A) are poor communicators
(B) lack courageous supporters
(C) fail to use logic
(D) are unpatriotic
(E) are drug addicts

55. In line 18, the expression "secret hearts" suggests that the "furious men" are

(A) hypocritical
(B) disloyal
(C) angry
(D) mysterious
(E) shy

56. According to the passage, the common man is able to sleep well because he

(A) feels safe
(B) is unconcerned
(C) deludes himself
(D) has religious faith
(E) takes medication

57. The author's main purpose in writing this passage most likely is to

(A) analyze the motives for war
(B) advise a nation not to bear arms
(C) warn the nation about the impending war
(D) explain the basis of a just war
(E) berate the nation that starts a war

Among those at the social gathering was a lawyer, a young man of about twenty-five. On being asked his opinion, he said:

"Capital punishment and life-imprisonment are
5 equally immoral; but if I were offered the choice between them, I would certainly choose the second. It's better to live somehow than not to live at all."

There ensued a lively discussion. The banker who was then younger and more nervous suddenly lost his tem-
10 per, banged his fist on the table, and turning to the young lawyer, cried out:

"It's a lie. I bet you a million dollars that you wouldn't stick in a cell even for one year."

"If you mean it seriously," replied the lawyer, "then I
15 bet I'll stay not one but fifteen."

"Fifteen! Done!" cried the banker. "Gentlemen, I stake fifteen millions."

"Agreed. You stake fifteen millions, I my freedom," said the lawyer.

So this wild, ridiculous bet came to pass. The banker, 20 who at that time had too many millions to count, spoiled and capricious, was beside himself with rapture. During supper he said to the lawyer jokingly:

"Come to your senses, young man, before it's too late. Fifteen millions are nothing to me, but you stand to lose 25 three or four of the best years of your life. I say three or four, because you'll never stick it out any longer. Don't forget either, you unhappy man, that voluntary is much heavier than enforced imprisonment. The idea that you have the right to free yourself any moment will poison 30 the whole of your life in the cell. I pity you."

And now the banker, pacing from corner to corner, recalled all this and asked himself:

"Why did I make this bet? What's the good? The lawyer loses fifteen years of his life and I throw away fifteen 35 millions. Will it convince people that capital punishment is worse or better than imprisonment for life? No, no! all stuff and rubbish. On my part, it was the caprice of a well-fed man; on the lawyer's, pure greed of gold."

58. The interest of this selection is, for the most part, attributable to

(A) the well-developed dialogue forming the plot of the story
(B) the skill of the writer in creating a mood of mystery
(C) the many leading questions that are asked throughout the selection
(D) the large sum of money that the banker has been willing to risk
(E) the writer's power of character portrayal

59. The word "capricious" (line 22) refers to a person who

(A) is conceited to the point that he believes no one is worthy of his company
(B) is commercial even in his dealings with friends
(C) hardly ever takes time out for recreation and relaxation
(D) lives as his fancy dictates
(E) has a desire to be the center of attention

60. We may infer from the passage that the lawyer was eager to make the bet primarily

(A) to teach the banker a lesson
(B) to win fifteen million dollars
(C) because he was strongly opposed to punishment
(D) because he enjoyed being indoors for long periods of time
(E) to make the banker feel inferior

Let's be honest right at the start. Physics is neither particularly easy to comprehend nor easy to love, but then again, *what*—or for that matter, *who*—is? For most of us it is a new vision, a different way of understanding
5 with its own scales, rhythms, and forms. And yet, as with *Macbeth, Mona Lisa,* or *La Traviata,* physics has its rewards. Surely you have already somehow prejudged this science. It's all too easy to compartmentalize our human experience: science in one box, music, art, and literature
10 in other boxes.

The Western mind delights in little boxes—life is easier to analyze when it's presented in small pieces in small compartments (we call it specialization). It is our traditional way of seeing the trees and missing the forest. The
15 label on the box for physics too often reads "Caution: Not for Common Consumption" or "Free from Sentiment." If you can, please tear off that label and discard the box or we will certainly, sooner or later, bore each other to death. There is nothing more tedious than the
20 endless debate between humanist and scientist on whose vision is truer; each of us is less for what we lack of the other.

It is pointless and even worse to separate physics from the body of all creative work, to pluck it out from
25 history, to shear it from philosophy, and then to present it pristine pure, all-knowing, and infallible. We know nothing of what will be with absolute certainty. There is no scientific tome of unassailable, immutable truth. Yet what little we do know about physics reveals an inspiring
30 grandeur and intricate beauty.

61. In line 14, the phrase "seeing the trees and missing the forest" means

(A) putting experiences into categories
(B) viewing the world too narrowly
(C) analyzing scientific discoveries
(D) making judgments too hastily
(E) ignoring the beauty of natural surroundings

62. According to the author, what does the label on the box for physics suggest about physics?

(A) It is a dangerous area of study.
(B) It is a cause for great excitement.
(C) It is uninteresting and pointless.
(D) It is too scholarly for the ordinary person.
(E) It is a subject that should be elective but not required.

63. What statement does the author make about physics?

(A) It should be recognized for its unique beauty.
(B) It is a boring course of study.
(C) It appeals only to the Western mind.
(D) It is superior to music, art, and literature.
(E) It is unpopular with people who are romantic.

64. What is the main idea of this passage?

(A) Scientists contribute more to mankind than do humanists.
(B) The Western mind is more precise than other minds.
(C) Complete vision needs both the scientist and the humanist.
(D) Humanists and scientists share no common ground.
(E) Physics is as important as other sciences.

65. In which manner does the author of this passage address his audience?

(A) affectionately
(B) arrogantly
(C) humorously
(D) cynically
(E) frankly

S T O P

IF YOU FINISH BEFORE TIME IS CALLED, YOU MAY CHECK YOUR WORK ON
THIS SECTION ONLY.
DO NOT WORK ON THE OTHER SECTION IN THE TEST.

SECTION 2   MATH ABILITY
50 MINUTES   50 QUESTIONS

In this section solve each problem, using any available space on the page for scratchwork. Then decide which is the best of the choices given and blacken the corresponding space on the answer sheet.

The following information is for your reference in solving some of the problems.

Circle of radius r: Area = πr^2; Circumference = $2\pi r$
The number of degrees of arc in a circle is 360.
The measure in degrees of a straight angle is 180.

Definitions of symbols:
=	is equal to
≠	is unequal to
<	is less than
>	is greater than

≦	is less than or equal to
≧	is greater than or equal to
‖	is parallel to
⊥	is perpendicular to

Triangle: The sum of the measure in degrees of the angles of a triangle is 180.
If $\angle CDA$ is a right angle, then

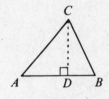

(1) area of $\triangle ABC = \dfrac{AB \times CD}{2}$

(2) $AC^2 = AD^2 + DC^2$

Note: Figures which accompany problems in this test are intended to provide information useful in solving the problems. They are drawn as accurately as possible EXCEPT when it is stated in a specific problem that its figure is not drawn to scale. All figures lie in a plane unless otherwise indicated. All numbers used are real numbers.

---

1. Which of the following is the closest approximation to 1.7999?

   (A) 2.00   (B) 1.80   (C) 1.79   (D) 1.78
   (E) 1.70

2. What is $\frac{1}{4}$ of the perimeter of a triangle if $\frac{2}{3}$ of its perimeter is 8?

   (A) 2   (B) 3   (C) 6   (D) 10   (E) 12

3. Every time they sit together in the same row of chairs Bill always sits next to Carrie but never next to Roni. Kristin always sits next to Bill. Which of the following could be a seating arrangement?

   (A) Bill, Carrie, Roni, Kristin   (B) Bill, Carrie, Kristin, Roni   (C) Roni, Carrie, Bill, Kristin (D) Roni, Bill, Carrie, Kristin   (E) Carrie, Bill, Roni, Kristin

4. If $y = 4$ is one solution of the equation $2y^2 + by - 4 = 0$, then find the value of b.

   (A) −7   (B) −4   (C) 2   (D) 4   (E) 7

5. If $y^2 - 8 = 17$, find $(y - 5)(y + 4)(y + 5)$.

   (A) 0   (B) 5   (C) 10   (D) 15   (E) 20

6. A drill on an assembly line works at a constant rate and drills 2,200 holes every 5 hours. At the same rate, how many hours will it take to drill 11,000 holes?

   (A) 20   (B) 25   (C) 30   (D) 35   (E) 40

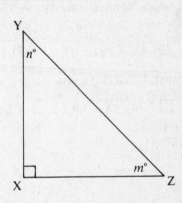

7. If m and n are integers in right triangle XYZ above, what is the greatest possible difference in values between m and n?

   (A) 179   (B) 178   (C) 89   (D) 88   (E) 1

8. For any number y, let its "counterpart" be $14-y$. What number y is equal to its counterpart?

   (A) 0   (B) 2   (C) 7   (D) 10   (E) 14

9. If m and n are positive integers less than 9, which of the following does *not* have to equal a number between 8 and 90?

   (A) $m + n + 9$ (B) $10m + n$ (C) $10n + m$
   (D) $10m + 10n$ (E) $m + n + 40$

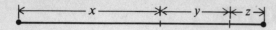

10. If $\frac{x}{2} = y$, $\frac{y}{2} = z$, and $z = 4$ in the figure above, find the value of $x + y + z$.

(A) $2\frac{1}{4}$ (B) $4\frac{1}{2}$ (C) 9   (D) 18   (E) 28

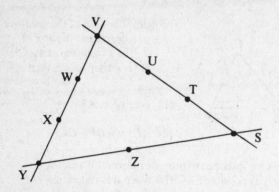

11. The three lines in the figure above contain eight lettered points as shown. How many new lines can be drawn which connect exactly two of the eight points?

(A) 7   (B) 9   (C) 11   (D) 13   (E) 14

12. If $x \div y = \square$, find $(3x) \div (4y)$.

(A) 12 $\square$ (B) 4 $\square$ (C) 3 $\square$ (D) $\frac{4}{3}$ $\square$

(E) $\frac{3}{4}$ $\square$

13. Of a group of 28 teachers, $\frac{3}{4}$ are women, and $\frac{1}{3}$ of these women are married. How many women in the group are married?

(A) 4   (B) 7   (C) 10   (D) 14   (E) 21

14. If a circle and a square intersect, what is the greatest possible number of intersection points?

(A) 4   (B) 7   (C) 8   (D) 9   (E) 10

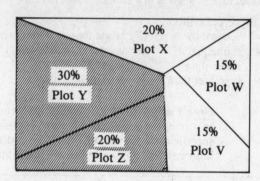

15. The figure above represents a rectangular piece of land divided into 5 plots. If the shaded plots indicate the swampy area of the land, what percent of the swampy area is Plot Z?

(A) 15%   (B) 20%   (C) 25%   (D) 40%
(E) 50%

Questions 16-32 each consist of two quantities, one in Column A and one in Column B. You are to compare the two quantities and on the answer sheet blacken space

    A if the quantity in Column A is greater;
    B if the quantity in Column B is greater;
    C if the two quantities are equal;
    D if the relationship cannot be determined from the information given.

Notes: 1. In certain questions, information concerning one or both of the quantities to be compared is centered above the columns.
        2. In a given question, a symbol that appears in both columns represents the same thing in Column A as it does in Column B.
        3. Letters such as x, n, and k stand for real numbers.

	EXAMPLES			
	Column A	Column B		Answers
E1.	2×6	$2 + 6$		● Ⓑ Ⓒ Ⓓ
E2.	$180 - x$	y		Ⓐ Ⓑ ● Ⓓ
E3.	$p - q$	$q - p$		Ⓐ Ⓑ Ⓒ ●

For E2 figure: angles $x°$ and $y°$ shown along a straight line.

	Column A	Column B
16.	$\dfrac{8}{13}$	$\dfrac{\frac{8}{13}}{\frac{8}{13}}$

$$y \neq 0$$

	Column A	Column B
17.	y	-4
18.	$3 + 3 + 3$	3^3
19.	$3(34 - 4)$	90

20. Line segment EF has its end points on a circle. A radius of the circle intersects EF at only point G, and the center of the circle is point D.

	Length of EG	Length of GF

	Column A	Column B
21.	25% of 90	$\frac{1}{2}$ of 45

	Column A	Column B
22.	1000 grams = 1 kilogram	

	Number of kilograms equal to 100,000 grams	100

	Column A	Column B
23.	$(3 + y)\,7$	$7y + 3$

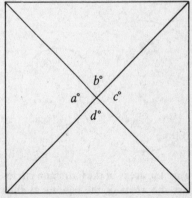

Note: Figure is not drawn to scale.

24. $c < d$

	Column A	Column B
	$a + b + c$	$b + c + d$

SUMMARY DIRECTIONS FOR COMPARISON QUESTIONS

Answer: A if the quantity in Column A is greater;
B if the quantity in Column B is greater;
C if the two quantities are equal;
D if the relationship cannot be determined from the information given.

Column A	Column B

25. $8 + 8n$ $9n$

26. The volume of a cone with radius r and height h is found by the formula $V = \frac{1}{3}\pi r^2 h$.

Volume of a cone with radius 6 and height 3   Volume of a cone with radius 3 and height 6

27. The average (arithmetic mean) of 10 consecutive negative multiples of 2   The average (arithmetic mean) of 10 consecutive negative multiples of 3

28. $(y - 4)^2 > 0$

y 4

29. Two dice each have faces numbered 1 through 6. When the dice are rolled at the same time, M is the probability that the sum of the two numbers rolled will be greater than 9, and N is the probability that the sum will be less than 4.

M N

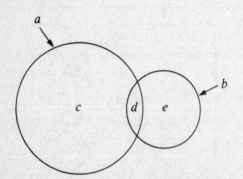

30. a and b are the areas of the indicated circles, and $c, d,$ and e are the areas of the regions as shown above. *Note: c, d,* and *e* do not overlap.

$2d$ $a + b - c - e$

Column A	Column B

31. $\dfrac{a}{b} = \dfrac{2}{3}$ and $\dfrac{b}{c} = \dfrac{5}{8}$

$\dfrac{a}{c}$ $\dfrac{5}{6}$

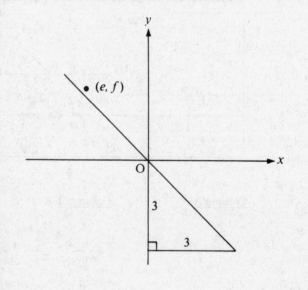

32. e^2 f^2

Solve each of the remaining problems in this section by using any available space for scratchwork. Then decide which is the best of the choices given and blacken the corresponding space on the answer sheet.

33. If $x - 3y \neq 0$, then $\dfrac{x(x-3y)}{6} \cdot \dfrac{3}{x-3y} =$

(A) $\dfrac{x}{2}$ (B) $\dfrac{x-3y}{3}$ (C) $\dfrac{x}{18}(x-3y)^2$

(D) $2x$ (E) $\dfrac{3}{x-3y}$

34. If each side of one square is of length 5, and each side of the other square is of length 2, what is the sum of the perimeters of the two squares?

(A) 8   (B) 15   (C) 25   (D) 27   (E) 28

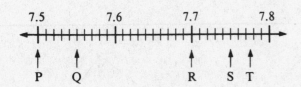

35. The figure above indicates that the arrow pointing to $7\dfrac{3}{4}$ is

(A) P   (B) Q   (C) R   (D) S   (E) T

36. By babysitting, Carol earned \$15, Ann earned $\dfrac{4}{3}$ the amount Carol did, and Nancy earned three times what Ann earned. What is the ratio of Carol's earnings to Nancy's?

(A) 1:4   (B) 1:3   (C) 1:2   (D) 2:3   (E) 4:3

37. Jazz represents $\dfrac{1}{9}$ of the total selection at a certain record store. If the total selection of the store is shown on a pie graph, what is the measure of the central angle of the graphed section representing jazz?

(A) 30°   (B) 40°   (C) 50°   (D) 60°   (E) 90°

38. Square WXYZ and line ℓ lie in the same plane. If $\ell \perp$ WX and ℓ bisects WX, how many right angles are created by the intersections of ℓ with the square?

(A) 2   (B) 4   (C) 6   (D) 8   (E) 9

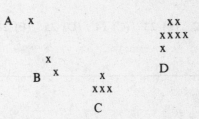

39. A, B, C, D, E, and F are children who are playing with jacks. If 36 jacks have been given out in accordance with the figure above, what is the least number of jacks that must be distributed so that each child will have the same number of jacks?

(A) 7   (B) 10   (C) 11   (D) 14   (E) 16

40. If the volume of a cube is equal to $27x^{27}$, then the length of each edge of the cube in terms of x is equal to

(A) $9x^9$ (B) $3x^9$ (C) $9x^3$ (D) $3x^3$ (E) $3x^{27}$

41. Which of the following is (are) always evenly divisible by 8?

I. The sum of three even numbers
II. The average (arithmetic mean) of three even numbers
III. The cube of an even number

(A) I only   (B) II only   (C) III only
(D) II and III only   (E) None

Questions 42–43 refer to the following chart of the watering of three plants.

WATERING PATTERNS FOR EIGHT DAYS

Plant	DAY*							
	1	2	3	4	5	6	7	8
U	Y	N	Y	N	Y	N	Y	N
V	Y	Y	Y	N	Y	N	N	N
W	N	Y	N	Y	N	Y	N	Y

*Assume these watering patterns repeat for at least 80 days. "Y" signifies that a plant was watered that day.

42. How many times would plant V be watered in the first 44 days?

(A) 22 (B) 23 (C) 24 (D) 25 (E) 28

43. During which of the first 80 days would all three plants be watered?

(A) 9th (B) 13th (C) 16th (D) 24th
(E) None

---

44. $5(5^x) + 5^x =$

(A) 5 (B) 5^x (C) 30^x (D) $6(5^x)$ (E) $5(6^x)$

45. Let y equal an integer. If $\frac{1}{4}$ is subtracted from the division of y by 4, and the result is then multiplied by 4 to yield a product P, what is y in terms of P?

(A) $P + 4$ (B) $P + 1$ (C) $P + \frac{1}{2}$ (D) $4P$
(E) None of the above

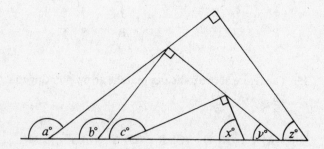

47. If $x + y + z = 150$ in the figure above, then find $a + b + c$.

(A) 320 (B) 360 (C) 385 (D) 420 (E) 450

46. $\sqrt{\dfrac{16}{25} + \dfrac{9}{4}} =$

(A) $\dfrac{7}{10}$ (B) $\dfrac{5\sqrt{29}}{29}$ (C) $\dfrac{36}{25}$

(D) $\dfrac{23}{10}$ (E) $\dfrac{17}{10}$

48. The operation ☆ is defined for all real numbers r and s by the equation $r ☆ s = rs^3$. Which of the following always makes $r ☆ s = s ☆ r$?

 I. $r \neq s$
 II. $r^2 = s^2$
 III. $r = 9, s = 0$

(A) I only (B) II only (C) III only
(D) II and III only (E) I, II, and III

49. The cost of a items is d dollars, and each item has the same price. How many dollars would b of these items cost?

(A) $\dfrac{bd}{a}$ (B) $\dfrac{ba}{d}$ (C) $\dfrac{ad}{b}$ (D) $\dfrac{a}{bd}$

(E) $\dfrac{d}{ab}$

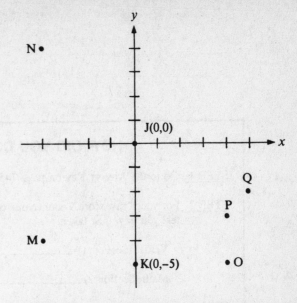

50. Points J and K are vertices of triangle JKL, which is not shown. Which of the following could *not* be the vertex of L if the area of triangle JKL is 10?

(A) M (B) N (C) O (D) P (E) Q

S T O P

IF YOU FINISH BEFORE TIME IS CALLED, YOU MAY CHECK YOUR WORK ON
THIS SECTION ONLY.
DO NOT WORK ON THE OTHER SECTION IN THE TEST.

HOW DID YOU DO ON THIS TEST?

STEP 1. Go to the Answer Key on page 745.

STEP 2. For your "raw score," count your correct answers in each of the test parts of the test you have just taken:

Verbal (Section 1) _____.

Math (Section 2) _____.

STEP 3. Refer to the "Self-Appraisal Chart" below.

THERE'S ALWAYS ROOM FOR IMPROVEMENT!

CHART FOR SELF-APPRAISAL BASED ON
THE PSAT PRACTICE TEST YOU HAVE JUST TAKEN

The Self-Appraisal Chart below tells you quickly where your PSAT strengths and weaknesses lie. Check or circle the appropriate box in accordance with the number of your correct answers for each area of the Practice Test you have just taken.

	20 Antonyms	15 Analogies	10 Sentence Completions	20 Reading Comprehension	50 Math Questions
EXCELLENT	17–20	13–15	9–10	17–20	42–50
GOOD	13–16	10–12	8–9	13–16	32–41
FAIR	9–12	7–9	5–7	9–12	20–31
POOR	5–8	4–6	3–4	5–8	10–19
VERY POOR	0–4	0–3	0–2	0–4	0–9

ANSWER KEY FOR PSAT PRACTICE TEST

Section 1—Verbal

1. D	11. E	21. E	31. A	41. E	51. C	61. B
2. B	12. B	22. E	32. E	42. B	52. D	62. C
3. E	13. A	23. B	33. C	43. D	53. D	63. A
4. A	14. C	24. A	34. D	44. C	54. B	64. C
5. C	15. E	25. A	35. B	45. A	55. A	65. E
6. C	16. C	26. C	36. C	46. A	56. C	
7. E	17. A	27. D	37. B	47. C	57. E	
8. B	18. D	28. E	38. E	48. B	58. A	
9. A	19. B	29. C	39. D	49. E	59. D	
10. D	20. D	30. D	40. A	50. A	60. B	

Section 2—Math

1. B	9. D	17. D	25. D	33. A	41. C	49. A
2. B	10. E	18. B	26. A	34. E	42. B	50. E
3. C	11. D	19. C	27. D	35. D	43. E	
4. A	12. E	20. D	28. D	36. A	44. D	
5. A	13. B	21. C	29. A	37. B	45. B	
6. B	14. C	22. C	30. C	38. D	46. E	
7. C	15. D	23. A	31. B	39. C	47. D	
8. C	16. B	24. B	32. B	40. B	48. D	

EXPLANATORY ANSWERS FOR PSAT PRACTICE TEST

Section 1: Verbal Ability

As you read these Explanatory Answers, you are advised to refer to "Using Critical Thinking Skills in Verbal Questions" (beginning on page 89) whenever a specific Strategy is referred to in the answer. Of particular importance are the following Master Verbal Strategies:

Sentence Completion Master Strategy 1—page 93.
Sentence Completion Master Strategy 2—page 94.
Analogies Master Strategy 1—page 89.
Antonyms Master Strategy 1—page 98.
Reading Comprehension Master Strategy 2—page 105

1. **(D)** Choice D is correct. *Capricious* means *erratic; whimsical*. The opposite of *capricious* is *steady*.

2. **(B)** Choice B is correct. *Abstemious* means *sparing; abstaining; moderate*. The opposite of *abstemious* is *greedy*.

3. **(E)** Choice E is correct. *Corroborate* means *support; strengthen; verify*. The opposite of *corroborate* is *undermine; weaken*.

4. **(A)** Choice A is correct. *Disputatious* means *argumentative; contentious*. The opposite of *disputatious* is *agreeable*.

5. **(C)** Choice C is correct. *Daunt* means *overcome with fear; intimidate*. The opposite of *daunt* is *encourage*.

6. **(C)** Choice C is correct. *Efface* means *wipe out; destroy*. The opposite of *efface* is *rebuild*.

7. **(E)** Choice E is correct. *Ephemeral* means *short-lived; brief; transient*. The opposite of *ephemeral* is *permanent*.

8. **(B)** Choice B is correct. *Fallow* refers to land which is *unseeded* or *uncultivated*. The opposite of *fallow* is *seeded* or *cultivated*.

9. **(A)** Choice A is correct. *Fraudulent* means *dishonest; cheating*. The opposite of *fraudulent* is *honest*.

10. **(D)** Choice D is correct. *Recalcitrant* means *resisting authority; not obedient; rebellious*. The opposite of *recalcitrant* is *easily managed*.

11. **(E)** Choice E is correct. *Vilification* means *slander; defaming; speaking ill of*. The opposite of *vilification* is *praise*.

12. **(B)** Choice B is correct. *Hilarity* means *boisterous gaiety; cheerfulness*. The opposite of *hilarity* is *sadness*.

13. **(A)** Choice A is correct. *Irascible* means *irritable; easily provoked to anger*. The opposite of *irascible* is *even-tempered*.

14. **(C)** Choice C is correct. *Paucity* means *scarcity; scantiness; insufficiency*. The opposite of *paucity* is *abundance*.

15. **(E)** Choice E is correct. *Penury* means *extreme poverty; destitution*. The opposite of *penury* is *wealth*.

16. **(C)** Choice C is correct. *Rescind* means *revoke; nullify; withdraw*. The opposite of *rescind* is *renew*.

17. **(A)** Choice A is correct. *Spurn* means *reject; scorn; despise*. The opposite of *spurn* is *accept*.

18. **(D)** Choice D is correct. *Sumptuous* means *luxurious; costly; entailing great expense*. The opposite of *sumptuous* is *shoddy; inferior*.

19. **(B)** Choice B is correct. *Turbulence* means *violent disorder; tumult; agitation*. The opposite of *turbulence* is *harmony*.

20. **(D)** Choice D is correct. *Mitigate* means *make less severe; become milder*. The opposite of *mitigate* is *make more severe*.

21. **(E)** Choice E is correct. See **Sentence Completion Strategy 4**. Note that the last part of the sentence contains an *opposition indicator* ("despite"). The word "adhere" in Choice E means "to stick" or "to cling." The Prime Minister's decision is in opposition to what the United States and its allies desire—that is, continuing to have United States jet fighters on Spanish soil. Also see **Sentence Completion Strategy 1**. Choices A, B, C, and D are incorrect because they do not contain the opposition idea expressed in the sentence.

22. **(E)** Choice E is correct. By using **Sentence Completion Strategy 2** we can eliminate Choice (B), "solitude ..." and Choice (C) "relaxation ..." because Hitler's actions could not have aroused either solitude or relaxation. Let us now consider the other three choices. The two words in Choice (E), "disgust ... abominable," make good sentence sense because Hitler's policies of mass murder were certainly abominable. Therefore, Choice E is correct. Choices A and D are incorrect because Hitler's policies of mass murder were certainly not sympathetic or considerate.

23. **(B)** Choice B is correct. See **Sentence Completion Strategy 1.** The word "solidified" means "strengthened," which makes good sense in this sentence. The other choices do not fit into the context of the sentence. See **Sentence Completion Strategy 1.**

24. **(A)** Choice A is correct. See **Sentence Completion Strategy 1.** The word "advocates"—as a noun —means "defenders" or "protectors." The consumer advocates are obviously defenders or protectors of the patients whom the doctors treat. Choices C and D are clearly incorrect because specialists and radiologists are themselves physicians. Choices B and E are incorrect because they are not pertinent.

25. **(A)** Choice A is correct. **Sentence Completion Strategy 2** will lead us to eliminate Choice (C) glaring ... and Choice (D) anticipatory ... because the story-telling could hardly be glaring or anticipatory. Now we shall consider the other 3 choices. The pair of words in Choice (A), interminable ... garrulous, gives us a logical example of cause and effect. The word pair in Choice (B) creates a contradiction in the sentence. So Choice B is incorrect. Choice (E), documented ... superstitious, simply tells us that the story-telling was documented and that the old man was superstitious. These facts do not explain why "we finally escaped from the old man." Therefore, Choice E is incorrect.

26. **(C)** Choice C is correct. See **Sentence Completion Strategy 2,** which refers to 2-blank questions. We may first eliminate Choice (B) tentative ... and Choice (D) scarce ... because it does not make sense to say that the math instructor is either "tentative" or "scarce." Before we go on to the other choices, refer to **Sentence Completion Strategy 4.** Note that we have an *opposition* situation here because of the "Even though" words which begin the sentence. Choices A and E do not make sense because the "polite" math instructor is not "gradual" and the "convincing" math instructor is not "conciliatory" in line with our *opposition* requirement. Choice C is the only correct choice because it makes sense to say that the math instructor, though "unfriendly," is "interested" in his students' getting a good grade.

27. **(D)** Choice D is correct. In the sentence, the word "scaled" is a verb which means to climb up or over. See **Sentence Completion Strategy 1.** The other choices do not make good sense for the sentence as it stands.

28. **(E)** Choice E is correct. See **Sentence Completion Strategy 1.** The word "sluggish" means "moving slowly," which completes the sentence satisfactorily. The other four choices do not fit into the context of the sentence.

29. **(C)** Choice C is correct. See **Sentence Completion Strategy 1.** The word "enthusiasm" (Choice C) makes good sense in the sentence because the painting sold for $53 million recently, and yet it was not appreciated wholeheartedly a hundred years ago.

30. **(D)** Choice D is correct. See **Sentence Completion Strategy 2.** Let us first eliminate Choices (A) impartial ... and (C) spiritual ... because we do not speak of "impartial" or "spiritual" changes. Now note that we have a *result* situation here as indicated by the presence of the conjunction "because" in the sentence. Choices B and E do not make sense because "unique" changes have nothing to do with "reflected" educational materials and "effective" changes have nothing to do with "interrupted" educational materials. Choices B and E certainly do not meet the *result* requirement. See **Sentence Completion Strategy 4.** Choice D is the only correct choice because it makes sense to say that there will be no "marked" changes in the scores because the books and other "necessary" educational materials are not available.

(Result relationship)

31. **(A)** Choice A is correct: When one spills, the result may be a stain. When one injures, the result may be a scar. See **Analogy Strategy 1.** Choice E may seem correct because when one wins, the result may be a reward. Note, however, that a reward is a positive or favorable result, whereas a stain and a scar are negative or unfavorable results. Also see **Analogy Strategy 4.**

(Result relationship)

32. **(E)** Choice E is correct. A star is part of a galaxy because a galaxy consists of a group of stars. An island is part of an archipelago because an archipelago consists of a group of islands. See **Analogy Strategy 1.** Choice D may seem to be correct because a shark is a type of fish. However, this is not a Part : Whole relationship required for the correct answer. See **Analogy Strategy 4.**

(Part-Whole relationship)

33. **(C)** Choice C is correct. We have here a Result relationship. The meal results in an eating experience which is *unpleasant*—a *tasteless* meal. The job results in a work experience that is also *unpleasant*—a *frustrating* job. See **Analogy Strategy 1.** The other four choices—Choices A, B, D, and E—are also Result relationships. However, these choices all have *pleasant* Result relationships. Therefore, these choices are incorrect. See **Analogy Strategy 4.**

(Result relationship)

34. **(D)** Choice D is correct. When a person is irritated, he is annoyed or disturbed. When he is furious, he is enraged or uncontrolled by anger. We have a relationship of Degree here. When something is damaged, it is hurt or impaired. When something is destroyed, it is reduced to useless fragments as by burning or smashing. See **Analogy Strategy 1.** Here again we have a relationship of Degree. Choices A, B, C, and E are incorrect because they do not have a Degree relationship.

(Degree relationship)

35. **(B)** A person who is ambitious is not likely to be indolent (lazy). A person who is reticent (disposed to be silent) is not likely to be outspoken. See **Analogy Strategy 1.** The relationship in each pair is an Opposite relationship. Choices A, C, D, and E are incorrect because they do not have an Opposite relationship.

(Opposite relationship)

36. **(C)** Choice C is correct. We have here a Cause and Effect relationship. Because of fatigue, a person may be sluggish (lacking in vigor). Because of bravery, a person may be honored. See **Analogy Strategy 1.**

(Cause and Effect relationship)

37. **(B)** Choice B is correct. An obstacle stands in the way of achieving a goal. A distraction interferes with (stands in the way of) maintaining attention. See **Analogy Strategy 1.**

(Action to Object relationship)

38. **(E)** Choice E is correct. A sprinter is associated with speed and a weightlifter is associated with strength. See **Analogy Strategy 1.** Note that in Choice C a hurdler may be associated with a leap. However, this choice is incorrect because the two words in this choice do not have the same Association sequence as the capitalized question stem and Choice E. See **Analogy Strategy 3.**

(Association relationship)

39. **(D)** Choice D is correct. An egg has a shell as a natural protective cover. A seed has a pod as a natural protective cover. See **Analogy Strategy 1.** Note that in Choice A, a sardine has a can as a protective cover, but a can is an *artificial* protective covering. Also note that in Choice B, a sword and a sheath are both *artificial* objects. Therefore, Choices A and B are incorrect. See **Analogy Strategy 4.** Choices C and E are incorrect because these choices do not have the Purpose relationship required for the correct answer.

(Purpose and Thing-Place relationship)

40. **(A)** Choice A is correct. The flesh of the pig used as food is called pork. The flesh of the deer used as food is called venison. See **Analogy Strategy 1.** Note that in Choice E, the fat found between the skin and muscle of the whale is called blubber, from which oil is made. Blubber is seldom, if ever, used as food. Therefore, Choice E is incorrect. See **Analogy Strategy 4.** Choices B, C, and D are incorrect because these choices do not have the Purpose relationship required for the correct answer.

(Purpose relationship)

41. **(E)** Choice E is correct. The purpose of an interpreter is to translate. The purpose of an arbitrator is to reconcile—to bring people together for an agreement. See **Analogy Strategy 1.**

(Purpose relationship)

42. **(B)** Choice B is correct. The tiger and the lion are land animals that belong to the cat family. The rabbit and the mouse are land animals belonging to the rodent family. See **Analogy Strategy 1.** Note that in Choice A, the horse and the elephant are also land animals but they are of different families. See **Analogy Strategy 4.**

(Part-Part relationship)

43. **(D)** Choice D is correct. A miser is unlikely to give charity. A dictator is unlikely to show kindness. See **Analogy Strategy 1.**

(Association relationship)

44. **(C)** Choice C is correct. When one appropriates, he takes something by force. When one demands, he requests something with insistence (force). See **Analogy Strategy 1.** Note that APPROPRIATE is a verb in this question. It is *not* an adjective (meaning "suitable"). See **Analogy Strategy 5.**

(Degree relationship)

45. **(A)** Choice A is correct. A scholar spends a good deal of his time engaged in research. A daydreamer spends a good deal of time in fantasy. See **Analogy Strategy 1.**

(Association relationship)

46. **(A)** Choice A is correct. The very fact that the author's mother began to cry when she got the news that FDR was dead (see lines 5–6) indicates that the family had a feeling of closeness with, and obligation toward, FDR. Choices B, C, D, and E are incorrect because none of these choices is stated or implied in the article.

47. **(C)** Choice C is correct. See lines 38–40. "Jackie Robinson ... did more to win equal treatment ... than anyone else." In regard to Choices B and E, these choices may be true but the article does not indicate that they are true. Choices A and D cannot be accepted on the basis of what the article states.

48. **(B)** Choice B is correct. In this passage, the expression "marching alone" means that Robinson was struggling to succeed even though the odds were heavily against him. See lines 14–21: "My father brought some rumors ... Jack Roosevelt Robinson was marching alone." Nothing in the passage indicates that any of the Choices A, C, D, or E is correct.

49. **(E)** Choice E is correct. Throughout the passage, the author tells us about how some insects benefit human society and how other insects are destructive and harmful. See line 6: "Man benefits from insects in many ways." Now see lines 28–29: "On the other hand, many insects are obnoxious or destructive." The titles given in Choices A, B, and D make sense but none of them expresses the main idea of the passage. The Choice C title, though interesting, requires documentation which the passage does not provide.

50. **(A)** Choice A is correct. Although the author explains that there are both beneficial and harmful insects, he specifies, in the last sentence of the passage: "In spite of the excessive attention paid to injurious insects ... the beneficial insects. . ." Accordingly, Choices B, C, D, and E are incorrect.

51. **(C)** Choice C is correct. See lines 41–43: "In spite of the excessive attention paid to injurious insects by ... entomologists in particular..." Choices A, B, D, and E are incorrect because the article gives no indication that these choices are true.

52. **(D)** Choice D is correct. See lines 18–20: "Insects are the sole or major item of food of many birds, fish, and other animals (including man in some parts of the world)." Although Choices A, B, C, and E may be true, there is nothing in the passage to imply that these choices are true.

53. **(D)** Choice D is correct. See lines 10–15. "Then the handful will shout louder ... and lose popularity." Choices A, B, C, and E are incorrect in accordance with what the author states in the passage.

54. **(B)** Choice B is correct. See lines 16–20: "Before long ... but do not dare to say so." The author does not suggest anything to indicate that Choices A, C, D, and E are acceptable. Therefore, these choices are incorrect.

55. **(A)** Choice A is correct. See lines 18–20. In these lines you will find that the "furious men" actually believe in "their secret hearts" what the anti-war speakers are saying, but these same "furious men ... do not dare to say so." Accordingly, they are hypocritical. Choices B, C, D, and E do not apply. So these choices are incorrect.

56. **(C)** Choice C is correct. See lines 25–31: ". . . every man will be glad ... grotesque self-deception." Choices A, B, D, and E are not suggested by the author. Therefore, these choices are incorrect.

57. **(E)** Choice E is correct. See lines 1–2: "There has never been ... instigator of the war." Also see lines 9–10: "It is unjust and dishonorable and there is no necessity for it." Choices A, B, C, and D are incorrect because none of these four choices expresses the main purpose of the passage.

58. **(A)** Choice A is correct. The reader can hardly wait for the next line of dialogue. The animated conversation of the banker and the lawyer keeps the reader in suspense. Choices B, C, D, and E are incorrect because there is nothing in the passage to indicate or imply that any of these choices are correct.

[The selection is from the short story "The Bet" by the Russian writer Anton Chekhov (1860–1904).]

59. **(D)** Choice D is correct. We get the meaning of "capricious" from the Italian musical term "capriccioso," which refers to a composition that has a free, irregular style. A capricious person is one who is changeable or erratic. Choices A, B, C, and E are incorrect because they do not fit the dictionary meaning for the word "capricious."

60. **(B)** Choice B is correct. See the last line, which indicates that the lawyer's interest in making the bet was his "pure greed of gold." Choices A, C, D, and E are incorrect because the passage contains no justification for any of these choices.

61. **(B)** Choice B is correct. The author is, in effect, saying that one must appreciate the forest as a whole—not merely certain individual trees. He therefore implies that we should not separate physics from the body of all creative work. See lines 23–24: "It is pointless ... all creative work." Choices A, C, D, and E are incorrect because they are not justified by the content of the passage.

62. **(C)** The two labels (lines 15–17) obviously have negative implications about the value of physics and thus indicate that physics is uninteresting and pointless. Accordingly, Choice C is correct. It follows, then, that Choice B—which states that physics "is a cause for great excitement"—is incorrect. Choices A, D, and E are incorrect because none of these choices is stated or implied in the passage.

63. **(A)** Choice A is correct. See lines 28–30: "Yet what little we do know ... grandeur and intricate beauty." Choices B, C, D, and E are incorrect because none of these choices is brought out in the passage.

64. **(C)** Choice C is correct. See lines 19–22: "There is nothing ... what we lack of the other." Also see lines 23–26: "It is pointless ... all-knowing and infallible." None of the other choices is indicated in the passage. Accordingly, Choices A, B, D, and E are incorrect.

65. **(E)** Choice E is correct. See the very first sentence of the passage: "Let's be honest right at the start." This frankness on the part of the author pervades the entire passage. Choices A, B, C, and D are, therefore, incorrect.

EXPLANATORY ANSWERS FOR PSAT PRACTICE TEST (continued)
Section 2: Math Ability

As you read these solutions, you are advised to do two things if you answered the Math question incorrectly:

1) When a specific Strategy is referred to in the solution, study that strategy, which you will find in "Using Critical Thinking Skills in Math Questions" (beginning on page 69).

2) When the solution directs you to the "Math Refresher" (beginning on page 199)—for example, Math Refresher #305—study the 305 Math principle to get a clear idea of the Math operation that was necessary for you to know in order to answer the question correctly.

1. (B) Choice B is correct. **(Use Strategy 15: Know how to eliminate certain choices.)**

We need to find the *closest* approximation for 1.7999. Rewrite the choices as 2.0000, 1.8000, 1.7900, 1.7800, and 1.7000. We can now immediately see that 1.8000 is only 0.0001 from 1.7999, whereas the second nearest number, 1.7900, is 0.0099 from 1.7999. Also, remember that we must round *up* if the last digit is 5 or greater, as it is in 1.7999.

(Math Refresher #609)

2. (B) Choice B is correct. **(Use Strategy 2: Translate from words to algebra.)**

Let P = perimeter of the triangle. $\boxed{1}$

Using $\boxed{1}$, we have been given that

$$\frac{2}{3} P = 8 \qquad \boxed{2}$$

(Use Strategy 13: Find unknowns by multiplication.)

Multiply $\boxed{2}$ by $\frac{3}{2}$. We have

$$\frac{\cancel{3}}{\cancel{2}}\left(\frac{\cancel{2}}{\cancel{3}} P\right) = \left(\cancel{8}^{4}\right) \frac{3}{\cancel{2}}$$

$$P = 12 \qquad \boxed{3}$$

The question asks for $\frac{1}{4}$ of the perimeter. **(Use Strategy 13: Find unknowns by multiplication.)** Multiplying $\boxed{3}$ by $\frac{1}{4}$, we have

$$\frac{1}{4} (P) = (12) \frac{1}{4}$$

$$= 3$$

(Math Refresher #111)

3. (C) Choice C is correct. **(Use Strategy 17: Use given information effectively.)**

We have been given that

Bill always sits next to Carrie	$\boxed{1}$
Bill never sits next to Roni	$\boxed{2}$
Kristin always sits next to Bill	$\boxed{3}$

Notice that the arrangement of

Roni, Carrie, Bill, Kristin

is the only one of the five choices in which $\boxed{1}$, $\boxed{2}$, and $\boxed{3}$ are all true.

(Logical Reasoning)

4. **(A)** Choice A is correct. **(Use Strategy 17: Use given information effectively.)**

We have been given that

$$y = 4 \quad \boxed{1}$$
$$2y^2 + by - 4 = 0 \quad \boxed{2}$$

Substitute $\boxed{1}$ into $\boxed{2}$:

$$2(4)^2 + b(4) - 4 = 0$$
$$2(16) + 4b - 4 = 0$$
$$28 + 4b = 0$$
$$4b = -28$$
$$b = -7$$

(Math Refresher #406)

5. **(A)** Choice A is correct.

We have been given that

$$y^2 - 8 = 17 \quad \boxed{1}$$

If we subtract 17 from both sides of $\boxed{1}$, we have

$$y^2 - 25 = 0 \quad \boxed{2}$$

We need to find $(y - 5)(y + 4)(y + 5)$. Do not multiply the three terms. **(Use Strategy 4: Remember classic expressions such as $x^2 - y^2$.)**

Instead, recognize that

$$(y - 5)(y + 5) = y^2 - 25 \quad \boxed{3}$$

Substituting $\boxed{2}$ into $\boxed{3}$, we know that

$$(y - 5)(y + 5) = 0$$

Zero multiplied by any quantity is zero, so

$$(y - 5)(y + 4)(y + 5) = 0$$

(Math Refreshers #401 and #409)

6. **(B)** Choice B is correct. **(Use Strategy 2: Translate words to algebra.)**

Set up a proportion:

$$\frac{5 \text{ hrs.}}{2,200} = \frac{x \text{ hrs.}}{11,000} \quad \boxed{1}$$

Cross-multiply in $\boxed{1}$ to get

$$\frac{55,000 \text{ hrs.}}{2,200} = x \text{ hrs.}$$

$$x \text{ hrs.} = 25 \text{ hrs.}$$

Alternatively, notice that 11,000 is $2,200 \times 5$. Therefore, the drill must take five times as long to drill 11,000 holes as it would to drill 2,200, which is 5×5 hrs. = 25 hrs.

(Math Refresher #120)

7. **(C)** Choice C is correct.

Given: m and n are integers. $\quad \boxed{1}$
$\triangle$ XYZ is a right triangle. $\quad \boxed{2}$

(Use Strategy 18: Know and use facts about triangles.) From $\boxed{2}$, we know that

$$m° + n° = 90° \text{ and} \quad \boxed{3}$$
$$m + n = 90 \quad \boxed{4}$$

To find the greatest difference in values between m and n, we must subtract the least possible value of n from the greatest possible value of m. From $\boxed{1}$, we know the least possible value of n:

$$n = 1 \text{ (smallest positive integer)} \quad \boxed{5}$$

Substituting $\boxed{5}$ into $\boxed{4}$, we have the greatest possible value for m:

$$m = 89 \quad \boxed{6}$$

(Use Strategy 13: Find unknowns by subtracting expressions.) Subtract $\boxed{5}$ from $\boxed{6}$:

$$m - n = 89 - 1$$
$$= 88$$

(Math Refresher #509)

8. **(C)** Choice C is correct.

We have been given that

$$\text{"counterpart" of } y = 14 - y \quad \boxed{1}$$

(Use Strategy 11: Use new definitions carefully.) To find which number y is equal to its counterpart, use the equation

$$y = \text{counterpart} \quad \boxed{2}$$

Substitute $\boxed{1}$ into $\boxed{2}$:

$$y = 14 - y \quad \boxed{3}$$

(Use Strategy 13: Find unknowns by addition.) Add y to both sides of equation $\boxed{3}$.

$$2y = 14$$
$$y = 7$$

(Math Refreshers #200, #406, and #431)

9. **(D)** Choice D is correct.

Given: m and n are integers   ⨵1⨵
$$0 < m < 9$$ ⨵2⨵
$$0 < n < 9$$ ⨵3⨵

From ⨵1⨵, ⨵2⨵, and ⨵3⨵, we know that the greatest possible value for m and n is 8, and the least possible value for m and n is 1.

(Use Strategy 8: When each choice must be tested, start with Choice E and work backward.)

Consider Choice E: $m + n + 40$ ⨵4⨵

To determine the range of values for ⨵4⨵, we must insert the greatest and least possible values for m and n into ⨵4⨵:

(greatest) $8 + 8 + 40 = 56$ ⨵5⨵
(least) $1 + 1 + 40 = 42$ ⨵6⨵

Both ⨵5⨵ and ⨵6⨵ are between 8 and 90. Now look at Choice D: $10m + 10n$ ⨵7⨵

The greatest possible value for ⨵7⨵ is

$$10(8) + 10(8) = 80 + 80$$
$$= 160$$

160 is not between 8 and 90, so Choice D is correct. The other choices do not have to be tested once the correct answer has been found.

(Math Refreshers #200, #419, and #431 and Logical Reasoning)

10. **(E)** Choice E is correct.

Given: $\dfrac{x}{2} = y$ ⨵1⨵

$\dfrac{y}{2} = z$ ⨵2⨵

$z = 4$ ⨵3⨵

(Use Strategy 17: Use given information effectively.)
Substitute ⨵3⨵ into ⨵2⨵ and solve for y:

$$\frac{y}{2} = 4$$

$$y = 8$$ ⨵4⨵

Substitute ⨵4⨵ into ⨵1⨵ and solve for x:

$$\frac{x}{2} = 8$$

$$x = 16$$ ⨵5⨵

We need $x + y + z$.   ⨵6⨵

(Use Strategy 3: The whole equals the sum of its parts.) Substitute ⨵3⨵, ⨵4⨵, and ⨵5⨵ into ⨵6⨵:

$$16 + 8 + 4 = 28$$

(Math Refresher #406)

11. **(D)** Choice D is correct. **(Use Strategy 17: Use given information effectively.)**

We cannot draw lines between points V, W, X, and Y or between S, T, U, and V, or between S, Z, and Y, because we can only draw lines between exactly 2 points. For example, a line connecting S and T would also include U and V.

(Use Strategy 14: Draw lines to make a problem easier.)

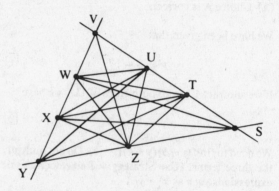

Z may be connected to the 5 points not on its line: T, U, V, W, and X.

Y may be connected to only U and T.

X may be connected to the 3 points not on its line: U, T, and S.

W may be connected to the 3 points not on its line: U, T, and S. (X and W have already been connected to Z.)

Total: 13 lines.

Note that it does not matter where we begin drawing lines, since the total is the same in all cases.

(Logical Reasoning)

12. **(E)** Choice E is correct.

Given: $\dfrac{x}{y} = \square$ ⨵1⨵

(Use Strategy 11: Use new definitions carefully.)

$$3x \div 4y = \frac{3x}{4y}$$

$$= \frac{3}{4}\left(\frac{x}{y}\right)$$ ⨵2⨵

Substitute $\boxed{1}$ into $\boxed{2}$:

$$3x \div 4y = \frac{3}{4}\ \square$$

(Math Refreshers #101, #111, and #431)

13. **(B)** Choice B is correct. **(Use Strategy 2: Translate from words into mathematical expressions.)**

Let T = number of teachers $\boxed{1}$
Let W = number of women teachers $\boxed{2}$
Let M = number of married women teachers $\boxed{3}$

Using $\boxed{1}$, $\boxed{2}$, and $\boxed{3}$, we can write the given information as

$$T = 28 \qquad \boxed{4}$$

$$\frac{3}{4}(T) = W \qquad \boxed{5}$$

$$\frac{1}{3}W = M \qquad \boxed{6}$$

Substituting $\boxed{4}$ into $\boxed{5}$, we can find W:

$$\frac{3}{\cancel{4}}(\overset{7}{\cancel{28}}) = W$$

$$W = 21 \qquad \boxed{7}$$

Substituting $\boxed{7}$ into $\boxed{6}$, we know that

$$\frac{1}{3}(21) = M$$

$$M = 7$$

(Math Refreshers #111, #200, and #406)

14. **(C)** Choice C is correct. **(Use Strategy 14: Draw a diagram to make a problem easier.)**

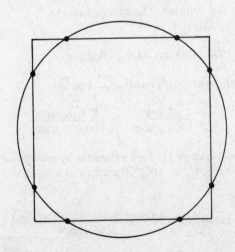

A straight line cannot cross a circle at more than 2 points. Since a square has 4 straight lines, the maximum number of intersection points is $4 \times 2 = 8$.

(Logical Reasoning)

15. **(D)** Choice D is correct. **(Use Strategy 17: Use given information effectively.)**

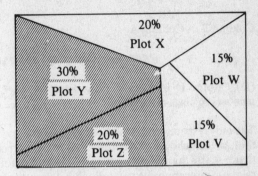

Given: Plot Z = 20% of all the land $\boxed{1}$
Plot Y = 30% of all the land $\boxed{2}$
Let S = swampy area

Since Plot Y and Plot Z form the swampy area, we add $\boxed{1}$ and $\boxed{2}$:

$$S = 50\% \text{ of all the land} \qquad \boxed{3}$$

Convert $\boxed{1}$ and $\boxed{3}$ to fractions.

$$\text{Plot } Z = \frac{20}{100} \text{ of all the land}$$

$$S = \frac{50}{100} \text{ of all the land}$$

To find what percent Z is of the swampy area, divide Z by S and multiply by 100. **(Use Strategy 19: Reduce and multiply.)**

$$\frac{\frac{20}{100}}{\frac{50}{100}} = \frac{\overset{2}{\cancel{20}}}{\cancel{100}} \cdot \frac{\overset{1}{\cancel{100}}}{\underset{5}{\cancel{50}}}$$

$$= \frac{2}{5}$$

$$= 0.4 \times 100 = 40\%$$

(Math Refreshers #107, #108, and #112)

16. **(B)** Choice B is correct. **(Use Strategy 19: Divide and reduce.)**

Column A	Column B
$\dfrac{8}{13}$	$\dfrac{\frac{8}{13}}{\frac{8}{13}}$

$$\text{Column B} \quad = \quad \frac{\frac{8}{13}}{\frac{8}{13}}$$

$$= \frac{\not{8}}{\not{13}} \cdot \frac{\not{13}}{\not{8}}$$

$$= 1$$

Column B > Column A

(Math Refreshers #101 and #112)

17. **(D)** Choice D is correct. **(Use Strategy C: Use numbers in place of variables.)**

The only restriction we have been given is that $y \neq 0$. Still, we can choose values for y that make y greater than -4, less than -4, or equal to -4. Thus, a definite relationship cannot be determined between the two columns.

(Math Refresher #419)

18. **(B)** Choice B is correct. **(Use Strategy 17: Use given information effectively.)**

Column A	Column B
$3 + 3 + 3 =$	$3 \cdot 3 \cdot 3 =$
9	27

Column B > Column A

(Math Refreshers #419 and #429)

19. **(C)** Choice C is correct. **(Use Strategy 12: Try not to make tedious calculations since there is usually an easier way.)**

$$\text{Column A} = 3\,(34 - 4) \qquad \boxed{1}$$

Simplify the expression in the parentheses in $\boxed{1}$ to get

$$3\,(30) = 90$$
$$\text{Column B} = 90$$

Remember to follow the order of operations. In other words, perform the operation within the parentheses in $\boxed{1}$ before attempting to multiply by 3.

(Math Refresher #409)

20. **(D)** Choice D is correct. **(Use Strategy 14: Draw a diagram to make a problem easier.)**

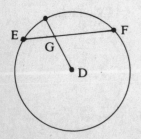
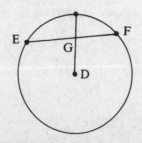

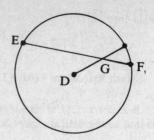

The three diagrams illustrate how EG may not be compared definitely with GF because of the infinite ways in which we can construct the diagram.

(Math Refreshers #200 and #524)

21. **(C)** Choice C is correct. **(Use Strategy 12: Try not to make tedious calculations since there is usually an easier way.)**

Column A	Column B
25% of 90	$\frac{1}{2}$ of 45
$\frac{1}{4} \times 90$	$\frac{1}{2} \times 45$
$\frac{90}{4}$	$\frac{45}{2}$
$\frac{45}{2}$	

Thus, Choice C is correct because the two quantities are equal.

(Math Refreshers #107, #108, and #111)

22. **(C)** Choice C is correct.

Let K = number of kilograms equal to 100,000 grams. $\qquad \boxed{1}$

Given: 1000 grams = 1 kilogram $\qquad \boxed{2}$

Set up a proportion using $\boxed{1}$ and $\boxed{2}$:

$$\frac{1 \text{ kilogram}}{1000 \text{ grams}} = \frac{K \text{ kilograms}}{100,000 \text{ grams}} \qquad \boxed{3}$$

(Use Strategy 13: Find unknowns by multiplication.)
Multiply $\boxed{3}$ by 100,000 grams and simplify:

$$\text{K kilograms} = \frac{(1 \text{ kilogram})\,(\overset{100}{\cancel{100,000} \text{ grams}})}{\cancel{1000} \text{ grams}}$$

$$K = 100$$

Column B = 100

(Math Refresher #120)

23. **(A)** Choice A is correct. **(Use Strategy A: Cancel numbers common to both columns by subtraction.)**

Column A		Column B
$(3 + y)\,7$		$7y + 3$
$21 + 7y$		$7y + 3$
21	$>$	3

(Math Refreshers #419 and #420)

24. **(B)** Choice B is correct.

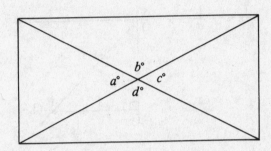

The figure above illustrates one way that c could be less than d, as given. **(Use Strategy 17: Use given information effectively.)**

$a = c$ ($a°$ and $c°$ are vertical angles) ☐1

$b = d$ ($b°$ and $d°$ are vertical angles) ☐2

Column A	Column B	
$a + b + c$	$b + c + d$	☐3

Change all variables to either c or d by substituting ☐1 and ☐2 in ☐3 :

$c + d + c$	$d + c + d$

(Use Strategy A: Cancel expressions common to both columns.) Cancel c and d from Column A and Column B:

$c + d + c$	$d + c + d$	
c	$<$	d (from the given)

(Math Refreshers #419, #501, and #503)

25. **(D)** Choice D is correct. **(Use Strategy C: Use numbers instead of variables.)**

Try $n = 1$: Column A = 16, Column B = 9
Try $n = 10$: Column A = 88, Column B = 90

Depending on whether $n < 8$, $n = 8$, or $n > 8$, $8 + 8n$ will be greater than, equal to, or less than $9n$, respectively. Thus, the relationship cannot be determined.

(Math Refresher #431)

26. **(A)** Choice A is correct.

Column A	Column B
$r = 6$	$r = 3$
$h = 3$	$h = 6$

Do not be intimidated by the complex formula. Merely substitute the given into the formula for the volume of a cone.

$$V = \frac{1}{3}\pi(6)^2(3) \qquad V = \frac{1}{3}\pi(3)^2(6)$$

(Use Strategy A: Cancel numbers common to both columns.)

$$V = \frac{1}{3}\pi(36)(3) \qquad V = \frac{1}{3}\pi(9)(6)$$

$$V = 108 \qquad\qquad V = 54$$

(Math Refreshers #200, #429, and #431)

27. **(D)** Choice D is correct.

Do not attempt to substitute numbers into both columns. The answer depends on how large the multiples of 2 are for Column A and how large the multiples of 3 are for Column B. Since this information is not given, we cannot compare the two columns.

(Math Refresher #200 and Logical Reasoning)

28. **(D)** Choice D is correct. **(Use Strategy C: Use numbers instead of variables.)**

Any real non-zero number, when squared, is greater than zero. Therefore, all we know from

$$(y - 4)^2 > 0$$

is that $y \neq 4$, else $(y - 4)^2 = 0$.

However, we do not know whether y is less than or greater than 4.

(Math Refreshers #419 and #431)

29. **(A)** Choice A is correct. **(Use Strategy 17: Use given information effectively.)**

The dice are numbered 1 through 6. Therefore, the sum of the two dice can be 2 through 12, or a total of 11 possible sums. ☐1

Given: M is the probability that the sum of the dice will be greater than 9. N is the probability that the sum of the dice will be less than 4.

$$M = \frac{\text{number of possibilities over 9}}{\text{total possibilities}} \quad ☐2$$

$$N = \frac{\text{number of possibilities under 4}}{\text{total possibilities}} \quad ☐3$$

There are 3 possibilities over 9 (10, 11, and 12). ④

There are 2 possibilities under 4 (2 and 3). ⑤

Substituting ①, ④, and ⑤ into ② and ③, we have

$$M = \frac{3}{11} \quad > \quad N = \frac{2}{11}$$

(Math Refresher #419 and Probability)

30. **(C)** Choice C is correct. **(Use Strategy 3: The whole equals the sum of its parts.)**

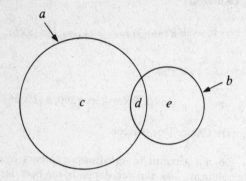

Notice that $a = c + d$ ①
and $b = d + e$ ②

Column A	Column B
$2d$	$a + b - c - e$ ③

Substitute ① and ② into ③:

$$\begin{array}{ll} 2d & \cancel{c} + d + d + \cancel{e} - \cancel{c} - \cancel{e} \\ 2d & 2d \end{array}$$

(Logical Reasoning and Substitution)

31. **(B)** Choice B is correct. **(Use Strategy E: Try to get the columns and the given to look similar.)**

We need to find $\frac{a}{c}$.

Given: $\frac{a}{b} = \frac{2}{3}$ ①

             $\frac{b}{c} = \frac{5}{8}$ ②

(Use Strategy 13: Find unknowns by multiplying equations.) Multiply ① by ②:

$$\frac{a}{\cancel{b}} \cdot \frac{\cancel{b}}{c} = \frac{\cancel{2}}{3} \cdot \frac{5}{\cancel{8}4}$$

$$\frac{a}{c} = \frac{5}{12}$$

$$\frac{5}{12} < \frac{5}{6}$$

(Math Refreshers #101, #111, and #419)

32. **(B)** Choice B is correct. **(Use Strategy 17: Use given information effectively.)**

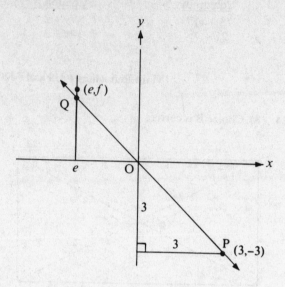

We know from the diagram that point P is (3, −3), since each leg of the right triangle is 3.

Slope of any line with points (x_1, y_1) and (x_2, y_2) is $\frac{y_2 - y_1}{x_2 - x_1}$.   ①

Line PO contains P (3, −3) and O (0,0).   ②

Substituting ② in ①, the slope of PO is

$$\frac{0 - (-3)}{0 - 3}$$

$$= \frac{3}{-3} \qquad ③$$

$$= -1$$

From ③ we know that every point on line PO must have x- and y- coordinates with the same value for the slope to have a value of −1.   ④

(Use Strategy 14: Draw lines in a diagram to make a problem easier.)

Note in our diagram that point Q has been added, as well as a line segment at x-coordinate e. Since Q is on line PO, we know from ④ that the coordinates for Q are

$$\begin{array}{ll} x = & e \\ y = & -e \end{array} \qquad ⑤$$

Since (e, f) is higher in the diagram than point Q, (e, f) has a greater y-coordinate. Therefore, from ⑤, $f^2 > e^2$.

(Math Refreshers #410, #416, #501, and #519)

33. **(A)** Choice A is correct. **(Use Strategy 19: Never multiply before reducing.)**

Avoid unnecessary work by canceling before multiplying:

$$\frac{x(x-3y)}{\underset{2}{\cancel{6}}} \cdot \frac{\cancel{3}}{x-3y}$$

$$= \frac{x}{2}$$

(Math Refreshers #108 and #111)

34. **(E)** Choice E is correct. **(Use Strategy 2: Translate words into mathematical expressions.)**

Let S = sum of both perimeters
Let P = perimeter of larger square
Let Q = perimeter of smaller square
Thus, S = P + Q   ☐1

The perimeter of a square is 4 times the length of any side. Thus,

$$P = 4(5)$$
$$= 20 \qquad \boxed{2}$$
$$Q = 4(2)$$
$$= 8 \qquad \boxed{3}$$

Substitute ☐2 and ☐3 into ☐1 :

$$S = 20 + 8$$
$$= 28$$

(Math Refreshers #200, #300, and #303)

35. **(D)** Choice D is correct. **(Use Strategy 16: Watch out for questions that are tricky. Beware of the "lure," Choice A.)**

Convert $7\frac{3}{4}$ to decimal form to match the number line.

$$\frac{3}{4} = 0.75 \qquad \boxed{1}$$
$$7\frac{3}{4} = 7.75$$

7.75 would be where Point S is, halfway between 7.7 and 7.8.

Do not carelessly choose Point P (7.5) after completing ☐1 .

(Math Refreshers #101 and #104)

36. **(A)** Choice A is correct. **(Use Strategy 2: Translate words into mathematical expressions.)**

Let C = Carol's earnings
Let A = Ann's earnings
Let N = Nancy's earnings

Given: C = $15   ☐1

$$A = \frac{4}{3}C \qquad \boxed{2}$$

$$N = 3A \qquad \boxed{3}$$

Substituting ☐1 into ☐2 , we have

$$A = \frac{4}{\cancel{3}}(\$\cancel{15}^{5})$$
$$= \$20 \qquad \boxed{4}$$

Substituting ☐4 into ☐3 , we have
$$N = 3(\$20)$$
$$= \$60 \qquad \boxed{5}$$

The ratio of Carol's earnings to Nancy's is ☐1 : ☐5 or $15 : $60, which reduces to 1 : 4.

(Math Refreshers #120, #200, and #406)

37. **(B)** Choice B is correct. **(Use Strategy 17: Use given information effectively.)**

Given: Fraction of $\frac{jazz}{total} = \frac{1}{9}$ ☐1

Total degrees in a pie graph = 360°   ☐2

The central angle representing jazz would be ☐1 times ☐2 :

$$\frac{1}{9} \times 360°$$

$$= 40°$$

(Math Refreshers #111 and #526)

38. **(D)** Choice D is correct. **(Use Strategy 14: Draw a diagram to make a problem easier.)**

Given: line ℓ bisects WX   ☐1
ℓ ⊥ WX   ☐2

Remember that a line is infinitely long.   ☐3

Now, we may draw a diagram using $\boxed{1}$, $\boxed{2}$, and $\boxed{3}$:

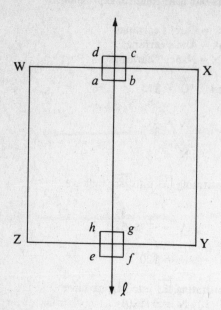

Since WX is parallel to ZY in a square, ℓ is also perpendicular to ZY. $\boxed{4}$

Thus, we know from $\boxed{2}$ and $\boxed{4}$ that the 8 right angles a, b, c, d, e, f, g, and h are formed.

(Math Refreshers #500, #501, and #520)

39. **(C)** Choice C is correct. **(Use Strategy 2: Translate words into mathematical expressions.)**

Given: Total number of jacks = 36 $\boxed{1}$
Total number of children = 6 $\boxed{2}$

If everyone is to have the same number of jacks, then

$$\frac{\text{number of jacks}}{\text{per child}} = \frac{\text{Total number of jacks}}{\text{Total number of children}} \quad \boxed{3}$$

Substitute $\boxed{1}$ and $\boxed{2}$ into $\boxed{3}$:

$$\frac{\text{number of jacks}}{\text{per child}} = \frac{36}{6}$$

$$= 6$$

Let us make a chart to determine how many jacks must be transferred.

Child	Number of jacks originally	Number of jacks desired	Number of jacks each must gain or lose
A	1	6	+5
B	2	6	+4
C	4	6	+2
D	7	6	−1
E	10	6	−4
F	12	6	−6

Notice that A, B, and C must gain 11, while D, E, and F must lose 11. Therefore, the least number of jacks that need to be distributed is 11.

(Math Refresher #200 and Logical Reasoning)

40. **(B)** Choice B is correct. **(Use Strategy 2: Translate words into mathematical expressions.)**

Let V = volume of the cube
Let e = length of an edge of the cube

Given: $V = 27x^{27}$ $\boxed{1}$

The volume of a cube is represented by the formula

$$V = e^3 \quad \boxed{2}$$

Substituting $\boxed{1}$ in $\boxed{2}$, we have

$$27x^{27} = e^3 \quad \boxed{3}$$

Take the cube root of $\boxed{3}$:

$$3x^9 = e$$

Remember that when taking the root of an exponent, divide the exponent by the root.

(Math Refreshers #200, #301, #313, and #430)

41. **(C)** Choice C is correct. **(Use Strategy 7: Use specific numerals to prove or disprove your guess.)**

The question asks which of the statements are always true. Therefore, if you can think of one example for which any of the statements is not true, then those statements are not correct.

Example for I:

$2 + 2 + 2$ is the sum of three even numbers, but
$2 + 2 + 2 = 6$. $\boxed{1}$

$\boxed{1}$ is not divisible by 8. Statement I is not correct.

Example for II: **(Use Strategy 5: Know how to manipulate averages.)**

The average of 2, 2, and 2 is

$$\frac{\text{sum of quantities}}{\text{number of quantities}} = \frac{2 + 2 + 2}{3}$$
$$= 2 \quad \boxed{2}$$

$\boxed{2}$ is not divisible by 8. Statement II is not correct.

Example for III:

Now consider the cube of an even number. An even number may be represented by $2k$, where k is any integer. Therefore, the cube of any even number is

$$(2k)^3$$
$$= 8k^3 \quad \boxed{3}$$

$\boxed{3}$ is obviously divisible by 8, so Statement III is correct.

(Math Refreshers #429, #601, #603, and #606)

42. **(B)** Choice B is correct. **(Use Strategy 17: Use given information effectively.)**

Since the 8-day pattern repeats, Plant V will be watered 4 times every 8 days. $\boxed{1}$

In 40 days, there will be 5 complete 8-day patterns. $\boxed{2}$

Multiplying $\boxed{1}$ by $\boxed{2}$, we have

$$4 \times 5 = 20 \text{ waterings} \quad \boxed{3}$$

In the next 4 days, there will be the same number of waterings as in the first 4 days, which is 3 waterings. $\boxed{4}$

The total number of waterings is $\boxed{3}$ added to $\boxed{4}$:

$$20 + 3 = 23$$

(Math Refresher #200 and Logical Reasoning)

43. **(E)** Choice E is correct. **(Use Strategy 17: Use given information effectively.)**

Note that in the first 8 days, there is no day during which all three plants are watered. Since the same pattern repeats for 80 days, there will be no day in the first 80 days during which all 3 plants are watered.

(Math Refresher #200 and Logical Reasoning)

44. **(D)** Choice D is correct. **(Use Strategy 16: Beware of tricky questions.)**

We are asked for $5(5^x) + 5^x$. $\boxed{1}$
Do not multiply: $(5 \cdot 5)^x + 5^x = 30^x$ (which is wrong). Rather, factor out the 5^x in $\boxed{1}$:

$$(5 + 1) 5^x$$
$$= 6(5^x)$$

(Math Refresher #409 and Distributive Property)

45. **(B)** Choice B is correct. **(Use Strategy 2: Translate from words to algebra.)**

$$\text{Given: } P = 4 \left(\frac{y}{4} - \frac{1}{4} \right)$$

$$P = \cancel{4} \left(\frac{y-1}{\cancel{4}} \right)$$

$$= y - 1 \quad \boxed{1}$$

(Use Strategy 13: Find unknowns by addition.) Solve for y by adding 1 to $\boxed{1}$:

$$P + 1 = y$$

(Math Refreshers #200 and #406)

46. **(E)** Choice E is correct. **(Use Strategy 16: Beware of tricky questions.)**

We cannot take the root of each number in a sum. We must find a common denominator and add the fractions *before* taking the root.

$$\sqrt{\frac{16}{25} + \frac{9}{4}}$$

$$= \sqrt{\frac{64}{100} + \frac{225}{100}}$$

$$= \sqrt{\frac{289}{100}}$$

$$= \frac{\sqrt{289}}{\sqrt{100}}$$

$$= \frac{17}{10}$$

(Math Refreshers #110 and #430)

47. **(D)** Choice D is correct. **(Use Strategy 18: Know facts about triangles.)**

$$\text{Given: } x + y + z = 150 \quad \boxed{1}$$

Remember that the exterior angle of a triangle equals the sum of the two remote interior angles. Therefore,

$$a = 90 + z \quad \boxed{2}$$
$$b = 90 + y \quad \boxed{3}$$
$$c = 90 + x \quad \boxed{4}$$

(Use Strategy 13: Find unknowns by adding equations.) Add $\boxed{2}$, $\boxed{3}$, and $\boxed{4}$:

$$a + b + c = 90 + 90 + 90 + x + y + z \quad \boxed{5}$$

Now substitute $\boxed{1}$ into $\boxed{5}$ to get

$$a + b + c = 90 + 90 + 90 + 150$$
$$= 270 + 150$$
$$= 420$$

(Math Refreshers #501 and #509 and Exterior Angles)

48. **(D)** Choice D is correct. **(Use Strategy 11: Use new definitions carefully.)**

Given: $r \,\mathord{\Leftrightarrow}\, s = rs^3$ $\boxed{1}$

From $\boxed{1}$, it follows that

$$s \,\mathord{\Leftrightarrow}\, r = sr^3 \qquad \boxed{2}$$

We need to find what values for s and r make $r \,\mathord{\Leftrightarrow}\, s = s \,\mathord{\Leftrightarrow}\, r$. $\boxed{3}$

Using $\boxed{1}$ and $\boxed{2}$ in $\boxed{3}$, we need to solve for the equation

$$rs^3 = sr^3 \qquad \boxed{4}$$

Subtract sr^3 from $\boxed{4}$:

$$rs^3 - sr^3 = 0 \qquad \boxed{5}$$

Factor $\boxed{5}$ to get

$$rs\,(s^2 - r^2) = 0 \qquad \boxed{6}$$

From $\boxed{6}$ we know that

$$rs = 0 \qquad \boxed{7}$$

$$\text{or} \quad s^2 - r^2 = 0$$
$$s^2 = r^2 \qquad \boxed{8}$$

$\boxed{7}$ establishes that Statement III is correct, and $\boxed{8}$ proves Statement II true.

(Use Strategy 7: Use specific numbers to disprove your guess.) Statement I can be shown to be false by proving it false in merely one instance.

Example: Select $\begin{array}{l} r \neq s \\ r = 1 \\ s = 2 \end{array}$ $\begin{array}{l} \\ \boxed{9} \\ \boxed{10} \end{array}$

Substitute $\boxed{9}$ and $\boxed{10}$ into $\boxed{4}$:

$$(1)(2)^3 \overset{?}{=} (2)(1)^3$$
$$1\,(8) \overset{?}{=} 2\,(1)$$
$$8 \neq 2$$

(Math Refreshers #409, #429, and #431)

49. **(A)** Choice A is correct. **(Use Strategy 7: Use specific numbers to prove your guess.)** This problem becomes extremely simple if you substitute numbers for the variables.

Example: 4 items cost \$10. $\boxed{1}$

1 item would cost $\frac{1}{4}$ of \$10. $\boxed{2}$

Substitute a for 4, b for 1, and \$ d for \$10 in $\boxed{1}$ and $\boxed{2}$:

a items cost d dollars.

b items would cost $\frac{b}{a}$ of d.
$$= \frac{bd}{a}$$

(Math Refreshers #111 and #431)

50. **(E)** Choice E is correct because Q could *not* be the vertex of L. **(Use Strategy 8: When each Choice must be tested, start with Choice E and work backward.)**

Given: Area of triangle JKL = 10 $\boxed{1}$

Recall the formula for the area of a triangle, where A is the area, b is the base, and h is the height:

$$A = \frac{1}{2}\,bh \qquad \boxed{2}$$

Let JK = b
$$\text{JK} = 5 \qquad \boxed{3}$$

When we substitute $\boxed{1}$ and $\boxed{3}$ into $\boxed{2}$, we have

$$10 = \frac{1}{2}\,(5)\,(h)$$
$$10 = \frac{5}{2}\,h \qquad \boxed{4}$$

(Use Strategy 13: Find unknowns by multiplication.)

Multiply $\boxed{4}$ by $\frac{2}{5}$:

$$\left(\frac{2}{5}\right)\,\cancel{10}^{\,2} = \left(\frac{2}{5}\right)\left(\frac{5}{2}\right)h$$
$$h = 4 \qquad \boxed{5}$$

From $\boxed{5}$ we know that the perpendicular distance from vertex L to line JK must be 4.

Note that M, N, O, and P are all 4 units along the x axis away from JK, which is on the y axis. Only Q is 5 units away from the y axis.

(Math Refreshers #301, #306, #406, #410, #500, and #514)